To one of my
friends and stepfathers

love
adam

TWENTY-FIVE

BEST PLAYS

OF THE

MODERN AMERICAN THEATRE

EARLY SERIES

EDITED WITH AN INTRODUCTION BY

JOHN GASSNER

NEW YORK
CROWN PUBLISHERS, INC.

Eleventh Printing, November, 1971

PRINTED IN THE UNITED STATES OF AMERICA

To the Memory

of

Burns Mantle
(1873—1948)

who was to the theatre

the most humane of critics and kindest of friends

CONTENTS

Note: Special introductions to plays and playwrights will be found on pages 2, 26-27, 58, 90, 124, 162, 214, 258, 294, 334, 372, 402, 444, 494, 530, 566, 612, 648, 686-687.

PREFATORY NOTE

The present volume represents a belated effort to fill a need left by the two previous collections of American plays published by Crown: *Twenty Best Plays of the Modern American Theatre,* which covered the period of the nineteen thirties, and *Best Plays of the Modern American Theatre: Second Series,* which presented the drama of the war crisis. With the present *Twenty-five Best Plays of the Modern American Theatre: Early Series,* the publishers now provide the general reader, the playgoer, and the student a living record of the period between 1919 and 1929, when our theatre arrived at maturity, and of the stirrings in the direction of modernity a few years earlier, as expressed by the Little Theatre movement through the production of ground-breaking one-act plays. The three volumes, taken together, now comprise a continuous account and anthology of the modern drama in America. The reader who wants a perspective on our stage history should start with the present book and then turn to *Twenty Best Plays of the Modern American Theatre* (1929-1939) and *Best Plays of the Modern American Theatre: Second Series* (1939-1946). Of course there are some gaps in the representation by plays in the series, but anthologists' apologies are already too numerous and since explanations are tedious, the editor politely foregoes them.

NOTE ON THE SELECTIONS

The selections, as will be seen, represent virtually every important playwright who made his impression before 1930. They also provide a cross-section of dramatic writing during the years covered by the book. Realism of one sort or another is exemplified by such selections, among others, as *Desire Under the Elms, What Price Glory?,* and *Street Scene,* normal fantasy by *Berkeley Square,* poetic symbolism by *Aria da Capo,* and expressionism variously by *"The Hairy Ape," Beggar on Horseback,* and *Machinal.* Folk drama is acknowledged through *Porgy* and one-acters, and social protest through *Gods of the Lightning.* Humor is presented on its two levels of "high" comedy in the case of *Paris Bound* and *The Second Man* and "low" comedy in the case of *The Front Page, Broadway,* and *Poor Aubrey.* The reader can make his own labels, if he wishes, and fit these and other plays into his private pigeonholes. In any case, *The Road to Rome* is offered as an example of the twenties' irreverent way with history, *Saturday's Children* as an example of how far the playwrights cared to travel the road of economic fact or fiction before 1930, and *Strictly Dishonorable* as simply fun, whatever else it may be construed to be.

Even so large a volume as this cannot, of course, exhaust the profitable and pleasant production of the play market of the decade, and it is very plain that O'Neill would have to be represented by several more plays than the two I am able to offer. A supplementary list of plays is given in the back of the book.

The one-acters presented collectively in the last section of the book should do some justice to the formative Little Theatre movement and the special regional theatre that leaned heavily on the one-act form. It may also serve to enlarge the representation of types and styles of dramatic composition during the period.

J. G.

Introduction

THE HAPPY YEARS, THE ADVANCING THEATRE

By John Gassner

In the brief chronicle of the modern American theatre, only one of its decades, that which ended ignominiously one late October day in 1929, was free from national anguish. One decade of unclouded skies is about as much as the children of the century have enjoyed anywhere, and we tend to look back upon it with a nostalgia that does not always seem quite so justified when a Broadway producer revives one of its plays. Skies were certainly not unclouded for the artists who found incentives for flight and scorn in the contentment of Main Street, which they were temperamentally incapable of sharing. And the one acknowledged genius of our theatre, O'Neill, glared balefully down on the scene of American prosperity with tragic perturbation and refused to be comforted.

Nevertheless, the sun did shine on a generally contented and confident people; and, for all the difficulties the exercise of art encounters and the distemper its practice produces or is produced by, our theatre did achieve a relatively undisturbed maturity. The sanguine disposition of the business man, so often deplored as "rotarianism" and the go-getting spirit, insinuated itself into the fledglings of the theatre more than they would have cared to admit. Combining with the *panache* of youth and with messianic intentions for the public in some psycho-chemical mixture, the "push" of the period gave birth to adventurous enterprises long enough to introduce new ideas and forms in staging and dramatic composition, to shake Broadway out of old ways and make it adopt new ones, and to set standards which stamped modernity upon our theatre. The story, which may be captioned "Genesis" in the annals of our stage, is a lusty one of playwrights and production groups springing up with rude strength or with bright-as-day cleverness, of battles fought in the name of self-liberation and art and frequently won on the fairy-tale field of commercial theatre. Although the book of beginnings cannot be read here in all its turbulence, we can at least flutter the pages.

It is not to be assumed, of course, that the American theatre was a desert on which nothing grew until a generation reaching its majority during the first World War began to eye it with ambitious intentions. Our perilously contracted Broadway theatre midway in the century can look back upon the period before 1917 with undisguised envy as one of expansion, of numerous playhouses later to be surrendered to motion picture exhibitors, of many more plays per season than we have today, of productions costing a fraction of what they must cost today. This was also the heyday of the touring company which brought theatre to the rest of the nation in a continuous stream, and the years 1900 to 1904 alone saw 308 plays on tour as compared with the insignificant dribble squeezed out of Broadway in the nineteen forties. Over five thousand professional theatres flourished on the American scene as against about two hundred and thirty in 1946, and this small number included opera houses. In the glorious twenties, as a matter of fact, the process of contraction had already set in as a result of costlier railroad transportation and of growing competition from the film industry. Nevertheless, the twenties must still look like bonanza years to the forties when we realize that the resurgent Broadway of 1946-47 had eighty-seven productions as against three hundred and two in 1927-28.

The recording angel will lift an eyebrow at the performance of the century before 1917 only if he sets quality above quantity. Yet even in this respect some circumspect reservations are in order. There had been stirrings of a sort in the American theatre since 1887 when Bronson Howard, who had ventured to brush the theme of capital and labor six years earlier in *Baron Rudolph,* treated Wall Street speculation with some realism in *The Henrietta.* By 1890, too, James A. Herne had written his *Margaret Fleming,* a noteworthy advance in realism with its story of a weakling embroiled in an extra-marital situation and a wife overriding convention by accepting his illegitimate child. William Dean Howells, champion of realism in the novel and himself a contributor to a new dispensation in American letters, was virtually acclaiming a new outlook in the theatre when he wrote of Herne's drama that, "It was common; it was pitilessly plain; it was ugly, but it was true," and William Archer, Ibsen's translator and exponent, could laud another play by Herne as "original American art." Ibsen was beginning to exert an attraction in our land, giving America's dean of cold-storage dramatic criticism, William Winter, a bad case of jitters as he protested that the explanation for Ibsen, as for Jonathan Swift, was a disordered brain.

In time, America adopted the problem play, of older inspiration than Ibsen but no doubt promoted by his example as well as by that of later playwrights across the Atlantic. Sacred cows were discreetly marked for sacrifice, as when, in 1911, Charles Klein, who made a business of grinding out popular fare, touched upon malefactors of great wealth in *The Lion and the Mouse* and when Edward Sheldon took note of political corruption in *The Boss.* Even Clyde Fitch, purveyor extraordinary of mild comedy of manners like *The Climbers* and *The Truth,* tried to heed his own complaint that "no one at present is getting the essence of his environment in thought, word, and deed" and contrived *The City,* in which he showed the veneer of respectability covering a corrupt public career. By the second decade of the century the American dramatist was catching up with *Pillars of Society,* if hardly going beyond Ibsen's early, and still Scribe-addicted, skirmishes of the eighteen seventies. The man and woman with a muckrake (Lincoln Steffens, Ida Tarbell) were at work in the nation and some of the sweepings fell on the stage. Theodore Roosevelt was wielding his big stick and its echoes reached the theatre. With the slums also becoming a concern of the social reformer, Edward Sheldon and Charles Kenyon moved into the congested city areas with *Salvation Nell* and *Kindling,* while the former even anticipated the racial problem plays and novels of later decades when he wrote *The Nigger.* Thematically, Sheldon in 1919 was not far behind the Sinclair Lewis of *Kingsblood Royal* in the nineteen forties.

Human relations, too, were undoubtedly beginning to be viewed with frankness rather than with the sentimentality usual in Victorian America. By 1909, Eugene Walters could dramatize the fluctuations of an immoral heroine in *The Easiest Way* and refrain from reforming her at the end. Perhaps Laura, the gentleman who keeps her, and the reporter who wants to marry her and bargains with his predecessor could not have been accepted by the public before being indurated to immorality by the Harry Thaw and other scandals that splashed the pages of the New York journals, but now a conservative critic like the late Alan Dale could concede that the play "gripped" even if it was "ugly, unpleasant, distressing" and "not a play for the Young Person." A play like Walters' had at last the status of a "slice of life," of the kind of *tranche de vie* exalted by the disciples of European naturalism several decades earlier. David Belasco, who produced the play, also complied with naturalistic requirements, making the most of the sordidness of the fallen Laura's furnished room, as well as doing his eye-filling best by her previous installation in a luxurious hotel. And three years earlier William Vaughn Moody, turning from poetry to prose drama in *The Great Divide,* had already made a rent in the curtain of prissiness that had veiled the theatre. In that play, he dramatized the thawing out of a proud New England woman who had been forced to yield to a bravo of the wild West fresh from his cups. A generation earlier the play, produced by the old-time manager Henry Miller and played by the stately Margaret Anglin, would have run to fustian melodrama and the "Unhand me, villain" type of sentiment. It would probably have ended with the self-immolation of the woman instead of her realization that she actually liked the man who had forced her. Here the sole concession to Pollyanna, from the viewpoint of bright Greenwich Villagers after 1914, was that the Westerner hustled the girl off to the nearest magistrate in spite of his intoxicated condition.

Finally, if we may omit as too tenuous the effort to achieve poetic drama in Percy Mackaye's *The Scarecrow* and Josephine Preston Peabody's *The Piper,* the new comedy was beginning to have its fling. On October 31, 1905, one of Bernard Shaw's "unpleasant comedies," *Mrs. Warren's Profession,* came to New York for a memorable evening before the watchdog of decency Mr. Comstock could intervene. The play, which was closed the next night, was too much in those days for even the liberal Norman Hapgood who lamented in the New York Herald that Arnold Daly had lifted the lid on indecency in the old Garrick Theatre. The only way to expurgate this insult to decency was to delete the entire text—"You cannot," declared Mr. Hapgood, "have a clean pig stye." His colleagues on other newspapers were no less outraged, and their reviews made liberal use of exclamation against "so vile and unnecessary a concoction," such "specious misrepresentation," such "mean and dirty action," and a subject so "decaying and reeking" that had no place in a theatre for mixed audiences. The comedies that began to thrust a mischievous head out of our native soil were understandably marked by greater caution than *Mrs. Warren's Profession.* Langdon Mitchell's *The New York Idea* was not "an unpleasant comedy" except to the diminishing number to whom the very idea of a divorce was still an abomination, but, like Shaw's play, it was irreverent toward the cloth and the marriage vows, and it had a pattern of wit that Brooks Atkinson found hardly faded in 1949. In 1906, when *The New York Idea* opened with a strong cast that included Mrs. Fiske and George Arliss, it could draw some snorts on the subject of the clever new generation from a Life reviewer. The latter also reflected ruefully that the author might have refrained from stirring up anarchy, and that divorcing one woman who had proved faulty in order to marry another was tantamount to avoiding the temperature of the frying pan by leaping into the fire. But he conceded the wit.

In 1914 Jesse Lynch Williams, who won the first Pulitzer Prize with *Why Marry?,* amused himself and others with the premise that the "new woman" could seriously, and from the purest motives, entertain the notion of love without marriage. He made his point even if he also managed to give her legal status at last in spite of her protestations. No one, so far as I know, rose up in arms against the comedy. (Eight years later Mr. Williams was to turn up again with *Why Not?* and show couples exchanging mates and amicably maintaining a *menage á quatre;* and so far had the relaxation of former standards gone that he could dispense with weighty arguments in support of his postulate.) In 1916, Clare Kummer breezed into the theatre with her frivolous antic *Good Gracious Annabelle;* and a year later in *A Successful Calamity* she contrived a mild plot with unusually Shavian dialogue. Around these early Arthur Hopkins productions swirled comedies by Rachel Crothers and others who whipped up the froth of such "modern" concerns as the "new woman" and her domestic experiments, while bedroom farces became more daring, if no more stimulating than could be expected. Even melodrama, that hardy staple of the American stage throughout the past century, acquired new wrinkles in such pieces as Bayard Veiller's 1912 thriller *Within the Law,* in which Jane Cowl avenged herself on her employer and on society for sending her to Auburn prison unjustly, and the same author's 1916 séance drama *The Thirteenth Chair,* as well as Elmer Rice's *On Trial.*

Nevertheless, American drama still stood many rungs below achievements in the novel, and was still some distance from qualifying as literature. Henry James had been writing masterpieces for several decades, Frank Norris had written *The Pit,* Theodore Dreiser in 1900 had turned out *Sister Carrie.* Nothing remotely comparable had been accomplished by the playwrights even when the best of them were at their best, and comparisons with their brethren abroad since 1880—with, let us say, Ibsen, Strindberg, Hauptmann, Becque, Chekhov, Shaw, and Synge—would have been too ridiculous to entertain. Insurgent youth in 1914 or 1917 could, moreover, have nothing but scorn for the hundreds of plays among which the few we have mentioned were isolated molehills of achievement. The general tenor of the drama produced by the flourishing theatre of the times, from which playgoers still demanded nothing but titillation, was of a diminishing species that later found a profitable haven only in the Grade B production units of Hollywood, where they could be tricked out by fancy camera work far more deceptively than by even David Belasco's sensational spectacles. The norm of playgoing was represented by *Peg O' My Heart, Kitty MacKay, Marie-Odile, The Cinderella Man, Daddy Long Legs,* and that apotheosis of the "Glad Girl" and *tour de force* for Patricia Collinge (later the Birdie of *The Little Foxes*) *Pollyanna.*

To these distilled sentimentalities, the better known of their kind, we may add a variety of other genres if we are to form some notion of the norm in playgoing. There was a ready and grateful market for the flow of melodramas from Owen Davis. Augustus Thomas was applauded in 1907 as a veritable modernist for *The Witching Hour* because it used mental telepathy as a plot contrivance. Pre-Freudian psychological technique had become fashionable in the theatre, and even William Vaughn Moody took a fling at hypnotism, in *The Faith Healer*. The first World War also spawned a considerable number of flag-waving exercises and spy melodramas. By comparison with the political innocents who wrote those pieces, a melodramatist like Herman Wouk writing *The Traitor* in 1949 could not feel secure until he supplemented his Geiger counter and Maxim silencer with disquisitions on liberalism and academic freedom. There were also plays that swung lightly like bungalow doors on the hinges of some plainly stated plot device, and playwrights plied their craft as a sort of game with the audience. This sport reached its climax with George M. Cohan's 1913 farce-melodrama *Seven Keys to Baldpate* and Frederick Ballard's popular Harvard prize play of the same year *Believe Me Xanthippe*. There were, finally, dialect farces like *Potash and Perlmutter* and romantic affairs like Edward Sheldon's *Romance*. Both were productions of the same *annus mirabilis*. They appeared on the eve of the first World War that was soon to destroy our pristine innocence.

2.

It does not follow that all the plays written or even produced after 1920 were immeasurably superior to the average product before 1917. That some have been just as bad, if not worse, will be attested by every reviewer who sat through *Grandma's Diary* in 1948. *Seven Keys to Baldpate,* for instance, held up in a revival later on with no great difficulty, and the late Laurette Taylor's vehicle *Peg o' My Heart* is still being played by summer theatre actors. *Abie's Irish Rose,* appearing in 1922, could roll up 2,327 performances during the sophisticated decade, although it could hardly have drawn such running fire of sarcasm from American critics in an earlier period as it received from Robert Benchley. Nor does it follow that most playwrights in the ever so progressive decades have not thought of their work as stage carpentry rather than as self-expression and literature. And, needless to say, it is impossible to set a date for the rise of a new dispensation in the theatre simply because the first World War ended in 1918.

The commercial theatre of the first post-war years simply fluttered around in its customary haphazard fashion, picking up straws in the wind of popular interest like the jackdaw it is. Pieces like *Three Wise Fools, The Charm School* and *Smilin' Through* continued to find a market for their sentimental wares, while George Jean Nathan breathed fire and the young generation tried to create its own theatre. At best, Winchell Smith and Frank Bacon turned out *Lightnin'* in 1918, and over twelve hundred performances attested its successful fusion of old contrived intrigue and sentiment with a lively penchant for local color and for a homespun hero. Don Marquis won hearts with *The Old Soak* as late as 1922, and J. C. Nugent's *Kempy,* of the same year, relied affectionately on the plight of a plumber who marries a girl only to discover that he loves her sister. Frank Craven thrived on the vagaries of the first year of a couple's marriage in *The First Year*. What Broadway did fairly expertly in these and similar plays was to weave old patterns with native thread, and it was the texture of the cloth rather than its design that deserved any sort of attention. Broadway's playwrights were actually doing what Augustus Thomas had attempted to do earlier, and ineptly, in such hinterland dramas as *In Mizzoura* and *Arkansas;* and what John Hay had done in his Pike Creek dialect ballads, Bret Harte in *The Luck of the Roaring Camp* type of fiction, and O. Henry in stories of urban life.

Melodramas dispensed with inflated language and used the surface of common reality or acquired pungency without being any the less dedicated to providing thrills. Plays about upper-class society became more vivid without being more drastic than Pinero had been when he wrote *The Second Mrs. Tanqueray*. Even as late as 1919 when Zoe Akins wrote *Déclassé,* her play about the descent of an impetuous lady from good society, Ethel Barrymore's performance in the play was more of a revelation than the content. Plays about bohemian life and the unconventional manners of its artists drew upon a phenomenon familiar to New York audiences, but revealed no particular penetration. The best of these treatments, as George Jean Nathan astutely realized, was the unsuccessful 1922 Zoe Akins comedy *The Texas Nightingale* in which shrewd characterization and a breezy amorality provided intelligent humor. Even here, however, the author made an easy accommodation by bringing together the boisterous and much-married opera singer with the noblest of her former husbands. Without rocking the intellectual cradle and without venturing innovations of style or form, the commercial theatre was, by and large, capitalizing on the victories of fiction and journalism, and using realism to flavor popular entertainment. Its policy was simply one of normal accommodation to public taste, which now demanded more authentic dialogue and background.

Another accommodation to the change of manners that started with the war-time flapper period and ended with the bathtub gin and speakeasy era, was the growing frankness of the stage. Before the twenties the theatre had found it necessary to wage a battle for this prerogative. The plays with which convention was first flouted ranged in quality from an inconsequential Bayard Veiller melodrama, *The Flight,* with one scene set in a house of prostitution, to *Mrs. Warren's Profession* and *Damaged Goods.* But their quality was less an issue of importance than the actual prevalence of a censorship as vigorous as that which was to be exerted in the motion picture industry later on. When the Broadway stage was relieved of this incubus it became possible for playwrights to function as free artists, and only in a few instances did they encounter efforts to suppress them in the twenties. In such cases, as in the battle fought over *Strange Interlude* in Boston, producers resisted intimidation. That the victory over censorship was worth winning, that it resulted not in license for sensation-monging but in freedom for significant drama, the theatre soon proved conclusively by the use it made of its liberty. The few tasteless numbers in musical revues that escaped suppression were a small price to pay for the possibility of producing *What Price Glory?* and O'Neill's dramas. One could reflect, besides, that when the censors take the field they invariably confuse art with immorality—and for the very good reason that art cuts deeply while licentious trash only titillates. As a rule, it is not against the massaging of the libido that the censorious rise up in arms, but against the surgery of the artist and the honest observer. The average mean sensual men who make good censors were more apt to make war on Bourdet's *The Captive* or O'Neill's *All God's Chillun Got Wings* and *Strange Interlude* than on "The Graphic" or the usual "girlie show." They were more inclined to protest against the spirituality of O'Casey's *Within the Gates* than to take up arms against bedroom farces and murder mysteries. One of the achievements of the nineteen twenties was the liberation of the stage from the proffered ministrations of blue-noses and bigots. If this liberation did not, and still does not, extend to every Main Street, the theatre was not materially deprived of whatever creativeness it could muster once Broadway became the initiator, test, and main mart of the American drama.

Whenever we deplore the centralization of the theatre in Manhattan that occurred during the period, we can reflect that this trend had advantages as well. History is entirely on the side of the assumption that important drama emerges only in metropolitan centers where a cosmopolitan outlook, a comparative freedom from taboos, and a degree of so-called sophistication rarely present in the provinces prevail. Euripides was unmistakably of Athens rather than of the villages of Attica, Shakespeare of London rather than of Stratford, Molière of Paris rather than of the towns he toured before turning from little farces to memorable comedy. Aiming at a Broadway production may have had deleterious effects on some playwrights who should have nourished themselves on native soil before flexing their muscles in megalopolis. It is also painfully true that overexposure to the average mentality of Broadway showmanship could vulgarize and cheapen. But it is questionable whether the talent so affected was anything that would have become sublime if it had remained in Zenith and had tuned its harp in Middletown's halls, and it is equally doubtful that O'Neill, Maxwell Anderson, and Sidney Howard offered sacrifices to Moloch in America's Carthage. If Hecht and MacArthur or Kaufman and his cohorts became expert entertainers, it would be difficult to determine what they lost as against what they and the stage of the moment gained by their adaptibility to Broadway idiom and tempo. In any case, the defense can "rest" until it is shown that any outlook useful to the drama failed to infiltrate professional playwriting from points west, north, and south, and until there is more evidence that Broadway-tainted plays have been resisted rather than snapped up by the rest of the country. The record of off-Broadway production during the past quarter of a century speaks contrariwise in spite of notable exceptions in Chapel Hill, Cleveland, Iowa City, Rose Valley (where Jasper Deeter's Hedgerow Theatre is located), and a few other places. In too many instances the theatre beyond the area bounded by Forty-second and Fifty-second streets has proved to be a borrower rather than a lender. and it has initiated less than it adopted.

3.

That was not the case between the years 1914 and 1920 when the non-professional stage constituted the vanguard. Without claiming for it a strict monopoly on ideas or courage and without attributing to it an exclusive role in modernizing American drama or stage production, it is no exaggeration to acknowledge its seminal importance. Although we tend to mistake an evolutionary process for a revolutionary one simply because its proponents call themselves revolutionists, the young men and women responsible for the so-called little theatre movement did introduce a new dispensation with their program and exertions.

As early as 1910, a Drama League of America dedicated itself to the encouragement of plays unacceptable to the commercial managements. If these could not be given lavish production, they could be introduced at least by special performances. A New York Stage Society was formed in 1912 by the élite of Manhattan, and three years later it proved sufficiently active to assure limited production to a play that ventured to attack religious hypocrisy under the irreverent title of *God and Company*. That year it also brought over Granville Barker from England to exhibit the new art of staging Shakespeare with a fluidity and imagination woefully absent in the Sir Henry Irving tradition of amputating texts and straitjacketing the bard in ponderous pseudo-realistic stage settings. The society then extended its sponsorship to Strindberg's *Easter* and other plays, Elizabethan and modern, at a considerable remove from the drama of Charles Klein and Clyde Fitch. Acting independently, as has been his wont since then, George Jean Nathan, then writing for the Smart Set, was speeding arrows of poisoned wit into the hide of the vested theatre interests and calling attention to the superior merit of the European drama. Other writers and lecturers Kenneth Macgowan, Hiram Motherwell, Walter Prichard Eaton, and Sheldon Cheney hammered away at the stage in workaday fashion, informing America of progress in stagecraft across the Atlantic, lecturing to groups, and founding a quarterly of advanced opinion, the Theatre Arts Magazine, in 1916.

A consciousness of dramatic art started bubbling in the colleges, where scholars had hitherto confined themselves largely to historical studies and where Scribe, Sardou, and other contractors of the "well-made play" were considered modern. In retrospect, the name of George Pierce Baker looms largest, as his Workshop 47, started discreetly at Radcliffe in 1903 and then transferred to Harvard, attracted students who were later to be identified with the new theatre. As Baker's book *Dramatic Technique* shows, the good Professor was hardly an iconoclast in matters dramatic, but he was iconoclast enough to initiate playwriting courses and experimental productions in the Yard at a time when theatre craftsmanship was not associated with literary study and when serious involvement in stage production by students was considered out of bounds. Professor Baker ministered to young people who were being educated in the humanities and who, largely thanks to his efforts, were actually to think of literature in connection with the stage, whereas it had been the usual practice to divorce the two. It is manifest that Victorian playgoers who could accept trashy farces and melodramas at the same time that they read Matthew Arnold, George Eliot, John Stuart Mill, and George Meredith made drastically divergent demands upon published books and stage productions. The same bill of divorcement between drama and literature was in force in the United States until the new generation, anticipated only by Henry James and Howells, insisted on a remarriage. Among the playwrights who were to try to meet the requirement were Baker students like Percy Mackaye and Edward Sheldon from the early classes, and later O'Neill, Sidney Howard, Lawson, Barry, and Behrman. They were to receive substantial support from other graduates; from the designers Robert Edmond Jones and Lee Simonson, the producers Theresa Helburn, Maurice Wertheim, and Winthrop Ames, and the critics Heywood Broun, Robert Benchley, and John Mason Brown.

Production on new levels, it is true, did not have to wait entirely for the full blossoming of the amateur theatre movement. An imaginative style of decor and staging, exemplified when Winthrop Ames imported Max Reinhardt's Japanese-styled production *Sumurun* in 1912, was becoming domesticated. Vibrations in the commercial field were evident when Hazelton and Benrimo's fantasy in the Chinese manner, *The Yellow Jacket,* was sponsored by the practical managements of Harris and Selwyn and the Coburns in 1912 and 1916 respectively. Winthrop Ames produced Granville Barker's and Laurence Housman's imaginative *Prunella* in 1913. Arthur Hopkins ventured upon stylization and artistry independently of the pioneering groups, aligning himself with Robert Edmond Jones some time before the association became notably successful with *Richard III, Hamlet* and the Edward Sheldon adaptation of Benelli's *The Jest* at the turn of the second decade. In 1916 John D. Williams, who was to present *Beyond the Horizon* in 1920 with some prompting from George Jean Nathan's critical corner, produced John Galsworthy's *Justice,* with John Barrymore playing the main role. As a result New York high schools started to assign the play to schoolboys for whom Charles Rann Kennedy's *The Servant in the House* was required reading in what was called modern drama.

A new age was dawning in America for a scenic art dedicated to poetic suggestiveness and symbolism, as opposed to flatfooted literalism or elephantine Belasco versions of realism. Joseph Urban, imported from Central Europe, designed new scenery for Boston's opera company and soon became an indispensable adjunct to Ziegfield's *Follies.* Robert Edmond Jones, returning from several years of study abroad, found an opportunity in 1915 to prove that he had been an apt scholar. His advent at Wallack's Theatre—on Broadway, I repeat, and not in the inconspicuous loft of some experimental stage group—was an assignment from Granville Barker to design the set for the Anatole France one-act play *The Man Who Married a Dumb Wife* which Barker used as a curtain-raiser to Shaw's *Androcles and the Lion.* Rejecting a conventional antiquarian accuracy for this medieval story, which would have called for heavy Gothic scenery, and responding instead to the mischievous *fabliau* spirit of the piece, Jones created a light as air design. He went so far in the effort to banish medieval gloom as to dispense with the Gothic arch in favor of square windows and of a flat balcony set on stilts. Jones, in short, put into practice what he was to announce in theory later on—the principle, namely, that scenery was to address itself to "the eye of the mind," and that "everything that is actual must undergo a strange metamorphosis, a kind of sea-change, before it can become truth in the theatre."

All this points, indeed, to a feature of the new movement usually ignored by those who adhere to the notion that the American stage came of age under the banner of realism. The facts speak otherwise. The insurgents in our theatre did not fight primarily under the banner of the middle-period Ibsen, Antoine, Brahm or Stanislavski but rather under the vaulting canopy of Max Reinhardt and Gordon Craig—and, whether they fully realized it or not, under the wings of that great Swiss visionary Adolph Appia, the father of modern lighting in the theatre. When the young artists of America went abroad, the experiments of Antoine's *Théâtre Libre* and Otto Brahm's *Die Freie Bühne* that had the good fight for realism were already regarded as outmoded. Even the Moscow Art Theatre had turned its face toward symbolism with productions like *The Blue Bird* and an invitation to Ellen Terry's son, Gordon Craig, who clamored for a theatre of dreams and poetic atmosphere. The "free theatres" had been displaced by the "art theatres" that specialized in theatrical magic rather than in verisimilitude. It was no longer enough to be true to plain fact, it was necessary instead to be true to the spirit or distilled essence of reality. America, which had skipped a truly realistic period in the evolution of the theatre except in so far as Belascoism gave a factitious imitation of it, never had a "free theatre" in any true sense of the term. America did develop an "art theatre" consciousness and did proliferate during the formative years in little "art theatres."

That something was lost in our missing an evolutionary stage was barely noticed for a while, and certainly not many steps were taken to make up the loss. Except in the case of the short-lived Actors' Theatre, we gave no such close attention as Stanislavski and his followers paid to acting as an art requiring inner development. We made only half-hearted and quickly abandoned efforts to perfect ensemble performance or, for that matter, to establish a genuine repertory system, Eva Le Gallienne's subsidized Civic Repertory Theatre being the only exception. The Theatre Guild could long follow the principle of starring no actor and could in 1926 establish a permanent repertory company with such players already distinguished or soon to achieve distinction as Alfred Lunt, Lynn Fontanne, Clare Eames, Dudley Digges, Edward G. Robinson and Frederic March, but the absence of stardom became merely a matter of nomenclature and the repertory idea was abandoned after two years. The roots for repertory simply had not been established in the formative period of modern American theatre. The new stagecraft tended to stress, instead, the virtuosity of the *régisseur* or director who, as in the case of Reinhardt, had to be followed obediently by his actors throughout his gyrations in the field of style. The new gospel tended even more to exalt the inanimate production component of scenery to which a strong animation was now being given. The vatic Gordon Craig could actually envision some future replacement of the living actor by a super-marionette more amenable to the demands of a super-director than brain cell and nerve-fibre.

That an impressive number of genuine actors did, nevertheless, arise between 1917 and 1929 is largely attributable to the contagious arduousness and idealism of the theatre. Their availability to a production was, nevertheless, rarely a substitute for a long trained ensemble, and it is something to wonder at how often since 1920 we have attributed acting genius to actors and actresses whose real stock in trade is an attractive stamp of personality. If it can be argued with some show of reason that personality, if distinctive enough, is also a legitimate commodity, it is nevertheless true that acting art was not a major achievement of our modernity. One may suspect that the enthusiasm our public lavishes upon British actors, a phenomenon frankly noted by Robert Morley while enjoying the success of *Edward, My Son,* is a compensatory mechanism. What really gave distinction to the new theatre was its improved décor and staging, as well as the better quality of imported and homegrown plays.

It was because the dissemination of the new art and the insemination of playwriting were most vigorously carried on by the uncommercial groups that sprang up by 1911 and reached their apogee by 1919 that the "little theatre" movement is considered so revolutionary in our stage history. Omitting early women's club theatricals that led in 1910 to the formation of the Drama League of America at Evanston, Illinois, we can take stock of a remarkable mushrooming of small enterprises throughout the United States, all of them dedicated to theatre art rather than business.

In this account, university theatres must not be slighted. A pioneer among these was Professor Baker's *47 Workshop Theatre,* established in 1912 and disestablished at Harvard in 1925; its value as a laboratory for young writers cannot be overlooked. A year earlier, the University of Wisconsin, where Thomas H. Dickinson took charge of dramatics, gave birth to the Wisconsin Dramatic Society. Renamed The Wisconsin Players, it soon performed both in Madison and Milwaukee and also provided facilities for fledgling playwrights. In 1914, Thomas Wood Stevens organized a laboratory theatre at Pittsburgh's Carnegie Institute of Technology and Frederick H. Koch formed the Dakota Playmakers at the University of Dakota. Theatre became a flourishing activity at Cornell University under Professor A. M. Drummond, the University of Iowa under Professor E. C. Mabie, Northwestern University, the University of Utah, the University of Washington under Professor Glenn Hughes, and numerous other schools. In 1918, Professor Koch created the Carolina Playmakers at the University of North Carolina where Thomas Wolfe, Paul Green, and others served an apprenticeship, and regional theatre won standing throughout the state and elsewhere as a result of the Playmakers' practice of touring widely. In time, such noteworthy plays as Paul Green's Pulitzer Prize play *In Abraham's Bosom* and *The House of Connelly* and Dorothy and DuBose Heyward's *Porgy,* as well as numerous one-act plays of distinction, emanated from Chapel Hill.

Later and well on into the present time, university theatres were to continue the good work at institutions too numerous to list here. Hallie Flanagan at Vassar became a galvanizing force in experimentation. Baker and his associates, notably Alexander Dean, turned out the director Elia Kazan and others at Yale who later won reputations. Milton Smith at Columbia University laid creative foundations and in association with the music department developed music-drama which was later to introduce Gian-Carlo Menotti's superb work *The Medium.* Garrett Leverton, Theodore Fuchs, and Lee Mitchell were to make Evanston a humming dramatic center. Mabie's enterprise at Iowa was to give us the playwright E. P. Conkle.[1] If the acting in all these ventures was unprofessional, the scenic art and the stage direction were not infrequently superior to ordinary professional produc-

[1] A large-sized volume could, indeed, be filled with reports of their work and that of Curtis Canfield at Amherst, N. Bryllion Fagin at the Johns Hopkins University, Sawyer Falk at Syracuse, Karl Wallace at the University of Illinois, Robert Gates Dawes at Ohio University, Kenneth Macgowan at UCLA, Hubert Heffner at Leland Stanford, E. J. West at the University of Colorado, Edwin Duerr at the University of California, Herschell R. Bricker at the University of Maine, Father Hartke and Walter Kerr at Catholic University, and many others after 1920.

tions. In time, too, the universities were to provide the best examples of modern theatre architecture, as at Madison, Amherst, and Williams, while Broadway was to content itself with half-antiquated structures and was to present a sorry contrast to the superb buildings that began to be constructed in continental Europe before the first World War.

Still, the most dramatic expression of the new theatre movement came from intrepid amateurs who proliferated without benefit of the academy. It was the groups they formed that impressed the nation with the simple facts that theatre should be an art practiced with the devotion that any artist brings to his work and that drama should be composed for self-expression and essential comment like any other form of literature.

Among the first ventures was the Chicago Little Theatre, founded in 1912 by Maurice Browne and Ellen Van Volkenburg. On ground slightly prepared by some earlier experimenters, the British-born Maurice Browne, who upon returning to England was later to collaborate on that first and still best atom-bomb drama *Wings Over Europe,* presented an uncompromising program of plays by Euripides, Ibsen, Strindberg, Schnitzler, Shaw and Synge that was to bankrupt his organization five years later. For five years Browne persisted in championing modernism with inadequate means and amateur players (perhaps professional actors could have broken the resistance of Chicago playgoers) but with admirable judgment of modern drama and good taste in scenery. Later, Browne continued the unequal battle at the Cornish Theatre in Seattle and elsewhere, and finally left America. A Toy Theatre in Boston served as a laboratory from 1912 to 1916, Los Angeles and Indianapolis acquired little theatres, and in Detroit the Arts and Crafts Theatre won considerable success for two years under the direction of that able Gordon Craig disciple Sam Hume, who combined experimentalism in staging with more cautious play selection. It was under the sponsorship of the Arts and Crafts Theatre that the influential Theatre Arts Magazine was founded. Hume helped to design a modern building and supervised all phases of production on the Craig theory that theatre must be a perfect synthesis stemming from a single individual's outlook and talent. His assistant Irving Pichel subsequently went on to the Berkeley Playhouse, Broadway, and Hollywood. Cleveland became an especially well nourished dramatic center after 1916 with the rise of the Cleveland Playhouse first under Raymond O'Neill and then, in 1921, with distinction under Frederic McConnell. At the Pasadena Community Playhouse, Gilmor Brown made a special point of involving the citizens; he acquired an excellent building and developed production facilities to such an extent that he was able to give a highly praised production of O'Neill's *Lazarus Laughed* whose inordinate physical requirements could well intimidate Broadway managements. Moving as far north as Seattle and as far south as Dallas, which reaped laurels in tournaments during the nineteen twenties (Dallas is now dramatically active once more in an arena theatre thanks to the dynamism of Margo Jones), the little theatre movement spread like wild fire.

In all probability, however, "art theatre" would not have made a strong dent in the Broadway of the Shuberts and the Frohmans but for three groups that established themselves in Manhattan, first at a discreet distance from the Main Stem. Of these, the Neighborhood Playhouse, founded in 1915, alone retained its amateur spirit to the end, which came in 1927. Located on the East Side and actually an outgrowth of the Adolph Lewisohn family's interest in social welfare, the Playhouse provided training for the talented young people of the neighborhood. But the Misses Alice and Irene Lewisohn's enterprise on Grand Street soon provided both entertainment and stimulation for the rest of New York by revealing resources of taste and style still largely absent in the uptown theatres. When professional acting began to appear at the Playhouse, a trip to the East Side became obligatory to art-loving New Yorkers. The organization was notable for productions like *The Dybbuk* and *The Little Clay Cart* as stylized as these plays respectively inspired by Jewish mysticism and fourth century Hindu traditionalism. Broadway could learn from this community theatre how to perform magic without ostentation. The organization experimented with dance drama and gave a new fillip to musical entertainment with impish intimate revues called *The Grand Street Follies.* Unfortunately it became impossible to sustain professional production in the small house without continual subsidy, but by the time the Neighborhood Playhouse stopped producing it had contributed a pleasant chapter to the chronicles of our theatre.

A greater destiny was in store for an enterprise that began with a number of Greenwich

Villagers in the autumn of 1914 and opened at the tiny Bandbox Theatre on East 57th Street early next year. A group of intellectuals—Lawrence Langner, a patent-lawyer whose taste for theatre had been whetted in London, the enthusiast and wit Philip Moeller, the unforgettable actress Helen Westley, Edward Goodman, and others—banded together to create theatre. Calling themselves the Washington Square Players, they attracted other artists, rebels, and bohemians to them. Among the several scenic designers were Rollo Peters and Lee Simonson, the Santayana-inspired Harvard prodigy only recently detached from his Paris atelier. Their manifesto took the usual swipes at commercial theatre and affirmed democracy in the theatre by establishing an admission charge of fifty cents. They called for public support and solicited subscribers. Although they refrained from setting up a rigid policy of play selection, they resolved to produce plays for which there was no place in the commercial theatre. They promised to give preference to works of American authorship but intended to include the writings of "well-known European authors which have been ignored by the commercial managers."

On Feb. 19, 1915 the Washington Square Players opened the first season with a program of three one-acters and a pantomime characteristically compounded of mischief, sophisticated comedy, and poetry. The pantomimed skit, called *Another Interior,* showed the human stomach in active operation while the protagonist of the piece, Gastric Juice, endured martyrdom. The two American one-acters, Edward Goodman's *Eugenically Speaking* and Lawrence Langner's *Licensed* provided avant-garde humor. The *pièce de résistance* was Maurice Maeterlinck's mood-drenched little tragedy *Interior.* Instead of adhering to the policy of giving only two performances, on Friday and Saturday evenings, the Players added a third performance when jaded critics and playgoers responded enthusiastically. Other productions of the season included Chekhov's vaudeville farce *The Bear* and one-acters by Rose Pastor Stokes and John Reed, who were to be better known as political radicals than as playwrights. The second season, the Players started paying the actors and playing seven times a week, and felt confident enough to set an admission price of one dollar instead of fifty cents. Frank Conroy and other professional actors began to augment the amateurs and it was not long before patrons noticed an appreciable improvement in the performances. Among the novitiates were Katherine Cornell, Roland Young, Glenn Hunter, and Rollo Peters.

Philip Moeller's clever spoof on a classic theme, *Helena's Husband,* won acclaim, as well it might since the public was ready for this type of irreverence toward historical figures. Another tribute to the new spirit was Alice Gerstenberg's *Overtones,* in which two women characters were supplied with their "other" selves, with inner and "real" alter egos whose candor was disconcerting. It is possible that some recollection of *Overtones* predisposed Lawrence Langner in favor of *Strange Interlude* when he persuaded his co-directors at the Theatre Guild to produce this unconventional compound of interior monologues. By the spring of 1916 the Players ventured to produce their first full-length play, Maeterlinck's *Aglavaine and Sylvette,* and followed it with Chekhov's *The Sea-Gull,* which was considerably beyond the reach of their acting company. With more courage than discretion they next moved closer to Broadway, renting the Comedy Theatre when the Bandbox proved too small for their needs. Here they adventured in 1917 with the Russian gloom and fatalistic symbolism of Leonid Andreyev's *Life of Man.* The play, in which the shadowy figure of Death follows the hero from the cradle to the grave, was certainly as experimental a play as any on which to cut baby teeth. They produced Ibsen's *Ghosts* during the same season, in defiance of William Winter's now receding thunder, and revived *Mrs. Warren's Profession* in 1918, without encountering Arnold Daly's difficulties with the police thirteen years earlier. Disinclined to abandon the one-act form, they also produced some of the best early American one-acters, Zona Gale's farm drama *Neighbors,* Susan Glaspell's stark *Trifles,* and O'Neill's *In the Zone.* But production costs were rising and America's entry into the war was depleting the Players' company of valuable personnel. In May 1918, after four flamboyant years during which the group had to its credit sixty-two short pieces and six full-length plays, the Washington Square Players ended their particular chapter—only to start another one with the founding of the Theatre Guild in 1919.

From the very start the Washington Square Players company charted a course to be followed not only by its successor, the Theatre Guild, but by the theatre of the twenties in general. It is a course not easily to be defined because it was improvisatory, wayward, and incalculable, as, for that matter, was the way of Max Reinhardt, the popularizer of art theatre on the European continent. It was characterized not by tenacious adherence to a program or art style but by marked eclecticism. Everything was grist to the producer's mill, even though the shrine kept scrupulously polished in the center was dedicated to the Unknown God, Art. Dramatic realism and even its extreme, naturalism, whose victories had been won decades ago in Europe, were mingled with poetic, symbolic and, later, expressionistic drama. All types of plays were produced with an equal sense of discovery and generosity toward the American public. The Players were earnest but at the same time urbane, and flexibility came easily to them. They would have no difficulty steadying themselves with alacrity in the quicksands of commercial theatre once they chose to make their stand on Broadway. Unreconstructed idealists of the little theatre were to observe their compromises ruefully, while grudgingly conceding the necessity of some of them and continuing to hope for a theatre in a receding future that would conform to the visions of Gordon Craig. That theatre was not to come in our time, as the twenties proved to be too giddy, the thirties too depressed and too filled with alarums, and the forties too anxious, bewildered, and full of military excursions.

The sister organization of the Washington Square Players which called itself the Provincetown Players was determinedly idealistic for a time and offered sturdier resistance to the temptation of facing toward Broadway. It became primarily a Playwrights Theatre, and the genius of its playwright, Eugene O'Neill, overshadowed any accomplishment in acting and production design. Although we are unlikely to forget Charles Gilpin's playing of "Emperor Jones," the stark production of O'Neill's sea-pieces under the collective title of *S.S. Glencairn,* and the stylized amenities of *Patience* and *Fashion,* it cannot be said that the Provincetown excelled in production. Its major contribution to the American theatre was Eugene O'Neill.

A playwrights' theatre was what we got in America and what, by and large, came to be expected by all but one or two of America's critics. The trend has continued to be discernible in American dramatic criticism which places its stress on the play rather than the performance. Our reviewers have vibrated with no particular sensitiveness to scenic design (often misjudging it indeed), and rarely have been impressed with directorial gymnastics. Our type of criticism has, in fact, disconcerted more than one European director in our midst. Some of the European craftsmen have actually prided themselves on having made extremely poor plays look like good ones by their exertions, but it is doubtful that they would have fared quite as well in New York as they did abroad. They would have earned at most a paragraph toward the end of the newspaper reviews informing the public that the director wasted his talent or that he struggled manfully with unrewarding material. If they had produced as well as directed the play, they would have reaped reproof and failure instead of praise and success.

An era of permanent repertory companies under the guidance of omnipotent artist-directors might well have changed our outlook, which is not confined to the fourth estate. And a case may be made out for a better understanding of production art both in front of the proscenium arch and behind it, since theatre not only includes but transcends the play text. Playwriting itself might have improved in the United States if writers had acquired greater awareness of the theatrical medium. O'Neill's preeminence is due in no small measure to the marriage of a novelist's and poet's insights to an actively theatrical imagination. It may be surmised, nevertheless, that concentration on the play had redeeming features not to be slighted. For one thing, we were spared the ignominy of swallowing soda pop under the illusion that it was champagne, our scenic artists were kept in hand, and our stage directors were saved from delusions of grandeur.

Sobriety was a special characteristic of the Provincetown Players, whose members could have come perilously close to bohemian dissipation of creativeness in Greenwich Village. Instead, devotion to the plain business of making art consumed their energies virtually from the start. The stalwarts were George Cram Cook and Susan Glaspell, Robert Edmond Jones, and Eugene O'Neill. They were joined by the playwright David Carb, the novelist and labor writer Mary Heaton Vorse, the story-writer Wilbur Daniel Steele, and others. On a wharf in Provincetown, Massachusetts, where Greenwich Village artists summered, a number of candidates for renown took over an abandoned fishhouse and staged their first production in 1915. One of their first playlets was Susan Glaspell's and George Cram Cook's *Suppressed Desires.* They returned to their wharf theatre the next two summers but also found city quarters in "the Village." Ultimately settling in a disused stable on Macdougal Street, they named it somewhat grandiloquently the Provincetown Playhouse. The hitching ring for horses was still fixed in the wall, and plainly the builder had not intended it for Pegasus any more than he had planned the interior for its riders. Remodelling and adjusting themselves to the cramped stage and the uncomfortable auditorium, the experimentalists made the unattractive building their workshop and temple from 1918 to 1929. A directorate composed of O'Neill, Robert Edmond Jones, and Kenneth Macgowan (a natural alignment of playwright, scene designer and critic), ultimately took charge of the Provincetown's destiny. The Provincetown lacked only a dominant stage director, who might have drawn disparate talents into a synthesis as Stanislavski, Copeau, and Reinhardt did abroad. Provincetown productions tended in consequence to be rather haphazard and improvisatory, falling short in this respect of the ideal of art theatre in the very process of fulfilling its proclaimed promise "to give American playwrights a chance to work out their ideas in freedom."

True to this avowed purpose the Provincetown produced plays by O'Neill, Glaspell, Paul Green, Theodore Dreiser, Virgil Geddes, Michael Gold, Lawrence Langner, Harry Kemp, Hatcher Hughes, Floyd Dell, Alfred Kreymborg, Maxwell Bodenheim, Edna St. Vincent Millay, Edmund Wilson, Stark Young, and others. The group also found room in the program for two of the most original plays of European modernism, Strindberg's *The Spook Sonata* and Hasenclever's *Beyond,* as well as for pert revivals of *Patience* and *Fashion.* Although it inclined somewhat toward realism in play selection, it gave the poets a hearing with such productions as Kreymborg's *Lima Beans* and Edna St. Vincent Millay's *Aria da Capo.* During 1923-25 the Provincetown operated both in the Macdougal Street cubicle and in the Greenwich Village Theatre on 4th Street near Washington Square, a comparatively commodious little building which was torn down in 1930. The latter displayed some of the most mature productions, *Desire Under the Elms, The Spook Sonata, Fashion,* and *All God's Chillun Got Wings.* In 1929 the Provincetown moved to Broadway. But before it could entrench itself there the economic depression exacted its toll, and after December, 1929 the Provincetown Players belonged to the ages.

4.

O'Neill was inevitably inherited by the Theatre Guild, since the Provincetown and Washington Square groups had made a common cause before 1920 and the latter had produced one of his sea-pieces early in his career. The Guild was, moreover, in a position to give America's leading experimentalist the production stagecraft he needed, as well as the largest possible audience. Founded in 1919 by Washington Square devotees and later arrivals who responded to Lawrence Langner's call for a reconstructed enterprise, the Guild had become the foremost theatrical organization in America. It is doubtful, indeed, whether American stage history would have been the same but for Mr. Langner, who had energy enough to create the Guild with his right hand and a flourishing law firm with his left. Trained in patent law and engineering in England before arriving here in 1913, consultant to the Ordnance Department during the war and on the Advisory Council of the American Committee at the Treaty of Versailles, he was a *bona fide* amateur. He became a playwright with two one-acters for the Washington Square Players, and he was later to write and adapt a number of plays, including the successful *Pursuit of Happiness* in collaboration with his actress-wife Armina Marshall. Combining practicality with enthusiasm and a flair for playwriting, he was largely instrumental in giving the new organization the habit of adaptability interrupted by flashes of inspiration and spurts of adventure that has carried the Guild through three decades of perilous Broadway production.

The Guild approximated some of the high hopes of the little theatre. It had, for one thing, a home of its own after 1925 at 245 West 52nd Street, a specially designed building that was the most modern on Broadway. The auditorium was spacious and comfortable without, however, exceeding the bounds of intimacy; "art theatre" always called for a close relation between the audience and the performance. Only the furniture and the décor looked back to a pre-modern epoch and acted, indeed, as a depressant. Taking its cue from European art theatres, the Guild also had a subscription audience that made the public a partner in its enterprises. The subscription system ensured money for productions, enabled the policy board to plan as many as six plays per season well in advance, and relieved the directors of the necessity of courting Broadway financiers for each individual production and of discarding plays for which money could not be raised among the "angels." This favorable position made experimentation possible whenever the Guild discarded the caution of the market place. Its 135 subscribers grew to 6,000 in October 1922 and to 23,000 in the fall of 1927. By the season of 1929-30 the Guild also had subscription audiences in Philadelphia, Chicago, Pittsburgh, Baltimore, Boston, Detroit, Cincinnati and St. Louis. A tour was thus assured for productions and the "road" was at last won over, in a measure, to modern drama far beyond the dreams of even the most ambitious little theatre that hoped to inseminate the land. By 1930, moreover, the Guild also successfully invaded England with touring companies of *Porgy, Strange Interlude,* and the Lunt-Fontanne vehicle of *Caprice.*

By virtue of the subscription basis and a commitment to produce a set number of plays each season the Guild was, in spite of private ownership by the directors, an organizational theatre. Its interest in dramatic literature and in advanced theatrical styles, its use of modern scenic design, and its attempt for a time to establish a permanent acting company and some form of repertory made it also an "art theatre." To meet the perquisites of an art theatre in full it lacked only the synthesizing rule of a director whose personal style would dominate every production, as in the case of European theatres ruled by a Stanislavski, Reinhardt, Copeau, Tairov, Meyerhold, Jessner, or Piscator. The American trend toward corporate responsibility, as well as our penchant for democratic procedure and the manner in which the Guild came into being, precluded this form of benevolent autocracy. Only the emergence of a brilliant stage director, Philip Moeller, and his collaboration with Lee Simonson, one of the two foremost American designers of the twenties, assured many productions a unity of style that would have been perfect if that other requirement, a permanent repertory company, had been maintained for a period longer than two seasons. The noteworthy productions that the Guild unfolded in the twenties grew in number as the crudities of acting associated with the little theatre movement were displaced by complete professionalism. With the Theatre Guild, the experimental stage grew up, and was able to compete against Broadway on equal and, more often than not, on superior terms. Its lasting power also proved unusual; new producers came and went or disappeared from the Main Stem for years, but the Guild went on, rain or shine. It has performed the miracle of weathering its thirtieth season at this writing.

A new period in American stage history began in 1919 when the Guild was founded. The Broadway theatre absorbed, to some degree, lessons learned abroad or taught by European visitors like Jacques Copeau's *Théâtre du Vieux Colombier,* advanced along lines laid down during the previous dozen years, and assimilated portions of the program of the little theatre movement. The Theatre Guild itself was not "little theatre" in any other sense of the word than that its directors retained some of the amateur's spirit in favoring the play of ideas and of literary distinction and in affecting the unusual in theatrical and dramatic style. The two most professional members of the directorate, Rollo Peters and Augustin Duncan, dropped out during the second season. The six who continued operations were, in addition to the Washington Square veterans (Langner, Moeller, Helen Westley), the painter Simonson who had helped them with occasional designs, the former Baker student and banker, Maurice Wertheim, who had occasionally advised the Players on financial affairs, and Theresa Helburn, who had written her first produced one-acter, *Enter the Hero,* for the Players and had published poetry. Bryn Mawr, Sorbonne, and Workshop 47 educated Miss Helburn, who had been writing criticism for The Nation, joined the Guild as "play reader," became a board member, and was later made executive director. Her usefulness did not end with her diplomacy, which was to steer the Guild through many a squall, for Miss Helburn had an uncanny ability to spot talent in all departments and to cast plays. She also retained an amateur's youthfulness longer than is usual; and this was apparent in 1943 when "Terry," as she is fondly called by half the theatrical world, arranged the union of Hammerstein and Rogers (just as she had earlier mated Lynn Fontanne and Alfred Lunt in *The Guardsman*) and initiated *Oklahoma!* In the late thirties and in 1940-41, Miss Helburn was also to play an unobtrusive role in advancing the early careers of Arthur Miller and Tennessee Williams, as well as helping a dozen more less prominent writers, through her Bureau of New Plays and a Playwriting Seminar at the New School. As the present writer was associated with her in these projects, he can testify that, so many years after the springtime of the amateur theatre, Miss Helburn was as eager to discover talent as any ardent neophyte could desire. It was characteristic, indeed, of the Guild's board members that, except in cases where the flesh had to pay its penalty to time, they would never quite lose the bloom of the amateur's capacity for enthusiasm and fresh experience.

Founded in the spring of 1919, the Guild cast about for plays to produce, and the search for material of literary value was, indeed, to be a major activity of the organization, which was to stand or fall more by the quality of the plays it produced than by any other factor. So far as I know, the Guild was at the time the only organization in America to maintain a play department. Josephine Meyer, Courtney Lemon, Ludwig Lewisohn, Ernest Boyd, Anita Block, Harold Clurman, Barrett Clark, and the present writer carried on the world-wide search with the aid of associates in London, Paris, Berlin, and Vienna. The Guild, at first inclined to favor European playwrights on its production schedule and criticized for this tendency during its early years, successively seemed to become the theatre of St. John Ervine, Shaw, Molnar, and other continental Europeans. It began its first season on April 19, 1919, with a stylized Spanish *commedia dell'arte* piece, *The Bonds of Interest* by Benavente, later a Nobel Prize winner. It was a *succés d'estime* but a commercial failure and the Guild, which could only rely on tokens of patronage from the philanthropist Otto Kahn, was in jeopardy.

Fortunately, Langner while hunting in Brentano's basement for printed plays came across *John Ferguson* and recalled that the author was someone with whom he had once debated as a boy in London. St. John Ervine's play, which cost the group under a thousand dollars to produce on May 12, earned a profit of forty thousand dollars and put the Guild on a paying basis. The *John Ferguson* production, staged by Augustin Duncan at the Garrick Theatre which Otto Kahn had made available, was not what Gordon Craig or his disciples had prescribed for the new art. It was "realism," but no one who saw Duncan, Westley, and the former Abbey Theatre actor Dudley Digges in the play was likely to cavil. The realism was that of an inner truth that had rarely been seen on Broadway. It is, indeed, of no small importance that the progressive movement that might have been mired in "artiness" and murky symbolism, if it had stuck to the modernism of the 1910's, leaned toward realism as much as to any other style. This was tantamount to recovering a step in the evolutionary process that had been overlooked by our commercial theatre and over-leaped by art theatre devotees. Inconsistency with the latter's program was in this respect the best thing that could have happened. The climate of America, and for that matter of the rest of the world after 1920, was not of a kind to out mode an honest or sensitive realistic style, for the pressure of common problems was to grow rather than diminish. Besides, selective realism could itself become a style. Nor did it have to dispense at all with poetic overtones and symbolism or suggestive detail, as realists had shown in *The Wild Duck, The Sea-Gull* and *The Cherry Orchard.*

The Guild's last but unsuccessful production in 1919 was a dramatization of William Dean Howell's realistic novel *The Rise of Silas Lapham* and the first production of 1920 was Tolstoy's masterly peasant drama, *The Power of Darkness.* St. John Ervine's *Jane Clegg,* which followed it, represented a dreary struggle among the English poor, and the next production, Strindberg's appalling *Dance of Death,* presented the sex duel of as unlovely a couple as any to be found in the Zola tradition of fiction or drama.

On November 10 of the same year the Guild gave the first professional production of Shaw's *Heartbreak House* on the English-speaking stage and subsequently was to produce fourteen other plays by the master. Five of the Guild productions were world premières, including an intrepid one of *Back to Methuselah* as a cycle, the parts of which were given on three successive evenings at a considerable sacrifice from the Guild's treasury. In rapid succession came successes and failures like Pinski's *The Treasure,* a new American play *John Hawthorne* by David Liebovitz, Milne's *Mr. Pim Passes By,* Molnar's *Liliom,* Verhaerren's *The Cloister, Ambush* by Arthur Richman, Andreyev's *He Who Gets Slapped,* Kaiser's expressionistic *From Morn to Midnight,* the robot-drama *R.U.R.,* Ibsen's *Peer*

Gynt, Elmer Rice's most experimental drama *The Adding Machine,* the Hungarian Vajda's *Fata Morgana,* and Molnar's *The Guardsman.*

On November 24, 1924, with *They Knew What They Wanted,* the Guild came of age so far as American playwriting is concerned. Sidney Howard won the Pulitzer Prize with the play and subsequently contributed *Ned McCobb's Daughter* and *The Silver Cord* to the Guild's program. On January 12, 1925, the organization unfolded the boldest American play of the period, exclusive of O'Neill's work, *Processional,* a jazz symphony of American life and class tensions by John Howard Lawson. It introduced our most brilliant writer of high comedy S. N. Behrman with *The Second Man* in the spring of 1927 after more bouts with European plays by Pirandello, Franz Werfel, Marcel Pagnol, and Shaw. In the fall of that year, the Guild also displayed the cream of American folk plays and the best product of the Southern regional theatre, *Porgy,* in a remarkable stage production by a new director—Rouben Mamoulian, who was to climax his career with *Oklahoma!* and *Carousel.* In 1925, to cast a backward glance, came the group's first venture into the musical field with *The Garrick Gaieties,* which brought the Columbia College graduates Richard Rodgers and Lorenz Hart to the fore, and it is not too much to attribute the introduction of wit into the field of American musical comedy largely to the three editions of this impudent intimate revue between 1925 and 1930.

Finally, on January 9, 1928, the Guild made itself O'Neill's theatre by producing his anti-Babbitt drama *Marco Millions* and substantiated that claim to distinction exactly two weeks later with *Strange Interlude.* The production of this nine-act play, with an intermission for dinner, was an unprecedented event and exceeded the venturesomeness any "little theatre" had displayed on the Western hemisphere. Miss Fontanne reached the peak of her career as a dramatic actress with it, and Philip Moeller's feat of brilliantly staging the mammoth psychological drama may be regarded as the most mature achievement of direction to come out of the "art theatre" movement this side of the Atlantic. Virtue in this particular case had its full terrestrial reward, and 432 consecutive performances in New York set a record for the Guild just as the decade, which had been a prosperous one not only for the Guild, came to an inglorious end.

A chronicle of the theatre of the twenties must not, however, create the impression that everything was the monopoly of little theatres that had ceased to be little. The period was simply too enterprising to belong solely to the Provincetown Playhouse and the Theatre Guild. Other aspiring groups and individual Broadway producers added substantially to the theatrical content.

Among the supplementary ventures perhaps the most notable was that of actors who in 1922 created The Actors' Theatre, first under the name of "Equity Players." Actors' Equity Association, greatly strengthened since the victorious actors' strike of 1919, provided the initial inspiration. One hundred and fifty Equity members helped to finance the first season, and the first board of directors was appointed by the Equity Council. The enterprise entered Broadway without preliminary skirmishes in the Village and rashly offered ten plays during its first season. Dedicated at first to producing only American plays, the company introduced John Howard Lawson with his socially charged expressionist drama *Roger Bloomer.* Other productions of some note were Jesse Lynch Williams' unconventional comedy *Why Not?* and Rachel Crothers' *Expressing Willie.* In the interests of experimentation, the group also gave special matinee performances, using a policy that the Theatre Guild also followed for a time with such plays as the Belgian Emile Verhaerren's symbolist drama *The Cloister* and Wilhelm von Scholz's *The Race With the Shadow.* The Actors' Company, however, made the strongest impression only after abandoning the all-American policy during its third season for want of good native material and turning to modern classics with *Candida, The Wild Duck,* and *Hedda Gabler.* Among these the Dudley Digges' production of *The Wild Duck,* with Henry Travers and Blanche Yurka in the cast, was the most memorable. Although short-lived, the Actors' Company set standards of ensemble acting that even the Theatre Guild was unable to maintain consistently after *John Ferguson.*

The effort of the actors to create a theatre of their own had its complement in a trend toward creating a theatre run by playwrights. A not particularly distinguished Dramatists Theatre made the first attempt. A second one by the New Playwrights Company, with assistance from Otto Kahn, was decidedly more unconventional and lasted three seasons. The novelist John Dos Passos contributed *The Moon Is A Gong,* a satirical expressionist piece with animadversions against Tammany, anti-radical legislation, prosperity-worship, and the Arrow Collar ideal of young manhood. The veteran Socialist Upton Sinclair took up the cudgels in behalf of imprisoned Western labor organizers in *Singing Jailbirds.* Paul Sifton, who was later to have productions from the Guild and the Group Theatre, deprecated the Ford transmission belt factory system in *The Belt.* John Howard Lawson unleashed another expressionist vaudeville, *Loud Speaker.* Em Jo Basshe, a new playwright, who had a greater talent than ever achieved fruition, charged a Negro folk drama with something more than conventional religious enthusiasm and folk humor in *Earth;* and Michael Gold, later a Daily Worker columnist but more notably the author of a vivid book about East Side life, splashed color in his Mexican drama *Fiesta.* The New Playwrights Company, which carried on an unequal battle with Broadway and called a halt in 1927, was an exotic bloom. It was a politically radical theatre with a Greenwich Village coloration. Since it anticipated somewhat the later drama of the depression, it reminds us that even the decade of prosperity was charged with social conflict. In general, however, as Joseph Wood Krutch correctly points out in *The American Drama since 1918,* "the radical who got a hearing was the radical whose criticism was directed rather at the culture than the political organization of America." It is also noteworthy that the thunder from the left in those days crackled, as a rule, with laughter rather than denunciation.

Finally, a large proportion of the period's meritorious productions came under the auspices of the commercial managements so utterly despised by art theatre apostles. Even at its progressive best, "Broadway," to be sure, functioned haphazardly, created no organizational theatres, and operated entirely according to the taste, whim, and financial status of the manager. But he was apt to be either a quick-witted or serious-minded individual. He was affected by the élan of the post-war years, especially by the growing sophistication and discrimination of the public. He followed its interest in psychological discoveries, its general scepticism, and its inclination to take a dim view of moral uplift. Since he was aware of advances in European stagecraft and of the experiments of the little theatre, especially when these began to "pay off" in the conspicuous case of the Theatre Guild, he was ready enough to take advantage of modern scenic design. He also adopted the new lighting that unified the stage picture, drenched it in the mood and spirit of the play, and gave expressive emphasis to the action by means of light and shade. When he found new playwrights, who had served apprenticeships in the little theatres or sprang full-grown upon the Broadway stage, he accepted their plays and often did as well by them as the institutional theatres. He was in fact in a good financial position to compete with artistic groups when it came to taking options on plays and promising expensive productions and large audiences. American business is rarely caught napping. The commercial theatre absorbed the taste, artistry, and even the venturesomeness of the so-called art theatre to a greater degree than the pioneers generally cared to admit.

The well-advertised conservatism of Brock Pemberton, for example, did not prevent him from producing two of Pirandello's most original ventures in playmaking, *Six Characters in Search of an Author* and *The Living Mask* (*Henry IV*), although it could be argued that these plays would have had more success if they had been produced by an artistically unified group. It was Brock Pemberton, too, who produced Maxwell Anderson's first poetic play, *White Desert,* in 1923. Anderson's and Stallings' *What Price Glory?,* which shattered precedents with its frankness and its anti-romantic treatment of war, was produced and directed by Arthur Hopkins. To Mr. Hopkins, in association with the *avant garde* artist Robert Edmond Jones, also goes the credit, as we noted earlier, for Tolstoy's *Redemption,* Benelli's *The Jest, Richard III,* and the Barrymore *Hamlet,* all of them high points in the art of the theatre. He also gave O'Neill his first popular success with *Anna Christie* after another Broadway individualist, John D. Williams, brought out his first full-length drama *Beyond the Horizon.* Mr. Hopkins furthered the career of Philip Barry with *Paris Bound,* and ventured with Sophie Treadwell's decidedly stylized *Machinal.* Winthrop Ames presented Galsworthy's candid social drama *Loyalties* and Philip Barry's first whimsy *White Wings.* Gilbert Miller was responsible for the unusual fantasy *Berkeley Square* and Herman Shumlin for John Wexley's powerful prison melodrama *The Last Mile.* Jed Harris, following a career in some respects the very apotheosis of "Broadway," produced vigorous Americana with *Love 'Em and Leave 'Em, Broadway, The Royal Family,* and *The Front Page.* Even Sam Harris, associate of George M. Cohan and definitely a deposit from an older stream of theatre, produced *Rain,* which was quite a departure for its time; *Icebound,* which marked a divorce from old-fashioned melodramas, for Owen Davis, Sr.; and Maurine Watkins' little less than excoriating satire *Chicago.* And it was William Brady, known for such antiquities as *Way Down East, The Two Orphans,* and *Trilby,* who accepted Elmer Rice's *Street Scene* after it had been turned down by all the progressive producing units. If neither critics nor playgoers in New York have felt any great obligation to behave benignly toward advanced groups that expect special dispensation for their productions, the reason is not necessarily philistinism. It merely happens that the producers that did not drape the flag of art across their shoulders could also play an honorable part in their hit and miss fashion.

It is characteristic of American life that it does not organize itself conspicuously for art. The twenties did not witness the development of mass subscription audiences like the *Volksbühne* under the Weimar Republic, did not encourage and hardly thought of developing state-subsidized theatres, and built no imposing temples to theatrical art. The decade was an optimistic scramble for success, in the theatre as much as in other kinds of business. The shortcomings of such disorganized activity were manifest then, and were to imperil the stage more than once in the next decades. Saroyan's *Time of Your Life* line, "No foundation—all the way down the line," applicable to much of life, could be echoed in nearly every playhouse. But the wayward state of the stage was somewhat mitigated by the existence of the Theatre Guild and the Provincetown Playhouse, and the vitality and effervescence of the age gave us the rest of a bouncing theatre. Europe could wonder at how things somehow got done in the land of wildcat enterprise. Europe had also lost its monopoly on progressive drama, and it was not long before the tide of dramatic production reversed itself sufficiently for European theatres to be quite as eager to import American plays as we had been to import theirs. Plays by O'Neill, Anderson, Rice, Treadwell, and others began to appear on their stages as frequently as those of Shaw, Milne, Molnar, Schnitzler, Werfel, and Capek appeared on ours. So far as the theatre is concerned, the American century was born in 1919.

5.

Whether the lively decade gave us many—or any—masterpieces is a question that need not detain us here. It would be difficult, in any case, to sustain the position that we had much or anything to set beside the best work of Shaw, Synge, O'Casey, and Chekhov as a gift to the century. And it would be rash to maintain that many of the plays that aroused enthusiasm have not lost their lustre or become threadbare. It is not for its isolated peaks but for a general elevation of the landscape that the period will be known. Nor is it necessary to insist that the iridescence of the flora was unfading to acknowledge the presence of bloom. Stringent criticism will indeed find cankers in many a rose and a more probing approach than this brief survey can afford would fill more than one solid volume. It has, in fact, already filled several.[1] It is more to the point here to review the characteristics of the decade's playwriting.

It must be noted from the start that the age was not distinguished in analysis and that its profundities will not exactly bear plumbing. The playwrights seized upon ideas and used them when, as a matter of history, most of them had already lost their novelty and had become commonplace. This was perhaps just as well, since it is easier for dramatists to assume a general understanding than to have to argue their points from a special outlook within the brief compass of a two and a half hour production. The few who have done so through the ages with any sort of success can be counted on one hand, and even they, including Shaw himself, will be found to have been less original than derivative in their thought. A few of our writers, O'Neill most conspicuously, did alight upon modern speculation with all the eagerness of neophytes, but even O'Neill had greater success in communicating feeling than thought, and made an impression largely through his aptitude for charged, sometimes surcharged, theatricality rather than through any revelations that he brought to us. Less ambitious playwrights were content to brush the flower of an idea in a carefree way and collect a little pollen which they promptly dropped on the stage platform with considerable insouciance.

[1] See the bibliography at the end of this book.

Freudian psychology proved attractive, especially as disseminated by popularizers like André Tridon. Havelock Ellis was avidly read, and Krafft-Ebing, Stekel, Adler, and Jung were dipped into. An oedipus complex, a regression to childhood, a slight case of sex inversion, a hypertrophied maternal instinct, or an undernourished or overfed libido was apt to win a nod or an embrace from playwrights and their public. This manifestation of the time-spirit is prominently represented in Sidney Howard's *The Silver Cord,* O'Neill's *Desire Under the Elms* and *Strange Interlude,* Virgil Geddes' *The Earth Between,* and Maxwell Anderson's *Gypsy.* War was waged within the theatre, as it was waged in books, against "Puritanism." The unhappiness and failures attributed to it were grist to every dramatic mill, and even an old-timer like Owen Davis, Sr. ground with it in *Icebound.* The chivalric code of the old South was also a subject for deprecation, and the George Abbott and Ann Preston Bridgers drama *Coquette* in 1927, which took note of it, provided Helen Hayes with one of her successful character roles. In *They Knew What They Wanted* Sidney Howard took a situation that the older theatre would have concluded with tragedy for the perpetrators of adultery and resolved it with an unwonted show of reasonableness on the part of the husband. George Kelly in *Craig's Wife* gave an accounting of the American middle-class woman that did not redound to her credit when he dramatized the displacement of love by compensatory possessiveness in her case. But there is no need to multiply examples of how the thread of the "new" psychology and morality ran through the content of dramatic composition. It is an indication that times had changed when the Pulitzer Prize, originally intended to encourage drama that best expressed American life, went to Howard's and Kelly's plays in the middle twenties.

As for the higher struggles of the spirit, which the great world theatre has presented ever since *Prometheus Bound,* more cannot be said than that the division in man's soul drew from O'Neill passionate and imaginative acknowledgments such as *The Hairy Ape, All God's Chillun Got Wings,* and *The Great God Brown,* as well as efforts better in intent than execution such as *Dynamo* and *Lazarus Laughed.* O'Neill also took note of the play of irony and fate in human life, as in *Beyond the Horizon,* and maintained a viewpoint that is hardly the exclusive discovery of the twentieth century.

Of social drama, in the strictly revolutionary sense in which the term was employed after 1930, there was little. There were few harangues on social justice and few blueprints for political salvation; there was little special pleading in the theatre and not much tipping of the scales in favor of a concrete program. The problem play, it can be said, was generally relieved of its sociological somberness; rather it was dispensed with the lightness of comedy of manners that appears in Philip Barry's *Paris Bound.* In an undoctrinaire sense, however, the drama was variously social minded. If the term is stretched sufficiently, a substantial part of the playwrights' output could be called social drama. It merely took forms and touched upon themes that latter-day conservatives have accepted as unexceptionable and latter-day radicals have considered inacceptably vague or mild.

Criticism, as previously noted, centered on puritanism and on narrow upper-class attitudes, as in Barry's *Holiday.* Attacks were made on the vulgarization of art, with special reference to popular entertainment, as in the Kaufman farces *Merton of the Movies* and *June Moon.* The theatre, in fact, nourished itself on all the absurdities of the age of yellow journalism, publicity-fanned murder trials, racketeering, prizefighting, prohibition-dodging and bootlegging. But the note of deprecation, when present at all, was implicit rather than explicit. We were, at least, spared the fingershaking of earlier decades when dramatists had to make a pretense of moralizing in case they wanted to make a dishonest dollar by vending sensationalism. The acceptable plays of the twenties were mercifully free of cant and hypocrisy. They were with few exceptions tough-fibred and unsentimental. It was also plain that the playwrights who described the antic aspects of the American scene derived a good deal of zest from them, even when they withheld approval. Whatever indignation they may have felt was sublimated into mockery. The truth is that they were half in love with what their minds despised, if they applied any mind at all to their material. As a rule, they had one foot, if not both feet, in the world that they criticized—a statement that applies perhaps as much to the novelists of the period (Scott Fitzgerald and Sinclair Lewis, for example) as to the Kaufman and Hecht type of merry-go-round *aficionado.* When a number of the playwrights sobered up in the next decade of economic neuralgia and political anxiety it was not always to the advantage of good playwriting and theatre.

An American type of farce-comedy, breezy, topical, and rough-edged, arose in contradistinction to suave continental humor and Shavian dialectics. Satire could thrive especially well on the life and the manners of Mr. & Mrs. Babbitt during the Harding-Coolidge jubilee, on the strenuous piety of revivalist preachers, on the rampaging rotarianism of the elect, on the lucubrations of the suburban mentality, and on the bland complacencies of supersalesmanship. Practical playwrights found profitable provocation for a snort or a chuckle in all the manifestations of a supremely confident materialism "on the make." The more affronted intellectual or artist winged his way to the left bank of the Seine on inflated European currency.

Writing in character (that is, suiting style and structure to the subject of crass worldliness and resilient aggressiveness), the American farceur perfected the racy "wisecrack" as an equivalent for literary wit. He maintained no consistent position in the plays, as if to stress the point that the characters had no consistency except in making inconsistency a way of life and honoring adaptibility as the supreme desideratum. He resolved situations with precisely those fortuitous occurrences which the characters, the vulgarians or "pushers," always expected from life. A nation indomitably resourceful and phenomenally successful had its exaggerated summation in these farces. The Broadway fables of a young hopeful's triumph were all metonymies of a nation confidently moving ahead toward "bigger and better" things. And even the fastidious observer could be swept from his critical pedestal by these farces long enough to enjoy a whirl with their uninhibited characters. If these were, moreover, anything but characters in any three-dimensional sense, they were very much "characters" in the colloquial sense of personalities whom we identify with some obtrusive trait. In a thousand years perhaps, when the distance between the sixteenth and the twentieth centuries will seem much shorter than now, historians may refer to these characters as figures in an American *commedia dell' arte* or in an American "comedy of humors."

It cannot be stressed too greatly for other nations, and it should not have to be stressed at all for countrymen, that the playwright of the twenties painted a picture not to be taken at face value. A sixteenth century Spaniard would have had a surprise in store for him if he had taken the measure of the English people from the cowards, braggarts, and eccentrics of Elizabethan comedies and pamphlets. The followers of Hitler, Mussolini, and Hirohito, we know, got a few surprises themselves from England and the United States; and any other nation that were to take theatrical versions of America for gospel truth might discover that it is feasible to make a distinction between fiction and reality. There is an art to understanding art that neither sociologists nor politicians seem to have quite mastered. Our farceurs saw America through a temperament, their own or Broadway's, and used ingredients of the national life for the purpose of creating theatre rather than sociology in any reliable sense of the term. Far more damning than anything they were inclined to say about our way of life would have been their being afraid to say it. Their uninhibited deviltry was itself a sign of the buoyant state of the nation that gave rise to their humor and not only condoned but enjoyed it.

The Kaufman relay teams were not alone in reaping reputation and monetary reward for tongue-in-cheek mimicry. High-pressure salesmanship and its invulnerable optimism gave George Kelly the matter and tone for *The Show-Off,* and for once this fundamental moralist who sometimes frustrated his vaudevillian talent rode herd on folly with abandon. One playwright proved that it was even possible, if not especially profitable, to create a poetry of madness out of this material: John Howard Lawson, who had one of the most brilliant if least disciplined talents in the theatre of the period, made his "jazz symphony" of America *Processional* an imaginative gambol as well as a mordant commentary; and his *Roger Bloomer* gave a nightmare quality to a young man's inability to join the carnival of the golden calf. For that matter, even George S. Kaufman, who is not usually associated with poetry, joined his wit to the Celtic whimsy of Marc Connelly and taking a cue from a German play, delivered an imaginative satire in the *Beggar on Horseback* phantasmagoria of big business. Francis Faragoh's contribution to the Neighborhood Playhouse, *Pinwheel,* made a gaudy kaleidoscope of the urban American scene, and Lawson's *Loud Speaker* turned it into a giddy extravaganza in 1927. When Elmer Rice considered the standardization of the average mind in an age of standardized mass production, he composed his best imaginative drama, *The Adding Machine.* The Theatre Guild made one of its most original productions, with brilliant settings by Lee Simonson, out of this Passion of Mr. Zero, the bookkeeper who was ultimately displaced by an adding machine after having become one himself. He murdered his employer and was duly executed, but when he found himself in an elysium he fled in horror because an afterworld of happiness offended his standardized notions of right and wrong. Finally, O'Neill wrote his best, if acrid, romantic play and his first comedy when he made the fabled Venetian traveler Marco Polo an avatar of babbitism in *Marco Millions*. Most of the writing in fantasy during the period was, in fact, inspired by an aversion to its realities. The only notable exception was John Balderston's *Berkeley Square,* in which the relativity of time was the dramatic device and part of the point, and in which fantasy was largely innocent of a social animus against modern times.

In spite of a soaring stockmarket and a determination to sell America as high as possible, there were, of course, poor people and disgruntled ones even then. Arthur Richman's *Ambush,* one of the first American plays to be produced by the Theatre Guild, dramatized the economic anxieties of an underpaid white collar worker. Maxwell Anderson wrote one of his best comedies, and a rueful one, on the problems of marriage for young people with incomes too meagre to sustain a romantic relation. In *Machinal,* Sophie Treadwell compassionately transmuted the struggles of a woman employee by means of the expressionist technique into a theatrical *tour de force*. And Elmer Rice wrote his *chef d'oeuvre* with his *Street Scene* cross-section of life in New York's slum tenements. It was as close as any American play would come to the "slice-of-life" ideal of European naturalism. Dramatic treatments of such themes in the thirties would have ended in a conversion to radicalism as in Odets' *Awake and Sing*. But the dramatist of the twenties, as in these instances, was more apt to take the facts and let the moral go. Salvation was, in any case, a theatrical discovery of the depression decade in America.

This was the case, by and large, even when the playwright joined the pitched battles of the period. Even then he did not feel obliged to adhere to a direct line of presentation and strictly Marxist formulations did not force themselves upon him. In extreme cases, he at least stylized his treatment, as did Lawson, in a fanciful manner that the insurgents of the next decade and the author himself came to regard as evasiveness. Stylization was an attribute even of Lawson's sanguine report on world revolution, *The International;* Joseph Wood Krutch has aptly called the writing "a sort of futuristic shorthand." Capital and labor at this time locked horns frequently, strikes sometimes flared into riots, the romantically anarcho-syndicalist "I.W.W." labor union was active on the West Coast and occasionally lynch mobs made up of respectable citizens went on a rampage. On the one hand, there were outcries against social wrong and perversions of justice; on the other, alarmed visions of bolsheviks, anarchists, and hoboes undermining our solid gold nation.

The end of the first World War and the Russian Revolution were followed for a time by red scares, repressions, and the application of anti-sedition laws against dissidents. These subjects cropped up in a number of the plays already mentioned, as in the strike scenes of *Processional* in which a strike leader is beaten up. The treatment is farcical, if also mordant, when his pockets are emptied of its contents by the vigilantes, whereupon a picture of the victim's mother falls into their hands and they draw themselves up to salute "His Mother." One conspicuous miscarriage of justice that the world has not been allowed to forget, the Sacco and Vanzetti case, inspired the period's most vigorous drama of social protest, *Gods of the Lightning,* which Maxwell Anderson wrote with the journalist, Harold Hickerson. Mr. Anderson was to return to the theme poetically in *Winterset* in the nineteen thirties. But, in spite of the tenor of *Gods of the Lightning,* which anticipated the journalistic propaganda type of drama that grew apace in the thirties, and probably more than either the author or admirers of his verse plays would care to admit, a poet's indignation lay at the core of the play. Playwrights also found a provocative subject in racial discrimination, although not quite so often as in later years. Paul Green, emerging out of regionalism with a social history of the Southern Negro, won a hearing in New York and a Pulitzer Prize for *In Abraham's Bosom,* and O'Neill treated the theme of miscegenation in *All God's Chillun Got Wings*. Still the treatment in each case distinguishes the plays from their successors after 1930. Mr. Green kept indignation in check, refrained from inflammatory preachment, and let his chronicle of a Negro's struggles for a good life speak for itself. Mr. O'Neill sublimated his story and turned the topical reality of racial division into a Strindbergian sex duel with a metaphysical wrinkle and with poetic overtones. His earlier drama *Emperor*

Jones merely recapitulated experiences of the race in the atavistic hallucinations of his Negro character, who far from being the immediate victim of oppression had himself so victimized his people that they turned against him.

Since, moreover, the first World War had been viewed with misgivings by many liberals who would virtually have been interventionists against Hitler in 1940, and since doubts turned to cynicism after Versailles, writers were particularly loud in making war on war. Yet it is characteristic of the playwriting of that time, that, except in Gilbert Emery's *The Hero* and Robert Sherwood's *Waterloo Bridge,* neither of them very successful, the tone of the campaign was exuberant rather than mournful or slashing. By contrast with the intense writers of fiction Dos Passos and E. E. Cummings who gave us *Three Soldiers* and *The Enormous Room,* not to mention both novelists and dramatists of the thirties, the playwrights were at their best in mockery. Robert Sherwood, who had been wounded in the war and was later to write trenchant drama in *Idiot's Delight* and *There Shall Be No Night,* was from the start among the most disillusioned. This did not prevent him from expressing his outlook in the comic pseudo-historical terms of *The Road to Rome.* And Laurence Stallings, a fighting marine who carried the mark of Armageddon on his body, wrote the most exuberant drama of the age in *What Price Glory?* His collaborator was Maxwell Anderson whose pacifism had lost him university and newspaper posts before he found himself ensconced in the offices of Pulitzer's New York World with Mr. Stallings. "Debunking" or the sport of deflating romantic notions and reputations was the special delight of the age. In the theatre, as to an even larger degree in published biographies of the great, debunking was processed with suave innuendo or with downright *Kitsch.*

Even in high comedy, the nap of which had hardly more than been creased in America before 1914, the playwright was either amiable or airy. In the thirties, S. N. Behrman was to front a harassed world with *Biography, Rain from Heaven, End of Summer, Wine of Choice,* and *No Time for Comedy.* In the twenties, Mr. Behrman was defeated in his effort to probe when he turned to megalomaniacal business symptoms in *Meteor.* But he just about wrote the purest and I believe still the best American high comedy, *The Second Man,* before he discovered social conscience as a theme. Edwin Justin Mayer made mischief his business in the Benvenuto Cellini story of *The Firebrand* and in the Henry Fielding, Jonathan Wild matter of *The Children of Darkness.* In the latter play, he performed the feat of even combining poetry with the "dry mock" and with comedy of eighteenth century manners. (This maverick drama, which is certainly not unflawed, had an unhappy career on the stage, but the present writer finds himself in distinguished, if isolated, company in agreeing with Mr. Krutch that it is a masterpiece.) Preston Sturges, who oddly enough came closest to turning out barbed social satire for the notoriously satire-shy motion picture industry, gave the twenties a politically innocent high comedy with *Strictly Dishonorable.* Philip Barry's best comedy of rebellion *Holiday* baited philistia in behalf of self-realization rather than a political program. Edward Childs Carpenter advanced as far as he and others could move from sentimentality even as late as 1928 when he brought detached amusement to the subject of illegitimacy in *Bachelor Born.* Clare Kummer, who had promised to go further on the road of satire, stopped in her tracks, and Rachel Crothers continued to pitch her problem comedies on the level of women's magazine fiction. High comedy of social excoriation and conflict of ideas such as Shaw had been writing for nearly thirty years was simply not in the cards for the American twenties.

At the opposite extreme of poetic drama, finally, the vista was full of unsuccessful effort at romanticism by Sidney Howard (*Swords*), Maxwell Anderson (*White Desert*), O'Neill (*The Fountain*), and others. Howard abandoned the effort in favor of the solid realism for which he became known, and Maxwell Anderson, whose prose is often extremely vivid, began to prevail with verse drama only in 1930 when *Elizabeth the Queen* succeeded. Mention might also be made of Dan Totheroh's prairie tragedy of love, *Wild Birds,* which won some esteem in 1925. The more acceptable results came chiefly from the field of folk drama. The examples of Lady Gregory and Synge and the desire to create drama of the soil inspired the regional theatres, and the years 1923 and 1924 gave accent to the trend with Broadway productions of Lulu Vollmer's *Sun-up* and Hatcher Hughes' North Carolina mountaineer drama *Hell-Bent for Heaven,* which received the then doubtful accolade of the Pulitzer Prize committee. But success was unqualified only in the case of one-act plays like Paul Green's *No 'Count Boy* and *White Dresses* and E. P. Conkle's *Minnie Field* and the other mid-western sketches published under the collective title of *Crick Bottom Plays.* It may be curious, in fact, though not inexplicable, that some of our noteworthy distillations of the folk spirit, such as Marc Connelly's *The Green Pastures* and Lynn Riggs' *Green Grow the Lilacs* (later *Oklahoma!*), should have been produced in the next decade when the disposition of the country was far from idyllic. When the folk dramatist of the twenties graduated from his regional apprenticeship, as Mr. Green did in *In Abraham's Bosom,* he was apt to cross over into the territory of social analysis while his purely local matter, as in *The Field God,* failed to capture Broadway. The sole and shining exception was *Porgy.* It was the purest, and perhaps for that reason the most colorful, product of the interest in folk drama.

The age, as a whole, was urban in outlook rather than rustic, realistic rather than romantic, sceptical rather than believing, and buoyantly worldly rather than moonstruck. The theatrical renaissance in an efficiently industrial and aggressively prosperous America was to be found at the opposite pole from the Celtic renaissance. It was rugged and brash by comparison with the British theatre, and remarkably good-humored, for all its strenuousness, by comparison with the often shrieking Central European, especially German, drama of the time. For all the Waste Land, "lost generation" clamor of the refined, the playwrights did not propose to end the world with either a bang or a whimper. Even O'Neill did not, by and large, represent doomsday as much as the struggle of souls toward integration. If his characters tried to weld what had been sundered by modernity with scant success, if they were unable to find a new connection with the universe when the old religious one had vanished, they twisted themselves at least into heroic gestures of defiance or pain. Even the foredoomed subintellectual stoker of *The Hairy Ape* was not another "Sweeney among the nightingales"; if he was a brute like T. S. Eliot's Sweeney, he was at least a questing one suffering on the rack of his own aspiration to become completely man. In the exception that occurs to me, *Beyond the Horizon,* where the main character is passive, doom came from the hand of fate and not from a social explosion. And if O'Neill set down dénouements of catastrophe on stony soil, as he did so hardily in *Desire Under the Elms,* he nevertheless affirmed the passionate nature of men and women. O'Neill had a good deal of that tragic sense of life that the hidalgo philosopher Unamuno considers a perquisite of greatness. When true greatness is denied to Mr. O'Neill by detractors of his talent, it is not for any want of courage but for want of language; not for any lack of vaulting content but for lack of consistent execution; not for any meagerness of spirit but for an insufficiency of discipline. Crushing the bitter grape against his palate, he had the intoxication of a tragedian. Even incompletely realized tragedy contains exaltations that merely querulous and complaining dramatists never feel and never communicate.

Although our stage was anything but unaware of frustration, whether caused by Fate, psychological complication or economics, it was decidedly not a whining theatre. Our dramatists, working in the diverse forms and styles natural to them or suitable to their aims, formed, on the whole, a bracing fellowship. The theatre that developed them and that they in turn helped so substantially to develop was, in the main, exhilarating. One does not have to place it beside the glorious climaxes of theatrical history to say that much for the twenties.

"The Hairy Ape"

BY EUGENE O'NEILL

First presented by the Provincetown Players, at the Provincetown Theatre, New York, March 9, 1922, with the following cast:

ROBERT SMITH "YANK"	Louis Wolheim
PADDY	Henry O'Neill
LONG	Harold West
MILDRED DOUGLAS	Mary Blair
HER AUNT	Eleanor Hutchinson
SECOND ENGINEER	Jack Gude
A GUARD	Harry Gottlieb
A SECRETARY	Harold McGee

Scene I. The firemen's forecastle of an ocean liner—an hour after sailing from New York.

Scene II. Section of promenade deck, two days out—morning.

Scene III. The stokehole. A few minutes later.

Scene IV. Same as Scene I. Half an hour later.

Scene V. Fifth Avenue, New York. Three weeks later.

Scene VI. An island near the city. The next night.

Scene VII. In the city. About a month later.

Scene VIII. In the city. Twilight of the next day.

THE O'NEILL PRODUCTION RECORD

Before 1920:

BOUND EAST FOR CARDIFF. (One-act play) Prod. by the Provincetown Players at Wharf Theatre, Provincetown, Mass., summer, 1916.

THIRST. (One-act play) Late summer, 1916, on a fourth bill of plays.

BEFORE BREAKFAST. (One-act play, a dramatic monologue) Prod. by the Provincetown Players at the Playwrights' Theatre (popularly known as the Provincetown), December 1916.

FOG. (One-act play) Prod. by the Provincetown Players, January 1917.

THE SNIPER. (One-act play) Prod. by the Provincetown Players, February 1917.

IN THE ZONE. (One-act play) Prod. by the Washington Square Players, October 1917.

THE LONG VOYAGE HOME. (One-act play) Prod. by the Provincetown Players, Nov. 2, 1917.

ILE. (One-act play) Prod. by the Provincetown Players, November 30, 1917.

THE ROPE. (One-act play) Prod. by the Provincetown Players, April 1918.

WHERE THE CROSS IS MADE. (One-act play) Prod. by the Provincetown Players, Nov. 1918.

THE MOON OF THE CARIBBEES. (One-act play) Prod. by the Provincetown Players, Dec. 1918.

THE DREAMY KID. (One-act play) Prod. by the Provincetown Players, October 1919.

After 1920:

BEYOND THE HORIZON. Prod. by John D. Williams at the Morosco Theatre, Feb. 2, 1920.

CHRIS CHRISTOPHERSON. (First version of *Anna Christie*) Prod. by George C. Tyler, Atlantic City, March 8, 1920.

EXORCISM. (One-act play) Prod. by the Provincetown Players, March 1920.

THE EMPEROR JONES. Prod. by the Provincetown Players, November 3, 1920.

DIFF'RENT. Prod. by the Provincetown Players, Dec. 27, 1920.

GOLD. Prod. by John D. Williams at the Frazee Theatre, June 1, 1921.

ANNA CHRISTIE. Prod. by Arthur Hopkins at the Vanderbilt Theatre, Nov. 2, 1921.

THE STRAW. Prod. by George C. Tyler at the Greenwich Village Theatre, Nov. 10, 1921.

THE FIRST MAN. Prod. at the Neighborhood Playhouse, March 4, 1922.

THE HAIRY APE. Prod. by the Provincetown Players, March 9, 1922.

WELDED. Prod. by Macgowan, Jones and O'Neill in association with the Selwyns at the 39th Street Theatre, March 17, 1924.

THE ANCIENT MARINER. (From the poem by Coleridge) Prod. by the Provincetown Playhouse, Inc., April 6, 1924.

ALL GOD'S CHILLUN GOT WINGS. Prod. by the Provincetown Playhouse, Inc., May 15, 1924.

S. S. GLENCAIRN. (A sequence of the sea-pieces: Moon of the Caribbees, Bound East for Cardiff, In the Zone, The Long Voyage Home) Prod. by the Barnstormers at Provincetown, Mass., in August 1924, then produced by Macgowan, Jones and O'Neill in New York.

DESIRE UNDER THE ELMS. Prod. by the Provincetown Players, Inc., at the Greenwich Village Theatre, Nov. 11, 1924.

THE FOUNTAIN. Prod. by Macgowan, Jones and O'Neill in association with A. L. Jones and Morris Green at the Greenwich Village Theatre, Dec. 10, 1925.

THE GREAT GOD BROWN. Prod. by Macgowan, Jones and O'Neill at the Greenwich Village Theatre, Jan. 23, 1926.

MARCO MILLIONS. Prod. by the Theatre Guild at the Guild Theatre, Jan. 9, 1928.

STRANGE INTERLUDE. Prod. by the Theatre Guild at the John Golden Theatre, Jan. 30, 1928.

LAZARUS LAUGHED. Prod. by the Pasadena Community Playhouse, Pasadena, Calif., April 1928.

DYNAMO. Prod. by the Theatre Guild at the Martin Beck Theatre, Feb. 11, 1929.

After 1930:

MOURNING BECOME ELECTRA. Prod. by the Theatre Guild at the Guild Theatre, Oct. 26, 1931.

AH, WILDERNESS! Prod. by the Theatre Guild at the Guild Theatre, Oct. 2, 1933.

DAYS WITHOUT END. Prod. by the Theatre Guild at the Guild Theatre, Jan. 8, 1934.

THE ICEMAN COMETH. Prod. by the Theatre Guild at the Martin Beck Theatre, Sept. 2, 1946.

A MOON FOR THE MISBEGOTTEN. Prod. by the Theatre Guild, 1947; withdrawn for recasting after "out-of-town" tryout.

(*See pages 26-27 for an introductory note on O'Neill.*)

SCENE ONE

The firemen's forecastle of a transatlantic liner an hour after sailing from New York for the voyage across. Tiers of narrow, steel bunks, three deep, on all sides. An entrance in rear. Benches on the floor before the bunks. The room is crowded with men, shouting, cursing, laughing, singing—a confused, inchoate uproar swelling into a sort of unity, a meaning—the bewildered, furious, baffled defiance of a beast in a cage. Nearly all the men are drunk. Many bottles are passed from hand to hand. All are dressed in dungaree pants, heavy ugly shoes. Some wear singlets, but the majority are stripped to the waist.

The treatment of this scene, or of any other scene in the play, should by no means be naturalistic. The effect sought after is a cramped space in the bowels of a ship, imprisoned by white steel. The lines of bunks, the uprights supporting them, cross each other like the steel framework of a cage. The ceiling crushes down upon the men's heads. They cannot stand upright. This accentuates the natural stooping posture which shoveling coal and the resultant over-development of back and shoulder muscles have given them. The men themselves should resemble those pictures in which the appearance of Neanderthal Man is guessed at. All are hairy-chested, with long arms of tremendous power, and low, receding brows above their small, fierce, resentful eyes. All the civilized white races are represented, but except for the slight differentiation in color of hair, skin, eyes, all these men are alike.

The curtain rises on a tumult of sound. YANK *is seated in the foreground. He seems broader, fiercer, more truculent, more powerful, more sure of himself than the rest. They respect his superior strength—the grudging respect of fear. Then, too, he represents to them a self-expression, the very last word in what they are, their most highly developed individual.*

VOICES. Gif me trink dere, you!
'Ave a wet!
Salute!
Gesundheit!
Skoal!
Drunk as a lord, God stiffen you!
Here's how!
Luck!
Pass back that bottle, damn you!
Pourin' it down his neck!
Ho, Froggy! Where the devil have you been?
La Touraine.
I hit him smash in yaw, py Gott!
Jenkins—the First—he's a rotten swine——
And the coppers nabbed him—and I run——
I like peer better. It don't pig head gif you.
A slut, I'm sayin'! She robbed me aslape—
To hell with 'em all!
You're a bloody liar!
Say dot again! (*Commotion. Two men about to fight are pulled apart.*)
No scrappin' now!
Tonight——
See who's the best man!
Bloody Dutchman!
Tonight on the for'ard square.
I'll bet on Dutchy.
He packa da wallop, I tella you!
Shut up, Wop!
No fightin', maties. We're all chums, ain't we?
(*A voice starts bawling a song.*)
"Beer, beer, glorious beer!
Fill yourselves right up to here."

YANK (*for the first time seeming to take notice of the uproar about him, turns around threateningly—in a tone of contemptuous authority*). Choke off dat noise! Where d'yuh get dat beer stuff? Beer, hell! Beer's for goils—and Dutchmen. Me for somep'n with a kick to it! Gimme a drink, one of youse guys. (*Several bottles are eagerly offered. He takes a tremendous gulp at one of them; then, keeping the bottle in his hand, glares belligerently at the owner, who hastens to acquiesce in this robbery by saying*) All righto, Yank. Keep it and have another. (YANK *contemptuously turns his back on the crowd again. For a second there is an embarrassed silence. Then——*)

VOICES. We must be passing the Hook.
She's beginning to roll to it.
Six days in hell—and then Southhampton.

Py Yesus, I vish somepody take my first vatch for me!
Gittin' seasick, Square-head?
Drink up and forget it!
What's in your bottle?
Gin.
Dot's nigger trink.
Absinthe? It's doped. You'll go off your chump, Froggy!
Cochon!
Whisky, that's the ticket!
Where's Paddy?
Going asleep.

Sing us that whisky song, Paddy. (*They all turn to an old, wizened Irishman who is dozing, very drunk, on the benches forward. His face is extremely monkey-like with all the sad, patient pathos of that animal in his small eyes.*)

Singa da song, Caruso Pat!
He's gettin' old. The drink is too much for him.
He's too drunk.

PADDY (*blinking about him, starts to his feet resentfully, swaying, holding on to the edge of a bunk*). I'm never too drunk to sing. 'Tis only when I'm dead to the world I'd be wishful to sing at all. (*With a sort of sad contempt.*) "Whisky Johnny," ye want? A chanty, ye want? Now that's a queer wish from the ugly like of you, God help you. But no matther. (*He starts to sing in a thin, nasal, doleful tone*):

Oh, whisky is the life of man!
Whisky! O Johnny! (*They all join in on this.*)
Oh, whisky is the life of man!
Whisky for my Johnny! (*Again chorus.*)
Oh, whisky drove my old man mad!
Whisky! O Johnny!
Oh, whisky drove my old man mad!
Whisky for my Johnny!

YANK (*again turning around scornfully*). Aw hell! Nix on dat old sailing ship stuff! All dat bull's dead, see? And you're dead, too, yuh damned old Harp, on'y yuh don't know it. Take it easy, see. Give us a rest. Nix on de loud noise. (*With a cynical grin.*) Can't youse see I'm tryin' to t'ink?

ALL (*repeating the word after him as one with the same cynical amused mockery*). Think! (*The chorused word has a brazen metallic quality as if their throats were phonograph horns. It is followed by a general uproar of hard, barking laughter.*)

VOICES. Don't be cracking your head wit ut, Yank.
You gat headache, py yingo!
One thing about it—it rhymes with drink!
Ha, ha, ha!
Drink, don't think!
Drink, don't think!
Drink, don't think! (*A whole chorus of voices has taken up this refrain, stamping on the floor, pounding on the benches with fists.*)

YANK (*taking a gulp from his bottle—good-naturedly*). Aw right. Can de noise. I got yuh de foist time. (*The uproar subsides. A very drunken sentimental tenor begins to sing.*):

"Far away in Canada,
Far across the sea,
There's a lass who fondly waits
Making a home for me——"

YANK (*fiercely contemptuous*). Shut up, yuh lousy boob! Where d'yuh get dat tripe? Home? Home, hell! I'll make a home for yuh! I'll knock yuh dead. Home! T'hell wit home! Where d'yuh get dat tripe? Dis is home, see? What d'yuh want wit home? (*Proudly.*) I runned away from mine when I was a kid. On'y too glad to beat it, dat was me. Home was lickings for me, dat's all. But yuh can bet your shoit no one ain't never licked me since! Wanter try it, any of youse? Huh! I guess not. (*In a more placated but still contemptuous tone.*) Goils waitin' for yuh, huh? Aw, hell! Dat's all tripe. Dey don't wait for no one. Dey'd double-cross yuh for a nickel. Dey're all tarts, get me? Treat 'em rough, dat's me. To hell wit 'em. Tarts, dat's what, de whole bunch of 'em.

LONG (*very drunk, jumps on a bench excitedly, gesticulating with a bottle in his hand*). Listen 'ere, Comrades! Yank 'ere is right. 'E says this 'ere stinkin' ship is our 'ome. And 'e says as 'ome is 'ell. And 'e's right! This is 'ell. We lives in 'ell, Comrades—and right enough we'll die in it. (*Raging.*) And who's ter blame, I arsks yer? We ain't. We wasn't born this rotten way. All men is born free and ekal. That's in the bleedin' Bible, maties. But what d'they care for the Bible—them lazy, bloated swine what travels first cabin? Them's the ones. They dragged us down 'til we're on'y wage slaves in the bowels of a bloody ship, sweatin', burnin' up, eatin' coal dust! Hit's them's ter blame—the damned Capitalist clarss! (*There had been a gradual murmur of contemptuous resentment rising among the men until now he is interrupted by a storm of catcalls, hisses, boos, hard laughter.*)

VOICES. Turn it off!
Shut up!
Sit down!
Closa da face!
Tamn fool! (*Etc.*)

YANK (*standing up and glaring at* LONG). Sit down before I knock yuh down! (LONG *makes haste to efface himself.* YANK *goes on contemptuously.*) De Bible, huh? De Cap'tlist class, huh? Aw nix on dat Salvation Army-Socialist bull. Git a soapbox! Hire a hall! Come and be saved, huh? Jerk us to Jesus, huh? Aw g'wan! I've listened to lots of guys like you, see. Yuh're all wrong. Wanter know what I t'ink? Yuh ain't no good for no one. Yuh're de bunk. Yuh ain't got no noive, get me? Yuh're yellow, dat's what. Yellow, dat's you. Say! What's dem slobs in de foist cabin got to do wit us? We're better men dan dey are, ain't we? Sure! One of us guys could clean up de whole mob with one mit. Put one of 'em down here for one watch in de stokehole, what'd happen? Dey'd carry him off on a stretcher. Dem boids don't amount to nothin'. Dey're just baggage. Who makes dis old tub run? Ain't it us guys? Well den, we belong, don't we? We belong and dey don't. Dat's all. (*A loud chorus of approval.* YANK *goes on.*) As for dis bein' hell—aw, nuts! Yuh lost your noive, dat's what. Dis is a man's job, get me? It belongs. It runs dis tub. No stiffs need apply. But yuh're a stiff, see? Yuh're yellow, dat's you.

VOICES (*with a great hard pride in them*).
Righto!
A man's job!
Talk is cheap, Long.
He never could hold up his end.
Divil take him!
Yank's right. We make it go.
Py Gott, Yank say right ting!
We don't need no one cryin' over us.
Makin' speeches.
Throw him out!
Yellow!
Chuck him overboard!
I'll break his jaw for him!

(*They crowd around* LONG *threateningly.*)

YANK (*half good-natured again—contemptuously*). Aw, take it easy. Leave him alone. He ain't woith a punch. Drink up. Here's how, whoever owns dis. (*He takes a long swallow from his bottle. All drink with him. In a flash all is hilarious amiability again, back-slapping, loud talk, etc.*)

PADDY (*who has been sitting in a blinking, melancholy daze—suddenly cries out in a voice full of old sorrow*). We belong to this, you're saying? We make the ship to go, you're saying? Yerra then, that Almighty God have pity on us! (*His voice runs into the wail of a keen, he rocks back and forth on his bench. The men stare at him, startled and impressed in spite of themselves.*) Oh, to be back in the fine days of my youth, ochone! Oh, there was fine beautiful ships them days—clippers wid tall masts touching the sky—fine strong men in them—men that was sons of the sea as if 'twas the mother that bore them. Oh, the clean skins of them, and the clear eyes, the straight backs and full chests of them! Brave men they was, and bold men surely! We'd be sailing out, bound down round the Horn maybe. We'd be making sail in the dawn, with a fair breeze, singing a chanty song wid no care to it. And astern the land would be sinking low and dying out, but we'd give it no heed but a laugh, and never a look behind. For the day that was, was enough, for we was free men—and I'm thinking 'tis only slaves do be giving heed to the day that's gone or the day to come—until they're old like me. (*With a sort of religious exaltation.*) Oh, to be scudding south again wid the power of the Trade Wind driving her on steady through the nights and the days! Full sail on her! Nights and days! Nights when the foam of the wake would be flaming wid fire, when the sky'd be blazing and winking wid stars. Or the full of the moon maybe. Then you'd see her driving through the gray night, her sails stretching aloft all silver and white, not a sound on the deck, the lot of us dreaming dreams, till you'd believe 'twas no real ship at all you was on but a ghost ship like the *Flying Dutchman* they say does be roaming the seas forevermore widout touching a port. And there was the days, too. A warm sun on the clean decks. Sun warming the blood of you, and wind over the miles of shiny green ocean like strong drink to your lungs. Work—aye, hard work—but who'd mind that at all? Sure, you worked under the sky and 'twas work wid skill and daring to it. And wid the day done, in the dog watch, smoking me pipe at ease, the lookout would be raising land maybe, and we'd see the mountains of South Americy wid the red fire of the setting sun painting their white tops and the clouds floating by them! (*His tone of exaltation ceases. He goes on mournfully.*) Yerra, what's the use of talking? 'Tis a dead man's whisper. (*To* YANK *resentfully.*) 'Twas them days men belonged to ships, not now. 'Twas them days a ship was part of the sea, and a man was part of a ship, and the sea joined all together and made it one. (*Scornfully.*) Is it one wid this you'd be, Yank—black smoke from the funnels smudging the sea, smudging the decks—the bloody engines pounding and throbbing and shaking—wid divil a sight of sun or a breath of clean air—choking our lungs wid coal dust—breaking our backs and hearts in the hell of the stokehole—feeding the bloody furnace—feeding our lives along wid the coal, I'm thinking—caged in by steel from a sight of the sky like bloody apes in the Zoo! (*With a harsh laugh.*) Ho-ho, divil mend you! Is it to belong to that you're wishing? Is it a flesh and blood wheel of the engines you'd be?

YANK (*who has been listening with a contemptuous sneer, barks out the answer*). Sure ting! Dat's me. What about it?

PADDY (*as if to himself—with great sorrow*). Me time is past due. That a great wave wid sun in the heart of it may sweep me over the side sometime I'd be dreaming of the days that's gone!

YANK. Aw, yuh crazy Mick! (*He springs to his feet and advances on* PADDY *threateningly—then stops, fighting some queer struggle within himself—lets his hands fall to his sides—contemptuously.*) Aw, take it easy. Yuh're aw right, at dat. Yuh're bugs, dat's all—nutty as a cuckoo. All dat tripe yuh been pullin'— Aw, dat's all right. On'y it's dead, get me? Yuh don't belong no more, see. Yuh don't get de stuff. Yuh're too old. (*Disgustedly.*) But aw say, come up for air onct in a while, can't yuh? See what's happened since yuh croaked. (*He suddenly bursts forth vehemently, growing more and more excited.*) Say! Sure! Sure I meant it! What de hell— Say, lemme talk! Hey! Hey, you old Harp! Hey, youse guys! Say, listen to me—wait a moment—I gotter talk, see. I belong and he don't. He's dead but I'm livin'. Listen to me! Sure I'm part of de engines! Why de hell not! Dey move, don't dey? Dey're speed, ain't dey! Dey smash trou, don't dey? Twenty-five knots a hour! Dat's goin' some! Dat's new stuff! Dat belongs! But him, he's too old. He gets dizzy. Say, listen. All dat crazy tripe about nights and days; all dat crazy tripe about stars and moons; all dat crazy tripe about suns and winds, fresh air and de rest of it—Aw hell, dat's all a dope dream! Hittin' de pipe of de past, dat's what he's doin'. He's old and don't belong no more. But me, I'm young! I'm in de pink! I move wit it! It, get me! I mean de ting dat's de guts of all dis. It ploughs trou all de tripe he's been sayin'. It blows dat up! It knocks dat dead! It slams dat offen de face of de oith! It, get me! De engines and de coal and de smoke and all de rest of it! He can't breathe and swallow coal dust, but I kin, see? Dat's fresh air for me! Dat's food for me! I'm new, get me? Hell in de stokehole? Sure! It takes a man to work in hell. Hell, sure, dat's my fav'rite climate. I eat it up! I git fat on it! It's me makes it hot! It's me makes it roar! It's me makes it move! Sure, on'y for me everyting stops. It all goes dead, get me? De noise and smoke and all de engines movin' de woild, dey stop. Dere ain't nothin' no more! Dat's what I'm sayin'. Everyting else dat makes de woild move, somep'n makes it move. It can't move witout somep'n else, see? Den yuh get down to me. I'm at de bottom, get me! Dere ain't nothin' foither. I'm de end! I'm de start! I start somep'n and de woild moves! It—dat's me!—de new dat's moiderin' de old! I'm de ting in coal dat makes it boin; I'm steam and oil for de engines; I'm de ting in noise dat makes yuh hear it; I'm smoke and express trains and steamers and factory whistles; I'm de ting in gold dat makes it money! And I'm what makes iron into steel! Steel, dat stands for de whole ting! And I'm steel—steel—steel! I'm de muscles in steel, de punch behind it! (*As he says this he pounds with his fist against the steel bunks. All the men, roused to a pitch of frenzied self-glorification by his speech, do likewise. There is a deafening metallic roar, through which* YANK's *voice can be heard bellowing.*) Slaves, hell! We run de whole woiks. All de rich guys dat tink dey're somep'n, dey ain't nothin'! Dey don't belong. But us guys, we're in de move, we're at de bottom, de whole ting is us! (PADDY *from the start of* YANK's *speech has been taking one gulp after another from his bottle, at first frightenedly, as if he were afraid to listen, then desperately, as if to drown his senses, but finally has achieved complete indifferent, even amused, drunkenness.* YANK *sees his lips moving. He quells the uproar with a shout.*) Hey, youse guys, take it easy! Wait a moment! De nutty Harp is sayin' somep'n.

PADDY (*is heard now—throws his head back with a mocking burst of laughter*). Ho-ho-ho-ho-ho——

YANK (*drawing back his fist, with a snarl*). Aw! Look out who yuh're givin' the bark!

PADDY (*begins to sing the "Miller of Dee" with enormous good nature*).

"I care for nobody, no, not I,
And nobody cares for me."

YANK (*good-natured himself in a flash, interrupts* PADDY *with a slap on the bare back like a report*). Dat's de stuff! Now yuh're gettin' wise to somep'n. Care for nobody, dat's de dope! To hell wit 'em all! And mix on nobody else carin'. I kin care for myself, get me! (*Eight bells sound, muffled, vibrating through the steel walls as if some enormous brazen gong were imbedded in the heart of the ship. All the men jump up mechanically, file through the door silently close upon each other's heels in what is very like a prisoners' lockstep.* YANK *slaps* PADDY *on the back.*) Our watch, yuh old Harp! (*Mockingly.*) Come on down in hell. Eat up de coal dust. Drink in de heat. It's it, see! Act like yuh liked it, yuh better—or croak yuhself.

PADDY (*with jovial defiance*). To the divil wid it! I'll not report this watch. Let thim log me and be damned. I'm no slave the like of you. I'll be sittin' here at me ease, and drinking, and thinking, and dreaming dreams.

YANK (*contemptuously*). Tinkin' and dreamin', what'll that get yuh? What's tinkin' got to do wit it? We move, don't we? Speed, ain't it? Fog, dat's all you stand for. But we drive trou dat, don't we? We split dat up and smash trou—twenty-five knots a hour! (*Turns his back on* PADDY *scornfully.*) Aw, yuh make me sick! Yuh don't belong! (*He strides out the door in rear.* PADDY *hums to himself, blinking drowsily.*)

CURTAIN

SCENE TWO

Two days out. A section of the promenade deck. MILDRED DOUGLAS *and her aunt are discovered reclining in deck chairs. The former is a girl of twenty, slender, delicate, with a pale, pretty face marred by a self-conscious expression of disdainful superiority. She looks fretful, nervous and discontented, bored by her own anemia. Her aunt is a pompous and proud—and fat—old lady. She is a type even to the point of a double chin and lorgnettes. She is dressed pretentiously, as if afraid her face alone would never indicate her position in life.* MILDRED *is dressed all in white.*

The impression to be conveyed by this scene is one of the beautiful, vivid life of the sea all about—sunshine on the deck in a great flood, the fresh sea wind blowing across it. In the midst of this, these two incongruous, artificial figures, inert and disharmonious, the elder like a gray lump of dough touched up with rouge, the younger looking as if the vitality of her stock had been sapped before she was conceived, so that she is the expression not of its life energy but merely of the artificialities that energy had won for itself in the spending.

MILDRED (*looking up with affected dreaminess*). How the black smoke swirls back against the sky! Is it not beautiful?

AUNT (*without looking up*). I dislike smoke of any kind.

MILDRED. My great-grandmother smoked a pipe—a clay pipe.

AUNT (*ruffling*). Vulgar!

MILDRED. She was too distant a relative to be vulgar. Time mellows pipes.

AUNT (*pretending boredom but irritated*). Did the sociology you took up at college teach you that—to play the ghoul on every possible occasion, excavating old bones? Why not let your great-grandmother rest in her grave?

MILDRED (*dreamily*). With her pipe beside her—puffing in Paradise.

AUNT (*with spite*). Yes, you are a natural born ghoul. You are even getting to look like one, my dear.

MILDRED (*in a passionless tone*). I detest you, Aunt. (*Looking at her critically.*) Do you know what you remind me of? Of a cold pork pudding against a background of linoleum tablecloth in the kitchen of a—but the possibilities are wearisome. (*She closes her eyes.*)

AUNT (*with a bitter laugh*). Merci for your candor. But since I am and must be your chaperon—in appearance, at least—let us patch up some sort of armed truce. For my part you are quite free to indulge any pose of eccentricity that beguiles you—as long as you observe the amenities——

MILDRED (*drawling*). The inanities?

AUNT (*going on as if she hadn't heard*). After exhausting the morbid thrills of social service work on New York's East Side—how they must have hated you, by the way, the poor that you made so much poorer in their own eyes!—you are now bent on making your slumming international. Well, I hope Whitechapel will provide the needed nerve tonic. Do not ask me to chaperon you there, however. I told your father I would not. I loathe deformity. We will hire an army of detectives and you may investigate everything—they allow you to see.

MILDRED (*protesting with a trace of genuine earnestness*). Please do not mock at my attempts to discover how the other half lives. Give me credit for some sort of groping sincerity in that at least. I would like to help them. I would like to be some use in the world. Is it my fault I don't know how? I would like to be sincere, to touch life somewhere. (*With weary bitterness.*) But I'm afraid I have neither the vitality nor integrity. All that was burnt out in our stock before I was born. Grandfather's blast furnaces, flaming to the sky, melting steel, making millions—then father keeping those home fires burning, making more millions—and little me at the tailend of it all. I'm a waste product in the Bessemer process—like the millions. Or rather, I inherit the acquired trait of the by-product, wealth, but none of the energy, none of the strength of the steel that made it. I am sired by gold and damned by it, as they say at the race track—damned in more ways than one. (*She laughs mirthlessly.*)

AUNT (*unimpressed — superciliously*). You seem to be going in for sincerity today. It isn't becoming to you, really—except as an obvious pose. Be as artificial as you are, I advise. There's a sort of sincerity in that, you know. And, after all, you must confess you like that better.

MILDRED (*again affected and bored*). Yes, I suppose I do. Pardon me for my outburst. When a leopard complains of its spots, it must sound rather grotesque. (*In a mocking tone.*) Purr, little leopard. Purr, scratch, tear, kill, gorge yourself and be happy—only stay in the jungle where your spots are camouflage. In a cage they make you conspicuous.

AUNT. I don't know what you are talking about.

MILDRED. It would be rude to talk about anything to you. Let's just talk. (*She looks at her wrist watch.*) Well, thank goodness, it's about time for them to come for me. That ought to give me a new thrill, Aunt.

AUNT (*affectedly troubled*). You don't mean to say you're really going? The dirt—the heat must be frightful——

MILDRED. Grandfather started as a puddler. I should have inherited an immunity to heat that would make a salamander shiver. It will be fun to put it to the test.

AUNT. But don't you have to have the captain's — or someone's — permission to visit the stokehole?

MILDRED (*with a triumphant smile*). I have it—both his and the chief engineer's. Oh, they didn't want to at first, in spite of my social service credentials. They didn't seem a bit anxious that I should investigate how the other half lives and works on a ship. So I had to tell them that my father, the president of Nazareth Steel, chairman of the board of directors of this line, had told me it would be all right.

AUNT. He didn't.

MILDRED. How naïve age makes one! But I said he did, Aunt. I even said he had given me a letter to them—which I had lost. And they were afraid to take the chance that I might be lying. (*Excitedly.*) So it's ho! for the stokehole. The second engineer is to escort me. (*Looking at her watch again.*) It's time. An here he comes, I think. (*The* SECOND ENGINEER *enters. He is a husky, fine-looking man of thirty-five or so. He stops before the two and tips his cap, visibly embarrassed and ill-at-ease.*)

SECOND ENGINEER. Miss Douglas?

MILDRED. Yes. (*Throwing off her rugs and getting to her feet.*) Are we all ready to start?

SECOND ENGINEER. In just a second, ma'am. I'm waiting for the Fourth. He's coming along.

MILDRED (*with a scornful smile*). You don't care to shoulder this responsibility alone, is that it?

SECOND ENGINEER (*forcing a smile*). Two are better than one. (*Disturbed by her eyes, glances out to sea—blurts out.*) A fine day we're having.

MILDRED. Is it?

SECOND ENGINEER. A nice warm breeze——

MILDRED. It feels cold to me.

SECOND ENGINEER. But it's hot enough in the sun——

MILDRED. Not hot enough for me. I don't like Nature. I was never athletic.

SECOND ENGINEER (*forcing a smile*). Well, you'll find it hot enough where you're goin.

MILDRED. Do you mean hell?

SECOND ENGINEER (*flabbergasted, decides to laugh*). Ho-ho! No, I mean the stokehole.

MILDRED. My grandfather was a puddler. He played with boiling steel.

SECOND ENGINEER (*all at sea—uneasily*). Is that so? Hum, you'll excuse me, ma'am, but are you intending to wear that dress?

MILDRED. Why not?

SECOND ENGINEER. You'll likely rub against oil and dirt. It can't be helped.

MILDRED. It doesn't matter. I have lots of white dresses.

SECOND ENGINEER. I have an old coat you might throw over——

MILDRED. I have fifty dresses like this. I will throw this one into the sea when I come back. That ought to wash it clean, don't you think?

SECOND ENGINEER (*doggedly*). There's ladders to climb down that are none too clean—and dark alleyways——

MILDRED. I will wear this very dress and none other.

SECOND ENGINEER. No offense meant. It's none of my business. I was only warning you——

MILDRED. Warning? That sounds thrilling.

SECOND ENGINEER (*looking down the deck—with a sigh of relief*). There's the Fourth now. He's waiting for us. If you'll come——

MILDRED. Go on. I'll follow you. (*He goes.* MILDRED *turns a mocking smile on her aunt.*) An oaf—but a handsome, virile oaf.

AUNT (*scornfully*). Poser!

MILDRED. Take care. He said there were dark alleyways——

AUNT (*in the same tone*). Poser!

MILDRED (*biting her lips angrily*). You are right. But would that my millions were not so anemically chaste!

AUNT. Yes, for a fresh pose I have no doubt you would drag the name of Douglas in the gutter!

MILDRED. From which it sprang. Good-by, Aunt. Don't pray too hard that I may fall into the fiery furnace.

AUNT. Poser!

MILDRED (*viciously*). Old hag! (*She slaps her aunt insultingly across the face and walks off, laughing gaily.*)

AUNT (*screams after her*). I said poser!

CURTAIN

SCENE THREE

The stokehole. In the rear, the dimly-outlined bulks of the furnaces and boilers. High overhead one hanging electric bulb sheds just enough light through the murky air laden with coal dust to pile up masses of shadows everywhere. A line of men, stripped to the waist, is before the furnace doors. They bend over, looking neither to right nor left, handling their shovels as if they were part of their bodies, with a strange, awkward, swinging rhythm. They use the shovels to throw open the furnace doors. Then from these fiery round holes in the black a flood of terrific light and heat pours full upon the men who are outlined in silhouette in the crouching, inhuman attitudes of chained gorillas. The men shovel with a rhythmic motion, swinging as on a pivot from the coal which lies in heaps on the floor behind it into the flaming mouths before them. There is a tumult of noise—the brazen clang of the furnace doors as they are flung open or slammed shut, the grating, teeth-gritting grind of steel against steel, of crunching coal. This clash of sounds stuns one's ears with its rending dissonance. But there is order in it, rhythm a mechanical regulated recur-

rence, a tempo. And rising above all, making the air hum with the quiver of liberated energy, the roar of leaping flames in the furnaces, the monotonous throbbing beat of the engines.

As the curtain rises, the furnace doors are shut. The men are taking a breathing spell. One or two are arranging the coal behind them, pulling it into more accessible heaps. The others can be dimly made out leaning on their shovels in relaxed attitudes of exhaustion.

PADDY (*from somewhere in the line—plaintively*). Yerra, will this divil's own watch nivir end? Me back is broke. I'm destroyed entirely.

YANK (*from the center of the line—with exuberant scorn*). Aw, yuh make me sick! Lie down and croak, why don't yuh? Always beefin', dat's you! Say, dis is a cinch! Dis was made for me! It's my meat, get me! (*A whistle is blown—a thin, shrill note from somewhere overhead in the darkness.* YANK *curses without resentment.*) Dere's de damn engineer crackin' de whip. He tinks we're loafin'.

PADDY (*vindictively*). God stiffen him!

YANK (*in an exultant tone of command*). Come on, youse guys! Git into de game! She's gittin' hungry! Pile some grub in her. Trow it into her belly! Come on now, all of youse! Open her up! (*At this last all the men, who have followed his movements of getting into position, throw open their furnace doors with a deafening clang. The fiery light floods over their shoulders as they bend round for the coal. Rivulets of sooty sweat have traced maps on their backs. The enlarged muscles form bunches of high light and shadow.*)

YANK (*chanting a count as he shovels without seeming effort*). One—two—tree—(*His voice rising exultantly in the joy of battle.*) Dat's de stuff! Let her have it! All togedder now! Sling it into her! Let her ride! Shoot de piece now! Call de toin on her! Drive her into it! Feel her move! Watch her smoke! Speed, dat's her middle name! Give her coal, youse guys! Coal, dat's her booze! Drink it up, baby! Let's see yuh sprint! Dig in and gain a lap! Dere she go-o-es. (*This last in the chanting formula of the gallery gods at the six-day bike race. He slams his furnace door shut. The others do likewise with as much unison as their wearied bodies will permit. The effect is of one fiery eye after another being blotted out with a series of accompanying bangs.*)

PADDY (*groaning*). Me back is broke. I'm bate out—bate—(*There is a pause. Then the inexorable whistle sounds again from the dim regions above the electric light. There is a growl of cursing rage from all sides.*)

YANK (*shaking his fist upward—contemptuously*). Take it easy dere, you! Who d'yuh tinks runnin' dis game, me or you? When I git ready, we move. Not before! When I git ready, get me!

VOICES (*approvingly*). That's the stuff!
Yank tal him, py golly!
Yank ain't affeerd.
Goot poy, Yank!
Give him hell!
Tell 'im 'e's a bloody swine!
Bloody slave-driver!

YANK (*contemptuously*). He ain't got no noive. He's yellow, get me? All de engineers is yellow. Dey got streaks a mile wide. Aw, to hell wit him! Let's move, youse guys. We had a rest. Come on, she needs it! Give her pep! It ain't for him. Him and his whistle, dey don't belong. But we belong, see! We gotter feed de baby! Come on! (*He turns and flings his furnace door open. They all follow his lead. At this instant the* SECOND *and* FOURTH ENGINEERS *enter from the darkness on the left with* MILDRED *between them. She starts, turns paler, her pose is crumbling, she shivers with fright in spite of the blazing heat, but forces herself to leave the* ENGINEERS *and take a few steps nearer the men. She is right behind* YANK. *All this happens quickly while the men have their backs turned.*)

YANK. Come on, youse guys! (*He is turning to get coal when the whistle sounds again in a peremptory, irritating note. This drives* YANK *into a sudden fury. While the other men have turned full around and stopped dumfounded by the spectacle of* MILDRED *standing there in her white dress,* YANK *does not turn far enough to see her. Besides, his head is thrown back, he blinks upward through the murk trying to find the owner of the whistle, he brandishes his shovel murderously over his head in one hand, pound-*

ing on his chest, gorilla-like, with the other, shouting.) Toin off dat whistle! Come down outa dere, yuh yellow, brass-buttoned, Belfast bum, yuh! Come down and I'll knock yer brains out! Yuh lousy, stinkin', yellow mut of a Catholic-moiderin' bastard! Come down and I'll moider yuh! Pullin' dat whistle on me, huh? I'll show yuh! I'll crash yer skull in! I'll drive yer teet' down yer troat! I'll slam yer nose trou de back of yer head! I'll cut yer guts out for a nickel, yuh lousy boob, yuh dirty, crummy, muck-eatin' son of a—— (*Suddenly he becomes conscious of all the other men staring at something directly behind his back. He whirls defensively with a snarling, murderous growl, crouching to spring, his lips drawn back over his teeth, his small eyes gleaming ferociously. He sees* MILDRED, *like a white apparition in the full light from the open furnace doors. He glares into her eyes, turned to stone. As for her, during his speech she has listened, paralyzed with horror, terror, her whole personality crushed, beaten in, collapsed, by the terrific impact of this unknown, abysmal brutality, naked and shameless. As she looks at his gorilla face, as his eyes bore into hers, she utters a low, choking cry and shrinks away from him, putting both hands up before her eyes to shut out the sight of his face, to protect her own. This startles* YANK *to a reaction. His mouth falls open, his eyes grow bewildered.*)

MILDRED (*about to faint—to the* ENGINEERS, *who now have her one by each arm—whimperingly*). Take me away! Oh, the filthy beast! (*She faints. They carry her quickly back, disappearing in the darkness at the left, rear. An iron door clangs shut. Rage and bewildered fury rush back on* YANK. *He feels himself insulted in some unknown fashion in the very heart of his pride. He roars.*) God damn yuh! (*And hurls his shovel after them at the door which has just closed. It hits the steel bulkhead with a clang and falls clattering on the steel floor. From overhead the whistle sounds again in a long, angry, insistent command.*)

CURTAIN

SCENE FOUR

The firemen's forecastle. YANK'S *watch has just come off duty and had dinner. Their faces and bodies shine from a soap and water scrubbing but around their eyes, where a hasty dousing does not touch, the coal dust sticks like black make-up, giving them a queer, sinister expression.* YANK *has not washed either face or body. He stands out in contrast to them, a blackened, brooding figure. He is seated forward on a bench in the exact attitude of Rodin's "The Thinker." The others, most of them smoking pipes, are staring at* YANK *half-apprehensively, as if fearing an outburst; half-amusedly, as if they saw a joke somewhere that tickled them.*

VOICES. He ain't ate nothin'.
Py golly, a fallar gat to gat grub in him.
Divil a lie.
Yank feeda da fire, no feeda da face.
Ha-ha.
He ain't even washed hisself.
He's forgot.
Hey, Yank, you forgot to wash.

YANK (*sullenly*). Forgot nothin'! To hell wit washin'.

VOICES. It'll stick to you.
It'll get under your skin.
Give yer the bleedin' itch, that's wot.
It makes spots on you—like a leopard.
Like a piebald nigger, you mean.
Better wash up, Yank.
You sleep better.
Wash up, Yank.
Wash up! Wash up!

YANK (*resentfully*). Aw say, youse guys. Lemme alone. Can't youse see I'm tryin' to tink?

ALL (*repeating the word after him as one with cynical mockery*). Think! (*The word has a brazen, metallic quality as if their throats were phonograph horns. It is followed by a chorus of hard, barking laughter.*)

YANK (*springing to his feet and glaring at them belligerently*). Yes, tink! Tink, dat's what I said! What about it? (*They are silent, puzzled by his sudden resentment at what used to be one of his jokes.* YANK *sits down again in the same attitude of "The Thinker."*)

VOICES. Leave him alone.
He's got a grouch on.
Why wouldn't he?

PADDY (*with a wink at the others*). Sure I know what's the matther. 'Tis aisy to see. He's fallen in love, I'm telling you.

ALL (*repeating the word after him as one with cynical mockery*). Love! (*The word has a brazen, metallic quality as if their throats were phonograph horns. It is followed by a chorus of hard, barking laughter.*)

YANK (*with a contemptuous snort*). Love, hell! Hate, dat's what. I've fallen in hate, get me?

PADDY (*philosophically*). 'Twould take a wise man to tell one from the other. (*With a bitter, ironical scorn, increasing as he goes on.*) But I'm telling you it's love that's in it. Sure what else but love for us poor bastes in the stokehole would be bringing a fine lady, dressed like a white quane, down a mile of ladders and steps to be havin' a look at us? (*A growl of anger goes up from all sides.*)

LONG (*jumping on a bench—hecticly*). Hinsultin' us! Hinsultin' us, the bloody cow! And them bloody engineers! What right 'as they got to be exhibitin' us 's if we was bleedin' monkeys in a menagerie? Did we sign for hinsults to our dignity as 'onest workers? Is that in the ship's articles? You kin bloody well bet it ain't! But I knows why they done it. I arsked a deck steward 'o she was and 'e told me. 'Er old man's a bleedin' millionaire, a bloody Capitalist! 'E's got enuf bloody gold to sink this bleedin' ship! 'E makes arf the bloody steel in the world! 'E owns this bloody boat! And you and me, Comrades, we're 'is slaves! And the skipper and mates and engineers, they're 'is slaves! And she's 'is bloody daughter and we're all 'er slaves, too! And she gives 'er orders as 'ow she wants to see the bloody animals below decks and down they takes 'er! (*There is a roar of rage from all sides.*)

YANK (*blinking at him bewilderedly*). Say! Wait a moment! Is all dat straight goods?

LONG. Straight as string! The bleedin' steward as waits on 'em, 'e told me about 'er. And what're we goin' ter do, I arsks yer? 'Ave we got ter swaller 'er hinsults like dogs? It ain't in the ship's articles. I tell yer we got a case. We kin go to law——

YANK (*with abysmal contempt*). Hell! Law!

ALL (*repeating the word after him as one with cynical mockery*). Law! (*The word has a brazen metallic quality as if their throats were phonograph horns. It is followed by a chorus of hard, barking laughter.*)

LONG (*feeling the ground slipping from under his feet—desperately*). As voters and citizens we kin force the bloody governments——

YANK (*with abysmal contempt*). Hell! Governments!

ALL (*repeating the word after him as one with cynical mockery*). Governments! (*The word has a brazen metallic quality as if their throats were phonograph horns. It is followed by a chorus of hard, barking laughter.*)

LONG (*hysterically*). We're free and equal in the sight of God——

YANK (*with abysmal contempt*). Hell! God!

ALL (*repeating the word after him as one with cynical mockery*). God! (*The word has a brazen metallic quality as if their throats were phonograph horns. It is followed by a chorus of hard, barking laughter.*)

YANK (*witheringly*). Aw, join de Salvation Army!

ALL. Sit down! Shut up! Damn fool! Sea-lawyer! (LONG *slinks back out of sight.*)

PADDY (*continuing the trend of his thoughts as if he had never been interrupted—bitterly*). And there she was standing behind us, and the Second pointing at us like a man you'd hear in a circus would be saying: In this cage is a queerer kind of baboon than ever you'd find in darkest Africy. We roast them in their own sweat—and be damned if you won't hear some of thim saying they like it! (*He glances scornfully at* YANK.)

YANK (*with a bewildered uncertain growl*). Aw!

PADDY. And there was Yank roarin' curses and turning round wid his shovel to brain her—and she looked at him, and him at her——

YANK (*slowly*). She was all white. I tought she was a ghost. Sure.

PADDY (*with heavy, biting sarcasm*). 'Twas love at first sight, divil a doubt of it! If you'd seen the endearin' look on her pale mug when she shriveled away with her hands over her eyes to shut out the sight of him! Sure, 'twas as if she'd seen a great hairy ape escaped from the Zoo!

YANK (*stung—with a growl of rage*). Aw!

PADDY. And the loving way Yank heaved his shovel at the skull of her, only she was out the door! (*A grin breaking over his face.*) 'Twas touching, I'm telling you! It put the touch of home, swate home in the stokehole. (*There is a roar of laughter from all.*)

YANK (*glaring at* PADDY *menacingly*). Aw, choke dat off, see!

PADDY (*not heeding him—to the others*). And her grabbin' at the Second's arm for protection. (*With a grotesque imitation of a woman's voice.*) Kiss me, Engineer dear, for it's dark down here and me old man's in Wall Street making money! Hug me tight, darlin', for I'm afeerd in the dark and me mother's on deck makin' eyes at the skipper! (*Another roar of laughter.*)

YANK (*threateningly*). Say! What yuh tryin' to do, kid me, yuh old Harp?

PADDY. Divil a bit! Ain't I wishin' myself you'd brained her?

YANK (*fiercely*). I'll brain her! I'll brain her yet, wait 'n' see! (*Coming over to* PADDY*—slowly.*) Say, is dat what she called me—a hairy ape?

PADDY. She looked it at you if she didn't say the word itself.

YANK (*grinning horribly*). Hairy ape, huh? Sure! Dat's de way she looked at me, aw right. Hairy ape! So dat's me, huh? (*Bursting into rage—as if she were still in front of him.*) Yuh skinny tart! Yuh white-faced bum, yuh! I'll show yuh who's a ape! (*Turning to the others, bewilderment seizing him again.*) Say, youse guys. I was bawlin' him out for pullin' de whistle on us. You heard me. And den I seen youse lookin' at somep'n and I tought he'd sneaked down to come up in back of me, and I hopped round to knock him dead wit de shovel. And dere she was wit de light on her! Christ, yuh coulda pushed me over with a finger! I was scared, get me? Sure! I tought she was a ghost, see? She was all in white like dey wrap around stiffs. You seen her. Kin yuh blame me? She didn't belong, dat's what. And den when I come to and seen it was a real skoit and seen de way she was lookin' at me—like Paddy said—Christ, I was sore, get me? I don't stand for dat stuff from nobody. And I flung de shovel—on'y she'd beat it. (*Furiously.*) I wished it'd banged her! I wished it'd knocked her block off!

LONG. And be 'anged for murder or 'lectrocuted? She ain't bleedin' well worth it.

YANK. I don't give a damn what! I'd be square wit her, wouldn't I? Tink I wanter let her put somep'n over on me? Tink I'm goin' to let her git away wit dat stuff? Yuh don't know me! No one ain't never put nothin' over on me and got away wit it, see!—not dat kind of stuff—no guy and no skoit neither! I'll fix her! Maybe she'll come down again——

VOICE. No chance, Yank. You scared her out of a year's growth.

YANK. I scared her? Why de hell should I scare her? Who de hell is she? Ain't she de same as me? Hairy ape, huh? (*With his old confident bravado.*) I'll show her I'm better'n her, if she on'y knew it. I belong and she don't, see! I move and she's dead! Twenty-five knots a hour, dat's me! Dat carries her but I make dat. She's on'y baggage. Sure! (*Again bewilderedly.*) But, Christ, she was funny lookin'! Did yuh pipe her hands? White and skinny. Yuh could se de bones through 'em. And her mush, dat was dead white, too. And her eyes, dey was like dey'd seen a ghost. Me, dat was! Sure! Hairy ape! Ghost, huh? Look at dat arm! (*He extends his right arm, swelling out the great muscles.*) I coulda took her wit dat, wit' just my little finger even, and broke her in two. (*Again bewilderedly.*) Say, who is dat skoit, huh? What is she? What's she come from? Who made her? Who give her de noive to look at me like dat? Dis ting's got my goat right. I don't get her. She's new to me. What does a skoit like her mean, huh? She don't belong, get me! I can't see her. (*With growing anger.*) But one thing I'm wise to, aw right, aw right! Youse all kin bet your shoits I'll git even wit her. I'll show her if she tinks she— She grinds de organ and I'm on de string, huh? I'll fix her! Let her come down again and I'll fling her in de furnace! She'll move den! She won't shiver at nothin', den! Speed, dat'll be her! She'll belong den! (*He grins horribly.*)

PADDY. She'll never come. She's had her belly-full, I'm telling you. She'll be in bed now, I'm thinking, wid ten doctors and nurses feedin' her salts to clean the fear out of her.

YANK (*enraged*). Yuh tink I made her sick, too, do yuh? Just lookin' at me, huh? Hairy ape, huh? (*In a frenzy of rage.*) I'll fix her! I'll tell her where to git off! She'll git down on her knees and take it back or I'll bust de face offen her! (*Shaking one fist upward and beating on his chest with the other.*) I'll find yuh! I'm comin', d'yuh hear? I'll fix yuh, God damn yuh! (*He makes a rush for the door.*)

VOICES. Stop him!
He'll get shot!
He'll murder her!
Trip him up!
Hold him!
He's gone crazy!
Gott, he's strong!
Hold him down!
Look out for a kick!
Pin his arms!

(*They have all piled on him and, after a fierce struggle, by sheer weight of numbers have borne him to the floor just inside the door.*)

PADDY (*who has remained detached*). Kape him down till he's cooled off. (*Scornfully.*) Yerra, Yank, you're a great fool. Is it payin' attention at all you are to the like of that skinny sow widout one drop of rale blood in her?

YANK (*frenziedly, from the bottom of the heap*). She done me doit! She done me doit, didn't she? I'll git square wit her! I'll get her some way! Git offen me, youse guys! Lemme up! I'll show her who's a ape!

CURTAIN

SCENE FIVE

Three weeks later. A corner of Fifth Avenue in the Fifties on a fine Sunday morning. A general atmosphere of clean, well-tidied, wide street; a flood of mellow, tempered sunshine; gentle, genteel breezes. In the rear, the show windows of two shops, a jewelry establishment on the corner, a furrier's next to it. Here the adornments of extreme wealth are tantalizingly displayed. The jeweler's window is gaudy with glittering diamonds, emeralds, rubies, pearls, etc., fashioned in ornate tiaras, crowns, necklaces, collars, etc. From each piece hangs an enormous tag from which a dollar sign and numerals in intermittent electric lights wink out the incredible prices. The same in the furrier's. Rich furs of all varieties hang there bathed in a downpour of artificial light. The general effect is of a background of magnificence cheapened and made grotesque by commercialism, a background in tawdry disharmony with the clear light and sunshine on the street itself.

Up the side street YANK *and* LONG *come swaggering.* LONG *is dressed in shore clothes, wears a black Windsor tie, cloth cap.* YANK *is in his dirty dungarees. A fireman's cap with black peak is cocked defiantly on the side of his head. He has not shaved for days and around his fierce, resentful eyes—as around those of* LONG *to a lesser degree—the black smudge of coal dust still sticks like make-up. They hesitate and stand together at the corner, swaggering, looking about them with a forced, defiant contempt.*

LONG (*indicating it all with an oratorical gesture*). Well, 'ere we are. Fif' Avenoo. This 'ere's their bleedin' private lane, as yer might say. (*Bitterly.*) We're trespassers 'ere. Proletarians keep orf the grass!

YANK (*dully*). I don't see no grass, yuh boob. (*Staring at the sidewalk.*) Clean, ain't it? Yuh could eat a fried egg offen it. The white wings got some job sweepin' dis up. (*Looking up and down the avenue—surlily.*) Where's all de white-collar stiffs yuh said was here—and de skoits—*her* kind?

LONG. In church, blarst 'em! Arskin' Jesus to give 'em more money.

YANK. Choich, huh? I useter go to choich onct—sure—when I was a kid. Me old man and woman, dey made me. Dey never went demselves, dough. Always got too big a head on Sunday mornin', dat was dem. (*With a grin.*) Dey was scrappers for fair, bot' of dem. On Satiday nights when dey bot' got a skinful dey could put up a bout oughter been staged at de Garden. When dey got trough dere wasn't a chair or table wit a leg under it. Or else dey bot' jumped on me for somep'n. Dat was where I loined to take punishment. (*With a grin and a swagger.*) I'm a chip offen de old block, get me?

LONG. Did yer old man follow the sea?

YANK. Naw. Worked along shore. I

runned away when me old lady croaked wit de tremens. I helped at truckin' and in de market. Den I shipped in de stokehole. Sure. Dat belongs. De rest was nothin'. (*Looking around him.*) I ain't never seen dis before. De Brooklyn waterfront, dat was where I was dragged up. (*Taking a deep breath.*) Dis ain't so bad at dat, huh?

LONG. Not bad? Well, we pays for it wiv our bloody sweat, if yer wants to know!

YANK (*with sudden angry disgust*). Aw, hell! I don't see no one, see—like her. All dis gives me a pain. It don't belong. Say, ain't dere a back room around dis dump? Let's go shoot a ball. All dis is too clean and quiet and dolled-up, get me! It gives me a pain.

LONG. Wait and yer'll bloody well see——

YANK. I don't wait for no one. I keep on de move. Say, what yuh drag me up here for, anyway? Tryin' to kid me, yuh simp, yuh?

LONG. Yer wants to get back at 'er, don't yer? That's what yer been sayin' every bloomin' hour since she hinsulted yer.

YANK (*vehemently*). Sure ting I do! Didn't I try to get even wit her in Southampton? Didn't I sneak on de dock and wait for her by de gangplank? I was goin' to spit in her pale mug, see! Sure, right in her pop-eyes! Dat woulda made me even, see? But no chanct. Dere was a whole army of plainclothes bulls around. Dey spotted me and gimme de bum's rush. I never seen her. But I'll git square wit her yet, you watch! (*Furiously.*) De lousy tart! She tinks she kin get away wit moider—but not wit me! I'll fix her! I'll tink of a way!

LONG (*as disgusted as he dares to be*). Ain't that why I brought yer up 'ere—to show yer? Yer been lookin' at this 'ere 'ole affair wrong. Yer been actin' an' talkin' 's if it was all a bleedin' personal matter between yer and that bloody cow. I wants to convince yer she was on'y a representative of 'er clarss. I wants to awaken yer bloody clarss consciousness. Then yer'll see it's 'er clarss yer've got to fight, not 'er alone. There's a 'ole mob of 'em like 'er, Gawd blind 'em!

YANK (*spitting on his hands—belligerently*). De more de merrier when I gits started. Bring on de gang!

LONG. Yer'll see 'em in arf a mo', when that church lets out. (*He turns and sees the window display in the two stores for the first time.*) Blimey! Look at that, will yer? (*They both walk back and stand looking in the jeweler's.* LONG *flies into a fury.*) Just look at this 'ere bloomin' mess! Just look at it! Look at the bleedin' prices on 'em—more'n our 'ole bloody stokehole makes in ten voyages sweatin' in 'ell! And they—'er and 'er bloody clarss—buys 'em for toys to dangle on 'em! One of these 'ere would buy scoff for a starvin' family for a year!

YANK. Aw, cut de sob stuff! T' hell wit de starvin' family! Yuh'll be passin' de hat to me next. (*With naïve admiration.*) Say, dem tings is pretty, huh? Bet yuh dey'd hock for a piece of change aw right. (*Then turning away, bored.*) But, aw hell, what good are dey? Let her have 'em. Dey don't belong no more'n she does. (*With a gesture of sweeping the jewelers into oblivion.*) All dat don't count, get me?

LONG (*who has moved to the furrier's—indignantly*). And I s'pose this 'ere don't count neither—skins of poor, 'armless animals slaughtered so as 'er and 'ers can keep their bleedin' noses warm!

YANK (*who has been staring at something inside—with queer excitement*). Take a slant at dat! Give it de once-over! Monkey fur—two t'ousand bucks! (*Bewilderedly.*) Is dat straight goods—monkey fur? What de hell——?

LONG (*bitterly*). It's straight enuf. (*With grim humor.*) They wouldn't bloody well pay that for a 'airy ape's skin—no, nor for the 'ole livin' ape with all 'is 'ead, and body, and soul thrown in!

YANK (*clenching his fists, his face growing pale with rage as if the skin in the window were a personal insult*). Trowin' it up in my face! Christ! I'll fix her!

LONG (*excitedly*). Church is out. 'Ere they come, the bleedin' swine. (*After a glance at* YANK'*s lowering face—uneasily.*) Easy goes, Comrade. Keep yer bloomin' temper. Remember force defeats itself. It ain't our weapon. We must impress our demands through peaceful means—the votes of the on-marching proletarians of the bloody world!

YANK (*with abysmal contempt*). Votes, hell! Votes is a joke, see. Votes for women! Let dem do it!

LONG (*still more uneasily*). Calm, now.

Treat 'em wiv the proper contempt. Observe the bleedin' parasites but 'old yer 'orses.

YANK (*angrily.*) Git away from me! Yuh're yellow, dat's what. Force, dat's me! De punch, dat's me every time, see! (*The crowd from church enter from the right, sauntering slowly and affectedly, their heads held stiffly up, looking neither to right nor left, talking in toneless, simpering voices. The women are rouged, calcimined, dyed, overdressed to the nth degree. The men are in Prince Alberts, high hats, spats, canes, etc. A procession of gaudy marionettes, yet with something of the relentless horror of Frankensteins in their detached, mechanical unawareness.*)

VOICES. Dear Doctor Caiaphas! He is so sincere!
What was the sermon? I dozed off.
About the radicals, my dear—and the false doctrines that are being preached.
We must organize a hundred per cent American bazaar.
And let everyone contribute one one-hundredth per cent of their income tax.
What an original idea!
We can devote the proceeds to rehabilitating the veil of the temple.
But that has been done so many times.

YANK (*glaring from one to the other of them—with an insulting snort of scorn*). Huh! Huh! (*Without seeming to see him, they make wide detours to avoid the spot where he stands in the middle of the sidewalk.*)

LONG (*frightenedly*). Keep yer bloomin' mouth shut, I tells yer.

YANK (*viciously*). G'wan! Tell it to Sweeney! (*He swaggers away and deliberately lurches into a top-hatted gentleman, then glares at him pugnaciously.*) Say, who d'yuh tink yuh're bumpin'? Tink yuh own de oith?

GENTLEMAN (*coldly and affectedly*). I beg your pardon. (*He has not looked at* YANK *and passes on without a glance, leaving him bewildered.*)

LONG (*rushing up and grabbing* YANK'*s arm*). 'Ere! Come away! This wasn't what I meant. Yer'll 'ave the bloody coppers down on us.

YANK (*savagely—giving him a push that sends him sprawling*). G'wan!

LONG (*picks himself up—hysterically*). I'll pop orf then. This ain't what I meant. And whatever 'appens, yer can't blame me. (*He slinks off left.*)

YANK. T' hell wit youse! (*He approaches a lady—with a vicious grin and a smirking wink.*) Hello, Kiddo. How's every little ting? Got anyting on for tonight? I know an old boiler down to de docks we kin crawl into. (*The lady stalks by without a look, without a change of pace.* YANK *turns to others—insultingly.*) Holy smokes, what a mug! Go hide yuhself before de horses shy at yuh. Gee, pipe de heine on dat one! Say, youse, yuh look like de stoin of a ferryboat. Paint and powder! All dolled up to kill! Yuh look like stiffs laid out for de boneyard! Aw, g'wan, de lot of youse! Yuh give me de eye-ache. Yuh don't belong, get me! Look at me, why don't youse dare? I belong, dat's me! (*Pointing to a skyscraper across the street which is in process of construction—with bravado.*) See dat building goin' up dere? See de steel work? Steel, dat's me! Youse guys live on it and tink yuh're somep'n. But I'm *in* it, see! I'm de hoistin' engine dat makes it go up! I'm it—de inside and bottom of it! Sure! I'm steel and steam and smoke and de rest of it! It moves—speed—twenty-five stories up—and me at de top and bottom—movin'! Youse simps don't move. Yuh're on'y dolls I winds up to see 'm spin. Yuh're de garbage, get me—de leavins—de ashes we dump over de side! Now, what 'a' yuh gotta say? (*But as they seem neither to see nor hear him, he flies into a fury.*) Bums! Pigs! Tarts! Bitches! (*He turns in a rage on the men, bumping viciously into them but not jarring them the least bit. Rather it is he who recoils after each collision. He keeps growling.*) Git off de oith! G'wan, yuh bum! Look where yuh're goin', can't yuh? Git outa here! Fight, why don't yuh? Put up yer mits! Don't be a dog! Fight or I'll knock yuh dead! (*But, without seeming to see him, they all answer with mechanical affected politeness.*) I beg your pardon. (*Then at a cry from one of the women, they all scurry to the furrier's window.*)

THE WOMEN (*ecstatically, with a gasp of delight*). Monkey fur! (*The whole crowd of men and women chorus after her in the *same tone of affected delight.)* Monkey fur!

YANK *(with a jerk of his head back on his shoulders, as if he had received a punch full in the face—raging)*. I see yuh, all in white! I see yuh, yuh white-faced tart, yuh! Hairy ape, huh? I'll hairy ape yuh! *(He bends down and grips at the street curbing as if to pluck it out and hurl it. Foiled in this, snarling with passion, he leaps to the lamp-post on the corner and tries to pull it up for a club. Just at that moment a bus is heard rumbling up. A fat, high-hatted, spatted gentleman runs out from the side street. He calls out plaintively.)* Bus! Bus! Stop there! *(And runs full tilt into the bending, straining* YANK, *who is bowled off his balance.)*

YANK *(seeing a fight—with a roar of joy as he springs to his feet)*. At last! Bus, huh? I'll bust yuh! *(He lets drive a terrific swing, his fist landing full on the fat gentleman's face. But the gentleman stands unmoved as if nothing had happened.)*

GENTLEMAN. I beg your pardon. *(Then irritably.)* You have made me lose my bus. *(He claps his hands and begins to scream.)* Officer! Officer! *(Many police whistles shrill out on the instant and a whole platoon of policemen rush in on* YANK *from all sides. He tries to fight but is clubbed to the pavement and fallen upon. The crowd at the window have not moved or noticed this disturbance. The clanging gong of the patrol wagon approaches with a clamoring din.)*

CURTAIN

SCENE SIX

Night of the following day. A row of cells in the prison on Blackwells Island. The cells extend back diagonally from right front to left rear. They do not stop, but disappear in the dark background as if they ran on, numberless, into infinity. One electric bulb from the low ceiling of the narrow corridor sheds its light through the heavy steel bars of the cell at the extreme front and reveals part of the interior. YANK *can be seen within, crouched on the edge of his cot in the attitude of Rodin's "The Thinker." His face is spotted with black and blue bruises. A blood-stained bandage is wrapped around his head.*

YANK *(suddenly starting as if awakening from a dream, reaches out and shakes the bars—aloud to himself, wonderingly)*. Steel. Dis is de Zoo, huh? *(A burst of hard, barking laughter comes from the unseen occupants of the cells, runs back down the tier, and abruptly ceases.)*

VOICES *(mockingly)*. The Zoo? That's a new name for this coop—a damn good name!
Steel, eh? You said a mouthful. This is the old iron house.
Who is that boob talkin'?
He's the bloke they brung in out of his head. The bulls had beat him up fierce.

YANK *(dully)*. I musta been dreamin'. I tought I was in a cage at de Zoo—but de apes don't talk, do they?

VOICES *(with mocking laughter)*. You're in a cage aw right.
A coop!
A pen!
A sty!
A kennel! *(Hard laughter—a pause.)*
Say, guy! Who are you? No, never mind lying. What are you?
Yes, tell us your sad story. What's your game? What did they jug yuh for?

YANK *(dully)*. I was a fireman—stokin' on de liners. *(Then with sudden rage, rattling his cell bars.)* I'm a hairy ape, get me? And I'll bust youse all in de jaw if yuh don't lay off kiddin' me.

VOICES. Huh! You're a hard boiled duck, ain't you!
When you spit, it bounces! *(Laughter.)*
Aw, can it. He's a regular guy. Ain't you?
What did he say he was—a ape?

YANK *(defiantly)*. Sure ting! Ain't dat what youse all are—apes? *(A silence. Then a furious rattling of bars from down the corridor.)*

A VOICE *(thick with rage)*. I'll show yuh who's a ape, yuh bum!

VOICES. Ssshh! Nix!
Can de noise!
Piano!
You'll have the guard down on us!

YANK *(scornfully)*. De guard? Yuh

mean de keeper, don't yuh? (*Angry exclamations from all the cells.*)

VOICE (*placatingly*). Aw, don't pay no attention to him. He's off his nut from the beatin'-up he got. Say, you guy! We're waitin' to hear what they landed you for —or ain't yuh tellin'?

YANK. Sure, I'll tell youse. Sure! Why de hell not? On'y—youse won't get me. Nobody gets me but me, see? I started to tell de Judge and all he says was: "Toity days to tink it over." Tink it over! Christ, dat's all I been doin' for weeks! (*After a pause.*) I was tryin' to git even wit someone, see?—someone dat done me doit.

VOICES (*cynically*). De old stuff, I bet. Your goil, huh?
Give yuh thc double-cross, huh?
That's them every time!
Did yuh beat up de odder guy?

YANK (*disgustedly*). Aw, yuh're all wrong! Sure dere was a skoit in it—but not what youse mean, not dat old tripe. Dis was a new kind of skoit. She was dolled up all in white—in de stokehole. I tought she was a ghost. sure. (*A pause.*)

VOICES (*whispering*). Gee, he's still nutty.
Let him rave. It's fun listenin'.

YANK (*unheeding—groping in his thoughts*). Her hands—dey was skinny and white like dey wasn't real but painted on somep'n. Dere was a million miles from me to her—twenty-five knots a hour. She was like some dead ting de cat brung in. Sure, dat's what. She didn't belong. She belonged in de window of a toy store, or on de top of a garbage can, see! Sure! (*He breaks out angrily.*) But would yuh believe it, she had de noive to do me doit. She lamped me like she was seein' somep'n broke loose from de menagerie. Christ, yuh'd oughter seen her eyes! (*He rattles the bars of his cell furiously.*) But I'll get back at her yet, you watch! And if I can't find her I'll take it out on de gang she runs wit. I'm wise to where dey hangs out now. I'll show her who belongs! I'll show her who's in de move and who ain't. You watch my smoke!

VOICES (*seriously and joking.*) Dat's de talkin'!
Take her for all she's got!
What was this dame, anyway? Who was she, eh?

YANK. I dunno. First cabin stiff. Her old man's a millionaire, dey says—name of Douglas.

VOICES. Douglas? That's the president of the Steel Trust, I bet.
Sure. I seen his mug in de papers.
He's filthy with dough.

VOICE. Hey, feller, take a tip from me. If you want to get back at that dame, you better join the Wobblies. You'll get some action then.

YANK. Wobblies? What de hell's dat?

VOICE. Ain't you ever heard of the I. W. W.?

YANK. Naw. What is it?

VOICE. A gang of blokes—a tough gang. I been readin' about 'em today in the paper. The guard give me the *Sunday Times*. There's a long spiel about 'em. It's from a speech made in the Senate by a guy named Senator Queen. (*He is in the cell next to* YANK's. *There is a rustling of paper.*) Wait'll I see if I got light enough and I'll read you. Listen. (*He reads.*) "There is a menace existing in this country today which threatens the vitals of our fair Republic—as foul a menace against the very life-blood of the American Eagle as was the foul conspiracy of Cataline against the eagles of ancient Rome!"

VOICE (*disgustedly*). Aw, hell! Tell him to salt de tail of dat eagle!

VOICE (*reading*). "I refer to that devil's brew of rascals, jailbirds, murderers and cutthroats who libel all honest working men by calling themselves the Industrial Workers of the World; but in the light of their nefarious plots, I call them the Industrious *Wreckers* of the World!"

YANK (*with vengeful satisfaction*). Wreckers, dat's de right dope! Dat belongs! Me for dem!

VOICE. Ssshh! (*Reading.*) "This fiendish organization is a foul ulcer on the fair body of our Democracy——"

VOICE. Democracy, hell! Give him the boid, fellers—the raspberry! (*They do.*)

VOICE. Ssshh! (*Reading.*) "Like Cato I say to this Senate, the I. W. W. must be destroyed! For they represent an ever-present dagger pointed at the heart of the greatest nation the world has ever known, where all men are born free and equal, with equal opportunities to all, where the Founding Fathers have guaranteed to each one happiness, where Truth, Honor, Liberty, Justice, and the Brotherhood of

Man are a religion absorbed with one's mother milk, taught at our father's knee, sealed, signed, and stamped upon in the glorious Constitution of these United States!" (*A perfect storm of hisses, cat-calls, boos, and hard laughter.*)

VOICES (*scornfully*). Hurrah for de
Fort' of July!
Pass de hat!
Liberty!
Justice!
Honor!
Opportunity!
Brotherhood!

ALL (*with abysmal scorn*). Aw, hell!

VOICE. Give that Queen Senator guy the bark! All togedder now—one—two—tree—— (*A terrific chorus of barking and yapping.*)

GUARD (*from a distance*). Quiet there, youse—or I'll git the hose. (*The noise subsides.*)

YANK (*with growling rage*). I'd like to catch dat senator guy alone for a second. I'd loin him some trute!

VOICE. Ssshh! Here's where he gits down to cases on the Wobblies. (*Reads.*) "They plot with fire in one hand and dynamite in the other. They stop not before murder to gain their ends, nor at the outraging of defenseless womanhood. They would tear down society, put the lowest scum in the seats of the mighty, turn Almighty God's revealed plan for the world topsy-turvy, and make of our sweet and lovely civilization a shambles, a desolation where man, God's masterpiece, would soon degenerate back to the ape!"

VOICE (*to* YANK). Hey, you guy. There's your ape stuff again.

YANK (*with a growl of fury*). I got him. So dey blow up tings, do dey? Dey turn tings round, do dey? Hey, lend me dat paper, will yuh?

VOICE. Sure. Give it to him. On'y keep it to yourself, see. We don't wanter listen to no more of that slop.

VOICE. Here you are. Hide it under your mattress.

YANK (*reaching out*). Tanks. I can't read much but I kin manage. (*He sits, the paper in the hand at his side, in the attitude of Rodin's "The Thinker." A pause. Several snores from down the corridor. Suddenly* YANK *jumps to his feet with a furious groan as if some appalling thought had crashed on him—bewilderedly.*) Sure—her old man—president of de Steel Trust—makes half de steel in de world—steel—where I tought I belonged—drivin' trou—movin'—in dat—to make *her*—and cage me in for her to spit on! Christ. (*He shakes the bars of his cell door till the whole tier trembles. Irritated, protesting exclamations from those awakened or trying to get to sleep.*) He made dis—dis cage! Steel! *It* don't belong, dat's what! Cages, cells, locks, bolts, bars—dat's what it means!—holdin' me down wit him at de top! But I'll drive trou! Fire, dat melts it! I'll be fire—under de heap—fire dat never goes out—hot as hell—breakin' out in de night—(*While he has been saying this last he has shaken his cell door to a clanging accompaniment. As he comes to the "breakin' out" he seizes one bar with both hands and, putting his two feet up against the others so that his position is parallel to the floor like a monkey's, he gives a great wrench backwards. The bar bends like a licorice stick under his tremendous strength. Just at this moment the* PRISON GUARD *rushes in, dragging a hose behind him.*)

GUARD (*angrily*). I'll loin youse bums to wake me up! (*Sees* YANK.) Hello, it's you, huh? Got the D. Ts., hey? Well, I'll cure 'em. I'll drown your snakes for yuh! (*Noticing the bar.*) Hell, look at dat bar bended! On'y a bug is strong enough for dat!

YANK (*glaring at him*). Or a hairy ape, yuh big yellow bum! Look out! Here I come! (*He grabs another bar.*)

GUARD (*scared now—yelling off left*). Toin de hose on, Ben!—full pressure! And call de others—and a straitjacket! (*The curtain is falling. As it hides* YANK *from view, there is a splattering smash as the stream of water hits the steel of* YANK's *cell.*)

CURTAIN

SCENE SEVEN

Nearly a month later. An I. W. W. local near the waterfront, showing the interior of a front room on the ground floor, and the street outside. Moonlight on the narrow street, buildings massed in black shadow. The interior of the room, which is general assembly room, office, and reading room, resembles some dingy settlement boys' club. A desk and high stool are in one corner. A table with papers, stacks of pamphlets, chairs about it, is at center. The whole is decidedly cheap, banal, commonplace and unmysterious as a room could well be. The secretary is perched on the stool making entries in a large ledger. An eye shade casts his face into shadows. Eight or ten men, longshoremen, iron workers, and the like, are grouped about the table. Two are playing checkers. One is writing a letter. Most of them are smoking pipes. A big signboard is on the wall at the rear, "Industrial Workers of the World—Local No. 57."

YANK (*comes down the street outside. He is dressed as in Scene Five. He moves cautiously, mysteriously. He comes to a point opposite the door; tiptoes softly up to it, listens, is impressed by the silence within, knocks carefully, as if he were guessing at the password to some secret rite. Listens. No answer. Knocks again a bit louder. No answer. Knocks impatiently, much louder.*)

SECRETARY (*turning around on his stool*). What the hell is that—someone knocking? (*Shouts.*) Come in, why don't you? (*All the men in the room look up.* YANK *opens the door slowly, gingerly, as if afraid of an ambush. He looks around for secret doors, mystery, is taken aback by the commonplaceness of the room and the men in it, thinks he may have gotten in the wrong place, then sees the signboard on the wall and is reassured.*)

YANK (*blurts out*). Hello.

MEN (*reservedly*). Hello.

YANK (*more easily*). I tought I'd bumped into de wrong dump.

SECRETARY (*scrutinizing him carefully*). Maybe you have. Are you a member?

YANK. Naw, not yet. Dat's what I come for—to join.

SECRETARY. That's easy. What's your job—longshore?

YANK. Naw. Fireman—stoker on de liners.

SECRETARY (*with satisfaction*). Welcome to our city. Glad to know you people are waking up at last. We haven't got many members in your line.

YANK. Naw. Dey're all dead to de woild.

SECRETARY. Well, you can help to wake 'em. What's your name? I'll make out your card.

YANK (*confused*). Name? Lemme tink.

SECRETARY (*sharply*). Don't you know your own name?

YANK. Sure; but I been just Yank for so long—Bob, dat's it—Bob Smith.

SECRETARY (*writing*). Robert Smith. (*Fills out the rest of card.*) Here you are. Cost you half a dollar.

YANK. Is dat all—four bits? Dat's easy. (*Gives the secretary the money.*)

SECRETARY (*throwing it in drawer*). Thanks. Well, make yourself at home. No introductions needed. There's literature on the table. Take some of those pamphlets with you to distribute aboard ship. They may bring results. Sow the seed, only go about it right. Don't get caught and fired. We got plenty out of work. What we need is men who can hold their jobs—and work for us at the same time.

YANK. Sure. (*But he still stands, embarrassed and uneasy.*)

SECRETARY (*looking at him—curiously*). What did you knock for? Think we had a coon in uniform to open doors?

YANK. Naw. I tought it was locked—and dat yuh'd wanter give me the once-over trou a peep-hole or somep'n to see if I was right.

SECRETARY (*alert and suspicious but with an easy laugh*). Think we were running a crap game? That door is never locked. What put that in your nut?

YANK (*with a knowing grin, convinced that this is all camouflage, a part of the secrecy*). Dis burg is full of bulls, ain't it?

SECRETARY (*sharply*). What have the cops got to do with us? We're breaking no laws.

YANK (*with a knowing wink*). Sure. Youse wouldn't for woilds. Sure. I'm wise to dat.

SECRETARY. You seem to be wise to a lot of stuff none of us knows about.

YANK (*with another wink*). Aw, dat's aw right, see. (*Then made a bit resentful by the suspicious glances from all sides.*) Aw, can it! Youse needn't put me trou de toid degree. Can't youse see I belong? Sure! I'm reg'lar. I'll stick, get me? I'll shoot de woiks for youse. Dat's why I wanted to join in.

SECRETARY (*breezily, feeling him out*). That's the right spirit. Only are you sure you understand what you've joined? It's all plain and above board; still, some guys get a wrong slant on us. (*Sharply.*) What's your notion of the purpose of the I. W. W.?

YANK. Aw, I know all about it.

SECRETARY (*sarcastically*). Well, give us some of your valuable information.

YANK (*cunningly*). I know enough not to speak outa my toin. (*Then resentfully again.*) Aw, say! I'm reg'lar. I'm wise to de game. I know yuh got to watch your step wit a stranger. For all youse know, I might be a plain-clothes dick, or somep'n, dat's what yuh're tinkin', huh? Aw, forget it! I belong, see? Ask any guy down to de docks if I don't.

SECRETARY. Who said you didn't?

YANK. After I'm 'nitiated, I'll show yuh.

SECRETARY (*astounded*). Initiated? There's no initiation.

YANK (*disappointed*). Ain't there no password—no grip nor nothin'?

SECRETARY. What'd you think this is—the Elks—or the Black Hand?

YANK. De Elks, hell! De Black Hand, dey're a lot of yellow backstickin' Ginees. Naw. Dis is a man's gang, ain't it?

SECRETARY. You said it! That's why we stand on our two feet in the open. We got no secrets.

YANK (*surprised but admiringly*). Yuh mean to say yuh always run wide open—like dis?

SECRETARY. Exactly.

YANK. Den yuh sure got your noive wit youse!

SECRETARY (*sharply*). Just what was it made you want to join us? Come out with that straight.

YANK. Yuh call me? Well, I got noive, too! Here's my hand. Yuh wanter blow tings up, don't yuh? Well, dat's me! I belong!

SECRETARY (*with pretended carelessness*). You mean change the unequal conditions of society by legitimate direct action—or with dynamite?

YANK. Dynamite! Blow it offen de oith—steel—all de cages—all de factories, steamers, buildings, jails—de Steel Trust and all dat makes it go.

SECRETARY. So—that's your idea, eh? And did you have any special job in that line you wanted to propose to us? (*He makes a sign to the men, who get up cautiously one by one and group behind* YANK.)

YANK (*boldly*). Sure, I'll come out wit it. I'll show youse I'm one of de gang. Dere's dat millionaire guy, Douglas——

SECRETARY. President of the Steel Trust, you mean? Do you want to assassinate him?

YANK. Naw, dat don't get yuh nothin'. I mean blow up de factory, de woiks, where he makes de steel. Dat's what I'm after—to blow up de steel, knock all de steel in de woild up to de moon. Dat'll fix tings! (*Eagerly, with a touch of bravado.*) I'll do it by me lonesome! I'll show yuh! Tell me where his woiks is, how to git there, all de dope. Gimme de stuff, de old butter—and watch me do de rest! Watch de smoke and see it move! I don't give a damn if dey nab me—long as it's done! I'll soive life for it—and give 'em de laugh! (*Half to himself.*) And I'll write her a letter and tell her de hairy ape done it. Dat'll square tings.

SECRETARY (*stepping away from* YANK). Very interesting. (*He gives a signal. The men, huskies all, throw themselves on* YANK *and before he knows it they have his legs and arms pinioned. But he is too flabbergasted to make a struggle, anyway. They feel him over for weapons.*)

MAN. No gat, no knife. Shall we give him what's what and put the boots to him?

SECRETARY. No. He isn't worth the trouble we'd get into. He's too stupid. (*He comes closer and laughs mockingly in* YANK'*s face.*) Ho-ho! By God, this is the biggest joke they've put up on us yet. Hey, you Joke! Who sent you—Burns or Pinkerton? No, by God, you're such a bonehead I'll bet you're in the Secret Service! Well, you dirty spy, you rotten agent provocator, you can go back and tell whatever skunk is paying you blood-money for betraying your brothers that he's wasting his coin. You couldn't catch a cold. And tell him that all he'll ever get on us, or ever has got, is just his own sneaking plots that he's framed up to put us in jail. We are what our manifesto says we are, neither more nor less—and we'll give him a copy of that any time he calls. And as for you—— (*He glares scornfully at* YANK, *who is sunk in an oblivious stupor.*) Oh, hell, what's the use of talking? You're a brainless ape.

YANK (*aroused by the word to fierce but futile struggles*). What's dat, yuh Sheeny bum, yuh!

SECRETARY. Throw him out, boys. (*In spite of his struggles, this is done with gusto and éclat. Propelled by several parting kicks,* YANK *lands sprawling in the middle of the narrow cobbled street. With a growl he starts to get up and storm the closed door, but stops bewildered by the confusion in his brain, pathetically impotent. He sits there, brooding, in as near to the attitude of Rodin's "Thinker" as he can get in his position.)*

YANK (*bitterly*). So dem boids don't tink I belong, neider. Aw, to hell wit 'em! Dey're in de wrong pew—de same old bull—soapboxes and Salvation Army—no guts! Cut out an hour offen de job a day and make me happy! Gimme a dollar more a day and make me happy! Tree square a day, and cauliflowers in de front yard—ekal rights—a woman and kids—a lousy vote—and I'm all fixed for Jesus, huh? Aw, hell! What does dat get yuh? Dis ting's in your inside, but it ain't your belly. Feedin' your face—sinkers and coffee—dat don't touch it. It's way down—at de bottom. Yuh can't grab it, and yuh can't stop it. It moves, and everything moves. It stops and de whole woild stops. Dat's me now—I don't tick, see?—I'm a busted Ingersoll, dat's what. Steel was me, and I owned de woild. Now I ain't steel, and de woild owns me. Aw, hell! I can't see—it's all dark, get me? It's all wrong! (*He turns a bitter mocking face up like an ape gibbering at the moon.*) Say, youse up dere, Man in de Moon, yuh look so wise, gimme de answer, huh? Slip me de inside dope, de information right from de stable—where do I get off at, huh?

A POLICEMAN (*who has come up the street in time to hear this last—with grim humor*). You'll get off at the station, you boob, if you don't get up out of that and keep movin'.

YANK (*looking up at him—with a hard, bitter laugh*). Sure! Lock me up! Put me in a cage! Dat's de on'y answer yuh know. G'wan, lock me up!

POLICEMAN. What you been doin'?

YANK. Enuf to gimme life for! I was born, see? Sure, dat's de charge. Write it in de blotter. I was born, get me!

POLICEMAN (*jocosely*). God pity your old woman! (*Then matter-of-fact.*) But I've no time for kidding. You're soused. I'd run you in but it's too long a walk to the station. Come on now, get up, or I'll fan your ears with this club. Beat it now! (*He hauls* YANK *to his feet.*)

YANK (*in a vague mocking tone*). Say, where do I go from here?

POLICEMAN (*giving him a push—with a grin, indifferently*). Go to hell.

CURTAIN

SCENE EIGHT

Twilight of the next day. The monkey house at the Zoo. One spot of clear gray light falls on the front of one cage so that the interior can be seen. The other cages are vague, shrouded in shadow from which chatterings pitched in a conversational tone can be heard. On the one cage a sign from which the word "gorilla" stands out. The gigantic animal himself is seen squatting on his haunches on a bench in much the same attitude as Rodin's "Thinker." YANK *enters from the left. Immediately a chorus of angry chattering and screeching breaks out. The gorilla turns his eyes but makes no sound or move.*

YANK (*with a hard, bitter laugh*). Welcome to your city, huh? Hail, hail, de gang's all here! (*At the sound of his voice the chattering dies away into an attentive silence.* YANK *walks up to the gorilla's cage and, leaning over the railing, stares in at its occupant, who stares back at him, silent and motionless. There is a pause of dead stillness. Then* YANK *begins to talk in a friendly confidential tone, half-mockingly, but with a deep undercurrent of sympathy.*) Say, yuh're some hard-lookin' guy, ain't yuh? I seen lots of tough nuts dat de gang called gorillas, but yuh're de foist real one I ever seen. Some chest yuh got, and shoulders, and dem arms and mits! I bet yuh got a punch in eider fist dat'd knock 'em all silly! (*This with genuine admiration. The gorilla, as if he understood, stands upright, swelling out his chest and pounding on it with his fist.* YANK *grins sympathetically.*) Sure, I get yuh. Yuh challenge de whole woild, huh? Yuh got what I was sayin' even if yuh muffed de woids. (*Then bitterness creeping in.*) And why wouldn't yuh get me? Ain't we both members of de same club—de Hairy Apes? (*They stare at each other—a pause—then* YANK *goes on slowly and bitterly.*) So yuh're what she seen when she looked at me, de white-faced tart! I was you to her, get me? On'y outa de cage—broke out—free to moider her, see? Sure! Dat's what she tought. She wasn't wise dat I was in a cage, too—worser'n yours—sure—a damn sight—'cause you got some chanct to bust loose—but me—— (*He grows confused.*) Aw, hell! It's all wrong, ain't it? (*A pause.*) I s'pose yuh wanter know what I'm doin' here, huh? I been warmin' a bench down to de Battery—ever since last night. Sure. I seen de sun come up. Dat was pretty, too—all red and pink and green. I was lookin' at de skyscrapers—steel—and all de ships comin' in, sailin' out, all over de oith—and dey was steel, too. De sun was warm, dey wasn't no clouds, and dere was a breeze blowin'. Sure, it was great stuff. I got it aw right—what Paddy said about dat bein' de right dope—on'y I couldn't get *in* it, see? I couldn't belong in dat. It was over my head. And I kept tinkin'—and den I beat it up here to see what youse was like. And I waited till dey was all gone to git yuh alone. Say, how d'yuh feel sittin' in dat pen all de time, havin' to stand for 'em comin' and starin' at yuh—de white-faced, skinny tarts and de boobs what marry 'em—makin' fun of yuh, laughin' at yuh, gittin' scared of yuh—damn 'em! (*He pounds on the rail with his fist. The gorilla rattles the bars of his cage and snarls. All the other monkeys set up an angry chattering in the darkness.* YANK *goes on excitedly.*) Sure! Dat's de way it hit me, too. On'y yuh're lucky, see? Yuh don't belong with 'em and yuh know it. But me, I belong wit 'em—but I don't, see? Dey don't belong with me, dat's what. Get me? Tinkin' is hard—— (*He passes one hand across his forehead with a painful gesture. The gorilla growls impatiently.* YANK *goes on gropingly.*) It's dis way, what I'm drivin' at. Youse can sit and dope dream in de past, green woods, de jungle and de rest of it. Den yuh belong and dey don't. Den yuh kin laugh at 'em, see? Yuh're de champ of de woild. But me—I ain't got no past to tink in, nor nothin' dat's comin', on'y what's now—and dat don't belong. Sure, you're de best off! Yuh can't tink, can yuh? Yuh can't talk neider. But I kin make a bluff at talkin' and tinkin'—a'most git away wit it—a'most!—and dat's where de joker comes in. (*He laughs.*) I ain't on oith and I ain't in heaven, get me? I'm in de middle tryin' to separate 'em, takin' all de woist punches from bot' of 'em. Maybe dat's what dey call hell, huh? But you, yuh're at de bottom. You belong! Sure! Yuh're de on'y one in de woild dat does, yuh lucky stiff! (*The gorilla growls proudly.*) And dat's why dey gotter put yuh in a cage, see? (*The gorilla roars angrily.*) Sure! Yuh get me. It beats it when you try to tink it or talk it—it's way down—deep—behind—you 'n' me we feel it. Sure! Bot' members of dis club! (*He laughs—then in a savage tone.*) What de hell! T' hell wit it! A little action, dat's our meat! Dat belongs! Knock 'em down and keep bustin' 'em till dey croaks yuh with a gat—wit steel! Sure! Are yuh game? Dey've looked at youse, ain't dey—in a cage? Wanter git even? Wanter wind up like a sport 'stead of croakin' slow in dere? (*The gorilla roars an emphatic affirmative.* YANK *goes on with a sort of furious exaltation.*) Sure! Yuh're reg'lar! Yuh'll stick to de finish! Me 'n' you, huh?—bot' members of this club! We'll put up one last star bout dat'll knock 'em offen deir seats! Dey'll have to make de cages stronger after we're trou! (*The gorilla is straining at his bars, growling, hopping from one foot to the other.* YANK *takes a jimmy from under his coat and forces the lock on the cage door. He throws this open.*) Pardon from de governor! Step out and shake hands! I'll take yuh for a walk down Fif' Avenoo. We'll knock 'em offen de oith and croak wit de band playin'. Come on, Brother. (*The gorilla scrambles gingerly out of his cage. Goes to* YANK *and stands looking at him.* YANK *keeps his mocking tone—holds out his hand.*) Shake—de secret grip of our order. (*Something, the tone of mockery, perhaps, suddenly enrages the animal. With a spring he wraps his huge arms around* YANK *in a murderous hug. There is a crackling snap of crushed ribs—a gasping cry, still mocking, from* YANK.) Hey, I didn't say kiss me! (*The gorilla lets the crushed body slip to the floor; stands over it uncertainly, considering; then picks it up, throws it in the cage, shuts the door, and shuffles off menacingly into the darkness at left. A great uproar of frightened chattering and whimpering comes from the other cages. Then* YANK *moves, groaning, opening his eyes, and there is silence. He mutters painfully.*) Say—dey oughter match him—wit Zybszko. He got me, aw right. I'm trou. Even him didn't tink I belonged. (*Then, with sudden passionate despair.*) Christ, where do I get off at? Where do I fit in? (*Checking himself as suddenly.*) Aw, what de hell! No squawkin', see! No quittin', get me! Croak wit your boots on! (*He grabs hold of the bars of the cage and hauls himself painfully to his feet—looks around him bewilderedly—forces a mocking laugh.*) In de cage, huh? (*In the strident tones of a circus barker.*) Ladies and gents, step forward and take a slant at de one and only—(*His voice weakening*)—one and original—Hairy Ape from de wilds of—— (*He slips in a heap on the floor and dies. The monkeys set up a chattering, whimpering wail. And, perhaps, the Hairy Ape at last belongs.*)

CURTAIN

Desire Under the Elms

BY EUGENE O'NEILL

First produced at the Greenwich Village Theatre, New York, November 11, 1924, with the following cast:

SIMEON CABOT	Allen Nagle
PETER CABOT	Perry Ivins
EBEN CABOT	Charles Ellis
EPHRAIM CABOT, their Father	Walter Huston
ABBIE PUTNAM	Mary Morris
A YOUNG GIRL	Eloise Pendleton
FARMERS	Romeyn Benjamin, Arthur Mack, William Stahl, John Taylor
A FIDDLER	Macklin Marrow
AN OLD WOMAN	Norma Millay
A SHERIFF	Walter Abel
DEPUTIES	Arthur Mack, William Stahl

The action of the entire play takes place in, and immediately outside of, the Cabot farmhouse in New England, in the year 1850.

Part I. The beginning of summer.

Part II. A Sunday, two months later.

Part III. Late spring of the following year.

Eugene O'Neill's career in the twenties may be arbitrarily divided into two phases. In one, represented by *Desire Under the Elms* (as well as by his one-act sea pieces, *Beyond the Horizon, Diff'rent, Anna Christie, The Straw, The First Man,* and *Welded*), he gave comfort to those who thought that our theatre needed a strong injection of realism. In the other phase, exemplified by *The Hairy Ape* (as well as by *The Emperor Jones, All God's Chillun Got Wings, The Great God Brown,* and *Strange Interlude*), he sustained the hopes of those to whom modernity meant departing from realistic style and finding other forms of expression. The division is an arbitrary one since O'Neill alternated his styles instead of adhering to one or the other for any length of time, and he even interposed another, romantic type of drama (*Gold, The Fountain, Marco Millions*) every now and then. O'Neill actually served under no star other than his own baleful one. It impelled him to employ a variety of styles for his work, which was, in many respects, a calvary of self-expression. That he could take many liberties as a prerogative makes him, indeed, ideally the representative of modernity in the twenties, when the theatre was willing to try almost anything at any time. It was a period when searching and experimenting were common even to playwrights who discovered a practical style acceptable to the public and profitable to themselves—as did Kaufman and Barry.

Since O'Neill's best plays exist on several levels simultaneously, his adoption of any particular technique or tone never was a complete or exclusive commitment. The realistic content and colloquial dialogue of the one-act sea plays (the *S.S. Glencairn* series) accommodated a poet's sense of fateful mystery in the universe as well as the actual environment, including the loneliness, toil, and misery, of sailors, wharf rats, and tarts. Although *Beyond the Horizon* dramatizes frustration by environment, sexual impulse, and by an ironic fate that deals out wrong careers to the players, the anguish in that play is fundamentally that of the bemused soul rather than of the carnal man on whom naturalism was wont to concentrate. If the colloquialism and background of *Anna Christie,* as well as the unsavory past of Anna, could be regarded in 1921 as the ultimate in American realism, its conclusion is romantic, as O'Neill's critics noted with some dissatisfaction; and more importantly, there are cosmic intimations even in that play from that "ole davil" the sea which represents the inscrutable malignity of fate for Chris Christopherson.

For all the "stark realism" usually lauded or deplored in the rustic tragedy of *Desire Under the Elms* (and it is indeed comparable to peasant tragedy in European naturalism, notably Tolstoy's *The Power of Darkness* and Hauptmann's *Before Sunrise*), the play is by both theme and mood a tragic poem. There is mystery in its straining heart. In part, it is the mystery of "ambivalence," of continual transformations of love into hate and of hate into love ever since the first member of the primitive horde fought his father or turned his eyes on the first woman beyond his reach—and ever since the first woman found love in him she feared. There is an oedipus complex, among much else, in *Desire Under the Elms,* but we are likely to understand very little about that, too, if we see only the formula. Freud himself saw all of human history in it, and every clinical case of his contains a complex human record for which the term is but a category and not an equivalent. Besides, Freud meant what he said when he used the word "complex" whereas shallow persons who adopted his terminology spoke as though he meant, *pace* Joyce, a "simplex." O'Neill, however, was not shallow in *Desire Under the Elms.*

All this is mingled in the play with the related complexities so long present in human nature: with the fact, for instance, that man both accepts and resents tribe and taboo, "father" and conscience; that his religion and economic activity are implicated in his passions, and that man desires beyond woman as he also desires beyond inanimate possessions. Simple attention to Eben and his father will reveal that much. For all its distinct localization in New England, the play belongs to man and not to a region. For all its suggestion that illicit passion lurks behind the facade of puritanism, so welcome a piece of information to "debunkers" of the period and so abhorrent to the watchdogs of respectability, *Desire Under the Elms* aspires to poetry and not to sociology. If it gave the impression of a "shocker" in the social and cultural context of the twenties, it was nevertheless the purest and best integrated expression of O'Neill's vision of human life. In this respect it is superior as dramatic art to the schematized and more openly formulated plays from *The Hairy Ape* and *The Great God Brown* to *Strange Interlude* and *Mourning Becomes Electra,* which seemed more imposing because they were either experimentally constructed or were spun out longer and with more diversified threads of complication.

Conversely, O'Neill's departures from realistic technique in the twenties had much matter pertinent to social fact, inquiry, and protest. *The Emperor Jones* and *All God's Chillun Got Wings* recapitulated some of the struggles of the Negro in America. *The Hairy Ape* suggested parallels of "class struggle." *The Great God Brown* implied that man's inner conflicts were caused, to a degree, by unhealthy religious training, the pressures of materialism, and a general unwholesomeness of environment. It is idle to try to remove O'Neill from the social scene, and even his own publicized efforts to disclaim interest in it remain unconvincing. O'Neill picked up the ideas of his time with the alertness of a young artist and he observed the world around him directly, responded to social currents, and had social sympathies along with his fellow artists.

The son of the successful actor James O'Neill (he was born in Manhattan's theatrical district in 1888) became very much part of the world after his suspension for a year from Princeton for a freshman prank. Instead of returning to college, he went prospecting for gold in the Honduras with a mining engineer. Sent home after contracting malaria, he toured with his father's acting company for a while as assistant stage manager. Tiring of this comparatively tame position, he shipped to Buenos Aires on a Norwegian boat and worked in Argentina for American companies like Westinghouse and the Singer Sewing Machine Company. Next, he enlisted on a steamer carrying mules to South Africa, on his return to Buenos Aires went "on the beach" there, traveled again as an able seaman, lived in a waterfront bar in New York, and finally settled down to a reporter's and columnist's job on the New London Telegraph in Connecticut. His health was undermined by then and he spent a term in a sanatorium for tubercular patients, reading the Greeks, Strindberg, and other moderns. His disease arrested, he joined Baker's Workshop 47 in 1914 and then spent a year among the insurgent intellectuals of Greenwich Village. Among those who made their headquarters there were George Cram Cook, Susan Glaspell, Edna St. Vincent Millay, the vagabond poet Harry Kemp, and the social idealists John Reed and Mary Heaton Vorse. Joining some of them on Cape Cod for the summer (and the diversity of their interests alone could have given him an education in modern ideas), he became one of the Provincetown Players, acted for them, and submitted plays to them. In the summer of 1916, they placed his one-act sea play *Bound East for Cardiff* on their second program, and from then on O'Neill's career belonged to theatrical history.

Except for *Marco Millions,* where a commentary on the American scene is explicit even if the subject is Marco Polo, O'Neill's romantic plays proved far less impressive than his expressionistic ones. In these he could use to the full extent his considerable theatricalizing faculty, for it has always been apparent that O'Neill's imagination has been even more theatrical than visionary and poetic. His magic as well as his violence, for which he has been accused of giving us melodrama in the guise of tragedy, his mastery as well as its aberrations, must be related to the fact that theatre came to him many-shaped and unconstrained when he sat down to write. A theatrical imagination was, however, his ally whenever he wanted to dramatize the division in men's souls. This is seen in the phantasmagoric vignettes of *Emperor Jones* and *The Hairy Ape,* and in his use of masks for *The Great God Brown* and of interior monologues for *Strange Interlude.*

Among the most stylized or "expressionist" of these experiments, *The Hairy Ape,* moreover, best illustrates the fact that even symbolism in O'Neill was double-faceted. Whereas another dramatist might have been content to make Yank, the stoker hero of the play, represent the working man trying to work out his disorientation and protest, O'Neill made him a symbol of Man looking for a connection with the universe once he emerges from a brutish unthinking state. (And this is only a partial explanation.) The social basis of the play, which is so plainly set down in several episodes, is here transcended poetically and, in a sense, metaphysically. If this is achieved not without the penalty of some mystification, and if this argues a want of integration in O'Neill's art (except in his congenial family comedy, *Ah, Wilderness!*), it is the very essence of the plays that they represent efforts to find unity. The effort was still being dramatized in *Days Without End* (1934) and in *The Iceman Cometh* (1939, produced in 1946), and may appear in plays O'Neill has until now withheld from Broadway. And from this point on, one would have to exhaust at least a chapter and preferably a book if one were to examine the problems O'Neill raises for criticism by his declared intention to carry the drama beyond "the banality of surfaces."

PART I

Scene One

Exterior of the Farmhouse. It is sunset of a day at the beginning of summer in the year 1850. There is no wind and everything is still. The sky above the roof is suffused with deep colors, the green of the elms glows, but the house is in shadow, seeming pale and washed out by contrast.

The south end of the house faces front to a stone wall with a wooden gate at center opening on a country road. The house is in good condition but in need of paint. Its walls are a sickly grayish, the green of the shutters faded. Two enormous elms are on each side of the house. They bend their trailing branches down over the roof. They appear to protect and at the same time subdue. There is a sinister maternity in their aspect, a crushing, jealous absorption. They have developed from their intimate contact with the life of man in the house an appalling humaneness. They brood oppressively over the house. They are like exhausted women resting their sagging breasts and hands and hair on its roof, and when it rains their tears trickle down monotonously and rot on the shingles.

There is a path running from the gate around the right corner of the house to the front door. A narrow porch is on this side. The end wall facing us has two windows in its upper story, two larger ones on the floor below. The two upper are those of the father's bedroom and that of the brothers. On the left, ground floor, is the kitchen—on the right, the parlor, the shades of which are always drawn down.

A door opens and EBEN CABOT *comes to the end of the porch and stands looking down the road to the right. He has a large bell in his hand and this he swings mechanically, awakening a deafening clangor. Then he puts his hands on his hips and stares up at the sky. He sighs with a puzzled awe and blurts out with halting appreciation.*

EBEN. God! Purty! (*His eyes fall and he stares about him frowningly. He is twenty-five, tall and sinewy. His face is well-formed, good-looking, but its expression is resentful and defensive. His defiant, dark eyes remind one of a wild animal's in captivity. Each day is a cage in which he finds himself trapped but inwardly unsubdued. There is a fierce repressed vitality about him. He has black hair, mustache, a thin curly trace of beard. He is dressed in rough farm clothes.*) (*He spits on the ground with intense disgust, turns and goes back into the house.*) (SIMEON *and* PETER *come in from their work in the fields. They are tall men, much older than their half-brother* [SIMEON *is thirty-nine and* PETER *thirty-seven*], *built on a squarer, simpler model, fleshier in body, more bovine and homelier in face, shrewder and more practical. Their shoulders stoop a bit from years of farm work. They clump heavily along in their clumsy thick-soled boots caked with earth. Their clothes, their faces, hands, bare arms and throats are earth-stained. They smell of earth. They stand together for a moment in front of the house and, as if with the one impulse, stare dumbly up at the sky, leaning on their hoes. Their faces have a compressed, unresigned expression. As they look upward, this softens.*)

SIMEON (*grudgingly*). Purty.

PETER. Ay-eh.

SIMEON (*suddenly*). Eighteen year ago.

PETER. What?

SIMEON. Jenn. My woman. She died.

PETER. I'd fergot.

SIMEON. I rec'lect—now an' agin. Makes it lonesome. She'd hair long's a hoss' tail —an' yaller like gold!

PETER. Waal—she's gone. (*This with indifferent finality—then after a pause.*) They's gold in the West, Sim.

SIMEON (*still under the influence of sunset—vaguely*). In the sky?

PETER. Waal—in a manner o' speakin' —thar's the promise. (*Growing excited.*) Gold in the sky—in the West—Golden Gate—Californi-a!—Goldest West!—fields o' gold!

SIMEON (*excited in his turn*). Fortunes layin' just atop o' the ground waitin' t' be picked! Solomon's mines, they says! (*For a moment they continue looking up at the sky—then their eyes drop.*)

PETER (*with sardonic bitterness*). Here —it's stones atop o' the ground—stones atop o' stones—makin'—stone walls—year atop o' year—him 'n' yew 'n' me 'n' then Eben—makin' stone walls fur him to fence us in!

SIMEON. We've wuked. Give our strength. Give our years. Plowed 'em under in the ground,—(*He stamps rebelliously.*) — rottin' — makin' soil for his crops! (*A pause.*) Waal—the farm pays good for hereabouts.

PETER. If we plowed in Californi-a, they'd be lumps o' gold in the furrow!

SIMEON. Californi-a's t'other side o' earth, a'most. We got t' calc'late——

PETER (*after a pause*). 'Twould be hard fur me, too, to give up what we've 'arned here by our sweat. (*A pause.* EBEN *sticks his head out of the dining-room window, listening.*)

SIMEON. Ay-eh. (*A pause.*) Mebbe—he'll die soon.

PETER (*doubtfully*). Mebbe.

SIMEON. Mebbe—fur all we knows—he's dead now.

PETER. Ye'd need proof.

SIMEON. He's been gone two months—with no word.

PETER. Left us in the fields an evenin' like this. Hitched up an' druv off into the West. That's plumb onnateral. He hain't never been off this farm 'ceptin' t' the village in thirty year or more, not since he married Eben's maw. (*A pause. Shrewdly.*) I calc'late we might git him declared crazy by the court.

SIMEON. He skinned 'em too slick. He got the best o' all on 'em. They'd never b'lieve him crazy. (*A pause.*) We got t' wait—till he's under ground.

EBEN (*with a sardonic chuckle*). Honor thy father! (*They turn, startled, and stare at him. He grins, then scowls.*) I pray he's died. (*They stare at him. He continues matter-of-factly.*) Supper's ready.

SIMEON *and* PETER (*together*). Ay-eh.

EBEN (*gazing up at the sky*). Sun's downin' purty.

SIMEON *and* PETER (*together*). Ay-eh. They's gold in the West.

EBEN. Ay-eh. (*Pointing.*) Yonder atop o' the hill pasture, ye mean?

SIMEON *and* PETER (*together*). In Californi-a!

EBEN. Hunh? (*Stares at them indifferently for a second, then drawls.*) Waal—supper's gittin' cold. (*He turns back into kitchen.*)

SIMEON (*startled—smacks his lips*). I air hungry!

PETER (*sniffing*). I smells bacon!

SIMEON (*with hungry appreciation*). Bacon's good!

PETER (*in same tone*). Bacon's bacon! (*They turn, shouldering each other, their bodies bumping and rubbing together as they hurry clumsily to their food, like two friendly oxen toward their evening meal. They disappear around the right corner of house and can be heard entering the door*).

THE CURTAIN FALLS

Scene Two

The color fades from the sky. Twilight begins. The interior of the kitchen is now visible. A pine table is at center, a cookstove in the right rear corner, four rough wooden chairs, a tallow candle on the table. In the middle of the rear wall is fastened a big advertizing poster with a ship in full sail and the word "California" in big letters. Kitchen utensils hang from nails. Everything is neat and in order but the atmosphere is of a men's camp kitchen rather than that of a home.

Places for three are laid. EBEN *takes boiled potatoes and bacon from the stove and puts them on the table, also a loaf of bread and a crock of water.* SIMEON *and* PETER *shoulder in, slump down in their chairs without a word.* EBEN *joins them. The three eat in silence for a moment, the two elder as naturally unrestrained as beasts of the field,* EBEN *picking at his food without appetite, glancing at them with a tolerant dislike.*

SIMEON (*suddenly turns to* EBEN). Looky here! Ye'd oughtn't t' said that, Eben.

PETER. 'Twa'n't righteous.

EBEN. What?

SIMEON. Ye prayed he'd died.

EBEN. Waal—don't yew pray it? (*A pause.*)

PETER. He's our Paw.

EBEN (*violently*). Not mine!

SIMEON (*dryly*). Ye'd not let no one else say that about yer Maw! Ha! (*He gives one abrupt sardonic guffaw.* PETER *grins.*)

EBEN (*very pale*). I meant—I hain't his'n—I hain't like him—he hain't me!

PETER (*dryly*). Wait till ye've growed his age!

EBEN (*intensely*). I'm Maw—every drop o' blood! (*A pause. They stare at him with indifferent curiosity.*)

PETER (*reminiscently*). She was good t' Sim 'n' me. A good Step-maw's scurse.

SIMEON. She was good t' everyone.

EBEN (*greatly moved, gets to his feet and makes an awkward bow to each of them—stammering*). I be thankful t' ye. I'm her—her heir. (*He sits down in confusion.*)

PETER (*after a pause—judicially*). She was good even t' him.

EBEN (*fiercely*). An' fur thanks he killed her!

SIMEON (*after a pause*). No one never kills nobody. It's allus somethin'. That's the murderer.

EBEN. Didn't he slave Maw t' death?

PETER. He's slaved himself t' death. He's slaved Sim 'n' me 'n' yew t' death —on'y none o' us hain't died—yit.

SIMEON. It's somethin'—drivin' him—t' drive us!

EBEN (*vengefully*). Waal—I hold him t' jedgment! (*Then scornfully.*) Somethin'! What's somethin'?

SIMEON. Dunno.

EBEN (*sardonically*). What's drivin' yew to Californi-a, mebbe? (*They look at him in surprise.*) Oh, I've heerd ye! (*Then, after a pause.*) But ye'll never go t' the gold fields!

PETER (*assertively*). Mebbe!

EBEN. Whar'll ye git the money?

PETER. We kin walk. It's an a'mighty ways—Californi-a—but if yew was t' put all the steps we've walked on this farm end t' end we'd be in the moon!

EBEN. The Injuns'll skulp ye on the plains.

SIMEON (*with grim humor*). We'll mebbe make 'em pay a hair fur a hair!

EBEN (*decisively*). But t'ain't that. Ye won't never go because ye'll wait here fur yer share o' the farm, thinkin' allus he'll die soon.

SIMEON (*after a pause*). We've a right.

PETER. Two-thirds belongs t'us.

EBEN (*jumping to his feet*). Ye've no right! She wa'n't yewr Maw! It was her farm! Didn't he steal it from her? She's dead. It's my farm.

SIMEON (*sardonically*). Tell that t' Paw —when he comes! I'll bet ye a dollar he'll laugh—fur once in his life. Ha! (*He laughs himself in one single mirthless bark.*)

PETER (*amused in turn, echoes his brother*). Ha!

SIMEON (*after a pause*). What've ye got held agin us, Eben? Year arter year it's skulked in yer eye—somethin'.

PETER, Ay-eh.

EBEN. Ay-eh. They's somethin'. (*Suddenly exploding.*) Why didn't ye never stand between him 'n' my Maw when he was slavin' her to her grave—t' pay her back fur the kindness she done t' yew? (*There is a long pause. They stare at him in surprise.*)

SIMEON. Waal—the stock'd got t' be watered.

PETER. 'R they was woodin' t' do.

SIMEON. 'R plawin'.

PETER. 'R hayin'.

SIMEON. 'R spreadin' manure.

PETER. 'R weedin'.

SIMEON. 'R prunin'.

PETER. 'R milkin'.

EBEN (*breaking in harshly*). An' makin' walls—stone atop o' stone—makin' walls till yer heart's a stone ye heft up out o' the way o' growth onto a stone wall t' wall in yer heart!

SIMEON (*matter-of-factly*). We never had no time t' meddle.

PETER (*to* EBEN). Yew was fifteen afore yer Maw died—an' big fur yer age. Why didn't ye never do nothin'?

EBEN (*harshly*). They was chores t' do, wa'n't they? (*A pause—then slowly.*) It was on'y arter she died I come to think o' it. Me cookin'—doin' her work—that made me know her, suffer her sufferin'—she'd come back t' help—come back t' bile potatoes—come back t' fry bacon—come back t' bake biscuits—come back all cramped up t' shake the fire, an' carry ashes, her eyes weepin' an' bloody with smoke an' cinders same's they used t' be. She still comes back—stands by the stove thar in the evenin'—she can't find it nateral sleepin' an' restin' in peace. She can't git used t' bein' free—even in her grave.

SIMEON. She never complained none.

EBEN. She'd got too tired. She'd got too used t' bein' too tired. That was what he done. (*With vengeful passion.*) An' sooner'r later, I'll meddle. I'll say the thin's I didn't say then t' him! I'll yell 'em at the top o' my lungs. I'll see t' it my Maw gits some rest an' sleep in her grave! (*He sits down again, relapsing into a brooding silence. They look at him with a queer indifferent curiosity.*)

PETER (*after a pause*). Whar in tarnation d'ye s'pose he went, Sim?

SIMEON. Dunno. He druv off in the

buggy, all spick an' span, with the mare all breshed an' shiny, druv off clackin' his tongue an' wavin' his whip. I remember it right well. I was finishin' plowin', it was spring an' May an' sunset, an' gold in the West, an' he druv off into it. I yells "Whar ye goin', Paw?" an' he hauls up by the stone wall a jiffy. His old snake's eyes was glitterin' in the sun like he'd been drinkin' a jugful an' he says with a mule's grin: "Don't ye run away till I come back!"

PETER. Wonder if he knowed we was wantin' fur Californi-a?

SIMEON. Mebbe. I didn't say nothin' and he says, lookin' kinder queer an' sick: "I been hearin' the hens cluckin' an' the roosters crowin' all the durn day. I been listenin' t' the cows lowin' an' everythin' else kickin' up till I can't stand it no more. It's spring an' I'm feelin' damned," he says. "Damned like an old bare hickory tree fit on'y fur burnin'," he says. An' then I calc'late I must've looked a mite hopeful, fur he adds real spry and vicious: "But don't git no fool idee I'm dead. I've sworn t' live a hundred an' I'll do it, if on'y t' spite yer sinful greed! An' now I'm ridin' out t' learn God's message t' me in the spring, like the prophets done. An' yew git back t' yer plowin'," he says. An' he druv off singin' a hymn. I thought he was drunk—'r I'd stopped him goin'.

EBEN (*scornfully*). No, ye wouldn't! Ye're scared o' him. He's stronger—inside—than both o' ye put together!

PETER (*sardonically*). An' yew—be yew Samson?

EBEN. I'm gittin' stronger. I kin feel it growin' in me—growin' an' growin'—till it'll bust out—! (*He gets up and puts on his coat and a hat. They watch him, gradually breaking into grins.* EBEN *avoids their eyes sheepishly.*) I'm goin' out fur a spell—up the road.

PETER. T' the village?

SIMEON. T' see Minnie?

EBEN (*defiantly*). Ay-eh!

PETER (*jeeringly*). The Scarlet Woman!

SIMEON. Lust—that's what's growin' in ye!

EBEN. Waal—she's purty!

PETER. She's been purty fur twenty year!

SIMEON. A new coat o' paint'll make a heifer out of forty.

EBEN. She hain't forty!

PETER. If she hain't, she's teeterin' on the edge.

EBEN (*desperately*). What d'yew know——

PETER. All they is . . . Sim knew her—an' then me arter——

SIMEON. An' Paw kin tell yew somethin' too! He was fust!

EBEN. D'ye mean t'say he . . . ?

SIMEON (*with a grin*). Ay-eh! We air his heirs in everythin'!

EBEN (*intensely*). That's more to it! That grows on it! It'll bust soon! (*Then violently.*) I'll go smash my fist in her face! (*He pulls open the door in rear violently.*)

SIMEON (*with a wink at* PETER*—drawlingly*). Mebbe—but the night's wa'm—purty—by the time ye git thar mebbe ye'll kiss her instead!

PETER. Sart'n he will! (*They both roar with coarse laughter.* EBEN *rushes out and slams the door—then the outside front door—comes around the corner of the house and stands still by the gate, staring up at the sky.*)

SIMEON (*looking after him*). Like his Paw.

PETER. Dead spit an' image!

SIMEON. Dog'll eat dog!

PETER. Ay-eh. (*Pause. With yearning.*) Mebbe a year from now we'll be in Californi-a.

SIMEON. Ay-eh. (*A pause. Both yawn.*) Let's git t'bed. (*He blows out the candle. They go out door in rear.* EBEN *stretches his arms up to the sky—rebelliously.*)

EBEN. Waal—thar's a star, an' somewhar's they's him, an' here's me, an' thar's Min up the road—in the same night. What if I does kiss her? She's like t'night, she's soft 'n' wa'm, her eyes kin wink like a star, her mouth's wa'm, her arms're wa'm, she smells like a wa'm plowed field, she's purty . . . Ay-eh! By God A'mighty she's purty, an' I don't give a damn how many sins she's sinned afore mine or who she's sinned 'em with, my sin's as purty as any one on 'em! (*He strides off down the road to the left.*)

Scene Three

It is the pitch darkness just before dawn. EBEN *comes in from the left and goes around to the porch, feeling his way, chuckling bitterly and cursing half-aloud to himself.*

EBEN. The cussed old miser! (*He can be heard going in the front door. There is a pause as he goes upstairs, then a loud knock on the bedroom door of the brothers.*) Wake up!

SIMEON (*startledly*). Who's thar?

EBEN (*pushing open the door and coming in, a lighted candle in his hand. The bedroom of the brothers is revealed. Its ceiling is the sloping roof. They can stand upright only close to the center dividing wall of the upstairs.* SIMEON *and* PETER *are in a double bed, front.* EBEN'S *cot is to the rear.* EBEN *has a mixture of silly grin and vicious scowl on his face*). I be!

PETER (*angrily*). What in hell's-fire . . . ?

EBEN. I got news fur ye! Ha! (*He gives one abrupt sardonic guffaw.*)

SIMEON (*angrily*). Couldn't ye hold it 'til we'd got our sleep?

EBEN. It's nigh sunup. (*Then explosively.*) He's gone an' married agen!

SIMEON *and* PETER (*explosively*). Paw?

EBEN. Got himself hitched to a female 'bout thirty-five—an' purty, they says . . .

SIMEON (*aghast*). It's a durn lie!

PETER. Who says?

SIMEON. They been stringin' ye!

EBEN. Think I'm a dunce, do ye? The hull village says. The preacher from New Dover, he brung the news—told it t'our preacher—New Dover, that's whar the old loon got himself hitched—that's whar the woman lived——

PETER (*no longer doubting—stunned*). Waal . . . !

SIMEON (*the same*). Waal . . . !

EBEN (*sitting down on a bed—with vicious hatred*). Ain't he a devil out o' hell? It's jest t' spite us—the damned old mule!

PETER (*after a pause*). Everythin'll go t' her now.

SIMEON. Ay-eh. (*A pause—dully.*) Waal —if it's done——

PETER. It's done us. (*Pause—then persuasively.*) They's gold in the fields o' Californi-a, Sim. No good a-stayin' here now.

SIMEON. Jest what I was a-thinkin'. (*Then with decision.*) S'well fust's last! Let's light out and git this mornin'.

PETER. Suits me.

EBEN. Ye must like walkin'.

SIMEON (*sardonically*). If ye'd grow wings on us we'd fly thar!

EBEN. Ye'd like ridin' better—on a boat, wouldn't ye? (*Fumbles in his pocket and takes out a crumpled sheet of foolscap.*) Waal, if ye sign this ye kin ride on a boat. I've had it writ out an' ready in case ye'd ever go. It says fur three hundred dollars t' each ye agree yewr shares o' the farm is sold t' me. (*They look suspiciously at the paper. A pause.*)

SIMEON (*wonderingly*). But if he's hitched agen——

PETER. An' whar'd yew git that sum o' money, anyways?

EBEN (*cunningly*). I know whar it's hid. I been waitin'—Maw told me. She knew whar it lay fur years, but she was waitin' . . . It's her'n—the money he hoarded from her farm an' hid from Maw. It's my money by rights now.

PETER. Whar's it hid?

EBEN (*cunningly*). Whar yew won't never find it without me. Maw spied on him—'r she'd never knowed. (*A pause. They look at him suspiciously, and he at them.*) Waal, is it fa'r trade?

SIMEON. Dunno.

PETER. Dunno.

SIMEON (*looking at window*). Sky's grayin'.

PETER. Ye better start the fire, Eben.

SIMEON. An' fix some vittles.

EBEN. Ay-eh. (*Then with a forced jocular heartiness.*) I'll git ye a good one. If ye're startin' t' hoof it t' Californi-a ye'll need somethin' that'll stick t' yer ribs. (*He turns to the door, adding meaningly.*) But ye kin ride on a boat if ye'll swap. (*He stops at the door and pauses. They stare at him.*)

SIMEON (*suspiciously*). Whar was ye all night?

EBEN (*defiantly*). Up t' Min's. (*Then slowly.*) Walkin' thar, fust I felt 's if I'd kiss her; then I got a-thinkin' o' what ye'd said o' him an' her an' I says, I'll bust her nose fur that! Then I got t' the village an' heerd the news an' I got madder'n hell an' run all the way t' Min's not knowin' what I'd do—(*He pauses—then sheepishly but more defiantly.*) Waal —when I seen her, I didn't hit her—nor I didn't kiss her nuther—I begun t' beller like a calf an' cuss at the same time, I was so durn mad—an' she got scared—an' I jest grabbed holt an' tuk her! (*Proudly.*) Yes, siree! I tuk her. She may've been his'n—an' your'n, too—but she's mine now!

SIMEON (*dryly*). In love, air yew?

EBEN (*with lofty scorn*). Love! I don't take no stock in sech slop!

PETER (*winking at* SIMEON). Mebbe Eben's aimin' t' marry, too.

SIMEON. Min'd make a true faithful he'pmeet! (*They snicker.*)

EBEN. What do I care fur her—'ceptin' she's round an' wa'm? The p'int is she was his'n—an' now she b'longs t' me! (*He goes to the door—then turns—rebelliously.*) An' Min hain't sech a bad un. They's worse'n Min in the world, I'll bet ye! Wait'll we see this cow the Old Man's hitched t'! She'll beat Min, I got a notion! (*He starts to go out.*)

SIMEON (*suddenly*). Mebbe ye'll try t' make her your'n, too?

PETER. Ha! (*He gives a sardonic laugh of relish at this idea.*)

EBEN (*spitting with disgust*). Her—here—sleepin' with him—stealin' my Maw's farm! I'd as soon pet a skunk 'r kiss a snake! (*He goes out. The two stare after him suspiciously. A pause. They listen to his steps receding.*)

PETER. He's startin' the fire.

SIMEON. I'd like t' ride t' Californi-a—but——

PETER. Min might o' put some scheme in his head.

SIMEON. Mebbe it's all a lie 'bout Paw marryin'. We'd best wait an' see the bride.

PETER. An' don't sign nothin' till we does!

SIMEON. Nor till we've tested it's good money! (*Then with a grin.*) But if Paw's hitched we'd be sellin' Eben somethin' we'd never git nohow!

PETER. We'll wait an' see. (*Then with sudden vindictive anger.*) An' till he comes, let's yew 'n' me not wuk a lick, let Eben tend to thin's if he's a mind t', let's us jest sleep an' eat an' drink likker, an' let the hull damned farm go t' blazes!

SIMEON (*excitedly*). By God, we've 'arned a rest! We'll play rich fur a change. I hain't a-going to stir outa bed till breakfast's ready.

PETER. An' on the table!

SIMEON (*after a pause—thoughtfully*). What d'ye calc'late she'll be like—our new Maw? Like Eben thinks?

PETER. More'n likely.

SIMEON (*vindictively*). Waal—I hope she's a she-devil that'll make him wish he was dead an' livin' in the pit o' hell fur comfort!

PETER (*fervently*). Amen!

SIMEON (*imitating his father's voice*). "I'm ridin' out t' learn God's message t' me in the spring like the prophets done," he says. I'll bet right then an' thar he knew plumb well he was goin' whorin', the stinkin' old hypocrite!

Scene Four

Same as Scene Two—shows the interior of the kitchen with a lighted candle on table. It is gray dawn outside. SIMEON *and* PETER *are just finishing their breakfast.* EBEN *sits before his plate of untouched food, brooding frowningly.*

PETER (*glancing at him rather irritably*). Lookin' glum don't help none.

SIMEON (*sarcastically*). Sorrowin' over his lust o' the flesh!

PETER (*with a grin*). Was she yer fust?

EBEN (*angrily*). None o' yer business. (*A pause.*) I was thinkin' o' him. I got a notion he's gittin' near—I kin feel him comin' on like yew kin feel malaria chill afore it takes ye.

PETER. It's too early yet.

SIMEON. Dunno. He'd like t' catch us nappin'—jest t' have somethin' t' hoss us 'round over.

PETER (*mechanically gets to his feet.* SIMEON *does the same*). Waal—let's git t' wuk. (*They both plod mechanically toward the door before they realize. Then they stop short.*)

SIMEON (*grinning*). Ye're a cussed fool, Pete—and I be wuss! Let him see we hain't wukin'! We don't give a durn!

PETER (*as they go back to the table*). Not a damned durn! It'll serve t' show him we're done with him. (*They sit down again.* EBEN *stares from one to the other with surprise.*)

SIMEON (*grins at him*). We're aimin' t' start bein' lilies o' the field.

PETER. Nary a toil 'r spin 'r lick o' wuk do we put in!

SIMEON. Ye're sole owner—till he comes—that's what ye wanted. Waal, ye got t' be sole hand, too.

PETER. The cows air bellerin'. Ye better hustle at the milkin'.

EBEN (*with excited joy*). Ye mean ye'll sign the paper?

SIMEON (*dryly*). Mebbe.

PETER. Mebbe.

SIMEON. We're considerin'. (*Peremptorily.*) Ye better git t' wuk.

EBEN (*with queer excitement*). It's Maw's farm agen! It's my farm! Them's my cows! I'll milk my durn fingers off fur cows o' mine! (*He goes out door in rear, they stare after him indifferently.*)

SIMEON. Like his Paw.

PETER. Dead spit 'n' image!

SIMEON. Waal—let dog eat dog! (EBEN *comes out of front door and around the corner of the house. The sky is beginning to grow flushed with sunrise.* EBEN *stops by the gate and stares around him with glowing, possessive eyes. He takes in the whole farm with his embracing glance of desire.*)

EBEN. It's purty! It's damned purty! It's mine! (*He suddenly throws his head back boldly and glares with hard, defiant eyes at the sky.*) Mine, d'ye hear? Mine! (*He turns and walks quickly off left, rear, toward the barn. The two brothers light their pipes.*)

SIMEON (*putting his muddy boots up on the table, tilting back his chair, and puffing defiantly*). Waal—this air solid comfort—fur once.

PETER. Ay-eh. (*He follows suit. A pause. Unconsciously they both sigh.*)

SIMEON (*suddenly*). He never was much o' a hand at milkin', Eben wa'n't.

PETER (*with a snort*). His hands air like hoofs! (*A pause.*)

SIMEON. Reach down the jug thar! Let's take a swaller. I'm feelin' kind o' low.

PETER. Good idee! (*He does so—gets two glasses—they pour out drinks of whisky.*) Here's t' the gold in Californi-a!

SIMEON. An' luck t' find it! (*They drink—puff resolutely—sigh—take their feet down from the table.*)

PETER. Likker don't pear t' sot right.

SIMEON. We hain't used t' it this early. (*A pause. They become very restless.*)

PETER. Gittin' close in this kitchen.

SIMEON (*with immense relief*). Let's git a breath o' air. (*They arise briskly and go out rear—appear around house and stop by the gate. They stare up at the sky with a numbed appreciation.*)

PETER. Purty!

SIMEON. Ay-eh. Gold's t' the East now.

PETER. Sun's startin' with us fur the Golden West.

SIMEON (*staring around the farm, his compressed face tightened, unable to conceal his emotion*). Waal—it's our last mornin'—mebbe.

PETER (*the same*). Ay-eh.

SIMEON (*stamps his foot on the earth and addresses it desperately*). Waal—ye've thirty year o' me buried in ye—spread out over ye—blood an' bone an' sweat — rotted away — fertilizin' ye — richin' yer soul—prime manure, by God, that's what I been t' ye!

PETER. Ay-eh! An' me!

SIMEON. An' yew, Peter. (*He sighs—then spits.*) Waal—no use'n cryin' over spilt milk.

PETER. They's gold in the West—an' freedom, mebbe. We been slaves t' stone walls here.

SIMEON (*defiantly*). We ain't nobody's slaves from this out—nor no thin's slaves nuther. (*A pause—restlessly.*) Speakin' o' milk, wonder how Eben's managin'?

PETER. I s'pose he's managin'.

SIMEON. Mebbe we'd ought t' help—this once.

PETER. Mebbe. The cows knows us.

SIMEON. An' likes us. They don't know him much.

PETER. An' the hosses, an' pigs, an' chickens. They don't know him much.

SIMEON. They knows us like brothers—an' likes us! (*Proudly.*) Hain't we raised 'em t' be fust-rate, number one prize stock?

PETER. We hain't—not no more.

SIMEON (*dully*). I was fergittin'. (*Then resignedly.*) Waal, let's go help Eben a spell an' git waked up.

PETER. Suits me. (*They are starting off down left, rear, for the barn when* EBEN *appears from there hurrying toward them, his face excited.*)

EBEN (*breathlessly*). Waal—har they be! The old mule an' the bride! I seen 'em from the barn down below at the turnin'.

PETER. How could ye tell that far?

EBEN. Hain't I as far-sight as he's near-sight? Don't I know the mare 'n' buggy, an' two people settin' in it? Who else. . . . ? An' I tell ye I kin feel 'em a-comin', too! (*He squirms as if he had the itch.*)

PETER (*beginning to be angry*). Waal—let him do his own unhitchin'!

SIMEON (*angry in his turn*). Let's hustle in an' git our bundles an' be a-goin' as he's a-comin'. I don't want never t' step inside the door agen arter he's back. (*They both start back around the corner of the house.* EBEN *follows them.*)

EBEN (*anxiously*). Will ye sign it afore ye go?

PETER. Let's see the color o' the old

skinflint's money an' we'll sign. (*They disappear left. The two brothers clump upstairs to get their bundles.* EBEN *appears in the kitchen, runs to window, peers out, comes back and pulls up a strip of flooring in under stove, takes out a canvas bag and puts it on table, then sets the floorboard back in place. The two brothers appear a moment after. They carry old carpet bags.*)

EBEN (*puts his hand on bag guardingly*). Have ye signed?

SIMEON (*shows paper in his hand*). Ay-eh. (*Greedily.*) Be that the money?

EBEN (*opens bag and pours out pile of twenty-dollar gold pieces*). Twenty-dollar pieces—thirty on 'em. Count 'em. (PETER *does so, arranging them in stacks of five, biting one or two to test them.*)

PETER. Six hundred. (*He puts them in bag and puts it inside his shirt carefully.*)

SIMEON (*handing paper to* EBEN). Har ye be.

EBEN (*after a glance, folds it carefully and hides it under his shirt—gratefully*). Thank yew.

PETER. Thank yew fur the ride.

SIMEON. We'll send ye a lump o' gold fur Christmas. (*A pause.* EBEN *stares at them and they at him.*)

PETER (*awkwardly*). Waal — we're a-goin'.

SIMEON. Comin' out t' the yard?

EBEN. No. I'm waitin' in here a spell. (*Another silence. The brothers edge awkwardly to door in rear—then turn and stand.*)

SIMEON. Waal—good-by.

PETER. Good-by.

EBEN. Good-by. (*They go out. He sits down at the table, faces the stove and pulls out the paper. He looks from it to the stove. His face lighted up by the shaft of sunlight from the window, has an expression of trance. His lips move. The two brothers come out to the gate.*)

PETER (*looking off toward barn*). Thar he be—unhitchin'.

SIMEON (*with a chuckle*). I'll bet ye he's riled!

PETER. An' thar she be.

SIMEON. Let's wait 'n' see what our new Maw looks like.

PETER (*with a grin*). An' give him our partin' cuss!

SIMEON (*grinning*). I feel like raisin' fun. I feel light in my head an' feet.

PETER. Me, too. I feel like laffin' till I'd split up the middle.

SIMEON. Reckon it's the likker?

PETER. No. My feet feel itchin' t' walk an' walk—an' jump high over thin's—an'. . . .

SIMEON. Dance? (*A pause.*)

PETER (*puzzled*). It's plumb onnateral.

SIMEON (*a light coming over his face*). I calc'late it's 'cause school's out. It's holiday. Fur once we're free!

PETER (*dazedly*). Free?

SIMEON. The halter's broke—the harness is busted—the fence bars is down—the stone walls air crumblin' an' tumblin'! We'll be kickin' up an' tearin' away down the road!

PETER (*drawing a deep breath—oratorically*). Anybody that wants this stinkin' old rock-pile of a farm kin hev it. T'ain't our'n, no sirree!

SIMEON (*takes the gate off its hinges and puts it under his arm*). We harby 'bolishes shet gates, an' open gates, an' all gates, by thunder!

PETER. We'll take it with us fur luck an' let 'er sail free down some river.

SIMEON (*as a sound of voices comes from left, rear*). Har they comes! (*The two brothers congeal into two stiff, grim-visaged statues.* EPHRAIM CABOT *and* ABBIE PUTNAM *come in.* CABOT *is seventy-five, tall and gaunt, with great, wiry, concentrated power, but stoop-shouldered from toil. His face is as hard as if it were hewn out of a boulder, yet there is a weakness in it, a petty pride in its own narrow strength. His eyes are small, close together, and extremely near-sighted, blinking continually in the effort to focus on objects, their stare having a straining, ingrowing quality. He is dressed in his dismal black Sunday suit.* ABBIE *is thirty-five, buxom, full of vitality. Her round face is pretty but marred by its rather gross sensuality. There is strength and obstinacy in her jaw, a hard determination in her eyes, and about her whole personality the same unsettled, untamed, desperate quality which is so apparent in* EBEN.)

CABOT (*as they enter—a queer strangled emotion in his dry cracking voice*). Har we be t' hum, Abbie.

ABBIE (*with lust for the word*). Hum! (*Her eyes gloating on the house without seeming to see the two stiff figures at the gate.*) It's purty—purty! I can't b'lieve it's r'ally mine.

CABOT (*sharply*). Yewr'n? Mine! (*He stares at her penetratingly. She stares back. He adds relentingly.*) Our'n—mebbe! It was lonesome too long. I was growin' old in the spring. A hum's got t' hev a woman.

ABBIE (*her voice taking possession*). A woman's got t' hev a hum!

CABOT (*nodding uncertainly*). Ay-eh. (*Then irritably.*) Whar be they? Ain't thar nobody about—'r wukin'—r' nothin'?

ABBIE (*sees the brothers. She returns their stare of cold appraising contempt with interest—slowly*). Thar's two men loafin' at the gate an' starin' at me like a couple o' strayed hogs.

CABOT (*straining his eyes*). I kin see 'em —but I can't make out. . . .

SIMEON. It's Simeon.

PETER. It's Peter.

CABOT (*exploding*). Why hain't ye wukin'?

SIMEON (*dryly*). We're waitin' t' welcome ye hum—yew an' the bride!

CABOT (*confusedly*). Huh? Waal—this be yer new Maw, boys. (*She stares at them and they at her.*)

SIMEON (*turns away and spits contemptuously*). I see her!

PETER (*spits also*). An' I see her!

ABBIE (*with the conqueror's conscious superiority*). I'll go in an' look at *my* house. (*She goes slowly around to porch.*)

SIMEON (*with a snort*). *Her* house!

PETER (*calls after her*). Ye'll find Eben inside. Ye better not tell him it's *yewr* house.

ABBIE (*mouthing the name*). Eben. (*Then quietly.*) I'll tell Eben.

CABOT (*with a contemptuous sneer*). Ye needn't heed Eben. Eben's a dumb fool—like his Maw—soft an' simple!

SIMEON (*with his sardonic burst of laughter*). Ha! Eben's a chip o' yew—spit 'n' image—hard 'n' bitter's a hickory tree! Dog'll eat dog. He'll eat ye yet, old man!

CABOT (*commandingly*). Ye git t' wuk!

SIMEON (*as* ABBIE *disappears in house—winks at* PETER *and says tauntingly*). So that thar's our new Maw, be it? Whar in hell did ye dig her up? (*He and* PETER *laugh.*)

PETER. Ha! Ye'd better turn her in the pen with the other sows. (*They laugh uproariously, slapping their thighs.*)

CABOT (*so amazed at their effrontery that he stutters in confusion*). Simeon! Peter! What's come over ye? Air ye drunk?

SIMEON. We're free, old man—free o' yew an' the hull damned farm! (*They grow more and more hilarious and excited.*)

PETER. An' we're startin' out fur the gold fields o' Californi-a!

SIMEON. Ye kin take this place an' burn it!

PETER. An' bury it—fur all we cares!

SIMEON. We're free, old man! (*He cuts a caper.*)

PETER. Free! (*Gives a kick in the air.*)

SIMEON (*in a frenzy*). Whoop!

PETER. Whoop! (*They do an absurd Indian war dance about the old man who is petrified between rage and the fear that they are insane.*)

SIMEON. We're free as Injuns! Lucky we don't skulp ye

PETER. An' burn yer barn an' kill the stock!

SIMEON. An' rape yer new woman! Whoop! (*He and* PETER *stop their dance, holding their sides, rocking with wild laughter.*)

CABOT (*edging away*). Lust fur gold—fur the sinful, easy gold o' Californi-a! It's made ye mad!

SIMEON (*tauntingly*). Wouldn't ye like us to send ye back some sinful gold, ye old sinner?

PETER. They's gold besides what's in Californi-a! (*He retreats back beyond the vision of the old man and takes the bag of money and flaunts it in the air above his head, laughing.*)

SIMEON. And sinfuller, too!

PETER. We'll be voyagin' on the sea! Whoop! (*He leaps up and down.*)

SIMEON. Livin' free! Whoop! (*He leaps in turn.*)

CABOT (*suddenly roaring with rage*). My cuss on ye!

SIMEON. Take our'n in trade fur it! Whoop!

CABOT. I'll hev ye both chained up in the asylum!

PETER. Ye old skinflint! Good-by!

SIMEON. Ye old blood sucker! Good-by!

CABOT. Go afore I. . . !

PETER. Whoop! (*He picks a stone from the road.* SIMEON *does the same.*)

SIMEON. Maw'll be in the parlor.

PETER. Ay-eh! One! Two!

CABOT (*frightened*). What air ye. . . .?

PETER. Three! (*They both throw, the

stones hitting the parlor window with a crash of glass, tearing the shade.)

SIMEON. Whoop!

PETER. Whoop!

CABOT (*in a fury now, rushing toward them*). If I kin lay hands on ye—I'll break yer bones fur ye! (*But they beat a capering retreat before him,* SIMEON *with the gate still under his arm.* CABOT *comes back, panting with impotent rage. Their voices as they go off take up the song of the gold-seekers to the old tune of "Oh, Susannah!"*)

"I jumped aboard the Liza ship,
And traveled on the sea,
And every time I thought of home
I wished it wasn't me!
Oh! Californi-a,
That's the land fur me!
I'm off to Californi-a!
With my wash bowl on my knee."

(*In the meantime, the window of the upper bedroom on right is raised and* ABBIE *sticks her head out. She looks down at* CABOT*—with a sigh of relief.*)

ABBIE. Waal—that's the last o' them two, hain't it? (*He doesn't answer. Then in possessive tones.*) This here's a nice bedroom, Ephraim. It's a r'al nice bed. Is it my room, Ephraim?

CABOT (*grimly—without looking up*). Our'n! (*She cannot control a grimace of aversion and pulls back her head slowly and shuts the window. A sudden horrible thought seems to enter* CABOT*'s head.*) They been up to somethin'! Mebbe—mebbe they've pizened the stock—'r somethin'! (*He almost runs off down toward the barn. A moment later the kitchen door is slowly pushed open and* ABBIE *enters. For a moment she stands looking at* EBEN. *He does not notice her at first. Her eyes take him in penetratingly with a calculating appraisal of his strength as against hers. But under this her desire is dimly awakened by his youth and good looks. Suddenly he becomes conscious of her presence and looks up. Their eyes meet. He leaps to his feet, glowering at her speechlessly.*)

ABBIE (*in her most seductive tones which she uses all through this scene*). Be you—Eben? I'm Abbie—— (*She laughs*). I mean, I'm yer new Maw.

EBEN (*viciously*). No, damn ye!

ABBIE (*as if she hadn't heard—with a queer smile*). Yer Paw's spoke a lot o' yew. . . .

EBEN. Ha!

ABBIE. Ye mustn't mind him. He's an old man. (*A long pause. They stare at each other.*) I don't want t' pretend playin' Maw t' ye, Eben. (*Admiringly.*) Ye're too big an' too strong fur that. I want t' be frens with ye. Mebbe with me fur a fren ye'd find ye'd like livin' here better. I kin make it easy fur ye with him, mebbe. (*With a scornful sense of power.*) I calc'late I kin git him t' do most anythin' fur me.

EBEN (*with bitter scorn*). Ha! (*They stare again,* EBEN *obscurely moved, physically attracted to her—in forced stilted tones.*) Yew kin go t' the devil!

ABBIE (*calmly*). If cussin' me does ye good, cuss all ye've a mind t'. I'm all prepared t' have ye agin me—at fust. I don't blame ye nuther. I'd feel the same at any stranger comin' t' take my Maw's place. (*He shudders. She is watching him carefully.*) Yew must've cared a lot fur yewr Maw, didn't ye? My Maw died afore I'd growed. I don't remember her none. (*A pause.*) But yew won't hate me long, Eben. I'm not the wust in the world—an' yew an' me've got a lot in common. I kin tell that by lookin' at ye. Waal—I've had a hard life, too—oceans o' trouble an' nuthin' but wuk fur reward. I was a orphan early an' had t' wuk fur others in other folks' hums. Then I married an' he turned out a drunken spreer an' so he had to wuk fur others an' me too agen in other folks' hums, an' the baby died, an' my husband got sick an' died too, an' I was glad sayin' now I'm free fur once, on'y I diskivered right away all I was free fur was t' wuk agen in other folks' hums, doin' other folks' wuk till I'd most give up hope o' ever doin' my own wuk in my own hum, an' then your Paw come. . . .

(CABOT *appears from the barn. He comes to the gate and looks down the road the brothers have gone. A faint strain of their retreating voices is heard: "Oh, Californi-a! That's the place for me." He stands glowering, his fist clenched, his face grim with rage.*)

EBEN (*fighting against his growing attraction and sympathy—harshly*). An' bought yew—like a harlot! (*She is stung and flushes angrily. She has been sincerely moved by the recital of her troubles. He adds furiously.*) An' the price he's payin' ye—this farm—was my Maw's, damn ye! —an' mine now!

ABBIE (*with a cool laugh of confidence*). Yewr'n? We'll see 'bout that! (*Then strongly.*) Waal—what if I did need a hum? What else'd I marry an old man like him fur?

EBEN (*maliciously*). I'll tell him ye said that!

ABBIE (*smiling*). I'll say ye're lyin' a-purpose—an' he'll drive ye off the place!

EBEN. Ye devil!

ABBIE (*defying him*). This be my farm—this be my hum—this be my kitchen——!

EBEN (*furiously, as if he were going to attack her*). Shut up, damn ye!

ABBIE (*walks up to him—a queer coarse expression of desire in her face and body—slowly*). An' upstairs—that be my bedroom—an' my bed! (*He stares into her eyes, terribly confused and torn. She adds softly.*) I hain't bad nor mean—'ceptin' fur an enemy—but I got t' fight fur what's due me out o' life, if I ever 'spect t' git it. (*Then putting her hand on his arm—seductively.*) Let's yew 'n' me be frens, Eben.

EBEN (*stupidly—as if hypnotized*). Ay-eh. (*Then furiously flinging off her arms.*) No, ye durned old witch! I hate ye! (*He rushes out the door.*)

ABBIE (*looks after him smiling satisfiedly—then half to herself, mouthing the word*). Eben's nice. (*She looks at the table, proudly.*) I'll wash up *my* dishes now. (EBEN *appears outside, slamming the door behind him. He comes around corner, stops on seeing his father, and stands staring at him with hate.*)

CABOT (*raising his arms to heaven in the fury he can no longer control*). Lord God o' Hosts, smite the undutiful sons with Thy wust cuss!

EBEN (*breaking in violently*). Yew 'n' yewr God! Allus cussin' folks—allus naggin' em!

CABOT (*oblivious to him—summoningly*). God o' the old! God o' the lonesome!

EBEN (*mockingly*). Naggin' His sheep t' sin! T' hell with yewr God! (CABOT *turns. He and* EBEN *glower at each other.*)

CABOT (*harshly*). So it's yew. I might've knowed it. (*Shaking his finger threateningly at him.*) Blasphemin' fool! (*Then quickly.*) Why hain't ye t' wuk?

EBEN. Why hain't yew? They've went. I can't wuk it all alone.

CABOT (*contemptuously*). Nor noways! I'm wuth ten o' ye yit, old's I be! Ye'll never be more'n half a man! (*Then, matter-of-factly.*) Waal—let's git t' the barn. (*They go. A last faint note of the "Californi-a" song is heard from the distance.* ABBIE *is washing her dishes.*)

THE CURTAIN FALLS

PART II

Scene One

The exterior of the farmhouse as in Part I—a hot Sunday afternoon two months later. ABBIE, *dressed in her best, is discovered sitting in a rocker at the end of the porch. She rocks listlessly, enervated by the heat, staring in front of her with bored, half-closed eyes.*

EBEN *sticks his head out of his bedroom window. He looks around furtively and tries to see—or hear—if anyone is on the porch, but although he has been careful to make no noise,* ABBIE *has sensed his movement. She stops rocking, her face grows animated and eager, she waits attentively.* EBEN *seems to feel her presence, he scowls back his thoughts of her and spits with exaggerated disdain—then withdraws back into the room.* ABBIE *waits, holding her breath as she listens with passionate eagerness for every sound within the house.*

EBEN *comes out. Their eyes meet. His falter, he is confused, he turns away and slams the door resentfully. At this gesture,* ABBIE *laughs tantalizingly, amused but at the same time piqued and irritated. He scowls, strides off the porch to the path and starts to walk past her to the road with a grand swagger of ignoring her existence. He is dressed in his store suit, spruced up, his face shines from soap and water.* ABBIE *leans forward on her chair, her eyes hard and angry now, and, as he passes her, gives a sneering, taunting chuckle.*

EBEN (*stung—turns on her furiously*). What air yew cacklin' 'bout?

ABBIE (*triumphant*). Yew!

EBEN. What about me?

ABBIE. Ye look all slicked up like a prize bull.

EBEN (*with a sneer*). Waal—ye hain't so durned purty yerself, be ye? (*They stare into each other's eyes, his held by hers in spite of himself, hers glowingly possessive. Their physical attraction becomes a palpable force quivering in the hot air.*)

ABBIE (*softly*). Ye don't mean that, Eben. Ye may think ye mean it, mebbe, but ye don't. Ye can't. It's agin nature, Eben. Ye been fightin' yer nature ever since the day I come—tryin' t' tell yerself I hain't purty t'ye. (*She laughs a low humid laugh without taking her eyes from his. A pause—her body squirms desirously—she murmurs languorously.*) Hain't the sun strong an' hot? Ye kin feel it burnin' into the earth—Nature—makin' thin's grow—bigger 'n' bigger—burnin' inside ye—makin' ye want t' grow—into somethin' else—till ye're jined with it—an' it's your'n—but it owns ye, too—an' makes ye grow bigger—like a tree—like them elums——(*She laughs again softly, holding his eyes. He takes a step toward her, compelled against his will.*) Nature'll beat ye, Eben. Ye might's well own up t' it fust 's last.

EBEN (*trying to break from her spell—confusedly*). If Paw'd hear ye goin' on. . . . (*Resentfully.*) But ye've made such a damned idjit out o' the old devil. . . ! (ABBIE *laughs.*)

ABBIE. Waal—hain't it easier fur yew with him changed softer?

EBEN (*defiantly*). No. I'm fightin' him—fightin' yew—fightin' fur Maw's rights t' her hum! (*This breaks her spell for him. He glowers at her.*) An' I'm onto ye. Ye hain't foolin' me a mite. Ye're aimin' t' swaller up everythin' an' make it your'n. Waal, you'll find I'm a heap sight bigger hunk nor yew kin chew! (*He turns from her with a sneer.*)

ABBIE (*trying to regain her ascendancy—seductively*). Eben!

EBEN. Leave me be! (*He starts to walk away.*)

ABBIE (*more commandingly*). Eben!

EBEN (*stops—resentfully*). What d'ye want?

ABBIE (*trying to conceal a growing excitement*). Whar air ye goin'?

EBEN (*with malicious nonchalance*). Oh—up the road a spell.

ABBIE. T' the village?

EBEN (*airily*). Mebbe.

ABBIE (*excitedly*). T' see that Min, I s'pose?

EBEN. Mebbe.

ABBIE (*weakly*). What d'ye want t' waste time on her fur?

EBEN (*revenging himself now—grinning at her*). Ye can't beat Nature, didn't ye say? (*He laughs and again starts to walk away.*)

ABBIE (*bursting out*). An ugly old hake!

EBEN (*with a tantalizing sneer*). She's purtier'n yew be!

ABBIE. That every wuthless drunk in the country has. . . .

EBEN (*tauntingly*). Mebbe—but she's better'n yew. She owns up fa'r 'n' squar' t' her doin's.

ABBIE (*furiously*). Don't ye dare compare. . . .

EBEN. She don't go sneakin' an' stealin'—what's mine.

ABBIE (*savagely seizing on his weak point*). Your'n? Yew mean—my farm?

EBEN. I mean the farm yew sold yerself fur like any other old whore—my farm!

ABBIE (*stung—fiercely*). Ye'll never live t' see the day when even a stinkin' weed on it 'll belong t' ye! (*Then in a scream.*) Git out o' my sight! Go on t' yer slut—disgracin' yer Paw 'n' me! I'll git yer Paw t' horsewhip ye off the place if I want t'! Ye're only livin' here 'cause I tolerate ye! Git along! I hate the sight o' ye! (*She stops, panting and glaring at him.*)

EBEN (*returning her glance in kind*). An' I hate the sight o' yew! (*He turns and strides off up the road. She follows his retreating figure with concentrated hate. Old* CABOT *appears coming up from the barn. The hard, grim expression of his face has changed. He seems in some queer way softened, mellowed. His eyes have taken on a strange, incongruous dreamy quality. Yet there is no hint of physical weakness about him—rather he looks more robust and younger.* ABBIE *sees him and turns away quickly with unconcealed aversion. He comes slowly up to her.*)

CABOT (*mildly*). War yew an' Eben quarrelin' agen?

ABBIE (*shortly*). No.

CABOT. Ye was talkin' a'mighty loud. (*He sits down on the edge of porch.*)

ABBIE (*snappishly*). If ye heerd us they hain't no need askin' questions.

CABOT. I didn't hear what ye said.

ABBIE (*relieved*). Waal—it wa'n't nothin' t' speak on.

CABOT (*after a pause*). Eben's queer.

ABBIE (*bitterly*). He's the dead spit 'n' image o' yew!

CABOT (*queerly interested*). D'ye think so, Abbie? (*After a pause, ruminatingly.*) Me 'n' Eben's allus fit 'n' fit. I never could b'ar him noways. He's so thunderin' soft —like his Maw.

ABBIE (*scornfully*). Ay-eh! 'Bout as soft as yew be!

CABOT (*as if he hadn't heard*). Mebbe I been too hard on him.

ABBIE (*jeeringly*). Waal—ye're gittin' soft now—soft as slop! That's what Eben was sayin'.

CABOT (*his face instantly grim and ominous*). Eben was sayin'? Waal, he'd best not do nothin' t' try me 'r he'll soon diskiver. . . . (*A pause. She keeps her face turned away. His gradually softens. He stares up at the sky.*) Purty, hain't it?

ABBIE (*crossly*). I don't see nothin' purty.

CABOT. The sky. Feels like a wa'm field up thar.

ABBIE (*sarcastically*). Air yew aimin' t' buy up over the farm too? (*She snickers contemptuously.*)

CABOT (*strangely*). I'd like t' own my place up thar. (*A pause.*) I'm gittin' old, Abbie. I'm gittin' ripe on the bough. (*A pause. She stares at him mystified. He goes on.*) It's allus lonesome cold in the house—even when it's bilin' hot outside. Hain't yew noticed?

ABBIE. No.

CABOT. It's wa'm down t' the barn—nice smellin' an' warm—with the cows. (*A pause.*) Cows is queer.

ABBIE. Like yew?

CABOT. Like Eben. (*A pause.*) I'm gittin' t' feel resigned t' Eben—jest as I got t' feel 'bout his Maw. I'm gittin' t' learn to b'ar his softness—jest like her'n. I calc'late I c'd a'most take t' him—if he wa'n't sech a dumb fool! (*A pause.*) I s'pose it's old age a-creepin' in my bones.

ABBIE (*indifferently*). Waal—ye hain't dead yet.

CABOT (*roused*). No, I hain't, yew bet—not by a hell of a sight—I'm sound 'n' tough as hickory! (*Then moodily.*) But arter three score and ten the Lord warns ye t' prepare. (*A pause.*) That's why Eben's come in my head. Now that his cussed sinful brothers is gone their path t' hell, they's no one left but Eben.

ABBIE (*resentfully*). They's me, hain't they? (*Agitatedly.*) What's all this sudden likin' ye've tuk to Eben? Why don't ye saying nothin' 'bout me? Hain't I yer lawful wife?

CABOT (*simply*). Ay-eh. Ye be. (*A pause —he stares at her desirously—his eyes grow avid—then with a sudden movement he seizes her hands and squeezes them, declaiming in a queer camp meeting preacher's tempo.*) Yew air my Rose o' Sharon! Behold, yew air fair; yer eyes air doves; yer lips air like scarlet; yer two breasts air like two fawns; yer navel be like a round goblet; yer belly be like a heap o' wheat. . . . (*He covers her hand with kisses. She does not seem to notice. She stares before her with hard angry eyes.*)

ABBIE (*jerking her hands away—harshly*). So ye're plannin' t' leave the farm t' Eben, air ye?

CABOT (*dazedly*). Leave. . . ? (*Then with resentful obstinacy.*) I hain't a-givin' it t' no one!

ABBIE (*remorselessly*). Ye can't take it with ye.

CABOT (*thinks a moment—then reluctantly*). No, I calc'ate not. (*After a pause —with a strange passion.*) But if I could, I would, by the Etarnal! 'R if I could, in my dyin' hour, I'd set it afire an' watch it burn—this house an' every ear o' corn an' every tree down t' the last blade o' hay! I'd sit an' know it was all a-dying with me an' no one else'd ever own what was mine, what I'd made out o' nothin' with my own sweat 'n' blood! (*A pause—then he adds with a queer affection.*) 'Ceptin' the cows. Them I'd turn free.

ABBIE (*harshly*). An' me?

CABOT (*with a queer smile*). Ye'd be turned free, too.

ABBIE (*furiously*). So that's the thanks I git fur marryin' ye—t' have ye change kind to Eben who hates ye, an' talk o' turnin' me out in the road.

CABOT (*hastily*). Abbie! Ye know I wa'n't. . . .

ABBIE (*vengefully*). Just let me tell ye a thing or two 'bout Eben! Whar's he gone? T' see that harlot, Min! I tried fur t' stop him. Disgracin' yew an' me—on the Sabbath, too!

CABOT (*rather guiltily*). He's a sinner—nateral-born. It's lust eatin' his heart.

ABBIE (*enraged beyond endurance—wildly vindictive*). An' his lust fur me! Kin ye find excuses fur that?

CABOT (*stares at her—after a dead pause*). Lust—fur yew?

ABBIE (*defiantly*). He was tryin' t' make love t' me—when ye heerd us quarrelin'.

CABOT (*stares at her—then a terrible expression of rage comes over his face—he springs to his feet shaking all over*). By the A'mighty God—I'll end him!

ABBIE (*frightened now for Eben*). No! Don't ye!

CABOT (*violently*). I'll git the shotgun an' blow his soft brains t' the top o' them elums!

ABBIE (*throwing her arms around him*). No, Ephraim!

CABOT (*pushing her away violently*). I will, by God!

ABBIE (*in a quieting tone*). Listen, Ephraim. 'Twa'n't nothin' bad—on'y a boy's foolin'—twa'n't meant serious—jest jokin' and teasin'. . . .

CABOT. Then why did ye say—lust?

ABBIE. It must hev sounded wusser'n I meant. An' I was mad at thinkin'—ye'd leave him the farm.

CABOT (*quieter but still grim and cruel*). Waal then, I'll horsewhip him off the place if that much'll content ye.

ABBIE (*reaching out and taking his hand*). No. Don't think o' me! Ye mustn't drive him off. 'Tain't sensible. Who'll ye get to help ye on the farm? They's no one hereabouts.

CABOT (*considers this—then nodding his appreciation*). Ye got a head on ye. (*Then irritably.*) Waal, let him stay. (*He sits down on the edge of the porch. She sits beside him. He murmurs contemptuously.*) I oughtn't t' git riled so—at that 'ere fool calf. (*A pause.*) But har's the p'int. What son o' mine'll keep on here t' the farm—when the Lord does call me? Simeon an' Peter air gone t' hell—an Eben's follerin' 'em.

ABBIE. They's me.

CABOT. Ye're on'y a woman.

ABBIE. I'm yewr wife.

CABOT. That hain't me. A son is me—my blood—mine. Mine ought t' git mine. An' then it's still mine—even though I be six foot under. D'ye see?

ABBIE (*giving him a look of hatred*). Ay-eh. I see. (*She becomes very thoughtful, her face growing shrewd, her eyes studying* CABOT *craftily.*)

CABOT. I'm gittin' old—ripe on the bough. (*Then with a sudden forced reassurance.*) Not but what I hain't a hard nut t' crack even yet—an' fur many a year t' come! By the Etarnal, I kin break most o' the young fellers' backs at any kind o' work any day o' the year!

ABBIE (*suddenly*). Mebbe the Lord'll give *us* a son.

CABOT (*turns and stares at her eagerly*). Ye mean—a son—t' me 'n' yew?

ABBIE (*with a cajoling smile*). Ye're a strong man yet, hain't ye? 'Tain't noways impossible, be it? We know that. Why d'ye stare so? Hain't ye never thought o' that afore? I been thinkin' o' it all along. Ay-eh—an' I been prayin' it'd happen, too.

CABOT (*his face growing full of joyous pride and a sort of religious ecstasy*). Ye been prayin', Abbie?—fur a son?— t' us?

ABBIE. Ay-eh. (*With a grim resolution.*) I want a son now.

CABOT (*excitedly clutching both of her hands in his*). It'd be the blessin' o' God, Abbie—the blessin' o' God A'mighty on me—in my old age—in my lonesomeness! They hain't nothin' I wouldn't do fur ye then, Abbie. Ye'd hev on'y t' ask it—anythin' ye'd a mind t'!

ABBIE (*interrupting*). Would ye will the farm t' me then—t' me an' it. . . ?

CABOT (*vehemently*). I'd do anythin' ye axed, I tell ye! I swar it! May I be everlastin' damned t' hell if I wouldn't! (*He sinks to his knees pulling her down with him. He trembles all over with the fervor of his hopes.*) Pray t' the Lord agen, Abbie. It's the Sabbath! I'll jine ye! Two prayers air better nor one. "An' God hearkened unto Rachel"! An' God hearkened unto Abbie! Pray, Abbie! Pray fur him to hearken! (*He bows his head, mumbling. She pretends to do likewise but gives him a side glance of scorn and triumph.*)

SCENE TWO

About eight in the evening. The interior of the two bedrooms on the top floor is shown. EBEN *is sitting on the side of his bed in the room on the left. On account of the heat he has taken off everything but his undershirt and pants. His feet are bare. He faces front, brooding moodily, his chin propped on his hands, a desperate expression on his face.*

In the other room CABOT *and* ABBIE *are sitting side by side on the edge of their bed, an old four-poster with feather mat-*

tress. He is in his night shirt, she in her nightdress. He is still in the queer, excited mood into which the notion of a son has thrown him. Both rooms are lighted dimly and flickeringly by tallow candles.

CABOT. The farm needs a son.

ABBIE. I need a son.

CABOT. Ay-eh. Sometimes ye air the farm an' sometimes the farm be yew. That's why I clove t' ye in my lonesomeness. (*A pause. He pounds his knee with his fist.*) Me an' the farm has got t' beget a son!

ABBIE. Ye'd best go t' sleep. Ye're gittin' thin's all mixed.

CABOT (*with an impatient gesture.*) No, I hain't. My mind's clear's a well. Ye don't know me, that's it. (*He stares hopelessly at the floor.*)

ABBIE (*indifferently*). Mebbe. (*In the next room* EBEN *gets up and paces up and down distractedly.* ABBIE *hears him. Her eyes fasten on the intervening wall with concentrated attention.* EBEN *stops and stares. Their hot glances seem to meet through the wall. Unconsciously he stretches out his arms for her and she half rises. Then aware, he mutters a curse at himself and flings himself face downward on the bed, his clenched fists above his head, his face buried in the pillow.* ABBIE *relaxes with a faint sigh but her eyes remain fixed on the wall; she listens with all her attention for some movement from* EBEN.)

CABOT (*suddenly raises his head and looks at her—scornfully*). Will ye ever know me—'r will any man 'r woman? (*Shaking his head.*) No. I calc'late 't wa'n't t' be. (*He turns away.* ABBIE *looks at the wall. Then, evidently unable to keep silent about his thoughts, without looking at his wife, he puts out his hand and clutches her knee. She starts violently, looks at him, sees he is not watching her, concentrates again on the wall and pays no attention to what he says.*) Listen, Abbie. When I come here fifty odd year ago—I was jest twenty an' the strongest an' hardest ye ever seen—ten times as strong an' fifty times as hard as Eben. Waal—this place was nothin' but fields o' stones. Folks laughed when I tuk it. They couldn't know what I knowed. When ye kin make corn sprout out o' stones, God's livin' in yew! They wa'n't strong enuf fur that! They reckoned God was easy. They laughed. They don't laugh no more. Some died hereabouts. Some went West an' died. They're all under ground—fur follerin' arter an easy God. God hain't easy. (*He shakes his head slowly.*) An' I growed hard. Folks kept allus sayin' he's a hard man like 'twas sinful t' be hard, so's at last I said back at 'em: Waal then, by thunder, ye'll git me hard an' see how ye like it! (*Then suddenly.*) But I give in t' weakness once. 'Twas arter I'd been here two year. I got weak—despairful—they was so many stones. They was a party leavin', givin' up, goin' West. I jined 'em. We tracked on 'n' on. We come t' broad medders, plains, whar the soil was black an' rich as gold. Nary a stone. Easy. Ye'd on'y to plow an' sow an' then set an' smoke yer pipe an' watch thin's grow. I could o' been a rich man—but somethin' in me fit me an' fit me—the voice o' God sayin': "This hain't wuth nothin' t' Me. Git ye back t' hum!" I got afeerd o' that voice an' I lit out back t' hum here, leavin' my claim an' crops t' whoever'd a mind t' take 'em. Ay-eh. I actoolly give up what was rightful mine! God's hard, not easy! God's in the stones! Build my church on a rock—out o' stones an' I'll be in them! That's what He meant t' Peter! (*He sighs heavily—a pause.*) Stones. I picked 'em up an' piled 'em into walls. Ye kin read the years o' my life in them walls, every day a hefted stone, climbin' over the hills up and down, fencin' in the fields that was mine, whar I'd made thin's grow out o' nothin'—like the will o' God, like the servant o' His hand. It wa'n't easy. It was hard an' He made me hard fur it. (*He pauses.*) All the time I kept gittin' lonesomer. I tuk a wife. She bore Simeon an' Peter. She was a good woman. She wuked hard. We was married twenty year. She never knowed me. She helped but she never knowed what she was helpin'. I was allus lonesome. She died. After that it wa'n't so lonesome fur a spell. (*A pause.*) I lost count o' the years. I had no time t' fool away countin' 'em. Sim an' Peter helped. The farm growed. It was all mine! When I thought o' that I didn't feel lonesome. (*A pause.*) But ye can't hitch yer mind t' one thin' day an' night. I tuk another wife—Eben's Maw. Her folks was contestin' me at law over my deeds t' the farm—my farm! That's why Eben keeps a-talkin' his fool talk o' this bein' his Maw's farm. She bore Eben. She was purty—but soft. She tried t' be hard. She couldn't. She never knowed me nor nothin'. It was lonesomer n' hell with her. After a matter o' sixteen odd years, she died. (*A pause.*) I lived with the boys. They hated me 'cause I was hard. I hated them 'cause they was soft. They coveted the farm without knowin' what it meant. It made me bitter 'n wormwood. It aged me—them coveting what I'd made fur mine. Then this spring the call come—the voice o' God cryin' in my wilderness, in my lonesomeness—t' go out an' seek an' find! (*Turning to her with strange passion.*) I sought ye an' I found ye! Yew air my Rose o' Sharon! Yer eyes air like. . . . (*She has turned a blank face, resentful eyes to his. He stares at her for a moment—then harshly.*) Air ye any the wiser fur all I've told ye?

ABBIE (*confusedly*). Mebbe.

CABOT (*pushing her away from him—angrily*). Ye don't know nothin'—nor never will. If ye don't hev a son t' redeem ye. . . . (*This in a tone of cold threat.*)

ABBIE (*resentfully*). I've prayed, hain't I?

CABOT (*bitterly*). Pray agen—fur understandin'!

ABBIE (*a veiled threat in her tone*). Ye'll have a son out o' me, I promise ye.

CABOT. How kin ye promise?

ABBIE. I got second-sight, mebbe. I kin foretell. (*She gives a queer smile.*)

CABOT. I believe ye have. Ye give me the chills sometimes. (*He shivers.*) It's cold in this house. It's oneasy. They's thin's pokin' about in the dark—in the corners. (*He pulls on his trousers, tucking in his night shirt, and pulls on his boots.*)

ABBIE (*surprised*). Whar air ye goin'?

CABOT (*queerly*). Down whar it's restful—whar it's warm—down t' the barn. (*Bitterly.*) I kin talk t' the cows. They know. They know the farm an' me. They'll give me peace. (*He turns to go out the door.*)

ABBIE (*a bit frightenedly*). Air ye ailin' tonight, Ephraim?

CABOT. Growin'. Growin' ripe on the bough. (*He turns and goes, his boots clumping down the stairs.* EBEN *sits up with a start, listening.* ABBIE *is conscious of his movement and stares at the wall.* CABOT *comes out of the house around the corner and stands by the gate, blinking at the sky. He stretches up his hands in a tortured gesture.*) God A'mighty, call from the dark! (*He listens as if expecting an answer. Then his arms drop, he shakes his head and plods off toward the barn.* EBEN *and* ABBIE *stare at each other through the wall.* EBEN *sighs heavily and* ABBIE *echoes it. Both become terribly nervous, uneasy. Finally* ABBIE *gets up and listens, her ear to the wall. He acts as if he saw every move she was making, he becomes resolutely still. She seems driven into a decision—goes out the door in rear determinedly. His eyes follow her. Then as the door of his room is opened softly, he turns away, waits in an attitude of strained fixity.* ABBIE *stands for a second staring at him, her eyes burning with desire. Then with a little cry she runs over and throws her arms about his neck, she pulls his head back and covers his mouth with kisses. At first, he submits dumbly; then he puts his arms about her neck and returns her kisses, but finally, suddenly aware of his hatred, he hurls her away from him, springing to his feet. They stand speechless and breathless, panting like two animals.*)

ABBIE (*at last—painfully*). Ye shouldn't, Eben—ye shouldn't—I'd make ye happy!

EBEN (*harshly*). I don't want t' be happy—from yew!

ABBIE (*helplessly*). Ye do, Eben! Ye do! Why d'ye lie?

EBEN (*viciously*). I don't take t'ye, I tell ye! I hate the sight o'ye!

ABBIE (*with an uncertain troubled laugh*). Waal, I kissed ye anyways—an' ye kissed back—yer lips was burnin'—ye can't lie 'bout that! (*Intensely.*) If ye don't care, why did ye kiss me back—why was yer lips burnin'?

EBEN (*wiping his mouth*). It was like pizen on 'em. (*Then tauntingly.*) When I kissed ye back, mebbe I thought 'twas someone else.

ABBIE (*wildly*). Min?

EBEN. Mebbe.

ABBIE (*torturedly*). Did ye go t' see her? Did ye r'ally go? I thought ye mightn't. Is that why ye throwed me off jest now?

EBEN (*sneeringly*). What if it be?

ABBIE (*raging*). Then ye're a dog, Eben Cabot!

EBEN (*threateningly*). Ye can't talk that way t' me!

ABBIE (*with a shrill laugh*). Can't I? Did ye think I was in love with ye—a weak thin' like yew! Not much! I on'y wanted ye fur a purpose o' my own—an' I'll hev ye fur it yet 'cause I'm stronger'n yew be!

EBEN (*resentfully*). I knowed well it was on'y part o' yer plan t' swaller everythin'!

ABBIE (*tauntingly*). Mebbe!

EBEN (*furious*). Git out o' my room!

ABBIE. This air my room an' ye're on'y hired help!

EBEN (*threateningly*). Git out afore I murder ye!

ABBIE (*quite confident now*). I hain't a mite afeerd. Ye want me, don't ye? Yes, ye do! An yer Paw's son'll never kill what he wants! Look at yer eyes! They's lust fur me in 'em, burnin' 'em up! Look at yer lips now! They're tremblin' an' longin' t' kiss me, an' yer teeth t' bite! (*He is watching her now with a horrible fascination. She laughs a crazy triumphant laugh.*) I'm a-goin' t' make all o' this hum my hum! They's one room hain't mine yet, but it's a-goin' t' be tonight. I'm a-goin' down now an' light up! (*She makes him a mocking bow.*) Won't ye come courtin' me in the best parlor, Mister Cabot?

EBEN (*staring at her—horribly confused —dully*). Don't ye dare! It hain't been opened since Maw died an' was laid out thar! Don't ye. . . ! (*But her eyes are fixed on his so burningly that his will seems to wither before hers. He stands swaying toward her helplessly.*)

ABBIE (*holding his eyes and putting all her will into her words as she backs out the door*). I'll expect ye afore long, Eben.

EBEN (*stares after her for a while, walking toward the door. A light appears in the parlor window. He murmurs*). In the parlor? (*This seems to arouse connotations for he comes back and puts on his white shirt, collar, half ties the tie mechanically, puts on coat, takes his hat, stands barefooted looking about him in bewilderment, mutters wonderingly.*) Maw! Whar air yew? (*Then goes slowly toward the door in rear.*)

SCENE THREE

A few minutes later. The interior of the parlor is shown. A grim, repressed room like a tomb in which the family has been interred alive. ABBIE *sits on the edge of the horsehair sofa. She has lighted all the candles and the room is revealed in all its preserved ugliness. A change has come over the woman. She looks awed and frightened now, ready to run away.*

The door is opened and EBEN *appears. His face wears an expression of obsessed confusion. He stands staring at her, his arms hanging disjointedly from his shoulders, his feet bare, his hat in his hand.*

ABBIE (*after a pause—with a nervous, formal politeness*) Won't ye set?

EBEN (*dully*). Ay-eh. (*Mechanically he places his hat carefully on the floor near the door and sits stiffly beside her on the edge of the sofa. A pause. They both remain rigid, looking straight ahead with eyes full of fear.*)

ABBIE. When I fust come in—in the dark—they seemed somethin' here.

EBEN (*simply*). Maw.

ABBIE. I kin still feel—somethin'. . . .

EBEN. It's Maw.

ABBIE. At fust I was feered o' it. I wanted t' yell an' run. Now—since yew come—seems like it's growin' soft an' kind t' me. (*Addressing the air—queerly.*) Thank yew.

EBEN. Maw allus loved me.

ABBIE. Mebbe it knows I love yew, too. Mebbe that makes it kind t' me.

EBEN (*dully*). I dunno. I should think she'd hate ye.

ABBIE (*with certainty*). No. I kin feel it don't—not no more.

EBEN. Hate ye fur stealin' her place—here in her hum—settin' in her parlor whar she was laid— (*He suddenly stops, staring stupidly before him.*)

ABBIE. What is it, Eben?

EBEN (*in a whisper*). Seems like Maw didn't want me t' remind ye.

ABBIE (*excitedly*). I knowed, Eben! It's kind t' me! It don't b'ar me no grudges fur what I never knowed an' couldn't help!

EBEN. Maw b'ars him a grudge.

ABBIE. Waal, so does all o' us.

EBEN. Ay-eh. (*With passion.*) I does, by God!

ABBIE (*taking one of his hands in hers and patting it*). Thar! Don't git riled thinkin' o' him. Think o' yer Maw who's kind t' us. Tell me about yer Maw, Eben.

EBEN. They hain't nothin' much. She was kind. She was good.

ABBIE (*putting one arm over his shoulder. He does not seem to notice—passionately*). I'll be kind an' good t' ye!

EBEN. Sometimes she used t' sing fur me.

ABBIE. I'll sing fur ye!

EBEN. This was her hum. This was her farm.

ABBIE. This is my hum! This is my farm!

EBEN. He married her t' steal 'em. She was soft an' easy. He couldn't 'preciate her.

ABBIE. He can't 'preciate me!

EBEN. He murdered her with his hardness.

ABBIE. He's murderin' me!

EBEN. She died. (*A pause.*) Sometimes she used to sing fur me. (*He bursts into a fit of sobbing.*)

ABBIE (*both her arms around him—with wild passion*). I'll sing fur ye! I'll die fur ye! (*In spite of her overwhelming desire for him, there is a sincere maternal love in her manner and voice—a horribly frank mixture of lust and mother love.*) Don't cry, Eben! I'll take yer Maw's place! I'll be everythin' she was t' ye! Let me kiss ye, Eben! (*She pulls his head around. He makes a bewildered pretense of resistance. She is tender.*) Don't be afeered! I'll kiss ye pure, Eben—same 's if I was a Maw t' ye—an' ye kin kiss me back 's if yew was my son—my boy—sayin' good-night t' me! Kiss me, Eben. (*They kiss in restrained fashion. Then suddenly wild passion overcomes her. She kisses him lustfully again and again and he flings his arms about her and returns her kisses. Suddenly, as in the bedroom, he frees himself from her violently and springs to his feet. He is trembling all over, in a strange state of terror.* ABBIE *strains her arms toward him with fierce pleading.*) Don't ye leave me, Eben! Can't ye see it hain't enuf— lovin' ye like a Maw—can't ye see it's got t' be that an' more—much more—a hundred times more—fur me t' be happy—fur yew t' be happy?

EBEN (*to the presence he feels in the room*). Maw! Maw! What d'ye want? What air ye tellin' me?

ABBIE. She's tellin' ye t' love me. She knows I love ye an' I'll be good t' ye. Can't ye feel it? Don't ye know? She's tellin' ye t' love me, Eben!

EBEN. Ay-eh. I feel—mebbe she—but—I can't figger out—why—when ye've stole her place—here in her hum—in the parlor whar she was—

ABBIE (*fiercely*). She knows I love ye!

EBEN (*his face suddenly lighting up with a fierce, triumphant grin*). I see it! I sees why. It's her vengeance on him—so's she kin rest quiet in her grave!

ABBIE (*wildly*). Vengeance o' God on the hull o' us! What d'we give a durn? I love ye, Eben! God knows I love ye! (*She stretches out her arms for him.*)

EBEN (*throws himself on his knees beside the sofa and grabs her in his arms—releasing all his pent-up passion*). An' I love yew, Abbie!—now I kin say it! I been dyin' fur want o' ye—every hour since ye come! I love ye! (*Their lips meet in a fierce, bruising kiss.*)

SCENE FOUR

Exterior of the farmhouse. It is just dawn. The front door at right is opened and EBEN *comes out and walks around to the gate. He is dressed in his working clothes. He seems changed. His face wears a bold and confident expression, he is grinning to himself with evident satisfaction. As he gets near the gate, the window of the parlor is heard opening and the shutters are flung back and* ABBIE *sticks her head out. Her hair tumbles over her shoulders in disarray, her face is flushed, she looks at* EBEN *with tender, languorous eyes and calls softly.*

ABBIE. Eben. (*As he turns—playfully.*) Jest one more kiss afore ye go. I'm goin' to' miss ye fearful all day.

EBEN. An me yew, ye kin bet! (*He goes to her. They kiss several times. He draws away, laughingly.*) Thar. That's enuf, hain't it? Ye won't hev none left fur next time.

ABBIE. I got a million o' 'em left fur yew! (*Then a bit anxiously.*) D'ye r'ally love me, Eben?

EBEN (*emphatically*). I like ye better'n any gal I ever knowed! That's gospel!

ABBIE. Likin' hain't lovin'.

EBEN. Waal then—I love ye. Now air yew satisfied?

ABBIE. Ay-eh, I be. (*She smiles at him adoringly.*)

EBEN. I better git t' the barn. The old critter's liable t' suspicion an' come sneakin' up.

ABBIE (*with a confident laugh*). Let him! I kin allus pull the wool over his eyes. I'm goin' t' leave the shutters open and let in the sun 'n' air. This room's been dead long enuf. Now it's goin' t' be my room!

EBEN (*frowning*). Ay-eh.

ABBIE (*hastily*). I meant—our room.

EBEN. Ay-eh.

ABBIE. We made it our'n last night, didn't we? We give it life—our lovin' did. (*A pause.*)

EBEN (*with a strange look*). Maw's gone back t' her grave. She kin sleep now.

ABBIE. May she rest in peace! (*Then tenderly rebuking.*) Ye oughtn't t' talk o' sad thin's—this mornin'.

EBEN. It jest come up in my mind o' itself.

ABBIE. Don't let it. (*He doesn't answer. She yawns.*) Waal, I'm a-goin' t' steal a wink o' sleep. I'll tell the Old Man I hain't feelin' pert. Let him git his own vittles.

EBEN. I see him comin' from the barn. Ye better look smart an' git upstairs.

ABBIE. Ay-eh. Good-by. Don't ferget me. (*She throws him a kiss. He grins—then squares his shoulders and awaits his father confidently.* CABOT *walks slowly up from the left, staring up at the sky with a vague face.*)

EBEN (*jovially*). Mornin', Paw. Stargazin' in daylight?

CABOT. Purty, hain't it?

EBEN (*looking around him possessively*). It's a durned purty farm.

CABOT. I mean the sky.

EBEN (*grinning*). How d'ye know? Them eyes o' your'n can't see that fur. (*This tickles his humor and he slaps his thigh and laughs.*) Ho-ho! That's a good un!

CABOT (*grimly sarcastic*). Ye're feelin' right chipper, hain't ye? Whar'd ye steal the likker?

EBEN (*good-naturedly*). 'Tain't likker. Jest life. (*Suddenly holding out his hand—soberly.*) Yew 'n' me is quits. Let's shake hands.

CABOT (*suspiciously*). What's come over ye?

EBEN. Then don't. Mebbe it's jest as well. (*A moment's pause.*) What's come over me? (*Queerly.*) Didn't ye feel her passin'—goin' back t' her grave?

CABOT (*dully*). Who?

EBEN. Maw. She kin rest now an' sleep content. She's quits with ye.

CABOT (*confusedly*). I rested. I slept good—down with the cows. They know how t' sleep. They're teachin' me.

EBEN (*suddenly jovial again*). Good fur the cows! Waal—ye better git t' work.

CABOT (*grimly amused*). Air yew bossin' me, ye calf?

EBEN (*beginning to laugh*). Ay-eh! I'm bossin' yew! Ha-ha-ha! See how ye like it! Ha-ha-ha! I'm the prize rooster o' this roost. Ha-ha-ha! (*He goes off toward the barn laughing.*)

CABOT (*looks after him with scornful pity*). Soft-headed. Like his Maw. Dead spit 'n' image. No hope in him! (*He spits with contemptuous disgust.*) A born fool! (*Then matter-of-factly.*) Waal—I'm gittin' peckish. (*He goes toward door.*)

THE CURTAIN FALLS

PART III

SCENE ONE

A night in late spring the following year. The kitchen and the two bedrooms upstairs are shown. The two bedrooms are dimly lighted by a tallow candle in each. EBEN *is sitting on the side of the bed in his room, his chin propped on his fists, his face a study of the struggle he is making to understand his conflicting emotions. The noisy laughter and music from below where a kitchen dance is in progress annoy and distract him. He scowls at the floor.*

In the next room a cradle stands beside the double bed.

In the kitchen all is festivity. The stove has been taken down to give more room to the dancers. The chairs, with wooden benches added, have been pushed back against the walls. On these are seated, squeezed in tight against one another, farmers and their wives and their young folks of both sexes from the neighboring farms. They are all chattering and laughing loudly. They evidently have some secret joke in common. There is no end of winking, of nudging, of meaning nods of the head toward CABOT *who, in a state of extreme hilarious excitement increased by the amount he has drunk, is standing near the rear door where there is a small keg of whisky and serving drinks to all the men. In the left corner, front, dividing the attention with her husband,* ABBIE *is sitting in a rocking chair, a shawl wrapped about her shoulders. She is very pale, her face is thin and drawn, her eyes are fixed anxiously on the open door in rear as if waiting for someone.*

The musician is tuning up his fiddle, seated in the far right corner. He is a lanky young fellow with a long, weak face. His pale eyes blink incessantly and he grins about him slyly with a greedy malice.

ABBIE (*suddenly turning to a young girl on her right*). Whar's Eben?

YOUNG GIRL (*eying her scornfully*). I dunno, Mrs. Cabot. I ain't seen Eben in ages. (*Meaningly.*) Seems like he's spent most o' his time t' hum since yew come.

ABBIE (*vaguely*). I tuk his Maw's place.

YOUNG GIRL. Ay-eh. So I've heerd. (*She turns away to retail this bit of gossip to her mother sitting next to her.* ABBIE *turns to her left to a big stoutish middle-aged man whose flushed face and starting eyes show the amount of "likker" he has consumed.*)

ABBIE. Ye hain't seen Eben, hev ye?

MAN. No, I ain't. (*Then he adds with a wink.*) If yew hain't, who would?

ABBIE. He's the best dancer in the county. He'd ought t' come an' dance.

MAN (*with a wink*). Mebbe he's doin' the dutiful an' walkin' the kid t' sleep. It's a boy, hain't it?

ABBIE (*nodding vaguely*). Ay-eh—born two weeks back—purty's a picter.

MAN. They all is—t' their Maws. (*Then in a whisper, with a nudge and a leer.*) Listen, Abbie—if ye ever git tired o' Eben, remember me! Don't fergit now! (*He looks at her uncomprehending face for a second—then grunts disgustedly.*) Waal—guess I'll likker agin. (*He goes over and joins* CABOT *who is arguing noisily with an old farmer over cows. They all drink.*)

ABBIE (*this time appealing to nobody in particular*). Wonder what Eben's a-doin'? (*Her remark is repeated down the line with many a guffaw and titter until it reaches the fiddler. He fastens his blinking eyes on* ABBIE.)

FIDDLER (*raising his voice*). Bet I kin tell ye, Abbie, what Eben's doin'! He's down t' the church offerin' up prayers o' thanksgivin'. (*They all titter expectantly.*)

A MAN. What fur? (*Another titter.*)

FIDDLER 'Cause unto him a—(*He hesitates just long enough.*) brother is born! (*A roar of laughter. They all look from* ABBIE *to* CABOT. *She is oblivious, staring at the door.* CABOT, *although he hasn't heard the words, is irritated by the laughter and steps forward, glaring about him. There is an immediate silence.*)

CABOT. What're ye all bleatin' about—like a flock o' goats? Why don't ye dance, damn ye? I axed ye here t' dance—t' eat, drink an' be merry—an' thar ye set cacklin' like a lot o' wet hens with the pip! Ye've swilled my likker an' guzzled my vittles like hogs, hain't ye? Then dance fur me, can't ye? That's fa'r an' squar', hain't it? (*A grumble of resentment goes around but they are all evidently in too much awe of him to express it openly.*)

FIDDLER (*slyly*). We're waitin' fur Eben. (*A suppressed laugh.*)

CABOT (*with a fierce exultation*). T'hell with Eben! Eben's done fur now! I got a new son! (*His mood switching with drunken suddenness.*) But ye needn't t' laugh at Eben, none o' ye! He's my blood, if he be a dumb fool. He's better nor any o' yew! He kin do a day's work a'most up t' what I kin—an' that'd put any o' yew pore critters t' shame!

FIDDLER. An' he kin do a good night's work, too! (*A roar of laughter.*)

CABOT. Laugh, ye damn fools! Ye're right jist the same, Fiddler. He kin work day an' night too, like I kin, if need be!

OLD FARMER (*from behind the keg where he is weaving drunkenly back and forth—with great simplicity*). They hain't many t' touch ye, Ephraim—a son at seventy-six. That's a hard man fur ye! I be on'y sixty-eight an' I couldn't do it. (*A roar of laughter in which* CABOT *joins uproariously.*)

CABOT (*slapping him on the back*). I'm sorry fur ye, Hi. I'd never suspicion sech weakness from a boy like yew!

OLD FARMER. An' I never reckoned yew had it in ye nuther, Ephraim. (*There is another laugh.*)

CABOT (*suddenly grim*). I got a lot in me—a hell of a lot— folks don't know on. (*Turning to the fiddler.*) Fiddle 'er up, durn ye! Give 'em somethin' t' dance t'! What air ye, an ornament? Hain't this a celebration? Then grease yer elbow an' go it!

FIDDLER (*seizes a drink which the* OLD

FARMER *holds out to him and downs it*). Here goes! (*He starts to fiddle "Lady of the Lake." Four young fellows and four girls form in two lines and dance a square dance. The* FIDDLER *shouts directions for the different movements, keeping his words in the rhythm of the music and interspersing them with jocular personal remarks to the dancers themselves. The people seated along the walls stamp their feet and clap their hands in unison.* CABOT *is especially active in this respect. Only* ABBIE *remains apathetic, staring at the door as if she were alone in a silent room.*)

FIDDLER. Swing your partner t' the right! That's it, Jim! Give her a b'ar hug! Her Maw hain't lookin'. (*Laughter.*) Change partners! That suits ye, don't it, Essie, now ye got Reub afore ye? Look at her redden up, will ye? Waal, life is short an' so's love, as the feller says. (*Laughter.*)

CABOT (*excitedly, stamping his foot*). Go it, boys! Go it, gals!

FIDDLER (*with a wink at the others*). Ye're the spryest seventy-six ever I sees, Ephraim! Now if ye'd on'y good eyesight . . . ! (*Suppressed laughter. He gives* CABOT *no chance to retort but roars.*) Promenade! Ye're walkin' like a bride down the aisle, Sarah! Waal, while they's life they's allus hope, I've heerd tell. Swing your partner to the left! Gosh A'mighty, look at Johnny Cook high-steppin'! They hain't goin' t'be much strength left fur howin' in the corn lot t'morrow. (*Laughter.*)

CABOT. Go it! Go it! (*Then suddenly, unable to restrain himself any longer, he prances into the midst of the dancers, scattering them, waving his arms about wildly.*) Ye're all hoofs! Git out o' my road! Give me room! I'll show ye dancin'. Ye're all too soft! (*He pushes them roughly away. They crowd back toward the walls, muttering, looking at him resentfully.*)

FIDDLER (*jeeringly*). Go it, Ephraim! Go it! (*He starts "Pop, Goes the Weasel," increasing the tempo with every verse until at the end he is fiddling crazily as fast as he can go.*)

CABOT (*starts to dance, which he does very well and with tremendous vigor. Then he begins to improvise, cuts incredibly grotesque capers, leaping up and cracking his heels together, prancing around in a circle with body bent in an Indian war dance, then suddenly straightening up and kicking as high as he can with both legs. He is like a monkey on a string. And all the while he intersperses his antics with shouts and derisive comments*). Whoop! Here's dancin' fur ye! Whoop! See that! Seventy-six, if I'm a day! Hard as iron yet! Beatin' the young 'uns like I allus done! Look at me! I'd invite ye t' dance on my hundredth birthday on'y ye'll all be dead by then. Ye're a sickly generation! Yer hearts air pink, not red! Yer veins is full o' mud an' water! I be the on'y man in the county! Whoop! See that! I'm a Injun! I've killed Injuns in the West afore ye was born—an' skulped 'em too! They's a arrer wound on my backside I c'd show ye! The hull tribe chased me. I outrun 'em all—with the arrer stuck in me! An' I tuk vengeance on 'em. Ten eyes fur an eye, that was my motter! Whoop! Look at me! I kin kick the ceilin' off the room! Whoop!

FIDDLER (*stops playing—exhaustedly*). God A'mighty, I got enuf. Ye got the devil's strength in ye.

CABOT (*delightedly*). Did I beat yew, too? Wa'al, ye played smart. Hev a swig. (*He pours whisky for himself and* FIDDLER. *They drink. The others watch* CABOT *silently with cold, hostile eyes. There is a dead pause. The* FIDDLER *rests.* CABOT *leans against the keg, panting, glaring around him confusedly. In the room above,* EBEN *gets to his feet and tiptoes out the door in rear, appearing a moment later in the other bedroom. He moves silently, even frightenedly, toward the cradle and stands there looking down at the baby. His face is as vague as his reactions are confused, but there is a trace of tenderness, of interested discovery. As the same moment that he reaches the cradle,* ABBIE *seems to sense something. She gets up weakly and goes to* CABOT.)

ABBIE. I'm goin' up t' the baby.

CABOT (*with real solicitation*). Air ye able fur the stairs? D'ye want me t' help ye, Abbie?

ABBIE. No. I'm able. I'll be down agen soon.

CABOT. Don't ye git wore out! He needs ye, remember—our son does! (*He grins affectionately, patting her on the back. She shrinks from his touch.*)

ABBIE (*dully*). Don't—tech me. I'm goin'—up. (*She goes.* CABOT *looks after her. A whisper goes around the room.* CABOT *turns. It ceases. He wipes his forehead streaming with sweat. He is breathing pantingly.*)

CABOT. I'm a-goin' out t' git fresh air. I'm feelin' a mite dizzy. Fiddle up thar! Dance, all o' ye! Here's likker fur them as wants it. Enjoy yerselves. I'll be back. (*He goes, closing the door behind him.*)

FIDDLER (*sarcastically*). Don't hurry none on our account! (*A suppressed laugh. He imitates* ABBIE.) Whar's Eben? (*More laughter.*)

A WOMAN (*loudly*). What's happened in this house is plain as the nose on yer face! (ABBIE *appears in the doorway upstairs and stands looking in surprise and adoration at* EBEN *who does not see her.*)

A MAN. Ssshh! He's li'ble t' be listenin' at the door. That'd be like him. (*Their voices die to an intensive whispering. Their faces are concentrated on this gossip. A noise as of dead leaves in the wind comes from the room.* CABOT *has come out from the porch and stands by the gate, leaning on it, staring at the sky blinkingly.* ABBIE *comes across the room silently.* EBEN *does not notice her until quite near.*)

EBEN (*starting*). Abbie!

ABBIE. Ssshh! (*She throws her arms around him. They kiss—then bend over the cradle together.*) Ain't he purty?—dead spit 'n' image o' yew!

EBEN (*pleased*). Air he? I can't tell none.

ABBIE. E-zactly like!

EBEN (*frowningly*). I don't like this. I don't like lettin' on what's mine's his'n. I been doin' that all my life. I'm gittin' t' the end o' b'arin' it!

ABBIE (*putting her finger on his lips*). We're doin' the best we kin. We got t' wait. Somethin's bound t' happen. (*She puts her arms around him.*) I got t' go back.

EBEN. I'm goin' out. I can't b'ar it with the fiddle playin' an' the laughin'.

ABBIE. Don't git feelin' low. I love ye, Eben. Kiss me. (*He kisses her. They remain in each other's arms.*)

CABOT (*at the gate, confusedly*). Even the music can't drive it out—somethin'. Ye kin feel it droppin' off the elums, climbin' up the roof, sneakin' down the chimney, pokin' in the corners! They's no peace in houses, they's no rest livin' with folks. Somethin's always livin' with ye. (*With a deep sigh.*) I'll go t' the barn an' rest a spell. (*He goes wearily toward the barn.*)

FIDDLER (*tuning up*). Let's celebrate the old skunk gittin' fooled! We kin have some fun now he's went. (*He starts to fiddle "Turkey in the Straw." There is real merriment now. The young folks get up to dance.*)

Scene Two

*A half hour later—Exterior—*EBEN *is standing by the gate looking up at the sky, an expression of dumb pain bewildered by itself on his face.* CABOT *appears, returning from the barn, walking wearily, his eyes on the ground. He sees* EBEN *and his whole mood immediately changes. He becomes excited, a cruel, triumphant grin comes to his lips, he strides up and slaps* EBEN *on the back. From within comes the whining of the fiddle and the noise of stamping feet and laughing voices.*

CABOT. So har ye be!

EBEN (*startled, stares at him with hatred for a moment—then dully*). Ay-eh.

CABOT (*surveying him jeeringly*). Why hain't ye been in t' dance? They was all axin' fur ye.

EBEN. Let 'em ax!

CABOT. They's a hull passel o' purty gals.

EBEN. T' hell with 'em!

CABOT. Ye'd ought t' be marryin' one o' 'em soon.

EBEN. I hain't marryin' no one.

CABOT. Ye might 'arn a share o' a farm that way.

EBEN (*with a sneer*). Like yew did, ye mean? I hain't that kind.

CABOT (*stung*). Ye lie! 'Twas yer Maw's folks aimed t' steal my farm from me.

EBEN. Other folks don't say so. (*After a pause—defiantly.*) An' I got a farm, anyways!

CABOT (*derisively*). Whar?

EBEN (*stamps a foot on the ground*). Har!

CABOT (*throws his head back and laughs coarsely*). Ho-ho! Ye hev, hev ye? Waal, that's a good un!

EBEN (*controlling himself—grimly*). Ye'll see!

CABOT (*stares at him suspiciously, trying to make him out—a pause—then with scornful confidence*). Ay-eh. I'll see. So'll ye. It's ye that's blind—blind as a mole underground. (EBEN *suddenly laughs, one short sardonic bark: "Ha." A pause,* CABOT *peers at him with renewed suspicion.*) What air ye hawin' 'bout? (EBEN *turns away without answering.* CABOT *grows angry.*) God A'mighty, yew air a dumb dunce! They's nothin' in that thick skull o' your'n but noise—like a empty keg it be! (EBEN *doesn't seem to hear.* CABOT'S *rage grows.*) Yewr farm! God A'mighty! If ye wa'n't a born donkey ye'd know ye'll never own stick nor stone on it, specially now arter him bein' born. It's his'n, I tell ye—his'n arter I die—but I'll live a hundred jest t' fool ye all—an' he'll be growed then—yewr age a'most! (EBEN *laughs again his sardonic "Ha." This drives* CABOT *into a fury.*) Ha? Ye think ye kin git 'round that someways, do ye? Waal, it'll be her'n, too—Abbie's—ye won't git 'round her—she knows yer tricks—she'll be too much fur ye—she wants the farm her'n—she was afeerd o' ye—she told me ye was sneakin' 'round tryin' t' make love t' her t' git her on yer side . . . ye . . . ye mad fool, ye! (*He raises his clenched fists threateningly.*)

EBEN (*is confronting him, choking with rage*). Ye lie, ye old skunk! Abbie never said no sech thing!

CABOT (*suddenly triumphant when he sees how shaken* EBEN *is.*) She did. An' I says, I'll blow his brains t' the top o' them elums—an' she says no, that hain't sense, who'll ye git t'help ye on the farm in his place—an' then she says yew'n me ought t' have a son—I know we kin, she says—an' I says, if we do, ye kin have anythin' I've got ye've a mind t'. An' she says, I wants Eben cut off so's this farm'll be mine when ye die! (*With terrible gloating.*) An' that's what's happened, hain't it? An' the farm's her'n! An' the dust o' the road—that's you'rn! Ha! Now who's hawin'?

EBEN (*has been listening, petrified with grief and rage—suddenly laughs wildly and brokenly*). Ha-ha-ha! So that's her sneakin' game—all along!—like I suspicioned at fust—t' swaller it all—an' me, too . . . ! (*Madly.*) I'll murder her! (*He springs toward the porch but* CABOT *is quicker and gets in between.*)

CABOT. No, ye don't!

EBEN. Git out o' my road! (*He tries to throw* CABOT *aside. They grapple in what becomes immediately a murderous struggle. The old man's concentrated strength is too much for* EBEN. CABOT *gets one hand on his throat and presses him back across the stone wall. At the same moment,* ABBIE *comes out on the porch. With a stifled cry she runs toward them.*)

ABBIE. Eben! Ephraim! (*She tugs at the hand on* EBEN'S *throat.*) Let go, Ephraim! Ye're chokin' him!

CABOT (*removes his hand and flings* EBEN *sideways full length on the grass, gasping and choking. With a cry,* ABBIE *kneels beside him, trying to take his head on her lap, but he pushes her away.* CABOT *stands looking down with fierce triumph*). Ye needn't t've fret, Abbie, I wa'n't t' kill him. He hain't wuth hangin' fur—not by a hell of a sight! (*More and more triumphantly.*) Seventy-six an' him not thirty yit—an' look whar he be fur thinkin' his Paw was easy! No, by God, I hain't easy! An' him upstairs, I'll raise him t' be like me! (*He turns to leave them.*) I'm goin' in an' dance!—sing an' celebrate! (*He walks to the porch—then turns with a great grin.*) I don't calc'late it's left in him, but if he gits pesky, Abbie, ye jest sing out. I'll come a-runnin' an' by the Etarnal, I'll put him across my knee an' birch him! Ha-ha-ha! (*He goes into the house laughing. A moment later his loud "whoop" is heard.*)

ABBIE (*tenderly*). Eben. Air ye hurt? (*She tries to kiss him but he pushes her violently away and struggles to a sitting position.*)

EBEN (*gaspingly*). T'hell—with ye!

ABBIE (*not believing her ears*). It's me, Eben—Abbie—don't ye know me?

EBEN (*glowering at her with hatred*). Ay-eh—I know ye—now! (*He suddenly breaks down, sobbing weakly.*)

ABBIE (*fearfully*). Eben—what's happened t' ye—why did ye look at me 's if ye hated me?

EBEN (*violently, between sobs and gasps*). I do hate ye! Ye're a whore—a damn trickin' whore!

ABBIE (*shrinking back horrified*). Eben! Ye don't know what ye're sayin'!

EBEN (*scrambling to his feet and following her—accusingly*). Ye're nothin' but a stinkin' passel o' lies! Ye've been lyin' t' me every word ye spoke, day an' night, since we fust—done it. Ye've kept sayin' ye loved me. . . .

ABBIE (*frantically*). I do love ye! (*She takes his hand but he flings hers away.*)

EBEN (*unheeding*). Ye've made a fool o' me—a sick, dumb fool—a-purpose! Ye've been on'y playin' yer sneakin', stealin' game all along—gittin' me t' lie with ye so's ye'd hev a son he'd think was hisn', an' makin' him promise he'd give ye the farm and let me eat dust, if ye did git him a son! (*Staring at her with anguished, bewildered eyes.*) They must be a devil livin' in ye! T'ain't human t' be as bad as that be!

ABBIE (*stunned—dully*). He told yew. . . . ?

EBEN. Hain't it true? It hain't no good in yew lyin'.

ABBIE (*pleadingly*). Eben, listen—ye must listen—it was long ago—afore we done nothin'—yew was scornin' me—goin' t' see Min—when I was lovin' ye—an' I said it t' him t' git vengeance on ye.

EBEN (*unheedingly. With tortured passion*). I wish ye was dead! I wish I was dead along with ye afore this come! (*Ragingly.*) But I'll git my vengeance too! I'll pray Maw t' come back t' help me—t' put her cuss on yew an' him!

ABBIE (*brokenly*). Don't ye, Eben! Don't ye! (*She throws herself on her knees before him, weeping.*) I didn't mean t' do bad t'ye! Fergive me, won't ye?

EBEN (*not seeming to hear her—fiercely*). I'll git squar' with the old skunk—an' yew! I'll tell him the truth 'bout the son he's so proud o'! Then I'll leave ye here t' pizen each other—with Maw comin' out o' her grave at nights—an' I'll go t' the gold fields o' Californi-a whar Sim an' Peter be!

ABBIE (*terrified*). Ye won't—leave me? Ye can't!

EBEN (*with fierce determination*). I'm a-goin', I tell ye! I'll git rich thar an' come back an fight him fur the farm he stole—an' I'll kick ye both out in the road—t' beg an' sleep in the woods—an' yer son along with ye—t' starve an' die! (*He is hysterical at the end.*)

ABBIE (*with a shudder—humbly*). He's yewr son, too, Eben.

EBEN (*torturedly*). I wish he never was born! I wish he'd die this minit! I wish I'd never sot eyes on him! It's him—yew havin' him—a-purpose t' steal—that's changed everythin'!

ABBIE (*gently*). Did ye believe I loved ye—afore he come?

EBEN. Ay-eh—like a dumb ox!

ABBIE. An' ye don't believe no more?

EBEN. B'lieve a lyin' thief! Ha!

ABBIE (*shudders—then humbly*). An' did ye r'ally love me afore?

EBEN (*brokenly*). Ay-eh—an' ye was trickin' me!

ABBIE. An' ye don't love me now!

EBEN (*violently*). I hate ye, I tell ye!

ABBIE. An' ye're truly goin' West—goin' t' leave me—all account o' him being born?

EBEN. I'm a-goin' in the mornin'—or may God strike me t' hell!

ABBIE (*after a pause—with a dreadful cold intensity—slowly*). If that's what his comin's done t' me—killin' yewr love—takin' yew away—my on'y joy—the on'y joy I ever knowed—like heaven t' me—purtier'n heaven—then I hate him, too, even if I be his Maw!

EBEN (*bitterly*). Lies! Ye love him! He'll steal the farm fur ye! (*Brokenly.*) But t'aint the farm so much—not no more—it's yew foolin' me—gittin' me t' love ye—lyin' yew loved me—jest t' git a son t' steal!

ABBIE (*distractedly*). He won't steal! I'd kill him fust! I do love ye! I'll prove t' ye. . . . !

EBEN (*harshly*). T'ain't no use lyin' no more. I'm deaf t' ye! (*He turns away.*) I hain't seein' ye agen. Good-by!

ABBIE (*pale with anguish*). Hain't ye even goin' t' kiss me—not once—arter all we loved?

EBEN (*in a hard voice*). I hain't wantin' t' kiss ye never agen! I'm wantin' t' forgit I ever sot eyes on ye!

ABBIE. Eben!—ye mustn't—wait a spell—I want t' tell ye. . . .

EBEN. I'm a-goin' in t' git drunk. I'm a-goin' t' dance.

ABBIE (*clinging to his arm—with passionate earnestness*). If I could make it—'s if he'd never come up between us—if I could prove t' ye I wa'n't schemin' t' steal from ye—so's everythin' could be jest the same with us, lovin' each other jest the same, kissin' an' happy the same's we've been happy afore he come—if I could do it—ye'd love me agen, wouldn't ye? Ye'd kiss me agen? Ye wouldn't never leave me, would ye?

EBEN (*moved*). I calc'late not. (*Then shaking her hand off his arm—with a bitter smile.*) But ye hain't God, be ye?

ABBIE (*exultantly*). Remember ye've promised! (*Then with strange intensity.*) Mebbe I kin take back one thin' God does!

EBEN (*peering at her*). Ye're gittin cracked, hain't ye? (*Then going towards door.*) I'm a-goin' t' dance.

ABBIE (*calls after him intensely*). I'll prove t' ye! I'll prove I love ye better'n. . . . (*He goes in the door, not seeming to hear. She remains standing where she is, looking after him—then she finishes desperately.*) Better'n everythin' else in the world!

Scene Three

Just before dawn in the morning—shows the kitchen and CABOT'S *bedroom. In the kitchen, by the light of a tallow candle on the table,* EBEN *is sitting, his chin propped on his hands, his drawn face blank and expressionless. His carpetbag is on the floor beside him. In the bedroom, dimly lighted by a small whale-oil lamp,* CABOT *lies asleep.* ABBIE *is bending over the cradle, listening, her face full of terror yet with an undercurrent of desperate triumph. Suddenly, she breaks down and sobs, appears about to throw herself on her knees beside the cradle; but the old man turns restlessly, groaning in his sleep, and she controls herself, and, shrinking away from the cradle with a gesture of horror, backs swiftly toward the door in rear and goes out. A moment later she comes into the kitchen and, running to* EBEN, *flings her arms about his neck and kisses him wildly. He hardens himself, he remains unmoved and cold, he keeps his eyes straight ahead.*

ABBIE (*hysterically*). I done it, Eben! I told ye I'd do it! I've proved I love ye—better'n everythin'—so's ye can't never doubt me no more!

EBEN (*dully*). Whatever ye done, it hain't no good now.

ABBIE (*wildly*). Don't ye say that! Kiss me, Eben, won't ye? I need ye t' kiss me arter what I done! I need ye t' say ye love me!

EBEN (*kisses her without emotion—dully*). That's fur goodby. I'm a-goin' soon.

ABBIE. No! No! Ye won't go—not now!

EBEN (*going on with his own thoughts*). I been a-thinkin'—an' I hain't goin' t' tell Paw nothin'. I'll leave Maw t' take vengeance on ye. If I told him, the old skunk'd jest be stinkin' mean enuf to take it out on that baby. (*His voice showing emotion in spite of him.*) An' I don't want nothin' bad t' happen t' him. He hain't t' blame fur yew. (*He adds with a certain queer pride.*) An' he looks like me! An' by God, he's mine! An' some day I'll be a-comin' back an' . . . !

ABBIE (*too absorbed in her own thoughts to listen to him—pleadingly*). They's no cause fur ye t' go now—they's no sense—it's all the same's it was—they's nothin' come b'tween us now—arter what I done!

EBEN (*something in her voice arouses him. He stares at her a bit frightenedly*). Ye look mad, Abbie. What did ye do?

ABBIE. I—I killed him, Eben.

EBEN (*amazed*). Ye killed him?

ABBIE (*dully*). Ay-eh.

EBEN (*recovering from his astonishment—savagely*). An' serves him right! But we got t' do somethin' quick t' make it look s'if the old skunk'd killed himself when he was drunk. We kin prove by 'em all how drunk he got.

ABBIE (*wildly*). No! No! Not him! (*Laughing distractedly.*) But that's what I ought t' done, hain't it? I oughter killed him instead! Why didn't ye tell me?

EBEN (*appalled*). Instead? What d'ye mean?

ABBIE. Not him.

EBEN (*his face grown ghastly*). Not—not that baby!

ABBIE (*dully*). Ay-eh!

EBEN (*falls to his knees as if he'd been struck—his voice trembling with horror*). Oh God A'mighty! A'mighty God! Maw, whar was ye, why didn't ye stop her?

ABBIE (*simply*). She went back t' her grave that night we fust done it, remember? I hain't felt her about since. (*A pause.* EBEN *hides his head in his hands, trembling all over as if he had the ague. She goes on dully.*) I left the piller over his little face. Then he killed himself. He stopped breathin'. (*She begins to weep softly.*)

EBEN (*rage beginning to mingle with grief*). He looked like me. He was mine, damn ye!

ABBIE (*slowly and brokenly*). I didn't want t' do it. I hated myself fur doin' it. I loved him. He was so purty—dead spit 'n' image o' yew. But I loved yew more—an' yew was goin' away—far off whar I'd never see ye agen, never kiss ye, never feel ye pressed agin me agen—an' ye said ye hated me fur havin' him—ye said ye hated him an' wished he was dead—ye said if it hadn't been fur him comin' it'd be the same's afore between us.

EBEN (*unable to endure this, springs to his feet in a fury, threatening her, his twitching fingers seeming to reach out for her throat*). Ye lie! I never said—I never dreamed ye'd— I'd cut off my head afore I'd hurt his finger!

ABBIE (*piteously, sinking on her knees*). Eben, don't ye look at me like that—hatin' me—not after what I done fur ye—fur us—so's we could be happy agen——

EBEN (*furiously now*). Shut up, or I'll kill ye! I see yer game now—the same old sneakin' trick—ye're aimin' t' blame me fur the murder ye done!

ABBIE (*moaning—putting her hands over her ears*). Don't ye, Eben! Don't ye! (*She grasps his legs.*)

EBEN (*his mood suddenly changing to horror, shrinks away from her*). Don't ye tech me! Ye're pizzen! How could ye—t' murder a pore little critter—— Ye must've swapped yer soul t' hell! (*Suddenly raging.*) Ha! I kin see why ye done it! Not the lies ye jest told—but 'cause ye wanted t' steal agen—steal the last thin' ye'd left me—my part o' him—no, the hull o' him—ye saw he looked like me—ye knowed he was all mine—an' ye couldn't b'ar it—I know ye! Ye killed him fur bein' mine! (*All this has driven him almost insane. He makes a rush past her for the door—then turns—shaking both fists at her, violently.*) But I'll take vengeance now! I'll git the Sheriff! I'll tell him everythin'! Then I'll sing "I'm off to Californi-a!" an' go—gold—Golden Gate—gold sun—fields o' gold in the West! (*This last he half shouts, half croons incoherently, suddenly breaking off passionately.*) I'm a-goin' fur the Sheriff t' come an' git ye! I want ye tuk away, locked up from me! I can't stand t' luk at ye! Murderer an' thief 'r not, ye still tempt me! I'll give ye up t' the Sheriff! (*He turns and runs out, around the corner of house, panting and sobbing, and breaks into a swerving sprint down the road.*)

ABBIE (*struggling to her feet, runs to the door, calling after him*). I love ye, Eben! I love ye! (*She stops at the door weakly, swaying, about to fall.*) I don't care what ye do—if ye'll on'y love me agen— (*She falls limply to the floor in a faint.*)

SCENE FOUR

About an hour later. Same as Scene Three. Shows the kitchen and CABOT'S *bedroom. It is after dawn. The sky is brilliant with the sunrise. In the kitchen,* ABBIE *sits at the table, her body limp and exhausted, her head bowed down over her arms, her face hidden. Upstairs,* CABOT *is still asleep but awakens with a start. He looks toward the window and gives a snort of surprise and irritation—throws back the covers and begins hurriedly pulling on his clothes. Without looking behind him, he begins talking to* ABBIE *whom he supposes beside him.*

CABOT. Thunder 'n' lightin', Abbie! I hain't slept this late in fifty year! Looks 's if the sun was full riz a'most. Must've been the dancin' an' likker. Must be gittin' old. I hope Eben's t' wuk. Ye might've tuk the trouble t' rouse me, Abbie. (*He turns—sees no one there—surprised.*) Waal—whar air she? Gittin' vittles, I calc'late. (*He tiptoes to the cradle and peers down—proudly.*) Mornin', sonny. Purty's a picter! Sleepin' sound. He don't beller all night like most o' 'em. (*He goes quietly out the door in rear—a few moments later enters kitchen—sees* ABBIE*—with satisfaction.*) So thar ye be. Ye got any vittles cooked?

ABBIE (*without moving*). No.

CABOT (*coming to her, almost sympathetically*). Ye feelin' sick?

ABBIE. No.

CABOT (*pats her on shoulder. She shudders*). Ye'd best lie down a spell. (*Half jocularly.*) Yer son'll be needin' ye soon. He'd ought t' wake up with a gnashin' appetite, the sound way he's sleepin'.

ABBIE (*shudders—then in a dead voice*). He hain't never goin' t' wake up.

CABOT (*jokingly*). Takes after me this mornin'. I hain't slept so late in. . . .

ABBIE. He's dead.

CABOT (*stares at her—bewilderedly*). What. . . .

ABBIE. I killed him.

CABOT (*stepping back from her—aghast*). Air ye drunk—'r crazy—'r. . . !

ABBIE (*suddenly lifts her head and turns on him—wildly*). I killed him, I tell ye! I smothered him. Go up an' see if ye don't b'lieve me! (CABOT *stares at her a second, then bolts out the rear door, can be heard bounding up the stairs, and rushes into the bedroom and over to the cradle.* ABBIE *has sunk back lifelessly into her former position.* CABOT *puts his hand down on the body in the crib. An expression of fear and horror comes over his face.*)

CABOT (*shrinking away—tremblingly*). God A'mighty! God A'mighty. (*He stumbles out the door—in a short while returns to the kitchen—comes to* ABBIE, *the stunned expression still on his face—hoarsely.*) Why did ye do it? Why? (*As she doesn't answer, he grabs her violently by the shoulder and shakes her.*) I ax ye why ye done it! Ye'd better tell me 'r . . . !

ABBIE (*gives him a furious push which sends him staggering back and springs to her feet—with wild rage and hatred*). Don't ye dare tech me! What right hev ye t' question me 'bout him? He wa'n't yewr son! Think I'd have a son by yew? I'd die fust! I hate the sight o' ye an' allus did! It's yew I should've murdered, if I'd had good sense! I hate ye! I love Eben. I did from the fust. An' he was Eben's son—mine an' Eben's—not your'n!

CABOT (*stands looking at her dazedly—a pause—finding his words with an effort—dully*). That was it—what I felt—pokin' round the corners—while ye lied—holdin' yerself from me—sayin' ye'd a'ready conceived—— (*He lapses into crushed silence—then with a strange emotion.*) He's dead, sart'n. I felt his heart. Pore little critter! (*He blinks back one tear, wiping his sleeve across his nose.*)

ABBIE (*hysterically*). Don't ye! Don't ye! (*She sobs unrestrainedly.*)

CABOT (*with a concentrated effort that stiffens his body into a rigid line and hardens his face into a stony mask—through his teeth to himself*). I got t' be—like a stone—a rock o' jedgment! (*A pause. He gets complete control over himself—harshly.*) If he was Eben's, I be glad he air gone! An' mebbe I suspicioned it all along. I felt they was somethin' onnateral—somewhars—the house got so lonesome—an' cold—drivin' me down t' the barn—t' the beasts o' the field. . . . Ay-eh. I must've suspicioned—somethin'. Ye didn't fool me—not altogether, leastways—I'm too old a bird—growin' ripe on the bough. . . . (*He becomes aware he is wandering, straightens again, looks at* ABBIE *with a cruel grin.*) So ye'd liked t' hev murdered me 'stead o' him, would ye? Waal, I'll live to a hundred! I'll live t' see ye hung! I'll deliver ye up t' the jedgment o' God an' the law! I'll git the Sheriff now. (*Starts for the door.*)

ABBIE (*dully*). Ye needn't. Eben's gone fur him.

CABOT (*amazed*). Eben—gone fur the Sheriff?

ABBIE. Ay-eh.

CABOT. T' inform agen ye?

ABBIE. Ay-eh.

CABOT (*considers this—a pause—then in a hard voice*). Waal, I'm thankful fur him savin' me the trouble. I'll git t' wuk. (*He goes to the door—then turns—in a voice full of strange emotion.*) He'd ought t' been my son, Abbie. Ye'd ought t' loved me. I'm a man. If ye'd loved me, I'd never told no Sheriff on ye no matter what ye did, if they was t' brile me alive!

ABBIE (*defensively*). They's more to it nor yew know, makes him tell.

CABOT (*dryly*). Fur yewr sake, I hope they be. (*He goes out—comes around to the gate—stares up at the sky. His control relaxes. For a moment he is old and weary. He murmurs despairingly.*) God A'mighty, I be lonesomer'n ever! (*He hears running footsteps from the left, immediately is himself again.* EBEN *runs in, panting exhaustedly, wild-eyed and mad looking. He lurches through the gate.* CABOT *grabs him by the shoulder.* EBEN *stares at him dumbly.*) Did ye tell the Sheriff?

EBEN (*nodding stupidly*). Ay-eh.

CABOT (*gives him a push away that sends him sprawling—laughing with withering contempt*). Good fur ye! A prime chip o' yer Maw ye be! (*He goes toward the barn, laughing harshly.* EBEN *scrambles to his feet. Suddenly* CABOT *turns—grimly threatening.*) Git off this farm when the Sheriff takes her—or, by God, he'll have t' come back an' git me fur murder, too! (*He stalks off.* EBEN *does not appear to have heard him. He runs to the door and comes into the kitchen.* ABBIE *looks up with a cry of anguished joy.* EBEN *stumbles over and throws himself on his knees beside her—sobbing brokenly.*)

EBEN. Fergive me!

ABBIE (*happily*). Eben! (*She kisses him and pulls his head over against her breast.*)

EBEN. I love ye! Fergive me!

ABBIE (*ecstatically*). I'd fergive ye all the sins in hell fur sayin' that! (*She kisses his head, pressing it to her with a fierce passion of possession.*)

EBEN (*brokenly*). But I told the Sheriff. He's comin' fur ye!

ABBIE. I kin b'ar what happens t' me —now!

EBEN. I woke him up. I told him. He says, wait 'till I git dressed. I was waiting. I got to thinkin' o' yew. I got to thinkin' how I'd loved ye. It hurt like somethin' was bustin' in my chest an' head. I got t' cryin'. I knowed sudden I loved ye yet, an' allus would love ye!

ABBIE (*caressing his hair—tenderly*). My boy, hain't ye?

EBEN. I begun t' run back. I cut across the fields an' through the woods. I thought ye might have time t' run away —with me—an'. . . .

ABBIE (*shaking her head*). I got t' take my punishment—t' pay fur my sin.

EBEN. Then I want t' share it with ye.

ABBIE. Ye didn't do nothin'.

EBEN. I put it in yer head. I wisht he was dead! I as much as urged ye t' do it!

ABBIE. No. It was me alone!

EBEN. I'm as guilty as yew be! He was the child o' our sin.

ABBIE (*lifting her head as if defying God*). I don't repent that sin! I hain't askin' God t' fergive that!

EBEN. Nor me—but it led up t' the other—an' the murder ye did, ye did 'count o' me—an' it's my murder, too, I'll tell the Sheriff—an' if ye deny it, I'll say we planned it t'gether—an' they'll all b'lieve me, fur they suspicion everythin' we've done, an' it'll seem likely an' true to 'em. An' it is true—way down. I did help ye—somehow.

ABBIE (*laying her head on his—sobbing*). No! I don't want yew t' suffer!

EBEN. I got t' pay fur my part o' the sin! An' I'd suffer wuss leavin' ye, goin' West, thinkin' o' ye day an' night, bein' out when yew was in—— (*lowering his voice*) 'r bein' alive when yew was dead. (*A pause.*) I want t' share with ye, Abbie —prison 'r death 'r hell 'r anythin'! (*He looks into her eyes and forces a trembling smile.*) If I'm sharin' with ye, I won't feel lonesome, leastways.

ABBIE (*weakly*). Eben! I won't let ye! I can't let ye!

EBEN (*kissing her—tenderly*). Ye can't he'p yerself. I got ye beat fur once!

ABBIE (*forcing a smile—adoringly*). I hain't beat—s'long's I got ye!

EBEN (*hears the sound of feet outside*). Ssshh! Listen! They've come t' take us!

ABBIE. No, it's him. Don't give him no chance to fight ye, Eben. Don't say nothin' —no matter what he says. An' I won't, neither. (*It is* CABOT. *He comes up from the barn in a great state of excitement and strides into the house and then into the kitchen.* EBEN *is kneeling beside* ABBIE, *his arm around her, hers around him. They stare straight ahead.*)

CABOT (*stares at them, his face hard. A long pause—vindictively*). Ye make a slick pair o' murderin' turtle doves! Ye'd ought t' be both hung on the same limb an' left thar t' swing in the breeze an' rot—a warnin' t' old fools like me t' b'ar their lonesomeness alone—an fur young fools like ye t' hobble their lust. (*A pause. The excitement returns to his face, his eyes snap, he looks a bit crazy.*) I couldn't work today. I couldn't take no interest. T' hell with the farm! I'm leavin' it! I've turned the cows an' other stock loose! I've druv 'em into the woods whar they kin be free! By freein' 'em, I'm freein' myself! I'm quittin' here today! I'll set fire t' house an' barn an' watch 'em burn, an' I'll leave yer Maw t' haunt the ashes, an' I'll will the fields back t' God, so that nothin' human kin never touch 'em! I'll be a-goin' to Californi-a—t' jine Simeon an' Peter— true sons o' mine if they be dumb fools —an' the Cabots'll find Solomon's Mines t'gether! (*He suddenly cuts a mad caper.*) Whoop! What was the song they sung? "Oh, Californi-a! That's the land fur me." (*He sings this—then gets on his knees by the floor-board under which the money was hid.*) An' I'll sail thar on one o' the finest clippers I kin find! I've got the money! Pity ye didn't know whar this was hidden so's ye could steal. . . . (*He has pulled up the board. He stares—feels —stares again. A pause of dead silence. He slowly turns, slumping into a sitting position on the floor, his eyes like those of a dead fish, his face the sickly green of an attack of nausea. He swallows painfully several times—forces a weak smile at last.*) So—ye did steal it!

EBEN (*emotionlessly*). I swapped it t' Sim an' Peter fur their share o' the farm —t' pay their passage t' Californi-a.

CABOT (*with one sardonic*). Ha! (*He begins to recover. Gets slowly to his feet —strangely*). I calc'late God give it to 'em —not yew! God's hard, not easy! Mebbe they's easy gold in the West but it hain't God's gold. It hain't fur me. I kin hear His voice warnin' me agen t' be hard an' stay on my farm. I kin see his hand usin' Eben t' steal t' keep me from weakness. I kin feel I be in the palm o' His hand, His fingers guidin' me. (*A pause—then he mutters sadly.*) It's a-goin' t' be lonesomer now than ever it war afore—an' I'm gittin' old, Lord—ripe on the bough. . . . (*Then stiffening.*) Waal—what d'ye want? God's lonesome, hain't He? God's hard an' lonesome! (*A pause. The Sheriff with two men come up the road from the left. They move cautiously to the door. The Sheriff knocks on it with the butt of his pistol.*)

SHERIFF. Open in the name o' the law! (*They start.*)

CABOT. They've come fur ye. (*He goes to the rear door.*) Come in, Jim! (*The three men enter.* CABOT *meets them in doorway.*) Jest a minit, Jim. I got 'em safe here. (*The Sheriff nods. He and his companions remain in the doorway.*)

EBEN (*suddenly calls*). I lied this mornin', Jim. I helped her do it. Ye kin take me, too.

ABBIE (*brokenly*). No!

CABOT. Take 'em both. (*He comes forward—stares at* EBEN *with a trace of grudging admiration.*) Purty good—fur yew! Waal, I got t' round up the stock. Good-by.

EBEN. Good-by.

ABBIE. Good-by. (CABOT *turns and strides past the men—comes out and around the corner of the house, his shoulders squared, his face stony, and stalks grimly toward the barn. In the meantime the Sheriff and men have come into the room.*)

SHERIFF (*embarrassedly*). Waal—we'd best start.

ABBIE. Wait. (*Turns to* EBEN.) I love ye, Eben.

EBEN. I love ye, Abbie. (*They kiss. The three men grin and shuffle embarrassedly.* EBEN *takes* ABBIE'*s hand. They go out the door in rear, the men following, and come from the house, walking hand in hand to the gate.* EBEN *stops there and points to the sunrise sky.*) Sun's a-rizin'. Purty, hain't it?

ABBIE. Ay-eh. (*They both stand for a moment looking up raptly in attitudes strangely aloof and devout.*)

SHERIFF (*looking around at the farm enviously—to his companion*). It's a jim-dandy farm, no denyin'. Wished I owned it!

THE CURTAIN FALLS

What Price Glory?

BY LAURENCE STALLINGS AND MAXWELL ANDERSON

First produced by Arthur Hopkins at the Plymouth Theatre, New York City, on September 3, 1924, with the following cast:

CORPORAL GOWDY ...... Brian Donlevy
CORPORAL KIPER .... Fuller Mellish, Jr.
CORPORAL LIPINSKY .... George Tobias
FIRST SERGEANT QUIRT. William Boyd
CAPTAIN FLAGG .... Louis Wolheim
CHARMAINE DE LA COGNAC .... Leyla Georgie
PRIVATE LEWISOHN .... Sidney Elliott
LIEUTENANT ALDRICH .. Fay Roppe
LIEUTENANT MOORE .... Clyde North
LIEUTENANT SCHMIDT .. Charles Costigan
GUNNERY SERGEANT SOCKKEL .... Henry G. Shelvey
PRIVATE MULCAHY ..... Jack MacGraw
SERGEANT FERGUSON ... James A. Devine
A BRIGADE RUNNER .... John J. Cavanaugh
MONSIEUR PETE DE LA COGNAC .... Luis Alberni
ANOTHER BRIGADE RUNNER .... Arthur Campbell
BRIGADIER GEN. COKELEY .... Roy La Rue
A COLONEL .... Keane Waters
A CAPTAIN .... William B. Smith
A LIEUTENANT .... Fred Brophy
ANOTHER LIEUTENANT .. Thomas Buckley
A CHAPLAIN .... John C. Davis
TOWN MAYOR .... Alfred Renaud
SPIKE .... Keane Waters
A PHARMACIST'S MATE .. Thomas Sullivan
LIEUTENANT CUNNINGHAM .... J. Merrill Holmes
LIEUTENANT LUNDSTROM .... Robert Warner

ACT I

Company Headquarters in a French village in the zone of advance.

ACT II

A cellar in a disputed town.

ACT III

The bar at Cognac Pete's.

When Laurence Stallings (1894) and Maxwell Anderson resolved to collaborate on *What Price Glory?* in 1924, they were both skeptical young men and regarded conventional treatments of the first World War as sheer pseudo-romantic fabrication. Of the two writers, Stallings, speaking from experience, could testify that war in the twentieth century was considerably different from anything to be read in Froissart's *Chronicles*. In 1917 he had written a cub reporter's piece on the U.S. Marine Corps and was sufficiently inspired by his own literary effort to join the "leathernecks." He rapidly advanced to a captaincy and was in the thick of the fighting in France when he was wounded at Chateau-Thierry and had to have his leg amputated. His fighting days over, he came back with the intention of preparing himself for a good sedentary profession like teaching and went so far as to obtain a Master's degree in science at the University of Georgetown. Instead, he returned to journalism, wrote the war novel *Plumes,* and was reviewing books on the old New York World when he met Mr. Anderson (1888). The latter's war-time experience had been less direct than his collaborator's. The son of a Baptist preacher, he became a pacifist during the war and in consequence met with a variety of minor disasters. He was dismissed from the staff of Whittier College and relieved of an editorial post on the San Francisco Bulletin. He, too, had found a haven in the offices of the New York World, which were then simply teeming with literary talent. Having already had his baptism in the theatre with *White Desert,* a modern tragedy in verse that failed in 1923, he seemed a likely collaborator to Mr. Stallings.

After the extraordinary success of *What Price Glory?,* the playwrights worked together on an Andrew Jackson play *First Flight* and on the pirate Henry Morgan romance *The Buccaneer*. Both plays were produced in 1925 and both failed, whereupon the collaborators parted ways. Mr. Anderson tried his hand alone at a dramatization of a Jim Tully book *Outside Looking In,* which the Provincetown Players produced at the Greenwich Village Theatre in the same year. He then won a considerable success with *Saturday's Children* in 1927, drew only moderate attention in 1928 with *Gods of the Lightning,* and failed with *Gypsy* in 1929. His best years were still to come. Mr. Stallings essayed collaborations on musicals with scant success (*Deep River* in 1926 and *Rainbow* in 1928, as well as *Virginia* in 1937) and did not fare very well with a dramatization of Ernest Hemingway's war novel *A Farewell to Arms,* but became a busy and thriving motion picture scenarist.

What Price Glory? made a strong impression on the generation of the twenties with its authentic treatment of soldiering and war. Its dialogue made it the most outspoken play of its time. The result was vivid and salty theatre, and it did more than any other dramatic piece to promote the cause of realism and freedom of speech on the American stage. Alexander Woollcott announced that compared with the characters in *What Price Glory?* all the other stage officers that had charged upon the public from Broadway's dressing rooms "seemed to step glistening from some magazine cover."

In its day, this comedy was also considered the last word in pacifism because the authors described fighting as a grimy business, employed considerable irony, and refrained from attributing exalted sentiments to its warriors. Nevertheless, Stallings and Anderson did not write a tract for the times, but a lively comedy of intrigue and manners—or lack of manners. Trench warfare as a subject recedes before the vigorous duel of a captain and a top-sergeant for the favors of a camp-following lady. And if war is presented without romantic persiflage, it cannot be said that soldiering is represented mournfully; the main characters are too exhilarating to be used for moral purposes. It is, indeed, far from certain that the authors were not themselves captivated by what they set out to deprecate. The truth is that their fundamental impulse was to make vivid theatre out of recollected experience. The standards of *All Quiet on the Western Front, Under Fire, Three Soldiers,* or *The Enormous Room,* not to mention *War and Peace,* are inapplicable to their showmanship. Their comment, which is hardly notable for analytical refinement, lies in the verisimilitude of their picture.

An excellent analysis of the play will be found on pages 29-41 of *The American Drama since 1918* by Joseph Wood Krutch.

ACT ONE

SCENE I

A room in a French farmhouse—now a U. S. Marine company headquarters. A couple of desks covered with maps and papers. Several scattered chairs. Three runners sit talking and smoking, very much at ease. LIPINSKY *is seated at one end of bench,* KIPER *at the other;* GOWDY *is sitting on a stool near* KIPER.

GOWDY. Well, where the hell did you come from?

KIPER. Who, me? I come from every place I've been to.

GOWDY. Yeah, well, where you been to?

KIPER. Me? I've been to China, Cuba, the Philippines, San Francisco, Buenos Ayres, Cape Town, Madagascar . . . wait a minute—Indiana, San Domingo, Tripoli, and Blackwell's Island.

LIPINSKY. Ever going home?

KIPER. Who, me? I can't go anywhere without going home.

GOWDY. By the time this war's over you ought to be pretty near ready to marry and settle down.

KIPER. There ain't going to be any after-this-war. Anyway, I got married after the last two wars and when I get through paying my debt to Lafayette, I'm through settling down. I never have settled down in so many hick towns in my life.

LIPINSKY. What became of them two broads?

KIPER. My wives?

LIPINSKY. Yeah.

KIPER. The first one never knew my last name, and when I left town she was out of luck.

GOWDY. And the next one?

KIPER. Ain't I signing the payroll for her every month? A twenty-dollar allotment, and she gives it to a fireman in Buffalo. Here I am saving democracy, and he's turning in a twenty-bell alarm the first of every month.

GOWDY. That's a waste of cash, the way I look at it. It stands to reason when a girl gets rid of one bozo she's looking for another. Now why does the late unlamented finance that little game? There's no justice in that.

KIPER. Who said it was justice? It ain't justice; it's alimony.

GOWDY. Well, alimony's all right if you're well fixed; hell, a girl ought to have some fun! I don't want a girl to quit living just because she ain't living with me, but the guy that's getting his ought to pay for it. What do you want to pay alimony for?

KIPER. What did you want to come to France for? It's the same reason why I pay alimony. So's to see the rest of the girls. Join the Marines and see the girls —from a porthole.

GOWDY. God! I came to France because I had a brain-storm one day and signed on the dotted line.

LIPINSKY. There ain't but one man in the world that came to France to see the mam'selles, and that's the skipper. When there's women around the skipper's got trick eyes like a horsefly.

KIPER. The old man? Say, he can't look at a mam'selle without blushing. Compared to me he's an amateur. He don't know the difference between a Hong-Kong honky-tonk and a Santo Domingo smoongy.

LIPINSKY. No, oh, no! I suppose women is an open book to you. You're damn well right—a code book.

KIPER. Yeah, you're damn well right. When I was in Turkey with that landing party the Sultan had to hunt through his harem with a flashlight to find a decent-looking girl, and when I left China the Yangtse was full of the bodies of virgins that drowned their beautiful selves because I was shipping over. And when I was in Spain the king of Spain put an ad in the paper offering a reward for the return of the queen.

GOWDY. What did you do?

KIPER. Took her back for the reward.

LIPINSKY. Huh! I notice you've got Cognac Pete's daughter, too.

KIPER. If I had the skipper's uniform and his Sam Browne belt, I could take that little wench away from him before you could say squads right! You ain't never seen it done. The skip's full of wind.

GOWDY. Anyway, Flagg's got Pete's kid sewed up—and she's as pretty a little frog as ever made a dish of frog's legs.

KIPER. Pete's kid! The poor little tart! What could she do? Ain't the skipper billeted there? God! I guess even Lippy could make a kid if she slept on the other side of a paper wall.

LIPINSKY. God! I don't know. Ain't it

the truth some guys just naturally walk away with women? Damned if I could ever do it!

KIPER. Take one good long look at yourself and you'll see why. There ain't many as unfortunate as you are. I guess there ain't anybody handicapped with features like them there.

LIPINSKY. Sometimes I think it's features, and sometimes I think it's luck. Once I spent three hundred dollars on a dame at Asbury Park in two days, and she keeping her damn chum with her all the time. Finally I got the extra one so drunk she couldn't tell her own name, and I ditched her. Then this broad I was trying to make insisted on riding on the merry-go-round. . . . God! the merry-go-round. Nothing else would satisfy her. She'd rung ducks till it rained ducks. She'd shot up more powder in shooting galleries than's been shot in this war, and she wanted to ride on the merry-go-round! So we got on the merry-go-round, and I threw her into a chariot and I piled on a horse. She hollers, "Whoopee, whoopee, let's do it again!" Jeez, I had spent three hundred bucks and I said, "Now, honey, let's not ride any more. Come on, let's do what you promised." She said she would after one more turn on the merry-go-round. So I, like a bloody fool, tries to save twenty cents by catching a brass ring. Son-of-a-bitch! I fall off and break my leg!

KIPER. My God!

LIPINSKY. Yes, sir. I broke my leg.

GOWDY. You certainly have had your share of tough luck.

LIPINSKY. So when the captain walks off with the top soldier's girl I say to myself, maybe there's luck in it. Maybe the breaks favored him. They never did favor me.

GOWDY. Any skipper can walk off with any top soldier's girl in my opinion. Say, maybe that's the lowdown on why the sergeant left.

KIPER. Naw—he was too damn good. Regimental took him. We'll probably get a lousy replacement. Probably get a corporal with ten years' experience chasing prisoners at Portsmouth. Soon's the new sergeant gets here the skip's going on ten days' leave.

LIPINSKY. Yeah? Where?

KIPER. Paris.

LIPINSKY. You going with him?

KIPER. Yep.

LIPINSKY. Some guys have all the luck.

(*The door opens.* SERGEANT QUIRT, *the very picture of an old-timer, enters and looks quickly around. All rise.*)

QUIRT. L. Company?

KIPER. Company Headquarters.

QUIRT. Where's the company commander?

KIPER. Just stepped down the street. Will be back soon.

QUIRT. He's going on leave?

KIPER. Right.

QUIRT. What's his name.

KIPER. Captain Flagg.

QUIRT. Whew!

KIPER. You know him?

QUIRT. Do you?

KIPER. Yes, sir!

QUIRT. Company Headquarters. Looks like a God damn reception room to me.

KIPER. We aim to please.

QUIRT. Yeah, to please yourself. Well, listen, I'm the new top soldier here. Who's the company clerk?

LIPINSKY. I am, sir.

QUIRT. Clear this jam out of here and let's have a look at what you're doing.

LIPINSKY. Will you get the hell out?—and don't come back till you're sent for. (KIPER *and* GOWDY *go out.*)

QUIRT. I've been ten kilometers west of you. Took the wrong turn.

LIPINSKY. Here's the map. That's the only road there is, and we can't use it. The damn thing is one long shell-hole from last May.

QUIRT. Jeez!

LIPINSKY. That's what they all say.

QUIRT. Don't you ever clean these galleys?

LIPINSKY. We don't do anything else.

QUIRT. You haven't got a police sergeant, I suppose?

LIPINSKY. We've got an acting corporal. Old Hennessey was bumped off last time up.

QUIRT. Spud Hennessey?

LIPINSKY. That's the soldier.

QUIRT. Tough for Spud to go. A grand soldier. Too damn finicky, though.

LIPINSKY. We've gone to hell for chow since he left.

QUIRT. That's queer. I never knew Flagg to let his men go to hell.

LIPINSKY. Not his fault. These cooks are no good. Hennessey was acting mess sergeant, too.

QUIRT. That's like old times.

LIPINSKY. Yeah?

QUIRT. Say, if the skipper's going ashore they'd better get him out of here before he gets too drunk to navigate. I've seen him shove off with a liberty party and spend a forty-eight-hour leave sleeping it off on the beach.

LIPINSKY. It's the same skip, all right. You know him.

QUIRT. I'll say I do . . . I think I'll look him up. Where's he likely to be?

LIPINSKY. Damned if I know. He might be at Pete's place. Anybody can tell you where that is—just this side of the river.

QUIRT. All right. I'll find it.

(*Goes out briskly. After he has gone* LIPINSKY *goes to the door and whistles.* KIPER *and* GOWDY *come in.*)

LIPINSKY. Did you take a slant at the amphibian?

GOWDY. Yeah.

KIPER. What of it?

LIPINSKY. He's our new papa.

KIPER. So he says.

LIPINSKY. He's soldiered with the skipper before. Says he never saw the chief sober.

KIPER. Is he hard-boiled?

LIPINSKY. There's only one place in the world they boil them as hard as that, and that's the Tropic of Cancer.

KIPER. What does he know?

LIPINSKY. This God damn army's going to run right from now on or get off on its ear.

GOWDY. He must have used some language on you?

LIPINSKY. Not a word, and I'm not going to give him a chance, either.

KIPER. Scared, huh?

LIPINSKY. You meet a top with two glass eyes, a slit across his face for a mouth and a piece out of his ear, and you might just as well heave out and lash up. That bird could curse the hide off a whole Senegalese regiment.

(CAPTAIN FLAGG *enters and comes to chair above table. He is a fine, magnificently endowed man.*)

FLAGG. 'Tenshun! (*Reading report which he picks up from table.*) Where's that first sergeant?

KIPER. Went out looking for you, sir.

FLAGG. Scatter and find him, a couple of you. (LIPINSKY, GOWDY, *and* KIPER *start out.*) Stay here, Kiper. (KIPER *comes back.*) Damn him, why couldn't he sit still? (LIPINSKY *and* GOWDY *go out.*) What's he like?

KIPER. Tough.

FLAGG. Yeah? I hope he damn well hangs the whole damn company up by the thumbs. About time we had a little discipline around here.

KIPER. Yes, sir.

FLAGG. "Yes, sir!" "Yes, sir!" Shut your trap, will you?

KIPER. Oh, yes, sir.

FLAGG. Go to hell! Everything packed?

KIPER. Absolutely.

FLAGG. Bike working? Side-car trimmed?

KIPER. Tuned it up this morning.

FLAGG. Well, we're going ashore as soon as I see the new top soldier, you understand? And we don't stop for anything smaller than shell-holes!

KIPER. Ay, ay, sir!

FLAGG. Go sit down! Go read a book! You make me nervous. (KIPER *sits.* CHARMAINE *slips in. She is a drab.* FLAGG, *who is busy at the desk, does not see her at first. He looks up impatiently.*) Well, hello! hello! What are you doing here? You better run along back to your papa. Listen, *mon amie,* you better beat it back to *le père,* understand?

CHARMAINE. Why?

(*She comes nearer.*)

FLAGG. Well, I'm busy.

CHARMAINE. You are going away.

FLAGG. So that's it. Kiper, did you tell the kid I was going away?

KIPER. No, sir, she saw me with your *musette* bag.

CHARMAINE. The sergeant went away. He is not coming back. Now you go away. You are not coming back.

FLAGG. As far as the sergeant's concerned, you're quite right, dearie; but as far as I'm concerned, you're dead wrong. The sergeant isn't coming back. We have a new sergeant, see? But I am coming back.

CHARMAINE. *Oui?*

FLAGG. *Oui, oui, oui!*

CHARMAINE. No. You are such a lovely liar. You don't want to make me cry. So you lie a little—*n'est-ce pas?*

FLAGG (*takes her by shoulders*). I'm not lying, Charmaine. I don't know how I can prove it to you, but I'm telling the solemn truth. (*A knock on the door.*) See who that is, and keep him out, whoever it is.

KIPER (*opens the door, goes out, and returns*). It's Lewisohn, third platoon replacement. He wants permission to speak with you, sir.

FLAGG. What about?

KIPER. Lost something, sir.

FLAGG. Let him in. (LEWISOHN *enters. He is a pale little boy.*) Let's have it quick, soldier.

LEWISOHN (*saluting*). Beg pardon, sir. (*Very much scared.*)

FLAGG. What do you want?

LEWISOHN. The truth is, sir, I've lost my identification tag.

FLAGG. What? What? Lost what?

LEWISOHN. My identification tag.

FLAGG. Well, I thought I'd been around a good deal, and I've had 'em ask me to show 'em where they live and button up their pants for them and put on their little night-drawers, but I'm a son-of-a-gun if this isn't the first time anybody has ever asked me to help him find his identification tag!

LEWISOHN. Sorry, sir. I—I thought it was—I. . . .

FLAGG. What did you think?

LEWISOHN. I thought it was important, sir.

FLAGG. And what, may I ask, made you think it was important?

LEWISOHN. In case I was—ah—hit, sir. They wouldn't know who I was. I thought maybe it would matter.

FLAGG. Matter?—to whom?

LEWISOHN. Well—to keep the records—or to my folks.

FLAGG. Listen, boy, why did you ever leave your home and come over here?

LEWISOHN. Why, to fight, sir.

FLAGG. Yeah. Well, you'll get a chance, don't you worry, and for God's sake learn to act like a man. Never mind your identification tag. If you want to know what your name is look in your hat.

LEWISOHN. Yes, sir.

FLAGG. By the way, what is your name?

LEWISOHN. Louis Lewisohn.

FLAGG (*to* KIPER). Make a note of that, Kiper. (KIPER *makes a note in the book he carries in his pocket.*) Now, anything else? Hope you got a good room with a view and running water and everything.

LEWISOHN. No, sir.
(*Swallowing a lump in his throat.*)

FLAGG. No? I'm surprised. Well, go on outside and swear at me a while. It'll do you good, and that's what I'm here for. I'm here to keep you in hot water till you're hard-boiled. See? You can go.

LEWISOHN. Yes, sir.
(*He salutes and goes.*)

FLAGG. Make a note of that, Kiper, and get him a new tag if they have to build a new factory in Hoboken to turn it out. The God-forsaken fool's dying of grief away from mother. Got it?

KIPER. Yes, Captain Flagg.

FLAGG. Then step outside and guard the door a minute. (KIPER *salutes and goes out, closing the door carefully.* FLAGG *then turns to* CHARMAINE.) Now, you little she-woman, what do you want?

CHARMAINE. You are going away.

FLAGG. Damn it, I'm not going away. I'm going to Paris—coming back in eight days. Eight days in Paris, see, then I come back.

CHARMAINE. The sergeant did not come back.

FLAGG. My God, child, get this! The sergeant is not coming back. I am coming back. We have a new sergeant, see?

CHARMAINE. *Oui?*

FLAGG. *Oui, oui.*

CHARMAINE. No. I think the captain does not love me, not any more?

FLAGG. Girlie, I love you fit to kill. I love you no end, same as always. Come here. (*She puts her arms around his neck.* FLAGG *takes her in his arms.*) You're as sweet as Burgundy, and you've got a kick like triple sec. Sure I love you. Everybody loves you. I love you, dearie girl, but I don't trust you.

CHARMAINE. You take me to Paris? Yes? Take me to Paris?

FLAGG. No. I guess not.

CHARMAINE. But I'm so unhappy when you go away.

FLAGG. Yes, you are! I wish you were. Why, you little Geisha. (*Chucking her under the chin.*) If I didn't wear captain's stripes you wouldn't know me from the K.P.'s.

CHARMAINE. No, dear Captain Flagg. (*Her arms on his shoulders. She runs a hand through his hair.*) It is true, I shall be so lonesome. I shall be all alone at the inn, crying every day to break your heart.

FLAGG. You'll be dancing all night and flirting all day with the Y.M.C.A. boys, you mean. Ain't it so?

CHARMAINE. *Oui.* But you could take me. I can't be good—unless you take me. I want to be good for you. We could have so good time—in Paris.

FLAGG. No, I can't take you. But listen.

(*Takes hold of her shoulders.*) While I'm gone you wait for me. Remember, you're my girl, see? Just my girl, and you wait for me, see?

CHARMAINE. *Oui,* I will.

FLAGG. And listen to this. (*Putting her away.*) If I find out you've been running with some one else, I'll break you in two, see? (*He makes the motion of breaking something.*) Now, will you be good while I'm gone?

CHARMAINE (*coming into his arms*). *Oui, monsieur.*

FLAGG. That's better. You know what I mean?

CHARMAINE. *Oui.*

FLAGG. That's right, little kitten, purr. . . . And remember, I don't trust you any further than I can see you. Now run along. (FLAGG *turns to table, but* CHARMAINE *follows him.*)

CHARMAINE. But you will take me to Paris?

FLAGG (*seating himself on edge of table, he beckons her with his finger and takes her on his knee, between his legs*). You ever been to Paris?

CHARMAINE. *Non . . .*

FLAGG. Well, there's a river in Paris.

CHARMAINE. *La Seine.*

FLAGG. Yeah, the Seine. That's where they drown little girls like you. Every time the police catch a little girl in Paris, they drown her in the Seine. You can't go there. They'd drown you.

CHARMAINE. It is not true.

FLAGG. It is true. I'll tell you another thing. There's nothing to eat in Paris, no food but horses; no wine, only water. No young girls, only old women. Some of the girls they drown in the Seine; some they make into sausages for the generals. Paris is full of generals that won't eat anything but young girls. You can't go to Paris.

CHARMAINE. You are full of lovely lies. Oh, it is not true.

FLAGG. Uh, you don't know Paris.

CHARMAINE. Oh, but I know these captains and sergeants! They do not ever put anything, what you say, past me. But, oh, I love you for a lovely liar! (*Embraces him.*) And I will be good; I will, *vraiment!*

FLAGG. That's a good girl. Now you go back to Papa Pete's. Stay home nights. Wait for Captain Flagg. Kiss me goodbye. (*She kisses him.*) Now run along. (*She goes.*) Kiper!

KIPER (*coming in*). Yes, sir.

FLAGG. Have you found that sergeant yet?

KIPER. He's coming with Lipinsky, sir.

FLAGG. Tell him to damn well get a wiggle on.

KIPER (*to* QUIRT, *outside*). He's waiting for you, sir.

(LIPINSKY *enters with* QUIRT.)

QUIRT (*saluting*). Captain Flagg?

FLAGG (*returning salute and remains seated, not even glancing at* QUIRT). Hello, Sergeant. Where've you been all day?

QUIRT. Ten kilometers west by mistake.

FLAGG. Do you know our lay-out?

QUIRT. I've got a general idea.

FLAGG. What kind of a hole were you in over there?

QUIRT. Much the same as yours, only we had a road.

FLAGG. Do you think you can handle this company? It's a rough crowd of old men and little baa-lamb recruits.

(*He still does not look up.*)

QUIRT. It's an army, ain't it? Sure.

FLAGG. I damn well hope you can. We're in a devilish sector here, and it's going to be worse when we move up again. We just hold half a town; the Heinies hold the other half. It rains grenades most of the time. About half our men are green replacements. They damned near ruined us in that last tour of duty. You'll have to whip some of 'em into shape before we go up. Close order drill is best.

QUIRT. Half of 'em raw?

FLAGG. Over half.

QUIRT. Well, I've seen worse.

FLAGG. Now, I'm going on leave, you see. Eight days. While I'm gone you feed 'em up and give 'em hell. Teach 'em where they are. Make 'em so bad they'll eat steel rather than get another dressing from you. Make 'em hard, but don't break 'em. Give 'em eats and about eight hours of drill and guns a day. They're mostly Bible Class boys, and God knows most of 'em haven't got long to live.

QUIRT (*takes step toward table*). Cut the comedy, Captain. You must know me.

FLAGG (*rising, looks at* QUIRT *for the first time*). Yeah? I'm a cuckoo if it ain't the old Hoppergrass!

QUIRT. Thought you didn't know me. Well, I'm glad to meet you again, Captain Flagg.

FLAGG. Kiper——

KIPER. Yes, sir.

FLAGG. Step out and tell all platoon commanders to report here at once.

KIPER. Ay, ay, sir.

(*Exits.*)

FLAGG. Well, Quirt, I'm glad to see you, because if there was ever a good soldier needed I need one here, and you're as good as there is; but I'm damned if I take any particular joy in meeting you again. You've been poison to me everywhere I've served with you.

QUIRT (*at right of table*). Same to you, I'm sure, and many of 'em. Personally I'd as soon meet a skunk in a dugout, and officially I don't think much of your crew. I broke you the first time in China, and you broke me in Cuba. You're in a position to break me now, and if you didn't need me worse than the wildcat needed what he didn't have, you'd break me again.

FLAGG. I'd see you in hell before I'd break you, and you know it. I'll give you exactly what you deserve, and as long as you're straight we'll get along, always providing we don't have to shake hands. If that's understood, why, take hold. The company's yours.

QUIRT. Well, before I take hold, let me get one more remark in the record. I wish to God I could jump your damn gang. I've heard of it all along the line. You've got a rabble, and I know it. I saw it coming into Is-sur-Tille once when you didn't see me. A shambling bunch of hams that wouldn't salute anything under a general.

FLAGG. All right, and what's my outfit's rating at regimental?

QUIRT. Oh, I got to hand it to you. You can hypnotize 'em. They'd start out to cut their way to Berlin if you gave the word. But, my God, they ain't much to look at, Captain Flagg.

FLAGG. Well, teach 'em to salute if it'll make you feel any happier, Hoppergrass. And before the platoon commanders get here, there's one thing I'd like to ask you. What did you do with the little girl?

QUIRT. What little girl?

FLAGG. You damn well know what little girl.

QUIRT. It's a small world, Captain Flagg, but the number of soldiers' sluts is numerous.

FLAGG. I was a corporal under you in China. You broke me to get her.

QUIRT. You were a damn fool. You'd have married her if it hadn't been for me, and be running a laundry now with the seat of your pants hanging down between your knees.

FLAGG. What happened to her?

QUIRT. What happened to the battleship *Maine?*

FLAGG. My God. . . .

QUIRT. I broke you in China. I admit I broke you for that little Chink. And when I served under you in Cuba you got even. That's why I'm still a sergeant. (*A knock at the door from* KIPER.) Let it go at that.

FLAGG. Kiper?

KIPER (*outside*). Ay, ay, sir!

FLAGG. Bring 'em in. (KIPER *opens the door and follows into the room* LIEUTENANTS ALDRICH, MOORE, *and* SCHMIDT, *and* GUNNERY SERGEANT SOCKEL. *They salute. They line up.*) Gentlemen, this is First Sergeant Quirt, who is in charge. This is Lieutenant Aldrich; this is Lieutenant Moore, and this is Lieutenant Schmidt, and you'll remember Sockel from Cuba. He's commanding the fourth platoon.

QUIRT (*turns to* SOCKEL). Hello, Joe. How's tricks?

SOCKEL. Pretty good. How's yourself.

(*They smile broadly, two old-timers among green lieutenants.*)

QUIRT. Ticking like a clock.

FLAGG. Aldrich, you're senior here, aren't you?

ALDRICH. Yes, sir. Two days ahead of the others.

FLAGG. You'll be in command here. Ask Quirt for any advice you need. I'll be back Wednesday week. . . . Now, men, Sergeant Quirt here is one of the best God damn soldiers that ever destroyed a memorandum receipt. I've soldiered with him around the world, and there isn't a finer, cleaner, smarter Marine afloat than Quirt—when he's sober. As long as he's sober, he'll run this outfit— whether I'm here or absent; but Quirt loves the bottle; and when he's drunk he's the lousiest, filthiest bum that ever wore a uniform. When drunk, he's worse than I am, and you know damn well I don't allow anybody to get as bad as that. If he tanks up I'll break him. I've broken him once, and he knows I'll do it again. The first raw crack he makes will find him drilling in the rear rank of Sockel's platoon, drilling like a tramp with a broom for a rifle. Get that, Aldrich; the first time you find him down in the square with a face in the dirt in front of all these young nipplenursers, you lock him up and keep him locked up till I return.

ALDRICH. Yes, sir.

FLAGG. Give him his head, and let him have anything he wants, and don't forget he's forgotten more about being a soldier than any of you college boys will ever know. But if you're wise you won't play cards with him, and before you lend him any money you'd better kiss it a last long farewell. That's all. Kiper, have you got the waterproofs in that side-car?

KIPER. Ay, ay, sir.

FLAGG. Give her a spin, and we'll shove off.

(*Picks up cap and stick from table and goes out, followed by all save* QUIRT. *Off stage, the motorcycle clatters. The* LIEUTENANTS *shout farewell.* QUIRT *goes up to right window, looks out, and then sits at table, takes out dice, and practices a few turns. He holds the dice up to his eyes and then spins.* QUIRT *whistles "Pretty Baby."*)

QUIRT. Seven, baby. (*He smiles with satisfaction.*) Look at those acrobats act. You got to treat the old man right, now. (*There is a light tap on the door to left.* QUIRT *puts dice in pocket and looks at map.*) Come in.

(CHARMAINE *enters.*)

CHARMAINE. *Le capitaine—il est parti?*

QUIRT. Just left. Don't cry, little one.

CHARMAINE. *Le nouveau sergeant. N'est-ce pas?*

QUIRT. *N'est-ce pas* is right.

CHARMAINE. I wanted to see the captain.

QUIRT. Just too late, sorry to say. (*Looks at her for first time.*) You one piecie captain's fella boy? You captain's fella?

CHARMAINE. *Le capitaine? Mais non!*

QUIRT. I'll bet it's *mais mon.* Say, ain't you Cognac Pete's daughter?

CHARMAINE. *Oui.* You stay at Pete's?

QUIRT. Sure. (*Pause.*) *Et vous?*

CHARMAINE. *C'est mon père.*

QUIRT. Uh-huh. I thought so. (*Rises; crosses to her.*) Well, baby, you better stick to me, and you'll have another papa.

(*A terrific commotion begins outside. A vociferous Irish voice is heard shouting over and over again, "I'll get that lousy German son-of-a-bitch, I'll get the German bastard," while* LIPINSKY *and* GOWDY *yell, "Cut it out, you loafer. Dry up, dry up or you'll get yours."* LIPINSKY *opens the door.* CHARMAINE *steps back. The shouting is audible only when door is open.*)

LIPINSKY. Sergeant, there's a drunken Mick named Mulcahy raising hell outside. Can't do a thing with him. Got blood in his eyes for a guy from Cincinnati.

QUIRT (*sternly out of the corner of his mouth, not looking at him*). Tell him to pipe down. (LIPINSKY *goes out. Door closes; shouting stops.* CHARMAINE *goes toward door.*) Better not go out there now, honey. Some rough language is taking place out there.

(LIPINSKY *re-enters. Shouting is started again.*)

LIPINSKY. Sergeant, the Mick's sitting on Gowdy, and I can't pull him off.

QUIRT (*quietly, as before*). Tell him to pipe down. (LIPINSKY *goes out. Shouting stops.* QUIRT *crosses to* CHARMAINE.) You going to promenade *avec moi* tonight? Down by the canal? Under the lime trees?

CHARMAINE. No. (*She is trembling.*)

QUIRT. No? Captain's own private darling, huh? Say, you're a damned pretty frog. For a frog, I don't know as I ever saw a prettier.

(*The hullabaloo redoubles outside.* LIPINSKY *comes in again.*)

LIPINSKY. Shall we lock him up, Sergeant?

QUIRT. Drag him in. (LIPINSKY *and* GOWDY *drag in a huge, red-faced Irishman and stand him groggily on his feet below* QUIRT.)

MULCAHY. That damn Nussbaum from Cincinnati is a German spy, and I'll have his guts out of him before I'm through.

QUIRT (*quietly*). Mulcahy, pipe down.

MULCAHY. I tell you that Nussbaum is a German spy! I'll get the lousy German and every German out of Cincinnati. . . .

(*The* SERGEANT *plants one squarely on* MULCAHY'S *jaw. He goes down like a log.*)

QUIRT (*still out of the corner of his mouth*). Drag him out.

(LIPINSKY *and* GOWDY *take him by arms, turn him around, and drag him out.* QUIRT, *rubbing his knuckles, crosses back of table to* CHARMAINE, *who is smiling at her wonderful hero with the powerful punch.*)

QUIRT. Why, hello, Pittsburgh, you love me?

(*They embrace and hold a long kiss.*)

CURTAIN

ACT ONE

Scene II

Late afternoon, eight days later. The scene is unchanged. LIPINSKY *is lying along bench, smoking a cigarette and trying to sleep at the same time.* KIPER *enters, singing at the top of his voice.* LIPINSKY'S *cap is down over his eyes.* POLICE SERGEANT FERGUSON *is at table toward back, working over papers; he is smoking a pipe.*

KIPER. "Mademoiselle from Armentiere, parlez-vous?
Mademoiselle from Armentiere, parlez vous?
Mademoiselle from Armentiere——"
Hullo, hullo—Jeezus.
(*Puts musette bags in corner.*)

LIPINSKY. Knock off that chat.
(*On bench; doesn't move.*)

KIPER. Say, are you running this God damn army?

LIPINSKY. You're damn well right, I'm running this army.

KIPER. Well, you had better God damn well snap out of it. You're relieved.

LIPINSKY (*sitting up*). Skipper come back?

KIPER. Almost. He's at the Last Chance.

LIPINSKY. Still soaked?

KIPER. He ain't soaked. He's just the drunkest bum you ever saw in your life.

LIPINSKY. Trying to whip the world?

KIPER. Naw, just quiet drunk. Looks out of those eyes of his like two red holes in the snow.

LIPINSKY. How's Paris?

KIPER. Never got that far. Washed ashore at Bar-le-Duc.

LIPINSKY. Yeah? Good time?

KIPER. Pretty good the first day.

LIPINSKY. What'd you do the rest?

KIPER. You see, it was this way. The skip and me was promenading, and he was swinging that damn little Pekin swagger-stick of his when up comes an M.P. "Sorry, sir," says the M.P.; "Corps commander's regulations, sir, no swagger-sticks." The skip says, "Well, and who, may I ask, is the corps commander? Tell him he can take his lousy army and sell it for cheese." "Sorry, sir," says the M.P. "Corps commander's regulations, sir, and I'll have to take that stick away from you." "All right," says the skip, whirling the stick around his head, "pitch in, soldier, pitch in!"

LIPINSKY. Did he take it away?

KIPER. Aw, take it away! Listen to the poor nut. I spent the next six days of my leave detained as a material witness for attempted manslaughter.

LIPINSKY. I guess the skip didn't draw much.

KIPER. Draw hell! Didn't I swear this yellow-bellied M.P. came up and knocked him into the road?

LIPINSKY. Yeah?

KIPER. And the court looks at this M.P. and says, "Right face! Take him away and give him ten days, bread and water."

LIPINSKY. Serve him right, the Boy Scout! They ought to take away those guys' whistles before they blow themselves to death. And speaking of whistles, this new top of our's don't do nothing else at all besides blow a whistle. It's been one bloody formation after another ever since you left.

KIPER. Is that the kind of hombre he is?

LIPINSKY. He's a sea-going son-of-a-bitch. He ain't sit down since he was here. He's got the first platoon down in the village now taking up the dirt from the courtyard with teaspoons. You can't get in the chow line until you catch twenty horse-flies. He seen Cooper pulling a fag at reveille this morning. What's Cooper doing now? Boy, following the ponies, following the ponies. *He's* out collecting apples.

KIPER. Well, the skip will make him cut that stuff. Me and the skip ain't going to see the little boys bullied.

LIPINSKY. You and the skip, yeah. But say, the skip and this top soldier are going to tangle pant-legs over another little matter before they have been together one day.

KIPER. What t'hell!

LIPINSKY. This horny pelican is going aboard the skip's old hooker every night.

KIPER. Down at Cognac Pete's house?

LIPINSKY. Parking his dogs in Pete's kitchen every night with that little black-eyed frog sitting in his lap lighting his pipe.

KIPER. If the skip finds that out there'll be a noise like you'd throw a tomcat in a dog-pound.
(*Enter* SERGEANT QUIRT.)

QUIRT (*to* KIPER). Where's Captain Flagg?

KIPER. Last Chance.

QUIRT. What the hell do you mean, coming in here without him? What do you think you're paid for?

KIPER. I tried to argue with him, Sergeant, and he picked me up and threw me out the window. Lucky for me it was open.

QUIRT. Go get him. Don't argue. Get him. Take Lippy along.

(LIPINSKY *and* KIPER *start, hesitate, and talk.* QUIRT *starts toward chair above table.* LIEUTENANT ALDRICH *enters.*)

ALDRICH. Heard the skipper was aboard.

QUIRT (*turning to* ALDRICH). Grounded on the last bar.

ALDRICH. Yeah?

QUIRT (*to* KIPER *and* LIPINSKY, *who hurry off*). Cast off, will you? Travel! Hit the deck! (*To* ALDRICH.) Sending out a salvage party. He's full to the scuppers.

ALDRICH. All I hope is he comes in mild and goes to sleep. He's got too damn much talent for raising hell to suit me.

QUIRT. You ought to seen him in China. Straight as a mast, muscled like a gorilla, Christian as hell. Good deal of liquor has flowed under his belt since then.

ALDRICH. Expect any trouble?

QUIRT. What do you mean?

ALDRICH. This here now little wild woman.

QUIRT. I don't know what's your game.

ALDRICH. Oh, all right! Just the same, you'd be a damn sight wiser to lay off, in my opinion.

QUIRT. Lay off what?

ALDRICH. Charmaine.

QUIRT (*turning to* ALDRICH). Are you thinking of making this a three-handed game?

ALDRICH. I am not.

QUIRT. Because if you are, all I got to say is, help yourself to whatever you can get. It's love in a manner of speaking, and it's certainly war. Everything dirty goes.

ALDRICH. Suit yourself. You've known him longer than I have.

QUIRT. He's got a grudge against me, I don't mind telling you. And I ain't wasting any ardent affection on him. If it hadn't been for him, I'd had a company of my own. I didn't know she was his meat when I first saw her. But when I found out, d'you think I'd apologize and back out the door out of deference to him? I says, Kippy-dope, you're mine!

ALDRICH. Yeah—but do you know what I heard at mess to-day?

QUIRT. Nope.

ALDRICH. Well, now listen. I didn't intend to mix into this unless it was necessary, but Schmidt got it straight yesterday that old Cognac Pete was going to prosecute some soldier or other for corrupting Charmaine's morals.

QUIRT. Charmaine's what? Jeez, that's good!

ALDRICH. Maybe so. Just the same, he's got a case.

QUIRT. He has not.

ALDRICH. No? Suppose he gets you before a court martial? It's a hanging matter if he wants to push it. You know the regulations.

QUIRT. You mean he's after me?

ALDRICH. I don't know who he's after. You—or Flagg. Has Cognac anything on you?

QUIRT. Well, they might hang me once as a sort of lesson to me.

(*Motorcycle clatters outside.*)

ALDRICH. Well, there you are. Suppose he takes it to headquarters? Where's Quirt then? Sitting pretty?

QUIRT. Well, I just resign all rights and interests in the ma'am'selle and avoid possible complications.

ALDRICH. Fine. There's Kiper already. If Flagg's with him, for God's sake use a little diplomacy.

(*Outside,* FLAGG *in drunken voice says, "Get out of my way, Kiper." Noise of* KIPER *being pushed.*)

QUIRT. Diplomacy, with that?

(FLAGG *enters, coat in hand and hair mussed. He still carries stick.* LIPINSKY *and* KIPER *follow. All stand at attention until the* CAPTAIN *is seated.*)

ALDRICH (*saluting*). How are you, Captain Flagg?

FLAGG. I'm a wreck, that's what I am! I'm an epoch-making disaster! You see before you, Mr. Aldrich, one of the seven great calamities of the world!

QUIRT. Hope you had a pleasant leave, sir.

FLAGG. Well, I didn't. Held for carrying a stick. Picked up the second day by one of Pershing's Sunday-School teachers. By God, he must think he's running a day nursery! . . . What's happened?

QUIRT. Not a thing.

FLAGG. Boys in shape?

QUIRT. They'll do. Three more days, and I'd risk them on the line.

FLAGG. Try and get three days. If we aren't digging in somewhere before then, I'll pay the Russian national debt out of my salary. How much do you think I spent in Bar-le-Duc?

QUIRT. How much did you have?

FLAGG. Eight hundred francs, and I got a chance to get rid of thirty. Here's the whole roll. Does anybody want it? Just my luck to have to move in again with seven hundred and seventy francs on me and get bumped off. (*A knock at the door by* BRIGADE RUNNER.) Come in. (*A* BRIGADE RUNNER *enters.*)

THE RUNNER. Captain Flagg?

FLAGG. Right here.

THE RUNNER. From Captain Simpson, sir. He wanted you to know the "G One" crowd is on the way over.

FLAGG. Tell him I'm much obliged. Anything else?

THE RUNNER. That's all. How do I get to the Twelfth?

FLAGG. Show him, Kiper. (KIPER *and* THE RUNNER *salute and go out.* FLAGG *starts to button his coat.*) Damn headquarters! It's some more of that world-safe-for-democracy slush! Every time they come around here I've got to ask myself is this an army or is it a stinking theosophical society for ethical culture and the Bible-backing uplift! I don't want that band of Gideons from headquarters. Now you watch that door. Watch it! In ten minutes we're going to have another of these round-headed gentlemen of the old school here giving us a prepared lecture on what we're fighting the war for and how we're to do it—one of these bill-poster chocolate soldiers with decorations running clear around to his backbone and a thrilling speech on army morale and the last drop of fighting blood that puts your drive over to glorious victory! . . . The side-whiskered butter-eaters! I'd like to rub their noses in a few of the latrines I've slept in, keeping up army morale and losing men because some screaming fool back in the New Jersey sector thinks he's playing with paper dolls. (*A knock.*) Well, come in, come in. (LIEUTENANT MOORE *enters.*) Hello.

MOORE. How are you, Captain Flagg? Hope you liked Bar-le-Duc?

FLAGG. Ever been there?

MOORE. Once.

FLAGG. Ever put in much time in the re-decorated chicken stable where they detain the A.W.O.L.'s?

MOORE. Afraid I never saw it, sir.

FLAGG. Well, you haven't missed a great deal. They whitewashed the damn shanty right over the hen manure. Phew! I can smell it yet. If I'd stayed there another day I'd have laid an egg.

MOORE. Tough luck! But what I really wanted to say, sir, was there's an old fellow outside here who wants to see you about his daughter. He seems to think somebody's taken advantage of her.

FLAGG. Somebody in this outfit?

MOORE. Yes, sir.

FLAGG. Took advantage of the girl, huh?

MOORE. That's what he says.

FLAGG. He means she took advantage of her opportunities and now he's taking advantage of his. What's the old boy's name?

MOORE. Can't quite make it out, but it seems to be Pete something or other. Are there any Pete's in France? Sounded like Cognac Pete.

FLAGG. Yeah?

MOORE. Sounded like it.

FLAGG (*rising, perturbed*). Well, wait a minute. Cognac Pete's, huh? Is the girl with him?

MOORE. No.

FLAGG. Hell!

QUIRT. Think fast, Captain. Think fast.

FLAGG. Quirt, do you know anything about this?

QUIRT (*starting to leave*). Not a thing.

FLAGG. You leaving us?

QUIRT (*unembarrassed*). A few orders to make out, sir. (*He grins.*) Can't very well work here, you see.

FLAGG. I'm damned if I see. Sit down and spill your ink. And if you've put up a game on me, you crawling crab. . . .

QUIRT. Me? What have I got to do with it? Think fast, Captain, think fast.

FLAGG. Damn it, send him in, and we'll see. (MOORE *goes out.*) Hell!

QUIRT (*laughing*). Think fast, Captain. Don't forget to think fast.

FLAGG. You sit where you are, you hyena; and laugh, damn you, laugh. (*Enter* COGNAC PETE, *an ancient nut-brown Frenchman, very police and humble, followed by* MOORE *and* KIPER. MOORE *and* PETE *stand by the table.* KIPER *sits on bench.*) Pete, what's this I hear about a complaint? What's the matter, huh? One of my men, huh?

PETE. *Oui, mon capitaine.*

FLAGG. I'm damned if I can leave this damn army half a day without hell breaking loose somewhere. Come on, let's have it; spit it out.

MOORE. Allay, Pete.

PETE (*speaking in an unintelligible rush of French*). *Ah, monsieur le capitaine, je suis un vieillard; mais j' ai vécu heureusement, et mes enfants on été toujours honnêtes, mais hélas, mon capitaine, quelque chose de terrible vient de passer, une calamité monstrueuse. . . .*

FLAGG (*to* MOORE). What's on the menu? Do you get anything out of that?

MOORE. He says something has happened.

FLAGG (*distressed*). Does it take all that vocabulary to say something has happened in French? Well, keep going, keep going.

MOORE. Allay, Pete.

PETE. *Mais, mon capitaine, voilà que les Américains arrivent. Ils sont grands et forts, et ils demandent tourjours ce qu'ils veulent. Ils ne s'accoutument pas à nos mœurs ni à nos habitudes, mais—nom de Dieu!—pourquoi choisissent—ils la seule fleur de ma vie, quand ils peuvent trouver n'importe où qu'ils vont des poules qui les desirent? Ma seule fleur, ma fleur Charmaine, ma fleur délicate!*

FLAGG. What language is he talking now?

MOORE. He says the soldiers take what they want, and they have trampled the one flower of his life.

FLAGG. Is that all he said?

MOORE. The rest is poetry.

FLAGG (*impatiently*). Well, tell him to omit flowers, see, omit flowers.

MOORE (*to* PETE). *Brèvement.*

PETE. *Ma fille. Ma fille bien-aimée. Elle est défleurée. Elle est dans la boue, elle est déshonorée.*

FLAGG (*to* MOORE). More flowers?

MOORE. No, sir. He says his daughter's been—ah—ruined. (*Pause.*) . . . so to speak.

FLAGG. Ruined, huh? Rape or seduction?

MOORE (*to* PETE). *S'est-elle soumise, ou l'-a-t-on forcée?*

PETE. *Les Américains sont si forts. Ils se forcent sur elle, ils ferment sa bouche de façon qu'elle ne peut donner l' alarme. Que peut faire la petite fille? L'Américaine est forte, elle peut se défendre, mais la Française, elle est gentille et modeste et craintive et ne sait se défendre.*

FLAGG (*to* MOORE). Now what's all that?

MOORE. Rape, sir.

FLAGG. Does he allude to any specific girl, or is he speaking of French wenches in general?

MOORE (*to* PETE). *Comment s'appelle ta fille?*

PETE. Charmaine.

MOORE. Charmaine, sir.

FLAGG (*very seriously*). Look here, Moore. You know as well as I do, this same little baggage has been pretty free with me. What's the old boy's game? And for God's sake, what do you think you're up to, bringing him in here?

MOORE. You mean you're . . . God, I didn't know that!

FLAGG. You didn't! You must go around here wearing blinders. You see the fix you've got me in?

QUIRT. Think fast, Captain, think fast.

MOORE. To tell the truth, I got the impression it was somebody else. Honest to God, I thought he said it was a soldier. . . . (FLAGG *hesitates and then gives* MOORE *a quick look.* MOORE *is embarrassed.*) I wasn't sure, but I got that impression.

FLAGG. Did he name anybody?

MOORE. No.

FLAGG (*turning away*). Well, damn her little soul. No, I know damn well it wasn't anybody else. (*Turns to* MOORE.) Ask him how much he wants.

MOORE. How much what?

FLAGG. Money, you highbrow, money! What do you think he wants?

MOORE. I don't know, but if I thought he wanted money I certainly would not have listened to him.

FLAGG. You're just a bleating babe in the woods, you are. That's what they all want.

MOORE. He told me he wanted the man to marry the girl.

FLAGG. Marry her!

PETE. *Elle était une petite enfant innocente, une fleur à demiouverte.*

FLAGG. What's that? Flowers again?

MOORE. He says she was an innocent child.

FLAGG. Listen. You tell him I'm sure she's still an innocent girl. Tell him Charmaine is one of the most virtuous and respectable ladies I've ever had the pleasure of meeting.

MOORE (*to* PETE). *Monsieur le capitaine dit que c'est impossible et que vous vous trompez, monsieur, parce que Charmaine est tout à fait honnête and vertueuse.*

PETE (*shaking his head*). *Non! non! non!—je ne me trompe pas—malheureusement c'est bien la vérité.*

MOORE. He's sure of it.

FLAGG. Ask him if he wants to bring charges.

MOORE. *Désirez-vous le faire passer au conseil de guerre?*

PETE. *Conseil de guerre? Ca se peut.*

MOORE. He says perhaps.

FLAGG. What does he mean, "perhaps"? Ask him how much he wants.

MOORE. *Il demande ce que vous voulez.*

PETE. *Mais la petite qui est défleurée—il faut qu'on la fasse honnête, et moi—est-ce donc que l'honneur de ma famille ne vaut rien? Il faut qu'ils se marient, et quant à moi—il faut me payer si je ne le fais pas passer devant le conseil de guerre. Il me faut cinq cent francs.*

FLAGG. Flowers?

MOORE. No, he wants the fellow to marry the girl—and he wants five hundred francs.

FLAGG. I see. That's better. Tell him he can have three hundred. Tell him he can pick any son-in-law he wants out of the whole damn army.

MOORE (*to* PETE). *Elle peut choisir n'importe qui qu'il soit de toute la compagnie —et vous—vous aurez trois cent francs.*

PETE (*suddenly wildly angry*). *Ca ne va pas! vous vous moquez de moi, vous officiers américains. Je connais le truc—moi —de vous voir m'insulter quand il s'agit de la rapace. Alors, messieurs, j'irai aur G.H.Q. et vous verrez. C'est la mort, et gare à votre peau! Me voilà qui vient vous voir ici, malheureux mais amical, et je ne reçois que des insultes. Cinq cent francs! Rien de moins, et il la marie.*

(*He starts for door.*)

FLAGG. Wait a minute. (ALDRICH *bars the door.*) What's wrong?

MOORE. He's insulted. Going to Headquarters. Five hundred, he wants; and it's a certain man, he says.

FLAGG. What man?

MOORE. *Quel homme?*

PETE (*turning, crosses in front of table; to* QUIRT, *dramatically*). *Le voilà! Alors je m'en vais. Vous vous moquez de moi! Laissez-moi partir.*

(QUIRT *rises, knocking over chair.*)

FLAGG (*taking a step toward* QUIRT). Quirt, what's the meaning of this?

QUIRT. Sorry, sir, I don't quite catch the drift myself.

FLAGG. Have you been around with Charmaine?

QUIRT. Charmaine? I don't think so, Captain. But I've got a poor memory for names.

FLAGG. You're a liar. You knew Charmaine was mine, and you couldn't keep your hands off her.

QUIRT. Yeah? It's getting to be a habit of mine, huh? Whaddye going to do about it, Captain Flagg?

FLAGG. Oh? What (*Walks to table.*) am I going to do about it?—I'm going to marry you to Charmaine and let you make an honest woman out of her! Quirt, you've taken the detail right off my shoulders, and it's your turn to think fast! (*Turns to* MOORE.) Mr. Moore, now tell the old man that the sergeant was making honest proposals and desperate love! Ask what church he belongs to, or whether he wants 'em married by the cashier of the bank. (*Turns to* QUIRT. MOORE *turns to* PETE; *they start toward the door.*) Sergeant, you arrived in the nick of time with replacements! You saved the day! The Marines have landed and have the situation well in hand! We're going to decorate you! We're going to let you hold the bag!

QUIRT. All very interesting, Captain. But how are you going to do it? I may have landed, but I don't remember seeing any article in what I signed saying you could pick my woman for me. Seems to me you'd learned that I pick my women for myself.

FLAGG. Quirt, you've signed on for a cruise with this woman, and you can't jump ship. I can tell Aldrich to stand out of the way and let that old man go to headquarters with his story about you . . . and what chance has a lousy Marine sergeant got before an army court-martial when ten majors start the iron ball rolling? Ten army majors back in Paris, who ain't going to let anybody do any seducing but themselves. Don't be a hayshaker, Quirt. You can't play guardhouse lawyer in this country. You're in the army now, with a lot of western shysters sitting in the judge advocate general's room.

QUIRT. And who's going to be witness against me? You couldn't get that little frog to swear anything. I'm too damned handsome a soldier. I'm strong with this little French broad. Told me last night, just before you come back, she never loved a soldier who loved like me. Said she wished the whole damned outfit would move away and leave us in peace. Why, she's jealous every time I have to go to formation.

FLAGG. Sergeant, in about five minutes you're going to be married; in about eight you're going to please this old man by leaving an allotment here for about two-thirds of your pay in regular army style. The more you talk, the more you hang yourself up by the thumbs.

QUIRT. This ain't talk. What do you say I go get this little baby and you ask her if she'll say anything about me that ain't praise and admiration? What do you say I go get her? What do I care a whoop in hell what this old bozo says about me? I ain't seduced *him!* He's after money. Well, I ain't got money. I don't have to carry money around in my love affairs. What do you say I go get her?

FLAGG. Of course, you'll go get her. And propose marriage to her on the way, because you'll meet the wedding detail when you get here. Gowdy, go to the Y tent and get the chaplain. (GOWDY *goes out.*) Aldrich, accompany Sergeant Quirt to the tavern and tell Charmaine that I'm giving away in marriage the handsomest sergeant in the corps. Tell her she's a woman in a thousand, because Quirt has already run away from a thousand; and if it weren't for my seeing justice done him, he'd run away from that many more. All right, Quirt, we'll be waiting for you. (QUIRT *and* ALDRICH *go out.* FERGUSON *fixes chair, returns to seat, and turns to* MOORE.) Mr. Moore, tell papa the wedding bells are going to ring, and there's money in it for him, money in it!

(MOORE *seats* PETE *on stool at window; then whispers. A knock at the door.* LIPINSKY *opens it.*)

LIPINSKY. Brigade runner, Captain Flagg.

FLAGG. Send him in.

(*The* RUNNER *enters.*)

RUNNER. Company commander?

FLAGG. What is it—shoving off?

RUNNER. Moving in an hour, sir.

FLAGG. In an hour?

RUNNER. Please initial.

(*Offers pencil and paper.*)

FLAGG (*signing*). You hear that, Moore?

MOORE. Yes, sir.

FLAGG (*up, and business-like*). Going in an hour. You know what that means.

MOORE. Yes, sir.

FLAGG. Pass the word to our platoon commanders to stand in heavy packs in thirty minutes. The *camions* are waiting at the crossroads with ammunition. (MOORE *goes out.*) Kiper, tell Quirt to salvage all rations in the square. (KIPER *starts for door but stops as* FLAGG *says,* "Wait a minute.") Don't let on to Quirt we're going in. We'll marry him to Charmaine and march the blushing bridegroom off to war.

(*Walks up and down.*)

FERGUSON. Afraid you can't marry them this evening, Captain Flagg. Chaplain very sticky on that point. Have to be married in the morning.

FLAGG. Well, then, the mayor could marry them, couldn't he? Lipinsky, go get the mayor. Who's seen the mayor today?

KIPER. Just saw him down by the bridge on a load of manure.

FLAGG. There you are, Lipinsky—load of manure, near the bridge. Get the mayor, dust him off, and bring him here toot pronto. If the chaplain can't do it, the mayor can.

(LIPINSKY *starts to go out but halts and calls* "Tenshun." PETE *still sits on stool. In walks a* BRIGADIER-GENERAL, *one* COLONEL, *one* CAPTAIN, *and two* LIEUTENANTS.)

THE GENERAL. Hello, Flagg. Haven't you received that order yet? Not a soul stirring on your damned street. (*All salute.*) Flagg, you run the most disreputable outfit of the brigade. I come into town to hold a staff conference and find the whole shebang asleep. What kind of platoon commanders have you got, anyway, sitting round here like a nest of hoboes when you're moving in forty-five minutes? (*The staff remains standing at attention.*)

FLAGG. Just got the order, General. We'll get off in time. Never missed a train in my life.

THE GENERAL. Well, I don't see how you do it. *Camions* back two miles at the crossroads. Your men will have ammunition there, and I want every man to carry two extra bandoliers.

FLAGG. If you don't mind my saying so, General, we're the refuse of the brigade back of the line and we carry extra bandoliers into it.

THE GENERAL. Well, I'll tell you why.

Division wants a line straightened that we're going to take over. Isn't straight enough for him. Where's that map? Map, Davis!

THE COLONEL (*turns*). Map, Tolbert!

THE LIEUTENANT. Map, Price.

THE CAPTAIN. Where's that map? (*Looks wildly around. The last* LIEUTENANT *to enter hands map to* PRICE.) Here's the map, sir.

(*Hands map to* GENERAL.)

THE GENERAL. Good boy, good boy. A map, after all, among you soldiers. Now, see here, Flagg. (*Pointing to map, which he spreads out on table.*) There she is, and here's the line. The corps wants it straightened out. It will take the steel, the cold steel. But they've got to have it straightened out. Give them the steel and you can do it. You'll hold the town—our half of it—and you'll get these fellows out if it takes a week. Your men are a bunch of tramps, but they can do this sort of thing.

FLAGG. Individualists, General, individualists.

THE GENERAL. Well, it's the penalty you pay for laxity. I admit it has its compensations. But you've got to give 'em the steel. You've got to run 'em down like rats. You give them the old cowering point. We've got to get them out. We want to go in there and run 'em out. We want to give 'em steel.

FLAGG. We? Staff going in there too, General?

THE GENERAL (*disconsolately*). No—they won't risk us fellows, curse the luck.

FLAGG. That's too bad, General.

THE GENERAL. But we'll be behind you, Flagg.

FLAGG. How far, General?

THE GENERAL. We'll probably be at Cemetery Farm. We haven't studied the indirect fire properly yet, but we'll be behind you.

THE COLONEL (*handing bundle of posters to* GENERAL). Beg pardon, sir; these posters.

THE GENERAL. And, Flagg, some Yankee Doodle back in Hoboken sends you some posters with his compliments.

FLAGG. Posters? What for?

THE GENERAL. To post behind the German lines—sent to all companies of this brigade.

FLAGG. My God! What are we advertising? Camels?

THE GENERAL. Oh, no! It's intelligence work. Explaining our mission over here to the German soldier. There are three hundred posters. Send a small detail through the German lines some night and tack 'em up all over the place.

FLAGG. How many men am I supposed to lose on that job?

THE GENERAL. Not one. We don't want to lose a man. But tack 'em up.

FLAGG. Yeah, that's easy to say. I'd like to tack up a few in Hoboken containing my sentiments on two-starred idiots who waste men on that kind of monkey-business.

THE GENERAL. Well, here is another thing, Flagg, the big G. one wants a prisoner out of that town of yours. Wants an officer from one of those Alsatian regiments where the deserters are filtering through. And I've got to get him.

FLAGG. Oh, don't say that, General, don't break our hearts. I've got to get him. I knew damn well you had a bolt of black crepe up your sleeve when you came in the door.

THE GENERAL. Hold down the losses, Flagg . . . and listen. If you send me one of those Alsatian officers in good condition I'll send your whole company back for a month's rest.

FLAGG. You mean it?

THE GENERAL. Mean it! You know me, Flagg. I'll do more if you get me an officer without a scratch. I'll give you eight days in any hotel in France. If you weren't such a bum, Flagg, I'd put you on staff.

FLAGG. I've been a bum, General, but I'm damned if I'd go on staff.

THE GENERAL (*at the door*). Hold down the losses, Flagg, and give 'em the steel—and don't forget those posters, for they're damned important—and if you fetch me that prisoner you get a month's rest and eight days' leave. (*The door opens. In walk the* CHAPLAIN, CHARMAINE *and* QUIRT, MAYOR, KIPER, *and* LIPINSKY.) Hullo! My God, what's this? A wedding party?

FLAGG. Why, yes, General. I don't suppose we ought to wait for it, but it's a sort of special case and won't take long.

THE GENERAL. *You* aren't getting married, are you, Flagg?

FLAGG. Not this trip; no, sir. It's Sergeant Quirt.

THE GENERAL (*turning to* QUIRT). Oh, yes, I remember Sergeant Quirt very well.

FLAGG. I didn't like to intrude company

matters when you were in haste, General, but the truth is, Sergeant Quirt has expressed a wish to marry the inn-keeper's daughter here, and her father was waiting to press charges; so, you see——

THE GENERAL. Oh! Charges? . . .

FLAGG. Personally, I'm opposed to Quirt's marrying at all, but he insists his intentions were honorable, and he's such a fine soldier I should hate to carry this old man to H.Q. with a complaint.

THE GENERAL. What's this, Sergeant?

QUIRT. A courtship, General; a love match from the start. Honorable intentions on both sides.

THE GENERAL. Sounds a little fishy to me, I must say, but go right ahead. Don't waste time.

(FERGUSON *comes forward.*)

PETE. *Monsieur le général, les Américains sont si forts—ils m'ont déshonoré—ma petite fille—ma fleur charmonte—ma fleur délicate . . .*

FERGUSON. In case of a marriage, Captain Flagg, a little allotment is regulation.

FLAGG. Thanks, Fergy; I almost forgot the allotment.

QUIRT. Hell, we don't need no allotment. This is a love match.

FLAGG. Of course, it holds us up a bit, but if the General doesn't mind?

FERGUSON. A little allotment is regulation, sir.

THE GENERAL. Go ahead, go ahead.

FLAGG. Ferguson, where are those allotment blanks?

FERGUSON. Right here, sir.

THE GENERAL (*to* FERGUSON). Make it out for two-thirds of the sergeant's pay, Ferguson.

FERGUSON (*sits and fills papers*). Yes, sir.

QUIRT (*standing, with* CHARMAINE). I don't know about this, General.

THE GENERAL. It's for your own good, Quirt. How do you plan to get out of it, otherwise?

QUIRT. Get out of it? Didn't I tell you it was a love match?

THE GENERAL. No more talk, Sergeant; sign up or stand trial.

FLAGG. For your own good, Quirt.

QUIRT. For whose good, Captain Flagg?

THE GENERAL. Sign up, Quirt.

(FERGUSON *gives paper to* FLAGG. QUIRT *reluctantly signs.*)

FLAGG. All in order. (*Looks over paper.*) Shipshape, Sergeant Quirt. Beautiful hand you write, sir. And now, Chaplain, Sergeant Quirt is next.

THE GENERAL. Let's get it over with. And here's her father ready to give her away.

PETE. *Merci, mon général.*

THE GENERAL. A regular church wedding, and Captain Flagg can be best man.

FLAGG. Get that, Sergeant Quirt? Charmaine—(*He crosses and hands her allotment papers with a bow.*)—keep this in a good safe place. It means money to you the first of every month.

CHARMAINE. *Merci.*

THE GENERAL. Turn on the ceremony.

CHAPLAIN. This is a little irregular.

THE GENERAL. Run it through. Sorry we can't wait to kiss the bride, Quirt. You have about twenty minutes, Flagg.

FLAGG. Right, sir.

THE GENERAL. One word, Quirt. You're going in to-night. You're going in in twenty minutes. If you take your men into the line in first-rate condition, looking like soldiers, you'll square yourself with me. Keep that in mind.

QUIRT. We're going in in twenty minutes?

THE GENERAL. Yes. We're off, men. So long, Flagg. Twenty minutes.

FLAGG. Good-bye, General.

(*All salute.* THE GENERAL *and his retinue file out at door.*)

CHAPLAIN. Do you, Charmaine, take this man for your husband, to love, honor——

QUIRT. She does not, I do not, we do not. So we're going in in twenty minutes, eh —and you were going to tie me up before I knew anything about it? And I suppose if I don't marry her you'll lock me up. If you think you can take your men in to-night without a first sergeant, you lock me up. I would like to see you take this gang of tiny tots across that last two miles without a sergeant. Well, if this sergeant goes in, he goes in single; so you God damn well better make up your mind what you're going to do.

FLAGG. Well, skunk, you've got me. You win. Hit the deck.

QUIRT. Sorry, Charmaine, but I've got work to do. I can't marry you to-night, I can't marry you any God damn time at all, and if I never see you again—why, then I never see you again, understand? What's more, don't you try cashing that allotment, or by God I'll pull something that'll stop my pay for good. Get out of my way.

(*He goes out. Instantly a whistle blows.*)

FLAGG. Sorry, Charmaine, but I need that sergeant. Shake a leg, you hayshakers. Pass the word for inspection in five minutes, and they'd better be shipshape. *Camions* at the crossroad. Extra bandoliers and V. B. grenades for the outside ranks. Don't let Quirt do all the work.

THE RUNNERS. Ay, ay, sir.

(*They go out hastily.*)

PETE (*angry*). *Sont-ils mariés? Ou votre sergeant, se mosque-t-il de moi?*

FLAGG. Sure, they're married.

PETE (*beats on table*). *Prenez garde! Je viendrai!*

FLAGG (*turns—speaks ominously*). Don't bother me. Don't get in my way, see? We're fighting a war with Germany. I don't give a damn whether he's married or not. Run along outside. (*Turns* PETE *around; spanks him.*) I'm busy. (PETE *goes out, stops near* CHARMAINE *and says, "Sale vache"; then goes out.* FLAGG *goes to table, gets his hat, turns toward the door.*) So long, Fergy. Take care of the stuff.

FERGUSON. Yes, sir.

(*Turns to desk.* FLAGG *starts out.* CHARMAINE *crosses to him.*)

CHARMAINE (*her hand on his arm*). I'm so sorry. You should have taken me to Paris. I told you to take me to Paris. I could not be good all alone.

FLAGG (*takes her by shoulders*). That's all right, Charmaine. You're a damn fine little animal. Go right on having a good time. It's a great life, and you've got a genius for it.

CHARMAINE. But you do not love me, not any more?

FLAGG. Sure I love you! Everybody loves you.

CHARMAINE. You think I am *pas bonne?*

FLAGG. Listen, Charmaine. Don't you worry any more about Quirt and me. It's a thousand to one you'll never see either of us again. I'm damned sorry I have to take your sergeant away, but this war's lousy with sergeants. There'll be thirty along in thirty days. Anyway you'll probably never see us again. Kiss me good-bye. (*They kiss.*) Now you forget me!

CHARMAINE. I never forget you.

(*A whistle blows outside.*)

FLAGG. You won't forget me? Well, if I get leave, Charmaine . . . you never can tell. (*The whistle blows twice.*) It's a hell of a war, but it's the only one we've got.

(*He goes out. She stands staring after him.*)

FERGUSON (*from his table; turning*). Well, little missy. You're a single woman *with* an allotment. There ain't many as fortunate as that.

CHARMAINE. He will come back?

FERGUSON. Which one?

CHARMAINE. The captain.

FERGUSON. Not likely. Not likely either of them will. A soldier hardly ever doubles on his trail in this war.

CHARMAINE. No?

FERGUSON. Hardly ever. And you're just as fortunate you didn't marry a soldier, darling. They're a bad lot to keep house for. I know. I've been keeping house for one regiment or another since I was as young as you are.

CHARMAINE. Oh, but they are beautiful.

FERGUSON. The girls always like them. I don't know why.

CHARMAINE. They go into hell to die—and they are not old enough to die.

FERGUSON. I shouldn't think it would matter much to you, dear. Some get killed, but plenty more come in to relieve them. Never any shortage of soldiers.

CHARMAINE. It's terrible!

FERGUSON. It's their business. Some of 'em get killed at it, same as in any trade.

CHARMAINE (*crosses to back of* FERGUSON'*s chair; leans over him*). Can I help you?

FERGUSON. No.

CHARMAINE. To-morrow?

FERGUSON. No.

CHARMAINE. You are unkind.

FERGUSON. Just because I'm the only man around here do you think I'm going to let you bother me? You run along home and pray God to keep you out of mischief a few days. It won't do you any harm.

(*He bends over his work.*)

CHARMAINE. *Bon soir.* (*He does not hear her.*) *Bon soir!*

FERGUSON. What?

CHARMAINE. *Bon soir.*

FERGUSON. Oh, yes, good night. (*She slowly crosses to door, looking back at him all the way. She quietly closes door, and just as she does so,* FERGUSON *very loudly says,* "Good night." *He bends over his desk, alone, writing and sings.*)

"The French they are a funny race, parlez-vous,
The French they are a funny race, parlez-vous . . ."

CURTAIN

ACT TWO

A cellar in a disputed town, a typical deep wine cellar of a prosperous farmhouse on the edge of a village in France. It resembles half of a culvert thirty feet in diameter, with a corresponding curved roof and walls. One end is open, and the other is walled up, admitting a narrow and rather low door in the center, through which a flight of stairs extends to the ground floor above. This cellar is lit dimly by two candles placed at either side of the front stage and held in bottles on small bully-beef boxes. The rear wall can only barely be discerned. Along the sides of this culvert are dirty white ticks stuffed with straw for sleeping quarters, the sort of ticks headquarters detachment men carry about with them. There are four on each side, arranged with all the litter of miscellany a soldier carries about tucked at their heads, and with the foot of these pallets extending into the center of the culvert. The effect is not unlike in design that of a hospital ward, with feet toward the center aisle. Back of FLAGG's *bunk all manner of stuff—first-aid kits, bandages, chocolates, sticks, pistols and rifles, notes, books of memoranda,* etc.

Two men are asleep, snoring gently—gas masks at alert on chests, tin hats on back of heads, and heads on floor. They are indescribably dirty, and with six or eight days' beard.

The two men are SPIKE *and* KIPER. KIPER *is on second bunk at left,* SPIKE *on third bunk at right.* GOWDY *enters. Stirs* SPIKE *with his foot.*

GOWDY. All right. Heave out and lash up. Lively now. Rations are in. Go draw for ten. At the gray stable to-night. Take that sack there.

(*Points to a muddy sack on the floor near by.*)

SPIKE. What time is it? Rations in?

GOWDY. You heard me, Spike. Shake a leg and go draw rations for ten men, at the gray stable near the square. It's after two o'clock.

SPIKE. Where's Captain Flagg?

GOWDY. Down tying up Mr. Aldrich.

SPIKE. So they got him. Bad?

GOWDY. I'll say they did. A ticket home. Right arm torn all to hell.

SPIKE. A damned dirty shame. He's lucky, though, to get out with an arm. I'd sell 'em mine, and at the same price. What was it—that one-pounder again?

GOWDY. No. Fuse cap from a grenade. Made a hell of a mess on Mr. Aldrich. He was crawling on the embankment near the railway station, and somebody inside threw him a present.

SPIKE (*now up and re-winding a spiral legging*). A damned swell officer, if you ask me. Taking him out to-night?

GOWDY. No. The skipper is bringing him here. Send him out to-morrow night. He's lost too much blood to walk it before dawn. God, it's getting on my nerves.

KIPER (*who has been awakened*). Who? Mr. Aldrich hit bad?

GOWDY. Pretty bad. Arm. Make a bunk for him, willya? Shake it down and pile another in the back. He'll want to sit up with it. Make up Harry's bunk.

SPIKE (*at door, about to go upstairs, turns at this*). Harry's bunk? Why, Harry?

GOWDY. Harry's through with bunk.

SPIKE. Bumped off?

GOWDY. Worse. In the belly crossing the square.

(SPIKE *goes out.*)

KIPER. Where is he?

GOWDY. The skipper rushed him back an hour ago. No use, though; Harry was unconscious—halfway—holding half his guts in his bare hands and hollering for somebody to turn him loose so he could shoot himself.

KIPER. Captain Flagg want me?

GOWDY. He said not to wake you. Might need you later on.

KIPER. A good job for me, I suppose. Jeez, with this daylight saving I ain't going to live forever, that's sure. I think I'll go crazy and get the doc to gimme a ticket.

GOWDY. Flagg's crazy now. Raving crazy. Hasn't slept for five nights. We'll be sitting on him in another night like he's had to-night.

KIPER. The whole damned universe is crazy now.

(KIPER *has come forward to* FLAGG's *bunk, smoking. Enter* PHARMACIST'S MATE, *with a large clothing roll trussed up in leather straps with a portmanteau handle. He is young, pink-faced, but horribly callous, probably some kid from a medical school of 1917.*)

MATE (*looking about in the dark as he approaches* KIPER). Flagg's company P.C.?

KIPER (*hostile;* GOWDY *sits up*). Yeah.

MATE. Where'd I better set up shop, soldier?

(*He looks about the cellar.*)

KIPER (*worried*). What do you want to set up shop for, sailor?

MATE (*sitting down on bunk; starts unpacking, takes off helmet*). How'd I know? This ain't my party. Flagg wants it here.

KIPER. What's he want it for to-night?

MATE. He's going to put on a little party before morning. (*He uncovers a litter of blue-rolled bandages on bunk; absorbent cotton, a jar of iodine which he unscrews, and some wooden sticks around which he begins to twist wisps of cotton for daubs.*) A little party.

KIPER. The whole damn company, I suppose, and all the engineers he can find to boot.

MATE (*professionally*). Oh, no. He ain't got arrangements here for that many. I'd say a small party, according to the stuff they gave me at the dressing station.

KIPER (*incredulous*). How small?

MATE (*with immense indifference, busy about his detail*). Oh, I'd say about two operating tables . . . (*A pause as he enjoys the effect on* KIPER.) A small party. About four couples for bridge.

KIPER. Yeah. (*Rather miserable.*) Low bridge around that lousy railroad station.

MATE. I guess so. They were passing out V. B. grenades down by the street to the station when I came through.

KIPER (*immensely friendly all of a sudden*). Look here, sailor. You are smarter than me. . . .

MATE (*interrupting*). Oh, no!

KIPER (*insistently*). Oh, hell, yes! Any man smart enough not to join in them four couples is smarter than I am. Even you're smarter. Now that being the case, tell me why the hell we want the Heinies out of that God damn railway station. Leave 'em there, I say. Let 'em sit where they damned well are. They ain't going anywheres.

MATE. I can't tell you.

KIPER. Nobody can. Like as not General Pershing himself couldn't tell you about it . . . and . . . oh, sweet baby, but last night down there I swore to God so long as I lived I'd never let another German in that railroad station throw a potato masher at me.

MATE. You can throw a grenade at him.

KIPER. Sure I can. But I don't want to no more. I pitched yesterday, and my arm is sore. I know I can do it, and it ain't fun any more. I know all about Flagg's invitations to parties. I know why they all got R.S.V.P. on 'em. Right smart of V.B. grenades provided. . . .

(*Enter* LIPINSKY, *who comes down; looks first at* KIPER.)

LIPINSKY (*immediately perceiving the litter*). Jeez, Kiper, I wish you'd keep the undertakers out of here. What's all this, Jack?

(*He waves to the mate's stuff.*)

MATE (*selecting a small bandage*). Well, this one is yours, and the rest is for your friends.

LIPINSKY (*cheerily*). Don't try to put the bug on me. I ain't no queen bee. They ain't made one that could burst alongside of me. If they'd made it, I'd be down with the daisies long ago. I'm proof now. It's down in the cards that I'll live to see the navy at Mare Island again. (*He lights a cigarette which he has taken from* FLAGG'S *bunk.*) Yes, sir, I'll live to beat the pants of that bird that sold me the wrist watch down by the main gate.

KIPER. How do you know you're going to live? Said your prayers, I suppose, and got an answer.

LIPINSKY. And who'd send me an answer?

KIPER. The great cosmic top sergeant who runs this world.

LIPINSKY. Well, I don't want any answer from that bird. He'd send the answer collect, and it would say, "Fall in and get the manure outa the French angels' backyards. Clean up heaven, you low-down Marine, so's the National Guard won't get typhoid when they all die and come here."

KIPER. There ain't any heaven. Paris is heaven enough. If I ever get outa hell, I'm certainly going to stay in heaven until I die.

LIPINSKY. Of course, there's a heaven.

MATE. On the level, now. You birds know your souls go somewheres. You've seen too many men die. A fellow is walkıg along, blood in his face and breath in ııis lungs, and whizz - eeee - zzzz, boom-mmmm . . . he's down on the ground and something's gone. Something's gone, I tell you. Something that was in that bird a minute before has left, and all you've got is a pack of bloody rags and a lot of dirt. Well, for the want of a better name, you call that something a soul . . . and you can't kid me . . . the soul's gone some-wheres.

KIPER. What of it? That soul ain't any of my business. It ain't got to eat, it ain't got to run; it ain't got to stand in line ten days a week to sign the payroll. I should get on my ear about where this doodlebug in my chest is going after I die. It ain't never helped me none. It can go to hell for all I care.

LIPINSKY. Jezz, Kiper, don't talk that way around me. (*Raises eyes.*) It wasn't me, God; it wasn't your little Vladysek Lipinsky. Not him. He knows too damn well if he was to talk that way you would certainly make him cover up and yell for mercy before morning.

KIPER. And you were the one wasn't go-ing to be hit a while ago.

LIPINSKY. That's why I ain't going to be hit. My little soul's all ready to turn out for every formation, boots blacked and buttons shined. A little sea-going soul that knows its top sergeant can give it a kick in the pants any time he gets ready.

KIPER. Well, if there is a God, he ain't got medicine big enough to worry me. Why the hell doesn't he win the war for one side or the other and get this mess over? I know plenty of men could win it. Flagg probably could, if you gave him the army and a barrel of whisky.

LIPINSKY. But you like the chaplain, Kiper. You said he was a swell bird the other day.

KIPER. Sure I like the chaplain. Gimme two packs of Camels two nights ago. If God was to show himself, now—come down with a bunch of angels driving a wagon-load of cigarettes, that would be something like it. The chaplain said my folks was all praying for me to come through, and for God to spare me after hearing their prayers. God, I ain't that dirty a coward! That's a case of saying, "Oh, God, don't kill our child. Kill every kid in the neighborhood, but bring the one marked Kiper safe back home. . . ." No, I don't want none of that for mine. . . . And you can take all your New Testa-ments with the khaki backs and throw 'em in the incinerator so far as I want anything out of 'em. I'd rather have a book of ciga-rette papers any time. . . . I ain't asking anybody for a damned thing in this war. And you can take all your Bible backers and psalm singers and hitch 'em to the ration wagons, if you ask me.

MATE. Well, this is all very pleasant, but I got business over in the next company now. Bad curve in the position there, and 'long toward daybreak they start holler-ing "First Aid" as regular as a clock. If I was you fellows I'd go out and sleep in different shell-holes to-night . . . see which one of you is right. . . . Tell your skipper I'll be back around three-thirty.

(*He steps on his cigarette and prepares to go out after* QUIRT *enters, which he does.* QUIRT *enters.* SERGEANT QUIRT *is tired.*)

QUIRT. Captain Flagg here?

GOWDY. Still in the orchard . . . digging those new rifle pits. We've got nine cap-tured Maxims there. Those birds can't change the belts, but they can tap a thou-sand rounds apiece by pressing the but-tons in the dark. Fifteen men could hold this half of the town, the way he's got the positions staked out.

QUIRT. There'll be about fifteen holding it if this business of reconnoitering pa-trols keeps up. I'd like to have that divis-ional staff in this town one night. Still bad in the square?

GOWDY. Pretty had. Rifles in box rest in the railway station . . . light automatics.

QUIRT. I thought Flagg got 'em out last night.

GOWDY. They filtered back in at dusk to-night. Our cross-fire couldn't stop 'em. The skipper says they are working them from pulleys from the first floor, and the railroad embankment covers them from us.

QUIRT (*stretching out and sighing as he takes off his tin hat and mops his fore-head*). Running rations down that ravine every night is the toughest job I've ever soldiered.

GOWDY. Lucky to-night?

QUIRT. Pretty lucky. Six out of ten come back. Them two Jameson boys got it from the same shell going down. Dutchy and the little Jew were hit right at the dump. Easy ones though. They'll be back in ten days.

(*A commotion at head of stairs. Enter*

CAPTAIN FLAGG *supporting* ALDRICH *by gripping* ALDRICH'S *uninjured wrist over his shoulder and easing him gently down steps.* ALDRICH *is not groaning. After all, it won't hurt for fifteen minutes or so. But he is weak from loss of blood and soaked through, and is in an indescribable mess of dried blood and dirt, which appears black.* FLAGG, *who is unkempt, has no leggings or laces in his breeches, these flapping in the most disillusioning fashion about his bare legs. His blouse, an old army blouse many sizes too big and without a sign of any insignia, is tied with a piece of twine. He is bareheaded—no tin hat and no accoutrements of any sort. He is a very weary-looking man. He wears belt and holster with automatic bound to leg. As* FLAGG *enters, followed by* MATE, GOWDY *jumps up and spreads blanket on bunk.*)

FLAGG. Right here, Aldrich. (*Lowers him down on bunk. The* PHARMACIST'S MATE *follows him.* FLAGG *kneels above* ALDRICH. *The* MATE *stands.*) Gimme a stick of that dope, Holsen.

MATE. They are quarter grains, Captain.

FLAGG (*to* ALDRICH, *lying down*). Take these two now. (*He puts two tablets from a tiny vial in the wounded officer's mouth.*) I'm putting these in your blouse. Get somebody to give you one every three hours until you are carried out.

ALDRICH. What are they?

FLAGG. Morphine—quarter grains——

ALDRICH (*not dramatic, just casual*). What if I take them all when your back is turned?

FLAGG (*turning his back and crossing to his own bunk down left; sits on bunk*). Go ahead. It's your affair.

(*After* FLAGG *is seated on his hunk a strange sob is heard at the head of the stairs.* LIEUTENANT MOORE, *last seen in company headquarters, rushes in and goes straight over to* ALDRICH, *where he stands and looks down at his arm, and not his face.*)

MOORE. Oh, God, Dave, but they got you. God, but they got you a beauty, the dirty swine. God DAMN them for keeping us up in this hellish town. Why can't they send in some of the million men they've got back there and give us a chance? Men in my platoons are so hysterical every time I get a message from Flagg, they want to know if they're being relieved. What can I tell them? They look at me like whipped dogs—as if I had just beaten them—and I've had enough of them this time. I've got to get them out, I tell you. They've had enough. Every night the same way. (*He turns to* FLAGG.) And since six o'clock there's been a wounded sniper in the tree by that orchard angel crying *"Kamerad! Kamerad!"* Just like a big crippled whippoorwill. What price glory now? Why in God's name can't we all go home? Who gives a damn for this lousy, stinking little town but the poor French bastards who live here? God damn it! You talk about courage, and all night long you hear a man who's bleeding to death on a tree calling you *"Kamarad"* and asking you to save him. God damn every son of a bitch in the world who isn't here! I won't stand for it. I won't stand for it! I won't have the platoon asking me every minute of the livelong night when they are going to be relieved. . . . Flagg, I tell you you can shoot me, but I won't stand for it. . . . I'll take' em out to-night and kill you if you get in my way. . . .

(*Starts sobbing again.* GOWDY *and* KIPER *sit up.*)

FLAGG (*rising quickly as though he might kill the man, and then putting his arm around the chap, who has clearly gone smash for a few minutes. He speaks in a quiet, chastening tone, with a gentility never before revealed*). Here, boy, you can't do this before all these men. (*Walks him.*) They are rubbed up, too. You are all tuckered out with your side of the line. Don't worry about your platoon. We'll get them out. You turn in here. (*Walks him to bunk on the left side of the room.* KIPER *crosses and throws blanket on him; stops at bunk nearest entrance.*) And dope off for a little while . . . that's it, give him a blanket, Kiper . . . and now take it easy a while, and you can go back to your platoon in time to stand to. Sleep it off, boy, sleep it off. . . . You're in a deep wide hole, and shells can't get you. Sleep it off.

(FLAGG *crosses to his own bunk, lights cigarette at candle. seats himself on bunk.* GOWDY *rests head on arm.* QUIRT *kneels on floor, gets a piece of chocolate out of his pocket; rises, as thought his legs were asleep. He carries his helmet. He crosses and tosses candy to* MOORE.)

QUIRT. Just a little chocolate I bought off a Y.M.C.A. wagon down at the base.

(QUIRT *is sympathetic and begins to talk nervously.*) I got hit myself once. In Nicaragua. We were washed up before we made a landing. I was a corporal, and when we were scrubbing down and putting on clean uniforms—doctors' orders, you know, so they wouldn't have to wash us when we were hit—(*Turns to* GOWDY.) —A bird said to me—it was old Smoke Plangetch, who was killed in 1913 in a chippie joint in Yokahama—Smoke said to me: "You'd better swab down, you son of a sea-bitch, because I dreamed last night they wrote your name on a bullet." I said to him, "The bullet ain't been cast that can shoot Micky Quirt." He said, "If your name is on one, it will turn the corner and go upstairs to find you." Jeez! That afternoon when we made a landing and hit the beach, the spigs was on a hill five hundred yards off shore. We started up the hill—they weren't many of us dropping—and I came to a log I had to jump (QUIRT *illustrates this.*) and I lost my balance and threw my hand up in the air. (QUIRT *extends his wrist.*) Look, right through the God damn fin, as pretty as a pinwheel . . . Smoke saw it. "Oh, yeah, you wisenheimer son of a Chinese tart," he says to me, "your name was on that one and you had to reach up for it." (GOWDY *laughs.* QUIRT *is obviously embarrassed by having spoken of himself so much. He turns and recollects his business and goes over to* FLAGG. *Crosses to the foot of* FLAGG'S *bunk.*) Rations detail in, sir. Lost the two Jameson boys in the ravine going down. Both badly hit. Lost Fleischman and Rosenthal in the dump. Both slight. Brought back all the ammunition and two sacks of bread, one of canned willie, French; I carried a sack of beet sugar on my back. Got a piece of shrapnel in it where they are shelling the crossroads—stopped it square. In the next war, I'm going to wear a suit of beet sugar and stand forest fire watch in the Rocky Mountains. (*He turns, and then remembers and comes back.*) Oh, I brought up two of these thirty-day wonder lieutenants from a training camp. Sent up by divisional for instruction.

FLAGG. By God, I won't stand for it. They wipe their damned dirty feet on this company. They can give my men all their damned good jobs. They can keep us in the line all during the whole damned war. But I'll be damned if my sergeants have got time to teach army lieutenants how to button their pants in the dark.

QUIRT. They are in my hole now, sir. Pretty badly shaken up by the ravine. First time up, you know. Shall I send them to you, sir?

FLAGG. Send them to me, and for God's sake, don't call me sir any more to-night.

QUIRT (*to* GOWDY). All right. You heard him. Hit the deck. You'll find 'em in my hole. (GOWDY *goes.*) Those Huns in the railway station again?

FLAGG. Try to cross the town square when there's a flare up, and you'll see.

QUIRT. You get a visit from brigade headquarters to-night. I saw their party in the ravine as we were going down to the dump.

FLAGG. The old man says we've got to drive them off the embankment. Huh! He can give me five general courts and I'll not waste another man at that business. It will take a brigade action to get them out for good.

QUIRT. Do you mind if I take a look around there now? I'd like to see this damned war some. For six days I've been a lousy bakery wagon—haven't seen a spiggoty yet, except stinking dead ones—I never see soldiers stink like these Heinies.

FLAGG. All right. Go get your blooming can blown off. But bury yourself, while you're about it. The burying detail is in for the night.

QUIRT. Gosh, I wish to hell I was home.

FLAGG. Go get one of those Alsatian lootenants then, and you'll get a leave.

QUIRT. I don't want to die yet, thanking you just the same. Well, here goes. (*Exit.*)

FLAGG. Well, keep your head down. I can't waste any grave-diggers on sergeants. (FLAGG *shrugs his shoulders and walks over to above* ALDRICH.) Sorry Moore blew up that way, Aldrich . . . you are a damned sight luckier than he is, but he doesn't know it. I'll have you out to-morrow night with the ration detail, and you'll be parking your body in a big white bed in another two days. Good luck . . . You've been a damned good man. I wish you could get a ribbon for this town.

(*As* FLAGG *leaves,* GOWDY *enters with two lieutenants. They are just like tailor's dummies of a Burberry outfit slicked to the notch and perky and eager. As they enter,* FLAGGS *steps on his cigarette and stands facing them. The* LIEUTENANTS *come down and stand side by side.*)

FLAGGS (*starts back in mock admiration and salaams deeply as they come forward*). So *this* is the last of the old guard, eh? In the name of the holy sweet Jumping, are you gentlemen bound for a masked ball, that you come disguised as officers? Or do you wish to save the snipers the trouble of picking you off with a glass, that you wear signboards? (*He goes nearer them, inspecting their clothes.*) Can't you go without those trench coats even to the trenches? How long will you last in those boots? Take 'em off before you even part your hair in the morning. . . . (*He changes to a thundering staccato.*) My name is Flagg, gentlemen, and I'm the sinkhole and cesspool of this regiment, frowned on in the Y.M.C.A. huts and sneered at by the divisional Beau Brummells. I am a lousy, good-for-nothing company commander. I corrupt youth and lead little boys astray into the black shadows between the lines of hell, killing more men than any other company commander in the regiment, and drawing all the dirty jobs in the world. I take chocolate soldiers and make dead heroes out of them. I did not send for you, Mister . . . (*He leans forward, and the first officer salutes and speaks: "Cunningham, sir"*) nor for you . . . (*"Lundstrom, sir," also salutes.*); and I confess I am in a quandary. Four days ago I should have been more hospitable, for I had four gunnery sergeants then. Now I have two, and can't spare them to teach little boys how to adjust their diapers. I've no doubt that one of you was an all-American half-back and the other the editor of the college paper, but we neither follow the ball nor the news here. We are all dirt, and we propose to die in order that corps headquarters may be decorated. I should be happy to receive suggestions as to what should be done with you. Ah, I have it! There are two German gunners over in the enemy railway station. Two bright young men might get them out and cut their throats before dawn; then no more could get in the station all day. Two bright young men, who know very little of anything just yet. I have two bright ones, but they are far too valuable. They are corporals with ten years' experience. (*The* LIEUTENANTS *are speechless. There is not a smile in the cellar.* CUNNINGHAM, *who is the bigger of the two, finally answers, in a slow southern drawl.*)

CUNNINGHAM. I'll do anything you will. Where is the railway station and the two bucks that have got you buffaloed?

FLAGG. Why, it's Frank Merriwell! All right, Frank. You and me will be playing ball in hell by three o'clock this morning.

LUNDSTROM. Put me in too, sir.

FLAGG. Oh, no, no, no! We must have officers left. Rule of the game. Must have officers. Men would get right up and go home, and then there wouldn't be any war at all. Besides, three would be a crowd, and I hate crowds early in the morning around the railway station. They are so noisy, and they die so fast. (*He turns to* GOWDY.) Gowdy! Take Mr. Lundstrom to the fourth platoon sergeant, and tell him that here's his new officer. (RUNNER *and* LUNDSTROM *move to door.* FLAGG *is all business now.*) And by the way, Mr. Lundstrom, they filter through and bomb twice a week, small parties slipping down that ravine you'll find on your left. Watch it closely, or you'll all have your throats cut before you know it. And let that sergeant sleep for the next two days. Remember, he'll do no details until he's rested. Of course you can wake him for advice. That's all. Shove off. (RUNNER *and* LUNDSTROM *salute, and go out.* CUNNINGHAM *sits down.* QUIRTS *enters with his helmet on, limping; steals forward quietly, and sits down on his bunk. There is a nice bloody mess on his right calf.* FLAGG *happens to turn, sees what's going on, sits up, watches* QUIRT. QUIRT *looks back, finally grins, then tries to open a first-aid pack.*)

FLAGG. What's the matter with you?

QUIRT. Got a can opener?

FLAGG. You crook!

QUIRT. I say, Captain, got a can opener?

FLAGG. Those things are supposed to be opened with the teeth.

QUIRT. You don't say! Well, this'n' wasn't. This here can was evidently made for the Red Cross by the Columbia Red Salmon Company. Like as not instead of bandages I'll find the God damnedest mess of goldfish in it.

FLAGG (*rises, crosses to* QUIRT, *takes can away from him*). Where were you? (*He comes over, strains at the tin. He is looking daggers.*) Where were you?

QUIRT. Just looking around.

FLAGG. Here.

(*Hands him tin, opened.*)

QUIRT. Thanks.

FLAGG. Where were you, I said.

QUIRT (*takes out bandage*). In the vegetable garden, pulling turnips.

(*Starts wiping leg.*)

FLAGG. God damn you, Quirt, I believe you stuck your leg out.

(*Goes back and sits on bunk.*)

QUIRT. Like hell I did. If I'd wanted to stick my leg out don't you think I've had plenty of chances to do it before? No, sir, I stuck my head out and some bird in the church tower took a shot at me. There she is. In and out without touching the bone. Just let me squeeze the juice out and she'll be all right. Ain't she the prettiest little damn puncture you ever saw, Captain? Ain't she a beauty?

FLAGG. I suppose you think you're going back to Cognac Pete's, huh?

QUIRT. How'd you guess it? Yes, sir, back to my little skookum lady you tried to make me a present of. Am I happy? Am I happy? Oh, boy! Ask me, Captain, am I happy?

FLAGG. You mean to say you aren't cured of Charmaine yet?

QUIRT. Cured of Charmaine? No, sir, I ain't even getting better. Oh, Captain Flagg, ain't you proud of yourself, ain't you a wizard? God, ain't I sorry to leave you all alone here in this mess? Think of her sitting on my lap, lighting my pipe in the kitchen, and you dodging machine guns. I wonder I don't bust out crying. You know, I wouldn't wonder if you got bumped off and never came back. As a matter of fact, I hope you damn well get your head blown off.

FLAGG. Yeah, you always did have a charming disposition.

QUIRT (*squeezing his wound gently*). Oh, pretty baby, papa doesn't mean to hurt you. Lookit, Captain. By God, I wouldn't take a hundred dollars Mex. for that little bumble-bee that flew in there.

FLAGG. Feel pretty cocky, don't you? Well, you can't go out to-night. I guess you can work all right with that. You'll wait here till Cunningham and I get back with that Alsatian shavetail from the railroad embankment. Then I get leave, the company gets a rest, and we go back together, see?

QUIRT. Not much, I don't see. I've got a very important engagement back to Pete's place. Can't be postponed, not even for the pleasure of your enjoyable company, such as it is. I don't wait for nothing in the world but a medical tag.

(*Enter* PHARMACIST'S MATE; *stands on steps, leans head in door.*)

MATE. Heard your first sergeant was hit in that turnip patch. (FLAGG *indicates* QUIRT. MATE *crosses to* QUIRT; *kneels.*) Let's have a look. Um. Night soil in that patch, and you, like a damned fool, crawl after they hit you, and now you're full of that muck. Can you walk, Sergeant?

QUIRT (*lying back*). Well, depends on what I see.

MATE (*helps up* QUIRT, *who carries helmet*). Go to the sick bay at once for a shot of tetanus, and then get out of here. (*Takes his arm, and both cross.*) You can reach a collecting station before you're done.

QUIRT. Ain't this heart-breaking, Flagg? Well, duty calls. But my eyes fill with tears at the thought of leaving my old company commander. I don't know as I can go through with it.

FLAGG. Make it snappy, Quirt, or you'll find the door locked.

QUIRT. Yeah? What door.

FLAGG. Charmaine's.

QUIRT. Are you wounded, too, Mr. Flagg?

FLAGG. No, but inside ten minutes I'm going to be wounded or bumped off or have that God damned prisoner for the Brig.

QUIRT. Try to get killed, will you? To please me—just this once?

(QUIRT *and the* MATE *go out.*)

FLAGG. Mr. Cunningham . . . I guess you thought I was joking when I proposed that little expedition to the railroad embankments?

CUNNINGHAM. I did not. When do we start?

(*Coming to* FLAGG.)

FLAGG. Well, I was. I was kidding hell out of you. I'd no more let you go in there, boy, than I'd knife you in the back. The air is full of steel this side of that embankment, and a green man has about as much chance as a cootie on Fifth Avenue.

CUNNINGHAM. You going?

FLAGG. I've got official reasons for going, see? The Brig. wants a prisoner, and he also wants that nest wiped out. Also, I got private and personal reasons for wanting to catch up with that baboon that got the little present through his leg.

CUNNINGHAM. If you're going, that suits

me. I ain't no green man. I can crawl on my belly.

FLAGG. Yeah?

CUNNINGHAM. I'm a locomotive engineer and I've been crawling under trains for fifteen years. Had several engines shot out from under me likewise. You think you can scare me with this here war? Christ! You ought to see a few railroad wrecks!

FLAGG. Well, Mr. Cunningham, I'm inclined to think you'll do.

CUNNINGHAM. You're God damn right, I'll do.

FLAGG. What do you say we black our faces and give a little party, now the guests will be asleep?

CUNNINGHAM. Sure. I like the curt of your jib, and you can lead me to it. Show me which one is the lootenant, so I won't hurt him.

FLAGG. You from Texas?

CUNNINGHAM. You hit it.

FLAGG. Now I get you. So we've got another damned Texan in this outfit, wanting to fight anybody that ain't from Texas.

CUNNINGHAM. Yep, and I ain't no God damn college boy, either.

FLAGG. Good stuff! Now throw away them fancy-dress clothes of yours and dip in here.

(*He offers a can of lamp-black.*)

CUNNINGHAM. Sure. (*Takes off overcoat.*) I was a locomotive engineer on the Louisiana Midland. Three wrecks in my division last year. Christ, but this war shore is a great relief to me. (*Both black their faces.*) I'm an engineer officer attached to infantry. My brother's still driving an engine back home. Had a letter last month from him. He says, "You dirty yellow sapsucker, quitting your job on the Louisiana Midland. I knew you always were a yellow dog, but I didn't think you'd go back on the road thataway."

FLAGG. Now if I only had a pretty little engine. (*Suddenly there is a scream upstairs, a shout in a burly strange tongue. "Heraus!" and three bombs explode.* FLAGG, *the* RUNNERS, *and all save* ALDRICH *dash for the door.*) Marines! Marines! Marines! (*The lieutenant who had been put to sleep stirs uneasily. After a brief tumult, the people of the cellar descend stairs,* FLAGG *holding a German officer by the collar. He takes him straight to the candle.*) Let me have a look at you, sweetheart, let me have a look! Boys, he's an Alsatian lieutenant! He couldn't wait for us to go after him, so he came over. (*He embraces his captive.*) Oh, sweetheart—you're the sweetest sight I've seen since Charmaine! Here, Kiper (*Pushes him to* KIPER.)—take care of him for me, and for God's sake don't scare him to death, because he's our ticket of leave!

LEWISOHN (*screams, outside*). Captain Flagg . . .

FLAGG. Who's that?

LIPINSKY. It's little Lewisohn, sir.

(LEWISOHN *is carried in by* GOWDY *followed by* PHARMACIST'S MATE, *and he is crying monotonously for* CAPTAIN FLAGG.)

LEWISOHN. Captain Flagg. Captain Flagg. Stop the blood. Stop the blood.

FLAGG (*takes him from* GOWDY *and puts him on floor*). I can't stop it, Lewisohn, I'm sorry.

(*He examines wound in left side.*)

LEWISOHN. Oh, Captain Flagg, stop the blood.

FLAGG. Fix him with your needle, Mate.

(MATE *gives him needle in arm.*)

LEWISOHN. Oh, Captain Flagg, can't you please, sir, stop the blood?

FLAGG (*puts hand behind* Lewisohn's *head and gently lowers him to floor*). You'll be all right, boy. You'll be all right. You'll be all right.

(LEWISOHN *sighs and relaxes his body.*)

CURTAIN

ACT THREE

A tavern known colloquially as Cognac Pete's. Evening, two days later. The outside door is in the rear, small bar at the right, stairway left, an inside door at right. Windows rear. FERGUSON *sits at long table smoking and playing solitaire, a bottle of Martell and a brandy pony at his elbow.* CHARMAINE *is in front of the table by the candles, sewing.* FERGUSON *is enjoying the luxury of talking to himself, for it is apparent that* CHARMAINE *is not following all he says.*

FERGUSON. I'm glad they're coming back here. (*He sips, between sentences.*) It's a good, quiet town . . . quiet . . . last time we were in a town where the M.P.'s and the mule skinners fought every night . . . glad they sent 'em back here. . . . *You* ought to be. . . . Your father'll do a land office business when the outfit gets here.

He better knock the bung in every barrel of red ink he's got. God, how they'll eat . . . what's left of 'em. When two hundred leave me behind with the stuff, I always get ready to mess two hundred when they return. Of course a hundred may not return . . . but they'll eat right through to the bottom of the kettle just the same. Now you take that big oakum-haired Swede named Swenson. I never see a Marine eat more than he did . . . I damn well hope Swenson gets back . . . I like to see him eat. There was a little Jew named Lewisohn that could out-eat him, weight for weight; but the Swede weighed twice as much. That Swede could eat anything but a horse collar. (*He chuckles and* CHARMAINE *smiles.*) Well, I'll say we've kept each other company. We sure have, even if you can't speak a white man's lingo; that is, not to say *speak* it. Now if you'd been a Spanish girl we could have got together a little better . . . I lived with a Spanish girl at Cavite back in '99 . . . in those days I was salty as hell, a sea-going buckaroo.

CHARMAINE. *Est-ce-que* . . . you are lonely?

FERGUSON. It ain't so bad, staying behind this way. It ain't so bad. Twenty years now I've had 'em leave me. When I was younger I believed some of the liars who said they liked to fight . . . liked being under fire . . . but it always bored me to sit around and be sniped at. Somehow I never did get angry. And you've got to get angry when a bird's shooting at you if you're going to enjoy it. So I didn't have a good time . . . Now you take Flagg there . . . there's the sort likes it. Flagg gets mad as hell if you don't even like him, let alone shoot at him. Flagg and me are different. Now Flagg——

CHARMAINE. Where is *le capitaine?*

FERGUSON. Pretty near here, I suppose.

CHARMAINE. Near here?

FERGUSON. He'll be here presently, General.

CHARMAINE. *Le Capitaine Flagg*—he has been wounded ever?

FERGUSON. Naw! Flagg ain't never been wounded. Never will, neither, if you ask me. You can't hurt his kind. When you see a man like Flagg, it's curious, but they always have the pleasure of drinking themselves to death . . . funny thing . . . I never knew a man who could float a load of liquor, didn't hold all the cards besides. Now you take Flagg . . . he'll be here in fifteen minutes mebbe—mebbe two hours—but just the same as ever . . . thirsty as hell, wishing he had forty geisha girls to play with.

CHARMAINE. Fifteen minutes. . . .

FERGUSON (*with elaborate gestures*). Le Capitany . . . ici . . . sank . . . min-use ici, sank min-use . . . Compree?

CHARMAINE. *Oui, oui, oui! Merci bien.* (*She runs upstairs.* FERGUSON *continues smoking, pouring a pony of brandy. Presently the door at rear opens slowly. Enter* SERGEANT QUIRT *in a major's army overcoat, with black braids and a leather-visored garrison cap. He is shaven, crafty-faced. Below the overcoat, which is bursting on his chest, may be seen rough army shoes, gray woolen socks pulled over the bottoms of striped outing-flannel pajamas. He looks exactly what he is, a slightly wounded soldier escaped from hospital in borrowed clothes.* FERGUSON *turns, and seeing him, comes to attention.* QUIRT *also has a bottle with about half a drink in it.*)

FERGUSON (*rising courteously*). Good evening, Major.

QUIRT (*pours what remains in the bottle he carries into* FERGUSON'S *glass; then, taking the full bottle, sets his empty one in its place*). Sit down. Fergy, and use your eyes. Help me to get out of this rigging.

FERGUSON (*sitting; irritated*). What are you doing in those gadgets, Quirt? Where's the outfit? Where you been to?

QUIRT. Listen. I ain't writing my memoirs of this war till it's over. All you need to know is, I got two M.P.'s on my trail, and I don't want to meet 'em in these.

(*He removes his coat and is found to be in striped pajamas. A small red cross on the jumper pocket.*)

FERGUSON. You come from the lines in that outfit, Quirt? In night-drawers?

QUIRT. I suppose you think I go 'round this way because I like it. (*He stows the overcoat and cap under the bench.*) Major, you're relieved. (*Takes slicker from peg on stair rail.*) Lend me your slicker, Fergy, I'll give it back if it thunders.

(*He goes to chair at table, seizes the cognac, pours out two ponies and swallows them, looks at* FERGUSON, *then pours a third drink; drinks it.*)

FERGUSON. Of course you're paying for

those, Quirt, even if you have gone cuckoo.

QUIRT. All right, all right! Don't get on your ear about it . . . and now you want to know where I've been.

FERGUSON. Oh, no, if a soldier wants to campaign in a pair of night-drawers, it ain't none of my parade. It takes all kinds of sergeants to make an army.

QUIRT (*drinking his third*). You're too hard-hearted, Fergy. I ain't in my right mind. I was wounded, and now I've got aspasia. (*Mysteriously.*) My name is Field Marshal von Hindenburg, and I'm looking for a wagonload of pants that got lost in shipment.

FERGUSON. Yeah?

QUIRT. Yeah, sure. I wandered outta a hospital about five miles over at a place called Noisy. It was damned well named too, Fergy. Noisy was no name for it when I came outta the ether after I'd shipped in there with a piece of pants driven through a bullet hole in my leg.

FERGUSON. Have to give you ether to take off your pants?

QUIRT. No. They gave me ether so the stretcher bearers could steal a gold watch and eight hundred bucks off me. I certainly put up a squawk when I woke up and found 'em missing. But a hell of a lot of good it did me. I went looking for the bird that got them and ran into a guy in a bar-tender's coat in the operating room. He tried to pipe me down and I hung a shanty on the bimbo's eye. (*Enjoying the picture himself.*) And when they washed him off he was a captain. So they locked me up, wound and all. And then I got aspasia, and here I am. You ain't seen me.

FERGUSON. No, I ain't seen you. (*Distant voices shouting "Fergy!" "When do we eat?" "Chow," etc. At this sound, very faint,* QUIRT *rises quickly, starting for the stairs with a skip and jump.*) Keep your drawers on, Quirt. They ain't no M.P.'s. That's the outfit. I've got old Pete and his brother down at the bridge, keeping coffee and slum hot for 'em. Better go and give yourself up to Flagg as soon as he drives in. You'll be safe then. I'd like to see a set of doctors take Flagg's first sergeant off him when he's just out of the lines. It surely would be a pretty sight afterwards, them doctors working on each other like monkeys. (*The voices come nearer. The cry, long drawn out like a wolf's, comes from many throats: "Ch-o-o-o-w-w!"*) That's me. They're calling for me. Well, old Fergy's got their chow, and hot too.

(*He goes.* QUIRT *limps quickly to door after* FERGUSON *goes.* CHARMAINE *comes down the stairs at the same time.*)

QUIRT (*turning to find* CHARMAINE). Hello, Pittsburgh.

CHARMAINE (*with a small cry, comes toward him*). You are wounded.

QUIRT. Sure I'm wounded. Ain't that enough to put me nine miles ahead of Flagg with you? I certainly beat him here.

CHARMAINE (*trying to put arms around his neck*). *Mais, mais . . . you are . . .*

QUIRT (*restraining her*). Don't embarrass me, darling, because I ain't clothed and in my right mind. I just been waiting for Fergy to leave so I could steal a uniform from him. Where's his room? (CHARMAINE *points to door.*) Wait a minute, dearie, until I salvage a pair of breeches. (*He goes out.* CHARMAINE *goes to the outside door, where voices are now heard.* QUIRT *reappears.*) Damn it, he's locked his chest! Gimme a ice pick.

(QUIRT *takes bottle from bar. There are steps and voices at the door, and* QUIRT *withdraws hastily to the right,* CHARMAINE *following. Enter* KIPER, GOWDY, *and* LIPINSKY. KIPER *spies the cognac bottle and holds it over his open gullet. The other two rush him. There is a tough scuffle.*)

KIPER. Lay off my bottle.

GOWDY. Say, don't drink it all! (*All then sit behind the table and deliberately begin a tremendous racket.*)

KIPER. Hey! *Vin rouge! Vin blanc!* You, Pete! *Venez ici.* Toot sweet!

LIPINSKY. Toot sweet—toot sweet—toot God damn sweet—*jambon? Des oeufs! Fromages! Vin! Vin!*

GOWDY. *Bière, bière, bière!*

(FLAGG *enters. The three jump up and push back their chairs. When he yells "Clear out," the tumult instantly ceases.* FLAGG *is cold sober, still in his old clothes and dusty, but recently shaven, and possessed of rolled leggings and an old brown shirt.*)

FLAGG. Clear out, you yapping hounds and tell the new platoon commander to billet every man down the moment he finishes mess. Tell him I don't want to see one of 'em around this tavern till that's done. (*Turns; crosses to bar.*) Tell them not to rag a man to-night. (*Takes bottle; turns to them.*) As soon as they know their billets, let 'em out. Let 'em drink. Let 'em fight. Get out.

THE RUNNERS (*gently; somewhat discouraged*). Ay, ay, sir.

(*They disappear.* CHARMAINE *enters quietly and stands leaning in the doorway.* FLAGG *pours a beaker and drinks it pleasantly, enjoyingly. Then he pours a second and walks around to chair at table and sits down.* CHARMAINE *has watched this from the doorway. He sees her at last.*)

FLAGG (*arising and bowing grandiosely, holding aloft the drink*). *Madame la comtesse de la Cognac!*

CHARMAINE (*embarrassed*). *Le grand capitaine de ma cœur.*

FLAGG. Yes, I'm the captain of your heart! Like hell I am. Why don't you come and kiss me? None but the brave, you know . . .

CHARMAINE. *Je ne comprends pas.*

FLAGG. Oh, no. You don't understand me. Well, I'm a weary man, and I don't want any finnagelling from you.

CHARMAINE (*at door*). You want me to kiss you?

FLAGG. Sure I want you to kiss me. Even though you played the dirtiest sort of trick on me. (*The liquor is beginning to deaden him.*) A dirty trick on your poor old Captain Flagg. (*Turns to her.*) If I weren't so kind and gentle I'd go out in the orchard, cut a cherry switch, and give you a tanning.

(*She crosses over, kisses him quickly, and draws back, a charmed bird before a snake.*)

CHARMAINE. You're a terrible man, *monsieur.*

FLAGG. I ain't terrible to you, honey. Come sit by your old man. (*She sits on the table and looks down into his eyes.*) Ain't I tired? Jeez, but I'm off war for life. It's all right with thirty or forty men in the hills who know their business. But there's so many little boys along with me ain't got any business here at all. (*He sighs and drinks the rest of the brandy.*) Ah! There ain't no strength in this stuff any more. (*Hands her his glass, which she places on table. He gets up unsteadily.*) Le's go walk by the canal. I wanna get away from these new lieutenants. Le's walk along that bicycle path.

CHARMAINE. *Non, non, non. Demain soir. Demain soir.*

FLAGG. To-morrow? All right. I'm tired anyhow. Never been so tired before. Liquor just takes the pins out of my knees. Gimme a bottle to drink in bed. I don't want to think to-night.

CHARMAINE (*bringing him a bottle from the bar, smiling*). *Ah, monsieur, vous êtes un grand soldat.*

FLAGG (*wandering to the door, suddenly apathetic.*) Nighty, sweetie. See you tomorrow.

(*He goes out at rear.*)

QUIRT (*entering stealthily, in a farmer's smock which comes to his waist*). So he's gone away. . . . What's the matter with the old boy?

(*He attempts to kiss her. She shudders.*)

CHARMAINE (*drawing away from him*). *Non, non, non! Merci.*

QUIRT. Why, what's the matter, Pittsburgh? Don't you love me no more?

CHARMAINE. *Oui—mais*——

QUIRT. Of course I understand. Seeing him that way sort of cut you up, especially when I was wearing such a lousy outfit, you liking them all in uniforms. Just wait, baby. When I git that brass lock off Fergie's box and turn out in his blues on sick leave, you'll forget this Flagg person. I understand. Sure. I been with soldiers' girls a lot, myself.

CHARMAINE. When you are beautiful, *mon sergeant,* then I love you——

(*She runs up steps.*)

QUIRT. Come back here!

(*She disappears, laughing.* KIPER *and* LIPINSKY *enter.*)

KIPER. Jeez, Sergeant, but you picked a funny outfit to be buried in.

QUIRT (*at foot of stairs—hostile*). Who's thinking of burying me?

KIPER. I expect Flagg'll make me bury you. But he's going to lay you out himself.

QUIRT. Is he looking for me? How did he know I'm here?

LIPINSKY. We just heard Ferguson telling him. I ain't never heard him swear so much since I been with him. We came to ask you to run away some more.

QUIRT. You did, eh? Well, you can go down to the bridge and head him off. You can tell him he passed up visiting this place just before the outfit shoved last time. You can tell him if he comes up here I'll cut his gizzard out for him. You can tell him I'm engaged to be married, and I ain't got no duty for him around here.

(FLAGG *enters, drunk and swaggering.*)

FLAGG. Who's the hay-shaker? Well, if it ain't Sergeant Quirt! A regular family reunion. Quirt, how are you? When you coming back to the factory?

QUIRT. Flagg, you're out of this here detail. Your hands off my business after that dirty trick you put over on me. If I kill you there isn't a court can touch me for it in this man's army.

FLAGG. Quirt, you're drunk.

QUIRT. Both of us.

FLAGG. Yeah, both of us.

QUIRT. Well, then, Flagg, you're drunk. What are you going to do about it?

FLAGG. I'm gonna have a drink.

(*Turns to bar and takes bottle; pours two drinks.*)

QUIRT. Both of us.

FLAGG. Yeah, both of us. (*They drink, first bowing to each other.*) Quirt, I got something I want to tell you.

QUIRT. The hell!

FLAGG. You want to hear it?

QUIRT. I ain't particular.

FLAGG. Well, this is it, Sergeant. you can go jump in the canal. I knew you'd head for Charmaine as soon as you got that bullet under your hide. You had half a day's start of me and you didn't beat me more than five minutes. You might just as well 'a' stayed on the bakery route. You ain't no more needed here than a third leg on a kangaroo. Have one on me.

(FLAGG *pours for both.*)

QUIRT (*they bow*). Delighted, I'm sure. (*They drink and replace glasses.*) You're a hell of an officer, Flagg. (QUIRT *wipes right hand on smock.*) And your views on me probably ain't worth a damn. On the other hand, it's only fair to warn you that I'm the sole survivor of seven catastrophes, any one of which was calculated to carry off every man-jack in the immediate neighborhood as was adjacent, and if there was to be a catastrophe of any dimensions in this here vicinity in the near future, I have expectations of survival exceeding your own. Have one on me.

(QUIRT *pours drinks.*)

FLAGG. Thank you, Quirt, I will. (*They drink, and* FLAGG *drunkenly points finger at* QUIRT *until he can get his mind to working.*) Your method of expressing yourself, Quirt, is complicated by your tongue being as thick as your God damn head. But if you mean trouble, let me point out to you that among other things, you forgot to bring your gun along. (QUIRT *feels for his absent weapon;* FLAGG *laughs heartily.*) Ain't you a neat little fool, Hoppergrass, and will you drink?

QUIRT. I will.

(FLAGG *pours. Both bow, then drink again; but* QUIRT *has taken a sip before he realizes he hasn't bowed.*)

FLAGG. Do you give up?

QUIRT. No.

FLAGG (*turns to bar and starts pouring*). Have another.

(*As* FLAGG *starts to pour,* QUIRT *leaps like a flash on his back.* KIPER *catches* QUIRT'S *wrists from behind.* LIPINSKY *drags* FLAGG *away. When* QUIRT *jumps* FLAGG, *he takes the gun out of* FLAGG'S *holster with his right hand; his left is in strangle-hold around* FLAGG'S *neck.* FLAGG *reaches back and holds* QUIRT *by back of neck. They scuffle until separated.*)

KIPER (*holding* QUIRT). What do you want done with him, sir?

FLAGG (*to* LIPINSKY, *who is holding him*). Let me go or I'll knock you for a row of G.I. cans. Take the gun away from him.

(QUIRT *throws the automatic on the floor.* FLAGG *puts his foot on it.*) Let go, all. (QUIRT *is turned loose.*) Well, bo, had enough?

QUIRT. I'll tell you what I'll do with you. I'll go outside with you and try two of them little toys at fifty yards.

FLAGG. And you, the best pistol shot in the corps, would put one through my carburetor as easy as pitching a penny in a well. Come again.

QUIRT. I'll take you on any way you can think of, you baboon. I can out-shoot you and out-think you and out-drink you. There ain't nothing I can't do better than you.

FLAGG. You're a liar, Quirt, and you know it. I could break you in two. You got my gun because you jumped me without warning. No soldier you ever soldiered with could head me when I got started . . . and by the way, Quirt, if you can out-drink me you ain't leading out very well to-night. You're talking thick and wild, Quirt, thick and wild. You'd better turn in somewhere and sleep it off.

QUIRT. Me? Sleep off a couple of drinks? I was living on cognac when all your buttons was safety pins.

FLAGG. Yeah, well, you can't carry it the

way you used to, then. You're getting old, Quirt. Old and feeble. Yeah, you're getting old.

QUIRT. Not me. *You* may be an old man, Flagg. Or an old woman if it suits you better, but not me. Captains and generals, they pass along. I've seen hundreds of 'em. Better men than you, Flagg. They passed along. But top sergeants is eternal. They don't never die.

FLAGG. Well, if you don't want to die, you top sergeant, don't fool with me. I've seen top sergeants go damn fast— Now, listen, Quirt, are you going to jump in that canal or are you going to need six pall-bearers to take you there?

QUIRT. It'll take more than six pall-bearers to put me in one of these French canals. I don't like the taste of them.

(CHARMAINE *re-enters.*)

FLAGG. Charmaine! Cognac!

(CHARMAINE *crosses behind table; gets bottle; pours drink for* QUIRT, *also for* FLAGG.)

CHARMAINE (*laying a hand on the* CAPTAIN'S *shoulder*). Is it now—friends again?

FLAGG (*putting an arm about her*). Best you ever saw, Charmaine. We'll drink to it, Quirt. Flagg and Quirt forever—till you get bumped off. Flagg and Quirt, the tropical twins! There ain't room for both of 'em in the whole world!

(FLAGG *pats* CHARMAINE *on hip.*)

QUIRT (*sets down his glass, hard*). Damn you, Flagg!

FLAGG (*setting down his glass*). What's the matter, Hoppergrass? Aren't you drinking?

QUIRT. I got here first, Flagg.

FLAGG. I know it. Nobody said you didn't.

QUIRT (*rising*). You take your hands off Charmaine.

FLAGG. Any time you want my hands off Charmaine, you come and take 'em off.

CHARMAINE. No. No! You must be friends.

FLAGG. With you around!

QUIRT. It strikes me there's only room for one of us in this shanty to-night. Do you plan on going somewhere, or not?

FLAGG. Did you ever see me leaving any place I didn't feel like leaving?

CHARMAINE (*touching the* CAPTAIN'S *sleeve*). Don't fight—please.

FLAGG (*not looking at her—pushing her back*). The hell you say! First time in six months I've had a good reason for fighting. The Germans don't want my woman. I been fighting them for eight dollars a day. . . . Go on back of the counter.

CHARMAINE. I—I love you both.

QUIRT. You get to hell outta here, Flagg. Dig up a broad of your own.

FLAGG. Sorry. Rejected.

QUIRT. You ain't man enough to shoot me for her. Well, here's what I'll do. I'll shoot you dice for her. (*Tosses out dice on table.*) High dice, aces low. (KIPER *and* LIPINSKY *take steps forward, interested.*)

FLAGG. Boys, is Quirt crooked with the bones?

(LIPINSKY *goes back to lean on platform.*)

KIPER. He's got a pair ought to be in a circus. (QUIRT *gives Kiper a bad look.*)

FLAGG. Then we'll deal a hand at blackjack.

QUIRT (*picks up dice; puts them back in pocket, while* KIPER *goes back with* LIPINSKY). And the guy that loses beats it for somewhere else.

FLAGG. What do you mean, beats it? We'll shoot, but my way. The man that wins gets a gun, and the man that loses gets a head start. Everybody wins, see? One gets the girl and the other gets a chance to stay in bed the rest of this war.

KIPER. Captain Flagg, I don't think you ought to do this.

FLAGG. Close your hatch. I'll try anything once, soldier. (*Briskly.*) Now for a game of blackjack for one automatic.

QUIRT. That's all right with me.

FLAGG. And the gun on the table between us.

(*He picks it up.*)

KIPER (*as he and* LIPINSKY *seize* QUIRT'S *arms*). Come quiet now, before he notices.

QUIRT (*writhing loose*). Keep off me, you swine!

(KIPER *and* LIPINSKY *fall back.*)

FLAGG (*having recovered gun, starts to straighten up.*) March out that door, both of you, and if you stick a neck in here before the game's over I promise to wreck you for life. Are you going, or do I demonstrate? (*They go out quickly.*) Charmaine! Upstairs!

(*She goes.* FLAGG *sits at table;* QUIRT *on table.* FLAGG *shuffles cards, and offering them to* QUIRT, *says "Cut."* QUIRT *fondles cards; says "Be good to me, babies, and I'll let moonlight into a captain." He cuts.* FLAGG *deals one to* QUIRT, *then one to him-*

self; then one to QUIRT, *and looks at the next one for himself.*)

QUIRT. What's that, a king?

FLAGG. How many you want? Make it snappy and knock off that guff. Here's looking down your grave. May you have many worms, Quirt.

QUIRT. Crawling, right out of your teeth, Flagg. Hit me.

FLAGG (*deals a card face up.*) A two-spot. Well, any more?

QUIRT. Hit me again.

FLAGG (*dealing one*). Well, you got a king that time. Remember, if you hold six cards without going bust you can empty the automatic at me.

QUIRT. Hit me again.

FLAGG. A king, by God! (QUIRT, *with one sweep turns over the table, with candles and chairs, and dives through the door; runs off.*) You double-dealing Chinaman! (FLAGG *finds the gun in the darkness and fires shot just outside the door. He is heard re-entering.*) Show a light, somebody, Charmaine!

(FLAGG *sets up the table.*)

CHARMAINE (*at the head of the stairs with a lamp*). What is it? You have killed him?

(*Goes up to door.*)

FLAGG. Killed hell! He knocked out the light and ran, the dirty hound! (CHARMAINE *looks out the door, shielding the lamp from the wind.*) Oh, he's gone.

CHARMAINE. Maybe you hit him.

(*Puts lamp on table; then crosses to* FLAGG.)

FLAGG. Don't you worry. He was halfway to the river, the rate he was going, before I found the door. Don't you weep, sweetheart. (*Puts her on his left knee.*) You're weeping for a skunk that'd run out on a game of cards. It's you and me to-night, lady. Listen, Charmaine. (*Putting his arm around her.*) I love you like the devil. I always did. You love me, Charmaine?

CHARMAINE. Only you.

FLAGG. God, I'm dead—I'm going to sleep for three days.

(FLAGG *rests head on her breast and sighs. Then* LIPINSKY *and* GOWDY *walk in.*)

LIPINSKY. Sorry to disturb you, sir.

FLAGG. My God, did you hear what I told you?

LIPINSKY. Got bad news, Captain Flagg.

FLAGG. Spit it out.

LIPINSKY. The outfit's going back. Battalion moving at once.

FLAGG. What? What?

LIPINSKY. We're ordered back. Ordered back in. Everybody's going back in. General movement.

FLAGG. Dammit, I'm on leave.

GOWDY. All leaves revoked, Captain Flagg.

FLAGG. Well, why couldn't you stay away from here? You knew where I was. Why in hell did you have to come and tell me?

GOWDY. Well, headquarters sent out, looking for you.

LIPINSKY. Kiper wouldn't come, Captain Flagg. He was for leaving you alone.

FLAGG. He was, was he? Well, Kiper's got sense. Look here, you never found me to give me the message, and I'm not going. Can you remember, or have I got to bury you to keep your mouth shut? What right have they got to offer a man leave and then revoke it? I gave them their prisoner! I've got their damn papers!

LIPINSKY. Well, you see, the company's going to shove off. What could we do?

FLAGG. You could have an attack of something, damn it to hell! You could fall and break your neck on the way here.

LIPINSKY. I was afraid not to let you know. You always wanted to know.

FLAGG. Well, you've got to do some tall lying to make up for it, because I'm not going. Tell them any story you think of, only I never got the news. I earned my leave, and it's signed, sealed, and delivered. That crowd at headquarters has got to live up to its end of the bargain. They can't take these men back in. I won't stand for it. (*Turns to* CHARMAINE.) Shall we stay here, Charmaine?

CHARMAINE. *Oui, ici.*

(*They embrace.* FLAGG *rests head on her breast.*)

FLAGG (*after a pause, shakes himself a bit*). No, I'll go. I may be drunk, but I know I'll go. There's something rotten about this profession of arms, some kind of damned religion connected with it that you can't shake. When they tell you to die, you have to do it, even if you're a better man than they are. Good-bye, Charmaine, put your money in real estate, and marry that cuckoo if you can. You'll never see me again. This town is a jinx for me. (*Again rests head on* CHARMAINE.) God Almighty, but I'm tired. (*He rises and crosses to where* FERGUSON *has entered.* CHARMAINE *sits in chair watching.*) Hello, Fergy. We're shoving off. Follow us, because we don't know where we're going. Nobody knows.

(*He goes out, staggering, tired.* FERGUSON *follows him out.* GOWDY *and* LIPINSKY *follow* FERGUSON. CHARMAINE *buries her head in arms on table.*)

QUIRT (*comes in upper floor stairway*). Hello, Pittsburgh!

CHARMAINE. You are not *killed?*

QUIRT (*coming downstairs to bottom step*). No. It's me all right. Everybody gone?

CHARMAINE. Everybody.

QUIRT. Outfit's going in again, huh?

CHARMAINE. *Oui.*

QUIRT. Well, well! I been upstairs. Climbed up the kitchen roof. Do you love your papa?

CHARMAINE. *Mais oui.*

QUIRT. Then you better kiss him goodbye. (*Pats her face; then kisses her. Staggers up to door.*) What a lot of God damn fools it takes to make a war! Hey, Flagg, wait for baby!

(CHARMAINE *watches from the table.*)

CURTAIN

THOSE who were impressed with the expression of a "new" morality in *They Knew What They Wanted* (1924) placed the emphasis on what least impressed the author himself. He claimed only to have retold the Paolo and Francesca story in the terms of a specifically contemporary environment and set of circumstances. Much of the attractiveness of this Pulitzer Prize drama stems from the limited extent of its author's aims. The higher his ambitions might have carried him, the more he might have tried to make progressive generalizations out of his particulars, the more factitious the play would have become. This is equally true of *Ned McCobb's Daughter* (1926), *Lucky Sam McCarver* (1925), *The Late Christopher Bean, Dodsworth,* and *Yellowjack*. He restrained himself even in his thesis drama *The Silver Cord* (1926) and in the rebellious play *Alien Corn* (1933). If Howard's preference for letting life speak for itself led at times to flatness and to an unsoaring kind of playwriting, it nevertheless gave his work considerable conviction and plain humanity. The adjectives "solid" and "sound" are apt to crop up in descriptions of his best writing. He himself claimed only a modest role for playwriting, maintaining that the merit of a play lay in its providing good parts for acting rather than in distinction of content or writing. Contending that playwrights were, in a sense, vicarious actors, he even doubted that many men of literary genius had written dramas. Consequently he tended to look upon himself as a journeyman of the theatre and did journeyman's work on a good deal of writing not original with him.

It should be noted, however, that even without using bold brush strokes, Howard managed to give considerable color to his canvas of common humanity. He had an ear for the individual and local idiom of his characters and an eye for distinguishing marks of personality. The specificity that he favored led him to always place his characters in some well-defined environment; in the grape-growing areas of California with their mixed population (*They Knew What They Wanted*), in Yankee Maine (*Ned McCobb's Daughter*), in the nightclub and business world of New York (*Lucky Sam McCarver*), for example. Without its highly colored environment and *dramatis personae, They Knew What They Wanted* would have had to rest on its argument and would have been no better, if no worse, than any ordinary problem play.

Sidney Howard was born in Oakland, California in 1891, was graduated from the University of California in 1915, and spent a year in Switzerland. He joined Professor Baker's playwriting class at Harvard in 1916 but left Workshop 47 to serve as an ambulance driver on the Salonika front. Transferred to the American air force in France, he advanced in rank rapidly enough to command a squadron before the war ended. He turned professional playwright only after proving himself a reliable reporter on such matters as narcotics rings, a coal miners' strike, and the then prevalent system of placing spies in labor unions, a subject he also treated in his book *The Labor Spy*. Perhaps it is to this apprenticeship that we may attribute his meticulous attention to detail, his ease and naturalness, and his clear play structure. His first play, *Swords* (1921), was a romantic drama and a failure, but in time, he became the most reliable of our playwrights, and he left well over twenty plays when he died in an accident in 1939.

Among these were a number of adaptations of foreign drama, such as *S.S. Tenacity* and *Michel Auclair* (by Charles Vildrac), *Morals* (by Ludwig Thoma), *The Last Night of Don Juan* (by Edmond Rostand) in 1925 for the Provincetown Players, and the highly successful comedy *The Late Christopher Bean* (by René Fauchois), 1932. His skill in fashioning plays out of non-fiction and fiction gave us the "yellow fever" drama *Yellowjack,* based on a chapter in Paul de Kruif's *Microbe Hunters* (written in 1928, first produced in 1934) and *Dodsworth,* a dramatization of the novel by Sinclair Lewis, 1934. His most impressive original work, however, belonged entirely to the nineteen twenties.

They Knew What They Wanted

BY SIDNEY HOWARD

First produced at the Garrick Theatre, New York City, by the Theatre Guild, on November 24, 1924, with the following cast:

JOE .... Glenn Anders
FATHER McKEE .... Charles Kennedy
AH GEE .... Allen Atwell
TONY .... Richard Bennett
THE R.F.D. .... Robert Cook
AMY .... Pauline Lord
ANGELO .... Hardwick Nevin
GIORGIO .... Jacob Zollinger
THE DOCTOR .... Charles Tazewell
FIRST ITALIAN MOTHER .... Frances Hyde
HER DAUGHTER .... Antoinette Bizzoco
SECOND ITALIAN MOTHER .... Peggy Conway
HER SON .... Edward Rosenfeld

Tony's farmhouse in the Napa Valley, California.

ACT I

Morning, in early summer.

ACT II

Evening. Same day.

ACT III

Three months later.

SCENE.—*The scene of the play is the home of an Italian winegrower in the Napa Valley in California. All of the action takes place in the main downstairs room which serves as general living and dining room.*

It is necessary to understand that the house is not in the least Spanish in its architecture. As a matter of fact, it would serve any respectable Middle-Western farmer as a fitting and inconspicuous residence. It was built in the 'nineties of wood, is painted white on its exterior, and has only one story.

A door at the back, the main one to the outer world, gives on the porch. Another door, to the right of the audience, gives on the kitchen. The kitchen is three steps above the level of the room and so placed that the audience can see into it. It is completely furnished. A third door, to the left of the audience, gives on a flight of steps which leads to the cellar of the house. A fourth door, also on the left and farther down stage, gives on the bedroom.

The back wall should also be broken by windows; on the right of the central door, a bay window, on the left, a double flat window.

The view from the house is over a valley and toward brown Californian hills. The landscape is checkered with cultivation. Some of the checkers are orchards. Most of them are vineyards. The foreground is all vines. Vines twine about the pillars of the porch. In the beginning of the play—it begins in summer—the grapes on the porch vines are small and green. In the last act—three months having elapsed—they are large and purple.

The back stage must be so arranged that people who approach the house from the highroad appear to mount the porch steps from a much lower level. At other times, however, it is required that the characters be able to go and come on the level of the house itself where the farmyard is.

Inside the room the wallpaper and the carpet are new and garish. The cheapest variety of lace curtains hangs in the windows. The furniture is new and includes a golden-oak dining table with chairs to match, a morris chair, another easy chair, a chest of drawers, a sideboard, a hat rack.

On one wall hangs a picture of Garibaldi. A picture of George Washington hangs over the central door. Other mural decorations include a poster of the Navigazione Generale Italiana, a still-life chromo, a religious chromo, and a small mirror.

On the hat rack hangs a double-barrelled shotgun draped with a loaded cartridge belt.

The whole impression must be one of gaiety and simple good living.

ACT ONE

The red, white and green of Italy combine with the red, white and blue of these United States in bunting, garlands of fluted paper, pompons and plumes of shredded tissue, to make up a scheme of decoration which is, to say the least, violent. The picture of Garibaldi is draped with an American flag, the picture of Washington with an Italian flag. The full glare of the early morning sun streams in through door and windows.

The room is fairly littered with boxes. Atop one of these, from which it has just been extracted, stands a handsome wedding cake, surmounted by statuary representing the ideal bride and groom in full regalia under a bell. The boxes are all addressed to

Tony Patucci,
R. F. D. Napa, Calif.

AH GEE *stands on a ladder on the porch outside the open entrance door, hanging Chinese lanterns. He is a silent, spare Chinaman, of age maturely indeterminate. He wears blue overalls and a black chambray shirt.*

JOE—*dark, sloppy, beautiful, and young—is busy opening a packing case in the center of the stage. His back is turned upon the door.*

JOE (*as he works, he half sings, half mutters to himself the words of "Remember," an I. W. W. song, to the tune of "Hold the Fort"*).
"We speak to you from jail to-day,
Two hundred union men,
We're here because the bosses' laws
Bring slavery again."

Through this the curtain rises and FATHER MC KEE *is seen climbing the porch steps. He wears the sober garb of a Catholic priest, not over clean, what with dust, spots, and all. He nods to* AH GEE *and comes into the doorway. He stands a moment to mop his large, pale face with a red bandana. Then he lowers lugubrious disapproval upon everything in sight. Then he yawns.*

He is one of those clerics who can never mention anything except to denounce it. And his technique of denunciation is quite special to himself. It consists in a long, throaty abstention from inflection of any kind which culminates in a vocal explosion when he reaches the accented syllable of a word upon which his emphasis depends. This word always seems to wake him up for an instant. Once it is spoken, however, he relapses into semi-somnolence for the remainder of his remarks. At heart, he is genial and kindly enough, quite the American counterpart of the French village curé.

FATHER MC KEE. Hello, Joe.

JOE. Hello there, Padre. What do you think?

FATHER MC KEE. Looks to me like a bawdy house.

JOE. It's goin' to be *some* festa. . . . Lily Cups! What do you know about that for style?

FATHER MC KEE. Where's Tony?

JOE (*nods toward the door of the bedroom*). In there gettin' dolled up. . . . Hey, there, bridegroom! The Padre's out here.

FATHER MC KEE. I come up to have a serious talk with Tony.

JOE. Well, for God's sake, don't get him upset no more'n what he is already. He's been stallin' around all mornin', afraid to go down and meet the bride. You better leave him alone.

FATHER MC KEE. I'm always glad to have your advice, Joe. I didn't look to find you still hangin' 'round.

JOE. Oh, didn't you, Padre?

FATHER MC KEE. Tony told me you'd decided to go away.

JOE. Well, Padre, I'll tell you how it is. (*He grins impudently.*) I don't believe in stayin' any one place too long. 'Tain't fair for me not to give the rest of California a chance at my society. But I ain't goin' before I seen all the fun, got Tony safely married, an' kissed the bride. (*He turns to the door and* AH GEE.) That's fine, Ah Gee. Better take these here Lily Cups in the kitchen when you get through.

(*Magnificently* TONY *enters from the bedroom. He is stout, floridly bronzed, sixty years old, vigorous, jovial, simple, and excitable. His great gift is for gesture. To-day we meet him in his Sunday best, a very brilliant purple suit with a more than oriental waistcoat which serves to display a stupendous gold watch chain. He wears a boiled shirt, an emerald-green tie, and a derby hat. He carries his new patent-leather shoes in his hand. He seems to be perspiring rather freely.*)

TONY. Looka me! I'm da most stylish fella in da world.

FATHER MC KEE. I come up to talk to you, Tony.

TONY. I'm glad you come, Padre. How you like my clothes, eh? Costa playnta good money! (*Attention is called to the shoes.*) For da feet. . . .

JOE (*a motion to the wedding cake*). How's it strike you, Tony?

TONY. Madonna! (*He throws his shoes into the morris chair. His hat assumes a terrific angle. He cannot keep his hands off that cake.*) Look, Padre! From Frisco! Special! Twelve dollar' an' two bits! Look! (*The miniature bride and groom particularly please him.*) Ees Tony an' his Amy!

JOE. Them lanterns is Ah Gee's personal donation.

TONY. Thank you, Ah Gee! Ees verra fine. Ah Gee, you go an' bring vino, now, for Padre, eh? (AH GEE *obeys the order, taking the Lily Cups with him into his kitchen.*)

JOE. Show some speed now, Tony. It's past nine. 'Tain't hardly pretty to keep the bride waitin'.

TONY (*as he sits down to the struggle with his shoes*). I'm goin' verra quick.

FATHER MC KEE. I got to have a word with you, Tony, before you go to the station.

JOE. The Padre's been tryin' to tell me you're scared to have me around where I can kiss the bride. (*He picks up a couple of flags and goes outside.*)

TONY (*in undisguised terror*). You ain't goin' be kissin' no bride, Joe. You hear dat?

JOE (*off stage he is heard singing*).

"We laugh and sing, we have no fear
  Our hearts are always light,
We know that every Wobbly true
  Will carry on the fight."

TONY. He's too goddam fresh, dat fella, with kissin' my Amy an' all dose goddam Wobbly songs. Don' you think so, Padre?

FATHER MC KEE. I didn't come up here to talk about Joe, Tony. I come up to talk about this here weddin'.

TONY. I'm glad you come, Padre. I'm verra bad scare'.

FATHER MC KEE. You got good reason for bein' scared, if you want to know what *I* think.

TONY. I got verra special reason.

FATHER MC KEE. What reason?

TONY. Don't you never mind! Da's my secret dat I don' tell nobody. You tell Joe he go away quick, Padre. Den, maybe, ees all right.

FATHER MC KEE. So that's it! Well, I don't blame you for that.

TONY (*deeply indignant at the implication*). Oh! . . . No, by God! You don' ondrastan', Padre. Joe is like my own son to me! Ees som'-thing verra different. Madonna mia! Ees som'thing I been doin' myself! Ees som'thing Tony's been doin' w'at's goin' mak' verra bad trouble for Tony.

FATHER MC KEE. I'll tell Joe nothin'. You've made your own bed and if you won't get off it while there's time, you got to lie on it. But I want you to understand that I don't like nothin' 'bout this here weddin'. It ain't got my approval.

TONY (*the first shoe slips on and he sits up in amazement*). You don't like weddin', Padre?

FATHER MC KEE. No, I don't. An' that's just what I come up here to tell you. I don't like nothin' about it, an' if you persist in goin' ahead in spite of my advice, I don't want you sayin' afterwards that you wasn't warned.

TONY. Dio mio! (*He amplifies this with the sign of the cross. Then his confidence rather returns to him.*) Aw . . . tak' a pinch-a snuff! You mak' me tire', Padre! You think festa is no good for people. You padre fellas don' know nothing. Work! Work! Work evra day! Den, by-an'-by, is comin' festa. After festa workin' is more easy. (*He resumes the shoe problem.*)

FATHER MC KEE. Tony, you know perfectly well that I ain't got no more objection to no festa than I have to any other pomp of the flesh. But I'm your spirichool adviser an' I been mullin' this weddin' over in my mind an' I come to the conclusion that I'm agin it. I don't like it at all. I got my reasons for what I say.

TONY (*does the Padre guess his secret?*). W'at reason you got?

FATHER MC KEE. In the first place, you ain't got no business marryin' no woman who ain't a good Cath'lic.

TONY (*immeasurable relief*). Ees no matter.

FATHER MC KEE. A mixed marriage ain't no better'n plain livin' in sin.

TONY. Ain' we got you for keep' sin away, Padre?

FATHER MC KEE. Why ain't you marryin' a woman out of your own parish instead of trapesin' all the way to Frisco to pick out a heretic?

TONY. Is no good womans in dees parish.

FATHER MC KEE. What's wrong with 'em?

TONY. Joe is sleepin' with evra one.

FATHER MC KEE. That ain't the point.

TONY (*enlisting the shoe to help his gesticulation*). Oh, ees point all right, Padre. Joe is told me 'bout evrathing. I been lookin' all 'round here at all da womans in dees parish. I been lookin' evra place for twent' mile. Ees no good womans for wife here. Joe is told me 'bout evra one. Den I'm gone to Napa for look all 'round dere an' in Napa ees no better . . . ees just da same like here. So den I go down all da way to Frisco for look after wife an' I find my Amy. She is like a rose, all wilt'. You puttin' water on her an' she come out most beautiful. I'm goin' marry with my Amy, Padre, an' I don' marry with nobody else. She's been tellin' me she is no Cath'lic. I say, w'at I care? By an' by, maybe, if we bein' patient, we bringin' her in da church, an' showin' her da candles and da Madonna, all fix up good with flowers and da big tin heart, an' evrathing smellin' so prett' an' you preachin' verra loud an' da music an' evrathing, maybe . . . by an' by . . . (*He turns again to his shoe.*) But now ees no mater. W'at I care?

FATHER MC KEE. It don't look good to me.

TONY. Ees all right. . . . If you don't want my Amy an' me gettin' married with good Cath'lic priest like you, den, by God—

FATHER MC KEE. I ain't said I wouldn't marry you.

TONY. Eh bene!

FATHER MC KEE. I'm only tryin' to tell you. . .

TONY. Ahi! Dio mio. . . . (*The shoe goes on, producing intense pain.*) He look much better as he feel!

FATHER MC KEE. There ain't no good in no old man marryin' with no young woman.

TONY. You think anybody marry with old woman? Tak' a pinch-a snuff!

FATHER MC KEE. I know one old man who married a young woman an' she carried on with a stage driver!

TONY. Dio mio!

FATHER MC KEE. He had knowed her all her life, too, an' you ain't knowed your Amy more'n 'bout five minutes.

TONY. Ees no matter.

FATHER MC KEE. An' I know another fellow who married one of them city girls like your Amy without bein' properly acquainted an' she turned out to be a scarlet woman.

TONY. My Amy don' do dat.

(AH GEE *enters from kitchen with two glasses and a bottle of wine.*)

FATHER MC KEE. Ain't you just now been tellin' me you're scared of her seein' Joe?

TONY. No, by God!

FATHER MC KEE. Joe ain't the only young fellow around, either!

TONY. Young fellas is no matter. Only Joe. An' I ain' scare' over Joe excep' for special reason. You tell Joe, Padre . . . (*He is returning to his old subject, but the wine distracts him.*) Ah-h-h!

FATHER MC KEE. Why didn't you get married forty years ago?

TONY. I think you know verra good w'y. Ees because I'm no dam' fool. . . . W'en I'm young, I got nothing. I'm broke all da time, you remember? I got no money for havin' wife. I don' want no wife for mak' her work all da time. Da's no good, dat. Da's mak' her no more young, no more prett'. Evrabody say Tony is crazy for no' havin' wife. I say Tony is no dam' fool. W'at is happen? Pro'ibish' is com'. Salute! (*A glass of wine.* AH GEE *has returned to his kitchen.*) An' wat I say? I say, "Ees dam' fool law. Ees dam' fool fellas for bein' scare' an' pullin' up da grape' for tryin' growin' som'thing different." W'at I'm doin'? I'm keep the grape, eh? I say, "I come in dees country for growin' da grape! God mak' dees country for growin' da grape! Ees not for pro'ibish' God mak' dees country. Ees for growin' da grape!" Ees true? Sure ees true! (*Another glass of wine.*) An' w'at happen? Before pro'ibish' I sell my grape' for ten, maybe twelve dollar da ton. Now I sell my grape' some'time one hundra dollar' da ton. Pro'ibish' is mak' me verra rich. (*Another glass of wine.*) I got my fine house. I got Joe for bein' foreman. I got two men for helpin' Joe. I got one Chink for cook. I got one Ford car. I got all I want, evrathing, excep' only wife. Now I'm goin' have wife. Verra nice an' young an' fat. Not for work. No! For sit an' holdin' da hands and havin' kids. Three kids. (*He demonstrates the altitude of each.*) Antonio . . . Giuseppe . . . Anna . . . Da's like trees an' cows an' all good people. Da's fine for God an' evrabody! I tell you, Padre, Tony know w'at he want!

FATHER MC KEE. Whatever made you think a man of your age could have children? (*This staggers* TONY.) I tell you, Tony, it ain't possible.

TONY. Eh? Tony is too old for havin' kids? I tell you, Tony can have twent' kids if he want! I tell you Tony can have kids w'en he is one hundra year' old. Dio mio! From da sole of his feet to da top of his hat, Tony is big, strong man! I think I ondrastan' you verra good, Padre. Tony is not too old for havin' kids. He's too rich, eh? (*This rather strikes home.*) Yah! Tony is rich an', if he don' have no kids, den da church is gettin' all Tony's money an' da Padre is gettin' Tony's fine house all fix' up good for livin' in, eh?

FATHER MC KEE (*a very severe shepherd*). Tony!

TONY (*the horns of the devil with his fingers*). Don' you go for puttin' no evil eye on Tony an' his Amy!

FATHER MC KEE. You're givin' way to ignorant superstition, which ain't right in no good Cath'lic.

TONY (*on his feet in a panic*). Dio mio! My Amy is comin' on dat train an' here you keep me, sittin', talkin'. . . .

FATHER MC KEE. You irreverent old lunatic, you, if you're bent on marryin', I'll marry you. (JOE *reappears in the doorway.*) But I don't want you comin' around afterwards squawkin' about it.

TONY. Eh, Joe! Da Padre don't want me gettin' marry with my Amy because he's scare' da church don' never get my money!

JOE. For cripe's sake, Tony, ain't you heard that whistle?

TONY. I go! I go!

JOE. Train's in now.

TONY. Porco Dio! Ah Gee!

JOE. Fix your tie.

TONY. I fix. . . . (AH GEE *comes from the kitchen for his master's order.*) Un altro fiasco. (AH GEE *returns to the kitchen.*)

JOE. You won't make no hit if you're drunk, Tony.

TONY. Not drunk, Joe. Only scare'. Verra bad scare'.

JOE. Bridegrooms is always scared.

TONY. Jes' Chris', maybe I'm sick!

JOE. No!

TONY. Santa Maria, I *am* sick!

JOE. What's wrong with you?

TONY. I don' know! I'm sick! I'm sick! I'm sick!

(AH GEE *returns with the wine bottle refilled.* TONY *seeks prompt solace.* AH GEE *goes back to his kitchen.*)

JOE. You'll be a helluva sight sicker if you don't lay off that stuff.

TONY. I canno' go for get my Amy, Joe. I canno' go. . . .

JOE. All right. I'll go . . .

TONY. Oh, by God! No! NO!

JOE. Tony, if you drive the Ford down the hill in this state of mind you'll break your dam' neck.

TONY (*more solace*). I feel good now. I drive fine. I don' want nobody for go for my Amy but only me. . . . (*Then he weakens again.*) Joe, I'm scare', I'm scare', I'm scare'!

JOE. What you scared of, Tony?

TONY. Maybe my Amy . . .

JOE. Come on, beat it!

TONY. I feel good now an' I don' want nobody for go for my Amy but only me. You bet! (*He starts.*)

JOE. That's the boy!

TONY (*another relapse*). Joe, you don't get mad if I ask you som'thing? I got verra good reason, Joe . . . Joe . . . how soon you goin' away, Joe?

JOE. You don't *want* me to go, do you?

TONY. I think ees much better.

JOS. What's the idea, Tony?

TONY. Joe . . . som'thing is happen', da's all. . . . You go, Joe. I been tryin' for three days for ask you dees, Joe, an' I been scare' you get mad. I pay you double extra for goin' to-day, for goin' now, eh? Joe? Verra quick?

JOE. An' miss the festa? Like hell!

TONY. Joe, you don' ondrastan'. . . .

JOE. Forget it, Tony.

TONY. Joe . . .

JOE. If you keep her waitin', she'll go back to Frisco.

TONY. Dio Mio! (*He goes to the door and turns yet once again.*) Joe . . . ? (*He catches* FATHER MC KEE'S *eye.*) Som'thing verra bad is goin' happen with Tony. . . . Clean evrathing clean before my Amy come. (*He is really gone.* JOE *follows him out and stands on the porch looking after him. A Ford motor roars and dies away into high speed.*)

FATHER MC KEE (*at the window*). Look at him!

JOE. He could drive the Ford in his sleep.

FATHER MC KEE. I don't hold with no old man gallivantin'.

JOE. Don't you fret, Padre. Didn't I tell you not to get him all worked up? (*This ruffles the good priest who makes to follow* TONY. JOE *intercepts him and forces him back into the room.*)

FATHER MC KEE. Well?

JOE. Sit down a minute. You been tellin' Tony what you think. Now I got some tellin' to do.

FATHER MC KEE. Have you, indeed? Well, I don't see no good—

JOE. Maybe *I* don't see much good, but what the hell!

FATHER MC KEE. Young man! That's the pernicious doctrine of Lacey Fairey.

JOE. What's that?

FATHER MC KEE. A French expression meanin' "Sufficient unto the day."

JOE. What of it? If folks is bent on makin' mistakes, an' you can't stop 'em, let 'em go ahead, that's what I say. I don't want nobody hatin' my guts for bein' too dam' right all the time, see? Not bein' a priest, I aim to get along with folks. That way, when they're in wrong, I can be some use.

FATHER MC KEE. That ain't in accord with the teachin's of Jesus!

JOE. A helluva lot you an' me know about the teachin's of Jesus.

FATHER MC KEE. Joe, if you ain't goin' to be rev'rent . . .

JOE. I'm talkin' now.

FATHER MC KEE. Oh, are you?

JOE. Yeah. I wouldn't have no harm come to Tony, not for anything in the world, see? An' I been agitatin' against this weddin' a lot longer'n you have an' I know what it's all about, see? I'm here goin' on five months, now, an' that's longer'n I ever stayed any one place.

FATHER MC KEE. Is it?

JOE. Excep' once in jail, it is. An' I been lookin' after Tony all the time since I come here. I come in to bum a meal an' I stayed five months. Five months I been workin' for Tony an' lookin' after him and he's treated me dam' good an' that's God's truth. I wouldn't have worked that long for him if he hadn't treated me dam' good, either. I ain't none too strong for stayin' put, you know. I like to move an' now I'm goin' to move. I'm what the papers call a "unskilled migratory" an' I got to migrate, see? Tony wants me to go an' I want to go. But, what I want to know is: who's goin' to look after Tony when I'm gone?

FATHER MC KEE. Ain't that his wife's place?

JOE. Sure it's his wife's place. But suppose this weddin' don't turn out so good? Are you goin' to look out for him?

FATHER MC KEE. Ain't Tony my spirichool charge an' responsibility?

JOE. All *right!* An' I ain't so sure you're goin' to have much trouble, either. Amy looks to me like a fair to middlin' smart kid an' she knows what she's in for, too.

FATHER MC KEE. You seem to be well informed, Joe! Do you happen to know the lady?

JOE. I ain't never laid eyes on her. (*Then the implication percolates.*) Oh, I may go chasin' women plenty, but I don't chase Tony's wife, see? An' I ain't fixin' to, neither. Just get that straight.

FATHER MC KEE. I'm glad to hear it, Joe.

JOE. But I happen to know about her. Didn't I have to write all Tony's letters for him? You wouldn't expect Tony to be writin' to no lady with *his* education, would you?

FATHER MC KEE. No, I can't say that I would.

JOE. Why, I even had to read him the letters she wrote back. That's how I got my dope. An' what I say is: she's got plenty of sense. Don't you fool yourself she hasn't. I'll show you. (*He goes to the chest of drawers for some letters and photographs. He brings them back to the* PADRE.) You can see for yourself. (*And he submits Exhibit A—a letter.*) Tony goes to Frisco lookin' for a wife, see? The nut! An' he finds Amy waitin' on table in a spaghetti joint. Joint's called "Il Trovatore." Can you beat it? He ain't even got the nerve to speak to her. He don't even go back to see her again. He just falls for her, gets her name from the boss an' comes home an' makes me write her a letter proposin' marriage. That's her answer.

FATHER MC KEE. It's good clear writin'. It's a good letter. It looks like she's got more character'n what I thought. But, just the same, it ain't no way to conduct a courtship.

JOE. There's worse ways.

FATHER MC KEE. She says she likes the letter you wrote.

JOE. The second time I wrote, I told her all about the farm an' just how she was goin' to be fixed. Oh, I was careful not to say nothin' about Tony's money. Only the Ford. I thought she ought to know about the Ford. (*He hands the second letter over.*) An' she wrote this one back.

FATHER MC KEE. She likes the country, does she? She wants Tony's photo.

JOE. Say, you ought to have seen Tony gettin' his face shot! By God! It took me a whole week to talk him into it. An' when I did get him down there—you know that place across from the depot?—dam' if he wasn' scared right out of his pants!

FATHER MC KEE. By what?

JOE. By the camera! Would you believe it? We had to clamp him into the chair, both of us, the photographer an' me! You ought to have seen the wop sweat! And when we try to point the machine at him, he gives a yell you could hear a block an' runs right out in the street!

FATHER MC KEE. No!

JOE. I couldn't get him back, only I promised to let the guy shoot me first. They was some pictures! Tony's (*He hands a specimen to the* PADRE.) sure looks like him, but she must have seen somethin' in it, because she sent hers right back. (*He studies* AMY's *photograph for a moment before submitting it.*) Here. Not bad, huh?

FATHER MC KEE (*a long and very pleased contemplation*). There ain't no explainin' women! (*He returns the photograph.*) Do you think she's straight, Joe?

JOE. What the hell! If she ain't, she wants to be. That's the main thing.

FATHER MC KEE. Maybe it won't turn out so bad, after all. There's always this about life: no man don't never get everything he sets out to get, but half the time he don't never find out he ain't got it.

JOE. Oh, if you're goin' off on that tack!

FATHER MC KEE. It's the tack life travels on, with the help of Almighty God.

JOE. What the hell! Life ain't so bad.

FATHER MC KEE. I'm delighted to hear you say so!

JOE (*he has returned the exhibits to the drawer*). I never put over anything half so good myself!

FATHER MC KEE. Do you think Tony's goin' to put it over?

JOE. Wait and see.

FATHER MC KEE. Well, I don't know how I can approve of this weddin', but I'm willin' to give it the benefit of my sanction an' do all I can to help it along an' look out for Tony. Does that satisfy you? . . . Just the same, I don't believe in unnecessary chances, Joe. Pull along out of here like Tony asked you to.

JOE. Say, you make me sore! Why, anybody 'ud think, to hear you talk, that I'm all set to . . .

(*The* R. F. D. *has appeared on the porch. He carries a dusty coat on his arm, and wipes the sweat from his brow with his blue handkerchief. He wears a gray flannel shirt, old trousers hitched to suspenders that are none too secure. His badge is his only sign of office. He is an eager, tobacco-chewing old countryman*).

THE R. F. D. Hey, Tony! Tony! (*As he reaches the door.*) Where's Tony? 'Mornin', Padre.

JOE. Tony's gone to town. You're early.

THE R. F. D. That's more'n Tony is. I got to get his signature on a piece of registered mail.

JOE. What is it?

THE R. F. D. It's his wife. (JOE *and the* PRIEST *rise astonished.*) Sure! I got her outside in the buckboard an' she's madder'n hell because Tony didn't meet her. She's some girl, too. I never heard the beat! Lands a girl like that an' don't even take the trouble to— (*The other two are already at the windows.*)

JOE. Where'd *you* find her?

THE R. F. D. I finds her pacin' up and down the platform an' I gives her a lift. I sure do hate to see a good-lookin' girl cry—an' she sure was cryin'. I reckoned Tony couldn't get the Ford started so—

FATHER MC KEE. He went down all right. I wonder what happened to him?

JOE. He must have took the short cut.

FATHER MC KEE. Didn't you pass him?

JOE. I knew I ought to have went instead.

FATHER MC KEE. He wasn't in no condition.

THE R. F. D. I'll have a look on my way back.

JOE. What are *we* goin' do to with her?

THE R. F. D. Ask her in.

JOE. Ah Gee! (*He goes out, calling.*) Giorgio! Angelo! (THE R. F. D. *follows him.* AH GEE *comes from his kitchen and evinces some confusion, but does not hold back from the summons.* FATHER MC KEE *arranges his costume and goes out last. The stage remains empty for a moment. A babble of voices is heard, voices that speak both English and Italian.* JOE *is heard shouting.*) Lend a hand with that trunk!

AMY'S VOICE. How do you do? I'm pleased to meet you. I certainly had some time getting here. I certainly expected somebody would meet me at the station.

FATHER MC KEE'S VOICE. The old man left all right.

JOE'S VOICE. He started a little too late.

THE R. F. D.'S VOICE. I'll have a look for him. (*The rest is lost in a babble of Italian as* AMY *comes on to the porch and the others follow her, not the least among them being the two Italian hands,* GIORGIO *and* ANGELO *whose volubility subsides only as* AMY *enters the room. As for* AMY, *she is all that* TONY *said of her and much more. She wears a pretty dress, new, ready-made, and inexpensive, and a charming and equally cheap hat. Her shoes are bright coloured and her handbag matches them. But her own loveliness is quite beyond belief. She is small and plump and vivid and her golden hair shimmers about her face like morning sunshine. She herself shines with an inner, constitutional energy. Her look is, to be sure, just a little tired. She probably is not more than twenty-two or -three, but she seems older. Her great quality is definiteness. It lends pathos to her whole personality. At the moment, her vanity is piqued by* TONY'S *remissness and she carries matters with a hand a little too high to be entirely convincing. She is embarrassed, of course, but she won't admit it.*)

AMY (*as she enters*). I must say it ain't my idea of the way a gentleman ought to welcome his blooming bride. I don't get it. I don't get it at all. What was the matter?

JOE. Why, nothin'.

FATHER MC KEE. He was scared.

AMY. Scared of me? Why didn't you come yourself?

JOE. I wanted to, but . . .

AMY (*the decorations have caught her eye*). Say, did you folks go and do all this for the wedding?

JOE. Sure we did.

AMY. Well, if that ain't the cutest ever! A regular wop wedding! Excuse me. I meant Italian. (*The "I" is long.*)

JOE. That's all right.

AMY. And here's the priest, too, all set and ready. Say! I can see right now I'm going to like it here.

JOE. I don't guess nobody's goin' to kick at that.

AMY. All right, then, I'll forgive you. That's the way I am. Forgive and forget! I always believe in letting bygones be bygones. And down at the station I was thinking: Well, if they ain't got enough sense of politeness to come after the bride, I'm going to hop the very next train back to Frisco. I'd have done it, too, only—would you believe it?—I didn't have the price of a ticket! I spent the last cent I had on this hat. Say, when I remembered that, maybe I didn't cry! That's what I was crying over when you come up. (*This to the* R. F. D.; *otherwise her eyes have scarcely left* JOE'*s face.*)

THE R. F. D. Pleased to have been of service, ma'am.

AMY. Well, you certainly was of service. But here I am alive and well, as they say, so I guess we don't need to fuss about that any more. I guess I'll sit down. (*She does so.*)

JOE. Here's the cook an' the hands to pay their respects.

ANGELO (*a deep obeisance to* AMY). Eh, la nostra padrona! Tanti auguri, cara Signora, e buona festa! Come sta? Ha fatto buon viaggio? (*Here* GIORGIO *adds his voice.*)

ANGELO (*together*)	GIORGIO
Siamo tanto contenti di vedevla. Speriamo che si troverà sempre bene e felice nella casa ospitale del nostro generoso padrone.	Sia la benvenuta, egregia Signora. Auguriamo la buona fortuna a lei, e al suo stimatissimo sposo. Che la Santa Madonna le dia la sua benedizione e che tutti i santi l'accompagnino nel matrimonio!

JOE. Hey, that's enough!

AMY. Now, that was very nice of them. I liked every word they said. I guess I better study up on the lingo. All I know is words like spaghetti and raviole. . . .

ANGELO *and* GIORGIO (*sotto voce*). Ah! La Signora parla Italiano!

AMY. . . . I guess you got plenty of that around. Well, you can't make me mad. I just love it. (*Then she sees* AH GEE'*s ceremonious obeisance.*) How do you do? Are you the cook?

AH GEE. Yes, missy. Velly good cook.

AMY. Say, I didn't know I drew a chef. You didn't tell me. (AH GEE *takes himself off.*) Say, my baggage is out there.

JOE. All right boys, lend a hand. (ANGELO *and* GIORGIO *go down the steps.*)

AMY. If you don't mind I'll just keep an eye on them. My wedding dress is in that trunk. I bet you didn't expect me to bring a wedding dress. Well, I didn't expect to, myself. And I don't know why I did. But I did! I just blew myself. I said: "You only get married once" and—I got a veil, too. I got the whole works. (*She hears her trunk en route.*) Go easy there! (*She is out on the porch.*)

THE R. F. D. Well, that's her.

JOE. (*as he goes to help*). She ain't bad.

FATHER MC KEE. No, she ain't half bad.

AMY (*calling down*). Not upside down! Be careful, can't you?

THE R. F. D. I don't hold much with city girls myself, but—

JOE (*calling down*). Careful, boys! Look out for that vine! Gimme the grip.

FATHER MC KEE. Oh, she's above the average.

THE R. F. D. (*nudging him*). Do you think she . . . ?

FATHER MC KEE. I wouldn't hardly like to say off-hand, but . . .

THE R. F. D. I wouldn't think so.

FATHER MC KEE. Joe, do you think she . . . ?

JOE. No. Not her. Not on your life. (*He puts grip down inside the bedroom door. At the same time* ANGELO *and* GIORGIO *carry in* AMY'*s pathetic little trunk, which they take into the bedroom.*)

THE R. F. D. Well, I got my deliveries.

FATHER MC KEE. I'll come along with you. You stay here an' keep things conversational, Joe.

JOE. No! I'll come, too.

THE R. F. D. Till the groom turns up, Joe. You don't want her to get all upset again, do you?

FATHER MC KEE (*as* AMY *comes along the porch to the door*). Shh! Don't get her worryin'.

AMY (*in the doorway, finishing the feminine touch of powder to the nose*). I thought a little of this wouldn't make me any harder to look at.

THE R. F. D. We'll have to be movin' on, ma'am.

FATHER MC KEE. Yes.

AMY (*shaking hands with him*). I'm pleased to have made your acquaintance.

THE R. F. D. I hope to have the pleasure soon again.

AMY. Why, ain't you coming to the wedding?

THE R. F. D. Sure I am, if I'm invited.

AMY. I'll never forgive you, if you don't. And I certaintly want to thank you for the lift. (*A handshake to him.*) Thank you. . . . Good-bye. . . . Good-bye. . . .

THE R. F. D. Good-bye, ma'am (*He shuffles out.* JOE *starts to follow.*)

AMY. You ain't going, too?

JOE. Well, I—

THE R. F. D. (*through the window*). Just the Padre an' me.

FATHER MC KEE (*as he goes, to* JOE). We'll send him right up.

THE R. F. D. (*as they disappear*). Good-bye, ma'am.

AMY. Good-bye. See you later. (*Awkward silence.*) I ain't sorry they went. I think they ought to have done it sooner and left us to get acquainted. They got me all fussed up staring that way. I just couldn't think of what to say next. A girl gets kind of fussed, coming off like this to marry a man she ain't never seen. I was a mile up in the air. I—I guess I must have sounded kind of fresh. I wouldn't want you to think I was fresh.

JOE. I didn't.

AMY. I'm glad you didn't. You know, I like it up here already. You got it fixed up so cute and— (*She discovers the cake.*) and that. . . . It was awful nice of you to think of that. And the view! Is them all vines?

JOE. Yeah. . . . (*An awkward pause.*)

AMY. It certainly is a pretty sight. Coming up I could taste the wind way down inside me. It made me think of where I used to live.

JOE. Where was that?

AMY. In the Santa Clara. You know, I wrote you.

JOE. Oh, yeah. In the Santa Clara. I forgot.

AMY. We had a big place in the Santa Clara. Prunes and apricots. Ninety acres in prunes and fifty in apricots. . . . (*Again an awkward silence.*) I guess I'll sit down. (*She does so.*) There ought to have been good money in prunes and apricots. But the prunes didn't do so good and the apricots got the leaf curl.

JOE. You're quite a farmer.

AMY. My old man was, but he got to drinking.

JOE. That's bad.

AMY. So we lost it after my mother died. But I used to love it there. In the spring, when the blossoms was out, I used to climb up on the windmill at night, when there was a moon. You never saw such a pretty sight as them blossoms in the moonlight. You could see for miles and miles all round—for miles and miles.

JOE. It must have been pretty. (*Awkward pause.*)

AMY. Ever been in the Santa Clara?

JOE. Sure. I worked there before I come here.

AMY. Where did you work?

JOE. Near Mountain View. I forget the guy's name.

AMY. I went to school in Mountain View. Our place was near there. Ever know Father O'Donnell?

JOE. No.

AMY. Thought you might have, being a Catholic and all.

JOE. I was organizer for the Wobblies.

AMY. The Wobblies?

JOE. I. W. W.

AMY. Say! You ain't one of them?

JOE. I used to be.

AMY. I sure am glad you gave that up. You don't talk one bit like an Italian.

JOE. I ain't. Only by descent. I was born in Frisco.

AMY. Oh, in Frisco? I see. . . . I'm Swiss by descent myself. My father was born in Switzerland and my grandfather, on my mother's side, he was born there, too. I don't know what that makes me—Swiss cheese, I guess. . . . (*She laughs.*

JOE *does not. This crushes her and there is another awkward gap.*) Our old house in the Santa Clara was bigger than this one, but it wasn't near so pretty. I must say you keep this house nice and clean for having no woman around. Our house got awful dirty toward the end. You see, my mother got to drinking, too. Hard stuff, you know. I got nothing against beer or vino, but the hard stuff don't do nobody any good. . . . That how you stand on prohibition?

JOE. Sure, I guess so.

AMY. I'm glad to hear that. I sure am. I don't want no more experience with the hard stuff. . . . That certainly is some view. Got the Santa Clara beat a mile. The Santa Clara's so flat. You couldn't get no view at all unless you climbed up on that windmill like I told you about. . . . Our old house had a cellar. Has this house got a cellar?

JOE. Sure, it has. Underneath the whole house. (*She goes to the cellar door to see.*)

AMY. I used to hide in our cellar when things got too rough upstairs. You could hear the feet running around over your head, but they never come down in the cellar after me because there was a ladder, and when you're that way you don't care much for ladders. . . . They always took it out on me.

JOE. Did they?

AMY. Yeah. I always had the cellar though. I used to play down there hot days. It smelt like apricots.

JOE. Our cellar smells like hell. It's full of vino.

AMY. That's a nice clean smell. It's sour, but it's healthy.

JOE. You're a regular wop, ain't you?

AMY. Well, after two years in a spaghetti joint! I like Italians. They always left me alone. Guess it wouldn't have done 'em much good getting fresh with me, at that. . . . Say, I'm getting pretty confidential.

JOE. Go right ahead.

AMY. All right. . . . I guess I ain't got much reason for being shy with you, at that. I wouldn't never have said I was going to marry an Italian, though. But I guess I just jumped at the chance. I got so tired of things. Oh, everything! I used to think I just couldn't keep on any longer.

JOE. Poor kid!

AMY. Oh, I usually know which side my bread's buttered on. I just said to myself: "He looks all right and I like the country and anyway it can't be no worse than this." And I said: "Why shouldn't I take a chance? He's taking just as much of a chance on me as I am on him."

JOE. That's fair enough.

AMY. Sure it is. And—maybe I hadn't ought to say it—but when I come in here and seen all you done, fixing things up for the wedding and all, and looked out the window, and smelt that wind, I said to myself, I said: "Amy, old kid, you're in gravy." Now, what do you think of that for an admission?

JOE. You're dead right. That's just what I said when I come here. I only intended to stay a few days. I'm that way, see? I been here goin' on five months now.

AMY. Is *that* all?

JOE. That's the longest I ever stayed any one place since I was old enough to dress myself.

AMY. You *have* been a rover!

JOE. I been all over—with the Wobblies, you see. Before I come here, that is.

AMY. What did you used to do?

JOE. Cherries an' hops—melons down in the Imperial an' oranges down South an' the railroad an' the oilfields. . . . Before I come here. When I come here I just stayed. Maybe I was gettin' tired of bummin'. Now I'm tired of this. But I don't mind.

AMY. Well, don't get too tired of it. I'm not a bit strong for moving myself. I had all I want of that in my time.

JOE. I guess you have.

AMY. I wonder what you think of me coming all the way up here like I did, all by myself, to marry a man I ain't never seen, only his photograph.

JOE. You couldn't have picked a better man.

AMY. Say! Don't get a swelled head, will you?

JOE. Who, me?

AMY. Oh, no, nobody! (AH GEE *passes along the porch*) I hope you're right that's all. And I guess you are, at that. And believe me, if I thought this wasn't a permanent offer, I wouldn't be here. I mean business. I hope you do.

JOE. Me?

AMY. Well, I certainly ain't referring to the Chink.

JOE. Say, who do you think . . . ?

AMY (*touching his sleeve with a kind*

gentle diffidence which is her first attempt at intimacy). Don't get sore. The minute I came in I knew I was all right. I am. Why, I feel just as comfortable as if we was old friends. There don't seem to be anything strange in me being here like I am. Not now, anyhow. It just goes to show you: you never can tell how things is going to turn out. Why, if a fortune-teller had told me that I would come up here like I did, do you know what I would have said to her? I'd have said, "You're no fortune-teller." Life sure is funny, though. It's lucky for me I can say that now and laugh when I say it. I ain't always been so good at laughing. I guess we'll get used to each other in time. Don't you think we will, Tony?

JOE. Tony? Say, I ain't . . . ! Oh, Jesus! (*His words are lost in the roar of a Ford motor as it approaches, and the motor, in turn, is drowned in wild cries of dismay from* GIORGIO *and* ANGELO.)

(*The tension between the two in the room is broken by the excited entrance of* AH GEE, *who has evidently seen, from his kitchen window, the cause of disturbance.*)

FATHER MC KEE (*calling from off stage*). Joe! Joe!

JOE (*following* AH GEE *toward the door*). What is it? (*From the porch he sees what it is.*) What—Is he dead? . . . Take that bench! (*He disappears in the direction of the disturbance which continues in both English and Italian.*)

AMY. What's the matter? Is somebody hurt?

(*The* DOCTOR, *with his fedora hat and his little black satchel, appears. He is the perfect young rural medico, just out of medical school and full of learned importance.*)

THE DOCTOR. I'll get the ambulance.

JOE (*following him in*). Is he bad, Doc?

THE DOCTOR (*as he goes into the bedroom*). Both legs above the knee—compound fractures.

JOE. Why didn't you take him to the hospital?

THE R. F. D. (*as he enters*). The Ford went right off the bridge.

FATHER MC KEE (*as he enters*). Not two hundred yards from here, Joe.

THE R. F. D. Must have fell twenty feet!

FATHER MC KEE. Never seen such a wreck! (*To* AMY.) We found him lyin' in two feet of water. The car was turned right upside down.

AMY. But who is it? I don't get it. I don't know what's happened.

FATHER MC KEE. Two broken legs, that's what's happened.

THE DOCTOR (*he reappears in his shirt sleeves*). Better lend a hand, Joe!

(*He vanishes again.* GIORGIO *and* ANGELO *appear, carrying the bench and apostrophizing the deity in Italian.* TONY *is recumbent and unconscious on this improvised stretcher. Much "Steady" from* JOE. *Much "There now, Tony" from the* R. F. D. *Much and prolonged groaning from* TONY.)

JOE (*as the bench is set down*). All right now, Tony.

TONY (*reviving*). AH-h-h! . . . Ees you, Joe?

JOE. Yeah. It's me. Amy's here.

TONY. Amy? Ees all right, Joe? You been makin' evrathing all right?

JOE. Sure. Everything's fine.

TONY. Where is my Amy? (*He sees her where she stands dumbfounded against the wall.*) Ah-h-h, Amy! . . . Amy, don' be standin' way off dere! Come over here for shake hands. (AMY *shakes her head.*) You ain' mad with me, Amy? . . . (AMY *shakes her head again.*) Amy ain' mad with me, Joe?

JOE. Nobody's mad. . . . Don't you worry.

TONY. Den we have da weddin' just da same? We have da weddin' just da same? (*The* DOCTOR *appears in the bedroom doorway, holding a hypodermic.*)

JOE. Sure, we will.

THE DOCTOR. All right, boys, bring him in. I want to give him another one of these and clean up his cuts.

JOE. Come on now, boys! Avanti! Careful there!

TONY. Amy! . . . Amy! . . . (*The jar of movement hurts him. He breaks down into groans and is carried into the bedroom. All others go with him except* JOE *and* AMY.)

JOE (*as he starts to go, a strangled sound from* AMY *arrests him. He turns and meets her gaze. He closes the door*). This is tough on you.

AMY (*almost voiceless with her terrible surmise*). Who—who is that old guy?

JOE. That? That's Tony. . . .

AMY. Tony?

JOE. It's too bad he never got to meet you. It's too bad he wasn't here when you come. (AMY *sways desperately a moment, then, with a choked cry, makes for the bedroom.*) You can't go in there.

AMY. I want my trunk.

JOE. Now, listen! It ain't Tony's fault he's had an accident. . . .

AMY. Of all the dirty, low-down tricks that was ever played on a girl!

JOE. An' it ain't his fault you made a little mistake.

AMY. What do you think you are—a bunch of Houdinis? (*She tears open her handbag which she put down on the table at her first entrance and produces a photograph.*) Is this your photo or isn't it?

JOE (*in amazement*). Where did you get it?

AMY. Where do you think I got it?

JOE. Good God, Tony didn't send you this, did he? For God's sake, tell me! Did Tony send you this?

AMY. Ain't I just told you?

JOE. By God, he must have been plumb crazy! By God, he was so dead gone on you he was afraid you wouldn't have nothin' to do with an old man like him. . . . He didn't have the nerve. . . . An' he just went an' sent you my photo instead of his. . . . Tony's like that, Amy. He ain't nothing but a kid. He's like a puppy, Tony is. Honest, Amy, it's God's truth I'm telling you. . . . I wouldn't have had nothin' to do with no such thing. Honest I wouldn't. I did write the letters for him, but that was only because he don't write good English like I do.

AMY. That ain't no excuse.

JOE. But there wasn't one word in them letters that wasn't God's own truth. I never knew nothin' about this photo, though. Honest to God, I never! An' Tony never meant no harm neither, Amy. Honest he never. An' he's been after me to beat it, too. Every day he has. . . . Sure it was a dirty trick an' he was crazy to think he could get away with it. I ain't denyin' it's the dirtiest trick I ever heard of. . . . Only he didn't mean no harm.

AMY. Oh, didn't he? Well, how about *my* feelings? How about *me?*

JOE. I'll do everything I can to square it. I'll drive you right down to the station now, and you can hop the first train back.

AMY. Oh, *can* I? And what do you expect me to do when I get there? Ain't I thrown up my job there? Do you think jobs is easy for a girl to get? And ain't I spent every cent I had on my trousseau?

JOE. I'll make Tony square it.

AMY. Oh, my God! Oh, my God! I got to go back and wait on table! What'll all those girls say when they see me? And I ain't even got the price of my ticket!

JOE. We can fix that.

AMY. I'll get a lawyer, I will! I wish to God I hadn't never heard of no wops!

JOE. Don't start cryin'. (*He tries to comfort her.*)

AMY. You take your hands off me and get my things.

JOE. All right. . . . (*He looks at her a moment, his distress quite evident. Then he gives it up and goes into the bedroom. As he opens the door, the* DOCTOR *and* TONY *are audible. He closes the door after him.*)

(AMY *picks up the few belongings she has left about the room. She stands a moment holding them, looking about her, at the four walls, at the country outside. Then her eye falls upon* JOE'*s photograph which still lies, face-up, on the table. She takes it in her hand and looks at it. Mechanically she makes as though to put it into the bosom of her dress. She changes her mind, drops it on the table and looks around her again. She seems to reach a decision. Her face sets and she pushes the photograph vigorously away from her.* JOE *returns with her satchel.*)

JOE. The doc's give him something to make him sleep. They're goin' to get an ambulance an' take him to the hospital. We can take the doc's Ford an' . . . It's a shame, but . . .

AMY. I ain't going.

JOE. What?

AMY. No. I ain't going. Why should I go? I like the country. This place suits me all right. It's just what I was looking for. I'm here and I might as well stick. I guess he ain't so bad, at that. I guess I could have done a lot worse. If he wants to marry me, I'm game. I'm game to see it through. It's nice up here. (*She pulls off her hat and sits, exhausted.* JOE *stares in mute admiration as the curtain falls.*)

ACT TWO

The scene remains unchanged. It is late evening of the same day. The lanterns out-of-doors have been burning so long that some of them have already guttered out. The room is lighted by two oil lamps.

TONY *lies groaning faintly on a cot, his*

legs encased in a plaster cast, his eternal wine bottle by his side. The DOCTOR *sits beside him.*

Outside, the festa is in full swing. A desperate Italian tenor is singing "La Donna è Mobile" from "Rigoletto" as the curtain rises. His tones ring frantically out.

A short pause follows the song. The hiss of a skyrocket is audible. The light from the rocket flares through the windows and a long "Ah" rises from the crowd out-of-doors.

TONY. Fireworks!

THE DOCTOR. Lie quiet.

TONY. Someone verra sick in bed. Povereto! Povereto! Tony miss festa. (*Gay voices outside call to children and children answer. The* DOCTOR *rises impatiently and goes to the door.* TONY *turns his head ever so slightly.*) Eh, Doc! W'ere you go?

THE DOCTOR. It's high time those coyotes went home.

(*Applause rings from the crowd. The tenor is again vigorously repeating the last phrase and cadenza of "La Donna è Mobile."*)

TONY. Dat fella is no coyot'! He is music artiste.

THE DOCTOR. It's a marvel to me the man has any lungs left. He's been howling for five hours.

TONY. You don't ondrastan' such music. Come è bella! Ees "Rigoletto!"

THE DOCTOR. Look here now, Tony! I let you out of the hospital to get married.

TONY. You bet your life! You think any goddam doc is stoppin' me from gettin' married?

THE DOCTOR. I'm talking medicine, not love.

TONY. You talkin' too goddam much. You been spoil evrathing.

THE DOCTOR. Now, be reasonable, Tony. I let them bring you in here where you could see your friends.

TONY. An' den you mak' all my friends go outside.

THE DOCTOR. You're a sick man.

TONY. Ahi! Tony is verra sick . . . verra sick!

THE DOCTOR. Enough's enough. Why, half of what you have been through today would have killed a white man! You wops are crazy.

TONY. I don't let nobody stop no festa in my house. You go outside an' have a good time.

THE DOCTOR. I don't sing and I don't dance and I don't talk Italian and I don't drink.

TONY. I'm surprise' how much you don' know, Doc. (*He laughs. The jar is painful. He groans. The* DOCTOR *comes over to his bedside.*) W'ere is my Amy?

THE DOCTOR. She's all right. Keep quiet.

TONY. You goin' look for my Amy, Doc? You goin' see if she is havin' fine time?

(*Mandolins, a guitar, and an accordion strike up a sentimental waltz outside.*)

THE DOCTOR. If you'll be quiet. (*Humoring him, he goes to the door.*) I can see her from here and she's having a splendid time. Does that satisfy you?

TONY. Now evrabody goin' for dance!

(*A brief silence filled by the dance music to which* TONY, *the incorrigible, beats time. Then* JOE *and* AH GEE *come along the porch pushing a wheelbarrow, a little flurry of the crowd in their wake. The* DOCTOR *shoos out the crowd.* JOE *and* AH GEE *come in.*)

JOE. How you makin' out, Tony?

TONY. Verra sick, Joe. Is festa goin' good?

JOE. Festa's goin' fine, Tony. Me and Ah Gee's after more vino.

TONY. Da's good! Da's good!

JOE. Sure it's good. But it's a wonder everybody ain't drownded already.

TONY. Italian fellas don't get drownded in vino. Is my Amy havin' good fun, Joe?

JOE. Sure, she is! She's playin' with the kids.

TONY. Ah! . . . You go in da cellar with Ah Gee, Joe, and bring back playnta vino. Den you come back here and mak' little talk with Tony.

JOE. That's the idea. . . . (*He goes into the cellar, followed by* AH GEE.)

THE DOCTOR (*in the door, a fractious eye on the festa*). Those mothers ought to be reported for keeping youngsters up this time of night. (*A pause filled with voices and laughter.*)

TONY (*crescendo*). Doc! Doc! Doc! (*The* DOCTOR *turns.*) You think I am well next week, Doc?

THE DOCTOR. I sincerely hope, Tony, that you may be well in six months.

TONY. Six month'?

THE DOCTOR. You don't seem to realize what a bad smash you had. (*As he sits down to his professional manner.*) Both tibia and fibula are fractured in the right leg. The femur is crushed in the left, and the ischium damaged as well. Now, if no systemic complications develop . . .

TONY. Oh, my God!

THE DOCTOR. . . . six months . . . .

TONY (*crescendo again*). Six month'! Six month'! Six month'!

THE DOCTOR. You won't make it any shorter by exciting yourself.

TONY. Da's right, Doc. Ees no good get excit'. I ondrastan'. But six month' . . . (*A pause.*) Doc, I'm goin' ask you som'-thing an' you goin' tell me just da truth, eh?

THE DOCTOR. I know what's on your mind, Tony. If you keep quiet and take care of yourself, you'll have all the kids you want.

TONY. How many?

THE DOCTOR. Ten, anyway!

TONY. Three is playnta.

(*The music is loud again as* JOE *and* AH GEE *come back from the cellar with the new barrel of wine. They load it on the wheelbarrow and* AH GEE *takes it off to the thirsty populace,* JOE *remains behind.*)

THE DOCTOR. In the meanwhile Amy's going to have her hands full, taking care of you.

TONY (*violently*). I don' marry with no woman for mak' her work. I don't want my Amy do nothing but only be happy an' fat.

JOE. There ain't nothin' too good for Tony. He marries a fine wife to play the piano for him an' he's goin' to rent a trained nurse to take care of him.

(AH GEE *is greeted with shouts of "Vino! Vino!" from the men and "Viva Antonio" from the girls.*)

TONY. You bet your life!

THE DOCTOR. Renting trained nurses is expensive, Tony.

TONY. I got playnta money.

(*The concertina and the mandolin begin playing the chorus of "Funiculi, Funicula!" The music is continued throughout the following scene.*)

JOE (*cigarette business*). You old son of a gun! Give us a light, doc.

THE DOCTOR. Not in here, Joe!

(JOE *takes his cigarette outside. He sits with a wave to the crowd, who answer, "Joe! Joe!"*)

TONY. Is my Amy havin' good fun, Joe?

JOE. Sure. She's dancin' with the postman.

TONY. Da's good! Ees verra funny weddin' for me, Joe, but my Amy must have good time.

THE DOCTOR. Tony's got it bad.

JOE. Don't blame him. She's some girl.

TONY. I got to talk verra secret with Joe, Doc. You go outside for talk with my Amy. You better get good acquaint' with my Amy, Doc.

(*Applause outside for the dancers.*)

JOE. You could do worse, an' that's a fact.

THE DOCTOR. Tony's got to go to sleep.

(*The crowd outside shouts vociferously.*)

JOE. I won't keep him up.

TONY. Just a little w'ile, Doc? Fifteen minute'?

THE DOCTOR. Well, don't make it any longer. I want some sleep myself. Anybody would think I haven't a thing to do but take care of Tony.

JOE. We know you're a busy baby, Doc.

THE DOCTOR. Busy is right. (*Very expansive.*) To-morrow, now, I've got two confinements I'm watching and an appendicitis, all up on the St. Helena road. Then, just the other side of town, I've got the most beautiful tumor you could hope to see. And the sheriff's wife! Operated her yesterday. Gallstones. Gallstones? They were cobblestones. I never saw such a case! And then, with my regular practice and my own scientific researches to keep up with things.

TONY. Corpo Dio, goddam, Doc; don' be tellin' me no more 'bout who is sick and w'at he's sick for! I'm sick playnta myself, an' I got playnta trouble here. You go outside an' leave me for talk with Joe.

THE DOCTOR. All right, but I won't have any more nonsense when I come back. (*He goes; to* JOE *on the porch.*) I cannot be responsible unless the patient enjoys complete quiet, after a shock like this to his nervous system.

JOE. Has Tony got a nervous system?

THE DOCTOR. Of course he has! (*He disappears. A shout welcomes him.*)

TONY. W'at is nervous system, Joe?

JOE. It's what make things hurt, Tony.

TONY. I got playnta.

(JOE *comes in and stands over* TONY *for a moment with a look of half-tender amusement on his face.* TONY *hums distractedly keeping time with one hand to the music of "Funiculi, Funciula." With the end of the music he drops his hands with a sigh.*)

JOE. What's on your mind, Tony?

TONY. Oh, Joe! . . . Joe!! . . . Joe!!

JOE. What's the matter, Tony. Ain't you feelin' good?

TONY. Ees Amy! . . .

(JOE *sits in the* DOCTOR's *chair, hitching it closer to the bed.*)

JOE. What do you want for a nickel? She married you, didn't she?

TONY. I'm scare', Joe. I'm scare' verra bad. I love my Amy, but my Amy don' love me.

JOE. Give her time, can't you? She wouldn't have married you if she wasn't all set to go through on the level.

TONY. You think?

JOE. Hell, I *know.*

TONY. W'at Amy say w'en she see me dees morning?

JOE. Oh, forget it, I tell you.

TONY. I got to know, Joe. You got to tell me. She's pretty goddam mad, eh?

JOE. Well, if she was, she got over it.

TONY. W'at I'm goin' to do for mak' evrathing all right, Joe? Da's w'at I want to know.

JOE. I tell you everythin' *is* all right, Tony. Oh, I ain't sayin' you ain't got to keep things movin' along easy an' friendly an' all. But that ain't goin' to be so hard. Just be good to her and take care of her. That's what Amy needs. She's tired, poor kid!

TONY. I'm all ready for tak' care like hell.

JOE. From what Amy was tellin' me this mornin', she's been a-havin' a helluva hard life for a girl, an' if she come through straight like she did, well, there ain't no credit due nobody but just only herself, and that's a fact.

TONY. You're a goddam smart fella, Joe.

JOE. I dunno how smart I am, Tony, but you can't tell me much. Not about women, you can't. Believe me, a girl gets a lousy deal any way you look at it. (*He reflects upon this for an instant before he illustrates.*) Take a fella, now, a young fella like me, see? It's goin' to do him good to knock around an' have his troubles an' all. (*A solemn shake of the head.*) But knockin' around just raises hell with a girl. She can't stand it. She can't stand it, because it ain't in her nature to get away with the whole show like a fella can. (TONY *is much impressed and signifies approval with a grunt.*) If a fella wants a meal, he swipes it, don't he? A girl can't be swipin' things. It 'ud make her feel bad. She'd think she was doin' somethin' wrong. (*This surprises* TONY, *but he is willing to take* JOE's *word for it.*) Gee, I sure would hate to be a woman!

TONY (*nodding agreement*). Nobody is wantin' to be woman, Joe . . . But ees playnta good womans like my Amy!

JOE. Sure, there's good ones an' bad ones. But that ain't exactly what I mean, Tony. What I mean is, as far as I can see, it don't make a helluva lot of difference what a woman is: good or bad, young or old . . .

TONY. I lik' best fat!

JOE. . . . all women is up against it, and it's a dirty shame, too, because women ain't so bad. They ain't much use, maybe, but they ain't so bad.

TONY. My Amy is goin' have evrathing she want.

JOE. Ever heard anythin' about this dam' women's rights stuff? You know. Equality of the sexes. Woman doin' a man's work an' all that bunk?

TONY. Da's crazy idea!

JOE. The idea ain't so bad.

TONY. Ees crazy idea! Looka me! You think any woman is goin' be doin' my work? No, by God! I tell you, Joe, woman is best for sit in da house an' love da husband.

JOE. The trouble with women is, there's too goddam many of 'em. Why, I was readin' in the paper only the other day about England havin' three and a half women to every man.

TONY. W'at you mean?—half a womans!

JOE. I'm only tellin' you what the paper said.

TONY. Ees crazy idea! Half a womans! I tell you, Joe . . .

JOE. I been lookin' women over from San Diego to Seattle an' what most of 'em is after is a home. A good safe home, whether they get any rights with it or not. You take my advice an' make everythin' nice an' comfortable for Amy an' you won't have no trouble. Amy's satisfied here. Don't you kid yourself she ain't. (*Outside the crowd is off again, the tenors leading them in "Maria Mari."*)

TONY. You're a good boy, Joe, you're pretty smart.

JOE. I'm just tellin' you the truth. You're dam' lucky you picked a girl like Amy.

TONY (*a moment of comfort; then despair again*). Ees no good, Joe—ees no good.

JOE. Oh, for cripe's sake, Tony!

TONY. I'm tellin' you, Joe, ees no good. I'm the most unhappy fella in the world. W'y? Because I been verra bad sinner an' God is goin' get me for sure! He's broke both my legs already an' he's not finish' with me yet! God is no cheap fella, Joe. God is lookin' out at Tony right now, and you know what he's sayin'? He's sayin': "Tony, you been one goddam sonuvabitch for playin' goddam dirty trick on Amy!" Da's w'at God is sayin', Joe, an' I know verra good wat God is goin' do more. Just for playin' goddam dirty trick like dat on Amy, Tony don' never have no kids, never! W'at you think is mak' me do such a thing, Joe?

JOE. Oh, hell, you always was crazy.

TONY. Ees no good, for such a bad fella like me gettin' married. God is goin' fix me playnta, all right.

JOE. I seen God let worse guys'n you get by.

TONY. You think?

JOE. If you want to square things, you better make Amy glad you done what you done.

TONY. You think? . . . Yes. . . . (*Pause.*) Look, Joe. . . . (*He draws a plush box from under his blanket.*) Ees present for Amy. You open him.

JOE (*obeying*). Say! Them's what I call regular earrings!

TONY. You bet your life! He's cost four hundra dollar'!

JOE. Are them real diamonds?

TONY (*nodding*). I guess Amy like 'em pretty good, eh?

JOE. She'll be crazy about 'em. You're a pretty wise old wop, Tony, ain't you? (*He hands the box back to* TONY, *who laughs delightedly.* JOE *looks at him for a moment then goes to door and calls out.*) Amy!

TONY. Eh, Joe!

JOE. You're goin' to make the presentation right away now. That'll settle your worries for you. . . . Amy, come here! Tony wants to see you!

TONY. You think is good time now?

JOE. *I know.* . . . Amy?

(AMY *appears in doorway. She wears her wedding dress and veil. The dress is undeniably pretty and only wrong in one or two places. The veil has been pulled rather askew. The whole picture is at once charming and pathetic.*)

AMY. What's the idea? (*Her voice is a little tired. She does not look at* JOE.)

JOE. Tony wants you.

AMY (*she comes in stolidly and takes the chair farthest from* TONY'*s cot. She sits there stiffly*). Well, here I am.

TONY (*ultra-tenderly*). My Amy is tire'!

AMY. You don't blame me, do you? I've had quite a day. Gee, them kids out there have been climbing all over me.

TONY. Da's good.

AMY. Oh, I don't mind kids if they go to bed when they ought to and know how to behave. Believe me, if I ever have any kids, they're going to behave.

TONY. You hear dat, Joe?

AMY. I said "if." (*A silence.*) I wouldn't object.

TONY (*amorously*). Amy . . . Come over here.

AMY (*rising quickly*). I guess I ain't so tired. I guess I better go back or they'll be wondering what's become of the blooming bride. Some bloom, huh? (*The fireworks hiss and flare again and* AMY, *very like a little girl, is out on the porch for the delight of seeing them. The enthusiasm of the crowd fairly rattles the windows.*) They sure do yell out there! When you get enough wops together and put enough vino in 'em, they sure can speak up! . . . I think I'll take off my veil. (*She does.*) Phew! That thing don't look like no weight at all, but it feels like a ton of bricks.

TONY. Amy, come over here.

AMY. I'm all right where I am.

TONY. Amy!

AMY. What?

TONY. You like earrings, Amy?

AMY. Earrings? I'm human, ain't I?

JOE. That's the idea.

AMY (*a real snarl*). I didn't speak to you. I was addressing Tony.

TONY. Ah, you call me Tony for da first time!

AMY. Expect me to call my husband mister? That'd sound swell, wouldn't it? Tony. Short for Antonio. Antonio and Cleopatra, huh? Can you beat it? You'll have to call me Cleo.

TONY. I like better Amy.

AMY. There ain't no short for Amy. It's

French and it means beloved. Beloved! Can you beat it? The boss in the spaghetti palace told me that the night he tried to give me a twelve-dollar pearl necklace. Twelve dollars! He was some sport. When he seen I couldn't see it that way, he give it to Blanche. She was the other girl that worked there. He had a wife and three kids too. (TONY *beckons again and* AMY *takes further refuge in conversation.*) I like that name Blanche. I used to wish my name was Blanche instead of Amy. Blanche got in trouble. Poor Blanche! Gee, I was sorry for that girl!

TONY. Come over here, Amy. (*He holds out the box.*)

AMY. What's that?

TONY. Ees my present for my Amy.

AMY. What you got there, Tony?

TONY. For you.

AMY. Something for me? (*By this time, she has got over to the cot. She takes the box.*) Honest? Well, now, if that isn't sweet of you, Tony. (*She opens it.*) Oh! . . . Oh!! . . . Oh!!!

TONY. Ees for mak' Amy happy.

JOE. They're real! Real diamonds!

TONY. You bet our life! Four hundra dollar'.

AMY. I . . . I . . . (*Tears come.*) Real diamonds. . . . (*She sits in the* DOCTOR's *chair and cries and cries.*)

TONY. Don' cry, Amy! Don' cry! Ees no' for cry, earrings! Ees for festa! Ees for marryin' with Tony!

AMY. I don't know what to say! I don't know what to do!

JOE. Put 'em on. (*He gets the mirror, brings it over to where* AMY *sits, and holds it for her while she begins to put the earrings on. Her sobs gradually subside.*)

AMY. I had another pair once, so I got my ears pierced already. Ma pierced my ears herself with a needle and thread. Only these kind screw on! Say, ain't they beautiful! My others were turquoises and gold. Real turquoises and real gold. But these here cost four hundred dollars! Oh, I never dreamed of anything so gorgeous! (*She takes the mirror from* JOE.)

TONY. Amy . . . Amy . . .

AMY. Can I wear 'em whenever I want?

TONY. You can wear 'em in da bed if you want!

AMY. Oh, thank you, Tony! (*She is just about to kiss him.*)

JOE. Now, everything's fine!

AMY (*furiously*). Say what's the idea? What have you got to do with this? You're always buttin' in. Say . . . (*Suddenly she remembers the momentous photograph which still lies on the table.*) Wait a minute. (*She picks it up and hands it quite violently to* JOE.) Here's your picture.

TONY (*watching in terror*). Santa Maria!

AMY. *Here!* You better take it! Take it, I tell you! I don't want it.

(JOE *looks first at the photograph, then at the lady.*)

JOE. I guess you ain't far wrong, Amy. I hope there ain't no hard feelin's.

AMY. Why should there be any hard feelings?

TONY. Benissimo!

JOE. All right. Only I didn't want you to think. . . . (*A long pause.*)

AMY (*very steadily*). You ain't got much of a swelled head, have you, Mr. Joe? (JOE's *face falls. The tension is snapped by a gesture from* TONY.)

TONY. Tear him up, Joe! Tear him up! (JOE *obeys.*)

AMY. Now we don't ever have to think of that again.

TONY. Madonna! . . . Da's verra good.

AMY. You see, that's the only way to do. There ain't no use of keeping things around to remind you of what you want to forget. Start in all over again new and fresh. That's my way. Burn up everything you want to put behind you. No reminders and no souvenirs. I been doing that regular about once a month ever since I was a kid. No memories for me. No hard feelings. It's a great life, if you don't weaken. I guess, if I keep at it long enough, I may get somewhere, some day. (*She turns and deliberately kisses* TONY *on the brow.*)

JOE (*to* TONY). Will that hold you? I guess you don't need to worry no more after that. I guess that fixes your troubles for good. I guess you better admit I was pretty near right.

TONY. Now you know for w'y I been wantin' you go away, Joe. Dat goddam picture photograph! But evrathing is fix' now. Evrathing is fine. You don' need go away now, Joe.

JOE. You don't need me now. I guess I can migrate now. You got Amy to take care of you.

TONY. No! No! I need you here for tak' care of my vineyard. I don' let you go away now. Amy don' let you go away now.

AMY. Is he thinking of going away, Tony?

TONY. He don't go now, Dio mio! Ees no good Joe goin' away and leavin' Tony sick in da bed with nobody for runnin' vineyard!

JOE. You'll get somebody.

AMY. When's he going?

TONY. He say to-morrow. You don't let him go, Amy?

AMY. I got nothing to say about it.

TONY. You hear dat, Joe. Amy is asking' you for stay here.

AMY (*scorn*). *Yes,* I am!

JOE. I got to go, Tony. I just plain got to go.

AMY. If he won't stay for you, Tony, he won't stay for me. It ain't the place of a lady to be coaxing him, anyhow. . . . (*She again turns malevolent attention upon* JOE.) Where you headed for?

JOE. The next place.

AMY. What's the idea?

JOE. I just got to be on my way, an' that's all there is to it.

TONY. Ees all dose goddam Wobblies, Amy. You tell him stay here w'ile Tony is so sick in da bed like dees. You don' go to-morrow, Joe. You and me is talkin' more by-an-by, in da mornin'.

JOE. Oh, what's the use? I'm goin', I tell you.

AMY (*smiling darkly*). It must be pretty swell, being free and independent and beating it around the country just however you feel like, sleeping any place the notion hits you, no ties, work a day and bum a week, here and there, you and the —what do you call 'em? Wobblies? Huh! I never could see much in it myself. Calling in at farmhouses for a plate of cold stew and a slab of last Sunday's pie. Down in the Santa Clara we used to keep a dog for those boys. I guess it's a fine life if you like it. Only I never had much use for hoboes myself.

TONY. Joe ain' no hobo, Amy!

AMY. Ain't he?

JOE (*completely discomfited*). I guess I'll say good-night.

FATHER MC KEE (*furiously shouting off stage*). You got no business callin' it sacramental, because it ain't got no sanction from the Church!

(TONY *looks at the pair of them in unbelieving horror.* JOE *starts to go.* AMY *smiles triumphantly. Then the situation is saved by a tumult of voices and the porch is suddenly packed with the guests of the festa: men, women, and children, old and young, fat and lean. They follow* THE DOCTOR *and* FATHER MC KEE, *who are engaged in a furious argument.*)

THE DOCTOR. Is the Church opposed to the law or is it not?

FATHER MC KEE. The Church is opposed to interfering with the divine gifts of Providence.

THE DOCTOR (*as he enters*). It's the greatest reform since the abolition of slavery.

FATHER MC KEE (*as he enters*). "The ruler of the feast calleth the bridegroom and sayeth unto him: 'Every man setteth on first the good wine'."

THE DOCTOR. Oh, hell!

FATHER MC KEE. You're a godless heretic, young man, or you wouldn't be talkin' such blasphemy! I ain't got no sympathy with drunkenness, but there's plenty of worse things. How about chamberin'? Ain't chamberin' a worse sin than drunkenness? You think you can put a stop to drunkenness by pullin' up all the grapes. I suppose you can put a stop to chamberin' by pulling up all the women!

JOE. There's an argument for you, Doc.

THE DOCTOR. Alcohol is a poison to the entire alimentary system whether you make it in a still or in a wine barrel. It's poison, and poison's no good for any man. As for the Church . . .

FATHER MCKEE (*beside himself*). It ain't poison if you don't get drunk on it, an' you don't get drunk if you're a good Cath'lic!

THE DOCTOR. I suppose that drunkenness is confined to such scientific heretics as myself?

AMY. You certainly was lappin' it up outside, Doc.

TONY. Don' fight!

FATHER MC KEE. You'll have to pardon me, Tony, but when I hear these heretics gettin' full on bootleg liquor and callin' it sacramental!

(*The rest of the arguments is drowned in the pandemonium of the crowd. At first* THE DOCTOR *tries to keep them out.*)

THE GUESTS. Buona notte! Buon riposo! Evviva Antonio! Tanti auguri! Felice notte! Tante grazie!

JOE. Festa's over.

THE GUESTS. Come sta Antonio? Come

vas Voglio veder la padrona! Grazie, Antonio! Buona notte! Tanti auguri! A rivederci!

THE DOCTOR (*to* JOE). Tell them to cut the row!

THE GUESTS. Grazie, Antonio! Mille grazie, Antonio! Buona notte, Antonio! Tanti auguri! A rivederci!

THE DOCTOR. Keep those wops out of here! There's been enough noise already with this bigoted old soak.

FATHER MC KEE. You heretical, blasphemin' . . .

TONY. Padre, Madonna mia, don' fight no more! (*To the crowd.*) Eh!

THE DOCTOR (*still holding the crowd back in the doorway*). No, you can't come in here!

THE GUESTS. Si, si, dottore! Si, si dottore! Prego, dottore!

THE DOCTOR. No! Tony's too sick!

TONY. Tak' a pinch-a snuff, Doc, an sit down. (*The guests surge in as* TONY *calls to them.*) Vieni! Vieni qui! Venite tutti! Venite tutti!

THE GUESTS. Come va? Sta bene? Sta meglio, Antonio? Ha tanto sofferto, poveretto! Poveretto!

TONY (*picking out a small boy*). Ecco il mio Giovannino! Ah, com' è grande e bello e forte! Quanto pesa?

GIOVANNINO'S MOTHER. Ah, si, è grande, non è vero? Pesa sessanta cinque libbre.

TONY. Sessanta cinque! (*To* AMY.) Amy, looka him! He weigh' sixty-five pound', an' he's only . . . (*To the mother.*) Quant' anni?

GIOVANNINO'S MOTHER. Soltanto nove.

TONY. He's only nine year' old an' he weigh sixty-five pound'!

ANOTHER MOTHER. Antonio, ecco la mia. (*A little girl runs to throw her arms around* TONY'S *neck and kiss him. Exclamations of delight.*)

TONY (*to the mother*). Ah! Come so chiama?

THE SECOND MOTHER. Maria Maddalena Rosina Vittoria Emanuela.

TONY. Maria Maddalena Rosina Vit— (*To* AMY.) Looka Maria Maddalena! Ah, Maria Maddalena is goin' grow up an' be a fine, beautiful lady like my Amy.

GIOVANNINO'S MOTHER. E il mio Giovannino! (*To* MARIA'S MOTHER.) Santa Madonna! Ella non è più bella che il mio Giovannino!

MARIA'S MOTHER (*furious*). Si è più bella! E molto più bella che un ragazzone come questo.

GIOVANNINO'S MOTHER. Non è ragazzone, senti!

MARIA'S MOTHER. Si! Ma, la mia carina.

THE MEN (*hilariously*). Giovannino! Giovannino!

THE WOMEN (*at the same time*). Maria Maddalena! Maria Maddalena!

THE DOCTOR. Come on, now, get out! We've had enough of this!

ANGELO *and* GIORGIO (*facing the howling mob*). Basta! Basta! Via! Via! Fuori! Avanti! Al diavolo!

(*Uproar and retreat.*)

AMY (*on the porch, she stops them*). No, wait a minute! I want to tell 'em all good-night. Good-night! Good-night! Thank you. I've had the very best wedding that ever was and I'm the happiest girl in the world because you've been so good to me. Come back to-morrow and see Tony and tell him all the news. Good-night and God bless you.

VOICES. Siamo molto contenti! Com' è gentile! Com' è bella! Com' è simpatica! Grazie tanto, Amy!

JOE. They say thank you and God bless you. . . . Beat it, now. Buona notte! Run along. Come back to-morrow.

(*As they go down the hill, tenor, concertina, and chorus strike into song.*)

TONY. Oh, Amy, I w'isper in your ear, Amy. You ain' goin' be mad with Tony for bein' so crazy-wild with love? You come in da house like da spring come in da winter. You come in da house like da pink flower dat sit on da window sill. W'en you come da whole world is like da inside da wine cup. You ondrastan', Amy? I canno' help talkin' dees way. I got for tell you, Amy, an' I ain't got no English language for tell you. My Amy is so good, so prett'! My Amy. . . . (*He fairly breaks down.* AMY *pats his hand.*)

JOE (*to* FATHER MC KEE). Look at the poor wop. (*He is just going.*)

THE DOCTOR. Don't go, Joe. I want a hand with Tony.

FATHER MC KEE. Listen. . . . (*He holds up his hand for them to attend to the music. He pours wine into a cup.*) Here's to the bridal couple!

JOE (*same business*). Doc?

THE DOCTOR. No, thanks.

AMY. Oh, Doctor!

TONY. Doc, you no drink Tony's health?

THE DOCTOR. Oh, all right! (*He drinks*

with the others). Nasty stuff. (*He drains his glass. They laugh, all of them.*) Off to bed with you now, Tony!

TONY. My leg is hurt too much. I canno' sleep.

THE DOCTOR. I've got something that'll make you sleep. (*He mixes a powder in water and presents it to* TONY *for consumption.*)

TONY. Jes' Chris'! I canno' drink water, Doc! (*With the* DOCTOR'S *consent he adds wine to the draught.*)

THE DOCTOR. That's right. . . . Drink up. . . . (*The potion is downed.*)

TONY. Amy, you lookin' sad!

JOE. Do you blame her? She's had some day. (*A pat on her shoulder. She shrinks angrily.*)

AMY. I ain't sad. . . . It was a swell wedding and everybody had a swell time. Hear that? They're still singing. Ain't it pretty? And I don't want to hear no more of what the Doc was telling me outside about bringing a trained nurse up here from Napa. I'm all the nurse Tony needs, and don't nobody be afraid of my working, because there's nothing I like better. And when Tony's good and strong and don't have to be in bed all the time, we'll have Giorgio and Angelo carry him out in the sun and I'll sit beside him and read the paper out loud and we'll look at the view and feel that nice wind and we'll just enjoy ourselves. And the doc'll come up and see us. And the Padre, too, if they can keep from fighting. And if Joe goes away—why—he goes away, that's all. Don't nobody fret about little Amy. She's going to be all right.

(*The* DOCTOR *and the* PRIEST *exchange approving glances.*)

FATHER MC KEE. Amy, you're a credit to the parish.

THE DOCTOR (*at the head of the cot*). Joe, take that end!

TONY (*still spellbound*). My Amy. . . .

AMY. Yes, Tony?

TONY. I'm sleepy.

THE DOCTOR (*as* JOE *and he lift the cot*). Not too high.

TONY (*groaning, he can still reach to take his bottle along*). Wait!

JOE. Steady! You hold the door, Padre.

THE DOCTOR. Easy now! Not too fast.

AMY. Watch out for his hand!

THE DOCTOR. Take shorter steps, Joe. Every man ought to be taught how to carry a stretcher. Why, when I was in France . . . (*He backs through the door.*) Lower your end, Joe! You'll give him apoplexy.

TONY. Oh! . . .

JOE. I got him. . . . (*He follows through the door with the foot of the cot. Another groan from* TONY. AMY *takes a step toward door.*)

FATHER MC KEE. Better give 'em a minute. (*He goes into the bedroom.* AMY *is left alone. She stands quite still for a moment; then, giddily, drops into a chair.* FATHER MC KEE *returns.*)

FATHER MC KEE. You're a fine brave girl.

AMY. Thanks.

FATHER MC KEE. We have our trials, all of us.

AMY. Sure, I know that.

FATHER MC KEE. If ever you need a word of comfort, call on me, my daughter.

AMY. Thanks.

FATHER MC KEE. You may not be a Cath'lic, but I'll do my best by you. (AMY *smiles wanly.*) I had my doubts of this here marriage, but God knows who's meant for who in this world. He ain't done a bad turn by either you or Tony.

AMY. I got no kick.

(*The* DOCTOR *enters, quietly closing the bedroom door after him.*)

FATHER MC KEE. Be patient with him. He's old enough to be your father, and no man ain't got no business marryin' at his age, but he's a good fella.

AMY. I guess I better go in there now.

THE DOCTOR (*wiping his hands medically on his spotless handkerchief*). He's asleep. I've never known the like. Never in all my years of practice. It's a case that ought to be written up for the whole, entire medical profession. Both legs broken in the morning. Tibia, fibula, femur, and ischium. X-rayed and set inside of an hour after the accident. Patient married at noon and survives ten hours of whooping Dago celebration with no apparent ill effects.

AMY (*grim*). Yeah! What do you want me to do, Doctor?

THE DOCTOR. Let me send up a nurse in the morning.

AMY. No.

THE DOCTOR. A man in a cast's a handful. It's going to be a long siege.

AMY. I can manage. (*Suddenly desperate.*) God! I got to have something to do!

THE DOCTOR. Well. . . . (*He shrugs his shoulders.*) If he wakes up to-night, give him another one of those powders in a little wine. Wine won't harm the drug and the water might kill the patient. Eh, Padre?

AMY. Is that all, Doctor?

THE DOCTOR. That's all. I'll come up early in the morning.

AMY. Thanks.

THE DOCTOR. Sure about the nurse? (*She nods.*) You take it pretty calmly.

AMY. Ain't much else I can do, is there?

THE DOCTOR. Good-night. Joe's fixing you up a bed. He'll be here if you want him.

FATHER MC KEE (*going with the* DOCTOR). I ain't kissed the bride.

THE DOCTOR. Come on! (*He pushes* FATHER MC KEE *in front of him and they go off. Their voices die away.*) (AMY *goes to the table and mechanically removes her earrings.* AH GEE *enters by the outer door with a tray of glasses.* JOE *enters from the bedroom, closing the door carefully after him.*)

JOE. You turn in, Ah Gee. I'm going to sleep in here. (AH GEE *goes to his kitchen.* JOE *watches* AMY *with the same puzzled frown he has worn since she first turned upon him.*) Amy . . . (*She stiffens.*) I got you fixed up in Tony's big bed. I'm goin' to sleep in here in case you want any help.

AMY. All right.

JOE. Well, good-night. (*He goes about making himself comfortable for the night.*)

AMY. Good-night, Joe.

JOE. Keep a stiff upper lip. Everything's going to turn out O. K. Good-night.

AMY. You certainly do think you're God Almighty, don't you?

JOE. I don't get you.

AMY. Oh, well, let it go. I guess I don't feel so good.

JOE (*still busy with his bed*). Maybe it's the vino. It don't agree with some folks.

(*A slight pause.*)

AMY. I guess I'm just nervous.

JOE. I'd be nervous myself if I'd just been married.

AMY. Would you?

JOE. If I was a girl, I would.

AMY. Maybe that's why I'm nervous.

JOE. Sure it is. I often think how it must be for a girl takin' a big, important step like gettin' married. Everything new an' diff'rent an' all that.

AMY. Yeah.

JOE. But I wouldn't let it worry me if I was you.

AMY. I won't, Mister Joe. (*She takes up one of the lamps.*)

JOE. That's the idea. Good-night.

AMY. Good-night. (*She turns and looks desperately at him.*)

JOE. Say, look here, Amy . . .

AMY. I don't remember of giving you leave to use my Christian name.

JOE. Excuse me . . . only . . . there's something I just got to say to you before I go away. Because I am going. I'm going in the morning just as soon as Tony wakes up so's I can tell him good-by. But there's something I just got to ask you.

AMY. What is it?

JOE. You like Tony all right, don't you?

AMY. I married him, didn't I? And I let him give me jewelry, too, didn't I? A nice, self-respecting girl don't accept jewelry from a man she don't like. Not real jewelry.

JOE. I know that . . . only . . . it ain't just what I mean. Because, Tony—oh, he's a nut an' a wop an' all that, but he's just the best old fella I ever knew. Regular salt of the earth, Tony is. I wouldn't like to see Tony in trouble or unhappy or gettin' his feelings hurt or anything in that line. . . .

AMY (*dangerously*). Oh, wouldn't you?

JOE. No. An' it's all up to you now. . . . An' . . . well, you see what a fine old fella he is, don't you?

AMY. I ain't been complaining about him that I remember. When I start in complaining there'll be plenty of time then for outsiders to butt in and make remarks.

JOE. Don't get sore.

AMY (*fury again*). Who's sore? Say, listen to me. I know what I'm about, see? I married for a home, see? Well, I got a home, ain't I? I wanted to get away from working in the city. Well, I got away, didn't I? I'm in the country, ain't I? And I ain't working so very hard, either, that I can notice. Oh, I know what's expected of me and I ain't going to lay down on my job. Don't you fret. You be on your way, and mind your own business.

JOE. Oh, all right!

AMY. I got all I bargained for and then

some. I'm fixed. I'm satisfied. I didn't come up here . . . like I did . . . looking for love . . . or . . . or anything like that.

JOE. All I got to say is it's a good thing you got so dam' much sense.

AMY. I'll thank you not to swear about me, too. . . .

JOE. You got me wrong, Amy. I apologize. Maybe I was only seein' Tony's side of the question. Some girls would have been sorer'n you was over what old Tony done to get you here. But you're a real sport, that's what you are. You're a great girl an' I'm all for you. (*He emphasizes his approval with another patronizing pat on her shoulder.*)

AMY. Oh, for God's sake, leave me alone, can't you?

JOE (*who can grow angry himself*). Sure, I can! Good-night!

AMY. Good-night! (*She stands quite still, so does he. Far, far away the irrepressible tenor resumes "Maria Mari."*)

JOE. I'm sleeping in here in case . . .

AMY. There won't be any need of you putting yourself out.

JOE. How do you know but what Tony. . . .

AMY. I can take care of Tony and the further off *you* keep yourself the better I'll be pleased. (*Their eyes blaze.*)

JOE. Well, if you feel that way, I'll go back to my own shack. (*He grabs his coat and makes for the door.*) That wop'll be singing all night. (*He is out on the porch.*)

AMY. Joe!

JOE. What? (*He returns.*)

AMY. Would you mind waiting just a minute? There's something I got to ask *you.*

JOE. Shoot. . . .

AMY. You got to tell *me* the truth this time. You just got to tell me the truth. . . . You really and honestly didn't know nothing about his sending me that photo of you instead of his own, did you? You didn't know nothing at all about that?

JOE. Honest to God, I didn't. . . . Honest to God. . . .

AMY. On your sacred word of honor?

JOE. Honest.

AMY. I'm glad. And I want to apologize to you for what I said just now . . . and for that other thing I said about your being a common hobo and all. . . . I'm sorry, Joe. Will you forgive me?

JOE. Oh, that's all right.

AMY. I wouldn't want to have you go away to-morrow thinking what a mean character I got.

JOE. Nothing like that.

AMY. You mean it?

JOE. Shake. (*They shake hands, standing in the doorway.*) You're cryin'! . . . What's the matter, kid?

AMY. Oh, I don't know. . . . Nothing. . . . I'm all right. . . .

JOE. Come on! Don't get upset. Just make the best of things.

AMY. It ain't that.

JOE. Well, just make the best of things, anyway.

AMY. I'm trying to! I'm trying to!

JOE (*his hands on her shoulders*). You're married to a good man. I know the weddin' was kind of funny with Tony all smashed up an' all. But you just hold on a while an' everythin'll be O. K. You'll see!

AMY. I bet all those people are laughing at me.

JOE. No, they ain't.

AMY. I bet you're laughing at me.

JOE. I ain't, Amy. I'm sorry. . . .

AMY (*moving back from him*). Leave me alone, can't you?

JOE (*his voice very low*). Say, you're all right, Amy. . . . You're plumb all right.

AMY. I always was all right till I come up here. Now I wish I was dead! I wish I was dead!

JOE. Don' talk that way. You're all right. . . . (*Clumsily, he takes her arm. She stumbles. He catches her. There is a moment of silence broken only by their deep breathing as the physical being of one is communicated to the physical being of the other. Suddenly and irresistibly he clutches her to his breast and kisses her. She struggles a moment, then abandons herself.*)

TONY (*calling out in the bedroom*). Amy! (*She breaks loose, sobbing hysterically.*)

JOE (*a whisper*). Jesus! (*She stifles a little cry and turns for the bedroom door.*) No, you don't. . . . (*He catches her.*)

AMY (*struggling*). Let me go!

TONY. Amy!

(*She breaks free, terrified, and runs out of the house.* JOE *stands listening a moment, then runs after her as the curtain falls.*)

ACT THREE

The scene is unchanged, but the woman's presence has made itself felt. Handsome, though inexpensive, cretonne curtains grace the windows. A garish jardinière of porcelain holds a geranium plant and stands upon a colored oriental tabouret. The lamps have acquired art shades: one of some light-colored silk on a wire form and adorned with roses of the same material in a lighter shade, the other of parchment painted with windmills and Dutch kiddies. New pictures selected from the stock-in-trade of almost any provincial "art department" hang upon the walls; one of them, perhaps, a portrait of a well-known lady screen star. These have replaced Washington and Garibaldi and the Italian Steamship Company's poster. Painted and elaborately befringed leather sofa cushions fill the large chairs. It is hoped that one of the variety showing the head of Hiawatha can be secured for this, as they say, "touch." A brilliantly embroidered centerpiece covers the dining-room table and the flowers in the middle are palpably artificial. A white waste-paper basket is girt by a cerise ribbon which makes some corner of the room splendid. A victrola graces another corner.

Three months have passed. It is mid-afternoon.

An invalid chair has been made by laying a board between the seat of the morris chair and the top of a box. In this TONY *reclines, his crutches lying on the floor by his side.* FATHER MC KEE *nods drowsily in another chair.* JOE *sits on the porch rail outside the window perusing the scareheads of an I. W. W. paper.*

FATHER MC KEE (*continuing the discussion*). Now, Joe, don't be tryin' to tell me that things is goin' to be any better for havin' a revolution, because they ain't. Gover'ment's always gover'ment no matter what you call it, an' no particular kind of gover'ment ain't no more'n a label anyway. You don't change nothin' by givin' it a new name. Stick a "peppermint" label on a bottle of castor oil an' then drink it an' see what happens to you. Castor oil happens!

TONY. I am work' just as much like Joe an' I don' want changin' nothing.

JOE. I suppose you both come over here in the first place because you was satisfied with everythin' just like it was in the old country?

FATHER MC KEE. Human nature ain't nothin' but human nature an' the only way you ever could make a gover'ment is by obedience. Scalliwaggin' around about grievances an' labels don't accomplish nothin'. An' the only way you can make a revolution anythin' but a mess to no purpose is to change the people's ideas an' thank goodness there ain't nobody can accomplish that. It can't be done.

JOE. They're changin' already, Padre.

FATHER MC KEE. I'm talkin' to you with the cassock off, Joe. I'm lettin' you in on the secrets of the Mother Church. She knows the stock of ideas the world over an' she knows they don't never change. The Mother Church just keeps hammerin' an' hammerin' the same old nails because she knows there ain't no new ones worth hammerin'.

TONY. People come in da Unita State' because ees good place. I been comin' for mak' money.

JOE. You certainly succeeded.

TONY. You don' ondrastan', Joe. You got crazy idea. I'm comin' here for mak' money an' you want tak' my money all away.

JOE. What's your idea of progress, Padre?

FATHER MC KEE. Improvin' yourself! Now, Joe, it comes to my notice that you been 'round here talkin' pretty uppity 'bout the U. S. gover'ment. 'Tain't no good just makin' slurrin' remarks 'bout the gover'ment when you ain't got the ability nor the power to do nothin' toward improvin' it. You have got the power to do somethin' toward improvin' yourself, but I don't see you doin' it.

TONY. W'at I care for gover'ment? Peoples is tellin' me king is no good an' freedom is verra fine. W'at I care for king? W'at I care for freedom? Evrabody say dees gover'ment is bad for havin' pro'ibish'. I say pro'ibish' mak' me dam' rich. Evra man got his own idea w'at is good for evrabody else.

JOE. You're a bloomin' capitalist, that's what you are!

TONY. You mak' me tire', Joe. Evra minute talkin' 'bout Russia. . . . Russia. . . . Tak' a pinch-a snuff an' shut up!

JOE. Russia's got the right idea.

FATHER MC KEE. Now, listen to me,

young man. If you had the energy an' the reverence for authority and the continence that Tony has, you wouldn't be carryin' on 'bout no revolutions in Russia. 'Tain't sense. I've read a-plenty of your radical literature an' if you ask me, it's just plain stupid. I may be a priest an' I may be a celibate, but that don't make me no less of a man. An' no real man ain't never got no use for carryin's on. You radicals, Joe, you're always an' forever hollerin' an' carryin' on 'bout your rights. How 'bout your duties? There ain't no one to prevent your doin' your duties but you ain't never done 'em in your life.

JOE. I'm savin' my duties for the brotherhood of man.

TONY. Dio mio!

FATHER MC KEE. You're talkin' a lot of balderdash. Mind your own business an' leave the brotherhood of man to me. Brothers is *my* job.

TONY. You think evrabody's goin' be brother like dat an' don' scrap no more? Ees crazy idea! You ain' got no good sense, Joe, you an' dos goddam Wobblies.

FATHER MC KEE. I been mullin' this over in my mind, Joe, ever since Tony asked me to come up an' talk to you. An' I come to the conclusion that capital an' labor'll go on scrappin' to the end of time and they'll always be a certain number of people that'll stand up for the underdog. I been standin' up for the underdog all my life . . .

JOE (*indignant, he comes into the room*). Yes, you have! A helluva lot of standin' up you ever done for anybody but yourself!

TONY (*talking at the same time*). Now, Joe, don' you be gettin' fresh! You listen to w'at da Padre's sayin'!

FATHER MC KEE (*talking at the same time*). . . . but I learned a long time ago that the dog on top needs just as much standin' up for as the other kind and I ain't got much use for either of 'em because both of 'em's always complainin' an' carryin' on.

TONY. I been 'Merican citizen for twent' year'. I been vote evra year—some times two times. Ees fine thing, vote! I like. He mak' me feel like I am good man an' patriotic fella. But w'at I know 'bout vote? I don't know nothing. I don' care nothing. You think you know so much, eh? You want for change evrathing an' w'en you got evrathing change' like you want, some other fella is comin' for changin' you. Ees no good. (*A defiant look about him.*) You look-a me an' do like I done. You marry with good wife like my Amy an' live quiet in a fine house an' gettin' rich like me an' . . . an' . . . an' raisin' playnta kids like I am goin' do. Da's w'at is for life. Not for runnin' evra place, goddam to hell gover' ment with goddam Wobblies!

JOE. Now you got Tony goin' on kids again. I sure am catchin' all that's comin' my way. But, just the same, I'm goin' to take my trip to Frisco an' see what's what.

FATHER MC KEE. Well, Joe, I can understand your wantin' to shake the dust of this place off'n your feet. But I got to tell you that the adventures of the spirit is a great deal more interestin' than the adventures of the flesh. No man can't do no more'n 'bout six things with his flesh. But he can have a heap of fun with his immortal soul.

TONY. Joe is dam' lucky havin' good job here. Last time he talk 'bout goin' away, he tak' my advice an' stay here for runnin' da vineyard. Dees time he better tak' my advice some more.

(FATHER MC KEE *is fingering* JOE'S *papers ominously.*)

JOE. I'll just trouble you for them papers, Padre.

FATHER MC KEE. If you take my advice you'll burn 'em.

TONY. Joe don't mean no harm.

JOE. Maybe I don't mean nothin' at all. Maybe I'm just restless an' rarin' to go. I read these things an' they make me think. A man ought to think if he can. Oh, not tall talk. Just what he could be doin' himself. I think how I could get into the scrap. I ought to have been in on the dock strike at San Pedro, but I wasn't. I don't want to miss another big fight like that, do I? You fellows don't understand, but that's the way it is. An' maybe you're right an' I'm wrong. I can't help that. Maybe when I get down to Frisco I'll hear the same old bull from the same old loud-mouths, just like it used to be. Maybe I'll get disgusted and beat it south for the orange pickin's, or maybe go back on the railroad, or maybe in the oilfields. But, what the hell! I been hangin' around here on the point of goin' for three months now. I might just as well pick up and clear out to-morrow or the day after. I'll come back some day,

Tony. Anyway, there ain't no use of expectin' anythin' out of a guy like me. Don't get sore. What the hell!

TONY. You goin' in da jail, sure!

JOE. I could go worse places. A guy went to jail up in Quincy, in Plumas County, awhile back, for carryin' a Wobbly card—like this one, see? (*He displays the famous bit of red cardboard.*) His lawyer pleads with the judge to go easy on the sentence. "Your honor," he says, "this chap served in France an' won the Croy de Gaire an' the Distinguished Service Cross." An' right there the guy jumps up an' says: "Don't you pay no attention to that stuff," he says. "I don't want no credit for no services I ever performed for no gover'ment that tells me I got to go to jail to stand up for my rights."

FATHER MC KEE. Do you want to go to jail?

JOE. There's worse places, I tell you. I been there before, too. That guy in Quincy got the limit an' I'd like to shake hands with him, I would. Tony says this is a free country. Well, Tony ought to know. He's a bootlegger.

TONY (*indignantly*). Hah!

JOE. What I say is: about the only freedom we got left is the freedom to choose which one of our rights we'll go to jail for.

FATHER MC KEE (*super-sententiously*). Joe.

TONY. Shhh! Here's Amy!

AMY (*off stage*). Ah Gee!

(JOE *rises;* FATHER MC KEE *pauses in his harangue;* TONY *beams;* AMY *enters. She wears a bright dress and a red straw hat which pushes her hair down about her face. A duster swings dashingly from her shoulders. Her market basket hangs from her arm. She has stuffed some late lupin in the top of it.*)

AMY. Scrapping again, are you? What's the matter, this time? Has Joe got another attack of the foot-itch? (*She sets the basket down on the table, doffs hat and duster, and, as she does so, sees* JOE'S *papers.*) Oho! So that's it. (*Patiently* JOE *folds the papers up.*) See them, Tony? (*She exhibits the lupin and begins to stuff it into the vase with the artificial flowers.*) Ain't they sweet? They're so pretty they might be artificial.

FATHER MC KEE. We been talkin' 'bout reformin' the social system.

AMY. Well, you got a fine day for it. (*She hugs* TONY'S *head and lets him pat her hand.*) Ain't the doctor come yet?

TONY. Doc don' come to-day.

AMY. Sure he does.

JOE. He comes on Thursday.

FATHER MC KEE. To-day's Wednesday.

AMY. Well, I never! Here they are reforming the world and they don't even know what day of the week it is. Ain't men the limit?

TONY. Nobody is so smart like my Amy. (*With a toss of her head she swirls off into the kitchen.*)

AMY. Don't let me stop you! Go right ahead. (*In the kitchen.*) Ah Gee . . . Oh, there you are. . . .

FATHER MC KEE. Thursday! It's my day to talk to the boys down at the parish school.

JOE. Hand 'em what you just been handin' me, Padre.

FATHER MC KEE. What I told you was confidential, Joe. I'm sorry you won't listen to it.

AMY (*she returns, carrying a dish with apples and a knife*). See them, Tony?

TONY. Apples!

AMY. Guess what for?

TONY. Apples pie?

AMY (*she sits beside* TONY *and falls to on the apples*). Well, the world may need reforming but I got no kick. The grapes is near ripe and ready for picking. The nights is getting longer, the mornings is getting colder, and Tony's getting better. Down town they're putting up the posters for the circus and I hear the show's going into winter quarters just the other side of Napa. I guess that's all the remarks I got to make now.

JOE. Here's the doc, now. . . .

(*A Ford motor.*)

THE DOCTOR (*off stage*). Hello!

AMY. Yoo hoo!

(*The* DOCTOR *appears, shakes hands with* AMY, *nods to* JOE *and the* PADRE, *and then he comes in to* TONY.)

THE DOCTOR. Well, how do the crutches go?

AMY. Just fine.

TONY. You want see me walkin', Doc?

THE DOCTOR. Perhaps, I do. Let's see. . . . (*He feels the injured legs.*) Tibia . . . Fibula . . . Feels all right.

TONY (*with a proud, anatomical gesture*). Ischium?

THE DOCTOR (*he rises and nods approvingly*). All right, Tony, show us what you can do. No jumping, mind! Lend him a hand, Joe.

(*He stands aside to watch.* JOE *assists* TONY. *Grunting,* TONY *stands on his crutches and grins proudly.*)

TONY. Ees hurtin' here. (*Indicating arm pits.*) But ees goin' fine! (*A few tottering steps.*)

THE DOCTOR. Steady! Whoa! (*Laughter as* TONY *barely makes a chair.*) You ought to be put on exhibition. If anyone had told me that day when I had you on the table that I should see you on crutches in three months! Well, all I can say is, it pays to know how to set a fracture.

AMY. I guess it makes you realize what a good doctor you are.

THE DOCTOR. He owes something to your nursing, ma'am.

FATHER MC KEE. It's like the layin' on of hands, her nursin' is.

AMY. Funny you're saying that, Padre. I once had my fortune told down in Frisco. Out of a palmistry book one of my friends had. Everything in your hand means something, you know. See those bumps? Ain't they funny? Well, the book said that those bumps mean you're a good nurse and can take care of anybody no matter how sick he is. That's why I wouldn't let you send for no trained nurse, Doc. I was afraid she wouldn't have my bumps. . . . Gee, I got funny hands! . . .

THE DOCTOR. I'm not sure that medical science pays much attention to the nursing bump, ma'am, but you have certainly got it. I'll admit that.

TONY. My Amy is da best nurse I ever see.

AMY. Oh, Tony!

THE DOCTOR. I'm going to put your patient outside in the sun. Is there a good level place?

AMY. Under the arbor! . . . Oh Tony!

TONY. After three month' in dees goddam house!

THE DOCTOR. Fix him up right with a big easy chair.

AMY. And plenty of pillows.

TONY. Amy, you ain' forgot how you promise' 'bout readin' da paper outside in da sun?

AMY. You bet I ain't forgot.

THE DOCTOR. Go on, now. I want to see you fixed.

TONY (*hobbles to the door and calls out*). Giorgio . . . Angelo . . . Eccomi!

(GIORGIO *and* ANGELO *arrive in a whirlwind of Italian.* TONY *hobbles out of sight.* AMY *follows with two pillows, looking back at the* DOCTOR *and laughing.* FATHER MC KEE *carries the board and box. The* DOCTOR *goes to the door as though he intended following them. He stands looking out and speaks without turning.*)

THE DOCTOR. Joe . . .

JOE. What is it?

THE DOCTOR. I hear you're going away.

JOE. Yeah. I'm really goin' this time.

THE DOCTOR. Where to?

JOE. Search me. Frisco first.

THE DOCTOR. Hadn't you better take Amy with you? (*He turns then and looks sternly into* JOE's *startled eyes.*)

JOE. What?

THE DOCTOR. You heard me.

JOE. I don't get you.

THE DOCTOR. Amy came to see me last week. I didn't tell her what the trouble was. I didn't have the heart. I put her off. . . . Oh, it's easy to fool a woman. But you can't fool a doctor, Joe. (*A step nearer* JOE *and eyes hard on his face.*) Tony isn't the father. . . . He couldn't be. (*A long pause.*)

JOE (*under his breath*). Oh, Christ!

THE DOCTOR. I thought so. (*Another long pause.*) I've been trying to figure out how to make things easiest for Tony. It upset me a good deal. Doctors get shocked more often than you'd think. . . . And a girl like Amy, too. . . . I didn't know what to do. I guess it's up to you.

JOE. Poor old Tony!

THE DOCTOR. You might have thought of him sooner—and of Amy, too, for that matter.

JOE. It wasn't on purpose. It was only once! But—honest to God, we wouldn't either of us have put anything like that over on old Tony. Not for a million dollars!

THE DOCTOR. You couldn't have wasted much time about it.

JOE. It was the first night.

THE DOCTOR. Good Lord!

JOE. It just happened. There was a reason you don't know about. I'm a swell guy, ain't I? To do a thing like that to a fellow like Tony.

THE DOCTOR. Shall I tell Tony? Or Amy?

JOE. No. . . . Gimme time to think.

THE DOCTOR. There's no concealing this.

Don't try anything of that sort. I won't have it.

JOE. No.

THE DOCTOR. This is going to come near killing him.

(JOE *nods fearsomely. The* DOCTOR *turns and is going when* AMY *appears, marshalling* ANGELO *and* GIORGIO.)

AMY. Just cut out the welcome to our city stuff and carry this chair down there under the arbor where the boss is. (*As they pick it up, she turns to the* DOCTOR.) Say! You'd think to hear 'em that Tony'd just been raised from the dead. (*She turns back to the two Italians.*) Put it in the shade. . . . Mind that varnish, you club-footed wops. . . . There. . . . (*She has seen the chair safely along the porch. She returns and makes for the bedroom, saying, as she goes.*) He wants a cover and everything you can think of. . . .

THE DOCTOR (*to* JOE). Let me know if I can do anything.

(AMY *returns carrying a great, thick quilt. She cuts for the door, muttering happily to herself. On the porch she stops to call through the window to the stricken* JOE.)

AMY. Joe—just hand me them newspapers, will you?

JOE (*obeying*). Here.

AMY (*in the doorway, her arms filled with papers and comforter, she sees his face*). Gee—you look something fierce.

JOE (*in a strangled voice*). Amy . . .

AMY. What is it?

JOE. I got to see you by an' by. . . . I got to see you alone . . . (*She starts to speak. He sees that he has frightened her.*) God damn . . . oh, God damn. . . .

AMY. What's the matter with you? What you scaring me this way for?

JOE. Amy. . . . Just a minute ago . . .

AMY. Make it snappy. . . . I don't like this being alone with you. . . . It makes me think . . . I want to forget all that.

JOE. Yeah . . . An' me . . . that's what I mean.

AMY. What?

JOE (*after an awful pause*). You're goin' to have a kid. (*She stares incredulously at him without making a sound.*) Yeah. . . . It's so, Amy. . . . I'm awfully sorry. . . . The doc just told me. . . . He found out when you was sick last week. . . . He knows all about it . . .

AMY (*she stands a moment without moving at all. Suddenly she lets quilt and papers slip to the floor and her hands clasp themselves over her abdomen*). Oh, my God! (*She picks the quilt and papers up very carefully and puts them on the table. She drops weakly into one of the chairs as though her knees had failed her, her face rigid with terror.*)

AMY. What am I going to do?

JOE. I got to think. . . .

AMY. If you go wrong, you're sure to get it sooner or later. I got it sooner.

JOE. That kind of talk won't help any.

AMY. I'm glad of it. It serves me right. . . .

JOE. There's ways, you know . . . there's doctor. . .

AMY (*shakes her head vigorously*). Them kind of doctors is no good.

JOE. But maybe . . .

AMY. They're no good. I'm too far gone anyway . . . I know . . . and anyway . . . doing that . . . It's worse than the other.

JOE. I'm sorry, Amy. . . .

AMY. You being sorry ain't got nothing to do with it, either. I'm thinking of Tony.

JOE. So'm I.

AMY. Tony's a white guy if he *is* a wop.

JOE. Yeah. . . .

AMY (*desperately loud*). What am I going to do? What am I going to do?

JOE. Hey! . . . Not so loud!

AMY. But I ain't got no money . . . only my earrings. . . .

JOE. I got money enough.

AMY. You?

JOE. Tony made me save it. It's in the bank. More'n two hundred bucks. That'll see you through.

AMY. Tony'll be crazy. . . . Tony'll be just crazy.

JOE. The doc said for me to take you away with me.

AMY. You?

JOE. Yeah. . . . An' believe me, Amy, I'll do anything . . .

AMY. Going away with you won't help things any.

JOE. I'll treat you right, Amy.

AMY. Poor Tony!

JOE. I'll do the right thing if it kills me.

AMY. I must have been crazy that night.

JOE. We both was . . . but there's no use sayin' that now.

AMY. No. . . . Tony'll be crazy. (*She lifts her head, recognizing the inevitable.*) I guess the doc's right. I guess I'll have to go with you. . . . Somebody's got to help me out. . . . There ain't nobody but you.

JOE. That's all right. . . . I'm willing. . . .

AMY. And afterwards . . . Oh, my God! . . . And Tony'll be thinking that all the time . . . you and me . . . Oh! (*This is an exclamation of unutterable disgust.*) Poor Tony! You don't know how good he's been to me. And all the time he was so crazy for a kid. . . . Oh, I can't stick around here now! I got to go. I got to go quick.

JOE. I'm ready, if you are.

AMY. I'll just pack my grip.

JOE. Don't take it too hard, Amy. (*He tries to take her hand.*)

AMY (*shaking him off*). None of that! I don't want no sympathy.

JOE. Excuse me.

AMY. You better get your own things.

JOE. All right. . . . I'll be back in a minute.

AMY. I'll get a move on, too.

(AH GEE *comes in with the dishes for dinner and begins to lay the table. Apparently* JOE *thinks of something more to say, but is deterred by* AH GEE'S *presence. He goes quickly.* AMY *hears* AH GEE *and watches him for a moment as though she were unable to understand what he is doing.*)

AH GEE (*as he puts down dishes*). Velly good dinner tonight, Missy. Beans an' roas' veal an' apple pie!

TONY (*calling from off stage*). Eh, Joe! Eh, JOE! W'ere you go like dat? Amy! W'ere are you, Amy? (*He comes up on to the porch.*) Ah! Here you are!

AH GEE. Oh, Bossy! Velly good dinner tonight. Apple pie!

TONY (*pleased*). Ah! Apples pie! (AH GEE *goes into his kitchen.* TONY *leans against door.*) Amy! W'y you no' come back?

AMY (*who has been clinging desperately to the back of a chair*). I don't know!

TONY. You leave me alone so long.

AMY. I just come in for the papers and . . .

TONY. . . . An' Joe is runnin' crazy wild an' don' say nothing w'en I'm askin' him, "Joe, w'ere you goin' like dat?"

AMY. Joe's going away.

TONY. He's no' goin' without sayin' goo'-by?

AMY. I dunno. . . . Maybe he is. . . .

TONY. That boy mak' me verra unhappy. I been lovin' Joe like he was my own son an' he's goin' away like dat. He's no good.

AMY. People who ain't no good ain't worth worrying about. The thing to do is let 'em go and forget 'em.

TONY. Da's no' so easy like you think, Amy. I been lovin' Joe like my own son.

AMY. Joe ain't no worse than other people I could mention.

TONY. I love Joe but he don' love me.

AMY. I love you, Tony! I love you!

TONY. I know, Amy, I know.

AMY. And you ain't never going to believe that I do again.

TONY. W'at you talkin' 'bout, Amy?

AMY. Something's happened, Tony!

TONY. Eh?

AMY. It's going to make you terrible mad.

TONY. Amy!

AMY (*nerving herself*). It's going to make you just crazy, but I'm going to tell you just exactly what it is, Tony, because I ain't going to have you thinking afterwards that I wasn't grateful or that I ain't been happy here . . . happier than I ever been in my whole life. . . .

TONY. Amy!

AMY. Wait a minute. . . . I got to confess, Tony. I got to tell you the whole business so's you won't be thinking I been any worse than just what I have. . . .

TONY. Amy!

AMY. Yeah. . . . And I don't want you blaming Joe no more'n what you blame me and anyway you're a-bound to find out sooner or later, an' it'll hurt you a lot less in the long run if I tell you the truth right now, and I got to tell you the truth anyway. I simply got to. Wait a minute, Tony! I'm going to tell you the truth and after I go away and you don't see me no more you can say: "Well she wasn't no good but it wasn't my fault." Because it wasn't your fault, Tony. Not one bit, it wasn't. You didn't have nothing to do with it. And I wouldn't be going away, neither, not for a million dollars I wouldn't, only for what's happened. . . .

TONY. Amy, w'at you talkin' 'bout goin' away?

AMY. That's what I'm trying to tell you, Tony, only you got to give me a chance because it ain't easy to tell you no more'n it's easy to go away. And I got to go. But it ain't because I don't love you. I do. And it ain't because I don't appreciate all you done for me. I ain't never going to forget none of it, nor you, nor this place. . . .

TONY. Amy!

AMY. Listen to me, Tony! You're going to kick me out when you hear what I got to say, but I don't care if you do. I'm going to have a baby, Tony . . . and it's . . . God help me! . . . it's Joe's baby.

TONY (*raising his crutch with a great cry of anger*). Ah!

AMY. Didn't I tell you you'd kick me out?

TONY (*faltering*). Dio mio! Dio mio! No! Amy, you fool with me? Eh?

AMY. No, I'm not fooling. It's so. And that's why I'm going away, Tony.

TONY (*pursuing her as she retreats*). You been Joe's woman!

AMY. I was crazy!

TONY. You been Joe's woman!

AMY. I was crazy!

TONY. You been lovin' Joe!

AMY. No . . . I ain't . . . I ain't . . . I never loved Joe. Honest, I never. I was crazy.

TONY. You been just like da Padre say you was. . . . You been a whore. . . .

AMY. I ain't! . . . I ain't! I been straight all my life! Only that one night. . . .

TONY. W'at night?

AMY. The first night I come here.

TONY. Da night you marry with me!

AMY. I ain't even spoke to Joe alone since that night.

TONY. You lyin'!

AMY. I swear to God I ain't! Not once! Not till to-day after the doc told him what was going to happen.

TONY. You lyin' to me! You been Joe's woman!

AMY. I ain't, Tony! That's what I'm trying to tell you. It's the truth I'm trying to tell you and now I'm going away.

TONY. You goin' away with Joe?

AMY. My God, what else can I do?

TONY (*furiously he forces her back into the corner where the shotgun is hanging, spluttering all the time with slobbering, half-intelligible rage*). I don' let you go! I don' let you go! By God, I'm goin' kill dat Joe! Questo bastardo, Joe! I'm goin' kill him an' keep you here for see me kill him! Goddam you! You goddam dirty . . . (*He has got the gun down, broken it, and is loading it.*)

AMY (*speaking at the same time*). No, you won't, Tony! Don't do anything like that, now, Tony! You'll be sorry if you do! You know what'll happen to you if you do that! You know what'll happen to you, Tony! That ain't no way to act! You'll see what you get! You'll see!

TONY. Goddam! . . . You wait, you dirty . . . (*He flourishes the broken gun. She covers her eyes with her hands.* JOE *arrives, sees what* TONY *is doing, gives a cry, springs on him, wrenches the gun away. The struggle upsets* TONY'S *balance and he topples headlong off his crutches.* AMY *screams.*)

AMY. Oh, his leg! (*Joe drops the gun and bends over him.*)

JOE. I tried to catch him. . . . (TONY'S *bellows are terrifying to hear.*) Did you hurt yourself, Tony? (*Tony's answer is untranslatable into speech.*)

AMY (*as she pulls a chair over*). For God's sake, pick him up, can't you?

JOE (TONY *fights him, trying to choke him, and sinks into the chair, howling with pain and fury*). All right now, Tony! Steady!

AMY. Tony. . . . Tony. . . . (*She kneels down by him.* TONY'S *roars subside into moans.*) I had to tell him! Oh, my God! I just had to tell him!

JOE. He didn't hurt himself much. (TONY'S *moans break into sobs.*)

AMY. This is awful.

JOE. Get your things. Let's pull out of here. We can send the Padre up to look after him.

AMY. I'm only taking my little grip, Tony. I'm leaving the earrings on the dresser. (*She goes quickly into the bedroom.* TONY'S *sobs keep up wretchedly and terribly.*)

JOE. Tony, I . . . (*Again* TONY *springs madly at* JOE'S *throat.* JOE *wrenches away and runs quickly to the table where he gets a glass of wine which he brings back to* TONY. TONY *pushes it away, spilling the wine over his shirt.* JOE *drops the glass.*)

TONY. Amy! Amy! Amy! Amy!

AMY (*she comes back, with her hat on and her coat over her arm. She has her yellow grip half open with clothes sticking out.* JOE *takes it from her*). Here I am, Tony. Here I am.

TONY. W'ere you goin' Amy? W'ere you goin' away from here?

AMY. I dunno . . . .Frisco, I guess. . . .

TONY (*bitter sobs*). You goin' be livin' with Joe?

AMY (*vague misery*). I dunno. . . . No,

I ain't going to live with Joe. . . . No matter what happens, I ain't.

TONY. Who is goin' be lookin' after you, Amy?

JOE. I am, Tony. I'll do the right thing if it kills me.

TONY. You? . . . You? . . . Oh, Dio mio! Dio mio! No! No!

JOE. Come on, Amy, for the love of Pete!

AMY. I'm coming.

TONY (*a hand out to stop her*). You ain't got no money, Amy.

AMY. It don't matter.

TONY. Yes!

JOE. I got plenty.

TONY. No! . . . No! . . . No! . . . Joe is no good for lookin' after womans an' baby!

AMY. Don't take on, Tony. . . . Please don't take on! Let me go, and forget all about me. There ain't no use in talking any more.

TONY. You goin' have baby!

AMY. God, I know I am!

TONY. How you goin' mak' money for keep him? Before you go, you tell me dat!

AMY. God knows. . . . I don't.

TONY. Pretty quick Joe is leavin' you desert, and den w'at is goin' happen?

JOE. I swear I'll stick, Tony!

TONY. No! *No!* NO!! Ees no good! My Amy havin' baby in da street. Ees no good.

AMY. Don't say that for God's sake, Tony, don't say that . . .

TONY. W'at is goin' happen, Amy? W'at's goin' happen with you?

AMY. Joe . . . I can't stand no more of this.

TONY (*frenzied*). No! *No!* NO!! NO!!!

AMY. Let go, Tony! Let go of my skirt!

TONY. You ain' goin', Amy! I don't let you go! You stayin' here with Tony!

AMY. Don't talk that way, Tony! It ain't no good.

TONY. No! No! You goin' listen to w'at Tony say now. You goin' listen, Amy. You don' love Joe. You love Tony. You been good wife, Amy. . . .

AMY. Good wife!

TONY. W'at is Tony goin' do without you?

JOE. Come on!

TONY. Amy, I get excite' just now, Amy. Excuse! Excuse! I think verra good once more. You ain' goin' with Joe. You stayin' here with Tony just like nothin' is happen', an' by an' by da little fella is come. . . .

AMY. Don't talk that way, Tony!

TONY. W'y not?

AMY. Because it ain't no way to talk!

TONY. Yes . . . yes . . . ees good sense! Ees w'at is evrabody wantin' here! You an' Joe an' me! . . . Looka Joe. Joe is wantin' go with Wobblies, eh? With goddam Wobblies. All right . . . Looka Amy . . . Amy is wantin' stay here nice an' safe in dees fine house with Tony. Is not true, eh? (AMY *nods through her tears.*) Sure is true. Look Tony, Dio mio, an' ask him w'at he want? Don' he want baby?

AMY. But not this baby, Tony?

TONY. W'at I care?

AMY. But, think of what people would say!

TONY. W'at I care w'at evrabody say? We tellin' evrabody he's Tony's baby. Den evrabody say Tony is so goddam young an' strong he's break both his leg' an' havin' baby just da same! . . . Ees good, eh? You don' go with Joe now, Amy? . . . Oh, Amy! . . .

AMY (*he has swayed her, but she looks at him as at a madman*). No. . . . It wouldn't work, Tony. . . . You wouldn't mean it afterward. . . . You're crazy. . . .

TONY (*a last frantic appeal*). No! No! No! (*Leaning back in his chair and looking around the room.*) W'at's good for me havin' dees fine house? W'at's good for me havin' all dis money w'at I got? I got nobody for give my house an' my money w'en I die. Ees for dat I want dis baby, Amy. Joe don' want him. Ees Tony want him. Amy, . . . Amy, . . . for God's sake don' go away an' leave Tony!

AMY. But, Tony! Think of what I done?

TONY. What you done was mistake in da head, not in da heart. . . . Mistake in da head is no matter.

AMY. You—you ain't kiddin' me, are you? . . . You're serious, ain't you—Tony? You'll stick to this afterwards, won't you, Tony? (*She walks slowly over to him. She throws her arms around his neck and presses his head against her breast. A prolonged pause.*) Well, Joe, I guess you better be going.

JOE. You mean?

AMY. I guess you'd better be going. (JOE *straightens in great relief.*)

JOE. All right. (*He picks up his knap-*

sack which he dropped when he came in.) I guess you're right. (*He pulls on his cap and stands a moment in the doorway, a broad grin spreading over his face.*) I guess there ain't none of us got any kick comin', at that. No real kick. (*He goes out slowly.*)

AMY (*lifting her face*). No.

(TONY *clutches her even closer as the curtains falls.*)

Beggar On Horseback

BY GEORGE S. KAUFMAN AND MARC CONNELLY

First produced by Winthrop Ames at the Broadhurst Theatre in New York City, on February 12, 1924, with the following cast:

DR. ALBERT RICE	Richard Barbee
CYNTHIA MASON	Kay Johnson
NEIL McRAE	Roland Young
MR. CADY	George W. Barbier
MRS. CADY	Marion Ballou
GLADYS CADY	Anne Carpenger
HOMER CADY	Osgood Perkins
A BUTLER	Pascal Cowan
JERRY	Edwin Argus
A BUSINESS MAN	Maxwell Selser
MISS HEY	Spring Byington
MISS YOU	Fay Walker
A WAITER	Charles A. House
A REPORTER	James Sumner
A JUROR	Paul Wilson
A GUIDE	Walker M. Ellis
A SIGHTSEER	Norman Sweetser
A NOVELIST	Bertrand O. Dolson
A SONG WRITER	Chappell Cory, Jr.
AN ARTIST	Henry Meglup
A POET	Hamilton McFadden

THE PANTOMIME—DURING PART TWO

A Kiss in Xanadu

The music of the pantomime, and all other music used in the play, composed by Deems Taylor.

H.R.H. THE CROWN PRINCE OF XANADU	George Mitchell
H.R.H. THE CROWN PRINCESS OF XANADU	Grethe Ruzt-Nissen
FIRST LADY IN WAITING	Spring Byington
FIRST LORD OF THE BED-CHAMBER	Drake DeKay
A LAMPLIGHTER	Tom Raynor
A POLICEMAN	Edwin Argus
CÆSAR AND POMPEY	J. Hamilton and H. James

IF THE UNIQUE quality of *Beggar on Horseback* is attributable to Marc Connelly's known taste for fancy, it is also plainly a product of George S. Kaufman's special flair for theatricality. The story, it is true, did not originate with either of the playwrights any more than did the style of expressionism. They derived the one from the comedy *Hans Sonnenstössers Höllenfahrt* by Paul Apel, brought to their attention by Winthrop Ames, and the other from the subjective or dream technique known as expressionism first cultivated by Strindberg in *The Dream Play* and *The Spook Sonata* and sociologized in the early twenties by Central Europeans like Kaiser, Toller, and the brothers Capek. But Connelly and Kaufman took Apel's sketchy picture of an artist's revolt against middle-class family ties and rounded it out with recognizably American life. Their treatment became original American showmanship. The play is a breezy and harum-scarum travesty in the form of a young composer's nightmare after he has considered marriage to a businessman's daughter. The serious underside of the fantasy is the pervasive question of how an artist is to maintain integrity in our time, of how he can survive as artist while hired to work at his craft: "You take our money and you live our life. . . . We pay the piper and we tell him what to play." Kaufman and Connelly were not alone in raising the question, and it was to be asked in the theatre and in fiction repeatedly. The authors are less to be commended for stating it than for the way they made vivid theatre out of it in the idiom of their time and place.

Beggar on Horseback was not their first collaboration. Connelly (1891) from McKeesport, Pa., and Kaufman (1899) from Pittsburgh, Pa., both became journalists after their respective schooling. (Kaufman was drama editor for The New York Times.) They first pooled resources when they came to write *Dulcy* (1921), a play based on the befuddled heroine of F.P.A.'s New York World column. Next came *To the Ladies* (1922), *Merton of the Movies* (1922), the musical *Helen of Troy, The Deep Tangled Wildwood,* and after *Beggar on Horseback* (1924) another musical *Be Yourself* (1924).

When they parted company, Connelly wrote the pleasant whimsy *The Wisdom Tooth* (1926), that memorable folk drama *The Green Pastures* (1930), *The Farmer Takes a Wife* (with Frank B. Elser, 1934), and other plays. Kaufman wrote *The Butter and Egg Man,* a comedy about show business, independently in 1925. He collaborated with the novelist Edna Ferber on *Minick* (1924), *The Royal Family* (1928), and *Stage Door* (1936), and with Ring Lardner on *June Moon* (1929), a farce on tinpan alley tunesmith business which has echoes of *Beggar on Horseback*. He achieved another fruitful partnership with Moss Hart in *Once in a Lifetime* (1930), *Merrily We Roll Along* (1934), the Pulitzer Prize comedy *You Can't Take It With You* (1936), the musical *I'd Rather Be Right* (1937), *The Man Who Came to Dinner* (1939), and *The American Way* (1939). He made musical comedy history with Morrie Ryskind in *Of Thee I Sing* and *Let 'Em Eat Cake* (1931, 1933). He wrote a number of other plays in collaboration, such as *The Dark Tower* (with Alexander Woollcott, 1933) and *First Lady* (with Katherine Dayton, 1935), and he dramatized John P. Marquand's *The Late George Apley* (1944).

Mr. Kaufman has been an extremely ingenious practitioner on Broadway. Although he has rarely risen measurably above its aims and requirements, he has enabled it to flourish as vivid, topical, and worldly theatre. His collaborators and he have been marvelous recorders of American surfaces, and they have occasionally penetrated beneath the surface long enough to suggest a critical outlook that they themselves were either disinclined or unable to carry to conclusions. Their mockery was barbed although they generally withdrew the arrow for the sake of amiability and a full box-office tiller. Their cynicism was often knowing, their flippancy amusing and at worst just a trifle too empty; only their sentiment, as a rule, was without any sort of merit other than good will.

PART ONE

The scene is NEIL MCRAE's *apartment in a comfortable, run-down and not very expensive building. It is plainly an artist's room, and furnished with as many good looking things as the occupant could afford—which are not many. The most luxurious piece of furniture in the room is a grand piano, which* NEIL *has probably hung on to with no little difficulty. It stands well down left. Down right is an easy chair—the only chair in the room that even suggests comfort—and against the rear wall is* NEIL's *desk. In front of the desk is a swivel chair, and two or three other chairs, stiff-backed, stand around the room. At the left of the stage, near the piano, is a window, hung with chintz curtains that have seen better days—curtains which come to life here and there in great splotches of red. Some of the same stuff hangs in a centre doorway—a doorway that leads to* NEIL's *bedroom and thence to a "kitchenette." The door into the apartment is at the right—somewhere beyond it is the elevator, and one needs only a look at the room to know that it is an elevator that requires four minutes to ascend the three floors.*

The time is about four-thirty of a Spring afternoon. The curtain rises on the room and nothing more; then, after a second, there comes a knock on the door. The knock is repeated, then the knob is cautiously turned and the door slowly opens. DR. ALBERT RICE, a young man of *thirty or so, peers inquiringly into the room through the widening crack, sees no one, and enters.*

ALBERT. Neil! (*There is no answer; he observes the room. Slightly to his surprise, he sees a sewing basket on the piano.*) Are you married? (*He goes up to the bedroom entrance and veers into the semi-darkness.*) Neil! (CYNTHIA MASON, *who seems to be about twenty-five, appears suddenly in the doorway at right. There is a moment of uncertainty as she and the doctor confront each other.*)

CYNTHIA. Are you looking for Mr. McRae?

ALBERT. Yes. The door was open.

CYNTHIA (*disturbed*). Really? Was it wide open?

ALBERT. It was closed, but it wasn't locked.

CYNTHIA. *Oh!* (*There is a pause of uncertainty.*) Was Mr. McRae expecting you?

ALBERT. No—I just got in from Chicago. Neil and I are old friends. My name is Rice.

CYNTHIA. Oh! You're not *Doctor* Rice?

ALBERT. Yes.

CYNTHIA (*laughing*). I'm so relieved! My name is Cynthia Mason, Dr. Rice. I know a great deal about *you.* (*They shake hands.*)

ALBERT. Of course Neil never writes letters, so you've been concealed from me. You didn't know him a few months ago, did you, when I left New York?

CYNTHIA. No, only since he moved here. I live across the hall.

ALBERT. Oh, I see.

CYNTHIA (*looking around*). There's that work basket. (*She takes it from the piano, then faces the doctor again.*) I hope you'll forgive me, when I tell you why I lingered.

ALBERT. You're forgiven.

CYNTHIA. Night before last we had burglars.

ALBERT. Really?

CYNTHIA. Not on this floor—the apartment below. The poor man lost three or four suits of clothes, so——

ALBERT (*with an understanding smile*). So Neil leaves his door unlocked.

CYNTHIA. Probably since early this morning. Though I'm afraid the burglar who took Neil's clothes wouldn't do very well.

ALBERT (*with a look around the room*). No, I suppose not.

CYNTHIA (*a pause; she turns, with an air of finality*). Well, he'll be here soon.

ALBERT. You're not going?

CYNTHIA. I must. Neil has some people coming to tea.

ALBERT (*bent on holding her*). Well—now, how do you know I'm *not* the burglar?

CYNTHIA. Because I don't believe there are such things as gentlemen burglars. (*She drops a half curtsy; turns again toward the door.*)

ALBERT. Oh, wait! What did Neil tell you about me?

CYNTHIA. Let me see. He said you were extremely brilliant. But too versatile.

ALBERT. Brilliant, yes. But versatile—on the contrary, I'm going to become a specialist.

CYNTHIA. Sometimes I wonder what's happened to all the young men who used to become just doctors.

ALBERT. They all died of starvation.

(*There is a pause;* CYNTHIA *looks at her watch.*)

CYNTHIA. I don't know why Neil isn't here.

ALBERT. You don't expect *him* to be prompt, do you?

CYNTHIA. But he has some people coming. You may know them—their name is Cady.

ALBERT. Cady? Not the Cadys from Livingston?

CYNTHIA. Yes—*do* you know them?

ALBERT. I'm not sure—I think I used to. You know, I lived in Livingston myself, a long time ago.

CYNTHIA. So Neil told me.

ALBERT (*puzzled*). The Cadys? What are *they* coming for?

CYNTHIA. Miss Cady is Neil's pupil.

ALBERT. You mean he's giving her music lessons?

CYNTHIA. He is.

ALBERT. But he's not a teacher. (*He waits for a denial.*) *Is* he?

CYNTHIA. He *must* do something.

ALBERT (*with a sigh*). Things aren't any better with him, then?

CYNTHIA. Well, he isn't ready to retire.

ALBERT (*with a shake of the head*). I suppose he'll always go on this way. He's so—utterly improvident, so——

CYNTHIA (*rallying to his defense*). Well—he's really improved in that way. He may surprise you.

ALBERT. He certainly would.

CYNTHIA. He's saving money! (*Her tone changes.*) But the trouble is—he's working so hard to get it.

ALBERT. You mean giving music lessons?

CYNTHIA. Worse. You've got to talk to him—he won't listen to me. He's been sitting up night after night——

NEIL (*heard in the hallway*). Halloo! (*He kicks open the door and enters. He is carrying a pile of books, and on top of the pile a music portfolio. He sees* ALBERT; *dumps the books abruptly into the easy chair.*) Albert! Well, I'll be damned! (*Tosses his hat into the bedroom; seizes* ALBERT'*s hand.*)

ALBERT. Mr. McRae, I believe?

NEIL. Where did you come from? Chicago?

ALBERT. This morning. Of course, you never told me you'd moved. How are you?

NEIL. Never felt better! Gosh, I'm glad you're back! You've met Cynthia?

CYNTHIA. Well, we've been talking. I thought I'd caught the burglar.

NEIL. Did you find him in here? (*To* ALBERT.) How did you get in?

ALBERT (*elaborately*). First I turned the knob of the door——

CYNTHIA. And, as you hadn't locked it, he had no difficulty in entering. (*She turns to the books in the easy chair.*) What are these?

NEIL. Why—just some books.

CYNTHIA (*takes one up*). "Life of Charles I." Neil!

NEIL. Well—I used to be very interested in history, and especially——

CYNTHIA (*severely*). The truth, Neil!

NEIL. I—I bought them, that's all.

CYNTHIA. Oh, Neil. After your promise!

NEIL. Well— (*To* ALBERT.) Just take a look at this binding.

ALBERT (*giving no encouragement*). Yes. I see it.

CYNTHIA (*determined*). Neil, where did you get them?

NEIL (*still to* ALBERT). There was a burglary downstairs, and this fellow lost all his clothes.

CYNTHIA (*resigned*). And you bought these books from him.

NEIL. Well—ah——

CYNTHIA. You work at these terrible orchestrations to *make* a little money, and then—did you go to bed at all last night?

NEIL. Of course I did.

CYNTHIA. Doctor, you *will* talk to him, won't you? (*She takes up her work basket.*) I'm sure he hasn't been sleeping—he hasn't been doing *anything* he should. (*She is heading for the door.*)

NEIL. You're not going?

CYNTHIA. I am. You have people coming to tea, remember.

NEIL. Good heavens, what time is it?

CYNTHIA. Nearly five. I suppose you have everything ready?

NEIL. Why, yes—I've got—that is, I think—— (*He smiles helplessly.*) Be a darling and help me, will you?

CYNTHIA. Are you sure you have everything? (*Knowing well that he hasn't.*)

NEIL. I think so.

CYNTHIA. He thinks so. (*This to* AL-

BERT, *with a smile, as she goes through the bedroom doorway.*)

ALBERT. She's charming, Neil.

NEIL. Isn't she? (*He moves his portfolio from the chair to the desk.*) She's a designer in one of the big dressmaking firms. Did she tell you how we met?

ALBERT. No.

NEIL. She lives across the hall. (*He raises his voice for* CYNTHIA's *benefit.*) She thinks she can play the piano.

CYNTHIA (*in the kitchen*). I can!

NEIL. You cannot! (*To* ALBERT.) One night I knocked on her door and asked her to stop. She did. We've been great pals ever since. (*Calling to* CYNTHIA.) Can I help you, Cynthia?

CYNTHIA. No, nor anyone else. (*She returns.*) Do you remember when you last had any tea?

NEIL. The other day.

CYNTHIA. You have three leaves left. (*She exhibits them.*)

NEIL (*inspects them*). Four!

CYNTHIA. And did you know that your toast machine was burnt out?

NEIL. Oh, yes—I forgot. But I'm sure there's some tea—I remember—no, I used the last of it early this morning. I'll run right out—— (*He is about to start.*)

CYNTHIA (*holding him*). Neil!

NEIL. What?

CYNTHIA. Then you *were* up all night?

NEIL. Why—not exactly.

CYNTHIA (*to the doctor*). He's been sitting up making orchestrations for a cheap little music publisher. Neil, it's like copying bad paintings. Doctor, you must make him stop.

NEIL. Well—I'll go out and get some tea.

CYNTHIA. No! You stay and talk to the Doctor. I'll bring everything over from my place. (*Again she picks up the basket.*)

NEIL. I can't let you do that. Let me help.

CYNTHIA. I will not. (*She goes.*)

NEIL (*more to himself than to* ALBERT). I could have sworn I had everything.

ALBERT. She'll take care of things. (*He is near the window.*) Come over here and let me see you.

NEIL. Now, you're not going to fuss over me just because I've been doing some work.

ALBERT. No. But I want to look at you. (*An orchestra, in a restaurant across the street, strikes up a jazz tune. It comes faintly through the window.*)

NEIL. Good Lord, that again!

ALBERT. What?

NEIL. That damned cabaret orchestra across the street. It begins at five every afternoon.

ALBERT. You *are* nervous, aren't you?

NEIL. Huh? No. I just don't like that music.

ALBERT. *Did* you work all night?

NEIL. Some of it.

ALBERT. It's bad business, Neil. (*He feels for his pulse.*) How many Cadys are coming to tea?

NEIL. Oh, did Cynthia tell you? You remember the Cadys?

ALBERT. Vaguely. I don't suppose they'd know me. Do they live here now?

NEIL. They moved East a few months ago. Gladys is my one and only music pupil.

ALBERT (*watch in hand*). Rich, I suppose?

NEIL. Lord, yes. Millions.

ALBERT. What did he make it in? (*He puts away the watch.*)

NEIL. Funny—I don't even know. Manufactures something.

ALBERT (*trying to remember*). Just the one daughter, isn't there?

NEIL. Yes. (*Adds, as an afterthought.*) There's a brother.

ALBERT (*recalls him, apparently none too pleasantly*). I remember him.

NEIL. I *had* to ask them. For heaven's sake, stay and help out.

ALBERT (*with a laugh*). Well, I'll stay a little while. (*Feels for his pipe.*)

NEIL. Try to get away. (ALBERT *laughs, lightly.*) Well, what's the verdict on *me?*

ALBERT. You're just a little tired, that's all. Sort of nervous.

NEIL. Nonsense.

ALBERT. Got any tobacco?

NEIL. Right there on the desk.

ALBERT (*fooling with the tobacco jar; unable to open it*). Have you been writing *anything* of your own?

NEIL. Well, no—only snatches of things. I'm going to get back at it soon, though.

ALBERT. That's good. (*The jar in hand.*) How do you open this thing?

NEIL (*takes up a paper knife from the piano—a knife of ivory, scimitar-shaped, and with a long black tassel hanging from it*). I use this. Give it to me. (ALBERT *hands it over;* NEIL *opens and returns it, all without a word.*)

ALBERT (*filling his pipe*). How old is the daughter now?

NEIL. Gladys?

ALBERT. Yes.

NEIL. Twenty-two or three—I don't know. Why?

(*He puts the knife back on the piano.*)

ALBERT. How soon will they be here?

NEIL. Any minute, I guess. Why all the questions?

ALBERT. I just wondered. (*Takes a medical case from his pocket and shakes out a pill.*) I want you to take one of these before they come, and another one later on.

NEIL. Good heavens, there's nothing the matter with me.

ALBERT. I know there isn't.

NEIL. What'll they do—make me sleep?

ALBERT. They'll quiet you.

NEIL. But I don't dare go to sleep. In the first place the Cadys are coming, and——

(CYNTHIA *re-enters. She is now hatless, and carries a folded table-cloth.*)

CYNTHIA. I hope you scolded him. (*She goes to the desk and begins to spread the cloth.*)

ALBERT. Not enough, I'm afraid. (*Pill in hand.*) Do you think you have a glass of water left?

NEIL (*starting*). Oh, of course!

ALBERT. No, no, I can find it. (*He goes into the bedroom.*)

CYNTHIA (*with a glance at the portfolio*). You didn't let them give you more to do?

NEIL. Why, hardly any. It's all right.

CYNTHIA. It *isn't* all right. Oh, I wouldn't mind if it were something decent! But it's perfectly sickening to think of your genius being choked to death in this way!

NEIL. I'll work on the symphony soon, honestly.

CYNTHIA. And then make up for it by mere hack-work. I wish someone would subsidize you.

NEIL. That would be nice. (ALBERT *comes back with the glass of water.*)

ALBERT. Here you are! (*Gives* NEIL *pill and glass.*)

NEIL. Oh, all right. But there's nothing the matter with me. (*He takes the pill.*)

ALBERT. How was it?

NEIL. I've tasted better. (*The orchestra across the street is heard in another outburst of jazz.*) Would you believe that people actually enjoy that? Wait! I've got one here that will be next month's national anthem. (*Searches for it in portfolio.*) There aren't any words to it yet, but it's going to be called "Sweet Mamma."

CYNTHIA. Don't, Neil. Play Dr. Rice the second movement of your symphony.

NEIL. Want to hear it?

ALBERT. You bet. (*He indicates the pipe.*) Do you mind?

CYNTHIA. Not at all.

NEIL. She calls it the second movement because there isn't any first.

CYNTHIA (*finding it*). Here! (*She spreads the manuscript on the rack.*)

NEIL. You understand this is just a movement. It's—(*He sees place that needs correction.*) Oh! (*Starts fishing for a pencil.*) Of course I never have a pencil. (CYNTHIA *gets one from his left vest pocket and hands it to him.*) Oh, thanks! (*He makes the correction.*) It's just a sketch. Not finished, you know.

CYNTHIA. But it's going to be—and soon.

(NEIL *starts to play, but is not far into it when the phone rings.*)

NEIL (*stops playing*). I'll bet that's the Cadys. (*Goes to the phone.*) Hello! (*To* CYNTHIA.) It is. Downstairs. . . . Send them right up, Jerry.

CYNTHIA. Good heavens, I'll have to bring the tea things in.

NEIL. Why not?

CYNTHIA. They don't want to meet me.

NEIL. Don't be foolish.

CYNTHIA. Well—I won't stay. (*She goes.*)

NEIL. I suppose I ought to clear things up a bit.

ALBERT (*with a glance at the books in the easy chair*). If you expect them to sit down. (NEIL *carries the books into his bedroom. He returns, counts the chairs, then tests a spindley-legged one that stands centre.*)

NEIL. I hope nobody heavy sits in this. (*Voices are heard in the hall, and* MR. *and* MRS. CADY, HOMER *and* GLADYS *appear at the open door.* MRS. CADY *enters first, then* GLADYS, *then* MR. CADY, *and* HOMER. *Together they make up an average Middle West family. They have no marked external characteristics except that* HOMER *is wearing a violent yellow tie.*)

MRS. CADY. Why, Neil!

NEIL. How are you, Mrs. Cady? Gladys.

MRS. CADY. After all these years!

GLADYS. Hello, Neil!

CADY. Well, well, Neil, my boy!

NEIL. Hello, Mr. Cady!

HOMER. Hello, there!

NEIL. How are you, Homer?

HOMER. Not so good.

NEIL (*feeling keenly his position as host*). Ah—this is Dr. Rice. Mr. and Mrs. Cady, and—Miss Cady and—Cady. (*His voice trails off. There are the indistinct greetings that follow an introduction.*)

MRS. CADY. Doctor, did you say?

ALBERT. Yes, ma'am.

MRS. CADY. Homer, here's a doctor.

HOMER. Yes?

MRS. CADY. Homer's had a good deal of trouble from time to time. Sit here, Homer—in this easy chair. (HOMER *takes the only easy chair.*)

NEIL (*delinquent*). Oh, yes—sit down, everybody. I'm sorry I—ah——

MRS. CADY. Oh, that's all right. We'll just settle ourselves. (*She sits in the swivel chair at the desk.*)

NEIL (*stirring up conversation*). Ah—Dr. Rice comes from Livingston, too.

MRS. CADY. Really?

CADY. That so?

ALBERT. Oh, a long time ago. We moved away when I was very young.

MRS. CADY. I wonder if I—(*There is a sneeze from* HOMER)—Are you all right, Homer?

HOMER. Yes. (*Something in his tone says that he is as all right as possible, considering where he is.*)

MRS. CADY (*blandly finishing*)—knew your people?

HOMER. *I* don't remember them. (*You gather that* ALBERT *just couldn't have had any people.*)

CADY (*at the telephone*). Mind if I use this?

NEIL. Oh, no, of course not.

CADY. Thanks. I left the office a little early. (*Takes the receiver off.*)

MRS. CADY (*bent on placing the doctor*). Let me see. *Old* Mrs. Rice——

CADY. Cortlandt 8262.

MRS. CADY. I guess you're not the same. (*There is a half-query in her voice.*)

ALBERT. Well, as a matter of fact, I moved away just after you came there.

MRS. CADY. Oh, I see.

GLADYS (*producing a box of candy*). I brought you some candy for your tea, Neil.

NEIL. Oh, thanks. (*To* MRS. CADY, *who is teetering in the desk chair.*) There's another chair if——

MRS. CADY. No, I like this. Feels like my rocking chair at home. (*She sways back and forth.*)

GLADYS. Mother's favorite chair is her rocker.

MRS. CADY. There's nothing like an old-fashioned rocking chair.

CADY (*at the phone*). Let me talk to Burgess.

MRS. CADY. Mr. Cady says I'm chair-bound. Just joking, you know. (*She explains elaborately, to* ALBERT.) Mr. Cady. Says I'm chair-bound.

ALBERT (*just the news he was waiting for*). Oh, yes.

SIMULTANEOUSLY

MRS. CADY. Let me see: there were two families of Rice out there, and I remember that one of them came here, just before we left. (*She finishes in a sibilant whisper, having been shushed by her husband.*)	CADY. Burgess? Any word from 653? . . . Hush, mother. . . . Well, I'll tell you what to do. We ought to send a tracer. . . . That's right. . . . Well, I'll tell you what to do—if you don't hear by six o'clock send a tracer. That's all.

(CADY *hangs up: turns to* NEIL.)

CADY. Much obliged. When I get a foot away from a telephone I'm lost. (*He starts for the weak chair;* NEIL *makes a movement.*) What is it?

NEIL. That chair isn't very strong.

CADY. Oh, I'll be careful.

NEIL (*not exactly at ease*). We're going to have some—tea and things—pretty soon now.

CADY (*has taken out a cigar*). Match?

NEIL (*starting*). How's that?

CADY. Match.

NEIL. Oh, yes! Right here. (NEIL *lights his cigar.*)

GLADYS (*taking in the room*). See, mama, isn't it cute?

MRS. CADY. Yes, indeed.

GLADYS. There's the piano over there.

MRS. CADY. Oh, yes. (*Everybody looks at the piano.*) Neil must play something for us. (*It is Remark No.* 80 *and purely perfunctory.*)

CADY. It's certainly very nice. We've been hearing quite a bit about you, Neil.

NEIL. Is that so?

CADY. Hear you've become quite a musician since you went away from Livingston.

NEIL. Oh, I don't know.

CADY. Well, Gladys has been telling us so. So we thought we'd come and find out for ourselves. Gave up a golf game to do it, too. Play golf?

NEIL. No, I don't.

CADY. Play golf, Doctor?

ALBERT. I'm sorry.

CADY. Well, everybody ought to. Great exercise. Keeps a man fit for business. I'd make Homer do it, if he wasn't so delicate. (HOMER *shifts in his seat.*)

MRS. CADY. Comfortable, Homer?

HOMER (*carelessly*). Um-hum.

(CYNTHIA *comes in with the tea things.*)

NEIL. Oh, here we are! I—I want you to meet Miss Mason. She's brought the things over from her place.

MRS. CADY. Oh, I see.

NEIL (*beginning again the weary round of introductions*). Mrs. Cady and—of course you know Gladys——

GLADYS. Yes.

CYNTHIA. How are you, Miss Cady?

NEIL. And Mr. Cady and—another Mr. Cady. (HOMER *does not rise. Mumbled greetings are exchanged.*) Miss Mason lives—just across the hall.

MRS. CADY. Yes, so Gladys has told us. Are you a musician, too, Miss Mason?

CYNTHIA. No, I'm not, Mrs. Cady.

MRS. CADY (*turning to her husband*). Don't she make you think of Elizabeth Merkle, Fred?

CADY. Well—I see what you mean.

HOMER (*ever the dissenter*). She don't me.

MRS. CADY. Of course Elizabeth's dark, but there's something about the shape of the face. (*To* NEIL.) *You* knew the Merkles, Neil. Mr. Merkle had the skating rink.

NEIL. Oh, yes. Elizabeth was a little girl when I knew her.

MRS. CADY. She's twenty-two or three. Twenty-three, isn't she, Fred?

CADY. Yes, I guess so.

HOMER. Lizzie Merkle's crazy. She's going to marry Lou Carmichael.

GLADYS. Oh, did grandma say when it was to be?

MRS. CADY. No, I don't think they know themselves. You knew Lou, didn't you, Neil? (CYNTHIA *is serving tea.*)

NEIL. Did they live over on Pine Street?

MRS. CADY. I think they did.

HOMER. No, they didn't.

GLADYS. Hush up! They did. They lived next door to Dr. Endicott.

HOMER. They did not. They've always lived on Mead Avenue.

GLADYS. Well, I guess I ought to know. Didn't I go and meet his sister once? Remember that tall girl, mama?

HOMER. You're crazy.

MRS. CADY. Lou used to take Gladys to dances a lot.

GLADYS. He was a wonderful dancer! (*She giggles.*)

MRS. CADY. He was with the telephone company.

HOMER (*scornfully*). Charlie Ferris nearly beat him up.

MRS. CADY. Remember when he and Charlie Ferris were crazy about Gladys? This girl's had more boys crazy about her, Neil. (CYNTHIA *gives tea to* CADY)

GLADYS. Oh, I never cared for either of them.

HOMER. You never let them *think* so.

GLADYS (*smugly*). Homer!

HOMER (*to* NEIL, *unpleasantly, as he passes tea to him*). No, thanks. Tea always sits on me.

CADY. Say, I hear your Uncle James is dead, Neil. Leave you anything?

NEIL. No—Uncle James never had anything.

CADY. Too bad. He was a fine man. Everybody was sorry when he moved to Boston.

MRS. CADY. He was nice. (*To* CYNTHIA.) We used to sing together in Sunday school when we were children.

NEIL. I remember you sang in the choir.

GLADYS. Mama still sings, when she lets herself go.

HOMER. We call her Galli-Curci.

MRS. CADY (*genially*). They're always joking me about my voice. But I do love old hymns. Your father was a good singer, too, Neil.

NEIL. I guess he was a better lawyer.

CADY. Yes, everybody had a great deal of respect for John McRae.

MRS. CADY. He was a beautiful character.

CADY. He'd give his money away to everybody. Afraid he never made very much, though. Lawyers don't, as a rule.

Neil, did you know that when I was a young man I studied law—right in the same office with your father?

NEIL. No? Did you?

CADY. Yes, sir. Had it all figured out to be a judge—Judge Cady—till I found out what was the most a judge could make. (*Puts his tea down, almost untasted.*)

CYNTHIA. Too strong?

CADY. No. I'm not much of a tea drinker.

MRS. CADY. I guess Gladys and I are the tea drinkers in our family. We have it every afternoon. (NEIL *is opening the candy box.*)

GLADYS. Neil's going to come up and have some with us next week. Tuesday.

NEIL. Candy? (MRS. CADY *takes a piece; so does* MR. CADY.)

MRS. CADY. That's nice. We'll have some people in. I want you to see the new house. My, I don't know what the folks would say back in Livingston if they could see it. Remember our house in Livingston, Neil?

NEIL. Yes, indeed. (*He passes the candy box to* HOMER, *who waves it disdainfully aside.*)

MRS. CADY (*trying to be bantering*). You ought to. You were there enough. Every afternoon, pretty near. Neil and Gladys would play together and I'd go out in the kitchen and make candy for them. (*She rocks.*)

GLADYS. Oh, yes! Wasn't it fun, Neil?

MRS. CADY. We always saved some pieces for Mr. Cady. All the Cadys are fond of candy. Aren't they, Fred? (*She taps his knee.*)

CADY. (*munching*). Guess that's right, mother.

HOMER. I'm not.

MRS. CADY. Except Homer. (*She resumes, largely to herself.*) All the Cadys eat candy.

CYNTHIA. And now—if you'll excuse me. (*Rises.*)

NEIL. Oh, you're not going? (HOMER *doesn't rise with the other men.*)

CYNTHIA. I'm afraid I must.

CADY. That's too bad.

MRS. CADY. Well, I hope we meet again.

CYNTHIA. I just ran in for a moment to be temporary hostess.

GLADYS. Goodbye, Miss Mason.

CYNTHIA (*to* ALBERT). I hope I'll see you again. (*Shakes his hand.*)

ALBERT. Oh, I'll be back in a few weeks. (*There are further goodbyes.* CYNTHIA *goes.*)

MRS. CADY (*looking after her*). She *is* like Elizabeth.

CADY (*noisily*). Well—how are things generally, Neil? Making a lot of money out of your music?

NEIL. No—with music you don't make a great deal of money.

CADY. I don't know about that. It's just like any other business. Maybe you're not giving them what they want.

MRS. CADY. I guess Neil's doing his best, aren't you, Neil?

CADY. We've all got to please the public. Eh, Doctor?

ALBERT. Oh, yes.

CADY. I've got to in my business. Of course I don't claim to know anything about music, but I think I represent about the average viewpoint. Now, what I like is a good lively tune—something with a little snap to it. As I understand it, though, you sort of go in for—highbrow music.

NEIL. It isn't exactly that.

CADY. Well, there's no money in it. You know what happened to your father.

MRS. CADY. Had to scrape all his life. (*Turn to* ALBERT.) Neil's father. Had to scrape all his life.

CADY. A young fellow's got to look out for his future, I claim—got to save up a little money.

NEIL (*puzzled*). Yes, sir.

MRS. CADY (*helping along what is clearly a prearranged conversation*). In some *business,* Mr. Cady means.

CADY. Yes. Now you take—well, my business, for example. We've always got an opening for—a bright young fellow.

NEIL. You mean—*me*—in your business?

CADY. Well, I just mentioned that for example.

NEIL. I—I'm afraid I wouldn't be much good in business, Mr. Cady.

MRS. CADY. Of course you'd be good.

NEIL. I did work once in an office, and I guess I wasn't—very——

CADY. That's all right. You'd learn. The idea is you'd be making money. Some day you'd maybe have a nice interest in the firm. 'Tain't as though you couldn't write a little music now and then in your spare time, and we'd be sort of all together. (*The jazz orchestra is heard again—this time louder.*)

MRS. CADY. Just like one big family.

GLADYS (*singing and swaying to the tune*). Oh, they're playing "The Frog's Party." (*To* NEIL.) Come on and dance!

NEIL. I'm sorry, but I don't dance.

GLADYS. Oh, so you don't—but I'm going to make you learn. I know a wonderful teacher. (*Turns to* ALBERT.) Dance, Doctor?

ALBERT. A little.

(GLADYS *and* ALBERT *take a few turns about the room.* MRS. CADY *hums the tune, not knowing the words.*)

CADY. Great song! A man I played golf with yesterday tells me that for the first six months of the fiscal year that song'll make a hundred thousand dollars. Write something like that and you're fixed. That's music.

HOMER. We got it on the radio last night.

ALBERT (*politely*). You don't say?

GLADYS (*near the piano*). Oh, Neil!

(*The three remaining* CADYS *are grouped with* ALBERT.)

SIMULTANEOUSLY

GLADYS (*holds up a piece of music, as* NEIL *crosses to her*). What's this?

NEIL. Just something I'm working on.

GLADYS (*sotto voce*). I want to talk to you.

NEIL. Oh!

GLADYS. Don't you want to talk to me?

NEIL. Oh, yes.

GLADYS. Neil. (*Points to a small photograph on piano.*)

NEIL. Yes?

GLADYS (*takes up the picture*). Can I have one of these?

NEIL. I'm afraid I haven't got another.

GLADYS. This was in the Musical Courier, wasn't it?

NEIL. Why, yes.

CADY. Couple of hundred miles away, wasn't it?

HOMER. Three hundred.

CADY. Think of that!

ALBERT. It's wonderful.

MRS. CADY. I was going to ask you, Doctor, if you're related to those other Rices. There were two daughters, I think.

ALBERT. No, I haven't any relatives left, there.

CADY. Live in New York, now, I suppose?

ALBERT. No, Chicago. I'm just here for a flying visit.

CADY. Chicago? Don't say? Well, that's a good town.

HOMER. Chicago a good town? Huh!

SIMULTANEOUSLY

GLADYS. I saw it. You're pretty well known, Neil. I'm proud of you. I wish I could have this one. Only I wish it were of you alone, instead of you and this other girl, whoever she is. (*Puts picture back.*)

NEIL. It's just a girl I met one summer. (*A pause.*)

GLADYS. Neil?

NEIL. Well?

GLADYS. Do you like me better than you do Miss Mason?

NEIL. Well, I think she's awfully nice.

GLADYS. Don't you think I'm nice, too?

NEIL. Yes, of course.

GLADYS. Because, I think *you* are. You know that, don't you, Neil?

NEIL (*nearly choking*). I'm—glad.

GLADYS. So, of course, I want *you* to think *I* am.

NEIL. I—do.

GLADYS (*suddenly*). Oh! That reminds me. (*Fishes in her handbag.*)

NEIL. What is it?

GLADYS (*bringing out four or five small samples of colored cloths*). I knew I wanted to ask you something. Which do you like best?

NEIL. Why, they're all very nice.

MRS. CADY. It would be nice if you could come up and see us, too, Doctor.

ALBERT. Thank you, but I'm going back soon.

MRS. CADY. Well, do come if you can. Any day after Thursday. Both our butlers are leaving, and I can't get any new ones to come until after the holiday. But we always like to have people from Livingston drop in. I always say if you don't keep in touch with your old home town, why your old home town won't keep in touch with you.

HOMER. I never want to go back there.

CADY. Well, I don't know as I do either.

MRS. CADY. Listen to that man. And to think he was president of the Board of Trade there for five mortal years.

CADY (*thoughtfully, to* ALBERT). You know, I think I've got you placed now. Was your father E. J. Rice in the lumber business?

ALBERT. No, he was an architect.

MRS. CADY. An architect — you don't say? Put up buildings, did he?

ALBERT. Yes, a few.

SIMULTANEOUSLY

GLADYS. But don't you like one best?

NEIL. I don't know. They're all sort of—ah—why—

GLADYS. Because I'd like to get the one you'd like.

(NEIL *is puzzled. She spreads the samples on his arm.*)

They're samples, silly! I'm going from here to the dressmaker's to pick one out.

NEIL. Oh, I see. (*He removes the samples.*)

GLADYS (*pouting*). Of course if you don't care what I wear, why, all right.

NEIL (*not enthusiastic*). I do care.

GLADYS (*eager again*). Well, which one would you rather see me in? The blue?

NEIL. Yes, that would be nice.

GLADYS. I like the pink one myself.

MRS. CADY. Put up any buildings in Livingston?

ALBERT. Why, yes.

CADY. Not the First National?

ALBERT. No, he designed the Mechanics' Building, right next door.

CADY. You don't say?

MRS. CADY. Well, that's a nice building, too.

HOMER. I remember it.

MRS. CADY. Mr. Cady had his offices in the First National Building.

ALBERT. Is that so?

CADY. I guess there's been quite a building boom since you were there. That whole block is pretty solid now.

ALBERT. Really?

MRS. CADY. My, yes. You wouldn't know the place.

CADY. Yes, sir! I guess there's been a good many million dollars invested there in the last five years.

ALBERT. You don't say?

MRS. CADY. Mr. Cady put up a building himself.

ALBERT. That so?

CADY. Just a warehouse. Of course we still have a plant there——

HOMER (*heard by himself*). It's half past, pop. (*Rises.*)

CADY. Yes, I guess we'll have to be going. (*Rises.*)

MRS. CADY. Ready, Gladys? (*Rises.*)

GLADYS. Yes, mama. (*Starts, then turns back to* NEIL.)

SIMULTANEOUSLY

GLADYS (*suddenly, to* NEIL). Oh, Neil!

NEIL. Yes?

GLADYS. I won't go home for dinner —if you don't want me to.

NEIL. Well, I did sort of think I'd do some work—

GLADYS. I'll go with *you* to a new restaurant I just heard about! I'll tell you what! I'll only be at the dressmaker's a few minutes. Then you can meet me.

NEIL. Well, I don't know exactly how I'll be fixed.

GLADYS. I'll telephone you the minute I'm finished.

NEIL. But, Gladys, I'm going to be tied up, I'm afraid, and——

GLADYS. Well, anyway, I'll phone.

MRS. CADY. Well, now, don't forget, Doctor! Come and see us, if you can.

ALBERT. Thank you.

CADY. Or have a round of golf with me some time. Play golf?

ALBERT. I'm sorry, I don't.

CADY. I remember—I asked you before.

HOMER (*impatient*). Oh, come on!

MRS. CADY. Just a second, Homer. Gladys is talking.

HOMER. She's always talking.

MRS. CADY (*to* ALBERT, *with a laugh*). Just like a brother, isn't he?

CADY. Well, goodbye, Doctor.

ALBERT. Goodbye, Mr. Cady.

CADY. Come on, Gladys.

GLADYS. All right. (*To* NEIL.) I'll telephone you from the dressmaker's when I'm through.

MRS. CADY. And, Neil—you're coming Tuesday, remember.

NEIL. Oh, thanks. I'm sorry I couldn't have had a nicer party for you.

MRS. CADY. It was elegant. Only next time we come, you must play something for us.

NEIL. I'll ring for the elevator.

MRS. CADY. Oh, that's nice. Come on, Homer.

(NEIL, MR. CADY *and* MRS. CADY *pass into the hall.*)

GLADYS. Goodbye, Doctor.

ALBERT. Goodbye, Miss Cady.

(GLADYS *follows them out;* HOMER *lingers with the Doctor.*)

HOMER. What about him? Do you know

him well? (*He takes out a box of powders.*)

ALBERT. Who? Neil?

HOMER. Yeh. Is he all right?

ALBERT. Why?

HOMER. Well, I just like to know things about a possible brother-in-law.

ALBERT. I see.

HOMER. Gladys is nutty about him. Thinks he's artistic, my God! And did you hear the old man? Just because his father was John McRae! (*Puts the powder on his tongue—takes a glass of water.*)

MRS. CADY (*in the hall*). Hurry, Homer!

HOMER (*calling*). All right! (*He swallows the words, drinking at the same time.*) So long. Well, I hope it don't happen. (*He strolls out.*)

ALBERT. So long.

(*The voices of the departing guests are heard in the hall.* NEIL *returns; looks back into the hall.*)

NEIL. What was all that about?

ALBERT. Oh, nothing in particular.

NEIL. How did you like the Cadys?

ALBERT. They seem to be all right. They must be richer than mud. Did you hear Mrs. Cady on her "butlers?"

NEIL. No.

ALBERT. I never heard of anybody having more than one butler before, but the Cadys seem to have 'em in pairs.

NEIL (*laughing*). I haven't been to their house yet. I'm going next week, though. (*His glance going to the door.*) Say! Homer's a dirty dog, isn't he?

ALBERT (*thoughtfully*). Neil, I want to talk to you.

NEIL. Good Lord, again?

ALBERT. In the first place, I want you to go to bed.

NEIL. At half past five o'clock?

ALBERT. You haven't slept for days.

NEIL. But I can't go to bed now. I've got work to do. (*A second's pause.*) You don't mean I'm sick?

ALBERT. No, but you need rest. I want you to put on your dressing gown and lie down for a while. And then take another one of these. (*Produces the pills.*)

NEIL. But I can't afford to go to sleep. I told you that. I've got work to do.

ALBERT. You can't work tonight.

NEIL. I must.

ALBERT. On those orchestrations?

NEIL. Yes.

(*A pause.*)

ALBERT. Neil.

NEIL. What?

ALBERT. I want to talk to you about something else.

NEIL. Good heavens!

ALBERT. All right, but—somebody has to. (NEIL *looks up, sensing something important.*) What are you going to do about your work?

NEIL. Huh?

ALBERT. Your *real* work, I mean. How much have you done since I went away?

NEIL. Well, what you heard. And Miss Mason and I are working out a little pantomime together. It's going to be a lot of fun——

ALBERT. How much of it is written?

NEIL. A lot. About half, I guess.

ALBERT. About half a movement of a symphony and about half a pantomime.

NEIL. I still have to eat.

ALBERT. But Neil, don't you see—you're wasting your genius!

NEIL. Genius, my hat!

ALBERT. You're wasting the best years you'll ever have doing odd jobs just to keep alive. You've got to be free to write.

NEIL. Well, maybe some day I'll write a popular song and make a million.

ALBERT. If you ever did you'd either burn it or sell it for ten dollars. You'll never make any money, Neil. You know that as well as I do.

NEIL. Then what's the answer? Are you going to subsidize me?

ALBERT. I wish to God I could! But there's no reason why you shouldn't subsidize yourself.

NEIL. What do you mean?

ALBERT. I mean the Cadys.

NEIL. What are you talking—Oh, don't be foolish!

ALBERT. Why is it foolish?

NEIL. Gladys would never—why, you're crazy!

ALBERT. Am I? Think back. How did she behave this afternoon? And Papa Cady? "Nice little share in the business?" And—well, I know what I'm talking about.

NEIL. You mean you're seriously advising me to ask Gladys Cady to marry me?

ALBERT. That's exactly what I'm doing. She's a nice girl, and pretty. You'd have comfort and money and time——

NEIL (*interrupting, with growing excitement*). Well, what about *me?* Do you think money and music and time would make up for everything else? No, sir! I'd rather keep on living right here—just as I am now—all my life long.

ALBERT. Now, now! Don't get temperamental! If you'll just——

(CYNTHIA *opens the door.*)

CYNTHIA. May a poor girl call for her dishes?

NEIL. I'm sorry—I should have brought them over.

CYNTHIA (*detecting a note in his voice*). Neil, there's nothing the matter?

ALBERT. I've been trying to persuade him to rest. (*To* NEIL.) Won't you go in and—get ready?

NEIL. I—I can't now.

CYNTHIA. Neil, please.

(*A pause.*)

NEIL. All right. But don't go away. I want to talk to you. (*He goes into the bedroom.*)

CYNTHIA. He *is* difficult.

ALBERT. Yes, he is.

CYNTHIA. I'm glad you've taken charge of him. (*She is collecting the tea dishes.*)

ALBERT. He'll be all right. Just needs sleep, that's all. I'm not worrying about him physically so much as—well, spiritually.

CYNTHIA. I know. I've been worrying about it for weeks.

ALBERT. You do see his genius, don't you?

CYNTHIA. Oh, yes! He has it, if anyone ever had.

ALBERT. And this hack-work—it must be killing his spirit.

CYNTHIA. When I think of his keeping on, year after year! And he's such a babe-in-arms about practical things. He *does* so need—(*She hesitates.*) We must do something, mustn't we?

ALBERT. Yes, we must. (*A pause.*) There *is* a possible way out, you know. (*A pause.*)

CYNTHIA (*slowly*). Yes, I know. (*A longer pause.*)

ALBERT. It's the only way, I'm afraid.

CYNTHIA. Oh, I've been thinking about it ever since she began coming here! You really *do* think it's the right thing for him? The wisest?

ALBERT. I'm sure of it.

CYNTHIA. But could he be happy?

ALBERT. That's the only way he *can* be happy, permanently—if he's free to write his music. That's the most important thing in the end.

CYNTHIA. It seems—and yet I'm afraid you're right.

ALBERT. We only hurt people by being sentimental about them. That's one of the first things a doctor learns. Let's put this through. Will you?

CYNTHIA. Oh, I couldn't!

ALBERT. You can do more than I can. You'll be here, and I've got to go away. And anyway, a woman can always do more than a man about this sort of thing. (*Holds out his hand to her.*) For Neil's sake. (*He takes a step away from her as he hears* NEIL *returning.* NEIL *comes back, wearing a dressing gown.*) That's right! Now!

NEIL. Of all the rot! Putting a grown man to bed at half past five!

ALBERT. Who ever accused you of being a grown man? Here! (*Produces a pill.*) Be brave. One swallow and it's over.

NEIL. Oh, all right—give it to me.

ALBERT. Here! (NEIL *takes it.*) And another before you go to bed. I'll put them here. (*He takes up his hat.*)

NEIL. You're going?

ALBERT. Got to—dining uptown. (*Taps* NEIL *lightly with his gloves as he passes.*) I'll look in in the morning. You'll be all right then. Good night, Miss Mason.

CYNTHIA. Goodbye, Doctor.

(ALBERT *goes.*)

NEIL (*to* CYNTHIA, *who is gathering the last of her dishes*). He's been talking to you about me, hasn't he?

CYNTHIA. Why—you and other things. (*Not looking up.*)

NEIL. What did he say?

CYNTHIA. Don't you wish you knew—curiosity!

NEIL. I *do* know. I know exactly. He said the same thing to me. He said I was a failure—practically. That I'd have to depend on other people all my life.

CYNTHIA. Neil, you're just exciting yourself. You're tired, and you know he wants you to——

NEIL. No, wait! We've got to talk about this, you and I. He said more than that. He said that I ought to ask Gladys Cady to marry me. (*A pause.*) Well! You don't seem—surprised.

CYNTHIA. No, I'm not.

NEIL. Don't you even think it's—funny, a little bit?

CYNTHIA. No.

NEIL. Cynthia! (*Looks at her for a mo-*

ment and then with a cry.) Oh, Cynthia —dear! (*Takes her hand.*)

CYNTHIA. Don't, Neil!—*Please* don't!

NEIL. But Cynthia, don't you know—without my telling you—that I love only you and no one else?

CYNTHIA. *Oh, Neil, please.* (*Then, with an attempt at lightness.*) This is so sudden!

NEIL (*hurt*). Oh, Cynthia, please don't!

CYNTHIA. Oh, please, don't *you!*

NEIL. You know I love you, Cynthia! Of course you know; you couldn't help knowing! I thought maybe you—don't you, at all, Cynthia?

CYNTHIA (*regaining control of herself*). Neil, let me tell you something. I *have* seen that you were growing to care for me, and I've—I've tried to think what I ought to do about it.

NEIL. Do about it! What can you do about it if——

CYNTHIA. You can do lots of things—if you're practical and sensible.

NEIL. Oh, my dear!

CYNTHIA. I said to myself, I think he's beginning to care about me more than he ought to, considering how we're both situated, and that nothing could come of it. And if I stay here I mightn't be sensible either. So, I'm going away.

NEIL. What!

CYNTHIA. I'm going to move uptown and live with Helen Noland. I'm going tomorrow.

NEIL. Cynthia—do you mean that you don't care about me at all?

CYNTHIA. Oh, yes, I do, Neil. I care about you very much. I think you're a great artist.

NEIL. Artist! (*He turns away from her.*)

CYNTHIA. And I think it would be the greatest possible misfortune for your music for you to go on this way, living from hand to mouth. So—when Dr. Rice suggested that you marry Miss Cady, it seemed to me a very sensible thing to do.

NEIL (*faces her again*). Cynthia—do you know what you're talking about?

CYNTHIA. Perfectly.

NEIL. You can't mean that music or no music I ought to marry Gladys.

CYNTHIA. I think you ought to do just that for the sake of your music.

NEIL (*hurt*). Oh! You're like Albert! You think my music is the only thing about me that's worth while! (*He again turns away.*)

CYNTHIA. Oh, Neil!

NEIL (*continuing*). It never *was* me that you cared about—only the music.

CYNTHIA. I want you to be happy, Neil.

NEIL (*laughs mirthlessly*). I certainly got it all wrong, didn't I? (*A pause.*) Well, goodbye, Cynthia.

CYNTHIA. Oh, Neil! Don't say goodbye like that.

NEIL. What other way is there? You're all being so sensible and practical. I might as well be practical and sensible too. (CYNTHIA *starts to speak, chokes up, goes out—stifling her tears. After a moment* NEIL *turns and sees that she is gone.*) My music! (*Then, less viciously.*) My music! (*The phone bell rings.* NEIL *looks toward it—plainly,* GLADYS *has finished at the dressmaker's. For a second he hesitates; then he makes up his mind and strides to the phone. There is grim determination in his voice, from the opening greeting.*) Hello, Gladys!

GLADYS (*over the phone*). Hello, Neil!

NEIL. Well, is the fitting over? (*He stifles a yawn; the pills are beginning to work.*)

GLADYS. Yes, but it wasn't a fitting.

NEIL. Well, whatever it was.

GLADYS. I took the pink one.

NEIL. The pink one. That's fine.

GLADYS. Oh, you don't care which at all!

NEIL. Of course I care which.

GLADYS. Can you meet me?

NEIL. Well, I don't think I can do that.

GLADYS. What?

NEIL. I say I can't go out. The doctor says I must stay in for a while.

GLADYS. Oh, my goodness! Are you sick?

NEIL. Oh, no. Just tired. Really, that's all. I have to—sleep for about an hour. (*He is growing momentarily more listless.*)

GLADYS. Oh, dear!

NEIL. Well, why don't you come up here instead?

GLADYS. Shall I?

NEIL. Of course.

GLADYS. Why?

NEIL. Well, there's something I want to say to you, to ask you—something we all want to—I mean something I want to ask you——

GLADYS. I wish I knew!

NEIL. Maybe you do know. We thought —that is, I thought—how would you like to marry a great composer? (*The receiver nearly falls from his grip.*)

GLADYS. Oh, darling! Do you mean it?

NEIL. Sure I mean it.

GLADYS. Of course I'll marry you!

NEIL. Would you, honestly?

GLADYS. Yes, indeed!

NEIL. Well, that's fine. We'll show them, won't we?

GLADYS. Who?

NEIL. Oh, everybody.

GLADYS. Can I tell them?

NEIL. Yes, tell them all. Homer and——

GLADYS. Oh, darling, I'm so happy!

NEIL (*his tone dull*). Well, I'm happy, too.

GLADYS. Let me hear you say "Sweetheart."

NEIL. Do I have to say it?

GLADYS. Of course.

NEIL (*barely audible*). Sweetheart.

GLADYS. Go ahead.

NEIL. Didn't you hear it?

GLADYS. No.

NEIL (*viciously*). Sweetheart!

GLADYS. Do you love me?

NEIL. Of course I do.

GLADYS. Well, I'll come over in about an hour.

NEIL. All right. (*A sleepy pause.*) In about an hour. You come, and—I'll sleep for an hour. I'll—sleep. (*He tries to replace the receiver, but is too sleepy. It dangles from its cord.* NEIL *rouses himself from the chair with difficulty.*) And that's that! (*Across the street the jazz orchestra begins again to play "The Frog's Party." It seems louder than before—already* NEIL'*s imagination is causing it to swell. He wheels toward the window.*) Now go ahead and play! (*He staggers to the easy chair and drops into it.*) Play the wedding march, damn you! Play the wedding march! (*The tune resolves itself into a jazzy version of Lohengrin's Wedding March. At the same time* NEIL *finally collapses into the chair, and the lights of the room begin to go down. As it grows dark the music swells. Then, after a moment, it begins to grow light again—but it is no longer* NEIL'*s room. It is a railway station, with the arch of Track 37 prominently visible, and other arches flanking it at the side. A muddled train schedule is printed on the station walls, with strange towns that never existed.* NEIL'*s piano, however, has remained where it was, and so has his easy chair. Then, down the aisles of the lighted theatre, there comes suddenly a double wedding procession. One section is headed by* MR. CADY *and* GLADYS—MR. CADY *in golf knickers and socks, knitted vest, and frock coat, with a silk hat prominently on his arm.* GLADYS *is the gorgeously attired bride, bearing proudly a bouquet that consists entirely of banknotes. Behind them stream four ushers—spats, frock coats, and high hats, to say nothing of huge bridal veils, draped over their heads. If you could peer beneath their veils, however, you would find that all four of them look just alike. The procession that comes down the other aisle is headed by* MRS. CADY *and* HOMER. MRS. CADY *wears a grotesque exaggeration of the dress that* NEIL *has seen her in, and* HOMER'*s yellow tie has assumed tremendous proportions. Behind* MRS. CADY *and* HOMER *are four bandsmen. Like the ushers, they all look alike, all wearing bridal veils, through which they play their instruments.*)

(*At the foot of the stage the processions halt; the music stops.* ALBERT *appears from nowhere in particular; he has turned into a minister.*)

GLADYS. Oh, Neil!

NEIL (*in his sleep*). Huh? (ALBERT *gently rouses him.*)

ALBERT. Neil! Did you forget that you were being married today?

NEIL. Oh! Why—I'm afraid I did. (*He looks wonderingly at the railway station, then turns and sees* GLADYS.) Oh, hello, Gladys! I'm sorry. (*The two processions stream up onto the stage. The ushers and the bandsmen line up behind the* CADY *family.*)

GLADYS. Neil, I want you to meet my ushers. They're all boys I used to know pretty well. (*As* GLADYS *begins the introductions the entire thing turns into a rhythmic chant, to an orchestral accompaniment.*) This is Alf and this is Georgie.

NEIL. Glad to meet you!

ALF. Glad to meet you!

GLADYS. This is Steve.

NEIL. I'm glad to meet you!

GLADYS. This is Fatty.

NEIL. How d'you do?

GLADYS. This is Lou.

LOU. I'm glad to meet you!

NEIL. Glad to meet you!

LOU. Glad to meet you!

GLADYS. And this last is Cousin Harry.

HARRY. Glad to meet you!

NEIL. How d'you do?

CADY. Hurry up, now! Let's get at it!

ALBERT. Take this man to be your huband?

(*A trainman, in uniform, enters through the gates of the railway station.*)

TRAINMAN. Wolverine, for Monte Carlo!

ALBERT. Have and hold him . . .

GLADYS. Yes, I do!

(*They all begin to rise and fall on their toes, to the beat of the music.*)

ALBERT. All your worldly goods and chattels. . . .

(*A trainboy, carrying the usual magazines, chocolates, etc., comes through the gates.*)

TRAINBOY. Latest magazines and papers!

MRS. CADY. Going off to leave her mama!

HOMER. Say, it's cold here! Ah, kerchoo!

(*The ushers begin to march around* GLADYS *and* NEIL, *faster and faster.*)

CADY. Train pulls out in just a minute!

ALBERT. Both for richer and for richer. . . .

TRAINMAN. Pasadena, Paris, London!

ALBERT. Better, worser . . .

GLADYS. Sure I will!

CADY. Special car Appolinaris!

(GLADYS *is kissing the ushers as they march.*)

TRAINBOY. Nothing sold after the train leaves!

MRS. CADY. Don't know *what* I'll do without her!

TRAINMAN. Show your tickets!

HOMER. Ma, keep still!

CADY. Get aboard! I'll tip the preacher!

TRAINMAN. Right this way, please! Right this way, please!

TRAINBOY. Huyler's chocolates and bonbons!

MRS. CADY. Oh, my baby!

HOMER. Oh, good Lord!

TRAINMAN. Lenox, Palm Beach, Narragansett!

ALBERT. I pronounce you—got the ring, Neil?

ALL THE USHERS. Bet he's lost it! Bet he's lost it!

GLADYS. Here's another!

TRAINMAN. All aboard!

(*The procession starts through the gates —*ALBERT *and* CADY *first, then the rest of the* CADYS, *then the ushers and the bandsmen. As they all file through the ushers continue the chant, calling out in unison:*)

Well, goodbye! Congratulations!
Goodbye, Gladys! Goodbye, Gladys!
Send us back a picture postal!
Hope you're happy!
Well, goodbye!

(GLADYS *tosses her bouquet back to them; the ushers scramble for the banknotes. As the last of the procession disappears through the doors the lights die down. A moment later they come up again, revealing a row of white marble columns, with crimson curtains hung between them.* NEIL'S *piano, however, is still incongruously in the left corner, and his easy chair stands at the right. Immediately* NEIL *and* GLADYS *enter through side curtains.* NEIL *is still wearing his bathrobe—a somewhat sad spectacle amid all this grandeur.* GLADYS *is no longer in bridal costume, but wears a pleated dress—an exaggeration of the dress that she has worn in real life, with great pleats several inches thick.*)

GLADYS. We're married, Neil!

NEIL. Yes.

GLADYS. I'm your little bride.

NEIL. My little bride.

GLADYS (*giggles*). Isn't it all just too wonderful? (*Runs into his arms.*) This is our beautiful home—see! (*The curtains behind the front columns part, revealing a magnificent interior consisting entirely of more marble columns and velvet curtains.*) You're going to have everything you've always needed! Mama and papa both say so!

NEIL. Oh! Do they?

GLADYS. Yes, indeed! You just wait—they'll be here any minute!

NEIL. They're coming here?

GLADYS. Of course they are! There's a lot of people coming—all coming to see our beautiful new home! Wait a minute—I'll show you! (*Calls.*) Butlers! (*Two butlers appear. They are exactly alike.*) Announce somebody!

THE TWO BUTLERS. Mrs. Cady and her chair and knitting!

(MRS. CADY *enters with a rocking chair attached to her. She begins knitting immediately. The two butlers depart.*)

MRS. CADY. Two little lovebirds! Gladys and Neil! Gladys and Neil! Are they happy? Oh, my dear, you never *saw* anyone so happy! I was saying to Mr. Cady, "Well, Mr. Cady, what do you think of your little daughter now? (*She sits.*)

How's this for a happy family?" And Mr. Cady says to me, "Well, I never would have believed it." And I says to Mr. Cady, and Mr. Cady says to me, and I says to Mr. Cady, and Mr. Cady says to me, and I says——

NEIL. *Stop!* (MRS. CADY *stops.*) So—so you're my wife's mother?

GLADYS. Why, of course she is! I think she's a pretty nice mother-in-law, don't you? Most people don't like their mothers-in-law, but I think *she's* pretty nice.

NEIL. But is *she* going to be—always——

GLADYS. Yes, indeed! Won't it be lovely? And that isn't all! (*Calls.*) Butlers! (*Four butlers enter.*)

THE FOUR BUTLERS. Mr. Cady, her father!

(MR. CADY *enters. He is in complete golf attire, and there is a telephone attached to his chest. As he enters the butlers depart.*)

CADY (*into the telephone*). Yep! Yep! Hullo! Well, I'll tell you what to do! Sell eighteen holes and buy all the water hazards. Yep! Yep! Hullo! Well, I'll tell you what to do! I expect caddies will go up any time now. How's the eighth hole this morning? Uh-huh. Well, sell it in three. Yes, sir. That's fine. Yep! Yep! Hullo! Well, I'll tell you what to do! Buy——

NEIL. No, no! (CADY *stops; looks at* NEIL.) You must stop—both of you! Do you know me?

CADY. My son! My new son! Well, Neil, how's the nice music and everything? Making a lot of money?

NEIL. Are we all going to live together?

GLADYS. Yes, indeed, darling.

CADY. Yes, indeed.

MRS. CADY. Yes, indeed.

GLADYS. And that isn't all. (*Six butlers enter. Of course they are all alike.*) I've *another* surprise for you!

THE SIX BUTLERS. Her brother, Homer. He makes me sick.

FIRST BUTLER. I don't think *he's* sick at all. (*The butlers go.* HOMER *enters—the yellow tie is bigger than ever.*)

HOMER. Oh, there you are, you dirty dog! I'm on to you! You married her just because Dad's got a lot of money, and you think you're going to have a cinch. But if you think you're going to get all of Dad's money, you're mistaken, because I'm going to get my share and don't you forget it. (*He makes straight for the easy chair, sits in it, and sneezes.*)

MRS. CADY. Now, Homer! Homer's sick.

CADY. Yes, he's sick.

GLADYS. It's all right, dearest.

NEIL. It isn't all right. I don't want the money. All I want to do is write my music. That's what I want to do—work. Do you think I'll be able to?

GLADYS. Why, of course you will, dear. We've just had this whole room done over for you to work in.

MRS. CADY. It's awfully pretty, Neil.

CADY. Cost a lot of money, too. (*His phone rings.*) Hello! . . . No—wrong number! (*He hangs up.*)

GLADYS. Don't you just love it, Neil, keeping house together? Say "Sweetheart!"

NEIL (*automatically*). Sweetheart.

GLADYS. And next week we're going to have everything done over in some *other* color. Here are the samples—the samples. (*She producers another set of samples, larger than those used in real life.*) Now which color would you like? It's going to be whichever color you like.

NEIL. Why, any one. (*He removes the samples from his arm.*)

HOMER. Make him pick one! Make him pick it!

GLADYS. Here, I'll tell you! You stop in and get them matched! Get some of this one, and some of that one, and maybe some of the other one—on your way home from business tomorrow. It'll give you something to do.

NEIL. Am I going to business tomorrow?

CADY. Yes, sir! Start right in at the bottom and work up. Learn all the ins and outs. Lots of people think the ins and outs don't amount to anything; but you can't get anywhere in business without them.

NEIL. But if I have to go to business tomorrow I'd like to work on my symphony now—if you'll only go.

HOMER. Huh! The symphony!

GLADYS. That old thing!

CADY. That's no good!

MRS. CADY. I wouldn't have it in the house!

NEIL. But it is good—and I've got to finish it.

CADY. Highbrow music—that's what it is.

NEIL. Well, then, I'll work on the pantomime—that's not so highbrow. (*He goes to the piano.*)

MRS. CADY. For my part I like hymns. There's nothing like the old familiar hymns. (*She sings—"Oh, Blessed Be the Tie That Binds."*)

GLADYS. Anyhow, you can't work now. It's tea time!

MRS. CADY (*to the tune of the hymn*). Yes, tea time! It's tea time! It's tea time!

CADY. So it is. (*Into his phone.*) Hello! . . . Don't disturb me now—I'm busy. . . . Tea!

CADY. Quite a crowd coming this afternoon.

MRS. CADY. Yes, coming to meet Neil! Yes, Gladys and Neil! Gladys and Neil!

GLADYS. Now, Neil, you be nice to everybody. I want you to make a nice impression. (*Eight butlers enter.*)

THE EIGHT BUTLERS. A friend of her family's. (*The butlers go. No one enters, but apparently the* CADYS *see someone. They greet the invisible guest.*)

GLADYS. How do you do?

CADY. How do you do? (*They bring her down to* MRS. CADY.)

MRS. CADY. How do you do? Oh, what a nice new ear trumpet!

GLADYS. I'm so glad you were able to come! (NEIL *peers, trying his best to see what it is all about.*)

MRS. CADY. Well, it's wonderful to see you again!

GLADYS. Doesn't she look well, mama?

MRS. CADY. You're the picture of health! No one would ever say *you* had an operation. I say—no one would ever say you had an operation. Yes, it always does it if you were heavy before. Oh, was it a year ago? Well, tempus does fugit, as Homer says. You remember Homer?

HOMER. I said hello.

MRS. CADY. Homer's sick.

GLADYS. Oh, Neil! I want you to meet an old friend of mama's. She's deaf. You'll have to talk loud.

(*Ten butlers enter.*)

THE TEN BUTLERS. Another friend of the family's! (*The butlers go.*)

GLADYS (*greeting the newcomer*). How do you do?

CADY. How do you do?

GLADYS. So glad to see you again. And little Hattie! Oh, look, mama! (CADY *and* GLADYS *bend over, as though greeting a child.*)

MRS. CADY. Why, if it isn't little Hattie! Look, Gladys! Isn't she cunning?

GLADYS. Isn't she? Those cute little curls! Do you want to meet your great big cousin Neilie? Neil, darling, this is your little cousin Hattie. Isn't she a big girl? Say something cute to her. (GLADYS *turns away from* NEIL *and he passes his foot over the spot where the child is supposed to be.*)

(*Twelve butlers enter.*)

THE TWELVE BUTLERS. A great many other friends of the family.

FIRST BUTLER. And all pretty terrible, if you ask me. (*They go.*)

CADY. Hello, Alf! You remember Mrs. Cady?

HOMER. Hello, Fatty.

MRS. CADY. How do you do?

CADY. Say, I called you up a couple times but couldn't get any answer.

GLADYS. Why, how do you do, Alf? I'm awfully glad you were able to come. Oh, Neil! I want you to meet an old friend of papa's. He's known me ever since I was—how high? Yes, but you couldn't lift me now. (*The invisible guest tries to lift her and fails. She giggles.*)

(*Butlers enter with imaginary trays.*)

MRS. CADY. And now we'll have some nice tea to drink.

HOMER (*probably to* FATTY). He married Gladys for her money.

MRS. CADY. And then Neil will play for us.

GLADYS. Oh, hello! Haven't seen you in a long time! No, I guess I wasn't engaged then.

(*It is a Babel. The* CADYS *are all speaking together, moving around and greeting guests.* NEIL *moves through it all, walking through guests, passing his hands through the butlers' trays—bewildered.*)

CADY. Oh, hello, Ralph. I want you to meet my new son-in-law. Neil, this is Mr. Umn.

GLADYS. Oh, have you been out to California? Did it rain much?

CADY. Yes, he's going to be very valuable to me in business, too.

HOMER. I'll bet he's rotten.

CADY. But after all there's nothing like business. It'll all be his when I retire—his and Homer's, his and Homer's. (*Slaps* NEIL *on back.*)

(*The following four speeches are spoken simultaneously.*)

MRS. CADY. Well, Miss Mmmm, you

know Mmm, don't you? He's a cousin of John's who knew Francis very well. She's Ted's aunt. Yes. It's such a long time since you've been to see us. Gladys is always saying: "Mama, why is it Mrs. Mmm doesn't come and visit us, or why don't we go out and see her?" and all like that. You know Mrs. Mmm, don't you? You've become very plump, or you've become very thin. You don't mind my not getting up, do you? Mr. Cady always says I'm chair-bound. But that's his way of making a joke. He's always making a joke. You know Neil, of course. Would you like to have Neil play for us? Would you like to have Neil play for us? Neil, play for us.

HOMER. Look at him, the dirty dog! He married her for her money all right, but if he thinks he's going to get it he's got another think coming. Pop's going to put him in the business! Huh! He thinks he's going to get the business, too. Well, I'll show him—the dirty dog! He isn't going to get the business away from me—not while I'm alive and kicking. All because he's a musician. Yes, he thinks he plays the piano. Well—let him play it and see if I care. I dare him to play it. Go on and play for us.

MR. CADY. Well, well, well! You know Judge Mmm of course. Old man, I want you to meet the Judge. Yes, they've got a very beautiful home here. Would you like a cocktail, eh? Yes, sir! Well, Judge, how's everything been going? Say, you know Mr. Mmm, don't you? How are you? How have you been all these years? Have a cocktail—that's the boy. Yes, she's a big girl now. Grown up—married. That's her husband there. That's the one I bought for her. Very talented. I'll get him to play. Neil, we'd like to hear you play. Come on, Neil, play something on the piano.

GLADYS. Oh, how do you do, Aunt Gertrude? You know Willie, of course. Willie, you remember Aunt Gertrude. Aunt Gertrude, you remember Willie. Yes, this is our beautiful home. My husband's very talented. No, you didn't interrupt him a bit. He's awfully glad you came. He wasn't going to do anything this afternoon. Anyway, we always have tea. And if it isn't tea, it's something else. We're always having such a good time, Neil and I. Yes, that's my husband there. He plays the piano beautifully. Shall I get him to play? I think he would if I ask him. Oh, Neil, darling, play something. Please, Neil! Neil, for my sake, you'll play, won't you?

(MR. *and* MRS. CADY, GLADYS *and* HOMER *reach the "Come on and play" lines simultaneously.*)

THE CADYS. Play something for us! Play something for us! Play something for us!

NEIL (*in quiet desperation*). All right. (*Crosses to piano, seats himself and turns on them.*) I'll play, but I'll play what I want to—and I don't think you'll like it. (*He plays—music that is soft and flowing, and reminiscent of* CYNTHIA. *The lights fade on the* CADYS *and their reception; the curtains fall. Through the window by the piano comes* CYNTHIA.)

NEIL (*as he continues playing*). Cynthia! I thought that would bring you—I hoped so.

CYNTHIA. Of course, Neil, dear.

NEIL. Cynthia, it was a mistake! I'm terribly unhappy!

CYNTHIA. I'm so sorry, Neil. Because I want you to be happy, always.

NEIL. But I can't be happy with these people. I should have married you, Cynthia. I wanted to, you remember? But you wouldn't. And now it's too late.

CYNTHIA. Yes, it's too late. And I'm sorry, too.

NEIL. I don't want you to be sorry, Cynthia. I don't want you to regret anything. It was all my own fault. (NEIL'S *music turns to jazz as he plays.*)

CYNTHIA. Oh, Neil, don't let your music do that! (*She begins to draw back into the window.*)

NEIL (*desperately, as the music becomes more and more jazzy*). I can't help it! It's these people. I'm trying—but I can't help it. (CYNTHIA'S *image begins to fade.*) No—no! Don't leave me, Cynthia! I need you! Don't leave me with these people! They don't understand! They never can understand! (*But* CYNTHIA *is gone now.* NEIL *ends the jazz music with a treble crash, and buries his head on the keyboard. Immediately* MR. CADY *enters—his hat on and a morning newspaper in his hand.*)

CADY (*as he passes*). Hurry up, Neil! Mustn't be late for business. (*An elevator man, the same who was the trainman during the wedding scene, enters from the other side and meets* MR. CADY *at center.*) Good morning, Jerry.

ELEVATOR MAN. Good morning, Mr.

Cady. Express elevator going up! Watch your step!

(NEIL *looks up. There is no elevator, but this time even* NEIL *is persuaded, and he believes that he sees it. Four business men, all with hats and newspapers, and all looking just alike, enter one at a time and step into the imaginary elevator.*)

CADY (*to the first of them*). Good morning! Made it in twenty-eight minutes this morning!

FIRST BUSINESS MAN. Good morning! I got the eight-six this morning!

SECOND BUSINESS MAN. Good morning! I missed the seven-forty-three.

THIRD BUSINESS MAN. Good morning! I always take the nine-two.

FOURTH BUSINESS MAN. Good morning! I thought you were on the eight-sixteen.

(NEIL *gets into the car; the men huddle together.*)

STARTER (*clicking his signal*). All right! Twentieth floor first stop!

CADY. No, sir, I wouldn't sell under a million five! No, sir, a million five! Oh, good morning, Neil!

NEIL. Well, I'm starting.

CADY. Good boy, Neil! I want you to meet some of my associates. This is my son-in-law, gentlemen. Just bought him for my daughter. Mr. Canoo, statistical department.

FIRST BUSINESS MAN. Four out!

(*As* MR. CADY *thus introduces him the* FIRST BUSINESS MAN *walks out of the elevator, and goes off, paying no attention to* NEIL, *who nods at his retreating back.*)

CADY. Mr. Deloo, traffic department.

SECOND BUSINESS MAN. Five out! (*He goes.*)

CADY. Mr. Meloo, tax department!

THIRD BUSINESS MAN. Six out! (*He goes.*)

CADY. Mr. Beloo, general department.

FOURTH BUSINESS MAN. Eight out. (*He goes.*)

CADY. Well, well, Neil, starting in to work? You'll like it. You'll learn the ins and outs in no time. Hey! Wait a minute. I said nine out! (*He goes.*)

NEIL. Excuse me, Jerry! Can you tell me where I can learn the Ins and Outs?

STARTER. Ins and Outs Department! Room three hundred and thirty-three and one-third. Try and find it. (*He goes.*)

NEIL. Thank you.

(*The curtains between the marble columns at right part. A small office is disclosed.* MISS HEY, *a stenographer, is typing at a small desk behind a railing.*)

NEIL. I beg your pardon?

MISS HEY. Well?

NEIL. I want a pencil.

MISS HEY (*still typing*). What is it?

NEIL. I want a pencil.

MISS HEY. Who sent you?

NEIL. I don't know. But I have to have a pencil. I worked in a place like this once before. I had a great deal of difficulty getting a pencil then, I remember.

MISS HEY. It's just as hard to get one here.

NEIL. I thought it would be. I suppose there's a lot of red tape to go through.

MISS HEY (*turning toward him*). Yes. Now as I understand it, you want a pencil.

NEIL. That's right.

MISS HEY. Of course you've filled out a requisition.

NEIL. No, I haven't. A piece of paper, isn't it? (*She hands him a tremendous sheet of paper. It is about twenty by thirty inches. He studies it.*) What I want is a pencil. There's a place for that to be put in, I suppose?

MISS HEY (*wearily*). Yes—where it says: "The undersigned wishes a pencil to do some work with." How old are you?

NEIL. Thirty-two.

MISS HEY (*taking the paper away*). That's the wrong form. (*She gives him another—a blue one this time.*) Parents living?

NEIL. No.

MISS HEY. What did you do with your last pencil?

NEIL. I didn't have any.

MISS HEY. Did you have any before that?

NEIL. I don't think I ever had any. (*He indicates the form.*) Is that all right?

MISS HEY. It isn't as regular as we like, but I guess it'll do.

NEIL. What do I do now? Go to someone else, don't I?

MISS HEY. Oh, yes. Sometimes you travel for days.

NEIL. Are we all crazy?

MISS HEY. Yes. (*She resumes typing.*) You might try Room E—right down the corridor.

(*The curtains close over her, and the curtains at the left simultaneously open, revealing another office, just like the first. Another stenographer,* MISS YOU, *is at work on a typewriter.* NEIL *approaches her, requisition in hand.*)

NEIL. Is this Room E?

MISS YOU (*mechanically*). Did you have an appointment?

NEIL. No—you don't understand. I'm trying to get a pencil.

MISS YOU. Well, what do you want to see him about?

NEIL (*handing over the requisition*). It's this. Somebody has to sign it.

MISS YOU (*takes requisition*). Oh! (*Looks at it.*) Mr. Bippy! The man is here to see about getting a pencil or something.

NEIL. It *is* a pencil.

MISS YOU. Did you see Mr. Schlink?

NEIL. Yes.

MISS YOU. Mr. Woodge?

NEIL. Yes.

MISS YOU. Mr. Meglup?

NEIL. Yes.

MISS YOU. What did *they* say?

NEIL. Why, they seemed to think it would be all right.

MISS YOU (*calls again*). Oh, Mr. Bippy! (*To* NEIL.) Belong to the Employes' Mutual Mutual?

NEIL. Oh, yes.

MISS YOU. Cady Golf and Building Fund?

NEIL. Yes.

MISS YOU. Well—all right. (*She stamps the requisition with an elaborate machine, which rings a bell as it works. She hands the paper back to* NEIL.)

NEIL. Oh, thanks. Do I get a pencil now?

MISS YOU. Oh, no! It has to be O.K.'d by the President. All requisitions have to be O.K.'d by the President.

NEIL. Is he around here some place?

MISS YOU. Oh, no! He's in a big office. Just keep going until you find a great big office.

NEIL. Where?

MISS YOU. Oh, somewhere in the new building. Mr. Bippy!

(NEIL *turns away. The curtains close.*)

NEIL. The new building. A big office. (*The center curtains open, revealing a larger office.* MR. CADY, *seated at a long table, is dictating, in alternate sentences, to* MISS YOU, MISS HEY, *and to a dictaphone which stands before him.*)

(NEIL *tries to attract* MISS HEY'S *attention.*)

SIMULTANEOUSLY

NEIL (*to* MISS YOU). I beg your pardon. . . . (*To* MISS HEY.) I beg your pardon . . . would you mind if I—is this the President's office? Excuse me. . . . Excuse me. MISS HEY (*to* NEIL). Well, what is it? NEIL. I want to see the President. MISS HEY. What do you want to see him about?	CADY (*dictating*). And so beg to state—yours of the 19th instant—hoping to receive your valued order—yours received and would say — our Mr. Mmm will call on you—in re our No. 2160 — yours sincerely—annual sales convention—beg to state—beg to state — beg to state — pursuant to your instructions of the 13th ultimo—F.O.B. our factory—beg to state—beg to state—beg to state—as per your terms and specifications—would say—would say—— (*By this time, hearing* NEIL'S *voice,* CADY *turns.*)

CADY. Why, Neil!

NEIL. Here I am—at work!

CADY. Yes, sir! Business! Big business!

NEIL. Yes, Big business. What business are we in?

CADY. Widgets. We're in the widget business.

NEIL. The widget business?

CADY. Yes, sir! I suppose I'm the biggest manufacturer in the world of overhead and underground A-erial widgets. Miss You!

MISS YOU. Yes, sir.

CADY. Let's hear what our business was during the first six months of the fiscal year. (*To* NEIL.) The annual report.

MISS YOU (*reading*). "The turnover in the widget industry last year was greater than ever. If placed alongside the Woolworth Building it would stretch to the moon. The operating expenses alone would furnish every man, woman and child in the United States, China and similar places with enough to last for eighteen and one-half years, if laid end to end."

CADY. How's that?

NEIL. It's wonderful!

CADY. And wait for September 17th!

NEIL. Why?

CADY. That's to be National Widget Week! The whole country!

NEIL. That's fine, but what I came up about——

CADY. Never mind that now—we've got more important things. Conferences, mostly. (*To* MISS HEY *and* MISS YOU.) Any good conferences on for today?

MISS HEY AND MISS YOU (*together*). One at 3:19 this afternoon. (*They go.*)

CADY. That's fine! Ever been to a conference, Neil?

NEIL. No, but I've heard a lot about them.

CADY. They're great! You make speeches and decide things, and nobody can get in while they're going on.

(MISS YOU *and* MISS HEY *re-enter excitedly.*)

MISS YOU AND MISS HEY. All ready! They're going to start the conference, the conference, the conference!

(*They rush out.*)

CADY. Fine! Come right in, gentlemen! (*Half a dozen business men enter. They wear clothes that suggest fatness and prosperity. They walk in stiffly, in a line, repeating the phrases "Overhead," "Turnover," "Annual Report," "Overhead," "Turnover," "Annual Report." They sit, in stiff poses.*) We are going to have a conference! (*Calls off.*) Bolt the doors, out there! Gentlemen—this is our annual quarterly meeting. (*He drops a gold piece in front of each man.*) I want to introduce a young man who has been showing great promise in our factory. I don't know what he will have to say to you——

NEIL. I know what to say! (*Rises.*) I remember now—I know exactly what to say!

CADY. Gentlemen, Mr. Neil McRae!

(*As* NEIL *rises to speak the men all fall into mechanical positions, reminiscent of the board of directors pictures in the advertisements.* NEIL *pounds the table occasionally during his speech, but there is no sound.*)

NEIL. I know you must be surprised to see so young a man stand up before you, but I have *trained* myself to occupy the position I am now in. I have learned my facts. That is how I happen to own my own home. It simply took up my spare time in the evenings. Then, one day, the head of the factory came through the room where I happened to be working on a very difficult piece of machinery. "Who is that?" he asked the foreman. "He seems to be brighter than the others." "Not at all," answered the foreman. "He has simply applied himself and I think we must raise his pay, if we want to hold him." A few weeks later I was able to solve in five minutes a problem that had puzzled the best brains in our organization. I am now the head of my department, and my old foreman is working under me. (NEIL *sits; there is applause; the men lean over and shake his hand, congratulating him.*)

BUSINESS MEN. Wonderful! Wonderful!

CADY. I knew he could do it! Gentlemen, he has saved us millions!

FIRST BUSINESS MAN. Why, he is going to be the biggest man in the organization.

OTHERS. Yes! The very biggest!

FIRST BUSINESS MAN. What do you say to signing up with us for ten years at half a million dollars a year?

SECOND BUSINESS MAN. And becoming sales manager?

CADY. How about a bonus?

FIRST BUSINESS MAN. Yes, a bonus!

SECOND BUSINESS MAN. Here's my check for one hundred thousand dollars!

CADY. And here's mine! Two hundred thousand dollars.

FIRST BUSINESS MAN. And mine for one hundred thousand!

OTHER BUSINESS MEN. And mine—one hundred and fifty thousand dollars!

NEIL. Oh, thank you, thank you! (*He looks at the checks; they are of various-colored paper—pink, blue, yellow.*) It's an awful lot of money, isn't it?

CADY. A million dollars!

NEIL. A million dollars!

CADY. Well, gentlemen, that was a dandy conference!

FIRST BUSINESS MAN. One of the best!

CADY. Let's have another!

SECOND BUSINESS MAN. Yes, another.

(CADY *hands out gold pieces again as the curtains close in.* NEIL, *however, has stepped out of the scene and stands facing the audience. Curtains fall behind him.*)

NEIL. Just think, a million dollars. (*He looks at the checks in his hand, but they have turned into samples of colored cloth.*) Blue and pink and yellow. Blue and yellow and pink. I was to match them. *I* know! I was to match them for——

GLADYS (*heard in the distance*). Oh, Neil!

NEIL. For Gladys! (*Then, mechanically.*) Sweetheart!

(GLADYS, *resplendent in evening dress and wrap, joins him.*)

GLADYS. Did you have a hard day at the office, Neil?

NEIL. Here they are. It's a million dollars—I think.

GLADYS. Oh, good. I always knew you'd be a big success, Neil.

NEIL (*dully*). But I'm not doing what I want to do. My music—I want to write my music.

GLADYS. Oh, not now! It's time to go somewhere! We're going to dance!

NEIL. No, no! I've got to write my music. I want to go home now!

GLADYS. Oh, nobody ever goes home. We're going to go and dance!

NEIL. But we've got to eat dinner first!

GLADYS. Of course! We're going to eat right here!

NEIL. In this restaurant again? But we were here last night, and the night before. You don't want to come here every night, do you?

GLADYS. Why, of course I do! Suppose it *is* expensive, you can afford it now! And nobody comes here but the best people! We'll come here every night from now on! They have the nicest little lamps on the tables!

(*A check-room boy enters from one side and a headwaiter from the other. A second glance reveals the fact that the headwaiter is* ALBERT. *The check boy takes* GLADYS'S *wrap and* NEIL'S *bathrobe.*)

ALBERT. Bon soir. (*Holds up two fingers.*) How many, please?

NEIL. Two.

ALBERT. Two?

NEIL (*counts them*). Two.

ALBERT. Two?

NEIL. Why, hello, Albert!

ALBERT. Hello, Neil!

NEIL. Oh, yes! You were a waiter at college, weren't you? You know Gladys?

GLADYS. Of course.

(ALBERT *and* GLADYS *shake hands. Then* ALBERT *immediately becomes again the formal waiter.*)

ALBERT. How many, please?

NEIL. Two.

ALBERT. Two?

NEIL (*looks around to see if a third has mysteriously appeared*). Yes—two.

ALBERT. I will see if I can find you a table. (*He consults his chart.*) All our reserved tables are reserved.

(*The center curtains part, revealing a gaudy cabaret interior. In the center, at the rear, is a window, set in a frame of wrought iron. There is a single table, set with much fancy glassware and two table lamps of the sort so dear to* GLADYS'S *heart. As this scene is revealed an unseen orchestra strikes up the jazz tune, "The Frog's Party."*)

Ah! Right this way, please! Here is a nice one—right by the window! (*He seats them with an elaborate flourish, simultaneously uttering the meaningless ritual of headwaiters everywhere.*) Yes, Madame! Yes, sir!

(*A cigarette girl, Spanish in attire, enters and circles around the table.*)

GIRL. Cigars and cigarettes! Cigars and cigarettes!

(ALBERT *presents the menu, a huge affair, to* NEIL.)

GLADYS. See, Neil! Isn't it wonderful? (*She sways to the music.*) Order! He's waiting! Hurry up—you've got to order!

NEIL (*scanning the card*). I—I can't decide right away.

GLADYS. Oh, that music! I can't stand it any longer! (*She rises and seizes* ALBERT.) Dance?

(*She whirls around the table with him, to the accompaniment of the jazz tune and the cigarette girl's chorus of "cigars, cigarettes."*)

ALBERT (*when the dance is over*). Perhaps Madame would care for some Bordelaise à la Bordelaise, or some Bordelaise à la Bordelaise, or some Bordelaise à la Bordelaise.

GLADYS. Why, yes—I'd like that!

ALBERT. And what will Monsieur have?

NEIL (*studying card*). What is Bordelaise à la Bordelaise?

ALBERT. Very nice, sir.

NEIL. Yes, I know, but what is it?

ALBERT. It's served in a little round dish—very nice.

NEIL. Can't I find out what it is?

ALBERT. I'll see if anybody knows, sir. (*He turns his back.*)

GLADYS. Neil!

NEIL. Well?

GLADYS. People don't do that—making a scene in a restaurant!

NEIL. I only want to know what it is.

GLADYS. But you must pretend that you *do* know! That's the thing!

(ALBERT *turns back to* NEIL.)

ALBERT. I'm sorry, sir—nobody knows.

NEIL. It doesn't matter. I'll take it.

ALBERT. Yes, sir. Thank you, sir.

(*Four waiters enter, with dishes.*)

GLADYS. Oh, here's dinner!

(*The waiters circle the table, clanking the lids of their dishes as they exhibit the food. They go slowly at first, then faster and faster, in time to the constantly accelerating music.*)

NEIL (*springing up*). Stop! I can't stand it! (*The waiters halt in their tracks; the music stops.*) Is it going to be like this always?

GLADYS. What?

NEIL. Our life!

(ALBERT *dismisses the waiters.*)

GLADYS. Why, I think it's wonderful! You're going ahead being a big success in papa's office, and every night we'll go out and dance! You'll have to learn!

NEIL. I won't dance! I don't want to dance! I wouldn't ever have had to dance if I hadn't married you! (*It gives him a thought.*) If I hadn't married you——

GLADYS. Well, I don't care whether you dance or not. *I'm* going to! Albert—(*She rises and seizes* ALBERT; *they dance off.*) If you hadn't married me you'd have starved to death—starved to death—starved to death—(*Her voice dies down in the distance as she and* ALBERT *dance off to the accompaniment of the jazz tune. As* NEIL *starts the next speech the jazz tune slowly changes into the* CYNTHIAN *theme, and at the same time the gaudy cabaret changes into a sunny cottage.*)

NEIL. I don't think so. I might have been poor, but we'd both have work to do. It's a small house, I know, but the sun finds it the first thing every morning. And flowers live longer in our windows than anywhere else, because she cares for them so.

(*The wrought-iron window has turned into a simple thing of chintzes; chintz curtains appear in the doorways, and a box of jonquils takes its place at the foot of the window. The table no longer contains restaurant silver and electric lamps, but is simply furnished with a few breakfast things, with a vase of jonquils to keep them company. The place is flooded with sunlight.*)

NEIL (*calling*). Cynthia!

CYNTHIA. I'm coming!

NEIL. *Are* you coming, or must I use force?

CYNTHIA. It's the toast machine. You sit down and begin.

NEIL. As though I ever begin without you! Besides, I have something beautiful for you. (CYNTHIA *enters, bringing a tray laden with breakfast.*) See what I've done!

CYNTHIA. What?

NEIL. Nothing at all! Merely created an utterly beautiful morning!

CYNTHIA. *You* did? I started it an hour ago.

NEIL. Perhaps; but see those little powder-puff clouds? *They* weren't there ten minutes ago.

CYNTHIA. They *are* nice, darling. I didn't think you were so clever.

NEIL. And wait till you see the sunset I'm planning.

CYNTHIA. You can't beat last night's. What a scarlet!

NEIL. It blushed because we flattered it so.

(*A pause.*)

CYNTHIA. Darling.

NEIL. What?

CYNTHIA. A letter.

(*They stare at the envelope corner.*)

NEIL. Didn't you dare open it?

CYNTHIA. No. But let's be brave. (*They hold hands and take a long breath.*) Now—one, two, three! (*They tear the letter open; read it in silence.*) Do you believe it? (*The voice is ecstatic.*)

NEIL. No! Do you?

CYNTHIA. Darling!

NEIL. Darling!

CYNTHIA. But it *must* be real—it's typewritten.

CYNTHIA AND NEIL (*reading in unison*). "Your symphony will be played by our orchestra on December the tenth."

NEIL. Darling!

CYNTHIA. Darling! They'll applaud and applaud! You'll have to come out and bow!

NEIL. I won't!

CYNTHIA. You'll have to have a new dress suit!

NEIL. And you'll have to have a new evening dress—yellow chiffon, too. I can do their damned orchestrations now. I can do a hundred of them between now and October.

CYNTHIA. No, you won't!

NEIL. But, my youngest child, we must continue to eat.

CYNTHIA. But, my dear, we're extremely wealthy. Have you seen my new housekeeping book?

NEIL. No.

CYNTHIA. Look! I ruled every one of those columns myself.

NEIL (*rises*). Oh! Sit down!

CYNTHIA. That's why my middle finger is all red. (NEIL *kisses her finger.*) This is serious. This is finance. Listen! (*Reading from book.*) "To Mrs. Neil McRae—debtor. Ninety-seven dozen eggs from the little red hen at seventy-nine a dozen—ninety-seven, seventy-nine. Four hundred and forty-six quarts of milk from the little dun cow at sixty-four—four hundred and sixty-four. Thirty-six pots of jonquils sold Mr. Frost, the florist, at thirty-six sixty-six—six sixty-six, sixty-six." And there's the total!

NEIL. But, Cynthia, that can't be right; it's impossible!

CYNTHIA. Add it up for yourself.

NEIL. Sixty-three and eight are forty-two——

CYNTHIA. Neil, you may be one of the minor gods, but you can't add. (*Takes pencil.*) There! Look!

NEIL. But that means——

CYNTHIA. It means we're billionaires, that's all.

NEIL. We have a hundred and seventy-seven dollars and—seventy-seven cents?

CYNTHIA (*nods*). And we can keep on just as we have been doing.

NEIL. Cynthia, do you suppose *any* two people *ever?* (*He kisses her.*)

CYNTHIA. No, I don't believe *any* two people *ever.*

(*The voice of* GLADYS *comes out of the distance, faintly.*)

GLADYS. Oh, Ne-il!

CYNTHIA. What is it, dear?

NEIL. I thought I heard someone calling.

CYNTHIA. You did that last night at tea time. I'm frightened.

NEIL. You mustn't be—there are no fears in this house.

GLADYS (*louder this time—the same old call*). Oh, Ne-il!

NEIL. Cynthia, it's calling me!

CYNTHIA. What?

NEIL. I don't know. I must go to it.

(*He steps out of the cottage.*)

CYNTHIA. I'll go along!

(*The voice grows weaker as* GLADYS'S *gets stronger.*)

NEIL. You can't, my dear! It's too absurd.

(*The curtains close on the cottage; the jazz begins again.*)

GLADYS. Oh, Ne-il!

CYNTHIA (*faintly*). O-o-o-h!

NEIL. Yes, what is it?

GLADYS. Oh, Neil!

(GLADYS *enters—so do the check boy, the cigarette girl,* ALBERT, *and the four waiters. They stand in a line with outstretched palms.*)

NEIL. Yes, what is it?

(GLADYS, *as she speaks, dances with each waiter in turn.*)

GLADYS. Come on, sweetheart! We're going home now! Tip the waiters! Tip the waiters!

NEIL. For heaven's sake, stop that dancing!

GLADYS. I should say not! Tip the waiters! Tip them big! Tip them big!

(*She dances off with the last of the waiters.*)

(NEIL *hands out large bundles of money to the waiters, then as he proceeds along the line, he comes suddenly to* ALBERT.)

NEIL. Albert! (*The music stops.*) You got me into this! You've got to tell me how I'm going to get out of it!

ALBERT. What's the matter?

NEIL. I can't stand it! I can't live with Gladys any longer. What am I going to do about her?

ALBERT. Why, that's easy.

NEIL. What do you mean?

ALBERT. Just kill her—that's all.

NEIL. Kill her?

ALBERT. Of course. It's simple and practical.

NEIL. Do you know I never thought of that? I'm not very practical, am I?

ALBERT. No, you're not.

NEIL. Of course, I wouldn't like to do it unless it were absolutely necessary.

ALBERT. Still, it's worth thinking about.

(*He leaves him with this thought.*)

NEIL. Yes, it is.

(*The music starts;* GLADYS *and the waiter dance on again.*)

GLADYS. We're going home now! Tip the waiters! Did you tip them all? We're going home! Mama and papa will be there, and Homer!

(*The waiters are now gone, and the curtains reopen on the Cady home of pillars.* HOMER *is working a radio set;* MR. CADY *is playing golf with an imaginary ball;* MRS.

CADY *rocks, knits and sings. All is pandemonium.*)

CADY. Fore! Everybody, fore!

HOMER. I've got the radio fixed! Listen!

RADIO. Stock market reports! Stock market reports! (*Ad infinitum.*)

GLADYS. Oh, Neil! Isn't it nice to be in our own home again? (*She leaps into his lap.*)

MRS. CADY (*singing*). "Bringing in the sheaves! Bringing in the sheaves!"

CADY. Give me the niblick! Give me the niblick!

NEIL. I wish you'd all keep still.

GLADYS. What, darling? Wait! Wait! (*Everyone subsides.*) I hear them! The dancing teachers! The dancing teachers! *Now* you'll learn to dance.

NEIL. I won't, I tell you!

GLADYS. Oh, yes, you will! Here they are! The dancing teachers! Come in, dancing teachers! Now you'll learn to dance! (*Six dancing teachers enter—exquisite gentlemen, one like another.*)

NEIL. Gladys, I won't!

GLADYS. You've got to! Look! Aren't they wonderful? Here he is—my husband! You're to teach him to dance!

LEADER OF THE DANCING TEACHERS. Ah! (*He circles around* NEIL, *about to pounce.*)

NEIL. Gladys, I warn you! If you go ahead with this, you'll be sorry!

GLADYS. Teach him to dance! Teach him to dance!

LEADER (*advancing upon* NEIL). You've got to dance! We teach the world to dance! We make it dance. (*He seizes him.*) We've got him.

GLADYS. *Now* you'll learn to dance!

LEADER. Now watch me! One foot out and one foot in! One foot out and one foot in!

GLADYS. He's learning to dance! He's learning to dance!

ALL THE DANCING TEACHERS (*forcing* NEIL'S *arms, shoulders and feet*). One foot out and one foot in! One foot out and one foot in! Now your shoulder, now your elbow! Now your shoulder, now your elbow! One foot out and one foot in! One foot out and one foot in. Now your shoulder——

NEIL (*tears himself loose*). No! No! I tell you! Get out! All of you! (*They fall back.*) Get out, every one of you! I won't learn to dance! (*They have disappeared.*)

GLADYS. Neil!

NEIL (*the* CADYS *meantime unconcernedly continue their customary occupations, but in subdued tones*). Thank God! Now I'm going to write!

GLADYS. Neil, do you realize how you're behaving?

NEIL. I do! I won't go on with this any longer! If this is to be our life together then I can't stand it! I won't! That's all—I won't!

GLADYS. Neil! After all I've done for you! After all papa's done for you!

NEIL. Done for me? You've ruined me, that's all! You've given me a lot of money that I didn't want, and you won't let me do the one thing I want to do! Well, now I'm going to write my music! I'm going to finish my symphony!

GLADYS. Oh, no, you're not! (*Crosses quickly to the piano and tears up the manuscript.*) There's your old symphony! Now, what have you got to say?

NEIL. You tore it up! It was the only reason I married you, and you tore it up! All right—there's only one thing to do! (*He takes up the paper knife from the piano—it is about twice the size that it was when the audience last saw it.*)

GLADYS. Neil, Neil! What are you going to do?

NEIL. I'm going to kill you!

(*She stands looking at him, transfixed. He stabs her, and she falls dead.*)

MRS. CADY (*quietly*). Now you've done it!

NEIL. It was her fault! She killed my work!

MRS. CADY. She was a sweet girl. The police will get you. (*She sings "Bringing in the Sheaves."*)

NEIL. Stop that singing!

MRS. CADY. I won't!

NEIL. And stop that damned knitting!

MRS. CADY. I won't! "Rock of Ages, cleft for me."

(NEIL *stabs her. She dies, falling over backward, chair and all.*)

CADY (*blandly continuing his golf game*). This is outrageous! The idea of killing a man's daughter and wife! I'm ashamed of you!

NEIL. You're to blame, too! Just as much as the others! Look!

CADY. What is it?

NEIL. *You're* dead, too.

CADY. Oh! (MR. CADY *dies.*)

NEIL. Thank God, they're out of the way! Peace! I can work at last!

THE RADIO. Stock market reports! Stock market reports!

HOMER (*coming from behind the radio machine*). Is that so? I guess you forgot all about *me*, didn't you?

NEIL. Forget you? Indeed I didn't! Homer, my boy! (*He stabs him;* HOMER *crumples up on the floor.*) I guess that ends that! Free! Free!

HOMER (*sitting up*). Free nothing! We'll sue you for this, you dirty dog! (*He falls dead again.*)

NEIL. It won't do you any good! Not when they know why I did it! Not when I show them what you killed! Not when I play them my music!

(*Half a dozen newspaper reporters enter. They are dressed alike and look alike; each has a pencil expectantly poised over a piece of paper.*)

THE REPORTERS (*speaking one at a time, as they surround* NEIL). The Times! The World! The Post! The Globe! The Sun! The News! The Times! The World! The Post! The Globe! The Sun! The News!

NEIL (*indulging in a gesture with the paper knife*). Gentlemen, this is purely a family affair. I don't think I should say anything at this time, but do come to my trial.

THE REPORTERS (*again speaking one at a time*). A statement! A statement! A statement! A statement! A statement! A statement!

NEIL. Well, gentlemen, it's a long story. (*Instantly a dozen newsboys rush down the aisles of the theatre, crying "Extra! Extra! All about the murders!" The din is terrific. Simultaneously the theatre lights up; the audience turns for a second to look at the newsboys, and in that second the curtain falls. The newsboys pass out copies of The Morning-Evening, containing a full account of the quadruple murder.*)

PART TWO

The scene is now a courtroom. Against curtains of black stand three major objects of red—the same red that appeared fitfully in NEIL'S *chintz curtains, and again as draperies for the pillars in the Cady home. Squarely in the center is a block of twelve seats mounted on a platform. They are designed, obviously, for the jury, but instead of being the customary jurors' chairs they are of the kind found in theatres.* NEIL'S *piano and easy chair, of course, remain in their accustomed places. At the right, also vividly red, is the judge's bench, and against it leans a frame of photographs, of the sort that you see in theatre lobbies. The pictures show* MR. CADY *in various costumes and poses. The witness's box is at the left, and beside it a ticket taker's box, presided over by the ubiquitous* JERRY. *Near him is a hat-check boy recognizable as the same youth who took* NEIL'S *robe in the restaurant, and who also sold chocolates during the wedding ceremony. A couple of ushers, girls, stand chatting beside the jury box.* NEIL, *of course, is also present, walking up and down somewhat nervously, and consulting his watch. The jurors are beginning to arrive as the curtain ascends—three or four are streaming in. To* NEIL'S *surprise they all turn out to be dancing teachers.*

TICKET TAKER (*as the curtain ascends*). Oyez! Oyez! Oyez! (*He takes the tickets of the jurors, returns the stubs, and drops the remainder into his box.*)

CHECK BOY. Check your coat! Check your coat!

1ST JUROR. I guess we're early.

NEIL. Excuse me, but are you some of the jurors?

2ND JUROR. We certainly are.

NEIL. But—but you're dancing teachers, aren't you?

1ST JUROR. Best in the world.

NEIL. Are you going to try me? My music?

1ST JUROR. That's what.

NEIL. But it doesn't seem fair. I'm afraid you'll be prejudiced against something really good.

(*The* SECOND *and* THIRD JURORS *meet and automatically shake hands.*)

2ND JUROR. Hello, Ed!

3RD JUROR. Hello, Ed!

2ND JUROR. Well, you old son-of-a-gun!

3RD JUROR. Well, you old son-of-a-gun!

2ND JUROR. Glad to see you!

3RD JUROR. Glad to see you. (*They put their hands in their pockets simultaneously.*)

2ND JUROR. Fine! How's every little thing?

3RD JUROR. Fine! How's every little thing?

2ND JUROR. Well, glad I saw you!

3RD JUROR. Well, glad I saw you!

2ND JUROR. Goodbye, Ed!

3RD JUROR. Goodbye, Ed!

1ST JUROR (*at the frame of photographs.*) Say, who's this?

NEIL. That's the judge. It's the opening night of my trial, you know. That's the way he appeared in several famous cases.

2ND JUROR (*joining them and pointing to a picture*). Oh, yes! That's the way he looked in the Watkins trial. He was terrible good. Did you see it?

(*A fourth juror is shown to a first row seat by an usher.*)

1ST JUROR. No, I was out of town. (*Points to another picture.*) There he is in the Ferguson case! Gosh, he was good in that!

NEIL. Yes, I heard he was.

2ND JUROR. Was he funny?

1ST JUROR. Funny? He had that courtroom roaring half the time.

2ND JUROR. I don't know another judge in the country who can deliver a charge to a jury like he can. Pathos, comedy, everything.

1ST JUROR. They say this will be the best trial he's ever done. I hear they were sold out last Monday.

(*More jurors are entering.*)

TICKET TAKER. Tickets, please!

HAT-CHECK BOY. Coats checked! Check your coat!

(*The* THIRD JUROR *presents his ticket stub to an usher.*)

USHER. Other aisle, please! (*He crosses to the other side of the jury box and presents the stub to the other usher.*)

USHER. Other aisle, please! (*He returns to the* FIRST USHER.)

USHER. Right this way! (*She indicates a seat in the middle of the box.*)

3RD JUROR (*looking at the stub*). Ain't this an aisle seat?

1ST USHER. No, sir. Fourth seat in.

3RD JUROR. After paying all that money to a speculator! (*He takes his seat in the middle of the back row.*)

4TH JUROR. There ought to be a law against them. (*Other jurors are being seated.*)

(NEIL, *at the footlights, catches the attention of the orchestra leader.*)

NEIL. Now, the overture to the trial, please.

(*The orchestra plays the overture—a few bars of cheap musical comedy strains, the modulation from one tune to another being most elaborate. As the orchestra plays, more jurors are seated, leaving empty only the seat next the Judge's bench for the foreman, and another in the middle of the first row. The jurors look at their programs, talk, adjust opera glasses, etc. As the overture ends,* ALBERT *enters, a camera slung over his shoulder.*)

NEIL. Why, hello, Albert!

ALBERT. Hello, Neil!

NEIL. What are you doing here?

ALBERT. I'm covering the trial.

NEIL. "Covering" it? For a newspaper?

ALBERT (*nods*). I'm a reporter on the Illustrated.

NEIL. Oh, yes! You used to write, didn't you?

ALBERT. I understand they're going to try some of your music?

NEIL. Yes. You'll give it a fair criticism, won't you—in the paper?

ALBERT. In what paper?

NEIL. Why, your paper.

ALBERT. The Illustrated? We don't use any writing. It's an *illustrated* paper. Didn't you ever see it—in the subway?

NEIL. Of course! I remember—just pictures. But how do people know what they are?

ALBERT. Oh, we always have a few simple words, saying what the picture is about. A good many of our subscribers can read, and they tell the others.

(*A* CANDY SELLER *appears. He has the usual tray of chocolates and peppermints seen in the theatres.*)

CANDY SELLER. Chocolates and bon-bons! Fresh chocolates and bon-bons! Assorted chocolates!

1ST JUROR (*leaning out of the jury box*). Here you are. (*Buys a box of candy.*)

(*The* CANDY SELLER *goes out again. There is a sudden burst of activity in the jury box.*)

NEIL. What's all that?

ALBERT. They are getting ready to elect a foreman for the jury.

(*There is something like a cheer from the jury box. At one end a sign appears reading: JONES FOR FOREMAN. At the other side: SMITH FOR FOREMAN. The* FIRST JUROR *rises to speak. He receives hearty applause.*)

1ST JUROR. Mr. Chairman and ladies and gentlemen of the Fifth Jury District: I don't think anybody here has to be told at this late date that Harry J. Smith, retired, is the logical man for foreman of this grand jury. I guess everybody here knows Mr. Smith's record. You have all known him since childhood. He is an old Eighth Ward boy and will give a jury a business administration.

OTHER JURORS. Hooray!

(*The* FIRST JUROR *sits. The* SECOND JUROR *immediately demands attention.*)

2ND JUROR. Mr. Chairman and ladies and gentlemen of the Fifth Jury District: I don't think anybody here has to be told at this late date that Thomas A. Jones, retired, is the logical man for foreman of this grand jury. I guess everybody here knows Mr. Jones's record. You have all known him since childhood. He is an old Eighth Ward boy and will give the jury a business administration.

VOICE. What about Ireland?

(*There are cries of "Throw him out!"*)

(NEIL *holds up a hand for silence.*)

NEIL. Wait! (*He goes into the witness box.*) Ladies and gentlemen of the Fifth Jury District: I know it is late to be putting forward a new candidate for foreman of this grand jury, but this is my trial, and it is my music that you're going to hear. Both of the candidates who are now up before you are good dancers, but it is only fair that there should be someone on the jury who knows good music.

JURORS. Hooray!

NEIL. Therefore, when the light on the Times Building swings on tonight, I want it to be a steady red light, which will show that we have elected the Hon. Albert Rice, of Chicago, a man of the people, for the people, and by the people, and the stars and stripes forever in the good old U. S. A.!

JURORS. Hooray!

(*Almost immediately a red light shines across the group, and the orchestra strikes up Sousa's march, "Stars and Stripes." The jurors, cheering, march around the jury box, carrying American flags, banners, noise-makers, etc. There are cries of "Rice Wins! Hoorah for Rice!" Albert, still mindful of the fact that he has been sent to get the news, makes ready his camera and calls on the crowd to halt.*)

ALBERT. Hold it, please!

(*They stop—there is a scurrying to get into the photograph.* ALBERT *snaps them.*)

NEIL. Hold it! (He takes the camera *and* ALBERT *automatically prepares to have his own picture taken. One of the ushers tries to slip into the picture, but* NEIL *waves her aside. He snaps* ALBERT.) Will they be out soon?

ALBERT. Soon? They are out! (*He pulls a copy of the Illustrated from his pocket —a newspaper covered with a front page crowded with photographs, but entirely blank elsewhere.*) I brought one with me.

NEIL. They're on the front page.

ALBERT. Sure! We put everything on the front page. (*He points.*) There's a picture of the judge delivering his charge.

NEIL. But he hasn't delivered it yet.

ALBERT. Well, we have to get things quick. Our readers expect it.

(ALBERT *takes his place in the jury box. The other jurors lean over and shake his hand.*)

NEIL. The Hon. Albert Rice assumes office as thousands cheer.

(*He waits for the cheer—it does not come. He motions to the jury. They clap their hands perfunctorily.*)

ALBERT. Thank you, gentlemen.

TICKET TAKER (*announcing*). His Honor, the Judge!

(*Everyone rises. The orchestra begins the Soldiers' Chorus from "Faust." The Judge enters. He is* MR. CADY, *his golf suit handsomely covered by an enormous red robe. He also wears an enormous Judge's wig. He throws away all dignity, however, by lifting the skirts of his gown and skipping into view. The music ends on a long note in the brasses, such as attends the finish of an acrobat's trick.* CADY *curtsies toward the jury box in response to unanimous applause, and blows a kiss. He goes up to his chair and holds the picture of a satisfied actor as he waits for another burst of applause to subside.*)

CADY (*at last—to* NEIL). Got a match?

NEIL. What?

CADY. Got a match?

NEIL. Oh, yes! (*He strikes a match. Although several feet away from the cigar, the cigar lights.* MR. CADY *and jury are about to sit when* NEIL *hisses.*) Look out!

CADY. What is it?

NEIL. That chair. It isn't very strong, you know.

CADY. Oh, I'll be careful. (*He sits. The jurors sit.*)

TICKET TAKER. Oyez! Oyez! Oyez!

(*The final juror enters and presents his ticket.*)

CADY. Ladies and gentlemen, I——

NEIL (*noticing the tardy juror*). Just a

minute! He's late. (*To the juror.*) Can't you people ever be on time? (*The tardy juror gives his seat check to an usher, who starts to lead him to his place, in the middle of the second row, but finds somebody already in it.*)

CADY (*blandly*). Ladies and gentlemen, I declare the Court— (*The confusion makes him break off again.*)

USHER (*leaning far over*). May I see your check, please?

CADY. I declare the Court——

USHER. May I see your check?

JUROR (*searching his pockets*). I had it here some place. Ah! (*Gives stub to the* USHER.)

(*The* USHER *examines the ticket stub.*)

USHER. Oh, you belong in the row ahead. This gentleman has a ticket for this seat.

(*People in both rows have to stand up while the exchange is made. It is a good deal of trouble, to put it mildly.*)

NEIL (*to* CADY). All right now. I'm sorry.

CADY. I declare the Court to be in session. (*There is a round of applause.* CADY *bows.*) The business of the day is the trial of Neil Wadsworth McRae for murder. (*There is more applause.* NEIL *is finally compelled to bow.* CADY *again addresses* NEIL *confidentially.*) Am I right?

NEIL. Yes. And don't forget, I'm going to play my symphony. That was the reason I did it, you know.

CADY. Yes, I remember. (*He is quite conversational.*) Now, the first thing to be done, I should say, is to have the prosecuting attorney make a sort of general charge. (*To* NEIL.) What do you think?

NEIL. I guess that's right. How about it, Albert?

ALBERT (*looking up from his program*). Yes, that's right. (NEIL *nods to the* TICKET TAKER.)

TICKET TAKER (*announcing*). The prosecuting attorney!

(HOMER *enters to the tune of "Tammany." He wears a long black robe. He receives a hearty round of applause, with a few hisses.*)

NEIL. Oh, it's you!

HOMER (*quietly*). I'll get you now, you dirty dog!

NEIL. I think not.

CADY. Come, come, we can't be all day at this. I've got to get back to the office. Now, just what were these murders all about?

HOMER (*reads from document. As* HOMER *begins to read* USHER *and* CHECK BOY *begin a whispered conversation that soon dominates the scene.*)

SIMULTANEOUSLY

HOMER. "On such and such a blank date, the defendant, Neil Wadsworth McRae, did brutally murder, maim, assault, destroy, stab, injure, kill and cause the death of Gladys Virginia Cady, his wife; Mr. Cady, her father; Mrs. Cady, her mother, and Homer Cady, her brother, destroying one and all of the aforesaid Gladys Virginia Cady, his wife; Mr. Cady, her father; Mrs. Cady, her mother, and Homer Cady, her brother—by the use of a large paper knife, of bone manufacture and curious design, a picture of which appeared in the newspapers at the time." (*Hands the newspaper containing the picture to* CADY.)	USHER. Did you sell much candy? CHECK BOY. Sure—enough to buy a couple seats for the movies. USHER. Oh, let's see the one up the street! CHECK BOY. Oh, that's punk! You always want to see the sad ones. USHER. I hate comedies. CHECK BOY. Well, I hate sad ones. NEIL. Quiet, please; some of us would like to hear the show! (*They grudgingly leave the room.*)

CADY. Yes, I saw it. A great, big, long one. Exhibit A. (*He hands it to the foreman.*)

ALBERT. Exhibit A!

(*Passes it to the other jurors.*)

(*The other jurors repeat "Exhibit A," passing the newspaper from one to another.*)

HOMER. Having caused the death of the aforesaid and aforementioned people, I therefore call upon the Court to punish said Neil Wadsworth McRae in one of two ways prescribed by law—death or hard labor for life, whichever they do in this state.

CADY (*realizing that maybe it's serious after all*). Oh, no! Is that so?

NEIL (*lightly*). Just wait!

CADY (*to* HOMER). Yes. Just wait, please.

1ST JUROR (*leans toward his neighbor, with open program, and reads from it, as though confiding a bit of real news.*) Say, this courtroom, with every seat occupied, can be emptied in less than three minutes.

CADY. Silence in the court!

(*A pause.*)

HOMER. The State rests.

(*He sits in the easy chair and is immediately seized with a fit of coughing.* MRS. CADY *instantly appears behind* HOMER; *she has her knitting, but no chair.*)

MRS. CADY. Are you all right, Homer?

HOMER. I guess so.

MRS. CADY (*to the jury*). Homer's sick. He was always delicate. But he was a good boy though. When Homer wanted to be he was as good a boy as you'd find in a month of Sundays. There was no reason on earth why Neil shouldn't have allowed him to live, just like a lot of other people are allowed to live. (*The jurors applaud her.*)

CADY. You are his mother?

MRS. CADY. Yes, sir.

(CADY *shakes her hand, sympathetically.*)

CADY. You were also a victim, I believe?

MRS. CADY. That's right. (CADY *shakes her hand again.*) You heard how he did it? With a paper knife.

CADY. Oh, yes! You see, we're trying him today.

MRS. CADY. For the murders?

CADY. Yes.

MRS. CADY. Oh, I beg your pardon! (*Begins to back away in confusion.*) I wouldn't have intruded, if I'd known.

NEIL. Wait a minute! I'd like to have Mrs. Cady take the stand, please.

MRS. CADY (*flustered*). Who? Me?

NEIL. If you don't mind.

HOMER. What! Going to make her take the stand? A mother? (*There are hisses from the jury.*)

NEIL. Over here, please! (*Leads her to the witness box.*) Do you swear to tell the truth—the truth—and—the truth?

MRS. CADY. Yes.

NEIL. You can't tell the truth unless you raise your hand, you know.

MRS. CADY. No?

NEIL. No. (*She puts up her hand.*) You're Mrs. Cady, aren't you?

MRS. CADY. Yes. (*To* MR. CADY.) Is that right, Fred?

CADY. Yes—that's all right.

NEIL (*suddenly wheeling on* MRS. CADY). Now then. (MRS. CADY *jumps.*) Where were you on Friday, June third?

MRS. CADY. Knitting. (*She suits the action to the word.*)

NEIL. But you used to sing in the choir, didn't you?

MRS. CADY. Oh, yes. (*Sings.*) "Just as I am, without one plea." (*The jurors stand and join in.* CADY *stops smoking for a moment and also sings a bar or two.*)

CADY (*suddenly rapping for order*). Silence in the court!

NEIL (*waves a warning finger at* MRS. CADY, *as though to intimate that another question is about to come*). Prove an alibi!

HOMER. I object, Your Honor!

CADY. Objection sustained and overruled! (*To* MRS. CADY.) Answer the question! (NEIL *smiles mockingly at* HOMER.)

MRS. CADY. What was it?

NEIL. Prove an alibi!

MRS. CADY. What kind?

NEIL (*to* CADY.) I didn't know there were different kinds.

CADY. Oh, yes—there are several kinds of alibis.

NEIL. Then prove any kind.

HOMER. Your Honor, I object!

CADY. You object?

HOMER. Yes! (*He goes to* NEIL *and looks sinisterly at him.*) I object to his looks!

NEIL. Why, what's the matter with them?

CADY. (*it is apparently a point of great import*). An objection has been raised to the prisoner's looks. (*Looks at* NEIL *carefully.*) Hm! Have you anything to say?

NEIL. Sir?

CADY (*quite casual*). Have you anything to say about your looks?

NEIL. Why—I think they're all right. (*There is a weighty pause.*)

CADY. This is a serious question. (*He removes his wig. The jury breaks out in chatter;* CADY *raps.*) Order, please! Now, the prisoner thinks that his looks are all right.

HOMER. But he can't prove it!

CADY (*to* NEIL). *Can* you prove it?

NEIL. Why— (*Here's an awful situation!*)

CADY. You see, this is a court of law. Everything has to be proved.

NEIL. Well, well—can't the jury tell by

looking? (NEIL *looks toward the jury, which peers at him closely, but is puzzled. The jurors shake their heads, uncertain.*)

CADY. You see, it's illegal for a jury to know anything until it's been instructed. Now, as I understand it, the point is that you think your looks are all right?

NEIL. Yes.

CADY. But you can't prove it?

NEIL (*if he can only have a moment's peace in which to think it over!*). Oh, Lord! (*One of the jurors is noisily unwrapping a candy box.*) Quiet! Good heavens—how can I think if they're going to— Your Honor, they *must* be quiet!

CADY. Quiet!

THE JUROR. But it's candy! (*It is a big box full and it is passed up to the Judge.*)

CADY. Oh, really? (GLADYS *enters in a brilliant dinner gown and an ornate cloak.*)

GLADYS. Oh, candy! (*She crosses to the Judge's stand and begins rifling the box.*) Hello, Neil! I didn't mean to interrupt! I just ran in to get the boys! We're going dancing! (*Some of the jurors rise; one or two even begin climbing over the railing to join her.*) There's a big new place opening tonight and they're going to take me there! Got some money, papa?

CADY. Ten thousand enough? (*He gives her a handful of bills.*)

GLADYS. Oh, thanks. Come on, boys. (*The jurors make further gestures toward going.*)

NEIL. No, wait! (*All movement is suspended.*) You mean you want to take—*them*—away with you?

GLADYS. Of course!

NEIL. But—but I'm being tried for the murders. And if you take the jury away——

GLADYS. I'm sorry, Neil, but I couldn't miss the opening, could I? Are you ready? (*The jurors step toward her.*)

NEIL. No, no! (*Again the jurors halt.* NEIL *appeals to* CADY.) She can't do that, can she?

CADY (*who has been eating so much candy he has had little time for the trial's new aspect*). What?

NEIL. Take the jury away, right in the middle of things?

CADY (*licking his fingers*). She can if it's habeas corpus.

NEIL (*not at all sure*). Well—is it?

CADY (*he licks his fingers*). It's beginning to look that way.

NEIL. But it isn't fair! They've got to hear my music. I know what I'll do! (*He faces* CADY.) I'll take it to a higher court!

CADY (*just a bit hurt*). Oh, don't you like this court?

NEIL. It isn't that. It's a good court, I guess, and the people are lovely, but——

CADY. About how high a one would you want?

NEIL. I'd want the highest I could get.

CADY. All right. (JUDGE CADY *slowly goes up in the air, as his stand grows two or three feet higher.*) Is this high enough for you?

NEIL. I guess so. Is this the superior court?

CADY. Oh, yes. Much superior. And more up-to-date. We send out all our verdicts by radio.

NEIL. She can't take them away with her now, can she—in this court?

CADY. Oh, no! You see, in a higher court the lower court is reversed.

NEIL. Good! (*The jurors resume their old positions.*)

GLADYS. Oh, the devil! Well, then I'll take Albert. He's only the foreman. (*She grabs* ALBERT *by the hand and leads him out of the courtroom.*)

CADY (*sucks a sticky thumb*). Well, are the rest of you ready to bring in a verdict? All in favor will say——

NEIL. No, wait! I'm not through—you haven't heard the music yet.

CADY. Oh, that's right! You're going to play for us.

NEIL. Of course. That's why I killed them, you know—on account of the music. I want to prove that I was justified. Listen! (*He goes to the piano.*) You won't blame me when you've heard the music. (*He strikes a chord.*) This is a symphony in C Minor. (*He starts to play. The result is disconnected, meaningless. There is a budding hissing from the jurors.* NEIL, *with a cry, jumps to his feet, holding up the torn sheet of music. He finds it almost impossible to speak.*) She destroyed it! She tore it up, and now I can't play it! Cynthia! Cynthia!

(CYNTHIA *appears at the piano. She is calm and sympathetic, as always.*)

CYNTHIA. Yes, dear?

NEIL. Cynthia, she tore up the symphony! I can't remember it, and they're waiting for me to play!

CYNTHIA. You still have the pantomime, haven't you?

NEIL. Yes.

CYNTHIA. Then play that for them instead. (*She finds the pantomime music.*) They'll think it's better, anyhow. (*Puts the music before him.*)

NEIL. But it isn't finished.

CYNTHIA. Well, now you *can* finish it.

NEIL. Can I?

CYNTHIA. Of course. It'll be all right, dear—you'll see.

NEIL. You—you think we ought to do it?

CYNTHIA. Of course.

NEIL. All right. (*He faces his inquisitors.*) Ladies and gentlemen, instead of the symphony, we're going to play a little pantomime, called "A Kiss in Xanadu" —written by Cynthia Mason and Neil McRae. We'll need quite a lot of room, so if you don't mind clearing the court— (*The Judge's dais and the witness box disappear. The jury box, too, moves into blackness.*) The scene is the royal palace in Xanadu. It's a night in June—one of those spring nights that you find only in Xanadu. Now, if you're all ready—music! (*The music of the pantomime begins.*) Cynthia, we ought to have a window to show what kind of night it is.

(*In the distance a great open window appears. Beyond a moonlit balustrade are flowers and trees and stars.*)

CYNTHIA. It's coming!

NEIL. Thanks! The scene is the bedchamber of the Prince and Princess. On the right is the bed of the Princess and on the left is the bed of the Prince.

(*Two fairy-tale beds appear from the darkness. They are canopied in pink. Above them are flower-draped testers that rise to golden points.* NEIL *and* CYNTHIA *seat themselves at the piano and the pantomime begins.*

A LORD OF THE BEDCHAMBER *and a* LADY OF THE BEDCHAMBER *enter and bow to each other ostentatiously. They are followed into the room by two small black pages, carrying tiny bed tables. The one for the Princess' bed bears a small lamp with a dainty shade. The Prince's has a candle and shade, and a small phonograph. As the* LORD *and* LADY *examine the room the pages go out and return with a pillow, which is placed at the foot of the Princess' bed, and a costumer, which is for the convenience of the Prince. The attendants convince themselves there are no intruders under the beds and depart. A clock strikes nine.*

The PRINCESS *enters. She is very beautiful, but very bored. The lovely night lures her to the window. She goes out on the little balcony and sighs. She is a married Princess. She returns to the bedchamber and snappishly commands the* LADY *to undress her. Nothing to do but go to bed! The* LADY *draws the curtains and leaves.*

The PRINCE *enters with his* LORD. *He would like to be a Gay Dog Prince and he twirls his mustache bravely. He, too, would like to find romance again, but here he is—a married Prince! A page puts his royal dressing gown and crown on the costumer. The* LORD *attaches curlers to the royal mustache and leaves the* PRINCE. *The* PRINCE *turns on the phonograph and tries to do his Nightly Dozen. But the night outside distracts him. He goes to the window. It is too much for him. A second attempt to exercise is abandoned. He will go out to Adventure. If he turns the royal dressing gown inside out it should make a rather good disguise. He does so. The lining of the crown makes a serviceable cap. He tiptoes to the other bed. The* PRINCESS *is asleep. He draws the canopy across his own bed and steals out the window.*)

CYNTHIA. But the Princess wants to go adventuring, too. I know! Let's have the moon wake her.

NEIL. Yes! Come on, moon! (*The moon obligingly sends its beams across the bed of the* PRINCESS.) Thank you!

(*The pantomime proceeds. The* PRINCESS' *heads pops through the draperies. It is such a beautiful night! She observes the closed canopy of her lord's bed. He is asleep—the dull, conventional husband. She goes to the window. What a night! Romance lies out there. She hesitates. She decides. Frightened, but determined, she takes a cover from her bed. An excellent shawl it makes! But something is wrong. She stands undecided, her hands touching her lovely hair. The music stops.*)

NEIL. We skipped a place here. We're got to disguise the Princess. She mustn't be recognized, either, you know.

CYNTHIA. Of course not. I have it! Let her put on her lamp-shade for a bonnet!

NEIL. And she can use the Prince's candle-shade for a mask!

(*The music starts again and the* PRINCESS

dons the lamp-shade and puts two finger holes through the candle-shade. She is very happy and goes out to the trees and stars. There is darkness—and here we are in a public park in Xanadu. There are a good many flowery bushes to be seen, but they are not noticed by the PRINCE, *who sits, depressed, on a park bench, under a street lamp. A* POLICEMAN, *a* LAMPLIGHTER *and two small attendants enter on patrol, and sedately go about their business. The* PRINCESS *comes into the park. A man, a romantic-looking man, even if he is masked by that upturned coat collar! A girl, a charming girl, even if she is holding a small mask before her eyes! She skips away, but returns. She drops her handkerchief. She quietly and politely sneezes. He springs to her aid with her handkerchief. She sits beside him on the bench. He plucks a rose from the bush behind them and offers it timidly. She tosses it away. The light in the lamp is much too bright. A mighty puff from the* PRINCE *and it goes out. But the* WATCH *returns. The lamp is relighted. The* PRINCE *and the* PRINCESS *sit a little closer. He offers another rose. This time she accepts it. But that lamp! He has a permanent solution. He breaks the lamp in two. Masks are not needed in the darkness, but the moon comes up. He waves it away. She kisses him. A clock strikes five. The sun rises. The adventure is over. She runs away. He calls, but she does not answer. He picks up the rose she spurned. His grief is covered by considerate darkness.*

Once more it is the Royal bedchamber. The PRINCESS *creeps into the room and into bed. The* PRINCE *steals in a moment later. He goes to the* PRINCESS' *bed. Still asleep! He goes to his bed. The clock strikes eight. The* LORD *and* LADY *arrive. The pages fetch a breakfast table. The royal pair are awakened. They sit down to eat. She starts to pour her husband's coffee. Oh, yes, she had forgotten! She rises and offers a cheek to be kissed. He mechanically obliges. They sit down again. But they cannot eat. The music of the night is still with them. They steal wistful looks at the window. The* PRINCESS *looks at the rose He gave her. The* PRINCE *looks at the one She first refused. The flowers are stealthily put away. The* PRINCE *and the* PRINCESS *unfold their napkins. It is the humdrum life once more.*)

(*The curtain falls, slowly. Then, slowly, the footlights go down, plunging the auditorium into complete darkness. Immediately we hear the verdict from the vastly Superior Court—sent out, as* JUDGE CADY *had said, by radio. It comes, through magnifiers, from the rear of the auditorium, and takes the form of loud and derisive laughter, punctuated by cries of "Rotten!" "No good!" "Highbrow!" "Terrible!" In the darkness the curtain again rises. Seated cross-legged on* NEIL'S *piano, still in the red wig and with a red light playing on him, is* JUDGE CADY. *As always, he is smoking a cigar.* NEIL *sits facing him on the piano stool.*)

CADY (*to the invisible voices*). Silence! (*The voices stop.*) Now, was that what you wanted to show us?

NEIL. Yes, sir.

CADY. Well, of course we don't want to hurt your feelings, Neil, but I'm afraid it's a little bit highbrow. Don't you think so?

NEIL. No, sir. Not very.

CADY. Well, I don't think it's what they want. (*To the unseen jurors.*) How about it?

(*A single voice comes over the radio. It says "Rotten!"*)

CADY. Are you ready to bring in a verdict?

FIRST JUROR'S VOICE. Yes, I move we bring in a verdict!

SECOND JUROR'S VOICE. I second the motion!

FIRST JUROR'S VOICE. It is moved and seconded that we bring in a verdict. Remarks? (*A pause.*) All those in favor say "Aye."

CHORUS OF VOICES. Aye!

FIRST JUROR'S VOICE. Opposed—"No?" (*Pause.*) The motion is carried.

CADY. Well, what sort of a verdict do you want to bring in? There are several kinds of verdicts.

FIRST JUROR'S VOICE. I move we bring in a verdict of guilty!

SECOND JUROR'S VOICE. I second that motion!

FIRST JUROR'S VOICE. It is moved and seconded that we bring in a verdict of guilty. Remarks? All those in favor say "Aye."

CHORUS OF VOICES. Aye!

FIRST JUROR'S VOICE. Opposed—"No?" (*Pause.*) Well, I guess the motion's carried.

CADY. See, Neil? I told you so.

NEIL. Well—well, what are you going to do with me?

CADY. This thing of using the imagination has got to stop. We're going to make you work in the right way. You see, your talents belong to us now, and we're going to use every bit of them. We're going to make you the most wonderful song writer that ever lived.

NEIL. But I can't write that kind of music! You know I can't!

CADY. You can do it by our system. You are sentenced to be at the Cady Consolidated Art Factory at eight o'clock tomorrow morning!

NEIL. Art factory?

CADY. At eight o'clock tomorrow morning!

(*The lights slowly dim and fade out, and instantly there is a burst of noise. Pianos are playing discordantly; there is the sound of machinery in the distance, a voice is singing a jazz tune, and other voices are heard in loud declamation. The lights go up again on a tier of four cells. In the first a man is dictating to a stenographer; in the second* NEIL *is working away at a piano, while a youth in a belted coat and a straw hat, atilt on his head, sings to the accompaniment of* NEIL'S *music; in the third cell an artist works before an easel, and in the fourth a young man is loudly reciting poetry, apparently moved to do so by the posturings of two other youths who are in the cell with him. After a moment of this pandemonium a guide enters, followed by three visitors. All four are dancing teachers, so far as outward appearances go, but they are marked apart by the fact that the guide wears an official-looking cap, and the visitors carry umbrellas and open Baedekers. The guide raises his voice for silence; a gong sounds somewhere, and all activity ceases. The figures in the cages come down to the bars and stand waiting.*)

GUIDE. Now this, gentlemen, is the manufacturing department. In this studio —(*He indicates the first.*)—we have Walter Carp Smith, the world's greatest novelist——

NOVELIST (*more or less routine*). How are you?

GUIDE (*passing to the second cage*). In this studio, Neil McRae, the world's greatest composer!

NEIL (*listlessly*). How are you?

GUIDE (*at the third cage*). In this one, Finley Jamison, the world's greatest magazine artist!

ARTIST. How are you?

GUIDE (*at the fourth cage*). And in this, James Lee Wrex, the world's greatest poet!

POET. How are you?

GUIDE (*indicating the unseen cages beyond*). The studios beyond are devoted to science and religion. Mr. Cady was the first person in the world to put religion up in ten-cent packages, selling direct to the consumer.

FIRST VISITOR. You don't say so!

GUIDE. He also prides himself on having the largest output of literature and music in the world. He's going to open two more plants the first of the month. Now, would you like to see how these men work?

FIRST VISITOR. Yes, indeed! (*Goes toward the first cage.*) Did you say this was the novelist?

GUIDE. The world's greatest. Author of more than two thousand published works.

FIRST VISITOR. What an imagination!

GUIDE. Yes, sir, none at all. Now if you're ready, I'll show you how he works. Go!

NOVELIST (*begins at once to dictate from a book in his hand*). "Something closely resembling a tear fell from the old patrician's cheek. 'Margaret,' he cried, 'the people of the West have learned to love you, too.' 'Jackie boy,' she whispered. 'They have made you governor after all.' Far off on the—the—" (*He hesitates; the stenographer takes up the story.*)

STENOGRAPHER. "—desert, the caravan faded away. Night took them in its arms and a great hush fell on the forest. The two lovers——"

GUIDE. Stop! (*He turns to the visitors.*) There you are!

FIRST VISITOR. Was *she* writing it?

GUIDE. Oh, no! Sometimes she gets a little ahead of him, that's all.

FIRST VISITOR. Isn't he wonderful!

GUIDE. Forty-five minutes after he finishes a novel we have it printed and assembled and on its way to the movie men.

FIRST VISITOR. May we talk to him?

GUIDE. Certainly.

FIRST VISITOR (*to the novelist*). I've enjoyed your novels very much.

NOVELIST. Thank you.

FIRST VISITOR. I see you're writing a new

one.

NOVELIST. Of course. I'm under contract.

FIRST VISITOR. What's that? (*Indicating the book in the novelist's hand.*)

NOVELIST. It's my last one.

FIRST VISITOR. But weren't you just dictating from it, for your new one?

NOVELIST. Yes. They like it that way.

GUIDE. Under the old system they wrote it all new each time. Here—let the gentleman have it as a souvenir.

FIRST VISITOR (*reading the title*). "Eternal Love." What's your new one called?

NOVELIST. "Love Eternal."

GUIDE. Don't forget—you're lecturing at three o'clock at Wanamaker's.

SECOND VISITOR. Say, will you show us how the artist works?

GUIDE. Certainly. What will you have—a cover or an advertisement?

SECOND VISITOR. What's the difference?

GUIDE. There isn't any.

SECOND VISITOR. Well, then, I'll take an advertisement.

GUIDE. All right. Go! (THE ARTIST *draws without looking at the canvas. He hands it to the guide, who hands it to the visitor. The canvas is blank.*) There you are!

SECOND VISITOR. What beautiful eyes!

THIRD VISITOR. Wonderful!

GUIDE. Do you want to talk to him?

SECOND VISITOR. Oh, thanks. I suppose it'll be used on a magazine?

ARTIST. Oh, yes—thousands.

SECOND VISITOR. Must be worth five or six hundred dollars.

ARTIST (*bored to death*). Thirty-five hundred.

FIRST VISITOR. You don't say so!

GUIDE. And here, gentlemen, is our poet. His "Jolly Jingles" are printed in three million newspapers a day.

FIRST VISITOR (*pointing to the men in back*). Who are those men?

GUIDE. Those are his models. He is the only poet in the world who works from living models. That's why all his poetry is so true, so human. He'll show you. Go!

POET. I will now write a friendship poem. (*Motions to his models.*) Friendliness No. 3, please. "Friendship."

(*The* MODELS *strike a pose, hands clasped.*)

(*The* POET *recites.*)

"Goodbye, old pal; hello, old pal; the greatest pal I ever knew.
A dog's your finest friend, my lad, when all the world is blue."

SECOND VISITOR. Ain't it human?

GUIDE. And here, gentlemen, is Mr. Neil McRae, America's foremost composer.

FIRST VISITOR. Who's that in back?

GUIDE. That's his lyric writer. You will now see how they work. What kind of a song will it be, McRae?

NEIL. A pathetic. (*Sits at the piano.*)

GUIDE. A pathetic. Go! (NEIL *plays.*)

SINGER (*in a horrible voice*). "You've broken my heart like you broke my heart, So why should you break it again?"

(NEIL *comes to the bars again.*)

GUIDE. That will sell one and one-half million.

SECOND VISITOR. I suppose you write other kinds of songs, too?

NEIL. Oh, yes—mammies, sweeties and fruit songs. The ideas are brought from the inspiration department every hour on the hour. After I turn them into music they are taken to the purifying department, and then to the testing and finishing rooms. They are then packed for shipment.

FIRST VISITOR. A wonderful system!

THIRD VISITOR. I should say so!

SECOND VISITOR. Do you work all the time?

NEIL. No, the night shift comes on at eight.

FIRST VISITOR. How long have you been here?

NEIL. For years and years.

SECOND VISITOR. Say, will you write another song for us—just as a souvenir?

NEIL (*desperately*). Oh, why don't you all go away?

GUIDE. What's that? What was that? You get busy there and write another song!

NEIL. No! I've been writing forever—I'm tired of it.

GUIDE. Do you want me to call Mr. Cady?

NEIL. I don't care! I don't care what you do!

GUIDE. I'll give you one more chance.

NEIL. No! I won't!

GUIDE. All right, then! Mr. Cady! Mr. Cady!

(*The* GUIDE *rushes out. The visitors slink away. A gong sounds. Those in the cages huddle in fear.* MR. CADY *appears behind the cages. He carries a large snake whip.*)

CADY. What's the matter here?

GUIDE. McRae says he won't go on!

CADY. He won't, eh? Well, we'll see

about that!

NEIL. I can't go on! I'm tired!

CADY. What's that got to do with it? You've got to go on!

NEIL. I *can't*, I tell you. I *can't* keep on at this sort of thing.

CADY. You know your sentence, don't you? You've got to work our way until you die.

NEIL (*dully*). Yes, I know.

CADY. We own you now. The family. The family owns you. (*He falls into rhythmic measure.*)

You take our money and you live our life,
  We own you, we own you.
You take our money and you live our life,
  We own you, we own you.
You take our money and you live our way,
  We pay the piper and we tell him what to play.
You sold your soul and you can't get away,
  We own you, we own you.

(*The* CADY *family and others enter at back, and weave back and forth joining in the chant, reaching through the bars at* NEIL.)

NEIL. Until I die! I can be free from you if I die! I *can* die! You can't keep me from it! That's how I can get away from you! Open the door! Open the door! (*He shakes the door on the audience's side of the cage. It opens.*) It was never locked! (*He steps out and closes the door.* CYNTHIA *enters.*) Cynthia, Cynthia, I'm free! I can die! (*Those in the background disappear.*) Cynthia, how are we going to do it?

CYNTHIA. We'll go to an executioner. I know a good one. You mustn't be afraid. It won't hurt. (*An* EXECUTIONER *appears masked, with a black robe and a huge paper knife.*) See—it's Jerry!

JERRY. Hello, Mr. McRae. (*Takes off his mask and cap.*)

NEIL. Oh, hello, Jerry! You're going to do it, are you?

JERRY. Sure. (*Feels the edge of his knife.*)

NEIL. Oh, that's good.

CYNTHIA. Do we have to wait long?

JERRY. No—you're next.

NEIL. Oughtn't we to have a block?

CYNTHIA (*moving the armchair*). We'll use this. It'll be more comfortable.

NEIL. Oh! And you'll stay with me?

CYNTHIA. Always. (*She stands beside him.*) But it won't hurt. (ALBERT *enters, wearing a short medical apron and jacket.*) Albert will give you a pill.

NEIL. Oh, yes! Hello, Albert!

ALBERT. Hello, Neil! Got a glass of water?

CYNTHIA (*glass of water in hand*). We're ready, Doctor. (ALBERT *goes to the chair; tests its strength.*)

ALBERT (*to the* EXECUTIONER). Is the light all right? (*The cabaret orchestra is heard in the distance.*)

JERRY. I think so.

NEIL. There's that music again.

ALBERT. You're nervous, that's all. Here! (NEIL *swallows a pill.*)

CYNTHIA. Now it can't possibly hurt you.

ALBERT (*motions* NEIL *to the chair*). Here we are! (NEIL *sits.*) That's it—way back. (*To* JERRY.) Right?

NEIL. Shall I take off my collar?

ALBERT. Oh, no. There's room, I think.

NEIL. Just a once-through, please.

ALBERT. Of course. It'll be all over in a minute.

NEIL. Cynthia!

CYNTHIA. Yes.

NEIL. I was afraid you'd gone.

CYNTHIA. No, dear. (JERRY *taps his knife on floor.*) Are you ready, Neil?

NEIL. Yes, except for that music. Charles the First didn't have any music. (*The lights begin to fade.*)

CYNTHIA. He's ready, Doctor.

NEIL. Don't go away, Cynthia!

ALBERT. All ready. (JERRY *taps the knife again on the floor.*)

NEIL. Goodbye! I'll see you soon.

CYNTHIA. Are you comfortable?

NEIL. Yes. You'll be with me always, won't you, Cynthia? (*There is darkness, save for a cloudy moving light on* NEIL.)

CYNTHIA. Always.

ALBERT. All right.

NEIL. Cynthia, are you there?

CYNTHIA. Yes, darling.

(*There is a hum of voices. Presently one can discern several chanting, "You take our money and you lead our life."* MRS. CADY *is heard saying, "Homer's sick."* MR. CADY *is apparently telephoning somewhere. He is shouting, "Well, I'll tell you what to do!"* HOMER'S *voice repeats, "You dirty dog!"* GLADYS *shrilly calls out, "He's learning to dance!" The voices become a chant, finally unintelligible. The lights slowly go up again. We are back in* NEIL'S *apartment. He is asleep in his chair. It is sunset. There is a knock, a real knock, on the door.*)

NEIL (*half asleep*). Yes? (CYNTHIA *enters.*)

CYNTHIA. Is anything the matter, Neil? I thought I heard you talking.

NEIL. It didn't hurt. Was it a success?

CYNTHIA. Neil, are you all right?

NEIL (*takes her hand*). I need you, Cynthia!

CYNTHIA. Oh, Neil, do you? Are you sure you do? I—I couldn't stay away, Neil. I tried to, but I couldn't. Because I need you, too. I just couldn't give you up to anyone else on earth.

NEIL. Cynthia, dear.

CYNTHIA. It wouldn't have worked, Neil—with those people. Don't you know it wouldn't?

NEIL. I think I do.

CYNTHIA. I've been sitting out on a bench in the square, trying to think out what it would mean—what it would do to you.

NEIL. I know. Widgets.

CYNTHIA. That would be worse for you than any amount of poverty.

NEIL. Poverty in our cottage.

CYNTHIA. Did you think of a cottage, too?

NEIL. Of course—I lived there.

CYNTHIA. We could manage. I know quite a lot about raising chickens.

NEIL (*reminiscently*). A little red hen and a little dun cow.

CYNTHIA. Yes, we might have a cow. Have you been thinking about it, too? (*Rises.*)

NEIL. Well—let's say dreaming. (*He rises and goes to the desk.*) It was terrible, Cynthia—do you know, I dreamed I was married to *her*?

CYNTHIA. To Gladys?

NEIL. When I thought you didn't care, I was hurt and angry. And I dreamed she telephoned—(*Sees the receiver off the hook.*) My God! Did she telephone! Oh, Cynthia, it's real! I *did* do it! I did!

CYNTHIA. Did what?

NEIL. I did ask her to marry me!

CYNTHIA. Neil! You didn't! And she—accepted you?

NEIL. Yes.

CYNTHIA. Oh, Neil.

(*A knock at the door.* JERRY *puts his head in. He wears a uniform somewhat like the one that accompanied him through the dream.*)

JERRY. It's me, Jerry. I've been ringing your phone for the last five minutes. Yeh, I thought so—you left it off the hook again. (NEIL *replaces the receiver.*) The young lady that came before was waiting, so I brought her right up.

GLADYS (*in the doorway*). It's me, Neil—may I come in? (*Enters.*) Oh, hello again, Miss Mason!

CYNTHIA. I—I forgot my tea things. (*Half choking, she takes up her tray of tea things.*)

GLADYS. Well, here we are. Isn't it exciting! We're engaged.

NEIL. Yes.

GLADYS. Did you have a good nap?

NEIL. Yes, thank you.

GLADYS (*obviously something on her mind*). Do you love me a lot, Neil? Enough to do me a great big favor?

NEIL. What?

GLADYS. It's a big one, and maybe you won't want to do it.

NEIL. What is it?

GLADYS. Well, it's this way. Coming back from the dressmaker's I met Walter Craig. I told you about him, didn't I? He's a boy that sort of used to like me.

NEIL. Oh, yes.

GLADYS. Now, mind you, Neil, you can say "No" to this if you want to, but—he said, "What are you doing tonight?" Now, you won't be angry, Neil?

NEIL. No, no.

GLADYS. Well, then he said he didn't know any other girl in New York, and would I sort of play around with him this week. So all I wondered was—well—you know how a fellow is—if he thinks a girl's engaged, why, he won't come near her at all. Now mind, you don't have to do it—and I won't be a bit hurt if you don't, but what I thought was—if we could start being engaged, say, a week from today—you wouldn't mind, would you, Neil? Of course, next week, after we *are* engaged, we'll just go everywhere together.

NEIL. I see.

GLADYS. I know a dozen people, pretty near, that'll give big parties for us. It's an awful lot of fun, being engaged.

NEIL. Is it? I'm afraid I wouldn't fit in with that sort of thing.

GLADYS. Why, half the fun of being engaged is—well——

NEIL. Gladys, just what is your idea of

being engaged?

GLADYS. Why—I've just been telling you. (NEIL *smiles.*) What's the matter?

NEIL. Well, it's just that your idea of an engagement is different from mine.

GLADYS. What is yours?

NEIL. I think I'd want to be somewhere alone, just the two of us, where we could talk.

GLADYS. Talk about what?

NEIL (*with a meaning look*). I don't know.

GLADYS. You don't mean you'd *always* be like that, do you? I mean, when you're married?

NEIL. I might.

GLADYS. Well, where would I come in? Do you mean you'd expect *me* to sit around *every* evening and—just talk? I did think you'd be willing to—play around the way other people do.

NEIL. I see.

GLADYS. But, of course, if you wouldn't —well—why—there doesn't seem to be much sense in our being engaged, does there?

NEIL. It's to be just as you say, Gladys.

GLADYS. Well, I don't think we're exactly suited to each other—if you think it over. Honestly, I don't. Do you?

NEIL. No, Gladys.

GLADYS. I noticed the difference the minute I saw Walter again! I can kind of let myself go with Walter. You're sure you don't think I'm a quitter?

NEIL. I think you're all right.

GLADYS. And we'll still be friends, won't we? I've always thought you were nice, Neil. (*She gives a sigh.*) It's a sort of a relief, isn't it?

NEIL. Yes, it is—rather.

GLADYS. Well, goodbye. I've got to go because I left Walter downstairs. (*She departs.*)

NEIL. Oh! (*Laughs. Starts to call out.*) Cyn—(*Looks across the hall, crosses to the piano and begins to play the music of the pantomime.*)

(*After a moment* CYNTHIA *comes slowly into the room.*)

CYNTHIA (*hesitatingly*). Want me, Neil?

NEIL. Do I want you? (*He continues playing as he hears her approaching.*)

CURTAIN

It is doubtful whether George Kelly (born in Philadelphia in 1890) would have felt flattered if anybody had congratulated him on exposing the average American middle-class woman. Disapproval of her, as well as of her husband, in the middle twenties appeared often enough in belles-lettres and fiction to be considered fashionable. Mr. Kelly's Pulitzer Prize play *Craig's Wife* became identified with a criticism of American life, and its heroine was to stand for years as the representative of emotionally inadequate Main Street women. If a generalization based on her character could only be a half-truth, it did, nevertheless, have some application to a way of life that filled homes with bric-a-brac and conveniences and kept husbands' noses to the grindstone of business. Harriet Craig herself suggests an economic factor in her calculations when she confides "I saw to it that my marriage should be a way toward emancipation for me. I had no private fortune. . . . So the only road to independence for me that I could see, was through the man I married." Although she adds that "It isn't financial independence that I speak of particularly," her absorption in everything material contradicts her qualification. Surely she was not, and is not, alone in making the "cash nexus" a major feature of marital relationships, and even Marxist historians of marriage would not have had to be more explicit in statement and demonstration than Kelly was.

Mr. Kelly is a playwright who keeps his own counsel. But if one may presume to speak for him, one may not fall wide of the mark in saying that he had not intended to write a social report but was concerned only with individual human character and with the timid and unloving heart. His own stress is on the psychological compulsion that makes Harriet calculate and behave as she does. One cannot, however, avoid making suppositions concerning his work since he invites them by being somewhat tight-lipped and cryptic as a rule, moralistic in tone at times, and meticulously specific about everyday details, which makes it appear that he is a very close observer of middle-class life. In *Craig's Wife,* as in several other plays, moreover, Mr. Kelly has a way of constructing a play as though he were a first-rate prosecuting attorney bent on getting a hanging verdict against the culprit Harriet Craig. He piles up the evidence with cold relentlessness. This also happens to be the main limitation of the play, as well as the source of its power. Whenever George Kelly got hold of a subject he was not likely to relax his grip.

Mr. Kelly qualified as a rather grim and mordant realist, and a reserved but doggedly persistent one. This distinguishes *Craig's Wife* (1925), *Daisy Mayme* (1926), *Behold the Bridegroom* (1927), *Maggie the Magnificent* (1929), *Philip Goes Forth* (1931), *Reflected Glory* (1936), *The Deep Mrs. Sykes* (1945), and even the softer and warmer *Fatal Weakness* (1946) from the fast and glib but actually less stringent exposés of his more Broadway-minded colleagues. Even his comic structure and constrained, deliberately flattened out idiom have a somewhat forbidding quality. His style and his way with characters, at whom he so often looks with wry detachment, is personal. His animus may seem to be other writers' property at first glance, but it proves to be uniquely his own. It is not even certain that his kind of writing is realism in the accepted meaning of the term. He sees with merciless clarity and yet seems to peer at us through the window-pane of a temperament that collects a haze from his breath now and then. It is as if he saw the human comedy as a movement of figures slightly doomed to madness, fatal weakness, and sins of selfishness, instability, or *hubris.* He makes his commonplaces of observation and even his platitudes go further than one would expect; they go decidedly further than when others propel less stereotyped people or actions and use much brighter words.

He is, by the same token, one of the most genuine, if puzzling, artists who arose in the theatre of the twenties and have remained there ever since. Even his seeming stiffness and naïveté wear a Silenic mask. George Kelly's way with the majority of his plays is, moreover, particularly odd since, as an ex-vaudevillian, he showed early that he could outcontrive and outrun any of the fabricators and mile-a-minute runners in Broadway's steeplechase. This was apparent in his early sketch *Poor Aubrey* (see page 721), in his ebullient satire on amateur theatricals *The Torchbearers* (1922), and in *The Show-Off* (1924), which, in spite of a happy conclusion wholly unexpected, is the most devastating picture of super-salesmanship and overconfidence ever drawn in the American theatre, not exclusive of John Howard Lawson's *Success Story* (1932). For its equal one would have to go to American fiction like John O'Hara's *Pal Joey* (turned into an acidulous musical comedy in the thirties) and Jerome Weidman's *I Can Get It For You Wholesale.*

Craig's Wife

BY GEORGE KELLY

First presented by Rosalie Stewart at the Morosco Theatre, New York City, on October 12, 1925, with the following cast:

MISS AUSTEN	Anne Sutherland
MRS. HAROLD	Josephine Williams
MAZIE	Mary Gildea
MRS. CRAIG	Chrystal Herne
ETHEL LANDRETH	Eleanor Mish
WALTER CRAIG	Charles Trowbridge
MRS. FRAZIER	Josephine Hull
BILLY BIRKMIRE	Arling Alcine
JOSEPH CATELLE	Arthur Shaw
HARRY	J. A. Curtis
EUGENE FREDERICKS	Nelan Jaap

The entire action of the play transpires between five-thirty in the evening and nine o'clock the following morning in the living room in the home of Mr. Walter Craig.

fanatical orderliness

ACT ONE

The entire action of the play transpires between five-thirty in the evening and nine o'clock the following morning, in the living room in the home of MR. WALTER CRAIG. *This room, like all the other rooms in the house, reflects the very excellent taste and fanatical orderliness of its mistress. It is a kind of frozen grandeur, in dark, highly polished wood—strewn with gorgeous, gold-colored rugs and draped in rich brocaded satins. The piano scarf and the scarf on the oblong center table are canary-colored, and the draperies on the bay window at the left, and on the curving window on the stair landing at the back, are dark green. This curving window has a beautiful built-in window seat, with lovely cushions, and there is another built-in seat at the right of the staircase, from which the balustrade curves upwards. On the right, at the back, there is a wide door hung with brown velvet portières; and the rest of the room at the right is taken up with an ornamental mantelpiece, fancy mirror and fireplace. In front of this fireplace there is a beautiful high-backed chair. There is another big chair at the left of the center table, a small fancy chair beside the piano, and a chair at either side of the room, forward. There are two fancy benches, one immediately above the center table, and one in front of the center table. There is sufficient room between the table and this forward bench to permit of the business of passing between them. Up at the left there is a glass vestibule, one door of which opens into the room and the other out on to the front porch. As* MRS. CRAIG *enters, she appears to have been dressed for this particular room. She wears an extremely fashionable fawn-colored ensemble suit, brown slippers and stockings, and a small, dark brown velvet toque. She carries a brown leather pocket-book and a brown silk umbrella.*

MISS AUSTEN *hurries down the stairs and out through the portières at the right.* MRS. HAROLD *comes in through the door up at the left, carrying the evening newspaper and some tabourette doilies, and moves down towards the center table.*

MRS. HAROLD (*stopping halfway to the table and peering out after* MISS AUSTEN). Is there something you wanted, Miss Austen?

MISS AUSTEN. No, thanks, dear, I'm just looking for that pattern that I sent for the other day. I wanted to show it to Mrs. Frazier.

MRS. HAROLD. Lift up the lid of that worktable there, Miss Austen; I think I saw a pattern of some kind in there this morning. (*Continuing to the table and putting down the newspaper and doilies.*)

MISS AUSTEN. Yes, here it is, I have it. (*There is a sound from the right.*) I knew I left it right here somewhere.

(*She hurries in through the portières and up the stairs.*)

MRS. HAROLD (*moving up to the door at the left*). I gave those roses she brought to Mazie to put in some water.

MISS AUSTEN. Oh, did you—thanks ever so much.

MRS. HAROLD. She's gettin' a vase for them.

MISS AUSTEN. They're lovely, aren't they?

MRS. HAROLD. Yes, they're handsome.

(*She goes out on to the porch again, and* MAZIE *comes in through the portières, carrying a vase of pink roses, which she puts on the upper corner of the small grand piano at the left.*)

MAZIE (*calling out through the French windows to* MRS. HAROLD). Did the paper come yet, Mrs. Harold?

MRS. HAROLD. Yes, I just brought it in, —it's there on the table.

(MAZIE *turns and comes back to the table, picks up the paper, and strolls forward, holding it up as though to allow the light from a window at the right to fall upon it.*)

MAZIE. More rain again to-morrow.

MRS. HAROLD (*answering her from the front porch*). Does it say so?

MAZIE. Unsettled to-night and Friday —probably thunder showers. Slightly cooler, with moderate winds.

MRS. HAROLD (*coming in*). I don't know where all the rain is comin' from.

MAZIE. It isn't very nice weather for Mrs. Craig, is it?

MRS. HAROLD (*moving forward to the piano*). You can't tell; it might not be rainin' in Albany. Aren't these roses beautiful?

MAZIE. Yes, they're lovely.

(MRS. HAROLD *smells the roses.*)

MRS. HAROLD (*crossing to the foot of the*

stairs). I heard her telling Miss Austen she's got over two hundred rose bushes in her garden.

MAZIE (*turning and looking at* MRS. HAROLD). Is she still upstairs?

MRS. HAROLD. Yeh. I guess she's talkin' poor Miss Austen to death. (MAZIE *laughs and resumes her paper, and* MRS. HAROLD *gives an eye around the room.*) Bring that paper out with you when you're comin', Mazie; don't leave it layin' around in here.

MAZIE. All right.

MRS. HAROLD (*moving up to the door at the left and looking out*). It'ud be just like the lady to walk in on us.

(MAZIE *turns sharply and looks at her.*)

MAZIE. Mrs. Craig, do you mean?

MRS. HAROLD. She might, you can't tell.

MAZIE. I thought you said she wouldn't be back before Saturday.

MRS. HAROLD (*coming back to the table and picking up the doilies*). That's what she told me when she was goin' away. But it's just as well to keep a day or two ahead of a woman like Mrs. Craig, Mazie (*She flicks the dust from the table with the doilies.*) If she gets an idea up there that there's a pin out of place around here,—she'll take the first train out of Albany. (MAZIE *makes a sound of amusement and resumes her paper and* MRS. HAROLD *starts for the door at the right.*) Oh, there's plenty like her—I've worked for three of them; you'd think their houses were God Almighty.

(*She goes into the other room.*)

MAZIE. Didn't you tell me, Mrs. Harold, that you worked out on Willows Avenue one time?

MRS. HAROLD (*calling from the other room*). Yes, I worked out there for two years, at Doctor Nicholson's.

MAZIE. Did you know any people out that way by the name of Passmore?

MRS. HAROLD (*appearing between the portières*). By the name of what?

MAZIE. Passmore. Capital P-a-double s-m-o-r-e. Mr. J. Fergus Passmore and wife.

MRS. HAROLD (*coming forward at the right*). No, I don't remember anybody by that name; why?

MAZIE. Nothing.—It says here they were both found dead this morning in their home on Willows Avenue.

MRS. HAROLD. Oh, Lord have mercy on them! What happened to them?

MAZIE (*reading*). Why, it sez: "Fashionable Willows Avenue Residence Scene of Double Tragedy—Bodies of J. Fergus Passmore and Wife, Socially Prominent in This City, Found Dead in Library from Bullet Wounds—Empty Revolver Near Fireplace—Cause of Death Shrouded in Mystery—Police Working upon Identity of Gentleman Visitor Seen Leaving Premises in Automobile Shortly After Midnight." (MAZIE *looks fearfully at* MRS. HAROLD, *who shakes her head dolefully.*) "About eight o'clock this morning upon entering the library in the home of Mr. J. Fergus Passmore of 2214 Willows Avenue, Miss Selma Coates, a colored maid—"

MRS. HAROLD. Twenty-two fourteen must be out near the lake. (*The front doorbell rings incisively.*) See who that is, Mazie.

(MRS. HAROLD *disappears into the other room and* MAZIE *crosses up to the door at the left, putting down the newspaper on the table as she passes.*)

MRS. CRAIG (*out on the porch*). We can leave these right here, Ethel,—Mazie'll bring them in.

MAZIE. Oh, how do you do, Mrs. Craig.

MRS. CRAIG. Hello, Mazie.

MAZIE (*going out*). You're back a little ahead of time.

(MRS. HAROLD *comes in through the portières, peering out toward the front porch.*)

MRS. CRAIG. Yes, a little. Will you take these things, Mazie?

MAZIE. Yes, Ma'm.

(MRS. HAROLD *sees that it is* MRS. CRAIG, *gives a quick glance around the room, snatches up the paper from the table, and, with another glance over her right shoulder toward the front door, vanishes into the other room.*)

MRS. CRAIG. And will you see that that catch is on that screen door, Mazie—

MAZIE. Yes, Ma'm.

MRS. CRAIG (*appearing in the door*). It was half open when I came in. (*She comes into the room, sweeping it with a narrow eye, and crosses to the table to put down her handbag and umbrella.* ETHEL *wanders in after her and stands at the upper corner of the piano. The screen door closes outside.*) Take your things off, dear, and sit down; you look tired. (*She moves across to the mirror over the mantelpiece at the right, and* ETHEL *puts her handbag on the piano and commences to remove her coat and hat.*) I think there's nothing in the world so exhausting as train riding. (MAZIE *comes in, carrying a lady's satchel and a suitcase.* MRS. CRAIG *turns.*) You may as well take those things right upstairs, Mazie.

MAZIE. Yes, Ma'm.

MRS. CRAIG (*crossing up and over to* ETHEL). Put that suitcase in the corner room, Mazie—Miss Landreth'll occupy that room for the next few days.

MAZIE (*going up the stairs*). Yes, Ma'm.

MRS. CRAIG (*taking* ETHEL's *hat and coat*). I'll take them, dear.

ETHEL. Thanks.

MRS. CRAIG. I'll have Mazie take them right up to your room.

(*She puts them down on the table carefully and* ETHEL *crosses down towards the mirror, settling her hair.*)

ETHEL. I suppose I look terrible, don't I?

MRS. CRAIG (*crossing and taking* ETHEL's *bag from the piano*). No, dear, you look quite all right. Would you like a drink of something?

ETHEL. I would like a drink of water, yes, if you don't mind.

(MRS. HAROLD *appears between the portières.*)

MRS. CRAIG. Hello, Mrs. Harold.

MRS. HAROLD. I see you're back again.

MRS. CRAIG. This is Mrs. Harold, Ethel.

ETHEL. How do you do.

(MRS. HAROLD *bows and* ETHEL *moves back again to the roses on the piano.*)

MRS. CRAIG. Miss Landreth will be staying here with us for a week or two, Mrs. Harold, so I wish you'd see that everything is all right in that corner room.

MRS. HAROLD. All right, I will.

(MAZIE *comes down the stairs.*)

MRS. CRAIG (*moving down to the mirror, removing her coat*). And will you bring a glass of water, please, Mrs. Harold.

MRS. HAROLD. Yes, Ma'm. Just one glass?

MRS. CRAIG. Yes, I don't want any.

(MRS. HAROLD *goes out again.*)

ETHEL. Aren't these roses beautiful. (MRS. CRAIG *shifts her eyes from* MAZIE, *who is gathering* ETHEL's *things up from the table, and looks steadily at the roses.*) I don't think I've ever seen such lovely roses.

MRS. CRAIG. Yes, they're very nice. Take those things upstairs, Mazie.

MAZIE (*starting up the stairs*). Yes, Ma'm.

MRS. CRAIG. And I wish you'd use that back way when you go up and down stairs, Mazie.

MAZIE (*coming down again*). I always keep forgettin' that.

(ETHEL *turns and looks at* MAZIE, *and* MRS. CRAIG, *laying her coat across* MAZIE's *arm as she passes her, moves up to look at the stairs closely.* MAZIE *goes out at the right.*)

MRS. CRAIG. This stairway'll soon look the way it did before, with everybody tramping up and down it every five minutes. (*She turns to* ETHEL *with a kind of apologetic smile, and commences to remove her gloves.*) It doesn't seem ever to occur to anybody in the house, Ethel, to use the back stairway. It's the funniest thing you've ever seen in your life, really. We might just as well not have one. No matter how many times they have to go up or down stairs, they must go tramping up and down this front way. And you know what stairs look like after they've been tramped up and down a few times. (MRS. HAROLD *comes in with a glass of water on a small silver tray.*) Thanks, Mrs. Harold.

ETHEL (*picking up a framed photograph from the piano*). Isn't this Mother's picture, Aunt Harriet?

(MRS. HAROLD *goes out.*)

MRS. CRAIG (*crossing to* ETHEL). Yes, that's your mother.

ETHEL. I thought it looked something like her.

MRS. CRAIG (*taking the picture*). She had it taken at Lakewood one summer, and I always liked it. I like that dress; it never seemed to get old-fashioned.

ETHEL (*starting to cry*). It doesn't look much like her now, does it?

(*She moves forward to the chair beside the piano and sits down.*)

MRS. CRAIG (*putting the picture back on the piano*). Now, Ethel dear, you mustn't start that. Your mother's been through this very same kind of thing many times before.

ETHEL. But, I should *be* there, Aunt Harriet. Supposing something should happen.

MRS. CRAIG. But, nothing is going to happen, dear child. I haven't the slightest doubt but that your mother will come through this little spell just as she's come through all the others.

ETHEL. I don't think the others have been as serious as this, though.

MRS. CRAIG. Listen, Ethel dear, I've seen your mother at least a dozen times at what I was perfectly sure was the point of death, and she's always come around all right.

ETHEL. Well, why did Doctor Wood send for me, if he didn't think it was serious?

MRS. CRAIG. Because your mother asked him to, I suppose, dear; just as she asked him to send for me. But he certainly couldn't have thought it was so very serious when he suggested you come away with me.

ETHEL. It wasn't the doctor that suggested that, Aunt Harriet, it was the night nurse,—I heard her tell him so. She said it upset Mother too much to see me, and if I were there she'd want to see me.

MRS. CRAIG. Well, that's very true, dear; but you know how she cried when you came in. And there's nothing in the world so upsetting to the heart as crying.

ETHEL. But, I should be there; it seems terrible to me now to have walked away and left Mother in that condition.

MRS. CRAIG. But, what could you do if you'd stayed, dear?

ETHEL (*with a touch of desperation*). I'd at least know what was going on.

MRS. CRAIG (*handing her the glass of water, and putting her arm around her shoulder*). Now, don't upset yourself, Ethel. Here, take a sip of this water. I'm perfectly sure you're magnifying the seriousness of your mother's condition, dear. And I most certainly should never have come away myself only that I've seen this same thing over and over again. (*She turns and settles the photograph on the piano.*) Besides, there isn't a solitary thing we could do if we'd stayed; those nurses won't allow it. (*Taking the glass from* ETHEL.) And the doctor said I was upsetting your mother,—simply because I told her a few things I thought she should be told.

(*She crosses to the table and sets down the glass.*)

ETHEL. There was something I wanted to tell her, too, but he said he thought I'd better wait.

MRS. CRAIG. Well, I'd have told her anyway, if I'd been you.

ETHEL. I'm rather sorry now I didn't,—I think it would have made her easier in her mind.

MRS. CRAIG (*taking her handkerchief from her bag*). Was it something important?

ETHEL. It was about Professor Fredericks, at school. Mother met him last year when she was up there at Commencement, and she liked him very much. And when we got home she said if he ever said anything to me, she'd be glad if I could like him well enough to marry him. She said she'd feel easier about me, in case anything ever happened to *her*. And I wanted to tell her.

MRS. CRAIG. You mean he *had* said something?

ETHEL. Yes, he asked me to marry him right after Easter. But I didn't write anything about it to Mother; I thought I'd wait until she'd be up there in June for my Commencement, and then I'd tell her.

MRS. CRAIG. I don't know why your mother should be so panicky about your future, Ethel; you're only nineteen.

ETHEL. She said she'd like to feel that I'd *have* somebody.

MRS. CRAIG. Why does a person need anybody, dear, if he has money enough to get along on? (*She turns and crosses to the mirror to remove her hat.*) And, as a matter of fact, you wouldn't be left absolutely desolate even if something *did* happen to your mother. You'd always have me—I'm your mother's sister. So that, really, I think you're a very foolish girl, Ethel, if you allow your mother's apprehensions to rush you into marriage. Unless, of course, it were an advantageous marriage.

ETHEL. She didn't want to rush me into it—she simply said she thought it would be better for me to be settled.

MRS. CRAIG (*bringing her hat back to the table, and taking a powder puff from her bag*). Well, naturally, I can understand that, of course. But, after all, simply being settled isn't everything, Ethel—a girl can be a great deal worse off being settled than when she was unsettled. And, personally, I can't conceive of being very much worse off than married to a college professor—stuck away in some dreadful place like Poughkeepsie or Northampton—with not a ten-cent piece to bless yourself with—unless you used your own money. I'm constantly reading agitations in the newspapers about the poor pay of college professors. And your marrying one of them will hardly improve the situation. (*She flips the bag back on to the table, and moves forward to a small ornamental bench in front of the center table, where she kneels.*) Did you accept this man when he asked you?

ETHEL. Practically, yes. We'd rather thought of being married sometime during the summer.

MRS. CRAIG. Then, you mean you're engaged to him?

ETHEL. Yes. I knew Mother liked him, for she said so. The only thing was, she wanted me to be sure that *I* liked him.

MRS. CRAIG. Well, that's all very nice, Ethel, but simply liking a man isn't going to go very far toward keeping things going, is it?

ETHEL. Well, I have money of my own, Aunt Harriet.

MRS. CRAIG. I know that, dear child, but surely he isn't marrying you because of that?

ETHEL. No, of course not; he doesn't know anything about that.

MRS. CRAIG. Well, I hope not—he surely wouldn't expect you to use your own money to keep *his* house going. If a man marries a girl he certainly must expect to support her, at least.

ETHEL. Well, he does expect to support me, naturally.

MRS. CRAIG. How, dear—on a professor's salary?

ETHEL. Why, lots of professors are married, Aunt Harriet.

MRS. CRAIG. But their wives are not living the way you've been accustomed to living, Ethel: not the wives of young professors, at least. And I suppose this man is young, isn't he?

ETHEL. He's twenty-seven.

MRS. CRAIG. Well, there you are. He's very lucky if he's getting two hundred dollars a month: unless he's some very extraordinary kind of professor; and he can scarcely be that at twenty-seven years of age.

ETHEL. He's professor of the Romance Languages.

MRS. CRAIG. Naturally. And I suppose he's told you he loves you in all of them.

ETHEL. Well, I certainly shouldn't care to think about marriage at all, Aunt Harriet, unless I were at least in love with the man.

(MRS. CRAIG *gives a little smile of pained amusement, and moves towards* ETHEL.)

MRS. CRAIG. That is your age, Ethel darling: we all pass through that. It's the snare of romance,—that the later experience of life shows us to have been nothing more than the most impractical sentimentality. (*She arranges the piano scarf more precisely.*) Only the majority of women are caught with the spell of it, unfortunately; and then they are obliged to revert right back to the almost primitive feminine dependence and subjection that they've been trying to emancipate themselves from for centuries.

(*She crosses to the big chair at the left of the center table and straightens it.*)

ETHEL. Well, *you* married, Aunt Harriet.

MRS. CRAIG (*leaning on the back of the chair*). But not with any romantic illusions, dear. I saw to it that my marriage should be a way toward emancipation for *me*. I had no private fortune like you, Ethel; and no special equipment,—outside of a few more or less inapplicable college theories. So the only road to independence for *me*, that *I* could see, was through the man I married. I know that must sound extremely materialistic to *you*, after listening to the professor of romantic languages;—but it isn't really; because it isn't financial independence that I speak of particularly. I knew that would come—as the result of *another* kind of independence; and that is the independence of authority—*over* the man I married. And that doesn't necessarily imply any dishonesty of attitude toward that man, either. I have a full appreciation of Mr. Craig—he's a very good man; but he's a husband—a lord and master—*my* master. And I married to be independent.

ETHEL. Independent of your husband too, do you mean?

MRS. CRAIG. Independent of everybody. I lived with a stepmother, Ethel, for nearly twelve years, and with your mother after she was married for over five; I know what it is to be on some one else's floor. And I married to be on my own—in every sense of the word. I haven't entirely achieved the condition yet—but I know it can be done.

(*She turns and glances up the stairs and out through the portières, to assure herself that no one is listening.*)

ETHEL. I don't understand what you mean, exactly, Aunt Harriet.

MRS. CRAIG (*turning to* ETHEL *again*). I mean that I'm simply exacting my share of a bargain. Mr. Craig wanted a wife and a home; and he has them. And he can be perfectly sure of them, because the wife that he got happens to be one of the kind that regards her husband and home as more or less ultimate conditions. And my share of the bargain was the security and protection that those conditions imply. And I have *them*. But, unlike Mr. Craig, I can't be absolutely sure of them; because I know that, to a very great extent, they are at the mercy of the *mood* of a *man*. (*She smiles knowingly.*) And I suppose I'm too practical-minded to accept that as a sufficient guarantee of their permanence. So I must secure their permanence for myself.

ETHEL. How?

MRS. CRAIG. By securing into my own hands the control of the man upon which they are founded.

ETHEL. How are you ever going to do a thing like that, Aunt Harriet?

MRS. CRAIG. Haven't you ever made Mr. Fredericks do something you wanted him to do?

ETHEL. Yes, but I always told him that I wanted him to do it.

MRS. CRAIG (*half-sitting on the arm of the big chair*). But there are certain things that men can't be told, Ethel; they don't understand them; particularly romantic men; and Mr. Craig is inveterately idealistic.

ETHEL. But, supposing he were to find out sometime?

MRS. CRAIG. Find out what?

ETHEL. What you've just been telling me—that you wanted to control him.

MRS. CRAIG. One never comprehends, dear, what it is not in one's nature to comprehend. And even if it were possible, what about it? It's such an absolutely unprovable thing; that is, I mean to say, it isn't a thing that one does or says, specifically; it's a matter of—interpretation. (*She is amused.*) And that's where women have such a tremendous advantage over men; so few men are capable of interpreting them. But, they can always interpret themselves, if they're so disposed. And if the interpretation is for the instruction of a romantic husband, a woman can always keep it safely within the exigencies of the moment. (*She laughs a little, and moves over to* ETHEL, *resting her hand on* ETHEL'S *shoulder.*) I know you're mentally deploring my lack of nobility.

ETHEL. No, I'm not at all, Aunt Harriet.

MRS. CRAIG. Yes, you are, I see it in your face. (*She crosses to the front of the center table.*) You think I'm a very sordid woman.

ETHEL. No, I don't think anything of the kind.

MRS. CRAIG (*turning to* ETHEL). Well, what *do* you think?

ETHEL. Well, frankly, Aunt Harriet, I don't think it's quite honest.

MRS. CRAIG. But it's very much safer, dear—for everybody. Because, as I say, if a woman is the right kind of a woman, it's better that the destiny of her home should be in *her* hands—than in any man's. (MRS. HAROLD *appears between the portières.*) Did you want to see me about something, Mrs. Harold?

MRS. HAROLD. It'll do after a while, Mrs. Craig; I thought the young lady had gone upstairs.

MRS. CRAIG. No, not yet, she's going up immediately. (*Turning to* ETHEL.) That's what I want you to do, Ethel—go upstairs and lie down for an hour or so; you'll feel ever so much better. I'll call you in time for dinner.

(ETHEL *rises and moves towards the stairs.*)

ETHEL. I don't think I'll be able to eat any dinner, Aunt Harriet.

MRS. CRAIG (*guiding* ETHEL *towards the stairs*). Well, now, you might feel very different after you've had a bit of a rest.

ETHEL. I'm so terribly worried, Aunt Harriet.

MRS. CRAIG. I know, dear child, it's very trying; but it's one of the things we've got to go through with, I suppose. Besides, worrying can't possibly help her, dear.

(MRS. CRAIG *continues with* ETHEL *up to the landing, and* ETHEL *goes on up the stairs.*)

ETHEL. Oh, how can I help worrying.

MRS. CRAIG. You can't help it, of course, dear; that's the reason I want you to lie down for a while. I'll be up in a few minutes—just as soon as I've seen to a few things down here. It's the room straight down the hall, to the right. Mazie's very likely in there now. And don't worry,

dear. (ETHEL *disappears at the head of the stairs, and* MRS. CRAIG *looks closely at the landing, to see if she can discover any fresh scratches upon it.* MRS. HAROLD *comes in at the right.*) What was it you wanted to see me about, Mrs. Harold?
(*She comes down into the room again.*)

MRS. HAROLD. Why, I wanted to tell you, Mrs. Craig, that the cook left on Thursday. She went away and didn't come back.

MRS. CRAIG. Did she get her wages?

MRS. HAROLD. I paid her up till Tuesday.

MRS. CRAIG. Did she take her things with her?

MRS. HAROLD. Why, she only had a suitcase and a small graphophone; she took *them.* But I didn't think anything about it, because she took *them* every Thursday.

MRS. CRAIG. Have you been doing the cooking since, Mrs. Harold?

MRS. HAROLD. Yes, we've been managin' between us. Mazie's a pretty good cook. I called up the Camac Agency on Saturday to send somebody out, but Miss Hewlitt said she wanted to see you first. (MRS. CRAIG *looks at her.*) She sez she's sent so many, she wants to find out what's the matter before she sends any more.

MRS. CRAIG (*crossing to the piano*). She ought to have a few of them cook for her; she'd *know* what was the matter. Where did these roses come from, Mrs. Harold?

MRS. HAROLD. Why, that woman across the street brought them over to Miss Austen.

MRS. CRAIG. Mrs. Frazier, you mean?

MRS. HAROLD. Yes, Ma'm, she brought them over to the porch—Miss Austen was sitting out there sewing.

MRS. CRAIG. Well, you'd better take them out of here, Mrs. Harold: the petals'll be all over the room.
(MRS. HAROLD *moves across to the roses, and* MRS. CRAIG *busies herself with the draperies in the bay window beyond the piano.*)

MRS. HAROLD. You didn't have to stay away as long as you thought, did you?

MRS. CRAIG. Well, I suppose I *could* have stayed away indefinitely, if I had allowed myself to become sentimental. But I'm afraid I haven't very much patience with sick people, Mrs. Harold.
(MRS. HAROLD *takes the vase of roses and starts back across towards the portières.*)

MRS. HAROLD. Well, I suppose it takes all kinds to make a world.

MRS. CRAIG. I suppose so.

MRS. HAROLD (*stopping, and turning*). Where do you want these roses put, Mrs. Craig?

MRS. CRAIG. I don't care where you put them, Mrs. Harold, as long as they're not in the rooms; I don't want to be picking up petals every two minutes.

MRS. HAROLD. Maybe Miss Austen 'ud like them in her room.

MRS. CRAIG (*moving down to examine the spot where the vase stood*). Maybe she would; you can ask her. Is she up there now?

MRS. HAROLD. Yes, Ma'm; Mrs. Frazier is showing her something about a pattern that she has.
(MRS. CRAIG *looks at her.*)

MRS. CRAIG. Do you mean to tell me that Mrs. Frazier is upstairs, Mrs. Harold?

MRS. HAROLD. Yes, Ma'm, she's up there.

MRS. CRAIG. And how did she happen to *get* up there?

MRS. HAROLD. Well, I don't know, I'm sure, Mrs. Craig, unless Miss Austen asked her.

MRS. CRAIG. All right. (*She crosses to the foot of the stairs and looks up, and* MRS. HAROLD *goes out through the portières.*) Have there been any letters or messages for me, Mrs. Harold, since I've been away?

MRS. HAROLD. Why, there were two letters, yes; I left them in your room. (*Coming into the room again.*) One came this morning, and one came Tuesday. And there was a gentleman called Mr. Craig last night about eight o'clock, but he'd gone out. So I gave him the telephone number that Mr. Craig gave me in case anybody called him.

MRS. CRAIG. Who was the gentleman? Did you get his name?

MRS. HAROLD. Yes, Ma'm, he said his name was Birkmire.

MRS. CRAIG. Do you know if he got Mr. Craig all right?

MRS. HAROLD. Yes, Ma'm, he did; because when I told Mr. Craig this morning about him calling, he said it was all right, that he'd talked to him last night. (MRS. CRAIG *nods and moves down to the center table.*) And then he called again this afternoon about half-past four.
(MRS. CRAIG *turns and looks at her.*)

MRS. CRAIG. Mr. Birkmire did?

MRS. HAROLD. Yes, Ma'm; he said he wanted Mr. Craig to get in touch with him as soon as he came in.

MRS. CRAIG. What number was it Mr. Craig gave you last night, Mrs. Harold, to have Mr. Birkmire call him at?

MRS. HAROLD. Why, it was Levering three, one hundred. I wrote it down on a piece of paper, so I wouldn't forget it.

MRS. CRAIG. All right, Mrs. Harold, I'll tell him when he comes. (MRS. HAROLD *goes out.*) And will you get another vase for those roses, Mrs. Harold, before you take them up—

MRS. HAROLD. All right, I will.

MRS. CRAIG. That one belongs down here. (*She stands and thinks quietly for a second; then, with a glance up the stairs and out after* MRS. HAROLD, *she moves to the telephone and picks it up.*) Give me Information, please.

(*She waits, glancing toward the other room and up the stairs.* MAZIE *comes down the stairs.*)

MAZIE. Miss Landreth sent me down for her bag.

MRS. CRAIG. It's there on the table. (MAZIE *picks up the bag from the table and starts for the stairs again.* MRS. CRAIG *looks steadily at her and is about to speak when* MAZIE *thinks of herself and turns back, crossing towards the portières.*) Take that glass out, too, Mazie.

MAZIE (*picking up the glass from the table as she goes*). Yes, Ma'm.

MRS. CRAIG (*into the telephone*). Information? Why, could you give me the address of the telephone number, Levering three, one hundred? Oh, don't you?—All right, it isn't important—thank you very much.

(*She stands thinking for a second. Then the screen door outside bangs, and she sets down the telephone and moves towards the door.* MR. CRAIG *comes in briskly, wearing a Panama hat and carrying a newspaper.*)

CRAIG. Well, look who's here, bright and smiling!

(*He advances, removing his hat, and she moves a step or two towards him.*)

MRS. CRAIG. You almost beat me home.

CRAIG. How did this happen? (*He kisses her affectionately.*) When did you get in, Harriet?

MRS. CRAIG (*taking his hat and the newspaper from him and putting them on the table*). A few minutes ago. I left Albany at noon.

CRAIG (*tossing his gloves on the piano*). And how is it you didn't wire or something?

MRS. CRAIG (*picking up her own gloves from the table and straightening out the fingers*). I never thought of it, to tell the truth; there was so much to be done around there—getting Ethel's things together, and one thing and another.

CRAIG. Was Ethel there?

MRS. CRAIG. Yes, Estelle insisted that she be sent for last Saturday. And for the life of me I don't know why she did such a thing; for it upset her terribly. So the doctor said he thought the best thing to do would be to get Ethel out of her sight for a few days: so I brought her back with me. She's upstairs, lying down.

CRAIG. How *is* Estelle?

MRS. CRAIG. Why, I couldn't see that there was anything the matter with her—any more than usual. But you'd think from her letter she was dying. And then I have to walk out, and leave my house for a whole week, and go racing up to Albany.

CRAIG. Has she a trained nurse?

MRS. CRAIG (*picking up his hat from the table*). My dear, she's had two of them, for over six weeks. But you know what trained nurses are.

CRAIG. Well, I'm sorry to hear Estelle is so bad.

MRS. CRAIG (*handing him his hat*). Here, take this, Walter.

CRAIG (*drawing her back into his arms*). But I'm glad to have you back again.

MRS. CRAIG (*laughing lightly*). Stop it, Walter.

CRAIG. Seems you've been away a month instead of a week.

(*He kisses the side of her head.*)

MRS. CRAIG. Don't break my bones, Walter!

CRAIG. That's what I think I'd like to do sometimes.

MRS. CRAIG (*laughing*). Now, stop it. (*He releases her and she straightens up, touching her hair.*) Stop. Here, take this hat and put it out where it belongs. (*He takes the hat and crosses above her towards the portières.*) And take this paper out of here too; this room's a sight. (*He steps back and takes the paper, then goes on out into the other room.*) Your aunt's company will be scandalized.

CRAIG (*from the other room*). Has Auntie Austen got some company?

MRS. CRAIG (*moving up to arrange the pillows on the fancy seat at the right of the stairway*). So Mrs. Harold says. She's upstairs with her.

CRAIG (*reëntering, and crossing directly over to the bay window at the left*). Who is it?

MRS. CRAIG. The lady of the roses, across the street there.

CRAIG. Mrs. Frazier?

MRS. CRAIG. Yes. She's getting very sociable.

CRAIG. She certainly has some beautiful roses over there, hasn't she?

MRS. CRAIG. She ought to have; she has nothing to do but look after them.

CRAIG. Those ramblers make a pretty effect, down at the side there, don't they?

MRS. CRAIG. Wait till you see them a week from now.

CRAIG (*turning to her*). Why?

MRS. CRAIG. Why there'll be petals all over the place over there.

CRAIG. That ought to be prettier than the way it is now.

MRS. CRAIG. Well, you might not think it was so pretty if you had to sweep them up.

CRAIG (*taking some papers from his inside pocket, and moving to the chair beside the piano*). I wouldn't sweep them up. (MRS. CRAIG *makes a sound of vast amusement.*) I can't think of anything much prettier than to have rose petals scattered all over the lawn.

(*He sits down.*)

MRS. CRAIG (*straightening the big chair in front of the fireplace*). You'd have a nice looking place, I must say.

CRAIG. It's a wonder she wouldn't bring a few of those roses over here to Auntie Austen.

MRS. CRAIG. I guess she has sense enough to know that if we wanted roses we could plant some. (*She starts across towards him, above the center table, glancing toward the head of the stairs.*) Listen; she's apt to be down here any minute, Walter, and if I were you I wouldn't be sitting there when she comes; for if she sees you you'll never get away till she's told you her entire history. I've just escaped it twice.

(*She gathers her things together on the table.*)

CRAIG. I've talked to her a couple of times on the way up from the garage.

MRS. CRAIG. You mean she's talked to you.

CRAIG. No, she was out there fixing the roses when I came by.

MRS. CRAIG. Of course she was. That's where she is most of the time. (*Becoming confidential, and moving towards him, below the table.*) And the funny part of it is, Walter, I don't think she realizes that people know exactly why she does it. Really, it's the most transparently obvious thing I've ever seen in my life.

CRAIG. Well, why do you think she does it?

MRS. CRAIG. Why do I think she does it?

CRAIG. Yes.

(MRS. CRAIG *laughs, with a shade of amused impatience.*)

MRS. CRAIG. Well now, Walter—why do certain women go about all the time with a child by the hand, or a dog on a leash. To facilitate the—approach. (*She returns to the table and puts her gloves in her pocketbook; and* CRAIG *sits looking at her, mystified.*) Only the lady upstairs uses roses. So, really, I wouldn't be sitting there when she comes down, if I were you, Walter; you know there *is* a danger in propinquity.

CRAIG (*resuming his letters*). I guess she could have gotten plenty of men if she'd wanted them.

MRS. CRAIG. But she may not have been able to get the kind she wanted. And *you* may be the kind. (*He looks at her and laughs.*) And this little visit this afternoon, laden with flowers, may be simply the initial attack in a very highly premeditated campaign.

CRAIG. Did you say she brought some flowers over this afternoon?

MRS. CRAIG. I said, "highly premeditated." I believe you told me you'd stopped a number of times to talk to her.

CRAIG. I've stopped twice, as a matter of fact.

MRS. CRAIG. And admired her roses?

CRAIG. There was nothing much else to talk about.

MRS. CRAIG. Of course there wasn't; that's the point. And if there hadn't been any roses, there wouldn't have been anything at all to talk about. And you wouldn't have stopped, and talked. (*She looks at him directly and smiles.*) But since you did, why—it isn't at all inconceivable that she should conclude that you probably liked roses. And that you might regard it as a very charming little gesture if she were to just bring a few over sometime—to your aunt—when your wife was out of the city.

CRAIG (*leaning back against the piano and looking at his letters*). What are you trying to do, kid me, Harriet?

MRS. CRAIG. Not at all. Don't lean back against that piano that way, Walter, you might scratch it.

CRAIG. My coat won't scratch it.

MRS. CRAIG (*crossing hurriedly*). Well, there might be something in your pocket that will. (*She pushes him away from the piano.*) Now, sit up. (*She gives him a little slap on the back.*) Sit over there.

(*She indicates the big chair at the left of the center table, and he rises good-naturedly and crosses to it. Then she busies herself examining the spot on the piano where he leaned, and settling the piano scarf carefully.*)

CRAIG. Yes, sir, I think that's what you're trying to do, Harriet, just kid me.

MRS. CRAIG. Well now, do you think what I've been saying is at all improbable?

CRAIG. No, it isn't improbable; it's just funny.

MRS. CRAIG (*crossing back to the table and gathering all her things up*). The flowers were on the piano when I came in.

CRAIG. Well, if they were they were for Auntie Austen.

MRS. CRAIG. Maybe they were. I sent them up to her room, anyway. So Mrs. Frazier probably thinks I *thought* they were for Auntie Austen. (*She starts for the portières at the right, and he looks after her and laughs. She turns and looks at him.*) What are you laughing at?

CRAIG. You.

MRS. CRAIG. Really?

CRAIG. You're very amusing to-night.

MRS. CRAIG (*coming forward at the right of the table*). And I think you're just a little bit reckless, Walter—sitting there tempting the temptress.

CRAIG. You know, I think you're getting jealous of me, Harriet.

MRS. CRAIG (*amused*). Not at all, dear boy; I'm simply suspicious of rich, middle-aged divorcees, who specialize in wayside roses.

(*She leans on her umbrella.*)

CRAIG. Mrs. Frazier isn't a divorcee.

MRS. CRAIG. Isn't she?

CRAIG. No, her husband was killed in an automobile accident in 1915. She told me so herself. She was in the car with him.

MRS. CRAIG. And how is it she wasn't killed?

CRAIG (*laughing a little*). Well now, does everybody have to be killed in automobile accidents?

MRS. CRAIG. No, there's always the Galveston Flood, for husbands. You're a very guileless young man, Walter; and I'm sorry your mind doesn't work just a little bit more rapidly.

CRAIG. It works pretty thoroughly, though, when it sees the point.

MRS. CRAIG. But, that's a very slight advantage, Walter, if the point is made before you see it.

CRAIG. Do you know, I'd like to be able to see just what's going on in your mind to-night.

MRS. CRAIG. Well, if you could, I dare-say you'd find something very similar to what's going on in the minds of most of our neighbors these days.

CRAIG. Now, just what do you mean by that?

MRS. CRAIG. They have eyes, Walter; and they use them. And I wish you'd use yours. And I also wish you'd tell me whose telephone number Levering three, one hundred is.

CRAIG. Fergus Passmore, why?

MRS. CRAIG. Nothing, I was just wondering. Mrs. Harold told me you gave her that number last night in case any-body wanted you, and I was wondering where it was.

(*She moves towards the door again.*)

CRAIG. *Fergus* Passmore's. I was playing cards out there last night. I ran into him yesterday in front of the First National, and he asked me to come out there last night and play a little poker.

MRS. CRAIG. What did Billy Birkmire want you for?

CRAIG. Why, a—

MRS. CRAIG. Mrs. Harold said he called you up.

CRAIG. Yes, Fergus told me to get hold of him, too, and bring him out there; so I did; but he called me up later to tell me that his father had just come in from St. Paul, and he wouldn't be able to make it. I wasn't here when he called, so I talked to him from there.

MRS. CRAIG. I hope you're not going to get into card-playing again, Walter.

CRAIG. Why, I never gave up card-playing.

MRS. CRAIG. Well, you haven't played in nearly a year.

CRAIG. Well, I suppose that's because *you* don't play. And most of the folks know that, so they don't ask *me*. I don't suppose Fergus would have asked me yesterday, only that I happened to mention that *you* were away.

MRS. CRAIG. Was his wife there?

CRAIG. She was for a while, but she didn't play; she was going out somewhere.

MRS. CRAIG. I suppose that's the reason Fergus asked you, wasn't it?

CRAIG. What do you mean?

MRS. CRAIG. Why, you know how insanely jealous of her he used to be.

CRAIG. Well, I'm sure he was never jealous of me.

MRS. CRAIG. He was jealous of everybody, from what I could see.

CRAIG. Oh, don't be silly, Harriet.

MRS. CRAIG. Well, you wouldn't know it, Walter, even if he were.

CRAIG. Well, I'm glad I wouldn't.

MRS. CRAIG. And you come to find out, I'll bet that's just the reason Billy Birkmire dodged it. I'll bet that's just what he called you up to tell you.

CRAIG. He didn't call me up to tell me anything of the kind, now, Harriet; he simply called me to tell me that his father had come in unexpectedly from—

MRS. CRAIG. I don't mean last night; I mean when he called you to-day.

CRAIG. He didn't call me to-day.

MRS. CRAIG. He did, this afternoon, around four o'clock.

CRAIG. Here?

MRS. CRAIG. So Mrs. Harold told me. Said he wanted you to get in touch with him as soon as you came in.

CRAIG (*rising, and crossing to the telephone*). Wonder why he didn't call the office.

MRS. CRAIG (*moving towards the portières*). Probably he did, and you'd gone.

CRAIG. What's Birkmire's number, do you know?

MRS. CRAIG (*turning at the door*). Park 840, isn't it? Unless they've changed it.

CRAIG. I think it is.

MRS. CRAIG (*lowering her voice*). And I'm really serious, Walter, about that woman upstairs.

CRAIG (*into the telephone*). Park 840. (*There is a laugh from* MRS. FRAZIER, *at the head of the stairs.*)

MRS. CRAIG. So if I were you I wouldn't be here when she comes down.

(*He silences her with a gesture; and, with a glance towards the head of the stairs, she goes out at the right.*)

MRS. FRAZIER. I used to have considerable difficulty myself, when I first started to use them.

CRAIG. Hello—Park 840?

MISS AUSTEN (*at the head of the stairs*). Well, I think I understand it now.

CRAIG. Is Mr. Birkmire there? (MRS. FRAZIER *and* MISS AUSTEN *come down the stairs.*) Oh, that's too bad; I just missed him, didn't I?

MRS. FRAZIER. Well now, please don't hesitate to call me, Miss Austen, if there's anything you don't understand,—

CRAIG. Yes, this is Mr. Craig speaking.

MISS AUSTEN. I will, I'll let you know.

MRS. FRAZIER. Because I haven't a solitary thing to do.

(*She sees* MR. CRAIG *at the telephone, and turns to* MISS AUSTEN, *laying her finger on her lips.*)

CRAIG. Then, he'll probably be here pretty soon. (MRS. FRAZIER *comes down into the room, and* MISS AUSTEN *stops on the landing, looking at* MR. CRAIG.) Thanks—that's fine. Thank you very much.

MISS AUSTEN. Hello, Walter.

CRAIG. Hello, Auntie. How are you?

MISS AUSTEN (*coming down from the landing*). I didn't know you were home.

CRAIG. Just got in this minute. How do you do, Mrs. Frazier.

MRS. FRAZIER. How do you do, Mr. Craig.

MISS AUSTEN. Mrs. Frazier was kind enough to come up and show me something about a new pattern that I just bought.

CRAIG. That so?

MISS AUSTEN. Mrs. Harold tells me that Harriet is home.

CRAIG. Yes, she just got in ahead of me.

MISS AUSTEN. Did she say how Mrs. Landreth was?

CRAIG. Pretty bad shape, I imagine, from what she says.

MISS AUSTEN. Where is Harriet, upstairs?

CRAIG. Yes, she's just taken her things up.

MRS. FRAZIER. Miss Austen was telling me that Mrs. Craig's sister has heart trouble.

CRAIG. Yes, she's had it a long time.

MRS. FRAZIER. Poor woman.

MISS AUSTEN. Nearly ten years.

MRS. FRAZIER. How unfortunate. I suppose Mrs. Craig is very much upset, isn't she?

CRAIG. Yes, I suppose she is.

MRS. FRAZIER. Is she her only sister?

CRAIG. Yes, there are just the two of them.

MRS. FRAZIER. Too bad. But, that's the way it seems to go as a rule, doesn't it?

CRAIG. Yes, that's true.

MISS AUSTEN. Walter, you should see all the wonderful roses Mrs. Frazier just brought me over.

(MRS. FRAZIER *gives a little deprecating laugh and moves towards the piano at the left.*)

CRAIG. Oh, yes?

MISS AUSTEN. They're perfectly beautiful.

MRS. FRAZIER. Not a very generous giving, I'm afraid, when there are so many of them.

CRAIG AND MISS AUSTEN (*speaking together*). CRAIG: Well, I'm sure we appreciate it very much. MISS AUSTEN: I think it's very charming of you to remember us at all.

MRS. FRAZIER. Sometimes I think perhaps I am a bit foolish to have so many of them, because it *is* a lot of work.

MISS AUSTEN. It must be; I often say that to Walter.

MRS. FRAZIER. Yes, it is. But, you see, they were more or less of a hobby with my husband when he was alive; and I suppose I tend them out of sentiment, really, more than anything else.

MISS AUSTEN. How long has your husband been dead, Mrs. Frazier?

MRS. FRAZIER. He'll be dead ten years this coming November. Yes. Yes, he died the twenty-third of November, 1915. He was injured on the second, in an automobile accident at Pride's Crossing, Massachusetts: we were on our way back from Bar Harbor—I was telling Mr. Craig about it. And he lingered from that until the twenty-third. So, you see, the melancholy days have really a very literal significance for me.

MISS AUSTEN. I should say so, indeed.

MRS. FRAZIER. Yes, that is the one month I must get away. I don't care where I go, but I must go somewhere; I couldn't stand it here; I have too many memories. So every year, as soon as ever November comes around, I just pack up my things and go out to Dayton, Ohio. I have a married daughter living out there; her husband is connected with the National Cash Register Company. And, of course, she makes all manner of fun of my annual pilgrimages to Dayton. She says instead of being in England now that April's there, with me it's in Dayton now that November's there. (*She laughs faintly.*) We have great fun about it. But, of course, her husband's business is there. And I think sometimes perhaps I should spend more time with her; I think it would help us both. But the trouble is, when I go out there, it's so very difficult for me to get away again. She has the most adorable baby—just fifteen months old; and he thinks there's nobody in the world like his grandmother. And, of course. *I* think there's nobody in the world like *him*. Although, to tell the truth, I did resent him terrifically when he was born—to think that he'd made me a grandmother. But he's quite won me over; and I suppose I'm as foolish now as all the other grandmothers.

MISS AUSTEN. Is she your only daughter, Mrs. Frazier?

MRS. FRAZIER. Yes, she was my only child.

CRAIG. Then, you live alone over here, Mrs. Frazier?

MRS. FRAZIER. All alone, yes.

MISS AUSTEN. Is that so?

MRS. FRAZIER. Yes, I've lived alone now for nearly four years—ever since my daughter was married. Alone at fifty. (*She laughs lightly.*) Rather a premature desolation, isn't it?

(*She laughs again, a little.*)

CRAIG. Certainly is.

MISS AUSTEN. I should say so.

MRS. FRAZIER. I remember reading a story by that name one time, a number of years ago; and I remember thinking then, how dreadful that would be—to be left alone—especially for a woman. And yet the very same thing happened to me before I was fifty.

MISS AUSTEN. Well, didn't you ever think of going out and living with your daughter, Mrs. Frazier?

MRS. FRAZIER. Well, of course, she has never given up trying to persuade me to do that; but I always say to her, "No, darling, I will live out my days in your father's house—even though he isn't there." I say, "I have my memories, at least; and nobody can take those from me." Of course, she says I'm sentimental; (*She laughs.*) but I'm not, really—not the least bit. Because if I were, I should have probably married again; but I feel that—

CRAIG. I should think you would have married again, Mrs. Frazier.

MRS. FRAZIER. Well, I suppose that would have been the logical thing to do, Mr. Craig; but, I don't know—I suppose perhaps I'm one of those one-man women. There are such women, you know.

MISS AUSTEN. Yes, indeed there are.

MRS. FRAZIER. Just as there are one-woman men. And I think it's particularly unfortunate when anything happens to the attachment of a person of that kind—whether it's death, or disillusionment, or whatever it is—because the impairment is always so absolutely irreparable. A person of that type can never care very greatly again, about anything.

MISS AUSTEN (*looking away off*). That's very true, Mrs. Frazier.

MRS. FRAZIER (*falling into a mood*). Never. (*She shakes her head slowly from side to side; then starts.*) Well, I think I'd better go, or you'll be agreeing with my daughter that I'm sentimental.

(*They follow her towards the door.*)

MISS AUSTEN AND CRAIG (*speaking together*). MISS AUSTEN: Oh, not at all, Mrs. Frazier; I agree with you perfectly. CRAIG: I think a little bit of sentiment is a very nice thing sometimes.

MRS. FRAZIER (*turning at the door*). And I do hope you'll tell Mrs. Craig that I was inquiring about her sister.

CRAIG. I will, Mrs. Frazier, thank you very much.

MRS. FRAZIER. I hope she'll be better soon. Good afternoon, Mr. Craig.

(*She goes out.*)

CRAIG. Good afternoon, Mrs. Frazier. I hope you'll come over again very soon.

MRS. FRAZIER (*calling back*). Thanks ever so much, I shall be delighted to.

MISS AUSTEN (*following her out*). And thanks again for the roses.

(CRAIG *turns away from the door and goes up the stairs.* MRS. CRAIG *appears between the portières, looking darkly towards the bay window at the left, where* MRS. FRAZIER *can be seen passing across the lawn.*)

MRS. FRAZIER. Oh, don't mention it, dear child, I should have brought you twice as many.

MISS AUSTEN. And I'll let you know if there's anything I don't understand as I go along.

MRS. FRAZIER. Please do, now, Miss Austen; don't hesitate to call me.

MISS AUSTEN. I will, I'll let you know.

MRS. FRAZIER. Good-by.

MISS AUSTEN, Good-by, Mrs. Frazier.

(*The screen door slams.* MRS. CRAIG *moves forward to the mirror over the mantelpiece at the right.*)

MRS. CRAIG. The silly creature.

(*She stands looking in the mirror, touching her hair.* MISS AUSTEN *comes in.*)

MISS AUSTEN (*stopping just inside the door*). Oh, Harriet, I was just going up to your room. How did you find your sister? Mrs. Harold told me a moment ago that you were back.

MRS. CRAIG (*without turning*). Yes, I'm back. (*Turning, with a touch of challenge in her manner.*) And I think it's about time I *came* back, don't you?

MISS AUSTEN. Why, dear?

MRS. CRAIG. Why?

MISS AUSTEN. Yes, I don't understand what you mean.

MRS. CRAIG. Well, from the looks of things, if I'd stayed away much longer, I should have probably come back to find my house a thoroughfare for the entire neighborhood.

MISS AUSTEN. You mean Mrs. Frazier being here?

MRS. CRAIG. You know perfectly well what I mean, Auntie Austen; please don't try to appear so innocent. (*She moves up to the foot of the stairs, to assure herself that* MR. CRAIG *is not within hearing distance.* MISS AUSTEN *gives her a long, narrow look and moves forward at the right of the piano. There is a pause; then* MRS. CRAIG *comes forward to the center table in a perfect fury.*) That's exactly what that woman's been trying to do ever since we've been here; and the minute you get my back turned you let her succeed—

just for the sake of a lot of small talk. How did she happen to get in here?

MISS AUSTEN. Why, I asked her in, of course; you don't suppose she walked in of her own accord.

MRS. CRAIG. I wouldn't put it past her, if she knew I was away. (MISS AUSTEN *looks at her.*) I know Mrs. Frazier's type better than you do. (*She settles the things on the table.*) What did you do; go over after her?

MISS AUSTEN. No, I did not. I was sewing on the porch there, and she brought me some roses over, which I think was very thoughtful of her.

MRS. CRAIG. Very thoughtful.

MISS AUSTEN. And I happened to mention the dress that I was making, and that the pattern that I'd bought for it wasn't quite clear to me. And she seemed to know from my description just what pattern it was, and very kindly offered to help me.

MRS. CRAIG. Of course; and you walked right into the trap.

MISS AUSTEN (*turning to her*). Well, why do you think she should be so anxious to get in *here,* Harriet?

MRS. CRAIG. For the same reason that a lot of other women in this neighborhood want to get in here—to satisfy their vulgar curiosity; and see what they can see.

MISS AUSTEN. And, why should you care if they do see?

MRS. CRAIG. I wouldn't gratify them—I don't want a lot of idle neighbors on visiting terms. Let them tend to their houses, and they'll have plenty to do: instead of wasting their time with a lot of silly roses. (*She crosses down to the mirror again.*) Mrs. Frazier is very likely one of those housekeepers that hides the dirt in the corners with a bunch of roses.

MISS AUSTEN. You know nothing about her house, Harriet.

MRS. CRAIG. I know what her lawn looks like,—that's enough for me. (*Turning.*) And you had to bring her upstairs, too, for fear she wouldn't see enough down here.

MISS AUSTEN. I don't suppose the woman knows what you've got in your house, Harriet.

MRS. CRAIG. Oh, Auntie Austen! Really, I wish you were as guileless in certain other respects as you seem to be in the matter of visiting neighbors.

MISS AUSTEN. A good neighbor is a very good thing sometimes, Harriet.

MRS. CRAIG. Well, you may have them; I don't want them running in and out to me.

MISS AUSTEN. None of them has ever run in and out to you so far that I remember.

MRS. CRAIG. One of them has just left.

MISS AUSTEN. She wasn't here to see you.

MRS. CRAIG. She was in my house, wasn't she?

MISS AUSTEN. And in your husband's house.

MRS. CRAIG. Oh—(*She gives a little laugh of mirthless amusement.*) Well, she was hardly here to see my husband, was she?

(MISS AUSTEN *holds her eye for a second.*)

MISS AUSTEN. No, she was not; although I've no doubt you'd attempt such an interpretation if you thought there was any possibility of Walter's believing it. I don't think any extremity would be too great for you, Harriet, as long as it kept people out of the Temple of the Lord. This Holy of Holies. It's a great wonder to me you haven't asked us to take off our shoes, when we walk across the carpet. (MR. CRAIG *coughs, somewhere upstairs, and* MRS. CRAIG *moves suddenly to the foot of the stairs and looks up.*) Mrs. Frazier was here to see *me,* your husband's aunt. And I made her welcome; and so did he. And asked her to come back again. And I don't think you'd find him very much in accord with your attitude, if he knew about it.

MRS. CRAIG. Well, you'll probably tell him.

MISS AUSTEN. Oh, I've got a lot of things to tell him, Harriet.

MRS. CRAIG. I've no doubt you have.

MISS AUSTEN. I've had plenty of time to think about them during the past two years, up there in my room. And they've been particularly clear to me this past week that you've been away. That's why I've decided to tell Walter; (MRS. CRAIG *turns sharply and looks at her*)—because I think he should be told. Only I want you to be here when I tell him, so that you won't be able to *twist* what I say.

MRS. CRAIG (*coming forward to the table*). You have a very good opinion of me, haven't you, Auntie Austen?

MISS AUSTEN. It isn't an opinion I have of you at all, Harriet; it's *you* that I have.

MRS. CRAIG. Well, whatever it is, I'm not at all interested in hearing about it. And I want you to know that I resent intensely your having brought Mrs. Frazier in here.

MISS AUSTEN (*turning away*). Oh, be honest about it, at least, Harriet!

MRS. CRAIG. What do you mean?

MISS AUSTEN. Why particularize on Mrs. Frazier?

MRS. CRAIG. Because I don't want her here.

MISS AUSTEN. You don't want anybody here.

MRS. CRAIG. I don't want *her*.

(*She strikes the table with her knuckles.*)

MISS AUSTEN (*looking directly at her*). You don't want your husband—(MRS. CRAIG *starts slightly and then stands rigid.*)—only that he's necessary to the upkeep here. But if you could see how that could be managed without him, his position here wouldn't be as secure as the position of one of those pillows there.

(*She indicates the pillows on the seat at the right of the stairway.*)

MRS. CRAIG. Well, I must say, Miss Austen, that's a very nice thing for you to say to me.

MISS AUSTEN. It's the truth, whether you like to hear it or not. You want your house, Harriet, and that's all you do want. And that'll all you'll have, at the finish, unless you change your way. People who live to themselves, Harriet, are generally left to themselves; for other people will not go on being made miserable indefinitely for the sake of your ridiculous idolatry of house furnishings.

MRS. CRAIG. You seem to have borne it rather successfully.

MISS AUSTEN. I did it for Walter's sake; because I knew he wanted to have me here; and I didn't want to make it difficult. But I've been practically a recluse in that room of mine upstairs ever since we've been here; just to avoid scratching that holy stairway, or leaving a footprint on one of these sacred rugs. I'm not used to that kind of stupidity. I'm accustomed to *living* in rooms; (MR. CRAIG *comes quietly down the stairs and stands on the landing, looking inquiringly from one to the other.* MRS. CRAIG *sees him out of the corner of her eye, and drifts forward to the mirror at the right.*) And I think too much of myself to consider their appearance where my comfort is concerned. So I've decided to make a change. Only I want my reasons to be made perfectly clear to Walter before I go—I think I owe it to him; for his own sake as well as mine.

(MISS AUSTEN *becomes aware of* CRAIG'*s presence on the stairway and turns and looks at him. There is a dead pause. Then she turns away, and* CRAIG *comes down into the room and forward at the left of the table.*)

CRAIG. What's the matter?

MRS. CRAIG (*turning*). I haven't the faintest idea, I'm sure. But from what Auntie Austen has just been saying, she seems to think there are quite a few things the matter.

CRAIG. What is it, Auntie?

MRS. CRAIG. She tells me she's going to leave us.

(*He looks at his wife, then at his aunt.*)

MISS AUSTEN. It's nothing very new, Walter.

CRAIG (*to his wife*). Going to leave the house, you mean?

MRS. CRAIG. So she says.

(*He looks at* AUNTIE AUSTEN *again.*)

CRAIG. You didn't say that, did you, Auntie?

MRS. CRAIG. Haven't I just told you she said it?

MISS AUSTEN. I am leaving to-morrow, Walter.

CRAIG. But, why? What's happened?

MRS. CRAIG. She says she finds my conduct of affairs here unendurable.

MISS AUSTEN. I'll be obliged to you, Harriet, if you'll allow me to explain the reasons for my going; I know them better than you do.

MRS. CRAIG (*turning to the large chair in front of the fireplace and sitting down*). You haven't any reasons that I can see; except the usual jealous reasons that women have—of the wives of men they've brought up.

MISS AUSTEN. You'll have plenty of time to give your version of my leaving after I've gone.

MRS. CRAIG. Well, sit down, then, and let us hear *your* version of it.

MISS AUSTEN. I prefer to stand, thank you.

MRS. CRAIG. Just as you please.

MISS AUSTEN (*glancing at the chair at the left, below the piano*). I doubt if I'd know quite *how* to sit in one of these chairs.

CRAIG. Why, what do you mean, Auntie? I can't believe that you've had any difficulty with any one; and especially with Harriet—who thinks the world of you. (MISS AUSTEN *smiles dryly.*) Now, you know she does, Auntie. Harriet is just as fond of you as I am. (*Turning to his wife.*) Why, it's incredible, positively.

MRS. CRAIG. I'm glad you're here—to hear some of this.

CRAIG. I suppose there *are* little irritations come up around a house occasionally, just as there are in any other business; but I'm sure you're too sensible, Auntie, to allow them to affect you to the extent of making you want to leave the house. Why, what would we do around here without you. It wouldn't seem to me that we had any house at all. What was it you said to Auntie, Harriet?

MRS. CRAIG. I haven't said anything to her, of course; she's simply using her imagination.

CRAIG. Then, it isn't anything that Harriet has said to you, Auntie?

MISS AUSTEN. Oh, no—Harriet never *says* anything. She simply acts; and leaves you to interpret—if you're able. And it takes a long time to be able—until you find the key. And then it's all very simple—and very ridiculous, and incredibly selfish. So much so, Walter, that I rather despair of ever convincing you of my justification for leaving your house.

CRAIG. Well, what has Harriet done, Auntie?

MRS. CRAIG. I'll tell you what I did, Walter—I objected to Auntie Austen's having brought that woman across the street there in here while I was away.

CRAIG. You mean Mrs. Frazier?

MRS. CRAIG. Yes, I mean Mrs. Frazier.

CRAIG. Why, what's the matter with Mrs. Frazier?

MRS. CRAIG. She's a vulgar old busybody, that's what's the matter with her—that's been trying to get in here ever since we've been here.

CRAIG. What do you mean, she's been trying to get *in* here?

MRS. CRAIG. You wouldn't understand if I told you, Walter. It's a form of curiosity that women have about other women's houses that men can't appreciate.

MISS AUSTEN. Harriet is chiefly provoked, Walter, because she has allowed herself to be tempted off form for a moment. She would much prefer to have excluded Mrs. Frazier by the usual method—that has been employed in the exclusion of every other man and woman that has ever visited here. But since she's blundered, she must attempt to justify herself now by arraigning Mrs. Frazier as everything from a vulgarian to a busybody—and even to insinuating that her visit here this afternoon was inspired by an interest in you.

MRS. CRAIG. I insinuated nothing of the kind. I simply asked a question in answer to an insinuation of yours.

MISS AUSTEN. The details are unimportant, Harriet; I know the principle.

MRS. CRAIG. Well, tell the truth about it, at least.

MISS AUSTEN. That is exactly what I am going to do—even at the risk of Walter's disfavor.

CRAIG. I don't think you could very well incur that, Auntie.

MISS AUSTEN. You're a man, Walter; and you're in love with your wife. And I am perfectly familiar with the usual result of interference under those circumstances.

CRAIG. Well, I hope I'm open to conviction, Auntie, if you have a grievance.

MISS AUSTEN. It isn't my own cause I'm about to plead; it doesn't matter about me. I sha'n't be here. But I don't want to be witness to the undoing of a man that was by way of becoming a very important citizen, without warning him of the danger.

CRAIG. I don't understand what you mean, Auntie.

MISS AUSTEN. That is probably the greater part of the danger, Walter—that you *don't* understand. If you did it would be scarcely necessary to warn you.

CRAIG. Of what?

(*There is a pause; and* MISS AUSTEN *looks right into his eyes.*)

MISS AUSTEN. Your wife.

(MRS. CRAIG *breaks into a mirthless laugh, at the absurdity of* MISS AUSTEN'S *implication.* CRAIG *turns and looks at her.*)

CRAIG. What are you laughing at, Harriet?

MRS. CRAIG. Why, don't you think that's very amusing?

CRAIG. I don't know that I think it's so very amusing.

MRS. CRAIG. Well, wait till you've heard

the rest of it; you'll probably change your mind.

MISS AUSTEN (*looking steadily at* MRS. CRAIG). Harriet isn't really laughing, Walter.

MRS. CRAIG. What *am* I doing, crying?

MISS AUSTEN. You are whistling in the dark.

MRS. CRAIG (*vastly amused, and rising*). Oh, dear!

(*She touches her hair before the mirror.*)

MISS AUSTEN. You're terrified that your secret has been discovered.

(MRS. CRAIG *turns sharply and faces her.*)

MRS. CRAIG. Really? And what *is* my secret?

MISS AUSTEN. I think it's hardly necessary to tell you that, Harriet.

MRS. CRAIG. But, I'm interested in hearing it.

MISS AUSTEN. Well, you can listen while I tell it to Walter.

MRS. CRAIG. Very well.

MISS AUSTEN. But, I want you to know before I tell him that it didn't remain for your outburst against Mrs. Frazier here a few minutes ago to reveal it to me; I knew it almost as soon as Walter's mother knew it.

(*There is a pause: then* MRS. CRAIG *moves a few steps towards her husband.*)

MRS. CRAIG (*with a touch of mock mysteriousness*). She means that I've been trying to poison you, secretly, Walter.

MISS AUSTEN. Not so secretly, either, Harriet.

(MRS. CRAIG *laughs lightly.*)

MRS. CRAIG (*going up towards the portières*). Well, I'm sorry I must go, for I'm sure this is going to be very amusing.

MISS AUSTEN. I've asked Harriet to stay here, Walter.

(MRS. CRAIG *turns sharply at the portières.*)

MRS. CRAIG. Well, I don't intend to stay.

MISS AUSTEN. I didn't think you would.

CRAIG. Why not, Harriet?

MRS. CRAIG. Because I have something more important to do than listen to a lot of absurdities.

MISS AUSTEN. Then I shall have to regard your going as an admission of the truth of those absurdities.

MRS. CRAIG. Well, you may regard it as you please: only I hope when you've finished discussing me, you'll be as frank in letting Walter know something of what *I've* been putting up with during the past two years.

(*She goes out through the portières.*)

MISS AUSTEN. Playing the martyr as usual. (CRAIG *takes a step or two towards the portières, and they stand for a second looking after her. Then he turns and looks at his aunt.*) I could have almost spoken those last words *for* her, Walter; I know her so well.

CRAIG (*coming down to the front of the table*). I wish you'd tell me what's happened here, Auntie.

MISS AUSTEN (*crossing to him*). That isn't so easy to tell to a man, Walter; it requires a bit of elucidation.

CRAIG. What is it?

MISS AUSTEN. Walter—why do you suppose your mother asked you to promise her, when she was dying, that you'd take me with you when you married?

CRAIG. Why, I think that was a perfectly natural request, Auntie, considering what you'd been to both of us during her illness.

MISS AUSTEN. But, it wasn't as though I should *need* a home—for she knew I preferred to travel,—that that's what I was preparing to do when she was first stricken. And I never told you, Walter, but she asked *me* to promise her that I should accept your invitation when you made it. You see, she knew her woman, Walter,—the woman you were going to marry.

CRAIG. You mean that Mother didn't like Harriet?

MISS AUSTEN. Nobody could like Harriet, Walter; she doesn't want them to.

CRAIG. I like her.

MISS AUSTEN. You're blinded by a pretty face, son, as many another man has been blinded.

CRAIG. Well, what has Harriet done?

MISS AUSTEN. She's left *you* practically friendless, for one thing; because the visits of your friends imply an importance to you that is at variance with her plan: so she's made it perfectly clear to them, by a thousand little gestures, that they are not welcome in her house. Because this *is* her house, you know, Walter; it isn't yours—don't make any mistake about that. This house is what Harriet married—she didn't marry you. You simply went with the house—as a more or less regrettable necessity. And you must not obtrude; for she wants the house all to herself. So she has set about reducing you to as negligible a factor as possible in the scheme of things here.

CRAIG. You don't really believe that, Auntie, do you?

MISS AUSTEN. That is her plan concerning you, Walter, I'm telling you. That is why the visits of your friends have been discouraged.

CRAIG. I can't think that Harriet would discourage my friends, Auntie.

MISS AUSTEN. Does any of them come here?

CRAIG. Why, most of them have been here at one time or another, yes.

MISS AUSTEN. Not within the last eighteen months; and you've only been married two years.

CRAIG. Well, why shouldn't Harriet want my friends here?

MISS AUSTEN. For the same reason that she doesn't want anybody else here. Because she's a supremely selfish woman; and with the arrogance of the selfish mind, she wants to exclude the whole world—because she cannot impose her narrow little order upon it. And these four walls are the symbol of that selfish exclusion.

CRAIG (*turning away, and crossing towards the right*). I can't believe that, Auntie.

MISS AUSTEN (*extending her arms towards the front door*). Can you remember when any one has darkened that door—until here to-day, when Mrs. Frazier came over?—And you see the result of that. And why do you suppose that people have so suddenly *stopped* visiting you? They always visited you at home. It can hardly be that you've changed so radically in two years. And I daresay all those charming young men and women that used to have such pleasant times at home, thought that when you married your house would be quite a rendezvous. But they reckoned without their—hostess, Walter—just as they are beginning to reckon without you. (*He turns and looks at her.*) You never go out any more.—Nobody ever asks you.—They're afraid you might bring her; and they don't want her.—Because she's made it perfectly clear to them that she doesn't want *them.* (CRAIG *turns away again slowly.*) And just as your friends are beginning to reckon without you in their social life, so it is only a question of time till they begin to reckon without you in their *business* life. (*He looks at her again, and she moves across towards him.*) Walter—why do you suppose your appointment as one of the directors of the local bank never materialized?

CRAIG. Why, I think Littlefield had something to do with that; he's been high-hatting me a bit lately.

MISS AUSTEN. Because Harriet insulted his wife here; I saw her do it.

CRAIG. When?

MISS AUSTEN. The week after New Year's, when Mrs. Littlefield called.

CRAIG. What did Harriet do?

MISS AUSTEN. Nothing—what Harriet always does. It was a little feline subtlety—that would sound too incredible in the ears of a man. But Mrs. Littlefield appreciated it, for all her stupidity. I *saw* her appreciate it—and you were not appointed. (CRAIG *looks away.*) And I want to tell you something else that I saw the other day in the city, or rather heard. I was having luncheon at the Colonnade, and two of your old Thursday-night poker crowd came in, and sat at a table within hearing distance of me. And presently a man and his wife came in and sat down at another table. And the wife immediately proceeded to tell the man how he should have sat down; and how he should sit now that he *was* down, and so on. And I distinctly heard one of your friends say to the other, "Listen to Craig's wife over here." (CRAIG *turns his head and looks right into* MISS AUSTEN'S *eyes. There is a slight pause. Then he crosses in front of her, and continues over to the piano at the left. She moves towards the left also, going up above the table.*) That is a little straw, Walter, that should show you the way the wind is blowing. Your friends resent being told where they shall sit, and how; so they are avoiding the occasion of it—just as I am going to avoid it. But you cannot avoid it, so you must deal with it.

CRAIG. How? How should I deal with it?

MISS AUSTEN (*taking hold of the back of the chair at the left of the table*). By impressing your wife with the realization that there is a *man* of the house here, as well as a woman; and that *you* are that man. And if you don't, Walter, you are going to go the way of every other man that has ever allowed himself to be dominated by a selfish woman.—Become a pallid little echo of her distorted opinions; believing finally that every friend you ever had before you met her was trying to lead you into perdition—and that she rescued you, and made a man of you. (*She makes a little sound of bitter amusement, and turns away towards the foot of the stairs.*) The irony of it. And yet they can do it.

CRAIG (*crossing back towards the right*). Harriet could never turn me against my friends.

MISS AUSTEN (*turning at the foot of the stairs, and speaking with level conviction*). Walter—they can make men believe that the mothers that nursed them—are their arch enemies. (*She comes forward suddenly and rests her left hand on the table.*) That's why I'm warning you. For you're fighting for the life of your manhood, Walter; and I cannot in conscience leave this house without at least turning on the light here, and letting you see what it is that you're fighting against.

(*She starts for the stairs, and* CRAIG *turns suddenly and follows her.*)

CRAIG. Auntie, I can't see you leave this house!

MISS AUSTEN (*stopping on the second step*). But, if I'm not happy here.

CRAIG. Well, why have I been so blind that I haven't seen that you were not happy, and fixed it so that you would be!

MISS AUSTEN (*quietly*). Because you haven't *seen* your wife, Walter.

CRAIG. Oh, I can't be convinced that there isn't an enormous element of misunderstanding between you and Harriet. (MISS AUSTEN *closes her eyes and shakes her head from side to side.*) Oh, I'm not disputing that she has a peculiar disposition—she may be all that you say of her;—but I really can't see the necessity of your leaving the house; the thing must be susceptible of some sort of adjustment.

(MISS AUSTEN *lays her right hand on his shoulder.*)

MISS AUSTEN. No house is big enough, Walter, for two women who are interested in the same man.

CRAIG (*crossing over to the left*). I'll never have a minute's peace if you leave here; I'll reproach myself.

MISS AUSTEN. You have nothing to reproach yourself with, Walter; you've always been very kind and very good to me.

CRAIG. What will you do if you leave here?

MISS AUSTEN. What I've always wanted to do—travel—all over the world—far and wide: so that I shan't become—little. I have such a deadly fear of that after these past two years.

CRAIG. But, I promised Mother that you'd always have a home with me, and if you go, I'll feel somehow that I'm breaking that promise.

MISS AUSTEN. You haven't a home to offer me, Walter. (*He looks at her.*) You have a house—with furniture in it—that can only be used under highly specified conditions. I have the impression somehow or other, when I look at these rooms—that they are rooms that have died—and are laid out.

(*She turns and starts up the stairs.*)

CRAIG. Well, whatever they are, they'll seem less if you leave them. I don't think I'd feel worse if it were Mother herself that were leaving.

(MISS AUSTEN *turns, with her hand on the balustrade.*)

MISS AUSTEN. Be glad that it isn't your mother, Walter; she would have left long ago.

(*She goes on up the stairs, and he stands looking after her. There is a ring at the front door. He turns and looks out through the French windows, then moves to the middle of the room and looks out through the portières. The bell rings again; then* MAZIE *comes down the stairs.*

CRAIG. There's a little boy at the front door, Mazie.

MAZIE. Yes, sir, I heard the bell.

CRAIG. I'm expecting a gentleman, too, Mazie, in a few minutes; I'll be upstairs.

MAZIE. All right, Mr. Craig, I'll call you when he comes.

(MAZIE *goes out to answer the bell, and* CRAIG *goes up the stairs. He stops halfway up and thinks.*)

BOY'S VOICE (*at the front door*). Why, Christine, up at the corner, sez if you're goin' to the Society to-night, would you mind payin' her dues for her; she sez she can't go to-night.

(CRAIG *disappears.*)

MAZIE. Oh, sure, tell her I'll be glad to.

BOY'S VOICE. She sez the card's in the envelope there with the money.

(MRS. HAROLD *comes in through the portières and crosses towards the door, looking out keenly.*)

MAZIE. All right, dear, tell her I'll tend to it.

(*The screen door slams and* MAZIE *comes in.*)

MRS. HAROLD. Did you answer that door, Mazie?

MAZIE (*crossing below the table to the mantelpiece*). Yes, it was the tailor's little boy, up at the corner, with Christine's Society money. He sez Christine can't go to-night.

MRS. HAROLD. Is to-night Society night again already?

MAZIE (*putting an envelope back of the center ornament on the mantelpiece*). It's the third Friday.

MRS. HAROLD. I can never keep track of that old Society.

MAZIE. Do you want me to pay your dues for you?

MRS. HAROLD (*moving to the foot of the stairs*). No, dear, I'm paid up to the first of July. (MAZIE *turns from the mantelpiece and moves towards her.*) Where did Mr. Craig go—upstairs?

MAZIE. I guess so, unless he's out there somewhere.

MRS. HAROLD (*glancing towards the front porch, and taking a step or two towards* MAZIE). No, he's not out there.

MAZIE. Why, what's the matter?

MRS. HAROLD (*laying her hand on* MAZIE'S *arm, and lowering her voice*). I think the old lady's goin' to leave.

(*She tiptoes to the portières,* MAZIE *watching her.*)

MAZIE. Miss Austen?

(MRS. HAROLD *nods; and then looks out through the adjoining rooms.*)

MRS. HAROLD (*turning to* MAZIE). The lady made a row about Mrs. Frazier being here.

(*She looks out again.*)

MAZIE. Did she?

MRS. HAROLD (*coming back*). She was furious. I knew it was coming by the face on her when she told me to take the roses out of the room. So as soon as I heard Mrs. Frazier goin', I went right up to the library; you can hear every word up there, you know, over near the radiator.

MAZIE. Yes, I know you can. Was *he* here?

MRS. HAROLD. He wasn't at first, but I think he must have come down while they were at it. I heard *her* say she didn't want her house made a thoroughfare for the neighborhood.

MAZIE. Can you imagine it—as though anybody ever came *in* here.

MRS. HAROLD. That's what *I* felt like sayin'. But Miss Austen told her.

MAZIE. Did she?

MRS. HAROLD. I should say she did. It didn't take Mrs. Craig long to get out of the room once Miss Austen got started. (*A door closes upstairs, and* MAZIE *darts to the center table and settles the table scarf.* MRS. HAROLD *steps to the big chair in front of the mantelpiece and feigns to be occupied in setting it straight.* MAZIE *glances over her right shoulder up the stairs, then steps up to the foot of the stairs and glances up. Then she hurries forward to* MRS. HAROLD *again, glancing through the portières as she goes.*)

MAZIE. What did Mrs. Craig do, walk out of the room?

MRS. HAROLD. Yes. She said she had something else to do besides listenin' to a lot of silly talk. (MAZIE *raises her eyes to heaven.*) I felt like sayin' I'd like to know what it was she had to do.

MAZIE. So would I.

MRS. HAROLD. I've been here nearly a year now, and *I* have my first time to see her do anything—only a lot of snoopin'—after somebody else has finished.

MAZIE. It's too bad Miss Austen didn't tell her that while she was at it.

MRS. HAROLD (*raising her hand, with a touch of solemnity*). She told her enough. (*She goes up to the foot of the stairs and looks up.*)

MAZIE. Well, didn't he say anything?

MRS. HAROLD. Not very much; Miss Austen done most of the talkin'. (*She comes down to* MAZIE'S *left, confidentially.*) She told him if he didn't do something very soon, his wife 'ud make him look like an echo.

MAZIE. She will, too.

MRS. HAROLD. He said she had a peculiar disposition—and that Miss Austen didn't understand her. Well, I felt like sayin' if Miss Austen don't understand her, I do. And I'd soon tell her how well I understand her, too, only that she gives me a wide berth.

MAZIE. I feel kind of sorry for him sometimes, though.

MRS. HAROLD. Yes, it's a pity for *him*. (*Lowering her voice, and speaking with great conviction.*) She could build a nest in his ear, and he'd never know it.

(*She turns to the table and settles the various ornaments.*)

MAZIE. She certainly is the hardest

woman to please that I've ever worked for.

MRS. HAROLD. Well, I don't know whether she's hard to please or not, Mazie, for I've never tried to please her. I do my work, and if she don't like it she has a tongue in her head; she can soon tell me, and I can go somewhere else. I've worked in too many houses to be out of a place very long. (*Straightening up and resting her left hand on the table.*) Did I tell you about her wanting me to dust the leaves off that little tree in front of the dining-room window last week?

MAZIE. Dust the leaves?

MRS. HAROLD (*looking to heaven for witness*). That's the honest God's fact. And me with the rheumatism at the time.

MAZIE. Can you imagine such a thing?

MRS. HAROLD. Well, you know how I done it, don't you?

MAZIE. What'd you say to her?

MRS. HAROLD. I told her right up; I said, "I'll dust no tree for nobody."

MAZIE. You done right.

MRS. HAROLD. She sez, "You mean you refuse to dust it?"—"Yes," I sez, "I refuse, and," I sez, "what's more, I'm goin' to stay refuse." "Well," she sez, "it needs dusting, whether you dust it or not." "Well," I sez, "let it need it," I sez. I sez, "A little dust won't poison it." I sez, "We'll be dust ourselves some day, unless we get drownded."

(*She goes to the portières.*)

MAZIE. You done right.

MRS. HAROLD. Oh, I told her.

(*She glances out through the rooms.*)

MAZIE. I think the worst kind of a woman a girl can work for is one that's crazy about her house.

MRS. HAROLD. I do, too; because I think they *are* crazy half the time. You know, you can go crazy over a house, Mazie, the same as you can over anything else.

MAZIE. Sure you can.

MRS. HAROLD. Doctor Nicholson's wife was one of them; although she wasn't as generous a woman as this one.

MAZIE. No, that's one thing you've got to say for Mrs. Craig; she's not stingy.

MRS. HAROLD. No, that's true, she isn't.

MAZIE. I don't think I've ever worked in a house where there was as good a table for the help.

MRS. HAROLD. That's right; you always get whatever they get.

MAZIE. And you never have to ask for your wages, neither.

(*The doorbell rings.*)

MRS. HAROLD. No, she's very good that way.

MAZIE (*going to answer the door, settling her cap and apron*). I guess that's that gentleman Mr. Craig's expectin'.

MRS. HAROLD. Come out when you come in, Mazie.

(*She goes out through the portières.* MR. CRAIG *comes down the stairs.*)

BIRKMIRE (*at the front door*). Good evening. Is Mr. Craig in?

MAZIE. Yes, sir, he's in.

(*The screen door is heard to close, and* BIRKMIRE *enters.*)

CRAIG (*coming in*). Hello, Billy, how are you?

BIRKMIRE (*shaking hands earnestly*). Hello, Walt.

(*He looks right into* CRAIG'*s eyes.*)

CRAIG. I called your house a little while ago; (BIRKMIRE *turns to the piano with his raincoat and hat.*)—there was a message here for me when I got in, saying you'd called.

(MAZIE *comes in and crosses towards the portières.*)

BIRKMIRE. Yes, I've been trying to get hold of you since four o'clock.

CRAIG. Let me take those things out of your way.

(MAZIE *stops near the portières and looks back, to see if they want her to take* BIRKMIRE'*s things.*)

BIRKMIRE. No, thanks, Walter, I've got to get right back to the house.

(MAZIE *goes out; and* CRAIG *moves down towards the table.*)

CRAIG. Your father still here?

BIRKMIRE. Yes, he'll be here for a day or two yet.

(*He looks keenly out through the portières, stepping up towards the back of the room.*)

CRAIG (*watching him curiously*). What's the matter? (BIRKMIRE *makes a deft gesture, signifying that* MAZIE *may be within hearing distance.*) What is it?

BIRKMIRE (*stepping down close to* CRAIG *and laying his hand on his sleeve*). What about it, Walt?

CRAIG. About what?

BIRKMIRE. About Fergus and his wife. You were out there last night, weren't you?

CRAIG. Sure. That's where I talked to *you* from.

BIRKMIRE. Well, my God, what happened out there, Walter?

CRAIG. What do you mean?

BIRKMIRE. Haven't you seen the evening papers?

CRAIG. Not yet, no. Why?

BIRKMIRE (*smothering an exclamation, and stepping to the piano to get a newspaper out of his pocket*). Jesus, how did you miss it!

CRAIG. Why, what's happened?

BIRKMIRE. Fergus and his wife are dead.

CRAIG. What!

BIRKMIRE. Found them this morning in the library.

CRAIG. Passmore, you mean?

BIRKMIRE (*handing him the paper*). Here it is on the front page of the *Telegraph.*

CRAIG (*crossing down to the right*). What are you saying, Billy?

BIRKMIRE (*stepping over towards the portières and looking out*). It's in every paper in town.

CRAIG. Where is it?

BIRKMIRE (*coming forward at* CRAIG'S *left and indicating a certain headline*). Fergus Passmore and wife found dead in library.

CRAIG. My God!

BIRKMIRE. I happened to see it over a man's shoulder coming down in the elevator in the Land Title Building about four o'clock, and I damned near had heart failure. (*He turns away to the left and takes a cigarette from a case.*) I've been trying to get you on the 'phone ever since. And I saw *her* myself at the Ritz last night at twelve o'clock. I was talking to her. I took the old man over there for a bit of supper after the show, and she was there with that military gent she's been stepping it with lately. (*Suddenly laying his hand on* CRAIG'S *arm.*) That's my hunch on this thing, Walter. I think she's been playing this soldier fellow a little too much lately and Fergus has heard of it and probably called it when she got in last night, and busted up the show. You know, he was always jealous as hell of her.

(*He takes a step or two towards the back and glances through the portières.*)

CRAIG. There must be a catch in this thing somewhere, Billy.

BIRKMIRE (*coming forward again*). How could there be a catch in it, Walter? Do you think they'd print that kind of stuff for a joke.

CRAIG. Well, my God, I was out there last night till twelve o'clock.

BIRKMIRE (*tearing the cigarette between his fingers*). Well, evidently this thing happened after you got away from there. Did she get in before you left there last night?

CRAIG (*looking up from the paper*). What?

BIRKMIRE. I say, did Adelaide get in last night before you left out there?

CRAIG. No, but she was there when I got out there, about nine o'clock. She was going out somewhere.

BIRKMIRE. Yes, and I know who it was she was going out *with,* too; that's the third time I've run into her with that bird lately. And I want to find out what his name is right away quick, too, for he might be in on this thing.

CRAIG. Have you been out there yet?

BIRKMIRE. Out to Fergus', you mean?

CRAIG. Yes.

BIRKMIRE. Sure, I hopped right out there as soon as I read it; but you can't get near the place.

CRAIG. I think I ought to get in touch with Police Headquarters right away, Billy.

BIRKMIRE. Well, that's why I wanted to get hold of you. It says there they're looking for a man seen leaving the house after midnight.

CRAIG. Sure, that's me.

BIRKMIRE. Well, not necessarily you, Walter.

CRAIG. That's the time I got away from there.

BIRKMIRE. That doesn't mean anything. Only I think it 'ud be a good thing to let them know right away.

CRAIG (*turning suddenly and going up to the telephone*). Sure, I'll call up right away.

BIRKMIRE (*following him up*). Well, now, wait a minute, Walter, don't move too fast; you know a thing like this can take a thousand and one turns, and we don't want to make any false move. This kind of thing 'ud be pie for the newspapers, you know; and the fact that we were invited out there to play cards wouldn't read any too well.

CRAIG. Well, *you* weren't out there.

BIRKMIRE. I know that; but I'm not

sitting back in the corner in this thing, you know, Walter. It just so happened that I *wasn't* out there. But I talked to you on the telephone out there last night, from my house, and in a thing of this kind they trace telephone calls and everything else.

CRAIG (*looking at the paper again*). My God, this is a terrible thing, though, isn't it, Billy.

BIRKMIRE (*turning away to the left, and passing his hand across his brow*). I haven't got it myself yet.

CRAIG. Terrible.

BIRKMIRE. It'll be a jar to your wife when she hears it, won't it?

CRAIG. Awful.

BIRKMIRE. She'll very likely see it in the paper up there in Albany.

CRAIG. She's back from Albany.

BIRKMIRE. Is she?

CRAIG. She got in a while ago.

BIRKMIRE. Well, she doesn't know anything about this yet, does she?

CRAIG. I don't think so; unless she happened to see the paper I brought home. I suppose it's in it.

BIRKMIRE. Sure, it's in all of them.

CRAIG. I just took it from the boy and put it in my pocket.

BIRKMIRE. Where is Harriet?

CRAIG. She's upstairs.

BIRKMIRE (*lowering his voice*). Does she know you were out there last night?

CRAIG. I don't know, I guess she does. Yes, I think I mentioned it a while ago.

BIRKMIRE (*stepping to* CRAIG'S *side, and laying his hand on his arm*). Well, now, listen, Walter—If she doesn't happen to see the paper, what she doesn't know won't bother her. And this thing is apt to clear itself up over night. It might be cleared up now, for all we know; for I suppose the police have been working on it all day. But, I think the wise move for us is just to hop out there and try to find out what's going on; and if they haven't found anything out yet, just get in touch with Police Headquarters and let them know where we're at.

CRAIG (*tossing the newspaper on to the seat beside the telephone table*). Yes, let's do that. Wait till I get my hat.

(*He goes through the portières.*)

BIRKMIRE (*crossing to the piano for his things*). I've got my car out here; we can cut across the park and be out there in ten minutes.

(*He throws his raincoat across his arm, picks up his hat, and steps quickly across to get the newspaper that* CRAIG *left on the seat. He glances up the stairs and out through the portières. Then he sees* CRAIG *coming through the adjoining room, and starts for the front door.*

CRAIG (*entering, wearing his hat, and carrying the newspaper he brought home*). I'll take this paper with me; keep it out of sight.

BIRKMIRE. I've got the other one here in my pocket.

(BIRKMIRE *goes out.*)

CRAIG (*glancing about the room as he crosses to the front door*). We take the *Globe* here in the afternoon, but I don't see it anywhere around out there.

(*He goes out.*)

BIRKMIRE (*outside*). I've got the car right out here.

CRAIG (*outside*). I guess across the park will be the quickest.

BIRKMIRE. Yes, we can be over there in ten minutes.

(*There is a dead pause. Then a clock somewhere out at the right strikes half-past six, with a soft gong. There is another slight pause, and then* MRS. CRAIG *sweeps through the portières, carrying an open newspaper. She sees that no one is in the room, and rushes to the forward window to see if she can see* MR. CRAIG *anywhere about. Then she starts for the front door, but changes her mind and rushes up to the landing of the stairway.*

MRS. CRAIG (*calling up the stairs*). Walter!—Walter!—Are you up there, Walter? (*She hurries down into the room again and over to the portières.*) Mazie!—Mazie!

(*She runs across to the front door and out.* MAZIE *comes in through the portières and looks about, then starts towards the front door.* MRS. CRAIG *hurries in again.*)

MAZIE. Were you calling me, Mrs. Craig?

MRS. CRAIG. Yes, Mazie. Have you seen anything of Mr. Craig?

MAZIE. Why, he was here a few minutes ago, Mrs. Craig, with a gentleman.

MRS. CRAIG. What gentleman? Who was he?

MAZIE. I don't know who he was, Mrs. Craig; I never saw him before.

MRS. CRAIG. Didn't you catch his name?

MAZIE. No, Ma'm, I didn't. He came in an automobile.

MRS. CRAIG. Well, did Mr. Craig go away with him?

MAZIE. I don't know whether he did or not, Mrs. Craig. I didn't know he'd gone.

MRS. CRAIG (*turning* MAZIE *around quickly by the shoulder and urging her towards the portières*). See if Mr. Craig's hat's on the rack out there.

MAZIE (*hurrying out*). Isn't he up in his room?

MRS. CRAIG. No, he isn't. (*She turns breathlessly and looks towards the bay window at the left.*) Oh, Lord! (*Turning to the portières again.*) Is it?

MAZIE (*from somewhere out at the right*). No, Ma'm, it isn't.

MRS. CRAIG. Well, listen, Mazie, run over to the garage there and see if he's there! No, no, come this way, it's quicker. (*She waits frantically until* MAZIE *rushes through the portières and across towards the front door.*) And if he's there tell him to come over here immediately; I want to see him.

MAZIE. Yes, Ma'm.

(*The screen door slams after her, and she hurries past the bay window at the left.*)

MRS. CRAIG. Hurry now, Mazie. Tell him I want him right away. (*She turns in the door and leans against the jamb, looking straight out, wide-eyed, and holding the newspaper against her bosom.*) Oh, my God! (*She hurries across above the center table and down to the window, forward, at the right.*) Oh, my God! (*She stands looking eagerly through the window, toward the left, as though watching* MAZIE *running down the street.*)

THE CURTAIN DESCENDS SLOWLY

ACT TWO

Ten Minutes Later

Mrs. Craig is standing at the window, forward, reading the newspaper. She stops reading, glances out the window, and then moves with a kind of controlled desperation to the bay window at the left, where she looks out again eagerly. Mrs. Harold comes in from the right.

MRS. HAROLD. Is Mazie here, Mrs. Craig?

(MRS. CRAIG *turns nervously.*)

MRS. CRAIG. No, she isn't, Mrs. Harold; I've sent her on an errand; she'll be back in a minute.

MRS. HAROLD (*turning to go out again*). I told her I thought I heard you calling her.

(*Telephone bell rings.*)

MRS. CRAIG. See who that is, Mrs. Harold, will you, please.

(MRS. HAROLD *comes back and picks up the telephone.*)

MRS. HAROLD. Hello?—Hello?

MRS. CRAIG. What's the matter; don't they answer?

MRS. HAROLD. No, Ma'm, they haven't answered yet. Hello!

MRS. CRAIG (*turning to the window again*). Never mind it, Mrs. Harold; it's probably a mistake.

MRS. HAROLD (*hanging up the receiver*). It does that sometimes when it's a long-distance call.

(MRS. CRAIG *turns sharply.*)

MRS. CRAIG. They didn't say it was long distance, did they?

MRS. HAROLD. No, Ma'm, they didn't say anything; nobody answered at all.

MRS. CRAIG. Well, if they want us they'll ring again.

MRS. HAROLD. Will you tell Mazie I want her when she comes in, Mrs. Craig, please?

MRS. CRAIG. Yes, I'll send her out to you as soon as she comes back.

(MRS. HAROLD *goes out through the portières, and* MRS. CRAIG *crosses over and down to the window, forward, and looks out. She sees* MAZIE *hurrying back from the garage, and steps quickly up to the door at the left.* MAZIE *can be seen running past the bay window. The screen door slams, and* MAZIE *rushes in.*) Isn't he over there, Mazie?

MAZIE. No, Ma'm, he isn't.

MRS. CRAIG. Are you sure?

MAZIE. Yes, Ma'm, I looked all around.

MRS. CRAIG. Did you go round to the back?

MAZIE. Yes, Ma'm, I looked everywhere. Old Mr. Foster was standin' over there; I ast him if he'd seen anything of Mr. Craig, but he said he hadn't.

MRS. CRAIG. Is the garage locked?

MAZIE. Yes, Ma'm, I tried the door.

MRS. CRAIG. Well, could you see whether or not the car was in there?

MAZIE. Yes, Ma'm, they're both in there, the little one, too; I looked through the glass. (MRS. CRAIG *turns away to the right, with a troubled expression, and moves down towards the mirror, and* MAZIE *moves towards the door at the right.* MRS. CRAIG *glances out the window, forward.*) I guess maybe he musta went away with that gentleman that was here.

MRS. CRAIG. He probably did. You say that gentleman came in a car, Mazie?

MAZIE. Yes, Ma'm, I think it was his; it was standin' right in front of the house when I opened the door for him.

MRS. CRAIG. All right, Mazie. Mrs. Harold wants you for something.

MAZIE (*going out*). Oh, does she?

(MRS. CRAIG *leans against the mantelpiece and thinks hard. The telephone bell rings. She turns and looks at the telephone; it rings again. Then she moves to answer it.* MAZIE *comes in.*)

MRS. CRAIG. I'll answer it, Mazie.

MAZIE. Oh, all right.

(*She withdraws, and* MRS. CRAIG *starts to pick up the telephone.*)

MRS. CRAIG (*in a subdued voice*). Mazie.

MAZIE. Yes, Ma'm?

MRS. CRAIG. Come here for a minute. (MAZIE *appears between the portières.*) Go up and see that Miss Landreth's door is closed.

MAZIE (*withdrawing*). Yes, Ma'm.

MRS. CRAIG. Be very quiet about it, now, Mazie, and don't disturb her if she's asleep.

MAZIE. All right.

(*Telephone bell rings again.*)

MRS. CRAIG. Hello?—Yes?—All right. (*She glances up the stairs, and then waits.*) Hello?—Yes—(*In a louder voice.*) Hello! Yes—this is *Mrs.* Craig at the telephone—Mr. Craig isn't here just now, if you wanted *Mr.* Craig. Oh—why-a-Miss Landreth is lying down just now. Who is this speaking, please?—Oh, I see. Why—not a thing in the world, Mr. Fredericks, except that she's very tired—We've only just now gotten in from Albany, and I suggested that she go upstairs and lie down for a while. Yes—Am I going to do what? No, I didn't understand what you said, Mr. Fredericks. Why, yes, of course, I'd go back with her if anything unforeseen developed—otherwise she can go back herself. We're simply waiting now to hear something from her mother's physician up there.—Yes, of course I'm sure. Why, why should you put yourself to that trouble, Mr. Fredericks?—There wouldn't be anything you could do when you get here.—Well, I'd much rather not call her, if you don't mind, Mr. Fredericks; she's lying down. —Well, can't you tell me what it is you want to tell her—and I can give her the message? Well, probably it would, Mr. Fredericks;—it's very nice of you to be so solicitous about her, but I don't care to disturb her just now. I'm very sorry.

(*She hangs up abruptly, and glances toward the head of the stairs.* MAZIE *appears between the portières.*)

MAZIE. The door was closed, Mrs. Craig.

MRS. CRAIG. All right, Mazie. (MAZIE *withdraws, and* MRS. CRAIG *moves forward, thoughtfully. There is a tap at the front door bell.* MAZIE *turns and crosses to answer the door.* MRS. CRAIG *is looking sharply toward the front door.*) See what those gentlemen want, Mazie.

MAZIE. Yes, Ma'm.

CATELLE (*at the front door*). Mr. Craig in?

MAZIE. No, sir, he's not in just now; he went out about twenty minutes ago.

CATELLE. What time do you expect him back?

MAZIE. Why, I couldn't say for certain; but I guess he'll be back in time for dinner, about seven o'clock.

CATELLE. Is his wife in?

MAZIE. Yes, sir, she's in.

CATELLE. I'd like to speak to her for a minute if I could.

(MRS. CRAIG, *who has been standing very still, listening, vanishes through the portières, looking over her shoulder apprehensively towards the front door.*)

MAZIE. Yes, sir. Will you just step in? (*The screen door closes; and immediately* MAZIE *hurries into the room.*) If you'll just take a chair for a minute I'll call her. (CATELLE *wanders in, removing his hat, followed by* HARRY, *who also removes his hat as he enters.* CATELLE *moves down to the center table, puts his hat down, and takes a small leather notebook from his inside pocket; and* HARRY *comes forward and sits in the chair beside the piano. There is a pause.*)

HARRY. They didn't get this place with a pound of tea.

CATELLE. A lot of money. Phoenix Fire Insurance people. This lad's old man used to be the president of the Company. Died about twelve years ago. I guess this gent's in line for the old man's job, if he lives.

(MRS. CRAIG *enters through the portières.* HARRY *rises and* CATELLE *turns to her.*)

MRS. CRAIG. Good evening.

HARRY. Good evening.

CATELLE. Good evening, Ma'm. I called to see Mr. Craig.

MRS. CRAIG. Mr. Craig isn't in just now, I'm sorry.

CATELLE. Are you Mrs. Craig?

MRS. CRAIG. Yes.

CATELLE. Have you any idea what time Mr. Craig'll *be* in?

MRS. CRAIG. Why, I'm expecting him any minute; he was here less than a half-hour ago, when I went upstairs; so he must be right here in the neighborhood somewhere.

CATELLE (*consulting his watch*). I see.

MRS. CRAIG. He'll certainly be back for his dinner, at seven o'clock, if you'd care to call back.

CATELLE. Well, I've got to be over the other side of town at seven o'clock,—so it may be that you could give me the information I am looking for, as well as Mr. Craig. Would you sit down for a minute?

MRS. CRAIG. Yes, certainly.

(*She turns to the chair in front of the mantelpiece and sits down.* HARRY *resumes his chair beside the piano, and* CATELLE *sits on the small bench immediately above the center table.*)

CATELLE. I thought I'd like to speak to *Mr.* Craig first, but I don't suppose it makes a great deal of difference.

MRS. CRAIG. I thought he might be over at the garage—I wanted him myself a few minutes ago; but the maid says he isn't over there.

CATELLE. Well, I'll tell you what it is I wanted to see him about, Mrs. Craig. I suppose you've seen in the evening paper about this unfortunate affair out here on Willows Avenue?

MRS. CRAIG. You mean that shooting affair?

CATELLE. Yes, at the Passmore home.

MRS. CRAIG. Yes, isn't that a dreadful thing!—I've just been reading it here.

CATELLE. Yes, it's a very sad affair.

MRS. CRAIG. They're *both* dead, aren't they?

CATELLE. Yes, they're both dead.

MRS. CRAIG. Isn't that terrible. That's what I wanted to see my husband for; I wanted to ask him if he knew that man.

CATELLE. He probably did; they're pretty well known people here in town.

MRS. CRAIG. Yes, they must be, according to the paper. I haven't had a chance to read it all yet, I've just gotten in from Albany.

CATELLE. It's a rather peculiar case.

MRS. CRAIG. Was it a robbery or something?

CATELLE. No, there wasn't anything taken. Of course, it could have been a foiled *attempt* at robbery, but that' ud hardly explain certain other circumstances.

MRS. CRAIG. Are you gentlemen working on the case?

CATELLE. Yes, Ma'm, we're from Police Headquarters. But, that doesn't need to alarm *you,* Mrs. Craig; there's no particular connection between that and our visit *here.*

MRS. CRAIG. Well, I'm very glad to know that.

CATELLE. No, this Passmore affair looks to me pretty clearly a matter of jealousy motive. Of course, there are one or two attendant circumstances, as there usually are in cases of this kind, but they don't mean anything, as far as the actual shooting is concerned. There was a man seen leaving the house shortly after midnight in an automobile—One of the neighbors happened to see him; but it was too dark to establish any identification. Besides, that wouldn't account for the death of *Mrs.* Passmore; because she didn't get in until after three o'clock, and the man left there between twelve and one.

MRS. CRAIG. I see.

CATELLE. But, of course, as you understand, Mrs. Craig, it's part of our business to follow up any little outside clue that we happen to get hold of that might throw some additional light on a case.

MRS. CRAIG. Yes, of course.

CATELLE. And that's what I wanted to see Mr. Craig about.

MRS. CRAIG. You mean you think Mr. Craig might be the man that was seen leaving there last night.

CATELLE. No, that circumstance is really not being seriously considered; a house of that description might have had any number of visitors during the evening.

MRS. CRAIG. That's very true.

CATELLE. But, we've had a report late this afternoon, Mrs. Craig, from the

Lynnebrooke Telephone Exchange, where your light comes in, that there was a call made on your telephone here at five-twenty-seven this evening, asking for the address of the telephone number Levering three, one hundred; and that happens to be the number of the telephone at Mr. Passmore's home.

MRS. CRAIG. You mean that somebody called from here?

(*She indicates the telephone.*)

CATELLE. On this telephone, yes, Ma'm. Oakdale, six, two, three. That's the number of your telephone here, isn't it?

MRS. CRAIG. Yes, that's our number.

CATELLE. That's what I've got here.

MRS. CRAIG. But I can't imagine who it would be that called.

CATELLE. The report says it was a woman's voice.

MRS. CRAIG. Who was it that reported it, do you know?

CATELLE. I couldn't tell you that, Mrs. Craig.

MRS. CRAIG. I mean to say, would it be possible that the person who reported it could have made a mistake in the number?

CATELLE. No, they're usually pretty careful in an affair of this kind.

MRS. CRAIG. And the call was made at five o'clock this evening, you say?

CATELLE. Five-twenty-seven, my report says. The operator didn't give the address, of course; it's against the telephone company's rules. And the party rang off.

MRS. CRAIG. Well, that's extraordinary. Although it might have been one of the servants—probably saw it in the evening paper and was curious to know where it was. (*Rising.*) I'll ask them.

CATELLE. Well, I could understand that curiosity if the address wasn't published; but it is; and the telephone number *isn't*. And I was interested in finding out why any one 'ud have that particular 'phone number to-day and not know the address —when it's been in all the newspapers since two o'clock this afternoon. And this call wasn't made till after five.

MRS. CRAIG. It does seem strange, doesn't it?

CATELLE. I haven't been able to figure it out.

MRS. CRAIG. But, I dare say there's some very simple explanation of it.

CATELLE. Has this telephone here been used at all, to your knowledge, Mrs. Craig, since five o'clock this afternoon?

MRS. CRAIG. Why, I *answered* a call, a few minutes ago, from Northampton, Massachusetts.

CATELLE. A long-distance call, you mean?

MRS. CRAIG. Yes. It was a Mr. Fredericks, at Smith College there, calling my niece, to inquire about her mother. Her mother is ill in Albany.

CATELLE. I see.

MRS. CRAIG. That's where we've just come from.

CATELLE. You don't know whether or not anybody from the outside has been in here since five o'clock?

MRS. CRAIG. Not to my knowledge; except a neighbor from across the avenue there, Mrs. Frazier. She brought some roses over to my husband's aunt. She was here when I got in; although I scarcely think she would have used the telephone. But, I'll ask Miss Austen if you like.

CATELLE. I wish you would, please, if you don't mind.

MRS. CRAIG (*going to the stairway landing*). Not at all. She's up in her room I believe.

CATELLE. Would you mind asking her to step down here for a few minutes?

MRS. CRAIG. Yes, certainly. (*Calling.*) Miss Austen!—Miss Austen!

(*There is the sound of a door opening somewhere upstairs.*)

MISS AUSTEN (*from upstairs*). Is some one calling me?

MRS. CRAIG. Yes,—it's me, Miss Austen. Would you mind coming down here for a minute or two, Miss Austen? I'd like to speak to you.

MISS AUSTEN. All right, I'll be down in a moment.

(MRS. CRAIG *turns to come down.*)

MRS. CRAIG. If you will, please. She'll be right down.

CATELLE. Thank you very much.

MRS. CRAIG (*moving towards the portières*). I suppose I'd better call the servants too, hadn't I? They'll probably know something about it.

CATELLE. Yes, I'd like to see them for a minute.

MRS. CRAIG (*going through the portières*). I'll call them right away.

(CATELLE *looks at his watch and rises.*)

CATELLE (*crossing towards the por-*

tières). What time have you got there, Harry?
(*He watches keenly through the portières.*)

MRS. CRAIG. Mazie!

HARRY. Just seven.

MAZIE (*out at the right*). Yes, Ma'm?

MRS. CRAIG. Would you come here for a minute?

CATELLE. Do you mind if I use this 'phone here, Mrs. Craig?

MRS. CRAIG. They'll be right in.
(*She enters.*)

CATELLE. Do you mind if I use this 'phone here for a minute?

MRS. CRAIG (*moving forward*). Not at all, go right ahead. I didn't hear what you said.

CATELLE. I've got a call to make at seven o'clock.

MRS. CRAIG. That's quite all right.
(*He stands holding the telephone, and* MRS. CRAIG *listens keenly.*)

CATELLE (*into the telephone*). Spring 4000.—Right.
(*There is a stillness: then the clock strikes seven, with a soft gong.* MAZIE *enters, on the third gong.*)

MAZIE. Did you want me, Mrs. Craig?
(MRS. CRAIG *motions to her to be silent;* MAZIE *stands looking from one to the other in a state of positive bewilderment.*)

CATELLE. Thielens? Catelle.—That so? —I got away from there before six. Period? Righto, Chuck. What are you trying to do, break Harry's heart? (*He gives a rather dry little laugh.*) All right, Chuck, I'll be right over. (*He hangs up and crosses to the table for his hat.*) We'd better get right out there, Harry. (*Harry rises and moves up to the door.*) I won't have to bother you any more right now, Mrs. Craig; there's been a bit of additional information come in over at headquarters that'll hold things up temporarily.

MRS. CRAIG (*moving towards the center table*). Well, do you want me to have Mr. Craig get in touch with you when he comes in?

CATELLE. No, we'll get in touch with him if it's necessary.

MRS. CRAIG. And you don't want to question the rest of the people now, either?
(HARRY *goes out.*)

CATELLE. Not just now, Mrs. Craig, thank you very much.
(*He starts for the door.*)

MRS. CRAIG. You're welcome, I'm sure. All right, Mazie.
(MAZIE *withdraws reluctantly, her eyes fastened upon* CATELLE.)

CATELLE. I'm sorry to have had to trouble you.

MRS. CRAIG (*following him to the door*). That's quite all right.

CATELLE (*turning at the door*). You can explain the circumstances to Mr. Craig, if you will.

MRS. CRAIG. Yes, I will. He'll probably know something about it.

CATELLE (*going out*). Very likely he will.

MRS. CRAIG. And if he doesn't, I'm sure one of the others will.

CATELLE. All right, thank you very much, Mrs. Craig.

MRS. CRAIG. You're very welcome, I'm sure.

CATELLE. Good evening.

MRS. CRAIG. Good evening.
(*The screen door closes, and* MRS. CRAIG *turns slowly and lifts her closed hands in a quiet panic. Then she hurries forward and across to the window and watches the two detectives going down the street.* MISS AUSTEN *comes down the stairs quietly, and stands on the landing, looking at her.*)

MISS AUSTEN. Did you want to see me about something, Harriet?
(MRS. CRAIG *starts slightly and turns.*)

MRS. CRAIG (*going out through the portières*). No, not now, Miss Austen; it isn't necessary. I'm sorry to have troubled you.
(MISS AUSTEN *stands for a second looking after her; then she moves forward to the window, to see what it was that had so engaged* MRS. CRAIG'S *attention. Then she moves up towards the telephone, glancing through the portières.*)

MISS AUSTEN (*into the telephone*). Will you give me Clearfield, six, two,—six, two?—Please? (*She waits, glancing towards the portières and out the window.*) Hello? Is this the Mowers Express Office? Well, how early could I have some things taken away to-morrow morning? Six hundred and eighty Belmont Manor. Yes, just a square from the Park. Well, eight o'clock would be time enough. Miss Irene Austen. That's right. Thank *you.*
(*She hangs up, and goes up the stairs.* MRS. CRAIG *comes through the portières, glances towards the head of the stairs, and moves to the foot of the stairs to look up. Then she steps to the telephone table and*

settles everything precisely. MAZIE *appears between the portières.)*

MRS. CRAIG. What is it, Mazie?

MAZIE. Why, Mrs. Harold wants to know if she'll serve the dinner now, Mrs. Craig.

MRS. CRAIG (*moving forward, thoughtfully*). Tell her not yet for a little while, till Mr. Craig gets here; I'm expecting him any minute.

MAZIE. Yes, Ma'm.

(*She goes out; and* MRS. CRAIG *stands thinking hard for a second. The screen door closes sharply, and she wheels round with a rapid movement, crossing above the center table towards the door.* CRAIG *enters, removing his hat.)*

MRS. CRAIG. Walter! Where have you been?

CRAIG. Out with Billy Birkmire. Why?

MRS. CRAIG (*indicating the outer door of the glass vestibule*). Shut that door.

(*He turns and shuts it, and she moves along the foot of the stairway, glancing up and out through the portières.)*

CRAIG (*coming into the room again*). What's the matter?

(MRS. CRAIG *turns and crosses back towards him.)*

MRS. CRAIG. My God, haven't you seen the evening paper about Fergus Passmore and his wife!

CRAIG. Yes, I've seen it.

MRS. CRAIG. Well, what about it, Walter?

CRAIG (*putting his hat down on the piano*). I don't know any more about it than you do, Harriet.

MRS. CRAIG. My God, isn't that a terrible thing! I've been nearly out of my mind for the last half-hour. I happened to see it in the paper there when I came downstairs, and I couldn't find you anywhere.

CRAIG. I went out with Birkmire.

MRS. CRAIG. Was that Birkmire that was here?

CRAIG. Yes, he wanted to see me about it.

MRS. CRAIG. I didn't even know whether you knew it or not; because you hadn't said anything about it when you came in this evening.

CRAIG. I didn't *know* it when I came in this evening.

MRS. CRAIG (*pointing at the paper on the table*). It's on the very front page of the paper there.

CRAIG. I didn't see the paper this evening till Birkmire showed it to me.

MRS. CRAIG. Well, why didn't you call me then, and not go rushing out of the house?

CRAIG. I didn't want to upset you.

MRS. CRAIG (*moving forward and across in front of the center table*). Well, I certainly couldn't have been any more upset than I have been. (*Turning to him.*) Mazie said there's been a man here, and that you'd gone away with him in an automobile—so, of course, I didn't know what to think. I thought probably you'd been arrested or something.

(*He looks at her sharply.)*

CRAIG. What would I be arrested for?

MRS. CRAIG. Why, in connection with this thing, of course. (*Taking a step towards him.*) The Police are looking for you; you know that, don't you?

CRAIG. Who says the Police are looking for me?

MRS. CRAIG. Two of them have just left here, not five minutes ago.

CRAIG. Policemen?

MRS. CRAIG. They said they were from Police Headquarters; that's all I know.

CRAIG. And what are they looking for me for?

MRS. CRAIG. Well, now, why do you suppose they're looking for you, Walter?

CRAIG. I don't know.

MRS. CRAIG. Doesn't it say in the paper there that you were seen leaving Passmore's at twelve o'clock last night?

CRAIG. It doesn't say that *I* was seen leaving there.

MRS. CRAIG. It says there was a man seen leaving there, and who else could it have been but you? You were out there, weren't you?

CRAIG. Yes.

MRS. CRAIG. Well, that's enough, isn't it?

(*She turns away to her left, and crosses above the table towards the portières.)*

CRAIG. But *they* don't know that.

MRS. CRAIG. Oh, don't be absurd, Walter.

CRAIG. Who saw me?

MRS. CRAIG (*coming back towards him.)* Somebody always sees in a case of this kind.

CRAIG. Who could it have been?

MRS. CRAIG. The butler saw you, didn't he?

CRAIG. What if he did?—he didn't

know me from Adam. He says so there in the paper, doesn't he?

MRS. CRAIG. He could identify your picture, couldn't he?

CRAIG. Who's going to give him my picture?

MRS. CRAIG. Don't talk so loud.

(*She steps back towards the portières, to assure herself that neither of the servants is listening.*)

CRAIG (*moving forward at the left of the center table*). Anyway, I don't believe he'd recognize my picture if he *did* see it; he only came into the library for a couple of minutes to serve some drinks, and went right out again. And he didn't get my name, because Fergus was sitting on the lawn when I got there and took me in himself. And the butler was in bed when I left there.

MRS. CRAIG (*coming forward at the right of the table*). Didn't any of the other servants see you?

CRAIG. Not that I know of.

MRS. CRAIG (*coming very close to him and lowering her voice*). Didn't you tell me that Billy Birkmire called you on the telephone out there last night?

CRAIG. Yes, I talked to him out there.

MRS. CRAIG. Well, didn't the butler get your name then?

CRAIG. No; Fergus answered the 'phone himself, on the extension in the library.

MRS. CRAIG. Well, those men have been here, anyway.

CRAIG. Well, what did they want?

MRS. CRAIG. Haven't I just told you what they wanted? They wanted to see *you*.

CRAIG. Did they say they knew it was I that was out there last night?

MRS. CRAIG. I don't remember *what* they said, exactly; I was too upset. But they wanted to know where you were, and, of course, I couldn't tell them; because you were here when I left the room, and then you suddenly disappeared. (*Turning away to the right.*) I was never placed in such a position in my life. I'm sure those men must have thought I was evading them. (*Turning back to him again.*) But *I* didn't know what to say to them—except that you'd probably taken a little walk around the neighborhood here; because I'd sent Mazie over to the garage to look for you as soon as I saw the paper, and she said both the cars were in there.

CRAIG. I went out in Birkmire's car.

MRS. CRAIG. Where did you go with him?

CRAIG. Over to Fergus' house.

MRS. CRAIG. And what in heaven's name did you do a thing like that for, Walter!

CRAIG. Why not?

MRS. CRAIG. Supposing you'd run into somebody out there?

CRAIG. And what if I did?

MRS. CRAIG. Do you want your name to be dragged into this thing?

CRAIG. My name 'll be dragged into it anyway, won't it?

MRS. CRAIG. Why will it?

CRAIG. You say those men have been here already.

MRS. CRAIG. And what if they have? That doesn't mean anything.

CRAIG. It means that they must have associated my name with it already, doesn't it?

MRS. CRAIG. No, it doesn't mean anything of the kind; they were simply looking for information.

CRAIG. But it was to me they *came* for that information.

MRS. CRAIG. Because you were a friend of Passmore's.

CRAIG. Exactly. And they'll very likely come back here again.

MRS. CRAIG. But, you don't have to go out looking for them, do you?

CRAIG (*turning away and going up towards the door at the left*). You can't be playing any game in a thing like this, Harriet.

MRS. CRAIG (*following him up*). No, and you don't have to go rushing out to meet a lot of scandalous publicity, either. I should think your own common sense would show you what it would mean to have your name even mentioned in a thing of this kind. (*Turning away and down towards the center table.*) Why, it 'ud be in every newspaper in the country.

CRAIG (*coming forward at the right of the piano*). That wouldn't bother me in the least.

MRS. CRAIG (*aghast*). It wouldn't bother you!

CRAIG. Not the least bit—My conscience is clear.

MRS. CRAIG (*stepping to his side*). Oh, don't be so absurdly romantic, Walter!

CRAIG. It isn't a question of romanticism at all.

MRS. CRAIG. No, and it isn't a question of conscience, either. It's simply a matter of discretion. If you've had nothing to do with this thing, what's the use of becoming involved?

CRAIG. What do you mean, *if* I've had nothing to do with it?

MRS. CRAIG (*with sudden temper*). Oh, now don't start picking me up on every word! (*She turns away to the left and crosses above the center table towards the portières.*) I've had cross-examination enough in the last fifteen minutes. (CRAIG *takes a cigarette from a case and closes the case with a snap.* MRS. CRAIG *turns and sees that he is about to smoke.*) Now, don't smoke in this room, Walter. (*He throws the cigarette across the room to the fireplace.* MRS. CRAIG *looks at it in astonishment, and then at him.*) Well, that's a nice place to throw it, I must say.

(*She goes down to the fireplace and picks it up.*)

CRAIG (*sitting in the chair at the right of the piano*). Oh, what does it matter!

MRS. CRAIG. Don't you want it?

CRAIG. What good is it, if I can't smoke it?

MRS. CRAIG (*crossing above the table towards the front door, holding the cigarette away from her, between her thumb and finger*). There are plenty of other places in the house to smoke, if you want to smoke.

CRAIG. I don't know where they are.

MRS. CRAIG (*going out the door*). You can smoke in your den, can't you?

CRAIG. If I shut the door. (*He sits thinking, deeply. The screen door slams, and* MRS. CRAIG *comes in again, looking keenly towards the portières.*) Did those men say when they'd be back here?

MRS. CRAIG. I don't remember whether they did or not;—I suppose they did. They said they'd get in touch with you if it was necessary. (*Coming forward to his side, and lowering her voice.*) But, if they *do* come back here, Walter, don't give them any more information than I did.

CRAIG. Well, I certainly won't deny that I was a friend of Fergus'.

MRS. CRAIG. You don't have to deny that you were a friend of his; but you certainly don't have to submit to a lot of cross-examination by detectives, either, simply because you happened to be a friend of his. (*She turns away and moves to the front of the center table.*) Let them go and cross-examine some of his other friends; you weren't the only friend he had.

CRAIG. Why did you submit to their cross-examination?

MRS. CRAIG (*turning to him*). Because I didn't know at the time to what extent they were justified in questioning me. I thought probably they had some information about your having been out at Passmore's last night. And I was at my wit's end, trying to keep from saying something that would imply an admission of it. I told them right away that I'd just gotten in from Albany, so I suppose they assumed that I didn't know where you'd been last night.

CRAIG. How long did they stay here?

MRS. CRAIG. About fifteen minutes, I imagine; but it seemed like a year.

CRAIG. What were they talking about all that time?

MRS. CRAIG. About you, and Fergus Passmore, and where you were, and when you'd be back, and all kinds of questions. (*She goes to the piano and picks up his hat, settling the piano scarf.*)

CRAIG. Did they say they'd been to any other of Fergus' friends?

MRS. CRAIG. I don't remember, they may have. They said something about him being very well known here socially, so they probably have.

(CRAIG *thinks for a second, then rises abruptly and crosses below the center table and up to the telephone.*)

CRAIG. I think I'll call Birkmire up and see if they've been to see him.

MRS. CRAIG (*with a panicky movement towards him*). Now, wait a minute, Walter! (*She puts his hat on the table as she crosses above it.*) You're not going to do anything of the kind.

CRAIG. Why not?

MRS. CRAIG (*taking the telephone from him*). Now, go away from this 'phone. (*She draws him forward by the arm, away from the telephone.*) Let me tell you something.

CRAIG. What's the matter?

MRS. CRAIG. Don't you realize that that telephone is being watched—and that they are probably watching Birkmire's too?

CRAIG. Who is?

MRS. CRAIG. Why, the Police, of course. Haven't you any realization of your position in this affair?

CRAIG. I evidently haven't the same realization that you have.

MRS. CRAIG. Well, it's time you did have.

CRAIG. It is?

MRS. CRAIG. Yes, it is.

CRAIG. And what realization have you of my position?

MRS. CRAIG. Never mind what realization I have; that doesn't matter now. I simply know that the very first thing the Police do in a case of this kind is to watch the telephone calls to and from the house.

CRAIG. Not from this house.

MRS. CRAIG. I mean from Fergus' house.

CRAIG. I wasn't going to call Fergus' house.

MRS. CRAIG. You were going to call Billy Birkmire, weren't you?

CRAIG. At his own house, yes.

MRS. CRAIG. Well, what difference does it make, Walter. Do you think those detectives can't put two and two together? Birkmire called you last night at Passmore's, didn't he?

CRAIG. Yes.

MRS. CRAIG. And there's undoubtedly a record of the call.

CRAIG. That wouldn't involve my name, would it?

MRS. CRAIG. It would if the operator listened in.

CRAIG. And do you think she has nothing to do but listen in on calls?

MRS. CRAIG. She listened in on this one, didn't she?

CRAIG. On which one?

MRS. CRAIG. What? (*She steps back from him suddenly, and touches her hair, in an effort to appear casual.*) What did you say?

CRAIG. Which call do you say the operator listened in on?

MRS. CRAIG. I don't know which one she listened in on. But some one must have listened in on something or those men wouldn't have come here, would they?

CRAIG. Did they say the operator had reported on a call from here?

MRS. CRAIG. I don't remember what they said, distinctly. One of them kept rambling something about a telephone call, but I assumed it was the one that Birkmire made to you last night out at Fergus'.

CRAIG. Didn't they say when the call was made?

MRS. CRAIG. What does it matter when it was made, Walter?

CRAIG. It matters a lot.

MRS. CRAIG. The fact remains, doesn't it, that that telephone is undoubtedly being watched *now.*

CRAIG (*whirling round and picking up the telephone again*). Well, I want to know *why* it's being watched.

MRS. CRAIG (*springing to his side and seizing the telephone*). Now, listen to me, Walter Craig; you *must* not use that telephone. (*She looks him straight in the eyes, then moves back several steps and looks at him defiantly.*) I will not allow you to drag my name into a notorious scandal.

CRAIG (*whipping the receiver off and putting it to his ear*). I've got to find out where I'm at in this thing!

MRS. CRAIG (*raising her voice threateningly*). If you speak over that telephone I'll leave this house! (*He takes the receiver from his ear and looks at her steadily. There is a pause.*) And you know what construction 'ud be put upon that, under the circumstances.

(*He slowly hangs up and sets the telephone back onto the little table, holding her eyes steadily. Then he moves slowly towards her.*)

CRAIG. What do you mean, you'll leave this house?

MRS. CRAIG (*stonily*). I mean exactly what I said. Do you think I could stay in this neighborhood twenty-four hours after my name had been associated with a thing of this kind?

CRAIG. And haven't you any appreciation of the necessity of my knowing what's happening in this case?

MRS. CRAIG. I have no appreciation of any necessity except the necessity of keeping still.

CRAIG. But supposing something developed that would reveal absolutely the fact that I had been out there last night—

MRS. CRAIG. What *can* develop, if you keep still?

CRAIG. But, supposing something did? Wouldn't it be very much better for me to have been open and aboveboard from the beginning, instead of having played a waiting game, and probably create an attitude of suspicion where there are no grounds for any?

MRS. CRAIG. There *are* grounds for suspicion, Walter; don't evade the issue.

CRAIG. What are they?

MRS. CRAIG. The fact that you were out there last night.

CRAIG. That doesn't mean a thing.

MRS. CRAIG. Evidently not, to you.

CRAIG. Does it to you?

MRS. CRAIG. What does it matter what it means to me? It isn't for me to determine the degree of your guilt or innocence. I'm not interested.

CRAIG. You're not interested!

MRS. CRAIG. I'm interested only in the impression on the popular mind,—and the respect of the community we've got to live in.

CRAIG. You mean you'd rather know I was involved in this thing and *keep* the respect of the community, than know I was a victim of circumstances, and lose it?

(MRS. HAROLD *appears between the portières.* MRS. CRAIG *sees her over* CRAIG'S *shoulder, and crosses quickly below him.*)

MRS. CRAIG. What is it, Mrs. Harold?

MRS. HAROLD. I'm sorry to bother you, Mrs. Craig, but I'm afraid the dinner'll be spoiled.

MRS. CRAIG (*going down to the mirror*). All right, Mrs. Harold, put it up; I'll be right out.

(CRAIG *moves forward to the upper right-hand corner of the center table.*)

MRS. HAROLD (*withdrawing*). All right.

CRAIG. Mrs. Harold.

MRS. HAROLD (*stopping*). Yes, sir?

(*She comes back a few steps towards him.*)

CRAIG. Mrs. Harold, do you know if anybody has called that number that I gave you last night here, to-day, on this telephone?

MRS. HAROLD. You mean the number you gave me to have Mr. Birkmire call you at?

CRAIG. Yes, Levering three one hundred.

MRS. HAROLD. No, sir, I don't know that anybody has. I only gave it to Mr. Birkmire over the telephone last night when he called.

CRAIG. *You* haven't had occasion to call that number to-day on this telephone, have you, Mrs. Harold?

MRS. HAROLD. No, sir, I haven't, Mr. Craig.

CRAIG. All right, Mrs. Harold, thanks very much.

(*She starts to go, then stops and turns again.*)

MRS. HAROLD. I never even thought about it to-day until Mrs. Craig asked me for it when she came in this evening.

(*There is a pause.* CRAIG *shifts his eyes to his wife, who raises her arm slowly and touches her hair before the mirror.*)

CRAIG. All right, Mrs. Harold, thank you very much. (MRS. HAROLD *withdraws, and* CRAIG *moves up slowly towards the portières and watches her out of hearing distance. Then he turns and looks at his wife. She stands very still. He moves a step or two slowly towards her.*) It was you that made that call. (*She turns and looks at him, with a touch of defiance.*) What were you doing, checking up on me?

MRS. CRAIG (*starting up towards the portières*). Don't flatter yourself, Walter.

CRAIG. That's what you were doing, wasn't it?

MRS. CRAIG. Don't flatter yourself. The man hasn't been born yet that I'd bother checking up on.

CRAIG. Why didn't you tell the truth?

MRS. CRAIG (*whirling upon him*). Because I anticipated an attack of your romantic conscience.

CRAIG. You were playing safe; that was it, wasn't it?

MRS. CRAIG. Exactly!

CRAIG. And at my expense!

MRS. CRAIG. I knew the necessity of it with you!

CRAIG (*turning away to the left, crossing in front of the center table*). God!

MRS. CRAIG (*following him up*). I knew if I told you I made that call, you'd be on the telephone in five minutes telling the Police.

CRAIG (*turning sharply*). I intended doing that anyway.

MRS. CRAIG. You silly fool!

CRAIG. That's where I went this evening, with Birkmire, when I left here—to Police Headquarters.

MRS. CRAIG (*aghast*). Oh!

CRAIG. And the only reason I didn't tell them then was that the man in charge of the case had gone to his dinner and wouldn't be back till eight o'clock. But he'll be told *then!*

(*He swings up to the front door.*)

MRS. CRAIG (*leaning across the center table, and speaking threateningly*). Well, if you do, you'll explain my leaving you, too.

CRAIG. That wouldn't worry me in the least, Harriet.

MRS. CRAIG. Well, it might worry *them.* (*He turns sharply and looks at her, dismayed.*)

CRAIG (*coming back to the table*). Listen to me, Harriet. Why weren't you at least *honest* with me in this thing, and not try to make it appear that *I* was responsible for the visit of those detectives?

MRS. CRAIG. Because I knew exactly what you'd do if I told you. And that would mean an explanation of why I had called up; and the next thing would be an admission of the fact that you are the man the Police are looking for.

CRAIG. But it's *you* those detectives are looking for.

MRS. CRAIG. Oh, you needn't try to turn it on to me! They wouldn't be looking for either of us if you'd stayed at home last night, instead of being out card-playing with a lot of irregular people. (*She turns down to the mirror.*)

CRAIG. What was there irregular about Fergus Passmore?

MRS. CRAIG (*turning to him, in a wrath*). There must have been some irregularity, or this thing wouldn't have happened. Everybody that knew Fergus Passmore knew that he was insanely jealous of his wife; and then *you* have to go out visiting them. (*She crosses below the table to the piano.*) I felt in my bones up there in Albany that something 'ud happen while I was away; that was the reason I didn't stay up there any longer than I absolutely had to. I knew as soon as ever my back was turned you'd be out with your friends again. (*He looks at her, under his brows; and there is a pause.*)

CRAIG. And what has your back being turned got to do with my visiting my friends?

MRS. CRAIG. Never mind what it has to do with it; only you wouldn't have *been* visiting them if I'd been here.

CRAIG. How would you have stopped me?

MRS. CRAIG. I'd have stopped you all right, one way or another.

CRAIG. What would you have done—locked the door on me?

MRS. CRAIG. It wouldn't have been necessary to lock the door on you. (*Turning and looking at him directly.*) You haven't *been* visiting them in the last eighteen months, have you?

CRAIG. No, I haven't.

MRS. CRAIG. And they haven't been visiting you, either?

CRAIG. No, they haven't.

MRS. CRAIG (*turning away*). Well—

CRAIG (*after a slight pause*). You mean you've kept them out of here?

MRS. CRAIG (*turning to him again and looking him straight in the eyes*). Well, if I did the end justified the means; you at least haven't been in the shadow of the law in the last eighteen months.

(*He holds her eye for a second, then moves forward to the front of the table.*)

CRAIG. You're certainly running true to form, Harriet.

MRS. CRAIG. Well, I'm glad of it if I am.

CRAIG. My aunt said here a while ago that you'd driven all my friends away from this house.

MRS. CRAIG (*with level significance*). There are ways of getting rid of people without driving them away from the house.

(CRAIG *makes a little sound of bitter amusement.*)

CRAIG. And I thought she was imagining things at your expense.

MRS. CRAIG. Well, you see she probably had better perception than you'd given her credit for.

(*He turns and looks at her darkly.*)

CRAIG. Probably she had; for she perceived something else, Harriet, that may be equally true.

MRS. CRAIG. Is that so?

CRAIG. She said you were trying to get rid of me too—(*She darts a look at him.*) without actually driving me away from the house. (*She laughs derisively, and moves across towards the portières. He follows her up, raising his voice.*) And I believe that's true, too.

MRS. CRAIG. Keep your voice down! Do you want everybody in the house to hear you?

CRAIG. You've admitted it, by your attitude in this affair this evening.

MRS. CRAIG (*looking at him, and moving forward to the mantelpiece*). I don't know what you're talking about.

CRAIG (*coming forward and leaning on the table*). Very well, you know what I'm talking about. And you knew what my aunt was going to talk about too, here a while ago; that's the reason you left the room before she started.

MRS. CRAIG. I'm sorry I didn't stay here now.

CRAIG. No danger of your staying here, Harriet; you couldn't bear it. (*She laughs, and he moves forward to the left.*) My God, how perfectly she knows you, Harriet! She couldn't have read you any better if you'd written it out for her. And I felt rather sorry listening to her, thinking she was probably getting a little old and suspicious; particularly when she said you had excluded my friends.

MRS. CRAIG. Do you think I wanted my house turned into a tavern?

CRAIG. My friends never turned my mother's house into a tavern.

MRS. CRAIG. They didn't play poker at your mother's house till all hours of the morning.

CRAIG. Every Thursday night for ten years; till two o'clock, if they felt like it.

MRS. CRAIG. Well, evidently, your mother and I had very different ideas of a house.

CRAIG. Very different indeed, Harriet; there was more actual home in one room of my mother's house than there'd be in all of this if we lived in it a thousand years.

MRS. CRAIG. Why didn't you stay in it, then, if you found it so attractive?

CRAIG. Now you're talking, Harriet; why didn't I do *just that*. (*He turns away to the left, then turns suddenly back.*) But, don't make any mistake that I think you didn't want my friends here simply because they played cards; you wouldn't have wanted them if they'd come here to hold prayer meetings. You didn't want them because, as my aunt says, their visits implied an importance to *me* that was at variance with your little campaign—the campaign that was to reduce me to one of those wife-ridden sheep that's afraid to buy a necktie for fear his wife might not approve of it.

(*He goes up towards the front door.*)

MRS. CRAIG. Oh, don't try to make yourself out a martyr; you've had your share of this bargain.

(*He turns suddenly and looks at her, then comes forward again to the front of the table.*)

CRAIG. I never regarded this thing as a bargain.

MRS. CRAIG. Did you expect me to go into a thing as important as marriage with my eyes shut?

CRAIG. I wanted you to go into it honestly, as I went into it—fifty-fifty—And you've been playing safe right from the start.

(*He turns away towards the piano.*)

MRS. CRAIG. I've been doing nothing of the kind.

CRAIG. Don't tell me what you've been doing; I see your game as clearly as my aunt sees it. (*He turns and comes back towards her.*) You've been *exploiting me,* consistently, in your shifty little business of personal safety. And you'd throw me right now to the suspicion of implication in this double murder—to preserve that safety.

(*He goes back towards the piano again.*)

MRS. CRAIG (*almost crying*). I've been trying to preserve my home.

CRAIG. That's all I've heard from you since the day I married you.

MRS. CRAIG. Well, what else has a woman like me *but* her home?

CRAIG (*turning to her*). Hasn't she her husband?

MRS. CRAIG. She could lose her husband, couldn't she?—As many another woman has.

CRAIG. Couldn't she lose her home too?

MRS. CRAIG. She couldn't if she knew how to secure it.

CRAIG (*raising his finger solemnly*). That's the point in a nutshell, Harriet; if she knew how to *fix* it for herself.

(*He turns away and rests his hands on the piano.*)

MRS. CRAIG. Well, what if I have fixed things for myself? You haven't lost anything by it, have you? If I've fixed them for myself I've fixed them for you too. Your home is here. And maybe if I hadn't played the game so consistently it wouldn't *be* here. And I wouldn't be the first woman that's lost her home, and her husband too, through letting the control of them get out of her hands. (*She moves up towards the back of the room, in a crying temper.*) I saw what happened to my own mother, and I made up my mind it 'ud never happen to me. (*She turns and comes forward again.*) She was one of those "I will follow thee, my husband" women—that believed everything my father told her; and all the time he was mortgaging her home over her head for another woman. And when she found it out, she did the only thing that women like her *can* do, and that was to die of a broken heart—within six months; and leave the door open for the other woman to come in as stepmother over Estelle and me. (*She turns to the mantelpiece.*) And then get rid of us both as soon as Estelle was marriageable. (*Turning to him suddenly.*) But the house was never mortgaged over *her* head, I'll promise you that; for she saw to it that it was put in her name before ever she took him; and she kept it there, too, right to the finish. (*She sweeps up towards the back of the room again.*)

CRAIG. Why didn't you ask me to put this house in your name?

MRS. CRAIG (*whirling upon him*). Because I didn't *want* it in my name!

CRAIG. It would have been more honest.

MRS. CRAIG (*coming forward to the right end of the table*). I haven't done anything that wasn't honest!

CRAIG. How would you know, Harriet?

MRS. CRAIG. I've simply tried to be practical; but, with your usual romanticism, you want to make me appear like a criminal for it.

CRAIG. I'm not reproaching you at all.

MRS. CRAIG. Well, you shouldn't reproach me; for there's nothing to reproach me about.

CRAIG. You simply married the wrong man, Harriet.

MRS. CRAIG (*witheringly*). I married a romantic fool! (*He looks at her narrowly, and she holds his eye.*) *That's* what I married. (*She turns away and goes up to the portières to look out.*) And I'm seeing it more every day I live.

(*There is a pause. Then* CRAIG *breaks into a hard little laugh.*)

CRAIG. How well we understand each other now, Harriet.

MRS. CRAIG (*coming forward to the mantelpiece again*). Well, I understand you, anyway, whether you understand me or not. (*Speaking directly to him.*) And you ought to thank your God that I do, for I don't know what 'ud become of you if I didn't.

(*She turns to the mantelpiece, and suddenly sees the card that* MAZIE *left back of the center ornament. She picks up the little envelope deftly, takes the card out and reads it. Craig regards her icily; and after a pause, he speaks— in a level, rather dangerous tone.*)

CRAIG. The brass of you—and the presumption.

(*She looks at him.*)

MRS. CRAIG. What?

CRAIG. I'm just wondering how you *get* that way.

MRS. CRAIG. How I get what way?

CRAIG. So brazenly presumptuous, as to say such a thing to me.

MRS. CRAIG. What have I said? I don't know what you're talking about.

CRAIG (*moving slowly away a step or two from the piano*). What have you ever done, or a million others like you, that would warrant the assumption of such superiority over the men you're married to?

MRS. CRAIG. Nobody's assuming any superiority.

CRAIG. Doesn't your remark admit it?

MRS. CRAIG (*turning and moving up to the portières*). Don't get yourself into a temper.

CRAIG. That you don't know what 'ud become of me only that *you* understand me.

MRS. CRAIG (*glancing through the portières*). Neither I do.

CRAIG. The presumption of you.

MRS. CRAIG. What are you standing there for, Mazie?

MAZIE AND CRAIG (*speaking together*).

MAZIE. Why, Mrs. Harold sent me in to see if you were coming in to dinner.

CRAIG. That you should set yourself about to control the very destiny of a man,—

MRS. CRAIG. Yes, I'm coming right away.

MRS. CRAIG *and* CRAIG (*speaking together*).

MRS. CRAIG. But I want to see you for a minute first, Mazie.

CRAIG. As though I were some mental incompetent.

MAZIE. Yes, Ma'm.

MRS. CRAIG (*turning and going towards* CRAIG, *lowering her voice, and trying to silence him with a gesture*). Don't make a show of yourself in front of Mazie. (MAZIE *comes through the portières, and* MRS. CRAIG *turns to her.*) Mazie, what is this card here?

MAZIE. Why, it's the Society card, Mrs. Craig, of the Mutual Benevolent.

MRS. CRAIG. And what is it doing here?

MAZIE. Why, Christine sent it down about an hour ago, with the tailor's little boy, to know if I'd pay her dues for her.

MRS. CRAIG. And couldn't you find any place for it but back of that ornament?

MAZIE. Why, I was—

MRS. CRAIG. After all the times I've told

you never to put anything on that mantelpiece.

MAZIE. Yes, you *have* told me, Mrs. Craig, but when I came in—

MRS. CRAIG. Then, why do you do it? Must I keep telling you the same thing indefinitely? You know perfectly well I never allow anybody even to *dust* that mantelpiece but myself. I even bought a special little brush for those ornaments, because I wouldn't trust them to anybody else. And yet the minute you get my back turned you must use them as a catchall for everything in the house.

MAZIE. Mrs. Harold asked me something when I came in, and—

MRS. CRAIG. I am not interested in what anybody asked you; that does not excuse you. (MAZIE *takes a handkerchief from the pocket of her apron and touches it to her eyes.*) I have told you over and over again *never* to put anything back of those ornaments; and you deliberately disobey me. You simply will *not* do as you are told. And when a girl will not do as she is told, the best thing for her to do is to go some place where she will be *made* to do it. So I want you to get your things together to-night and leave this house to-morrow morning. (MAZIE *looks at her, then turns away to leave the room.*) Here's the card. And find some place for it besides back of an ornament. (MAZIE *takes the card and withdraws.*) And tell Mrs. Harold to put up the dinner, I'll be down in two minutes; (*She starts for the stairs.*) I'm going up to see what my niece wants for *her* dinner. (*She goes up the stairs haughtily. Halfway up she turns, but without stopping, and addresses* CRAIG *coldly.*) You'd better go out there and get your dinner, before it's cold.

(*She disappears at the head of the stairs, and* CRAIG *stands looking at the floor. His eyes wander up the stairs after her, and then down the right side of the room. They settle upon the ornament on the mantelpiece, and he looks at it hard; then crosses slowly and picks it up. He holds it in his hand, looking at it curiously: then suddenly lifts it in the air and smashes it on the bricks in front of the mantelpiece. He stands looking at the shattered pieces for a moment; then takes a cigarette from his case and strolls back across the room towards the piano. He taps the cigarette on the case, then takes out a match and lights it, tossing the burned match on to the floor. Then he leans against the piano and smokes thoughtfully.* MRS. HAROLD *hurries in through the portières.*)

MRS. HAROLD. Did something get broke in here, Mr. Craig? (*He indicates the shattered ornament with a nod, and* MRS. HAROLD *looks towards the mantelpiece. She sees pieces of the shattered ornament, and raising her hands and eyes to Heaven, takes a step or two towards them.*) Glory be to God this day and this night, how did that happen, Mr. Craig! Did it fall off the mantelpiece?

CRAIG (*without moving*). No, I smashed it, Mrs. Harold.

MRS. HAROLD (*puzzled*). On purpose, do you mean, Mr. Craig?

CRAIG. Yes.—I didn't like it.

MRS. HAROLD. I wish you'd tell Mrs. Craig it was you that done it, Mr. Craig; if she sees it she might think it was one of us that broke it.

CRAIG. I'll tell her all about it, Mrs. Harold; don't you worry about that.

(*He straightens up and starts across slowly towards the big chair in front of the mantelpiece, and* MRS. HAROLD *moves a step or two towards the portières.*)

MRS. HAROLD (*turning to him*). Will I get the dustpan and sweep that up, Mr. Craig?

CRAIG. No, don't bother about it now, Mrs. Harold; go out and get your dinner.

(*She moves towards the portières, then stops again.*)

MRS. HAROLD. Ain't you comin' to your dinner, Mr. Craig?

CRAIG (*sitting down*). No, I don't want any dinner to-night, Mrs. Harold.

MRS. HAROLD. Don't you want nothing at all?

CRAIG. Not a thing.

(*She withdraws; and he sits smoking and thinking.*)

MRS. CRAIG (*from the head of the stairs*). Are you down there, Walter?

CRAIG. Yes.

MRS. CRAIG. Listen—did something *fall* down there a minute ago?

CRAIG. No.

MRS. CRAIG. Are you sure?

CRAIG. Yes, I'm sure.

MRS. CRAIG. Well, it sounded up here as though the house fell down.

CRAIG (*after a slight pause*). Maybe it did, Harriet—I'm just sitting here won-

dering.
(*He sits smoking. His gaze wanders up, and out, and away off.*)

THE CURTAIN DESCENDS SLOWLY

ACT THREE

SCENE: *Same as preceding act—the following morning, about eight-thirty.* CRAIG *is still sitting in the big chair before the fireplace, asleep. After a pause,* MRS. HAROLD *enters through the portières, carrying a dustpan and hand brush. She sees* CRAIG, *looks at him curiously, and also observes the pieces of the shattered ornament and the cigarette butts at his feet. She turns and puts the dustpan and brush down on the seat at the right of the stairway, and, with a glance up the stairs, crosses and unlocks the front door and goes out. The screen door slams after her and* CRAIG *wakes. He looks around, glances at his watch, gets up and settles himself before the mirror.* MRS. HAROLD *tiptoes in, bringing the morning paper.*

CRAIG. Good morning. Mrs. Harold.

MRS. HAROLD (*stopping above the center table*). Good morning, Mr. Craig.

CRAIG. I must have made a night of it sitting here.

MRS. HAROLD. Yes, I was wondering if you'd been there all night.

CRAIG. I must have fallen asleep.

MRS. HAROLD. You must feel pretty tired, don't you?

CRAIG (*turning to her*). No, I'm all right. Is that the morning paper you have there, Mrs. Harold?

MRS. HAROLD. Yes, sir, I was just bringing it in.

CRAIG. Let me see it, will you?

MRS. HAROLD. Yes, sir. (*He takes the paper; and, stepping to the window, forward, reads it eagerly.*) Would you like a cup of coffee, Mr. Craig?

CRAIG. Yes, I'll take a little coffee if you have it.

MRS. HAROLD (*starting for the portières.*) It's all made;—I'll just turn on the percolator for a minute.

(*She goes out; and he stands reading. There is the sound of a door opening somewhere upstairs. He glances towards the head of the stairs, then crosses quickly up to the front door and out on to the porch.* MRS. HAROLD *comes in again; and, picking up the dustpan and brush, comes forward to the mantelpiece and starts to sweep up the ornament and cigarette butts.* MRS. CRAIG *appears on the stairway.*)

MRS. CRAIG. Mrs. Harold.

MRS. HAROLD (*straightening up*). Yes, Ma'm?

MRS. CRAIG. Has the morning paper come yet?

MRS. HAROLD. Yes, Ma'm, I just gave it to Mr. Craig; he's reading it there on the front porch.

MRS. CRAIG (*puzzled, and coming down the stairs*). What is *he* doing up so early?

MRS. HAROLD. I don't think he's been in bed at all, Mrs. Craig; he was sitting in this big chair here when I came in this morning, and he was sitting here last night when I locked up.

(MRS. CRAIG *crosses to the bay window at the left and looks out on to the porch; and* MRS. HAROLD *resumes her sweeping.* MRS. CRAIG *becomes aware of what* MRS. HAROLD *is doing, and turns to her.*)

MRS. CRAIG. What is that you're sweeping up there, Mrs. Harold?

MRS. HAROLD (*straightening up*). Why, it's that center ornament that was here, Mrs. Craig.

(MRS. CRAIG *crosses down in front of the center table, looking wide-eyed at the vacant place on the mantelpiece.*)

MRS. CRAIG. What!

MRS. HAROLD. It got broke last night.

MRS. CRAIG. Oh, my God, Mrs. Harold, don't tell me that that's that beautiful statuette!

MRS. HAROLD. Mr. Craig said that he broke it.

MRS. CRAIG (*looking at the shattered pieces in the dustpan, which* MRS. HAROLD *is holding*). Oh, my God, look at the way it's broken!—It's smashed into a thousand pieces.

MRS. HAROLD. It must have fallen on the bricks here.

MRS. CRAIG. Oh, that never simply fell, Mrs. Harold; it's absolutely shattered—look at the size of the pieces. It's out of the question even to think of having it mended.

MRS. HAROLD. No, I don't think it could ever be mended now.

MRS. CRAIG (*almost crying*). That beautiful thing—that I wouldn't even allow anybody to go near; and look at it now.

MRS. HAROLD. It certainly is too bad.

MRS. CRAIG. And, of course, I might just as well throw those others away now, for they're absolutely meaningless without this one. (*She turns away, in a pang of grief, and moves a few steps towards the left, then suddenly turns again to* MRS. HAROLD.) How on earth did it ever happen, Mrs. Harold?

MRS. HAROLD. I don't know, I'm sure, Mrs. Craig.

MRS. CRAIG. I suppose Mazie broke it for spite, didn't she?— Because I reprimanded her last night for putting things back of it.

MRS. HAROLD. No, she didn't break it, Mrs. Craig, for she was out there in the kitchen with me when we heard it fall.

MRS. CRAIG (*turning away and crossing below the center table*). Well, send her in here now, I want to speak to her.

MRS. HAROLD. Mr. Craig said that *he* broke it. (MRS. CRAIG *turns and looks at her.*) He said he didn't like that ornament.

MRS. CRAIG. Tell Mazie I want to see her.

MRS. HAROLD. She isn't here, Mrs. Craig; she's gone.

MRS. CRAIG. You mean she's left already?

MRS. HAROLD. Yes, Ma'm, she left right after she had her breakfast.

MRS. CRAIG. Of course she did, the contemptible little devil.

MRS. HAROLD. Mr. Craig said that he'd tell you all about it.

MRS. CRAIG. Where did Mazie go?

MRS. HAROLD. She said she was goin' to her married sister's for a while.

MRS. CRAIG. Did you pay her her wages?

MRS. HAROLD. Yes, Ma'm, I paid her last night.

MRS. CRAIG (*turning away towards the front door*). All right, Mrs. Harold. (MRS. HAROLD *goes out through the portières, taking the dustpan and brush with her.*) Walter, come in here for a minute, will you? (*She glances over her shoulder, to see that* MRS. HAROLD *is out of earshot, then turns and waits till* CRAIG *comes in. He enters, carrying the newspaper.*) What does the paper say this morning about the Passmore thing?

CRAIG (*handing her the newspaper*). You're quite safe.

(*He comes forward and across in front of the center table to the mirror, and straightens his tie.*)

MRS. CRAIG (*stepping forward to the piano and spreading the paper out eagerly*). What does it say?

CRAIG. His brother got in last night from Pittsburgh, with a letter that Fergus had written him, intimating his intentions.

MRS. CRAIG. Then, Fergus did it himself?

CRAIG. So it appears.

MRS. CRAIG. I always told you he was jealous of his wife.

(CRAIG *turns and looks at her.*)

CRAIG. He did it because she was dishonest.

MRS. CRAIG (*reading*). I suppose this telegram here from his brother about Fergus' letter was the additional information that that detective spoke about here last night. (*She straightens up and speaks directly to* CRAIG.) He called Police Headquarters from here about seven o'clock, and then he said it wouldn't be necessary to bother us any more for a while,—that there'd been some additional information come in on the case: so I suppose that's what it was; for it says here the telegram was received at Police Headquarters at six forty-five.

CRAIG (*moving with a wearied air towards the portières*). What does it matter now, Harriet?

MRS. CRAIG. It doesn't matter *now,* but it would have mattered—only that I kept my head last night, and didn't allow you to telephone, and make a show of us all. (*He laughs bitterly.*) You can laugh, as much as you like; but you can thank me that your name isn't in every paper in the city this morning.

(*She resumes her reading.*)

CRAIG. Oh, I can thank you for more than that, Harriet.

MRS. CRAIG. Well, you can thank me for that, anyway.

CRAIG. I can thank you for having given me a new name last night—that fits me so perfectly that I've decided to continue its use. You called me a romantic fool.

MRS. CRAIG. Fergus must have known about this man that Adelaide's been going around with; for it says here he'd mentioned him once before in a letter to his brother.

(MRS. HAROLD *appears between the portières.*)

MRS. HAROLD. The coffee's ready, Mr.

Craig.

CRAIG (*turning quietly towards the portières*). All right, Mrs. Harold.

(*She withdraws, and he follows her.* MRS. CRAIG *looks up suddenly and crosses towards him.*)

MRS. CRAIG. Listen, Walter, come here for a minute.

(*He turns.*)

CRAIG. What?

MRS. CRAIG. Listen. (*She glances over his shoulder after* MRS. HAROLD, *then lowers her voice.*) Billy Birkmire 'ull very likely want you to go out there with him to Fergus' funeral; but don't you do it. And you'd better tell him not to go around there either; for one of you is apt to say something. And if that butler out there sees *you,* he might recognize you. And there's no use starting anything now, when the thing's all over.

(*He looks at her steadily.*)

CRAIG. Is that all you wanted to tell me?

MRS. CRAIG. Well, it's the thing to do, isn't it? It certainly wouldn't help matters *now* to say anything, would it? What are you smiling at?

CRAIG. At your wanting to help matters.

MRS. CRAIG. So I *have* wanted to help them.

CRAIG. Since when?

MRS. CRAIG (*turning away to the center table*). Well, don't let's go into all that again. I've been wanting to help *you* principally, but you don't seem to have sense enough to appreciate it.

CRAIG. Is that all you want me for?

MRS. CRAIG (*turning to him again*). No, it isn't all I want you for. I want to know about that ornament there that was broken here last night.

CRAIG. What about it?

MRS. CRAIG. I don't know *what* about it; that's the reason I'm asking you. Mrs. Harold tells me here this morning that you told her last night that you'd broken it.

CRAIG. So I did.

MRS. CRAIG. Well, you ought to be proud of yourself.

CRAIG. I was for a moment.

MRS. CRAIG. What were you doing—leaning against the mantelpiece again as usual?

CRAIG. No, it wasn't an accident; I did it deliberately.

MRS. CRAIG. What do you mean, you did it deliberately?

CRAIG. I mean that I smashed it purposely.

MRS. CRAIG. What for?

CRAIG. I became suddenly heroic.

MRS. CRAIG. I don't believe you.

CRAIG (*turning away*). Very well, that's that.

MRS. CRAIG. Why would you deliberately break a beautiful, expensive ornament like that?

CRAIG (*turning back*). I didn't break it.

MRS. CRAIG. Well, you said you did.

CRAIG (*bitterly*). I said I smashed it—into a thousand little pieces, right here on these bricks here. And then I smoked one cigarette after another, till I had your sanctum sanctorum here absolutely littered with ashes and cigarette butts. I was positively a hell of a fellow around here for about an hour last night; you should have seen me.

MRS. CRAIG. What did you do, go out of your mind or something?

CRAIG. No, I was particularly clear in my mind, strange to say. You made a remark here last night, Harriet, that completely illuminated me; and illuminated you. And suddenly I saw—for the first time—everything—just as one sees an entire landscape at midnight in a flash of lightning. But, unfortunately, the lightning struck my house—and knocked it down; and I sat here all night wondering how I might build it up again.

MRS. CRAIG. What remark are you talking about?

CRAIG. You said that a woman might lose her husband but not her home, if she knew how to secure it.

MRS. CRAIG. Well, hasn't many a woman lost her husband?

CRAIG. And many a man has lost his life too, Harriet, because his wife has never made a sufficiently illuminating remark. But you did make it. And that other remark—when you said there were ways of getting rid of people without driving them away from the house. (*He smiles bitterly.*) I saw your entire plan of life, Harriet, and its relationship to me. And my instinct of self-preservation suggested the need of immediate action—the inauguration of a new régime here: so I smashed the little ornament there—as a kind of opening gun. And I was going to smash all the other little ornaments—and Gods you had set up in the temple here, and been worshipping before me. I was going to put my house in order, including my wife; and rule it with a rod of iron. (MRS. CRAIG *turns away, faintly amused.*) I don't wonder that amuses you; it amused me; particularly when I suddenly remembered the truth of what you called me last night; and in view of that, the absurdity of my trying to sustain such a rôle indefinitely. It made me laugh— But I'm rather sorry you couldn't have seen me, anyway; I think you would at least have appreciated the sincerity of my *attempt* to continue here as your husband.

(*He turns slowly and moves towards the portières.*)

MRS. CRAIG. What do you mean, your attempt to continue here as my husband?

CRAIG. The rôle is not *for* me, Harriet; I can only play a romantic part.

(*She turns her head quietly and looks at him; and he holds her eye for a second, then goes out through the portières; and she stands looking after him. Then she moves slowly to the portières and stands, thinking. The doorbell rings, but evidently she doesn't hear it. She moves forward slowly, still thinking narrowly.* MRS. HAROLD *comes through the portières hurriedly.*)

MRS. CRAIG. There's some one at the door, Mrs. Harold.

(*The doorbell rings again.*)

MRS. HAROLD (*hurrying across to answer the door*). I guess maybe it's the man for Miss Austen's things.

MRS. CRAIG. Is Miss Austen leaving already?

MRS. HAROLD (*stopping near the door*). I think so; she said last night she was going first thing in the morning.

MRS. CRAIG. Is she up?

MRS. HAROLD. Yes, Ma'm, she asked me to call her at seven.

(*She goes out, and* MRS. CRAIG *crosses after her.*)

MRS. CRAIG. Well, if that's the man for her things, Mrs. Harold, have him go around to the side door and bring her things down the back stairway; I don't want him dragging trunks down these front stairs.

(*She steps to the bay window at the left and looks out at the expressman.*)

EXPRESSMAN (*at the front door*). Trunks ready?

MRS. HAROLD. Yes, they're ready. Would you mind going around to the side door; you can bring them down the back way.

EXPRESSMAN. Around this way?

MRS. HAROLD. Yes, up the steps; I'll open it for you.

(*The screen door slams, and she hurries in again, crossing towards the portières.*)

MRS. CRAIG. Are Miss Austen's things ready, Mrs. Harold?

MRS. HAROLD. Yes, Ma'm, I helped her pack last night.

MRS. CRAIG. Did she say where she was going?

MRS. HAROLD (*stopping*). Yes, Ma'm; she sez she's going to the Ritz-Carlton Hotel now, but after that she sez she's going to travel. (*Continuing to the portières.*) I must open the door for that man.

(*She goes out, and* MRS. CRAIG *stands looking after her, thinking. She moves across towards the portières and stops again, looking out through the portières.* ETHEL *hurries down the stairs, with her hat and coat on.*)

MRS. CRAIG. Ethel, dear child, what are you doing up so early?

ETHEL. I haven't been asleep all night. I've been waiting to hear some one else up.

MRS. CRAIG. You're not ill, are you, dear?

ETHEL. No, but I must go home immediately, Aunt Harriet; I'm too troubled in my mind to stay here any longer.

MRS. CRAIG. But you can't go immediately, dear.

ETHEL. I must go, Aunt Harriet.

MRS. CRAIG. But there's no train, dear, until the nine-seventeen.

ETHEL. Well, it's nearly that now, isn't it?

(MRS. CRAIG *looks at her watch.*)

MRS. CRAIG. It isn't a quarter of nine yet.

ETHEL. Well, it'll take that time to get to the station, won't it?

MRS. CRAIG. It doesn't take ten minutes, dear, in a taxicab; and I can have one here in five minutes.

ETHEL (*putting her bag on the table and crossing down to the mirror*). Well, will you call one, please?

MRS. CRAIG (*moving after her*). Certainly, dear; but there's no use calling it already, you'd only have to wait around the station there.

ETHEL. I'm so worried, Aunt Harriet.

MRS. CRAIG. I know, dear child; but I'm sure you're upsetting yourself unnecessarily; we certainly would have heard something if anything had happened.

ETHEL (*turning to* MRS. CRAIG). I really should call Mr. Fredericks on the long distance, Aunt Harriet; he'll be wondering what on earth is the matter. Because I rushed away as soon as ever I got Dr. Wood's wire, and simply left a note that Mother was very ill. And he's probably called me up at home by this time and found that I'm down here; and he won't know what to think of it.

MRS. CRAIG. Well, I wouldn't worry myself too much about what he'll think, dear.

ETHEL. But he'll think it's funny that I should be down here if Mother's so ill. (*There is a sound upstairs of a trunk being moved.*)

MRS. CRAIG (*dashing towards the stairs and up on to the landing*). He probably hasn't given it a thought.

ETHEL (*moving across above the table and looking out the bay window*). Oh, don't say that, Aunt Harriet, I know he has.

(MRS. CRAIG *claps her hands briskly, to attract the expressman's attention.*)

MRS. CRAIG. Please be careful of that floor there, Mr. Expressman, will you?

EXPRESSMAN. This baby got away from me. I thought it was lighter than it is.

MRS. CRAIG. Well, please try to keep it away from that wall there; I don't want that wall all scratched up; I only had it painted in April. (*There is a sound of the trunk being dragged along the hallway to the back stairs, and then a heavy thud.* MRS. CRAIG *closes her eyes in an agony of suffering and leans heavily upon the banister to keep from fainting. Then she turns and comes down into the room again.*) Mr. Craig's aunt is sending some luggage away to be mended; and those expressmen are so careless they don't care if they tear down the house.

ETHEL. I haven't had a chance to speak to Miss Austen yet.

MRS. CRAIG. I suppose she's getting dressed.

ETHEL. I haven't seen Uncle Walter yet, either.

MRS. CRAIG. He's out there having some coffee, I believe. Don't you want to come out and have some too, dear?

ETHEL. I don't think I could touch a thing, Aunt Harriet.

MRS. CRAIG. You could take a sip of coffee.

ETHEL. I don't want Uncle Walter to see me looking so terrible.

MRS. CRAIG. What does it matter, darling; he understands the circumstances. And you really shouldn't start on that trip back home without something. And when you do go back, Ethel, I want you to consider seriously what I've been saying to you about Mr. Fredericks. You're not married to him yet; and if there's anything to be done, it's now that it must be done. You can't come back and undo a thing like marriage.

ETHEL. Oh, I don't know what to do, Aunt Harriet.

MRS. CRAIG. Well, there's no hurry about doing anything just now. And don't let him hurry you. Just think it over—for his sake as well as for your own. You don't want to be a burden to him, do you?

ETHEL. Certainly not.

MRS. CRAIG. Well, what else would you be to him, dear—unless you used your own money? And that isn't conducive to respect for a man. And, in any case, you'd find in time that he'd come to resent your independence of him.

MISS AUSTEN (*at the head of the stairs*). Yes, I have it here in my bag, Mrs. Harold.

MRS. CRAIG (*drawing* ETHEL *towards the portières*). So just think it over. And come on out to the breakfast room and let me get you something.

(*They go out through the portières.* MISS AUSTEN *comes down the stairs, dressed for the street. She glances through the portières and picks up the telephone.*)

MISS AUSTEN (*into the telephone*). Will you give me Market, three, three, three, three, please? Please. (MRS. HAROLD *comes down the stairs, dressed for the street, and carrying a suit case and a smaller bag.*) I think you might as well take those right out on to the porch, Mrs. Harold.

MRS. HAROLD (*going out*). Yes, Ma'm.

MISS AUSTEN. Have them ready when the cab comes. (*Into the telephone.*) Hello.—Will you please send a taxicab to six hundred and eighty Belmont Manor, right away, please? Yes. (*She sets the telephone down and* MRS. HAROLD *comes in.*) It'll be here in a few minutes, Mrs. Harold. Are you all ready?

MRS. HAROLD. Yes, Ma'm, I'm ready.

MISS AUSTEN. Hadn't you better speak to Mrs. Craig about your keys, Mrs. Harold?

MRS. HAROLD. I left them with yours up on her dressing table.

MISS AUSTEN. I think you'd better tell her, Mrs. Harold.

MRS. HAROLD. Do you want me to tell them *you're* going?

MISS AUSTEN (*going towards the door*). No, it isn't necessary, Mrs. Harold; I'll write to Mr. Craig. But, I think you'd better tell them that *you're* going.

MRS. HAROLD. I did tell Mr. Craig I was going; I told him this morning.

MISS AUSTEN. Well, I think you'd better tell Mrs. Craig, also.

MRS. HAROLD. Yes, Ma'm.

MISS AUSTEN. There might be something she'd want to ask you.

MRS. HAROLD. All right, I'll tell her.

MISS AUSTEN. I'll sit here on the porch till the taxi comes.

(*She goes out, and* MRS. HAROLD *goes to the mirror and straightens her funny hat.*)

MRS. CRAIG (*coming through the adjoining room*). Are you in there, Mrs. Harold? (MRS. HAROLD *moves up to the foot of the stairs and stands facing the portières.* MRS. CRAIG *comes in.*) Oh, I've been looking for you out there, Mrs. Harold; I wanted you to give my niece a little breakfast.

MRS. HAROLD. I've left everything ready out there, Mrs. Craig.

MRS. CRAIG. Where are you going, Mrs. Harold?

MRS. HAROLD. Why, I'm going with Miss Austen, Mrs. Craig.

MRS. CRAIG. Indeed?

MRS. HAROLD. She was tellin' me last night she was goin' to leave here, and I said I thought I'd be leavin' pretty soon myself; so she said if I was goin' anyway soon, she'd like very much to have me go with her.

MRS. CRAIG. And where are you going with her?

MRS. HAROLD. Why, we are goin' to the Ritz-Carlton first, and after that she sez she's goin' to travel for a few years.

MRS. CRAIG. Well, that ought to be a very good experience for you.

MRS. HAROLD. Yes, I've never been many places outside of here and Long Branch, and I thought I'd better take the chance while I had it.

MRS. CRAIG. And do you think it's very considerate of you, Mrs. Harold, to walk away this way without giving me any notice?

MRS. HAROLD. You didn't give Mazie much notice last night, Mrs. Craig.

MRS. CRAIG. Mazie didn't deserve any notice; she was a very disobedient girl. She absolutely refused to do what I told her.

MRS. HAROLD. Well, I haven't always done exactly what you told me to do, either, Mrs. Craig,—so maybe I deserve to go as well as Mazie.

MRS. CRAIG. Well, of course, you can suit yourself about going, Mrs. Harold, but you understand I shall have to tell Miss Hewlitt about your leaving without notice.

MRS. HAROLD. Miss Hewlitt knows all about my leaving, Mrs. Craig; she's surprised that I didn't leave long ago, to tell you the truth.

MRS. CRAIG. And why didn't you leave?

MRS. HAROLD. Well—there were no children—and it's near church. But Miss Hewlitt told me when I came here that if I stayed a month I'd be the first out of seven that did.

MRS. CRAIG. Miss Hewlitt has sent some very unsatisfactory women here.

MRS. HAROLD. A lot of them have worked in some pretty fine places.

MRS. CRAIG (*turning away, and moving down to the mirror*). Well, of course, that depends upon what a person's idea of a fine place is. And I suppose the next *batch* she sends me won't be any more satisfactory than the rest.

MRS. HAROLD. I think you're very foolish to have her send any more, Mrs. Craig, if you ask me.

MRS. CRAIG. One person can't do everything.

MRS. HAROLD. I've heard you say yourself more than once that you had to do over again everything that any woman that ever worked for you did,—so why not save the money?

(MRS. CRAIG *turns from the mirror and comes towards her.*)

MRS. CRAIG What about the keys?

MRS. HAROLD. I left them all on your dressin' table upstairs; and Miss Austen's, too.

MRS. CRAIG. Wasn't there anything else to be left?

MRS. HAROLD. Yes, Ma'm, I left the

money that I had over with the week's list in an envelope with the keys.

MRS. CRAIG (*turning to the portières*). All right.—I hope you enjoy your world tour.

MRS. HAROLD (*going towards the front door*). It'll be a change, anyway.

(MRS. CRAIG *turns at the portières.*)

MRS. CRAIG. And I hope when you come back, you'll be able to find a place that'll be as easy as this one has been.

MRS. HAROLD (*stopping at the door and turning*). Don't worry about me, Mrs. Craig; nobody belongin' to me ever died in the poorhouse.

(*She goes out on to the porch, and* MRS. CRAIG *looks after her stonily. The front doorbell rings incisively, and* MRS. CRAIG *steps forward at the right and looks keenly towards the front door.*)

FREDERICKS (*at the front door*). How do you do?

MRS. HAROLD. How do you do?

FREDERICKS. I should like to see Miss Landreth, if I could. My name is Fredericks.

(MRS. CRAIG *makes a rapid movement of consternation, then looks at the portières.* ETHEL *comes through the portières.*)

ETHEL AND MRS. HAROLD (*speaking together*).

ETHEL. I think I'd better get my things, Aunt Harriet; it must be nearly nine o'clock.

MRS. HAROLD. Oh, come in, please. I think Miss Landreth is just having her breakfast.

(*The screen door slams.*)

ETHEL AND FREDERICKS (*speaking together*).

ETHEL. Would you mind telephoning for a taxicab?

FREDERICKS. I suppose I am a bit early.

(ETHEL *hears his voice and stops at the foot of the stairs.* MRS. CRAIG *glides out through the portières.* MRS. HAROLD *comes in at the front door.*)

MRS. HAROLD. Oh, I was just comin' to call you, Miss Landreth; there's a Mr. Fredericks here to see you.

(*He comes in.*)

FREDERICKS. Hello, Ethel.

(MRS. HAROLD *passes to the door, back of him, and goes out again.*)

ETHEL. Gene, there isn't anything happened to Mother?

FREDERICKS. Not a thing in the world, dear, that I know of.

ETHEL. You're sure?

FREDERICKS. 'Pon my word, Ethel. I haven't been to your house.

ETHEL. Well, why did you come away down here, then, at this hour of the morning?

FREDERICKS (*taking a step to her*). I wanted to see *you.* (*She begins to cry, and he takes her in his arms.*) I thought maybe you were ill or something. Don't cry, darling; I give you my word there isn't a thing wrong at home. I simply telephoned you as soon as I got your note, and they told me you'd left for here: so then I called you on the long distance. But I couldn't get any satisfaction on the long distance, and I didn't know what to think. So I just jumped on the night train and got in here at eight-twenty.

ETHEL (*straightening up and touching her hair*). I'm going back right away, Gene; there's a train at nine-seventeen from the station down town.

FREDERICKS. I'll go back with you.

ETHEL. I don't know why I ever came away in the first place.

FREDERICKS (*guiding her to the chair at the right of the piano*). Sit down here for a minute, dear; you look terribly pale. (*He puts his hat on the piano.*)

ETHEL. I haven't closed my eyes since I've been here, I've been so worried.

FREDERICKS. I've been worried about *you,* too, ever since I got your note.

ETHEL. And then I told Aunt Harriet about our engagement, and that upset me more than ever.

FREDERICKS. Why?

ETHEL. Oh, she didn't seem to approve of it exactly.

FREDERICKS. Why not?

ETHEL (*rising*). Oh, for several reasons, Gene,—I'll tell you on the train.

(*She starts for the foot of the stairs.*)

FREDERICKS (*taking her hand as she passes him*). I wish you'd tell me now, Ethel.

ETHEL (*turning to him*). There isn't time, dear.

FREDERICKS. But you make me uneasy.

ETHEL. It's nothing, Gene, particularly. She simply said she thought perhaps I hadn't considered the thing sufficiently.

FREDERICKS. What is there to consider, darling, in a thing of this kind—except that we love each other.

ETHEL. But she said a thing like marriage should be considered more practically.

FREDERICKS. I don't accept that argument, Ethel; I've seen too many carefully reasoned marriages turn out badly. It's simply a chance that one has to take, more or less. And I have a good way of getting along.

ETHEL. As a single man, yes.

FREDERICKS. And even as a married man.

ETHEL. You don't know that yet, Gene, whether you have or not.

FREDERICKS. But other fellows marry, darling, and get along, on a great deal less salary than I'm getting.

ETHEL. I know that, Gene; but, as Aunt Harriet says, their wives are not living the way I've been accustomed to living. Not that I'd mind that in the least, dear; only I wouldn't want you to feel that I was making any sacrifices. And she says you might feel that in your present circumstances.

FREDERICKS. But haven't you any faith in my ability to improve those circumstances?

ETHEL. Of course; but I wouldn't want to be a burden to you in the meantime.

FREDERICKS. But you're the kind of burden I need, Ethel. You know I've had three promotions since I've known you.

ETHEL. Yes, I know you have.

FREDERICKS. Well, I attribute it to nothing but the incentive that the thought of marrying you has given me. I've worked like a dog these past two years, with just that in mind; and if it were removed,—well, I just don't think beyond that, that's all.

(*He turns away to the left a few steps and stands looking straight out. She crosses and lays her hand on his arm.*)

ETHEL. I hadn't thought of not marrying you, Gene; I was just thinking whether or not it would be wise to postpone it.

FREDERICKS (*turning to her*). It *wouldn't* be wise, Ethel; it isn't a good thing to postpone a thing like marriage —so many things can happen. (*He suddenly takes her in his arms.*) And I don't want anything to happen.

ETHEL. What else have I got, Gene, if anything happened to Mother?

(*She buries her face in his shoulder and cries hard.*)

FREDERICKS. Nothing's going to happen to her, sweetheart. And if it did, you wouldn't feel any worse than I'd feel if anything happened to this.

(*She continues to cry for a second, then straightens up and presses her handkerchief to her eyes.*)

ETHEL. We'd better go, Gene, it must be nearly nine o'clock.

(*She starts across below the table towards the mirror, and* FREDERICKS *starts across above the table towards the telephone.* CRAIG *comes through the portières.*)

FREDERICKS. I'd better call a taxi, hadn't I?

ETHEL. Oh, Uncle Walter,—this is Mr. Fredericks.

(FREDERICKS *continues over to shake hands with* CRAIG, *and* ETHEL *moves up to* FREDERICKS' *left.*)

CRAIG (*shaking hands*). I'm glad to meet you, Mr. Fredericks.

FREDERICKS. How do you do, Mr. Craig?

ETHEL. Mr. Fredericks is the young man I'm engaged to be married to.

CRAIG. Well, I *am* glad to meet you.

FREDERICKS. Pretty lucky fellow, don't you think, Mr. Craig?

CRAIG. I'd say you were. And is it all set?

FREDERICKS. I hope so; although Ethel seems to feel a little nervous about it.

CRAIG. What are you nervous about, Ethel?

ETHEL. I'm not nervous—it isn't that. But I was telling Gene that I'd been discussing it with Aunt Harriet, and she seemed to think that probably I hadn't considered it enough.

(FREDERICKS *looks at* CRAIG.)

CRAIG. What did she want you to consider?

ETHEL. Well, she said on account of my age she didn't think I appreciated the practical side of marriage enough.

CRAIG. That's the one side of marriage that should not be appreciated too much, Ethel; it's a lack of faith in each other.

FREDERICKS. That's what I tell Ethel.

CRAIG. The only thing I think you need to consider really seriously—is whether or not you are both absolutely honest with each other. (FREDERICKS *looks at* ETHEL, *and* CRAIG *crosses below them towards the stairs.*) It doesn't seem to me that there's very much else to worry about.

ETHEL. We're going back on that nine-seventeen, Uncle Walter; do you know the number of the taxicab company?

CRAIG (*starting up the stairs*). You won't need a taxi, I'm going right down past the station.

ETHEL. Are you going now?

CRAIG. Right away, yes. I'll get my hat. You have plenty of time; I can get you down there in less than ten minutes.

ETHEL. Uncle Walter, will you bring my satchel down when you're coming?

CRAIG. Yes, I'll get it.

ETHEL. It's on the chair there, right inside my door. (*Picking up her bag from the table and crossing down to the mirror to fix herself.*) We won't have to call a taxi.

(FREDERICKS *glances out through the portières, then comes forward, lowering his voice.*)

FREDERICKS. Did your aunt tell you I called you last night?

(ETHEL *turns and looks at him.*)

ETHEL. On the long distance, you mean?

FREDERICKS. Yes, I called you from Northampton as soon as I got your note. I called you at home first, of course, and they gave me this address.

ETHEL. And you called here?

FREDERICKS. Yes, about seven o'clock. Didn't she tell you?

ETHEL No, she didn't, Gene.

FREDERICKS. I talked to her. She said you were asleep.

ETHEL. I couldn't have been asleep, Gene.

FREDERICKS. I asked her to call you to the telephone, but she didn't seem to want to do it. She said you'd just gotten in and you were tired out.

ETHEL. Well, I *was* tired, but she could have called me; she might have known I'd want to talk to you. Because I didn't know what you'd think of my being down here, after leaving word that I was going home.

FREDERICKS. Have you seen her this morning?

ETHEL. Yes, but she didn't say anything about it. And I was talking to her here this morning about you, too. I was saying that I ought to call *you* on the long distance, that you'd be wondering what was the matter.

CRAIG (*hurrying down the stairs with* ETHEL'S *satchel*). I'll run over and get the car.

FREDERICKS. Can I take that, Mr. Craig?

CRAIG. I'll leave it out here on the porch. I'll be back in two minutes. You have lots of time.

FREDERICKS (*going to the piano for his hat*). Are you ready, Ethel?

ETHEL. Yes, I'm ready, Gene. I'd better say good-by to Aunt Harriet.

FREDERICKS. Will I wait for you outside?

ETHEL. Don't you want to meet her, Gene?

FREDERICKS. I don't think she wants to meet me, Ethel.

ETHEL. Why not?

FREDERICKS. After what you've been telling me.

ETHEL. Oh, that's nothing, Gene.

FREDERICKS. She hung up on me last night.

ETHEL. Yes, I want to ask her about that call.

FREDERICKS (*going out*). I think I'd better wait for you outside.

(ETHEL *glances through the portières, then comes forward thoughtfully at the right. There is a slight pause. Then* MRS. CRAIG *glides through the portières and across to the bay window to look out.* ETHEL *watches her narrowly, then moves to the right end of the center table.*)

ETHEL. I'm just going, Aunt Harriet.

(MRS. CRAIG *turns, slightly startled.*)

MRS. CRAIG. Oh, I thought you'd gone. (*She comes back towards* ETHEL.) I didn't hear anybody in here, and I was wondering if you'd gone without telling me.

ETHEL. No, I'm just going.

MRS. CRAIG. Where are Mr. Craig and Mr. Fredericks?

ETHEL. Mr. Fredericks is there on the porch. (MRS. CRAIG *turns to the front door and glances out.*) Uncle Walter's gone over to get the car.

MRS. CRAIG. Oh, he's going to drive you in.

ETHEL. Yes.

MRS. CRAIG. Well, that'll be fine,—you won't have to bother calling a taxi. (*Coming forward to* ETHEL *again.*) Did Mr. Fredericks have any word about your mother?

ETHEL. No, he hadn't been home.

MRS. CRAIG. Why don't you call him in, Ethel; I should like to meet him.

ETHEL. He thought probably you wouldn't care to meet him.

MRS. CRAIG. Why, how absurd. Why not?

ETHEL. I was telling him about what you said last night, when I told you I was going to marry him.

MRS. CRAIG. Well, my dear child, I was simply talking in a general way. My remarks weren't directed against Mr. Fredericks particularly. I'm sure he'd appreciate the logic of what I said himself.

ETHEL. He doesn't, Aunt Harriet; I told him what you said, and he takes quite the opposite view.

MRS. CRAIG. Well, of course, he has considerable to gain by the transaction, Ethel, you must remember that.

ETHEL. Well, Uncle Walter has nothing to gain by it, and he agrees with him.

MRS. CRAIG. Well, you remember I told you last night that Mr. Craig was extremely romantic.

ETHEL (*becoming very stony*). Why didn't you call me last night, Aunt Harriet, when Mr. Fredericks telephoned?

MRS. CRAIG. Because you were asleep, dear.

ETHEL. I couldn't have been asleep. I haven't closed my eyes since I've been here.

MRS. CRAIG. Well, I thought you were asleep, Ethel; I sent Mazie up to your room and she said your door was closed.

ETHEL. Well, she could have rapped.

MRS. CRAIG. Well, what was the sense of upsetting you, dear?

ETHEL. Because it was important to me.

MRS. CRAIG. I asked him if it was important, and if there was any message he wanted to leave, and he said no.

ETHEL. And you hung up on him.

MRS. CRAIG. Because he insisted upon talking to you; and you were not in any condition to be talked to.

(*She turns and moves towards the bay window.*)

ETHEL. Why didn't you tell me this morning that he'd called—when I said I should call him?

MRS. CRAIG (*turning coldly*). Now, please, Ethel dear—I shan't answer any more questions about Mr. Fredericks. (*She goes to the bay window to look out.*) I've had quite enough to worry me this morning without thinking about Mr. Fredericks. He's going back with you, I suppose?

ETHEL (*crossing up to the front door*). Yes.

MRS. CRAIG (*turning to her*). Well, I'm glad you won't have to make the trip alone. Good-by, dear. (*She kisses her.*) I hope you'll let me know right away how you find your mother.

ETHEL (*holding her hand*). Aunt Harriet—

MRS. CRAIG. What, dear?

ETHEL (*after a pause, and holding her eye*). Aunt Harriet, is Uncle Walter *leaving* you?

MRS. CRAIG. Why, what on earth ever put that into your head, Ethel?

ETHEL. Something he was saying when I came to the head of the stairs to come down this morning.

MRS. CRAIG. And what was he saying?

ETHEL. Something about your having made a remark that made it impossible for him to continue here as your husband.

MRS. CRAIG. I'm sure I haven't the faintest idea what you're talking about, Ethel.

ETHEL. And then a while ago here, when I told him I was going to be married to Mr. Fredericks, he said the only thing we needed to consider seriously was whether or not we were absolutely honest with each other. And I was wondering if he'd found out.

MRS. CRAIG. Found out what?

ETHEL. That that you told me last night,—when I said I didn't think it was honest.

(*There is a movement on the front porch. The screen door slams, and* MRS. CRAIG *turns away quickly and looks out the bay window.*)

CRAIG (*outside*). All set?

FREDERICKS (*outside*). All set. Ethel's inside.

ETHEL (*going out*). Good-by, Aunt Harriet.

MRS. CRAIG (*turning and following her to the door*). Good-by, dear.

ETHEL. I'll write you as soon as I get home.

MRS. CRAIG. Do, dear; let me know how your mother is.

ETHEL. Yes, I shall.

(*The screen door slams.*)

CRAIG. Ready, Ethel?

ETHEL. Yes, I'm coming, Uncle Walter.

(MRS. CRAIG *turns nervously and moves across and down to the mantelpiece.*)

CRAIG. Your satchel's in the car. I'll be with you in a minute.

(*He comes in, taking a little leather key

case from his pocket, and crosses to the portières.)

MRS. CRAIG. Are you going to the office now?

CRAIG. Yes, it's nearly nine o'clock.

(He goes through the portières, and MRS. CRAIG *moves up to the portières.)*

MRS. CRAIG. Mrs. Harold says you haven't been in bed all night; you won't feel much like sitting at a desk all day.

CRAIG *(from the other room)*. I'll have plenty of time to rest after a bit.

*(*MRS. CRAIG'S *eyes narrow, in an attempt to fathom this remark. She comes forward again at the right, slowly and thoughtfully.* CRAIG *enters, fastening the little key case, and crosses towards the front door, picking up his hat from the table as he passes.)*

MRS. CRAIG. Did you find what you were looking for?

CRAIG. I wasn't looking for anything—I was just leaving the key to your car and the garage, with some other things I've left there for you. *(He turns at the door.)* If you should want me for anything during the next week or two, Harriet, I'll be at the Ritz.

(She turns suddenly and makes a rapid movement to the center table.)

MRS. CRAIG. Now, listen to me, Walter Craig, you're surely not serious about leaving this house.

CRAIG. Why, I should think that decision would please you very much.

MRS. CRAIG. Well, it doesn't please me at all; it's absolutely ridiculous.

CRAIG. But it's so absolutely practical.

MRS. CRAIG. Oh, don't try to be funny.

CRAIG. And you've been deploring my lack of practicality so long.

MRS. CRAIG. I'd like to know what's practical about a man walking out and leaving his wife and his home.

CRAIG. I have no wife to leave,—for you neither loved nor honored me.

MRS. CRAIG. Well, you married me, whether I did or not.

CRAIG. I never saw you before in my life, Harriet—until last night.

MRS. CRAIG. You married me, didn't you?

CRAIG. And you married a house; and if it's agreeable to you, I'll see that you have it; and that you can go on having it, just as though I were here.

MRS. CRAIG *(turning away towards the mantelpiece)*. You'll be here; unless I'm very much mistaken.

CRAIG. You don't know your man, Harriet.

MRS. CRAIG. I know him well enough for that, anyway.

CRAIG. Oh, you knew me pretty well, I'll grant you that; particularly when you said my mind worked very slowly.

MRS. CRAIG. It's working pretty slowly now, when you don't appreciate the absurdity of a move of this kind.

CRAIG. But you failed to reckon with the thoroughness of my mind, Harriet, when it *does* work. And it appreciates this situation so thoroughly that it has no illusions about the impossibility of my continuance here.

MRS. CRAIG. What is there so impossible about it?

CRAIG. We've shown our hands, Harriet, and the game is up.

MRS. CRAIG. What did I do last night that was so terrible?

CRAIG. You simply showed your hand, that was all.

MRS. CRAIG. I simply kept you from making a fool of yourself; that was all I did.

CRAIG. But you also showed me how I could keep from making a fool of myself in the future.

MRS. CRAIG. Well, you're certainly not beginning very auspiciously, I can tell you that.

CRAIG. But I shall be at least a self-respecting fool; and that's something I could never be if I stayed here. There's something in a man, Harriet, that I suppose is his essential manhood; and you insulted that last night. And I should be too embarrassed here, under your eye, knowing that you had no respect for that manhood. I should remember my lover's ardors and enthusiasms for our future; and you bearing with me contemptuously, for the sake of *your* future. I couldn't stand it.

MRS. CRAIG. You're not telling the truth; I always respected you; and I never had anything but respect for your plans, either.

CRAIG. Don't try to soften the blow, Harriet; I assure you it isn't necessary.

(He turns towards the door, and she makes a move towards him.)

MRS. CRAIG. Where are you going when you leave here?

(He turns and looks at her.)

CRAIG. That 'ud be rather interesting to know, Harriet—where a lot like me are going.—Out of fashion, possibly.

MRS. CRAIG. Well, what about your things?—Aren't you going to take anything with you?

CRAIG. You may send them to me if you like.

MRS. CRAIG (*turning away*). Well, I won't send them to you; for you'll very likely be back again within a week.

CRAIG. Perhaps it will be just as well if you don't send them to me, Harriet,—for I'm rather sentimental about things; and I might look back, and be turned into a romantic fool.

MRS. CRAIG. Oh, I suppose you'll never forgive me for calling you that.

CRAIG. No, there isn't a thing in the world I don't forgive you for, Harriet; that's the reason it won't be necessary for me to come back here any more; there's nothing to adjust. I guess possibly I'm just a bit of an old-fashioned man—I must be trusted—and you never trusted me.

MRS. CRAIG. I wouldn't trust any man after what I've seen.

CRAIG. I don't blame you. But I wonder that, with all your wisdom, it never occurred to you that one cannot play a dishonest game indefinitely.

MRS. CRAIG. I haven't played any dishonest game.

CRAIG. Possibly not, according to your standards; but I think you have. And I think you know you have. And that's the rock that you and I are splitting on, Harriet. If this affair at Passmores' hadn't revealed you, something else would: so my going may as well be to-day as to-morrow. Good-by, Harriet.

(*He goes out; she leans on the table. The screen door slams. She moves over to the bay window and watches him get into the automobile: then she comes forward to the window at the right and watches him down the street. After he has passed beyond her vision, her gaze wanders into the room again, and she becomes conscious of two tiny pieces of the broken ornament near the mantelpiece. She stoops and picks them up, flicking away with her foot any other invisible particles that may be about. Then she looks at the two remaining ornaments on the mantelpiece and tries to come to some conclusion about their arrangement. She places them equi-distant from each other and the ends of the mantelpiece, and stands off to observe the effect. The front doorbell rings sharply. She turns and crosses to answer it.*)

BOY'S VOICE (*at the front door*). Telegram for Mrs. Walter Craig.

(*She signs for the telegram, the screen door slams and she comes in, opening the telegram. She reads the telegram, looks straight ahead for a second, thinking—looks at the wire again, and bursts into tears—sinking into the chair at the right of the piano. She cries hard for a moment, then smooths the telegram out and reads it again.* MRS. FRAZIER *appears in the door, dressed in gray, and carrying an armload of white roses. She comes forward inquiringly.*)

MRS. FRAZIER. Good morning, Mrs. Craig. (MRS. CRAIG *doesn't hear her.*) Good morning. (MRS. CRAIG *looks at her, startled, gets up nervously and moves across to the front of the center table, touching her eyes and her hair.*) I do hope you'll pardon my walking in without ringing, but I thought Miss Austen 'ud be on the front porch, and I wanted to bring her these roses. (*She hands* MRS. CRAIG *the roses.*) I was telling her yesterday I'd bring her over some; she was saying she admired white roses so much; and I have so many of them over there just now.

MRS. CRAIG. I haven't seen her yet this morning.

MRS. FRAZIER (*preparing to go*). Well, if you'll just tell her I left them.

MRS. CRAIG. Yes, I shall; thanks ever so much.

MRS. FRAZIER (*turning back*). Oh, have you had any word about your sister this morning, Mrs. Craig? Miss Austen was telling me yesterday she was quite ill.

MRS. CRAIG (*starting to cry again*). She died this morning at six o'clock.

MRS. FRAZIER. Oh, dear me, how sad.

MRS. CRAIG. I just had this wire.

MRS. FRAZIER. Dear, dear, dear, isn't that too bad!

MRS. CRAIG. I had no idea she was so ill or I should never have come back.

MRS. FRAZIER. Dear, dear, dear, I'm so sorry. I shouldn't have bothered you at all.

MRS. CRAIG. That's quite all right.

MRS. FRAZIER. I'm sure you have my sympathy.

MRS. CRAIG. Thank you.

MRS. FRAZIER. I do hope you'll let me know, Mrs. Craig, if there's any way I can be of any service to you.

MRS. CRAIG. Thank you very much; I don't think there's anything anybody can do.

MRS. FRAZIER. I suppose you'll have to go right back up there again, won't you?

MRS. CRAIG. I don't know whether I shall be able to or not, to tell you the truth, Mrs. Frazier; it's been such a strain.

MRS. FRAZIER. Yes, those long illnesses are dreadful. But I hope you won't hesitate to let me know if there's anything I can do.

MRS. CRAIG. That's very kind of you. I'll give these roses to Miss Austen when I see her.

MRS. FRAZIER. If you will, please. (*She starts for the door.*) I'm terribly sorry. I'll run over again.

(*She goes out; and* MRS. CRAIG *stands very still until she hears the screen door close. Then she steps up to the door and clicks the latch. Then she turns, comes forward a few steps into the room again, and stands, holding the roses against her bosom and looking straight out. A clock out in one of the adjoining rooms strikes nine with a mournful gong. After the fourth gong her eyes wander in the direction of the clock and she moves slowly across towards the portières. Then she comes forward at the right, wandering, and crosses below the table to the piano. Several rose petals flutter to the floor. She stands at the piano for a moment, looking out through the bay window, then retraces her steps. She looks unseeingly at the scattered petals, continues up towards the portières, looks out through the deserted rooms, and finally stops. A few more petals drift to the floor. The curtain commences to descend, very, very slowly. She turns desolately and wanders back towards the piano again, clutching the roses close, her eyes wide and despairing.*)

CURTAIN

George Abbott is generally considered America's specialist in the popular arts of farce and melodrama. In *Broadway,* he was able to apply the two genres with extraordinary success to the subject of prohibition and gang warfare. With the addition of a display of "hoofing," *Broadway* proved to be sensational theatre, and it is a cultural vestige of considerable interest to us. It is "Americana" that we may not care to display abroad as an example of the best in American civilization, but its robustness is of a kind that only America has displayed in the theatre. Salty and loud, it is a testament to some sort of vitality and to democratic *élan* gone berserk.

Mr. Abbott's collaborator was Philip Dunning, born in 1892, who started an apprenticeship to the theatre at an early age by running away from his Meriden, Connecticut family home to join a carnival show and then to work in vaudeville, for which he also wrote skits. After contributing to soldier shows during the first World War, he stagemanaged for a Marilyn Miller musical show at the New Amsterdam Theatre, and it was there he was to be found shepherding *Sunny* when *Broadway* opened on September 16, 1926 at the Broadhurst a few blocks north. Among his later solo efforts and collaborations, which fared less well than his initial effort, were *Get Me in the Movies* (with Charlton Andrews), 1928, *Night Hostess,* 1928, *Sweet Land of Liberty,* 1929, *Lilly Turner,* 1932, *Kill That Story* (with Harry Madden), 1934, *Page Miss Glory* (with Joseph Frank), 1934, and that nostalgic comedy of adolescence and mainstay of amateur theatricals, *Remember the Day* (with Philo Higley), 1935.

Mr. Abbott, born in 1889 in Forestville, N. Y., took a B.A. from the University of Rochester in 1911, studied with Professor Baker at Harvard in 1912, and became an actor in 1913. He has since then been identified with the stage and screen in virtually every capacity. He has been singularly successful as producer, director, and collaborator on numerous plays. Among these are: *The Fall Guy* (with James Gleason), 1925, *Love 'Em and Leave 'Em* (with John V. A. Weaver), 1926, *Broadway, Coquette* (with Ann Preston Bridgers), 1927, and *Three Men on a Horse* (with John Cecil Holmes), 1935. He has also been successfully active in the field of musical comedy (*On Your Toes, Best Foot Forward, Billion Dollar Baby,* etc.), and he produced such successes not written by himself as *Boy Meets Girl, Brother Rat, Room Service, What a Life,* and *Kiss and Tell.*

To call *Broadway* dramatic literature of any importance would be a gross exaggeration. But it belongs inescapably to the theatre of the twenties by virtue of its brassy and insouciant representation of an era, its tumultuous pace, and its surface of sophistication, which proves naive enough upon scrutiny yet has enough cheek to look exceedingly worldly wise. By inviting imitation, it promoted a Broadway type of entertainment that did not go undercover after 1929 simply because the nineteen-thirties discovered a social conscience and found some rather definite formulations for it.

Broadway

BY PHILIP DUNNING AND GEORGE ABBOTT

First produced by Jed Harris at the Broadhurst Theatre, New York City, on September 16, 1926, with the following cast:

NICK VERDIS	Paul Porcasi
ROY LANE	Lee Tracy
LIL RICE	Clare Woodbury
KATIE	Ann Preston
JOE	Joseph Spurin-Calleia
MAZIE SMITH	Mildred Wall
RUBY	Edith Van Cleve
PEARL	Eloise Stream
GRACE	Molly Ricardel
ANN	Constance Brown
BILLIE MOORE	Sylvia Field
STEVE CRANDALL	Robert Gleckler
DOLPH	Henry Sherwood
"PORKY" THOMPSON	William Foran
"SCAR" EDWARDS	John Wray
DAN McCORN	Thomas Jackson
BENNY	Frank Verigun
LARRY	Millard Mitchell
MIKE	Roy R. Lloyd

Gangsters, Waiters

The action takes place in the private party room of the Paradise Night Club, New York City.

ACT I

A spring evening, just before the first show.

ACT II

Half an hour later.

ACT III

The next night.

ACT ONE

The rising curtain discloses the orange-lit, tinsel magnificence of the private party-room at the Paradise Night Club. To the tinny obligato made by "LIL" RICE *at the piano, five chorus girls are in line singing and dancing one of the numbers from the revue. The rehearsal is under the direction of* NICK, *a middle-aged Greek, mercenary and hard.*

LIL, *the prima donna of the cabaret, at the piano, a heavy, middle-aged woman with a certain amount of good looks, which, however, have long since lost their bloom. She rolls her own, and removes tight slippers from swollen feet whenever occasion permits.*

ROY LANE, *a typical song and dance man, with his coat off, sleeves rolled up, is leading the number. The chorus girls,* MAZIE, GRACE, RUBY, PEARL, *and* ANNE *are in line behind* ROY.

Some of the girls are in street clothes, others in practice clothes. One or two have their skirts pinned up so as to give their legs freedom for the dance. Some of the girls' coats, hats, wraps, etc., are hanging on hooks or thrown on chairs or tables.

JOE, *an Italian waiter, enters from cabaret, takes pin-wheel effect to cabaret.*

NICK (*as they dance*). Hey, straighten your line—you—straighten it up—— Now listen, don't forget to smile, Pearl—some pep. (*Girls continue to dance in straightened line.*) Shake it, shake it. (*Shouts.*) No, no! Stop! (*They all stop guiltily.*) Pearl, watch what you're doing.

PEARL (*under her breath, as she turns away*). Go fry an egg.

ROY (*to* PEARL). You went into that step on the off beat, girlie.

NICK (*to the dancers*). For God's sake, think what you're doing, will you? Now once again, the finish.

LIL. Where from?

ROY (*singing the cue music*). Ta da-ta-tadada-ta-ta.

(*They finish the dance—and break formation. The orchestra is rendering dance music in the cabaret. This continues at intervals throughout the play. Colored lights play upon the swinging doors.*)

(NICK *watching coldly.*)

NICK (*as they stand waiting for a decision*). No good. Nothing like it. It ain't only ya dance with your feet, ya gotta smile—show the teets— (*He illustrates.*) Last night—oh—hoo. (PEARL *and* RUBY *start to whisper. Makes a noise of disgust.*) Rotten. Will you pay attention? (PEARL *looks guilty.*) I say smile. Show the teets. Like this.

ROY. I guess ya got it now, ain't ya, girls?

MAZIE. Sure, we have.

NICK. Last night a gentleman gets up in the middle of the first number. He says to me, "Outside your place it says: 'Paradise Club—Best Cabaret in New York'—that's what it *says*"—and then he walks out.

LIL. Wise-crackin' rounder—

RUBY. Had to be smart.

NICK. He was right. This show ain't bad, it's lousy. Say, look—I pay you—and I can't even look at it. The show's too tame —I have to undress you. Live it up—

ROY. The show is good, what there is of it, Boss, but you ought to get in more people.

NICK. Yeh?

ROY. Sure. *Variety* says the Golden Slipper is doing a nifty biz, but they got fourteen weenies and six performers. Now, if you ask me—

NICK. Well, I don't ask you—I don't ask nobody, y'understand?

ROY. Well, if you don't want good advice, that's your loss.

RUBY. Anyhow, I should think you might save some of your raspberries for the one that caused the whole trouble.

PEARL. That's what I say.

GRACE *and* ANN. Yeah. That's what I say.

MAZIE. Hey, easy.

ROY (*to them*). Nix, nix.

RUBY. How can we get it right if Miss Billie Moore don't take the trouble to come to rehearsals?

ROY (*under his breath.*) Hey, don't be a kibitzer.

RUBY. Who the hell does she think she is—keep us waiting for her?

ROY. Well, I tell you, Mr. Verdis, I don't think she knew there was a rehearsal.

RUBY. She was standing right alongside me in the dressing room last night when you called it.

ROY. No, she had gone.

MAZIE. Certainly she had.

ANN. No, she heard it—she was in the room.

GRACE. Sure. I saw her.

MAZIE. You're crazy—I say she was gone.

LIL. Oh, for God's sake. (*They stop their chatter and look at her.*) Listen, you poor bunch of baby saps—if you spent half your time minding your own business instead of watching other people—

ROY. So says I.

LIL. When I was your age, before I got fat—(RUBY's *razz*)—yeh, fat—I kin say it myself—I was so busy tryin' to get somewhere, trying to get out of the chorus, I didn't know whether anybody was in the dressing room or not. If you're going to rehearse this, do it. If you ain't, tell me, 'cause I ain't supposed to sit here and pound this music box—I sing here and I am just doing this for Nick.

RUBY. You ain't so fat you can't talk—are you—

LIL (*starts to get up*). Say, listen, Owl. I'll pull all the sawdust out of you if you ain't nice. (*Movement and ad lib.*)

NICK. Here, here, here! What is this? Lil is right—gals today ain't nothin' but a lot of jumpin' jacks. Come on,—we'll do it again.

GRACE. Oh, please—I'm tired.

NICK. You're tired! My God, I got better girls in a dump once.

ROY. Aw, quit ridin' 'em, will ya, Mr. Verdis?

NICK. Ah, shut your face. I run this place.

ROY. They been rehearsin' since eight-thirty tonight—

RUBY. Yeh, and don't forget we can't get this right 'till Billie gets here.

ANN. That's what I say.

PEARL. Why make us the goat?

GRACE. How am I gonna give a performance?

NICK. Quit it. I don't need no advice what to do with girls that come late.

ROY. Listen, Mr. Verdis, Billie's only been in this game a short while—

NICK. And she won't be in it a hell of a while longer. (JOE *enters from hall with drink which* NICK *takes.*) As soon as she comes in, she goes out. (LIL *plays "How Dry I Am."* NICK *pauses as he is about to drink and looks at her.*) Joe, get Lil a drink.

(*He drinks. The girls lounge about the room, smoking, using nail files, etc.* JOE *exits to hall.*)

ROY. Gee, Mr. Verdis, it's not like Billie to fall down on the job. Why, that kid is one of the best lookers and neatest workers you got. You'll make one big mistake if you let her out. She's a mighty nifty little trick.

NICK. Why all the talk? You don't work for her—you work for me.

ROY. God knows I know that.

NICK. Whadda ya mean?

ROY. Well— Not to pin any bouquets on myself, but where could you get a guy to do what I'm doing for the coffee and cake money you're paying me?

RUBY. He's off again.

ROY. You see, it ain't only I can dance, but I got personality—

MAZIE. Huh!

ROY. Personality plus—

MAZIE (*to* GRACE). Ain't he a darb?

GRACE. He hates himself.

NICK. Somethin' else ya got is a terrible swell head.

ROY. Who, me? Nothin' swell-headed about me, Boss. I could 'a' been that way long ago, if I'd wanted to.

(KATIE, *a cigarette girl, enters down hall.*)

NICK. Aw, cut out the bellyachin' and quit any time you want.

KATIE. Mr. Verdis—

NICK. Don't bother me. Can't you see I'm busy?

RUBY. In conference.

NICK. What? (*He glares at the wrong girl. Then turns back to* KATIE.) Well, why don't you go?

KATIE. It's for Mr. Crandall.

NICK (*manner changes*). Oh—well—he ain't here yet. Who is it? Who wants him?

KATIE. The two same gentlemen that was in last night.

NICK. All right. I'm coming out. Tell 'em I'm coming. (KATIE *exits to hall.*) Don't go to your dressing rooms till I come back—we ain't done rehearsing yet. (*Exit down hall.*)

(RUBY *thumbs her nose at his back and the girls break into a clamor.*)

ANN. Gee, it's about time.

GRACE. He's a slave driver.

MAZIE. Thank God!

PEARL. Don't he ever get tired?

ROY. Oh, lay dead.

GRACE. Oh, gee, I can't rehearse any more.

ANN. Well, you're gonna have to, whether you can or not, so don't start squawking about it.

RUBY. Ah, I think I'll quit this dump, anyhow.

PEARL. I'm gonna buy everybody a drink.

ANN. Big hearted.

LIL. My God, it can talk.

PEARL. What?

LIL. That's the first time I heard you speak since you been working here—I always supposed you was a deaf and dumb girl up to now.

PEARL. I worked in night clubs before—it don't pay to talk too much.

ROY. Like to see anybody stop me talking.

MAZIE. So would I. (*They all laugh.*)

GRACE. Say, what about this drink?

PEARL. Does he let you have the waiter come in here?

ANN. Sure—Joe can go anywhere.

GRACE. Come on, girls. Let's go down the hall to the bar—

RUBY. Wait a minute— Maybe Pearl doesn't have to pay for mine. Four to one—a dollar or nothing. (*Puts coin in poker machine; pushes lever and watches the numbers spin. Is disappointed.* ANN, GRACE, RUBY *and* PEARL *start out hall.*)

PEARL (*to* LIL). Ain't you coming? (ROY *waves her aside.*)

LIL. They're bringing mine.

MAZIE. I gotta 'phone. (*The girls exeunt.*)

LIL. Where the hell is Joe with my drink? He must be down in the laundry making it. (*Picks up a copy of "Variety."*) If your girl friend gets late to another rehearsal like this, she's gonna get a piece of my mind.

ROY. They must be some good reason why Billie ain't here. Listen, Lil, don't put it into Nick's head to give her the air, will you? 'Cause she needs the do-ray-me pretty bad—she's got a mother and sister over in Trenton.

LIL. I never knew a jane in this business that didn't have.

ROY. On the level. I met 'em.

MAZIE. I room with her and I happen to know she's a good kid.

ROY. And believe me, it pays to be good.

MAZIE. Sure, but not much.

LIL (*wisely—to* ROY). So you met the family, eh?

ROY. Yeh, I went out there one Sunday. You see, I take a sort of brotherly interest in that kid.

LIL. Brotherly—?

ROY. You heard me. Anyhow, I and her are fixing up a little vaudeville act together.

LIL. Say, sweetheart, why don't you get hip to yourself?

ROY. What do you mean?

LIL. Ain't you wise that she's given you the bum's rush? Why, that guy's got her so dizzy she don't know you're alive.

ROY. Who? Crandall? No—no—not at all. She'll get over that. She ain't used to going to such swell places, that's all. She's got more sense than to care a thing about Crandall himself personally—it's just the buggy ride. I seen it happen lots of times—young kids get taken out by a rich guy—everything swell; music, lights—they get baffled. You know what I mean, dazzled—and then suddenly they get wise to themselves that the whole works is a lot of boloney and they realize where the real guys in this world is at—

LIL. Hoofing in cabarets.

ROY. Yeah. That's no kid, neither. (MAZIE *grunts derisively and crosses to phone.*) Billie's ambitious to get ahead in this game. I guess she'd want to stick with somebody could learn her something, huh? (MAZIE *puts coin in phone.*)

MAZIE. Pennsylvania 5000.

ROY. Her and me ain't long in this joint, anyhow. I'm going to make her something besides a chorus girl.

LIL. What's coming off?

ROY. As soon as I get Billie ready, we're all set for a lot of nice booking on the big time.

LIL. Soon as you get Billie ready? Are you—all ready?

ROY. Who—me? Well, that's a funny question—you're lookin' at me every night. You can see. I don't belong here.

MAZIE. Pennsylvania 5000.

(JOE *enters from hall with drink.* LIL *throws cigarette on floor and steps on it preparatory to taking drink.*)

JOE. I couldn't find Pete and he had the keys—that's what kept me.

LIL. That's all right. The longer it stands, the better it is. It was only made this afternoon.

JOE. Not this stuff. That's last week's.

MAZIE. Operator, I want Pennsylvania five— (JOE *exits to hall.*) What? I did give you my nickel. Wonder if we could get Pullman service with this phone. (*Placated. Sits back of chair.*) Pennsylvania 5000.

LIL (*offering glass*). Want a piece of this?

ROY. No—I can't drink and do what I do.

LIL (*drinking*). I see. You ain't never played any of the big time yourself, have you, Personality?

ROY. No—but then, I've been waiting—but you know as well as I do—it's just the breaks. Look at all the loafers in this man's town—getting by— Getting by big. Have they got anything on me? I ask you, have they? This big Greek Nick is always—cracking about Jack Donahue—there ain't a thing that guy's doin' that I can't do—yeh—and mebbe I done some of those steps first—but Jack got the breaks and mine ain't here yet.

MAZIE. Pennsylvania 5000.

ROY. Listen, when I was out on the Gus Sun time, couple years ago—the manager in McKeesport comes back to my dressing room and tells me—that never did anybody do the stuff I was doing.—And the road show of the Follies was only there the week before. But the act with Billie is a sure thing. And then you'll see the old names—with a big ad in *Variety,* telling 'em—look who's here. God, I dreamed about it years.

MAZIE. Pennsylvania Hotel? Listen, I want to speak to Mr. Manuel Tellazar—

LIL. My God, you can't find a guy with a name like that in a hotel—he's in Ellis Island, dearie.

MAZIE. Oh, for God's sake— (*Hangs up in disgust.*)

(BILLIE *enters back door. She is a beautiful little creature, despite the obvious commonplaceness of her clothes. She enters breathlessly.*)

LIL. Here she is now.

MAZIE. Where you been, kid?

ROY. Gee whiz, Billie—

BILLIE. Is Mr. Verdis sore?

LIL. Oh, no, nobody's sore—we're just curious.

ROY. He was kinda sore till I talked him out of it. He may say a little something, but don't pay no attention to him. Where the hell you been?

BILLIE. Mr. Crandall said he'd keep track of the time.

LIL. Hah!

ROY. Oh, him.

MAZIE. You been out with Steve?

BILLIE. I didn't think there was anything wrong.

MAZIE. There ain't.

ROY (*referring to corsage of orchids*). Did Crandall give you them dandylions?

MAZIE. Listen, Billie, if you was out with Steve, you got nothing to worry about, 'cause Nick won't dare say a word to you.

BILLIE. I didn't mean to be late, honest I didn't—but it was just so wonderful and the orchestra was playing special numbers that he asked 'em to play just for me—and I just seemed like I was in a dream or something.

LIL. And ain't it hell when you wake up?

BILLIE. I just don't know where the time went, that's all. Roy, here's some more coupons.

(*He accepts the cigar coupons sulkily and adds them to a large roll which he carries in his pocket held together by a rubber band.*)

MAZIE (*looking at the phone*). I wonder if that banana gave me a phoney name.

BILLIE. When Mr. Crandall asked me to go to dinner with him, I told him I had a rehearsal and he promised to get me here.

ROY. Where's the big stiff?

BILLIE (*resentful of his tone*). He's outside parking the car.

ROY. I guess maybe it's time I give you a piece of advice, Billie—lay off these sugar daddies—I seen a lot of these big cabaret spenders—they're only after one thing. Don't let your head get turned by a lot of soft gab—bowing you out of a taxi like you was Texas Guinan or somebody, don't think that— Say, where do you s'pose he got his money, anyhow?

BILLIE. In Florida real estate.

LIL. Listen, Personality—what difference does it make in this man's town where you get the sugar so long's you got it?

(RUBY, ANN *and* GRACE *enter from hall. At sight of* BILLIE *they sputter out their indignation.*)

RUBY. Oh, so you finally showed up, eh? Say, you got a nerve.

ANN. That's what I say.

GRACE. What'd you think we are?

(PEARL *enters from up hall.*)

BILLIE. I'm awfully sorry.

(NICK *enters from down hall.*)

NICK. Well—so—you did come— What you got to say for yourself—no, don't say it. Of all the damn nerve—

(STEVE *appears in back door. He is a tall*

man, handsome in a hard sophisticated way.)

STEVE. Evening, Nick.

NICK (*his manner changing to one of deference*). Well, look who's here! Good evening, Mr. Crandall. Glad to see you.

STEVE. Hello, girls.

GIRLS. Hello.

STEVE. Hallo, Lil. (*She bows grandly.*) Hope I didn't keep Billie from rehearsal, Nick.

NICK. I was just gonna ask her where she was—

STEVE. Guess it didn't put you out much, did it?

NICK. No, no, it didn't make so much difference.

RUBY (*bitterly*). I should say not.

NICK. What?

RUBY. I didn't say anything.

BILLIE (*to girls*). Well, gee, I'm awfully sorry.

NICK. You and me can talk about that later.

LIL. Well, are we going to rehearse some more or ain't we? I been sitting here for three hours and my feet hurt like hell—

NICK. Billie can rehearse separate with Jack Donahue here.

ROY. No trouble at all.

NICK. So that's all for the rest of you.

RUBY. Thank God!

STEVE. Oh, by the way, I'm tossing a little party tonight, and I'd like to have you all stay.

(*The girls crowd around him except* PEARL *who starts toward stairs.*)

MAZIE. That's us.

ANN. Sure we will.

GRACE. You tell 'em.

RUBY. Yes, we'll come.

STEVE (BILLIE *crosses below armchair*). How about it, Pearl?

PEARL (*pausing*). I don't think I can, Mr. Crandall.

STEVE. You old cross-patch, I got some Chicago friends just dying to meet you.

NICK. She'll be there.

PEARL. Sure, I'll be there.

STEVE. Fine. I can get the party room, can't I, Nick?

NICK. Anything you say, Mr. Crandall.

STEVE. Bye, bye, little one, and thank you again for a very pleasant evening.

(*He kisses* BILLIE'S *hand gallantly.* ROY *makes derisive sound known as "the bird." Girls snicker.* STEVE *looks around, not quite sensing what happened.* NICK *hastens to dismiss them.*)

NICK. Come on, now. Get made up, girls. (*They start toward stairs. He turns to* STEVE.) Dolph and Porky are outside waiting for you.

GRACE. Gawd, I'm all in. I'm going to hit the hay tonight——

RUBY. If you was a rich man's darling, you wouldn't have to rehearse.

MAZIE. The trouble with you is, you're jealous 'cause he don't take you out no more.

RUBY (*pausing on stairs*). Say, where do you get off to jump me?

MAZIE. If you don't stop passing remarks about Billie, I'll jump you, all right—I'll knock your block off.

RUBY. You and who else?

LIL. Shut up. (*Pushes past them.*) Why don't you two hire a hall? (ANN, PEARL, GRACE, LIL *and* RUBY *exeunt upstairs.*)

STEVE. Tell 'em I'll wait for 'em here—— (NICK *exits down hall.*)

MAZIE. I'm going to bust everything God gave her some night—all but her teeth. I'll take them out and give them back to her dentist.

(MAZIE *and* BILLIE *exeunt upstairs.*)

ROY (*who has been standing watching* STEVE). Have a nice ride this afternoon?

STEVE (*after looking him over, amused*). Lovely. Sorry you weren't along.

ROY. Say, tell me something, will you?

STEVE. Shoot.

ROY. I been knocking around cabarets, dance clubs, vaudeville, everything for a long time, and what I can't get through my head is this—why is it that all the guys like you are never satisfied with the hundreds of janes that will do anything you want—all the rummies and bums you can have, and by God—you'll quit 'em all to go after one girl that you know is good—why is that, huh?

STEVE. Do you know some that are good?

ROY. I know one that's good.

STEVE. Who is that?

ROY. That's Billie.

STEVE. You're sure she's good?

ROY. I'll give you odds she is.

STEVE. Where the hell do you get the idea that no one can speak to this Moore girl but you? Who are you? What can you do for her?

ROY (*almost pleading*). I can do a lot

for her, Mr. Crandall. I can put her in the Palace Theatre—inside six months.

STEVE. Doing what?

ROY. Doing a swell dancing act. Now there's my cards on the table, Mr. Crandall, that's what I'm going to do for her. We can't lose. She's got looks, a shape, and with my personality——

STEVE. Your personality. Oh, I see, that's what you're going to sell. Well, Kid, that's a great idea—just an idea. By the way, I guess I'll have you do a little clowning for a few minutes for my friends tonight. I'm not inviting you to remain on the party, understand, because there won't be dames enough to go around. I'll give you a ten spot.

ROY. Sure. I'll do some stuff I ain't done here, seeing how you want some laughs. (NICK *enters down hall, bringing* DOLPH, *a dark, wiry man, and* PORKY, *placid and bald-headed—both in evening clothes.* ROY *sees them coming—starts upstairs.*)

DOLPH. Hello, Steve.

STEVE. Hello, boys. Get Joe in here, Nick. Let's have a drink. (NICK *goes up hall.*)

DOLPH (*kidding* ROY). Well, if it ain't old Fred Stone himself.

ROY. That ain't no insult neither. For his own kind of stuff, he's a hundred percenter, that guy. We can all learn something from him, believe me, even the best of us.

PORKY. Yeh, but I like your stuff much better.

ROY. That's all right. Just keep your eye on me. Pretty soon you'll see my name in lights. It's in the boy. I can't lose. (*Exit upstairs.*)

STEVE. Never leave any strychnine around. This guy is just dying to commit suicide. (*They laugh.*) The poor nut.

DOLPH. I got the bracelet, Steve.

STEVE. Good. I'll look at it later.

PORKY. Let's sell this load of stuff to Nick—

STEVE (*warningly*). All right—— (PORKY *stops abruptly.* NICK *enters up hall.*)

STEVE (*casually*). For Christ's sake, Nick, where's all your chairs? (*They all hasten to get him a chair.*)

DOLPH. Here you are, Steve.

NICK. We moved them back for rehearsing. It's all your fault, too, keeping that gal out all day.

STEVE. Ain't sore, are you, Baby?

NICK. A lot good it would do me. (*They all laugh.*)

PORKY (*as they sit*). Had a lucky break last night, Nick.

NICK. Yeh, you fellas is always lucky.

PORKY. I'll say so.

DOLPH. Got hold of some great stuff.

NICK. Yeh?

DOLPH. You bet, fresh from the boat.

NICK (*on his guard*). Didn't know you had any boat coming.

PORKY. We didn't. . . .

DOLPH. But Scar Edwards did. (*They laugh.*)

NICK (*protesting*). This hi-jacking is no good.

DOLPH. But it's luck for you just the same, eh, kid?

NICK. I don't know—— (JOE *enters with drinks which he passes around.*) Some day you get in trouble.

PORKY. Let Steve do the worrying about that.

DOLPH. Ah, here we are. (PORKY *holds nose and drinks.*) If Steve wasn't a big-hearted guy, he'd never sell you this stuff at the same price.

NICK. Good, eh?

DOLPH. It's the real thing, Nick, no kid.

NICK. No, I got quite a lot on hand. (JOE *exits.*)

STEVE. You got nothin' but cut stuff. You better get in on this—White Horse in the clear—not white mule, neither. You can get twenty buck a quart for it.

NICK. No, they drank bum stuff so long they don't know when it's good. Anyhow, if I take booze you hijacked off Scar Edwards, he'll come down here and raise hell.

STEVE. I'll take care of Scar.

NICK. If you fight with his mob—then I'll get it in the neck. Of course they won't make no trouble if you keep below 125th Street.

STEVE. Roll over—trade is where you find it.

DOLPH. You tell 'em.

STEVE. My connections are better than any man in this town.

DOLPH. You bet you.

STEVE. In that same we got people on our list with streets named after them.

PORKY. That's no lie either.

STEVE. You don't think I am going to let a greasy lot of Polish second-story men tell me where to head in, do you? I'm telling you that I want to clean up this order quick and I think I got a right to count on you.

DOLPH. Sure. Where would you be today if it wasn't for Steve?

PORKY. Yeah,—a waiter.

STEVE. Never mind that—where would *you* be, as far as that goes?

DOLPH. Ain't that what I'm sayin'?

STEVE. It ain't what you was—it's what you are. I cleaned spittoons in my time, fella, and I'm proud of it—that's when Porky tried to make a box fighter out of me. Eh, Porky?

PORKY. I always said you had stuff in you—and now I'm workin' for you.

STEVE. Say, boys, this business of peddling booze is the second largest industry in the United States right now. Give me a year more at it and we'll all retire.

NICK. Listen, Steve. I'm on your side.

STEVE. Well, good God! Would I be sitting here talking to you if I thought you wasn't?

NICK. But the Edwards' gang might shoot things up.

STEVE (*quietly*). They ain't got a monopoly on it, have they?

PORKY. Oh, Nick—— (*Waves him laughingly away.*)

NICK. You're too quick with the gun, Steve. Some time you might get in trouble. Anyhow, it's no good. A lot of murders—very bad for business. Scar might get me raided again——

STEVE (*hard*). Listen, Nick—you never got poor taking my tips yet——

PORKY. Damn right he didn't.

STEVE. And I wouldn't advise you to change right now.

NICK. Oh, no. (*Depreciating the idea vehemently.*)

STEVE. Listen, Nick, if my trade is going to grow I got to crush a little competition now and then. I'm taking Scar's booze when I can lay my hands on it, and I'm taking his territory. It's just business, that's all. Are you with me or not? You gotta declare yourself in or out.

NICK. All right—send me what you want. I'll pay for it.

(JOE *enters, gets glasses, exits.*)

PORKY. Now you got sense.

DOLPH. Sure.

STEVE (*takes hat off*). Now, Nick, this party I'm giving is for the Chicago gang that hits town tonight. They're all itching to show what they can do, and if Edwards starts anything they'll be very handy—see.

NICK. Well, I'm counting on you.

STEVE. Sure, you can count on me, 'cause I got everything fixed. Now, Porky, you go to the hotel, and as soon as the gorillas land, get 'em dressed up and bring 'em around.

PORKY. Sure.

STEVE. I want all the girls to stay. Make it right, and tell Joe champagne, flowers and all the rest of it.

DOLPH. Hot dog!

NICK. Anything you say, Steve.

STEVE. Now go down the cellar and check up your stuff and see if you can't make this order a record. Eh, old timer?

NICK (*crosses to cabaret door*). Anything that's for you, I want to do it. Come on, Porky—— (*Peeks through doors.*) Not so good for Friday night. (PORKY *and* NICK *exeunt to hall.*)

DOLPH (*as they are out of hearing*). That's the way to handle him, all right. He's got a nerve to argue after all you've done for him.

STEVE. Well, we'll spend a lot of money tonight, anyhow—make Nick feel good. Let's see the bracelet. (DOLPH *passes it and stands watching.*) Who owned it?

DOLPH. The fence wouldn't tell me. But he says it was lifted off one of the classiest mammas in this town.

STEVE. How much?

DOLPH. Five yards. He wanted a grand at first. I beat him down.

STEVE. All right—we'll keep it. It'll look nice on the kid—eh, Dolph?

DOLPH. You tell 'em. You certainly have fell for that baby, ain't you? I never seen you waste so much time on a jane, Steve. (*Plays poker machine.*)

STEVE (*coolly*). Don't see too much.

DOLPH (*apologetically*). You know me, Boss.

STEVE. Got to handle each one different. Wouldn't want me to show my technique first thing, would you?

DOLPH. Not if you mean what I think you mean.

STEVE. This gal is a nice kid.

DOLPH. She won't be after she knows you long.

STEVE. That's all right, too. (DOLPH *plays the machine.*) But you gotta use your head.

DOLPH. Jesus! This machine is crooked——

(SCAR EDWARDS *enters back door. He is a*

tense man—slightly overdressed in Broadway fashion.)

STEVE. You see, she don't belong in this cage at all—consequently you got to treat her different.

DOLPH (*turning and seeing* SCAR). Well, for God's sake.

STEVE. Hello, Sweetheart.

SCAR. How are you? (DOLPH *closes cabaret door.*) I thought this is where I'd find you.

STEVE. What made you think that?

SCAR. Do you think Steve Crandall is the only bird in town that's got ways of findin' things?

STEVE. Well, I'll tell you, Scar, I wouldn't advise you to do it often.

SCAR. No?

STEVE. No. In fact, I think you got a hell of a nerve to come bustin' in this way.

SCAR. Not much busting about it.

STEVE. Next time, knock—see——

SCAR. You don't always knock when you come to visit me.

STEVE. I don't visit you, Scar.

SCAR. You visit in my neighborhood sometimes, don't you, Steve?

STEVE. Do you own it?

SCAR. All depends on how you look at it.

STEVE. I'm just telling you for your own good, Scar. Come gum-shoeing in the back way of a strange place—you know, somebody might take you for a burglar.

SCAR (*closes in*). I ain't scared of you guys. I come down here to have a showdown—alone—with no gun. (*Pats pocket to show he is unarmed.*) So let's talk turkey.

STEVE. All right, Edwards, but listen to what I tell you—next time you better let us know when you're coming or you may wish you'd brought your gun.

SCAR. You don't let me know when you're coming.

STEVE. Meaning what?

SCAR. I s'pose you don't know.

STEVE. You heard me ask you.

SCAR. Aw, you know god-damn well what I mean—you been poaching on me, Steve—you been cutting in on my territory and it's got to stop.

DOLPH. Will you listen to that——

STEVE. You own everything above 125th Street, do you?

SCAR. We stocked that territory and we got a right to it. My mob worked for four years to get things the way we got 'em—and *nobody*—get that—nobody is goin' to cut in from down here and spoil a nickel's worth of it. You hi-jacked another truck-—(STEVE *rises*)—load last night. Yes, and you been spillin' more jack round for protection than we can afford. We ain't never come down here to horn in on your Broadway trade, but you're ruinin' our game up there and I'm here to tell you that you can't get away with it.

STEVE. If you knew me a little better, you'd know that yelling wouldn't get you much.

DOLPH. That's just what I was goin' to say.

SCAR. Peddle your papers, will you? (DOLPH *walks away squelched. In the cabaret the orchestra can be heard playing George Olsen's Battle Number.*) I'm talking to the boss now. I come here for a showdown with you guys, see.

STEVE. All right. I don't mind a little showdown myself once in a while. You're looking for trouble, is that it?

SCAR. No, I ain't lookin' for trouble. Nothin' like that. Not that my friends ain't capable of holding up their end, if it comes to that. But I say they's plenty of business for everybody and them what works up the trade should be the ones to get it.

STEVE. And supposing I say that I'll sell any damn place I can get away with it?

SCAR. Then I'm warning you that it's dangerous for you to do business in Harlem, 'cause from now on 125th Street is the dead line. Get me?

STEVE. Yeah?

SCAR. Yeah.

STEVE. Well, that's just dandy, Scar. Thanks for the tip-off. Now if you've spoke your piece you can take the air. I don't care about having a public fight with the likes of you, because everybody in this place don't know my business yet, and I don't care to have you stand around and broadcast it.

SCAR. There's a lot of things I can broadcast, if I have to.

DOLPH (*comes to the other side of* SCAR.) You heard what the boss said, didn't you?

SCAR. You, too—the both of you—since you're looking for tips, I'll give you another one. I happen to be the guy who can clean up a few murder mysteries in this town. I suppose you don't know who knocked O'Connell off!

DOLPH. What are you talking about?

SCAR. And who dumped his body up in Harlem so my mob would get blamed for it.

STEVE. What the hell are you driving at?

SCAR. This is what I'm driving at.

DOLPH. Wait a minute.

SCAR. I've waited long enough. Now get this— You guys stay down here in your own territory and you leave my trucks alone. See—cause I got the dope on you, Steve—you croaked O'Connell.

DOLPH. Look here—— (*Grabs* SCAR.)

SCAR. Take your hands off me or I'll bust your god-damn face. You guys can't put me out of business.

(SCAR *is facing* DOLPH. STEVE *quickly pulls out his gun, presses it against* SCAR's *back and fires.* SCAR *pitches forward.* DOLPH *catches him in his arms.* SCAR's *hat falls off.*)

DOLPH. Jesus Christ, Steve, what have you done?

STEVE (*remaining cool*). Get hold of him under the arms. Quick—walk him out of here—— (*Orchestra still playing battle number—trumpets and shots.* DOLPH *on one side of* SCAR *and* STEVE *on the other hold him up as they would a drunken man.*) Wait a minute. (*Gets* SCAR's *hat and puts it on* SCAR's *head. As* STEVE *and* DOLPH *are walking the dead man toward back door under stairs,* ROY *and* BILLIE *come downstairs from dressing room.*)

ROY. Come on. I'll run through the number with you—we got time. (BILLIE *and* ROY *look over railing and see* STEVE *and* DOLPH *with* SCAR *between them.*) Who's the drunk?

STEVE. Just one of the boys we're helping home.

(SCAR, DOLPH *and* STEVE *exeunt back door, closing it after them.*)

ROY. It's powerful stuff Nick dishes out.

PEARL (*appears at top of stairs*). Billie, was there a shot?

ROY (*laughs*). That's the band——

BILLIE. They're doing the battle number——

(*Orchestra just finishing Battle Number.*)

PEARL. I'm nervous as hell tonight. (*Exits to dressing room.*)

ROY (*to* BILLIE). Come on, now. Ready —let's do it together. One—two—three—— (*They dance.*)

(NICK *enters from hall and stands watching* BILLIE *and* ROY. BILLIE *senses his presence and stops dancing.*)

BILLIE. You didn't want to see me, did you, Mr. Verdis?

NICK. I did—but now I don't. All the same, you shouldn't miss that rehearsal——

BILLIE. I'm awfully sorry.

NICK. Don't let this happen some more.

BILLIE. I won't—thank you, Mr. Verdis.

NICK. See if you can dance better tonight.

BILLIE. Yes, sir.

ROY. She will. I just came down to skate over it with her. (*He takes off coat, revealing the fact that his cuffs are sewed into the coat sleeves and that he is bare-armed and a bit ragged underneath.*) One —two—three—four—— (NICK *exits to office.*)

BILLIE. Wasn't he nice to me, though?

ROY. Sure, he was afraid he'd lose me if he gave you the gate. The last step where you went into the side kick is where it got muddled last night. Now I'll count it slow— Watch me—— (*He hums the tune and they both dance as he counts — One — two — three — four.* BILLIE *gets mixed up on one of her kicks.*) No—no—— That's where you went wrong last night. Second time you do it with the left foot. Ready again—go— (*They do the dance again—this time correctly.*) You can't wish a number on—you got to rehearse 'em. (*She does the dance alone while he hums and counts.*) Fine. That's it. You just keep picking up a little each day and improving and you'll be going fine before long—you'll be as good as I am soon—— (*She demurs.*) Honest. Then we'll tie the merry old can to this saloon, eh, kid?

BILLIE. I s'pose so.

ROY. What do you mean—I s'pose so?

BILLIE. Well, that's what I mean—only Mazie says not to count on it, that's all. She says, well, I s'pose she's just kiddin'—but she says it's a pipe dream.

ROY. Yeh, no wonder she never gets anywhere with that kind of a outlook, huh? (*She limbers up by putting her foot on piano and bending down.*) That's right. Don't forget what I told you. The act is just as good as booked and you'll make a great partner, too. We'll soon be copping three hundred a week—one hundred for you and two hundred for me. You could send fifty or so home to your old lady every week instead of ten.

BILLIE. I hope it comes true.

ROY (*puts coat on*). Come true? It's just as good as if I was handing you the money right now. (*She stops exercise and starts for stairway.*) Is that all you're going to do? Say, Billie, you're still strong for the act, ain't you?

BILLIE. Sure, why not?

ROY. Well, you been wasting quite a lot of time lately.

BILLIE. Oh, I don't know.

ROY. We used to get in early and have a special rehearsal. Now you been staying out to dinner with some guy or other.

BILLIE. Well, I don't mean to do what's not right. I'll rehearse—only a person ought not to miss wonderful opportunities. I mean, I ought not to miss a chance to go out with Mr. Crandall.

ROY. You ought not to miss a chance to go out with me neither.

BILLIE. Well, of course, you're different.

ROY. I'll say I am. (*Imitates* STEVE.) Bye, bye, little one. Thank you for a very pleasant evening—huh! That's the parrot's cracker—that stuff.

BILLIE. Mr. Crandall has been very nice to me—(ROY *grunts.*)—Well, he has, Roy—— And I don't like you making fun of him.

ROY. Well, I don't like him interfering with our act.

BILLIE. He isn't. I'll rehearse any time you say.

ROY. It ain't only a matter of rehearsing—you gotta keep your mind on your work. Don't be thinking about hotels and things like that. Be thinking about your partner.

BILLIE. Well, I do.

ROY. Do you? Say, Billie, suppose we go out after, tie on the feed bag and talk over the act, huh?

BILLIE. To-night?

ROY. Oh, I remember, this is the night you go home to see your old lady, ain't it?

BILLIE. Well, this is the night I usually do.

ROY. Give her and your sister my love. By the way, Maloney Brothers are breaking in their new act over in Trenton, the last half. If you see 'em around, tell 'em I was asking for 'em.

BILLIE. Well, I don't know as I'll go.

ROY (*clouds*). Oh!

BILLIE. I thought maybe I ought to stay to Mr. Crandall's party.

ROY. Can't they get soused without you?

BILLIE. Mr. Crandall asked me first one of all—he said it would be just flat and stale without me.

ROY (*laughs up sleeve*). That would be tough. Pardon me while I laugh—ha-ha. I'm tellin' you to go home. Suppose anything ever happened like your old lady kicking the bucket?

BILLIE (*walking away*). You would!

ROY. Listen, Billie, tell me something straight, will you?

BILLIE. Sure.

ROY. Are you falling for this guy?

BILLIE (*stalling*). I never thought of such a thing.

ROY. Are you falling for anybody?

BILLIE. Mr. Crandall never thinks of me that way at all. He just considers me like a friend or just a kind of pal.

ROY. I suppose he's going to adopt you. Just a big brother. You wait a couple of days and I'll give you the low-down on him. I'm gonna do a little detective work myself. Florida real estate—hah!

BILLIE. Now, Roy.

ROY. I'm thinking of your career, that's all.

BILLIE (*flirting*). Is that all? I thought you might perhaps be thinking about me.

ROY. I take a personal interest in you, too. After all, we're going to be partners, ain't we?

BILLIE. Sure, on the stage.

ROY (BILLIE *and* ROY *start upstairs*). Sure. And I know what's best for you. Just think of your career. Here you got the opportunity to hook up with me in the act—we mustn't let nothing get in the way. You got talent, kid, when I bring it out. We're likely to be the sensation of vaudeville—everybody talking about us. Why, I can see our names in lights now—Roy Lane and Company. (*Exit upstairs.*) (*The back door opens and* STEVE *enters quietly. He holds door open and waits for* DOLPH. *The latter is frightened. His hat has been pushed to the back of his head. He walks past* STEVE *and stands waiting.* STEVE *closes the door—puts hat on piano.*)

STEVE (*nodding head toward cabaret*). You better go in there for a while.

DOLPH. What'll I do?

STEVE. Why, get yourself something to eat, kid.

DOLPH. You sure everything's all right?

STEVE (*smiles, faintly scornful*). Ain't got any appetite, huh? (*Jovially.*) You yellow bastard, I didn't think a little thing like that would bother you.

DOLPH. Say, nothing bothers me if I know what's coming. Gee, I never seen nothing like this before.

STEVE. That's why it's good. I've often thought it would be a nice thing if Scar—was out of the way. And look at the way it broke for us. Ever see anything prettier in your life? Now if Scar's mob has got any sense, I'll hook up the two gangs and run this town right—all the protection in the world, plenty of profits for everybody.

(PORKY *enters from down hall.*)

PORKY. Well, I got the Chicago boys out there.

DOLPH (*jumps at voice*). Oh, that you, Porky?

PORKY. All yelling for ringside seats, so they could see the dimples.

DOLPH. Well, I guess I'll have a drink. (DOLPH *exits to hall.* PORKY *watches him, puzzled. Turns and senses something eery in* STEVE's *over-deliberate lighting of a cigarette.*)

PORKY. What's the matter, Steve? (STEVE *blows out flame of lighter.*)

STEVE. Not a thing in the world, Porky.

PORKY. You act kind of——

STEVE. Kind a what?

PORKY. I don't know.

STEVE. Neither do I. (LIL *enters on stairs in silk kimona.*) I'll go ask Nick if he knows.

PORKY (*looking at* LIL). Well, I guess I'll stay out here.

STEVE. Go to it. (*Starts out.*) Lil, have you met my friend, Mr. Thompson?

LIL. I don't know as I have. How are you?

PORKY. Pleasure. (*Nods.*)

STEVE. Great admirer of yours. (*Exit to office.*)

PORKY. I've seen you before, Miss Rice.

LIL. That so?

PORKY. Yes, from out in the audience—out in front, I guess they calls it. You might have noticed me last night after your last song—I was applauding and——

LIL. They was two of you.

PORKY. I mean, you know, extra loud—and yelling, too—I yelled, Bravo! Bravo!

LIL. Was that what you yelled? If I'd known that, I'd 'a' done an encore.

PORKY. I hadn't been in to see Nick since you joined the troupe. Steve—that is, Mr. Crandall—my business associate—he's in here quite a lot—and I dropped in and I thought your stuff was extremely good——

LIL. Well, I certainly am flattered, Mr. Thompson. Who the hell's been monkeying with my props?

PORKY. Very interesting, the life back stage.

LIL. All depends on how you look at it. Of course it's nicer here than in a regular theatre, 'cause here there's nobody can drop scenery on you—all we got to dodge is the stuff out front.

PORKY. Well, I'm going to be out in front looking at you.

LIL. Don't look at me—just listen to me. I guess when that squab scenery comes out, you won't pay much attention to the old timers. (*On stairs.*)

PORKY. Whadda you mean, old timers? I'm an old timer myself. Me. I'm allus strong for the guy that's been somewhere and seen something.

LIL. That takes me in—I've seen a lot.

PORKY. Here too——

(DOLPH *enters down hall.*)

LIL. There's your boy friend. I'll take the elevator.

PORKY. Well, Miss Rice, I'd like to see some more of you, some time.

LIL. Stick around. (*Exits upstairs.* DOLPH *opens office door and jerks his head to* STEVE *to come out.*)

PORKY. Hey, listen, there's a gal I could fall for. No skinny-legged slat-sided baby pigeons like you guys pick. Me, I like a dame that can sit in a Morris chair and fill it.

DOLPH. Say, Porky, you know Dan McCorn?

PORKY. I speak to him—I ain't never been arrested by him.

DOLPH. Cut the comedy. He's out here. Keep an eye on him for a second till I come back, will you?

PORKY (*impressed*). Sure. (*Exit down hall.*)

(STEVE *enters from office.*)

DOLPH. There's a bull out there.

STEVE. What of it?

DOLPH. Maybe there's something up.

STEVE. Go home and go to bed.

DOLPH. There might be.

STEVE. Do you know him?

DOLPH. Sure. Dan McCorn.

STEVE (*taking a little interest*). Homicide Squad. What's he doing?

DOLPH. Sitting there reading a newspaper.

STEVE (*impressed*). That don't look so good. (JOE *enters from hall and goes toward office.* STEVE *takes him by the arm.*) Joe.

JOE. Yes, sir.

STEVE. Just run upstairs and ask Miss Moore—Billie Moore—to step down here.

JOE. Sure, Mr. Crandall. (*Exits upstairs.*)

STEVE. You better go out and cool off.

DOLPH. Don't think I'm shaky, but—

STEVE. Go on, now. Keep out of sight for a while.

(JOE *appears at head of stairs.*)

JOE. She ain't changed yet.

STEVE. Tell her it's important. (JOE *disappears.*)

DOLPH. Listen, you better fix the hoofer, too.

STEVE (*impatient*). Keep away from him or you will get me in trouble—I know how to handle this.

DOLPH. Listen, you still got that rod on you—let me get rid of it.

STEVE. Oh, for God's sake, don't have a panic. Who do you think I am, Johnnie the Dope? Should I have my pockets sewed up or something because a bull's in the next room? (JOE *comes downstairs followed by* BILLIE *in costume for opening number.*) (*To* DOLPH.) Beat it. (DOLPH *goes out down hall.* JOE *goes up hall.*)

BILLIE. I haven't quite dressed yet.

STEVE. I won't keep you a minute. Just a little something I want to ask you. (*She comes to him hooking dress.*) Listen, cute fella, I want to ask you a favor.

BILLIE. Why, Mr. Crandall, of course——

STEVE. 'Tisn't so much. I want you to forget you saw Dolph and me helping that drunken fellow out of here a while ago.

BILLIE. What drunken fellow? Oh, I know—out there—I remember.

STEVE. Well, I want you to be a good kid and promise to forget to remember.

BILLIE. All right.

STEVE. You see, he's a big politician—if it got out it might cause a lot of trouble—just thought I'd warn you so that—you know—if you happened to talk you might get yourself in a bad jam.

BILLIE. Oh, I wouldn't say anything.

STEVE. I can count on you, then.

BILLIE. Positively.

STEVE. Oh, by the way, here's something else I just happened to think of. (*Takes out handkerchief in which he had wrapped bracelet.*) Guess what?

BILLIE. Why, Mr. Crandall—how should I know?

STEVE. Birthday present for you.

BILLIE. But, Mr. Crandall, I had my birthday.

STEVE. Be smart and have two of them.

BILLIE. Oh, Steve—oh, I never *saw* anything— Oh, Mr. Crandall—why, it's beautiful!

STEVE. I'm glad you like it.

BILLIE (*without too much conviction*). But I couldn't take it.

STEVE. Now, listen, don't give me any of that silly talk—why, it's just a little trinket that doesn't amount to anything. (*Buzzer sounds and lights flash.*)

BILLIE. Oh, my goodness, there's the opening.

(MAZIE *enters on stairs, with costume, followed by* ROY, GIRLS *in costume.*)

MAZIE. Hey, kid, you forgot part of your props.

BILLIE. Oh, did I? Thanks, Mazie.

ROY. Come on, girls. There's the opening. Make it snappy, now.

ANN (*snatching cigarette from* GRACE). Gimme a drag on that weed before you kill it.

RUBY. Say, Grace, you better remember what I told you about cutting in front of me in this number.

GRACE. I will.

RUBY. See that you don't.

MAZIE. Aw, tie it outside.

RUBY. Who's talking to you?

ROY. Get your places. (*Pulls* BILLIE *away from* STEVE. NICK *enters from office.*) Every night a first night. They all paid for their seats. Heavy cover. We got to be good.

NICK. Now, girls, tonight some pep, and for God's sake, remember, smile at the men.

RUBY. Smile at 'em—it's all we can do to *keep from laughing* at 'em.

(*With a swell of music* ROY *and girls exeunt to cabaret. As each one reaches the door, she picks up the dance step and sings, changing her manner from boredom to pep. The music becomes faint as doors close.*)

NICK (*sits*). According to my bookkeeping, I owe myself money—I don't know.

STEVE. Well, I've heard that before. How much, Nick? (DAN MC CORN *enters from hall door. He is a man about thirty; mat-*

ter of fact and rather well dressed.) Well, good old Dan McCorn.

DAN. Hello, boys. (*He turns to look at poker machine.* NICK *has risen alarmed—* STEVE *motions him to sit.*)

NICK. What you want in here?

DAN. Oh, just dropped in.

STEVE. You're unusually sociable, ain't you?

DAN. Well, mebbe—I paid the rent to-day and two grocery bills—that always makes me feel good.

NICK. Grocery bills shouldn't worry you if you would listen.

STEVE. A square dick, huh?

DAN. Figure it out yourself. (JOE *comes from hall with two drinks—sees* MC CORN *and quickly exits.*) Well, Nick, how's business?

NICK. Can't complain.

DAN. How's your business, Steve?

STEVE. So so——

DAN. Extending your trade a little, ain't you?

STEVE. How do you mean?

DAN. Kinda moving up town.

STEVE. Where do you get that idea?

DAN. Oh, I hear everybody's troubles.

NICK. And they got a lot of 'em, I bet you.

STEVE (*deliberately*) Say, Dan, you don't suppose for a minute——

DAN. That you can't peddle it where you please? No, I ain't sayin' that, only ain't it likely to cause trouble?

STEVE. Trouble?

DAN. That's a bad bunch up there. Some of 'em two-term men——

NICK. Some of them gorillas of Steve's ain't such a sweet bunch either.

DAN. That's what I say—that's why it looks like fireworks. (STEVE *glares at* NICK.)

NICK. Wouldn't you think, with all the trouble it is to get it—they wouldn't fight over who sells it?

STEVE. Well, some people ain't never satisfied.

DAN. By the way, seen Scar Edwards lately?

STEVE (*with mild surprise—as though he hadn't quite caught the question*). Speaking to me?

DAN. Well, not exactly. Have you?

STEVE. About two weeks ago I saw him —at the races.

DAN. Speaking to him?

STEVE. Sure—why not? I gave him a tip that paid 20 to 1.

DAN. Yeah? You didn't see him, then, when he was here to-night?

NICK. Huh?

STEVE. Here? Who?

DAN. You didn't, Steve? Huh?

STEVE (*long pause*). Your arm is swelling, Dan. What did you put in it?

DAN. Scar Edwards was here, wasn't he?

STEVE. Listen, Dan. Scar Edwards and me are personal friends, but we don't do business together.

DAN. Maybe that's why he came.

STEVE. Don't be silly.

DAN. I'm not.

NICK. He wouldn't come to my place.

DAN. Well, he was in this neighborhood, anyway—anyway—that much I know, 'cause I saw him myself.

STEVE. You saw him? Where?

DAN. Under a blanket in a Westcott Express truck, just a block and a half from here—lying on his face with a slug in his back.

NICK. For God's sake!

STEVE. So they got him, eh? That's too bad— Scar wasn't a bad sort when you knew him.

DAN. I hope to tell you.

STEVE. Well, that's a tough break—I'm sorry to hear it.

DAN. Now that I don't sound so silly—who pulled that off?

STEVE. How the hell should I know?

DAN. Funny part of it all is, he didn't have a rod on him.

NICK. You find him——

DAN. No, the Westcott driver found him, when he came out of the lunch room. I got there shortly after.

STEVE. Can you imagine that driver.

DAN. Yeh, lucky thing he found him so soon, still warm when I got there——

STEVE (*casually*). What time was it?

DAN. Must have been—say—twenty minutes or half past ten.

STEVE. Well, I've been here all evening, haven't I, Nick?

DAN. I didn't ask you for an alibi, but since you mention it—let's have it—who was with you?

STEVE (*revealing just a flash of chagrin at his slip, he controls himself and speaks calmly*). Why, Porky Thompson and Nick here part of the time. Billie Moore—one of the girls—most anybody could tell you they all saw me.

(PORKY *comes in from hall.*)

PORKY (*to* DAN, *surprised*). Oh, you're here—I was looking at the show and—yeah—how are you?

DAN. Thompson, what time were you here with Steve and Nick tonight?

PORKY (*hesitatingly.* STEVE *motions with his hands*). I came in—about—five after nine—(STEVE *signals again*)—yes, sir—five minutes after ten.

(STEVE *walks away with satisfied expression.*)

DAN. Why so positive?

STEVE (*cutting in*). I happened to ask him for the correct time when he came in.

DAN. You didn't have a watch?

STEVE. Sure. But I wanted to see if I was right.

DAN. When he told you—then you knew you were right—is that it?

STEVE (*righteous indignation*). Where the hell do you get off to sweat me?

PORKY. What's the matter—what's up?

NICK. Someone killed Scar Edwards.

PORKY (*smiles*). Well, well—— (*Sees* STEVE'S *look—changes mood.*) Gee, that's too bad.

DAN. You guys ain't thinking of goin' in mourning, are you?

(ROY *and girls come back in line with swell of music and faint applause.* LIL *enters on stairs.*)

ROY. Holy gee, but the orchestra put that number on the fritz—a bunch of plumbers—they're off the beat like a night watchman.

LIL. Why ain't you guys out there giving the kids a hand?

ROY. All set, Lil. I'm going to announce you.

LIL. Anybody out there?

ROY. Not yet. They don't come in as a rule till just before my big number (*Exit to cabaret. Heard announcing:*) Miss Lillian Rice! (LIL *exits to cabaret as orchestra plays blues.*)

(*The girls change into the other costumes which they have left on the prop table.*)

DAN. Nice looking bunch, Nick.

NICK. You got your eyes open, eh, Dan. Would you like to know one of 'em?

DAN. That red-headed one sort of appeals to me.

STEVE. Don't introduce him to Billie. I'm taking no chances.

BILLIE (*hears her name*). What?

STEVE. Don't have anything to do with these handsome cops.

NICK (*brings* PEARL *down*). Pearl, I want you to be nice to my old friend, Dan McCorn, here.

PEARL. How are you?

DAN. I was thinking I'd seen you somewhere before.

PEARL. That's an old one.

DAN. On the level. You used to be dancing at—the Golden Bowl, didn't you?

PEARL. No, sir, not me. (*She goes back to her dressing table.*)

DAN (*shakes hands with* NICK). Well, boys, I guess there's nothing else I can talk about just now—sorry to have took so much of your time.

STEVE (*shakes with* DAN). Hell, Dan, glad to give you all the time we got—only wish I could help you. I know you got your job same as I got mine.

NICK. Sure, it's best everybody get along.

DAN. Well, so long.

NICK. So long, Dan.

STEVE. Come again, Dan.

DAN. Sure. (*Exits to cabaret.*)

STEVE. Porky, take a stroll out. (PORKY *follows* DAN.)

MAZIE (*seeing bracelet*). Hey, will you look at that. (ALL GIRLS *crowd around.*)

ANN. Let's see. Where'd you get it?

RUBY. Where'd you s'pose she got it?

MAZIE. Oh, gee, the Knickerbocker Ice Company. Gee, you got him *going strong.*

ROY (*enters from cabaret*). Well, Boss, they're eating it up out there.

RUBY. Well, hoofer, I guess you'll be looking for a new partner.

ROY. What?

PEARL. Oh, boy, when'd he give it to you?

GRACE. Some rocks!

ROY (*pushes his way through girls and looks at bracelet*). What you got there?

ANN. Steve gave it to her.

ROY. You ain't gonna keep it?

MAZIE. Certainly she is.

ROY. Give it back to him.

BILLIE. Now, Roy——

ROY. Listen, Billie, don't be a fool. You know what everybody'll be saying about you.

BILLIE. Don't tell me what to do!

ROY. I tell you, give it back to him.

BILLIE. Listen, General Pershing.

ROY. You do what I say.

BILLIE. Mind your own business.

ROY. Please, Billie, I'm telling you something straight from the heart——

NICK (*pushes* BILLIE). Hey, hey, what

you gonna do—have some heart talks instead of doing your number?

ROY. No, sir, Mr. Verdis. I'm right here waiting to do my stuff. Nobody can say I don't give the customers one hundred percent every performance. The night my old man died, I went out at the Regent Theatre in Danbury and give as good a performance as I ever done in my life—(*Turns and looks at* BILLIE.) And even if a jane I'd put my hope and trust in was going to hell, I could still go out and give 'em my best. (*Cross up.*) Line up, kids. (PORKY *enters from hall.*)

PORKY. Dan McCorn is sittin' out there waitin'. What the hell's—the matter?

ROY. There's the cue. Give it to 'em. Cut 'em deep and let 'em bleed. Here we go. Here we go. Let's mop up

(*While the two men stand looking at each other inquiringly, the cabaret doors open, the music swells,* ROY *puts on a little hat with a feather in it, and dances out behind the girls.*)

CURTAIN

ACT TWO

Half an hour later.

Music off in cabaret.

PORKY *sits picking his teeth—shakes his head pessimistically. He tosses a coin—is dissatisfied with the result.*

STEVE *enters from hall; closes the double doors.*

———

STEVE. Good thing I went out there and calmed down them Chicago gorillas. If they kept on talking shop so loud, I'd lose my reputation as a butter and egg man from Florida.

PORKY. Dan McCorn still out there?

STEVE. He's talking to one of the pickups.

PORKY. Wish to God he'd go for good.

STEVE. I don't know—he seems to be having a good time.

PORKY. I seen 'em act that way before. Believe me, I think he's getting all set to make a pinch.

STEVE. Cut that out. Don't be so jumpy. What makes you so jumpy every time somebody gets bumped off?

PORKY. Well, I was thinkin', maybe he's got a lot of bulls hanging around the block, for all we know. (STEVE *lights a cigarette.*) Say, Steve, tell me on the square, you know who done it, don't you?

STEVE. I haven't the faintest idea.

PORKY. Well, you know it ain't healthy for you to hang around here after Scar's been killed, don't you?

STEVE. Are you talking to me?

PORKY. Sure thing I am.

STEVE (*stops him with look—then speaks casually*). A gang shooting is no novelty in this burg. The cops will be glad he's out of the deck.

PORKY (*summoning up his courage*). But, Steve, you done it, didn't you?

STEVE. I don't know a thing about it. Me and the deceased was great friends. We'll spare no expense in giving him a swell funeral. Flowers—all kinds—we'll make it the biggest event of the season—a great success—and tell the boys I want 'em all to turn out for it.

PORKY. Say, you talk like it was his wedding.

STEVE. Not much different, at that.

(*Knock on back door. Pause.* STEVE *gestures to* PORKY. PORKY, *fearful but obedient, peeks through shutters.*)

PORKY. It's Dolph. (*Opens door and* DOLPH *comes in.*) What's the matter?

STEVE. I thought I sent you out for air.

DOLPH (*pulls tabloids out from under coat*). The morning papers just came out.

STEVE. Yeah?

DOLPH. A lot of stuff about Scar Edwards' bump off.

PORKY (*takes paper*). What's it say?

STEVE (*takes paper*). Let's see.

PORKY (*reading*). "Gang leader murdered. Story on Page 4."

STEVE. Pictures and everything. Say, that's quick work, ain't it? Dan McCorn himself only knew it about two hours ago. Wonderful what they do nowadays. We should be very thankful for these modern inventions, boys—keeps us posted on the underworld.

DOLPH. Believe me, all that stuff ain't gonna be so good for somebody—all this talkin' and chewin' about it.

PORKY. "Harlem Gang Leader's Body Found in Roaring Forties. Old Gang Feud Likely to Break Out."

STEVE. Read to yourself——

DOLPH (*tensely*). It says the cops have got some hop tips.

STEVE. Sure they have. Here's the real dope, though. Now listen—this is good, see. (*Read.*) "It is learned from confidential sources that the police suspect one of Edwards' own gang who is said to have nursed a grudge against his leader. An arrest is expected within twenty-four hours."

DOLPH. What do you know about that—— (*He takes the paper from* STEVE *and reads as it trembles in his hands.*)

STEVE. Smart boys, them cops. Yes, sir, Porky, you want to be very careful how you conduct yourself in the future, because them fellows don't let nothing get by.

DOLPH. It says they suspect one of Scar's own crowd, huh?

STEVE. That's what it says. Well, that's my theory. It's a good hunch, don't you think so, Dolph?

DOLPH (*dumfounded*). Sure.

PORKY. But even if the cops don't bother us—they's something in that gang-war talk all right——

STEVE. What do I care? I got you two boys to protect me.

DOLPH. Listen, Steve, this ain't as sweet as it looks.

PORKY. Dolph is right.

STEVE. Oh, shut up. (*Quietly.*) I certainly get a lot of co-operation out of you two. For the love of Mike, pull yourselves together.

PORKY. We're together.

STEVE. Anybody'd think you was a couple of Staten Island hicks trying to find the Subways.

DOLPH. Well, what's the matter? I was just tipping you what was going on——

PORKY. He was just thinking about your safety, Steve. (DOLPH *crosses to door under stairs, peeks out.*) Wish I knew who done it—I'm worried.

STEVE (*steps toward* PORKY). Will you shut up, or will I crown you with a gun butt?

PORKY. I'm shut—— (STEVE *strolls away.*) But I'm worried, just the same. What if the Edwards' outfit bump me off?

DOLPH. Me too.

STEVE. Well, what of it? You only have to die once. You got nothing to worry about—— I'll bury you right—I may get a special professional rate from Campbell's if they get the both of you. (*Laughs.*) Say, quit worryin'. I wish they *would* start something. We'll go up to Harlem in a couple of fast cars and let these Chicago boys show off some of their machine-gun stuff.

DOLPH. No, Steve, on the dead, whyn't you go out of town till this blows over?

STEVE (*sits*). I got something here that interests me.

PORKY. Take her with you.

DOLPH. I hate to see this chorus amitshure playing you for a sucker. Why don't you take her for a ride and then stop off at Little Ed's roadhouse?

PORKY. Sure, we might all get in trouble if you stay here.

STEVE. Say, have you both lost all your sense? If I wanted to get myself accused of the murder of Scar Edwards, the surest way to do it would be to blow town. No, I'm staying here because *I am innocent.*

(*The cabaret doors open. The music swells to a finale with a crash of cymbals. There is applause, and the girls in Hawaiian costume, and* ROY, *enter. They go to the prop tables, in perfunctory fashion, and gather up their belongings.* KATIE *follows* PEARL, *hands her a note and stands waiting for an answer.*)

STEVE. That's intermission. You go out now and keep the visitors from coming back here, and don't be rubbering at McCorn—act unconcerned.

PORKY. Sure.

STEVE. You, too, Dolph.

PEARL (*as she finishes reading note*). Tell him I'll come as soon as I've changed. (PORKY *and* DOLPH *go to cabaret.*)

STEVE. Billie, I've been waiting here for half an hour trying to get a word with you. (MAZIE, *seeing that* STEVE *wants to be alone with* BILLIE, *takes her props and costumes and goes upstairs and out with the others knowingly.*) In fact, ever since I was out in front looking at you and saw that something was missing. Didn't you like the bracelet?

BILLIE. Oh, of course I did—awfully—I thought it was lovely.

STEVE. Then why don't you wear it?

BILLIE. Well—I—Mr. Crandall, I'll explain about it a little later when we've got time.

STEVE. We've got time now. This is the intermission, isn't it?

BILLIE. Yes, but I—I mean——

STEVE (*takes her hand*). No, really, I want to know. I'm proud of you, little fella—so I thought it would be nice for you to wear my bracelet——

BILLIE. I did wear it for a while.

STEVE. If you don't like it, I'll take it back to Tiffany's and change it.

BILLIE. Oh, I'm just crazy about it.

STEVE. Then why'd you take it off?

BILLIE. Well, Ruby began making some dirty cracks about it—and then I got wise to what it really meant——

STEVE. What does it mean?

BILLIE. I guess you know.

STEVE. No, tell me. I just thought it was a good-looking bracelet and you were a good-looking kid, and the two of you looked awfully well together.

BILLIE. It's a slave bracelet, isn't it?

STEVE. I guess that's what it's called.

BILLIE. That's what they said—and they said if a rich man gives you one and you wear it, then that's a sign that you belong to him.

STEVE (*quietly*). I don't mind if they say that.

BILLIE. Well, I do.

STEVE. You like me, don't you? I know you like me—I can tell——

BILLIE. Yes.

STEVE. And I sure like you—and—I want to be able to do things for you and——

BILLIE. It isn't fair to you—that—I mean I can't take this bracelet off you because it wouldn't be fair.

STEVE. Don't you think I'd treat you right?

BILLIE. I s'pose I shouldn't have let you take me out at all, Mr. Crandall, because I know it sounds silly, but I'm not that kind of a girl, that's all.

STEVE. Maybe that's why I like you.

BILLIE. I know there's nothing wonderful about being the way I am—I mean being virtuous, I s'pose you call it—I know lots of the best-hearted girls in the world that aren't, so it isn't that; but I mean it isn't fair for me to keep your bracelet because that's the way I am.

STEVE. Well, listen, baby, have I ever tried to pull any rough stuff?

BILLIE. No, you haven't, and that's what I always say——

STEVE. Then why haven't I got as much right to hang around you as some of these other yaps?

BILLIE. Well, you're married, of course, and——

STEVE. No, I'm not.

BILLIE. They said you was.

STEVE. No, I'm divorced—I'm all right—I'm divorced—twice. Just because you're here in the show, don't think I regard you in a light way—no, indeed—I'm no fly-by-night—I'm a very sincere sort of person, Baby, and I want you to understand how I feel about you. I'm crazy about you. Honest, no foolin'. (*Draws her to him a little.* ROY *enters on stairs.*) Don't listen to nobody but me, kiddie—'cause I'll treat you right——

ROY. Mazie wants to see you right away, Billie.

BILLIE. Oh, does she? All right—excuse me. (*She goes up and out.* ROY *summons up his courage and comes downstairs, trying to look unconcerned.* STEVE *stands grimly waiting for him.*)

STEVE. Say, listen, actor—— (ROY *stops.*) Did anyone ever hit you right on the nose?

ROY. Yeh, once—come to think of it—twice. Why?

STEVE. I was wondering if you'd like to have it happen again.

ROY. What did I ever do to you?

STEVE (*recovering his calm*). Nothing—you couldn't. I was a sucker to get sore. Forget it. (*He exits to cabaret.*)

(MAZIE *and* BILLIE *enter at top stairs.*)

MAZIE. Hey, oilcan, what is this?

BILLIE. She never said she wanted me at all. You had no right to say that, Roy.

ROY. What I done was for the best—I had to get you out of hearing so I could chase that twenty-five-cent guy out of here.

MAZIE (*coming downstairs*). Listen to what's a yapping about twenty-five cent guys.

ROY. He ain't a fit companion for Billie and from now on I'm making it my business to see that he don't have nothing to do with her.

MAZIE. Where's your wings?

BILLIE (*following them*). Well, Roy, it seems to me you're taking an awful lot for granted without consulting anybody.

MAZIE. And picked out an exciting job for himself, too.

ROY. In the first place, you ain't going to stay to his party to-night.

MAZIE. She certainly is.

ROY. It's no place for a nice girl like Billie.

MAZIE. Oh, I see. But it's perfectly all right for me, though, eh?

ROY. Well, maybe you know how to handle gorillas—you know your goolash. She don't.

MAZIE. Billie'll be all right. Steve's a fine fellow and he's just out for some innocent fun——

ROY. Says you——

MAZIE. Says I——

ROY. This staying up all night, running wild, drinking poison, don't get you a thing. I'm no prude. I'm for light wines and beer—but if a girl wants to get ahead in this racket, she shouldn't start out her career partying with rough-necks. In the second place—you're going to give back that bracelet.

MAZIE. Give it back—— Ha! Ha! I'll tell one. Why, she could get five hundred for it in hock. Listen, Small Time, this little novice has got a great chance to grab off a millionaire if she works her points. Are you going to stand around and try to gum it?

ROY. I certainly am.

MAZIE. Then you ain't the gentleman I thought you was. He might marry her. Did you see that cracked ice—— When Steve gives up like that, he's gone, hook, line and sinker.

ROY. Marry!

MAZIE. I'm telling you—hand-embroidered night-gowns and everything——

BILLIE. Now, if you're all done discussing me, perhaps I could say a word myself.

ROY. Well, if there's any thought of his trying to get away with that marriage stuff, it's time for me to do something definite.

MAZIE. Sure it is—bow yourself out of the picture.

ROY. Is that the way you feel about it, Billie?

BILLIE. No.

ROY. All right. Then I'd like to speak to you about something very private. (*To* MAZIE.) Would you kindly leave us?

MAZIE. Go to it. I got to get in some work on a sandwich, anyhow. Don't believe a word he says, Billie. (*Exit upstairs.*)

BILLIE (*comes to him*). Roy, I wish you wouldn't keep acting that way.

ROY. What way is that?

BILLIE. Just going around arguing with everybody and making trouble.

ROY. I'm going to save you from getting into a lot of trouble.

BILLIE. I didn't ask you to.

ROY. I know you didn't. And take it from me, I ain't achin' to play the hero in this picture myself, but there's nothing else to do. Now first, I'm going to put a plain proposition to you. (*He comes toward her, half appealingly. She sits, looking up at him.*) I guess you know pretty well that I'm very strong for you, but I ain't said nothing about matrimony on account of my old man has just recently died. But since this big four-flusher is talking about a wedding ring, I'll play my own ace. Listen, honey, how about getting hitched up?

BILLIE (*faintly*). Roy, I don't know.

ROY. It would be better for the act, wouldn't it?

BILLIE. I never thought much about it.

ROY. I s'pose I should of tipped you off how I felt before, but anyhow there it is in black and white.

BILLIE (*distressed*). Gee, I don't know what to say.

ROY. Take your time. I know it's kind of sudden. But I sort of thought you was wise to how I felt anyhow.

BILLIE. Well, I did think you liked me —I mean I hoped you liked me.

ROY. Well, now that you know how much I like you, what do you think about the idea?

BILLIE (*rises*). I don't know what to say.

ROY. I always thought, way down in our insides, we knew we was for each other. God knows I'm for you, Billie girl, so just say the word that you're for me and I won't let out no yells or nothing, but I sure would feel just like doing that little thing. (*She doesn't answer.*) What do you say?

BILLIE. Well, Roy, of course I'd have to think a thing like this over and——

ROY. Nothing doing. Just as easy to say it now as some other time.

BILLIE. How can I say it, when I don't know for sure whether I'm in love with you or not.

ROY. Well, we certainly get on well together.

BILLIE. Oh, I know we do, just wonderful.

ROY. Well, when you see me coming to say hello to you in the morning, don't your heart never beat no faster?

BILLIE. Yes, it does.

ROY. Well, that's it. That's what they call love at first sight, kid. It's wonderful. I'm the same way.

BILLIE. But I don't know if we ought to talk about marrying when we're so poor——

ROY (*he comprehends her reason for hesitating*). Oh—— (*Turns away from her, hurt and tense.*) You want a rich guy——

BILLIE. I didn't say that.

ROY (*contemptuously*). A gold digger.

BILLIE. I'm not. I'm not. But I don't want to be foolish and say something that I'll be sorry for afterwards. All I say is that I ought to think about a thing like this.

ROY. Aw, you want to think.

BILLIE. Yes.

ROY. All right, my duty's plain. Go on upstairs and think.

BILLIE. Well, don't talk to me that way or I never will marry you.

ROY (*dismissing her*). Sure. Talk it over with you next week. (*She bites her lip to keep back the tears and runs upstairs.* ROY *watches her until she's off, then goes to phone and drops a nickel in slot.*) Hello—I want long distance. (*Gets returned nickel.*) Long distance? I want to get Trenton, New Jersey. I want the Capitol Hotel there and I want to speak to one of the Maloney Brothers. No, not Baloney—Maloney — Maloney — M-a-l-o-n-e-y—Maloney. "M" as in matrimony. Yes, that's right. Maloney—there's two of them in the act and any one of them will do. Make it snappy, girlie, will you, 'cause this is a very important call. How much will this set me back? What? Gee—— Well, all right. This is Roy Lane. Circle 5440. (*During the latter part of his speech* BILLIE *enters from dressing room and comes downstairs hesitatingly.*) Now do me a favor, sister, and put this call through right quick, will you, please?

BILLIE (*pleadingly*). Roy—— (ROY *hangs up.*)

ROY. What do you want?

BILLIE. I ought to explain.

ROY. Now, listen. I told you where I stood. All you got to do is say yes or no.

BILLIE. First you ought to give me a chance to explain.

ROY (*comes closer*). Hey, you've got your make-up all streaked. You been crying.

BILLIE. Yes, I have.

ROY. One of the first things every artist should learn is, never cry during a performance.

BILLIE. I cried because of the way you talked to me.

ROY. Forget it, forget it. I'm wise now to how you feel—that's what I wanted to know. I got my duty that's all.

BILLIE. But you don't know how I feel. You never gave me a chance——

ROY. I got the idea and just now I'm expecting a phone call, so——

BILLIE. You make me feel terrible. I don't want a rich man, but I know that it's just awful to be poor.

ROY. Well, to-morrow——

BILLIE (*almost in tears*). All my life everybody I've known has been poor, and my mother always says, whatever you do, don't marry a poor fellow——

ROY. Well, for God's sake, haven't I told you what they get on the big time vaudeville and productions? (*Phone rings.*) All right. Now get out of here, willya? This is a business call. (*She exits upstairs.* ROY *at phone.*) Hello.—Yes, I'm trying to get Trenton. All right. (*Drops quarters in slot.*) There you are, sister. Hello—hello—This one of the Maloney Brothers? Jack? Oh, Babe—Babe, this is Roy—— How's the act going? Yeah. Got you opening the show, eh? Well, don't worry, Babe. I'll take a peek at it—I'll probably make some suggestions that will fix it O.K. That's duck soup for me, you know. What? Oh, nothing's wrong with me. Everything's O.K. But listen, Babe——

(*Lights flash. Buzzer sounds.* RUBY, GRACE *and* MAZIE, *in school-girl costume, enter from dressing rooms, come down stairs talking.*)

ROY (*lowers voice*). Listen, can you hear me? I want you to do me a big favor—listen—— Have you got a pencil? (*Continues talking—speaking low.*)

RUBY. Sure, we'll have to stay for Steve's party. Who's yowling about it?

GRACE. Oh, Billie.

(GRACE *gets school books and slates from prop table.*)

RUBY. That one. Guess one party won't spoil her.

MAZIE. How many did it take to spoil you?

RUBY. You ought to know—I saw you at the first. (*They all wrangle at once.*)

ROY (*at phone—turns to them*). Hey, take it easy.

MAZIE. Steve's passed you up like a white chip, ain't he, dearie?

RUBY. Say, want me to haul off and knock you down?

MAZIE. If you do, I'll bounce up and *separate your ideas* from *your habits!*

GRACE. There's the cue. (*The three girls quickly form in line and exit to cabaret singing with baby voices, "M-i-s, s-i-s, s-i-p-p-i," etc.*)

ROY (*at phone*). You're a life-saver—do as much for you some time. So long. (*To* PEARL *who appears on stairs in pirate costume.*) Want the phone?

PEARL. No, I gotta meet a John.

ROY. I got a John I'm going to meet pretty soon and bust him right square in the beak. (*Grabs hat and books.*)

PEARL. Say, Roy.

ROY. Yeah?

PEARL. You been extra sweet to me since I been around here, and let me tip you off to something. Don't monkey with the Crandall fellow. You might get hurt.

ROY. Him? I'll have him in Sing Sing before I get through. (*Runs to door to listen for cue, but finds he has plenty of time and comes back.*) You know what I think he really is?

PEARL. What?

ROY. A bootlegger!

PEARL (*with assumed surprise*). No? You don't say so.

ROY. Wait and see. (*Exit to cabaret in posture of Professor, while girls' voices are heard singing "School Days."*)

(PEARL, *finding herself alone, goes to phone, drops coin in slot.* DAN *enters from up hall.* PEARL *quickly hangs up receiver, turns from phone.*)

DAN. Hello.

PEARL. Oh!

DAN. You got my note all right, did you?

PEARL. Sure.

DAN. Was you going to telephone?

PEARL. No, nothing important.

DAN. Positive?

PEARL. Didn't I tell you? (*Waits, then adds, impatient to be away from him.*) I gotta get ready for my number in a minute.

DAN. I won't keep you long. (PEARL *stops, back towards* DAN. *Pause.*) Seen Scar Edwards lately?

PEARL (*turns*). What?

DAN (*ignoring her bluff*). Have you?

PEARL. What's the idea?

DAN. You know who I am?

PEARL. Sure, you're a cop.

DAN. Well, I know who you are, too. You're the girl I seen palling around with Scar Edwards when you were dancing up in the Golden Bowl.

PEARL. You never saw *me*.

DAN (*turns her to face him*). Oh—yes—I—did—didn't I?

PEARL. Well, that's no crime, is it?

DAN. Not exactly, but why are you working down here?

PEARL (*dropping bravado*). You ain't going to give me away to Nick, are you?

DAN. Not a bit. What I'm asking you is for my own information, see. It don't go any further. Are you on the outs with Scar?

PEARL. No, and if it's all the same, would you mind calling him Jim?

DAN. Excuse me. (*Looks at her steadily.*) You're keeping tabs on this bunch for Scar?—I mean Jim. Is that right?

PEARL (*appeals to him*). He didn't want to put somebody down here he couldn't absolutely trust, for fear they'd double cross him—a lot of dirty skunks. They wouldn't stop at nothing.

DAN. But Jim Edwards trusts you, eh?

PEARL. Sure—(*With a sudden burst of confidence.*) We're gonna be married as soon as he gets his final papers.

DAN (*walking away*). That's too bad.

PEARL. What is? (*Pause.*) Has he done something you want him for?

DAN. No, I haven't a thing on him, lady.

PEARL. Well, tell me straight—has something happened? You act so kind of funny.

DAN. You gotta finish this show tonight? Sing and everything?

PEARL. Sure, I go on again.

DAN. Well, I won't take up any more of your time, then. I just wanted to know if you'd seen Edwards to-night.

PEARL. No, I ain't seen him since breakfast, but— (*Again decides to trust him.*) I don't know why I shouldn't tell you—he told me he was coming down here to-night to have a show-down with Steve.

DAN. Oh, oh, he told you—— Well, I'll be going along about my business. Thanks, Mrs. Edwards.

PEARL (*pleased*). In three weeks.

DAN. You just keep this under your hat, won't you?

PEARL. Will I? (ROY *enters, followed by girls, singing "Farmer in the Dell."*) If I want to get out of here with all my neck, I will.

DAN. Pleased to have met you. (*Strolls out cabaret arch, then turns to his left and goes down hall.* PEARL *is puzzled—depressed—tries to shake off her fear—walks to stairs and exits.* ROY *grabs up a prop.*)

ROY. After this, a little more room, girls, when I make that side kick.

GRACE. All right.

RUBY. In your hat. (ROY *exits to cabaret, dancing; the girls start upstairs.*) Which one of you tarts got on my slippers, huh?

MAZIE. These must be yours, dearie. They're a mile too big for me.

(*Girls go upstairs to dressing room.* NICK *and* PORKY *enter from hall.*)

PORKY. I can't look at that hoofer no longer—a different suit, but the same old dance.

(BILLIE *comes down stairs with telegraph blank and goes left.*)

NICK. It's the best I can do for the money. (*To* BILLIE.) Where you going?

BILLIE. I'll be back in time for my number.

NICK. That ain't what I asked you.

BILLIE (*at cabaret door*). I want to give this telegram to the doorman to send my mother. If I'm going to stay to the party, I have to tell her. (NICK *gestures to go ahead. She exits up hall.*)

PORKY. Is that the one that Steve is nuts about?

NICK (*shrugs*). Yeh, I don't know why—but that's it. He says she got best looking legs in New York——

(LIL *enters on stairs.*)

PORKY. Legs—ain't all one size—some is lean—some is fat.

LIL (*at foot of steps*). And how do you like 'em, Mr. Thompson?

(PORKY *is embarrassed.* NICK *exits to office.*)

PORKY. Me? If a woman's got sense, I never see her legs.

LIL (*cross to piano, puts box on it*). Ain't you a comfort.

PORKY. Well, my friends say they liked your act very well.

LIL. Yeah? Did you like it?

PORKY. Sure I did. Didn't you see me out there?

LIL. Yeah—but I was a little bit discouraged when I looked down and seen you was asleep.

PORKY. What? Oh, my God, lady—no. No, that's the way I get—you know—carried away—I shut my eyes when I'm terribly interested.

LIL. I guess you didn't shut your eyes when the weenies was out there.

PORKY. No. I wasn't interested. They wasn't nothing worth listening to, so the least I could do was to look at 'em. But your singin' was—well, I can't express it—it's like I says to a friend of mine sittin' next to me—I says, "I consider that she's got one of the finest voices of her sex," I says.

LIL. Well, I'm generally in key.

PORKY. Sure you are, and that is more than a lot of these opera singers can say, too. Listen, I want you to tell me how you do that singin' some time—a long personal talk, if you know what I mean. You're stayin' to Steve's party to-night, ain't you?

LIL. I will—(*Smiles.*)—if you do.

PORKY. Sure.

LIL. Only don't ask me to sing, 'cause I don't know a single dirty song,—that is, not dirty enough for that bunch.

PORKY. This ain't no singing party. That bunch all lost their voices asking for bail. (*Buzzer.*)

LIL (*starts out*). Well, there goes the whistle. I gotta step out now and hit a couple of high ones.

(ROY *enters from cabaret.*)

PORKY. I'm coming too.

LIL. Sit where I can see you

PORKY. Sure—I'll be right at your feet.

(LIL *exits to cabaret, followed by* PORKY *down the hall.*)

(ROY *stands looking after them.* BILLIE *enters from hall. He turns away from her, goes to prop table and begins to undress.* BILLIE *starts upstairs, expecting him to speak, but he doesn't. She pauses.*)

BILLIE. All I've got to say is, if you always treated me like you have to-night, you'd make a terrible husband.

ROY. Oh, that's all you got to say, huh?

BILLIE. I should think that would be enough.

ROY. Not for me. (*She starts up.*) Come here a minute!

BILLIE. If you have anything to say, you know where to find me.

ROY. I gotta make a quick change, you know that.

BILLIE (*comes to him*). What is it?

ROY. Was you out there taking a drink?

BILLIE. No.

ROY. I'm glad to hear that, anyways.

BILLIE. I was sending a telegram to my mother.

ROY (*startled*). What?

BILLIE. You tried to boss me so much, I just thought I'd find out if I had a mind of my own. So I just went and telegraphed that I wouldn't be home to-night 'cause I'm going to the party.

ROY. Well, I'm sorry you done that. (*Takes off trousers.*) Listen to me, kiddie, if it's just to spite me you're doing this, why, I'll eat mud.

BILLIE. It's not only that—it's because I have an obligation.

ROY (*throws trousers over arm and goes to her*). Listen, partner. I've been your pal, anyhow, and I got some right to talk to you. Who have you got the greatest obligation to in this world, huh—a big rounder like Steve Crandall, who's got no respect for pure womanhood, or your poor old gray-haired mother who is sitting at home alone waiting for you?

BILLIE. But she's not alone—my sister's with her.

ROY. Oh. (*In disgust he throws his trousers on chair.*)

BILLIE. If you don't think I got enough character to be decent at a party, you better look for somebody you got confidence in.

(PORKY *enters from hall.*)

PORKY. Your shirt-tail's hanging out. (*Exit to office.*)

ROY (*paying no attention to him*). That ain't the life for you. (*Getting on trousers while he pleads earnestly.*) You don't want to be pegged with them bags, do you? They think they're wiser than Almighty God, the guy that wrote the book,—but when they're hittin' the home stretch for Potter's Field, they'll be wiser still. For God's sake, think of all the plans we made. Billie. Don't be a dumb-bell.

BILLIE. I'm not.

ROY. You're giving a good imitation of one.

BILLIE. I'd go, if for nothing else, just to show you good and proper that I don't belong to you.

ROY. If you did, I'd spank you.

BILLIE. Oh, you would—would you?

ROY. You bet I would—and if I catch you inhaling any of that poison, I'll spank you before the whole mob.

BILLIE. Then I *would* be finished with you.

ROY. I don't care if you never spoke to me again. I gotta do my duty by my partner—first the artist, that's me—and second, the human bein'. (*Buzzer.*) I done everything I could to appeal to your better instincts. I pulled every wire I knowed to keep you decent—and we ain't heard from all the precincts yet. (*Tries out comedy hat.*) I told you just what my feelings for you is. Nothing up the sleeve, so far as I'm concerned, so if you want to be sore, I guess that's how it'll have to be, that's all. (*Dances into cabaret in comic position.*)

(PORKY *comes in from office—stops a second in door, talking into office.*)

PORKY. Sure you're right. Sure you are. (PORKY *sees* BILLIE, *who has started upstairs, shuts door and crosses to middle of room.*) Say, little girl, did you see . . . ? (*The party doors open and* DAN *appears.*) Ah, yeah— well, never mind. I'll talk to you about it some other time. (BILLIE *looks over railing to see who it is, then exits.*) Well, hello, Dan. What you doin' in here? I thought you was out with one of the frails.

DAN (*coming down*). Well, I'm broadminded. I go in for everything. Got a light?

PORKY (*lights match*). Sure. (PORKY'S *hand shakes.*)

DAN. What are you shaking about?

PORKY. I'm not shaking.

DAN (*laughs*). Sure you are. Look—— (*He holds* PORKY'S *wrist.*)

PORKY. That's the way I always get.

DAN. When a cop's around?

PORKY. No, when I'm in love.

(DOLPH *enters from hall. Stops, alarmed at seeing* PORKY *and* DAN *together—then hurries back down hall.*)

DAN. Ever been accused of murder?

PORKY (*inarticulate with fear*). Me? Listen, Dan. Don't get me wrong—that stuff ain't in my line.

DAN. Oh, no, no—I didn't mean that—I was thinking about a fella I knew—it's tough, that's all—it's tough.

PORKY. Oh, very tough.

DAN. The fella would 'a' been all right if he'd told what he knew in the first place —but he tried to hold out.

PORKY. Oh, gee, what a mistake—always come clean, that's me—always come clean.

DAN. He was mixed up with kind of a sour crowd and——

PORKY. That's another thing. Bad company, that's something we all should avoid, Dan—eh? Ain't that right? Listen, Dan . . . (STEVE *enters from down hall, followed by* DOLPH, *who hovers in the background.*) I didn't have nothing to do with this thing—I——

STEVE. What the hell you trying to do, Mac, crab my party?

DAN. No, I am waiting for someone who saw Scar Edwards when he was here.

STEVE. Well, we've all told you he wasn't here.

DAN. You might be mistaken.

STEVE. No one around here has got any reasons for holding out on you. If I saw him, I'd say so—why not?

DAN. You might forget.

STEVE. Bushwah.

PORKY. I think some of his own crowd done it that got jealous.

DAN. I figger different. You see he didn't have a gun on him and he was shot in the back, which looks to me like he come peaceful to have a show-down—and just for that one reason he didn't carry his cannon.

PORKY. Well, I said once—and I'm willin' to repeat it—I didn't know him.

DAN (*sharply*). How do you know you didn't see him since you don't know him?

PORKY. Well—I—there wasn't anyone here when I came in.

DAN (*slowly*). No one?

STEVE. Well, I was—but I was in the office.

DAN (*without looking around*). Oh, and you were where, Dolph?

DOLPH. I was out riding with a couple of janes,—and if you want me to bring 'em into court and tell about it, I'll be glad to oblige you—— (*Innocently.*) Why? What's happened?

DAN. No matter what it is, you got your alibi all fixed now, eh?

DOLPH (*advancing*). What do you mean?

STEVE (*pulling him back*). Dan don't mean a thing, Dolph. Treat him civil even if he is a dick.

DAN. When did you get here to-night, Dolph?

DOLPH. Early, then I left Steve here and went out for the ride.

DAN. You left Steve alone?

STEVE. No, Porky was here.

DAN (*to* DOLPH). When you left?

DOLPH. No, I was——

PORKY. I was just coming in when he was going out.

DAN (*slowly*). Oh, now I got it—Steve was here when Porky comes in, but Porky didn't see him cause Steve was in the office—— (*To* PORKY.) Well, how did you know Steve was in the office if you didn't see him?

PORKY. Why——

STEVE (*stepping toward* DAN *belligerently*). He could hear me talking—— The door was open. Say for God's sake, Dan, you been all over this once. Now listen, if you think any of us here had anything to do with it, why go ahead and make the pinch, let's get some bail fixed and get it over with. But don't stand around here and make a coroner's inquest out of the place. I got a party on here tonight.

DAN. Well, now listen, sweetheart, why get excited? You know it's my business to ask questions, ain't it? I know you guys didn't have anything to do with it, but I got to make a report and I'm workin' at this from a couple of angles.

PORKY. Sure, Dan—that's right.

DAN. Trouble with you, Steve, is that you've had so much business with a lot of half-baked federal dicks, you ain't used to talking to just a plain old New York cop any more.

STEVE (*placated*). Well, maybe you're right.

DAN. I ain't always—— I been wrong lots of times, but this case of Edwards interests me—terribly. You see, whether a guy shoots square or not—according to the law—ain't always it—but no matter what he's done, to me, he should have a break, and somebody shot this guy in the back. (*Starts out.*)

(BENNIE, *a thug in a dress suit, enters from hall.*)

BENNIE. Hey—fellows—— (DAN *looks him over.*)

DAN. Well, Bennie, you're out in Chicago, now, eh?

BENNIE. Huh? What's the idea?

(DAN *exits down hall.*)

DOLPH (*between his teeth, going to hall door*). The son of a bitch.

BENNIE. Who's that guy?

PORKY. Dan McCorn.

STEVE. What you doing back here, Bennie? We ain't ready for you yet.

BENNIE. The boys want to be with the lingerie. (*Buzzer.*) The nerve of that big stiff looking at me that way! (GIRLS *start coming down stairs, dressed in Pirate costumes.* GRACE *and* BILLIE *cross to piano, then* PEARL, *then* ANN, RUBY *and* MAZIE *enter steps.*) What's the idea anyhow?

STEVE. Nothing that concerns you, Bennie.

RUBY. Ready, Pearl?

PEARL. Sure, I'm ready.

STEVE. A local nuisance by the name of Scar Edwards got bumped off tonight, that's all.

(PEARL *at the mention of* SCAR *halts her descent. As the sentence is finished, she gives a scream, loses her grip on the stair rail and falls down the steps in a faint.*)

GRACE. What—what's the matter? My God.

MAZIE (*hurrying to her*). Pearl.

STEVE. What happened?

RUBY. What the hell happened——

ANN. What happened; what's the matter?

BILLIE. Pearl! But, dearie, you must of——

PEARL. I'm all right.

MAZIE. What is it, Pearl?

PEARL (*trys to push them away*). I tell you I'm all right.

MAZIE. Gee Christmas, kid——

STEVE. What'd you do?

PEARL. I tripped on the stairs. That's all.

RUBY. I thought you fainted.

PEARL. Fainted? Fer what? Twisted my ankle, that's all.

(BILLIE *helps* PEARL.)

STEVE. Sure you're all right?

PEARL. Sure I am.

MAZIE. She'll be all right.

STEVE (*turns back dismissing the incident*). All right, Bennie. Bring your bunch back. Pretty near time, anyhow. Go ahead, Dolph. (*Exit* DOLPH *and* BENNIE *down hall.*) Come on girls. I want to buy you a drink. What say?

MAZIE. We can't now, Steve. We're on for this flash, you know.

STEVE. Well, I'll have a flock of them waiting for you as soon as you come off. All ready for a big night?

MAZIE. Try us.

STEVE. I am going to. Now here you are —girls—see these hundred-dollar certificates? Well, you each get one of them. (*They crowd around, except* PEARL *and* BILLIE.)

GIRLS. One for each.

GRACE. Atta boy.

PEARL. You tell 'em.

ANN. Me for you.

RUBY. Go to it.

STEVE. Wait a minute—this is the way we do it. I'll tear 'em in half and give each one of you your bit. Now if you're all good babies, when the party is over I'll tack the other half on. Fair? (*He tears the bills in half, passing each girl half.*

MAZIE. Sure it's fair.

GRACE. Three cheers for Steve.

ANN. This sure looks like a good start.

RUBY. Everything is hotzy-totzy.

STEVE. Just be yourselves with these friends of mine and the sky is the limit. This party will be nobody's business. Here, Pearl, if you make good you get the other half——

PEARL. Don't worry. I'll make good.

STEVE. Atta baby. Here, Billie. (BILLIE *won't take hers.* STEVE *laughs.*) I'll keep it for you.

(ROY *enters from cabaret.*)

ROY. Come on, girls. Give 'em your best. This is a short one. I just got a flash at a guy standin' in the back that I thought was Al Jolson.

GIRLS (*excited*). Oh!

ROY. On your toes—alley op. (*Doors open. They exit, with daggers in mouth.*)

PORKY (*crossing to* STEVE). Did I say the right things?

STEVE. What do you mean?

PORKY. To Dan McCorn.

STEVE. Sure, don't worry about him. Forget it—

PORKY. I do, but——

(JOE *opens doors of party room. It is now brightly lighted—the table set—the waiters hurrying about making final preparations.*)

STEVE (*calling to party room*). Joe, fix up some highballs and make mine a strong one. (BENNIE *and* DOLPH *come in from hall with Chicago mob.* PORKY *does comedy lockstep.* BENNIE *kicks* PORKY *in fun.*) Come on in, boys. What do you think of it, huh?

MIKE. Class, all right.

STEVE. Nothing like this in the Loop.

LARRY. This is get together week in old Manhattan.

BENNIE. The place you got to go through to get to Chicago.

DOLPH. Wait till you're here awhile.

BENNIE. Looks like a big night.

LARRY. How long before we meet the dames?

STEVE. They'll be here in a minute. (*Cheers.*) Now remember, boys, no shop talk tonight. Everybody here don't know our racket.

DOLPH. Steve, you better be the one to serve out the introductions.

PORKY. And don't let anyone sing the prisoner's song or we'll all be in tears. (*They laugh.*)

(*Girls come rushing in from cabaret.*)

DOLPH. Here they come. Come on, boys. Step up. Don't be bashful.

STEVE. Here we are. Now how about the drinks?

MAZIE. Not yet, Steve. This is the quick change for the finale.

RUBY. The parade of the nations.

DOLPH. Step up, fellows. Don't be bashful.

(*The Chicago mob get an eye-full. Girls keep right on with their change. They now change to flag costume.*)

STEVE. Let me present you fellas. Boys, this is Miss Billie Moore—and this is Mazie——

MAZIE. Just Mazie? I got another name.

STEVE. Excuse me—Miss Mazie Smyth.

MAZIE. *Smith*—ordinary Smith.

STEVE. Fxcuse me again—common, ordinary Smith.

MAZIE. Ordinary, but not common. (*All men laugh.*)

STEVE. And here's Ruby—Pearl—Grace. (*To* ANN.) What's your name, Baby?

ANN (*weakly*). Ann. (*All laugh.*)

STEVE. Sure—Ann it be. Girls, my friends from Chicago.

RUBY. My Gawd, from way out there in Montana?

LARRY. Illinois.

PORKY. She's kiddin'.

(NICK *enters from office.*)

STEVE. And here's the old chief himself, boys. This is Nick Verdis, a regular. He's paid so many fines, he owns stock in the White House.

LARRY. Glad to get in wid youse.

BENNIE. Ya got some swell frills—yes, sir.

DOLPH. I could use one right now.

LARRY. Split one with you.

DUKE (*shaking hands with* NICK). I heard of you, fellow.

NICK. Any friends of Steve's is K.O. with me. Come on in here, and we can set down.

(*Some of the men mingle with the girls and begin to get intimate.*)

BENNIE. Sit down and leave all this lingerie? Am I crazy?

STEVE. They got to finish the show yet. We'll see 'em all afterwards.

MAZIE (*getting position*). Well, I hope to tell you.

DOLPH. Me for you.

MAZIE. Be generous—your friends may like me.

ROY (*rushes in from cabaret, out of breath*). Ready to unravel the last one, kids?

(*The girls start parading out four steps apart, very regally.*)

STEVE. And fellows, this is Roy Lane, better known as Personality——

ROY (*making change to Uncle Sam costume*). In person—not a moving picture.

STEVE. Possibly the greatest living song and dance artist who never played the Palace. (*Crowd laugh.*)

ROY. There's a lot of time, Wisenheimer. I ain't worryin' about my future. (*He follows girls to cabaret.*)

NICK. Don't get him started now.

STEVE. He's a character. I'm going to have him stay for a little while. He'll hand you a million laughs——

NICK. Come on, Chicagoes. I'll buy the first one.

(NICK *leads way to party room.*)

LARRY. We ain't exactly what you call broke ourselves, you know. (*They all laugh and start drinking.* LIL *enters from cabaret.*)

PORKY. Wait a minute, gang. Here's one you ain't met yet. This is Lil, the silver-toned song bird——

LIL (*kidding*). Give the little girl a big hand.

PORKY. Maybe we can get her to wobble something——

DOLPH. How about "Silver Threads Amongst the Gold"?

BENNIE. Nix—nix——

PORKY. One of these guys knows you, Lil—says he heard you sing at Jim Tomasso's joint in Chicago seven years ago.

BENNIE (*yells*). I said seventeen years ago.

LIL. What do you mean? That was my mother.

(*The girls and* ROY *enter from cabaret. Everyone laughs.* DOLPH *hands* LIL *a drink. The Chicago mob kid* PORKY *and* STEVE *ad lib, while drinking and eating. There is substantial applause.*)

MAZIE. Well, that's over.

GRACE. Now for the big feed.

RUBY. And my Gawd, how I could use a drink.

MAZIE. One of them guys is kinda good lookin'.

RUBY. What great eyesight you got.

ANN. She saw his pocketbook.

MAZIE. Oh, you're waking up, too.

(ROY *has started upstairs carrying his costumes and props.*)

DOLPH (*steps out*). Come on, girls—let's have fun. In here, everybody. (PEARL *sits down overcome for the moment.*) Hey, young fellow, have a drink.

ROY. No, thanks. I just had my hair cut. (*Exits. Piano in party room is heard.*)

NICK (*to* PEARL). What's the matter with you?

PEARL (*recovering herself—tough*). I'm waiting for someone to bring me a drink. (BENNIE *and* LARRY *rush for* PEARL.)

LARRY. I saw you first, redhead. We'll get Lil to sing (*Crowd makes noise.*)

NICK (*turns off lights*). Not so much noise. (*He exits to hall.* BENNIE *chases* BILLIE *from party room.*)

BENNIE. Come on. Jazz it up, blue eyes. (BILLIE, *frightened, runs toward* STEVE. STEVE *pushes* BENNIE *back.*)

STEVE (*throws* BENNIE *back.*) Bennie, cut it. Get to hell in there——

(DOLPH *closes the party room doors, leaving* BILLIE *alone with* STEVE. *We hear the piano dimly.* BILLIE *rushes to* STEVE *for protection.*)

STEVE. It's all right, Billie. Don't be scared. Everything's all right.

BILLIE. Oh, Steve, what'll I do?

STEVE (*holding her*). I won't let anybody bother you—— (*He looks at her tenderly. Is suddenly overcome by his passion.*) I love you—kid. (*Holds her close to him.*) God, I love you. I'd do murder for you. (*He kisses her passionately. She tries to break away.*)

BILLIE (*frees herself and goes to chair*). Steve, please don't.

STEVE. All right—I'm sorry. Listen— (*Kneels beside her—contrite.*) Billie, just to show you that I appreciate what a real nice girl you are, you don't need to stay to the party. You can go home if you'd be happier about it.

BILLIE. No, I ought to stay because I owe that much to you, and anyhow—(*Looking upstairs after* ROY.)—I said I'd stay and I'm going to.

STEVE. But you're such a little peach I want to make you happy—see. Listen, to-morrow night, after the show, let's get in the car—go for a ride and have a good talk. Will you? (BILLIE *nods.*) All right, that's a date. We'll stop at Ed's place and get a nice little supper and I've got something important to tell you. (*He fondles her.*)

BILLIE. Make your hands behave, Steve,

STEVE (*drawing back.*) All right. I'm just as meek as a lamb, see! Whatever you say.

(*The door opens from party room and* MAZIE *chases* RUBY *out. Others follow with great clamor.*)

MAZIE. I'll make your shirt roll up your back like a window-shade.

RUBY (*drunk*). I'll step on you. I'll spit in your eye——

DOLPH. Cut it out—— (*Separates them.*)

NICK. Hey, hey! Quiet! Quiet! Shut up that noise.

MAZIE. No phoney blond with store teeth can pull that on me and live.

NICK. Shut it. Shut it. Take 'em back.

STEVE. All right. I'll handle this.

LIL (*to* PORKY). Andrew, dance for mama.

(PORKY *dances Charleston. Fight breaks up, as couples begin to dance.*)

STEVE. Inside. It's all right, Nick. I'll pay for the noise, too, so keep your shirt on.

GRACE. Where's my boy friend?

NICK (*to* STEVE). McCorn is sitting just outside there. (STEVE *herds them back.*)

STEVE. Listen, folks. The party is on the inside—nobody is to come out here without a permit from the Chief—that's me. (ANN *jumps on* STEVE. *They exit to party room.*)

ANN. Hail the Chief. (*Cheer from party.* JOE *enters from hall with more drinks.*)

JOE. I never seen such a thirsty gang.

STEVE. Excuse me a minute, Billie. (*He shuts doors to party room, leaving only the two girls and* NICK *outside.*)

NICK (*going*). What do they think this is, Ike Bloom's? (*Exits to hall.*)

MAZIE (*going to* BILLIE). Ain't you having a good time?

BILLIE. I'm all right.

MAZIE. Come on, have some fun. You're only going to live once.

BILLIE. You go ahead—don't pay any attention to me.

MAZIE. Don't be afraid. Nothin'll happen to you. Listen, Billie, crack wise. It ain't so serious. Just kid 'em along, that's all, kid 'em along. It ain't so bad as it looks. I wouldn't give you a bum steer, kid, honest I wouldn't—but you don't always want to pay too much attention to what people say. Take me, for instance, you think I'm a pretty tough character. Sure I am, in a way—(KATIE *enters from hall.*)—But I seldom give up—very seldom.

KATIE. Say, Miss Moore, here's a telegram for you.

BILLIE (*taking it*). Me?

KATIE. The hostess told me to bring it in.

BILLIE. Thanks.

KATIE. 'S all right. (*Exit to cabaret.*)

BILLIE (*to* MAZIE). Gee whiz. I'm scared of telegrams. Ain't it crazy?

MAZIE. Once I got an offer of a job that way.

BILLIE. Yeah?

MAZIE. Sure. And it can't talk, so you gotta read it. (BILLIE *tears it open—reads —looks at* MAZIE, *terrified.*) What's the matter, kid? It ain't bad news? (BILLIE *nods, bites her lip and begins to weep.*) What is it?

BILLIE (*passes her the wire, trying not to sob*). It's mamma.

MAZIE (*reads*). "Mother very low—come at once. Mary."

BILLIE. Oh, Mazie, and to think I'm acting like this and she's maybe dying.

MAZIE. Now, Billie, maybe it ain't nothing at all. Now you get hold of yourself, Billie. (ROY *enters on stairs, in street clothes.*) Roy, Billie's got some bad news.

ROY. What is it?

MAZIE. Her mother.

BILLIE (*going to him impulsively*). Oh, Roy—she must of had a stroke or something. She was all right last week—a telegram from Mary—maybe she's dying. Oh, dear! Oh, how could I have acted this way.

MAZIE. You didn't do anything, darling. (*Pulls* BILLIE *from* ROY *and puts her arms about her.*)

ROY (*takes her back in his arms*). It's all right, Kid. Everything's all right now. You're among friends. We'll take care of you. (*She weeps more uncontrollably.*) There. There.

MAZIE. Gee, I can't stand seein' her like that.

ROY. It'll come out all right. Take it from me. Everything's goin' to be all right, Billie.

BILLIE. I want to go home.

ROY. Of course you do, and I'm right here to take you, too, honey. The sooner the better, so stop your crying now. Just leave it to me. Come on, let's get out of here fast.

BILLIE. You're so good to me.

ROY. You bet I'm good to you. Why wouldn't I be? Ain't we pals through thick and thin? That's us, Kid. Now you hurry and jump into your traps, honey, and we'll be on the train for Trenton in twenty-five minutes.

(STEVE *enters from party room. Inside they are singing and dancing.*)

MAZIE. Oh, Steve, Billie's got to go home—her mother's sick.

BILLIE (*to* STEVE). I'm awfully sorry. Mazie, have you got a handkerchief? (MAZIE *shakes her head, calling attention to her undress.* ROY *dries her eyes.*)

STEVE. Well, that's tough luck, but we'll see what we can do. To hell with the party. I gotta get you home. Hurry up now. The car's out back. I'll have you out there in no time.

(KATIE *enters from hall.*)

ROY. You don't need to bother, Mr. Crandall. Everything is already arranged, see?

KATIE. Here's another one, Miss Moore.

BILLIE. What? (STEVE *takes it and opens it.*)

KATIE. Almost like an opening night, or something. (*Exit to hall.*)

STEVE (*reads to himself, then grunts*). Huh.

BILLIE. What's it say? She's not——?

STEVE (*reads*). "Your wire received. Stay to party and have good time. Mother." (*They all look at each other.*)

ROY. She must a got better.

MAZIE. Ain't that peculiar?

BILLIE. I don't see. . . .

ROY. Sometimes those things gets mixed.

MAZIE. I'll say they do.

STEVE. Well, everything's all right anyhow, isn't it? See? All that worry for nothing. So dry up those tears and powder the little nose and join the bunch.

ROY. I think, as long as we planned to go, Billie, the best thing would be to—start out now and see for sure if everything's all right. I'll take you home. (STEVE *and* ROY *both pull* BILLIE.)

STEVE. Of course she ain't going home.

ROY. It seems to me, it's the wisest thing to do.

STEVE (*takes her with him*). No, she's going to stay. Come along, Billie. You come on too, Lane. Do your clowning.

ROY. I'm particular what kind of society I'm seen with——

STEVE. Wait a minute.

(NICK *enters hall.*)

ROY. I don't know as I will.

STEVE. What do you mean?

ROY. I mean Billie ought to get out of here—and as for me, I wouldn't stay and entertain your gang of goofers if you kissed my foot in Macy's window at high noon.

STEVE. Why, you dancing tramp!

ROY. I know all about you. It's guys like you give New York a bad name.

STEVE. You waxed-floor bum!

NICK. Steve, easy.

STEVE (*controlling himself*). Tell him to get.

NICK. Get.

MAZIE (*grabs* STEVE, *looking at telegrams*). Say, I just thought of something. This last wire is an answer to Billie's. Now, the other one is an answer to something else. I'll bet my winter hat the boy-scout framed it himself.

ROY. You're full of chestnuts.

STEVE. What?

NICK. Framed what?

MAZIE. He was telephoning long distance. Billie, you told me yourself.

ROY. Maloney Brothers, that's all.

(DOLPH *opens the party doors looking for* STEVE; *he senses something wrong and waits—others join him.*)

MAZIE. He got the Maloney Brothers to send the wire.

RUBY. What is it?

PEARL. What's going on?

GRACE. What's the riot?

ANN. They got drinks out here?

BILLIE. Roy, you didn't?

ROY. Certainly I didn't.

MAZIE. You certainly did.

STEVE. So you framed a wire on her? That's the kind of tricks you're up to, eh?

BILLIE. Roy, you wouldn't scare me like that——

ROY. Don't pay any attention to any of 'em. (*Wavering.*) Anything I done I guess I'd know if I done it.

BILLIE (*seeing the truth in his eyes*). You did. (*Wounded beyond expression.*) That's the dirtiest trick anybody could ever do. Oh, Roy, making me think—— (*Turns away.*)

ROY. Now, Billie, listen——

BILLIE. I don't want to listen—I don't want anything to do with you—you big sap.

ROY (*almost ready to cry*). Suppose I did do it? I did it for you, didn't I? I know these kind of guys, and you can't be right if you run with guys like Steve Crandall—he's just out to grab you—and he don't care what means he uses. I'm tellin' you he's just plain no good, and I don't give a damn who knows it!

(*There is a growl from the men. They move toward* ROY *threateningly, but* STEVE *stops them.*)

DOLPH. Hey, wait a minute.

PORKY. What'll we do to him?

RUBY. What do you think of that?

MAZIE. You're going fine——

GRACE. Look who's here.

(STEVE *gives* PORKY *a quick instruction and stands waiting for the girls to be taken out.*)

NICK. No more. Nobody. Get back in the room. There's still peoples out there.

PORKY (*downstage pushes girls into party room*). Come on, girls. I want to tell you a bedtime story. Come on, now. All the girls in with me. Come on, Billie. (*Exits with girls to party room.*)

(JOE *enters, closes party room doors and stands there.*)

STEVE. Now, you lousy little bum, I got you where I want you. (*Hits him and knocks him down.*)

ROY. Thanks. (*Getting up.*) Ain't you a brave guy, though. That's all right, but look out for this one.

(ROY *rushes at* STEVE. STEVE *pulls his gun.*)

STEVE. And look out for this one!

DOLPH. Don't shoot. They'll hear you.

JOE. Cheese it.

DOLPH. Look out, the dick.

(DOLPH *grabs his arm, twisting his wrist. In the struggle the gun is dropped. Before it can be recovered, they become aware that Dan McCorn has come in from cabaret. They are frozen into quiet. Roy picks up the pistol defensively, without realizing he has it.*)

DAN. What's the matter, boys?

STEVE. Little argument, that's all.

DAN. *Little* argument?? (*Goes to* ROY.) So little you pull this? (*Takes gun from* ROY.)

ROY. That ain't mine.

DAN. No? Whose is it, then?

STEVE. It's his, all right—he pulled it on me just now.

ROY. You big liar!

NICK. Liar yourself, Lane. We all saw you do it.

(NICK *closes cabaret doors.* JOE *stands guard at party doors.*)

GANG. Yes, sure—we saw him.

DAN (*to Roy*). You got a permit to carry this?

ROY. No, of course not——

DAN. Oh, you're the boy that——

ROY. I'm the chief performer here,

Mister, Roy Lane.

DAN. Oh, yes.

ROY. Singing and dancing specialties; this is just a filler-in.

DAN. Ever hear of the Sullivan Act?

ROY. What time is it playing?

DAN. This Sullivan Act is a law—it gives you plenty of time for carrying one of these.

LARRY. you said it. . . . (*The gang laughs.*)

ROY. I tell you it ain't mine.

DAN. No—then I'll keep it till I find out who owns it. You better come along with me now. (*Pulls* ROY *up, puts gun in his pocket.*)

DOLPH (*aside to* STEVE). He's just stallin' about the hoofer. He wants the gun.

STEVE. Shut up.

LARRY. Who the hell is this guy, Steve?

STEVE. He's a dick.

BENNIE. The one I was telling you about.

LARRY. Well, what the hell——

BENNIE. What's the idea hornin' in—what's the idea——

STEVE. Give him back his rod, Dan—I can settle my own arguments with him.

LARRY. I'll say we can——

DOLPH. You tell him.

BENNIE. You bet you can.

DAN. So these are your friends from Chicago?

STEVE. Listen, Mac. What the hell are you tryin' to do? You been gumshoeing around here all night. For what? Now you come buttin' in here around my party. Understand, *mine*. . . . You ain't got a warrant to go tearing around here as you like. This room is private. Now I'll thank you to run along and call it a day—and give the kid back his cap pistol. I can settle my own arguments with him. (DAN *stands surrounded.*)

DAN. I said I'd keep the gun.

LARRY. You said what?

BENNIE. Not if Steve says to give it back you won't.

DOLPH. Yeah—you bet you won't.

LARRY. Not while we're here.

STEVE. Better give it up, Dan, while you're able and take the ozone.

DAN (*sees he's in tight place—changes his tone*). Well, Steve, you're a damn fine ungrateful guy for the finish—I'll say that. So I been gumshoeing around here all night, have I?

STEVE. I'll say you have.

DAN. Shall I tell you why? You know Scar Edwards was bumped off to-night. You know, the minute his mob heard it, they got together, didn't they? And where would they head for? Right here—and who would they be looking for—why, for you—so I phoned over to the house and gets seven of the boys to lay around outside in case that mob of Scar's show up. (STEVE *relaxes his aggressive pose a bit, and the others follow suit.*)

STEVE. You did? You did that, Dan?

DAN. Just to protect you. There's three of my men wasting good time out there in back now.

STEVE. Dan, I didn't know that.

DAN. Besides, maybe I saved you from getting shot up by this Indian. (*Indicates* ROY.) And you yelling your head off about me buttin' in.

STEVE. But you been hangin' around all night, asking questions and acting like you really thought I might have had something to do with Scar's bump-off.

DAN. Well, I gotta ask questions, Steve, but that don't say I suspect you.

ROY. Well, I suspect him.

NICK. Oh, shut him up!

ROY. And I got a good reason, too——(*Points to* DOLPH.) I saw this guy and Steve helping a fellow with a scar on his face—out the back door there—to-night.

DOLPH. Who, me?

STEVE (*starts for* ROY). You're a liar!

DAN (*holds arm up—keeps* STEVE *from hitting* ROY). Wait! Wait a minute, Steve—take it easy. (*Pause—to* ROY.) What time did you see Steve with Scar?

ROY. Before the show—about ten o'clock.

STEVE. He's lying, Dan.

DOLPH. Sure he is.

DAN (*to* ROY). Would you know this guy with the scar if you saw him again?

ROY. Sure I would. I saw them and Billie Moore saw them, too. They were taking him out that door. I asked, "Who's the drunk?" and Steve said, "One of the boys we're helping home." If you don't believe me, ask Billie—she'd never tell nothing but the truth—ask her.

STEVE. Dan, this kid is sore at me—he's jealous—he made up that rotten lie to get me in bad.

DOLPH. Sure. Dan can see through him.

DAN. Verdis, call in the Moore girl.

(NICK *glances at* STEVE. STEVE *makes sign, so* NICK *goes up, opens door of party room.*)

DOLPH (*during above, speaks to* DAN

confidentially). Don't believe nothin' this hoofer says. I tell you, he's nuts.

DAN (*impressed*). Yeah?

NICK. Billie—hey, Billie—come—want to see you a minute.

DOLPH. Sure—ask anybody—he's an awful liar.

(BILLIE *comes in. Some of the girls come to doorway, curious.*)

BILLIE. What do you want me for?

GRACE. What's the matter?

MAZIE. Why ain't you guys paying us attention—

RUBY. Shut up. Look what's going on.

DAN. Miss Moore—— (*They become quiet.*) Miss Moore, about ten o'clock to-night, before the show started, when you came down here to rehearse with the dancer here, did you see Steve and this gentlemen—(*Points to* DOLPH.)—helping a drunken man out the back door?

BILLIE (*unable to grasp the situation*). Why——

ROY. Tell the truth, Billie.

DAN. Did you? A man with a scar on his face. (STEVE *turns and looks at her—she catches his eye—turns back to* DAN—*pause.*)

BILLIE. No. (STEVE *shrugs, satisfied, as though to say, "I told you."*)

DOLPH. I told you that kid was nuts.

DAN (*to girls*). Did any of you see Scar here to-night?

GIRLS. No. (PEARL *steps forward, starts to speak, then walks towards stairs.*)

ANN. Who? Somebody else coming?

NICK. I'm here all the time. I didn't see him.

STEVE. Now are you satisfied?

DAN. Yes.

MAZIE. Say copper, will you do me a favor? Take Personality with you before he tries to make any more trouble here.

STEVE. Is that all you want, Dan?

DAN. That's all for now. (*Pulls* ROY *by the arm.*) Come on, Lane. I'll tell you some more about the Sullivan Act.

ROY. You can't take me like this, Officer. Who's going to look after Billie? She don't know what kind he is—— (*Crowd starts back to party room.*)

DAN. Come on——

ROY (*desperately*). No. Wait a minute. For God's sake, give me a chance. She's only a kid. She don't know what she's up against. Mazie, tell him. This Crandall guy is out to grab her——

STEVE. Take him along.

ROY. I'll fix you! (*Breaks away; rushes at* STEVE. BENNIE *grabs him.*) I'll kill you if you touch her—I will, God damn you . . . . (DAN *recaptures him; yanks him toward back door.*) Lil—somebody—why don't you say something? I don't care what you do to me—— Oh, God, Billie! (*The music starts up.* DAN *is dragging* ROY *out.*)

CURTAIN

ACT THREE

In the cabaret the orchestra is just finishing the Battle number. JOE *sits on a chair, center, asleep.*

DOLPH *comes down back and looks around—sees* JOE.

DOLPH (*growling to himself*). Hey! (*Kicks* JOE *on the sole of the foot waking him with a start.*) What's the idea?

JOE. I'm resting.

(NICK *enters on stairs.*)

NICK. What's the matter?

DOLPH. I come in here and find this guy asleep.

JOE. The show didn't start yet.

NICK. That's enough—Joe. (JOE *exits, muttering.*)

DOLPH. Now, listen, Nick, I gotta get outa here fast. Steve phoned me to drop in and tell you that the stuff will be here at three o'clock.

NICK. What's the rush? I wasn't expecting it to-night. Where's Steve, anyway?

DOLPH. I don't know where he is just now, Nick. He might be goin' out of town for a couple of days. He phoned me to tell you about the truck.

NICK. Some trouble come up?

DOLPH. No, no, everything's all right.

NICK. Listen, Dolph, you shouldn't hold out on me. Now, tell me straight, what is it? If Steve is in trouble, then I should be the one to know as much as anybody——

DOLPH. Everything is all right, Nick—everything is perfectly all right.

NICK. That hoofer done some pretty wild talking last night and——

DOLPH. Hey, don't pay no attention to him. He was sore at Steve, that's all—even McCorn could see that.

NICK. Yeh, but he might tell a lot of lies. They got him in jail—and——

DOLPH. No, they ain't.

NICK. No?

DOLPH. They turned him loose. They

give him the air a couple of hours ago.

NICK. Yeh?

DOLPH. Sure—they could see he didn't have no sense—he was just a false alarm, so they threw him out.

NICK. Then why don't he come back to work? I gotta give a show tonight. Half my actors didn't turn up.

DOLPH. I don't anything about that. I just wanted to tell you about the truck, that's all. (RUBY *appears on stairs in kimono.*) Hello, Baby—— Well, Nick—three bells it is, remember. So long. (*Exit down hall.*)

RUBY. Got any news yet? (*He looks up —shrugs shoulders.*) Well, what do'y say? (*She comes down and sits on armchair*). Looks like we get a night off, then—huh?

NICK (*looks at watch*). Where the hell do you think they is?

RUBY. Sleeping it off.

(JOE *enters from up hall, with a slip of paper.*)

JOE (*apathetically*). Want to O.K. this?

NICK. Don't bother me. (JOE *leans against the door and waits—bored.*) Got to think someways to give some kind of a show tonight—Pearl not here, Billie not here, Lil not here, the hoofer not here—every other time he's around so much I don't want to see the sight of him—tonight when I need him, where is he? Go on, let me alone. (JOE *exits to hall again.*)

RUBY. Steve's party sure busted up the show for fair. That Chicago spendthrift I drew must have been born in Scotland. (ROY *enters back door in street clothes.*) Here's God's little gift to the night clubs now. (NICK *looks at him, waiting for explanation.* ROY *ignores him—walks to the prop table and begins to collect his belongings.*)

NICK. Jesus whiz, you're late.

ROY. Late for what?

NICK. For work.

ROY. Ease off, Greek, you didn't think I came back to this bucket of blood to work, did you?

NICK. Why not?

ROY. After what you slipped me last night?

NICK. I don't know what you're talking about.

ROY. You thought we parted good friends, did you?

NICK. Oh, a little thing like that—we forget—it's just like I says to Steve last night—I says, don't be mad at the hoofer, he can't help it—he's just a little nutty. Now here it is pretty near time for show to go on—I need you, you need me——

ROY. No, I don't need you—all I need is what dough I got coming and a chance to pick up my traps and get out of here. After the raw deal I got last night—me keep on working in this shooting gallery?

NICK. Listen, Lane—you gotta work—just to-night——

ROY (*turns away*). What a chance.

NICK (*seeing that nothing can be gained this way,* NICK'S *manner changes to one of oily flattery*). It ain't for me I ask you to stay—I can get another hoofer—but it's because of the peoples that come here especially to see you, see?

ROY (*interested*). What?

NICK. Already big party come in—they ask me how long before that young fella comes on with that wonderful personality —they say——

ROY. Well, wait a minute—you say that —what kind of looking people?

NICK. I don't know who they was—very important people—I say, Mr. Lane, he's not in yet, but he's sure to come because he don't never disappoint his public.

ROY. I never disappointed my public yet.

NICK. That's what I said—I told 'em about that time in Danbury, Massachusetts. I told 'em what I always said, that you're a real artist, and, that no matter what happens, I could always count on you, for the very best that's in you.

ROY. *Listen,* I'll go on tonight.

NICK. Good.

ROY. But I'm leaving at the end of the week—and the doorman can tell anybody that's interested where to find me.

RUBY. Mills Hotel.

NICK. I knew I could count on you, Lane—— Now I'll go out in front and see what I can do—— Use the big brain figgerin' how to give a show—— Lil not here—nor Billie—nor Pearl—I'll be back. (*Exit to cabaret.*)

ROY. They ain't showed up yet, huh?

RUBY. That's how I heard it.

ROY. I wouldn't go back in this dump, neither, if I didn't think it was my duty. (RUBY *gives him the bird.*) My big chance will come; I figure I might as well be eating while I'm waiting for it. Billie's usually on time—wonder what's keeping her tonight?

RUBY. The same guy that kept her last night.

ROY. Now I ask you, is that nice?

RUBY. You going to worry about her after the royal raspberry she slipped you? She's got you goin' around like a top.

ROY. I'm thinkin' about the good of the show, that's all. Didn't Nick call up the agents to get a gal to shout in Lil's place?

RUBY. Sure, he called 'em, but the agents are no damn good when you want 'em.

ROY. It's me that knows that, Sister.

RUBY (*stringing him*). Well, how was the dear old jail?

ROY. That's all right.

RUBY. Come on, spill it, how'd your act go in the night court?

ROY. Aw, that don't concern you.

RUBY. A mysterious guy. Yeah, if Nick hadn't got you off——

ROY. The big baloney never had nothing to do with it. I got myself off.

RUBY. What'd you say to 'em?

ROY. I told 'em a few things.

RUBY. Didn't you even get a fine?

ROY. No, I wouldn't stand for it. I give 'em a little spiel.

RUBY. I bet you made quite an impression.

ROY. I told 'em who I was—there was a guy there had seen me play on the Poli time and of course that was in my favor. I gave 'em a rough idea what I thought of Steve, too. And that cop that was here—I and him got to be very good friends. He was wise from the start that that wasn't my gun—just a stall to get me out.

RUBY (*drawing him out*). Go on.

ROY. Sure. And it was a stall about them other bulls laying outside, too. He's a smart cop, that fella; he knows his oats.

RUBY. And then they just turned you loose?

ROY. Well, listen—— (*Comes closer and lowers voice.*) McCorn told me to keep this under my hat, but I guess it wouldn't get no further with an old-time trouper like you——

RUBY. No.

ROY. Listen, they took me to the morgue to identify the other guy.

RUBY. Yeah?

ROY. Gee, the way these gangsters pop each other off. Well, I guess it's nothing but a lucky break kept me from occupying the slab right next to him.

(BILLIE *enters back door. She and* ROY *face each other without speaking.* NICK *enters down hall.*)

BILLIE. Ruby.

RUBY. So you decided to come.

NICK. All right—I won't say anything—go on—get made up.

BILLIE. I'm terribly sorry—the Trenton train had a break-down.

RUBY. Hah! (*Gets up and starts toward stairs.*) She wants to have us believe she's been out to see her mother. God, if ever I seen a professional virgin, she's it.

NICK. Don't start nothing now—things is worse 'nough.

RUBY. All right, sweetheart, but Faith, Hope and Charity is waiting here for news—do we give a show tonight or don't we?

NICK. Sure we give a show—we gotta.

RUBY. All right, I'll go up and tell the other inmates (*To* BILLIE.) Come on, Purity. (RUBY *exits upstairs*—NICK *turns and hurries into the office.* BILLIE *has been waiting, hoping that* ROY *will speak to her —he ignores her and walks to stairs.*)

BILLIE (*pleadingly*). Roy. (*He stops.*) Roy, I'm terribly glad to find out you didn't get hurt or anything.

ROY (*without turning around*). Sure. See you again some time.

BILLIE. I don't think that's a very nice way to act—all I says was I'm glad you didn't get hurt.

ROY. It's no thanks to you I didn't.

BILLIE. Everything would have been all right, if you hadn't tried to boss me.

ROY. Well, I'm done trying to boss you now. Course I feel kind-a sorry on account of the act.

BILLIE. What do you mean?

ROY. On account of it's being busted up, I mean.

BILLIE (*weakly*). Is it busted?

ROY. Sure.

BILLIE. Oh.

ROY. Of course, when a fella's worked like I have to get together the best dancing act in the business, and gets all ready for bookings, he hates to see it go blooey just because a big stiff that's rancid with coin comes along and cops his partner.

BILLIE. What right have you got to say that he's copped me?

ROY. Last night you lied to save him and against me.

BILLIE. Yes, but I didn't know—you got no right talking that way—all the girls around here are always saying I'm too good—and you're saying I'm too bad. I hate this damn place.

ROY. And another thing—last night you called me a sap in the presence of several witnesses.

BILLIE (*almost in tears*). Oh, shut up. That's what you are.

NICK (*enters from office*). All right—all right—get made up.

(BILLIE *starts upstairs, so agitated that she scarcely senses* NICK's *presence. She pauses and leans over the banister.*)

BILLIE. And I'll tell you something else, and it's most likely the last thing I'll ever tell you—the reason I went to my mother's was to ask her, if a girl was terribly in love with a person, so much it was like regular love at first sight, was it all right to marry 'em even if they was poor—that's what. Now, how'd you like to go to hell? (*Exits upstairs.*)

ROY (*gazes after her dumfounded*). They pick up that language quick around this honky-tonk.

NICK. She's right. Don't be interfering with her.

ROY. Well, they's a lot of personal things mixed up here you don't understand. But I'll tip you off to one thing—my next partner is going to be a man.

NICK. Fine. Now, I want to tell you about something. (*Sits down.*) If Steve comes, don't start yowling at him.

ROY (*gives* NICK *a look of mild surprise*). I wouldn't.

NICK. You done it last night.

ROY. I got wise to a lot of things since then—I didn't know those guys would shoot you right out in public.

NICK. Well, don't argue with him.

ROY. I ain't going to. I don't carry any gatlin' gun. The Sullivan Act is O.K. with me—and for one thing—I wouldn't think it was fair to you for me to get in any argument with him, 'cause if he put a hole in me, your show'd be out in the alley. Of course, if Mr. Crandall cares to meet me over in the Y. M. C. A. gym, I'd just as leave tell him what I think about him.

NICK. He's all right, Lane. Good customer. Look—last night the party alone cost him two thousand dollars, you understand?

ROY. I wasn't saying nothing to Steve anyhow—I was showing Billie the truth about him. He had a fall out of every girl in the place. Why couldn't he leave her alone?

NICK. 'Cause all men like what's hard to get.

ROY. She had the chance of a lifetime if she'd only have stuck. It's pretty tough after I had a swell double act framed. Oh, well—nobody never got their name in lights by getting discouraged. (*Tries to snap out of his depression.*) Say, what I want to ask you, Boss, what we gonna do for a solo in Lil's spot tonight?

NICK. That's what I want to ask you. You sing it.

ROY. I might fake up a mammy song at that.

NICK. Sure. (*Slaps his back.*) You'll be the whole show tonight.

ROY. I am every night. If you don't think so, you're crazy. On the level, Boss, I don't know what you'd do without me.

(PORKY *and* LIL *enter back door, drunk but dignified.*)

LIL. Hello.

PORKY. I told you this was the place.

ROY. We been looking for you, Lil.

LIL. I was looking for you, too. (*Goes to* NICK *unsteadily.*) Shake hands, Nick, and guess who I am.

NICK. Minnie Stew, that's who you are. What I ought to do is slap a good stiff fine onto you. (PORKY *bristling.*)

PORKY. Slap? (LIL *stops him, forces him into chair, center, takes hat off and puts in his lap.*)

LIL. Don't pay any attention to Nick, baby, he don't mean anything—it is just the way these foreigners talk. (*Pats his face.*)

NICK. Now you are here, would you hurry a little—*please?*

LIL. We been hurrying, Nick—we hurried and hurried. We been the longest time getting here, haven't we, Andrew?

PORKY. That's right, dearie.

NICK. For God's sake, where you been? What's happened to you?

LIL. Almost everything—we're married. (PORKY *goes asleep.*)

ROY. Holy Gee.

NICK. What?

LIL. That's the reason we're so proud.

ROY. Oh, is *that* what you are!

LIL. That joke's on you. You'll all have to give up presents and everything.

NICK. Well, going to work tonight?

LIL. Did I return for these purposes?

NICK (*helping her toward stairs*). Then go up and lie down. I'll send up some coffee—and we'll find a place in the office for Porky.

LIL. Andrew—if you please——

NICK. All right, Andrew. (*Motions to* ROY *to take* LIL.) Go ahead, Lane.

ROY. Come on, Lil, I'll fix you a couch. (*Whispers to* LIL.) You ain't got anything on your hip, have you?

LIL. Only a birthmark, and you're the first guy that's asked me about it.

(NICK *shakes* PORKY. *He wakes suddenly, rising as* NICK *walks him to office.*)

PORKY. I think I'm married.

(NICK *and* PORKY *exeunt to office.* NICK *comes right out and goes to cabaret—meantime* ROY *is struggling to get* LIL *upstairs.*)

ROY. Come on, Lil—I'll help you.

LIL. I feel so damn foolish.

ROY. Cut it out—lemme help you.

LIL. Sure. You help me and I'll help you. (*Nearly knocks him downstairs.*)

ROY. Behave yourself, will you? You wouldn't want to have anybody say you missed a performance. Come on, now, Lil; this is serious business. (LIL *exits, singing.* ROY *stops to pick up her handbag which has fallen in the scuffle.* DOLPH *comes in back door.*)

DOLPH (*to* ROY). Hello, nut—where's Nick?

ROY. Find out, wise guy—I dance here. I ain't a waiter. (*Exits to dressing room.*)

(DOLPH *is followed in by* STEVE, *who is evidently laboring under considerable repressed excitement.* JOE *comes in from hall with coffee and crosses to stairs.*)

JOE. Good evening, Mr. Crandall.

STEVE. Hello, Joe. (*To* DOLPH.) Get outside and do as I told you. (DOLPH *exits.* STEVE *turns to* JOE.) Listen, Joe—I'm not here to *anyone* tonight. Get that. And tip me if McCorn or any dick blows in (JOE *starts to leave.*) Wait a second. Don't be in such a hurry. Here—— (*He hands* JOE *a bill.*)

JOE. Thanks, Mr. Crandall.

STEVE. And tell the doorman to turn away anybody he don't know, and give him this. (*Hands* JOE *another bill.*) Some of Scar Edwards' playmates might try to crash in, looking for trouble. (NICK *comes in from hall.*) I got my own lookout men planted, but I'm taking no chances.

NICK. Hurry along with that, Joe. (JOE *goes upstairs.*) Hello, Steve. (JOE *exits upstairs.*) What's the matter? You look sick.

STEVE (*he has lost his hard assurance—he is nervous—his face almost twitches—he can't stand still. He speaks very quietly*). I ain't feeling as well as I could.

NICK. No?

STEVE (*takes off his hat*). Look at that lid.

NICK. Huh?

STEVE. Look at that hole!

NICK. Sure, I see it—— Cigarette?

STEVE. No—bullet.

NICK (*impressed*). For God's sake!

STEVE. Just a minute ago. I'm standing down here in the middle of the block—in front of the Midtown Garage—talking to Dolph, when buzz—— (*Puts hat on.*)—it goes through my hat.

NICK. Mmm! (*To show his concern.*) Who done it?

STEVE. That's the hell of it. I don't know.

NICK. I mean, where'd it come from?

STEVE. That's what I'm telling you—there wasn't a sound—whoever took a crack at me must of had a silencer on his gat——

NICK (*guttural exclamation*). Ohoo!

STEVE. There wasn't anyone on the street—that is, anyone but what seemed to be walking along minding his own business—but just as the shot went through my lid, a taxicab across the street started up and went toward Sixth Avenue like a bat out of hell—but there was only a woman in it.

NICK. A woman?

STEVE. Yeh—it couldn't been her—I don't think—it must have come from some of those windows on the second floor—Scar Edwards' mob, I guess—they use silencers——

NICK. Whoo—that's bad, Steve—extra bad.

STEVE. An inch lower and it would have been a lot worse. It's good—I planned to get out of here when I did.

NICK. You goin' tonight?

STEVE. Yeh. (*Walks toward back door—restless.*) Get me a drink, will you? (NICK *goes into office and comes out with bottle.* JOE *comes downstairs and goes to hall.*) Joe—don't forget to give that bill to the doorman.

JOE. No, sir. (*Exits down hall as* NICK *enters from office with bottle and glass.*)

NICK. And—a—where you going?

STEVE (*comes to* NICK—*takes drink*). I'll lay in with some friends up in Montreal for the time being.

(PEARL *enters back door. She comes in fearfully, sees them and pulls herself together.* STEVE *turns quickly at sound of door—but seeing who it is, relaxes again.*)

NICK. About time!

STEVE (*perfunctorily*). Hello, Pearl.

NICK. Hurry up, you're late; don't waste

any time. (PEARL *hurries up stairs.*)

NICK. If you didn't croak Scar Edwards, what you blowin' for?

STEVE (*walking away*). I can make my plans without your help, Nick.

NICK. Sure. (*Watches him.*) You taking Billie with you?

STEVE. That's some more of your business.

NICK. I want to know if I gotta get a new gal, that's all.

STEVE (*crosses to* NICK, *who pours another drink and passes it to him*). Well, I'm taking her, all right, but she don't know it yet, so you don't need to advertise. I prefer to get 'em without being rough—but I'm pressed for time, so I'll have to try Dolph's stuff this crack. (*Drinks.*) Now—I gotta get hold of Porky.

NICK. He's here.

STEVE. He is?

NICK. In there. Drunker than hell—he got married.

STEVE. He got what?

NICK. Sure, to Lil. They both come in while ago stewed to gills.

STEVE. To Lil? Gee! Well, will you tell me why he fell for that big horse?

NICK. Maybe she ain't your kind—but them big broads that's been all through the war sometimes make pretty women at home.

STEVE. Oh, I ain't boosting for Porky—at that I think Lil got the worst of it. Let's take a lamp at him. I want to see what he looks like married. (*As they start to enter office,* STEVE *sees* BILLIE *coming downstairs. He gestures to* NICK *to go ahead.* NICK *exits*—STEVE *comes back to meet* BILLIE.) Hello, beautiful. Well, you look as sweet as sugar— How's tricks?

BILLIE. All right. (BILLIE *is ill at ease with him. She hurries up to the table with her props, trying to be casual, but betraying a new manner toward* STEVE, *that almost amounts to suspicion.*) I came in late and then I hurried so—that I'm about the first one ready.

STEVE. Found the folks all right, did you?

BILLIE. Oh, fine.

STEVE. That's good. That gives me a great deal of pleasure. Of course we missed not having you stay for the finish of the party last night.

BILLIE. Well, you were awfully nice about letting me go home, Mr. Crandall.

STEVE. Well, I'll tell you, Billie girl, any time I'm not nice, you remind me and I'll get nice, 'cause as far as you're concerned, that's the way I want to be, see?

BILLIE. Of course I don't understand about the detective and everything.

STEVE. Of course you don't, Girlie, but I'll explain it to you. It's just politics . . . that's all. I'll tell you all about it after the show tonight. It'll be very interesting. You're going for a ride with me tonight, you know. (*Takes her hand.*)

BILLIE (*steps away from him*). Well, I don't know.

STEVE. You haven't forgotten. That was a promise—you wouldn't try to go back on that.

BILLIE. Well——

STEVE (*quite frantic*). You did promise—don't forget that——

BILLIE. I wouldn't go back on my promise——

(MAZIE *enters on stairs.*)

MAZIE. Hello, Steve.

STEVE (*mutters*). Hello, Mazie. (MAZIE's *presence drives him away. He starts for office then turns back and touches her arm as though he wanted to assure himself that she were still there—almost reverently.*) Don't forget now—— (*Exits to office.*)

MAZIE (*comes downstairs*). I see he's still friends.

(RUBY *enters stairs.* ROY *and* GIRLS *come downstairs. They all wear the costumes for opening number as in Act One.*)

RUBY. Yeh, she promised to come early and shave my neck.

(NICK *enters from office.*)

MAZIE. Well, here we are for the merry-merry.

NICK. Now, remember, some pep tonight.

MAZIE. I'm full of pep and no control.

ROY (*starts to cabaret*). Save your pep, kid—you may need it—— (*Cabaret doors open.*) Good evening, folks. (*Exit. Doors close behind him.*)

RUBY. If that's pep, I never smelled gin.

MAZIE. Listen, Dizzy—you won't smell anything again—'cause I'm going to *bust your smeller.* (*She starts.*)

BILLIE. Mazie, behave yourself.

GRACE. What is this, Grand Street?

ANN. My head aches.

RUBY. Wait till the show's over—I'll show you.

(BILLIE *pulls* MAZIE. GRACE *pulls* RUBY.)

MAZIE. Why wait? (ROY *comes back*

from cabaret and pushes between them.) That's enough of that. You can't go out there scrapping like that. I don't want my stuff spoiled. I got friends out there—agents and managers—looking me over every night.

MAZIE. Oh, I forgot—I ain't used to working with these headline acts.

ROY. Well, there's lots worse than me headlining, sister——

MAZIE. Well, for Gawd's sake, what did I say?

(*Buzzer sounds—lights flash.*)

ROY. Come on—quit it—line up. Let's unravel our daily dozen. *Every night's* a first night. Give 'em your best.

(*The music swells as the doors open and they dance out. As* ROY *is going through the doors,* STEVE *enters from office*—ROY *thumbs his nose at him and exits.*)

STEVE (*looks out after him*). You'd think last night would a-took all the freshness out of that hoofer, wouldn't you?

NICK. Hu—forget it. I'm going to fire him.

STEVE. You don't need to bother—I'll tend to him myself when I get the time. I don't want to have it happen too quick after his visit with McCorn. (*Moves about nervously.*) He hasn't been around tonight, has he?

NICK. Who?

STEVE. McCorn.

NICK. No. Why? You want to see him?

STEVE. That's just what I don't want to do. I thought he might come snoopin' around again.

NICK. You afraid of him—Dan McCorn?

STEVE. Me? What for? He ain't got nothing on me—not a thing.

NICK. Sure he ain't—so why get excited?

STEVE. Well, I'll tell you, Nicholas—a guy like McCorn gets on my nerves—he don't say anything—he don't make any accusations, but that damn rotten slow way of talking he's got and that dirty smile—you know—sorta gets me ragged. Now what the hell did he want to take my gun for last night?

NICK. Well, after all, Steve, none of us ain't got no right to carry—a gat——

LIL (*comes from dressing room, starts downstairs*). Where's my husband?

(STEVE *looks her over and shakes his head and exits to office.*)

NICK. He's all right, Lil.

LIL. Tell him his little wife—— No, I'll tell him myself. (*She finds that coming downstairs backward is lots easier.*)

NICK. Feel better now, Lil? All ready for going on?

LIL. Say, Nick, please can I cut my first number—I can do it, if I have to, but I ain't just set.

NICK (*resigned*). All right—go on out—sit down, drink some more black coffee and see the show.

LIL. Thanks, old timer—you're a true friend. That's just what I said to Andrew—I says, if ever your little Lillie had a true friend—it's that greasy Greek, Nick Verdis. (PORKY *enters from office.* LIL *croses to* PORKY.) I'm going out and see the show, darling.

PORKY. I'll go with you, dearie.

LIL. Take my arm, sweetheart, and keep the hell off my feet.

(*They exeunt to cabaret.* GIRLS *and* ROY *come in from cabaret.* GIRLS *put props on table.*)

ROY. Well, we ruined 'em, Boss——

NICK. Listen, Lane, Lil ain't able to work—— Listen, I gotta find something to fill that spot.

ROY. Better give 'em an orchestra specialty.

NICK. They'll get sick of that, too, before the night's over—— Listen, I been thinking—I'll take a chance—how'd you like to break in your act with Billie—huh?

ROY (MAZIE *pokes* BILLIE, GIRLS *show interest*). What?

NICK. You can do it for the next number.

ROY. No—the act is split—it's off—all busted up.

NICK. Listen, you been talkin' about it—rehearsin' and everythin'—now I give you a chance——

ROY. I'd like to do it for you, Boss, but I ain't got my partner, I——

NICK (*to* BILLIE). What's the matter? You won't work?

BILLIE. I didn't say I wouldn't. He don't want me any more.

NICK. Go on. (*To* BILLIE, *who exits up stairs.*) Just because I need the two of you, you're busted up. Come on, I ask it for special favor. There's a orchestra number first, so you got lots of time. This is a chance for you. I'll give the agent a good report no matter how rotten it is.

ROY. As long as Miss Moore wants to do it, I'm willing to, just to keep the show going.

NICK. Fine. (*To others.*) We'll do the Hawaiian number after that. Go on now, get ready. (*They start.*)

ROY. We didn't rehearse today. (ROY *starts warming up with some dance steps.*)

MAZIE. Can we go out to the tables and watch, Mr. Verdis?

NICK. Sure, go ahead.

RUBY (*as she exits upstairs*). They'll die standing up.

MAZIE (*as* PEARL *starts upstairs*). Come on, Pearl, and watch 'em, why don't you?

PEARL. I'll change first and be right out.

ROY. Mazie, tell Brophy to play my introduction music when this orchestra number is over—he'll know what you mean.

MAZIE. Sure.

(*Exeunt* MAZIE, GRACE *and* ANN *to hall.* NICK *takes pencil and paper and plans his program.* ROY *in the midst of his dancing suddenly gets a thought. He walks over to* NICK *importantly.*)

ROY. Boss, there's gotta be a better understanding—about the money in the future——

NICK. Maybe after you do this act you have no future. (*Laughs.*)

ROY. Razzin' me, eh? All right, after tonight you gotta struggle along without me. How do you like them grapes?

NICK. Aw, you can't take a joke. You and me, Lane, we're friends. Go on, now, like a good fellow. Maybe I'll have a sign fixed with your name in lights.

ROY. Well, how big a sign?

NICK. I'll tell you after I see the act. (*Exits to hall.* BILLIE *enters stairs in special dance costume.*)

BILLIE. We might as well go on and try it, now that we rehearsed it so much, even if you don't like me any more.

ROY (*he hooks her dress*). It ain't a question of liking you. But when I get a throw-down like last night, I get wise to myself.

BILLIE. Well, when I get a throw-down like I just got today, I'm wise to myself, too. But lots of people that don't like each other, they still work together. I mean, if you still think we'd make a good team, then it's just a business proposition. A couple can be in the same act without being crazy about each other.

ROY. Well, I used to think we'd make about the best combo I could imagine—but I'm the kind of a guy I don't want to butt in where I ain't wanted. You want to run over a few of them steps? (BILLIE *nods.*) Just remember your routine, that's all you got to do.

BILLIE. Let's try the finish—that's where we got mixed up at the last rehearsal.

ROY. All you gotta do is follow me. watch me out the corner of your eye and you can't go wrong. (*Takes place to do steps. She puts her arms around his neck, pulling their cheeks together. He puts her hand down to his waist.*) Down here.

BILLIE. The last time we did it this way.

ROY. Well, that was the last time. We'll do it now the old way. (*Stops acting and looks away from her.*) You see, it's kinda spoiled it for me, thinkin' you might have had your arms around Steve that way.

BILLIE. I haven't. (*Pause.*) And when I lied last night about the drunken man, it was because I had promised Steve to say that, and I didn't know a thing about that you'd said the opposite. And I went home alone last night.

ROY (*looks at her—melts*). We'll do the finish the new way—like this. (*Puts her arm around his neck.*) Billie, you know that, what you asked your mother when you went home today—about marryin' a poor fellow?

BILLIE. Yeah——

ROY. Well. (*Buzzer. They jump apart.*) Never mind. You can tell me later. We gotta think of our work now. On your toes, baby—don't get nervous. (*At door.* BILLIE *at armchair.*) Listen, Mr. Verdis is makin' an announcement — sensational newcomers—Roy Lane and Company. Oh, boy, don't that make you feel proud?

BILLIE (*overcome with sudden panic*). Roy—I'm scared——

ROY. Don't be scared—remember, I'm right beside you. It'll all be over 'fore you know it.

BILLIE. Roy, I don't believe I can go on. Can't we wait till tomorrow till we have a chance to rehearse?

ROY. Pull yourself together. We can't have no stage fright gummin' our act. I'll give you a sock in a minute. There's our music. We'll finish in a blaze of glory. Lots of snap now. We'll show 'em. (*Pulls her to entrance—blesses himself—doors open. They exit to cabaret, dancing gaily.*)

(DAN MC CORN *enters hall.* JOE *follows.*)

JOE. No strangers allowed back here—Mister.

DAN. That's all right, Aloy-ius. I'm no stranger.

JOE. Well, you can't——

(NICK *enters from other end of hall.*)

DAN. Oh, yes, I can.

JOE. No, you can't.

NICK. Joe! (*Signals him to go.* JOE *exits to hall sulkily.*) What you doin' back here?

DAN. Just thought I'd drop in and say hello. Steve around?

NICK. Nope, I ain't seen him all day.

DAN. He'll be in later, though, won't he?

NICK (*sits*). No—he won't come tonight. He had such big night last night—y'understand. You want to see him?

DAN. Nothing in particular. They'll be lots of other chances. Have a good time last night?

NICK. No, them kinda things make me sick. You gotta do it, understand, but it ain't no fun. When I get drunk for pleasure, that's one thing—but when I get drunk for business, daugh! No—no.

DAN. Sure. All the girls stay?

NICK. Yes, I guess so. I don't know. I got cock-eyed awful soon. I ain't sure of nothing last night.

DAN. Well, guess I'll blow. My partner's waiting for me outside.

NICK. Is he waiting like them other bulls you told Steve about last night?

DAN (*smiles*). No, he's waiting.

NICK. You're a pretty slick guy, Mac—you put it over on me, too.

DAN (*still smiling*). Oh, you're all wrong, Nick—they were there.

NICK. Yeah, like hell—well, it's all right with me—put me in awful bad—them Chicagoes started everything.

DAN. That's a bad bunch a bail hoppers, Nick, on the level. I could a grabbed a couple of 'em—but it wouldn't get me anything. We don't want 'em here in New York.

NICK. Steve tells me they're goin' back to Chicago in a couple of days——

DAN. I thought you said you didn't see Steve all day?

NICK (*pause—caught*). I didn't—he called me on the phone—he told me——

DAN. Oh! (*Pause.*) Well, see you later.

NICK. You ain't coming round again?

DAN. Oh, I don't mean tonight.

NICK. Well, that's good—— You're a fine fellow, Mac, but every time you come in my cabaret, 'bout twenty people goes out.

DAN. You got nothing to fear from me, Nick.

(RUBY *and* PEARL *enter from dressing rooms. They have changed to next chorus costume. They come down the stairs.*)

NICK. I know that, but it looks bad when you're round so much.

RUBY. My Gawd, this place is getting like Headquarters—every time you come into a room around here, you fall over a badge.

NICK. Mac's just visiting. Beside, you shut up.

RUBY (*going toward hall*). Is that act out there so bad you can't look at it?

DAN (*as* PEARL *crosses toward cabaret*). Hello, there.

PEARL. Hello (GIRLS *exeunt to cabaret.*)

DAN. She's still around, huh?

NICK. Why not?

DAN. I thought that party last night would be too much for her.

NICK. These kids I got are tanks—they can drink any ten men under.

DAN. Well, be good. I'll take a peek at this new act of yours. (*Exits to hall.*)

(NICK *peeks out to be sure* DAN *is not coming back, turns to office.* STEVE *opens door and comes out, almost twitching with nervousness.*)

STEVE. Damn him, what does he want?

NICK. Nothing important, he says. Just asked for you. I said you wasn't here like you told me.

STEVE. He's got nothing on me. Not a thing—— (PEARL *walks down hall quickly, just glancing in as she passes double doors and disappears.*)

NICK. Say, listen, what the hell's the matter with you? Soon as somebody mentions this dick, McCorn, you go—up in the air. What's the reason for this?

STEVE. I'm all shot, I tell you. Too much booze last night, I guess, and—oh, a lot of things—— (*There is a noise of someone trying back door under stairs, then a knock.* STEVE *rises, controls himself, and sits again.*) Take a look first!

NICK (*peeks out*). It's Dolph. (NICK *unbolts the door, opens it.* DOLPH *enters.*)

STEVE. What's the matter?

DOLPH (*frightened*). Why—I—a——

STEVE. What the hell is it?

DOLPH. There's a guy out there been walking up and down—passed by a dozen times—makes me all nervous.

STEVE. A dick?

DOLPH. Either that or one of Scar Edwards' bunch—nobody I seen before.

NICK. There's a lot of people walk up

and down—it's a free country almost. What's to be afraid of? You guys ain't done nothing.

DOLPH. Ain't there some way to get out of here, Steve—now—before——

STEVE. No, I'm not ready yet. I'll break cover in an hour. Go on, wait out there.

DOLPH. But it ain't safe out there. One of the Edwards crowd might take a shot at me, with a silencer.

STEVE. Go on out—stick by that back entrance, like I told you to. You're my right hand man, ain't you? (*Slaps him on back. Pushes him out.*)

DOLPH. Sure; all right. (*Exits out back door.* STEVE *closes door and bolts it.*)

NICK. I don't get this business, Steve.

STEVE. Listen, Nick, you and I been best kind of pals for a long time. I'd shoot the works for you and I hope you would for me.

NICK. Sure I would. What you want?

STEVE. I am going to blow tonight. I don't want to have any slips. This damn bull McCorn is getting too curious. He thinks some of my mob got Edwards.

NICK. Did they?

STEVE. No, they didn't. Now, listen, I want you to get Joe or someone you can trust to beat it over to Charlie's and tell him to bring his car, *not mine,* they know mine—and leave it at the back entrance for me.

NICK. You can phone him.

STEVE. No, these dicks might have the wires tapped. Sending Joe is safer. After the show, I'll take Billie and a couple of these broads and pile in the car. Looks like we're going for a joy ride, savvy? Then if they trail us, when I get 'em out on the Post Road, I can lose 'em, see, but they won't think I'm going to blow, so long as I got the girls with me. I can get rid of the ones I don't want later on.

NICK. You go to lots of trouble just 'cause a bull's asking questions. My Gawd, Steve, where is your guts?

STEVE. You think I'm yellow, huh? I don't want no man thinking that. Listen, Nick. (*They look at each other intently. Grabs* NICK'*s arm.*) I did that job myself. (NICK *motions quiet with both hands.*) Now, they can't get me for it—they got nothing on me but that gun—but it's getting on my nerves—I'm getting ragged and I want to get out of here—— Now, have you got it?

NICK. Sure, I understand. But don't bump anybody else off in here——

STEVE. You won't get in trouble—I'll fix that—now send for the car.

NICK. Sure, right away—you wait in the office, Steve. (*He hurries into cabaret.* STEVE *goes to big door under stairs, peeks out cautiously through peep hole—then crosses to cabaret doors. Closes them. As he does so, the party door opens, and* PEARL *steps into room with a pistol in her hand. It has a silencer affixed.*)

PEARL (*soft*). Turn around, rat! (*He wheels about.*) I don't want to give it to you like you did him—in the back.

STEVE (*he can't move*). For Christ's sake, don't.

PEARL. I'm giving you more chance than you gave him—I'm looking at you—and the last thing you see before you go straight to hell is Jim Edwards' woman, who swore to God she'd get you.

STEVE (*backing away*). Don't—don't kill me—don't——

PEARL. Whine, you rat—I knew you would. (*She fires. There is just a pish as the gun goes off, a slight curl of smoke.* STEVE *lurches toward office and falls out of sight as he clutches at the door.* PEARL *stands paralyzed by the violence of her act. Then she thrusts the pistol into her handbag and scurries upstairs like a frightened rabbit. Before she is out of sight,* RUBY *opens the cabaret doors and comes in laughing derisively.*)

RUBY. Ha! A total loss!

(*The other girls follow down hall as* BILLIE *and* ROY *rush in from cabaret. There is some applause.*)

MAZIE. Them guys don't know a good act when they see it.

ROY. Come, Billie, it's good for a bow. (BILLIE *and* ROY *run back.*)

RUBY. And they even steal a bow.

ANN. And they rehearsed it, too.

(BILLIE *and* ROY *enter.*)

BILLIE. How do you think it went?

GRACE. That bunch are full of novocain.

RUBY. You'd be a riot in the Palace.

ROY. We could have grabbed another. That detective and Nick crabbed our act with their argument. How could we get attention, everybody watching them. Gee, what a rotten break. Well, go on up, kids; make your change. I'll give the leader a buzz—see how they like it. (*He exits down hall while girls start upstairs.*)

BILLIE. I did my best.

MAZIE. Sure you did, kid; cheer up. I

don't think it's as bad as they say it is.

(*The girls go out.* DAN *and* NICK *are heard arguing. They enter from hall.*)

NICK. Dan, you're getting me sore, y' understand—I gotta right to send any of my waiters any place I want—without any advice from you.

DAN (*pulling him around*). Now, listen to me, Greek—I been pretty nice to you in a lotta ways—now, you get this—you don't want to be accused of helping some guy that's wanted for murder, do you?

NICK. No, but I——

DAN. Then listen to me, before you do any more for Steve Crandall I want to have a talk with him—and after that you can do as you please. I been waiting around here until your show was over before I started something—as I didn't want to give your dump any worse name than it's got. So keep out of my business and you won't have to sit in a witness chair. Now, I happen to know Steve's here; come on, where is he? Where is he? (NICK *motions toward office.*) Tell him I want to see him. (NICK *goes reluctantly to office. He opens door and draws back with a gasp.*) What's the matter? (DAN *runs to door, sizes up situation, and steps past him into the room.*) Come in. Shut the door. (*They go to office.* NICK *fearfully —the door is shut.*)

(RUBY *enters, half dressed, followed by* MAZIE, *who catches her on stairs and chokes her—bending her over the banisters.*)

MAZIE. Now you're going to eat mud.

RUBY. Quit.

MAZIE. Now what am I the son of?

RUBY. You're an angel.

MAZIE. Say uncle——

RUBY. Uncle.

MAZIE (*releases her*). Now, get back. I'd drop you over if I wasn't feeling so good-natured.

(RUBY *exits.* MAZIE *dusts off her hands as* ROY *enters with a rush. He has supper card in his hand.*)

ROY. Look, Mazie—look at this—I got this from Mike Shea—he just caught our act.

MAZIE. Who's he?

ROY. He's one of the biggest booking agents in New York—he wrote me on this supper card——

MAZIE. Mike Shea—never heard of him.

ROY (*at top of stairs*). Listen, what he wrote. At last I got a break. I got to show it to Billie. "I can offer you and partner Chambersburgh and Pottsville next week"—— Billie, Billie! (*Runs out to dressing room.*)

MAZIE (*laughs*). That's one for the book! (*Follows him.*)

(NICK *comes out of office, looking under great stress*—DAN *follows.*)

DAN. He's dead, all right. (NICK *moans.*) Right through the old pump.

NICK (*suddenly*). Lane, the hoofer. He's the one. He killed Steve. I'll betcha. He was out to get him.

DAN. The actor, you mean?

(PEARL *enters on stairs. She starts down—hears the voices and halts.*)

NICK. Sure, he's been tryin' to get him. He's been lyin' about him.

DAN. No, it wasn't Lane—it was suicide.

NICK. Suicide?

DAN. Sure. (*Fascinated,* PEARL *comes slowly down stairs, her hands against the back wall.* DAN *talks to* NICK, *his eye on the girl.*) Here's Steve's own gun—with one chamber empty.

NICK. I thought you had that?

DAN. I gave it back to Steve today.

NICK. But Steve said——

DAN. I said I gave it back to him today. He knew I was going to pinch him, so he took the shortest way out. I'm calling up headquarters to report it suicide—so that's what it is.

NICK. All right—all right—whatever you say.

DAN. Give me the key to this door. (PEARL *sits at piano.* NICK *gives him key to the office door.* DAN *locks it.*) I want to keep everyone out of there till the Coroner gets here. I'll wait for him out back. (*He starts to back door; as he passes* PEARL *he speaks disinterestedly—out of the corner of his mouth.*) Pull yourself together, kid. (*Exits back door.*)

(PEARL *lets her head fall forward, weak with relief, as* DAN *exits and the other girls and* ROY *enter on stairs, laughing and joking excitedly.*)

MAZIE. Pottsville and Chambersburgh. Gawd, Billie, you must love this guy.

BILLIE. I certainly do.

ROY. I been so busy gettin' the act framed, I ain't had time to show you how much I love you. But here goes.

(ROY *and* BILLIE *embrace.*)

ANN. My Gawd, in front of every body——

GRACE. When do you two play the matrimonial circuit——

MAZIE. Break—time——

RUBY. Look at 'em.

(GIRLS *laughing and pulling* BILLIE *and* ROY *apart.*)

NICK (*bursting out suddenly—his nerves unable to stand their hilarity*). Cut out this noise—I—er—we gotta cut it out, y' understand.

(*They stand dumfounded by his violence. The buzzer sounds—and* ROY *snaps back to his job.*)

ROY. There goes the gong again—all ready, girls? Come on, Pearl. Gee, I'm happy. Our names will be in bright lights soon, *Roy Lane and Co.* Remember you're all artists. Here we go—here we go——

(*The girls form in line and dance into cabaret singing as* NICK *crosses himself and prays leaning against the door as though half fainting.*)

CURTAIN

Paris Bound

BY PHILIP BARRY

First produced by Arthur Hopkins at the Music Box Theatre, New York City, on December 27, 1927, with the following cast:

MARY HUTTON .... Madge Kennedy	JAMES HUTTON .... Gilbert Emery
JIM HUTTON .... Donn Cook	RICHARD PARRISH ..... Donald Macdonald
NORA COPE .... Ellen Southbrook	PETER COPE .... Edwin Nicander
HELEN WHITE .... Martha Mayo	NOEL FARLEY .... Mary Murray
FANNY SHIPPAN .... Hope Williams	JULIE .... Marie Bruce

ACT I

The upstairs sitting room of a house in the country near New York.

ACT II

The music room on the top floor of a house in uptown New York, near the East River.

ACT III

Same as Act II.

When, after making a debut on Broadway with three fairly romantic comedies (*You and I,* 1923, *The Youngest,* 1924, and *In a Garden,* 1925), Philip Barry turned out *Paris Bound* in 1927 he approached the altitudes of high comedy which had not been conspicuous in the American theatre. It required a certain degree of detachment from sentiment, whether moral or romantic, to suggest that adultery was not necessarily a sound reason for divorce. If Mr. Barry's religion may have inspired this judgment it, nevertheless, has its origin in the older religion of the Comic Muse—namely, common sense. Joseph Wood Krutch aptly calls it "that morality of compromise which is the essence of the comic spirit," although I am not sure how this applies to Ben Jonson, Gogol, or Shaw. But he who wants guidance had better read all that Mr. Krutch has written on *Paris Bound* (in *The American Drama since 1918,* pages 165-67). Without some understanding of the nature of high comedy which has become rare even among the educated of our time, *Paris Bound* is apt to strike the reader as mild or commonplace in spite of much well-turned dialogue.

As for the reader who believes that nothing is quite "important" unless it occurs below the upper strata of society (an assumption I have confronted in university courses on the novel as well as the drama, and not only in classes), let him transpose the situation of *Paris Bound* to ordinary life. He will find the wisdom and experience of the common man fighting on Mr. Barry's side. But, of course, it is the very essence of this author's best work in comedy that he is merely observing rather than "fighting" for anything.

The well-educated author, who was born in Rochester in 1896, came to the theatre after studying at Catholic schools, Yale University, and Baker's Workshop 47 at Harvard, and working for the State Department in Washington and London. He followed the success of *Paris Bound* with *Holiday* in 1928. It impressed his public as an even better comedy than its predecessor, an opinion with which we may differ. It expressed the then fashionable revolt of the younger generation against the worship of business success. It said nothing particularly incisive about the problem of making money or wanting it in modern society, but as a comedy of manners *Holiday* was an extremely smooth and charming piece of writing.

In the twenties, Mr. Barry also made efforts to cultivate other gardens than those of comedy. He did not succeed with the religious drama *John* in 1927 and he raised a whimsy somewhat too arch in conception and naive in execution, *White Wings* (1926), which made fun of human resistance to change. His other departures from comedy of manners came after the twenties with *Hotel Universe* (1930), *Here Come the Clowns* (1938), and *Liberty Jones* (1941)—the last two being allegories on the subject of contemporary tensions. He returned to comedy more successfully with *Tomorrow and Tomorrow* (1931), *The Animal Kingdom* (1932), *Without Love* (1942), and *The Foolish Notion* (1945), and very successfully with *The Philadelphia Story* (1939), which may be read with profit in conjunction with *Paris Bound* as another contribution to comedy's morality of compromise. His other plays to date have been *A Punch for Judy,* first produced in Workshop 47 in 1921, *Cock Robin* (a collaboration with Elmer Rice, 1928), *The Joyous Season* (1934), *Bright Star* (1935), the adaptation *Spring Dance* (1936), and another adaptation *My Name is Aquilon* (1949). He is also the author of a novel *War in Heaven* which provided the basis for *Here Come the Clowns.*

ACT ONE

SCENE.—*The upstairs sitting-room of a house in the country near New York. July, six years ago.*

The sitting-room is a spacious, comfortable room, of no particular period. There is a table and there is a chaise-longue. There are two or three chairs. The entire back wall is bowed into large windows, shaded by awnings from the bright noon-day sun.

Entrance from the hall is at right.

Entrance into the bedroom is at left.

At Rise: JULIE, *about 45, a housemaid of a superior type, is listening attentively at the hall doorway. From downstairs, a dance orchestra is heard playing the concluding strains of a tune. The music stops and for a moment there is a dead silence. It is followed by a sudden rush of shouts, cheers, laughter and the sound of two people running upstairs. The orchestra breaks into one triumphal phrase of the wedding-march, and concludes abruptly. Another silence, interrupted by a shout: "She's going to throw it!" Then impatient cries of "Throw it!" "Throw it!" "Why don't you throw it?" Again, a silence, briefer this time, then more cheers and laughter.* JULIE *crosses to the bedroom and goes out, closing the door after her. For a moment the room is empty, then, hand-in-hand in the hall doorway, appear* JIM *and* MARY HUTTON. JIM *is twenty-six and* MARY *twenty-two. They have been married two hours. The wedding-breakfast is over, but the guests still remain to see them off.* MARY *is lovely in her wedding-dress and* JIM *almost handsome in cutaway and white waistcoat. Both are flushed with excitement, and very happy.*

JIM. How long do you think you'll be?

MARY. Twenty minutes. What about you?

JIM. Ten at the outside.

MARY. Good.

JIM. Are your bags ready?

MARY. They will be.

JIM. Peter's to take mine out the back way and stow 'em in the motor. We'll drop yours down through the window.

MARY. That will be nice.

JIM. —Only hurry.

MARY. All right. Will you come back for me here?

JIM. Sure. (*A pause.*) Mary—

MARY. What?

JIM. —Fun.

MARY. I've never enjoyed a wedding so much in my life.

JIM. Me neither.

MARY. And I always enjoy weddings.

JIM. Me too.

(*They gaze at each other for a moment, smiling, fascinated. Finally:*)

MARY. Jim—you know something?

JIM. What?

MARY. —I'm a fool about you.

JIM. Dear, you've got nothing on me.

MARY (*a concession*). —Say fifteen minutes.

JIM. That's better.

MARY. Good-bye, then—

JIM. Good-bye.

MARY. Mind you hurry!

JIM (*from the hallway*). Mind you do!

(MARY *comes into the sitting-room. She calls:*)

MARY. Julie! Where are you, Julie?

(*She goes to a table and finds three telegrams on a tray. The bedroom door is opened and* JULIE *comes in.*)

JULIE. Yes, Mrs. Hutton?

MARY. —"Mrs—"—?—Don't do that, dear. Not yet. You'll throw me all off.—Still more telegrams?

JULIE. There were a few addressed to you personally. Miss Archer said to keep them here for you.

(MARY *opens and reads a telegram.*)

MARY. Oh dear—(*She reads another.*) —Dear, oh dear.—Julie, I could cry.

JULIE. You should be very happy, Miss.

MARY. I am. (*She opens the third telegram.*)—Everyone downstairs seemed to think you made a good job of me.

JULIE. You looked beautiful.

MARY (*reading the telegram*). Don't I still?

JULIE. Oh, indeed!

MARY (*absently*). Julie—

JULIE. Yes, Miss?

MARY. This morning Aunt Grace asked me if there was anything in this house I wanted to take with me for my house—and I said you.

JULIE. Ah, that was very kind.

MARY. We'll be back in two months. Would you like to come to me in town, in September?

JULIE. There's no one I'd as soon be with, Miss.

MARY. Then we'll call it settled, shall we?

I've got a room on the top floor there, for my music: I'll want you to keep just it, and my room, and me. Is that all right?

JULIE. Oh yes, Miss. Yes—anything—

(MARY *hesitates a moment, then tears up the telegrams and moves toward the bedroom.*)

MARY. I must rush into my things now. Are the bags locked?

JULIE (*following her*). —All but the small one. I have the checks for the trunks.

MARY. Don't let me forget them. I'm not remembering very well to-day.

(*She goes out into the bedroom.* JULIE *follows her and closes the door after them. A moment, then the hall door is again opened and* NORA COPE *enters. She is a pretty girl of about twenty-three, dressed as a wedding-attendant.*)

NORA. Will you come in here, Mrs. White?

(HELEN WHITE *enters from the hall. She is a woman of forty-five, slender and distinguished.*)

HELEN. Oh thank you—I can't imagine what came over me.

NORA. It *was* hot in that garden. I feel rather wilted myself.

HELEN. I think it was standing so long in the line.

NORA. Can't I get you some water or whisky or something?

HELEN. Oh no—no thank you. This is all I need—(*She seats herself upon the chaise-longue.*)—just to rest a moment.—Let me see, now—you were maid-of-honor, weren't you?

NORA. —Matron. I'm Nora Cope.—That funny-looking usher who went up first—he's my husband.

HELEN. A great friend of my son's, then.

NORA. Oh yes—Peter and Jim are just like *that.*

HELEN (*smiling*). It's—rather trying for a mother to be a stranger at her own son's wedding.

NORA. Jim was so touched at your coming such a long way for it.

HELEN. The dear boy.

NORA. —But you knew Mary, didn't you?

HELEN. —For the first time, two hours ago.

NORA. Oh, I see.—How does she strike you?

HELEN. She seems to be such a sweet, attractive girl.

NORA. She's all of that, Mrs. White.

HELEN. I'm so glad.—And Jim *is* a nice boy, isn't he?

NORA. Heavens, yes. Jim's a first-rater.

HELEN. I'm sure they will be very happy.

NORA. I think they've a good chance at it.

HELEN. —A chance, only?

(NORA *shrugs.*)

NORA. What more can you say for anyone? (*She smiles.*)—Any two, that is.

(FANNY SHIPPAN *enters from the hall, in bridesmaid's dress. She is about* NORA'S *age, bluff, smart, likable.* NORA *greets her.*) Hello, Fanny.

FANNY. Listen: where the devil's Mary? I've looked everywhere except—(*She sees* MRS. WHITE.) Oh—

NORA. You've met Jim's mother, haven't you? (*To* MRS. WHITE.) This is Miss Shippan—

HELEN. How do you do?

FANNY. How do you do, Mrs. Hutton. Wasn't it the loveliest—? Oh, I beg your pardon—

(HELEN *smiles faintly.*)

HELEN. "Mrs. White," it is now.

FANNY. Of course.—Trust me to forget it, though. (*To* NORA.) Where *is* the girl?

NORA. In there. (FANNY *crosses toward the bedroom door.*) Fanny—

FANNY. Yes, chick?

NORA. Is Noel all right?

FANNY. Well, not so very—

NORA. I'm worried sick about her.

FANNY. So am I. She acts as if she'd never seen champagne before.

NORA. What's to be done?

FANNY. Peter's keeping an eye on her.

NORA. Much good that'll do.

FANNY. I'll go down again myself, in a minute.

NORA. Don't let on to Mary.

FANNY. I should say not. (*She knocks at the door.*) Oh Mrs. H.! Mrs. H.!

(MARY'S *voice is heard from inside.*)

MARY. Is that you, Fanny?

FANNY. Yes, Mrs. H.

MARY. Come in, idiot. What's the matter?

(FANNY *goes out, into the bedroom.* JAMES HUTTON *enters from the hall. He is 47, of youthful figure, and with a fine face, rather humorous about the eyes and mouth.*)

JAMES. —Resting after the battle, Nora?

NORA. Wasn't it superb, Mr. Hutton? Weren't you proud of them?

JAMES. —Good-looking son I've got, eh?

NORA. But why not? Look at the parents.

JAMES. That's the girl.

(NORA *moves toward the bedroom.*)

NORA. I'll—uh—I'll just go see if—(*She knocks on the door.*) Mary! It's Nora.—Anything I can do?

MARY (*from the bedroom*). Come in, darling! I was just shouting for you.

(NORA *goes out, into the bedroom.* JAMES *lights a cigarette, watching* HELEN. *Finally:*

JAMES. Cigarette?

HELEN. No thank you.

(*A pause.*)

JAMES. Do you feel any better?

HELEN. Very much. The—heat bothered me frightfully.

JAMES. Is that all that bothered you, Helen?

HELEN. You mean seeing you again?

JAMES. No, I didn't mean that.

HELEN. Extraordinary, how completely we've escaped each other. How long is it?

JAMES. This is nineteen hundred and—: fifteen years.

HELEN. That's quite a time, in a world of this size.

JAMES. You don't come home very often, do you?

HELEN. Home? America?—Never when I can avoid it.

JAMES. Why did you marry White?

HELEN. Because I wanted to.

JAMES. I met him once. I thought him an exceptionally dull man.

HELEN. That depends on how you look at him.—What is it you think "bothered" me?

JAMES. The whole thing: the sight of your boy being married, quite as lovingly, quite as hopefully, as you married me.

HELEN. Oh. (*She reflects.*) I can only hope they make a better job of it than we did.

JAMES. I'm sure they hope so.

HELEN. I'm told they're very well suited to each other.

JAMES. So were we.

HELEN. —Except in certain particulars.

JAMES. Jim is like me in a great many ways, Helen.

HELEN. Then I suppose I should be sorry for her.

(JAMES *rises and bows slightly.*)

JAMES. Madame. (*And seats himself again.*)—I'm very fond of Mary. I was rather afraid he was going to marry Noel—not that there's ever been anything between them, but I've always sensed a kind of—

HELEN. —Noel?

JAMES. Noel Farley—one of the bridesmaids—the prettiest, in fact. Pat Farley's girl—you remember Pat and Alice—

HELEN. I thought she was behaving rather cheaply downstairs.

JAMES. Don't be unkind, Helen. I don't think I've ever seen more tragic eyes in a young girl's head.

(*She smiles.*)

HELEN. Trust you to note the tragic eyes, James.

(*He looks at her curiously for a moment. Then:*)

JAMES (*small talk*). —Charming wedding, wasn't it? Charming house, charming garden, charming breakfast—

HELEN. Quite. Her aunt must have money.

JAMES. She has.

HELEN. Is Mary well-off, too?

JAMES. I believe her father left her considerable.

HELEN. Did both parents die young?—She looks strong enough.

JAMES. They went within two weeks of each other, with influenza.

HELEN. How sad. Jim told me next to nothing in his letter. (*A moment.*) Between them they'll have plenty, then.

JAMES. Helen, I'm amazed at you.

HELEN. Why so?

JAMES. Your coldness. Your utter worldliness.

HELEN. Don't let it distress you too much.—Does Jim like his business?

JAMES. Enormously—and works very hard at it.

HELEN. —Youth, health, love, money and an occupation—they seem to have the odds on their side, at any rate.

JAMES. So did we.

HELEN. —So "More shame to us"?

JAMES. More shame to you, let us say.

(*A brief pause.*)

HELEN. The years haven't put wrinkles in your cheek, have they, James?

JAMES. Cheek?

HELEN. Cheek.

(JAMES *shakes his head over her.*)

JAMES. —Still bitter. It's amazing.

HELEN. Poor dear, life is such a constant

surprise to you.—As I remember, you were amazed when I divorced you.

JAMES. That was an act of resentment on the part of a raw young girl. You're past forty now, and should know better.

HELEN. You still don't accept the impossibility of my living with you after what you did—

JAMES. I shan't ever accept it.

HELEN. Well, I give up. In fact I gave up, some time ago, didn't I?

JAMES. I know: that's one of your troubles.

(*She rises.*)

HELEN. I'm afraid I must—

JAMES. —Duck—dodge again—get out from under. All right, my dear.

(*She turns on him.*)

HELEN. Jim, I—! (*She stops abruptly and sinks down into another chair. Then:*) Which of us was in the wrong—you or me?

JAMES. —You were. I may have committed adultery, Helen, but I never committed divorce.

HELEN. When you had your affair with —with that woman—

JAMES (*amused*). Mrs. Bliss, her name was—Kitty Bliss—pretty name—

HELEN. —And a pretty affair! Just pretty enough to destroy our marriage.

JAMES. I think it was you who did the destroying, Helen.

HELEN. How do you figure that?

JAMES. —Through what you made of it. Because, you know, all that *we* had—you and I—*our* province was never touched by it.

HELEN. That's easy enough to say.

JAMES. It's gospel.

HELEN. I'm afraid I don't understand these separate provinces of yours.

JAMES. Mine?—Everyone's!

HELEN. I don't understand them.

JAMES. Well, here's your son Jim: he is attractive to women. His wife Mary is attractive to men. He's twenty-six, she is twenty-two. Is he never to know another woman, or she another man?

HELEN. Know them? But of course!

JAMES. Well, love them, then.

HELEN. Even love them—in a way.

JAMES. —Provided they "behave"—

HELEN. Naturally.

(*He smiles.*)

JAMES. —Provided they behave naturally—

HELEN (*indignant*). I didn't say—

JAMES. Well, I don't think it's very important whether they do or not.

HELEN. Then why any marriage at all?

JAMES. Simply because marriage of one woman to one man for a lifetime is the most civilized and beautiful idea poor humanity has ever conceived of.

HELEN. Imagine your thinking so.

JAMES. I've never thought otherwise.—And any two people, I don't care who they are, who marry for love as we did—as most do—and live before the world as man and wife, create between them something they can never get away from and never hope to duplicate.

HELEN. I wonder if they can't.

JAMES. You know they can't.—It's an entity as real as any child is and it's born without them knowing it, simply of the fact that a man and woman in love have elected to face *all* the facts of life together, from under one roof.

HELEN. So I denied our spiritual child—is that it?

JAMES. That will do, yes.

HELEN. It was for that that I left *you,* Jim.

JAMES. You left me because you found out that I had gone with another woman —*found it out.*

HELEN. Wasn't that almost enough?

JAMES. No. It didn't begin to be.—For following a physical impulse which I share with the rest of the animal kingdom, you destroyed a spiritual relationship which belonged only to us. For an act which in reality was of little or no importance to you, you did me out of my marriage and my home, of the daughter I've always longed for—very nearly out of the son I already had. You did a good, thorough job. And after all, where did it land you?

HELEN. Really, James—

JAMES. Yes really.—I should like to know.

HELEN (*rising*). I think I've had about enough of this, if you don't mind.

JAMES. I suppose that's the real trouble with you: you can't stand very much. You've dodged things all your life. So now you're soft where you should be hard, and hard as nails where you should be soft. I think you might have struck a better balance if you'd weathered that one rough stretch, as you should have. You might still be the once-wronged wife, but you'd be ten times the person you are now.

HELEN (*furious*). —To-day of all days, from you of all people—you who left a young wife who trusted you utterly for a—for some rotten affair.

JAMES. My God, Helen—what *is* all this stuff about—?

HELEN. I'll tell you what it is! It's—

(*She stops abruptly, as the bedroom door opens and* FANNY *re-enters, talking back through the open door, into the bedroom:*)

FANNY. My dear, I'm the ninth richest woman under thirty in North America, and if I can't give pianos for wedding-presents, I don't know who can. (*She closes the door, and crosses toward the hall, smiling amiably at* JAMES *and* HELEN.) Hello, Mr. Hutton—are you taking care of Mrs. *White* all right? (*Her hand flies to her mouth.*) Oh my Lord— (JAMES *laughs.* FANNY *accelerates her pace toward the hall door, which opens to admit* JIM, *now dressed for departure.*)

JIM. Hi, Fanny. What's the report?

FANNY (*passing him*). She's almost ready.—Another day or two ought to see you off.

(*She goes out.* JIM *enters, stopping in surprise at the sight of his father and mother.*)

JIM. Well, hello! (*He looks at them amusedly.*)—Happy reunion?

HELEN. Come here, Jim. (*He goes to her. She kisses him.*)—I think she's lovely.

JIM. I have luck, don't I?

HELEN. I think you both have.

JIM. Lord, I feel good. (*He looks at his watch, then calls in the direction of the bedroom door.*) Oh, *Mary!*

MARY (*from inside*). Hello, Angel!

JIM (*to* JAMES). You see? She adores me— (*To* MARY.) What about those fifteen minutes?

MARY. I'm coming!

JIM. I guess we wait.

(*He slumps down into a chair, clasps his hands over his waist, watches* JAMES *and* HELEN, *and begins to whistle a popular song, off-key.*)

MARY. Jim!

JIM. Hello!

MARY. Don't do that!

JIM. What?

MARY. Whistle.

JIM. Why?

MARY. It's horrible.

(JIM *looks at* JAMES *in pretended surprise.*)

JIM. What can she mean?

JAMES. Do you still take cold baths in the morning, Jim?

JIM. Yes, why?

JAMES. —And do you sing in them?

JIM. Sure, I suppose so.

JAMES. I think I'd give it up, if I were you.

(JIM *stares for a moment, then laughs.*)

JIM. What do you advise, Mother?

HELEN. Well, with a musician for a wife I should imagine that simple gasps are better.

JIM. His voice died in his throat.

JAMES. Anything more I can do for you, Son?

JIM. Nothing possibly. You've been a brick.—I told you what I thought about your coming on for it, Mother.

HELEN. I'd have gone around the world, Jimmy.

JIM. You're a great pair, you two.

JAMES. Do you think so?

JIM. I know it. (*A pause.*)—I'm not sure of the ethics of a situation like this, but I'd like to make an inquiry—

JAMES. Go ahead.

JIM. What's it like to be together again? (*He smiles.*)—Excuse me, but I'm in the publishing business.

JAMES. Well, I find it very agreeable.

(JIM *looks to* HELEN.)

HELEN. Your father was always an attractive man.

JIM (*suddenly*). Why'd you leave him, Mother?

HELEN. Why I—that is, I—

JIM. I didn't mean to blurt it out quite like that, but I've always wondered.

JAMES. You mean to say you don't know?

JIM. No.—Of course I suppose you just didn't hit it off. But—

JAMES. We hit it off perfectly—

(JIM *looks to* HELEN.)

JIM. Then I don't see—

JAMES. —Except in one respect.

(HELEN *turns away.*)

JIM. Oh. Never mind—I'm sorry. (*He looks at his watch again.*) Why doesn't that girl hurry? I hate to wait for people.

JAMES. —It happened that I was once what your mother calls "unfaithful" to her.

JIM (*incredulously*). You mean you wanted to quit Mother, and—?

JAMES. Oh no—no, never for a minute.

(*A brief pause.* JIM *turns to his mother.*)

JIM. But you—?

HELEN (*coldly*).—But I.

JAMES (*after a moment*). Well, what do you think of it, Jim?

JIM. Would *you* like to know, Mother?

HELEN. If you like.

JIM. Well, it strikes me it was quite short-sighted, and pretty unjust, to boot. (*A pause. Then:*)

HELEN. —I imagine, however, that Mary would not think so.

JIM. I'm certain she'd think the same. (*There is an awkward silence.* JIM *adds:*) —Marriage is a pretty big job, of course. But it seems to me that if both people use their heads, they can manage it.

JAMES. You may be sure they can.

JIM. I'm not worried. I think *we'll* stay put, all right.

HELEN. That, I've no doubt, will be largely up to you.

JIM. Oh no—it'll be up to Mary. Nothing'd ever unmarry me.

HELEN. I think you would do well, however, to learn to profit by your father's mistake.

JIM. Aren't you being a little rough on him, Mother? (*He smiles engagingly.*)—I tell you what: I'll do that, if you'll teach Mary to profit by yours.

(*The bedroom door opens and* MARY *comes in in her "going-away dress."* JIM *springs up and rushes to her.*)

JIM. Oh, what a handsome wench! Can this be mine? (*He takes her hand and turns her around to* JAMES *and* HELEN.)—Is my wife making a good impression?

JAMES. We are speechless.

MARY (*to* JIM). You *can* whistle, if you like.

(JIM *whistles two notes.*)

JIM. Is that enough?

MARY. Plenty.

JIM. —Just now and again, to assert my rights.

(MARY *goes to* HELEN *and* JAMES.)

MARY. You've been sweet, both of you.

HELEN. So have you, Mary.

JAMES. Stay that way, will you?

MARY. We'll try, won't we, Jim?

JIM. I will. You don't need to.

(*She sinks down into a chair, with a sigh.*)

MARY. Ladies and Gentlemen, this is the happiest day of my life.

JIM. Don't you believe it.

(*He seats himself on the arm of the chair, and takes her hand.*)

JAMES (*to* HELEN). I think we'd better go down again, don't you?

MARY. Oh no, not yet! We aren't leaving till—Peter!

(PETER COPE *enters from the hall. He wears a cutaway, with a white flower in the button-hole, and carries a tray with a bottle of champagne and several glasses. He is about twenty-eight, robust and amiable. At present he is also pleasantly exhilarated.*)

PETER. —Just the day for a picnic. (*He places the tray and napkin on a table near them.*)

MARY. Oh Peter—marvellous—

JIM (*simultaneously*). Good man, Peter.

PETER. They said I couldn't make the stairs with it: I said I could.—Where's my wife, Nora?

MARY. —In there, helping Julie.

PETER. I must speak with my good wife, Nora. (*He moves toward the bedroom, stopping for a moment beside* MARY. *He scowls at* JIM.) Leave go that lady's hand, you naughty navy man. (*He drops his hand gently upon* MARY'S *head.*)—Nice girl. Always remember what Granny says, and don't trust a navy man. (*He calls at the bedroom door:*) Nora?

(NORA *replies from inside:*)

NORA. Yes?

PETER. Let down the drawbridge!

(*He goes out into the bedroom.* JAMES *has filled the glasses. He gives one to* MARY *and one to* HELEN.)

JAMES. Well, my dears,—here's to a happy, happy life for you.

(*He and* JIM *take glasses.*)

JIM (*raising his*). Here's to one for all of us.

MARY. Yes.

JAMES. Yes.

(*They sip the wine. The strain is now gone. They are all friends together. Their talk runs with a new animation.*)

HELEN. What *are* your plans, Jim?

JIM. —From now, you mean?

JAMES. Yes.

JIM. Well, we ought to make town in two hours and a half at the outside.

MARY. I'll drive part of the way.

JIM. You *will* not.—We'll go straight to the hotel. Peter's reserved rooms.—Where do you want to dine, Darling?

MARY. Have we got a sitting-room?

JIM. Yes.

MARY. There, then. It's less trouble.

JIM. That's my idea.—I wired the man at the club to see what revues he could get seats for, and then to get two for the one he couldn't.

MARY. That sounds promising.

JIM. The boat sails at midnight.—When are *you* going back, Mother?

HELEN. Early next month.

JIM. Be in London, will you?

HELEN. I expect so.

JIM. With him?

HELEN. With my husband, yes.

JAMES. —"White" is the name—pretty name.

JIM. We might try to join up for a day or two. I'd like to meet him.

HELEN. Let's arrange to, by all means.

JIM. The Company wants me to make a yearly trip over, starting next May. So I'll be seeing you regularly, I hope.

HELEN. I do hope so, Dear.

JAMES (*to* MARY). What *I* should like to know is, am I to be called Father, or am I not?

MARY. Yes, Father, you are. (*To* HELEN.) —Did you hear what he's given us for our house in town?

HELEN. Tell me.

MARY. Another floor.

HELEN. —Another f—?

JIM. —Floor. And a top floor, at that. Roofs cost like hell.

MARY. It's to be for my music.

HELEN. But how very nice.—And is Jim to be allowed in it?

MARY. Only on rare occasions. The library's his province.

JAMES (*to* HELEN). "Province."

HELEN. Be still, James.

JIM. What's the joke?

HELEN. Never mind. (JULIE *enters from the bedroom with two bags, which she places near the center window.* HELEN *rises, goes to* MARY *and kisses her.*) Good-bye, Mary.)

MARY. Good-bye, dear. Thanks for coming and thanks for that whopping cheque and I love you, I really do.

(HELEN *smiles, pats her cheek, turns to* JIM *and kisses him.*)

HELEN. Good-bye, Jimmy. Be a good boy.

JIM. Bet your life, Mother. Thanks from me, too.

JAMES (*kissing* MARY). Good-bye, daughter. I shan't fret about you two.

MARY. Don't you do it.

(JULIE *goes out again, into the bedroom.* JAMES *shakes hands with* JIM.)

JAMES. Have a good trip, son.

JIM. Yes, sir.—See you in the autumn, eh?

JAMES. That's right! (*He holds out his arm to* HELEN.) Come—we must dance together now, and scandalize the guests. We owe it to them. (HELEN *takes his arm. They move toward the hall.* JIM *and* MARY *stand together watching them. At the door,* JAMES *stops and turns to them once more.*) I've only one thing to say to both of you: if at first you don't succeed, don't try again.—Do you second that, Helen?

HELEN. No, I do not. (*She tightens her arm in his.*)—Are you coming?

(JAMES *smiles back at* JIM *and* MARY.)

JAMES. —She does, though.

(*They go out into the hall. Waltz music is heard from downstairs until the door closes again after them.* MARY *stands staring at the door. A silence. Then:*)

MARY. Oh Jim—how awful—

JIM. I know, Dear—but don't you worry.

MARY. Oh, let's be careful, let's be *careful!*

JIM. We will, Sweet.

(*She sinks down into a chair and gazes in front of her for a moment.* JIM *lights another cigarette.*)

MARY (*suddenly*). You know, it occurs to me I've married you under fairly false pretences.

JIM (*amused*). Oh? Such as—?

MARY. I've got a lot of bum theories about marriage. You've never heard them.

JIM (*grinning*). Let's save 'em up for the long winter evenings, shall we?

MARY. I'm afraid I'll forget them.

JIM. —How do they go?

MARY. Well, for one thing, I don't believe much in monopolies.

JIM. No?

MARY. Not for us, anyhow. We're too fond of—people.

JIM. You and me and the great throbbing heart of America—that'll be all right.

MARY. —Not quite so general as that, maybe.

JIM. I shall like you best, Mary.

MARY. So will I you.—But the point is, I don't expect never to see another man, and I don't expect you never to see another girl.—We've simply got to *make* ourselves see them! Then there won't ever be the danger of them getting to be—to be—

JIM. —Novelties to us?

MARY (*gratefully*). Exactly.—And I like

to be alone a lot. I may seem sullen, but it won't mean anything, really it won't.

JIM. I'll look the other way.

MARY. —"Respect each other's privacy." Oh, that sounds terrible. Hints to the Lovelorn.

JIM. All theories are terrible.

MARY. Of course they are. But what are you going to do?

JIM. Dunno. (*A brief pause.*)—One thing: we're being nice and sensible and modern, aren't we?

MARY. Oh, Jim, we've got to be! (JIM's *smile fades.*) I mean it. We've simply got to be a success. All my life I've seen nothing but—

(*She averts her head.*)

JIM. —But how can we help but be?! *You—? Me—?*

MARY. It isn't as easy as that, Jim. There's where people make the mistake. It takes work, and they won't work. *I know it takes work.*

JIM. Mary—

MARY. What?

(*His smile reasserts itself.*)

JIM. —Beads of sweat'll be standing out on my forehead.

(*She laughs, and holds her hand out to him in a quick gesture. He takes it and kisses it.*)

MARY. I'm a fool.

JIM. Nope. Not a bit.—But I think we'll be all right.

MARY. I know we shall.

(*From the bedroom* NORA *enters, followed by* PETER, *who carries a bag in each hand, and a third under one arm. He goes to the window with them.*)

NORA. Listen: Peter says Noel Farley's in a dreadful state downstairs.

PETER. I said—

MARY. How do you mean?

JIM. Noel? What's she doing?

PETER. Well, she keeps laughing all the time, and very loud.

NORA. I was wondering if we oughtn't to do something about her.

(*A pause. Finally.*)

MARY. What could we?

JIM. Oh Noel's all right. She's just excitable. (*He goes to the center window.*) How are we to get these bags down, Pete?

PETER. I've got Tom down there under the window. (*He calls.*) Are you ready there, Tom?

(*A voice replies from below:*)

VOICE. Right here, sir.

PETER. Here are the bags! (*He turns to the others.*)—And here's the rope. It's a clothesline. Happy Days, from the laundress.

MARY. Do be kind to my lovely new luggage.

NORA (*to* PETER). Will it reach?

PETER. Why, its reach exceeds its grasp.

NORA. Hurry up, Stupid, and quit talking.

(*She continues to look troubled over Noel.* PETER *is tying one end of the line to two bags.*)

PETER. Don't cross me. Never cross a Cope.

(JIM *leans out of the window and calls cautiously.*)

JIM. All right, Tom?

VOICE (*from below*). All right, sir.

PETER. —Scratch a Cope, and you find a wife-beater.

JIM. Heave, Petey.

PETER. What've you got in here, Mary—sand?

MARY. My grandfather was a puddler in a steel-mill. It's the old family tools.

PETER (*lifting the bag to the window-sill*). —Well, I didn't stroke the Vassar crew for nothing.

JIM. What about our get-away, Pete?

PETER. What about it?

MARY. Jim means, can we get away with it?

PETER. I've arranged it all myself, with these two bare hands. You wait here, with the craven bridegroom. When everything's set, I'll tell the orchestra to crash into something appropriate—

MARY. What?

PETER. Well, say "The Bastard King of England."

NORA (*impatiently*). *What,* Peter?

PETER. "Mary is a Grand Old Name."

NORA. They won't know it.

PETER (*defiantly*). But it *is* a grand old name.

JIM. Have them play something I'll recognize.

MARY. What would you?

JIM (*after a moment's thought*). Dardanella, or the wedding-march.

PETER. It's an inspiration: I'll have them play the wedding-march.

NORA. *That's* settled.

PETER. —Then you join hands and scurry down the stairs through the hall and out the door, amid rice and rose-petals. Then buckety-buckety up the drive.

way toward the car you're supposed to take. You'll recognize it by its decorations and wall-mottoes, mostly very obscene. I printed them out myself, last night.—Sure you wouldn't rather go in that car?

MARY. No, no, idiot!

PETER. Then cut across the tennis-court to the south drive, where Tom'll be with my high-powered Pope-Toledo.

MARY. It's miles.

PETER. Rome wasn't built in a day.

MARY. Can we trust him, Nora?

NORA. Look here, Peter—(PETER *turns to her. She examines his face searchingly.*) Yes.

PETER. —Thanks for the vote of confidence. (*He calls out the window.*)—The South road, near the tennis-court. Forty paces from the old pine. Have you got that, Tom?

VOICE. Yes, sir.

JIM. I'm going to drive, you know.

PETER. He understands.—Now, my boy, I want *your* bag, and I mean to have it. (*He calls again through the window.*) One more to come, Tom!

VOICE. Right, sir.

PETER. I'll meet you with it in the pantry.—Where is it, Massa Jim?

JIM. I'll show you.

(*They move together toward the hall. The door opens and* FANNY *enters.*)

FANNY. Listen: something radical's got to be done about Noel.

JIM. Why? What's the matter?

FANNY. I'm afraid Love has reared its ugly head, Jim.

(JIM *turns away, abruptly.*)

JIM. You're talking through your hat. (*To* PETER.) Come on—

MARY. Wait a minute.—What's she doing, Fanny?

FANNY. Oh, laughing and carrying on in a generally outrageous manner.

PETER. I saw her glass filled four times at the breakfast.

FANNY. Now all the younger boys are cutting in on her. It's rotten, really.

NORA. Hasn't anyone spoken to her?

FANNY. Jerry and Cooper did. So did I. I've never had such a stare from anyone in my life. Her mother's in the library, dying of mortification.

JIM. You might go down, Pete, and take her for a walk around the garden.

PETER. I tried to. She wouldn't come.

(*A pause.*)

FANNY. I'm afraid it'll end by her making some wretched scene or other, and I like Noel.

NORA (*sharply*). Of course you do. So do we.

(*A pause. Finally:*)

FANNY. We're all friends, aren't we? (*She looks at the faces around her.*)—Yes. Well, I saw her maid in the dressing-room. She said Noel hadn't slept a wink in three nights. Why, she didn't know.

(*There is a long silence. Then:*)

MARY. You go down, Fanny, and tell her Jim wants to see her up here for a moment before we leave.

JIM. Oh *listen,* Mary—!

MARY. You've got to.

FANNY. I think it's the only thing that'll make her pull up, I really do.

JIM. But I tell you—!

MARY. Jim—

JIM. What?

MARY. I don't want anything unpleasant to happen to-day. It's been too lovely.

JIM. But what on earth can *I* say to her?

FANNY. Just tell her to snap out of it.

JIM. Didn't you?

FANNY. I'm not you, Jimmy.

MARY (*to* FANNY). Go on, will you?

JIM. No—wait a minute.

MARY. Please, Jim. I'm asking it. (JIM *shrugs helplessly.*) You hold up the signals a few moments, will you Peter?

PETER. Sure.—But about that bag—

JIM. Come on—we'll get it.

MARY. —And see if Aunt Grace is in her room as you go by.

(*At the door,* JIM *turns to her.*)

JIM. —I'll be right back.

MARY. Thanks, Jim.

(*He goes out, followed by* PETER.)

FANNY. You're a good soldier, Mary.

MARY. So is Noel.

FANNY (*kissing her*). Good-bye, if I don't see you again. Lots of luck.

MARY. Thanks, Darling. (FANNY *goes out into the hall.* MARY *begins to pull on her gloves. To* NORA:) Well, apparently it's happened.

NORA. Isn't it the devil? You'd think Noel would have sense enough.

(*The seam of a glove breaks.*)

MARY. There goes a glove. (*She goes into the bedroom, continuing from there:*) I was probably wrong to ask her to be bridesmaid.

NORA. I don't think so.

MARY. I thought it would put an end to all that wretched talk.

(NORA *seats herself upon the chaise-longue.*)

NORA. —Which it did.

MARY. Poor Jim now, though.

NORA. I know.

MARY. It *is* an assignment.

NORA. —He's the only one can do it. It'd be awful for Noel if she was let make a real scene.

(MARY *re-enters with fresh gloves.*)

MARY. You know, I think she loves him terribly.

NORA. She'll get over it.

(MARY *ponders.*)

MARY. —I wonder doesn't he love her at all—

NORA (*astounded*). What!?

MARY (*calmly*). —It's quite possible. I could understand that. And I don't think I should mind—much.

(NORA *laughs.*)

NORA. —You say that to-day. Wait a bit —in a month you'll be for scratching out the eyes of anyone who looks at him sideways.

(MARY *seats herself beside her.*)

MARY. I should hate to feel like that.

NORA. You won't be able to help it. It's what we all come to. You get a sense of ownership, or something. It starts to work before you know it.

MARY. But I believe Jim has the right to know as many women as he wants to.

NORA. Know them? How?

MARY. In every sense.

NORA. Big-hearted Mary.

MARY. I mean it. It certainly needn't interfere with me—with us.

NORA. Where'd you get all this, anyhow?

MARY. Some of it, talking to Mr. Hutton one night. Most of it by myself.

NORA. Oh, what a fine about-face you're in for, Mary.

MARY. I don't think so.

NORA. —How about your right to know a few men?

MARY. But of course!

(NORA *looks at her curiously for a moment. Then:*)

NORA. Another once-loving pair bound for Paris.

MARY. It's one way of avoiding it, Nora —one good way.

(JIM *comes in from the hall.* NORA *rises.*)

JIM. Mary, your Aunt Grace is in there, about to burst into tears.

(MARY *rises.*)

MARY. Did you tell her good-bye?

JIM. Yes.

MARY. I'll go right in.

JIM. Don't be long.

(MARY *goes out into the hall.*)

NORA (*to* JIM). Good-bye to you, young man. Best of luck.

JIM. Good-bye, Nora. You've been wonderful.

(*He kisses her cheek.*)

NORA. You know how we feel about you and Mary, don't you?

JIM. —Just as we do about you and Pete, I should imagine.

NORA. It'll be great fun, the four of us.

JIM. Lord! Won't it, though!

(*There is a sound at the door.* NORA *glances at it.*)

NORA. It's Noel. Mind your step, Jimmy.

JIM. Don't you worry.

(NORA *goes swiftly to the door, which opens to admit* NOEL FARLEY. *She is twenty-two, and lovely.*)

NORA (*to* NOEL). Have you seen Peter anywhere?

NOEL. Not for—not for a few minutes, no.

NORA. I must find the man!

(*She goes out, closing the door after her.* NOEL *stands just within the room, looking directly at* JIM, *without moving.*)

JIM. Hello, Noel.

NOEL. Fanny said—

JIM. Yes. We—uh—we wanted to see you before we left.

NOEL. That was sweet of you. Where is Mary?

JIM. Farewells to Miss Archer. She'll be here in a minute. (*A brief pause.*) Noel—

NOEL. What?

JIM. Will you do something for us?

NOEL. Why of course, Jim. What is it?

JIM. —After—after you see Mary, quit the party and go on home.

(*There is a silence. Then:*)

NOEL (*in a low voice*). Would you like me to go out the back way?

JIM. I don't think that's necessary, no.

NOEL. —Perhaps it would be better just to hide somewhere, till the rest go.

JIM (*turning away*). You can do as you like, Noel.

NOEL. That's very kind. Thanks.

JIM. I'm sorry to have disturbed you. Forgive me, will you?

NOEL. I don't know. Does it matter?

JIM. No.

NOEL. That's all right, then. (*They stand looking at each other for a long moment.*

Finally:) Do you enjoy it, Jim?

JIM. Do I enjoy what?

NOEL. —Standing there, kissing me.

JIM. My God, Noel.

NOEL. —Mine too, Jim.—It's what you've been doing for a long while now—each time we've been together. What's it matter that you've never been much closer to me than this—so long as you've thought it and wished it?

JIM. You've—had a good deal to drink, haven't you?

NOEL. Yes.—But I've been drunker than this before on no wine at all. And so have you, my dear, dear, dear—

JIM. Oh quit it, quit it, will you?

NOEL. I love you, Jim, and I die hard. There should have been two of you, you know—one for me.

JIM. Listen: have I ever said or done the slightest—

NOEL. —I think there *are* two of you—and one *is*.—No, you haven't. But you want me, and I want you and if it keeps up, someday there'll be hell to pay. I'm telling you.

JIM. Noel—

NOEL. I know. You've always behaved with the most praiseworthy restraint. That's been splendid of you, I suppose, though I rather wish you hadn't. But you can't fool anyone as Irish as me about love. I couldn't have felt as I do about you, if you didn't feel much the same about me. It doesn't happen that way. It takes two.

JIM. I'm sorry, but I don't agree with you.

NOEL. You don't have to.—Nor need you think for a minute that I'm not aware how terribly you love your Mary, and how utterly different it is to what you feel for me. I envy her, but she need never envy me. Not if she's wise.

JIM. How do you mean, wise?

NOEL. *She* knows.

JIM. Noel, I haven't the remotest idea of what you're driving at, I really haven't.

NOEL. Well, great intelligence never was your long-suit, was it? (*A brief pause. She adds:*)—And, *I've* done a tall lot of thinking, these last few weeks. I've damn well had to.

JIM. I can't see you've got very far.

NOEL. I've gone a tremendous way. I'll tell you where I've arrived, if you like.

JIM. You needn't mind.

NOEL. I'd rather—if *you* don't. (*She waits. He is silent.*) It's my little pleasure to acknowledge, now, that I'm yours, heart and soul—

JIM. Noel—

NOEL. —But you needn't let it upset you: I'm inclined to glory in it. A day like today is fairly rough-going, of course, but I imagine I'll survive it. Because you see I'm just as sure as I am of my name, that part of you is mine. I can't make head or tail of it—I'm still frightfully balled-up in every direction, but of what's between us, I'm quite sure. I wish we'd been something—important to each other. I wish something actual, had happened. Our chances for pulling out of it would be better, then. But we weren't—and nothing has. So here we are, and here we'll be—and you'd better shun me as you would the devil.

JIM. When you see me running from someone, you'll know it.

NOEL. That's the boy!—Spoken like a Yale man.

JIM. Oh, shut up.

NOEL. You can't be indifferent to me, Jimmy Hut—so don't try. (*She softens in an instant.*) Oh come here a minute—let me look at you. Never mind—I'll come there. (*She moves toward him. Her voice breaks:*) Jim—Jim—

JIM. Quit it, Noel.

(*But she does not:*)

NOEL. What a handsome groom you were, Jim—I was proud of you, truly I was. I could feel my heart swell to see you, really I could—so straight, and so well turned-out, and so cock-sure of yourself, and so much in need of a beating. I didn't kiss you when the others did, did I? Here—I shall—

(*She puts her hands upon his shoulders, and leans up to him. He turns away, speaking in an agonized voice:*)

JIM. Noel—Oh *damn* it, Noel—this is my wedding-day!

(*She drops her head upon his breast with a sudden sob, then turns and leaves him, tears bright in her eyes.*)

NOEL. Stupid—stupid—we'd have had a much better chance, if you'd let that go—. Well—(*A pause. She composes herself.*) Is this someone's wine? (*She lifts a full glass from the tray.*) Here's to your great happiness—and may I share in it. (*She drains the glass. There is a knock at the door and a tentative twist of the knob. With an exclamation,* NOEL *sets the glass down upon the tray, dashes the back of her hand across her mouth, leans back on both arms against the table, facing the door, and calls clearly:*) Come in, won't you?

(MARY *enters.*)

MARY. Oh hello.—I didn't know who—

NOEL. What do you think, Mary?—Jim's been having me over the coals for enjoying the party too much.

MARY. —Really?

(*She goes to get her handbag from the table.*)

NOEL. Yes—can you believe it? But I've sworn I'll be a good giri now. (*She and* MARY *look at each other.* MARY *wins.* NOEL *drops her bantering tone and speaks lowly, honestly:*)—I love you both, Mary. I do love you very much.

MARY. So do we you, Noel.

NOEL. —You know, you have the wisest eyes I've ever seen.

(*There is a silence. Then* MARY *laughs, preferring to laugh.*)

MARY. Run along, child. (*She kisses her, briefly.*) We've got to scoot. Good-bye.

NOEL. Good-bye, Jim. Have a good trip.

JIM. Thanks, Noel.

NOEL (*lingering*). Good-bye, Mary—

MARY. Good-bye, dear.

(NOEL *moves in the direction of the hall.*)

NOEL. I—I'll just go—and get my wrap—

(*She goes out. A moment, then* MARY *turns to* JIM.)

MARY. I think that was a good thing to do.

JIM. I don't know. Anyway, it's done.

MARY. Thanks. (*She smiles at him.*)—Is it still me, Jim?

JIM (*darkly*). Mary, I'll—

(*She laughs.*)

MARY. Never mind! (*She glances at her watch.*)—You know, *I'm* about ready to start.

JIM. Tugging at the leash, that's what I am.

MARY. I do hope Peter doesn't muff the signals.

JIM. We'll give him three minutes: after that we'll duck anyway.

MARY. —In the meantime, let's form a group called "Alone at Last," shall we?

(*With a sigh, she seats herself on the chaise-longue.* JIM *drops down beside her, his arm around her.*)

JIM. Lord knows I'm willing.

(MARY *closes her eyes.*)

MARY. —I'm just so tired, and so happy.

JIM. So am I.

MARY. It's like a warm bath.

JIM. It's better.

MARY. I don't expect to have another serious thought for months on end, now.

JIM. If you feel one stealing up on you, fight like hell.

(MARY *opens her eyes again.*)

MARY. —All that silly talk of mine about theories and strategems and what-nots generally—don't mind it. It's just that when I think anything awful might happen to you and me, my heart slides right down to my toes in a panic. It's just—wanting desperately to guard the most precious thing I've ever had or shall have.

JIM. I know, Darling. That goes for me, too.

MARY. Then it's on—

JIM. You bet it is.—Let's make just one blanket agreement, shall we?

MARY. What is it?

JIM. —Whatever happens, never quit each other.

(*She presses her cheek against his.*)

MARY. Never, never.

JIM. —Never in this world.

MARY. In any world. (*A pause. Then suddenly she starts forward.*) What's that music!?

(JIM *goes to the hall door, opens it a crack, listens, then exclaims disgustedly.*)

JIM. Dardanella.

MARY. —It may be by way of warning. —You haven't forgotten anything, have you?

JIM. Not a thing.

MARY. As for me— (*Silently and thoughtfully, she ticks seven items off on her fingers, then exclaims:*) Oh!

JIM. What is it? Anything important?

(MARY *rushes to the bedroom door and opens it.*)

MARY. Heavens, yes! (*She calls into the bedroom.*) Julie!

JULIE (*from within*). Yes, Miss?

MARY. Please be sure to tell Aunt—Miss Archer—that I'd like my piano in the house by the time we get back. I don't care about the other things, but I would like the piano.

JULIE. I'll tell her, Miss.

MARY. Thanks!—Good-bye, dear! (*She closes the door, and returns to* JIM.) There. That's— (*Suddenly.*) Shh!

JIM. What?

MARY. It's *it!*

JIM. Is it?

MARY. Yes! Listen!

(*And it is the wedding march.*)

JIM. You're right.

MARY. Come on, Sweet!

JIM. Where's my hat?

MARY. Oh never mind your hat.

JIM. All right, the hell with it.

MARY. Give me your hand!

JIM. —Give me yours. I'm the man.

(*Their hands fumble for each other.*)

MARY. Quit fooling! Hurry up, or they'll murder us!

JIM. What's the rush? We've got fifty years.

MARY. *Are you coming!?*

(*He leans and kisses her cheek, hastily.*)

JIM. To Mary from Jim, with love. Here we go!

(*He takes her hand and rushes for the hall. From downstairs, rising above the wedding march, comes the sound of shouts and cheers and laughter. From outside the house, motors starting, electric horns blowing. Through it all, is heard a call from different voices, men's and women's: "Good Luck!" "Best of Luck!" "Good Luck!"*)

CURTAIN

ACT TWO

SCENE.—*The music-room, on the top floor of the Huttons' house, in uptown New York, near the East River. May, of this year. Eleven o'clock in the morning.*

The music-room is unlike most music-rooms, in that it is comfortable, attractively furnished in the modern style and very sunny. Just off center at back, is a high and broad studio-window. There is a fire-place in the right wall, center, of very simple design, in white plaster. The walls are of smooth gray, without pictures. The floor is dark, and bare except for two or three small rugs of plain color. The furniture is low and comfortable. The curtains at the window are of green, in some lively material. There is a bowl of white flowers on a large piano. There are no wall-brackets, the room being lighted at night entirely by four lamps, two made of silvered globes with plain, low shades of coral paper, two of glass globes filled with water, with shades of the same color as the curtains.

Entrance is from the hall, down left.

At Rise: RICHARD PARISH *is seated at the piano, playing from a handwritten score on the stand before him.* MARY *leans against the piano, listening.* RICHARD *is a few months younger than* MARY, *that is to say between 27 and 28. He has no manners but natural manners, no graces but a natural grace. This, plus the particular spirit which moves him from within, must be the sum of his charm, for he is not at all handsome, not in the least well-dressed and with no gift whatever for making pretty speeches. He plays for a moment or two without speaking. Then:*

RICHARD (*as he plays*). This is for the wood-winds. There's no brass at all in the first part. Do you think I need it?

MARY. Wait a minute. (*He plays on a little further.*) No.

RICHARD. I didn't think so.

(*He goes on playing.*)

MARY (*suddenly*). There! *That's* what I don't like.

RICHARD. This?

MARY. Yes.

RICHARD. What's the matter with it?

MARY. It's sloppy.

RICHARD. Sloppy!—The way I play it?

MARY. The way you wrote it.

(*Scowling,* RICHARD *tries several variations of the same theme. Finally he repeats one.*)

RICHARD. —Is that "sloppy"?

MARY. No.

RICHARD. Neither was the first. I think the first was better.

MARY. That's a pet idea of yours. It isn't always right.

RICHARD. A musician needs a man with a hammer just the way a painter does.

MARY. —Man with a hammer?

RICHARD. —To hit him over the head when a thing's finished.

MARY. Don't fool yourself that *you* do.

RICHARD. You think I'm lazy—

MARY. Maybe.

RICHARD. Mary—

MARY. What?

RICHARD. Oh hell.

MARY. Richard, *I* know the gift you have— Oh yes, it is a gift!—And I've told you you can have this room and this piano every morning you want and all morning and all alone. I don't ever come hanging around except when I'm expressly asked to. And—

RICHARD (*grinning*). You're invited.

(*He leaves the piano, and seats himself facing her.*)

MARY. Thanks— How long do you figure it will take you to finish your wretched ballet?

RICHARD. About two months. Less, if you'll help me.

MARY. —*If* I'll—?—It's a godsend.

RICHARD. How's that?

MARY. Jim's off for his trip abroad pretty soon, and I'd like something to help me stand it. Even the children aren't enough. I want a job.

RICHARD. Why don't you go with him?

MARY. I don't know. I just never do. Once I did, the first year. Then the next year I was about to have a baby, and the next year Aunt Grace was about to have an appendix, and the next year I'd just had another baby, and last year both of them had whooping-cough and this year, when I could go, I won't.

RICHARD. Don't you want to?

MARY. Heavens, yes. But I've got some crazy notion that married people need holidays from each other, so I'm making a firm stand. Six weeks. That's no picnic, you know.

(*She seats herself upon the sofa.*)

RICHARD. You're a funny pair.

MARY. We're a nice pair, don't you think?

RICHARD. —Sure, very nice.—Terribly in love, too, aren't you?

MARY. Oh yes, terribly.

RICHARD. How long is it?

MARY. Six years the tenth of July.

RICHARD. Pretty good.

MARY. It keeps getting better.

RICHARD. I suppose you aren't likely ever to crash now unless one of you falls in love with someone else.

MARY. I don't think Jim and I could crash even on that.

RICHARD. No?

MARY. No.

RICHARD. Well, there's not much chance it'll happen, is there?

MARY. It might. To Jim, it might.

RICHARD. And if it did—?

MARY. My one fear in the world is that he wouldn't quite understand how little it meant to me.

(*A silence.*)

RICHARD. I guess there's nothing to be said to that.

MARY. There it is.

RICHARD (*after a moment*). D'you know, I can't tell you how much I grant you two. And it's a funny thing, because you're the kind of people I've resented all my life. I never expected to believe that you could be so—so damned valuable. I used to curse into my beard whenever I passed a house like this. I used to spit on the pavement whenever a decent-looking motor-car passed me. I don't anymore, because I've found two among you whom I know to be of absolutely first importance in all the ways I value. You're hard in the right places, you're wise with a most beautiful wisdom and for your life as you live it, I've nothing but salutes and cheers. You're a revelation to me, Mary.

MARY (*overcome*). Why Richard—

RICHARD. Why, your grandmother. It's true, and I mean it. (*He rises and goes to the piano.*) What about this bollicking ballet? Do you really want to help me get it down?

MARY. I ask for nothing better. The babies are in the country with Aunt Grace. They're thriving. I'll spend four days a week in town and you can come out for week-ends. She's got a Knabe. It's old, and the lacquer's cracked, but it's sweet as a nut.

RICHARD. When does Jim sail?

MARY. Saturday. He was to have gone on the *Paris* to-day but he couldn't get a cabin. Now it's not until the *France,* May fifteenth. I can go to work on the sixteenth.

RICHARD. Lord, it'd be wonderful. You know you *have* got a pretty good ear.

MARY. I've got a first-rate ear, and I can write the stuff down like a house on fire.

RICHARD. Imagine finishing it!

(*A brief pause. Then:*)

MARY. How many things *have* you finished, Richard?

RICHARD. Oh be still. (JULIE *enters with a tray containing a glass of milk and a plate of sandwiches.* RICHARD *frowns at it.*)—Speaking of babies, I think I can live without this milk every morning.

MARY. It builds you up. See what a big girl I am. (JULIE *places the tray on a low table beside* RICHARD.)

JULIE. Miss Shippan just telephoned to—

MARY. Fanny Shippan? Telephoned—!?

JULIE. She arrived last evening, and she wished to know if you were lunching at home, and if so—

MARY. I hope you told her Yes, by all means.

JULIE. I did, Miss.

MARY. Thanks, Julie. Set two extra places, then, will you?

JULIE. She said she would not be able

to stay. She just wanted to come in for a moment.

MARY. I'll persuade her.

JULIE. Very well, Miss.

(*She goes out.*)

MARY (*to* RICHARD). That's terribly exciting. She was one of my bridesmaids. I haven't seen her in two years.

RICHARD. Where's she been?

MARY. Oh all over.

RICHARD. I get a feeling in this house that everyone's either just going up a gang-plank or just coming down one—

MARY. That doesn't go for me. I wish it did.—Richard—tell me the way the story goes—of the ballet, I mean.

RICHARD. I don't want you getting the story mixed up with it. *You're* to listen to *notes.*

MARY. Do you suppose for a minute I can think of anything else when I hear them?

(*He looks at her sharply.*)

RICHARD. No. As a matter of fact, I don't believe you can.

MARY. Then tell me.

RICHARD. 'Tisn't all worked out yet. It probably never will be.

MARY. Don't you believe it won't!

RICHARD. Probably never get put on, anyway. Probably cost a fortune to put it on.

MARY. Isn't the Russian Ballet rich?

RICHARD. I'd rather an American did it. —No—not the Metropolitan nor any of the Art Boys, either. I'd like some good, hard-boiled revue-manager. Then they'd dance, by God, not waddle around picking dream-flowers off the ground-cloth. And I'd have an orchestra for whom the world didn't end with Debussy.

MARY. I should think you could find a manager.

RICHARD. My only hope is that it *might* be amusing.

MARY. Do tell me how it runs.

RICHARD. Well, to begin with, it's for children.

MARY. Entirely?

RICHARD. Yes. It's a downright fairy-story. If older people want to like it, that's their look-out.

MARY. I see.

RICHARD. It's called "The Friendly Germ." Of course the whole thing is completely cock-eyed, but I think it adds up to make sense.

MARY. What's in it?

RICHARD. Well, there's a lot of religion in it, and a lot of test-tubes and microscopes and down-town at lunch-hour and Madison Square Garden with a hockey-match and that joint in Harlem where I've got a new job playing the piano from twelve to two—it's a swell place, really—and oh, Lord, there's a lot in it really.

MARY. Is there any form to it?

RICHARD. Of course there's form to it. What do you mean, "Is there any form to it"?

(*He rises.*)

MARY. How does it *run,* I say!?

RICHARD. Well, the first scene's at the Church Conference in the Middle Ages to decide how many angels could dance on the point of a needle. That's the Gregorian stuff you get in the opening movement. My mother used to wheeze it out on an old harmonium in a frame-church at Single River, in Minnesota, and didn't I soak it up, though. That, and the music my father's saw-mill made, and the water. Well, I see the entire chorus in the same wooden robes you see in primitives, and they move like wood, and oh Lord, it sounds terrible—

MARY. No it doesn't.

RICHARD. Then the second scene's in the top tower of the American Needle Building on lower Broadway. A thin white room, sort of a conical shape, up to a point. They've developed a needle with the finest point in the world. They're going to measure it under a microscope and broadcast the happy news to God's whole great big monkey-house. What you hear is the music from the street below: curb brokers, street-cars, motors, feet, frosted chocolate milk-shakes being sucked through straws—

MARY. Exciting!

RICHARD. 'Think so?—Well, they march up to the microscope, take a peek and fall back in astonishment. For cat's sake what is it? The celestial music begins—curtain—then curtain up again on the field of the microscope—

MARY. What?!

(RICHARD'S *gestures become broader.*)

RICHARD. —The field of the microscope —round—enormous—just as you'd see it —a big ground-glass disc, measured off into square areas, tilted back a little.

MARY. Richard!

RICHARD. It's alive with angels, dancing —no wings, you know,—they just know how to use their arms. The germ's a very peculiar individual, with very dancy feet. The angel named Mike, who's our hero, if there is a hero in the cock-eyed thing—he's trying to ride the germ. Finally, just as he gets on his back, you see an enormous instrument come down like that, and separate 'em from the others and push 'em up on a glass-slide and off the scene. So far so good?

MARY. I love it. But watch out that your angel doesn't go whimsical on you.

RICHARD. Not a chance.

MARY. That's the danger, though.

RICHARD. This angel is a real guy. He's superb, this angel. He's a kind of Lindbergh.

MARY. Poor thing—what do they do with him?

RICHARD. He and the germ are taken home by the president of the Needle Works to his apartment.—There sits his lovely daughter, who has been ailing, poor girl. She's being dosed with thyroid extract, with no results. Here's something new to amuse her. All right: Mike and his funny friend get in among the thyroid and grow up to life size.

MARY. Does it work that way?

RICHARD. Ask a doctor.—You see, the germ—

MARY. You might call him Pat—

RICHARD. I intend to. Pat's the germ of the dance: he infects everyone within reach with it. The two of 'em become a sensation. Talk of the town, talk of the country, talk of the world. Mike can do anything—he's the perfect man. Big promoters try to syndicate him. Flying for profit. Dowagers cut each other's throats to get him to dine. Come and meet our Winged Lion. Drawing-room flying at nine, by the celestial Mike. Come and get bitten by Pat, and feel your old legs stir again. Then the girl begins to want Mike all for her very own—the way you want Jim all for yours—the way everyone in love turns fool and says "No shares! This is all mine!"

MARY. They don't, though.

RICHARD. Oh yes they do!—But Mike can't stand it. She gets desperate. All mine! All mine!—There's a chase across the roof of the apartment. They go over the edge—

(*He stops, as* JIM *enters.*)

MARY. Why Jim! Hello!

JIM. Hello, Darling. Hello, Parish. How are you?

RICHARD. Fine, thanks. I've just been boring Mary stiff with a couple of Tales of Hoffman.

MARY. He *has* not.—Jim, who do you think telephoned? Fanny. She got in last night. She's coming for lunch, I hope.

JIM. Good. Only I won't be here.

MARY. Why? Where are you off to?

JIM. London first, then—

MARY. What do you *mean?!*

JIM. The French Line telephoned they had a cancellation just this morning, and could put me on the *Paris.*

MARY. Jim!

JIM. She sails at one. Julie's packing bags. I've got to go on account of Proctor. He's off for some other god-forsaken place on the twentieth. I've cabled him I'm coming with a contract for his next three books. He's too good to miss, really.

MARY. I hate his stuff, I hate it!

JIM. He sells, though. If it was really good stuff, I could put the trip off a year.

MARY. But one o'clock!

JIM. It isn't twelve yet. I've got lots of time. Father'll be up with some papers to be signed in a minute, then we'll tear for the river. Do you want to come to the dock?

MARY. Do I want to come to the dock! Oh, I'll kill you, I'll—!

RICHARD (*rising*). Here I go.—Lunch some other day, Mary.

MARY. Do you mind?

RICHARD. Not a bit. (*To* JIM.) Good-bye. Have a good trip.

JIM. Thanks. Anything I can do for you in Paris?

RICHARD. You might tell the Art Boys on the Left Bank not to talk quite so much.

JIM. All right, I will.

MARY. I'll telephone you, Richard.

RICHARD. Will you do that? Fine! Good-bye.

MARY. Good-bye! (RICHARD *goes out,* MARY *rushes into* JIM'*s arms.*) Oh Jim, I hate it! It was bad enough not going last year. Now it's worse.

JIM. Come on with me, darling. It's a big cabin.

MARY. No. I can't.

JIM. We'd have fun.

MARY. Shut up, shut up!

JIM. I think this is all rot, you know—this enforced-holiday business.

MARY. Maybe it is.—When will you be

back?

JIM. By July—the tenth surely, now. Where's your party for the anniversary to be—here or in the country?

MARY. Here. I'm going to keep the house open till the fifteenth anyway. Do make it in time, Jim. It's important to me. I'm a fool about Christmas and birthdays and things like that.

JIM. You leave it to me. I'll be here. (MARY *smiles.*)

MARY. —I've always said if we got safely past the sixth—

JIM. It's been a good go, hasn't it, darling?

MARY. Hasn't it, though?

JIM. I'd do it again, wouldn't you?

MARY. Oh, maybe I wouldn't!

JIM. Kiss me, please. Very small: I've got a boat to catch.—Thanks.

MARY. Are you sure you've everything you'll need?

JIM. No, but I'll manage. I made a list and told Julie most of it. She's—(*The telephone rings.*) That must be the country. I put the call in downstairs—

MARY. Aunt Grace won't be there, you know.

JIM. I wanted to tell Jimmy good-bye. (*He goes to the telephone.*)

MARY. You're sweet, Jim.

JIM. So's Jimmy. (*He takes the telephone.*) Hello. All right. (*A moment.*) Hello—Is that you, Frederic? Yes.—Tell Sabina to bring young Jim to the telephone, will you? Thanks—(*He turns to* MARY.) Come here, Darling. Don't stay so far away. (*She comes to him. He stands with his arm around her, and the receiver to his ear. They talk on at random until* SABINA *comes to the telephone.*) How's your special account? All right?

MARY. Bursting.

JIM. What are you going to do about that garden on the roof here?

MARY. Gravel costs enormously.

JIM. Let's have it, anyway.

MARY. I'll order it then.

JIM. Is Collins behaving himself better?

MARY. Some. He's hauled the manure up, at least.

JIM. Tell him I said we're very fond of him, but this next month decides it.

MARY. I did, yesterday.

JIM. Did it ever occur to you that Sabina might drink?

MARY. No. Of course she doesn't.

JIM. I don't like that nose much.

MARY. It's the weather does that. Once I tried to get her to take some brandy for a stomach-ache, and she nearly left in a pet.

JIM. See if you can't get her to work regularly on Mimsie's legs. Massage or something.

MARY. But my dear, *all* babies' legs are like that!

JIM. I'm scared of her growing up with fat legs. Girls ought to have thin legs.

MARY. She will.

JIM. —If she's any daughter of yours.

MARY. —If she's any daughter of mine.

JIM. Don't have any vaccinations or anything till I get back, will you?

MARY. I wasn't planning any.

JIM. Just keep cool with Coolidge.

MARY. You betcha.

JIM. What'll you be doing all the time?

MARY. Music with Richard, mostly. He's got a grand idea for a ballet.

JIM. Where'd you find him, Mary?

MARY. —Richard? He was at the Rosalskys' that night. Don't you remember?

JIM. Oh, yes. (*A moment.*)—He's not the kind that makes passes, is he?

MARY. Richard?—Not in the least.

JIM. If anyone does, haul off and paste him one for me.

MARY. No one will.

JIM. *I* would.

MARY. Most men have more manners.

JIM. Mary.

MARY. What?

JIM. I'm in love with you.

MARY. —But what about my children?

JIM. Forget 'em. Come with me in my death-car.

MARY. When do we leave?

JIM. How would, say, twelve-thirty do? We could— (*He turns to the telephone.*) Sabina? Yes. I'm going off to-day instead of next week, Sabina, and I'd like to say good-bye to Jimmy. Is his face clean enough? Yes. Oh yes indeed. I will, Sabina—and Matthew and Mark and Luke, too. Thanks very much.—Hello, Jimmy! How are you? Good! What have you been doing, riding Punch? Does he go any faster? Well, he's still pretty stiff, you know—it was a hard winter.—What's that? He didn't! You tell him for me he's old enough to know better than that, and if he doesn't he can't *come* on the front lawn. That's right. Listen, Jimmy: I'm going on the big boat this morning.—No, darling—next time maybe. I'm awfully sorry, but they almost didn't have room for me, even. What shall I bring you? Yes.—Yes— Yes, if I can find one. Yes. Yes. Is that all?—Well, anything else you think of, just tell your Mother, and she'll write me. Good-bye, darling—(*He smacks a resounding kiss.*)—Did you get it? (*A moment.*) Yes, so did I. Good-bye, Jimmy. You be a good boy and I will too. Kiss Mimsie good-bye for me and tell her to keep that thumb out of her mouth or I'll beat the tar out of her.—Of course there's tar in her! There's tar in everyone. Why, I knew a man once, and—

MARY. I want to speak with Sabina a minute.

JIM. —And he was nothing *but* tar!—Call 'Bina, will you Jim? Your Mother wants to tell her something—Good-bye, Angel.—You bet I won't! I'll bring a bag-ful.

(MARY *takes the telephone.* JIM *begins to consult a list.*)

MARY. Good-bye, Darling. Yes, to-morrow, sure. No—after your nap. Yes, he understands. Of course, he'll tell the Captain. He'll—Sabina? Yes.—Is everything all right? Mimsie? Where? Oh dear. Have you got some of that boric-powder? That's right. And we'd better cut down on the vegetables to-morrow and Sunday. No—the milk of magnesia—just a little in the formula. I'll be out early to-morrow afternoon. If she starts running a fever telephone me, and I'll motor out to-night. Good-bye. (MARY *puts down the telephone and turns to* JIM.) I'll see that Julie's got everything straight.

JIM. She has, I'm sure. Stay, dear. I'll go down myself when Fanny comes.

MARY. What's that? A list?

JIM. Yes. Checked, mostly. Oh, would you tell Peter I can't play golf with him Wednesday—

MARY (*a mental note*). —Peter—golf—Wednesday.

JIM. Let's see, now: (*He reads the list and checks the items.*) "Telephone Father" —check. "Telephone country"—check. "Kiss Mary"—(*He kisses her.*)—check. "Don't forget passport"—(*He feels for it.*) "Tell Julie plenty underwear"—check. "Tell Mary love her"—(*He turns to her.*)—Love you.

MARY. You are good, and kind.

JIM. Check. "About liquor supply—"—If you need anything, telephone Trotter at the Club.

MARY. Trotter?

JIM. Trotter.

MARY. —Liquor—Trotter—Club.

(JIM *looks at the list silently for a moment. Then as he folds it up:*)

JIM. "Keep out of draughts, Don't eat starchy foods, pump up bicycle-tires and be at foot of West 14th Street at ten minutes to one."

MARY. Ten minutes to one. Six weeks. Jim, Jim, Jim, Jim.

JIM. Aw Mary—

MARY. I'm going to weep.

JIM. Blink your eyes. Swallow.—That's the girl.

MARY. Write me all the time. Cable me every minute.

JIM. You bet I will.

MARY. Don't have a French doctor even for a cold.

JIM. No.

MARY. —If the ship starts to sink, kick all the women and children out of the way and grab the biggest life-belt and—

JIM. You bet.

MARY. —Say your prayers night and morning—and—(*Suddenly she clings to him.*) Oh Jim—Jim—

JIM. Oh cut it out, will you?

(*He kisses her. A moment, then* JAMES HUTTON's *voice is heard from the hall*).

JAMES. Jim? Mary? (MARY *leaves* JIM's *arms. He goes swiftly to the window, and stands there with his back to the room, composing himself. There is a silence. Then again* JAMES's *voice, nearer:*) Are you up here, Mary?

MARY. Yes. Hello, Father. So's Jim. Come on in! (*Then softly, to* JIM.) Darling—come here—

(JIM *comes to her.* JAMES HUTTON *appears in the doorway.*)

JIM. Hello, Father.

JAMES. I—er— There was a young woman on your doorstep. She asked me to announce her: A Miss F—

(FANNY *bursts in from the hall.*)

FANNY. —It's Fanny! Whoopee! It's Fanny!

MARY. I don't believe it!

(*They embrace.*)

FANNY. My dear girl, what fun!

MARY. But you look simply stunning!

FANNY. —If that means fat, I'll have your heart out and— Hello, James, my boy. (*She goes to* JIM *and shakes his hand.*) How is the book business?

JIM. Hello, Fanny. It's great you're back.

FANNY. I'm staying for years. (*She seats herself.*) This rock shall stir from its firm base as soon as I.

JIM. What's the matter? Didn't you like the life among the British?

FANNY. Listen: if ever we have another war with England, I want it understood right here and now, *I* was the one that fired the first shot.

MARY. But my dear—the papers were full of you!

FANNY. I had a salon. I honestly had a salon. I can't tell you what I've been through. Last night when I saw Fifth Avenue, I cried into my lap for fully twenty minutes. It's a nice little city you've got here, friends. It's going to grow. (*To* JIM.) You're not really sailing for that place to-day?

JIM. At one o'clock.

FANNY. Well you're simply crazy, that's all. How are your babies, Mary?

MARY. Wonderful.

FANNY. —Still, it's nice to be in an uninteresting condition again—wot?

MARY. My dear, I've gone mad: I'm supporting three dressmakers.

FANNY. I'm dying to see the new one. Boy or child? I forget.

MARY. Child. Name of Mary. Her mother was a dancing-girl. Come out with me to-morrow, will you? I'll hold a one-man exhibit.

FANNY. I'd love it.—Isn't she pretty, Mr. Hutton?

JAMES. I've always contended that.

FANNY. —I was afraid I might find just a mother. (*To* JIM.) You poor boy, going off on a boat. Don't let them put you at the Captain's table. I was—and the strain was too much: my wrists gave way. Twice I spilled gruel on my bib. It was a fearful trip. Lord knows I'm no beauty, but I'm young and I'm sound, and yet the only real attention I called forth from the whole big *Aquitania* was from a middle-aged professor at Tulane University, named Regan. I said that I was happy as a lark, and he said, But is a lark really happy? Can you bear it?

MARY. Stop, Fanny! We were just feeling so nice and sad over parting.

FANNY. —New York. My Lord, its wonderful. You forget how wonderful it is. Who'll put me up for the Chamber of Commerce? For the last three months I've been unfurling American flags from my blouse on every occasion. From now on I'm going to be just a home girl. No more nasty, drafty castles for Fanny.

JIM. You weren't presented at Court, were you? There was a rumor.

(*He rises, and moves toward the hall.*)

FANNY. James, I was there with ostrich-plumes in my hair. It was a riot. The queen swooned, and the king was carried out screaming. They say that down in White-Chapel the boys were—oh, goodbye—

JIM. Don't stop. I'm just going downstairs a minute to close a bag or two.

MARY (*rising*). I'll—

JIM. No darling—really—I'll be right up. Have you got those letters, Father?

JAMES. Miss Anderson's in the library. She'll take your signature.

(FANNY *is groping in her handbag.*)

JIM. Good.

FANNY. 'Wait a minute, Jim. 'Arf a mo'. Presents—pretty presents. (*She gives a small box to* MARY.) These are for you, Mary.

MARY (*opening the box*). "These?" That means earrings.

FANNY. I got them in Venice, for a certain popular song.

(MARY *holds up the earrings.*)

MARY. Fanny!

FANNY. Tush, child. I could give pearls, and never feel it.

MARY. You angel. They're simply gorgeous.

(*She puts them on.* FANNY *offers a larger box to* JIM.)

FANNY. —And these, James, are for you, to hold your pants up. (JIM *takes the box.*)—Hand-painted braces, for the unexpected guest. I think the scene is from Manon.

JIM. Fanny, you're a girl after my own heart.

FANNY. No, Darling—I was once, but Mary was too quick for me.

JIM. I'll sail in them.

(JAMES looks at his watch.)

JAMES. You don't sail at all, if you go on this way.

(JIM *looks at his watch.*)

JIM. There's something in what you say.

(*He goes out.*)

FANNY. —Lovely boy, really lovely.—Honestly, Mary, I never saw two happier looking people in my life.

MARY. We're pretty sunk over this trip, just at present.

FANNY. —Most people I know would be cheering. You're in luck. You don't realize it.

MARY. Oh yes we do!

FANNY (*to* JAMES). It isn't just put-on, is it?

JAMES (*smiling*). I don't think so.

FANNY. I've got a little skeptical about marriage: me, who had such faith. Paris is simply alive with people you know, getting divorces.

MARY. Well, *I* think it's sickening.

FANNY. —So do I. What I hate most, is what it does to their what-do-you-call-its—souls—characters. Honestly, just listening to their tales, I felt like Bad Fanny, the wickedest woman in Bridgeport. I claim it shows in their faces. You wouldn't know Susie Price.

MARY. *She* isn't, too!

FANNY. Indeed she is!—Her precious little individuality was being stifled.

MARY. Her what?!—I didn't know she had one.

FANNY. Home-life developed it.—But of course as soon as the decree is handed down, she's going to try again with some fifth-rate Englishman. She's living with him now in the South of France somewhere.

MARY. It *is* vile.

FANNY. —Just thank your stars, Girlie. Because there's something awfully wrong with marriage.

MARY. There's something awfully wrong with the people who *get* married.

FANNY. How are Peter and Nora? Are they all right?

MARY. Now don't go *looking* for trouble, Fanny.

FANNY. Catch me! These days I spread oil wherever I go. You have to.

JAMES. Did *you* get to the South at all, Fanny?

FANNY. —Of France? No, worse luck. (*To* MARY.) Oh but I must tell you. Zoe Evans was at Cannes, and—

MARY. I don't know her.

FANNY. I know you don't. But she knows Jim and she said she saw you and him two or three times at—what's the name of that little place up in the mountains back of Antibes? St. Paul du—something—St. Paul du Var! And she was going to speak to you, only—

MARY (*carefully*). When was that?

FANNY. Last May.

MARY (*more carefully*). Oh yes.

FANNY. —Only she couldn't get Jim's eye and you both looked so devoted, she concluded you were there to escape Americans. So she didn't. They thought at the inn you were a run-away couple, living in —well, it isn't sin to the French, is it? They'd whipped up quite a nice illicit romance about you. Clever Mary. It must have been fun. Zoe said the *patrone* told her you'd taken the sweetest little studio-place with actually a bathroom. I didn't even know you were over. Why didn't you look me up?

MARY. Well, it was—

FANNY. You *were* trying to avoid Americans!

(*A moment.*)

MARY. It was the shortest kind of a trip.

FANNY. You didn't run into Noel, did you? Someone told me she was down there somewhere on the Riviera—or maybe it was Rome.

MARY. No, we didn't.

FANNY. Apparently she's got an idea that she can write or paint or something—

MARY. And can she?

FANNY. I doubt it. There's a girl I never could make out.

MARY. Couldn't you, Fanny? I don't think Noel's hard.

FANNY. I must admit, I never worked much over her.—Your house is just as sweet as ever, Mary.

MARY. I love it.

FANNY. You've changed this room.

MARY. I'm forever changing it.—We're going to put gravel on the roof and make a garden.

FANNY. —Divine.—What time are you going out to-morrow?

MARY. How's three o'clock?

FANNY. That's fine for me.—Sure you want me?

MARY. I should say I do. It's too marvellous, having you back. Are you at the apartment?

FANNY. Yes.

MARY. I'll stop by for you at three, then.

FANNY. I'll be hanging out the window. What time is it now? Oh good lord!—Good-bye, Mr. Hutton—come and dine some night with Mary, will you?

JAMES. I should be glad to.

FANNY (*to* MARY). Don't come down with me, dear—honestly. I'm going on the run.

MARY. All right, I shan't.—Shout to Jim as you go by. His room's just below.

FANNY. I'll do that.—The poor lamb, having to leave his Mary.

MARY. Oh he doesn't mind.

FANNY. His face *looked* it.

MARY. Thanks a thousand times for the earrings.

FANNY. There are no two ears I'd sooner see 'em hang from, Dearie. (*She kisses her.*) Three o'clock, then.

MARY. Three o'clock.

(FANNY *goes out.* MARY *turns slowly, thoughtfully, and stands looking into space. There is a long silence.* JAMES *is watching her. Finally:*)

JAMES. Mary—

MARY. Yes?

JAMES. I don't think I should jump to any silly conclusions, if I were you.

MARY. Wouldn't you, Father?

JAMES. No.

MARY. Jim went abroad alone last year. I wasn't with him.

JAMES. No—nor was anyone else.

MARY. You don't think so.

JAMES. I'm sure of it. (*A pause. Suddenly* MARY *goes to the telephone and takes up a telephone-list. She finds the number and puts the receiver to her ear.* JAMES *rises.*) What are you doing?

(MARY *does not answer. Another pause. Then:*)

MARY. Plaza 2476.

JAMES. Whom are you calling, Mary?

(MARY *does not answer. Another pause. Then:*)

MARY. Hello, is this Plaza 2476?—May I speak with Mrs. Farley, please.—Mrs. Hutton, Mrs. James Hutton. Oh.—Well perhaps *you* could tell me—I wanted to ask Mrs. Farley for Miss Noel's address. Yes.

JAMES. Mary, this is utterly ridiculous. It wasn't Jim at all. The Evans girl was simply mistaken. And even if she wasn't—

MARY (*to the telephone*). Yes? "Villa May." Yes. "St. Paul—St. Paul-du-Var—Alpes Maritimes"—Yes, I have it. Thanks very much. No—that's all I wanted. Thank you.

(*She replaces the receiver and stands looking down at the table.*)

JAMES. You know, this isn't fair at all. This is—

MARY. I know Jim, Father, and I know Noel. And if they were there together—(*She cannot finish.*)

JAMES. That's a very hasty conclusion, my dear, and so far as I can see, entirely without foundation.

MARY. It's true, Father.

JAMES. How do you know it's true?

MARY. I feel it in my bones. (*She averts her face. Her breath escapes her in a cry.*) Oh—horrible—

JAMES. I can't for the life of me see how you can assume any such thing on any such evidence.

MARY. It's true, it's true!

(*A pause.*)

JAMES. —And suppose it were—then what?

MARY. Then it's not me he wants. He wants her.

JAMES. Good heavens, Mary—

(*She turns on him sharply.*)

MARY. What do you think, then? Is it both of us he wants?

JAMES. Jim loves you as few women are loved.

MARY. He could hardly love me—and go with her, could he?

JAMES. Couldn't he, Mary?

MARY. No.

JAMES. —It's not conceivable, is it?

MARY. If it were, I shouldn't let it be!

JAMES. Ah—I see.

MARY. I'm not doing any sharing—I'm not going any halves with—with—oh, I can't say her name, now.

JAMES. You'll never be called upon to share what you and Jim have.

MARY. He's taken the whole beautiful thing in his hands and done that with it. (*With a gesture of breaking it in two.*)

JAMES. If what you suppose has happened *has* happened, one good crass fact explains it.

MARY. —It might have once. Not now.

(*A moment. He watches her. Then:*)

JAMES. But Mary you must know—

MARY. I know that six years ago Jim and I were married.

JIM (*from the hall below*). Oh Mary! (*She does not answer.*) Darling—!

(*She goes to the doorway and calls:*)

MARY. Yes?

JIM. Where are those shiny new studs of mine?

MARY. They're on the dressing-table in my room.

JIM. Right!—You're all ready, aren't you?

MARY. Yes, I'm ready.—We ought to leave in two minutes!

(*She presses the button at the door.*)

JIM. Oh damn it! Let's make it *three*—

(MARY *comes back into the room.*)

JAMES (*softly*). —Don't you see, Mary, that *that's* the real thing—and the other just a—? (*Her gesture cuts him short. A moment, then:*) May I ask what you intend to do?

MARY. I don't know, yet. I'll have a month to myself to think in. When he comes back, I'll know.

JAMES. Surely you'll say nothing now.

MARY. I'll say nothing now. (*She closes her eyes in pain, and averts her head.*) I'll say less than nothing.

JAMES. —If you're wise, my dear, you'll say nothing ever.

(JULIE *comes in from the hall with a hat and the coat to* MARY'S *dress.*)

JULIE. Was it these you rang for, Mrs. Hutton?

MARY. Yes. Thanks, dear. (*She puts on the hat before a mirror.* JULIE *holds the coat for her.*) Tell Therèse just Mr. Hutton's father for lunch, will you?

JULIE. Very well, Miss.

JAMES. I can—

MARY. No—it's all right, really. (*To* JULIE.) I'm going right out to the country from the dock. Telephone Miss Shippan before dinner and tell her I had to go out to-day, on account of the children. Tell her I can't have her this week-end after all. I'll see her here in town Monday or Tuesday. It's the same apartment. The number's on the card there.

JULIE. Yes, Miss.

(JIM *comes in, with a box of flowers.*)

JIM. Is the motor here, Julie?

JULIE. Yes, sir.

JIM. Tell Tom to get the bags down, will you?

JULIE. Very well, sir.

JIM. Good-bye, Julie.

(*He shakes her hand.*)

JULIE. Good-bye, Mr. Hutton. I hope you'll have a very pleasant trip.

JIM. Thanks.—Look after her well, won't you?

JULIE. As well as ever I can, sir.

JIM. That's the girl. (*To* MARY.) Everything's set, dear. We'd better be on our way.

(*He gives her the box of flowers.*)

JAMES (*looking at his watch*). I think you had.

MARY. What's this?

(*She opens the box.* JULIE *goes out.*)

JIM. I sent Therèse to the corner for them.

MARY. That was sweet.

JIM. You can't go to a boat without flowers.—What's the matter. darling?

MARY. Why, nothing. Why?

JIM. You look—are you sure you *want* to come to the dock?

MARY. Yes, I'm quite sure. (*She pins the flowers upon her coat.*) These are sweet. They smell sweet—

JAMES. Don't work too hard, will you, son?

JIM. Not me. It'll probably be pretty tough going in London for awhile. I thought I might run over to Cannes or Antibes for a few days before sailing. That is, if I've time.

MARY (*a breath over the flowers*). —Awfully sweet. (*A brief pause.*)—I thought you hated the Riviera. You did when we were there.

JIM. That was in season.

MARY. I didn't know you'd ever been there out of season.

JIM. They say it's another place after the crowds go.—Father, would you tell the bank to cable a couple of thou' to my credit in London?

JAMES (*making a note on an envelope*). Have you got enough now?

JIM. Plenty, thanks.

MARY. Here you are—

(*She sets in* JIM'S *buttonhole a flower from her bouquet.*)

JIM. Oh thanks, Darling.

JAMES. If you see your Mother, give her my love.

JIM. I'll do that.

JAMES. When is it you're coming back?

JIM. I count on catching the *Mauretania* at Cherbourg. She's due here July ninth.—Good-bye, sir! You're a grand guy.

(*They shake hands.*)

JAMES. Thanks, so are you! Hurry, will you? It's twelve-thirty!

JIM (*to* MARY). Come on, Angel—

MARY. Here I am.

JIM. Just take Jimmy's hand—(*He holds his hand out to her. She puts her hand in it.*)—And away we go!

MARY. —Away we go.

JIM. Wait a minute.—I must have one good last look.

(*He takes her other hand, faces her about and looks at her. She returns his gaze, smiling.*)

MARY. Is that all right?

JIM. Father—am I in luck, or am I not?

JAMES. I think you're in great luck, Son. (*Swiftly,* JIM *bends over and kisses each of the hands in his. Then he tucks one of them through his arm.*)

JIM. —And don't I know it! (*To* MARY. *as they go out.*) Listen, Sweet, I've got a great idea—

MARY. What is it, dear?

JIM. —This stupid enforced-holiday—why not make it only four weeks? You could take a fast boat, and we'd have ten days in Paris, and then come back together. No, but seriously I don't see any reason why we shouldn't have at least a week there, and a *little* holiday together after this idiotic month of—

(*His voice has faded out until it is no longer heard.* JAMES *stands alone, looking after them, shaking his head.*)

CURTAIN

ACT THREE

SCENE.—*The music-room, six weeks later. A little after eleven on an early July night.*

The windows are opened wide and two of the lamps are lighted. On a small table at back, there is a tray containing a whisky-decanter, a bowl of cracked ice, some bottles of soda and a plate of sandwiches.

At Rise: At the piano, sits MARY *in a day dress of some soft, cool material. Some sheets of the ballet-score are before her. Others are strewn on the top of the piano, with pen and ink nearby. She plays a brief passage twice over, then a buzzer above the door sounds twice. She goes to the door, presses a button beside it several times, opens the door part way, listens intently then goes back to the piano. After a few moments* JAMES HUTTON *enters from the hall.*

MARY. Hello, Father. (*She rises, and goes to him.*) Thanks for coming. (*She kisses him.*) How are you, anyway?

JAMES. Fine, thanks.—*You* look a little white and wan—

MARY. It's the heat.

(*She reseats herself at the piano. He remains standing.*)

JAMES. I couldn't get a train till seven.

MARY. I'm terribly glad you didn't wait. (*She plays a few notes. Their talk is somewhat constrained.*) Have you been having fun?

JAMES. I've been lying in the sunshine hours a day, trying to get the neuritis out of my shoulder.

MARY. With results, I hope.—Have a cigarette—

JAMES. Thanks, I've got one.—Superb results.

MARY. I thought when you left we'd soon be reading about a smart suicide on Bailey's Beach.

JAMES. So did I. How are the children?

MARY. Simply thriving. I've concluded I fuss over them too much. The less I'm with them, the better they are. Jimmy was thrilled over those fire-works you sent him for the Fourth. He'd never seen such big ones.

(JAMES *smiles. A pause. Then:*)

JAMES. It's quite cool up here.

MARY. The river's a great blessing, and I keep the blinds closed from noon to sundown. It's the only way.

(*There is another and more strained pause.* JAMES *clears his throat.*)

JAMES. You've decided you prefer town, then.

MARY. Not exactly—but I've had to be in such a lot. I've been working like mad.

JAMES. Music?

MARY. Yes.

JAMES. Whom have you got here with you—Julie?

MARY. No. She's at Aunt Grace's with Sabina and the babies. She needed a rest. No one's with me.

JAMES. But doesn't the house seem rather large to you?

MARY. I live in this room. It's like an apartment. I've had an electric-arrangement put on the front-door, so that when it buzzes up here I can open it without going down.

JAMES. I'm not sure how safe that is.

MARY. Oh I don't press the button unless I hear the right signal—two short ones—buzz-buzz—like that. You happened to get it right.

JAMES. You'll have all the postmen in New York in on you.

MARY. I like postmen.

(*Another silence. Then:*)

JAMES. I suppose you've heard from Jim.

MARY. There was a radio this morning:

"Giant Liner Battered By Storm. Floating Palace Twelve Hours Late. Much Love."

JAMES. No hope of disembarking passengers before morning, I presume.

MARY. The office said not.—She's not due at Quarantine till midnight.

JAMES. I see.

MARY. I wired back I wouldn't try to meet him, and to come right here.—About breakfast-time, I expect.

JAMES (*at length*). Well, Mary—?

MARY. Have a whisky-and-soda, won't you?

JAMES. Shall I need it?

(MARY *laughs shortly.*)

MARY. You can't tell!

(JAMES *looks at her closely, but does not move.*)

JAMES. I'm sorry I didn't get your message till so late.

MARY. I didn't know about your fishing-trip.

JAMES. Anyhow, I came running back, didn't I?

MARY. You were sweet.

(*A brief pause. Then:*)

JAMES. Your note was not. (*Another pause.*) *Well,* Mary—?

(MARY *hesitates. Then:*)

MARY. I promised to let you know as soon as I did.

JAMES. Yes.

MARY. After Jim left I hoped for awhile that I'd been mistaken about—about Noel and him. I've found out since that I was not. I've found it out definitely.

JAMES. From Jim?

MARY. Oh, no!

JAMES. —But you've written him? What have you said?

MARY. I've said nothing. You know, and I know. No one else. I shall tell him as soon as he comes in, in the morning.

JAMES. To-morrow is the tenth, Mary.

MARY. I'm—aware of that—

JAMES. An anniversary, isn't it?

MARY —Six years is six years. I suppose, as things go, we've done rather well.

JAMES. Don't talk like that. Talk of that sort doesn't belong to you.

(MARY *shrugs.*)

MARY. Average, anyway.—What *is* the average, do you know? Less than six, or more?

JAMES. Stop it, Mary.

MARY. I'm sorry. I'm only speaking as I feel.

JAMES. You're actually going to leave Jim?

MARY. Yes.

JAMES. But only temporarily—not a real separation—

MARY. I'm going to divorce him, Father. (JAMES *stares at her for a moment, incredulously. With deliberation, she begins to play a passage from the ballet. He goes to the table and makes himself a drink. He turns to her with it in his hand. She stops playing, rises, and meets his gaze steadily. He shakes his head.*)

JAMES. Mary, Mary—

MARY. It's too bad, I know. But you see it's all gone, now.

(*Now she is standing against the piano, facing him.*)

JAMES. What is? Your love for him?

MARY. I don't know about that. I can't tell about that, yet awhile. But my life with him—that's gone, all right.

JAMES. Only if you let it go.

MARY. I'm afraid I'm not much good at hanging on to things, once they've begun to slip from me. I'm afraid I don't want them much, after that.

JAMES. What a fine, deep love it must have been, eh? (*She looks at him. He explains:*) To chuck the whole thing overboard so lightly, so easily.

MARY. I haven't had much ease these last weeks, Father. And I don't feel light, precisely. But if I mean no more to him than that—

JAMES. —Than what?

MARY. —If his love for me wasn't strong enough to—

JAMES. Listen to me, Mary: if you're going to quit Jim, quit him. But in heaven's name don't let it do this to you.

MARY. —Do what to me?

JAMES. —Fog your intellect, fog your reason—make an honest, fearless, first-rate woman into a softy.

MARY. I beg your pardon?

JAMES. "If I mean no more to him—" —"If his love for me wasn't strong enough—" Really, for you, of all people, to talk that kind of second-rate trash, is about the limit.

MARY. That's going it pretty stiff, don't you think?

JAMES. Yes, I do. And I'm amazed to think you need it.—What on earth has one misstep of Jim's to do with you?

MARY. It has a great deal to do with me.

JAMES. Nonsense!—If your hatred of

the Farley girl, or your jealousy of Jim is stronger than anything else you feel, all right. But this sense of grievance—personal injury—good heavens, what can Noel Farley do to *you?* If Jim has been anything to her—*he* may lose by it, but what *you* lose, I can't see.

MARY. I neither hate Noel nor am I jealous of Jim nor do I feel that I've been injured. But I've lost about everything I had, I think.

JAMES. How so?

MARY. Jim belonged to me. Jim was all my own.

JAMES. Don't glory in your sense of possession, Mary. It's the lowest instinct you've got.

MARY. I'm glorying in very little, now. It's—rather awful to know you're not loved. You miss it terribly.

JAMES. Jim loves you as he always has. I'm as sure of that as I am of my name.

MARY. In any event, I don't feel called upon to share him.

JAMES. I doubt if you've shared anything. If you have, it's the least important element in your whole relationship.

MARY. It seems not to be.

JAMES. I don't mean to belittle sex. It holds a high and dishonored place among other forms of intoxication. But love is something else again, and marriage is still another thing—

MARY (*bitterly*). Yes, and a great thing, isn't it?—Man's most divine conception—pure poetry—religion—sacrament—

JAMES. By heaven, it ought to be!

MARY. I was rather for it myself, if you'll remember. It was church to me, all right. But now, you see, I'm left with all the candles out, and rosy windows smashed and rotten ragtime playing through my church, where there was nothing but plain chant and Palestrina all the whole day long. I think I *have* lost something—

JAMES. Come here, Mary—

(*She goes to him and stands with her head against his shoulder.*)

MARY. It's gone, Father. It's gone, it's gone—

JAMES. Only if you let it. Think, child! Why, you used to say that nothing—

(MARY *raises her head.*)

MARY. Yes, I know: theories are fine, before things happen. But once they have, you find you don't think straight, if you're a woman. You can't—you only feel straight.

JAMES. You've had a bad shock, Mary. You've been jolted back into a state of mind you outgrew years ago. These straight feelings you talk of are twisted every which way by all the rubbish about love and marriage they taught you before you learned to think. They're a lot of old words and phrases, that's all.—"Trust betrayed," "deception," "infidelity."—Watch out for them.

MARY. He went from me to her. He chose her over me.

JAMES. There's no choosing to it. You ought to know that physical attraction isn't limited to one man or one woman. It never has been and never will be.

MARY. It must have been more than that.

JAMES. All right, capacity for love, then.

MARY. This isn't just any case of man—wife—mistress, Father. Mistresses are a different kind of person, as a rule. I can understand that sort of compromise, hateful as it would be. But Noel is a person like myself. I've known her all my life.

JAMES. Noel's no more like you than I'm like Lincoln. Mistresses are *always* a different kind of person, Mary, and so are lovers.—Will you tell me something?

MARY. Anything you like.

JAMES. When Jim came back a year ago, did you sense any change in him?

MARY (*after a moment*). No. (*Then suddenly.*)—If only he had told me! If only he had been honest! It's so—insulting—

JAMES. Jim is as honest as the day is long: you know that. The fact that he *didn't* tell you—the fact that you felt nothing in your bones, as you say—isn't that evidence enough for you that in his eyes it encroached in no way upon your province?

MARY. —And what about *my* eyes!?

JAMES. Oh Mary, I wish you might be twenty years older for one moment.

MARY. I should see it the same.

(*There is a silence. Then:*)

JAMES. —So you've convinced yourself there's only one thing to do.

MARY. I've tried to convince myself there wasn't.

JAMES. —Paris, with the rest of the defeated sisterhood—ten thousand dollars in hand for some wretched lawyer to bribe mean little French officials with—*you,* Mary—

MARY. —If that's the way it's done. How

else?

JAMES. Are you asking me? (*She gestures, lifelessly.*) Then I say not only put divorce completely out of your head but never by so much as one word let him know what you know. Refuse to admit it, Mary. Refuse, even to yourself, to admit it. Above all, don't speak of it. If there's one destructive thing in this world, it's words—spoken—

MARY. I shall tell him the first moment that I see him.

(*A moment. Then:*)

JAMES. —Well, it's quite beyond me. I counted on great things for you and Jim. When I stood there beside that boy in that hot little country church six years ago, and saw you coming up to him, I can't tell you what I felt about you both. It seemed to me that you had everything: strength, beauty, youth and wisdom—minds as open as any ever I've encountered—enormous gaiety—a great joy in each other, and in life. Such a wedding-garment as you two brought to your marriage, I've never known.

MARY. Well, it's in rags now, all right.

JAMES. And why?—If you and Jim had spent the last five years at each other's throats, that would be one thing. Actual, hopeless incompatibility I can understand. Drunkenness — cruelty — insanity —. But this, *this*—

MARY. —About the best reason there is, I think.

JAMES. Mary, it wasn't three months ago that all of you came to me for Easter. Jim arrived late. You hadn't seen him in three days—three whole days. I heard your voices from the next room. You chattered on about nothing until morning. You laughed a great deal. It was great music, Mary. There was more love in it than in all the sighs and picked-up roses in this world.

MARY. It's no use, Father.

JAMES. No?—Then all that's left for me to say is that a most uncommon marriage is about to go to smash because a once wise woman has become vain and selfish, because a good, hard mind has nicked its edge off on as rotten and false a conception as ever yet existed. You're going to quit Jim because he had "relations," as they say, with another woman—well, suppose he did, what of it? How big a part does that play in *your* life? Do you describe your marriage in those terms alone? I'm appalled you set so slight a value on yourself. I'm appalled that you accept defeat so easily, and on such a count.

MARY. I hoped you would understand me. Evidently you don't. If ours had been just any ordinary, halfway-happy marriage, perhaps it might survive this. But it was so perfect for so long, it can't. It goes from all to nothing.

JAMES. —Talk. (*She confronts him angrily.*) Yes! Everything you've told me to-night confirms my first suspicion: that it's the physical fact alone you can't escape. All you've said has been just one repeated statement that to you the most important thing in your whole marriage has been your physical relation to your husband.

MARY. —You think so!

JAMES. —Over and over you've said it. And now, because you insist on a monopoly of that particular thing, and find you haven't it, you take the lowest possible advantage of your ample means to indulge yourself in a luxury the lucky poor cannot afford. Bid up vanity! Bid up revenge! (*The buzzer sounds twice.*)—Well, do it, and you're a failure, Mary—a complete failure—not only in your marriage—but in every last department of your life.

MARY. That's enough, I think.

JAMES. I am ashamed of you. I cannot believe—

MARY. —*Quite* enough.

(*He looks at her intently. There is a silence. Then he bows slightly.*)

JAMES. Very well. Good-night, my dear.

MARY. Good-night.

(*A brief pause, then:*)

JAMES (*a last appeal*). Mary—

MARY. —Good-night.

(*The buzzer sounds again. He turns and goes out, stopping at the doorway long enough to press the electric button in response to the buzzer.* MARY *stands for a moment, rigid, then goes to the piano. Her fingers follow the ballet-score, but soundlessly.* RICHARD *enters.*)

RICHARD. H'lo.

MARY. Where are the Copes?

RICHARD. How should I know? (*He goes to the window.*)—Hot. Oh my God, how hot—(*He looks out.*) Look at that river to-night, will you—

MARY. I have been.

RICHARD. If ever I get any money, I'm going to buy a small tug and paint her up and live on her.

MARY. That's a divine idea. Let me make the curtains.

RICHARD. I think I'll go on a boat-trip myself to-morrow.

MARY. Oh? Where to?

(*He returns from the window.*)

RICHARD. Quite a way. (*He throws himself into a chair and sits with his head back, his eyes closed.*) It's wonderful to be able to breathe again.

MARY. Have you had dinner?

RICHARD. Of course I've had dinner. What do you think I live on? Air?

MARY. You've been known to, at times. —How much have you had to drink?

RICHARD (*starting forward*). I've had nothing to drink!

MARY. —Then make yourself a whisky-and-soda, won't you? There are the things—

(RICHARD *stares at the tray, then slumps back again into his chair.*)

RICHARD. Later, maybe.

(MARY *looks at him curiously, then:*)

MARY. What's the matter, my dear?

RICHARD. Don't say "my dear" to me. Don't say anything to me. Just let me sit here a minute, and then I'll go.

(*There is a long silence.* MARY *rises, picks up a sheet of the ballet-score and frowns over it.*)

MARY. —I wanted to ask you: this bit before the policemen come on in the last scene—it sounds to me like—

RICHARD. Oh don't talk about the ballet! Let the ballet alone.

MARY. But it isn't finished!

RICHARD. Let it stay where it is. It's as far as it'll get.

(*A pause. Then:*)

MARY (*quietly*). —And precisely what does that mean, may I ask?

RICHARD. Try thinking it out. That helps sometimes.

MARY (*chilling*). I'm afraid it's a little deep for me.

RICHARD. I'm sorry, if it is. You can console yourself it's deeper still for me.

(*There is an ominous silence. Finally:*)

MARY. —After all these weeks, and all the work we've done together—you won't put in one good half-hour more and finish it? You actually mean that?

RICHARD. Actually I do.

MARY. —One half-hour.

RICHARD. Who says it'd be only that?

MARY. It needn't be more. Not if it comes.

RICHARD. Well, it won't come.

MARY. How do you know?

RICHARD. I know. (*Suddenly he bursts out:*) What the devil does it matter, anyway? It hasn't a snowball's chance. It never had.

MARY. —So you quit on it.

RICHARD. Sure.

MARY. What do you suppose it means to me? Nothing?

(*He shrugs.*)

RICHARD. Oh—agreeable occupation gone — pleasant diversion — you'll find something else.

(*A silence. Then:*)

MARY (*in a small voice*). —Would you mind going now, please? (*He turns to her quickly. Her voice rises.*) Will you please go?

(*He makes a quick movement toward her, then stops, and murmurs:*)

RICHARD. All right.

MARY (*with intense feeling*). Richard, how can you do it!?

RICHARD. —How *can't* I do it, you mean.

MARY. Well?

RICHARD. Mary—listen, dear—

MARY (*impatiently*). What? *What?*

RICHARD. —Jim—his boat's late, isn't it?

MARY. Yes, why?

RICHARD. I've got to talk to you.

MARY. Then go ahead and talk.

RICHARD. —Talk for a long time—to-night—

MARY. I don't see how it's to be arranged, do you?

RICHARD. It can be.

MARY. Peter and Nora are coming. They ought to be here now.

RICHARD. Don't answer when they ring.

MARY (*directly*). But I must.

RICHARD. Why?

MARY. I must.

RICHARD. What is it you're afraid of, Mary?

MARY (*frowning*). —Afraid of?

RICHARD. Yes.

(*She looks at him steadily for a moment. Then:*)

MARY. Good-bye, Richard. (*He does not answer. She concludes, contemptuously.*) And sometime, if you can manage it, I wish you'd finish *something*.

RICHARD (*softly*). Oh damn you—

MARY (*in a burst*). —And damn you! Go and tune pianos, that's where *you* belong! A fine artist *you* are—lazy, dabbling, worthless—

(*He seizes her by the shoulders. She stops. They gaze at each other, tense, furious. At last he speaks.*)

RICHARD. I can't finish that ballet, because that ballet's you and me, and we aren't finished and never shall be. So *it* won't.

MARY (*after a moment, comprehending*). You can let go my shoulders now.

RICHARD. I won't, though.

MARY. What's it all about, Richard?

RICHARD. I love you, Mary.

MARY. I think you love music, my dear.

RICHARD. You and it—you're one to me.

MARY. Thanks. That's very sweet.

RICHARD. Oh, don't talk like such a fool.

MARY. I don't know what to say to you. What do you want me to say?

RICHARD. Something I'll—Anything you want to.

MARY. —I like you very much—so much, so much. And I shall miss you horribly.

RICHARD. We've been together all the time for weeks—so will I you.

MARY. I shan't know what to do with myself.

RICHARD. But you'll find something, won't you?

MARY. I'll try awfully hard.

RICHARD. Oh, don't you feel a thing for me—not anything at all?

(*She looks at him, a little startled.*)

MARY. I never thought—

(*A moment, then:*)

RICHARD. *I* think you do, Mary.

MARY. —Do you suppose?

RICHARD. Yes.—Don't *you?*

(*She moves away from him.*)

MARY. —It would be very funny if I did.

RICHARD. —And would you laugh a great deal?

MARY. I think I'd cry my eyes out.

RICHARD. Then never mind.

(*She turns to him again, swiftly.*)

MARY. Oh, you dear person, you—

RICHARD. Mary—come here to me a moment—

MARY. I can't.

RICHARD. —You don't want to—

MARY (*lowly*). I—didn't say that—

RICHARD. Then why—?

MARY. I don't know. It just seems to me I can't.

RICHARD (*after a moment*). All right.—Good-bye. Thanks ever so much for—ever so many things.

MARY. Oh, *don't* say that! It's I, who—

RICHARD (*an estimate, without self-pity:*) I expect when you take me all in all, I'm just a bum.

MARY. You're a pretty important bum, I think. To me you are, anyhow.

RICHARD. That'll do nicely. Good-bye—(*He holds out both his hands to her, smiling. She hesitates one instant, then moves directly into his arms, and kisses him. The breath leaves his body in a gasp. His arms tighten about her. She is rigid for a moment, then something within her gives way and she slumps against his breast, her face averted.*) Look up at me!

MARY. No, no—

RICHARD. Look up!

MARY. No—(*She makes a half-movement to leave him, but cannot. She lifts her face to his. They kiss. Again she averts her head, with a choked cry.*) Richard—!

RICHARD. I love you so terribly.

MARY. You—(*She cannot finish. A moment. Then:*) Oh, this isn't me! It can't be—

RICHARD. It *is* you!

MARY. No, no.

RICHARD. For the first time, it's you.

MARY. It's—just something raging inside me. It isn't me—it isn't—

RICHARD. It's *my* you.—It's the you *I* know.

(*She shakes her head.*)

MARY. Go quickly—dear Richard—go quickly—

RICHARD. I'm going to stay here with you.

MARY. You're—? But that's—that's not possible. You must go at once.

RICHARD. Oh Mary—

MARY. Please go, please go:—Peter and Nora—they'll be coming.

RICHARD. —When they ring, let them ring. Don't answer.

MARY. I must.

RICHARD. No.—You were tired waiting, weren't you, Mary?

MARY. —Was I?—I don't know.

RICHARD. —Don't say anything for a moment. Just stay close to me. Don't speak. (*A long silence. She remains in his arms. At last he speaks, very slowly.*) I can feel your heart beating. It wouldn't beat like that.

(*With a faint cry she strains against him. Another silence. Then:*)

MARY. It isn't mine.

RICHARD. It is—and you want me, too—

don't you, don't you, Mary?

MARY. —Impossible—it's not possible—

RICHARD. —*Don't* you, Mary? (*She does not answer, but her arms tighten around him.*)—Then where's the difference? Where is it, dear?

MARY. There *is* one. There's a great one.

RICHARD. I don't see it—

MARY. You've got to go—oh, *go,* will you?

RICHARD. —You think it will be just the beginning of something. It won't. It'll be the end. You're always saying things must be finished. So must this, Mary. It must be finished, Sweet, really it must, or we'll haunt each other our whole lives long. We'd never get away from it then, never, never. Oh, why won't you see that, Mary?

MARY. I can't. All I can see is that I'd hate the thought of you, of both of us.

RICHARD. No!

MARY. Yes.—It would—simply blast everything in my whole life. (*She leaves him.*)—Oh, how is it I can love him so, and still feel this for you? I don't understand it.

RICHARD (*following her*). —But we aren't three people—you and he and I. We're four people: you and he, and you and I. *His* you can't ever in this world be mine, any more than my you can be his.

MARY. —I don't understand it—

RICHARD. It has nothing to do with anyone or anything but us and our life. Don't you know that, Mary?

MARY (*dully*). Hasn't it, Richard?

RICHARD. I promise you!

MARY (*almost inaudibly*). Do you, Richard—

RICHARD. It won't be taking anything from anyone. You have enough love in you to give me—you keep making it, making it all the time—love and more love.

MARY. —I don't understand this, I don't understand it.

RICHARD. But it's our life, Mary, it really is—there's no one else in it but you and me—there's no one could come into it. Haven't you always said—?

MARY. I've said a lot of things.

RICHARD. Well, there's no need to say anything anymore. Just stay close to me—

(*Once more she is in his arms.*)

MARY. No—keep talking—keep on talking—(*He shakes his head, silently. She cries:*) You must! Talk! Talk! Will you *talk?!*

(*Again he shakes his head. There is a silence, finally broken by two sharp rings from the buzzer. She stirs in his arms.*)

RICHARD. Let it ring.

(*She is quiet once more. The buzzer sounds again.*)

MARY. Oh—floods are breaking all in and around us, and you won't even help me up out of them.

RICHARD. No.

(*The buzzer sounds again, long, insistent. He holds her closer to him. The buzzer stops. She speaks again, this time with despair in her voice.*)

MARY. I shouldn't think you'd want me this way. It won't be me at all—it will be —just *any* woman. (*A moment. He raises his head slowly, holds her off from him and looks at her intently. Her face is contorted, her eyes imploring.*)—That's true, you know. It *is* true!

(*There are two short and final signals from the buzzer. He turns his head abruptly away from her and stares at the door. Then, in a swift movement, he leaves her, goes to the door and presses the button beside it. With an exclamation, she covers her face. He goes to the piano and seats himself. Then:*)

RICHARD. In a few minutes I'll go, Mary. I'll walk down the stairs and out and up along the river to Eighty-ninth Street. I'll sit there on a bench for one half-hour. That's about what they'll stay. Then I'll come back.

MARY. Don't come back.—If you do love me, don't—

(RICHARD *begins to play the piano aimlessly.*)

RICHARD. —I'll come back. By then you'll have had time to think, and you can let me in or not, as you like. Before you do, look in the glass at your face and see that it *is* you—*my* you. Then, if you want me, I'll be here.—Is that fair?

MARY. I—suppose so.

RICHARD (*playing*). All right.—Now go to the top of the stairs and call down to them. They're coming up. (MARY *manages to light a cigarette.*) That's it.

MARY (*with difficulty*). Richard—anyhow—I want to tell you: I think you are—

RICHARD. There aren't any anyhows yet, my dear. (*He jerks his head in the direction of the door.*) Go ahead—

(MARY *goes to the door, opens it and calls:*)

MARY. Hello there!

RICHARD. Good girl.

(NORA's *voice is heard in protest from below.*)

NORA. Well!

MARY. Oh, I can't stand their chatter now! I simply can't.

RICHARD. You've damn well got to.

MARY. Keep playing, won't you?

RICHARD. Sure.

(MARY *goes to a mirror and hastily brushes back her hair and dabs powder upon her face.* NORA *enters.* RICHARD's *playing becomes louder.*)

MARY. Nora!—How are you?

NORA. We couldn't be worse. We've been ringing ten minutes. What on earth's been the matter?

MARY. You can't hear anything up here, with the piano going.

FANNY (*entering*). —Then throw the piano out. We're important people. (*She throws herself into a chair.*) Whew!—Hello, Parish—

RICHARD. Hello, Shippan.—How was the show?

NORA (*fanning herself with a handkerchief*). Not bad.

RICHARD. Sorry I couldn't—

FANNY. *I* never cracked a smile.

RICHARD. —make it.

(PETER *comes puffing in. He and* FANNY *and* NORA *are in evening clothes.*)

PETER. Fanny, why are you so tight with your money? Why don't you give these people an elevator? (*He mops his brow.*) —It's a little bit of heaven, and they call it a top-floor. (*He turns pompously to* MARY.) However do you do, my dear?

MARY. All hot and happy, thanks.

(*He turns to* RICHARD.)

PETER. Evenin', Massa Parish.

RICHARD (*playing*). Hello.

(*All the voices are pitched high, against the music.*)

MARY (*to* FANNY). I nearly gave you up. Where have you been?

FANNY. In a cellar on Forty-ninth Street, drinking white wine and seltzer.

PETER (*moving toward the whisky*). —The seltzer was good.

(*He pours himself a drink.*)

NORA. Peter won his case against old man Burke this morning.

MARY. You didn't!

NORA. Isn't he bright?

PETER. —I'm glad I did it. He was a beast.

MARY. But no wonder you're celebrating!

PETER. Celebrating? Me? Don't be silly. (*He stirs the ice noisily in his glass.*)

NORA. Peter, will you kindly stop that eternal clash, clash, clash!

FANNY. Poor lamb, it's her old wound again.

NORA (*fanning herself*). I'll die.

FANNY. Not in the house, darling.

PETER. —In the open air, seeking water. (*He raises his glass.*)—*Whisky* and water.

NORA. Don't speak of it.

MARY. Don't speak of what?—That doesn't make sense.

NORA. What does? Can you tell me?

(RICHARD *rises from the piano, takes off his coat and throws it across the bench beside him.*)

PETER. —Now there's a good idea.

NORA (*irritably*). What? What?

PETER. —Of Parish's. He cast his coat aside like an old coat.

(RICHARD *reseats himself and continues playing but at lower pitch.*)

NORA. We're moving on in one minute, so don't *you* start undressing. (*To* MARY.)—We thought we'd go and dance somewhere.

(MARY *does not answer.*)

FANNY. Are you coming?

(*Still* MARY *hears nothing but* RICHARD's *music. A moment, then:*)

NORA. Whoo-hoo! Mary! (MARY *turns to her.*)—Are you listening, darling?

MARY. Of course I am. (*To* FANNY.) What, darling?

FANNY. Come along with us to hell and Rector's, will you?

MARY. Well I should say not.

NORA. Why not?

MARY (*absently; still listening to* RICHARD). It's too hot, and I want some sleep.

FANNY (*to* NORA). —So she'll look her prettiest when the great big steamboat brings Daddy home to-morrow.

MARY (*smiling*). Yes. That's it.

(NORA *and* FANNY *are on the sofa.* MARY *stands near the piano, thinking.* PETER *paces, with his whisky.*)

PETER. What news of the lad?—Any news is good news.

MARY. He lands at about nine in the morning.

PETER. I can't stay up that long. It's impossible.

NORA (*to* FANNY, *watching* MARY). It'll be good to have Jim back, won't it?—If only to get Mary out of her doldrums.

FANNY. "Doldrums"—there's a funny word. It sounds quite lewd.

NORA. But have you seen Mary much lately?

FANNY. My dear, she sees no one.

NORA. Is she ill, do you think?

FANNY. It were better if she were.

NORA. Not having an affair with some-one!

FANNY. Mary? Oh no!

NORA. What is it, then?

FANNY. They say in Poictesme that she loves her husband.

PETER. Will the gray hordes never cease? God! Are we too late?

FANNY. Six weeks without him is just too much to bear, it's too much to bear.

NORA. Never mind. To-morrow we'll have our old Mary back again.

PETER. She had charm, that girl. Always a smile for everyone.

FANNY. And now it's a curse or a blow.

PETER. Love is like that.

MARY. What is it you're playing, Richard?

RICHARD. Listen—

(FANNY *and* NORA *look at each other.*)

FANNY. I—uh—I do hope we're not intruding.

MARY. Don't be silly.

PETER. Watch out, Parish, or the young master will thrash you roundly.

RICHARD. Yes?

NORA (*suddenly*). Mary, if you don't give that party to-morrow, I'm off you for life.

FANNY. So am I.

MARY. What party is that?

FANNY. Listen to it! "What party!"

NORA. You aren't actually going to let an anniversary pass without a celebration?

PETER. Say it ain't so, Mary.

NORA. I suppose they'll just dine alone together. That's what she really wants.

FANNY. Don't. My heart's breaking.

MARY. I want nothing of the sort. It's simply that I haven't any servants in town.

NORA. Why not get them in?

PETER. —The railroad, or steam-demon, as it was then called, was invented by Martin Luther in 1821. Since then—

FANNY. I'll lend you a butler with whiskers, if you like.—Or I tell you what! *I'll* give the party!

MARY. No you won't, darling.

FANNY (*to* NORA). What can you do with her?

RICHARD. Listening, Mary?

MARY. Yes.

(FANNY *looks from one to the other.*)

FANNY. Would you mind telling me what goes on here?

NORA (*bursting out*). —Well, *I* think it's a crime! You could get every single one that was in the wedding.

PETER. I saw Johnny Scott down town this very noon. "Hello, Johnny," said I. "How are you, Peter?" said he—

NORA. —All except Noel, anyway.

PETER. —Then we went and had a drink.

FANNY. —Noel, too. She's staying with the Potters. I saw it in the Times.

(*A brief pause. Then:*)

MARY. Oh, she's back, then—

FANNY. She must be.

PETER (*reflectively.*) —Noel Farley—I can see her now—

NORA. Can you? I never could.

PETER. Where's she been all the time?

FANNY. —Living somewhere in a little house-by-the-sea, with only her pets for companions.

PETER. Noel? Like hell she has. (*An afterthought:*) *What* pets?

NORA. Mary, it does seem such a shame. You and Jim can dine alone together for the rest of your lives.

FANNY. —And probably will.—What *I* always say is, one should share one's happiness with one's friends. It makes for better feeling.

MARY. I'm sorry, but I can't face a party.

PETER (*wistfully*). I've got a dandy new bird-call to do with the soup: it's the yellow-bellied wagtail.

MARY. You're all terribly kind, but I simply can't face it.

(*There is a pause.*)

PETER. Well that, I should say, is that.

MARY. I'm sorry, but I'm afraid it is.

NORA (*bursting out once more*). Honestly, if you aren't acting queerer than anyone I've ever known—

MARY. I'm sorry, Nora.

(FANNY *looks significantly from* MARY *to* RICHARD.)

FANNY (*to* PETER *and* NORA). What do you think?—Perhaps we'd better just tiptoe quietly out.

(*Suddenly* MARY *breaks:*)

MARY. Fanny, will you *kindly* stop talking like such a fool!

FANNY. Why, you saucy puss. (*She stares at her for a moment, then rises and turns to* NORA.) Come on, will you? I can't stand much more of this.

NORA. Wait a minute. (*To* MARY.) Now look here, darling, I—(*The buzzer sounds once.* MARY *starts in surprise.* RICHARD *stops playing and listens.*)—Who is it you're expecting?

MARY (*rising*). Why—no one—

RICHARD. A telegram, most likely.

(MARY *goes to the door.*)

FANNY. *I'm* going.

MARY. Please wait. I don't know who it is. (*She presses the button and opens the hall door, then turns to* FANNY.) I'm sorry, Fanny—I didn't mean to be rude.

FANNY. Oh, that's all right.

(MARY *presses her fingers against her temples.*)

MARY. It's just so damned hot.

PETER (*cheerfully*). Sure it is!—That's what it is: hot.

(RICHARD *is staring at the hall doorway.*)

FANNY. —All I want to know is, can we expect some little change after to-morrow. —In you, I mean.

(MARY *looks at her curiously, then laughs shortly. A brief pause. Then:*)

MARY. Fanny, after to-morrow you can expect a big change. I promise you you can.

(NORA *has gone to the hall doorway, where she stands listening.*)

FANNY. That's all right, then. Mummy understands.

NORA. —Do you want him to come up, whoever it is? Because he's coming.

MARY. —If it's a tel—

(NORA'S *sudden cry cuts her short:*)

NORA. Jim!

(*Steps are heard bounding up the stairs.* MARY *stands frozen against the wall by the door.* RICHARD'S *head bends lower over the piano and his hands drop once more upon the keys, which he fingers without sound.* JIM *enters past* MARY.)

JIM. Where's Mary? For the love of—! (*He turns and sees her, catches his breath in joy, and says:*) Hello, Mary.

MARY. Hello, Jim.

(*In an instant he is at her side, and has taken her into his arms.*)

NORA (*after a moment*). Well, if it isn't little friendly-face home again.

(JIM *looks over* MARY'S *shoulder at them.*)

PETER. You low cad. You come here with your fine clothes and your city manner, and—

JIM. Hello, Copes!

NORA. It's nice you're back.

FANNY (*pushing into view*). —And this is that attractive Shippan girl.

JIM. Fanny! How are you?

FANNY (*archly*). Need you ask, dear?

(JIM *laughs.*)

PETER. —All de Eighty-foist Streets togedder again—ain't it grand?

JIM. Oh Lord, if it's not!—Hello, Parish!

(MARY *leaves his arms.*)

RICHARD. —Good trip?

JIM. Terrible. The day before yesterday up came a monsoon or something and nearly blew us out of the water.

FANNY. You just can't tell about ole davvil Sea.

JIM (*to* MARY). How are the babies?

MARY. They said you wouldn't land until morning.—They're simply blooming.

PETER. How'd you work it, Jim?

JIM. —Bribery and corruption. I came in on the mailboat.

PETER. Just Hutton grit, that's all.

JIM. —And I wasn't above bringing some champagne with me, either.

PETER. —But that's against the law. It's against every decent—where is it?

JIM. No you don't! It's for to-morrow night, to drink the bride's health in—isn't it, Mary?

(MARY *smiles, but does not answer. There is a brief pause.*)

NORA. Oh, is there to be a party?

JIM. Of course there's to be a party!

FANNY. Thank God, the militia.

JIM. —And you're all invited.—How about you, Parish? Can you come, too?

RICHARD. I'm sorry. I won't be here.

JIM. Oh? Are you off somewhere?

RICHARD. Yes. I'm going boating.

FANNY. Where? Central Park?

RICHARD. No. Farther.

MARY. What's all this, Richard?

RICHARD. I know the purser on one of the United Fruit Boats. He says he can get me on board as one of the loading-crew. Six in the morning at the Battery. Sail at seven.

FANNY. Just like that!

PETER. Jim—(JIM *looks at him.* PETER'S *gesture includes* MARY *and* RICHARD.)—That's your luck, son.

(JIM *looks incredulous for a moment, then lights a cigarette, watching* RICHARD.)

MARY. When did you decide this, Richard?

(*He shrugs.*)

RICHARD. To-night.

NORA. Is it to be a long trip?

RICHARD. Not terribly: four or five months.

PETER. I knew a fellow did that once. It was years afterwards before he could even take orange-juice.

JIM (*casually*). —But how about this ballad you and Mary have been writing—

FANNY. —Ballet, idiot.

JIM. Well, ballet, then.—Is it finished?

RICHARD. I've just been playing the end of it. (*He rises and goes to* MARY.) I'll bat it out on paper to-night and send it to you in the morning, Mary.

MARY. That would be perfect.

RICHARD. —When the police finally follow Mike and the girl across the roof of the apartment and they go over the edge, and they look down after them, do you know what they find below in the courtyard?

MARY. You—hadn't decided.

RICHARD. I have now: two bodies.

MARY (*lowly*). I see.

(*There is a silence. Finally:*)

JIM (*lightly*). I should think—

FANNY (*simultaneously*). You know, they've been on a regular musical orgy, these two.

RICHARD (*to* JIM). It's a nice practical little ballet. It wouldn't cost more than a hundred thousand or so to put on.

JIM. Well, good luck with it, anyhow.

RICHARD. Thanks. I've had that already. (*To* PETER, FANNY *and* NORA.) Good-bye.

NORA. Good-bye. Come to see us when you get back.

FANNY. Good-bye. I think you're sweet.

PETER. Good-bye. They say the bananas are the worst.

RICHARD. I'll watch out for them.—Good-bye, Hutton.

JIM. Good-bye, Richard. (*They shake hands.*) Have a good trip.

RICHARD. Thanks, Jim. Good-bye, Mary—

(MARY *gives him her hand.*)

MARY. Write to me, won't you?

RICHARD. Sure! (*He bends toward her. She lifts her face to his. He kisses her.*) Good-bye—

(*He is gone. There is a silence.*)

FANNY. Was that fresh, or wasn't it?

MARY. No, Fanny. It was not.

PETER. I've got no technique for that fellow. He makes me feel about as appropriate as a French soldier sitting at a soda-fountain singing Boola-Boola.

NORA. Mary would say that it's because he's an artist and you're not.

PETER. Well, maybe she'd be right.—Anyone have a sandwich?

(*He takes one.*)

JIM. Mary, how long are these confounded people going to hang around here?

MARY. They're hopeless.

PETER. I know a hint when I hear one. Come, Nora—

(NORA *and* FANNY *rise.*)

JIM. We'll see you all to-morrow, sure.

NORA. Mary said there wasn't to be any party.

JIM (*frowning*). But I thought it was all—

MARY. I don't want a party, Jim.

FANNY. I know, but we do.

PETER (*to* MARY). Who are *you,* anyway? Just a guest in your own house.

JIM. Really don't you, Mary? (MARY *shakes her head.* JIM *turns to the others.*) Then there's no party—

PETER. —Telephone us in the morning —a good night's sleep will do you both good. You're tired, Hutton. You have never learned to spare yourself. Remember, mens sana in corpore sano.

(JIM *laughs uncertainly.*)

JIM. Get out!

NORA. Good-night! (*To* MARY.) It's great he's back.

MARY. Isn't it?

(PETER, FANNY *and* NORA *move toward the hall.*)

NORA. Don't bother to come down with us.

JIM. We wouldn't think of it.

(NORA *goes out,* FANNY *follows her, calling back:*)

FANNY. Thanks for the spinach!

PETER (*following* FANNY). But my dear —it wasn't here you got the spinach.

(*They are gone.* MARY *stands leaning against the piano, fortifying herself against the ordeal to come: she must tell* JIM *that she knows about* NOEL*—but then what, then what?* JIM *re-enters, uncertainty still upon him: what had* PETER *meant when he said of* RICHARD's *departure "That's your luck, Son?" What had that whole curious situation he came in on—what had that meant?*)

JIM. Well, darling—?

MARY. Jim—

JIM. What is it, dear—

MARY. I've got something I—want to talk to you about.

(JIM *looks at her: But it's not possible! Mary? Richard?*)

JIM. I'm not certain I want to hear it.

MARY. But it's—it's—

JIM. I'm certain I don't want to hear it! —Come and sit beside me—(*He takes her hand and leads her to the sofa.*) How's Father? Have you seen him?

MARY. Yes. He's all right. Jim—

JIM. *You* look a little white—

MARY (*slowly*). I've had to be in town a great deal—(*Then, in sudden determination.*) Listen to me Jim! I—

JIM (*as suddenly*). —I'm terribly glad you had that music-thing to work on. I think it's rotten not to be busy, when—. Oh, I saw Mother—I went down for the week-end. She's all right, but how she endures that man White, I don't know.

MARY. Is he awful?

JIM. He's such a damn bore. And he's forever taking care of himself. If she had to quit Father, I'd rather she'd married the black sheep of the Jukes family, I swear I would. (MARY *laughs.*) Did you get the roof fixed?

MARY. Jim, it's too perfect.

JIM. I thought you planned to have the party there.

MARY. I did, originally.

(*A pause.*)

JIM. How has Sabina been?

MARY. Angelic.

JIM. Did Collins straighten out all right?

MARY. No. He left and took the grass-cutter with him. But I've got a more reliable one now.

JIM. Grass-cutter?

(MARY *laughs.*)

MARY. No, Stupid. Gardener.

JIM. Business went marvellously.

MARY. I don't care.

JIM (*smiling*). I know you don't.

MARY. Did you get down to Cannes at all?

JIM. I hadn't time. Oh listen—all the presents, yours and the children's too—they're in my bag—I'll have to send to the dock for it. I'll (*Suddenly he catches her hand.*) Oh Mary, *do* you?

MARY (*lowly*). —What, Jim?

JIM. —Love me, Mary—? (*She turns away with a cry, half sob, of pain.*) Why what's the matter, dear?

MARY. I don't know—

JIM. Nothing's—really troubling you?

MARY. Jim, you've got to listen to me. I—

JIM. Stop it! (*Then.*) Look here, darling—I don't ever want to hear any bad news about us, do you understand? (*She nods, dumbly.*)—There's nothing ever can affect *us*, you know—nothing in this world.—Is there?

MARY (*after a long moment*). No. I expect there's not.

JIM. Then—there'll never be anything but good news, will there? (*She looks at him and shakes her head.*) That's right! (*He lifts her face to his.*)—Mary from Jim. Much love.

(*He kisses her. She murmurs:*)

MARY. —Much love.

JIM. Now about this party—

MARY. I haven't done a thing about it.

JIM. There's lots of time.

MARY. It couldn't be very elaborate.

(*Now they are chattering happily.*)

JIM. It needn't be. Let's keep it small. That's more fun. Where's your wedding-dress?

MARY. In the top tray of my old trunk. Why?

JIM. Oh do wear it!

MARY. It's miles too long now.

JIM. You could take a hitch in it.

MARY (*doubtfully*). I—

JIM. What are pins for?

MARY. Well—

JIM. —And all the men in cutaways.

MARY. They'll be in camphor in the country.

JIM. We'll give a camphor ball.

(MARY *laughs.*)

MARY. I'll feel a thousand.

JIM. You'll look six.—I wish we could bring the babies in for it.

MARY. —They might come out of a pie and turn handsprings.

JIM. Are they really blooming?

MARY. Wait till you see them!

JIM. Mary—

MARY. What?

JIM. Where's the motor?

MARY. In the garage, why? (JIM *goes to the telephone.*)—What are you doing?!

JIM (*to the telephone*). Rhinelander 0890.—That's right.

MARY. Jim!

JIM. Yes.

MARY. You're a madman. It's two o'clock.

JIM. What's the difference? (*To the telephone.*) Hello—

MARY. It'd be four by the time we got there.

JIM. Four's early.

MARY. It certainly is.

JIM (*to the telephone*). Hello, is this the garage? Is that you Sam? Hello, Sam, this is Mr. Hutton—

MARY. Wait a minute! Wait a *minute!*

JIM (*to the telephone*). —Just to-night. Half an hour ago. You bet I'm glad. Look here, Sam, it's hot in this attic and we think we need some air—

MARY. Will you *listen* to me!

JIM. Shhh! How can I talk with all this jabber-jabber? (*To the telephone.*)—That's right. Send the roadster right over, will you? Thanks, Sam. See you soon. Make it quick. That's the boy! Good-bye! (*He replaces the telephone and smiles at* MARY.)

MARY. Jim—really—I'm a woman of thirty.

JIM.—Not quite. Come on—

MARY. But they don't wake up until six.

JIM. While we wait we'll pick flowers and match pennies.

(MARY *laughs. Then:*)

MARY. I'm not dressed.

JIM. Where's your wrap?

MARY. It's downstairs.

JIM. I love to see them when they're asleep.

MARY. Honestly, Jim, this is ridiculous.

JIM. Tie something round your head and come on. Here—

MARY. Jim, I tell you, I—!

JIM (*severely*). You will do as I say.

MARY. It *would* be fun, you know.

JIM. Fun—? My dear girl, it's our duty! (*He ties a chiffon scarf around her head.*) There! All you need is the dress now. Come on, sweet.

MARY. Oh, the lights—

JIM. Never mind the lights.

MARY. All right, I won't.

JIM. You haven't forgotten anything, have you?

MARY. Not a thing. Just my dignity.

JIM. That's not serious.

MARY. Who said it was?—Give me your hand.

JIM. You give me yours. (*Their hands fumble for each other. They laugh and move toward the hall.*) Here we go, then—

MARY. Oh, here we go!

(*They go out. Their laughter is heard from the hall.*)

CURTAIN

THE distinguished career of Robert Sherwood is mainly a phenomenon of the thirties and forties. To these decades belong his highest achievements in comedy (*Reunion in Vienna,* 1931; the adaptation, *Tovarich,* 1936) and in serious drama (The *Petrified Forest,* 1935, *Idiot's Delight,* 1936, *Abe Lincoln in Illinois,* 1938, *There Shall Be No Night,* 1940, and *The Rugged Path,* 1945), as well as his activities as friend and adviser of Franklin Delano Roosevelt, assistant to the Secretaries of War and Navy, and director of the overseas branch of the O.W.I. in 1944. He won three Pulitzer Prizes with his plays in 1936, 1939, and 1941 and received a gold medal for his work in the drama from the National Institute of Arts and Letters in 1941. Another Pulitzer award came to him in 1949 for his book *Roosevelt and Hopkins.*

In the twenties, Mr. Sherwood was still trying his wings without conspicuous success in the case of *The Love Nest* (1927), a dramatization of a Ring Lardner story about the rebellion of a movie director's wife, and *The Queen's Husband* (1928). His 1929 melodrama *Waterloo Bridge,* failed to duplicate the success it had had in London, although it was intense in its animadversions on the futility of the first World War. But his very first contribution to the stage, *The Road to Rome* (1927), displayed a lively intelligence and wit, as well as an abhorrence of wars of conquest, which were to stand him in good stead in later years. This comedy also happened to constitute a summation of the effervescent theatre of the twenties by virtue of its irreverence toward historical reputations, anti-heroic outlook, and Freudian concern with repressions and compensation mechanisms, with sex the object of suppression and the drive to power and glory as the compensation.

Mr. Sherwood was born in 1896 in New Rochelle, New York, entered Harvard in 1914, and withdrew in his senior year to join the Canadian Black Watch regiment in 1917. Wounded in France and discharged from the army, he returned a confirmed pacifist, as *The Road to Rome* would indicate. He was to shed his pacifism only after considerable heart-searching in the late nineteen thirties, but not before expressing some mordant fatalism in *The Petrified Forest* and *Idiot's Delight.*

Having edited a "Vanity Fair" number for the Harvard Lampoon during college days, Sherwood naturally turned to journalism after his return to the United States. As a journalist he proved himself vigorous and bright, and he has the distinction of having written the first serious motion picture criticism published in any large magazine when he reviewed films for Life. He was subsequently motion picture editor for the New York Herald Tribune. He first joined Vanity Fair, and served there as drama editor. In the gallant company of Robert Benchley, he left Frank Crowinshield's publication over an issue of freedom of the press involving another employee, Dorothy Parker, and became an editor of Life and Scribner's Magazine. Mr. Sherwood has been a strenuous liberal ever since. But this does not appear to have impaired his sense of humor at all, as *The Road to Rome* and *Reunion in Vienna* proved, and as the musical comedy he is currently preparing for the summer of 1949, *Miss Liberty,* is likely to prove again.

The Road to Rome

BY ROBERT EMMET SHERWOOD

Presented by Messrs. William A. Brady, Jr., and Dwight Deere Wiman at the Belasco Theatre, Washington, D. C., January 17th, 1927; the Broad Street Theatre, Newark, N. J., January 24th, and the Playhouse, New York, January 31st, with the following cast:

VARIUS	Fairfax Burgher
META	Joyce Carey
FABIA	Jessie Ralph
FABIUS MAXIMUS	Richie Ling
AMYTIS	Jane Cowl
TANUS	Peter Meade
CATO	William Pearce
SCIPIO	Charles Brokaw
DRUSUS	William R. Randall
SERTORIUS	Lionel Hogarth
TIBULLUS	Alfred Webster
SERGEANT	Jock McGraw
CORPORAL	Lewis Martin
FIRST GUARDSMAN	Clement O'Loghlen
SECOND GUARDSMAN	Ben Lackland
THIRD GUARDSMAN	Walter A. Kinsella
FOURTH GUARDSMAN	John McNulty
FIFTH GUARDSMAN	Willard Joray
THOTHMES	Lionel Hogarth
HASDRUBAL	Louis Hector
MAHARBAL	Alfred Webster
CARTHALO	Harold Moffet
MAGO	Barry Jones
HANNIBAL	Philip Merivale
BALA	Gert Pouncy

ACT I

Courtyard in the home of Fabius Maximus in Rome: a June evening in the year 216 B.C.

ACT II

Hannibal's headquarters in a temple, about a mile east of Rome: an hour later.

ACT III

The same as Act II: the next morning.

ACT ONE

The curtain rises, disclosing a scene in the courtyard, or atrium, in the home of FABIUS MAXIMUS *in Rome. It is early evening, just before sunset, of a June day in the year 216 B.C.*

The house, which surrounds the courtyard on all three sides, is one story in height. It is simple and unostentatious in design, being representative of Rome in the period of the Republic, when the sterner virtues of economy and almost Spartan frugality were practised.

There are four entrances: one (downstage right) which leads to the kitchens and slave quarters; another (upstage right) which leads to the street—this being the main entrance to the house; a third (downstage left) which leads to the sleeping quarters, and a fourth (upstage left) which leads, through a passageway, to the street.

The scene is divided in half, laterally, by a row of columns. Over the front part of the stage is stretched a painted awning, or peplum; behind the columns, the atrium is open, the blue Italian sky being visible above the rear wall of the house. In this open space is a small pool; flowers and shrubs are growing in earthenware pots; there is a shrine in a niche in the rear wall.

At the right, in the foreground, is a table, with three chairs and a stool. Behind it, against the columns, is a sort of serving-table on which are goblets, bowls, pitchers, etc. At the left is another chair and a bench.

When the curtain rises, VARIUS, *a slave, is engaged in setting the table for the evening meal. He is a fair young man, obviously not a Latin, with the air of one who has known better circumstances than these. He is supremely contemptuous of his Roman masters, and inclined to be rebellious.*

VARIUS *pours some wine into a goblet, peers about cautiously to make sure that he is unobserved, and then tastes the wine.*

VARIUS (*calling off to the right*). This wine is terrible. Haven't we anything better in the house?

META (*off stage*). No. That's all we have. (META, *a slim, lovely young girl, enters, bearing a bowl of grapes which she deposits on the table.*) And there's none too much of that!

VARIUS. I wish they'd hurry up and settle this war so that we could have something to eat and drink.

META. It's not for a slave to criticize his master's wine.

VARIUS (*sitting down at the table*). Oh, I know it—but I'm fed up with keeping my place. (*He stands up, hastily.*)

META. Perhaps I'm fed up, too, Varius. Being a slave in Rome isn't quite the pleasantest occupation imaginable. . . . But I should like to know what's to be done about it.

VARIUS. Slaves sometimes escape.

META (*alarmed*). Don't speak of that again, Varius. You mustn't dare to try that. You know what the chances are. If you were caught, it would mean instant death!

VARIUS. Wouldn't you prefer death to this?

META. No—I can't say that I would.

VARIUS. You're better off than I am. You're close to her. She gives you some sympathy. She understands.

META. She understands us because she's an alien herself.

VARIUS. Yes, and in Rome the attitude toward all aliens is, "If you don't like it here, why don't you go back where you came from"—knowing damned well that we can't.

META. Cheer up, Varius. (*She puts her arm about him and strokes his hair.*) It might have been worse—it might have been much worse. Suppose we had been separated when they captured us?

VARIUS. I know. But why can't we have our love? Why are we compelled to smother our natural impulses? We belong to each other—but we can't have each other, because we're slaves!

META. In Rome, it's wise for a slave to forget that he is a human being.

VARIUS. If you weren't here, I might be able to forget it. (*He takes her in his arms.*) But when I look at you, I can't remember anything—except that I love you.

META. And I love you, Varius. I shall always love you. (*She backs away from him, nervously.*)

VARIUS (*vehemently*). We must escape, Meta! We must get away from Rome, and be free!

META. We can't get away from Rome, Varius. Rome is everywhere. Rome will soon be the whole world.

VARIUS. If we could only reach Apulia, we could join with the Carthaginians.

META. Even that's hopeless. The Roman army has cornered them at last. I heard the master say that he expected news of Hannibal's defeat any day.

VARIUS. The master doesn't always know what he's talking about.

META. Of course he doesn't know what he's talking about. He's not supposed to. He's a Senator. . . . But I couldn't go and leave her. She needs us, Varius. She's bored to death in Rome. . . .

VARIUS. She can't be blamed for that.

META. We're her only friends. She clings to us.

VARIUS (*excitedly*). Perhaps she'd escape with us!

META. If she knew of any way of escape from Rome, she would have taken it herself, long ago. . . . Now please put the thought out of your mind, Varius. We can't escape—ever.

VARIUS. There must be some way out for us. (*She kisses him tenderly.*)

(FABIA *comes in suddenly from the sleeping-quarters at the left, and gasps, with horrified indignation, at the sight of the two slaves embraced.* FABIA *is the mother of* FABIUS*—a cross, narrow-minded old lady, whose world is her home. For all her seventy-three years, she is brisk and vigorous, and she rules the establishment with an iron hand.*)

FABIA (*astounded at this breach*). What on earth do you two think you're doing? (*Hastily they separate, with sheepish self-consciousness.*) Why, I never heard of such loose, shocking behavior—never in all my life. How dare you kiss each other—right here in the atrium, of all places? I don't look for much delicacy among slaves, but you know as well as I do that this sort of thing is forbidden. You'll be punished for this.

META (*abjectly*). We're very sorry that it happened, my lady.

FABIA. I declare, you slaves are becoming more insolent every day. You're a problem, that's what you are. How dare you insult your master's house with such conduct?

VARIUS. We were making love to each other, my lady. It's an old custom in our country.

FABIA. Oh, it is, is it? Well, you're not in your country now. You're in Rome! Furthermore, you're slaves. If the people in your country had spent less time making *love*, and more at good, honest, hard work, perhaps our Roman armies wouldn't have conquered you so easily.

META. Yes, my lady.

FABIA. Is dinner ready?

META. It is, my lady.

FABIA. See that it's nicely served. (*The bolt on the outer door is heard.*) And I don't care to hear of any more *love*-making in this house. Do you understand?

VARIUS. We do, my lady—perfectly.

(FABIUS *enters from the right—the street entrance.*)

META (*to* VARIUS). The master!

(FABIUS *is a typical Senator—pompous, unctuous, consciously important and 100 per cent Roman. His most casual utterance is delivered, as it were, from the eminence of the rostrum. He is not, however, just an old wind-bag—inflated, for purposes of this play, merely to be punctured. On the contrary, he should convey a definite sense of authority, distinction and real power. He is, at the moment, at the head of the Roman state; he must "fit the picture-frame."*)

FABIA. Ah, my poor son! (*She anxiously scans his face.*) You look tired.

FABIUS. Yes, mother. I've had a hard day at the forum. (*He sinks down on the bench at the left.* META *goes out at the right.*) These are trying times, mother, trying times. Rome faces a grave crisis.

FABIA. What is the crisis now, my son?

FABIUS. The people are worried about Hannibal. He has the most irritating habit of winning victories, and our generals have been unable to check his advance. There is a demand in the Senate for positive action.

FABIA. Oh, don't listen to these old Senators. They're always talking. Talk—talk—talk! That's all they know how to do.

FABIUS. To-day the Senators really accomplished something, mother—something big. They took constructive, intelligent measures to combat the Carthaginian menace.

FABIA. What did they do?

(META *enters quietly from the right, carrying a pitcher of water.*)

FABIUS. I am proud to say that they recognized your son's long and not undistinguished career as a public servant of Rome.

FABIA (*excitedly*). They promoted you?

FABIUS (*rising*). They proclaimed me Dictator, with full power to conduct the state and the armies as I see fit.

FABIA. My boy! The Dictator of all Rome. (*She smothers him with congratulatory caresses.*) You have brought new glory to the Fabian name. You are the greatest man in the world. (*She turns to the slaves.*) Here, you slaves! Do you realize the honor that has come to our house? Your master is Dictator of all Rome. (*The two slaves bow politely.*)

FABIUS (*deprecatingly*). Oh, come, come, mother. I'm afraid it isn't quite so much as all that. Just a war-time measure, for purposes of—of expediency.

FABIA. Ah—but you are modest. You begrudge yourself the satisfaction of knowing that all Rome must bow before you now. (*She contemplates the possibilities.*) When I walk out into the streets of the city, everyone—even the best families —will bow before *me,* and say, "She is the mother of Fabius Maximus, the Dictator of all Rome!"

FABIUS. My dear, loyal mother. (*He pats her hand patronizingly.*) I'm rather anxious to see how Amytis takes this bit of news.

(FABIA's *brow clouds.*)

FABIA. Oh, she'll be delighted, of course.

FABIUS. I hurried home from the Forum to tell her about it. Where is she?

FABIA. She should have been here long ago. It is past the hour of dinner.

FABIUS. Meta, where is your mistress?

META. She has been down at the market-place.

FABIUS (*rising*). At the market-place? What for?

META. There is a merchant there, lately arrived from Antioch.

FABIUS. From Antioch, eh? What business has he in Rome?

VARIUS. I think he came here in the hope that he might make some money.

FABIUS. Or perhaps to pick up some valuable information. Antioch and Carthage are close allies. He may even be spreading Carthaginian propaganda. . . . I'll run the fellow out of town.

FABIA. *You* can do it, Fabius. *You're* the dictator!

(FABIUS *goes over to the table and dips his fingers in the bowl of water which* META *holds out to him, drying them with the towel which she also offers.*)

FABIUS. It doesn't look well for my wife to be patronizing a dirty foreign peddler. I wish she'd come home.

FABIA. Perhaps we'd better start dinner and not wait for her.

(FABIUS *and* FABIA *sit down at the table and start eating.* VARIUS *goes out.* FABIA *leans over to speak to* FABIUS, *confidentially.*)

FABIA. I'm very much worried about those slaves. They're becoming more and more insolent all the time.

FABIUS. In what way?

FABIA. Just now, I caught them making love . . .

FABIUS. Making *love?*

FABIA. They were *kissing* each other!

(META, *realizing that she is not supposed to overhear this conversation, tactfully goes out.*)

FABIUS. I hope you spoke to them about it.

FABIA. I reprimanded them—but not so severely as I should. It isn't entirely their fault.

FABIUS. Why not? (*The door bolt is heard again.*)

FABIA. Because they're continually being encouraged to violate the rules of discipline.

FABIUS. By whom?

(AMYTIS *enters from the right, upstage. She is followed by* TANUS, *a slave, who carries garments and materials of brilliant colors.*)

FABIA (*with a gesture toward* AMYTIS). By her!

(AMYTIS *is young, beautiful, gracious, and obviously civilized. She has an air of culture, sophistication, and refinement that is not evident in any of the Romans. Her mother was an Athenian Greek—her father a Roman officer—and within her are combined the worthiest characteristics of these two widely contrasted races: superficially, she is frivolous, frothy, apparently oblivious of the more serious problems with which her distinguished husband is continally wrestling; but behind this surface artificiality are profound depths of sympathy and understanding. Her external fluffiness and levity are masks for an essential thoughtfulness. She gives the impression, to* FABIUS *and his friends, that she is weak and inconsequential; actually, she is strong, and brave and wise.*)

AMYTIS (*talking rather fast*). I'm so sorry to be late, but there was a merchant from Antioch who had the most *fascinating* things, and I couldn't tear myself away.

(META *takes* AMYTIS' *cloak, and carries it out at the left, returning presently.*)

FABIA. Amytis, your husband has some great news for you.

AMYTIS (*not having heard*). Look at this. (*She takes a fragile garment from the slave's arms.*) It's a Phœnician nightgown, from the Court of Antiochus the Great. The merchant told me that it was made for the emperor's favorite concubine.

FABIUS. Amytis! There are servants present.

AMYTIS. And this piece of material. Isn't it gorgeous? Isn't it ravishing? See how it shimmers when you hold it to the light. No Roman loom could have woven fabric like that!

FABIA (*to* FABIUS). Tell her what happened at the Senate. . . .

AMYTIS (*going right ahead*). I don't know how I'll use it just yet, but it's bound to come in handy some time or other.

FABIUS. Amytis, the Roman Senate conferred a singular honor on your husband to-day. . . .

AMYTIS (*taking another garment from the slave*). But here's the real prize—a peacock-green dress from Damascus—made of silk. Think of it! Real silk! The merchant told me that it came from the farthest reaches of the Orient. It was carried on the backs of camels across the desert—"all for you, fair lady"—those were his very words. . . . Isn't it beautiful!

FABIUS. Yes, I suppose so. But do you think—do you think it's quite the sort of thing to be worn by a lady of your position?

AMYTIS. *My* position? I have no position. I'm just the wife of an ordinary Roman Senator—and, certainly, that doesn't mean much.

FABIA (*bristling*). The wife of an ordinary Roman Senator, indeed! Do you realize what happened in the Senate to-day?

AMYTIS. Now, *don't* tell me they passed another law.

FABIA. To-day the Roman Senate proclaimed your husband, Fabius Maximus, Dictator.

FABIUS. Yes, my dear, they have placed me at the head of the Roman state.

AMYTIS. Isn't that nice. . . . Tanus, put those things in my room. Go on with dinner. I'll be right back. (*She goes out at the left, with hurried instructions to* TANUS *to "lay them out on the bed so that I can see them all at once."* META *follows her out.*)

FABIUS. She took it calmly.

FABIA (*bitterly*). She doesn't understand what it means. After all, she's only a Greek.

(FABIUS *resumes his meal.*)

FABIUS. You mustn't be too hard on Amytis, mother. She has those queer Athenian ideas inbred in her, and she can't get rid of them. It isn't her fault. . . . The Athenians know nothing of the principles of government that have made Rome what it is to-day.

FABIA. Yes—and look at Athens now.

(META *re-enters.*)

FABIUS (*between mouthfuls*). Completely gone to seed. No state can survive unless it is founded on good, sound military strength and a policy of progressive conquest.

FABIA. Have we conquered Hannibal yet?

FABIUS. No, we haven't exactly conquered Hannibal as yet. But he's on the run.

FABIA. All Rome looks to you, my son.

(AMYTIS *comes in and goes to the table.*)

FABIUS. I hope that I shall not be undeserving of my countrymen's trust.

AMYTIS. Well—what have you two been talking about? (*As she speaks, she dips her fingers in the bowl which* VARIUS *holds.*)

FABIA. We've been talking about Hannibal.

FABIUS. I was just telling my mother that we have him on the run.

AMYTIS (*sitting down at the table*). Everyone seems to be talking about Hannibal these days, and I'm sick and tired of the sound of his name. . . . By the way, who is he?

(FABIUS *and* FABIA *are astounded at this confession of ignorance.*)

FABIUS. My dear Amytis—you're not serious!

AMYTIS. Why not? How should I know who Hannibal is? I'm not a member of the Senate.

FABIUS. Amytis—Hannibal is the arch-enemy of Rome, the invader of Italy. He has threatened the very sanctity of our homes.

AMYTIS. Where does he come from?

FABIUS. From Carthage.

AMYTIS. Really. I've heard that Carthage is a very beautiful city.

FABIUS. Quite possibly. But Carthage happens to be at war with Rome, and Hannibal is in command . . .

AMYTIS. Now, please don't ask me to keep track of our wars, or just who our enemies happen to be at the moment. With one war after another—and sometimes two or three wars at a time—I can't follow them. The mental effort is too great.

FABIUS. Perhaps you'd take a more lively interest if Hannibal marched into Rome, with his army of Africans and Spaniards and Gauls. How would you like to see this house burned down about you, and your loved ones slaughtered before your eyes? Would that amuse you?

AMYTIS. It might serve to break the monotony of life in Rome.

FABIA. I have lived in Rome for seventy-three years. I have not found it monotonous.

AMYTIS. But, my dear mother, you must remember that you've never been anywhere else. I had the misfortune to be born in Athens, where gaiety is not listed among the unpardonable sins.

FABIA. It was bad luck for you that your mother married a Roman officer.

FABIUS. Sometimes I wish that you had inherited more of your father's traits.

AMYTIS. Perhaps I did. Perhaps my Athenian frivolousness is purely superficial. Perhaps, in the depths of my soul, I am a stern, relentless, world-beating Roman!

FABIUS. I'm afraid I know nothing about the depths of your soul, Amytis.

AMYTIS. I'm afraid you don't.

FABIUS. You'll never believe that I am in sympathy with you.

AMYTIS. The trouble with me is—I'm bored. And I don't like it. Being bored is so—so snobbish.

FABIA. It is your own fault if you are bored. There are many subjects of interest in Rome.

FABIUS. My mother is right, Amytis. Rome to-day is the liveliest, most progressive city in the world. Why, just consider the population figures. Ten years ago . . .

AMYTIS. That's just it. Rome is too busily engaged in the great work of expanding to think about such trivial matters as happiness or even contentment. If we could only stop being successful for a change—if we could only *lose* a war, now and then, just for the sake of variety . . .

FABIUS. Our community life is well organized. Why don't you associate with the wives of my friends?

AMYTIS. Now, really, Fabius, you know that Senators themselves are dull; you ought to know that, having to listen to them make speeches all day. But even Senators are marvels of intellectual brilliance compared to their wives.

FABIA (*with obvious scorn*). I've noticed that you don't care to associate with ladies of the better class. You seem to prefer the companionship of *slaves.*

FABIUS. Please, mother. We needn't mention that.

AMYTIS. Fabius . . .

FABIUS. What is it, my dear?

AMYTIS. Couldn't we go out somewhere this evening?

FABIUS. Go *out?* Where?

AMYTIS. Oh, just somewhere. To a play, perhaps . . .

FABIA. I see no occasion for going to a play.

FABIUS. Is there a play?

AMYTIS, I believe there is. There's a company of players here; they come from Athens . . .

FABIUS. Oh! I've heard about *them.*

AMYTIS. They're giving "Œdipus Rex."

FABIUS (*incredulously*). And you want to see "Œdipus Rex"?

FABIA. Probably one of the coarsest plays ever written!

AMYTIS. Oh, but I *love* it! I adore a good, exciting tragedy.

FABIUS. But why?

AMYTIS. I love to cry. I like to go into the theatre and just sob.

FABIA (*horrified*). But "Œdipus Rex" . . .

AMYTIS. What's wrong with that?

FABIUS. To tell you the truth, Amytis. I've never seen the play—but I've heard that it's—well, that it's rather questionable.

AMYTIS. You can't very well judge as to that until you've seen it yourself.

FABIUS. I'm afraid I can't go out again, my dear.

FABIA. Of course you can't, my poor boy. You're terribly tired.

AMYTIS. Then please let me go, anyway.

FABIA. *Alone?*

AMYTIS. Why not?

FABIUS (*hastily*). That wouldn't do at all, my dear. I could never consent to that.

AMYTIS. Then what shall we do this evening—just sit around?

FABIUS. No. I shall not just "sit around." I am worn out. I shall go to bed presently.

AMYTIS. That will be fun.

FABIA. You can clear the table, Varius. (VARIUS *and* META *remove the remains of the meal.*)

AMYTIS. Is dinner over? (FABIUS *rises.*)

FABIA (*belligerently*). Did you expect anything more?

AMYTIS (*vaguely*). I didn't know . . .

FABIA. Of course you didn't know. How could you know? You never take the trouble to *order* the meals.

AMYTIS. I'm no good at housekeeping.

FABIUS (*with characteristic diplomacy*). There's no reason why Amytis should attend to the housekeeping, mother—not while you do it so well.

FABIA (*with elaborate scorn*). Oh, I wouldn't expect her to do any *work* around the house. Oh, no! But it isn't for her to complain.

AMYTIS. I only wanted something sweet. There doesn't seem to be any dessert.

FABRIA. Here! Eat a grape. (*She thrusts the bowl of grapes toward* AMYTIS, *who bites one and makes a wry face.*)

AMYTIS. Ugh! Those grapes are sour. (*She motions them away with an expression of disgust.*)

FABIUS. You don't realize that this is war-time, my dear. We have to deny ourselves some of the luxuries, for the sake of our brave boys at the front.

AMYTIS. Is that why there's no dessert?

FABIUS. Yes. This is sweetless Saturday. (*The meal is now over. The two slaves have cleared the table and gone out, followed by* FABIA, *who superintends their activities. When* FABIUS *and* AMYTIS *are alone,* FABIUS *paces up and down for a few moments, as though trying to find an opening for an embarrassing subject.*)

FABIUS. It is always difficult for me to talk to you, Amytis. Sometimes I feel that you and I don't speak the same language.

AMYTIS. Are you angry with me because I spent so much money in the market-place?

FABIUS. No—it isn't that—although, I must say, that Phœnician nightgown seems a little—perhaps——

AMYTIS. Indecent? What of it? None of the Senators will see me in that, will they? I bought that in the hope that it might be just the least bit stimulating to you.

FABIUS. And then that green dress—the one that the camels carried—do you intend to wear that in the streets of Rome?

AMYTIS. Of course. It will make all the women in Rome envious, and cause them to complain to their husbands that the wife of Fabius Maximus is not quite respectable.

FABIUS. But that's what we must avoid. We can't afford to have that sort of talk going on. Don't forget that you are now the first citizeness of Rome.

AMYTIS. And therefore the arbiter of fashion, the leader of thought, the ultimate authority in all matters relating to feminine deportment.

FABIUS. Of course, of course. You are the dictator's wife—and for that very reason, you are expected to set a good example in all the more desirable virtues.

AMYTIS. Such as?

FABIUS. Well—ah—respectability, modesty, economy, devotion to duty, reverence, chastity, and—and . . .

AMYTIS. Mediocrity! I see.

FABIUS. It is in the best interests of the state as a whole. Do you understand?

AMYTIS. I understand perfectly, and I shall do my best to be a model of all that is most virtuous and most thoroughly uninteresting.

FABIUS. And there is one other thing, Amytis.

AMYTIS. I suppose I am to be more regular in my attendance at the temple.

FABIUS. That goes without saying. What I wished particularly was to influence you to take a more lively interest in public affairs. For instance, I was shocked to learn that you know nothing of Hannibal.

AMYTIS. Why should I know anything about Hannibal? Remember, you confessed to me the other day that you had never heard of Aristotle.

FABIUS. That's quite true, my dear. But, after all, you must admit that Aristotle never did anything to make himself famous.

AMYTIS. What has Hannibal done? Has he contributed anything to the advancement of science or philosophy or art?

FABIUS. I'm afraid not. But he has led an army of foot-soldiers, cavalry, and elephants from Africa to Spain, from Spain to Gaul, across the Alps and into Italy—a distance of over three thousand miles. Hannibal is cruel, he is treacherous, he is a menace to our Roman civilization, but he is a great soldier. We must be generous with him and concede him that much.

AMYTIS. You say he is cruel. Is there any soldier who is otherwise?

FABIUS. Hannibal has spread destruction wherever he has gone. His army has burned homes, destroyed crops, butchered men, and despoiled women.

AMYTIS. That is the immemorial privilege of the conqueror . . .

FABIUS. Hannibal has taken undue advantage of that privilege. Last winter, when his army was quartered in Cis-Alpine Gaul, there was a veritable epidemic of pregnancy.

AMYTIS. Good for Hannibal! He sounds like a thoroughly commendable person.

FABIUS. Amytis! Please don't say such things, even in fun.

AMYTIS. Why not? Is it wrong for me to admire good, old-fashioned virility in men? I certainly haven't seen any too much of it in my own life.

FABIUS (*falteringly*). What do you mean?

AMYTIS. You know perfectly well what I mean, Fabius. . . . Has there been any epidemic of pregnancy around here?

FABIUS. I wish you wouldn't harp on that subject, Amytis. You know that I've been working hard lately. I've had so many worries. It's the state that demands all my time—all my energy . . .

AMYTIS. Of course—the state! What else is there in life but the state, and the state's business, and the state's public brawls . . .

FABIUS. We can have no other thought until Rome rules the world.

AMYTIS. When that happens, I suppose the orgies will start.

FABIUS. The splendid morale of the Roman people will never weaken.

AMYTIS. Morale—there's no such thing in Rome. There's nothing here but a narrow-minded, hypocritical morality. You Romans call it godliness; it's nothing but worldliness, of the most selfish, material kind.

FABIUS. Amytis! I can't bear to hear you talk that way. It—it's cruel.

AMYTIS. Oh—I'm sorry, Fabius. I don't mean to hurt you. Don't pay any attention to the things I say. My ideas don't fit in Rome, anyway. . . . (*She strokes his hair. He is easily mollified.*) Now! Go ahead and tell me all about your success in the Senate, and whatever it was they made you today.

FABIUS. (*expanding*). Dictator. They proclaimed me Dictator of All Rome. I control everything.

AMYTIS. Everything except Hannibal.

FABIUS. I'll have him under control before long. His head will be mounted on a spear in the center of the market-place, as a warning to all those who lack faith in the glorious destiny of Rome.

(AMYTIS *is sitting on the edge of the table and* FABIUS *on the stool before it. Toward the end of the preceding speech,* FABIUS, *warming to his subject, starts to rise with finger pointed upward in a characteristically oratorical gesture.* AMYTIS *places her hands on his shoulders and gently pushes him down again, murmuring, "now, Fabius, please sit down."*)

AMYTIS. All the hopes—all the aspirations of Rome are centered in you—aren't they, Fabius?

FABIUS. Yes, the gods of Rome have called upon me to conquer this ruthless African invader, who has trampled our virgin soil under the dread heel of oppression. (*Again* FABIUS *starts to rise, and again* AMYTIS *restores him to his seat.*)

AMYTIS. Splendid! Did you use that line in your speech of acceptance?

FABIUS. Yes, I believe I did voice some such sentiments.

AMYTIS. And the Forum rocked with applause, I'm sure.

FABIUS. I'm happy to say that my remarks were well received. After I had spoken, all the leaders of the Senate clustered around to congratulate me. . . . Would you like to know what else I said?

AMYTIS. Of course I should.

FABIUS (*standing up and achieving an attitude*). I said: "Fellow Romans, the hour approaches . . ." (*For the third time,* AMYTIS *pushes him back to the stool, saying, "Now please, darling— you mustn't get so excited."*)

FABIUS. I pointed with pride to our policy of delay, which has worried Hannibal and forced him to take up a defensive position in Apulia, two hundred miles from Rome. We have caught him in a trap. The army, under the command of Paullus and Varro, confronts the Carthaginians, and is ready to attack. Hannibal's mob is disorganized. His original force has melted to almost nothing, and he has bolstered it up with mutinous, unseasoned barbarians recruited in Spain and Gaul. (*He rises.*) Furthermore, our army outnumbers his by two to one. Our discipline is better, our equipment is better, our morale is better!

AMYTIS. I can just hear the cheers.

FABIUS. The time has come for us to strike—and to strike *hard!*

AMYTIS. Poor Hannibal! After travelling three thousand miles, he has to die ingloriously and be exhibited in the marketplace as a horrible lesson to little children.

FABIUS. Waste nc sympathy on Hannibal, my dear. He courted disaster when he embarked on this foolhardy enterprise.

AMYTIS. Why do you suppose he did it?

FABIUS. For obvious reasons: he wished to obliterate Rome.

AMYTIS. But why? What has Hannibal against Rome?

FABIUS. He's afraid of us. He knows that unless he destroys Rome first, Rome will ultimately destroy Carthage.

AMYTIS. That seems rather silly.

FABIUS. It may seem silly to you, my dear. The feminine mind can never comprehend the true significance of war.

AMYTIS Other women do. Whenever one of our armies start out, all the wives and mothers and sweethearts cheer themselves hoarse. And while the men are away, fighting battles and spreading Roman civilization with the sword, the womenfolk sit at home and talk about the great sacrifices they're making. I've heard them. (*She sits down in a chair beside the table.*)

FABIUS. I'm happy to say that the women of Rome have always rallied splendidly in the hour of peril— and I mean no offense to you, my dear. You just don't understand what war is.

AMYTIS. Fabius . . .

FABIUS. Yes?

AMYTIS. How old is Hannibal?

FABIUS. He's just a young man—thirty years of age, or thereabouts.

AMYTIS. How tragic!

FABIUS. Why tragic?

AMYTIS. I was thinking how wasteful it is to sacrifice a young man who has the genius to lead a troop of elephants across the Alps. Just think—if he were allowed to live, some day he might do something useful.

FABIUS. If he were allowed to live, Amytis, he might some day cause the downfall of Rome.

AMYTIS. And so you, my husband, are to be celebrated throughout all history as the man who conquered Hannibal and saved Rome.

FABIUS (*greatly pleased*). Yes, my dear —I suppose I shall be accorded some measure of recognition.

(*There is a slight pause, during which* AMYTIS *gazes off dreamily into space.*)

FABIUS. What are you thinking about now, my dear?

AMYTIS. I was just wondering what it would be like to be despoiled.

FABIUS. Amytis! Is that a proper subject for a lady's thoughts?

AMYTIS. Not proper, perhaps—but certainly not unusual.

FABIUS. You'd know what it is like, soon enough, if Hannibal's army ever marched into Rome.

AMYTIS. I suppose there are no chances of that . . .

FABIUS. No chances whatever, I'm happy to say.

AMYTIS. Are there any women in Rome who have had the misfortune to encounter Hannibal's army?

FABIUS. Oh, yes—we have a great many refugees in the city—pitiful creatures they are, too.

AMYTIS. I'd like to ask some of them up to dinner some time. Their comments might be interesting.

FABIUS. Hannibal will be made to pay for his atrocities.

(*From the far distance, a bugle call is heard—a shrill, weird, barbaric sound, repeated twice in quick succession.* AMYTIS *starts as she hears it, and looks up curiously.*)

AMYTIS. What was that?

FABIUS (*yawning*). Oh, probably some shepherd . . . (FABIA *enters.*) . . . bringing his flocks in from the fields. (*He sits down wearily at the left.*)

FABIA. Fabius, my son, you are tired. You must go to bed and rest. Remember that every ounce of your vigor must be conserved.

AMYTIS. Yes, Fabius—you *must* conserve your vigor.

FABIA. For now you belong to Rome.

FABIUS. Very well, mother dear. I have no choice but to obey. (*He rises and goes to* AMYTIS.)

AMYTIS. Good-night, Fabius, and don't be too annoyed at my ignorance. I'll try to learn. And when Hannibal's head is mounted in the market-place, I shall be there to jeer at his sad face.

FABIUS. Of *course* you will, Amytis. For all your talk, you're just as patriotic as any one. Isn't she, mother?

FABIA (*without enthusiasm*). I'm sure she is.

FABIUS. Good-night, Amytis, my love. (*He kisses* AMYTIS *and crosses to* FABIA.) Good-night, mother dear. (*He starts to go out at the left. At the door, he pauses and turns.*) Some day, perhaps, we'll all go to a play. (*He goes out.*)

FABIA. But it will not be "Œdipus Rex." (*She addresses* AMYTIS). Are you going to bed? (AMYTIS *doesn't answer.*) Are you going to bed?

AMYTIS. I think I'll stay out here for a while. The air is very pleasant.

FABIA. I advise you to put something around your shoulders. Good-night.

AMYTIS. Good-night, mother—and sweet dreams to *you*.

(FABIA *goes out.* META *and* VARIUS *come in timidly from the right.*)

META. My lady . . . Varius and I would like to go for a little walk. May we?

AMYTIS. Of course you may. I wish I could go with you—but I'm afraid it wouldn't look quite right.

VARIUS (*smiling*). I'm afraid not, my lady.

AMYTIS. You two would like to be married, wouldn't you?

VARIUS. Yes, my lady, we would. Our fathers destined us for each other when we were small children.

META (*hastily*). But it's out of the question, now, of course.

AMYTIS. I know. Slaves aren't allowed to marry in Rome. That's one of our best laws.

(VARIUS *steps forward, with sudden determination.*)

VARIUS. Might I speak to you, my lady . . .

META (*sensing his purpose*). No, Varius—you mustn't . . .

AMYTIS. Why, of course you may, Varius.

VARIUS. We want to get away . . .

META (*terrified*). Varius. Don't! Please don't say it . . .

VARIUS (*desperately*). We want to escape, my lady. We want to be free.

AMYTIS (*caressingly*). You want to be free!

META. We know it can't be done, my lady. (*Angrily*) Varius—you're a fool to say these things.

AMYTIS. Not at all, Meta. You and Varius can say anything you please—to me. You needn't be afraid that I'll tell . . . (*She glances toward the left.*) . . . anyone.

VARIUS. Then you'll help us to escape?

AMYTIS. I'm afraid that's quite another matter. If I could help you, I would do so. You know I would. But where can you go? Where can you find freedom?

META. I told him that, my lady. I told him it was hopeless. But he would blurt this out.

VARIUS. There are the Carthaginians, my lady. They're friendly to all enemies of Rome.

AMYTIS. The Carthaginians themselves will soon be slaves, Varius. They're to be conquered, like all the others who have tried to argue with Roman supremacy. . . . Rome can't be beaten—not yet. There's an air of destiny about this place, an intimation of empire—and it can't be subdued.

VARIUS. Then there is no hope for us?

AMYTIS. No. We have the misfortune to be thoughtful people—and there's no place for us in the world, as Rome is organizing it. We haven't that air of destiny, nor the self-confident strength that it gives. Thoughtful people are never very successful.

(*The distant bugle call is heard again.* AMYTIS, VARIUS, *and* META *pause to listen to it; there is a sense of vague, suppressed excitement.*)

AMYTIS. There's that strange sound again. What *is* it? (*A loud knocking is heard at the left.*)

AMYTIS. See who that is, Varius.

VARIUS. Yes, my lady.

AMYTIS. Whoever it is, I've gone to bed. (*She goes hurriedly into the sleeping quarters at the left.* VARIUS *goes out at the left, upstage. He is heard to unbolt and open the door, and then to say, "What is it, Cato?"* CATO *replies, excitedly, "You can see them plainly from the walls—*

thousands of our men." They are both speaking together, and their words are therefore indistinct. VARIUS *returns with* CATO, *an excited youth.*)

CATO (*to* META). There are hundreds of camp-fires off to the east.

(VARIUS *climbs up one of the columns so that he can see over the top of the low roof.*)

META. What can it be?

VARIUS. The army must have returned.

META. But I thought the army was away, fighting Hannibal.

CATO. They were. This must mean that they've conquered him, at last.

META. Poor Hannibal! (*Another loud summons is heard at the left.*)

VARIUS (*climbing down*). Open the gate, Cato.

(CATO *goes out at the left, and again a confusion of voices is heard*—CATO *saying, "What's happened, sir? You're wounded," and* SCIPIO *saying, "Is Fabius here? I must see Fabius, at once!"* SCIPIO *comes in, with* CATO *following.* SCIPIO *is a handsome young man, wearing the helmet, breastplate, etc., of a Roman officer. His cloak is torn, dirty, and spotted with blood. His left arm is bandaged. He is a fine, upstanding type of soldier—earnest, sincere, intense—one of the men who aided materially in Rome's conquest of the world.*)

SCIPIO (*steadying himself against a column*). Summon your master at once.

(VARIUS *exits into the sleeping quarters.* SCIPIO *crosses to the table and slumps down wearily into a chair.* META *hands him a goblet of wine.*)

META. We have seen the camp-fires, sir. Has the army returned?

SCIPIO. Some of it has returned.

(FABIUS *comes in, drawing his toga about him. He is followed by* VARIUS.)

FABIUS. Scipio, why are you here? What does this mean?

SCIPIO. It means that the Roman army has suffered a terrible defeat.

FABIUS (*bewildered*). Defeat? Where?

SCIPIO. At Cannæ. We were routed—disgraced!

(VARIUS *again climbs up the column to look out.*)

FABIUS (*aghast*). And Hannibal—where is he?

SCIPIO. Hannibal is at the gates of Rome!

VARIUS (*excitedly*). Then those are Hannibal's camp-fires!

FABIUS. But—but it can't be! It's impossible! Hannibal is two hundred miles from Rome.

SCIPIO. I tell you, Hannibal is at the gates!

META. Do you hear that, Varius? Hannibal is at the gates!

(FABIUS *sits down helplessly.*)

FABIUS (*almost sobbing*). Hannibal—at the gates—at the gates of Rome. What is it, Scipio? What has happened?

SCIPIO. The Roman army has been wiped out. Our strength and our prestige are gone. Hannibal rules the world.

FABIUS. What shall we do? What shall we do?

SCIPIO (*rising*). You are the dictator, Fabius. It is for you to decide.

FABIUS (*dully*). Yes, I am the dictator. It is for me to decide. (*He stands up, making a tremendous effort to pull himself together.*)

FABIUS. Go, Cato, and summon Sertorius, Tibullus, and Drusus, if you can find them.

CATO. Yes, sir!

FABIUS. Tell them to come here at once.

CATO. Yes, sir! (*He runs out.* FABIA *appears, greatly annoyed at this unusual disturbance.*)

FABIA. What *is* all this racket? Varius, what are you doing up on the roof?

VARIUS. I'm looking at Hannibal.

FABIA. Is Hannibal up there, on the *roof?*

FABIUS. Hannibal is at the gates of Rome.

(AMYTIS *comes in hurriedly, from the left.*)

AMYTIS. What's all this about Hannibal?

FABIUS (*desperately*). Do I have to say it again?

SCIPIO. Our army has been defeated. Hannibal has marched to Rome. He will occupy the city at any moment.

AMYTIS (*apparently delighted*). You don't *mean* it!

VARIUS. It's true, my lady. The sky is dark with the smoke of his camp-fires.

AMYTIS. So Hannibal got here, after all.

FABIUS. Yes—and it means death to us all—the end of everything for Rome.

AMYTIS. Think of it. . . . Hannibal!

FABIUS. Rome has been betrayed by the gods.

AMYTIS. Why don't you sit down, Scipio? You must be fearfully tired.

SCIPIO (*ungraciously*). I'm perfectly able to stand, thank you. (*It is obvious that he bears no love for* AMYTIS, *an attitude that is not uncommon among the friends of* FABIUS.)

FABIUS. Is there any remnant of the army left, Scipio?

SCIPIO. None, Fabius. We were annihilated at Cannæ. A few of us cut our way back to Rome, but even then we travelled no faster than Hannibal with his entire army. He is a superman—a god—against whom mortal strength is of no avail.

AMYTIS. A god!

FABIUS. But I can't understand it, Scipio. Superman or no superman—we outnumbered his army two to one. I thought we had him caught in a trap.

SCIPIO. Hannibal let us think so. He forced us to attack the center of his line, where his weakest troops were massed. He allowed us to drive through—and then surrounded us, with his infantry and Numidian cavalry.

FABIUS. More of his damnable deception.

AMYTIS. We would never have resorted to such foul tactics—would we, Fabius?

FABIUS. Never!

AMYTIS (*sits*). No—we wouldn't have thought of them.

(FABIUS *paces up and down in a turmoil of baffled rage, nervous apprehension and utter bewilderment.*)

SCIPIO. I saw Hasdrubal, the Numidian cavalry leader, cut down dozens of our men with his own sword. He fought like a fiend, sent down by the gods to punish us.

AMYTIS. And did you see Hannibal?

SCIPIO. I saw him in the distance.

AMYTIS. What was he doing?

SCIPIO. He was standing on a little hill . . .

FABIUS. Laughing, I suppose?

SCIPIO. No—he was not laughing. He was watching the battle as though it were a play that he had written, being performed by actors in a theatre.

AMYTIS. Is Hannibal good-looking?

SCIPIO. Hannibal's personal appearance did not interest me at the moment.

FABIUS. This is a serious matter, Amytis. I must ask you not to bother us with irrelevant questions now . . .

AMYTIS. But this isn't irrelevant. It is very important for Hannibal to be handsome. Think of the statues.

FABIUS. What else happened, Scipio?

SCIPIO. They closed in on us and butchered us . . . and all through the battle their terrible African war drums kept on beating—louder—louder . . .

AMYTIS (*without enthusiasm*). It must have been thrilling!

SCIPIO. Our army was a confused mass of struggling, writhing men—battling against an enemy that attacked from every side. The slaughter was unspeakably awful. . . . When it was over, at last, seventy thousand Romans lay dead on the field of Cannæ.

AMYTIS (*slowly*). Seventy thousand! Why did they die?

SCIPIO (*bitterly*). Ask Hannibal why they died.

FABIUS. Seventy thousand! What horror! What is this terrible thing the gods have done to us, Scipio—to us who have made our sacrifices regularly in the temple and have spared no effort to show our gratitude for past favors. I can't understand it.

AMYTIS. Perhaps Hannibal was nice to the gods, too.

FABIUS (*vehemently*). Hannibal's gods are false gods!

AMYTIS. Oh—I see.

SCIPIO. You must take immediate action, Fabius. Hannibal may advance on the city at any moment.

AMYTIS. Can't you possibly keep him out?

FABIUS. No. Rome is doomed. We have no more than five thousand men to defend the walls—and what are five thousand men against Hannibal?

SCIPIO. Every Roman is prepared to fight to the last.

FABIUS. But our women—what of them? You must escape, both of you, while there is still time. My mother and my wife must be spared.

AMYTIS. Spared from what?

FABIUS. From the bestiality of Hannibal's men.

AMYTIS. And are all the Carthaginians so—so extremely warm-blooded?

FABIUS. They're all utterly ruthless. When they enter the city, not one of our women will escape.

AMYTIS. It ought to be quite an experience for the women of Rome.

FABIUS. You must leave the city at once, Amytis.

AMYTIS. And how about you, Fabius?

FABIUS. I am prepared to die—but I am a man.

FABIA. And I, too, am prepared to die. I am a Roman! Here I was born, here I have lived and borne children, here I shall die.

AMYTIS (*rises*). Well, I am *not* prepared to die! I am not a Roman. I was not born here—and I have certainly borne no children, here or anywhere else. I shall go to Ostia and join my mother.

SCIPIO (*scornfully*). Spoken like a true Greek.

AMYTIS. Oh, I know it, Scipio—I'm a contemptible coward, but I can't help it. I love life, even monotonous life, and I can't bear to part with it. . . . Do you feel bitterness against me, Fabius, because I am not as brave as your mother?

FABIUS. No, Aymtis—but it would be beautiful if we were to die together.

AMYTIS. I'm sorry, Fabius, but that's not my idea of beauty. I must confess that I shudder at the thought.

FABIA (*coming forward*). At last I have an excuse to tell you what I think of you. I've tried to see the best in you, because you were my son's wife. But there is no best in you. You, who were honored with the love of a good man, have thrown it aside, flippantly. You have put on the airs of a goddess, and displayed the morals . . .

FABIUS. Mother!

FABIA. I hate you—I hate you—and I'm glad that the clean streets of Rome are not to be soiled with your vile blood.

FABIUS. Mother! You mustn't say such things to Amytis. She's sensitive.

AMYTIS. No, Fabius, I'm not sensitive. I don't mind. In fact, I'm glad that your mother has finally had the chance to deliver herself on this subject. It's been worrying her for a long time. I've noticed that.

FABIA. Oh, you've pulled the wool over my poor son's eyes. You've fooled him, all right, with your artificial beauty and your false Athenian superiority. Now, thank the gods, he sees you as you are—a heartless, soulless traitor!

(FABIUS *forces her into a chair at the left.*)

AMYTIS. I may be a traitor to Rome, but am not a traitor to my own convictions. I didn't start this war. I've never given it my support or encouragement. I have no axe to grind with Hannibal. Why should I sacrifice my life merely because the Roman army has failed to subdue a weaker enemy?

FABIUS (*wearily*). If you feel that way about it, you'd better go.

AMYTIS. I'm afraid I must, Fabius. You wouldn't want me to stay and be—whatever you call it, would you?

FABIUS. Don't speak of it, Amytis. It's unthinkable.

AMYTIS. Yes—one must draw the line somewhere. . . . Varius, go bring out the horses—the fastest horses in the stable.

VARIUS. Yes, my lady. (*He dashes out.*)

AMYTIS. Meta, come and help me make ready for the journey. We mustn't waste a moment.

FABIA. Luckily, Rome does not have to suffer because of your cowardice.

AMYTIS. Yes, mother—and Rome would gain nothing by my bravery if I were to stay and offer up my beautiful white body. . . . Come on, Meta. (*She and* META *go out at the left.*)

FABIUS. Go see if you can help her, mother.

FABIA. I'll do nothing of the kind. I shall go to the kitchen, and with my own hands I shall prepare some broth for you, my son—my true, Roman son. (*She embraces him and goes out at the right.*)

FABIUS (*in desperation*). I can't face this calamity, Scipio. Somehow, it doesn't seem right. The gods know we've done nothing to deserve this.

SCIPIO. Hannibal is greater than the gods. We may despise him as an enemy—we may do all in our power to discredit him—but no Roman sword will ever cut the laurel wreath of genius from his brow. (*The rattle of the bolt on the street door is heard.*)

FABIUS. I could well afford to see Hannibal, laurel wreath and all, at the bottom of the Tiber. (*Enter* SERTORIUS, *an elderly senator, and* DRUSUS, *an equally elderly general. They greet* FABIUS *formally.*) Have you heard the terrible news from Cannæ?

DRUSUS. All Rome has heard it by now. Every house in the city is draped with mourning for the dead, and great crowds are gathered in the market-place, weeping hysterically and sending up cries for mercy to the gods.

FABIUS. It will do them no good. The gods are in Hannibal's camp today.

SERTORIUS. There is no telling what horrors the people may commit in their madness. What are we to do?

FABIUS. What *is* there to do? Hannibal holds us in the hollow of his hand.

(TIBULLUS *comes in, followed by* CATO. TIBULLUS *is obviously agitated.*)

TIBULLUS. You must take decisive action, Fabius. You must *do* something!

FABIUS. If we could only delay for a few days, we might recall our army from the siege of Capua.

TIBULLUS. Delay is out of the question. Hannibal will attack before morning!

DRUSUS. We couldn't possibly get our army back from Capua in less than two weeks.

SERTORIUS. By that time, Rome will be a mass of smoking ruins.

FABIUS. I suppose it's hopeless.

(AMYTIS *enters, followed by* META, *who carries a large bundle.*)

AMYTIS. Good evening, gentlemen. I hope that you are all enjoying this fine day.

SERTORIUS. Unfortunately, the smoke of Hannibal's campfires interferes with the view.

AMYTIS. Well, I must be off for the sea coast, to spend a quiet holiday with my mother. I hope to find you all here when I get back.

FABIUS. Amytis! How can you be so callous?

AMYTIS. Can you blame me for being cheerful in the face of danger? You might try it yourself. If Hannibal should march into Rome, and find you all laughing, he might forget what he came for and join in the merriment.

SCIPIO. Hannibal does not laugh.

(VARIUS *enters from the left.*)

VARIUS. The horses are ready, my lady.

AMYTIS. Then we must start.

FABIUS (*tremulously*). Good-bye, Amytis. I'm afraid I shall never see you again.

AMYTIS. Don't say that, Fabius. Hannibal hasn't conquered Rome yet. There is still hope.

FABIUS. Hope is a poor defense against the Numidian cavalry.

AMYTIS. It's the only defense you have, isn't it?

FABIUS. Yes, I suppose so. We're doomed.

AMYTIS. Had you ever thought of treating with Hannibal?

DRUSUS. What do you mean?

AMYTIS. I mean—why don't you go out, under a flag of truce, meet Hannibal and talk the thing over in a civilized manner. He sounds to me like the type of man who might listen to reason.

FABIUS. I wonder if he would?

SCIPIO (*indignantly*). Nonsense! Hannibal talks only on the field of battle, with words of steel. The Roman does not live who can argue with him successfully there.

DRUSUS. Scipio is right. We'll have to fight it out.

SERTORIUS. We can at least show him that Romans know how to die. (*From a distance, the faint sound of many drums is heard, beating rhythmically, ominously.*)

FABIUS (*starting*). What's that?

SCIPIO. It's the drums—the African war drums.

TIBULLUS (*hysterically*). O, gods of Rome—save us! Save us!

FABIUS. The gods can't hear you, Tibullus.

AMYTIS. In that case, I had better hurry. I don't even know how to die gracefully. . . . (FABIA *enters from the right.*) Good-bye, my husband. Don't eat too much starchy food while I'm away. Good-bye, mother. Good-bye, gentlemen. Good-bye, good-bye. . . . (*She goes out with the two slaves at the left.* FABIA *is still standing at the right, gazing after the departed* AMYTIS.)

FABIUS. Now let's get down to business. (*He sits down, surrounded by the others. The sound of the drums becomes slightly louder, more emphatic.*) We must concentrate our infantry outside the city walls, prepared to withstand the first shock of assault . . .

FABIA. Fabius . . .

FABIUS (*paying no attention*). Our cavalry, such as it is, can be held within the city, prepared to make a sortie through the east gate when the situation becomes desperate . . .

FABIA. Fabius . . .

FABIUS (*still not listening*). You, Drusus, will take command of the infantry on the left . . .

FABIA (*louder*). Fabius!

FABIUS. And you, Scipio. . . . What is it, mother?

FABIA. Did you notice anything about Amytis when she left?

FABIUS. She seemed to be in a hurry.

FABIA. Did you notice anything strange in her appearance?

FABIUS (*impatiently*). No, I did not.

FABIA. She was wearing that new green silk dress!

FABIUS (*not interested*). She was, was she? . . . Now, if Hannibal attacks up on the right, you, Scipio, will move forward to meet him in pitched battle. If he concentrates on the left. . . . The—the green dress, eh! Isn't that a rather strange costume for travelling. . . . (*In the distance, the war drums continue to beat their weird tattoo as the*

CURTAIN FALLS.)

ACT TWO

Three bugle calls are heard—the curtain rising during the third call.

The scene is HANNIBAL'S *headquarters in a temple, about a mile east of Rome. The temple, normally open, has been converted into a sort of tent by means of rich, crimson draperies, which form the background of the scene. These draperies have been parted so as to form a wide entrance, upstage and slightly to the right, through which the Italian landscape is dimly visible. Characters coming through this entrance walk up two steps to reach the stage.*

There is another entrance at the extreme right, downstage. At the left, downstage, a corner of the inner temple juts out. This is used as HANNIBAL'S *sleeping quarters, and is entered through a door. There is a fourth entrance, upstage left, between the corner of the inner temple and the draperies at the back.*

To the left, and slightly upstage, is a huge column; there are two other columns, of equal size, at either side of the main entrance, although these are largely masked by the draperies.

At the right are a triangular table and two chairs, painted in weird colors and designs. By the column, at the left, are a chair and a massive chest. There is another chest at the back, to the left of the main entrance.

It is night—an hour later than the conclusion of Act I—and two braziers are burning dimly, one at the left and another at the right.

Although the scene is a Roman temple, and although it is probable that HANNIBAL *did not carry many household effects with him on his long march, strict realism and logic may be sacrificed for purposes of dramatic effectiveness in this scene. The barbaric splendor of Carthage itself must be reflected in all the trappings in this distant camp; the audience must feel that the action of the play has shifted from the virtuous but unimaginative simplicity of Rome to the Oriental opulence of its enemies.*

The headquarters guard, consisting of a CORPORAL *and five stalwart Carthaginian privates, is lined up for inspection by the* SERGEANT, *who is examining their breastplates and swords to see that the metal is well polished, and their hands and faces to make sure that they are clean.*

The SERGEANT *is a rough, husky, brutal veteran, whose counterpart is to be found on every drill ground from Quantico to Aldershot.*

The GUARDSMEN *are fine, upstanding soldiers—young, vigorous, confident, and cheerful. By their immediate appearance, they must suggest an emphatic contrast to the hopeless depression of* FABIUS *and the other old men in Rome. There is an eloquently triumphant air about them. In their speech they are tough and hard-boiled, exactly in the manner of the corporals in "What Price Glory," it being not unreasonable to assume that professional soldiers twenty-one hundred years ago did not differ materially from the professional soldiers of today. Their uniforms are neat, but they show signs of long and arduous wear.*

The SERGEANT *passes down the line, starting with the* CORPORAL *at the left, and ending with the* FIRST GUARDSMAN *at the right. He inspects the swords and equipment of the men. One helmet is on crooked; the* SERGEANT *unceremoniously straightens it.*

At the table sits THOTHMES, *the Egyptian clerk, a wizened little old man who laboriously inscribes characters with a brush on sheets of papyrus, paying no attention to the others.*

SERGEANT (*to the* FIRST GUARDSMAN). Look at the rust on that sword. Haven't you been in the army long enough to know how to keep your arms clean?

FIRST GUARDSMAN (*very weakly*). Yes, Sergeant. I cleaned it thoroughly this morning. It got rusty during dinner.

SERGEANT. During dinner! Were you *eating* with it?

FIRST GUARDSMAN. No, Sergeant. I was cutting oranges. You can't imagine how those oranges stain the steel.

SERGEANT. Never mind about the oranges. See that it's clean before the chief gets here. If he catches you with a sword like that, you'll do a turn with the elephants.

FIRST GUARDSMAN. Yes, Sergeant.

(*The* SERGEANT *notices something about the* SECOND GUARDSMAN'S *face. He steps up to him for closer scrutiny.*)

SERGEANT. Did you wash your face?

SECOND GUARDSMAN. Yes, Sergeant.

SERGEANT. When? While we was crossing the Alps, I suppose. . . . It's about time you went over it again.

SECOND GUARDSMAN. Yes, Sergeant.

SERGEANT. Now listen to this, you men. The commander-in-chief is inspecting the army, and he'll be through any minute now. There's going to be a meeting here of the general staff, Hannibal, Hasdrubal, and all the rest. You've got to be on the job, do you get that? You'll act as runners when you're needed. You'll be in charge, Corporal, 'till I get back.

CORPORAL. Yes, Sergeant.

SERGEANT. Keep two of the men on post outside headquarters, and see that the rest behave themselves. (*He addresses the* FIRST GUARDSMAN.) And *you*—don't you litter up this place with no orange peels, neither.

FIRST GUARDSMAN. No, Sergeant.

(*The* SERGEANT *stalks out, this being the signal for general relaxing by the guardsmen.*)

THIRD GUARDSMAN (*sweetly*). Good-bye, Sergeant. Come back soon.

(*The* CORPORAL *steps out of line and faces the squad.*)

CORPORAL (*to* FOURTH *and* FIFTH GUARDSMEN). You men follow me. The rest of you, fall out. (*He goes out at the left with the two guardsmen. The other three break ranks and sit down.*)

FIRST GUARDSMAN (*drawing his sword and exhibiting it*). Look! He calls that rusty.

THIRD GUARDSMAN. Well, I wouldn't exactly call it spotlessly clean myself.

FIRST GUARDSMAN (*polishing his sword*). It's a fine army, all right. They expect you to mop up the whole of Italy and keep clean at the same time.

THIRD GUARDSMAN. That's all right. You heard what the Sergeant said about the chief. If *he* catches you with a rusty sword, you'll be doing a turn with the elephants.

FIRST GUARDSMAN. I don't do no turn with no elephants, see? Not while old Hannibal is running this army. I'm Hannibal's little favorite, I am. He's very, very fond of me. Hannibal wants me right here on headquarters staff where I can look out for him.

SECOND GUARDSMAN. I'm certainly glad to hear that. I always wondered who was really the brains of this army.

THIRD GUARDSMAN. Just the same, I'd arrange to keep that knife clean, if I was you. Them elephants need a lot of attention—and Hannibal don't like to have 'em neglected.

SECOND GUARDSMAN. Sure. He put his own brother in command of the elephant brigade, didn't he? His own brother.

FIRST GUARDSMAN. Oh, I know why Mago got that assignment. Hannibal didn't want anyone to think he's playing favorites. He gives his own brother the rottenest job in the army just to show how impartial he is.

THIRD GUARDSMAN. I've felt sorry for the poor kid. He's been wet nursing those damned elephants now for two years.

FIRST GUARDSMAN. At first, he seemed to be fond of 'em.

SECOND GUARDSMAN. Yeh—I was with the elephant brigade when we was quartered on the Rhone. Well, it seems that there was some sort of funny business among the elephants, and one of the females got—you know—in a family way . . .

THIRD GUARDSMAN. She *did?*

SECOND GUARDSMAN. Well, we got orders to move across the river, and young Mago comes up to the chief and says, "Hannibal," he says, "we can't move yet. One of my elephants is about to become a mother." And Hannibal says, "That's interesting, but what are we going to do about it? Do you think we ought to hold up the army 'till the child is born?" And young Mago says, "Yes, brother, I think we should, because that elephant ought not to be moved, not in her condition." Well, sir, Hannibal tried not to laugh, and he finally told the kid, "Mago," he says, "we've got a very important war on our hands, and however much we may sympathize with this poor, wayward elephant, I'm afraid we can't afford to wait for her. . . ." You know how long it takes an elephant to come across, don't you?

FIRST GUARDSMAN. No.

SECOND GUARDSMAN. Seven years!

THIRD GUARDSMAN. We'd have been there yet. . . . I guess young Mago has felt sorry sometimes that he *is* Hannibal's brother. The chief keeps his eyes on him too much. Mago would like to have some fun with the women like the rest of us, but Hannibal won't let him.

FIRST GUARDSMAN. Hannibal thinks his own brother ought to be above such things.

THIRD GUARDSMAN. Ah—the chief don't know what it is to have a good time.

FIRST GUARDSMAN. Well, it's all right with me, as long as us privates can have it —when we can get it.

SECOND GUARDSMAN. If you ask me, Mago and the rest of the officers ain't been missing much. The women around here in Italy are terrible. They ain't got no originality at all!

THIRD GUARDSMAN. Just wait 'till I get back to Carthage!

FIRST GUARDSMAN. Yes—just wait. We've been on the road for four years now, and it don't look as if this war would ever be over.

THIRD GUARDSMAN (*sauntering over to the right*). Don't you worry about that. This war is over now. (*He points out at the right.*) Do you see what's over there on them hills? Do you know what that is? That's Rome! That's the place we've come all this way to get—and we're going to get it! When we've cleaned up that job, we're all going home.

SECOND GUARDSMAN. Don't talk to me about Rome. It's the biggest disappointment of my life. Why, I expected to see a real city, with big palaces, all made out of marble and gold and jewelry. I thought I'd take home enough souvenirs to keep me and the missus in luxury for the rest of our lives . . . and just look at the little dump! We'll be lucky to pick up a square meal in the whole town.

FIRST GUARDSMAN. It's your own fault, soldier. You *would* see the world.

(*The* THIRD GUARDSMAN *has wandered over to the table where* THOTHMES *is writing. He looks over the Egyptian's shoulder.*)

THIRD GUARDSMAN. What are you writing at now, Gyppy?

THOTHMES (*in a very deliberate, precise manner*). I am compiling the official record of the battle of Cannæ.

SECOND GUARDSMAN. You've got a fine job, Gyppy. We fight the battles, and you write 'em.

THOTHMES. *Some*body has to do this work in the army.

FIRST GUARDSMAN. Yes—and they always manage to find some damned Egyptian to do it.

THIRD GUARDSMAN. And somebody else has to do the dirty work—and wouldn't you know they'd pick on me for a job like that!

THOTHMES. You young men should realize that these records of mine have intense historical value. I have here the entire story of Hannibal's march.

SECOND GUARDSMAN. Don't talk to me about history. I'm getting pretty damned sick of parading around the world making history for somebody else to read.

THIRD GUARDSMAN (*looking about him*). Say—what kind of a place is this, anyway?

FIRST GUARDSMAN. It's a temple, ain't it, Gyppy?

THOTHMES. It's the temple of the Vestal Virgins. Each year the Roman High Priests select six maidens to guard the sacred flame——

THIRD GUARDSMAN. Vestal Virgins, eh! (*He starts toward the door, left.*) Well—let's have a look around. (*He opens the door and peers in.*)

SECOND GUARDSMAN. He lookin' for virgins. *There's* an optimist—You'd better keep out of there, soldier. That's Hannibal's sleeping quarters. (*The* THIRD GUARDSMAN *closes the door hurriedly.*)

(*Enter the* CORPORAL.)

CORPORAL. Watch yourselves, boys. Old Hasdrubal is coming up the hill. There's going to be one of them conferences here. 'Tshun! (*He salutes as* HASDRUBAL *strides in.* HASDRUBAL *is the second in command of the Carthaginian army—a dark, ominous, explosive, fire-eating cavalry officer, who moves with a jerky rapidity that indicates intense nervous energy. He glares at the three guardsmen.*)

HASDRUBAL. Is Hannibal here yet?

CORPORAL. No, sir. He hasn't come yet. He's down . . .

HASDRUBAL (*barking out his words*). What are you men doing here? Why aren't you out making yourselves useful?

CORPORAL. We were posted here by the

Sergeant, sir.

HASDRUBAL (*with withering sarcasm*). Oh—I see. This army is being commanded by sergeants, eh?

CORPORAL. That seems to be the general impression, sir—among the sergeants.

HASDRUBAL. You can convey my humble apologies to the Sergeant. Tell him I thought you might be more useful digging latrines, or any other damned thing you can think of. But DON'T STAND AROUND! Do you grasp that?

CORPORAL. Yes, sir.

HASDRUBAL. Very well, then. Get out!

CORPORAL. Yes, sir. Hup! (*The* CORPORAL *and the three guardsmen march out.* HASDRUBAL *turns to* THOTHMES, *who is still writing laboriously.*)

HASDRUBAL. And you, too. You'll have to find some other place to do your home work.

THOTHMES. But I was told . . .

HASDRUBAL. Never mind what you were told. I'm telling you something else. Get out!

THOTHMES. Very well, sir. (THOTHMES *gathers up his sheets of papyrus and his writing utensils.*)

(HASDRUBAL *sits down at the table and spreads out a map, which he proceeds to study.*)

(CARTHALO *and* MAHARBAL *enter.* CARTHALO *is a rough, bluff old warrior;* MAHARBAL *is a gaunt, hard, cynical strategist.*)

(THOTHMES *goes out, with an apprehensive glance toward* HASDRUBAL.)

CARTHALO. Hello, Hasdrubal. Is the chief here yet?

HASDRUBAL. No, there was no one here but some damned guardsmen. They told me they couldn't leave because they'd been posted by a sergeant. . . . Oh, how I hate staff sergeants!

MAHARBAL. We've got to have sergeants, Hasdrubal. That's just one of the many inconveniences of war.

CARTHALO. The chief has been down inspecting my division. He certainly does look tired.

MAHARBAL. He's been through the whole army since we pulled in this afternoon, examining the equipment and the food and talking to the men.

HASDRUBAL. I wish I had his patience. It seems to be a physical impossibility for me to talk to a private without losing my temper.

(*Enter* MAGO *wearily. He is* HANNIBAL'S *younger brother—a personable youth, well set up and handsome. At the start of the campaign, he had been terribly enthusiastic and overwhelmed by the craving for adventure, but most of the thrill has worn off by now. Nevertheless, he is still fresh and jaunty, with an irrepressible self-assurance.*)

CARTHALO *and* MAHARBAL. Hello, Mago . . .

MAGO. Hello, Hasdrubal—hello. . . . (*He sinks down wearily on a chair at the left.*)

CARTHALO. Well, Mago—how are the elephants?

MAGO. Don't speak of those damned elephants. I've just had 'em bathed, and fed, and their tusks polished. I've put 'em to bed, and sung 'em lullabies . . . and I'm tired out.

HASDRUBAL. Did you see Hannibal?

MAGO. Oh, yes. He's just been down inspecting us. He wants to make sure that the dear elephants are entirely comfortable.

CARTHALO. Never mind, Mago. You'll have your reward tomorrow. You and your elephants will be able to march into Rome.

MAGO. Do we go in tomorrow? Are we that near?

HASDRUBAL. Of course we are. There's Rome right over there.

MAGO (*jumping up and going to look*). So that's Rome, is it? It isn't so much, after all.

MAHARBAL. I wouldn't be too sure that we're going into Rome tomorrow.

HASDRUBAL. Why not? Why should we delay?

MAHARBAL. Hannibal may decide not to occupy the city just yet. He received a message from Capua today, asking for help. There's a Roman army there besieging our allies.

HASDRUBAL (*enraged*). Well, who gives a good goddam for our allies? We've come all this way to destroy Rome, haven't we? And now's our chance, isn't it?

MAHARBAL. You know Hannibal. He makes his own decisions for himself. He doesn't ask our advice.

CARTHALO. He doesn't need it.

HASDRUBAL. Hannibal is insane if he turns away from Rome now. The city is ours. They have only two legions to defend it. We could walk in this minute . . . and if we fail to destroy Rome now, you know what'll happen in Carthage, don't you? They'll turn against Hannibal. He'll be discredited—stripped of his power. . . . Oh, he can't make a mistake like this.

(*The* SERGEANT *is heard, off-stage, to shout "'Tshun!" The four officers snap to it and salute stiffly as* HANNIBAL *enters.*)

(HANNIBAL *is tall, thin, dark—quiet and surprisingly unemphatic in his speech—rather diffident in his manner. He is obviously terribly tired, but he has trained himself to such a point that he can readily ignore fatigue. He is the sort of man who is apparently none too powerful physically, but manages to exist on an inexhaustible supply of reserve strength. He provides not only the brains which direct his army, but the vitality which animates it. He is regarded with absolutely unqualified respect by his officers and men alike; his mildest whisper is instantly obeyed.*)

(HANNIBAL *returns the salute, and then removes his helmet and sword, which he hands to* BALA, *a gigantic Nubian slave, who follows him.* BALA *goes out at the left.*)

(HANNIBAL *walks to the table and sits down, relaxing easily in the chair.*)

HANNIBAL. Have you been looking at Rome?

MAGO. Yes, sir. It's not very impressive.

HANNIBAL. You'll have a closer view tomorrow.

HASDRUBAL (*excitedly*). Are we going in?

HANNIBAL. We attack the city on the morning.

HASDRUBAL. Thank the gods! We're going in at last!

(*The four officers are obviously delighted at the prospect.*)

MAHARBAL. I was afraid you might decide to turn off and raise the siege of Capua.

HANNIBAL. Capua can wait. The men need a little rest and recreation after all they've been through. The destruction of Rome will be in the nature of harmless diversion.

CARTHALO. Are we going to burn Rome to the ground?

HANNIBAL. I suppose so. That's what we came for, isn't it?

HASDRUBAL. Of course, it is! We'll show those damned Roman upstarts that they can't dispute the supremacy of Carthage. When we get through with Rome, there'll be nothing left of it but a memory.

HANNIBAL (*thinking of something else*). Nothing left but a memory.

MAGO. I suppose the elephant brigade, as usual, will miss all the fun.

HANNIBAL. On the contrary, Mago, the elephants will lead the procession into the city. I want you to put on your finest uniform, comb your hair, and shave carefully, because we expect you to look your best. We must convince these Roman upstarts, as Hasdrubal calls them, of our importance.

MAGO. I'll have those elephants painted every color in the rainbow.

HANNIBAL. I wouldn't exactly overdo it. We want the Roman citizens to think that we're an army. We mustn't look too much like a circus parade.

HASDRUBAL. They know we're an army, all right. They found that out at Lake Trasimenus and Cannæ.

HANNIBAL. Don't boast about your victories, Hasdrubal. You can save them for your wife when you get home.

HASDRUBAL. Damn it all, sir, you don't seem to get any satisfaction out of anything. You ought to feel proud that our army has beaten the Romans whenever we've met them. You ought to be like the rest of us and celebrate a victory, now and then. Sometimes, by the gods, I actually think you don't care whether we win or lose.

(HANNIBAL *stands up, and walks slowly across the stage during the following speech.*)

HANNIBAL. It's not quite as bad as all that, Hasdrubal. I *do* care whether we win or lose. I suppose it's the only thing I have to care about in the whole world. . . . But—if we win a victory, that's that. We have to go on to the next battle, then the next, and the next, until we've finished this war. Then we go home to Carthage and start looking for another.

MAHARBAL. You ought to take a rest, sir.

HANNIBAL. That's just the trouble with victory, Maharbal. You can't rest. You're only allowed to quit when you're losing. . . . Look at those seventy thousand Roman soldiers we butchered at Cannæ. They don't care now whether Rome is destroyed or not. Their work is done. They're at liberty to take a rest—a long rest.

HASDRUBAL. They can have their rest.

I'd rather go on fighting.

HANNIBAL. Of course, Hasdrubal. You're a soldier, and a damned good one. You live on cavalry charges, flank movements and counter-attacks; it's your whole existence.

HASDRUBAL. How about yourself, sir? I haven't noticed *you* signing any peace treaties.

HANNIBAL. I know it. But then, I have my oath to think of—undying hatred of Rome. I have had that with me ever since I was nine years old, and I can't very well get rid of it until there's no more Rome left for me to hate.

CARTHALO. That's the proper spirit, sir. It's much easier to kill a man if you hate him.

HANNIBAL. Very true, Carthalo, very true. I never thought of you before as a philosopher.

MAHARBAL. Have you any orders for tomorrow, sir?

HANNIBAL. Never mind them now, Maharbal. They're very simple, and we can talk them over in the morning. We all need some rest tonight.

MAHARBAL. You need it most of all, sir. How long is it since you've had any sleep?

HANNIBAL. Oh, I don't remember. What difference does it make?

MAHARBAL. It would make a great deal of difference to this army if you wrecked your health.

CARTHALO. We couldn't go on, sir.

HASDRUBAL. Don't be a damned fool, sir. For the love of Ba-al, take care of yourself.

HANNIBAL. I thank you, gentlemen, for the vote of confidence, but I can assure you that there's no cause for alarm. I fully expect to survive the destruction of Rome.

MAGO. After that's over, we can all go home, can't we?

HANNIBAL. I hope so.

MAGO (*reflectively*). I wonder what it will feel like to be back in civilian clothes.

HANNIBAL. You gentlemen can get back to your units, now. See that the men don't sit up all night drinking. They must get some sleep.

HASDRUBAL, MAHARBAL, *and* CARTHALO. Yes, sir. (*They salute and go out.* MAGO *stays behind.*)

MAGO. Can I stay for a while, Hannibal? I get so damned lonely down there with nobody to talk to except the elephants.

HANNIBAL. Yes, Mago, I want you to stay.

MAGO. Have you heard anything from home lately?

HANNIBAL. Yes—I got a letter from mother today. It was sent through Capua and forwarded on here.

MAGO. What does she say?

HANNIBAL. Oh, not much. Everything's just about the same in Carthage. They're all delighted at our victories . . .

MAGO (*bitterly*). Yes—they're so delighted that they won't do anything to help us. They expect us to get along without reinforcements or supplies or money. I wish some of those damned politicians could see what it's like over here. It might change their attitude about war a little.

HANNIBAL. I think we can manage without their assistance. (*He rings the gong.*)

MAGO. What else does mother have to say?

(BALA *enters.*)

HANNIBAL. She says that Uncle Hamilcar fell down and broke his hip again. . . . Here, do you want to read it? (*He hands* MAGO *the letter.*)

MAGO. Thanks.

HANNIBAL (*to* BALA). We'll have supper here whenever it's ready.

(BALA *bows and goes out.*)

HANNIBAL (*to* MAGO). I'm going to try to get clean. Call me when supper's ready. (HANNIBAL *goes out at the left.* MAGO *stands, reading the letter. The* SERGEANT *enters briskly and salutes.*)

MAGO. What is it, Sergeant?

SERGEANT. We've caught a spy, sir.

MAGO. Well, what of it? Cut his heart out.

SERGEANT. It isn't a he, sir. It's a woman.

MAGO. What sort of a woman?

SERGEANT. A young woman, sir. She says she's a Roman lady. Not bad-looking, either.

MAGO. Bring her in.

(*The* SERGEANT *goes to the back and calls, "Bring 'em in, Corporal." The* CORPORAL *enters with* AMYTIS, VARIUS, *and* META, *accompanied by the* FIRST *and* SECOND GUARDSMEN, *who have their swords drawn.* MAGO *continues to read the letter, paying little attention to the prisoners.*)

MAGO (*to* AMYTIS). They tell me you're a spy.

AMYTIS. Why, no, sir, I'm not exactly a spy—I . . .

MAGO. Who are those others?

AMYTIS. They're only my slaves—a delightful young couple from Sicily.

MAGO. Where did you find these people, Sergeant?

SERGEANT. Our sentries picked 'em up, sir. They was prowling around outside the camp—said they was refugees from Rome and got lost.

AMYTIS. We were trying to escape from the city, and took the wrong road.

MAGO. That sounds highly improbable. Have you anything more to say for yourself?

AMYTIS. I beg your pardon. Are *you* Hannibal?

MAGO. I am not.

AMYTIS. I didn't really think you were.

MAGO. I happen to be Hannibal's brother, in case you're interested.

AMYTIS. Where is Hannibal? I should love to meet him.

MAGO. I'm afraid that I must deny my brother that pleasure. Sergeant, take these damned Romans out and put 'em to death. (*The* SERGEANT *steps forward to seize* AMYTIS, *but hesitates when she speaks.*)

AMYTIS. To death! But you can't do that —it—it isn't fair.

VARIUS. You have no right to kill her. She's not an ordinary Roman, she's . . .

AMYTIS. Hush, Varius. (*To* MAGO.) I should like to know who gave you authority to sentence me to death, without a hearing, with no attempt at justice.

MAGO. You know the penalty. You took your chances when you came to spy on us.

AMYTIS. But I didn't . . .

MAGO. You're a Roman, aren't you?

AMYTIS. Of course, I . . .

MAGO. That's all I need to know. You're a Roman, an enemy of Carthage. You were caught snooping around within our lines. You'll have to die.

AMYTIS. Can't I even say a word in my own defense?

MAGO. You've said too much already.

AMYTIS. And I can't see Hannibal?

MAGO (*vehemently*). No! You can't see Hannibal. He has enough to worry about without having to listen to you.

AMYTIS. I suppose I shall have to take your word for it. (*She turns to* VARIUS *and* META.) I'm sorry that you must die.

META (*clasping* VARIUS' *hand*). We're not afraid.

AMYTIS. Of course you're not, you poor things. Roman slaves haven't much to live for.

VARIUS. But you—my lady—you're not ready to die.

AMYTIS. I'm always ready, Varius. . . . But it *is* a nuisance. . . . If I'd only stayed in Rome, I should have been acclaimed a heroine by my husband and Scipio and all those stuffy old Senators. Now, I must sacrifice my life and get no credit for it.

MAGO. We don't ordinarily bury spies with military honors, but we might make an exception in your case.

AMYTIS. I'm sure you'll do the right thing.

MAGO. All right, Sergeant.

SERGEANT. Hup! (*The* SERGEANT, CORPORAL, *and* GUARDSMEN *start to lead* AMYTIS, VARIUS, *and* META *out.*)

MAGO. Just a minute. Have you searched these people, Sergeant?

SERGEANT (*turning to* CORPORAL). Have you searched these people, Corporal?

CORPORAL (*turning to the* GUARDSMEN). Have you searched these people?

FIRST GUARDSMAN. Have you searched these people?

(*The* SECOND GUARDSMAN *turns his head slightly to see whether there is anyone to whom he can pass the buck.*)

SECOND GUARDSMAN. No, sir!

FIRST GUARDSMAN. No, sir!

CORPORAL. No, sir!

SERGEANT. No, sir!

MAGO. Then search 'em quickly. They may have despatches concealed.

(*The* CORPORAL *and the* GUARDSMEN *start to search* VARIUS *and* META. *The* SERGEANT *starts to search* AMYTIS.)

AMYTIS. Do I have to be pawed by this man?

MAGO. Never mind, Sergeant, *I'll* do the searching. (*The* SERGEANT *leads* AMYTIS *before* MAGO, *who starts to pat her all over, in the manner of a detective frisking a yegg for his gun.* MAGO *stands so that his back is to the left of the stage, which* AMYTIS *faces.* AMYTIS *giggles hysterically.*) What are you laughing at?

AMYTIS. You're tickling me!

(MAGO *completes the search without results, but he still holds* AMYTIS' *shoulders in his hands. He surveys her with interest.*)

MAGO. You know—you're rather beautiful.

AMYTIS. I always try to look my best when going to an execution.

MAGO (*significantly*). Maybe there won't be any execution, after all. Maybe

I'll take you down and show you the elephants. (*At this moment* HANNIBAL *comes in quietly at the left. He sees* MAGO *and* AMYTIS *in the center of the stage,* VARIUS, META, *and the soldiers at the back.* AMYTIS *sees him over* MAGO's *shoulder, but* MAGO *goes right on talking.*) You know, I've been waiting for a long time for someone like you to visit our camp. Hannibal won't let us officers associate with women who are our social inferiors, but you seem to be real aristocracy, as these things go in Rome. . . . Why do you keep poking me?

(AMYTIS *points to* HANNIBAL. MAGO *turns around, sees his brother, and starts guiltily away from* AMYTIS.)

MAGO (*lamely, as he salutes*). We caught a spy, sir—a Roman spy.

HANNIBAL. I was wondering . . .

AMYTIS. You're Hannibal, aren't you! (*A statement rather than a question.*)

HANNIBAL. I am. (HANNIBAL *walks past her and crosses to the table. Presently* AMYTIS *follows him.*)

AMYTIS (*surveying him*). So you're Hannibal. . . . You're not the way I pictured you, at all.

HANNIBAL (*politely*). I hope I'm not a disappointment.

MAGO. We caught this woman redhanded, sir. She and these others were trying to sneak through our lines.

HANNIBAL. That was highly injudicious of you, madam—I mean, to be caught.

AMYTIS. I realize that now.

MAGO. I cross-examined her.

AMYTIS. He did not. He tickled me.

MAGO. It was my duty, sir, to search her person for any documents that might be of value. She chose to interpret my actions as a personal advance.

AMYTIS. He told me he was going to take me down and show me the elephants —(HANNIBAL *laughs.*) Scipio told me you never laugh.

HANNIBAL. Scipio has happened to encounter me only in my less mirthful moments. (*He sits down at the table.*) I must apologize for my brother, madam. He's very young, and has much to learn about the gentle art of soldiering.

AMYTIS. Oh, that's all right. I understand perfectly. (*To* MAGO.) You're forgiven.

HANNIBAL. In this delightful conversation that went on between you two, was any mention made of the possible penalty for espionage?

MAGO. Of course there was. I sentenced all three of them to death.

HANNIBAL. Is there any particular reason why this ceremony should be delayed?

MAGO (*looking at* AMYTIS). There certainly isn't.

HANNIBAL. In that case, Sergeant, you may proceed in the usual manner.

SERGEANT. Come on you! (*He starts to lead her out.* AMYTIS *breaks away from him, goes to the table at which* HANNIBAL *is sitting, and speaks directly to him.*)

AMYTIS. I'm not asking for mercy, Hannibal. I know that there is no such thing in war.

SERGEANT (*starting for her*). I told you to come with me.

HANNIBAL. Stand back, Sergeant. Let her talk.

AMYTIS. I'm ready to die—for the glory of Rome, or whatever it is we're fighting for now. I'm not afraid—no, I mean that. I'm really not afraid. That's not heroism, either. It's just the attitude of stoicism that comes to everyone, I suppose. You soldiers who have been in battle must know what I mean.

MAGO. Must we listen to all this?

HANNIBAL. Go on.

AMYTIS. In Athens, when men were condemned to death, they were granted one last request—provided, of course, that it was within reason. If they wanted a sumptuous repast, they could have it. Or they might crave a last hour with their loved ones. They could have that, too. . . . Some of these men were murderers, some traitors, but all were accorded the same final favor. It didn't amount to much—it cost the state nothing. But it did help to send those poor creatures out with a somewhat less anguished conscience. . . . That's what I ask of you, Hannibal—one final favor.

MAGO. Don't listen to her, Hannibal. She's a bad woman.

HANNIBAL. What is it that you want?

AMYTIS (*hesitantly*). I can't tell you before all these people.

MAGO. I thought not. I tell you, Hannibal, she's dangerous. I wouldn't listen to a word she says.

HANNIBAL. Dismissed, Sergeant. Take these prisoners with you.

SERGEANT. Yes, sir. Hup!

(VARIUS *and* META *are led out by the* CORPORAL *and* GUARDSMEN.)

AMYTIS. Nothing will happen to them . . .?

HANNIBAL. Sergeant, you will be responsible for the safety of the prisoners.

SERGEANT. Yes, sir . . . (*He salutes and goes out.*)

MAGO. Well—what is it?

AMYTIS (*to* HANNIBAL). Does *he* have to stay?

HANNIBAL (*smiling*). You can go, Mago.

MAGO (*ominously*). I wouldn't do this, Hannibal.

HANNIBAL. Don't worry, Mago. I think I can take care of myself. She doesn't seem to be armed.

MAGO. She doesn't have to be. (*He goes out. For an instant,* HANNIBAL *regards* AMYTIS *in silence. Then he motions her gracefully to a chair across the table from his.*)

HANNIBAL. Won't you—sit down?

AMYTIS. Thanks. (*There is an awkward pause after she has seated herself.*)

HANNIBAL. I don't wish to seem peremptory, but I happen to be quite busy these days, and I therefore urge that you come to the point with the least possible delay . . . you'll forgive me, won't you?

AMYTIS. Don't mention it. I . . .

HANNIBAL. And before you start, I wish to impress upon you the fact that this indignity, to which you are necessarily submitted, is not intended as a personal affront. Not at all. We have nothing whatever against you as an individual; at the same time, we can't possibly ignore your status as a representative of Rome. It's this way: there happens to be a war on just at present, the contending parties being Rome, on the one hand, and Carthage on the other . . .

AMYTIS. Oh, yes. My husband told me all about that to-day.

HANNIBAL. Your husband should have told you something else before sending you out on this mission, whatever it is. He should have explained that there is an ancient law of warfare which prescribes instant death for all those caught in the act of espionage. If we violated that law, we should ourselves be guilty of delinquency, and Carthage would undoubtedly be expelled from the Mediterranean League.

AMYTIS. I appreciate the difficulties of your position.

HANNIBAL. I hoped you would. . . . Now, if you will be so good . . .

AMYTIS. You assume that my husband sent me on this mission. Do you know who my husband is?

HANNIBAL. I'm afraid I don't.

AMYTIS. He is Quintus Fabius Maximus.

HANNIBAL. Fabius Maximus, eh. . . . One of the consuls.

AMYTIS. One of the consuls nothing. He's the dictator!

HANNIBAL. Oh, I hadn't heard. Congratulations.

AMYTIS. My husband didn't send me on this mission. In fact, he doesn't even know I'm here. He thinks I'm on my way to Ostia to join my mother. . . . You know what's going on in Rome, of course.

HANNIBAL. I hear occasionally from my agents in the city.

AMYTIS. So you use spies, too.

HANNIBAL. Oh, we all do. One of my finest officers is in Rome this minute, posing as a merchant from Antioch.

AMYTIS. You don't *say* so. . . . Why, I bought this dress from him. Do you like it?

HANNIBAL. Charming!

AMYTIS. He has probably informed you that you are not a particularly welcome guest in these parts. Why, today, when the cry of "Hannibal is at the gates" went up, the whole population turned out to curse you and the gods that brought you here.

HANNIBAL. The gods are blamed for everything.

AMYTIS. I don't want you to think that I'm disloyal to Rome. I'm not really a Roman at all. I was born in Athens, and for some reason I've never been able to understand the Roman ideals of civic virtue. They think I'm an awful coward. . . . This evening they asked me to stay and die like a true Roman. . . .

HANNIBAL. To stay and die? Is the situation as hopeless as all that?

AMYTIS. We may as well be frank with each other, Hannibal. You know that the defenses of Rome haven't a chance against your army, and the Romans know it even better than you do. They've been desperately afraid of you ever since you crossed the Alps.

HANNIBAL. I suppose I should feel flattered.

AMYTIS. You should. Today, young Scipio described you as a superman, a god, against whom mortal strength is of no avail. I heard him say it—and that's why

I'm here.

HANNIBAL (*puzzled*). That's why you're here?

AMYTIS. I wanted, for once in my life, to see a superman. . . . When I left Rome in disgrace, I had no intention of going to visit my mother. That was just an excuse—I led my slaves along the wrong road, deliberately. When your sentries captured me, they wanted to put me to death at once. I told them I had a message for Hannibal.

(BALA *comes in, bearing a huge tray laden with food for* HANNIBAL *and* MAGO. *He sees* AMYTIS, *looks at her curiously, and then sets the tray down on the table.*)

HANNIBAL. I haven't yet heard what that message is.

AMYTIS. Oh, food! How nice! I'm simply famished! It was very thoughtful of you to have supper for me, Hannibal.

(BALA *serves the meal, and then takes up his position by the column, upstage.*)

HANNIBAL (*elaborately polite*). I must apologize for the simplicity of the meal. We're living on army rations, you know.

AMYTIS. Army rations! Why, it's de*lic*ious! We never have anything as good as this in Rome. We have to deny ourselves all luxuries on account of the war. . . . What marvellous wine!

HANNIBAL. Yes, the wine is rather good. It's a Spanish wine that we brought with us. There's very little of it left, but we hope to replenish our supply tomorrow.

AMYTIS. In Rome? (HANNIBAL *nods,* AMYTIS *laughs.*) You won't find much of that in Rome . . . or anything else, for that matter.

HANNIBAL. You don't seem to be particularly patriotic.

AMYTIS. That's what my husband has been telling me for five long years.

HANNIBAL. Your husband, I take it, is a true patriot.

AMYTIS. Oh, one hundred per cent—at least.

HANNIBAL. He might be a trifle annoyed if he knew that you were having dinner with the arch-enemy of Rome.

AMYTIS. It takes less than that to annoy him. Poor Fabius! But I can always talk him out of it.

HANNIBAL. He must be very fond of you.

AMYTIS. Oh . . . I suppose so. It's never really been what you'd call an ideal love match. My father left me under Fabius' protection, and our marriage was the inevitable result. Not that I cared, particularly. Being only a half-breed Roman, I had no choice in the matter.

HANNIBAL. Have you never fallen in love with anyone?

AMYTIS. No. . . . I worshipped all the heroes of mythology, of course—but that doesn't mean anything.

HANNIBAL. Your husband must be a hero in Rome.

AMYTIS. Possibly. . . . I know I should have been more appreciative. He's been a good, kind, considerate husband. We've got along well together. He's had his interests and I . . . well, I suppose it's my own fault that I haven't had mine . . .

HANNIBAL. Any children?

AMYTIS. That's a subject we don't discuss.

HANNIBAL. I beg your pardon.

AMYTIS. Am I boring you with all this?

HANNIBAL. Not at all. It's a rare treat. We have so few opportunities for polite conversation in the army. . . . But I'm afraid that the Sergeant is growing a trifle impatient out there . . .

AMYTIS. I'd almost forgotten about the Sergeant. And my slaves, they're out there, too. Poor things—they must be dying of hunger. Couldn't you . . .?

HANNIBAL. Of course! Bala, see that supper is served for the two prisoners, at once. They won't have much more time!

AMYTIS. And some of that Spanish wine, too. They'd love that.

HANNIBAL. Yes, Bala—get them some of the Spanish wine, by all means.

(BALA *bows and goes out.*)

AMYTIS. I've completely forgotten what we were talking about.

HANNIBAL. As I remember, we discussed plans for putting you to death and you asked . . . that's it! You were going to ask for one final favor.

AMYTIS. Of course!

HANNIBAL. Are you ready now to issue a statement on that subject?

AMYTIS. Before I do, I should like to ask you just one question. It may seem like a rather trivial question, but I hope you'll answer it—not as a Carthaginian conqueror speaking to a Roman victim—but as one civilized human to another.

HANNIBAL. What is the question?

AMYTIS. It is this: Why have you done it?

HANNIBAL. Why have I done it? Why

have I done what?

AMYTIS. Oh, everything that you've done—fighting wars, winning battles . . . why?

HANNIBAL (*after a moment's pause*). That's a strange question.

AMYTIS. You must know the answer. You must have had some definite motive to inspire you.

HANNIBAL. But who cares about my motives? It's only my actual accomplishments that count.

AMYTIS. I care about your motives.

HANNIBAL. Why?

AMYTIS. I just happen to be curious, that's all.

HANNIBAL. I should think that my reasons would be fairly obvious. I came here to destroy Rome. Isn't that reason enough?

AMYTIS. Is it enough to satisfy you?

HANNIBAL. I can't see that that makes any difference.

AMYTIS. Oh—but it does. It makes an enormous difference. You know, some day you'll have to reason this thing out with yourself. Some day, you'll say to yourself, "Here, I've marched three thousand miles, and crossed mountains and things, and spilt a lot of blood—and what good has it done?" It would be most embarrassing if you suddenly realized that you'd been wasting your time.

HANNIBAL. I'm not supposed to think about such things. I'm a soldier. I have to content myself with a soldier's rewards.

AMYTIS. As, for instance?

HANNIBAL. Well—when I get back to Carthage, I shall receive medals, and testimonial documents, and I shall be the guest of honor at state banquets, and . . .

AMYTIS. Yes, and they'll give you the key to the city. I know all about that. My husband once was given the key to the city. We have it at home, somewhere. Take my word for it, it doesn't do you any good.

HANNIBAL. I suppose not. But it's a nice sentiment.

AMYTIS. So that's what you've been striving for—fighting for all these years. A nice sentiment!

HANNIBAL. If you choose to put it that way—yes.

AMYTIS. No. I don't believe it. You'll have to offer a better reason than that.

HANNIBAL. I'm beginning to sympathize with your husband. . . . By the way, what is your name?

AMYTIS. Amytis. But why do you sympathize with my husband?

HANNIBAL. I shouldn't care to live with a woman who asked so many questions.

AMYTIS. If you'd only give me an intelligent answer, I'd stop.

(HANNIBAL *rises and crosses to the left.*)

HANNIBAL. Perhaps I can't explain my actions.

AMYTIS. You don't even know yourself?

HANNIBAL. That question of yours disturbed me a little. . . I've asked myself that same thing so many times.

AMYTIS. I rather imagined that you had.

HANNIBAL. One morning we were camped on the banks of the Rhone River. It was swollen with the spring floods. I had to get my army across—eighty thousand infantry, cavalry, elephants—with all their supplies. We had no boats of our own; there were no bridges. Across the river, a howling mob of Gauls was waiting to slaughter us as we landed. From the south, a large Roman army was advancing to attack us. . . . I sent a small body of men upstream to get across as best they could and to attack the Gauls on their right flank. I was waiting for the signal from that detachment, and wondering whether I should ever set foot on the opposite bank. . . . As I stood there, I asked myself, "Why do I do this? Even if a miracle occurs, and we do cross the river, what then? What will we have gained?" I didn't know.

AMYTIS. But you did cross the river, didn't you, Hannibal?

HANNIBAL. Yes—we routed the Gauls, and tricked the Romans, and marched on to the Alps. . . . Have you ever tried to lead an elephant over a snow peak?

AMYTIS. No—that's one of the many adventures I've missed.

HANNIBAL. Our men, who were accustomed to the fierce heat of Africa, had to plod through the Alpine snows, many of them in their bare feet. They had to drag the elephants and all the machinery of war with them, while the natives pushed avalanches down on our heads. . . . When we came to the last line of mountains, and saw Italy spread out at our feet, I asked myself that same question. . . . I've never been able to find an answer. I've watched our men slaughter the Romans in one terrible battle after another. Through all these years, I've seen nothing but death—death—and I've never been able to find an answer. (*He crosses over to the right and stands gazing off toward Rome.*)

AMYTIS. Not even in the key to the city?

HANNIBAL. For ten years I've followed the road that leads to Rome—and it's a hard road to travel, Amytis. It's littered with the bones of dead men. Perhaps they know why they died. I don't.

(AMYTIS *rises and stands behind him.*)

AMYTIS. And now you've come to the end of that road, Hannibal. There's your goal—before you. You can see the lights of Rome clearly, can't you? Even the lights seem to tremble with fear of Hannibal. . . . They know that tomorrow they'll be snuffed out forever. . . . Poor little Rome . . .

HANNIBAL. The Romans think that I'm a cruel, merciless enemy. . . . Well, I am.

AMYTIS. You're terribly proud of that, aren't you?

HANNIBAL (*turning to face her*). Proud of what?

AMYTIS. Of the thought that you're cruel—merciless—a big, terrifying brute.

HANNIBAL. The Romans have inflicted that reputation on me.

AMYTIS. And you're trying hard to live up to it, aren't you?

HANNIBAL. I'm not sorry to have my enemies afraid of me.

AMYTIS. Do you want me to be afraid of you?

HANNIBAL. I should like it better if you were the least bit more respectful.

AMYTIS. Have you any idea why *I* came here?

HANNIBAL. I assume that you're a spy . . . if you are, your methods of gaining information are inexcusably crude.

AMYTIS. I'm not a spy. Can't you believe that? I didn't come here to learn any military secrets. This is nothing but a pleasure trip.

HANNIBAL. A pleasure trip! With swift, violent death staring you in the face?

AMYTIS. I saw the smoke from your camp this afternoon.

HANNIBAL. Well?

AMYTIS. I saw the smoke—and I decided that I should like to see the fire.

HANNIBAL. Evidently you didn't consider the possibility that you might be burned.

AMYTIS. Oh, yes—I thought of that! It made it all the more exciting.

HANNIBAL. You should have waited in Rome. There'll be fire there tomorrow—the fire of divine vengeance.

AMYTIS. Divine vengeance! So you're doing this as a special favor to the gods.

HANNIBAL. The gods are on our side. That's why we're winning.

AMYTIS. You mean, that's why the gods are on your side.

HANNIBAL. I suppose you know that that's sacrilege.

AMYTIS. Call it sacrilege or truth—it's all the same thing. . . . You're afraid of the truth, Hannibal. You're afraid to face it, because the gods tell you to look the other way.

HANNIBAL (*scornfully*). Are the gods afraid of the truth?

AMYTIS. Of course they are; and they don't want us mortals to be too intimate with it. When we know the truth, we can't know fear—and without fear, there can be no gods. . . .

HANNIBAL (*moving toward the gong on the table*). I'd better send for the Sergeant. You've lived long enough.

AMYTIS (*hastily*). No, Hannibal—not yet. I'm not quite ready to die.

HANNIBAL. Are you afraid—you who know so much about truth?

AMYTIS. I don't want to die until I have lived. That's perfectly reasonable, isn't it?

HANNIBAL. I can give you death—but I can't give you life.

AMYTIS. How do you know you can't?

HANNIBAL. I don't know what it is. I don't want to know.

AMYTIS. I do want to know. I came here because I was determined to find out.

HANNIBAL. Mago was right, Amytis—you're dangerous.

AMYTIS. That's what they said of me in Rome. But it isn't so. I'm not dangerous. I'm only real.

HANNIBAL. You might be dangerous to me.

AMYTIS. Because you're afraid I might make *you* real.

HANNIBAL. You can't do it. No one can. When I was a child, my father laid me on the altar of Ba-al and consecrated me to the destruction of Rome. Since that moment, I've never been an individual—I've been a force, divinely inspired to crush the enemies of Carthage.

AMYTIS. You're using the gods again—as an excuse for your own murders

HANNIBAL. Those who kill for the glory of the gods are not murderers.

AMYTIS. Who told you that? One of the high-priests, I suppose.

HANNIBAL. Ba-al himself has spoken to me. Throughout my life I have been driven forward by his voice, saying, "Go on, Hannibal, go on, with sword and flame, until you have destroyed the glory of Rome."

AMYTIS. That wasn't the voice of Ba-al, Hannibal. That was the voice of the shopkeepers in Carthage, who are afraid that Rome will interfere with their trade. . . . Hatred, greed, envy, and the passionate desire for revenge—those are the high ideals that inspire you soldiers, Roman and Carthaginian alike . . . and when you realize the shameful futility of your great conquests, you turn around and attribute it all to the gods. . . . The gods are always convenient in an emergency . . .

HANNIBAL (*slightly nettled*). What, may I ask, is the object of all this conversation? Do you think you can talk me away from Rome?

AMYTIS. I don't care *what* happens to Rome. I'm trying to find something in you, something great, something noble, something exciting.

HANNIBAL. And you expect to accomplish this by insulting me, by calling me a rotten murderer, blaspheming my gods.

AMYTIS. Good! You're getting angry at last. That's an encouraging sign!

HANNIBAL. I'm beginning to entertain an extreme dislike for you. If you'll forgive me for saying so, you're becoming something of a pest.

AMYTIS. I've tried to be interesting.

HANNIBAL. You've succeeded in being exceptionally irritating. I don't want to hear any more. You'll have to die.

AMYTIS. Right this minute?

HANNIBAL. Yes. I'll be glad to get it over with.

(*In the subsequent speeches,* AMYTIS *betrays signs of tremulousness. Much of her amazing assurance is gone.*)

AMYTIS. But isn't this very unusual?

HANNIBAL. The execution of an enemy? No, I'm sorry to say that it is entirely according to regulations.

AMYTIS. Oh, I know that. But you ought not to kill me at once. without—without——

HANNIBAL. Without what? I've given you a meal, I've answered your damned questions—what more can I do?

AMYTIS. There's a certain—a certain ceremony to be gone through with, isn't there?

HANNIBAL. What sort of a ceremony?

AMYTIS. But it—it's so embarrassing to put it into words.

HANNIBAL. I'll count five. If you can't find words in that time, I'm afraid the subject—whatever it is—will have to remain closed forever. . . . One. . . . Two. . . . Three. . . . You'd better hurry. . . . Four. . . .

AMYTIS. I can't say it, Hannibal. You'd better call the Sergeant.

(*There is a long pause, while* HANNIBAL *studies her expression of mute but eloquent desperation.*)

HANNIBAL. Oh! (*He backs away from her.*) Is *that* the ceremony you had in mind?

AMYTIS. But no soldier ever kills a woman until he . . . and es*pec*ially if she happens to be attractive.

HANNIBAL. You rather fancy yourself, don't you?

AMYTIS. Naturally, I shouldn't have come here at all if I had been lacking in a certain amount of self-confidence.

HANNIBAL. I'm sorry to disappoint you. I should have been delighted to justify your confidence if the circumstances had been more favorable for a—an event of this kind.

AMYTIS. More favorable! How could any circumstances be more favorable. Here you are—alone, in the night—with your triumphant army behind you, with Rome cringing at your feet. Here you are, Hannibal—and here am I!

(*He makes a step forward, toward her, and for a moment there is the suggestion that he has weakened. But he braces himself, and again steps back.*)

HANNIBAL. I'll have to decline your kind offer and put you to death . . . and this time you won't be allowed to talk your way out of it. (*There is a piercing shriek off-stage at the left, followed by an incoherent rumble of gruff voices.* META *dashes in from the left. She is sobbing hysterically.* AMYTIS *rushes to her and takes her in her arms, attempting to calm and comfort her.*) What is it? What's happened?

META (*wildly*). Varius—save him . . .

AMYTIS (*to* HANNIBAL). You gave me

your word . . .

(VARIUS *rushes in, considerably dishevelled. He is followed by the* SERGEANT *and the* FIRST *and* SECOND GUARDSMEN.)

HANNIBAL. What is this, Sergeant?

SERGEANT. He started a fight, sir . . .

VARIUS (*breathlessly*). One of the soldiers tried to attack her . . .

AMYTIS (*gasping with rage*). What did he do?

META (*between sobs*). He tried to carry me away with him . . .

VARIUS. I went after him, my lady . . .

AMYTIS. I hope you killed him.

VARIUS. I knocked him down.

META. Then I ran here . . .

AMYTIS. You poor darling.

VARIUS. Then they all went after me.

AMYTIS (*to* HANNIBAL). Is this the way your men obey orders?

HANNIBAL (*to the* SERGEANT). I told you that you were to be responsible . . .

(MAGO *breezes in.*)

MAGO (*briskly*). What's all this?

AMYTIS (*flaming*). *You* were the one. *You* attacked her—you *beast!*

MAGO (*startled*). Why, I did *not.* I . . .

AMYTIS. Don't try to lie out of it. I know your licentious ways.

MAGO (*bewildered*). Why—I don't even know what happened. How could I . . .

AMYTIS. You'd have done the same thing to me if Hannibal hadn't stopped you.

MAGO (*to* HANNIBAL). What *is* going on here, anyway?

HANNIBAL. I should like very much to know. Sergeant, who attacked this girl?

AMYTIS. *He* did it. I know he did it—the beast!

MAGO. I'm *not* a beast.

HANNIBAL. Never mind about that. What happened, Sergeant?

AMYTIS. He's a disgrace to the army!

SERGEANT. It was one of Hasdrubal's men, sir.

MAGO. There! Do you hear that?

SERGEANT. He crept up in the darkness, sir, when we wasn't looking, and tried to carry her off.

(META *breaks out with a fresh burst of sobs.* AMYTIS *still holds her in her arms and comforts her.*)

AMYTIS. There, there, dear—it's all right. He can't touch you now. (*She looks at* MAGO *as she says this.*)

MAGO. Will you please be quiet and listen to the Sergeant?

SERGEANT. This man (*referring to* VARIUS) went after her before we knew what was up, and we figured we'd better get him calmed down before he tried to fight the whole army.

HANNIBAL. Where is the soldier who committed this indiscretion?

SERGEANT. He ain't woke up yet, sir.

AMYTIS. Good for you, Varius!

VARIUS. I lost my temper, my lady.

MAGO. Well—are you satisfied that it wasn't I?

AMYTIS. I wish it had been.

HANNIBAL. The soldier will be put to death, Sergeant.

MAGO. For a little thing like that?

HANNIBAL. It's not a little thing. Misconduct of this sort is not to be tolerated. There's been too much of it in our army. It's got to stop! (*As he says this, he glances meaningly at* AMYTIS.)

AMYTIS. You're quite right, Hannibal. That sort of thing ought to be discouraged.

HANNIBAL. You may go, Sergeant.

SERGEANT (*indicating* VARIUS *and* META). And how about them, sir?

HANNIBAL. Take them with you.

SERGEANT. Come on.

META (*quailing*). I—I'm afraid.

VARIUS. You mustn't be afraid, Meta. I won't leave you.

HANNIBAL. You'll wait for my orders, Sergeant. In the meantime, these prisoners are to be guarded more carefully. Do you understand?

SERGEANT. Yes, sir.

VARIUS. Come on, Meta. (*He puts his arm about her and leads her out, followed by the* SERGEANT *and* GUARDSMEN.)

AMYTIS. If anyone so much as lays a finger on her, I—I'll . . .

MAGO. You'll do *what?*

AMYTIS. Oh—are you still here?

MAGO. Yes—but I'm going. And you're coming along with me. Isn't she, Hannibal?

HANNIBAL. Yes, you can take her out.

AMYTIS. Is it all over, Hannibal? Am I going to die?

HANNIBAL. You're going to die.

MAGO. Come on. (*He takes her toward the steps.*)

AMYTIS (*turning*). You'll be sorry, Hannibal. (*She turns and is about to go down the steps.*)

HANNIBAL. Wait a minute, Mago.

MAGO. We mustn't delay any longer.

HANNIBAL. Bring her here.

MAGO. You haven't changed your mind?

HANNIBAL. Give me your sword. (MAGO *draws his sword, a long dagger, and hands it to* HANNIBAL.) I'm going to kill her myself. I'll send for you when it's over.

(*There is a shrill bugle call. Outside, the* CORPORAL *is seen changing guard. When this is over, the* CORPORAL *stands by the curtains at the back, prepared to lower them.*)

MAGO (*crestfallen*). Can't I stay and watch?

HANNIBAL. Go on, Mago.

MAGO (*to* AMYTIS). It's an honor to die by the hand of Hannibal. Perhaps you deserve it. (*There is a note of admiration in his voice. He goes out. The* CORPORAL *lowers the curtains, and as he does so the lights are dimmed.* HANNIBAL *and* AMYTIS *face each other.*)

HANNIBAL. You've called me a murderer. You say that I glory in my reputation for cruelty. Now I'm going to justify that reputation. I shall give you the final satisfaction of knowing that Hannibal, the merciless conqueror of Rome, is not a myth. . . . Come here . . .

(*She advances to him, slowly but without hesitation. He clutches her throat with his left hand. His right hand holds the dagger.*)

AMYTIS. Why do you choose to have me die, this way?

HANNIBAL. I couldn't trust Mago to do this. You might have told him some of the things you have told me. He might have weakened.

AMYTIS. Yes—Mago is a man. You, of course, are a god. . . . Perhaps some day you'll discover that you're a man, too, Hannibal—and not ashamed to weaken. . . . . Perhaps, some day, you'll realize that there's a thing called the human equation. It's so much more beautiful than war.

HANNIBAL. The human equation does not interest me.

AMYTIS. Because you don't know what it is. If you could ever find it, you'd know that all your conquests—all your glory—are only whispers in the infinite stillness of time—that Rome is no more than a tiny speck on the face of eternity—that the gods are the false images of the unimaginative . . . and then you'll wish that all that you've done could be undone.

HANNIBAL. Where can I go to find this human equation?

AMYTIS. It is here—on earth—not on the heights of Olympus.

HANNIBAL. Perhaps I'll find it—but never with you. You must die. (*He is very close to her.*)

AMYTIS. War is death, Hannibal. Rome is dying, Carthage is dying—but we're alive. . . . You can conquer men, Hannibal. You can conquer armies. But you can't conquer life.

HANNIBAL. You must die.

AMYTIS. Go out and destroy the wind, Hannibal. Destroy the stars, and the night itself—if you can. Then come back and kill me.

(*A bugle is heard, blowing the Carthaginian version of "taps"—softly, slowly.*)

(HANNIBAL, *using all his strength, tries to thrust her away from him and lifts the dagger higher, preparing to plunge it in her heart. She clings desperately to his arms.*)

HANNIBAL (*his voice now tremulous*). You're going to die!

AMYTIS. Yes—I'm going to die . . . but not until to-morrow. . . . (*Her face is close to his—too close. He kisses her.*)

(*Presently,* AMYTIS *draws away from him and gazes, unsmilingly, into his eyes.* HANNIBAL *raises the sword, thinks better of it, and throws the sword away, vehemently. Again he seizes her in his arms and kisses her.*)

CURTAIN.

ACT THREE

(*The Scene is the same as ACT II—the time, early the following morning.*)

(*There is a roll of drums as the curtain rises.* MAHARBAL, CARTHALO, *and* HASDRUBAL *are grouped around the table, in conference. The* SERGEANT *and the* FIRST *and* SECOND GUARDSMEN *are at the back.*)

MAHARBAL. Wouldn't it be wise to assemble some siege machinery before we start?

HASDRUBAL. Machinery be damned! The Romans know they're beaten already—that's the main thing. We don't need machinery to break down resistance that doesn't exist.

CARTHALO. The Roman walls are thick.

We'll need battering rams at least.

HASDRUBAL. I suppose you think you know more about it than Hannibal does. If he wanted any battering rams, he'd make 'em.

MAHARBAL. Then it will be up to the infantry to storm the walls.

HASDRUBAL. You won't need the infantry after I've attacked.

CARTHALO. Our infantry has the right to occupy the city first. We've earned that privilege.

(HANNIBAL *enters from the left and stands behind the column, so that he is unseen by the others.*)

MAHARBAL (*hotly*). How about my men? Do you think we're going to follow the cavalry in?

HASDRUBAL (*even more hotly*). What are you talking about? The Numidian cavalry corps is going in first, and by the gods . . .

CARTHALO (*cutting in*). They will not! The infantry has done all the heavy work in this war . . .

HASDRUBAL (*cutting in*). The heavy work, eh! Who did the heavy work at Trasimenus—who did the heavy work at Cannæ—who . . .

MAHARBAL (*cutting in*). The infantry, not the cavalry. We deserve to go into Rome first.

CARTHALO. Of course we do. You always want all the honors for your damned cavalry.

(HANNIBAL *steps from behind the column.*)

SERGEANT. 'Tshun! (*He and the three officers salute.*)

CARTHALO. You can settle this, sir.

HANNIBAL. Settle what?

HASDRUBAL. It's these damned infantry officers, sir. They think they're going to occupy the city first. The infantry!

MAHARBAL. It's the infantry's job. The cavalry is only supposed——

CARTHALO. And besides, my men can be trusted to do it right. They——

HANNIBAL. I think this can be settled without bloodshed.

HASDRUBAL. The cavalry goes in first.

MAHARBAL. The infantry won't stand for it.

HANNIBAL. We'll do it this way. You'll attack the city from the west, Hasdrubal. You attack from the south, Carthalo, and you from the north, Maharbal. We can send Mago against the east gate. All the Romans will concentrate there, to watch the elephants. The rest of you will break in easily.

CARTHALO. But which of us is to go in first?

HANNIBAL. You can all start at the same time—and the first one to reach the Forum—will win a prize.

HASDRUBAL. What is the prize?

HANNIBAL. I'll have to decide about that later. In the meantime, you can fall your men in.

MAHARBAL. Yes, sir.

HANNIBAL. Wait for further orders.

CARTHALO. Yes, sir.

(*The three of them salute and go out.*)

HASDRUBAL (*as they go*). The cavalry will go in first!

CARTHALO. Not by a damned sight . . .

MAHARBAL. We'll see who wins that prize . . .

(*They are all talking at once as they disappear from view.*)

HANNIBAL. Pack up this equipment, Sergeant.

SERGEANT. Yes, sir! Get busy, you!

(*The* FIRST *and* SECOND GUARDSMEN *start to pack up the maps, armor, etc., placing them in a large chest, which they carry out.*)

HANNIBAL. Have your men ready in half an hour.

(BALA *comes in bearing a tray of food, which he deposits on the table.*)

SERGEANT. Full marching order, sir?

HANNIBAL. No. Put their packs on the wagon.

SERGEANT. Yes, sir. (*He salutes and goes out.*)

HANNIBAL. Get your kitchen packed up, Bala. Then come back here and get my things. (BALA *bows and starts.*) And Bala . . . send those Roman slaves in to me.

(BALA *goes out.* HANNIBAL *is standing by the table, eating bread and drinking wine, this being his hasty breakfast. The change in his manner must be apparent: he is now gay, buoyant, carefree, and reluctant to concentrate on the serious business at hand. He has the air of one who doesn't much care whether school keeps or not. He glances toward the left.* VARIUS *and* META *come in, hesitantly. Their hands are tightly clasped, as though they are clinging to each other in the face of a common danger.*)

VARIUS. You sent for us, sir?

HANNIBAL. Yes! You're wanted in there.

(*He nods toward the left.* VARIUS *and* META *go out.*)

(*During this, and subsequent scenes, there is almost constant movement outside the temple. The* GUARDSMEN *pass to and fro, hurriedly, carrying equipment of various kinds. There must be the sense of intensive action—of rapid but systematic preparation for the battle that is imminent.*)

(MAGO *comes in quietly at the back, leans against one of the pillars, folds his arms, and looks at* HANNIBAL, *who is still standing, hastily gulping his breakfast.* MAGO *is attired in a shiny new uniform.*)

MAGO. Well . . . ?

HANNIBAL (*turns and sees* MAGO). Oh, hello—Mago.

MAGO. You're a *fine* example, you are. (*He comes down stage.*) What have you got to say for yourself now?

HANNIBAL. Nothing, Mago. It would take years to explain this.

MAGO. You're darned right it would.

HANNIBAL. What did you think had happened last night?

MAGO (*indignantly*). What did I think had happened! What else *could* I think? I stood out there, for hour after hour, waiting for you to send for me.

HANNIBAL. You shouldn't have waited.

MAGO. When I finally looked in here, the room was empty. . . . Even my own supper was all eaten up.

HANNIBAL (*with a glance toward the left*). She ate it.

MAGO. Of all the damned outrages!

HANNIBAL. You can eat breakfast here, if you want, to make up for the supper you missed. The army moves in half an hour.

MAGO. The elephants are ready.

HANNIBAL. And incidentally—perhaps it would be just as well if . . .

MAGO. Oh, don't worry about that. I won't say a word.

HANNIBAL (*laughing*). Thanks.

MAGO. I can't understand it, Hannibal. It's the first serious mistake you've ever made.

HANNIBAL. I've made many mistakes, Mago—but this isn't one of them. (*He goes out, munching an apple.*)

(*A bugle call is heard.*)

(MAGO *sits down at the table and starts to eat. He chuckles to himself.* AMYTIS *comes in through the door at the left. She is wearing the Phœnician nightgown, and a brilliant blue cloak. She passes behind the column, going to the right to gaze out after* HANNIBAL. MAGO *has not seen her. She turns to him.*)

AMYTIS. Good morning.

(MAGO *starts.*)

MAGO (*with no enthusiasm*). Oh! Good morning.

AMYTIS. Having breakfast?

(AMYTIS *is also a changed person. There are no evidences of her cheerful flippancy. She is langourous, meditative, reserved.*)

MAGO. Yes. . . . Can't I persuade *you* to have a little something to eat?

AMYTIS. Thanks, I will. (*She sits down at the table with* MAGO *and joins in the repast.*) What were you laughing at when I came in?

MAGO. I was just thinking what Rome will look like tonight, after we've finished with it.

(*Another bugle call is heard.*)

AMYTIS. There'll be nothing left, will there?

MAGO (*finishing a mouthful*). Nothing. First, we'll slaughter the men. When we've got them out of the way, we'll start plundering and see what we can pick up in the way of loot. After that, we'll set fire to the houses. . . . And then . . .

AMYTIS. Oh, I know what comes next.

MAGO. Exactly. After we've disposed of everything else, we'll turn to the women. . . . Are there any attractive women in Rome?

AMYTIS (*after a moment's thought*). Oh —any number of them. A trifle unimaginative, perhaps—but still, attractive.

MAGO. Do you think they'll be attracted to me?

AMYTIS. I don't quite see how they can avoid it. After all . . .

MAGO. Oh, I know what you mean. You mean, they won't dare refuse.

AMYTIS. That's about it, isn't it?

MAGO. Personally, I don't like that sort of thing—force, I mean. I like to feel that it's sort of—sort of mutual. Do you understand?

AMYTIS. I do, indeed.

MAGO. I mean to say—I like to think that they're giving in cheerfully.

AMYTIS. There's no question of that. You look magnificent in that gorgeous new uniform.

MAGO. Do you really think so? As a matter of fact, I've been saving that up for the entry into Rome. (*He stands up and draws himself to his full height.*) Today, the women of Rome will feast their eyes on a real Carthaginian soldier.

AMYTIS. I'm sure that the women of Rome will be duly appreciative.

MAGO (*sitting down again*). Hannibal will probably make me change back to my old uniform. He's always telling me not to show off.

AMYTIS. Tonight, when you run wild in Rome, will Hannibal join in the general merriment?

MAGO. If you'll allow me to say so, I think Hannibal has started that already.

(*The* SERGEANT *comes in quickly and salutes.*)

SERGEANT. Beg pardon, sir.

MAGO. What is it?

SERGEANT. Some Romans, sir.

(MAGO *springs up.*)

MAGO. Some *Romans?* Attacking?

SERGEANT. No, sir. It's a delegation of 'em, under a flag of truce.

MAGO. Send for Hannibal, quick! He's down conferring with Hasdrubal.

SERGEANT. Yes, sir. (*He goes to the back and calls out to the* THIRD GUARDSMAN.) Hey, you! (*The* THIRD GUARDSMAN *appears.*) Run down to Hasdrubal's tent and tell the commander-in-chief that there's a delegation of Romans here—and make it fast!

(*The* THIRD GUARDSMAN *dashes off.*)

MAGO (*turning to* AMYTIS). Do you know anything about this?

AMYTIS. I haven't the faintest idea what . . .

MAGO. It's some damned trick, and you're part of it. Are they armed, Sergeant?

SERGEANT. Oh, no, sir. We went all over 'em carefully.

MAGO. What did they say?

SERGEANT. They just said they'd like to see the commander-in-chief.

MAGO. Did you get their names?

SERGEANT. Only the leader—said his name was Fabius Maximus.

AMYTIS (*terrified*). My husband! (*She jumps up.*)

MAGO. A—ha! So you *do* know something?

AMYTIS. I've got to get out of here. (*She hurries toward the left.*)

MAGO. You'd better not try to communicate with your husband.

AMYTIS (*hastily*). Don't worry. I won't. (*She goes out through the door.* MAHARBAL *appears at the back.*)

MAGO (*muttering*). Damn her soul. I'd like to . . .

(MAHARBAL *comes in.*)

MAHARBAL. What do you suppose they want?

MAGO. I don't know. It looks pretty suspicious.

MAHARBAL. They'd better not try any of their tricks on Hannibal.

SERGEANT. Shall I bring 'em, sir?

MAHARBAL. Yes, bring them in.

(BALA *unobtrusively removes the breakfast tray and goes out.*)

CARTHALO (*entering*). The runner just told me.

MAHARBAL. Is Hannibal coming?

CARTHALO. Yes.

MAGO. I tell you, Maharbal, we'll have to stand by Hannibal now.

MAHARBAL. Nonsense. This doesn't mean anything. These Romans are just making a last desperate attempt to save themselves.

CARTHALO. It's their only hope.

MAGO (*desperately*). But I tell you, Hannibal is not himself. . . . He . . .

MAHARBAL (*reassuringly*). Calm down, Mago, calm down. It'll be *all* right. Hannibal is still Hannibal.

(*The* SERGEANT *appears. There is a roll of drums, which continues until* HANNIBAL's *entrance.*)

SERGEANT. This way . . .

(FABIUS *enters, followed by* SCIPIO, DRUSUS, *the* CORPORAL, *and four* GUARDSMEN. *The Romans salute; the Carthaginians return the greeting. The* GUARDSMEN, *with swords drawn, take up positions by the columns at the back, remaining there, rigidly at attention, throughout the ensuing scene.*)

(FABIUS *is obviously nervous, moving as one who expects to be stabbed in the back at any moment. He looks apprehensively toward* MAGO, MAHARBAL, *and* CARTHALO, *who are at the right.* SCIPIO *also regards them, but there is a belligerent flash in his eye. He had objected strenuously to this attempt at compromise, and during the parley he shows his impatience and dissatisfaction with the whole proceeding.*)

FABIUS (*clearing his throat*). Which of you is Hannibal?

CARTHALO. Hannibal will be here directly.

MAHARBAL. You're wasting your time, Romans. You'd better go back and defend your city.

SCIPIO. Do you hear that, Fabius? He's right!

DRUSUS. Hush, Scipio! Let Fabius do the talking.

SERGEANT. 'Tshun!

SCIPIO. There he is!

(HANNIBAL *enters, followed by* HASDRUBAL. *The Carthaginians and Romans salute, sharply.* HANNIBAL, *very erect and very serious, confronts his enemies.*)

HANNIBAL. Which one of you is Fabius Maximus?

FABIUS (*pleased*). I am.

HASDRUBAL (*barking*). When you speak to Hannibal, say "Sir!"

HANNIBAL (*gazing intently at* FABIUS). So you're Fabius Maximus. . . . That explains a great deal. (*He sits down at the table. The others remain standing.*)

HASDRUBAL. Come on, speak up! What do you want?

FABIUS. We came here under a flag of truce. We felt that we might talk this over in a civilized manner.

HANNIBAL. I can see no objection to that.

FABIUS (*getting over his first nervousness*). Here you are, Hannibal, at the gates of Rome, with a mighty army—an admirable army. Even though we are your enemies, we'll cheerfully admit that.

HASDRUBAL. Never mind the soft soap. What do you want?

FABIUS (*expanding*). For years, Rome and Carthage have been at each other's throats, in a death struggle, gentlemen, a death struggle. Thousands upon thousands of men—on *both* sides—have sacrificed their lives. It has all been most unfortunate. Just at present, the conflict seems to have reached what I may reasonably call a crisis.

HANNIBAL. You are not overstating it.

FABIUS. As I have already pointed out, here you stand at the gates of Rome, confronting our army, which is of sufficient strength to defend the city for months.

HASDRUBAL. That's a damned lie. You couldn't hold out for an hour.

HANNIBAL. Never mind that, Hasdrubal. . . . Go on . . .

FABIUS. You may not realize the full strength of our defending force. We now have, within the city, twenty war-strength legions, fully armed and prepared . . .

HASDRUBAL. Don't listen to him, Hannibal. Twenty legions! Do you expect us to believe that? Why, you have two legions, at the outside, and home guard at that. There's not a man in 'em who isn't a great-grandfather, at least.

HANNIBAL. Keep quiet, Hasdrubal. I'll hold up our end of the conversation. . . . Now, what else have you to offer?

FABIUS. I need not enlarge upon the physical advantages of our position. You must know that the walls of Rome are practically impregnable.

HANNIBAL. Well?

FABIUS. Well, then—what will be gained by a long, arduous, painful siege? Nothing, my dear sir, but acute suffering on both sides. We will sacrifice the lives of many gallant young soldiers, and so will you. And at the same time, there are the innocent victims to be thought of—the women, and the little children. What of them? This is not their war, Hannibal. They didn't start it. They have no axe to grind with you. . . . Why must they be made to pay the terrible price of pitched battle?

HANNIBAL. What do you suggest we do about all this?

FABIUS. I suggest that you abandon the idea of capturing Rome. The attempt would cost you heavily and would be doomed to ultimate failure.

HASDRUBAL. In other words, we're to lay down our arms and go home. (*He laughs heartily.*)

FABIUS. Oh, no—not exactly that. We realize that the war must be brought to a logical conclusion. But we do suggest that you move to some spot, not *quite* so near the city, where we can meet you honorably on the field of battle.

HASDRUBAL. How about those twenty legions of yours? Why don't you send them out here and let us fight it out?

FABIUS. We shall be glad to do that, in due time.

HASDRUBAL. Do you hear that? In due time! He wants us to wait until he can get his armies back from Capua and Spain. (HASDRUBAL, MAHARBAL, *and* CARTHALO *laugh.*)

HANNIBAL. Have you any further suggestions?

FABIUS. No—I think that's about all.

HASDRUBAL. Well, it isn't enough. If you think you can beg us off with a few hollow words, you're damned well mistaken. Our army is mobilized at this minute—forty thousand men, waiting for the order to move. Within an hour we'll have surrounded Rome—and then we'll see what sort of defense your twenty legions can put up.

SCIPIO (*bursting at this*). Twenty legions or not—we'll show you that we can fight better than we can talk!

DRUSUS. Keep out of this, Scipio. Leave it to Fabius.

SCIPIO. I can't keep out of it. I've fought against you, Hannibal, at Trasimenus and Cannæ, and by the gods, I'll fight against you again!

FABIUS Scipio—*please!*

SCIPIO. Hasdrubal is right. We can't stand them off with hollow words. We never should have come out here in the first place. Let them come to us.

DRUSUS. Hold your tongue, Scipio. You'll spoil everything.

HANNIBAL. I seem to detect a slight note of dissension.

FABIUS. Oh, no—not at all. Scipio just felt that it was unwise for us to talk this over with you . . .

HASDRUBAL. Scipio seems to be a real soldier. It's too bad you haven't more of them in Rome.

SCIPIO (*to* FABIUS). I told you not to listen to that damned woman. She put the idea into your head.

HANNIBAL (*interested*). What damned woman?

FABIUS. It was just a personal matter, I assure you.

SCIPIO. She was the one who suggested it.

HANNIBAL. Who was?

FABIUS. As a matter of fact, sir, it was my wife.

HANNIBAL. Oh! Your wife!

MAGO. I thought so. It was his *wife!*

HANNIBAL. Keep quiet, Mago.

FABIUS. She had the idea that you might consider this matter reasonably . . .

SCIPIO. She's a cowardly Greek, herself, and she succeeded in converting Fabius to her point of view.

HANNIBAL. Fabius must be a model husband. . . . But, after all, these domestic affairs are not of vital importance to us at the moment.

HASDRUBAL. You're damned right they aren't. Send these men back, Hannibal. The army is ready to attack. We can't wait.

HANNIBAL. We'll have to wait. I want time to think some things over.

HASDRUBAL. You don't have to give this a second thought—why, it's ridiculous on the face of it.

HANNIBAL. Nevertheless, I intend to think it over. . . . Mago, take these gentlemen down and show them the elephants. They might be interested.

FABIUS (*apprehensively*). You're not going to violate the flag of truce?

HANNIBAL. No—no. You'll be as safe here as you are in Rome . . . safer.

MAGO (*reluctantly*). Come on. (*He leads the three Romans out. They are followed by the* CORPORAL *and the* THREE GUARDSMEN.)

HANNIBAL (*to the other officers*). You gentlemen get back to your units. Be ready to move at a moment's notice.

HASDRUBAL. You're not going to be taken in by what those damned Romans said, are you? You can't delay the destruction of Rome another day. It would mean mutiny . . .

HANNIBAL. You heard your orders. (HASDRUBAL, MAHARBAL, *and* CARTHALO *go out. Three bugle calls are heard.*) You can wait outside, Sergeant.

(*The* SERGEANT *goes out.* AMYTIS *comes in.*)

AMYTIS. Don't believe a word of it, Hannibal. They haven't twenty legions in the city, or anything like it.

HANNIBAL. I know all that.

AMYTIS. Poor Fabius. I can just picture him brooding over that suggestion of mine. I made it quite casually. He probably worried about it all night, trying to persuade himself and Scipio and the others that I was right.

HANNIBAL. Why did you make that suggestion? Why did you think I'd listen to reason?

AMYTIS. I don't know. Why did I think so last night, for that matter?

HANNIBAL. You seem to guess right most of the time.

AMYTIS. I have one more favor to ask, Hannibal.

HANNIBAL. Is it as reasonable as the first one?

AMYTIS. It's about my slaves—I want them to go back to their homes—to be free. Will you take them with you?

HANNIBAL. Where do they come from?

AMYTIS. From Sicily.

HANNIBAL. I can send them there.

(AMYTIS *goes to the left and summons* VARIUS *and* META, *who come in at once.*)

AMYTIS. Hannibal is going to send you to Sicily. You're to be free.

META. Free—to go home?

VARIUS. And to be married?

AMYTIS. You'll be free to do anything you please.

HANNIBAL. You'll find Bala outside.

META. Good-bye, my lady—and thank you.

VARIUS. May the gods bless you for being good to us.

AMYTIS. Be good to each other—and forget that you were ever slaves in Rome.

META. We shall never forget you, my lady—or your kindness.

AMYTIS. Good-bye, both of you. I want you to be happy. (*They go out.*) I'm glad they're to be saved.

HANNIBAL. You too can be saved, Amytis—if you choose.

AMYTIS. If I choose?

HANNIBAL. Did you hear my conversation with your husband?

AMYTIS. Yes—I heard it all.

HANNIBAL. I delayed my decision—because I wanted to give you your choice. Last night, I should have put you to death. I shouldn't have listened to a word of protest or persuasion. But I did listen—and you didn't die. . . . This morning, it is different. . . . I can't destroy Rome until I know what your choice is to be. . . . I will spare your husband's life. You can go back to him, and I'll see that you both are allowed to escape—to go wherever you please . . . that's one part of your choice, Amytis.

AMYTIS. And the other part?

HANNIBAL. To go with me. To forget Rome—to forget Carthage—to be with me, forever . . .

AMYTIS. And if I agree to that part of it, will Rome be spared?

HANNIBAL (*emphatically*). No! Whatever your choice, Rome must be destroyed.

AMYTIS. Then I choose to go back to my husband. . . . Go ahead with your great work, Hannibal. Burn Rome to the ground; obliterate it. Keep your army here forever, to make sure Rome stays destroyed. Instruct your men to crush any blade of grass, any flower that dares to thrust its head above the ashes of the dead city. Prolong your victory. Glory in it till your dying day. . . . But don't ever look to me, or to my memory, for sympathy or applause.

HANNIBAL (*angrily*). I think I understand you at last. You came here to save Rome. If you fail in that, you're prepared to die. For all your talk, you care nothing for me.

AMYTIS. You mustn't believe that, Hannibal.

(*There is a shrill bugle call.*)

HANNIBAL. You thought you could save Rome from the destiny that is ready to overwhelm it! You have tried to build walls of words as a defense against my army.

AMYTIS. I'm not trying to save Rome, Hannibal. I'm trying to save you.

HANNIBAL. Why do you imagine that I'm worth saving?

AMYTIS. Because I want to have you—always—as my possession. Let Rome and Carthage remember you as a great general. I want to remember you as a conqueror who could realize the glory of submission.

HANNIBAL (*challenging*). And does Rome realize the glory of submission?

AMYTIS. No, and for that very reason Rome will destroy itself. Success is like a strong wine, Hannibal; give a man enough of it, and he'll drink himself to death. Rome will do that, too, if you leave it alone.

HANNIBAL. So I'm to leave Rome—and to leave you. Is that your choice?

AMYTIS. Yes, Hannibal—to leave me with something beautiful—something that is worth remembering. I don't want you to spoil that.

HANNIBAL. And what shall I have to remember? That I marched three thousand miles—and failed.

AMYTIS. Ah, but that's just the point, Hannibal. You haven't failed.

HANNIBAL. I came to conquer Rome. Anything short of that is failure.

AMYTIS. Are you sure of that? Are you sure that you didn't come all this way to find your own soul?

HANNIBAL. My own soul doesn't matter, Amytis. I myself amount to nothing. All of us amount to nothing. . . . We stand aside and watch ourselves parade by! We're proud of the brave manner in which we step forward, and of the nobility of our bearing, and the sparkle of divine fire that is in our eyes—and actually we have no more idea of where we're going, no more choice in the matter, than so many drops of water in a flowing river.

AMYTIS. Yes, and at the end of that river is an endless sea of things that are passed. It is called history. When you reach that sea, other drops of water may murmur respectfully, "Here comes Hannibal, the conqueror of Rome." But you won't care. You'll only be thankful for the interludes that you have known—the moments when you drifted from the main current and found peace and contentment in the deep, quiet pools.

(*They are standing close together, facing each other. With sudden, fierce strength,* HANNIBAL *takes her in his arms.*)

HANNIBAL. I'll turn away from Rome now, Amytis, if you'll come with me. . . . Rome can live, Amytis. You can save it . . .

AMYTIS. I don't want it to be that way . . .

HANNIBAL. I'll bury my sword before the gates of Rome. I'll hand over my command to Hasdrubal. I'll do the one thing I thought was impossible: I'll quit when I'm winning. But I can't do this alone . . . I can't . . .

AMYTIS. No, Hannibal. I don't want it to be that way. I don't want Rome to be saved because I made this choice . . . I want you to do it—to make the decision—to prove that you are stronger than your own victorious army . . .

HANNIBAL. If I recognize your truths, I'll have to believe that all my life has been wasted—that all those men who have fallen along the road to Rome have died for nothing. Do you want me to believe that?

AMYTIS. I do! I do! I want you to believe that every sacrifice made in the name of war is wasted. When you believe that, you'll be a great man. (*Gently, she strokes his hair.*) I want you to be a great man.

(*He kisses her, desperately.*)

MAGO (*offstage*). Hannibal! (MAGO *comes in, sees them embraced, and turns away.*)

(HANNIBAL *slowly relinquishes his grip on* AMYTIS *and steps back.*)

HANNIBAL. You were right, Mago. I should have let you put her to death without further delay.

MAGO. I'm glad you realize that at last. You see—I've had a lot more experience in these matters than you've had. I understand the risks.

HANNIBAL. Evidently.

MAGO. It isn't too late to punish her, even now.

(HANNIBAL *crosses to the table.*)

HANNIBAL. Perhaps it isn't too late. (*He beats the gong.*)

MAGO. The Romans are waiting for your decision.

(BALA *enters.*)

HANNIBAL. Send Thothmes here.

(BALA *bows and goes out.*)

MAGO. And the Romans?

HANNIBAL. Bring them here to me.

MAGO. Yes, sir. (*He goes out.*)

AMYTIS. I must go. My husband mustn't find me here—he—he'd die of shame.

(*The* FIRST *and* SECOND GUARDSMEN *enter, taking positions at either side of the main entrance.*)

HANNIBAL. Put that woman under arrest.

(*The two* GUARDSMEN *take her arms and hold her. She is at the left, upstage.*)

(THOTHMES *comes in.*)

AMYTIS. Hannibal—you can't do this. . . . Let me go!

THOTHMES. You sent for me, sir.

HANNIBAL. Have you your records with you?

THOTHMES. Yes, sir. They're all here.

(MAGO *comes in, followed by the* CORPORAL, *three* GUARDSMEN, *and the three Romans. As* FABIUS *enters,* AMYTIS *shrinks back, so that he does not see her at first.*)

HANNIBAL. Did you see the elephants?

FABIUS. Oh, yes, indeed. It was quite a treat.

DRUSUS. We don't see elephants around here very often.

(FABIUS *sees* AMYTIS.)

FABIUS. Amytis! (*He starts toward her, but the* CORPORAL *stops him.*) In the name of all the gods, what are you doing here?

AMYTIS. Fabius! I didn't want you to . . .

HANNIBAL (*harshly*). Our sentries arrested this woman. She represented herself as your wife.

FABIUS. She is my wife! Amytis, why did you come here?

HANNIBAL. She told me that she was concerned for your safety. She came to find you.

FABIUS. Amytis! My true, my loyal wife. Do you hear that, Scipio, she came to find *me!*

AMYTIS. I can't let you believe . . .

HANNIBAL (*quickly*). She evidently told us the truth. There is no reason why we should suspect the wife of Fabius Maximus. You may release her.

(*The* GUARDSMEN *release* AMYTIS *and she goes to* FABIUS' *side, standing before the column, where she remains until the end.*)

(HASDRUBAL, MAHARBAL, *and* CARTHALO *come in briskly, followed by the* SERGEANT.)

HASDRUBAL. The army is ready to attack.

HANNIBAL (*to* FABIUS). I'm issuing an order in which you may be interested.

FABIUS (*tremulously*). You're not going to . . .

HANNIBAL. The Carthaginian army will proceed at once to Capua.

HASDRUBAL (*wildly*). We're not going into Rome?

HANNIBAL. No—we are not.

HASDRUBAL. What in the name of all the gods is the matter with you? Have you lost every atom of judgment?

HANNIBAL. I've lost nothing, Hasdrubal—except a few perverted notions about various things. I could afford to lose those.

HASDRUBAL. I won't stand for it. Do you hear that? I won't stand for it! You can take your god-damned army to Capua. My cavalry will attack Rome this morning——

MAHARBAL. I'll go with you, Hasdrubal.

CARTHALO. So will I.

HASDRUBAL. There! Do you hear that? The two finest officers in your army. They know what it would mean to turn back now. They haven't lost control of their senses.

MAHARBAL (*angrily*). The trouble with you, sir, is that you know how to gain victories but not how to use them . . .

CARTHALO. Hasdrubal is absolutely right, sir. You'd better do as he says . . .

(*Both men are speaking at the same time, so that there is a jumble of angry voices.*)

FABIUS. Gentlemen—gentlemen! Might I say a word?

HASDRUBAL. Shut up!

HANNIBAL. So you propose to destroy Rome by yourselves?

HASDRUBAL. We do—and by the gods, we'll take you with us. You've led us all this way. And you'll see it through, if we have to force you into it at the point of a sword.

(HASDRUBAL *draws his sword and confronts* HANNIBAL.)

HANNIBAL (*quietly, but with tremendous emphasis*). Hasdrubal—you'll do as I say.

(HASDRUBAL *steps back a pace.*)

HASDRUBAL (*hoarsely*). We can't do it, Hannibal. Even if we gave the orders, the men wouldn't move away from Rome now. After four years of steady fighting, they won't be cheated out of their reward.

HANNIBAL. You and Maharbal and Carthalo and all the others in this army have the misfortune to be soldiers. You can't break away from the habit of obedience. You'll do as I say.

HASDRUBAL. Don't put that order through, Hannibal. Don't—*don't!* It'll be the end of all of us—of Carthage itself—and a rotten, humiliating end, too.

HANNIBAL. The army moves to Capua at once. Go tell your men to fall in.

HASDRUBAL. I've never disobeyed an order, Hannibal. What's more, when you've given me a command, I've never even stopped to ask why you gave it. I've accepted everything from you, as though it were the word of Ba-al himself. . . . But this is different. I won't move from this spot until you tell me why we are turning away from Rome.

HANNIBAL (*vaguely*). Everyone seems to be so damned curious about my motives.

HASDRUBAL. You owe that much to me—to every man in this sweating army. Tell us why—why?

(HANNIBAL, *suddenly collected, steps forward toward* HASDRUBAL.)

HANNIBAL. I'll tell you why, Hasdrubal . . . I've had a portent. (*He says this mysteriously.*)

HASDRUBAL (*awed*). A portent?

CARTHALO (*even more awed*). From the gods?

HANNIBAL. Yes—a portent from the gods.

MAHARBAL. From Ba-al?

HANNIBAL. No—from Tanit, the daughter of Ba-al. (*This last with a furtive glance toward* AMYTIS.)

HASDRUBAL. Then there is no hope. If Ba-al has sent his daughter to rule our destiny, then we are lost, forever.

HANNIBAL (*speaking now directly at* AMYTIS, *as though they again were alone*). She told me to look for the human equation. . . . When you have found that, she said, you will know that all your conquests, all your glory, are but whispers in the infinite stillness of time—that Rome is only a speck on the face of eternity.

CARTHALO. The gods speak strangely.

HANNIBAL. She told me that I must realize the glory of submission . . . I could only obey.

HASDRUBAL. The gods are cruel.

HANNIBAL. Cruel—but convenient, in an

emergency. . . . (AMYTIS *smiles tenderly.*) . . . We're going to Capua—to rest. We need rest, more than we need Rome. . . . Get to your posts!

(HASDRUBAL *steps forward and confronts* FABIUS, *menacingly.*)

HASDRUBAL. The Carthaginian army retreats, for the first time. But don't try to take credit for that, you Romans! Don't ever forget that it was only the gods themselves who saved Rome from the strength of our swords. (*He turns, salutes* HANNIBAL, *and strides out, followed by* MAHARBAL *and* CARTHALO.)

(MAGO *ambles in a leisurely manner across the stage and faces* AMYTIS.)

MAGO. So Hannibal had a portent, did he? (*He turns to* HANNIBAL.) That's a new name for it. (*He salutes and goes out.*)

HANNIBAL. Fall in the guard, Sergeant.

SERGEANT. Yes, sir. Hup!

(*The* SERGEANT, CORPORAL, *and* GUARDSMEN *march out.*)

HANNIBAL (*to* THOTHMES). Give me your records, Thothmes. (THOTHMES *hands him the records.*) You may go. (THOTHMES *goes out. Three bugles are heard.* HANNIBAL *looks through the sheets of papyrus, and then turns to the Romans.*) I have here a complete record of our march, from Carthage to the gates of Rome. I need hardly explain to you that this is a document of great historical importance. That being the case . . . (*He tears the sheets into small pieces.*) It is now no longer a document of any importance whatever. The exploits of Hannibal's magnificent army will live only as long as our own memory survives. That's the end of the story, gentlemen.

FABIUS. Hannibal—you've destroyed a chapter of History.

HANNIBAL. What difference does it make? In the end, there'll be more than enough history to go 'round.

SCIPIO. I have seen you before, Hannibal —in battle. Gods or no gods—it is not like you to do this—to retreat.

HANNIBAL. I'm leaving Rome to an enemy that is crueller even than I am. . . . I shall allow Rome to destroy itself.

SCIPIO. Perhaps we'll have the chance to fight it out some day.

HANNIBAL (*bowing*). I'm afraid so. (*He walks slowly to the back, then turns.*) Fabius, I wish happiness and prosperity to you, your wife, and your sons.

FABIUS. Thank you—but I have no sons.

HANNIBAL. You may have . . . and if you do, I hope that your first-born will inherit the qualities of greatness that were so evident in his father—that he will duplicate his father's signal triumphs and that he, too, will ultimately discover the human equation. . . . (*He turns to* AMYTIS.) It is so much more beautiful than war.

AMYTIS (*in a whisper*). Hannibal! You're a great man.

(*He takes an indecisive step toward her, as she stands before the column; the impulse, however, is only momentary. He steps back.*)

HANNIBAL. Good-bye, gentlemen. I wish you luck with your conquest of the world. (*He goes out.*)

(BALA *comes in from the left, picks up* HANNIBAL'S *shield, and follows his master out. There is a shrill bugle call.*)

FABIUS. What was all that he said about "the human equation?"

(DRUSUS *goes down the steps at the right, standing at the back—still visible—and gazing out after* HANNIBAL.)

SCIPIO. Hasdrubal was right. Hannibal has gone mad. (*He goes to the back to join* DRUSUS.)

FABIUS. Let this be a lesson to doubters. Hannibal, with all his elephants and all his men, could not subdue the high moral purpose of Rome.

AMYTIS. Virtue is rewarded—isn't it, Fabius?

(*The African war drums start beating. The bugles come in, with a suggestion of wild, barbaric marching music.*)

FABIUS. Virtue, my dear, is the one perfect defense against all the evil forces on this earth.

SCIPIO. Look, Fabius—the army has started to move!

(FABIUS *goes to the back and looks off toward the left.* AMYTIS *remains alone before the column.*)

FABIUS. What a glorious sight!

SCIPIO. There's Hannibal — riding away . . .

(*The terrifying sound of the drums and bugles swells in volume, the bugles seeming to shriek a final message of savage defiance to Rome. . . .* AMYTIS *goes to the top of the steps at the back, so that she is behind* FABIUS *and the others. She smiles sadly, and waves her hand to the departing Carthaginians.*)

CURTAIN.

The Second Man

BY S. N. BEHRMAN

First produced by The Theatre Guild at the Guild Theatre, New York City, on April 11, 1927, with the following cast:

MRS. KENDALL FRAYNE . . Lynn Fontanne
CLARK STOREY . . . . Alfred Lunt
AUSTIN LOWE . . . . Earle Larrimore
MONICA GREY . . . . Margalo Gillmore
ALBERT . . . . Edward Hartford

The scene of the play is laid in the living room of Clark Storey's studio in New York City.

ACT I

4:30 P.M.

ACT II

Scene 1.—8:30 P.M.
Scene 2.—11 P.M.

ACT III

3:30 the following afternoon

GENUINE high comedy in the twenties, as in later decades, was sufficiently rare in the American theatre to make any attainments in that field singularly gratifying. It is certain that the edge of high comedy was not then dulled by anything like the familiarity from which low comedy or farce came to suffer at last, driving its practitioners to ever more strenuous exertions ultimately subject to the law of diminishing returns. (Successful farces have been very much rarer on the stage since 1937, the year of *Room Service,* and also less original.) Efforts by Philip Barry and S. N. Behrman to write distinguished comedy rarely went unheeded by the discriminating. Even their failures were likely to be greeted with more poignant regret than the fiasco of farces which merely indicated that someone had failed to please the public taste to which he had pandered. For one thing, Mr. Barry and Mr. Behrman, as well as their less successful associates, tried to create literature and to make a valid comment, through their work.

Unquestionably, the most exquisite example of "high comedy" procedure will be found in *The Second Man.* In the low comedies of the period, the starry-eyed heroine would have reformed the novelist who is the object of her infatuation, and she would have taken him permanently in tow with assistance from the marriage license bureau. The accommodating playwright would have given her a workable strategy or would have seen to it that her mature rival is exposed as inexcusably debased or designing. The author of our hypothetical farce would have been, in short, immoral as an artist in order to gratify popular morality. In *The Second Man,* on the contrary, Behrman is moral as an artist and, therefore, leaves the immoral relationship between the novelist and the older woman intact. At the same time, Mr. Behrman is also on the side of intelligence and common sense, since it is plain that his self-indulgent and sceptical man is not a fit companion for the romantic girl. Had he succumbed to her, moreover, he would have done violence to the only integrity that he has—the integrity of his intellect and self-scrutiny. Since in telling this tale with perception and conviction the author sketched the manners and outlook of a segment of urbane society, *The Second Man* is also authentic social drama—in the sense in which all comedy of manners is "social." Moreover, in order to score his points and draw his picture Behrman, like Barry, operated in a world where even folly wears the mask of good manners or at least polished ones, and where raffishness is *de trop.*

Mr. Behrman's talent is all the more remarkable for not having been cradled and nurtured in upper-class American or European circles. He was born in Worcester, Mass., in 1893, of a simple middle-class Jewish family which he has sketched charmingly for the New Yorker. In Worcester he was attracted to the theatre by a local stock company and its leading ladies. Under that inspiration, he wrote a one-act play while still in high school, sold it to a vaudeville circuit, and even performed in it. Since his family had aspirations of a different nature for him, he was sent in 1912 to Clark University. After two years at Clark he went to Harvard and took his B.A. in 1916. In 1918 he also acquired a master of arts degree from Columbia University. Later in the year, he became assistant to the editor of the New York Times Book Review section and contributed reviews, articles, and short stories to the New Republic, Smart Set, The Seven Arts Magazines, The Masses, The Freeman, and the New Yorker. By a curious irony of contrast, he was also for a time a press agent for *Broadway,* the one play one would never associate with any of his own contributions.

When Behrman wrote *The Second Man* (1927), he was "discovered" by the Theatre Guild. Next came a frail collaboration with Kenyon Nicholson, *Love Is Like That* (1927) and a delightful dramatization, *Serena Blandish* (1929). By then, too, Mr. Behrman began to cultivate a vein of social phenomenology which was to have interesting results in the thirties. In the fading twenties his interest took the form of an unsuccessful, if provocative, psychological study of a business Napoleon, *Meteor* (1929). After a clever comedy of marriage, *Brief Moment* (1931), he devoted himself with frequent success to comedies concerning the conflict of ideas and political beliefs in our time, reflecting the tensions of the depression period and the second World War. These plays were: *Biography* (1932), *Rain From Heaven* (1934), *End of Summer* (1936), *Wine of Choice* (1938), *No Time for Comedy* (1939), *The Talley Method* (1941), and *Dunnigan's Daughter* (1945). He also wrote *Jane,* a dramatization of Somerset Maugham's short story which has been produced thus far only in England. In addition, he made successful adaptations of Giraudoux' *Amphitryon 38* (1937), Fulda's *The Pirate* (1942), and Werfel's *Jacobowsky and the Colonel* (1944). No one devoted to comedy in our theatre has written with comparable distinction.

ACT ONE

The SCENE *is the living-room of a suite in a studio building on the West Side of New York City.*

It is a comfortable room, its furnishings leaning a little to the exotic.

At the center at back is an arched opening with a hall-way beyond it lighted by a window at its upper end, the window being in tinted glass.

To the right and left of this window are doors in the walls of the hall, one of them, that on the left, leading to the outside of the building, the other being a service door.

On the left of the arch to the hall is another opening, to the left of which can be seen the foot of the stairs, and facing the stairs is another door which leads to the kitchenette.

A handsome fireplace is set in the upstage angle of the wall right, and below this is a large recessed window with a deep seat running round it.

A baby grand piano stands near the left wall placed so that the player faces the audience. It is draped with a rich embroidery and on the wall above it is an old tapestry.

On the right side of the piano there is a low bench.

Beyond the foot of the stairs, against the back of the recess, is a high, old Spanish chest on legs upon which are brass candlesticks which should be wired for lights.

At the left of the arched opening to the hall is a high bookcase. In the hall at its left down-stage corner is a wall table and above this a hat-rack with a broad shelf, and facing this the wall is almost covered with a large bookcase.

Above the fire to its left is a sideboard. An easy chair is set below it and a table below its left corner. Another easy chair to the right of the fire and below it books again.

A chesterfield settee is placed at an angle up and down stage right center, with a narrow table behind it. To the left of the settee and near to its up-stage end is a tabouret standing beside a comfortable, low, lounge chair right center.

Across to the left center is another chair with a high back.

Electric-light brackets on either side of the fire, and on the wall above the piano. A hanging lamp in the hall.

There are books and magazines in profusion everywhere.

When the CURTAIN *rises,* MRS. KENDALL FRAYNE *is discovered walking nervously about in front of the fire. She is a tall, handsome, beautifully dressed woman, about thirty-five. She might be described as "majestic"; she has a fine face; her voice is beautifully modulated and restrained even when she speaks under the stress of deep feeling. She is nervous and angry, and keeps looking at her watch. She takes up the manuscript of a story from the table left of the armchair above the fireplace, and drops it when she sees she has already read it. Finally she makes up her mind to leave; she grasps her fur wrap, lying on the chair below fire, and goes up to door. At the door she stops, and returns to the table left of armchair above the fire and takes up the telephone, throwing her wrap into the chair. Her voice is calm as she asks for the number.*

KENDALL (*at the telephone*). Gramercy 4304, please—yes—may I speak to Mr. Storey, please?—I believe he lunched at the Club and I thought he might still be there—thank you so much—(*She holds the receiver to her ear, sitting on the arm of the chair.*)—yes— about how long ago? —thank you. (*She takes up her wrap again with a sweeping gesture. This time she really means to go. She goes up stage; the telephone tinkles. She comes back quickly, quite excited, and answers the call.*) Yes. Yes, the line *was* busy—who?—no, Mr. Storey is not in—this—this is a friend of his—is there any message?—oh, Miss Grey—this is Mrs. Frayne—how do you do?—yes—he *was* here but he went out—he'll be back in a few minutes—I'm leaving now, but I'll leave the message for him. Not at all. Good-bye.
(*She hangs up the receiver. She is thoroughly angry, humiliated. She takes up pad and notes the message, and is beginning to go when* CLARK STOREY *rushes in.*)

STOREY (*meeting her in entrance hall*). Awfully sorry.

KENDALL. I'm leaving.

STOREY. Oh, come! I'm not *so* late. (*He throws his hat to rack on his* L.)

KENDALL. Only an hour.

STOREY. The distinguished Englishman *insisted* on my dropping into his hotel with him. We got to talking——

KENDALL. I'm leaving. (*She tries to pass him.*)

STOREY. Honestly, Kendall, I rushed up here as fast as I could. Had a fight with one taxi-driver and it took me hours to find another. (*She passes him on his* R. *towards door.*) Please don't be angry. (*He turns, standing behind her.*) I'm full of things to tell you——

KENDALL. This always happens. (*She comes into the room again reluctantly, standing at the top of the large table* R.C.)

STOREY. Besides, I thought you'd be quite comfortable. I left my new story for you to read. (*He follows to a little above her,* C.)

KENDALL (*as she moves across him*). That took exactly fifteen minutes. (*She walks up, and then down stage to piano.*)

STOREY. Only that? Really, I must write a novel. Then I can be late with impunity. (*At chair* C.) Great idea for a publisher's blurb: "This novel is so absorbing that a jealous woman, waiting for the author to keep an appointment, forgot all about him——"

KENDALL (*turning to him from her position at the piano*). Really, you've got to stop treating me like this!

STOREY (*leaning on the back of chair*). I swear I only stayed on so long because I thought it would amuse you to hear about the great English novelist. I kept saying to myself: "This will amuse Kendall——!" (*He advances to* L.C.)

KENDALL. Don't talk like that to me. It's all right for Monica Grey. It's transparent to me. She just telephoned you, by the way.

STOREY. What did she want?

KENDALL. You—— It was humiliating. I had to say you had gone out. Of course she understood that I was waiting for you.

STOREY. Oh, well, everybody in town was at that luncheon. The great novelist is tall and thin and has a red beard. I suspect that if he shaved it would be discovered that he has no chin. And I was delighted to find what I already suspected from reading his novels—he has no sense of humour.

KENDALL. Because he didn't find your flippancy amusing?

STOREY. It's as good a test as any.

KENDALL. He's a genius. It shows on nearly every page of his writing.

STOREY. I dare say he is a genius. Sad thing about geniuses—almost invariably lack humour. It's true. Genius is a sort of fanaticism——

(*The telephone rings.*)

KENDALL (*turning on her* R. *with a movement up stage*). I'm going.

STOREY (*backing a step, with his hand out to check her—then turning and going to the 'phone*). Please—just a minute—— (*At 'phone.*) You're doing it—who is this?—oh, hullo there, Austin—what about?—Monica again?—I thought you were all set—oh, you take her too seriously —I'm busy just now—Mrs. Frayne—oh, sure—say twenty minutes—bye-bye. (*He hangs up.*) Austin Lowe. All burned up about Monica Grey.

KENDALL (*who, as* STOREY *is speaking at the 'phone, has crossed in front to window* R.). And she's burned up about you.

STOREY (*as he comes to the top of the settee*). Nonsense. A baby. Doesn't know what she wants.

KENDALL. I think she does. (*Casually.*) Why don't you marry her?

STOREY. I have other plans.

KENDALL (*as she turns a step towards the lower end of the settee*). Meaning?

STOREY. Meaning you.

KENDALL (*turning and sitting on the upper corner of the window-seat*). Why should you want to marry me? Outside of the fact that—you love comfort and I am —rich.

STOREY (*coming in front of the settee and sitting on its lower arm facing* KENDALL). Outside of the fact that I love comfort—and that you are rich—I like you very much. I like you enormously. You're the most intelligent woman I know.

KENDALL. Not so intelligent. I discovered that—just—now—waiting for you.

STOREY. How?

KENDALL. I was—jealous.

STOREY (*wickedly*). Of the celebrated English novelist? You misunderstand me, Kendall.

KENDALL. Jealous of your independence of me, your self-sufficiency. I saw you there talking, enjoying yourself, revelling in your own fluency. I realized perfectly well that you must have forgotten me or, if you did think of me, that you must be saying: "Oh, she'll wait——" I was jealous, Storey.

STOREY (*getting off the arm of the sofa and throwing himself into the easy chair in front of it*). You too! My last hope is gone.

KENDALL. You see, Storey, you aren't the least bit in love with me.

STOREY. I feel a much rarer, more stable emotion—friendliness and all sorts of affection and——

KENDALL. I know.

STOREY. I was hoping we—you and I—might demonstrate the triumph of the loveless marriage.

KENDALL. How old are you, Storey? (*She rises and advances to the lower end of the settee.*)

STOREY. What did I tell you the last time you asked me?

KENDALL. I believe you said twenty-eight.

STOREY. I lied. I'm thirty.

KENDALL. I'm thirty-five.

STOREY. Delightful age.

KENDALL. When I'm forty-five you won't be any older than you are now.

STOREY. Won't I!

KENDALL. Suppose you fall in love? (*She sits on lower end of settee.*)

STOREY. I've done with that sort of thing.

KENDALL. You sound so young sometimes—so naïve.

STOREY. But I've been through that sort of thing. I know.

KENDALL. I can't imagine you really in love.

STOREY. But I assure you I was. It lasted two years. I suffered. I agonized.

KENDALL. Who was she?

STOREY. No one you know. She's married now. Has children and a dull husband, a dull home. I see her occasionally. And I wonder at myself. Was it for her I felt that base emotion—jealousy? Was it for her I used to wait in a torment of anxiety and anticipation? It seems impossible now. Such a nice, unimaginative, plodding creature. I see her and I wonder.

KENDALL. It may happen again—without warning.

STOREY. I doubt it. I'm fed up with love. It's a mirage, an illusion. Attain love and it vanishes—vanishes into the thin air or solidifies into such things as comfort and affection—things which you and I would have from the start, my dear.

KENDALL (*doubtfully*). All this is very pretty——

STOREY (*the 'phone rings*). That damn telephone—— (*He rises and going up* L. *of his chair takes up the receiver.*) Yes—hullo Monica—how are you?—yes, Mrs. Frayne told me—I'd just gone out to buy her a magazine with a poem of mine in it—oh, a trifle—not one of my major works—you've got to see me?—Austin just rang me up and told me the same thing—what've you been doing to him?—now don't be a silly child—you're lucky to have him—it's no good your coming to see me—I shan't coddle you. No, don't come; I shan't be here—I—— (*She has rung off. In disgust.*) Crazy kid!

KENDALL. Gracious! You *are* pursued by women!

STOREY (*as he comes down* C. *and stands* L. *of chair*). Now there's a case—Monica Grey! Poor as a church mouse. Mother at her wits' end to keep up the pretence of a conservative gentility. And here's Austin Lowe absolutely dotty about her. A millionaire and a great man to boot——

KENDALL (*gently*). He *is* dull, Storey.

STOREY. Dull! The most promising young chemist in America. Under thirty and he's actually discovered something new—an element. He's an F.R.S.! If there's one man on earth I envy it's Austin Lowe. If I had his money and his brains—the vices I'd encourage—the secrets I'd explore——!

KENDALL. In that case I'm glad you haven't his money and I'm certainly glad you haven't his brains.

STOREY. Just because he's not glib, like I am! (*As he crosses to the front of settee.*)

KENDALL. He never has anything interesting to say——

STOREY (*sitting above* KENDALL *on the settee*). I can talk, can't I? And that impresses you. But Austin's a great man who's made a contribution to science while I'm an imitative poet and a second-rate short-story writer.

KENDALL. You *are* a dear, Storey.

STOREY. Well, it's true!

KENDALL. I'll make a great sacrifice: Monica can have the great man. I'll take the second-rate short-story writer.

STOREY. You'll get your preference. Austin can't see any one in the world but Monica.

KENDALL. She doesn't care much for him, though.

STOREY. She will. I'll let you into a little secret——

KENDALL. Yes?

STOREY. Yes?

STOREY. Austin and Monica are engaged.

KENDALL. Really? It's not announced, is it?

STOREY. It just happened yesterday. Austin telephoned me in a perfect ecstasy.

KENDALL. I expect he's in less of an ecstasy to-day——

STOREY. Oh, Monica's a crazy kid. And being completely in love with her Austin's at her mercy.

KENDALL. She is rather adorable.

STOREY. Really an innocent. A Tennysonian *ingénue* with a Freudian patter.

KENDALL. Likes to be—audacious—doesn't she?

STOREY. Actually she has all the picture-book illusions of a *Saturday Evening Post* heroine.

KENDALL. Something appealingly wistful about her.

STOREY. But she's picked up the vocabulary of the intelligentsia. Don't let it deceive you.

KENDALL. Are you urging her to marry Austin?

STOREY. Urge her? My dear, I insist on it.

KENDALL. Why?

STOREY. Why? Because Austin'll make an admirable husband for her. She'll settle down and have babies and live in luxury. Her mother'll spend her old age in comfort. And—so shall I!

KENDALL. You're incorrigible.

STOREY. I have enormous respect for money. You can't appreciate it. It can only be felt by those whose past was poverty-stricken and whose present—is precarious.

KENDALL. You could make a fortune if you worked harder.

STOREY. I doubt it. (*He rises and crosses to the piano* L., *takes up box of cigarettes.*) I'm too intelligent to write commercial truck and incapable of writing great stuff. It's unfortunate. No, my dear. The only solution for me is to persuade you to marry me.

KENDALL. Would you want to marry me if I were poor?

STOREY. That would be presumptuous.

KENDALL. Presumptuous?

STOREY (*re-crossing to* KENDALL *and offering cigarettes. She shakes her head*). I am afraid you are a luxury I couldn't afford.

KENDALL. You're awfully mercenary.

STOREY. I'm mature. But I am honest as well as mercenary. If you do marry me—I promise—I absolutely promise—not to live above your income——

KENDALL (*amused*). I can't be angry with you. (*Rising and turning up* R. *of settee, to the fire.*)

STOREY. Why should you be angry with me?

KENDALL. Keeping me waiting an hour.

STOREY. At least I wasn't with another woman.

KENDALL (*as she moves above table and settee towards* C.). I suppose that will come too.

STOREY. I'll always come back to you.

KENDALL. You make me feel like a—terminal.

STOREY. Like a terminal?

KENDALL. Honestly, I wish I'd never met you. (*She sits on the* L. *arm of chair* L. *of the settee.*)

STOREY (*who has not left his position by the settee, only turning to follow her action*). You don't mean that. Think of the nice times we've had together.

KENDALL. I feel you'll make me very unhappy.

STOREY. Only momentarily. And never wilfully.

KENDALL. Anyway, I wish I weren't in love with you.

STOREY. You won't be—long. (*He crosses* L. *to the piano, places the cigarette box on it and sits at the keyboard lighting his cigarette.*) Love is like Poe's idea of poetry. It can't last beyond a moment or two.

KENDALL. It's lasted now—three years.

STOREY. But most of that time your husband was alive.

KENDALL (*after a moment*). Storey—apart from being in love with you—I'm very fond of you. I feel such fine things in you.

STOREY. Oh, now, Kendall, don't you be fooled too. Don't you go on having illusions about me. You're mistaken. I know my limitations. Nor have I any craving for immortality. When I'm rich—when I'm married to you—I probably shan't write at all. I'll be—what I've always wanted to be—a prosperous dilettante.

KENDALL. I never can tell when you're joking——

STOREY. I assure you I'm perfectly serious now. What this country needs is a dilettante class, interested in art with no desire to make money out of it. Why shouldn't there be an amateur class in art, as there is in sport?

KENDALL. Is this a pose with you?

STOREY. I assure you it isn't. Quite the contrary. At least you can't say afterwards that I married you under false pretences. I tell you now I'm an adventurer—intellectually and morally—an *arriviste* with one virtue—honesty.

KENDALL. Well, I've got you on my hands. I suppose I'll have to make the best of you.

STOREY. You'd better—— (*He rises, and coming to her* L. *kisses her lightly and arranges her wrap about her.*) Very pretty.

KENDALL (*amused*). I gather you're dismissing me.

STOREY. Well, I have to do some work. (*With a gesture towards the table up* R.C.)

KENDALL (*laughing*). What?

STOREY. I haven't touched that since this morning. And Austin's coming in——

KENDALL. Ah, ha! and Miss Grey. (*She rises and turns up* C.)

STOREY. You heard me tell her I wouldn't be at home.

KENDALL. I heard her say she was coming.

STOREY (*as he follows* KENDALL *to up* L.C.) What can one do? It'll be a relief to me when these two are married off.

KENDALL. To me, too.

STOREY. Are you going out to-night?

KENDALL. I don't think so.

STOREY. Suppose I ring you—5.30ish. You might dine here. I'll order dinner from downstairs.

KENDALL. All right. By the way, Storey—

STOREY. Yes?

KENDALL. It's—the end of the month and I bet you haven't a cent. I've a cheque here—somewhere.

STOREY. Ken, you demoralize me.

KENDALL. You can pay me when your ship comes in. (*She hands him the cheque and turns up into the passage way* C.) (STOREY *crosses to the top of the table behind the settee* R.C., *and lays the cheque down.*)

STOREY. You *are* a darling! I suppose it's dreadful to take money from a woman. But why it's worse than taking it from a man I don't know. (*He turns up to her* R.) Do you?

KENDALL. It all depends——

STOREY. Really, Kendall, you've got to marry me right away—to save my self-respect.

KENDALL. What do you want your self-respect for?

STOREY. I haven't the least idea——

KENDALL. Good-bye.

STOREY. Good-bye. 5.30 I'll call you. (*He walks with her to door* L.U.E. *and they go out. He returns a moment later and goes straight to the telephone.*) Restaurant, please—Mr. Storey speaking—I want dinner for two for to-night—seven thirty —up here. Oysters, small ones—clear soup —suprême of chicken with mushrooms—salad—yes—yes—thank you, Frederic—— (*He hangs up receiver, takes off his coat, which he throws into the chair* R. *of the telephone table and, taking from the back of the same chair an elaborate yellow dressing-gown, lined with silk with wide sleeves and brilliant sash, puts it on. He then takes the drawing-board from the side of the chair, his manuscript and a pencil from the small table, and coming down to the chair* L. *of the settee sits, putting the drawing-board across its arms, making a bridge on which he places the writing-paper and starts to create. Inspiration is halting; he lights a cigarette. The door-bell rings. He gets up and goes to door, admitting* AUSTIN LOWE. AUSTIN *is rather fat, serious and woe-begone.* STOREY'S *manner to him is extremely friendly.*)

STOREY (*as* AUSTIN *appears*). Hello, Austin! (AUSTIN *enters, crossing* STOREY *at the door and moving to the* R. *in the hallway.* STOREY *closes the door and precedes* AUSTIN *to* L.C. *Then with a wave towards his work:*) I was in the middle of an immortal sentence . . . (*Turns to the piano and knocks ash from cigarette into tray.*)

AUSTIN (*coming* C.). I'm sorry, old man. I *had* to see you.

STOREY. You look seedy.

AUSTIN. Didn't sleep a wink last night.

STOREY. Cocktail?

AUSTIN (*miserably*). Nothing.

STOREY. Do you good.

AUSTIN. I couldn't, really. Couldn't even eat my lunch.

STOREY (*leaning against the piano*). What's the matter? Don't tell me that discovery you made turned out to be old stuff.

AUSTIN. It's nothing to do with that. (*Sits in chair* L.C.)

STOREY. There's an idea. Scientist works twenty years on a scent—finally gets it.

Rushes to the Science Club or wherever scientists rush when they've found something. When he gets there the boss tells him: "Sorry, old man, but Professor Funkenwangler got this yesterday—here's his cable——" (*Hands* AUSTIN *box of cigarettes.*)

AUSTIN (*irritably waving the box away*). I tried to get you twenty times to-day. Last night, too. Where the devil've you been?

STOREY (*returning the box to piano and crossing behind* AUSTIN *to his chair* R.C.). Been? Let's see—where the devil have I been? Oh, last night I went to a party Charmian Drew gave. (*Sits.*) Know her?

AUSTIN. No.

STOREY. Very pretty girl. Got back at six this morning. Got up in time to go to lunch to meet Stryker Collins, the English novelist. Know his stuff?

AUSTIN. No.

STOREY. Vastly over-rated, if you ask me. The heroines are always throwing things at the heroes. Never saw such nasty women.

AUSTIN. I'm awfully low to-day, Storey, old man.

STOREY (*affecting surprise*). Low? Really? You seem so gay——

(AUSTIN *gives him a woeful look.*)

AUSTIN. It's about Monica.

STOREY. Monica?

AUSTIN. She's thrown me over.

STOREY. Nonsense.

AUSTIN. Says she won't marry me.

STOREY. You take that child too seriously, Austin.

AUSTIN. But she means it this time, Storey. Told me last night. Says it's all over. Gave me back—the ring. See. Here —— (*Shows him the ring, with which he fumbles miserably.*)

STOREY (*looking critically at the ring*). I'm glad she did. I never was crazy about that ring. Neither, I imagine, was Monica. You can return it now and get her something less—conventional. I'll go with you to Cartier's. The other day I saw a stunning oblong emerald——

AUSTIN. But don't you see! She doesn't want my ring. Any ring. She doesn't want me.

STOREY. What's her reason? For suddenly——

AUSTIN. Said when she promised to marry me she yielded to outside pressure——

STOREY. Her little mother.

AUSTIN. Said she acted against her better nature. Now she says she realizes she doesn't love me—that she never could love me. What shall I do now, Storey?

STOREY. Leave her alone: she'll come back.

AUSTIN. The worst of it is——

STOREY. What?

AUSTIN. She loves somebody else.

STOREY. She said so?

AUSTIN. Yes.

STOREY. Who?

AUSTIN. Wouldn't tell me.

STOREY. I don't believe it.

AUSTIN. Why not?

STOREY. She'd have told *me.*

AUSTIN. You think so?

STOREY. Certainly.

AUSTIN. She would, unless——

STOREY. Unless what?

AUSTIN. Unless the man she loves--is you.

STOREY. I? You're crazy, Austin.

AUSTIN (*breathless*). She likes you. She likes you better than me, that's plain. It's a wonder to me you *don't* marry her.

STOREY. Austin, you're losing your sense of humour. Fancy my being married to Monica! She'd leave me in six months. Or I should certainly have left her.

AUSTIN (*wanting to be contradicted*). I don't see why.

STOREY. She's penniless, for one thing. She couldn't stand the poverty of my ménage and—neither could I.

AUSTIN. I can't understand it. You're not in love with her?

STOREY. There speaks the eternal lover. I think it strange you *are* in love with her. She's pretty—I grant you that. But, great Heavens, man—so *young.*

AUSTIN (*rapt*). She *is* young.

STOREY. And so full of spirits!

AUSTIN. Isn't she?

STOREY. Always laughing. Like the constant ringing of chimes.

AUSTIN. It is like chimes.

STOREY. You've certainly got it badly, Austin.

AUSTIN (*rising to* R. *of his chair and restlessly pacing up* C.). I can't think of anything else. It—it—obsesses me. (*Coming to the back of* STOREY'S *chair.*)

STOREY (*a bit wickedly*). After all, you have your science.

AUSTIN (*moving aimlessly, to the piano*). You think that means anything to me now? When I've lost her? I tell you

I can't work since I've known Monica.

STOREY. Your researches?

AUSTIN (*coming down to the back of his chair* L.C.). They're all nothing. I can't do a thing. I don't give a damn. It's only—Monica.

STOREY (*shaking his head*). What an illusion that is about the cold mastery of scientific men! Look at you—helpless as a baby.

AUSTIN (*moves to front of chair* L.C. *and sits again*). And the worst of it is there's nothing to do. It's not like a problem—that you can work at. She just doesn't love me. And that's all there is to it. I'm sunk.

STOREY. If you want her—really want her—you can get her.

AUSTIN. That's what you always say. But it's not true.

STOREY (*rising and turning on his* R., *goes towards the fireplace and throws away cigarette end. Taking another from the case in his pocket and standing on the* R. *of the table behind the settee lighting it*). No doubt about it. I'm sure.

AUSTIN. But she told me—last night——

STOREY. A child. Doesn't in the least know what she wants. Won't till after she's married. That's up to you——

AUSTIN. But she's not attracted to me.

STOREY. She doesn't understand you. She has no appreciation of your intellectual gifts. (*Returns to his chair, passing below settee.*)

AUSTIN (*sadly*). That's true. My work means nothing to her.

STOREY. Why don't you make it mean something to her? Teach her to see how wonderful it is. Go on about the marvellous delicacy of your experiments.

AUSTIN. If I could only talk like you!

STOREY. That's easy.

AUSTIN. How?

STOREY. Cultivate superficiality.

AUSTIN. If she only understood me—as you do!

STOREY. She shall be made to.

AUSTIN. How?

STOREY. Maternal pressure. Monica's mother's perfectly cracked about the idea of having you for a son-in-law. Oh, it's not your scientific eminence. It's not even your family, though of course that has something to do with it. It's your money, my friend, your lucre, your multitudinous boodle——

AUSTIN. I can hardly believe——

STOREY. Sorry, but that's what it is. The Greys are mighty hard up. Monica's been dressing shamefully of late——

AUSTIN (*truculently*). She looks better——

STOREY. I know. Niftier in gingham than a fine lady in velvet.

AUSTIN. She looks wonderful in anything.

STOREY. How extraordinary that a little girl like Monica can make a man like you talk like a hack writer!

AUSTIN (*bristling*). Look here, I don't quite like your tone about Monica!

STOREY. Oh, I'm awfully fond of her. Don't misunderstand me. But she *is* a spoiled little minx, shallow as a platter. Her lack of appreciation of you proves that.

AUSTIN (*pathetically*). Well, she's only twenty. Sometimes I think I'm too old for her.

STOREY. You're only twenty-nine.

AUSTIN. It's not that alone. She's so gay, so full of fun. I can't—prattle, Storey. I can't follow her small talk.

STOREY. Her talk is not small. It is infinitesimal. Your microscopic training should help you.

AUSTIN. I don't do the things she likes—dance, play tennis—you know.

STOREY (*regarding him judicially*). You're not a jazz figure, Austin. But you'd better marry her anyway. If you don't she'll run away with a tenor or something.

AUSTIN. You keep telling me to marry her as if I didn't want to. Damn it, Storey, I'd give my soul——

STOREY. I don't think that will be necessary. But you might make one or two other sacrifices.

AUSTIN. I'll do anything——

STOREY. Take this thing more lightly, can't you? You've fallen in love like an awkward schoolboy—not like a man of the world.

AUSTIN. But I'm not a man of the world.

STOREY. Can't you act the base rôle? When Monica's around you get positively tongue-tied. All you can do is silently register adoration.

AUSTIN (*rising with a movement to* L.). I know it. I can't help it. When I do think of something to say it sounds so inadequate to me that I don't say it.

STOREY. If you'd only remember that everything's on your side. You've so much to offer.

AUSTIN. I wish I thought so. (*He moves up* C.)

STOREY. If you persist, you'll win her, as the military men say, by attrition.

AUSTIN (*moving to the back of chair* L.C.). She told me not to try to see her, nor to ring her up. I tell you, Storey, I don't know what to do with myself.

STOREY (*shaking his head*). You're a great argument against celibacy, Austin, old boy.

AUSTIN (*crossing to* STOREY'S L.). You know, Storey, I used to think—before I met Monica—that I'd never marry a girl unless she wanted me as much as I wanted her. But that was before I wanted anybody—as I want Monica. (*Passionately.*) I'd marry her on any terms, you understand? It's beyond—pride. You understand?

STOREY. Of course I understand. And I'll do everything I can to help you, believe me.

AUSTIN (*fervently*). You're a brick, Storey.

STOREY. I've got to do a little work. Why don't you go round the corner to the Chemists' Club, look over some of those fascinating magazines full of algebraic formulæ, and come back here to dine?

AUSTIN. That's awfully good of you, Storey, really. I hate to be alone.

STOREY. I know.

AUSTIN. You're the only person I can talk to.

STOREY. Come back—say in twenty minutes.

AUSTIN. You make it so easy for your friends to impose on you, Storey.

STOREY. Don't deceive yourself, old boy. I get a sadistic pleasure out of watching you writhe. And your pathetic reliance on me gives me a sense of superiority.

AUSTIN. Always joking!

STOREY. It's the grim truth.

AUSTIN. You're the finest—— (*Turning up* C. *towards the door.*)

STOREY. Come now, Austin, run along. See you in twenty minutes.

AUSTIN (*coming back to him*). Er—there's something else.

STOREY. Yes.

AUSTIN. I've been wanting to speak to you about it for some time.

STOREY. Well, spit it out.

AUSTIN. It's about money.

(STOREY *rises and sits on the* L. *arm of his chair.*)

STOREY. My favourite subject.

AUSTIN. Er—your writing. Does it—I mean to say—does it bring you in very much?

STOREY. Not much. I'm caviare to the general, Austin.

AUSTIN. That's what I thought. Well—you see—I mean to say—you see—well, damn it all, I'm so rich, Storey. Won't you let me help you out occasionally?

STOREY. Of course I will.

AUSTIN (*eagerly putting his hand into his pocket*). That's fine—I—— (*Turning a little to* L. *as he opens his pocket-book.*)

STOREY. Oh, not now. (*Rising and turning at the back of his chair to the top of the table behind settee.*) I've got a cheque on the table now—I don't even know how much it is—— (*Unfolds the cheque* MRS. FRAYNE *has left.*) Five hundred.

AUSTIN (*standing down* L.C., *turning towards* STOREY). For a story?

STOREY. Yes.

AUSTIN. That's more than we chemists get——

STOREY. But next time I'm broke—it'll probable be next week—I'll let you know.

AUSTIN (*as he crosses to* C.). Any time. It'll be a pleasure.

STOREY. It's a pleasure I shan't deny you. So long, Austin.

AUSTIN (*moving up to door* L.U.E.). Good-bye, old man. Awfully good of you to let me come back.

STOREY (*moving up with* AUSTIN). Don't mention it. (AUSTIN *goes out.*) (STOREY *comes down to a level with the small table up* R.C. *There is a smile on his lips. After a moment of meditation he takes up the telephone.*) Regent 2772—please—Mrs. Frayne—Mr. Storey—hullo, Ken!—I've changed my mind about dining here—let's go out somewhere—yes, I did order it, but I'm going to let two other people eat it—and—Kendall—will you ring me up in about twenty minutes—never mind what I say—just 'phone me. Comedy, my dear—tell you later—I'll come to your place about six-thirty—shan't dress, no—yes, I'm working now—oh, pretty well—not many sentences but distinguished. Good-bye, Mrs. Frayne, see you later. (*He hangs up the receiver, and coming down* C. *picks up the board which he has placed on the tabouret on the* R. *side of his chair with paper and pencil, sits and begins to write. After a moment he gets up and goes to bookshelf up* L.C. *for dictionary.*

Finds his word. Goes back to his board, writes a few lines when door-bell rings. He ignores it. It rings again, four short rings. Then, shouting:) Door's open!

(MONICA *bursts in.*)

MONICA (*coming down to his* L., *carrying a wrap over her arm. She has a purse and a small book*). Hullo, darling! Working? (*She is young, vibrant, utterly charming.*)

STOREY. Trying to.

MONICA. Sorry I came? (*Turning to the back of his chair.*)

STOREY (*dryly*). Well——!

MONICA. I don't care in the least. I'm delighted to see you. (*She strokes his hair.*)

STOREY. Don't mess me.

MONICA (*turning to* L. *of his chair again*). Just had to see you, Storey. The one person in the world I wanted to see.

STOREY. Everybody's told me that to-day. I begin to feel like a Father Confessor.

MONICA (*sitting on* R. *arm of chair* L.C.). Glad to see me? Tell the truth.

STOREY (*grumbling*). Been trying to work all the afternoon——

MONICA. You fib. You *are* glad. You know you are.

STOREY (*writing*). Oh, I don't mind you.

MONICA. I bet you're more than glad. I bet you're thrilled, excited.

STOREY. Modest creature.

MONICA (*jumping off the chair and going to him*). I'm sure you're in love with me, Storey, but you're too big a fool to tell me so.

STOREY (*continuing writing*). I thought we'd settled all that.

MONICA (*turning up* C.). You thought you did.

STOREY. Oh, do sit awhile.

MONICA. You thought I'd quietly succumb and marry Austin, but I'm not going to. (*As she takes off her hat and places it with her purse and book on wall-table* L. *of passage.*) Hear that, Storey? I'm not going to——

(*He finishes a page and starts a fresh one, putting the finished one on the tabouret beside him.* MONICA *comes down and looks over his shoulder.*)

STOREY. Can't you see I'm working?

MONICA (*taking finished page from the tabouret*). Oh, may I?

STOREY. Be through in a minute.

MONICA (*reading—as she moves to the settee*). Don't stop on my account.

STOREY (*grimly*). Oh, well, enough of creation—— (*He puts down his pencil, paper and board on tabouret.*)

MONICA (*absorbed*). Oh, this is awfully interesting. (*Sits in the middle of the settee.*)

STOREY (*same tone*). Think so, do you? (*He sounds suddenly weary.*)

MONICA. I love it. (*She mutters for a moment and then reads.*) "They had been dancing and he asked her to go outside with him. They stepped out through the open French windows, crossed the lawn and walked down a narrow path between high poplars. . . . The tree-tops made hedges in the sky between which the stars grew like buttercups." Buttercups. . . . That's lovely.

STOREY. Read some more.

MONICA. "It was a most curious moon, red-bronze in colour, wafer-thin, exquisitely curved, a shaving of a moon." (STOREY *rises to* L. *and turns.*) "Courtney allowed himself to speculate to the girl beside him. 'God,' he said, 'must be a curious person to fashion such a moon.' " (*She looks up at* STOREY. *He nods.*) "The girl thought it was slightly chilly and hadn't they better go back to the ballroom?" Oh, I think that's wonderful. So —ironic!

STOREY. You think it's wonderful?

MONICA. I think everything you write is wonderful. (*She places the MS. on the tabouret and then, putting her knee upon the settee, looks round at* STOREY.)

STOREY. I'm sorry I can't agree with you. Scented dish-water, that's what it is. Dishwater with eau-de-Cologne in it. (*He flings himself into the chair* L.C.)

MONICA. What a funny mood you're in!

STOREY. It annoys me when you keep prattling on that my stuff's wonderful. What do you know about it? Have you ever read anything except movie magazines? Have you——?

MONICA. Oh, now, Storey, please don't scold me. Not to-day. To-day I want you to be nice to me.

STOREY. What's this about you and Austin?

MONICA (*turning her head away*). I can't go through with it, Storey. That's all.

STOREY. But you told me—you definitely told me—you'd made up your mind to marry him.

MONICA (*whimpering a bit*). You're not a bit nice to-day.

STOREY (*crossing his legs*). You're an awful dumb-bell, Monica.

MONICA (*coming to him on the* R. *of his chair*). I'm not. You're a dumb-bell. (*She uncrosses his legs and sits on his lap.*) Storey— tell the truth—wouldn't you rather have me sitting on your lap like this than Mrs. Frayne?

STOREY. Don't get fresh, Monica.

MONICA. I can't imagine Mrs. Frayne sitting on anybody's lap.

STOREY. No one requires you to imagine that, my dear.

MONICA (*defiantly*). I don't like Mrs. Frayne.

STOREY. She likes you.

MONICA. I don't believe it. I'm sure she says nasty things about me.

STOREY. She doesn't discuss you. She thinks you're very pretty but adolescent.

MONICA (*with a wicked smile*). I may be young, but my thoughts are mature. (*She kisses him.*)

STOREY. What have you been reading?

MONICA. No, I don't like Mrs. Frayne. She's a bad influence on you.

STOREY. Will you please stop chattering about Kendall and tell me about you and Austin?

MONICA. You hate to have me criticize her. I know it.

STOREY (*putting her off his lap, crossing in front of her to the tabouret*). I'm really very busy, Monica.

MONICA. Busy! Bless your heart, you never do a thing.

STOREY. I might if you'd marry Austin and save me worrying about you. (*Picking up his MS.*)

MONICA (*incredulously*). Would you really let me marry him? (*Sinks on to* R. *arms of the chair* L.C.)

STOREY. Let you! I pray for it.

MONICA. You'd go to church—and—watch it happen——?

STOREY. Why not?

MONICA. And go home and rub your palms and say "That's that," I suppose. (*She turns round the back of her chair and goes up to the piano.*)

STOREY (*touched*). Oh, now, Monica! You know I'll always be awfully fond of you.

MONICA. *Fond——!*

STOREY. Mighty lucky for you I'm not in love with you.

MONICA (*leaning on the piano, looking round at him*). Oh, I wish you were. I'd be awfully happy if you were.

STOREY. We'd probably marry and that would be the end of us. The end of you at any rate. (*He sits in chair* R. *of settee.*)

MONICA. Why? We'd be a charming couple.

STOREY (*abruptly*). Tell me about you and Austin.

MONICA (*she crosses to his* L. *and sits on his lap again, cuddling up to him*). I will.

STOREY. Well? (*He jiggles his knees.*)

MONICA. Don't hurry me, darling. I'm going to stay here a long time.

STOREY. Unfortunately——

MONICA (*putting her hand over his mouth*). Unfortunately, nothing. I'm going to stay here and dine with you and then we'll have a long talk and after that —we'll take a walk——

STOREY. And after that?

MONICA. I'll come back with you if you like. Storey, if you ruin me will you make an honest woman of me?

(*They both laugh.*)

STOREY. I won't marry you, Monica, no matter what you do.

MONICA (*sighing*). My! Storey, you're hard to get.

STOREY. You *are* a sweet child. I'm not as indifferent to you as I pretend.

MONICA. Aren't you?

STOREY. Of course I'm not.

MONICA. Don't you want to kiss me? (*He pecks her three or four times on the tip of her nose.*) Oh, Storey, I'm so unhappy.

STOREY (*stroking her hair*). Why?

MONICA (*muffled*). Because nobody loves me.

STOREY. Austin loves you. He's crazy about you.

MONICA (*getting up and stamping her foot and crossing over to piano*). Oh, don't talk to me about Austin.

STOREY. Why shouldn't I?

MONICA. Because he bores me. He bores me to death. I never want to see him again. (*She sits on the* R. *end of the bench in front of piano. There is a pause.*)

STOREY (*rising and crossing to her, sitting below her on the bench*). Monica, I want to tell you something. Listen. Listen. I intend to be honest about Austin. You get me, don't you? He's so helpless—that I don't intend to take advantage of him.

Besides, he's a fine fellow. Awfully sincere. Awfully honest——

MONICA. He bores me. I don't like him.

STOREY. He's inarticulate, but he's a fine brain.

MONICA. I don't love him.

STOREY. You might learn. One can learn to love anybody.

MONICA. But I love you, Storey.

STOREY. Now don't be a silly child. What sort of life do you suppose we should have together?

MONICA. Cozy.

STOREY. And what'll we live on?

MONICA. I'll work.

STOREY. At what?

MONICA. I'll typewrite.

STOREY. What?

MONICA. Your stories. (*He makes a gesture of despair*). I'll go in the movies! I have a friend who's a director.

STOREY (*rises and moves at the back of chair* L.C. *towards* C.). Your mother would be delighted!

MONICA. By the way—I've told Mother.

STOREY (*turning*). You've told Mother what?

MONICA. That I can't marry Austin because I'm in love with you.

STOREY. You didn't——!

MONICA. Mother despises you, Storey.

STOREY (*very angry*). And you're fool enough to tell her——!

MONICA (*misunderstanding*). It doesn't matter to me that she doesn't like you. It just makes me love you all the more——

STOREY (*crossing down to below settee* R.). That's not the point. How dare you——

MONICA. Oh, that's not all I told her.

STOREY (*comes to* R.C.). It's quite enough——

MONICA (*in one breath*). I told her you loved me too, and that you'd asked me to marry you and that I'd said yes. I intend to make quite a campaign, you see.

STOREY. I've a good mind to spank you!

MONICA (*rising and coming down stage in front of chair* L.C. *towards* C.). I thought that if I told Mother you'd asked me that you would be—sort of compromised. You see, I'm trying to get it spread around—that we're engaged. (*He is about to speak.*)

STOREY. Now, Monica. (*Advancing, she puts her hand over his mouth to stifle his protest.*)

MONICA. For once don't talk and listen to me. The fact is that I'm doing all this for your good.

STOREY. Thank you!

MONICA. For your good, Mr. Storey.

STOREY. Would you mind telling me——!

MONICA. Of course I'll tell you. You see, I know, I'm just certain—that way down deep it's me you love—and not Mrs. Frayne or anybody else. Since you love me you ought to marry me. You admit that the only reason you *don't* ask me is because you're poor and you think I want all sorts of frivolous things. It's just like you—you're so splendid and always thinking of other people——

STOREY (*in despair*). Good heavens!

MONICA. But you misjudge me, Storey. Honestly you do. I could be awfully happy on just what you have.

STOREY (*turning away to the window-seat*). Perhaps. But *I* couldn't.

MONICA. You ought to marry a poor girl, Storey. It would stimulate you, make you work harder.

STOREY. Are you quite finished? (*He sits on the upper corner of the window-seat.*)

MONICA (*going to the lower end of the settee, kneeling upon it and leaning over the back of it towards him*). Not quite. I just got an idea. I think I'll 'phone an announcement of our engagement to the newspapers. (*She gets off the settee, turning on her* L. *and running round in front of the chair* R.C. *goes up towards the telephone.*)

STOREY (*jumping up, really frightened*). You'll do no such thing.

MONICA (*at the 'phone—lifting the receiver and laughing joyously*). I've got you, Storey—I've got you at last.

STOREY. Come here. Now, come here! Put that down! (*He goes up to her* L.)

MONICA. No way out of it for you, Storey. You're cooked.

(*He takes the receiver out of her hand, hangs it up, and putting his arm round her leads her gently from the 'phone a step or two down stage at the back of table* R.C. *and advances her in front of him towards the window-seat.*)

STOREY (*following her as he speaks*). Now sit down like a lamb and concentrate on what I'm going to tell you.

MONICA (*demurely*). All right, teacher. (*She takes a cushion from the lower end of the settee, as she speaks, and holds it to her with a little shake. Going to the window-seat she sits holding the cushion in her arms.)*

STOREY (*he sits below her on the upper corner of the seat*). How old are you, Monica?

MONICA. You know perfectly well. I'm twenty.

STOREY (*he takes the cushion from her and throws it on to the settee*). Now listen—this is serious. I'm thirty-one.

MONICA. Nice age for a man.

STOREY. Eleven years older than you. Just think when I'm forty-one——

MONICA. I'll be thirty-one. Think how attractive I'll be.

STOREY. Of course you will. And I'll be—bald and wrinkled and—— I know that's been said before.

MONICA. No, you won't. Your hair'll be just touched with grey. You'll look very distinguished.

STOREY. I'm too old for you, Monica.

MONICA. And yet you want me to marry Austin. He's as old as the hills.

STOREY. He's three years younger than I am.

MONICA. Well, he seems lots older. He's so correct—like an old parson.

STOREY. You talk outrageously before him.

MONICA. I love to shock him. He's such a Puritan!

STOREY. You've got to stop reproaching me, before him, for not having an affair with you. It gets on my nerves.

MONICA. I believe I shock you, too, Storey.

STOREY. Not in the least. But I hate to see the poor fellow suffer.

MONICA. Austin's so literal. Absolutely no glimmering of humour. Oh!

STOREY. Nobody in love has a sense of humour.

MONICA (*rising suddenly*). Oh! This will make you laugh. Wait till I show you. (*She runs round the lower end of the settee and up* C. *to the wall table on the* L. *of the hallway and gets the book she brought.* (*As she does so,* STOREY *rises and comes to the back of the lower end of settee.*) Look what he sent me. With an article by Austin in it. Look here. (*She returns down* C. *with the book as she is speaking and kneels on the end of the settee, facing* STOREY.)

STOREY (*taking the austerely covered pamphlet*). "Proceedings of the American Chemical Society——" (*Reading.*) "A new method of separating atoms and ions which are chemically similar but have different weights by diffusion—including the separation of radium from the barium residues." Tells you what to expect, doesn't it?

MONICA (*sitting back on her heels, laughing*). Now whatever do you think Austin thought I'd see in that?

STOREY (*intent on the article*) This is very touching, Monica. (*He hasn't removed his eyes from the article; she raises herself looking at it with him.*) Has a brilliant climax, this thing. It's an *equation*—can't you see!

MONICA. Oh, Storey, come now! I don't believe you have the faintest idea what it's all about.

STOREY. Of course I haven't. I've had a shallow literary education. But I *can* see this—you see—in this abracadabra—this forest of figures—Austin had scented, somewhere, an equation lurking. And he's found it, damn him, dredged it out of the morass, lifted it into clear light—and there it is!

MONICA. Oh, Storey!

STOREY. I'm perfectly serious, Monica. And I think it was very sweet of him to send you this—if you had any imagination you'd see—it's a tender, a beautiful gesture—this (*tapping book*)—this is *his lyric,* Monica.

MONICA (*getting bored*). I prefer lyrics that rhyme.

STOREY. An equation is a rhyme—a perfect rhyme, subtler and harder to find than any you'll see in *my* effusions—— How do you know what hope for the future is hidden in this little prose poem? (*He flings the book on to the table.*)

MONICA. You're so generous about others, Storey. I love you for it!

STOREY. Don't be too sure of my motive. Perhaps it's because I want to get conveniently rid of *you*!

(MONICA, *still seated on her heels before him, shakes her head stubbornly, her hands crossed behind her back.*)

MONICA. It's no good, Storey. You might as well give up!

STOREY (*comes round the end of the settee*). Now please be serious, Monica. Austin'll make you a wonderful husband. (*She makes a grimace and assumes a seated position on the settee—making room for* STOREY *beside her.*) You're lovely and his money will provide you with the exquisite background your beauty requires. . . . (*He sits on* MONICA's R.) And he's *good*!

MONICA (*piteously*). I just can't do it, Storey. Please don't ask me to.

STOREY. He won't bother you. Spends ages in his laboratory, you know.

MONICA (*rises and moves to* C., *keeping her back to him*). I'm sure he doesn't sleep in the laboratory.

STOREY. Oh now, Monica. Really, you're impossible.

MONICA. Am I so terrible, Storey? Don't *you* love me at all?

STOREY. I'm frightfully fond of you.

MONICA. Then why do you keep me in suspense like this?

STOREY (*rising and moving to her*). Monica, you're so young. I know so much more about life than you do. I know what would happen—I know this feeling you have for me now—won't last.

MONICA (*turning to him, placing her hands on his shoulders and looking up into his face*). But I swear—I'll never love anybody else. If you don't marry me—I'll go into a convent. I swear.

STOREY (*gently, putting her hands down*). I'm going to marry Mrs. Frayne—if she'll have me.

MONICA (*passionately*). Just because she's rich! You know you wouldn't think of marrying her if she weren't—the trouble with you is—you're damned selfish. (*She moves to* L.C.)

STOREY. Of course I am.

MONICA (*half turned from him*). Just admitting it doesn't do any good. You like to go about and be petted by people. And your silly little comforts. You see, I know, deep down, you're fonder of me than of any one. Just as I know that I'm fonder of you than I ever shall be of any one—— (STOREY *makes a sudden move towards her; is irresistibly attracted; stops. She turns to him—her arms extended.*) Obey that impulse!

STOREY (*for a moment stands irresolute, then he walks to the chair* R.C. *and sits*). It's ridiculous. Impossible. Ridiculous.

MONICA. Why not? (*Following to the* L. *of his chair.*)

STOREY. You're a silly child. (*A rather long pause.*) You don't know anything about anything. You don't know what you want, really.

MONICA. Yes, I do. (*Leaning over the* L. *corner of the back of chair.*)

STOREY (*disturbed*). I warn you, Monica—if you keep this up I *will* marry you.

MONICA. You ought to marry me for the sake of your art. If you marry Mrs. Frayne you'll be so comfortable you won't write a thing.

STOREY. I am thirty-one and in full possession of my senses. (*He rises and crosses to the window—his back to her.*)

MONICA. It isn't demoralizing to make you want to marry me.

STOREY. Yes, it is. It would be positively immoral for me to marry you.

MONICA (*she crosses to him*). But it would be more moral than anything else you could do to me.

(STOREY *turns and looks at her in perplexity.*) (*The door-bell rings.*)

STOREY. Thank goodness! Austin.

MONICA (*terrified, laying her hand on his arm*). Austin!

STOREY. Well, I think it's Austin.

(*The bell rings again.*)

MONICA. Don't answer. He'll go away.

STOREY. I couldn't do that. (*He crosses in front of the settee.* MONICA *follows quickly, trying to stop him.*)

MONICA. What a bore! Did you know he was coming?

STOREY. I wasn't sure.

MONICA. Promise you'll get rid of him—promise.

STOREY. I'll do what I can—— (*Bell rings.* STOREY *goes to the door* L.U.E. *and admits* AUSTIN. MONICA *takes up a book from the table and turns to the window-seat—sitting and pretending to read.*) Hello, Austin, what's the book?

AUSTIN. Just something I thought might interest you. (*Gives* STOREY *the book he carries and puts his hat and coat on the rack.*)

MONICA (*as* STOREY *precedes* AUSTIN *to a position* L. *of the telephone table.* AUSTIN *comes below him on his* L.). Hullo, Anti-Genesis!

STOREY. Anti what?

MONICA. Don't you know my little pet-name for Austin? Anti-Genesis-man.

STOREY. Why's that?

AUSTIN. Monica actually believed the world began in the Garden of Eden.

MONICA (*slyly*). Austin disillusioned me about the book of Genesis.

AUSTIN (*seriously*). She'd never heard of the Nebular Theory.

STOREY. Monica! It's the fashion nowadays to be flippant, Austin. Monica gets it from me—— (*The telephone rings.* STOREY *answers it, handing the book back to* AUSTIN *as he does so.* AUSTIN *places it on the wall-table and comes down stage to* L.C.) Yes—oh, hullo!—waiting for me?—why, our engagement was for Tuesday, wasn't it?—Dear me, is *this* Tuesday?—How awfully stupid of me—the truth is I've been so lost in my work—yes, I can make it easily by seven—I'll be there—Good-bye. (*He hangs up receiver.*) Certainly lucky you dropped in, Monica.

MONICA (*sensing something*). What's happened now?

STOREY (*coming down* C.). The fact is, I can't dine with you after all.

MONICA (*furious*). Oh, can't you?

STOREY. I had no idea it was Tuesday. I thought it was Monday.

MONICA (*bitterly*). Of course when one works as hard as you do one is apt to forget the day of the week!

STOREY (*to* AUSTIN). I've ordered dinner for two. Would you mind dining with Monica instead of me?

AUSTIN (*overjoyed*). Here?

STOREY. I've ordered a delicious dinner from downstairs.

AUSTIN. I'd love to. That is; if Monica——

MONICA (*mechanically*). Of course.

STOREY (*crosses up to rack* L. *of hallway, getting his hat and coat—putting coat on as he comes back to* AUSTIN). I've really got to dash. Austin, mind lending me a dollar for taxi fare? Don't believe I've got a cent with me.

AUSTIN (*eagerly*). Of course. (*He takes out a bill and hands it to* STOREY.)

STOREY. One thing about Austin. He's not one of those millionaires who never has any money with him.

AUSTIN. Can give you more. Here's a twenty.

STOREY. Well, perhaps I'd better. (*Takes it.*) So long, children. (*To* AUSTIN.) You'll find everything ready for a cocktail in the kitchenette.

(AUSTIN *turns up* L.C., *and goes into kitchenette up* L.)

MONICA. Are you coming back?

(*She rises and crosses up behind table* R.C. *to the* R. *of hallway.*)

STOREY. Might. I'll 'phone you.

AUSTIN (*calling off stage*). I'm not very good at mixing cocktails.

STOREY. And you a chemist! You'll find a recipe in there, too.

MONICA. This is a dirty trick, Storey. (*White with anger.*) You're dining with Mrs. Frayne.

STOREY. Yes. In five years you'll thank me. In less——

MONICA. All right for you, Storey!

STOREY. Be nice to him. Good-bye, darling.

(*He goes out with a disappearing,* "So long, Austin." MONICA *moves down stage to* L. *of chair* R.C. AUSTIN *reappears with a cocktail-shaker.*)

AUSTIN. It doesn't say how much absinthe or how much vermouth—— (MONICA *says nothing. Her face is set in misery.* AUSTIN *comes down a little. He stands awkwardly holding the cocktail-mixer by the neck.*) (*Wistfully.*) I don't know—do you put absinthe or do you put vermouth——

(*She turns away impatiently towards the window as the* CURTAIN *falls.*)

ACT TWO

Scene I

SCENE.—*The same room two hours later. 8:30 p.m.*

MONICA *and* AUSTIN *are seated at a table which is set a little* L. *of* C. MONICA *is smoking a cigarette.* AUSTIN *is on the* L., MONICA *is facing him. They have evidently finished dinner and the table has been cleared of all but its white cloth. Almost identically with the rise of the* CURTAIN, AUSTIN *leaves his chair and turning on his* R. *meets a* WAITER *who at the moment enters by the door* R.U.E. *at the top of the hallway, carrying a tray with coffee for two. Standing at the* L. *corner of the hallway,* AUSTIN *signs to the* WAITER *to place the tray on the wall-table* L. *of it. He then appears to direct the* WAITER *to remove the table* C.

The WAITER *comes to the table, bows and smiles to* MONICA *apologetically, who rises, turns and crosses to the window-seat, picks up a magazine and, returning with it, sits in the armchair* R.C.

The WAITER *goes up with the service table and as he passes* AUSTIN *the latter slips a dollar bill into his hand. The* WAITER, *putting the table down for a moment to pocket it goes out with the table by the service door at the top of the hallway* R.U.E.

The room lights are on and the window is blue with the night light.

AUSTIN, *standing at the wall-table, pours a cup of coffee. He brings it down to* MONICA *at the* L. *of her chair.*

Apparently things have been a little dull —he tries to brighten them up—but is serious about the way he attempts it.

AUSTIN (*crossing to her with cup*). Will you have some coffee?

MONICA. No, thanks.

(*There is another pause.*)

AUSTIN (*keeping the cup of coffee for himself, crosses in front of* MONICA *and sits on the settee*). It's—it's jolly dining up here.

MONICA (*mechanically*). Isn't it?

AUSTIN. It is for me, anyway. (*As she says nothing.*) I suppose you're—bored.

MONICA. Why, I'm not.

AUSTIN. I wish I knew how to amuse you, Monica.

MONICA. You're a dear, Austin. You're far too nice for me.

AUSTIN. Too nice for you . . . !

MONICA. You are, really. You're a great man. And awfully modest and nice. I'm just a restless little nobody who doesn't know what she wants.

AUSTIN. You're fairly certain about what you don't want. . . .

MONICA. I'm afraid I know what I want, too, Austin.

AUSTIN. I wish I could talk, like Storey.

MONICA. What would you say?

AUSTIN. I'd tell you how much I love you.

MONICA. But you've told me that. And I've told you that I don't admire your choice.

AUSTIN. I know.

(*There is a pause, during which he takes one sip of his coffee and then places the cup on the table behind him.*)

MONICA. There's no reason why we can't be friends.

AUSTIN. That's like telling a starving man—there's no reason he can't look at the food in a baker's window.

MONICA. Why, Austin, you're brilliant to-night.

AUSTIN (*emboldened by his success*). I feel that if I could find the words—somewhere there must be the words—that would say what I feel for you. And once you knew what I feel, I feel that you would love me.

MONICA (*half-listening*). I wonder. . . .

AUSTIN. Yes. I feel that. What I say to you is banal, trite. I have no gift of speech. I know it. I—I'm dumb. (*He leans forward, his hands between his knees, his head bent.*)

MONICA (*touched—patting his hand*). You *are* a dear, Austin. I'm very fond of you.

AUSTIN. Last night you said—you never wanted to see me again.

MONICA (*rising and walking about the room, she first turns up* C.). Last night?

AUSTIN. You said——

MONICA (*standing by the bookcase up* L.C.). Please, Austin, don't talk to me any more about last night.

AUSTIN (*meekly*). All right, Monica. (*One of those pauses.*) Would you—would you like to go to a theatre?

MONICA (*she comes down* L.C.). No, thank you.

AUSTIN. Storey says that Gertrude Lawrence——

MONICA (*turning up to the top of the piano and sitting on the stool*). I saw her.

AUSTIN. We could go to the opera. It's "Götterdämmerung." That would be fun, wouldn't it?

MONICA (*rising and coming down* L. *of chair* L.C.). Not to-night, Austin, thanks. (*A pause.*) Storey said he'd telephone, didn't he?

AUSTIN. Did he?

MONICA. I think he did. (*She walks up to the telephone.*)

AUSTIN. I believe Storey's dining with Mrs. Frayne.

MONICA (*she fidgets with things on the telephone table*). Is he?

AUSTIN. Yes.

MONICA. Austin?

AUSTIN. Yes?

MONICA. Do you like Mrs. Frayne?

AUSTIN. Yes. I think she's a lovely woman. Don't you?

MONICA. She probably was.

AUSTIN. She probably was.

AUSTIN. I wonder—will Storey marry her?

MONICA. I've no idea.

AUSTIN. I think she's in love with him.

MONICA. Why not?

AUSTIN. I think it would be a good match. Don't you?

MONICA. How can I tell?

AUSTIN. Storey sees her every day.

MONICA. Can't we really find anyone to talk about except Storey?

AUSTIN. Well, you're so keen about him.

MONICA (*turns quickly, taking a step to* C. *above chair* R.C.). What makes you think that?

AUSTIN. Aren't you?

MONICA. I despise him.

AUSTIN. But last night——

MONICA (*crossing to chair* L.C.). Last night doesn't matter. To-day does. I despise him. (*She slumps into the chair* L.C.)

AUSTIN (*rising from the settee and advancing to the front of chair* R.C.). Then, perhaps . . . (*He moves uncertainly, pauses, does not know what to say. She is lost in a dream and does not hear him.*) Then, perhaps——

MONICA. Perhaps what?

AUSTIN. If there's no one else . . . I mean, if you're not in love with Storey—or anyone else . . . perhaps——

MONICA (*almost in tears*). Please, Austin—don't make love to me.

AUSTIN (*sinking into the chair* R.C.). I can't help it. Isn't it awful? I can't make love to you and I mustn't make love to you—and I don't know what else to talk about.

MONICA. Talk to me—talk to me about evolution.

AUSTIN. But you said you preferred the Garden of Eden.

MONICA. To—primeval chaos. Yes. Don't you? Isn't a nice garden full of wild flowers better than a lot of slime?

AUSTIN (*he is now on his own ground*). But the Bible isn't true.

MONICA. What of it? Adam and Eve were such a *nice* couple.

AUSTIN. I can't see the use in talking about anything—that isn't true.

MONICA. That shuts out so many subjects.

AUSTIN (*hesitating*). Did you—did you get the—my—the article I sent you?

MONICA. Oh, yes, thanks! How awfully clever you are!

AUSTIN (*greatly flustered, blushing*). Oh—it was just—that's what I've been working on a good deal lately—a new method of separating radium.

MONICA (*gently*). Of course, I don't pretend to have understood it. . . .

AUSTIN. That's perfectly natural—if you don't know the vocabulary of science it doesn't mean much—like giving the score of a symphony to a person who can't read it.

MONICA. I know, I'm terribly ignorant, Austin.

AUSTIN (*earnestly*). You think what I do is awfully dull, don't you? If you'd come with me sometimes to the laboratory—I'd like to show you—it's really awfully interesting—it's exciting.

MONICA. Oh, for you!

AUSTIN. No, for anybody. . . . (*Wistfully.*) Monica, I wish you'd let me read you something.

MONICA. From your article?

AUSTIN. No. From a book I've bought you.

MONICA. Oh! What's the book?

AUSTIN (*rushing out to the hallway, gets the book from the wall-table and, coming down to her on her left, pulls the bench* R. *of piano close to her, excitedly*). It's by Bertrand Russell. . . .

MONICA (*apprehensively*). Oh!

AUSTIN. You know who he is, don't you?

MONICA (*doubtfully vague*). Well, I think I've *heard* of him.

AUSTIN. Well, he's just one of the greatest men alive, that's all.

MONICA (*touched by his eagerness, pats his arm*). Is he, Austin?

AUSTIN. I came across this passage the other day—I marked it—I thought—the minute I read it—"I must get this for Monica!"

(MONICA *peers over at the book.*)

MONICA. "Mysticism and Logic." What a nice title! Ordinarily you'd never think of putting those two together, would you? (*Her thoughts wander off to* STOREY.)

AUSTIN. There are a lot of essays—this one's about mathematics. . . . (*He looks up at her, notices her abstraction.*)

MONICA (*coming to, guiltily*). Oh! . . .

AUSTIN (*reading*). "Mathematics, rightly viewed, possesses not only truth but supreme beauty—a beauty cold and austere, like that of sculpture, without appeal to any part of our weaker nature, without the gorgeous trappings of painting or music, yet sublimely pure, and capable of a stern perfection such as only the greatest art can show. The true spirit of delight, the exaltation, the sense of being more than man, which is the touchstone of the highest excellence is to be found in mathematics as surely as in poetry." (*The cadence of* AUSTIN's *voice, his profound sincerity and the beauty of the passage it-*

self affect MONICA*—as a bit of sad music might. She is quite rapt, but* AUSTIN *feels suddenly unsure. Looking up.*) Interesting, isn't it?

MONICA. Isn't it?

AUSTIN (*continuing*). "Remote from human passions, remote even from the pitiful facts of nature, the generations have gradually created an ordered cosmos, where pure thought (*pause*) can dwell as in its natural home, and where one, at least, of our nobler impulses can escape from the dreary exile of the actual world." (*He stops for a moment to look at her and finds her eyes are full of tears.*)

MONICA. I wish I could do that.

AUSTIN. What?

MONICA. Escape from the dreary exile of the actual world.

AUSTIN (*fidgeting with the book*). Monica! You're crying! Aren't you happy, Monica?

MONICA. Not very. . . . Why don't you marry somebody else . . . somebody worthy of you?

AUSTIN (*still playing with the book, not looking at her*). Who?

MONICA. That awfully clever girl.

AUSTIN. Which?

MONICA. You know, that girl I met you with. You told me she was a research chemist. What's a research chemist?

AUSTIN (*very seriously*). A person who engages in chemical research.

MONICA. Oh!—Well, why don't you marry *her,* Austin? She seemed awfully nice.

AUSTIN. She *is* nice.

MONICA. And I suppose she adores you.

AUSTIN. Yes. She does like me.

MONICA. There you are!

AUSTIN (*shaking his head*). No.

MONICA. Why not?

AUSTIN. For one thing—she knows too much for me.

MONICA. Ho! You are vain!

AUSTIN. She wears woollen stockings.

MONICA. Oh, Austin, you *are* a funny man. (*Looking at him closely.*) You've no sense of humour, Austin. Sometimes—it's delicious.

AUSTIN. I prefer you, Monica.

MONICA. For a man who lives by his brain—you're awfully illogical, Austin.

AUSTIN. I know I am. I've tried to reason you—out of my—consciousness. I can't do it.

MONICA. Well, I'm as stupid as you are, Austin. Stupider.

AUSTIN (*still nervously fingering the book*). Why?

MONICA. For—loving him.

AUSTIN. Loving whom?

MONICA. Storey.

AUSTIN. Storey!

MONICA. Of course. Who else?

AUSTIN (*altogether bewildered*). But—but you just said—you despise him.

MONICA (*helplessly*). Oh, Austin. . . . (*She covers her face with her hands.*) (*A pause.*)

AUSTIN (*rising and crossing in front to the table* R.C., *puts his book down, picks up his coffee cup and takes a drink. Then, turning up* R. *of the table to the top of it, sees the cheque which* STOREY *has left there*). I don't understand you at all, Monica.

MONICA. You really shouldn't try, Austin. . . .

AUSTIN (*making conversation, and pointing out the cheque on table*). How careless Storey is—leaving a cheque lying about like this.

MONICA. A cheque? Didn't know he had a cheque.

AUSTIN (*taking out his cigarette case*). Five hundred dollars for a story.

MONICA. Five hundred! (*Rising and going up to* AUSTIN'S L., *picking up the cheque.*) Why didn't he tell me . . . ? (*Looks at it, sees* MRS. FRAYNE'S *signature. Her fingers clutch over it. Then casually.*) How do you know he got it for a story?

AUSTIN (*breaking the cigarette he has just taken from his case into small pieces*). He told me. I asked him whether he needed money.

MONICA. He did, of course!

AUSTIN. He said he didn't—because he'd just had this cheque.

MONICA (*bitterly, crumbling the cheque*). The highest bidder.

AUSTIN (*alarmed*). Here, what are you doing . . . ?

MONICA. I'm sorry. (*She throws it on the table and, coming down between the settee and chair* R. *of it, goes to the window.*) (AUSTIN *straightens out the cheque and refolds it neatly. In doing this he cannot avoid seeing the name. He looks over towards* MONICA, *who is standing by the upper corner of the window half turned from him, though able to see what he is doing. She does not look up at him. Having straightened the cheque he places it on the table again.*)

AUSTIN. Well . . . why not?

MONICA. I think it's—beastly.

AUSTIN. As they'll probably marry soon—I don't see any harm in it.

MONICA (*passionately*). They shan't marry!

AUSTIN. Monica—do you want to marry Storey yourself?

MONICA. Storey's in love with me.

AUSTIN. He isn't. He told me so.

MONICA. When?

AUSTIN. Just before you came.

MONICA. He lied.

AUSTIN. Why should he lie? I asked him to tell me the truth.

MONICA. He did lie. You wait. You'll see.

AUSTIN. He wouldn't take money from Mrs. Frayne—like this—if——

MONICA. You're naïve, Austin.

AUSTIN. I don't understand. I don't understand Storey. Why should he lie . . . ?

MONICA. She's trying to buy him.

AUSTIN (*a little bitterly*). He seems willing to sell.

MONICA. He has no character. Not an ounce.

AUSTIN. And yet—you want him.

MONICA. Yes. Worse luck. . . .

AUSTIN. I wish I'd never met you, Monica. (*He moves from the table towards* C.)

MONICA (*going up* R. *of the table and snapping up the cheque again*). Money—money, Austin. (*Abruptly.*) I've done with him.

AUSTIN. I should think you'd have more—pride.

MONICA. I'm off him for life. I swear.

AUSTIN. Oh, yes . . . !

MONICA. I swear it. Try me. Test me. (*She advances to him, standing above and a little to the* L. *of chair* R.C.)

AUSTIN (*facing her*). How do you mean?

MONICA. Make love to me. Do something. You'll see.

AUSTIN. You know, Monica, I—I'm crazy about you. I don't have to tell you. . . .

MONICA. Propose to me again.

AUSTIN. You know how I feel. . . .

MONICA. You want to marry me, don't you?

AUSTIN. Of course. What else?

MONICA. I have changed my mind. I'll marry you, after all.

AUSTIN. Monica! Really? (*He takes off his glasses as he speaks.*)

MONICA. Yes.

AUSTIN. You'll—marry me?

MONICA (*suddenly colourless, turning to the front of chair* R.C.). If you like, Austin.

AUSTIN (*overjoyed, advancing towards her*). Monica! Can I—can't I——?

MONICA (*drawing away and sitting on the settee*). No, Austin . . . !

AUSTIN. I mean—can I tell everybody?

MONICA. Oh. Of course. Why not?

AUSTIN. I'll try to make you happy, Monica.

MONICA (*with an impulse to cry*). Thanks, Austin.

(*The door-bell rings.*)

AUSTIN. I wonder who that is?

MONICA. Must be Storey.

AUSTIN. And Mrs. Frayne.

STOREY (*off*). It's only me. I rang the bell to warn you.

(*He comes in* L.U.E.)

AUSTIN (*turning up to meet him*). Hello, Storey!

STOREY (*throws hat and coat on rack*). Hello, Archimedes! Well, Miss Grey——(*Coming down on* AUSTIN'S L.) (MONICA *rises and turns up* R. *of table to the fireplace, turning her back on him.*) Nice dinner?

AUSTIN. Fine.

STOREY. Kendall and I dined at the Colony. (*Looking from one to the other.*) What are you depressed about? Eh?

AUSTIN. We're not depressed. That is—I'm not.

STOREY (*going up into the hallway and hanging up his coat and hat*). Well, you act like it. What's the matter, Monica?

(*As* AUSTIN *moves a little to* L.C., STOREY *comes to up* R.C.)

AUSTIN. Monica's just accepted me.

STOREY. What?

AUSTIN. We've made it up. We're engaged again.

STOREY. Really? No—really? (*Coming down to* R. *of* AUSTIN.)

AUSTIN (*doubtfully*). That's what she said.

STOREY (*shaking* AUSTIN'S *hand*). Splendid. I congratulate you, Austin. I congratulate you both. Austin—mind if I kiss the bride? (*He goes up above settee to fire as if to kiss her.*)

MONICA (*fiercely, turning away, and coming down into recess of window*). Don't come near me!

STOREY (*at the top of the table* R.C.). What's the matter with her?

AUSTIN. She's a little upset—who wouldn't be? Where's Mrs. Frayne?

STOREY (*coming* C.). Gone home to dress. Too bad Monica's in such a singular mood. Kendall wants us to make up a party.

MONICA (*turning to them*). I want to go home. Austin, take me home.

STOREY. Austin, exert your new-found authority. Make her behave.

AUSTIN. If she wants to go home——

STOREY. If you begin by giving her her own way she'll bully you, all your life.

MONICA (*bitterly*). Yes, Austin, listen to him. Do what *he* tells you! The authority! The philosopher! Tells everybody what to do, how to behave——

STOREY. Of course. My own behavior is so bad I can point the path of righteousness to other people. The drunkard lecturing on temperance—— (*He walks the drunkard's straight line to below settee—then turns to* AUSTIN.) The truth is, I'm a little tight. Ever get drunk, Austin?

AUSTIN. Once. Long time ago.

STOREY. Remember how it felt?

AUSTIN. Like *mal de mer.*

STOREY. Must have been bad stuff. Wait till you taste Kendall's champagne. It gives you ultimate sight, ultimate comprehension——

AUSTIN. And a head in the morning.

STOREY. But isn't it worth it? Wonderful illusions of grandeur——

AUSTIN. What's the good of illusions?

STOREY. Make reality bearable.

MONICA (*suddenly, as she turns up* R. *at back of table* R.C., *and crosses to get her hat and wrap which are now on rack*). I think they make it more difficult. (*To* STOREY.) Pay our respects to Mrs. Frayne. Tell her we're grateful for her invitation, but that we can't take advantage of her hospitality to-night.

STOREY (*moving to above chair* L.C. *and facing* MONICA). For pity's sake, Monica, stop talking like a book on etiquette!

AUSTIN (*as he crosses up* C. *to* L. *of telephone table*). Monica's right. It *would* be better——

STOREY. Oh, come now. Have a heart, both of you.

MONICA (*as she is handling her wrap*). I don't see why you want *us* when you have Mrs. Frayne.

STOREY. Of course I want you. I feel gay to-night.

MONICA. Be gay with Mrs. Frayne!

STOREY. Be nice, now, Monica. I've a peculiar feeling about to-night—that it's a sort of valedictory, a sort of farewell. After to-night, things won't be the same, life won't be the same.

AUSTIN (*gloomily*). I hope not.

(MONICA *at wall-table in the hall.* STOREY *above chair* L.C. AUSTIN *up* R.C.)

STOREY. You know what I mean—you and Monica'll get married—and, I hope, Kendall and I. We'll be stolid married people. We'll get old. We'll change. We'll drift apart. Am I getting sentimental? Well, why not? Be nice, Monica, for once. (*When* STOREY *speaks of marriage,* MONICA, *who has now put on her wrap and hat, comes down from the wall-table on a line with* STOREY. *It is here she makes up her mind about how she shall handle* STOREY *to prevent his marriage with* KENDALL.)

MONICA (*defiantly*). All right!

STOREY. You're a dear.

AUSTIN (*worried*). If you're tired, Monica——

MONICA. No; I've decided. (*Goes up to rack for her purse.*) I'm in great spirits now, Storey. Come on, Austin. (*She turns to the door* L.U.E.)

AUSTIN (*shaking his head as he passes* STOREY, *and going out into the hall for his hat*). I don't understand her.

STOREY (*going up behind* AUSTIN *as the latter gets his hat—to* MONICA'S R. *at door*). If you did—you'd disown her. . . . Come back soon. I'll be lonely.

MONICA. I'll be back. (*She goes out.*)

STOREY (*shaking his finger after her*). Don't you dare. (AUSTIN *with a nod to* STOREY *follows her.*) (STOREY *looks about, moves down into the room, touches things on the telephone-table, arranging them; sees cup on table* R.C. *and takes it to tray on wall-table. Then he comes down* L. *and replaces the bench by piano which* AUSTIN *has moved. Going over to chair* R. *of table he takes up his board and MS., and sits, thinks for a moment, then, having no inspiration, he jumps up and leaving the board across the chair goes up to the telephone, lifts it, and puts it down again. Going to the coffee service he pours out a cup and drinks it. Looking at himself in the mirror over the table, he finds a grey hair and pulls it out. He then goes towards the stairs, whistling "Silver threads among the Gold." As he is going up he hears the entrance door shut.*) (MONICA *enters and comes into the room.*) What do you do this for?

(*It is obvious that* STOREY *is a little frightened; he is very fond of her just now.*)

MONICA (*going to above chair* R.C.). I persuaded Austin, as he lives up-town and I live down, to let me go home alone.

STOREY (*leaving the stairs and going up quickly through the hall, looking out of the door and then closing it again and coming down to* MONICA's L.). You're crazy.

MONICA. I wanted to see you alone—to warn you——

STOREY. Suppose Austin saw you!

MONICA. It can't be helped.

STOREY. But it's cruel. You just told him you'd marry him.

MONICA. I had a moment of hating you, of utterly despising you.

STOREY. Go right away. I *warn* you.

MONICA. I saw that cheque.

STOREY. What cheque?

MONICA. Mrs. Frayne's for five hundred dollars. Is that your monthly stipend? Or is it weekly?

STOREY. Monica, go away. I've got to dress. (*He takes her by the arm and moves her towards the hallway.*)

MONICA (*aware of her hold on him, as he forces her up-stage, turns to face him*). What's the matter, Storey? (*She stands very close to him on his* R.) What's the matter? (STOREY *seizes her in his arms. He kisses her passionately. They are just under the arch of hallway.*) You do love me, don't you, Storey? It's me you love?

STOREY (*leaving her, comes down* C., *and goes* R. *to window-seat, sitting downstage end*). This isn't very nice, Monica. It's not at all nice.

MONICA. But, Storey, there's no reason in the world why we shouldn't.

STOREY. Austin.

MONICA (*moving down* C.). Oh, Austin!

STOREY. Kendall.

MONICA (*throws her wrap, hat and purse to chair* R.C. *In doing this the coloured scarf she wore at dinner with* AUSTIN *comes away with her wrap*). Oh, Kendall! (*She goes to* STOREY.)

STOREY. I feel funny about Austin. He's —so—helpless. He's so in love with you.

MONICA (*sits on window-seat, up stage and facing* STOREY). What about me?

STOREY. When I came in just now and you told me you were engaged—I—felt——

MONICA (*delighted*). Did you?

STOREY (*leaning to her*). I can tell you now. I *do* love you.

MONICA (*holds out her hands to him*). Tell me——

STOREY (*rising and sitting above her*). You're rare and exquisite, and——

MONICA (*both laughing softly*). You're always laughing at me.

STOREY. I know. You're never out of my mind. Your sadness, your youth. Your laughter . . . when you laugh, it's like the beginning of the world, before sorrow and death came. . . .

MONICA. Darling!

STOREY (*leaning back with low cry*). Oh! I am old!

MONICA. Old! You're not.

STOREY. I am. There's someone else inside me—a second man—a cynical, odious person, who keeps watching me, who keeps listening to what I say, grinning and sophisticated, horrid. . . . He never lets me be—this other man. . . .

MONICA. Kill him.

STOREY. I can't kill him. He'll outlive me.

MONICA (*nestling to him*). I'll kill him for you.

STOREY. You can't. Even now he's looking at me. He's mocking me. He's saying: "You damn fool, talking nonsense to this girl—pretending you want her above everything. You're making love to her because words come easily to you. But really you wouldn't get up early in the morning for her. You like to touch her because she's young and lovely. . . ."

MONICA. Don't, Storey. . . .

STOREY. "You wouldn't mind if she were once yours, but after that——"

MONICA. Storey, darling, I know you're fine and decent.

STOREY. He hears you say: "I'm fine and decent." And he says: "The illusion of an adolescent, of a love-struck girl."

MONICA. I'll beat him, Storey—I'll beat him.

STOREY. I wish you could.

MONICA. I just needed to know that you love me—tell me it again. Let me hear you say it again.

STOREY (*with an effort*). I love you.

MONICA. The way you said it before.

STOREY. I'm afraid I can't now.

MONICA. Storey . . . !

STOREY. You see how capricious I am.

MONICA. But you just said it. And when you did, I knew it was true.

STOREY. It probably was—then.

MONICA. A minute ago!

STOREY (*lightly*). A minute, a year, a century—what's the difference?

MONICA. But, Storey, I must believe in your love for me. I must!

STOREY. Why?

MONICA. Because I've got to believe in something. And if you don't love me—what is there?

STOREY (*rising and turning away from her, standing with his back turned at the foot of the table* R.C.). My dear child.

MONICA. Don't turn me down, Storey. (*There is a pause.* STOREY *considers.*)

STOREY. I want you to go away—and marry Austin—and don't see me alone again—ever.

MONICA. I won't. I tell you I won't.

STOREY. But don't you understand? I'm crazy about you. Do you think I'm made of wood?

MONICA. Why don't you take me, Storey?

(*A pause. He is nonplussed.*)

STOREY (*with a groan*). Oh—child . . . !

MONICA. I'd rather you married me, but if you don't want to——

STOREY (*crossing to* C.). Won't you allow me one shred of decency? I want to be loyal to Austin. I want to protect you. . . . (*He moves up to the piano.*)

MONICA. I don't want to be protected. Besides, it's all a pose. You want to marry Kendall Frayne so you can have lots of money.

STOREY. What's the use?

MONICA (*rising*). It's true. You talk about decency. With that cheque lying there—— (*She points to the head of table* R.C.) You ought to be ashamed, Storey.

STOREY. I'm not in the least ashamed. . . .

MONICA (*moving to below the settee*). You're just one of those men who goes around to smart dinners and having a good time—a parasite, Storey.

STOREY. That's what everybody's trying to be in one way or another. Mine's as good as any.

MONICA (*crossing to* C.). Instead of escaping from all this life and—fighting your own battles with me by your side to help you——

STOREY. Sounds like a popular song. . . . (*He sits at piano and improvises words and music.*)

"With you by my side to help me,
And no thoughts worth thinking of,
From morning till golden sunset,
But day-dreams of perfect love."

MONICA (*sobbing*). For pity's sake, Storey, how did you get this way? You couldn't have been always like this!

STOREY (*still seated at the piano*). Oh, no. I went through the idealistic stage. I used to sit in a garret and believe in Socialism. I could afford to then. I used to commit realistic fiction and moonlit poetry. I dreamed——

MONICA (*moving to the* R. *of chair* L.C.). I want to bring back those dreams.

STOREY. Why, what for?

MONICA. You must have been lovely then, Storey. . . .

STOREY. Oh, I was lovely.

MONICA (*hurt*). Storey!

STOREY (*rising and coming to the bench* R. *of piano*). Lovely. I dressed badly and followed the cults. It didn't take me long to find out how easy it is to starve on idealism. I had facility and there was a ready market for facility. I got five thousand dollars for writing a whitewashed biography of a millionaire sweat-shop owner. That started me. I took the money, and went to Italy, and I had a very good time. (*He sits on the bench.*)

MONICA (*leaning over chair* L.C.). But, Storey—you *must* believe in *something*. Don't you ever regret—don't you ever wish——?

STOREY. Regret? No. Not in the least. Why should I? I'd do it all over again.

MONICA. I can see that horrid second man in your eyes laughing now. . . .

STOREY. You amuse him.

MONICA (*going behind the chair* L.C. *and sitting above* STOREY *on the bench*). I'm going to beat him, in spite of you.

STOREY. He's got a terrific start on you, Monica.

MONICA. I'll beat him—trust me—just leave him to me. We'll be happy yet, sweetheart. (*She strokes the side of his face.*) (*A moment, and* STOREY *rises passionately, drawing her to him.*)

STOREY. Ah, child! I've done my best. (*They kiss. The moment breaks; he looks at her. They kiss again. The door-bell rings.*) Lucky for you, young lady! (*He puts her from him, goes quickly to the chair* R.C., *gets her hat, purse and wrap.*

MONICA *follows to* L.C.) Run home and dress . . . go out through the service door. (*Hands her her hat, which she puts on.*)

MONICA. All right. But I'm not worried about Kendall now. I'm not worried about anything. (*She takes her wrap and purse from him and goes up to the door* L.U.E. *Her coloured scarf is left in the chair.*)

STOREY (*following her*). No, no; out by the service door.

(*She turns and goes out* R.U.E.)

(STOREY *waits a moment, then calmly turns to door* L.U.E., *opens it, goes out and is heard speaking.*) From Mrs. Frayne! Thank you. (*He comes in with a hamper of wine, places it on the table* R.C., *opens it, takes out two bottles of champagne, sees a note and reads it.*) "For a good time for all!"

CURTAIN

Scene II

SCENE.—*The same. A lapse of two hours. It is now eleven o'clock.*

(*Before the rise of the* CURTAIN, KENDALL *is heard at the piano. She is discovered playing waltz from "Die Rosenkavalier." After a moment she stops and then plays a few bars of a popular sentimental song from music on the rest.*

The door-bell rings. She continues playing for a while. It rings again, when she rises and goes to open the door. She looks a splendid figure, graceful and distinguished in her black evening dress. She goes out into the hallway and returns in a moment, followed by AUSTIN. *He is in evening-dress. His manner with* KENDALL *at first is embarrassed and hesitant. Gradually, however, she puts him at his ease; she has that sort of manner.*)

KENDALL (*on* AUSTIN'S R., *as they come into the room*). STOREY'S dressing. I'm the first one here.

AUSTIN (*a little above her, putting hat and coat on rack*). Monica's not come yet?

KENDALL (*crossing to the piano*). No. Cigarette? (*Takes box from piano.*)

AUSTIN (*coming to back of chair* L.C.). Er—thanks. (KENDALL *holds the box to him.*) Thanks.

(*She puts the box back, taking a cigarette herself.*)

KENDALL. You and I are the only prompt ones.

AUSTIN. Yes. . . . (*He lights a match and holds it for her.*)

KENDALL (*after her cigarette is alight*). Do you know what time it is?

AUSTIN (*looking at his watch*). Ten minutes past eleven. (*He shakes out the match and turning up to telephone table puts it in ashtray, having lit his own cigarette.*)

KENDALL. I was here promptly at eleven. Storey hadn't even *begun* to dress.

AUSTIN (*turning*). He hadn't!

KENDALL (*she sits again on the piano stool*). I'm awfully glad you came. It was lonesome. (*She smiles at him.*)

AUSTIN (*going towards her*). I—I'm glad I found *you*.

KENDALL. Why do I never see you?

AUSTIN. Er—see me?

KENDALL. Storey talks about you all the time. You're one of the few people he respects. I always ask him to bring you to my house, but you never come.

AUSTIN (*turning a little down stage and towards* C.). I'm in the laboratory such a lot. (*He sees* MONICA'S *scarf—pauses a moment, and goes to chair* R.C. *on which it lays, taking up one end of it.*)

KENDALL. I know. Still, I do wish you'd come some time—and bring Miss Grey. . . . (*She notices him staring at* MONICA'S *coloured scarf which is lying across a chair.*) What is it?

AUSTIN (*with a step back, up stage, facing her*). That scarf!

KENDALL. Well?

AUSTIN. It's—it's Monica's.

KENDALL. You dined here with her—didn't you?

AUSTIN. Yes. I did.

KENDALL. Well, then——

AUSTIN. She wore it when I left with her.

KENDALL (*rising*). Didn't you take her home?

AUSTIN. She told me to go home alone—to save time.

KENDALL. Well, she probably ran back to tell Storey something. She's always running up here.

AUSTIN (*bitterly, as he crosses in front to the window*). She probably did. It must have taken a long time because—when you came, Storey hadn't even begun to dress.

KENDALL (*after a moment*). I think you can trust Storey.

AUSTIN (*comes to the foot of the settee*). Can I?

KENDALL. Didn't he tell me that—you and Miss Grey are engaged? (*She sits at piano again.*)

AUSTIN (*moving to the* R. *of chair* R.C., *looking at the scarf*). There's something funny about it.

KENDALL. There's something funny about most things.

AUSTIN (*moving to her* R., *warming to her*). Mrs. Frayne——

KENDALL. Call me Kendall.

AUSTIN (*sits on bench* R. *of piano*). Thank you. I wonder—I wonder if Storey tells me everything. I mean—about Monica and himself.

KENDALL. Perhaps he doesn't know everything.

AUSTIN. You mean—perhaps he's in love with her and doesn't know it.

KENDALL. Doesn't know it or won't admit it—even to himself. Perhaps. (*There is a pause.*)

AUSTIN (*abruptly*). Are you going to marry Storey?

KENDALL. I don't know.

AUSTIN (*naïvely*). I wish you would.

KENDALL. It would solve your problem, wouldn't it? It might complicate mine.

AUSTIN (*looks at scarf*). I'm not even sure it would solve mine.

KENDALL. It's comforting to know that even a scientific genius is not immune. It rather justifies a weak woman—like me.

AUSTIN (*rising and handling scarf on chair* R.C.). It's rotten to be this way. Wondering about everything, suspecting everything. Why should I care if Monica came back here or not? And yet—I do.

KENDALL (*slowly*). I care, too, Austin. Isn't it—stupid?

AUSTIN (*crossing to* R. *of chair* L.C.). Do you think Monica's in love with Storey?

KENDALL. You want me to tell you she isn't, don't you?

AUSTIN. Sometimes she tells me she loathes him. . . .

KENDALL. That's bad.

AUSTIN. Do you think so?

KENDALL (*still seated at piano*). Wouldn't it be nice if people were like molecules or electrons or whatever you work with? It would be nice for you because you would know all about them, then, wouldn't you?

AUSTIN (*moves up slowly to her*). Molecules are mysterious but they're more predictable than Monica. They obey some sort of law.

KENDALL (*amused and touched by his sincerity*). I think you're charming, Austin.

AUSTIN. Don't say that. I know better.

KENDALL. But you are!

AUSTIN. I'm dull and thick-witted and I—I have no words. I can't talk.

KENDALL. I think you do very well.

AUSTIN (*emboldened*). Well, that's because it's you.

KENDALL. I? (*She plays the piano.*)

AUSTIN. I find it easy to talk to you. Why is it?

KENDALL. Perhaps it's because——

AUSTIN. What's that?

KENDALL. Tchaikowsky.

AUSTIN (*sitting on bench* R. *of piano*). I feel I know where I am with you. With Monica I never know.

KENDALL (*rising and coming above him*). But you don't want to get anywhere with me. With me you don't have to make an effort. That's why you find me easy to be with.

AUSTIN. I—I'd like you to be my friend.

KENDALL (*puts her hand on his shoulder*). Of course.

AUSTIN. Won't you tell me—what to do?

KENDALL. Aren't you assuming—I'm wiser than I really am?

AUSTIN. But you *are* wise. You know all about the world and—you know—you're sophisticated. (KENDALL *is amused.*) You've had all sorts of—experiences.

KENDALL. I'm more experienced than you, I fancy. But no amount of experience can keep you from falling in love with the wrong woman. Or the wrong man. . . .

AUSTIN (*rising and going in front of chair* L.C. *to* R.C.). I know that Storey isn't the right man for Monica. I know that he won't make her—happy.

KENDALL (*crossing at back of chair* L.C. *to* C.). I think he's sufficiently honest to have told her that himself.

AUSTIN. But he should *convince* her. What's the good of all his talk if he can't convince her?

KENDALL (*still amused*). The more he talks the less convinced she probably is.

AUSTIN (*going to chair* R.C. *and fingering the scarf*). I don't see why she should have returned here.

KENDALL (*turning to chair* L.C., *shrugging her shoulders*). Some trivial reason, most likely.

AUSTIN. She must have been here quite

a time—if Storey wasn't dressed—when you came.

KENDALL (*sits in chair* L.C.). You know Storey. Never hurries. . . .

AUSTIN. It's funny——

KENDALL. I've said—I think you can trust Storey.

AUSTIN (*bitterly*). Can I?

KENDALL (*surprised at his tone*). Why, Austin . . . !

(*Enter* STOREY, *dressed, from upstairs. He speaks as he stands on the lower stair.* AUSTIN *remains fixed, and makes no move toward* STOREY.)

STOREY. Awfully sorry to keep you waiting. But then Monica isn't here yet, either.

KENDALL (*from the chair* L.C.). Two hours to dress. There's a fop for you, Austin.

STOREY (*to* AUSTIN, *as he comes down* C.). Fact is, I tried to write a little after you and Monica left.

AUSTIN (*stiffly*). Did you?

STOREY. A few lines—but distinguished. (*He goes up* R.C. *to the sideboard and brings a tray of glasses to the top of the table* R.C.)

KENDALL. You're getting industrious, Storey. What's the matter?

STOREY (*at the back of the table at its up-stage end*). I've decided to marry, settle down, cultivate the virtues.

(AUSTIN *goes over to the window.*)

AUSTIN. Marry?

STOREY. Don't you know I propose to Mrs. Frayne every day? And if I'm to support her in the style to which she's been accustomed I've got to work much harder.

(KENDALL, *leaving the chair* L.C., *crosses and picks up manuscript from chair* R.C. STOREY *goes up for wine in cooler by sideboard.*)

KENDALL. Don't you believe him, Austin. I looked at your manuscript before Austin came and there was only one sentence added to what I read this afternoon. (*She taps the manuscript.*)

STOREY (*coming back with a bottle of champagne*). But that one sentence was born of a travail—lasting two hours.

KENDALL (*picking scarf from chair, throws it on sofa*). "She rose and left him." Did it take two hours to write that?

STOREY (*as he opens wine*). I did brilliantly to write that in two hours. The exquisite simplicity of that sentence! The compactness of it! Think of the million things I might have written. Think of all the sentences in the world. And I picked that one. In two hours! The tremendous—celerity of the choice astonished me now I think of it. How did I do it?

KENDALL (*to* AUSTIN). Is he drunk?

STOREY. No, but it's a good idea. Kendall—— (*He brings a glass of champagne down between table and tabouret and hands it to* KENDALL. *As he returns to back of table, about to pour wine for* AUSTIN.) Austin——

AUSTIN. No, thanks.

STOREY. But you've got to. It's to celebrate your engagement to Monica. (*He fills two glasses.*)

AUSTIN. I don't feel like it.

STOREY. But I want us all to be gay tonight. I can't get comfortably drunk with a sober man in the party.

KENDALL. Don't make him drink if he doesn't want to, Storey.

STOREY. Do you know, he's only been drunk once in his life? (*To* KENDALL.) Imagine that!

KENDALL (*at chair* R.C.). If you're gloomy when you begin drink only intensifies your mood.

STOREY. Nonsense.

KENDALL. Well, so I've heard.

STOREY (*taking up a glass and coming down at the back of the table to* AUSTIN *at window*). Here, Austin. It's glorious stuff. Drink it and in ten minutes you'll feel imperial, omniscient. You'll know more about physics than Einstein . . . the Universe'll stretch out below you like a plaid.

AUSTIN. What's the use of a sensation like that?

STOREY. What's the use of love? (AUSTIN *takes the glass and* STOREY *returns to table for his.*) Hooray!

(*They lift their glasses.*)

KENDALL. Happy days!

STOREY. Happy days! (*They drink.*) (*Quoting.*) "The true, the blushful Hipprocrene."

KENDALL (*sitting in chair* R.C.). Nothing blushful about Roget. You're colourblind, Storey.

STOREY. Just an excuse to quote Keats. With beaded bubbles winking at the brim.

AUSTIN (*truculently*). Let's have another! (*He takes his glass to the table.*)

STOREY. That's the spirit. . . .

(*The door-bell rings.*)

KENDALL. Miss Grey. . . .

STOREY. I'll let her in. Fill the glasses, Austin. (*He goes up and opens the door* L.U.E.) (AUSTIN *fills his own and* STOREY'S *glass. He watches the door.* KENDALL *watches him.* MONICA *comes in. She looks charming in a simple evening frock, a picture of youthful loveliness.* STOREY *takes her wrap and puts it aside on rack. As they come into the room,* STOREY *pretends to blow a trumpet*—"Ta, ta, ta, ta-a-a.") (*Coming down to below chair* L.C.). May I present Miss Grey . . . ?

MONICA (*a little self-consciously comes to* KENDALL'S L.). Hello, Mrs. Frayne!

STOREY (*waving across to* AUSTIN). I believe you've met Mr. Lowe. . . .

MONICA. Hello, Austin!

AUSTIN. Good evening. (*He turns and sits in chair* R. *of fireplace.*)

STOREY (*crossing up to the sideboard, takes another bottle to the table*). Austin's on the loose to-night, Monica. Just guzzling champagne. . . .

KENDALL. Where would you like to go, Miss Grey? I haven't made a reservation anywhere. I wanted to know which dance-place you preferred.

MONICA. I am crazy about the music at the Trocadero.

KENDALL. Storey, will you telephone?

MONICA. Although you can't dance there. It's too crowded.

KENDALL. They're all crowded.

STOREY (*cross up for more wine*). I've heard of a marvellous coloured place.

MONICA. Oh, where?

STOREY. In the heart of Harlem.

MONICA (*excited*). Oh, let's go!

STOREY. I'm told you have to be a good shot——

(KENDALL *in chair* R.C., MONICA C. *to* KENDALL'S L. STOREY *opening wine at top of table* R.C. AUSTIN *in chair* R. *of fire.*)

KENDALL. Is that the place where the man was killed?

STOREY. Yes. It is, indeed.

MONICA. How exciting!

STOREY. Austin, you're marrying a savage.

AUSTIN. Oh, am I?

MONICA (*turning to* L.C.). Jilting me, Austin. Hear that, Storey? (*She makes her way to the bench* R. *of the piano.*)

KENDALL. If we're going anywhere, we'd better start.

AUSTIN (*rising to the table with his glass—a trifle desperately*). One more drink——

STOREY. Good! I always felt, Austin, if you ever got started—— (*Fills his glass.*)

MONICA (*sitting on the bench* R. *of piano*). A little one for me.

STOREY (*coming over to her with a glass and bottle of wine*). This is Roget '15.

MONICA. Is it? Well, then, a big one. (AUSTIN *takes his wine to the window.* STOREY *fills* MONICA'S *glass and turns to* KENDALL'S L. *offering wine.*)

KENDALL. None for me, Storey.

STOREY. Oh, please. (*He fills her glass, which she has kept in her hand.*) We'll drink a toast. (*He goes behind chair* R.C. *to top of table and pours for himself.*) To our married life . . . !

MONICA. But I haven't got one yet, Storey.

STOREY. But you will.

MONICA. Proposing to me?

STOREY. Don't flirt, Monica. To our married life. . . .

KENDALL. What a prosaic toast!

STOREY. Exactly. Wait a minute. (*Lifting glass.*) To our married life—may it be like the good prose of the English masters: solid, clear, sometimes hovering close to poetry—but in the main sensible and intelligent and—well-behaved.

(STOREY *points this: "Sensible" to* KENDALL. *"Intelligent" to* AUSTIN. *"Well-behaved" to* MONICA. *The "well-behaved" is a warning to her. They drink.*)

KENDALL. Nice toast, Storey.

MONICA. I don't think it's nice at all. I certainly don't want that kind of marriage.

STOREY. Let's drink to your kind.

MONICA. I'd like my marriage to be always like fine poetry—thrilling and exciting and lovely—and occasionally sensible and well-behaved—like prose.

STOREY. That's a large order!

AUSTIN (*bitterly to* STOREY). I suppose you mean that only you could fill it.

MONICA (*amazed*). Why, Austin . . . ? (*She rises.*)

(*There is an embarrassed pause.*)

KENDALL (*rising and putting her glass on the table* R.C. *across settee*). We'd better be starting. (*She turns on her* L. *and goes up a step.*)

STOREY. No, wait a minute. (*Coming down* R. *to* AUSTIN.) Are you angry with me?

KENDALL. It's the wine. . . .

AUSTIN (*sullenly*). No, it's not the wine.

STOREY. What is it, then? Come on—out with it. *In vino veritas!*

MONICA. What does that mean?

STOREY. It means that when you're tight, you tell your real name. (*He comes to* R.C. *below the settee.*)

MONICA. Oh, that's exciting! Everybody tell the truth—the absolute truth. (*Her last words are aimed at* STOREY.)

STOREY. We're not drunk enough for that.

(MONICA *comes to front of chair* L.C.)

AUSTIN (*to* MONICA). You might begin by telling me why you lied to me to-night.

KENDALL (*turning back to* STOREY). Now, you see, Storey——!

STOREY. You *have* had too much, Austin.

AUSTIN (*defiant*). I'll have as much as I like. (*He goes up at back of the table* R.C. *and pours himself another glassful and gulps it.* STOREY *and* KENDALL *turn to look at him. He still addresses* MONICA.) You told me you were going down-town. You came back here.

MONICA (*who has gone up* L.C.). Yes, I did!

AUSTIN. I found your scarf.

STOREY (*who has turned up between the settee and tabouret to the top of the table, pours himself a drink*). What of it?

AUSTIN. I suspected something. When she told me to go on alone—I came back and saw her go in. I hung around in the street——

KENDALL (*moving up* L. *of chair* R.C., *towards the hallway*). Do let's get started.

STOREY (*steps backwards from the table, holding out his left hand to stop her*). No, no, wait a minute. You hung around in the street. *You!*

AUSTIN. Yes, I did. It was all I could do to keep from bursting in on you. I hated you, Storey. I hate you now.

STOREY. Why?

AUSTIN. I resent you. I resent your fluency, your gift of words, your superficial . . . I resent you.

STOREY (*pouring wine into* AUSTIN's *glass*). Have another.

KENDALL (*coming behind* STOREY). Please, Storey . . . ?

STOREY. It's a rare moment. This sort of thing doesn't happen often. It'll be—revealing. (*Lifting his glass.*)

KENDALL. Something tells me we'll all be sorry for this. You, Storey, more than the rest.

STOREY (*recklessly*). I'll risk it. (*Lifting his glass.*) What did you think was happening in here?

AUSTIN. I saw her coming in here—going to you—I saw her looking up to you with love in her eyes—love that should have been meant for me. I saw . . . I wanted you to die!

STOREY. Sex reduces everybody to a common denominator. Here's Austin Lowe . . . whose knowledge makes him one man in ten million. And yet he stands in the streets looking up at that window and wanting to kill me because I'm kissing a girl! You're a Zulu, Austin.

AUSTIN. I suppose you're so damn civilized. (*He turns away to the bottom of the table.*)

STOREY. I? Not at all. When I came into this room to-night and you told me Monica was going to marry you, I felt a pang of resentment, too.

MONICA (*coming down to* R. *of chair* L.C.—*delighted*). Then it was *true*!

STOREY. Oh, it didn't spring from love for you. I felt: Why does *he* deserve her? I felt an impulse to take her away from you.

KENDALL (*who has moved to* C.). This is interesting, Storey.

STOREY (*to* KENDALL). It's not that I'm in love with Monica.

MONICA. Liar! (*Turns to the bench* R. *of piano and sits, sipping her wine.*)

STOREY (*ignoring her*). It's that I resent Austin. I'm jealous of him. I envy him the scientific eminence; I envy him his money. . . .

KENDALL. You might envy his integrity.

STOREY. I wouldn't have his integrity for worlds. It would destroy my amusements. I simply said to myself before: "Why should this mole-like creature"—meaning Austin—"possess this radiant girl?"

AUSTIN. I know that's what you think—I'm a mole, a scientific mole.

STOREY. Oh! Did I say that?

KENDALL (*coming down in front of chair* R.C. *and sitting on the settee*). Austin is a first-rate scientist. You're a third-rate writer.

MONICA. Storey's not third-rate.

STOREY (*moving to the back of chair* R.C.). But, my dear child, it's true. Artistically I'm third-rate. My mind is not as superficial as my work. . . .

KENDALL. Or as your life.

MONICA. Well, I don't care *what* you are . . . I love you, Storey.

AUSTIN (*like a small boy*). I don't think

I'll have a very good time at this party. I'm going home. (*He crosses in front of* KENDALL *and* STOREY, *going up to door* C.)

(STOREY *turns up stage with him, detaining him.*)

KENDALL. You are right, Austin. It appears we ought to leave Monica and Storey alone.

STOREY. I won't let you. That would be a calamity.

MONICA. I don't see where the calamity comes in. . . .

STOREY. You're too young to see. You're too much in love to see. But I see—for both of us. . . .

KENDALL. If Austin and I had any sense we'd leave you together.

MONICA. Why don't you?

KENDALL (*rising and crossing to* MONICA, *standing above the chair* L.C.). Why don't I?

(STOREY *and* AUSTIN *are up* C. *below the arch of hallway, the former on* AUSTIN'S R. KENDALL *above chair* L.C. MONICA *on the bench* R. *of piano.*)

MONICA (*challenging*). Why don't you?

KENDALL (*slowly*). Because——

MONICA. Because?

KENDALL (*advancing to above her and patting* MONICA'S *shoulder*). I'm afraid I should have a sleepless night.

STOREY (*with a slight movement to his* R. *towards the upper end of the settee*). If I were the cad you think I am, I would have an affair with Monica. But regrettably I am a Puritan. Can't help it. It's in my blood.

MONICA. Liar!

STOREY (*going to the top of the table, taking up his glass*). She's right. It is not Puritanism. It's prudence. I'd have to marry you. That would be fatal.

MONICA. Why?

STOREY. If you marry me, you would be happy for a year and unhappy for the rest of your life. If you marry Austin you'll be unhappy for a year and happy the rest of your life.

(AUSTIN *restlessly paces up and down the hallway.*)

KENDALL (*advancing to* L. *of* C. *a few steps beyond the chair* L.C.). And if I marry you?

STOREY. Your life will have the excitement of a perilous risk.

KENDALL (*coming nearer to* STOREY, *above the chair* R. *of table* R.C.). But I don't want excitement. I want—tranquillity. I want to be secure.

(AUSTIN *is now* L. *of* C. *below arch to hallway.*)

STOREY. Then you should marry Austin? Matrimonially he is as secure as a gilt-edged bond.

KENDALL (*turning on her* L. *to Austin*). What do you say, Austin?

AUSTIN (*moving down a little. He is befuddled with the champagne*). What do I say to what?

KENDALL. Shall we be sensible? Shall we get married—you and I?

MONICA. Say yes, Austin.

AUSTIN. But I'm in love with you.

KENDALL (*turning to* STOREY *again*). I'm out of luck, Storey.

STOREY. Don't weep over him. I'll take you on.

KENDALL. I accept you—not because you're worthy—but because I can't help it.

STOREY (*taking her in his arms*). You hear, everybody—she accepts me.

(*They kiss. He turns to the table, pours wine for* KENDALL *and gives her the glass.* MONICA *rises, about to shriek out* "Storey!" *but checking herself sinks on to the bench again, facing* L., *and breaks down.*)

KENDALL. I'll take a—flyer in you.

STOREY (*touching his glass to hers. She takes a sip of the wine*). And I'll try not to fluctuate too much. (*After he drinks.*) Now then, Austin. Your way is clear.

KENDALL (*turning to the others*). And now I really think we've talked enough nonsense. (*She turns up on her* L. *hand to hall.*) We'd better start.

STOREY. I'm just in the mood for a good jazz band. (*He joins her in the hallway.*)

KENDALL. Who'll carry the champagne?

STOREY (*at the hat-rack, preparing to get coat*). Austin.

AUSTIN (*in better spirits*). I'll take it. (*He crosses to the sideboard and lifts hamper.*) (KENDALL *and* STOREY *are talking in the hall.* STOREY *gets his coat as he talks to* KENDALL *but holds it in his hands.*) (*As he gets to* C. *with the hamper.*) Monica, I don't dance. Will you teach me? Come on, Monica. (*He goes with the hamper to* R. *of* KENDALL *in the hall and puts it down.*)

MONICA (*rising—speaking tensely—but only half turning to the room*). Before we go, there's something *I* want to say.

STOREY (*out in hall*). You'll tell us in the car.

MONICA. No. Here.

KENDALL. Another revelation?

MONICA. Yes.

(MONICA'S *voice and manner are very strained, like one keyed up to accomplish an almost impossible feat.*)

STOREY (*throwing his coat aside and coming to front of the chair* L.C.). What's the matter, Monica? Aren't you well?

KENDALL (*as she comes to* STOREY'S R.). You would start this.

AUSTIN (*coming down a little below* KENDALL *on her* R. *Very concerned*). Monica . . . !

MONICA (*moving from the bench a little further down* L.). Since everybody's telling the truth—why shouldn't I?

STOREY. Don't say anything you'll be sorry for.

MONICA. Even if I *am* sorry—I'm going to say it.

KENDALL. I really think we ought to go.

MONICA. I'll say it if it—kills me.

AUSTIN (*anxious*). What *is* it, Monica?

STOREY (*suspicious*). Think, child.

MONICA. I think you ought to know it, Mrs. Frayne. Austin and I think you ought to know it.

KENDALL. I know more than I want to know. There's been too much confession. Let's start. (*She moves up stage.*)

(AUSTIN *and* STOREY *each make a slight movement as if going.*)

MONICA. No; stop. All of you. (*They all face* MONICA.) I want you to know—that Storey—Storey is the father of my child—my unborn child.

(KENDALL *slightly up stage* L. *of* C. AUSTIN *down stage* C. STOREY *in front of chair* L.C. MONICA *below end of piano.*)

STOREY (*amazed*). Monica!

MONICA. There, now I've said it, I feel better. (*She turns to the end of the piano and holds to it, her back to the others.*)

(KENDALL *comes down between* AUSTIN *and* STOREY. AUSTIN *has involuntarily moved back a step* R. *They stare accusingly at* STOREY. *They are speechless.*)

STOREY. She's had too much champagne.

MONICA (*sullenly*). I haven't. I've had less than any of you.

STOREY. Monica—you're—— (*Turning to the others.*) Surely, you don't believe——

MONICA. If I had the courage to tell it—— (*She sways. She cannot finish. The strain has really made her faint. Clinging to the piano she sinks on to the bench.*)

KENDALL. I did think, Storey, that you observed *some* code.

STOREY. But I tell you, the child is—she's irresponsible. She's doing this——

(AUSTIN *rushes at him in front of* KENDALL. KENDALL *at his* R. *lays her hand on his arm.*)

AUSTIN (*almost screaming*). You cad! You damn, dirty cad!

KENDALL. No, no, Austin, will you take me home?

STOREY. She doesn't know what she's saying, I tell you.

MONICA. I do!

STOREY. Kendall, for pity's sake, listen.

(KENDALL *goes up to the hallway.* STOREY *follows up* L.C.)

KENDALL. I never want to see you again.

(STOREY *leans against the corner of wall* L. *of hall by the bookcase.*) Are you coming, Austin? (*She turns to the door* L.U.E.)

AUSTIN (*broken*). Monica, is it—true?

MONICA. Yes, Austin.

(KENDALL *goes out.*)

AUSTIN (*going up* C. *level with* STOREY, *looks at him*). Of course—why not? (*He takes his hat and coat from rack and putting on his hat follows* KENDALL *out* L.U.E.)

MONICA (*after a long silence, her back to him*). What've I done? (STOREY, *still leaning against the wall, stares at her.*) (*Pause.*) I had no idea they'd make such a fuss . . . but once I got started I couldn't back out, could I? (*As he does not speak.*) You're angry? After all, I saw you were letting me down. (*He still says nothing.*) Please say something, Storey. If you don't—I'll cry.

(STOREY *comes down to piano and takes a cigarette from box.*)

STOREY. You think you're smart, don't you? (*He crosses to chair* R.C. *and sits.*)

MONICA. I think I'm brave. Storey it's for you I did it, too. (*Long pause.*) Storey—don't you want me?

(*Pause.*)

STOREY. No.

MONICA. To-night—when I came back here—you made me feel you did. I was sure you did.

STOREY. That will pass and what will be left?

MONICA. Isn't there more to it than that, Storey?

STOREY. No.

MONICA (*rising*). I won't let you go, Storey. I'm going to fight for you—I'm going to bring you back—to what you were— (*She moves to the back of the chair* L.C.) to that youth you've let go. (*She moves to* C.) It's your one chance now, Storey—your last desperate chance. Don't you see, Storey?

STOREY. But I don't want to go back. I can't go back.

MONICA. It's such a little distance, Storey.

STOREY. Is it?

MONICA. These things you're selling yourself for—what good are they? Is this (*She includes the room in a gesture.*) what you *really* want? I can't believe it. Storey, dearest, I can see such a fine way we might live . . .

STOREY. I tell you it wouldn't work, Monica—even if I did try to be what you think I could be—it would be no use.

MONICA. I can't think of arguments like you can—I can't put things the way you can—I just know that if you had any bravery—if you had any courage . . . all these things you say are lies you've made up—lies to justify yourself, to prop you up—you're a pampered, weak thing, dawdling away your life on a sofa when you might be standing up straight on your own feet . . .

STOREY. Perhaps. Only I can see us now —five years from now—in a cheap flat—you looking blowsy—with little wrinkles under your eyes—and I in cheap shirts and cracked shoes—brooding in a room over a corpse of my genius . . . (*He gets up and goes to the piano and fills the glass still standing there.*) You can't have life on your own terms, Monica. I can't. Nobody can.

MONICA (*watching him, trembling—she is seeing him as if for the first time.*) I see I can't. . . .

STOREY. I'll marry you, Monica—but the joke's on you. (*He sits at the piano and plays, singing rather savagely the improvised catch*: "With me by your side to help you." *She falters to the chair, weeping piteously.*)

MONICA. Storey—stop—— (*But he plays on, cruelly, in an ecstasy of self-revealment —she huddled in the chair to escape the flagellation of sound, as the* CURTAIN *falls.*)

ACT THREE

SCENE.—*The same.*

TIME.—3.30 *the next afternoon.*

STOREY *is discovered in chair* R.C. *with the board across his knees, trying to work. He writes a sentence. Regards it. He is not pleased. With an impulse of disgust he tears several pages from his manuscript, crumpling them and throwing them on the floor.*

STOREY (*savagely*). Trash . . . trash . . . trash . . . trash . . . (*The door-bell rings.*) Damn . . . ! (*He springs up, tears the whole manuscript apart and scatters it into and about the fireplace.*) (*The bell rings again.*) (*Shouting.*) I'm not at home. . . . (*He goes up to the hall-door and admits* AUSTIN.) Hello! I say—you look done in. What's the matter? (*He draws back, facing* AUSTIN, *who passes him standing a little to the* L. *of the telephone table, almost* C. AUSTIN *does, in fact, look terrible. He has evidently been walking in the rain, his clothes are bedraggled. He hasn't slept. The champagne has made him ill all night. He is unshaved. His hands tremble. He is feverish and on the verge of being really ill.* STOREY *closes the door and comes down on* AUSTIN'S L., *looking at him. There is relief and a certain pleasure in his manner. He is glad* AUSTIN *has come.*) What's the matter? (*Going to the chair* L.C., *he moves it invitingly.*) Here—sit down. (AUSTIN *shakes his head as* STOREY *proffers the chair.*) You've been out in the rain. (*He moves a step to* AUSTIN.)

AUSTIN. Yes. (*He throws his hat on the telephone table.*)

STOREY. What doing?

AUSTIN. Walking.

STOREY. But my dear fellow! You shouldn't be doing that. You're obviously ill.

AUSTIN (*deadly serious*). This isn't a friendly visit.

STOREY. No?

AUSTIN. I've come to kill you.

STOREY. My dear Austin. You *are* ill!

AUSTIN. That's why I've come.

STOREY. I tell you there isn't a reason on earth why you should kill me.

AUSTIN. No reason!

STOREY (*moving in front of the chair* R.C. *towards the settee*). Last night was as unreal as a nightmare.

AUSTIN. Don't deny anything. It only makes you more—hateful.

STOREY (*sitting on the settee*). To-day Monica will probably tell you herself—it was a lie.

AUSTIN. Nothing can save you, Storey.

STOREY. My dear chap, let me get you a cup of tea. . . .

AUSTIN (*flaring*). Don't you laugh at me! (*Taking a step down, he whips out a gun and points it at him.*)

STOREY (*without flinching*). Is it loaded? Am I facing death? The situation is novel, but not as thrilling as I might have expected. Do you really mean to kill me, Austin?

AUSTIN. Why do you think I brought it?

STOREY. Did you go home for that thing? You needn't have. I have one upstairs. I'd have lent it to you.

AUSTIN (*with a quick movement to the back of the chair* R.C., *resting his right arm upon it, clenching the weapon, which is still directed at* STOREY). You don't believe I'll do it. That's why you're so flippant.

STOREY. Oh, I suppose you will. I suppose—at the Threshold of the Great Unknown, as they call it—I should be solemn. . . .

AUSTIN. Words!

STOREY (*leaning back*). Force of habit. Sorry. You press that thing—and no more words. Death is probably very commonplace. Disintegration. Resolution into original elements. Your province, Austin.

AUSTIN. Talker!

STOREY. Can't help it, old dear. It will wag.

AUSTIN. Not a real emotion, not a real feeling—even now!

STOREY. Real emotions and real feelings are destructive. I've learned to do without them. That's civilization.

AUSTIN. The old boast . . . !

STOREY. It's true. *You're* in the grip of a real emotion, a real feeling. What's it doing to you? (*Leaning a little forward.*) Listen a second. If you could empty your heart of its burden as easily as you can empty that cylinder there'd be some sense in curving your finger. But after I am lying there, silent for once, will you be happier?

AUSTIN. The world will be better off without you.

STOREY. Don't pretend this is a crusade. You want to shoot me because you think Monica's belonged to me. (*At* MONICA'S *name* AUSTIN *leans further forward across the chair-back, advancing the weapon.*) You want to shoot me because you're eaten by jealousy. You're not doing it to raise the general level of morality. Don't be a hypocrite, Austin.

AUSTIN. No matter what the reason—I can't endure your living——

STOREY. That I can understand. (*There is a pause.* AUSTIN *backs from the chair, raising his shaking hand as if to take better aim.* STOREY *grasps his board, holding it up between them as if to stop the shot from hitting him.*) Er—have you made any plans for the future?

AUSTIN. What is it to you?

STOREY (*shrugging his shoulders*). Curious. . . .

AUSTIN. First you—then myself.

STOREY. Oh, both of us? Teutonic efficiency. You *are* German, aren't you, Lowe? Lowe. Ja. (*He pronounces it with the umlaut.*)

AUSTIN (*in a knot of anger*). Be quiet. . . .

STOREY (*lowering the board*). It's rather a pity. Loss to the community. Yes, I mean you. I shan't matter. But *you*. It's a shame, really.

AUSTIN. Don't worry about me.

STOREY. But I do. (*Putting the board up again.*) (AUSTIN *backs away a little farther.*) (*Pursuing his vein.*) You might discover something perfectly tremendous —a cure for cancer or an escalator to Mars. (AUSTIN *backs again, lowering his pistol.*) Austin, do you mind not moving away from me? I admit—it makes me nervous.

AUSTIN. Have you nothing else to say?

STOREY (*putting the board away and going to the back of the chair* R.C.). Do you want a last speech? Dear me! I can't think of a thing. Isn't it funny? Now I'd like to say something brilliant I can't. I've often wondered how all those great men engineered their death-bed speeches. Made 'em up in advance, I bet. (AUSTIN *levels his gun.*) Wait! I've thought of something. . . .

AUSTIN. Say it quick. . . .

STOREY. His last words were: "Give my love to Monica. . . ."

AUSTIN (*wildly*). Damn you . . . ! (*He fires.*)

(STOREY *has dropped to the ground. The bullet goes three feet over his head.* AUSTIN *thinks he has killed him, and dropping the pistol, staggers, almost fainting, on to the bench right of piano.*)

STOREY (*as he gathers himself up* R. *of chair* R.C.). Good Lord, Austin! You nearly frightened the life out of me. Good heavens! (*He goes up to the sideboard and pours a drink of Scotch and gulps it. Comes down to* AUSTIN *with the glass and bottle, pouring whisky into the glass.*) Here. (AUSTIN *shakes his head.*) Do you good.

AUSTIN. Let me alone.

STOREY (*drinking it himself. Pours another for* AUSTIN). I saved your life, Austin, as well as my own. I give you back to Science. If you'd hit me they'd have sent you to jail for life . . . or . . . a valuable man like you. The jury system is one of the prime stupidities of democracy, don't you think? (AUSTIN *staggers to his feet and makes a movement up stage behind* STOREY *to* L.C. *He is pitiful.*) Where're you going? (*Quickly puts the bottle and glass on piano and follows* AUSTIN.)

AUSTIN. Home.

STOREY. You're in no condition to go home . . . you're ill. (*He takes* AUSTIN'S *left arm, turning him.*)

AUSTIN. Sorry. Made a fool of myself.

STOREY (*supporting him, brings him down* R. *of chair* L.C. *and puts him into it*). What did you do when you left here last night?

AUSTIN. Last night?

STOREY. Yes.

AUSTIN. Walked all night. Sick—not used to drinking. That champagne.

STOREY. Eaten anything to-day? (*He shakes his head.*) And you've been walking in all that rain? (*Moves behind chair* L.C. *to piano and gets glass.*) Look here, you've got to drink this. (*He comes to* L. *of* AUSTIN'S *chair and forces some whisky between his lips.*)

AUSTIN. Guess I'll go on. (*Pushing the glass away, he rises slowly and unsteadily.*)

STOREY. I won't let you go like this. (*Places glass on piano.*)

AUSTIN. Sorry to have—— (*He sways.*) (STOREY *turning in time to support him.*)

STOREY. That's all right. Shan't let you go out in this condition.

AUSTIN. Feel wobbly.

STOREY. Tell you what—you'll go in my room and lie down.

AUSTIN. Too much trouble.

STOREY. You've got to. (*He leads* AUSTIN *round* R. *of chair and up* L.C.) A little nap'll . . . this way—— (*He supports him and is taking him up the stairs when the door-bell rings. Shouts back.*) Come in. . . .

AUSTIN. I'll just lie down a minute. . . .

STOREY. A good sleep and a hot bath—— (*They go up the stairs.*)

(KENDALL *comes in. She looks around the room. The scattered papers at the fire attract her eye. Coming to* C., *she sniffs as if scenting the smell of the powder. Moving over towards the piano, she catches sight of the pistol which* AUSTIN *has let fall; picking it up, she places it on the piano. She turns in thought and, passing in front, sees* STOREY'S *crumpled manuscript on the floor in front of chair* R.C. STOREY *returns.*)

STOREY (*after a moment. Standing at the foot of the stairs*). Austin Lowe. He came to kill me and remained—to take a nap.

KENDALL (*without turning*). Poor fellow!

STOREY (*comes down to her* L.). Poor fellow! I like that. What about *me?*

KENDALL. You deserve it, Storey.

STOREY. What for?

KENDALL. We don't need to discuss it.

STOREY. You mean—last night. It's too silly. Even if it were true——

KENDALL. Don't deny it, Storey. Spare me that! (*She moves to* R.)

STOREY. Even if it *were* true—about Monica and me—one doesn't deserve death for that sort of thing.

KENDALL. I'm afraid I'm a very conventional person, Storey. By your standards, at any rate.

STOREY (*turning to piano, takes the glass and bottle and goes up with them to sideboard*). I leave standards to the moralists. I do the best I can. That's what everybody does—in the long run.

KENDALL. I didn't come here to reproach you, Storey.

STOREY (*coming down* C.). It's a mess, I know. It all comes—from trying to be intelligent.

KENDALL (*after a moment*). I came to say good-bye. . . .
(*A pause.*)

STOREY. Good-bye? (*He looks at her for a moment and then slowly moves over to the piano—taking a cigarette from the box.*)

KENDALL. I'm going abroad.

STOREY. When? (*His back to her.*)

KENDALL. Probably on the "Olympic." Sailing on the 10th. That will give me time to get my passports.

STOREY (*throws the cigarette back into the box and sits on bench* R. *of piano*).

You hate me, don't you?

(*There is a pause during which* KENDALL *moves to* C., *and a little up stage before she speaks.*)

KENDALL. I don't think so. I feel—dead about you. Just now—— (*Facing up stage.*)

STOREY. I tell you solemnly—that what Monica said last night—isn't true.

KENDALL (*turning to her* L. *to the* L. *side of chair* R.C. *Sees paper on floor*). Don't stoop to that, Storey. I see you've been throwing away your manuscripts.

STOREY. Yes.

KENDALL. I believe you might do good work—if you'd settle down.

STOREY (*ironically*). Monica's idea.

KENDALL. She must love you very much —to confess before everybody—the way she did last night.

STOREY (*wearily*). You don't know the half of it.

KENDALL (*turns to the chair* L.C. *and sits*). It's Monica—Miss Grey—I came to speak to you about—really.

STOREY. Yes.

KENDALL. At first I suppose it'll be a little hard for you—economically. Especially if you mean to do serious work. . . . I thought perhaps——

STOREY. You want to give us money—to start the new life on?

KENDALL. I have so much—and I'm alone.

STOREY. It's an excellent idea. But I'm afraid Monica—wouldn't see it.

KENDALL. She needn't know.

STOREY (*ironically*). Would you have us both start the new life—with a lie?

KENDALL. Always laughing. . . .

STOREY. Why not? Isn't life amusing?

KENDALL. You ought to turn over a new leaf, really, Storey.

STOREY (*pointing to fireplace*). Haven't I?

KENDALL. Perhaps that *is* a good sign.

STOREY. Nonsense. An impulse of irritation. The day after I marry I shall be regretting I tore it up. I shall be writing it again—from memory. I shall have to redouble my output because I shall have Monica to support and—you will be in Europe. In time Monica will come to see that I haven't in me the great works which she suspects are secreted in my brain. She'll begin to despise me a little bit. And I'll begin—to deceive her a little bit. And there we'll be—a typical married couple.

KENDALL. Poor Monica!

STOREY. It's too bad for both of us, really. You and I might have lived a civilized life. You have the two great requirements for the wife of a poor but intelligent man: money and tolerance.

KENDALL (*as she rises*). Unfortunately my tolerance doesn't extend—to this. (*She turns a little towards* C.)

STOREY (*rising to the* L. *of chair* L.C.). This—as you call it—is a lie. It doesn't exist.

AUSTIN (*off*). Storey, Storey!

KENDALL (*going up* C.). Good-bye, Storey.

STOREY (*above chair* L.C.). I tell you it simply isn't true.

KENDALL. Cheat!

STOREY. I should have thought Monica's —device—would be transparent to you.

KENDALL. Cad! Good-bye. I never want to see you again. . . . (*She sweeps to the door.*)

AUSTIN (*off*). Storey, Storey!

STOREY (*calling towards the stairs*). Coming . . . (*Following* KENDALL *as far as the arch to hall.*) Wait just a second, will you, Kendall?

KENDALL. I'm going.

(*The door-bell rings.*)

AUSTIN (*calling again.*) Storey!

STOREY (*to* KENDALL, *as he turns to the stairs in answer to* AUSTIN's *call*). Have a heart. (*He goes upstairs.*)

(KENDALL *is at the doorway* L.U.E. MONICA *opens the door.*)

MONICA (*hesitating in the doorway*). Oh! I'm sorry.

KENDALL. I'm just leaving.

MONICA. Is Storey home?

KENDALL (*uncertain how much to tell her*). He's—here.

MONICA (*passing* KENDALL *and turning to her*). I wanted to see him just for a minute. Please don't go.

KENDALL (*just above her*). I must. I only dropped in—to say good-bye to Storey.

MONICA. Good-bye?

KENDALL. I'm going abroad. I shall be gone a long time.

MONICA (*coming to the* R. *side of the telephone table, absently fingering a book upon it*). Oh! But you needn't go . . .

KENDALL (*coming to her* L.). My dear child. . . .

MONICA. And you needn't call me a child. (*Crossing* KENDALL *to* L.C.) I'm old

—now.

KENDALL (*a little down* C.). All of a sudden?

MONICA. Yes.

KENDALL. What's—aged you?

MONICA. Never mind. But I tell you—sincerely—if it's on my account, you needn't go. (*She goes to the* R. *of chair* L.C. *and sits.*)

KENDALL (*coming a little above her on the* R. *of the chair*). What inspires this mood—of renunciation?

MONICA. It's not renunciation. It's indifference.

KENDALL. I'm afraid—you're deceiving yourself.

MONICA. I'm not. Honestly. You'll see. I came—to tell that—to Storey.

KENDALL. I came once—to tell him that. I stayed though.

MONICA. This is different.

KENDALL. Oh, you're angry with him. That will pass.

MONICA. But I'm *not* angry with him. This is something else, I tell you—something else altogether.

KENDALL (*crossing to her below chair* L.C.). I think you'll be as happy as most people. Good luck. (*She holds out her hand to* MONICA.)

MONICA (*taking it*). You're very much in love with him, aren't you?

KENDALL. Yes, but I'm used to it. It's only uncomfortable— when I see him. But I'm going away now. (*She goes up a little.*) I enjoy travelling, and altogether I have a pretty good time.

MONICA. But I tell you, if it's on account of me—you needn't go.

KENDALL. You're worse off than I am, really. You're in love with a man who doesn't exist. I'm in love with one who does. That's why this sort of thing is less of a shock . . . if it ever happens to you. . . .

MONICA (*rising*). Mrs. Frayne, I must tell you—what I said last night—wasn't true.

KENDALL. Thanks, but one doesn't invent that sort of lie. (*She turns towards the hall.*) Good-bye.

MONICA (*follows to above chair* R.C.). But I swear to you I——

(*Enter* STOREY *from the stairs.*)

STOREY. Hello, Monica! Don't go, Ken. (KENDALL *is just below the archway.*)

MONICA. Hello, Storey!

(KENDALL *moves on towards the door.* STOREY *follows her.*)

KENDALL. Good-bye.

STOREY. Oh, don't go. . . .

KENDALL. I really must. . . . (*To* MONICA.) Good luck.

(*Smiling at* MONICA, KENDALL *goes out.*)

STOREY (*closing the door and coming back into the room*). Well, that's that.

MONICA (*crossing in front of* STOREY *to the* L.). She's—awfully nice.

STOREY. Oh, Kendall's one of the best. Understands everything.

MONICA. It hasn't done her much good, has it?

STOREY. How do you mean?

MONICA. She's not very happy.

STOREY. When it comes to that—who is? (*Crosses to papers on the floor at fire and starts to pick them up.*)

MONICA. You manage to have a pleasant time.

STOREY (*picking up paper and moving down behind table* R.C. *to below settee, while he is speaking*). I manage to behave as if I were having a pleasant time. One owes that to one's friends, I believe—just as one owes it them to be decently shaved and to wear clean linen. (*Picks up last of paper in front of chair* L. *of settee.*)

MONICA (*leaning on the back of the chair* L.C.). That's bunk. You have a good time because you're built that way. You're too selfish to worry about anything.

STOREY (*goes up to waste basket by telephone table*). I've reformed. I'm a better man now, Monica.

MONICA. Are you?

STOREY. Yes.

MONICA. How can you tell?

STOREY (*at basket*). Well, for one thing, I've torn up the story I was working on. There it is. (*Crams paper into basket.*)

MONICA. What made you do that?

STOREY. Last night after you left I had two hours of introspection.

MONICA. So did I.

STOREY. Henceforth I shall devote myself to the sincerities, the eternal verities, that sort of thing.

MONICA. Will you!

STOREY (*coming down* C.). It won't be easy. The trouble is the masses bore me, democracy bores me. I'd like to live in England on a private income. In a little cottage, with you.

MONICA. Poor Storey! I've robbed you of your subsidy.

STOREY. What do you mean?

MONICA. Mrs. Frayne. I just told her the truth about—last night.

STOREY. Did you?

MONICA. She said: "One doesn't invent that sort of lie."

STOREY. Well, it doesn't matter.

MONICA (*with sarcasm*). How generous you are!

STOREY (*crosses and sits in chair* R.C.). I dare say it'll be the finest possible thing for me to buckle down to hard work. I'll do hack-work to make a living, and the rest of the time——

MONICA. The rest of the time? (*Moves to* C.)

STOREY. The rest of the time I'll write sombre masterpieces, blood and tears. . . . I'll anatomize suffering. . . .

MONICA. But, Storey, you don't know anything about suffering.

STOREY. Most suffering *is* bunk, you know, Monica. Unintelligent people suffer because they want things beyond their limitations.

MONICA (*stamping her foot, turns away on her* L. *below chair* L.C. *towards the bench by piano*). How *can* you be so complacent?

STOREY. You're a victim of the popular prejudice in favour of agony. Why is a book about unhappy, dirty people better than one about gay and comfortable ones?

MONICA. But life *isn't* gay—or comfortable.

STOREY (*seriously*). Dear darling, life is sad. I know it's sad. But I think it's gallant—to pretend that it isn't.

MONICA. Poor Austin. . . . (*She sits on the bench.*)

STOREY. What makes you think of him?

MONICA. I've been thinking a lot of him —since last night. I'll never forget his face —the way he looked.

(*There is a pause.*)

STOREY (*rising and coming to chair* L.C., *turning it a little* L. *and sitting in it, his manner changing to one of sincerity*). Monica. . . .

MONICA (*out of a brown study*). Yes.

STOREY. If you take me on—I'll do my best. (*She stares at him with curiosity, fixedly.*)

MONICA. Will you?

STOREY. I'll try to be—what you think me.

MONICA. Thank you.

STOREY. Don't you believe me?

MONICA (*abstractedly*). What?

STOREY. Don't you believe me? That I'll try? What's the matter? Why are you staring at me?

MONICA. I'm trying to discover what it is.

STOREY. What *what* is? Why is everyone so cryptic to-day?

MONICA. I'm trying to discover what it is—that's changed everything. You *look* the same.

STOREY. The same face. . . .

MONICA. Is it only yesterday—that I loved you?

STOREY. This morning—1 a.m.

MONICA. I can't recall what it was like.

STOREY. What's this? Don't tell me you're fickle, too.

MONICA. It's not—fickle. It's that—you seem to me another person. Your voice is different.

STOREY. Slight cold.

MONICA. The things you say—sound hollow to me. I don't love you to-day, Storey.

STOREY. One can't have everything.

MONICA. I'll never be in love with you again, Storey. I'm sure. It's over. I'm dead. (*The two following lines overlap.*)

STOREY. How do you know? Tell me. I'm interested.

MONICA. I just—know it.

STOREY. The things I said to you last night?

MONICA. I suppose so. I see myself—all this time I've loved you—like a very little girl, a rather stupid little girl, reading a fairy-tale and believing it true—long after the other children knew it to be a lie.

STOREY. I always told you you idealized me.

MONICA. Last night you made me realize it. I saw you as you really are, mercenary, unadventurous and practical. I saw your soul. . . .

STOREY (*who has been leaning forward, now leans back in his chair*). *Must* we drag the soul into it?

MONICA. I saw it—a fat thing lolling in an armchair—with a brain ticking inside, like a clock. . . .

STOREY. But I'm not fat, Monica.

MONICA. Your body isn't and your brain isn't, but your soul *is,* Storey. You know it is. All night I saw you like that. I said to myself: "When you see him, when he stands in front of you—you'll forget all that, you'll feel as you did before." But I do see you. You do stand in front of me. And it doesn't matter.

STOREY. Don't talk like that. I'll fall in love with you.

MONICA (*rising and moving across* STOREY'*s chair to* C.). You're too clever for me, Storey. Your emotions are too complicated.

STOREY (*without moving from his position in the chair*). I wish I were like Austin. *His* emotions are as simple as those of a child.

MONICA (*tenderly*). As simple as those of a child.

STOREY (*rather bitterly*). No second man peering over *his* shoulder.

MONICA. He's a darling.

STOREY (*abruptly*). The darling almost shot me this morning.

MONICA. Shot you!

STOREY (*rising and taking the pistol from the piano*). He came here in a simple, uncomplicated mood. He's a rotten shot.

(MONICA *comes to him and takes the pistol out of his hand, horrified—she looks about her as if wishing to get rid of it and finally goes up* R.C. *and drops it into the waste-paper basket.*)

MONICA. Where'd he go?

STOREY (*moving across in front to the window*). He's upstairs taking a nap.

MONICA. How is he?

STOREY (*turns to her*). Feverish. He'd been up all night, walking in the rain.

MONICA. We ought to have a doctor.

STOREY. I don't think so. Champagne and jealousy.

MONICA (*coming to the top of the settee*). What did he say?

STOREY. He was incoherent. Had an idea he ought to avenge your honour, I suppose. Acted like a moving-picture hero and talked like an idiot. Really he was ridiculous. (*He restlessly punches the pillows on settee and window-seat into position.*)

MONICA. Didn't you tell him—that what I said last night . . . ?

STOREY (*crosses to down right*). Of course I told him. But he wouldn't believe me. Nobody'll ever believe the truth now. Really, Monica——

MONICA (*thinking only of* AUSTIN). Think what he must have gone through—to want to do that.

STOREY (*goes to right of table* R.C.). Can you imagine the trial if he'd succeeded? (*Tracing imaginary headlines.*) "Scientist Kills Writer Over Woman. Following an all-night champagne party in Clark Storey's luxurious West Side apartment . . ." The note of licentiousness and you on the witness-stand . . . the story of your confession . . . everybody's saying I got my deserts and Austin coming out a vindicated Saint George. . . .

MONICA (*turning from the top of the settee to the back of the chair* R.C., *leaning on it and facing away from* STOREY). Don't, Storey.

STOREY (*coming down* R. *and pacing over to* C.). But it's so *pretty,* Monica. It's almost a shame he didn't hit me. (*He walks backwards and forwards in front.*) Can't you see the humour of it, the lovely irony of it? What would you say on the witness-stand? Would you tell them the truth? That I never ruined you at all, that you lied, to save me from myself, as you call it, to prevent me from making a mercenary marriage. But if you did that you'd deprive the defence of a case. You'd send Austin to the chair. . . . (*He finishes* C. *on a line with* MONICA.)

MONICA. You're dreadful, Storey.

STOREY. And even if you said it was true —there might be difficulties. The prosecution would try to undermine you. They'd want proof beyond your statement. I believe you said you were the mother of my unborn child. Well, they'd want the child. Monica, you'd have to produce a child. . . . (MONICA *turns up* C. *to go. She is outraged by his facetiousness.* AUSTIN *appears at the foot of the stairs.*)

AUSTIN. Monica.

STOREY (*turning to face* AUSTIN). I thought you were asleep.

MONICA (*advancing a step to* L.). He is ill.

AUSTIN. Storey—Storey—I'm going now.

STOREY. You'll not. (*He goes up to* AUSTIN *and leads him down to chair* R.C.)

MONICA (*coming down between the settee and chair on* AUSTIN'*s* R.). Why, he's feverish——

STOREY (*to* AUSTIN, *making him sit*). You sit down. I'll get you something hot to drink.

(STOREY *goes out by the opening up* L.C. *and through door on its* R., *to the kitchenette.*)

AUSTIN (*to* MONICA). Did Storey tell you —what I——

MONICA (*just right of his chair*). Yes. He told me.

AUSTIN. Think if I had killed him, the

man you love—I'll never forgive myself, Monica.

MONICA. Whatever has happened is my fault.

AUSTIN. I've found out things about myself—what I really am. Look what I tried to do.

MONICA. Don't blame yourself. I can't bear it.

AUSTIN. You must know everything. I must tell you everything. You've got to know. I made up my mind to kill him. And do you know why? It wasn't alone because I hated him—but because I wanted to hurt you, Monica.

MONICA. I know.

AUSTIN. But all the time—it's hard for me to explain—I loved you. You were inside of me. I was desperate to tear you out. I see now I can't do it—I'll never do it. I have no existence apart from you. (*In his weak and shaken condition he is almost in tears.*)

MONICA. Austin, listen to me. You are trying to explain yourself to me. You needn't. I understand you. I understand you very well. You are clear to me. My trouble is—how will I make myself clear to you? How can I make you understand that what I said last night wasn't true?

AUSTIN. Not true?

MONICA (*turns and stands with her back to him at the settee*). It seemed to me—I thought that by saying it—I could change everything—make everything over—all in a second, it was so childish.

AUSTIN. You needn't tell me, Monica.

MONICA. How can I make you understand that it's all over now—that last night—yesterday—I loved Storey? That to-day I don't!

AUSTIN. I believe you. You don't owe me explanations, Monica.

MONICA. But I must. I want you to know everything that's in my thoughts. I musn't hold anything back from you. I still feel a pain about Storey, even now. But it isn't for him, do you understand, Austin? It isn't for losing him. It's for the feeling I had for him—that it should have been wasted—that feeling that will never come again—that can't come again.

AUSTIN. I suppose I'm luckier than you, Monica—because mine—remains.

MONICA (*turning and kneeling at his side*). Are you sorry? (*Crying.*)

AUSTIN. Oh, Monica, you here. Close to me. It's like being alive for the first time. (*Still seated, he takes her in his arms.*)

(STOREY *comes back, carrying a glass of punch.*)

STOREY (*from the opening up* L.). I had this finished five minutes ago. (*Enters.*) I drank it and made another. Here, Austin . . . nice of me, wasn't it? (*He comes down* L.C.)

AUSTIN (*rising*). I don't need it now, Storey, thanks.

MONICA (*rising, goes up between the settee and chair to* R. *corner of arch*). We're just leaving—together, Storey.

STOREY. Oh! (AUSTIN *moves up to above* STOREY.) (*Pause.*) Bless you, my children!

AUSTIN (*embarrassed*). Er—thanks. (*He turns up to* MONICA's L., *sees his hat and takes it up.*) Coming, Monica?

MONICA. Yes. Good-bye, Storey.

(AUSTIN *goes out into the hall.*)

STOREY. I'm awfully glad, Monica. Well, it's what I always told you to do. It's best for all of us, isn't it?

MONICA. I think so, Storey. Good-bye. (*She turns to* AUSTIN.)

STOREY. A happy ending. (AUSTIN *and* MONICA *go out together.* STOREY *follows and calls* "Happy Ending" *after them.*) (*After a moment—closing the door.*) That's that. . . . (*He puts down the glass of punch on the hall table. Then stares into the room—rather dazed. Pause—then he goes quickly to the 'phone.*) Regent 7577, please—is Mrs. Frayne there?—Hello—Kendall?—Storey—I'm frightfully low, Kendall—you've got to come and cheer me up—she's gone—certainly with Austin—we'll dance at their wedding, Kendall—what about dinner?—You're busy—what? — Oh, packing — oh, let's have dinner together—I haven't had a chance to say good-bye decently yet—Ken—Ken, I've never known you so stubborn—in common justice you ought to take me back on probation until Austin and Monica—that's the very least you can do—and, Kendall, I promise you—absolutely promise you—that if their baby—if their baby bears the *slightest* resemblance to me—thank God, Kendall, you're laughing—what?—No, why should you—keep your passport and get another—of course—for the southern route. Oh, yes, lovely this time of year——

(*The* CURTAIN *commences to descend.*)

—land at Naples and motor to Nice—certainly—heavenly trip——

Saturday's Children

BY MAXWELL ANDERSON

First produced by the Actor's Theatre, Inc. at the Booth Theatre, New York City, on January 26, 1927, with the following cast:

FLORRIE SANDS	Ruth Hammond
WILLY SANDS	Richard Barbie
MRS. HALEVY	Lucia Moore
BOBBY	Ruth Gordon
MR. HALEVY	Frederick Perry
RIMS O'NEIL	Roger Pryor
MRS. GORLIK	Beulah Bondi

ACT I

The Halevy's dining room—June.

ACT II

The O'Neils' kitchen-dining room—November.

ACT III

A bedroom in Mrs. Gorlick's boarding house in East 35th Street—three weeks later.

It is instructive to compare *Saturday's Children,* produced in 1927, with Frank Craven's earlier successful comedy *The First Year* (1920). Both plays concern the vicissitudes of a recently married young couple, their misunderstandings and conflicts. Quite apart from differences of timbre in the writing, we observe that Anderson's *Saturday's Children* takes notice of real economic facts in marriage, although without constituting an old-fashioned problem play, and ends on a note of high comedy with the married couple forced to behave like clandestine lovers and enjoying it. A refinement of spirit rarely known to older playwrights of the American theatre appears in Anderson's play. It indicates that the co-author of *What Price Glory?* belonged to that special breed of writers who brought individuality into a medium too often treated as a shooting gallery where authors were expected to aim at clay pigeons set up for public edification. One distinguishing mark of the twenties which brought Anderson to the fore is that a dramatist was no longer enslaved to shooting gallery practices. By straying from pigeons to people and from formulas to individuality of outlook, Anderson achieved a good deal of rueful sense.

By the same token, *Saturday's Children* also belongs to the area of anti-romanticism where many writers of the twenties prospected. The key to the comedy is contained in the young wife Bobby's protest: "What we wanted was a love . . . and what we got was a house and bills and general hell." One should not look for profundity here, and it is plain that through Bobby's complaint and the resolution of the play, the author was being anti-romantic in the cause of romanticism. And this, too, suggests a pattern for Mr. Anderson, who has been our theatre's most consistent romanticist.

He was to prove his right to that title when he returned to his first love, poetry, with the verse dramas and poetic prose plays that appeared after 1929: *Elizabeth the Queen* (1930), *Night Over Taos* (1932), *The Sea Wife* (produced at the University of Minnesota in 1932 but not produced on Broadway), *Mary of Scotland* (1933), *Valley Forge* (1934), *Winterset* (1935), *The Wingless Victory* (1936), *High Tor* (1937), *The Masque of Kings* (1937), the prose fantasy *The Star Wagon* (1937), *Knickerbocker Holiday* (1938), *Key Largo* (1939), *Journey to Jerusalem* (1940), *Candle in the Wind* (1941), *Eve of St. Mark* (1942), *Joan of Lorraine* (1946), and *Anne of the Thousand Days* (1948), as well as the radio plays *The Feast of Ortolans* and *Second Overture.* Taking an elevated view of humanity, of its errors as well as aspirations, but rarely overlooking realities of characterization and political background, Maxwell Anderson managed to give romanticism a new lease on life after it had been largely dismissed by 1920 as outmoded. This he accomplished, moreover, most successfully after 1930 when social realism was more highly prized than during the twenties.

Of all the plays written after 1930 only the Pulitzer Prize winner *Both Your Houses* (1933), *Storm Operation* (1944), and *Truckline Café* (1945) belonged altogether to prose realism. Among these only the first was entirely free of the romantic spirit, for the very good reason that it was a satire on politics in Washington, D. C.; yet even here the author leaned heavily on a somewhat romantic reformer.

Mr. Anderson began his career with the publication of a book of verse *You Who Have Dreams* and the tragedy in verse *White Desert* (1923). Literature has, indeed, echoed somewhat reminiscently in the work of this well-educated Pennsylvania-born playwright who took a B.A. at the University of North Dakota and an M.A. at Leland Stanford. He also taught English there in 1914 and at Whittier College in Southern California before mingling in public affairs on the Grand Forks Herald, the San Francisco Chronicle and San Francisco Bulletin (1918) and serving as an editorial writer on the New Republic, The New York Evening Globe, and The New York World. Anyone who noted Mr. Anderson's success with *What Price Glory?* in 1924 and observed the presence of the economic factor in *Saturday's Children* in 1927 might have predicted that the author was on the verge of becoming a social realist. He would have missed evidence to the contrary in Mr. Anderson's background and in much that did not appear on the surface of his work up to that time. If the prognosticator could have been again deceived by the next play, *Gypsy* (1929), because it drew the portrait of a dislocated modern woman, he would have been refuted a year later by the production of *Elizabeth the Queen.*

ACT ONE

The dining room of the HALEVY's *apartment. Large curtained window with window-seat right, beside which is large wing chair with standard lamp downstage of it. Upstage right is a large 1910 model Grand Rapids Buffet. Center stage is the dining room table with four chairs around it, and above that a small telephone table and chair. Upstage left center is a swinging door leading to the hall, the kitchen presumably being right and the front door left.*

WILLY SANDS *is seated in the arm-chair, left, reading the advertising sheet of the "Morning World." His wife,* FLORRIE, *is seated below the table, center, taking down the ads as he dictates them.* MRS. HALEVY *is at the end of the table.*

WILLY (*reading*). Cigar and stationery, poolroom, receipts $350 weekly, rent $80—good lease, large corner, good chance to build up—

FLORRIE. Wait a minute! Read slower!

WILLY. Oh, all right.—Cigar—stationery, poolroom, receipts $350—rent $80—

FLORRIE. And so with the young husband saving on his lunch like a dear and his little wife eking out the eggs and butter we just barely get through—and oh, we adore it, don't we, Willy?

WILLY (*reading*).—Good lease, large corner, good chance to build up large newspaper route, sacrifice, terms, going South. Federal Business Exchange, 1133 Broadway.

FLORRIE (*taking it down*). Well, you might answer your only love and darling pride instead of going on in that cold-blooded way, dearest—(*To* MRS. HALEVY.) And little Willy is really growing more adorable every day—I just grudge every hour away from him, and so does Willy, only he thinks it's unmanly for a father to talk about his child—you know, the way most men run on—don't you, dear?

WILLY (*reading*). Garage, Central Park West, 160 cars at $40 direct from owner. 230 Grand Street—

FLORRIE (*writing*). 230 Grand Street!—Darling, please, my arm's paralyzed—

WILLY (*interrupting her*). And say, get this—We collect quickly, bad bills, notes, checks, partnership frauds, stocks, schemes, business transactions confidentially investigated, investors protected, civil, criminal, commercial difficulties handled by clever experienced detectives, free advice, open evenings,—I'm going to sick that gang on a certain party tomorrow—

FLORRIE. On me, I suppose—

WILLY. I said, on a certain party, and she knows who I mean. I'm going to find out the truth about the strange dark man who carries ice into the basement and converses with my wife by way of the dumb waiter. It's been going on for over a year now and our child's three months old—draw your own conclusions—

FLORRIE. Willy! You obscene beast—just for that I do think Tony is the handsomest thing—

WILLY. Well, all I can say is I wish he was married off and salted away so I could go to work with an easy mind—

FLORRIE. Married! Darling, he has seven children—

WILLY. And still handsome? What a man!

MRS. HALEVY (*vaguely*). Who is it, dear?

FLORRIE. Oh, just the ice-man. Willy's always teasing me about him. I'm going to run away with him sometime but we've had to put it off because he hasn't any money. He has only the ice business, you know. So I'm living on with Willy and the baby for the present.

MRS. HALEVY. Oh, Florrie, I don't know whether you ought to joke about such things—

FLORRIE. Now, mother—

WILLY. It's no joke, you know. It's Florrie's romance. Everybody has to have his romance, and if your husband's a real estate agent you fall in love with the ice-man, and if your husband's an ice-man you probably run away with a real estate agent. I know how to handle her, though. I stay so damn poor she never has enough pocket money to run away with anybody.

FLORRIE (*laying down her pencil and addressing* MRS. HALEVY). Isn't he the most vicious!—Will you take that back?

WILLY. Nope.

FLORRIE (*baby talk*). Will you take it back?

WILLY. Nope.

FLORRIE (*her hands in his hair*). Will you take it back?

WILLY. Nope. Hey. Hey. Yep! Yep!

Sure!

FLORRIE. You take it all back?

WILLY. Sure! Say, leave me my hair—what there is of it.

FLORRIE. And does he love his Florrie?

WILLY. Sure, I do. I never said I didn't.

FLORRIE. And does his Florrie love him?

WILLY. Gosh, I hope so. If she does, she'll quit that. Quit it, you hear?

FLORRIE (*loosening her hold*). And is it a good little secretary?

WILLY. Sure thing.

FLORRIE. The best in the world?

WILLY. Best in the world.

FLORRIE. Because it's very vain of its stenography, you see, and it thinks a perfectly good little secretary is being perfectly thrown away being wife and mother for such a horrid beast! It does think so.

WILLY. Don't I know it?

FLORRIE. Don't you know what?

WILLY. Don't I know it thinks so?

FLORRIE (*with a ferocious yank*). And doesn't Willy think so?

WILLY (*climaxing with yell*). Sure I do. She's a love and a darling and hellcat and she can take two hundred to the minute and there ain't nobody like her! Now leggo.

FLORRIE. Will he give his secretary a kiss?— Just like he used to when she really was his secretary and there weren't any babies and ice-men?

WILLY. Come on, get it over with. (*He lets her kiss him.*)

FLORRIE. And will he take her over to the band concert, just the way he used to?

WILLY. Don't you think we'd better be getting home to that kid?

FLORRIE. Isn't that devotion? He knows perfectly well his angel child won't wake up till morning and the maid would take care of him if he did! Besides, I want to see Bobby, and she hasn't come home yet, stupid. Kiss me. (*She kisses him.*)

MRS. HALEVY. I don't know why Bobby isn't here. She's never as late as this. She must have had dinner downtown.

WILLY. Probably had dinner with her boss. Probably planning to marry her boss.

FLORRIE. She certainly could if she wanted to.

WILLY. If she's a sister of yours she could.

FLORRIE. Now, Willy, explain that quick!

WILLY. Me? Oh, I just meant—I just meant any relative of yours could do anything.

FLORRIE. Not good enough, darling. Try again.

WILLY. Well, you see, it's your fatal beauty that does it. They all fall for you. Realtors, icemen, princes of Wales and Sweden, bosses—bosses especially. I used to be a boss of one of you and look at me now.

FLORRIE. Mother dear, did father ever talk that way?

MRS. HALEVY. No, I don't think he did, Florrie. When we were young, nothing was the way it is now. But he's beginning to do it the last few years. He never even used to swear until you girls grew up—and then, he sort of learned it from you, I guess.

WILLY. I bet he had to. You keep a couple of girls in the house swearing blue rings around you from morning to night and it corrupts any man's morals. I'm getting so I swear myself.

FLORRIE. Well, I must say Bobby never did it much. She was the sweet little thing—

MRS. HALEVY. She's been making up for it since you left. I guess it's working in an office with all those men. I used to think it was terrible but she doesn't mean anything by it.

WILLY (*in the paper*). Well, when Florrie says damn—she means damn. You ought to hear her some morning when she breaks a tray of nursing bottles in the sink and spills the kid's formula over the ice-chest. Gee, you'd think she was a vice president.

FLORRIE. Well, that was only once, Willy.

WILLY. Once was enough. I learned a lot of new words that morning.

FLORRIE. You can read your paper now, dear.

WILLY (*who has been talking into his newspaper throughout this scene, and has not once changed his position*). Uh-huh.

FLORRIE (*sitting above table center*). Are you quite sure Bobby was coming home, mother?

MRS. HALEVY. Oh, she'd have telephoned.

FLORRIE. You know, mother, somebody ought to keep an eye on Bobby. It's so easy for a girl to drift into an affair—at that age.

MRS. HALEVY (*startled*). Bobby? Why, Florrie!—

FLORRIE. Yes, really, I mean it.

MRS. HALEVY. Bobby's a good girl, Florrie.

FLORRIE. Girls are awful hypocrites, mother. And the better they are the worse they can be. I'd feel a lot safer about her if she was married.

WILLY (*still deeper in paper*). Maybe we could kill two birds with one stone—fix something up between Bobby and our ice-man.

FLORRIE. You can read your paper, darling. You aren't so very funny.

WILLY. Yes'm.

FLORRIE. Did she turn Fred down, really? I mean, was it final?

MRS. HALEVY. Oh yes; but you couldn't blame her for that—he was—well, he was over thirty—and bald—

FLORRIE. I know. He wasn't a very romantic figure. Neither is old Helmcke, but he has got a lot of money. Is he ever here any more?

MRS. HALEVY. Yes, he's here, but he's deaf, and after all he's a widower. She's just sorry for him and doesn't want to hurt his feelings. You know he's getting so deaf you have to write out what you want to say to him.

FLORRIE. But he's got a lot of money. —And who else is there?

MRS. HALEVY. There's the O'Neil boy; —but he's going to South America—

FLORRIE. South America—! What for?

MRS. HALEVY. I don't know. Just some trip he got a chance to take. You know I did think it was getting serious, but he hasn't been here for a week or more and he's going day after to-morrow.

FLORRIE. Does Bobby mind?

MRS. HALEVY. I think she does, but her father doesn't—and she won't say a word.

FLORRIE. What a nuisance! To have him go away!

MRS. HALEVY. He is a nice boy.

FLORRIE. Does he make any money to speak of?

MRS. HALEVY. She told me he gets just as much as she does.

FLORRIE. Oh well, they couldn't live on his $40 a week. I wonder if Bobby sees him at the office.

MRS. HALEVY. I guess she sees him, but he's so busy about this trip—

FLORRIE. Well, I suppose that ends that—

WILLY (*from the paper*). Yep, looks like the boy's got away. (*The telephone rings.*)

FLORRIE. Never mind, mother. I'll get it. (*At the phone.*) Yes? Yes? . . . Rims? . . . Oh, this is her sister. . . . She hasn't come home yet. . . . Oh, Mr. O'Neil? Oh, yes. . . . Just a moment. It's Rims O'Neil asking for Bobby.

MRS. HALEVY. Tell him she'll surely be home.

FLORRIE (*musing*). I think I'd better make it interesting for him. Was Bobby going out tonight?

MRS. HALEVY. Oh, no!

FLORRIE. Hello. Why, Mr. O'Neil, she is going out to-night, but she'll have to be in shortly to dress, you know, and if you're nearby—yes—yes. . . . It must be a party or a dance because she couldn't get to the theatre now. . . . Oh, I know she'd like to see you but I'm afraid she won't have much time. . . . Well, that is a shame. . . . Oh, you are? Oh, I see. I'm sure she didn't know . . . yes, I would tell her, of course . . . yes . . . goodbye. (*She hangs up. A radio starts in the next room.*)

WILLY. Thin ice, my darling.

FLORRIE. Yes?

WILLY. What if they'd really had an engagement?

FLORRIE. As if I didn't find that out first! What an opinion he has of his secretary's brain! Here she thinks three answers ahead of him for years and years and that's all the good it does.

WILLY. Well, Jiminetti! You could tell the kid the truth, couldn't you?

FLORRIE. Why, Willy, you wouldn't want me to tell the truth to a perfect stranger? Think how it would sound.

MRS. HALEVY. It would have been better, Florrie— It would have been better.

FLORRIE. Now, mother, be a sport. I was just gambling. One last throw—Winner take all.

WILLY. What a dame!

FLORRIE (*caught by the music*). Isn't the old bear pleased with it? It's pleased with itself! It really is! (*Leaning over the back of the chair.*)

WILLY. You hate yourself, don't you?

FLORRIE (*moving towards right center, jazzily*). Don't it just?

It's vain of its face,
It's vain of its figger,
It's just fat enough
But it mustn't get—larger

WILLY. Rhyme it you dancing fool, *rhyme it!*

FLORRIE. Um— It never uses bad words. (*The radio wails.*) Poor Dad—he's got Chinatown on that two-syllable set of his. Run in and help him, Willy.

WILLY. I like it here, thanks.

FLORRIE. But supposing I wanted to talk to mother and you were in the way?

WILLY. Impossible.

FLORRIE. Oh, quite. You have finished with the dictation, Mr. Sands?

WILLY (*feeling the pressure*). That's all. (*He goes.*)

FLORRIE. Children, dishes and young husbands!

MRS. HALEVY. He's such a sweet boy, Florrie, you ought to be nicer to him.

FLORRIE. I'm a sweet girl and he ought to be nicer to me.

MRS. HALEVY. You really do like him, don't you, dear?

FLORRIE. I don't know. Yes, sometimes I think I do. But not often. —Mother, what do you really think about this Rims boy and Bobby? Is it kind of serious?

MRS. HALEVY. I don't know how it is with him—but Bobby's been crying her eyes out.

FLORRIE. You don't mean you've actually seen Bobby crying?

MRS. HALEVY. No, not seen her— But when she's been crying all night, I can tell in the morning.

FLORRIE. Well, if it's as bad as all that—

MRS. HALEVY. Oh, it is—

FLORRIE. Why, he'll probably keep her waiting for him for years, and then not come back at all—

MRS. HALEVY. I suppose so.

FLORRIE. Or else she'll just drift along waiting for somebody like him and the first thing we know she'll be an old maid and a public charge.

MRS. HALEVY. She's only twenty-three.

FLORRIE. Well, wasn't I married at twenty-three? It's easy to get married before you're twenty-five but afterwards try and do it. If only she wasn't such an egg!

MRS. HALEVY (*horrified*). Such a what?

FLORRIE. Such an egg!

MRS. HALEVY. Florrie!

FLORRIE. I know, but she's so unhatched, somehow—she doesn't know her way around the block—she never did.

MRS. HALEVY. People do wait sometimes —sometimes they wait for years—and then it comes out all right. We waited—

FLORRIE. Oh, I know, but that was different.

MRS. HALEVY. Yes, I suppose so. It was all different then.

FLORRIE (*a door closes outside*). Maybe that's her now. (*She goes toward the hall door.*)

FLORRIE. Bobby, dear, I haven't seen you for an age!

BOBBY (*entering*). Well, why should you, darling? Don't be sloppy. Ugh, I've just come from the subway! Let me at the bath-tub before you kiss me.

FLORRIE. We've been waiting to see you.

BOBBY. How's the baby?

FLORRIE. Wonderful.

MRS. HALEVY. Have you had dinner, dear?

BOBBY (*taking off an orchid*). I don't know. Yes, I guess so.

MRS. HALEVY. You don't know?

BOBBY. Yes—I was—I was in a place where they were eating. It must have been dinner.

FLORRIE. Fascinating company?

BOBBY. Just the boss. Mengle.

FLORRIE. Since when does Mr. Mengle take you to dinner?

BOBBY. Ever since six o'clock and it's been a long time.

FLORRIE. And his conversation was so charming you couldn't think of food?

BOBBY (*vague and a little bored*). I hope he didn't lay himself out to be charming because I didn't hear a word he said.

FLORRIE. Well, dearest, when you go to dinner with a man you ought to at least listen to him.

BOBBY. I'll get him to say it over again sometime. He won't mind. If he does he can always fire me.

FLORRIE. Well, you needn't have worried and spoiled poor Mengle's evening, for Rims did telephone, if that's what you want to know.

BOBBY. Rims? Rims telephoned?

FLORRIE. I think that's the name. Rims —Rims Murphy—

MRS. HALEVY. O'Neil, dear.

FLORRIE. Oh, yes, O'Neil.

BOBBY. What did he say?

FLORRIE. He wanted to know if you'd

be in this evening.

BOBBY. Oh.

FLORRIE. I said you were going to a dance or something, but if he came right over—

BOBBY. Oh, I'm not going anywhere.

FLORRIE. Well, why tell him that? You don't want him to think you're sitting home weeping about him?

BOBBY. Why should he think I'm weeping? Did you know I wasn't going out?

MRS. HALEVY. I told her you weren't, Bobby—

BOBBY. Then I don't see what occasion there was for—

FLORRIE. Child, you'll never know; you'll never, never know. You're just that innocent.

BOBBY. Oh—well, he'll know I wasn't going anywhere—because I'll be here.

FLORRIE. Couldn't you change your mind? At any rate you can't tell him you weren't going out because I told him you were.

BOBBY. Couldn't you be mistaken, dear? I think you could. I even think you were.

FLORRIE. You would!

BOBBY. I think it's perfectly silly.

FLORRIE. You're quite hopeless, darling —I doubt if I can do anything for you, but I can tell you this.

BOBBY. Yes?

FLORRIE. If you want a man to be interested in you, let him see you going out the door with another man. And if you want a man to come running, just let him imagine you at a dance with someone else.

BOBBY. You're pretty tiresome tonight, Florrie. If I cared enough about anybody to want to keep him— I'd care too much to want to keep him that way.

FLORRIE. My God, can anybody be as young as that and live!

MRS. HALEVY. Well, Bobby is right, Florrie—Bobby is right!

FLORRIE. Mother, you never grew up a day after you were married.

MRS. HALEVY. Well—I'm glad I've stayed young then.

FLORRIE. Do you know what I want you to do?

BOBBY. It doesn't matter. I wouldn't do it.

FLORRIE. I want you to put on your prettiest party dress. You were going to a dance, you see, and then Rims'll come in and you'll decide not to go. It just gives you a chance to look your best. Don't you see?

BOBBY. You must think I'm mad about this Rims.

FLORRIE. Aren't you, dear?

BOBBY. Not the least in the world.

FLORRIE. Oh, well, don't do it then. Because if you did he might ask you to marry him or something and then you'd have to turn him down and it'd be such a bother.

BOBBY. Yes, I know. There's nothing like a proposal to spoil an evening. I've been so unfortunate that way.

MRS. HALEVY. Well, you have had two in a week, Bobby.

BOBBY. Three, mother.

FLORRIE. Was it Mengle?

BOBBY. Yes, I think that's what he was talking about a good deal of the time— whenever he wasn't talking about the music business. The music business, by the way, is very good.

MRS. HALEVY. But Mr. Mengle's married, dear.

BOBBY. Oh, this wasn't a proposal of marriage. It was just a—proposal.

MRS. HALEVY. But Bobby—you can't work for a man like that!

FLORRIE. Oh, I wouldn't say that, mother.

BOBBY.—No—you see, I think probably I got the job because he had hopes of me. Hope springs eternal in the employer's breast.

MRS. HALEVY. What did you say to him?

BOBBY. I didn't disillusion him completely. It's better for Mr. Mengle's hopes to go on springing eternal.

MRS. HALEVY. He must be a beast—

BOBBY. He's a rather friendly old beast, and very considerate, really.

FLORRIE. He didn't mean anything, mother.

MRS. HALEVY. But it's really terrible— for a young girl—

FLORRIE. Will you put on the party dress?

BOBBY. I might if I had one.

FLORRIE. The pink one!

BOBBY (*she pauses, looking at* FLORRIE, *decides it is not worth arguing about. She reaches in her bag and pulls out a coin*). Heads or tails.

FLORRIE. Heads!

BOBBY (*flipping it*). You win.

FLORRIE. The pink dress.

BOBBY. Anything you say.

MRS. HALEVY. I must say she never would have done it if I'd asked her.

FLORRIE. Use just the right touch and you can get her to do anything. You see, mother, she's just a child. There's a psychologist writing for the American that says people don't really begin to think until they're nearly thirty. They walk around and talk and they seem human, but they're really practically unconscious.

MRS. HALEVY. I do wish you wouldn't read the American, dear.

FLORRIE. Well, sometimes I think it's really true. That's one reason why it's easy for a girl to get married young, and not so easy afterward. The idea is to catch your man while he's still unconscious. If he begins to think about it there really isn't any reason why he should get married at all. And so the psychologist says the only hope for a girl is to start thinking young and that's why girls have to be cleverer than men.

MRS. HALEVY. I don't know how people ever think of such things.

FLORRIE. He's paid to. I could think of nearly anything if I was paid to. (*There is a terrible crash of wood and metal in the next room.*)

MRS. HALEVY. Good Heavens! Merlin what did you do to it?

MR. HALEVY (*entering from left*). Nothing.

FLORRIE. But it sounded as if—

MR. HALEVY. It will sound no more, my darling. The infernal machine that wrecked our peace is forever silenced.

MRS. HALEVY. What have you *done?*

MR. HALEVY (*filling his pipe*). I have murdered the entire Philadelphia Symphony Orchestra, from Stokowski to the timpani player. I tried everything else on that Goddam machine and it didn't do any good, so I tried smashing it. From now on if we want any music we'll go where it is.

MRS. HALEVY. I don't know what's come over you, Merlin. You're so sudden lately.

MR. HALEVY. Yeah! Toward the end of his life the human male, having learned there is nothing to be gained by gentleness and compromise, begins to assert himself. You didn't want me to build a radio and I built it anyway. After I got it built I didn't like it so I smashed it. If you tell me to get another one I won't. If you tell me not to get another one I will. (WILLY *enters from left with a newspaper in his hand.*)

FLORRIE. It's best not to tell him anything, mother.

MRS. HALEVY. Goodness knows I never tried to tell him anything.

FLORRIE. As for Willy it wouldn't dream of trying to tell him anything, would it?

WILLY. Darling, how would I know anything if you didn't tell me?

FLORRIE. You wouldn't.

WILLY. Not a thing. (*The telephone rings.*)

FLORRIE (*answering it*). Hello! No. Oh, hello! Oh, yes. Mr. O'Neil? Oh, I see. Yes, she is . . . I think she's taking a bath— (BOBBY *pokes her head in at door up left.*) What? . . .

BOBBY. Who is it?

FLORRIE (*into the mouthpiece*). Just a moment. (*She covers the mouthpiece.*) It's this Rims fellow. The one you aren't mad about.

BOBBY. Let me talk to him.

FLORRIE. No, dear. You're supposed to be taking a bath. (*Into the phone.*) Hello, —why, she is in the tub and I hate to— yes— Why she seemed rather particular about this engagement, but I'm sure she'll wait if you put it that way.

BOBBY (*standing up left fixing belt of wrapper*). You fiend—give me that phone!

FLORRIE (*covering the mouthpiece*). Go away, dear. (*Into the phone.*) Just somebody cutting in, I guess.—

BOBBY (*grabbing phone*). Give me that phone. Hello, hello. . . . It's Bobby. . . . I was, but I heard the telephone, and . . . Oh, Rims, that's sweet of you, really. . . . I know you must be perfectly tied up . . . no, Rims, truly I'm not. . . . I haven't any engagement the least in the world. . . . It was just that infernal sister of mine. . . . I don't know, just her little joke, I guess . . . anyway, I'll be here —yes, good-bye.
(*She hangs up.*)

MRS. HALEVY. Florrie, what did you mean—

BOBBY. After this I'll answer the telephone for myself, thanks.

FLORRIE. Well, you've managed to ruin—

MR. HALEVY. What's the row about, girlies?

FLORRIE. Nothing whatever.

WILLY. I gather Florrie thinks Bobby's going out tonight and Bobby thinks she isn't.

MR. HALEVY. Well, Bobby ought to know.

MRS. HALEVY. Now, what's Rims going to think?

BOBBY. I'll tell him exactly what happened.

FLORRIE. Well, he won't believe you.

BOBBY. Of course he'll believe me.

FLORRIE. You mean to say you're coming out in that pink dress and tell him you weren't going anywhere?

BOBBY. I'm not wearing my pink dress—

FLORRIE. No? I thought I won the toss, my darling.

WILLY. Let us in on it. What's the gag?

BOBBY. It's too silly to talk about. I'm sure I don't know what Florrie thinks she's doing. I'm going to dress.

FLORRIE. We're all going over to the concert.

BOBBY. You mean you're maneuvering everybody out of the house just to—? Well, I won't have it— Dad, you won't go?

MR. HALEVY. Not if you'd rather I didn't, Bobby, but the radio's out of commission and I did want some music.

BOBBY. Oh, very well.

MR. HALEVY. But I'd just as soon stay, honey,—almost—

BOBBY. Never mind—

FLORRIE. The pink dress!

BOBBY. Very well. (*She goes into bedroom.*)

MR. HALEVY. What's up, Florrie?

MRS. HALEVY. Are we going to the park?

FLORRIE. Yes! Put something on, mother—he's coming right over. It's her Rims, dad—her marvellous Rims O'Neil—and we're just clearing out to give them elbow room—

MR. HALEVY. Well, if she doesn't want us to go—

FLORRIE. Of course she does. Only she thinks it looks too deliberate, as if he'd think of that—

MR. HALEVY. I thought he'd gone to South America—

FLORRIE. Well, he is going but he hasn't gone yet. That's the point, and the kids ought to have a chance to say goodbye.

MR. HALEVY. Well, if that's all—

WILLY (*coming out of paper*). Say, Florrie, listen!— You remember that little house on a hundred and forty-first—the one we wanted?—

FLORRIE. Of course, it remembers—

WILLY. Well, it's for rent—

FLORRIE. No, not the very one—

WILLY. Sure thing—the one we wanted—and reasonable too—

FLORRIE. How much?

WILLY. Sixty.

FLORRIE. Why that's less than our apartment. Now, why did we sign that lease?

MR. HALEVY. Sixty a month for a whole house?—

FLORRIE. Well, it's only two rooms and a kitchen, really—

WILLY. Sort of lost and forgotten among the apartment buildings—

FLORRIE. It's the funniest little place—

MR. HALEVY. Oh, well, if it's only two rooms.

FLORRIE. And a garden, dad, we simply adored it—

WILLY. We figured we could use part of the kitchen for a dining room, you see—

FLORRIE. Oh, well— (*To* MRS. HALEVY.) Listen, mother, I think I'd better wait a minute and make my peace with the kid. Take Willy with you and I'll meet you there—

MRS. HALEVY. Where we always sit?

FLORRIE. Yes, the same place.

WILLY. Come on, mother.

MR. HALEVY. You two run along. I'll catch up. I want to see her a minute myself—

WILLY (*going out with* MRS. HALEVY). Goodbye, Bobby!

BOBBY. Goodbye, Willy.

MR. HALEVY. Bobby! Dressed yet?

BOBBY (*entering left, still doing up the last few hooks of her dress*). Yeah!—what is it, dad?

MR. HALEVY. Anything the matter?

BOBBY. I guess not.

MR. HALEVY. I mean, is the kid happy?

BOBBY. Not very. Of course I'm happy.

MR. HALEVY. Well, be yourself, girlie. Don't let anybody run over you.

BOBBY. All right, dad.

MR. HALEVY. And, well,—don't do anything I wouldn't do—

BOBBY. Tell me something you wouldn't do.

MR. HALEVY. Not a damn thing I didn't feel like doing. So long. (*He goes out.*)

BOBBY. All right.

MR. HALEVY (*off stage*). Remember that.

BOBBY (*to* FLORRIE). Aren't you going?

FLORRIE. You don't like me much, do you?

BOBBY. No.

FLORRIE. Well, I'll run along.

BOBBY. Oh, stay if you want to.

FLORRIE. I was just trying to make things easier for you, dear. You're in love with Rims, aren't you?

BOBBY. No.

FLORRIE. Oh, well, then I'm sorry, and it was foolish. But, gee, kiddie, you're a rave in that dress. I wish somebody was coming you were in love with.

BOBBY. Thanks awfully.

FLORRIE. Will you make it up with me, dear? Because I really thought it was good fun—

BOBBY. Oh, why don't you go? Why didn't you go with the others?

FLORRIE. Bobby, you are in love with him.

BOBBY. I'm not in love with anybody that isn't in love with me.

FLORRIE. But he is.

BOBBY. No he isn't, if he was he'd have —well, it doesn't matter only I wish you'd go.

FLORRIE. It's all right, dear. I'll go the minute he comes. And listen—he is in love with you. I know by his voice over the phone. And if you want him, dear, don't you know you can have him?

BOBBY (*looking away*). He's going to Buenos Ayres to start a branch house. It may take two years.

FLORRIE. Don't let him.

BOBBY. If he wants to go, why shouldn't he?

FLORRIE. Because you're in love with each other, and you'd be much happier if he stayed here, wouldn't you?

BOBBY. It doesn't matter.

FLORRIE. You know what will happen? He'll fall in love with someone else.

BOBBY. Well, so will I, probably.

FLORRIE. You thought he was going to ask you to marry him, didn't you?

BOBBY. Yes.

FLORRIE. And if he'd stayed a little longer he would have, wouldn't he?

BOBBY. Yes.

FLORRIE. Then he'll ask you tonight.

BOBBY. No he won't. He's made up his mind not to.

FLORRIE. Darling, he didn't tell you that?

BOBBY. No, but I know.

FLORRIE. Oh, if I could only be in your shoes half an hour—just half an hour —wouldn't I get it out of him!

BOBBY. What would you do?

FLORRIE. I'd tease him—till he was wild.

BOBBY. Well, I won't.

FLORRIE. I guess you're just too good to live.

BOBBY. No, it isn't that. I like him too much to cheat him into anything.

FLORRIE. Darling, if you knew just half a dozen sentences to say that would make him propose to you, would you say them?

BOBBY. No, I wouldn't.

FLORRIE. It's so easy— When he asks if you weren't really going out with somebody, tell him you were going out with Fred—has he ever seen Fred?

BOBBY. No, but you're just wasting your time, Florrie. (FLORRIE *turns to table, rises, gets pad and pencil.*)

FLORRIE. Look, dear, I'm writing it down—can you read my shorthand?

BOBBY. I could if I wanted to—

FLORRIE. You're going with Fred to a dance or a supper-club—you see?—and then Rims will come in and ask you to stay with him this evening—and you'll say yes, you'll call it off when Fred telephones—and then I'll telephone—isn't it easy?

BOBBY. It doesn't interest me.

FLORRIE. Then he'll ask you to go somewhere with him and you'll suddenly take out your hanky and begin to cry a little and say you don't want to go anywhere.

BOBBY. Me—cry—me?

FLORRIE. Yes, darling, you. You'll weep a little and he'll ask you what's the matter and try to comfort you, and—

BOBBY. I can't cry on order—

FLORRIE. Oh, yes, you can, dear.

BOBBY. Anyway, I never cry.

FLORRIE. Well, he'll ask you what's the matter, and then you'll say, "Oh, I'm so tired of—of everything, Rims—and I'm afraid I'm not very good company,"— and he'll say, "Oh, yes, you are," and he'll put his arm around you—or would he?

BOBBY. How could he help it?

FLORRIE. Well, after that it gets easier all the time—you just say, "Rims dear, sometimes you're the only person in the world I can talk to—sometimes I can't bear to be with anybody else"—

BOBBY. I simply couldn't—

FLORRIE. But that's exactly what you've got to say—and then you go right on and say, "Rims, don't you ever get tired of poor me,—ever?"

BOBBY. And then he'd say "Never," of course.

FLORRIE. Of course—and you say, "You're such a darling—and it's going to be awfully hard"—

BOBBY. What is?

FLORRIE. That's exactly what he'll say—"What is?" and you'll say, "Marrying somebody else!" Then he'll draw back and say, "You getting married?" and you'll say, "Oh, Rims, a girl has to get married sometime, you know, while she's got chances," and he'll say, "How many chances do you get in a week?" or something like that, and you'll say, "I've had two every other week for two weeks," or something, and he'll say "Now kid, you don't mean you've set to marry somebody?" and then you'll say—

BOBBY. Oh, no, I won't—

FLORRIE. Yes, you will, dear, you'll say, "Fred wants me to marry him, and he's awfully in love with me and I don't want to go on working forever," and he'll say, "Well, if you're getting married this season, why not marry me?"—and there you are—

BOBBY. No, because he wouldn't say it—

FLORRIE. Why not?

BOBBY. Because he isn't such a sap for one thing, and for another I don't think it's fair and I wouldn't do it.

FLORRIE. My darling, how do you think people get married?

BOBBY. I don't know.

FLORRIE. I'll say you don't—

BOBBY. Honestly, do you think a person of any sense would fall for a deliberate trap like that?

FLORRIE. Why, honeybunch, hundreds of thousands of them fall for it every year. (*The doorbell rings.*) There's one coming now. I'm running along, dear. And, look, I'm leaving those notes—see?—

BOBBY. You'd better take them—

FLORRIE. Shut the note-book if you feel scrupulous—you'll probably remember the system anyway—it comes natural—Bye-bye! I'll just pass him in the door. (*She goes out.*) Oh, pardon me!

RIMS (*off-stage*). That's all right!

FLORRIE (*off*). I was just going out.

RIMS (*off*). Is Miss Halevy in?

FLORRIE (*off*). Miss Halevy? Oh yes.—Bobby!

BOBBY. Yes.

FLORRIE (*off*). Someone for you—

RIMS (*off*). O'Neil's the name—

FLORRIE (*off*). Mr. O'Neil—

BOBBY. Oh, Rims, come in!

FLORRIE (*off*). Goodbye, dear—

BOBBY. Goodbye, Florrie— (RIMS *enters.*) Hello, Rims.

RIMS. Hello, darling! Say!

BOBBY. You say it!

RIMS. Flaming youth! Bobby, you're a dream in that! Stand still and let me gaze at you!

BOBBY. You like it?

RIMS. Do I? Why haven't I seen you in that before!

BOBBY. I just made it.

RIMS. You made it? Say, I wish you'd make my clothes for me for a while. I'd have them falling for me from the third story windows!

BOBBY. Oh, any old clothes will do in Buenos Ayres. They say they fall easy down there.

RIMS. Yeah?

BOBBY. They say it's the climate.

RIMS. I'll bet the climate can't raise 'em any sweeter than you are because they don't come any sweeter— Say, you were stepping out somewhere, weren't you?

BOBBY. No, I wasn't.

RIMS. Sure, your sister said you had a heavy date on.

BOBBY. Well, I didn't.

RIMS. You're a poor liar, kid, if that's anything against you—

BOBBY. But I say I didn't have a date—

RIMS. What's the dress for—just trying it on?

BOBBY. No, it was to settle a bet—

RIMS. I'll bet it was— Anyway I'm sorry for the other guy and it's sweet of you to turn down a dance for me—

BOBBY. Wait a minute. I haven't turned it down yet—

RIMS. Is he coming for you?

BOBBY. He's going to telephone.

RIMS. Aw, give him the air, sweetheart. I want to talk to you. I haven't seen you for a week.

BOBBY. All right. Only it isn't my fault you haven't seen me, you know—

RIMS (*as he turns chair around and sits*

right center facing BOBBY). Gee, nobody's seen me. I haven't been able to see myself in the mirror the rate I was travelling. I've learned more about the Argentine in the last week than I ever knew about New York—principal cities, population, theatres, cabarets, rates of exchange, sheet music sales, what the girls like to dance to, how late they stay up—you ought to hear old Juan giving me a quiz—

BOBBY. So you're really going?

RIMS. It certainly looks that way—of course, the boss hasn't actually O.K.'d it yet but he seems to be sold on it—

BOBBY. Oh, so far as he's concerned it's going through.

RIMS. How do you know?

BOBBY. Well, I found out.

RIMS. Great stuff! Has he settled on me to go, do you know?

BOBBY. Oh, absolutely!

RIMS. You know I don't know a damn thing about it; old Juan's been coaching me but I'm pretty dumb, I guess. And there's a lot of fellows at the office that rank me for experience— But say, that's great, kid.

BOBBY. Of course, it's in confidence.—

RIMS. Sure thing. How'd you find out? Dictation?

BOBBY. He told me.

RIMS. He didn't talk it over with you?

BOBBY. I had dinner with him.

RIMS. Say, that's not so good, girlie. That bird's a pirate.

BOBBY. Well, I have to have dinner with somebody, don't I? And you haven't been giving anybody much competition—

RIMS. It wasn't because I didn't want to, though. You know every night I've thought maybe I could get away and then some damn complication fixed it so I couldn't.

BOBBY. Oh, I know.

RIMS. You know I haven't seen you since— Well—

BOBBY. Think hard.

RIMS. Gosh, it seems like a month.

BOBBY. Just a week ago tonight.

RIMS. You're right. And Mengle sprung this thing on me the next day. You mean I haven't seen you since that night on the bus?

BOBBY. Really, don't you remember?

RIMS. Gee, I'm a wash-out, girlie; this thing's wrecked me. Say, I wish you were coming along.

BOBBY. Maybe Mengle'll let you have a stenographer—

RIMS. No chance, I guess. He's doing this on a shoestring—the way he does everything. Anyway, I'm not the boss—Old Juan's in charge; I'm just a kind of super-cargo. They've got to have somebody that can write English . . . well . . . it was certainly a nice Spring while it lasted.

BOBBY. The best I ever had, Rims.

RIMS. Me too. You know Bobby, I'll never see a Fifth Avenue bus without thinking of you, never.

BOBBY. You won't see one for a while, though.

RIMS. That's true—but a postcard of Grant's Tomb or the Soldier's and Sailor's monument would do just as well—

BOBBY. I'll send you one with an X to mark the spot on it.

RIMS. Which spot, though? The route's sprinkled with 'em.

BOBBY. Well, where you said your poem to me, for instance.

RIMS. Yeah? Well, it wasn't much of a poem if you ask me.

BOBBY. Rims, it was a lovely poem!

RIMS. I thought it was pretty good at the time—but I guess it was pretty rank—I don't think I'm going to try poetry again for a while—

BOBBY. Not till you fall in love again, I suppose.

RIMS. No, that's the kind of thing only happens once.

BOBBY. Anyway, it's the only poem anybody ever wrote for me— (*She says it musingly.*)

When Bobby comes to the office
The boss takes off his frown;
She wears a coat of powder blue
And a powder blue gown.
She sits upon her office chair—

RIMS. You always make me think it's good, the way you can say it— (*The telephone rings.*) If that's your playmate tell him you're busy, will you?

BOBBY. Do you want to stick around, really?

RIMS. Sure I do.

BOBBY (*at the telephone*). Hello. Oh, yes. Why, Fred. (*She turns her back on* RIMS.) I'm awfully sorry, but I can't go. No, really I can't. No, don't come over, please. It isn't that. I'll tell you when I see you. I'm awfully sorry. Yes. Goodbye. (*She hangs up and turns to face him, radiant.*) There!

RIMS. You're a brick, Bobby. Are you sure you didn't want to go?

BOBBY. If I'd wanted to—I would have. (*There is a pause.*)

RIMS. I've been wanting to talk to you.

BOBBY. What about, Rims?

RIMS. Do you think it's a good thing—me going to South America?

BOBBY. It's an awfully good opening.

RIMS. Well, what I mean is, don't you think it's a good thing for a young fellow to see the world a little when he gets a chance—just so he can kind of make up his mind what he wants to do?

BOBBY. Surely.

RIMS. That's why I'm going, really. Oh, I'm not sure it's any great shakes of an opening, but I never have been much of anywhere and it's a chance—well, it's a kind of adventure, don't you see?

BOBBY. Surely.

RIMS (*at a loss*). That's why I'm going.

BOBBY. *Yes.* (*A pause.*)

RIMS. And, kid—

BOBBY. Yes?

RIMS (*placing a hand on her arm*). You certainly have been wonderful to me.

BOBBY. We did have a good Spring together, didn't we?

RIMS. You were certainly marvellous. (BOBBY *looks at him, and then turns away.*)

BOBBY. Well, it's Summer now.

RIMS. Yep. But that's no reason you shouldn't give me a kiss, is it?

BOBBY. I guess not. (*They kiss.*) Maybe you'd better run along, Rims.

RIMS. Why so, sweetie? The night's young.

BOBBY. Well— (*She looks down and her eye falls on* FLORRIE's *notebook. She looks at it fascinated. There is a pause.*)

RIMS (*lightly*). What you studying, Bobby?

BOBBY. Nothing. Only—oh, I'm so tired of everything, Rims, and I'm afraid I'm not very good company.

RIMS. Oh, yes, you are.

BOBBY. Rims, dear—

RIMS. Yes.

BOBBY (*she looks back at book*). Rims, sometimes you're the only person in the world I can talk to. Sometimes I can't bear to be with anybody else.

RIMS. Gee, kid.

BOBBY. Rims, don't you ever get tired of poor me, ever?

RIMS. Never, I should say not.

BOBBY. You're such a darling.

RIMS. Well, I wouldn't say that.

BOBBY. But you are. (*She turns and glances at the notebook.*) And it's going to be awfully hard. (*A pause.*)

RIMS. What is, sweetheart?

BOBBY. Marrying somebody else.

RIMS. You getting married? (*His hand drops from her shoulder.*)

BOBBY. Oh, Rims, a girl's got to get married sometime you know, while she's got chances.

RIMS. I suppose you get chances all right.

BOBBY. Yes.

RIMS. Do they come fast?

BOBBY. I've had two—every other week, for two weeks.

RIMS. Say, look here, you don't mean you're making up your mind to marry somebody in particular?

BOBBY. Well, Fred wants me to marry him, and he's awfully in love with me, and I don't want to go on working forever.

RIMS. I see. Yeah, I see. I didn't know you felt that way.

BOBBY (*breaking away*). Well, I don't, really. I was just—I was just joking. You'd better go, dear. I wouldn't marry anybody. I wouldn't marry—anybody. Not even you.

RIMS. You wouldn't?

BOBBY. No, I wouldn't!

RIMS. Oh, yes, you will. I mean—

BOBBY. Do you want me too?

RIMS. Sweetheart—I don't want anything else. (*They kiss.*)

BOBBY (*breaking away and crying on his shoulder*). But you're—you're going to South America—

RIMS (*still holding her*). South America can go to the devil—! Somebody else can go to South America!

CURTAIN

ACT TWO

The O'NEILS' *kitchen-dining room. There is the back door right, reached by passing through a shallow closet with props, brooms, pails, etc. Down right facing up center is a small chair. Up right is the stove and beside it a kitchen table. Next to the kitchen table is the sink with a rack of Gold Dust, Rinso, etc., above it. Left is an arch, with French-windows leading to living room, and front door. This has a table, a standard lamp, and an armchair visible. There are windows up right and up left.*

BOBBY *is standing left by table clearing the dishes away after supper.* RIMS *is off left in the living room.*

RIMS (*off left*). Where the devil are my pipe cleaners?

BOBBY. I should know.

RIMS. Well, I certainly put some here and I didn't move 'em.

BOBBY. Oh, dear, I took all the things off that desk because I had to set the lamp somewhere when the folks came—

RIMS (*off*). I knew you took 'em.

BOBBY. Why, Rims, I didn't take them. I moved them because I had to. What do you think I did with them?

RIMS (*off*). I give up.

BOBBY (*going in to help him*). Silly. I'll find them.

RIMS. Oh, hell, I'm all out of tobacco. Where's my cigarettes?

BOBBY (*re-entering*). Oh, here they are. Mine were all gone.

RIMS. Gosh, there's only one left.

BOBBY (*she picks up her cigarette*). That's all right. I've got one.

RIMS. Yeah, but I had half a package here.

BOBBY. I know. I asked you to bring me some last night, but I guess you forgot it.—

RIMS (*lighting cigarette*). Well, I didn't really forget it, only I was running so low on cash—

BOBBY. But you got paid to-day.

RIMS. Yeah, only I did forget 'em this afternoon.

BOBBY. You see. I thought sure you'd bring some, dear.

RIMS (*throwing match in ash tray, and smoking contentedly*). It's all right.

BOBBY. I don't see how you could be low in cash. You don't eat it all, do you?

RIMS. What do you expect on five dollars a week?

BOBBY. You never seem to have any money.

RIMS. Well, now, the truth is, I took a couple of passes at pinochle last week, and they ruined me.

BOBBY. But, Rims, if you do that—

RIMS. Hell, I'm not dead yet, you know.

BOBBY. We've got to stick to the budget, dear, or we'll never come out even. I've been over everything this afternoon and it's awfully close figuring.

RIMS. We're going to be lucky if we get by.

BOBBY (*flashing*). I wish you wouldn't talk that way, Rims. There's no luck about it. It's just figures. (*She gets out her account book.*) Listen—this is the way it adds up.

RIMS. Say, kiddie, spare me the horrible details.

BOBBY. No, it's the treasurer's report—you've got to hear it or we can't cooperate.

RIMS. You know I've tried that and it doesn't do any good.

BOBBY. But you didn't stick to it, then!

RIMS. Hell, I couldn't. Every time I thought I had it all worked out some damn thing would come along and sink me for a month. I know.

BOBBY. Well, listen, anyway.

RIMS. All right.

BOBBY. Well, we get $240 a month and when there's five weeks in a month we get $300.

RIMS. Sounds like too much money—how much is it in a year?

BOBBY. Don't interrupt. Two hundred and forty a month and out of that we pay sixty for rent, about thirty-five for groceries, forty on the furniture, twenty for your allowance, ten insurance, about six for gas and light, and about three for ice. And it comes to a hundred and seventy-four.

RIMS. You must have left something out.

BOBBY (*still intent*). Please! A hundred and seventy-four from two hundred and forty leaves sixty-six dollars—

RIMS. Then how do I happen to be broke all the time?

BOBBY. Of course, if it doesn't interest you—

RIMS. Sure it interests me, Bobby. You know, I've got a great idea, girlie. How about a little game of black jack for that sixty-six dollars?

BOBBY. Rims, you idiot! If you don't take me seriously I'll never—never— You can take care of your own dirty old money! I can earn some for myself!

RIMS. Ah, take it easy, Bobby. I was only fooling.

BOBBY. Will you really listen?

RIMS. Sure I will! Geez, I've been listening.

BOBBY. Oh, it isn't any use. You don't think it matters . . . but I *know* it does.

RIMS (*mock-serious*). Don't I know it matters? Why, kid, if you can figure out how we can save sixty-six a month—well —you're good.

BOBBY. I didn't say we could save that much. We have to use that for clothes and dentist and doctor's bills and extras—

RIMS. No, say, there's certainly something wrong here—

BOBBY. But just a minute. I *know* we'll just throw it away and never know where it goes if we don't use some system, so I want you to write down everything you spend and I'll do the same and every evening we'll go over it—

RIMS. I see a long row of pleasant evenings ahead—

BOBBY. But I mean it, dear. I've been thinking about it all day.

RIMS (*definite*). Well, that part's out.

BOBBY. What part?

RIMS (*he puts out his cigarette*). About writing it all down. That's out. No, thanks. I knew a guy that did that.

BOBBY. I think it's very sensible.

RIMS (*flaring up*). And make me accountable to you for every cent I spend?

BOBBY. Oh, is *that* the way you look at it?

RIMS. That's what it amounts to, isn't it?

BOBBY (*rising*). Well, then, I guess we won't discuss the matter any further. I'll finish the dishes. (*Pause.*)

RIMS. (*taking notebook and studying it*). No, wait a minute. There's something away out here.

BOBBY (*busy with the dishes*). It doesn't matter.

RIMS. Well, look here! Where do you get that two forty a month stuff? We don't get any two forty a month.

BOBBY. I've gone over and over everything.

RIMS. I know, but you're wrong. I get forty dollars a week. Four times forty's just 160 . . . (*A pause.*)

BOBBY. Oh! . . . oh . . . oh, what a fool! I know what I did—but I could never tell you—I must have put down sixty a week to start—but you'd never see how I could—

RIMS. It makes a hell of a big difference, I'll say—

BOBBY. Oh, I'm such a fool. It was just because Mengle had spoken of a raise—and I started to figure it on the basis of a new salary—and then I forgot and thought I'd started with forty dollars—no, I can't see how I did it! (*Suddenly face to face with it.*) Well, then, there's just no use, you see. We get 160 and our expenses are 174 and—

RIMS. Well, that's round numbers, you know.

BOBBY. We've just got to cut everything away down. Rims, we can't live on 160 a month.

RIMS. Well, some months it's more. Extra pay-days.

BOBBY. I suppose that's what's saved us so far.

RIMS. And then I'm going to get more, too, you know.

BOBBY. I hope so.

RIMS. And, I do—I do appreciate it—your taking the trouble to figure it all out—only it's a kind of a blow too. (*He rises.*) I didn't know it was so close. Gosh, I never used to have any money troubles to speak of—I just ran along—

BOBBY. Well, so did I. I wish I hadn't quit my job.

RIMS. Well, we both couldn't work in the same office after we got married. It doesn't go somehow.

BOBBY. It would have been embarrassing, but—it wouldn't really matter.

RIMS. Well, I'd mind if you didn't. It would make it look as if I weren't man enough to—to support my wife.

BOBBY. How I hate that word.

RIMS. What word?

BOBBY. Wife! I won't be a *wife!* It sounds so fat and stupid! I wish we hadn't *got* married! I wish you'd gone to South America.

RIMS.—Well, you haven't got anything on me.

BOBBY (*gently*). No, I didn't mean that, dear. It's not true.

RIMS. As a matter of fact, I meant to go to South America.

BOBBY. I know.

RIMS. And then I went to see you—and I guess I just had to have you—that's all.

BOBBY (*burying her head on his shoulder*). No, it was me. I had to—have you. It was my fault.

RIMS (*holding her close*). No, I knew what I was doing all right. And hell, I—I still feel that way. You look like a million dollars to me every time I see you.

BOBBY (*looking up at him*). Darling, you do love me, don't you?

RIMS. Honest, kid, nobody ever loved anybody the way I love you. I'm just silly about you. I think about you all day long. And then I come home at night and— (*He turns away*) we get into some goddam mess—and it just shoots the works—

BOBBY. I know. It's just the same way with me. I think all day how marvellous it's going to be when you come home—and then you get here—and I don't know—it isn't marvellous at all— It's just a house and we're just married people—and—sometimes I hate it—everything's getting spoiled—

RIMS. I guess it's mostly relatives and—money.

BOBBY. And pipe cleaners and clothes—and meals and—dishes—oh, I haven't touched those dishes yet—

RIMS. Anyway, you're marvellous, kid. You really are.

BOBBY. Even when I'm doing dishes?

RIMS. Even when you're doing dishes. And just to prove it I'm going to help you with them.

BOBBY. I don't want you to have to do dishes.

RIMS. Gee, I wish you didn't have to.

BOBBY. I even wish you never had to see me doing dishes. I almost wish I was somebody else's wife—so you could be my lover—and come to see me when he wasn't home—

RIMS. Well, I don't know about that—

BOBBY. No, not really, I mean: but don't you see it would be better—because you'd always like me then—and you'd always want to see me and we'd have to scheme and meet places and you'd hate the old brute that owned me.

RIMS. The only trouble is I'm the old brute that owns you—

BOBBY. Only you're not an old brute—but if you were—oh, I'd have the handsomest, dearest lover—just like you!

RIMS. I guess you mean it for a compliment so it's all right—

BOBBY. Oh, I do. He'd be wealthy, you see—

RIMS. Who would?

BOBBY. The brute would, and I'd have all the men in the world to choose from—and I'd take Rims.

RIMS. If you feel that way, what do we care if we're poor.

BOBBY. Ain't it the truth?

RIMS. (*his arms round her*). And you can lose my pipe-cleaners and add up wrong and have relatives to dinner and smoke my cigarettes forever and I won't get mad.

BOBBY. I guess it was me got mad. I always do.

RIMS. Compared to me you never get mad.

BOBBY (*smiling and going back to the dishes*). Only I don't think my relatives are so very terrible, do you?

RIMS. I guess not. No more'n most relatives.

BOBBY. And they don't come here so very often, do they?

RIMS. Well, they were here last night.

BOBBY. Yes.

RIMS. And the night before that. *And* the night before that.

BOBBY. Yes, it is true. It's partly because Florrie helped plant the garden.

RIMS. You know the old man's all right, but that sister of yours does kind of give me the pip, and what that Willy boy ever married her for is more than I can figure out. They actually think they own this place just because they saw it first.

BOBBY (*going to him*). Darling, as soon as the lease runs out we'll move.

RIMS. When do we pay the rent?

BOBBY. It's due day after tomorrow.

RIMS. Could it wait?

BOBBY. It won't have to. With to-day's money we can just do it.

RIMS. Well, I was going to ask you—they're having a stag blow-out for old Juan—he's just back from South America and he's retiring and the boys are getting him something, chipping in, you know. Do you think I could take five out of the rent money? It's two dollars a plate and they're chipping in about three.

BOBBY. Now, why should you give Juan anything?

RIMS. Well, he was pretty good to me, Bobby—and after the way I dropped out of the South America thing I don't want to look like a crab.

BOBBY. When is it?

RIMS. Wednesday.

BOBBY. Wednesday? Really?

RIMS. Yeah.

BOBBY. That's funny.

RIMS. Why?

BOBBY. Guess who called me up today?

RIMS. Fred?

BOBBY. No. . . . Mengle.

RIMS. The boss—? What did he want?

BOBBY. Well, first he wanted to know if I'd come back and work for him—

RIMS (*belligerently*). Oh, he did, did he? I'd like to see you—

BOBBY. Well, I said no, and he said, "Come down and see me sometime," and I said, "All right," and he said "Why don't you come and have dinner sometime," and I said, "No, thanks," and he said, "How about Wednesday night?"

RIMS. What did you tell him?

BOBBY. I told him I'd call up and let him know.

RIMS. Why didn't you tell him to go to the devil?

BOBBY. Well, I'd been going over these figures and I thought if our income was doubled—how easy it would be—and if I just took my job back—

RIMS. Get this from me right now, kid. I won't have you sitting in Mengle's private office taking dictation. It was bad enough before we were married.

BOBBY. Well, I guess I'll do as I please about that, my dear.

RIMS. You will not! You'll do as I tell you.

BOBBY (*icily*). I might if you asked me nicely, but—

RIMS. I'm not asking you! I'm telling you, and that's once for all! And you won't go to dinner with him, either!

BOBBY. I didn't intend to go to dinner with him, but if you say you won't let me, I certainly will.

RIMS. Oh, no, you won't.

BOBBY. Yes?

RIMS. Yeah, that'd put me in a nice position, wouldn't it? Me at the banquet and you dining alone with Mengle.

BOBBY. Well, I've had dinner with him before and it didn't seem to hurt your position much.

RIMS. That was before we were married!

BOBBY. Well, good God, what's the difference?

RIMS. You know damn well what's the difference.

BOBBY. Oh dear, we're quarreling again—over nothing.

RIMS. You call that nothing! Anyway, what the hell do I care if we are? I come home here every evening just because you're here—and what thanks do I get for it? They had a game going over at Perry's and I certainly wish I'd gone.

BOBBY. I certainly wish you had. I suppose you come home every evening just to keep me company—because you're afraid I'll be lonely—

RIMS. Sometimes I do.

BOBBY. Well, go to your game. I won't be lonely. Any time you don't come home I can amuse myself plenty.

RIMS. All right!

BOBBY. I had a bid out myself to-night if you want to know.

RIMS. Who was it?

BOBBY. Don't you wish you knew?

RIMS. Was it Mengle?

BOBBY. No it was Fred. He said he was all alone at the club party to-night and he wished I was going to be there.

RIMS. Are you going?

BOBBY. Why, darling, I was staying home *to keep you company*. But I wouldn't mind seeing another man once in a while—now that's the truth. (*The door-bell rings.*) I wonder who that is?

RIMS. You know all right. It's that sister of yours and her Willy boy. That's who it always is.

BOBBY. Rims! (*She goes out to open the door.* RIMS *puts on his coat and drops a paper from his pocket.*)

FLORRIE (*at the front door*). Oh, there you are. We were just going round to the back.

BOBBY (*in the front room*). Hello, Florrie. Hello, Willy.

WILLY (*off*). I didn't want to come, Bobby, but she made me.

FLORRIE. (*off*). Willy, you're making me furious!

WILLY (*off*). I know damn well they don't want a lot of old married folks running in on 'em at all hours.

BOBBY (*off*). Come on out to the kitchen—we're just finishing the dishes. (BOBBY *re-enters, bringing* FLORRIE *and* WILLY.)

FLORRIE. Hello, Rims, darling.

RIMS (*over his shoulder*). Hello.

WILLY. Hello, Rims.

RIMS. Hello.

FLORRIE. Such a heavenly night you never saw! And a lovely, lovely moon.

WILLY. That wasn't any moon. That was a street lamp.

FLORRIE. Oh, all right, grumpie, there wasn't any moon. There, doesn't that prove I love him? Because there really is a moon.

WILLY. There is not.

FLORRIE. I know, dear. I'm always

wrong. And all the North and South streets *do* run east and west, and the sun *does* rise over New Jersey, just as you said. What did you ever marry me for if you don't like me?

WILLY. Yeah, this is a fine time to ask me that.

FLORRIE. I wish I had a perfect husband like Rims, that never got sulky. Rims, when I get my divorce, will you marry me? Shall we fly together?

RIMS. I'm going out and get some cigarettes.

WILLY. Mind if I come along?

RIMS. Nope.

FLORRIE. Well say, come back after me, do you hear?

WILLY (*following* RIMS *out*). Yeah!

FLORRIE. Well, darling. Did I hear sounds of family revelry,—and is the husband in a vile mood?—not really?

BOBBY. What did you hear?

FLORRIE. Only the breaking of furniture and the fall of crockery. Who wins this evening?

BOBBY. Who wins?

FLORRIE. Why yes. The evening row.

BOBBY. I guess neither of us won. I guess we both lost.

FLORRIE. Then it's a draw, stupid. Only why take it seriously. It's the one that takes it seriously that loses.

BOBBY. It's not funny, Florrie.

FLORRIE. You child—it is funny. You're going through a period of adjustment and it's always funny. There's a man writing for the American—

BOBBY. Yes, I know—

FLORRIE. Well, he says, there's always a period of adjustment before it's settled who's to boss the other one, and the period of adjustment is just one long series of rows.

BOBBY. I see.

FLORRIE (*sighing*). Willy and I are nearing the end of our period of adjustment. Willy still struggles.

BOBBY. Then—I guess I don't want to be married. If it's like that.

FLORRIE. Of course you want to be married, my dear. We all want to be married. We want somebody to take care of us. Women can talk all they please about living their own lives— I don't believe it. It's all sour grapes.

BOBBY. It isn't sour grapes with me. It—it just kills me to quarrel with him —and it's always happening! Florrie, I don't know what to do.

FLORRIE. There's nothing to do. It's quite usual.

BOBBY. You mean people always quarrel when they're married, even when they're in love, madly in love?

FLORRIE. Well, I never knew a case where they didn't.

BOBBY. It can't be true.

FLORRIE. Naturally you don't go on being madly in love forever. Not if you're married to the person.

BOBBY. But why?

FLORRIE. Silly, you get to know him so well and he knows you so well. You can be sort of in love with your husband but not madly in love with him.

BOBBY. Then I don't want to be married. Because I want to be madly in love.

FLORRIE. No doubt you wish Rims had gone to Buenos Ayres.

BOBBY. No.

FLORRIE. Well, he's yours, my dear, and he was the one you wanted, so why worry about it?

BOBBY. I know it can't go on the way it is. He'll leave me or I'll leave him— or something will happen. We want to be together and then as soon as we are together,—it's no use. (*She rises.*) We always say the wrong things—

FLORRIE. Then, do you know what I think?

BOBBY. No.

FLORRIE. I think it's time for you to begin having a baby.

BOBBY. But if we don't get along together now—

FLORRIE. It makes everything different. It makes you so much more important, don't you see?

BOBBY. I don't want to be important.

FLORRIE. You want to be important to Rims, don't you?

BOBBY. Yes.

FLORRIE. Well, if you're having his baby you instantly become the most important thing in the world to him. Men are funny that way. They take so much credit and they feel so responsible, it's pathetic. So long as you don't have a baby Rims is really free, you see—and he might get tired of you—but just you tie him down with two or three good fat ones—and he'll stay. Willy used to get rebellious, but not any more. Not since the baby.

BOBBY. But that's terrible.

FLORRIE. What is?

BOBBY. To keep a man that way.

FLORRIE. It's been going on a long time, my dear. I wasn't the first to think of it.

BOBBY. You mean that's why women have children?

FLORRIE. Why, surely.

BOBBY. But they want to have them.

FLORRIE. Oh, yes. I suppose, partly they want to keep their husbands because they want to have children, and partly they want to have children because they want to keep their husbands. Anyway, it works.

BOBBY. It wouldn't—with us.

FLORRIE. You're just like the rest of us. It's a scientific fact. It works. Some morning you'll tell Rims it's going to happen, and all of a sudden everything will change. He'll bring you things and mother you, and smother you with kisses, and he'll be humble and happy and—well, you see, there's no arguing about a thing like that—

BOBBY. Oh, but I couldn't let it happen without telling him first.

FLORRIE. Why not?

BOBBY. He might not like it.

FLORRIE. He'll like it after it happens.

BOBBY. But I couldn't. It wouldn't be honest.

FLORRIE. Of course, he mustn't ever know it wasn't an accident.

BOBBY. We'd have to talk about it.

FLORRIE. Really.

BOBBY. Yes.

FLORRIE. Well, he'd say no, and that would be the end of that.

BOBBY. That's what I think.

FLORRIE. Unless—unless you did it—in a special way.

BOBBY. Is it another scheme?

FLORRIE. Scheme?

BOBBY. Like the—the questions on the pad?

FLORRIE. Well, didn't that one work out?

BOBBY. Yes, only I wish I'd never done it. I wish it had happened some other way.

FLORRIE. It couldn't have and you know it. Wait till some time when he's just crazy about you—you know—and then say—

BOBBY. Don't say it, *please!*

FLORRIE. If you think he'd see through it, dear, you're wrong. It's appalling what they never see through.

BOBBY. Oh, I wish we hadn't talked about it!

FLORRIE. Well, it may not be necessary yet. But any time you're really afraid of losing him, I'd say— (*The door bell rings.* BOBBY *goes into the living room to answer it.*)

FLORRIE. Well, I've got to go anyway.

MR. HALEVY (*in the living room*). Just the old man.

BOBBY (*still outside*). Oh, hello, Dad! I couldn't think who it would be—Where's mother? (FLORRIE *rises, finds on the floor the paper* RIMS *dropped from his pocket, and reads it.*)

MR. HALEVY (*outside*). She was tired. She went to bed early.

BOBBY (*outside*). Come on out. Florrie's here.

MR. HALEVY (*entering*). Hello, Florrie. (BOBBY *enters behind him.*)

FLORRIE. Hello, grandfather.

MR. HALEVY. Shut up that grandfather stuff!

FLORRIE (*in her sweetest baby talk*). Why, you precious old dear, are you ashamed of being a grandfather?

MR. HALEVY. Wait till you're a grandmother, and you'll know how I feel. If there's anything more humiliating than having squalling children it's having squalling grand-children.

FLORRIE. But he doesn't squall!

MR. HALEVY. Of course not. He *coos*.

FLORRIE. He's really a love, daddy. Imagine your never coming to see him! Not that I mind really. Bobby, I'll have to run along without Willy. You can tell him when he comes back. Something I found on the floor. (*She hands* BOBBY *the paper.*)

BOBBY (*laying it down*). Thanks,—I'm sorry you have to go.

FLORRIE. You'd better look at that. It's an I. O. U. Somebody owes Rims some money.

BOBBY (*looking at the thing*). Owes Rims money?

FLORRIE. Well, it's an I. O. U.

BOBBY. Oh.

FLORRIE. Don't let the boy gamble, dear. Well, goodbye. Why don't you come over sometime? We always come to see you and you never come to see us.

BOBBY. We will, Florrie, goodbye. (FLORRIE *goes.*)

MR. HALEVY (*lighting a cigar*). Well, kiddie, how's things?

BOBBY. Dad, what's an I. O. U. for?

MR. HALEVY. You mean you don't know?

BOBBY. I knew people gave them—but how would Rims happen to have one.

MR. HALEVY. I'd say he's lucky—if it's any good.

BOBBY. He couldn't have lent anybody money—because he didn't have it to lend.

MR. HALEVY. Then he won it.

BOBBY. But he didn't tell me.

MR. HALEVY. Why should he tell you everything, child? Do you think you own the boy just because he's married to you?

BOBBY. But it's for twenty-seven dollars, and to think of his not saying a word about it and we've been talking budget all evening—

MR. HALEVY. Well, ask him, ask him.

BOBBY. Dad—

MR. HALEVY. Yes?

BOBBY. Do you think—? I don't know—

MR. HALEVY. All right—what's on your mind?

BOBBY. Do you think—I ought to have a baby? (*A pause.*)

MR. HALEVY (*a whisper*). What!

BOBBY. Do you think I ought to have a baby? (MR. HALEVY *looks at her—then looks away and smiles.*)

MR. HALEVY. Jesus look down! How old are you, girlie?

BOBBY. Please don't be foolish.

MR. HALEVY. Yes, I suppose you are old enough. That was the wrong thing to say. But looking back at my beautiful wasted youth—why anybody should want to have a baby—why anybody should even want to get married—is more than —I can ever understand.—From me, my dear, I fear you will get nothing but ribald advice and evil counselling. I'd better go home.

BOBBY. No, don't go. This is serious!

MR. HALEVY. Bobby. I married young and brought up two lovely children. I can't say I regret it, but there are moments, and those moments occur more frequently now that I'm a grandfather, when it appears to me that Don Juan and Casanova chose the better part.

BOBBY. Yes, I suppose that's true if you're a man, but I'm not.

MR. HALEVY. I used to wish you were.

BOBBY. Why?

MR. HALEVY. Now, don't ask me to talk seriously on this topic, my dear. After all, I'm your father and I know my duty. If I said, "No, don't have any babies," you'd ask me if I was sorry we had you and Florrie, and I couldn't think of an adequate reply. Anyway, fathers shouldn't confide in their daughters. It isn't hundred per cent—. No doubt it would be considered a kind of intellectual incest. But I can tell you lies by the yard—

BOBBY. Then you think having a baby —would be a mistake?

MR. HALEVY. I didn't even want you to get married.

BOBBY. You didn't say anything—

MR. HALEVY. I came near it—the night you and Rims fixed it up. I was afraid it was going to happen.

BOBBY. Oh.

MR. HALEVY. Do you know how fathers feel about their daughters when they're growing up?

BOBBY. No.

MR. HALEVY. Well, they think—when they think about it—here I have two good-looking virtuous girls, and I'm putting in my whole life raising them up, feeding them, sending them to school—and for what? All for the service and delight of two unknown and probably disagreeable young men. So I used to wish I had sons, because they could have a good time at any rate. And then it occurred to me there was no reason why girls shouldn't have a good time.

BOBBY. How do you mean?

MR. HALEVY. Fall in love—have your affair—and when it's over—get out!

BOBBY. Oh!

MR. HALEVY. I told you I'd better go home.

BOBBY. But why not have a love affair —and get married?

MR. HALEVY. Marriage is no love affair, my dear. It's little old last year's love affair. It's a house and bills and dishpans and family quarrels. That's the way the system beats you. They bait the wedding with a romance and they hang a three-hundred-pound landlord around your neck and drown you in grocery bills. If I'd talked to you that night I'd have said—if you're in love with him, why have your affair, sow a few oats. Why the devil should the boys have a monopoly on wild oats?

BOBBY. Yes, I see.

MR. HALEVY. No, I shouldn't say that. Marriage is fine, kiddie, it's grand. It's the corner stone of progress. It's the backbone of civilization. Don't you believe anything against it.

BOBBY. Please, dad.

MR. HALEVY. But if I had talked to you that night, I'd have said, you're too young to get married. You haven't had any fun yet. He hasn't money enough to support you. Why should he support you? You're his economic equal.

BOBBY. Maybe I should have gone on working.

MR. HALEVY. Yes, and if you had gone on working and he didn't support you, why take his name and label yourself? I don't see it. . . . No, I shouldn't talk that way. I take it back.

BOBBY. I might have lost him.

MR. HALEVY. Not so surely as you'll lose him now. It used to be a love affair, didn't it?

BOBBY. Yes.

MR. HALEVY. What is it, as is?

BOBBY. Grocery bills—mostly.

MR. HALEVY. I'm—I'm sorry.

BOBBY. Then—then why didn't mother lose you?

MR. HALEVY. Well, maybe she did. And maybe I lost her. Of course we stayed around. We had children.

BOBBY. And—didn't you like having children?

MR. HALEVY. Now, to be honest—children do get you—they do get you. I have to admit that,—and I suppose a man wants to have children—just to prove he's all right. Before you have children you're afraid something's the matter with you—yes, and after you have them, you're sure of it. But—you don't go away. You see, you start one baby, just as a kind of experiment, and then you find it's a life sentence. (*Pause.*) For both of you.

BOBBY. But—if you have a husband—and you want to keep him all your life long—then maybe a baby is the best thing—isn't it?

MR. HALEVY. You scheming little devil!

BOBBY. It's true, isn't it?

MR. HALEVY. Oh, yes, it'll hold him, and you too.

BOBBY. You don't understand me, dad. I'm young and foolish—and Rims is everything in the world to me and I'm afraid I'll lose him. I can't help being young and foolish. (*The door bell rings.*)

MR. HALEVY. No, I suppose not.

BOBBY. So I guess I'll make it—a life sentence.

MR. HALEVY. All right.—Only think it over. (*The bell rings again.* BOBBY *goes out to the door.*)

FLORRIE (*outside*). Hello, Bobby. It's only us again.

BOBBY. Why Florrie, come in.

FLORRIE. I just happened to meet Willy and he said he had a message for you. (*She enters, followed by* BOBBY *and* WILLY.) That is, Rims asked him to tell you he'd be home late.

BOBBY. Oh. Oh, yes.

WILLY. Why, you see, he got a chance to get into a little game, so he told me to tell you to look for him when you saw him coming—

BOBBY. Oh.

FLORRIE. Never mind, dear. They all get that way sometimes. Give him rope.

WILLY. Sure, give him plenty of rope. That's always the best plan. And, by the way, Florrie, I may be out late tomorrow night. Don't look for me—

FLORRIE. No, you don't, darling.

WILLY. I thought not.

FLORRIE. Why, Willy, you know you always go out when you really want to—

WILLY. Well, as I often say, I wouldn't have known it if you hadn't told me.

BOBBY (*in her father's arms*). Dad!

MR. HALEVY. It's all right, dear.

BOBBY. I—I don't think he likes me any more.

MR. HALEVY. Sure, he likes you. He'd better like you, or I'd horsewhip him. Upstart cub!

BOBBY. Oh, no, dad, he's—

MR. HALEVY. I'd like to know what he's ever done to deserve a girl like my Bobby.

BOBBY. No,—I'm not good enough for him, dad—you don't know him.—(RIMS *enters by the back door.*)

MR. HALEVY. I don't have to know him.

FLORRIE. Why, Rims—Hello!

RIMS (*crossing to the living room*). Hello.

FLORRIE. Well, can we do anything for you, Rims? Kill a fatted calf, or something? (*There is no answer. A chair falls over, and a pile of books slide to the floor.*)

RIMS (*in living room*). God damn it!

BOBBY (*going to the door*). Can't I help you?

RIMS. No.

BOBBY (*going into the living room*). There's nothing in that closet but your overcoat—

RIMS. I'm just looking for something.

BOBBY. All right. (*She re-enters and picks up the I. O. U.* RIMS *comes in, evidently hunting for something.*) Were you looking for this, Rims?

RIMS. Where was it?

BOBBY. Why—

RIMS. Yeah, I know damn well where it was and so do you! It was in my coat pocket!

BOBBY. Maybe it was. I don't know.

RIMS. I'll bet you don't.

FLORRIE. Why, Rims, darling, what a thing to say to little wifie!

RIMS (*turning on her*). Baby talk!

FLORRIE. And I suppose you never talk baby talk.

RIMS. No!

MR. HALEVY (*turning to leave*). It was on the floor, Rims. You ought to take better care of your valuable papers. Well, Bobby, I'll be running along. (*He goes.*)

RIMS. Oh, stay! Spend the night! I'm going.

FLORRIE. What a charming manner he has with guests.

WILLY (*going out*). Keep out of it, can't you? It's none of your affair.

FLORRIE. Bobby, I'll run along! And Rims, you're just a love, just a perfect love. (*She goes out.*)

RIMS. Yeah, I always liked you too! You've got a grand family, take it all round . . . can't understand why your mother wasn't here . . . well. So long. (*He crosses to the door, then pauses.*) You probably want to know where I got that I. O. U.

BOBBY (*looking away*). No.

RIMS. Well, I'll tell you anyway. I got it playing blackjack. I guess I've got a right to a game even if I am married . . . you don't need to look so tragic. I always played cards and I'll do it some more.

BOBBY. I don't mind anything except you said you needed money—and you had some.

RIMS. Sure. I know. You think you've got a mortgage on everything I get. . . . That's why you want me to write it down on a book. So you won't miss anything.

BOBBY. Why do you have to be nasty about it?

RIMS. I'm not being nasty. I'm telling you a few things. You do as you please, you go to dinner with Mengle, you take back your job with him and as good as tell me if I don't like it I can go chase myself. Well then, by God, I'll do as I please. . . . Anyway, I didn't get that twenty-seven free and clear. I got an I. O. U. for 27 and I gave one for 29. I was two dollars in the hole . . . I didn't tell you because I didn't want to . . . I'm not used to telling anybody everything.

BOBBY. Well, don't worry about it, dear. Run along, and have a good time—

RIMS. You know, I haven't got anything against you—only I'm just not used to it, that's all.—I guess it's all right. I'm the earning end and you're the paying end and we've got to work together. Only it comes kind of hard. . . .

BOBBY. It surely comes hard to me, Rims.

RIMS. Aw, I'm not going. (*He throws his hat on a chair.*)

BOBBY. Why not? Run along. Have a good time.

RIMS. How can I have a good time—if you don't say goodbye to me?

BOBBY. Goodbye.

RIMS. Ah, kid . . . kiss me goodbye. (*She is silent. He turns again.*)

BOBBY. Rims! (*He drops his hat again and she throws herself into his arms.*)

RIMS. You know, I think it's that sister of yours. Every time she comes in the house, I see red. I don't like your family. That's the truth.

BOBBY. I wish I didn't have any family. I wish there was just you and me—

RIMS. Everybody ought to be born orphans.

BOBBY. Rims, do you really like me, or are you just being kind to me?

RIMS. You know darn well I'm crazy about you. But, hell, the way everybody goes blooey—

BOBBY. Well then I don't care how things go.

RIMS (*holding her*). Sweetheart! . . . Well, I guess I ought to be getting along, kid. The fellows are waiting for me.

BOBBY. Don't—don't go quite yet—

RIMS. All right.

BOBBY. Don't you think, there must be something wrong, dear? Or else we'd be happier?

RIMS. I don't know. We're pretty happy.

BOBBY. No,—no, we're not.

RIMS. Well, maybe you're right.

BOBBY. Maybe—maybe we ought to have a baby.

RIMS. Good God, girl! I guess we've got trouble enough—you think I want to join the chain gang? A baby! Say, did you ever see a kid you didn't want to run from?

BOBBY. I just thought maybe—we'd like each other better—

RIMS. For the love of Mike! . . . Say, kid, are you—? Are you?

BOBBY. No; oh, no!

RIMS. Well, I'm glad of that. That would—make it different.

BOBBY. Would it, dear?

RIMS. Would it?

BOBBY. Rims—if you knew what I wanted, more than anything else, would you let me have it?

RIMS. I guess it—it would depend.

BOBBY. Rims, dear, when a woman's truly in love with a man—and believes in him, why then what she wants most of anything—is to have a baby with him—a baby that would be just ours—

RIMS. Why, darling—gosh, kid—why—you see, we couldn't afford—say, I didn't know you felt that way—but if you—if you do—

BOBBY. No, I can't do it! I can't go through with it!

RIMS. What do you mean?

BOBBY (*turning on him*). What do I mean? I was roping you in. That's what I mean—and I can't do it! I was afraid I might lose you, that's all, and I thought I could keep you if we—if there was a—

RIMS. Oh, you were roping me in?

BOBBY. Yes, but I won't do it. I won't keep you that way. If I can't keep you on the level, why, I'll just have to lose you—

RIMS. I see.

BOBBY. Because—I love you too much—

RIMS. Did somebody put you up to that or did you invent it for yourself?

BOBBY. No.

RIMS. No what?

BOBBY. I just—thought of it.

RIMS. No you didn't. It's not like you. Somebody put you up to it.

BOBBY. Well, forget it.—I've been keeping you—

RIMS (*fiercely*). If it was that sister of yours—

BOBBY. Well, what if it was? I'm being honest with you now anyway. I'm going to be so honest it hurts. It isn't the first time I tried to trick you. I tricked you into marrying me.

RIMS. When?

BOBBY. When you asked me to marry you. Didn't you see it?

RIMS. No.

BOBBY. Well, it was obvious enough.

RIMS. Did she put you up to that too?

BOBBY. It doesn't matter. I did it.

RIMS. All right, I've got her number. And yours too. It's the last time you put anything over on me—

BOBBY. I don't want to put anything over on you. If I'd wanted to, I could have, couldn't I?—and I didn't!

RIMS. Listen, kid—I think we're going to have a showdown right here and now! A fellow gives up a lot when he gets married. As long as he's single, he owns the earth, but when he's married his money's not his own, his time's not his own, he's got to keep on working whether he wants to or not, and there's hell to pay if he spends an extra dime. Whenever I tired of my job I used to quit—if I didn't like one town I tried another—and now I can't—

BOBBY. Why not?

RIMS. Because I've got a wife—because I've got a family?

BOBBY. Good God—am I a family? I won't be a wife—I won't be a family! I'm just me!

RIMS. All right, be yourself!

BOBBY. All right, I'll be myself—and if you think a man gives up a lot when he gets married, a girl gives up something when she gets married, and don't you forget it! I spend the whole day here taking care of this damned house for you and cooking your meals and washing your dishes and never going anywhere because we can't afford it—and every time I get a dime for myself I have to ask for it! It's degrading!

RIMS. It's your own home.

BOBBY. It's not mine. It's all yours. You earn the money so it's all yours! I tell you it's despicable! Asking!

RIMS. Throw it up to me I don't earn enough! That's right!

BOBBY. Well, you don't!

RIMS. You knew how much I was earning when you married me. If you don't like it, why see what you can do about it!

BOBBY. Oh! Oh! Well I know what I can do about it!

RIMS. Well, you won't work for Mengle! If it's my house I'm going to have my way in it, and I won't have my wife working for Mengle! I give up a good deal to keep this damn place going and it's going to be the way I want it from now on—

BOBBY. Oh, it will! Well, I still know my way to the front door! I guess I know when I've got enough! (*She goes into front room.*)

RIMS. Where are you going? (BOBBY *stops in the arch, turns, and faces him.*)

BOBBY (*screaming*). You can wash your own dishes! The hot water's in the right hand tap! I'm running along! And I'm not coming back! (*She storms out.*)

RIMS (*calling*). You mean you're leaving me?

BOBBY (*in the living room*). If you don't believe it, you watch me!

RIMS (*picking up his hat and coat*). All right. Suits me. Two can play at that game. I'm not stopping you. Got any money?

BOBBY (*re-entering with her coat and hat on*). I've got the rent money.

RIMS. If you go to work for Mengle I quit him!

BOBBY (*picking up her pocket book*). I don't care where you work. It's a free country. Goodbye. (*She goes out through the living room; the door slams.*)

RIMS. Goodbye. (*He goes out the back door, slamming it. After a moment he comes in, shaken and humbled.*) Bobby! (*There is no answer. He turns off the kitchen light and goes out. The light in the living room still burns.* BOBBY *comes back through the living room.*)

BOBBY. Rims! Rims, dear! (*No answer. She turns slowly, crosses to the living room and goes out again, switching off the light. The front door closes.*)

CURTAIN

ACT THREE

Three weeks later. A bedroom in MRS. GORLIK'S *boarding house in East 33rd St. There is an entrance door at the left, a closet at the right. Near the closet an open window reveals a moonlit night and a fire-escape. There are a couple of ancient chairs, a dresser and an iron bed. The paper on the wall has been there—well, as long as the carpet on the floor. The stage is altogether dark save for the light outside the window. A breeze blows the curtains gently. There is a knock at the door.*

MRS. GORLICK (*outside*). Are you in yet, miss? (*She enters, switches on the lights and goes across to close the window, muttering.*) Never knew a girl wasn't a born fool. Leaves her window up with all these robberies—gets all my curtains dirty—(*She inspects a pair of stockings drying on a towel rack.*) T'ain't decent! (*A door bell rings below.*) (*She looks at the second pair.*) Another pair.

A VOICE (*from the basement*). Mrs. Gorlik!

MRS. GORLIK. What do you want?

VOICE (*from basement*). Man on his way up to see Miss Halevy.

MRS. GORLIK. What?

VOICE. Man here to see Miss Halevy.

MRS. GORLIK. She ain't here.

VOICE. He's on his way up.

MRS. GORLIK. Well, tell him the second floor.

VOICE. Second floor, mister!

MR. HALEVY (*on the stairs*). Looking for Miss Halevy's room.

MRS. GORLIK. This is her room, but I don't know when she'll be in.

MR. HALEVY (*entering*). That's all right, I'll just wait for her. I suppose I can wait for her?

MRS. GORLIK. You mean you'll wait here?

MR. HALEVY. Well not necessarily here—if you'd rather I waited somewhere else.

MRS. GORLIK. I don't know when she's coming back, and I don't know as you'd better wait.

MR. HALEVY. What's that?

MRS. GORLIK. I said, I don't know as you'd better wait.

MR. HALEVY. Well you see I always decide these matters for myself, my dear Miss—

MRS. GORLIK (*positive*). Mrs. Gorlik.

MR. HALEVY. Yes. Well you see, Mrs. Gorlik, I'm Miss Halevy's father. Now, if you'd rather I waited in the parlor—

MRS. GORLIK. There ain't any parlor.

MR. HALEVY (*smiling*). Don't apologize, Mrs. Gorlik. And don't worry about me. I'm perfectly all right.

MRS. GORLIK. Well, if you're her father—

MR. HALEVY. I am.

MRS. GORLIK. Then I should say it's a very good thing you came.

MR. HALEVY. Yes? (*He takes out his pipe.*)

MRS. GORLIK. Because she needs looking after.

MR. HALEVY. You don't say.

MRS. GORLIK (*seeing his pipe*). You can't smoke here, you know. Not a pipe.

MR. HALEVY. I beg your pardon. And so you think she needs looking after?

MRS. GORLIK. She certainly does.

MR. HALEVY. What makes you think so?

MRS. GORLIK. I can tell. When they come here looking for rooms late at night and when they have middle-aged gentlemen to call like she done last night—and when they smoke cigarettes—well—I can tell. (*The door-bell again.*)

MR. HALEVY. Then you—you won't mind if I wait—

VOICE (*from the basement*). Mrs. Gorlik.

MRS. GORLIK. What do you want?

VOICE. Another gentleman to see Miss Halevy.

MRS. GORLIK. I'll be right down! (*She goes out.*)

VOICE. He's coming up!

MRS. GORLIK (*outside*). Are you the gentleman to see Miss Halevy?

RIMS (*outside*). Miss Halevy hell, I'm here to see Mrs. O'Neil. (*He enters and sees* MR. HALEVY.)

MRS. GORLIK. There ain't any Mrs. O'Neil here. And besides— (*She stops, seeing they know each other.*)

MR. HALEVY. Hello, Rims.

RIMS. Hello. (MRS. GORLIK *goes.*)

MR. HALEVY. Bobby coming in soon?

RIMS. I don't know.

MR. HALEVY. Because if she is I'll run along. I didn't know you two'd got together.

RIMS. Me? I haven't seen her.

MR. HALEVY. Oh, I see.

RIMS. Yeah. I came in on the chance she might be here.

MR. HALEVY. So did I.

RIMS. You know when I first came in, I thought you were Mengle.

MR. HALEVY. Well, how is Mengle for looks?

RIMS. I'm no judge. I hate the face off him.

MR. HALEVY. What made you think he might be here?

RIMS. That's all right.

MR. HALEVY. Maybe you under-estimate Bobby.

RIMS. You think so?

MR. HALEVY. Or, maybe I under-estimate you. What made you think Mengle might be here?— (RIMS *doesn't answer.*) All right!

RIMS (*rising*). Listen, do you think I've been having an easy time these last three weeks?

MR. HALEVY. I don't know.

RIMS. Maybe you think I've been having the time of my life. My wife's left me. Now's my chance to step out, I suppose—why not? She does.

MR. HALEVY. That's funny!

RIMS. Yeah!

MR. HALEVY. Because if there was any one thing in the world she wanted it was you.

RIMS. How do you know?

MR. HALEVY. I know.

RIMS. Listen, Mr. Halevy. I called her up. She said I can't see her. Then I tried having some fun, but it wasn't any good. I don't want to play cards. I don't want anything else in the world except her. And—she's gone. She doesn't need me. She's having a good time.

MR. HALEVY. You'll have to prove that to me.

RIMS. Prove it! I hung around the office last night. I had to see her. And what happened? She comes out with Mengle—and they went to dinner together—Jeez—

MR. HALEVY. Well—?

RIMS. Well— She didn't see me. So I followed them. And after dinner she let him bring her home. He brought her here in a private car—with a chauffeur. I guess that's what she wants. I don't earn enough. She's got to have a private car—with a chauffeur.

MR. HALEVY. Oh, no—no—no.

RIMS. Well, anyway, I waited outside. And pretty soon he went away. God, I don't know what's the matter with me. I used to have a little sense. About girls, anyway. Now I act like a damn dummy. You don't know what it's like!

MR. HALEVY. Don't I?

RIMS. Does everybody go crazy this way?

MR. HALEVY (*lighting his pipe*). Every last one of us.

RIMS. You know, when I came in and thought Mengle was here, I was going to beat him up.

MR. HALEVY. No, no—that wouldn't do

any good, you know.

RIMS. No. but it'd be a lot of fun.

MR. HALEVY. You're lucky, Rims. You young fellows don't know how lucky you are. When a man's young he makes love—when he's middle-aged he makes money—or tries to—and when he's old he makes his soul. I never could make any money to speak of, so I suppose it's about time I began to make my soul. But I'd rather be young—and make love to a girl that was in love with me. There's nothing like it.

RIMS. She's not in love with me, Mr. Halevy. That's the hell of it. If she were, she wouldn't have gone away.

MR. HALEVY. Well, you went away, too, didn't you? And you were in love with her?

RIMS. Yeah. But—

MR. HALEVY. Maybe she left you because she was in love with you. (RIMS, *more or less taken aback at this idea, pauses for a moment, then reaches for his hat.*) Where are you going, Rims?

RIMS. I'm going to take a walk around the block. (*He starts to the door and meets a chauffeur who is carrying a package.*)

THE CHAUFFEUR. I've got a package for Miss Halevy.

RIMS. You mean Mrs. O'Neil. She's not here.

THE CHAUFFEUR. They said the second floor.

RIMS. Yes, this is her room, but she's not here. Anything I can do for you?

THE CHAUFFEUR. No. This thing's got to be delivered personally.

RIMS. Then I guess you'll have to come back.

THE CHAUFFEUR. Yeah?

RIMS. Yeah!

THE CHAUFFEUR (*he disappears*). All right!

RIMS. Now what the hell is going on?

MR. HALEVY. What do you think?

RIMS. Well, that's Mengle's chauffeur, isn't it? Must deliver to her personally. What the hell does that make me? (*He starts to go.*)

MR. HALEVY. Wait a minute! Shall I tell her you were here?

RIMS. No! (*He goes, bumping into* MRS. GORLIK. *She holds the door open.*)

MRS. GORLIK. You'll have to leave the door open, young man, (*She follows him down the hall and calls.*) Matty!

THE VOICE. Yes, Ma'am! (MR. HALEVY *puffs vigorously on pipe.*)

MRS. GORLIK (*outside*). See that that door is closed after that young man leaves. All the draughts in these halls is— (MRS. GORLIK *enters left.*) You'll have to leave the door open with gentlemen call— (*Seeing that* BOBBY *is not there.*) Oh, she ain't come in yet?

MR. HALEVY (*hiding the pipe*). No!

MRS. GORLIK. And the young man didn't wait?

MR. HALEVY. No!

MRS. GORLIK. You'll have to excuse me opening the door. It's not one of the things I like to do—going around opening girls' doors with gentlemen calling, Mr. Halevy. It is Mr. Halevy, ain't it?

MR. HALEVY. It is.

MRS. GORLIK. But I have to do it, much as I don't like to. (*Noticing he has sat down she does the same on edge of bed.*) If I was ever going into this business again, I wouldn't take girls, only gentlemen. True, gentlemen do get drunk and smash things. But I will say this for them. They do know how to take care of themselves, and you don't have to watch them.

MR. HALEVY. Why do you have to watch the girls?

MRS. GORLIK (*turning to him, breathless*). Why, my dear Mr.— Well—if you knew the kind of goings on, and what was thought of girls that close their doors with gentlemen callers—well, you wouldn't want it said about your daughter.

MR. HALEVY. You mean they get drunk and break things? (*The door-bell rings.*)

MRS. GORLIK. I guess you know what I mean, all right.

THE VOICE. Mrs. Gorlik—

MRS. GORLIK (*rising*). Well what is it?

THE VOICE. There's a special delivery letter.

MRS. GORLIK. Well, sign for it. Oh, never mind, I'm coming right down. (MR. HALEVY *resumes his pipe.*)

BOBBY (*outside*). Hello, Mrs. Gorlik.

MRS. GORLIK (*outside*). How do you do? There's a gentleman to see you that says he's your father. (BOBBY *enters.* MR. HALEVY *rises.*)

BOBBY (*kissing him*). Dad! Hello!

MR. HALEVY. Well, darling, I stayed away as long as I could.

BOBBY (*closing the door*). I'm glad you came. Do you like my place?

MR. HALEVY. It certainly looks familiar.

BOBBY. You don't mean it looks like home?

MR. HALEVY. No. But I lived in a lot of places like this before I was married. They haven't changed the carpet on the stairs of any one of them.

BOBBY. It must be different, though.

MR. HALEVY. My dear, there's nothing new about these places except the girls and boys that live in them— But, I'm certainly not crazy about this.

BOBBY. Well, I'm not either. But they won't take girls many places and I liked their scale of prices. (*She hangs up her coat.*)

MR. HALEVY. You know, I walked past that little house of yours this afternoon, and it looked pretty lonely. And I felt pretty lonely, and I thought three weeks of this was about enough. So I decided to come over and ask you what about it.

BOBBY. Well, I wanted to be alone, and I have been.

MR. HALEVY. You know, you could have your old room—at home—any time?

BOBBY. Dad, I'll never go home. It would be like going around in a circle. I'd be right back where I started.

MR. HALEVY. I'm afraid it was partly my fault.

BOBBY. No. I did it all with my little hatchet. I cannot tell a lie. I've gone back to work, dad—and I'm living here.

MR. HALEVY. What about poor Rims?

BOBBY. What about poor me? I had to be alone, dad! I didn't dare see Rims. If I had I might have gone back to him—and then—well, we'd be right back where we were. (*A knock at the door,* BOBBY *opens it.*)

RIMS (*entering*). Hello!

BOBBY. Hello, Rims!

MR. HALEVY. Good evening.

RIMS. Good evening, sir.

MR. HALEVY. Don't you sir me, young man. I'm only twice your age and I don't look that. And boy, do you want to meet a nice girl? My daughter, Mr. O'Neil. A working girl, but she has class. She— (*He stops, crosses to the door, and goes out.*)

RIMS. I guess you didn't want me to find you.

BOBBY. Oh, I don't mind.

RIMS. Well, I'll tell you about that first, so you'll know how it happened. I didn't ask anybody where your room was. I followed you home last night.

BOBBY. Followed me? I had dinner with Mengle.

RIMS. I know you did. Christ, kid, I've been out of my head. I hung around the office last night to see you, and who did you come out with?

BOBBY. You waited—at the office?

RIMS. Yes—

BOBBY. I didn't see you!

RIMS. And then he came home with you. He even stayed around a while.

BOBBY. I was just lonely.

RIMS. You didn't look very lonely to me. I can't stand that. After all, you are my wife.

BOBBY. Oh, was that why you came?

RIMS. No, it wasn't. I wanted to see you. You managed to make it lovely for me!

BOBBY. Did you come to see me or did you come to lecture me about Mengle?

RIMS. Well—you had dinner with him, didn't you?

BOBBY. It was just Mengle, wasn't it? That was all you wanted to see me about?

RIMS. No, it wasn't.

BOBBY. Then—what was it?

RIMS. Oh, I guess it does not matter.

BOBBY. That's what does matter.

RIMS. Yeah?

BOBBY. Don't you think so?

RIMS. I don't know.

BOBBY (*sitting down*). You might—have a chair.

RIMS (*he sits*). Thanks.

BOBBY. You have a new job I hear.

RIMS. Yeah!

BOBBY. How's it going?

RIMS. Pretty well.

BOBBY. Oh.

RIMS. Well—not bad!

BOBBY. Jobs are all pretty much alike.

RIMS. Sure.

BOBBY. What—what business is it?

RIMS. Automatic mooring winches.

BOBBY. Oh. Oh, yes!— Are there many of them used?

RIMS. What?

BOBBY. These—

RIMS. Automatic mooring winches?

BOBBY. Yes—

RIMS. You'd be surprised. . . . Same salary.

BOBBY. Truly?

RIMS. Yes.

BOBBY. Why that's marvellous, Rims—to change jobs and get the same salary the first thing. It is—marvellous.

RIMS. Not a very nice place, is it?

BOBBY. It's inexpensive.

RIMS. It ought to be.

BOBBY. You don't like it?

RIMS. Well, you're here, of course.

BOBBY. Thanks, Rims.

RIMS (*rising*). Say, Bobby—

BOBBY (*rising, and putting the chair between them*). Yes—?

RIMS. Are you really as hard-hearted as —as all this kind of implies?

BOBBY. When was I ever hard-hearted?

RIMS. You know, I came over here all primed to say something, and I'm damned if I know how to say it.

BOBBY. What was it?

RIMS. I came to ask you—if you hadn't enough of it—and—maybe you'd come home now—

BOBBY. Back to the house?

RIMS. Where else?

BOBBY. No.

RIMS. What are we going to do with the house, then?

BOBBY. I guess Florrie and Willy are going to take it off our hands.

RIMS. What are you going to do?

BOBBY. Live here.

RIMS. And what am I going to do?

BOBBY. I don't know. (*There is a knock.*) Come in. (*She opens the door and finds the chauffeur with his package.*)

THE CHAUFFEUR. I've a package for you, Miss Halevy.

BOBBY. Oh! thank you. (*She takes it.*)

THE CHAUFFEUR. You're welcome! (*He goes.* BOBBY *closes the door.*)

RIMS. So, it's flowers Mengle's sending you, huh? Well, you better open it.

BOBBY. I don't want to.

RIMS. Sure, open it. Why ruin the flowers—just on my account.

BOBBY. It isn't flowers!

RIMS. Then what is it?

BOBBY (*opening it*). It's really something for Mrs. Gorlik.

RIMS. It's a bolt!—

BOBBY (*laughing*). Yes—for the door!

RIMS (*taking out a screw driver and a hammer*). And a hammer, and a screw driver to put it on with.

BOBBY. Well—he said he was going to send me a bolt—but I thought he was joking. You see, when Mengle was here last night, the landlady seemed to think he was a shady character and kept opening the door all the time—

RIMS. Hey! Wait a minute! Let me get this straight!

BOBBY. I suppose he thought it would be funny. And I really did want a bolt.

RIMS. Yeah, go right ahead and explain. You're making it better all the time.

BOBBY. Rims—

RIMS. Yeah, explain some more! Did you ask him for it?

BOBBY. I didn't tell him he couldn't send it.

RIMS. Oh, you didn't? Well, all right—

BOBBY. You mean you think I haven't any right to let Mr. Mengle send me a bolt for my door?

RIMS. I mean it looks damned funny to me, and it is damned funny!

BOBBY. Certainly it's funny! That's why he did it? Don't you see?

RIMS. Do I see? I'll say I see! (*He starts for the door.*)

BOBBY (*stepping in front of him*). Rims, if you go now, it's the last you see of me as long as you live. (*There is a pause.*)

RIMS. Well, what I can't understand is why you'd let Mengle come to your room.

BOBBY. Well, why not, if I feel like it? It's my room. I can take care of myself.

RIMS. I doubt it.

BOBBY. Listen, Rims. I did want you to come. I've been waiting for you to come. But if you're going to begin to tell me what I can do and what I can't do—

RIMS. If you don't know enough to keep clear of Mengle, you shouldn't be at large.

BOBBY. That's just the point. I do know enough to keep clear of Mengle. Only I'm on my own now, and I'm going to use my own judgment.

RIMS. Such as it is.

BOBBY. Exactly. Such as it is. You use yours such as it is, and you haven't any guardian.

RIMS. What's the idea, anyway.

BOBBY. The idea is, I'm a free agent. Just as free as you are.

RIMS. You don't care about me any more?

BOBBY. Yes, I do.

RIMS. Well, it's all right about Mengle. I can see how it was.

BOBBY. It did look queer, I know.

RIMS. Only any time you want a bolt on your door, I wish you'd ask me.

BOBBY. I will—if you're around.

RIMS. You know damn well I'd be around if I thought you wanted me.

BOBBY (*smiling*). Well, I wasn't sure you would.

RIMS. (*coming close to* BOBBY). Listen, dear—about that house! That isn't a bad little house—as houses ago.

BOBBY. Any house is bad enough.

RIMS (*pleading*). You won't try it again?

BOBBY. No. . . . You see— Oh, I wonder if I can tell you— What we wanted was a love affair, wasn't it? Just to be together and let the rest go hang—and what we got was a house and bills and general hell. Do you know what I think a love affair is, Rims? It's when the whole world is trying to keep two people apart —and they insist on being together. And when they get married the whole world pushes them together so they just naturally fly apart. I want my love affair back. I wanted hurried kisses and clandestine meetings, and a secret lover. I don't want a house. I don't want a husband. I want a lover.

RIMS. So that let's me out.

BOBBY. Does it, dear? (*A knock. The door opens and* MRS. GORLIK *appears.*)

MRS. GORLIK. You'll have to leave the door open with gentlemen callers.

BOBBY. Oh, yes, Rims. I forgot to tell you. The door should be open.

MRS. GORLIK. Of course, I understand the gentleman last night was your boss, and the old one was your father and I daresay this one's your husband.

BOBBY. No. Oh, no.

MRS. GORLIK (*icily*). Then the door stays open.

BOBBY. Very well.

MRS. GORLIK. It's ten o'clock and I suppose you know there's no gentlemen callers allowed after ten.

BOBBY. Mr. O'Neil was just going.

MRS. GORLIK. Yes, the gentlemen are always just going!—It's ten o'clock! (*She goes.*)

BOBBY. I guess you'll have to go, Rims.

RIMS (*taking his hat*). All right.

BOBBY. Goodnight, dear.

RIMS. So we're not married any more?

BOBBY. No.

RIMS. That's nice.

BOBBY. It is, isn't it?

RIMS. When do I see you?

BOBBY. Whenever you like.

RIMS. And how do I see you? By appointment?

BOBBY. I'm not very busy—if we never had been married and I was just a girl you wanted to see sometime—how would you manage it?

RIMS. I could call you up tomorrow and take you for a bus-ride, I suppose. And dinner at Child's. Wouldn't that be grand?

BOBBY. I'd like it. Why don't you?

RIMS. Well, I don't want to go bus-riding— Aw Bobby, what's it all leading up to anyway. Are we going to get a divorce?

BOBBY. If you like.

RIMS. Will you marry me again if we do?

BOBBY. Oh, Rims, you are a darling! You are! Would you really do it all over again?

RIMS. Sure I would.

BOBBY. But you never really wanted to get married, did you? Now tell the truth—

RIMS. I wanted you.

BOBBY. Of course you did, but you didn't want a house. I wanted you but I didn't want a house. And I don't now.

RIMS. How do I know you won't fall for somebody else sometime? If I leave you here?

BOBBY. You don't.

RIMS. Oh.

BOBBY. How do I know you won't fall for somebody else? I don't. I don't want to. You aren't to see me unless you just can't keep away. You used to know me so well you didn't like me. You used to know where I was and what I was doing all the time. It was positively indecent, and we won't have any more of it. It's like not wearing any clothes.

RIMS. Well. All right.

BOBBY. So—now we're really free.

RIMS. I said all right. I don't give a whoop about that.

BOBBY. What do you give a whoop about?

RIMS (*close to her*). About you, you little fool! Can't you see it? Don't you see I can't get along without you? I can't stand being away from you all the time. I keep waking up in the night wanting you.

BOBBY. So do I.

RIMS. I want to see you to-night.

BOBBY. Well—?

RIMS. And the house is standing there

waiting for us.

BOBBY (*turning away*). It'll just have to wait, then. I got you into it in the first place—and you didn't like it—and I didn't like it. And now, thank God, we're out of it.

RIMS. I don't know what you want.

BOBBY. I don't either. I only know what I don't want.

RIMS. All right! (*He puts on his hat and goes out.*)

BOBBY. Goodbye. (*There's no answer. She stands still for a moment, then closes the door and sits disconsolately on the edge of the bed. There is a knock and she turns to the door. It's only* MRS. GORLIK.)

MRS. GORLIK. Have all the gentlemen gone?

BOBBY. Yes, Mrs. Gorlik. I'm sorry—but all the gentlemen have gone.

MRS. GORLIK. (*looking behind the door*). I'm just seeing for myself. Don't you try any tricks. I try to run—

BOBBY (*over her shoulder, annoyed*). I know—a respectable house.

MRS. GORLIK. Don't try any tricks. (*She goes out, closing the door.* BOBBY *sits for a moment, disconsolate, then gets her night things from the closet and climbs on a chair to turn out the wall-lamp. She starts to undress, then falls on the bed, sobbing.* RIMS *appears outside the window in the moonlight. He opens the window, climbs in softly, and tiptoes to the package containing the bolt. As he places the bolt against the door in the semi-dark he startles* BOBBY *with the metallic click.*)

BOBBY (*looking up*). Oh, Rims!

RIMS (*pointing to the screw driver on chair*). Bring me the screw driver, will you, dear?

BOBBY (*bringing it to him*). Hush! (RIMS *starts to fit the bolt to the door.*)

CURTAIN

Porgy

BY DOROTHY AND DUBOSE HEYWARD

FROM THE NOVEL BY DUBOSE HEYWARD

First produced by The Theatre Guild at the Guild Theatre, New York City, on October 10, 1927, with the following cast:

MARIA .... Georgette Harvey
JAKE .... Wesley Hill
LILY .... Dorothy Paul
MINGO .... Richard Huey
ANNIE .... Ella Madison
SPORTING LIFE ... Percy Verwayne
SERENA .... Rose MacClendon
ROBBINS .... Lloyd Gray
JIM .... Peter Clark
CLARA .... Marie Young
PETER .... Hayes Pryor
PORGY .... Frank Wilson
CROWN .... Jack Carter
CROWN'S BESS .... Evelyn Ellis
A DETECTIVE ..... Stanley de Wolfe
TWO POLICEMEN .. Hugh Rennie, Maurice McRae
UNDERTAKER ...... Leigh Whipper
SCIPIO .... Melville Greene
SINN FRAZIER .... A. B. Comathiere
WILSON .... G. Edward Brown
ALAN ARCHDALE .. Edward Fielding
THE CRAB MAN ... Leigh Whipper
THE CORONER .... Garrett Minturn

The action takes place in a Charleston, South Carolina tenement neighborhood known as Catfish Row, and in a palmetto jungle near by.

NONE of the efforts to create folk drama during the nineteen twenties reaped such attractive and lasting results as the South Carolina Negro fable *Porgy*. For once, the folk spirit appeared in our theatre without being spoiled by crudity, banality, or condescension toward lowly characters. Like all good folk stories, it also contained ingredients of local color and folk music of which the Theatre Guild and its director Rouben Mamoulian availed themselves generously. The singing and staging of the Negro spirituals in *Porgy* accounted to a considerable degree for the warm feeling and charm, as well as the success, of the production. When, later on, in 1935, *Porgy* was given musical treatment by George Gershwin, it became the first successful folk opera in the American theatre. Its music, based on Negro song and rhythm, discovered unexpected possibilities in the popular jazz music of the twenties for which few people had entertained such high hopes as were realized in *Porgy and Bess*.

Porgy is the masterpiece of one of the theatre's most admirable couples, the Heywards. Du Bose Heyward, a native of Charleston, South Carolina, was born in 1885 and embarked upon a career in literature after having achieved a successful one in the insurance business. He established a Poetry Society of Charleston and published a volume of poems, *Carolina Chansons* (1922), with Hervey Allen, who is most likely to be identified as the author of *Anthony Adverse*. Another collection of Heyward's poetry, *Skylines and Horizons,* appeared in 1924; still another, *Jasbo Brown,* in 1931. A year later was published his affectionate novel of Negro life *Porgy,* which Mrs. Heyward and he turned into a play noteworthy in itself and later to be even better known as the basis for the George Gershwin folk opera *Porgy and Bess*. Mr. Heyward wrote a number of other books before his death in 1940. Among them were *Peter Ashley* (1932), a Civil War chronicle; *Star Spangled Virgin* (1939), a study of the bewildered response of the Virgin Islanders to the New Deal; and another folk novel about a devoted Negro mother, *Mamba's Daughters* (1929).

Mrs. Heyward (*nee* Dorothy Hartzell Kuhns, born in Worcester, Ohio in 1890) completed a dramatization of the last-mentioned book in 1939, and Ethel Waters distinguished herself in the Broadway production. Educated at Radcliffe and a student of playwriting at Harvard and Columbia Universities, Miss Kuhns married Du Bose Heyward in 1923. She won a prize for playwriting at Harvard in 1924, and had her first production, *Nancy Ann,* in that year. After her husband's death she wrote, in addition to novels, a war play with anti-racialist connotations, *South Pacific* (1944), in collaboration with Howard Rigsby, and *Set My People Free,* a drama dealing with an early slave rebellion, which was produced by the Theatre Guild in 1948.

ACT ONE

Scene I

Before the rise of each curtain, the bells of St. Michael's, adjacent to the Negro quarter of old Charleston, chime the hour. The chimes are heard occasionally throughout the play.

Before the rise of first curtain, St. Michael's chimes the quarters and strikes eight.

The curtain rises on the court of Catfish Row, now a Negro tenement in a fallen quarter of Charleston, but in Colonial days one of the finest buildings of the aristocracy. The walls rise around a court, except a part of the rear wall of the old house, which breaks to leave a section of lower wall pierced at its center by a massive wrought-iron gate of great beauty which hangs unsteadily between brick pillars surmounted by pineapples carved of Italian marble.

By day, the walls of the entire structure present a mottled color effect of varying pastel shades, caused by the atmospheric action of many layers of color wash. A brilliant note is added by rows of blooming flame-colored geraniums in old vegetable tins on narrow shelves attached to each window sill. All of the windows are equipped with dilapidated slat shutters, some of which are open, others closed, but with the slats turned so that any one inside could look out without being seen. The floor of the spacious court is paved with large flagstones, and these gleam in faintly varying colors under their accumulated grime.

Beyond the gate and above the wall, one sees a littered cobbled street, an old gas street lamp, and, beyond that again, the blue expanse of the bay, with Fort Sumter showing on the horizon. Over the wall can be seen masts and spars of fishing boats lying on the beach.

By night, the court depends for its illumination upon the wheezing gas lamp, and the kerosene lamps and lanterns that come and go in the hands of the occupants of the Row.

At left front is PORGY'S *room (door and window), and beyond it, an arch letting on an inside yard. The pump stands against the wall right back; then, on around right wall,* SERENA'S *doorway, with her window above it, two more doors, then the door to* MARIA'S *cookshop. Center right is seen* SERENA'S *wash bench, and near right wall, well down front, is table on which* MARIA *serves her meals during the warm weather.*

As the curtain rises, revealing Catfish Row on a summer evening, the court reëchoes with African laughter and friendly banter in "Gullah," the language of the Charleston Negro, which still retains many African words. The audience understands none of it. Like the laughter and movement, the twanging of a guitar from an upper window, the dancing of an urchin with a loose, shuffling step, it is a part of the picture of Catfish Row as it really is—an alien scene, a people as little known to most Americans as the people of the Congo.

Gradually, it seems to the audience that they are beginning to understand this foreign language. In reality, the "Gullah" is being tempered to their ears, spoken more distinctly with the African words omitted.

It is Saturday night, and most of the residents of Catfish Row are out in the court, sitting watching the crap shooters or moving to and fro to visit with one neighbor, then another. Among those present are:

MARIA, matriarch of the court, massive in proportions and decisive in action.

ANNIE, middle-aged, quiet, and sedate.

LILY, loud, good-natured, the court hoyden.

CLARA, who has her baby in her arms. She is scarcely more than a girl and has a sweet, wistful face.

JAKE, CLARA'S husband. A successful captain of the fishing fleet; good-looking, good-natured.

"SPORTING LIFE," bootlegger to Catfish Row; a slender, overdressed, high-yellow Negro.

MINGO, young and lazy.

JIM and NELSON, fishermen.

SCIPIO, a boy of twelve, one of the numerous offspring of ROBBINS and SERENA.

ROBBINS *and* SERENA *are still in their room on the second floor,* SERENA *is seen occasionally as she moves back and forth past her lighted window. She is a self-respecting "white folks" Negress, of about thirty.*

The men are gathering for their Saturday-night crap game. They are grouped between gate and PORGY'S *room.* JAKE *is squatting right,* MINGO *center rear, and* SPORTING LIFE *is left, forming triangle. A smoking kerosene lamp is in center of group, and the men are tossing and retrieving their dice in the circle of light.*

JAKE (*rolling*). Seems like dese bones don't gib me nuttin' but box cars tonight. It was de same two weeks ago, an' de game broke me. I ain't likes dat luck.

(SPORTING LIFE *produces his own dice, and throws with a loud grunt and snap of his fingers.* MINGO *snatches the dice and balances them in his hand.*)

SPORTING LIFE. Damn yu', gib me dem bones.

(MINGO *holds him off with one hand while he hands the dice to* JAKE.)

MINGO. Whut yo' say to dese, Jake?

JAKE (*examining them*). Dem's de same cock-eye bones whut clean de gang out las' week. Ef dey rolls in dis game, I rolls out. (*Hands the dice back to* SPORTING LIFE.) Eberybody rolls de same bones in dis game, Sportin' Life—take 'em or leabe 'em.

(ROBBINS *comes from door, rear right. He is a well-set-up Negro of about thirty. The window above him opens, and* SERENA *leans from sill.*)

SERENA (*pleadingly*). Honey-boy!

ROBBINS. Now, fuh Gawd's sake, don't start dat again. I goin' play—git dat.

SERENA. Ef yo' didn't hab licker in yo' right now, yo' wouldn't talk like dat. Yo' know whut yo' done promise' me las' week.

ROBBINS. All right, den, I wouldn't shoot no more dan fifty cents. (*Joins the group.*) (CLARA *paces up and down the court, singing softly to her baby.*) Dat ole lady ob mine hell on joinin' de buryin' lodge. I says, spen' um while yo' is still alibe an' kickin'. (*Picks up dice. Throws them with a loud grunt.*) I ain't see no buzzard 'round her yit.

(JIM, *a big, strong-looking fellow, saunters over to the group of crap players. A cotton hook swings from his belt.*)

JIM. Lor', I is tire' dis night. I'm t'inkin' ob gettin' out ob de cotton business. Mebby it all right fo' a nigger like Crown dat Gawd start to make into a bull, den change He min'. But it ain't no work fo' a man.

JAKE. Better come 'long on de *Sea Gull.* I gots place fo' nudder fishermans.

JIM. Dat suit me. Dis cotton hook hab swung he las' bale ob cotton. Here, Scipio, yo' wants a cotton hook?

(*Throws the hook to* SCIPIO, *who takes it eagerly, fastens it at his waist, and goes about court playing that he is a stevedore, lifting objects with the hook and pretending that they are of tremendous weight.* CLARA *passes the group, crooning softly.*)

CLARA.

"Hush, li'l baby, don' yo' cry.
Fadder an' mudder born to die."

JAKE (*standing up*). Whut! dat chile ain't 'sleep yit. Gib 'um to me. I'll fix um fo' yo'. (*Takes baby from* CLARA, *rocks it in his arms, sings.*)

"My mammy tells me, long time ago,
Son, don' yo' marry no gal yo' know.
Spen' all yo' money—eat all yo' bread,
Gone to Savannah, lef' yo' fo' dead."

(*Several of the men join in on the last line.* JAKE *rocks the baby more violently and begins to shuffle.* CLARA *watches anxiously.*) "Spen all yo' money. Steal all yo' clothes. Whut will become of yo', Gawd only knows." (*The light leaves* SERENA'S *window.* JAKE *swings the baby back to* CLARA.) Dere now! Whut I tells yo'. He 'sleep already. (*The baby wails. The men laugh.* CLARA *carries baby to her room. Closes door.* SERENA *comes from her door with a lamp which she sets on her wash bench. She sits beside it and looks anxiously toward crap players.*)

MARIA (*to* SERENA). Whut worryin' yo', Serena? Yo' gots one ob de bes' mens in Catfish Row. Why yo' ain't let um play widout pickin' on um?

SERENA. He gots licker in um tonight, an' Robbins ain't de same man wid licker.

(MINGO *is rolling and retrieving the dice. While he does so, he looks and laughs at* ROBBINS, *then sings at him.*)

MINGO (*singing*).

"My mammy tell me, long time ago,
Son don't yo' marry no gal yo' know."

(*Speaking to* ROBBINS) Ought to be single like Porgy an' me. Den yo' kin shoot bones without git pick on.

ROBBINS. Oh, my lady all right; only 'cep' she don' like craps. She born a w'ite folks nigger. She people b'long to Gob'nor Rutledge. Ain't yo' see Miss Rutledge come to see she when she sick?

MARIA (*overhearing, to* SERENA). Oh, dat Miss Rutledge come to see yuh?

SERENA. Sho! yo' ain' know dat?

MARIA. She eber sell any ob she ole clothes?

SERENA. Not she. But sometime she gib 'em away to de nigger'.

MARIA (*sighing*). I wish I could git a dress off she. She de firs' pusson I eber see whut hipped an' busted 'zac'ly like me.

ROBBINS (*boasting*). Yes, suh! my lady —Yo' bes' sabe yo' talk fo' dem dice. Bones ain't got no patience wid 'omen.

MINGO. Dat's de trut'. Course dey can't git along togedder. Dey is all two atter de same nigger money.

JAKE. Annie dere likes de single life, ain't it, Annie? Whut become ob dat ole fisherman used to come fo' see yo'?

ANNIE. He ain't fisherman.

JAKE. Whut he do?

ANNIE. Him ain't do nuttin' mos' all de time. Odder time, him is a shoe carpenter.

(*The voice of* PETER, *the old "honey man," is heard in the street, drawing nearer and nearer.*)

PETER. Here comes de honey man. Yo' gots honey?—Yes, ma'am, I gots honey. —Yo' gots honey in de comb?—Yes, ma'am, I gots honey in de comb.—Yo' gots honey cheap?—Yes, ma'am, my honey cheap.

(PETER *enters gate and closes it behind him. He is a gentle, kindly Negro, verging on senility. A large wooden tray covered with a white cloth is balanced on his head.*)

LILY (*going to meet him*). Well, here come my ole man. (*Takes tray from his head and shouts in his ear.*) Now gimme de money. (*He hands her some coins. She points to bench.*) Now go sit an' res'. (*He does as he is told. She places tray in her room and returns to circle.*)

MARIA. Yo', Scipio! Here come Porgy! Open de gate fo' uh!

(PORGY *drives up to the gate in his soapbox chariot. He is a crippled beggar of the Charleston streets, who has done much to overcome his handicap of almost powerless legs by supplying himself with a patriarchal and very dirty goat, which draws a cart made of an upturned soap box, on two lopsided wheels, which bears the inscription,* "WILD ROSE SOAP, PURE AND FRAGRANT."

PORGY *is no longer young, and yet not old. There is a suggestion of the mystic in his thoughtful, sensitive face. He is black, with the almost purple blackness of unadulterated Congo blood.*

SCIPIO *reluctantly interrupts his performance on a mouth organ, shuffles across court, and opens one side of the ponderous gate.*

PORGY *drives through and pulls up beside the crap ring.*)

JAKE. Here de ole crap shark.

PORGY. All right, Mingo! Jake! Gib' me a han' out dis wagon. I gots a pocket full ob de buckra money, an' he goin' to any man whut gots de guts fo' shoot 'em off me!

(MINGO *and* JAKE *help* PORGY *from wagon to a seat on ground at left front of circle.*

SCIPIO *leads goat away through arch at rear left.*)

(JIM *saunters to gate and looks out.*)

ROBBINS. All right, mens! Roll 'em! We done wait long 'nough.

JIM (*returning to group*). Yo' bes' wait for Crown. I seen um comin', takin' de whole sidewalk, an' he look like he ain't goin' stan' no foolin'.

PORGY. Is Bess wid um?

JAKE. Listen to Porgy! I t'ink he sof' on Crown's Bess! (*All the men laugh.*)

PORGY. Gawd make cripple to be lonely. T'ain't no use for um to be sof' on a 'oman.

MARIA. Porgy gots too good sense to look twice at dat licker-guzzlin' slut.

LILY. Licker-guzzlin'! It takes more'n licker fo' sati'fy Crown's Bess.

SERENA. Happy dus'! Dat's what it take! Dat gal Bess ain't fit for Gawd-fearin' ladies to 'sociate wid!

SPORTING LIFE. Sistuhs! You needn't worry! Gawd-fearin' ladies is de las' t'ing on eart' Bess is a-wantin' for 'sociate wid.

PORGY. Can't yo' keep yo' mout' off Bess! Between de Gawd-fearin' ladies an' de Gawd-damnin' men, dat gal ain't gots no chance.

JAKE. Ain't I tells yo' Porgy sof' on um? (*More laughter.*)

PORGY. I ain't neber swap one word wid she.

(CROWN *and* BESS *appear at gate.* CROWN *is lurching slightly and* BESS *is piloting him through the entrance.*

CROWN *is a huge Negro of magnificent physique, a stevedore on the cotton wharfs. He is wearing blue denim pants and tan shirt with a bright bandanna about his neck. From his belt hangs a long gleaming cotton hook.*

BESS *is slender, but sinewy; very black, wide nostrils, and large, but well-formed mouth. She flaunts a typical, but debased, Negro beauty.*
From the occupants of Catfish Row there are cries of, "Here comes Big Boy!" "'Low, Crown!" "'Low Bess," etc.)

CROWN (*to* SPORTING LIFE). All right, high stepper. Gib us a pint, an make it damn' quick. (SPORTING LIFE *pulls a flask from his hip pocket and hands it to* CROWN. CROWN *jerks out cork and takes a long pull.*) (*To* BESS.) Pay um, Bess!

(BESS *settles for the bottle, then takes her seat by* CROWN, *ignoring the women of the court.*
CROWN *hands her the flask, from which she takes a long pull. She meets* SERENA'S *eyes, laughs at their hostility, and at once extends the bottle to* ROBBINS)

BESS. Hab one to de Gawd-fearin' ladies. Dere's nuttin' else like 'em—t'ank Gawd!

(ROBBINS *tries to resist, but the fumes of raw liquor are too much for him. He takes a deep drink.*
CROWN *snatches the bottle from him, gulps the entire remaining contents, and shatters it on the flags behind him.*
The crap circle is now complete. The positions are as follows:

Rear

X BESS   X CROWN
                              X DADDY PETER
X MINGO   X SPORTING LIFE
X JAKE
X ROBBINS   X PORGY

Footlights

(CROWN *throws coin down before him.*)

CROWN. I'm talkin' to yo' mans. Anybody answerin' me?

(*They all throw down money.*)

ROBBINS (*to* JAKE). An' dem fine chillen ob mine!

CROWN. Shet yo' damn mout' an' t'row.

ROBBIN (*taken aback and rolling hastily*). Box cars again! (*They all roar with laughter.*)

MINGO, Cover 'em, brudder, cover 'em.

ROBBINS. Cover hell! I goin' pass 'em along an' see ef I kin break my luck.

MINGO. He lady ain't 'low um but fifty cent, an' he can't take no chance wid bad luck.

(*All laugh at* ROBBINS.)

BESS (*with a provocative look at* SERENA). Dat all right, Honey-boy, I'll stake yo' when yo' four bits done gone.

SERENA (*to* ROBBINS). Go ahead an' play, yo' ain't need no charity off no she-devils.

BESS (*to* ROBBINS). See whut I git fuh yo'. De she-gawds is easy when yo' knows de way.

(CROWN *claps his hand over* BESS'S *mouth.*)

CROWN. Shet yo' damn mout'. Yo' don' gib Mingo no chance to talk to de bones.

(JAKE *has cast and lost, and the dice are now with* MINGO, *who is swinging them back and forth in his hand. Sings.*)

MINGO. "Ole snake-eye, go off an' die. Ole man seben, come down from Heaben." (*Grunts, throws, and snaps fingers.*) Seben! (*Scoops up dice.*)

CROWN. I ain't see dat seben yit. (*Snatches* MINGO'S *hand and open fingers. Looks at dice.*) Yo' done tu'n um ober.

MINGO (*to Circle*). Whut I t'row?

(*Cries of "Seben," "Jus' as he says," etc.* MINGO *pulls in pot.*)

CROWN. Well, dere's more'n one nigger done meet he Gawd fuh pullin' 'em in 'fore I reads 'em. See? An' I'm a-sayin' it ober tonight. (*All ante again.*)

MINGO. Come home again to yo' pappy. (*Shoots.*) Four to make! Come four! (*Shoots.*)

(*Cries of "Seben," "Crapped out," etc.* MINGO *passes dice to* CROWN.)

CROWN. Come clean, yo' little black-eyed bitches! (*Shoots. Cries of "Six," "Six to make," etc.* CROWN *takes up bones and produces rabbit foot from pocket. He touches dice with it.*) Kiss rabbit foot. (*Shoots.*)

SPORTING LIFE (*reaching for dice*). Crapped out! Come to your pappy.

(CROWN *extends a huge arm and brushes him back. He tries to focus his eyes on dice.*)

ROBBINS. Crown too cock-eyed drunk to read um. What he is say, Bess?

BESS. Seben.

CROWN (*scowls at* ROBBINS, *then turns to* SPORTING LIFE). I ain't drunk 'nough to read 'em, dat's de trouble. Licker ain't strong 'nough. Gimme a pinch ob happy dus', Sportin' Life.

(SPORTING LIFE *takes from his pocket a small folded paper.*)

BESS. Don' gib' um dat stuff, Sportin' Life. He's ugly drunk already.

CROWN. Yo' is a good one to talk! Pay um and shut up.

(*Takes the paper from* SPORTING LIFE, *unfolds it, and inhales the powder.*
BESS *pays* SPORTING LIFE. DADDY PETER *takes his pipe from his mouth and crowds in between* CROWN *and* SPORTING LIFE, *putting a hand on the arm of each.*)

PETER. Frien' an' dice an' happy dus' ain't meant to 'sociate. Yo' mens bes' go slow.

(CROWN *draws back his fist. Cries of "Leabe Uncle Peter be!" "He ain't mean no harm!" etc.* CROWN *relaxes.* SPORTING LIFE *picks up the dice.*)

SPORTING LIFE. Huh, seben! Huh, seben! Huh, seben! (*Shoots.*) 'Leben! Come home, Fido! (*Whistles, snaps fingers, and pulls in pot.*)

(*All ante.*)

CROWN. Gawd damn it. I ain't read um yet.

(*All laugh at him. Cries of "Crown cockeye drunk." "Can't tell dice from watermillion," etc.*)

CROWN (*growling*). All right. I'm tellin' yo'.

SPORTING LIFE (*shooting*). Six to make! Get um again! (*Shoots.*) (*Cries of "Seben," "Crapped out," etc.* PORGY *takes up dice and commences to sway, with his eyes half closed. He apostrophizes dice in a sort of sing-song chant.*)

PORGY. Oh, little stars, roll me some light. (*Shoots.*) 'Leben little stars, come home. (*Pulls in pot.*) (*All ante*). Roll dis poor beggar a sun an' moon! (*Shoots.*)

MINGO. Snake eyes!

PORGY. Dem ain't no snake eyes. Dey is a flock ob mornin' an' ebenin' star. An' jus' yo' watch um rise for dis po' beggar. (*Shoots.*)

(*Cries of "Made um," "Dat's he point," etc.* PORGY *pulls in pot.*)

CROWN. Roll up dat nigger sleeve. (PORGY *rolls up his sleeves.*) Well, yo' gots dem damn dice conjer den.

(*All ante.* PORGY *rolls. Cries of "Snake eyes," "Crapped out!" All ante.* ROBBINS *takes up bones, whistles, shoots, snaps them back up very rapidly.*)

ROBBINS. Nine to make! (*Whistles, shoots, snaps fingers.*) Read um! Nine spot! (*Sweeps them up, and reaches for money.* CROWN *seizes his wrist.*)

CROWN. Tech dat money an' meet yo' Gawd.

ROBBINS. Take yo' han' off me, yo' lousy houn'! (*Turns to* JAKE.) Han' me dat brick behin' you'.

(JAKE *reaches brickbat and puts it in his free hand.* CROWN *jerks his cotton hook out of his belt and lunges forward, bowling* ROBBINS *over, and knocking brick from his hand.* CROWN *then steps back and kicks over lamp, extinguishing it.*
The stage is now dark except for the small lamp at SERENA'S *wash bench. This lights up the woman's terrified face as she strains her gaze into the darkness.*
MARIA, CLARA *and the others of her group stand behind her.*
From the crap ring come cries and curses. Suddenly, shutters are thrown open in right and left walls of building, and forms strain from the sills. As the shutters are banged open, shafts of light from them flash across the court, latticing it with a cross play of light.
CROWN *and* ROBBINS *are revealed facing each other:* CROWN *crouched for a spring with gleaming cotton hook extended;* ROBBINS *defenceless, his back to the wall. Then* ROBBINS *lunges under the hook and they clinch. The fight proceeds with no distinguishable words from the combatants, but with bestial growls and breath that sobs and catches in their throats. In and out of the cross-play of light they sway—now revealed, now in darkness. The watchers move back and stand around the wall. They commence a weird, high-keyed moaning that rises as the figures take the light, and subsides almost to silence when they are obscured. Suddenly, out of the dark,* CROWN *swings* ROBBINS *into a shaft of light.* CROWN *is facing the audience and is holding* ROBBINS *at arms' length. With a triumphant snarl, he swings the hook downward.* ROBBINS *drops back toward audience into darkness, and* CROWN *stands in high light. There is dead silence now. In it* CROWN *looks down at his hands, opening and closing them. Then he draws his arm across his eyes.*
The silence is shattered by a piercing scream, and SERENA *runs across the court and throws herself on the body.*
BESS *appears in the light beside* CROWN. *She shakes him violently by the arm.*)

BESS. Wake up an' hit it out. Yo' ain't got no time to lose.

CROWN (*looking stupidly into the gloom at* SERENA *and the body of her man.*) Whut de matter?

BESS (*hysterically*). Yo' done kill Robbins, an' de police'll be comin'. (*She starts to pull him toward the gate.)*

CROWN. Whar yo' goin' hide? Dey knows you an' me pulls togedder.

(In the half light, it can now be seen that the court has been deserted, except for SERENA, *who sits beside the body with her head bowed, and sways from side to side with a low, steady moaning.*

A match is scratched and held in PORGY'S *hand. He is crouched on his doorstep. He looks toward* ROBBINS'S *body, and his face shows horror and fear. He gives a whimpering moan, and as the match burns out, he drags himself over his threshold and closes the door.)*

BESS. Dey wouldn't look fuh me here. I'll stay here an' hide. Somebody always willin' to take care ob Bess.

CROWN *(now at gate)*. Well, git dis: he's temporary. I'se comin' back when de hell dies down.

BESS. All right. Only git out now. Here, take dis. *(Thrusts the money into his hand. She pushes him out of gate. He disappears into the shadows. She turns around and faces the court. It is silent and empty except for the body and* SERENA. SPORTING LIFE *steps out of the shadows under* SERENA'S *steps, startling her.)* Dat yo', Sportin' Life? Fo' Gawd's sake, gib' me a little touch happy dus'. I shakin' so I can hardly stan'. *(Suddenly remembering.)* Oh, I done gib' all de money to Crown. I can't pay fo' um. But, for Gawd's sake, gib me jus' a touch!

SPORTING LIFE. Yo' ain't needs to pay fo' um, Bess. *(Pours powder into her hand.)* Sportin' Life ain't go back on a frien' in trouble like dese odder low-life nigger'. *(*BESS *quickly inhales the powder. Sighs with relief.)* Listen! I'll be goin' back up to Noo Yo'k soon. All yo' gots to do is to come wid me now. I'll hide yo' out an' take yo' on wid me when I go. Why, yo' an' me'll be a swell team! Wid yo' looks an' all de frien's I gots dere, it'll be ebery night an' all night—licker, dus', bright lights, an' de sky de limit! *(He looks apprehensively toward gate. Takes her arm.)* Come 'long! We gots to beat it while de beatin's good. *(*BESS *draws away sharply from his grasp.)* Nobody 'round here's goin' to take in Crown's Bess. Yo' bes' go wid yo' only frien'.

BESS. I ain't come to dat yet.

SPORTING LIFE. Well, de cops ain't goin' find me here fo' no 'oman! *(Slinks out gate.)*

*(*BESS *looks desperately about for shelter. She advances timidly and takes up lamp from the wash bench. She starts at rear left, and tries all of the doors as she goes. They are either locked, or slammed in her face as she reaches out to them. She comes to* MARIA'S *shop door, and as she reaches it, it is jerked open and* MARIA *confronts her.)*

MARIA *(in a tense voice)*. Yo' done bring trouble 'nough. Git out 'fore de police comes.

BESS. Yo' wouldn't hab' a heart, an' let me in?

MARIA. Not till hell freeze!

(A light is lit in PORGY'S *room, showing at window and crack in door.)*

BESS *(indicating* PORGY'S *room)*. Who lib ober dere?

MARIA. He ain't no use to yo' kin'. Dat's Porgy. He a cripple an' a beggar.

*(*BESS *seems to agree with* MARIA *that* PORGY *is of no use to her. Crosses to gate, hesitates. Then she turns slowly toward* PORGY'S *room and crosses, shuddering away from* SERENA *and the body, which she must pass on the way. She reaches the door, puts her hand on the knob, hesitates, then slowly she opens it, enters, and closes it behind her.)*

CURTAIN

SCENE II

ST. MICHAEL'S *chimes the quarters and strikes seven.*

The curtain rises on SERENA'S *room, a second story room in Catfish Row, which still bears traces of its ancient beauty in its high panelled walls and tall, slender mantel with Grecian frieze and intricate scroll work. The door is in left wall at back. Near the center of back wall a window looks toward the sea. The fireplace is in right wall. Over the mantel is a gaudy lithograph of Lincoln striking chains from the slaves.*

The room is vaguely lighted by several kerosene lamps, and is scantily furnished: a bed against the back wall at left, and a few chairs.

ROBBINS'S *body lies upon the bed, completely covered by a white sheet. On its chest is a large blue saucer. Standing about the bed or seated on the floor are Negroes, all singing and swaying and patting with their large feet.*

SERENA *sits at the foot of the bed swaying dismally to the rhythm.*

They have been singing for hours. The monotony of the dirge and the steady beat of the patting has lulled several into a state of coma.

"Deat', ain't yuh gots no shame, shame?
Deat', ain't yuh gots no shame, shame?
Deat', ain't yuh gots no shame, shame?
Deat', ain't yuh gots no shame?

"Teck dis man an' gone, gone,
Teck dis man an' gone, gone,
Teck dis man an' gone, gone,
Deat', ain't yuh gots no shame?

"Leabe dis 'oman lone, lone,
Leabe dis 'oman lone, lone,
Leabe dis 'oman lone, lone,
Deat', ain't yuh gots no shame?"

(*The door opens and* PETER *comes in. Doffs his old hat, crosses, and puts coins in saucer. The singing and swaying continue. He finds a seat at right front and begins to sway and pat with the others.* SERENA *reaches over, gets saucer, and counts coins. Replaces saucer with a hopeless expression.*)

JAKE. How de saucer stan', Sistuh?

(*The singing dies gradually as, one by one, the Negroes stop to listen, but the rhythm continues.*)

SERENA (*dully*). Fourteen dolluh and thirty-six cent.

MARIA (*encouragingly*). Dat's a-comin' on, Sistuh. Yo' can bury him soon.

SERENA. De Boa'd ob Healt' say he gots to git buried tomorruh.

CLARA. It cost thirty-four dolluh for bury my grandmudder, but she gots de three carriage'.

SERENA. What I goin' to do ef I ain't gots de money?

PETER (*understanding that they refer to saucer*). Gawd gots plenty coin' fo' de saucer.

SERENA. Bless de Lo'd.

PETER. An' He goin' soften dese nigger heart' fo' fill de saucer till he spill ober.

SERENA. Amen, my Jedus!

PETER. De Lord will provide a grabe fo' His chillun.

CLARA. Bless de Lo'd!

(*The swaying gradually changes to the rhythm of* PETER's *prayer.*)

PETER. An' he gots comfort fo' de widder.

SERENA. Oh, my Jedus!

PETER. An' food fo' de fadderless.

SERENA. Yes, Lo'd!

PETER. An' he goin' raise dis poor nigger out de grabe.

JAKE. Allelujah!

PETER. An' set him in de seat of de righteous, Amen.

SERENA. Amen, my brudder.

(*They all sway in silence.*)

ANNIE (*looking toward the door*). What dat?

CLARA. I hear somebody comin' up de steps now bringing much penny fo' de saucer.

(MARIA *opens the door and looks out.*)

SERENA. Who dat?

MARIA. It's Porgy comin' up de steps.

JAKE (*starting to rise*). Somebody bes' go help um.

MARIA. He gots help. Crown's Bess is a-helpin' um.

SERENA (*spring to her feet*). What's she a-comin' here fo'? (*They are all silent, looking toward door.* PORGY *and* BESS *enter.* PORGY *looks about; makes a movement toward corpse.* BESS *starts to lead him across room.* SERENA *stands defiant, silent, till they have gone half the way.*) What yo' bring dat 'oman here fo'?

PORGY. She want to come help sing. She's a good shouter.

(BESS, *self-possessed, leads* PORGY *on toward saucer. He deposits his coins. Then* BESS *stretches her hand toward saucer.*)

SERENA. I don' need yo' money fo' bury my man. (BESS *hesitates.*) I ain't takin' money off he murderer.

PORGY. Dat ain't Crown's money. I gib um to Bess fo' put in de saucer.

SERENA. All right. Yo' can put um in.

(BESS *drops the money in saucer and leads* PORGY *to a place at left front. They sit side by side on the floor.* SERENA *stands glaring after them.*)

PETER (*trying to make peace*). Sing, Sistuh, sing! Time is passin', an' de saucer ain't full.

SERENA (*to* PORGY). She can sit ober dere in de corner, ef she want to. But she can't sing!

(BESS *sits with quiet dignity; seeming scarcely to notice* SERENA's *tone and words.*)

PORGY. Dat all right. Bess don' want fo' sing, anyway.

(*The spiritual begins again.*)

"Leabe dese chillun starve, starve,
Leabe dese chillun starve, starve,
Leabe dese chillun starve, starve,
Deat', ain't yuh gots no shame?"

MINGO (*looking upward*). Dat rain on de roof?

JAKE. Yes, rainin' hard out.

PORGY. Dat's all right now fo' Robbins. Gawd done send He rain already fo' wash he feetsteps offen dis eart'.

LILY. Oh, yes, Brudder!

SERENA. Amen, my Jedus!

(*The spiritual continues. The swaying and patting begin gradually and grow. Slowly* BESS *begins to sway with the others, but she makes no sound.*

The door is burst suddenly open and the DETECTIVE *enters.* TWO POLICEMEN *wait in the doorway.*

The spiritual ceases abruptly. All the Negroes' eyes are riveted on the white man and filled with fear. He strides over to the corpse, looks down at it.)

DETECTIVE. Um! A saucer-buried nigger, I see! (*To* SERENA.) You're his widow?

SERENA. Yes, suh.

DETECTIVE. He didn't leave any burial insurance?

SERENA. No, boss. He didn't leabe nuttin'.

DETECTIVE. Well, see to it that he's buried to-morrow. (*Turns away from her. Slowly circles room, looking fixedly at each Negro in turn. Each quails under his gaze. He pauses abruptly before* PETER. *Suddenly shouts at him.*) You killed Robbins, and I'm going to hang you for it!

(PETER *is almost paralyzed by terror, his panic heightened by the fact that he cannot hear what the* DETECTIVE *says. His mouth opens and he cannot find his voice.*)

LILY (*to* DETECTIVE). He ain't done um.

PETER (*helplessly*). What he say?

LILY (*shouting in* PETER'S *ear*). He say yo' kill Robbins.

DETECTIVE (*laying his hand on* PETER'S *shoulder*). Come along now!

PETER. 'Fore Gawd, boss, I ain't neber done um!

(*The* DETECTIVE *whips out his revolver and points it between* PETER'S *eyes.*)

DETECTIVE. Who did it, then? (*Shouting.*) You heard me! Who did it?

PETER (*wildly*). Crown done um, boss, I done see him do um.

DETECTIVE (*shouting*). You're sure you saw him?

PETER. I swear to Gawd, boss. I was right dere, close beside um.

DETECTIVE (*with satisfied grunt*). Umph! I thought as much. (*Swings suddenly on* PORGY *and points the pistol in his face.*) You saw it, too! (PORGY *trembles but does not speak. He lowers his eyes.*) Come! Out with it! I don't want to have to put the law on you! (PORGY *sits silent. The* DETECTIVE *shouts with fury.*) Look at me, you damned nigger!

(PORGY *slowly raises his eyes to the* DETECTIVE'S *face.*)

PORGY. I ain't know nuttin' 'bout um, boss.

DETECTIVE (*angrily*). That's your room in the corner, isn't it? (*Points downward toward left.*)

PORGY. Yes, boss. Dat's my room.

DETECTIVE. The door opens on the court, don't it?

PORGY. Yes, boss, my door open on de cou't.

DETECTIVE. And yet you didn't see or hear anything?

PORGY. I ain't know nuttin' 'bout um. I been inside asleep on my bed wid de door closed.

DETECTIVE (*exasperated.*) You're a damned liar. (*Turns away disgusted. Saunters toward door. To* POLICEMEN, *indicating* PETER.) He saw the killing. Take him along and lock him up as a material witness.

(FIRST POLICEMAN *crosses to* PETER.)

FIRST POLICEMAN (*helping* PETER *to his feet*). Come along, Uncle.

PETER (*shaking with terror*). I ain't neber done um, boss.

POLICEMAN. Nobody says you did it. We're just taking you along as a witness. (*But* PETER *does not understand.*)

SERENA. What yo' goin' to do wid um?

POLICEMAN. Lock him up. Come along. It ain't going to be so bad for you as for Crown, anyway.

SECOND POLICEMAN (*to* DETECTIVE). How about the cripple?

DETECTIVE (*sourly*). He couldn't have helped seeing it, but I can't make him come through. But it don't matter. One's enough to hang Crown—(*With a short laugh.*)—If we ever get him.

MARIA (*to* FIRST POLICEMAN). How long yo' goin' lock um up fo'?

FIRST POLICEMAN. Till we catch Crown.

PORGY (*sadly*). I reckon Crown done loose now in de palmetto thickets, an' de rope ain't neber made fo' hang um.

DETECTIVE. Then the old man's out of luck. (*To* SERENA.) Remember! You've got to bury that nigger tomorrow or the Board of Health will take him and turn him over to the medical students.

PETER. I ain't neber done um, boss.

DETECTIVE (*to* FIRST POLICEMAN). Come on! Get the old man in the wagon.

(PETER, *shaking in every limb, is led out. The* DETECTIVE *and* SECOND POLICEMAN *follow. A moment of desolated silence.*)

MARIA. It sho' pay nigger to go blin' in dis world.

JAKE. Porgy ain't got much leg, but he sho' got sense in dealin' wid de w'ite folks.

PORGY (*slowly, as though half to himself*). I can't puzzle dis t'ing out. Peter war a good man. An' dat nigger Crown war a killer an' fo'eber gettin' into trouble. But dere go Peter fo' be lock up like t'ief, an' he're lie Robbins wid he wife and fadderless chillun. An Crown done gone he was fo' do de same t'ing ober again somewheres else.

(*The Negroes begin to sway and moan.*)

CLARA. Gone fo' true! Yes, Jedus!

(*A voice raises the spiritual, "What de Matter, Chillun?" It swells slowly. One voice joins in after another. The swaying and patting begin and grow slowly in tempo and emphasis. As before,* BESS *sways in silence.*)

"What' de mattuh, chillun?
What' de mattuh, chillun?
What' de mattuh, chillun?
Yuh can't stan' still.
Pain gots de body.
Pain gots de body.
Pain gots de body.
An' I can't stan' still.
"What de mattuh, Sistuh?
What de mattun, Sistuh?
What de mattuh, Sistuh?
Yuh can't stan' still.
Jedus gots our brudder,
Jedus gots our brudder,
Jedus gots our brudder,
An' I can't stan' still."

(*The door opens and the* UNDERTAKER *bustles into the room with an air of great importance. He is a short, yellow Negro with a low, oily voice. He is dressed entirely in black. He crosses to* SERENA. *The song dies away, but the swaying continues to its rhythm.*)

UNDERTAKER. How de saucer stan' now, my sistuh? (*Glances appraisingly at saucer.*)

SERENA (*in a flat, despairing voice*). Dere ain't but fifteen dollah.

UNDERTAKER. Umph! Can't bury um fo' fifteen dollah.

JAKE. He gots to git buried tomorruh or de Boa'd ob Healt' 'll take um an' gib um to de students.

SERENA (*wildly*). Oh, fo' Gawd's sake bury um in de grabeyahd. (*She rises to her knees and seizes the* UNDERTAKER'S *hand in both hers. Imploringly.*) Don' let de students hab um. I goin' to work Monday, an' I swear to Gawd I gon' to pay yo' ebery cent.

(*Even the swaying ceases now. The Negroes all wait tensely, their eyes riveted on the* UNDERTAKER'S *face, pleading silently. After a moment's hesitation, the* UNDERTAKER'S *professional manner slips from him.*)

UNDERTAKER (*simply*). All right, Sistuh. Wid de box an' one carriage, it's cost me more'n twenty-five. But I'll see yo' t'rough. (*An expression of vast relief sweeps into every face.* SERENA *silently relaxes across the foot of the bed, her head between her outstretched arms.*) Yo' can all be ready at eight tomorruh. It's a long trip to de cemetery.

(*The* UNDERTAKER *goes out door. The Negroes gaze silently after him with eyes filled with gratitude. There is a moment of silence after his departure. Then, carried out of herself by sympathy and gratitude,* BESS, *forgetful of the ban laid upon her, lifts her strong, beautiful voice triumphantly.*)

BESS. "Oh, I gots a little brudder in de new grabeyahd
What outshine de sun,
Outshine de sun,"

(PORGY'S *voice joins hers.*)

"Outshine de sun."

(*By the fourth line, many of the Negro voices have joined in, and the song grows steadily in volume and fervor.*)

"Oh, I gots a little brudder in de new grabeyahd
What outshine de sun,
An' I'll meet um in de Primus Lan'."

(BESS'S *voice is heard again for one brief moment alone as it rises high and clear on the first line of the chorus.*)

"I will meet um in de Primus Lan'!"

(*Then a full chorus, with deep basses pre-*

dominating, crashes in on the second line of the refrain. SERENA, *last of all, joins enthusiastically in the chorus.*)

"Oh, I'll meet um in de Primus Lan'!
I will meet um, meet um, meet um,
I will meet um, meet um, meet um,
I will meet um in de Primus Lan'!
"Oh, I gots a mansion up on high
What ain't make wid' han',
Ain't make wid han',
Ain't make wid han',
Oh, I gots a mansion up on high
What ain't make wid' han',
An' I'll meet um in de Primus Lan'!"

(*The beautiful old spiritual beats triumphantly through the narrow room, steadily gaining in speed.*

SERENA *is the first to leap to her feet and begin to "shout."* * *One by one, as the spirit moves them, the Negroes follow her example till they are all on their feet, swaying, shuffling, clapping their hands.* BESS *leads the "shouting" as she has the singing, throwing her whole soul into an intricate shuffle and complete turn. Each Negro "shouts" in his own individual way, some dancing in place, others merely swaying and patting their hands.*

"Allelujahs" and cries of "Yes, Lord" are interjected into the singing. And the rhythm swells till the old walls seem to rock and surge with the sweep of it.)

CURTAIN

ACT TWO

Scene I

ST. MICHAEL'S *chimes the quarters and strikes one. Morning.*

The court is full of movement, the Negroes going about their tasks. At right front a group of fishermen are rigging their lines. They are working leisurely with much noisy laughter and banter. Occasionally, a snatch of song is heard.

PORGY *is sitting at his window. The soap-box car stands by his door, the goat is inside the room. Occasionally looks out door.*

JAKE. Fish runnin' well outside de bar dese days.

* "Shouting" is the term given by the Carolina Negroes to the body rhythms and steps with which they accompany their emotional songs.

MINGO (*an onlooker*). Hear tell de Bufort mens bring in such a catch yesterday dat de boat look like he gots floor ob silber.

JIM. I hears dey gots to t'row away half de catch so as not glut de market.

JAKE. Yes, suh! Fish runnin' well, an' we mens bes' make de mores ob it.

JIM. Dats de trut'. Dem Septembuh storm due soon, an' fish don' like eas' win' an' muddy watuh.

ANNIE (*calling across court*). Mus' be you mens forget 'bout picnic. Ain't yo' know de parade start up de block at ten o'clock?

MINGO. Dat's de trut', Sistuh.

(*The men begin to gather up their fishing gear.*)

PORGY (*at window. Solicitously*). Bess, ain't you wants to go to de picnic after all? Yo' know I is membuh in good standin' ob "De Sons and Daughters ob Repent Ye Saith de Lord."

BESS (*unseen within room*). I radder stay home wid yo'.

PORGY. Yo' gots jus' as much right to go as any 'oman in Catfish Row.

BESS (*in unconvincing voice*). I ain't care much 'bout picnic.

(PORGY *is troubled. Sits in silence.*)

SPORTING LIFE (*who has sauntered over to group of fishermen*). All yo' mens goin' to de picnic?

JAKE. Goin' fo' sho'. How come yo' t'ink we ain't goin'?

SPORTING LIFE. I jus' ask. Don' hab no picnic in Noo Yo'k. Yo' folks still hab yo' picnic on Kittiwah Islan'?

JIM. Listen to Sporting Life. He been six mont' in Noo Yo'k, an' he want to know ef we still hab we picnic on Kittiwah! (*They laugh.*)

(SPORTING LIFE *moves off. Sits at* MARIA'S *table.* LILY *joins the group of men.*)

JAKE. All right, mens. I'm all fuh ridin' luck fur as he will tote me. Turn out at four to-morruh mornin', an' we'll push de *Sea Gull* clean to de Blackfish Banks 'fore we wets de anchor. I gots a feelin' we goin' be gunnels under wid de pure fish when we comes in at night.

LILY. Yuh goin' fuh take de *Sea Gull* out beyond bah? (*She laughs. Calls out to* NELSON, *who is on far side of court.*) Heah dis, Nelson. Dese mens aimin' fuh take de *Sea Gull* to de Blackfish Banks!

(NELSON *joins the group.* CLARA, *overhearing, slowly approaches, her baby in her arms.* LILY *turns to the others.*) Yo' mens bes' keep yo' ole washtub close to home. Wait till yo' gets a good boat like de *Mosquito* 'fore yo' trabble. (*All the men and* LILY *laugh delightedly.*)

JAKE. Mosquito born in de water, but he can drown jus' de same.

(*All laugh,* LILY *slapping* NELSON'S *shoulder in her appreciation.* CLARA *has stood silently beside them with anxious eyes.*)

CLARA. Jake! Yo' ain't plannin' to take de *Sea Gull* to de Blackfish Banks? It's time fuh de Septembuh storms.

JAKE (*laughing reassuringly*). Ain't yo' know we had one stiff gale las' yeah, an' he nebber come two yeah han' runnin'.

CLARA. Jake, I don' want yo' fuh go outside de bah!

JAKE. How yo' t'ink we goin' gib dat man child college edication?

(*They all laugh, except* CLARA.)

CLARA. Deys odder way fuh make money 'sides fish.

JAKE. Hear de 'oman! Mebbe yo' like me to be a cotton nigger! Huh? (*The men laugh.* SCIPIO *is playing about the court with a broad red sash pinned across his breast from shoulder to waist. It bears the legend, "Repent Ye Saith the Lord." From the boy's breast flutters a yellow ribbon with the word "Marshal." He struts about court leading an imaginary parade.* JAKE, *looking about for change of subject, sees* SCIPIO *and starts to his feet.*) Heah, Scipio! Who sash dat yo' gots? (SCIPIO *backs away.* JAKE *pursues.*) Come heah, yo'! Jus' as I t'ought. Dat's my sash!

(*Not watching where he is going,* SCIPIO, *in his flight from* JAKE, *runs straight into* MARIA, *who delivers him to* JAKE.)

MARIA. Heah yo' is, Jake.

JAKE. T'ank yo' kindly, Sistuh. (*To* SCIPIO, *while he rescues his sash and badge.*) How yo' t'ink I goin' lead dis picnic parade atter yo' been ruin my sash? (*Pins ribbons on his own breast. Sits on washing bench. Lights pipe.*)

(*The crowd begins to break up with noisy laughter and joking.* SERENA *comes in at gate, wearing a neat white apron and a hat. Crosses to* PORGY'S *door, greeting her friends as she passes them.*)

SERENA (*to the men*). Fine day fuh de picnic.

JIM. Fine fuh true, Sistuh.

(SERENA *knocks at* PORGY'S *door.* BESS *opens it.* SERENA *pays no attention to her.*)

SERENA (*looking through* BESS). Porgy! (*Sees him at window. Crosses to him.*) Oh, dere yo' is. I gots news. I done been to see my white folks 'bout Peter.

PORGY. What dey say?

SERENA. Dey say dey gots a white gentleman frien', name ob Mistah Archdale, who is lawyer an' he can get um out. I tells um yo' is de pusson fo' um to talk to 'cause yo' gots so much sense when yo' talks to w'ite folks. An' dey say he'll come fo' see yo' 'cause he pass right by here ebery day, an' yo' is cripple. (*Turns away, ignoring* BESS. *Crosses, sits beside* JAKE, *takes out and lights her pipe.* MARIA *is serving a late breakfast to* SPORTING LIFE. JIM *and* MINGO *have joined him at table. St. Michael's chimes the quarter hour.* MARIA *crosses to pump to fill kettle. After a few puffs,* SERENA *whispers loudly to* JAKE.) It's a shame when good Christian 'omans got to lib under de same roof wid a murderin' she-debil like dat Crown's Bess.

JAKE. She don' seem to harm nobody, an' Porgy seem to like to hab she 'roun'.

MARIA. Porgy change since dat 'oman go to lib' wid he.

SERENA. How he change?

MARIA. I tell yo' dat nigger happy now.

SERENA. Go 'long wid yo. Dat 'oman ain't de kin' fo' make cripple happy. It take a killer like Crown to hol' she down.

MARIA. Dat may be so, but Porgy don't know dat yet. An', 'sides, ef a man is de kin' what need a 'oman, he goin' be happy regahdless.

JAKE. Dat's de trut', Sistuh. Him dress she up in he own eye, till she stan' like de Queen ob Sheba to he.

MARIA. Porgy t'ink right now dat he gots a she-gawd in he room.

SERENA. Well, dere is gawds and gawds, an' Porgy sho' got de kin' what goin' gib um hell. Much as I likes Porgy, I wouldn't swap a word wid she.

MARIA. Dat all so, Sistuh. But yo' keep yo' eye on Porgy. He use to hate all dese chillen, but now he nebber come home widout candy ball fuh de crowd.

JAKE. I tells yo' dat 'oman——

(BESS *crosses to pump with bucket.*)

SERENA. Sh!

(*The three are silent watching* BESS. *She is neatly dressed, walks with queenly dignity, passes them as though they did not exist, fills her bucket, swings it easily to her head, turns from them with an air of cool scorn, and recrosses to her own door. The three look after her with varying expressions:* MARIA *interested,* SERENA *indignant,* JAKE *admiring.*)

JAKE. Dat's de t'ing. She sho' ain't askin' no visit ofen none ob she neighbors.

SERENA. Yo' poor sof'-headed nigger! Ain't yo' shame to set dere 'fore me an' talk sweet-mout' 'bout dat murderin' Crown's Bess? (*Making eyes at him.*) Now, ef I was a man, I'd sabe my sof' wo'd fuh de God-fearin' 'omans.

JAKE. Ef yo' was a man—— (*Pauses, looking thoughtfully at her, then shakes his head.*) No, it ain't no use. Yo' wouldn't understan'. Dat's somethin' shemale sense ain't goin' help yo' none wid. (*Knocks ashes from his pipe.*)

(MARIA *has turned toward her table. She suddenly puts down her kettle, strides to the table, seizes* SPORTING LIFE's *hand, opens the fingers before he has time to resist, and blows a white powder from his palm.*)

SPORTING LIFE (*furiously*). What yo' t'ink yo' doin'! Dat stuff cos' money.

(MARIA *stands back, arms akimbo, staring down at him for a moment in silence.* SPORTING LIFE *shifts uneasily in his chair.*)

MARIA (*in stentorian tones*). Nigger! I jus' tryin' to figger out wedder I better kill yuh decent now, wid yo' frien' about yo'—or leabe yo' fuh de white folks to hang atter a while. I ain't say nuttin' no matter how drunk yo' gets dese boys on you' rot-gut whisky. But nobody ain't goin' peddle happy dus' roun' my shop. Yo' heah what I say?

SPORTING LIFE. Come now, ole lady, don't talk like dese ole-fashioned, lamp-oil niggers. Why, up in Noo Yo'k, where I been waitin' in a—hotel——

MARIA. Hotel, eh? I suppose dese gal' yo' tryin' to get to go back to Noo Yo'k wid yo' is goin' to be bordahs! (*Shouting*). Don' yo' try any ob yo' Noo Yo'kin' roun' dis town. Ef I had my way, I'd go down to dat Noo Yo'k boat an' take ebery Gawd's nigger what come up de gangplank wid a Joseph coat on he back an' a glass headlight on he buzzum an' drap um to de catfish 'fore he foot hit decent groun'. Yes! my belly fair ache wid dis Noo Yo'k talk.

(*Bangs table so violently with her fist that* SPORTING LIFE *leaps from his chair and extends a propitiating hand toward her.*)

SPORTING LIFE. Dat's all right, Auntie. Le's you an' me be frien'.

MARIA. Frien' wid you'! One ob dese day I might lie down wid rattlesnake, an' when dat time come, yo' kin come right 'long an' git in de bed. But till den, keep yo' shiny carcass in Noo Yo'k til de debble ready to take cha'ge ob um.

(SIMON FRAZIER, *an elderly Negro dressed in black frock coat, comes in at the gate, looks about, crosses to* MARIA's *table.* MARIA *is still glaring at* SPORTING LIFE *so ferociously that* FRAZIER *hesitates.* MARIA *looks up and sees him. She is suddenly all smiles.*)

MARIA. Mornin', lawyer. Lookin' fuh somebody?

FRAZIER. Porgy live here, don't he?

MARIA. Sho' he do. Right ober dere he room.

FRAZIER. T'ank yo', Sistuh. (*Crosses toward* PORGY's *door.*)

LILY (*who is near* PORGY's *door*). Porgy! Lawyer Frazier to see yo'.

(MARIA *gives* SPORTING LIFE *final glare and enters shop.* BESS *helps* PORGY *on to doorstep and returns to room.*)

FRAZIER. Mornin', Porgy.

PORGY. Mornin', lawyer.

FRAZIER. I come to see yo' on business fo' one ob my w'ite client'.

PORGY. Huh?

FRAZIER. I been in to see Mistah Alan Archdale yesterday an' he gib' me message fo' yo'.

PORGY. Who he?

FRAZIER (*in disgust*). Who he? Yo' ain't know who is Mistah Alan Archdale? He lawyer, same as me.

PORGY (*uneasily*). Whut he wants wid me?

FRAZIER. I been in to see um on private business like we lawyers always has togedder. An' he say to me, "Mistah Frazier, do yo' know dat black scoundrel dat hitches his goat outside my window ebery mornin'?" I sez: "Yes, Misteh Archdale, I knows um." An' he say: "Well, when yo' goes out, tell um to mobe on." When I comes out, yo' is gone, so I come heah fo' tell yo'. *Mobe on.*

PORGY. Why he don't tell me heself?

FRAZIER. Yo' t'ink Misteh Alan Archdale gots time fo' tell nigger to mobe on? No, suh! He put he case in my han', an' I is authorize fo' tell yo' yo' gots to fin' nudder hitchin' place.

PORGY (*unhappily*). I been hitch on dat

corner mos' a mont' now. Why he don't want me 'roun'?

FRAZIER (*scratching his head*). I ain't quite make dat out. He say sompen 'bout de goat an' de commodity advertise on de chariot. (*Pointing to cart.*) "Pure an' fragrant." Dat's soap, ain't it? I gather dat he t'ink yo' goat need soap.

PORGY (*astonished*). Whut a goat want wid soap?

FRAZIER (*also puzzled*). I ain't know ezac'ly.

(BESS *comes to doorway and stands behind* PORGY. FRAZIER *resumes his authoritative tone.*) All I knows is yuh gots to *mobe on!* (FRAZIER *looks up and sees* BESS.) How yo' do? (*Looks at her, scrutinizing.*) Ain't yo' Crown's Bess?

PORGY. No, suh, she ain't. She's Porgy's Bess.

FRAZIER (*sensing business.*) Oh! I guess den yo' goin' be wantin' divorce.

PORGY. Huh?

FRAZIER. Ef de 'oman goin' stay wid yo', she gots to hab divorce from Crown or else it ain't legal.

(*Takes legal-looking document from pocket. Shows it to* PORGY. PORGY *looks at it, much impressed. Passes it to* BESS.)

PORGY. How much it cos'?

FRAZIER. One dollah, ef dere ain't no complications. (PORGY *looks dubious.* FRAZIER *quickly takes huge seal from his coat-tail pocket. Shows it to* PORGY.)

FRAZIER. When yo' gits divorce, I puts dis seal on de paper to show you has paid cash.

PORGY. Bess, yo' likes to hab divorce?

BESS (*with longing*). Whut yo' t'ink, Porgy?

(*The other Negroes are gradually edging nearer to listen.*)

PORGY. I goin' buy yo' divorce. Bring me my pocketbook.

(BESS *goes into room and returns immediately with a number of small coins tied up in a rag, hands it to* PORGY. *He laboriously counts out a dollar in nickels and pennies. In the meantime,* FRAZIER *is filling in document with fountain pen. Group of Negroes now listening frankly.* FRAZIER *takes coins from* PORGY. *Counts them.* BESS *holds out her hand for document.*)

FRAZIER (*pocketing coins*). Wait a minute. 'Tain't legal yet. (*Holding paper in hands, lowers glasses on his nose. Begins in solemn tones.*) Yo' name?

BESS. Bess.

(FRAZIER *makes note.*)

FRAZIER. Yo' age?

BESS. Twenty-six yeah.

FRAZIER. Yo' desire to be divorce from dis man Crown?

BESS. Yas, boss.

FRAZIER. Address de co't as Yo' Honor.

BESS. Yas, Yo' Honor.

FRAZIER. When was yo' an Crown marry?

(BESS *hesitates.*)

BESS. I don' rightly 'member, boss—Yo' Honor.

FRAZIER. One yeah? Ten yeah?

BESS. Ain't I done tell yo' I don' remember?

LILY. She ain't neber been marry.

FRAZIER. (*to* BESS). Dat de trut'?

BESS. Yas, Yo' Honor.

FRAZIER (*triumphantly*). Ah, dat's a complication.

BESS. I ain't know dat mattered.

PORGY. Yo' can't gib she divorce? Gib me back my dollah.

FRAZIER. Who say I can't gib she divorce? But, under circumstances, dis divorce cos' two dollah. It take expert fuh divorce 'oman whut ain't marry.

BESS. Don't yuh pay um no two dollah, Porgy. It ain't wuth it.

FRAZIER. Berry well, den, ef yo' wants to go on libin' in sin. (*Takes coins from pocket and begins to count. Seeing that they do not weaken, he pauses abruptly in his counting.*) Seein' that we is ole frien', I goin' make dis divo'ce dollah an' er half.

(*Again takes out impressive seal.* PORGY *eyes seal, greatly impressed. Begins counting out more pennies.* FRAZIER *affixes seal. Hands it to* PORGY. *Pockets extra money.*)

FRAZIER. Dat ain't much money considerin' whut yo' gets. One dollah an er half to change from a 'oman to a lady.

BESS (*happily*). T'ank yo' kindly, Yo' Honor.

FRAZIER. Glad to serbe yo'. When yo' ready to buy license, come to me.

PORGY. Whut she want wid license? She gots divorce, ain't she?

FRAZIER. Well, yo' ought to be stylish like de white folks, an' follow up divorce wid marriage license. (PORGY *and* BESS *look quite depressed at prospect of further complications.*) Well, good mornin', Missus Porgy. (*Turns to go. To* MARIA.) Yo' gots de cup coffee fo' sweeten my mout'?

MARIA. Sho' I is. Step right ober.

(*She and* FRAZIER *enter cookshop. The court is alive with noisy laughter and action. A fish vendor is calling his wares. St. Michael's is chiming the half hour.* MARIA *is bustling back and forth serving the men at her table.* SERENA *is pumping water and calling to her friends.* ANNIE *is holding* CLARA'S *baby, rocking and tossing it.* CLARA *is rearranging sash with motto "Repent Ye Saith the Lord" across* JAKE'S *breast, and consulting the others as to the proper angle. The sash adjusted,* JAKE *bursts into song. "Brer Rabbit, whut yo' da do dey!"* LILY *answers with second line of song. The duet continues.* SCIPIO *runs in at gate. Runs to* SERENA.)

SCIPIO. Dey's a buckra comin'. I heah um axin' outside ef dis Catfish Row.

(*The Negroes suddenly break off in their tasks.* JAKE *ceases to sing.*)

NELSON (*calling to* SERENA). Whut he say?

SERENA (*in guarded voice, but addressing the court in general*). W'ite gen'man.

(*There is a sudden deep silence, contrasting strangely with noise and movement that preceded it,* ANNIE *gives* CLARA *her baby, goes quickly inside her own door.* JAKE *removes sash, puts it in pocket.* SERENA *retreats behind her tubs. The men at table give absorbed attention to their food.* MARIA *serves them in silence without looking up.* SCIPIO *becomes engrossed in tinkering with an old barrel hoop.* BESS *goes inside.* PORGY *feigns sleep.* ALAN ARCHDALE, *a tall, kindly man in early middle age, whose bearing at once stamps him the aristocrat, enters the court, looks about at the Negroes, all ostensibly oblivious of his presence.*)

ARCHDALE (*calling to* SCIPIO). Boy! (SCIPIO *approaches, reluctant, shuffling.*) I'm looking for a man by the name of Porgy. Which is his room? (SCIPIO *shuffles and is silent.*) Don't you know Porgy?

SCIPIO (*his eyes on the ground*). No, suh.

ARCHDALE. He lives here, doesn't he?

SCIPIO. I ain't know, boss.

(CLARA *is nearest.* ARCHDALE *crosses to her. She listens submissively, her eyes lowered.*)

ARCHDALE. I'm looking for a man named Porgy. Can you direct me to his room?

CLARA (*polite, but utterly negative*). Porgy? (*Repeats the name slowly as though trying to remember.*) No, boss, I ain't nebber heah ob nobody 'roun' dese parts name Porgy.

ARCHDALE. Come, you must know him. I am sure he lives in Catfish Row.

CLARA (*raising her voice*). Anybody heah know a man by de name Porgy?

(*Several of the Negroes repeat the name to one another, with shakes of their heads.*)

ARCHDALE (*laughing reassuringly*). I'm a friend of his, Mr. Alan Archdale, and I want to help him.

(SERENA *approaches. Looks keenly at* ARCHDALE.)

SERENA. Go 'long an' wake Porgy. Can't yo' tell *folks* when yo' see um?

(*A light of understanding breaks over* CLARA'S *face.*)

CLARA. Oh, you means *Porgy!* I ain't understan' whut name yo' say, boss. (VOICES *all about the court: "Oh, de gen'man mean Porgy. How come we ain't onderstan'!"* CLARA *crosses to* PORGY'S *door, all smiles.*) A gen'man come fuh see Porgy (PORGY *appears to awake.* ARCHDALE *crosses to him.*)

PORGY. How yo' does, boss?

ARCHDALE. You're Porgy? Oh, you're the fellow who rides in the goat cart. (*Sits on step.*)

PORGY. Yes, boss, I gots goat.

ARCHDALE. Tell me about your friend who got locked up on account of the Robbins murder.

PORGY (*his face inscrutable*). How come yo' to care, boss?

ARCHDALE. Why, I'm the Rutledge's lawyer, and I look after their colored folks for them. Serena Robbins is the daughter of their old coachman, and she asked them to help out her friend.

PORGY (*a shade of suspicion still in his voice*). Peter ain't gots no money, yo' know, boss; an' I jus' begs from do' to do'!

ARCHDALE (*reassuringly*). It will not take any money. At least, not much. And I am sure that Mrs. Rutledge will take care of that. So you can go right ahead and tell me all about it.

(PORGY'S *suspicions vanish.*)

PORGY. It like dis, boss. Crown kill Robbins, an' Peter see um do it. Now Crown gone he ways, an' dey done gots ole Peter lock up.

ARCHDALE. I see, as a witness.

PORGY. Till dey catch Crown, dey say, but ef dey keep um lock up till den, dat ole man gots er life sentence.

ARCHDALE (*under his breath*). The dirty hounds! (*He is silent for a moment, his face set and stern.* PORGY *waits.* ARCHDALE *turns wearily to him.*) Of course, we can go to law about this, but it will take no end of time. There is an easier way.

(*Across the sunlit walls of Catfish Row falls the shadow of a great bird flying low, evidently just out of range of vision of audience. There is a sudden great commotion in the court. Cries of "Drive um away," "Don't let um light," "T'row dis brick." Brooms are waved at the bird overhead. Bricks thrown.* PORGY *looks up in anxiety.* BESS *comes to door with broom.* ARCHDALE *rises in perplexity.*)

PORGY. Dribe um off, Bess! Don't let um light.

ARCHDALE. What is it? What's the matter?

(*The shadow rises high. The commotion dies down.*)

PORGY. Dat's a buzzard. Yo' don' know dat bird like fo' eat dead folks?

ARCHDALE. But there's no one dead here, is there?

PORGY. Boss, dat bird mean trouble. Once de buzzard fold he wing an' light ober yo' do, yo' know all yo' happiness done dead.

(*With relief, the Negroes stand watching the bird disappear in the distance.* ARCHDALE *also looks after it.*)

SERENA (*leaning from her window and surveying court*). It sho' make me 'shamed to see all dese superstitious nigger' makin' spectacle ob demself befo' de w'ite gentlemans. Ain't we all see dat buzzard sit smack on Maria's table day fo' yesterday? An' whut happen? Nuttin'! No bad luck 'tall.

MARIA (*indignantly*). Bad luck! Whut dat 'oman call bad luck? Ain't I had more drunk customer' yesterday dan any day dis mont'? Dey fair bus' up my shop. (*Goes into shop muttering indignantly.*)

ARCHDALE (*turning back to* PORGY). Now listen. Peter must have someone to go his bond. Do you know a man by the name of Huysenberg who keeps a corner shop over by the East End wharf?

PORGY (*his face darkening*). Yes, boss, I knows um. He rob ebery nigger he git he han' on.

ARCHDALE. I see you know him. Well, take him this ten dollars and tell him that you want him to go Peter's bond. He hasn't any money of his own, and his shop is in his wife's name, but he has an arrangement with the magistrate that makes him entirely satisfactory. (*Hands* PORGY *a ten-dollar bill.*) Do you understand?

PORGY. Yes, boss. T'ank yo', boss.

(ARCHDALE, *about to go, hesitates, looks at goat-cart.*)

ARCHDALE. Porgy, there's another little matter I want to speak to you about. The last few weeks you've been begging right under my office window. I wish you'd find another place. (*Noticing* PORGY's *troubled expresion.*) There are lots of other street corners.

PORGY (*sadly*). I done try all de oder corner, boss. Ebery time I stop fo' beg, somebody tell' me to keep mobin'. But I been beggin' under yo' window fo' t'ree week' now, an' I beginnin to say to myself, "Porgy, yo' is fix fo' life. Mus' be yo' is found a gentlemans whut got place in de heart fo' de poor cripple."

ARCHDALE. I have a place in my heart for the cripple but not for the goat.

PORGY. Dis bery nice goat, boss. Lawyer Frazier say yo' t'ink he need soap. But I don't see how dat can be, boss. Two week han' runnin' now dat goat eat up Serena's washin' soap.

ARCHDALE. He doesn't need it inside.

PORGY (*mystified*). Whut goat want wid soap outside? (*Suddenly enlightened.*) Oh, yo' don' like to smell um? (FRAZIER *comes from shop. Sees* ARCHDALE. *Approaches. Stands waiting, hat in hand.* PORGY *is now all smiles.*) Dat all right, boss. By tumorroh I goin' hab' dis goat wash till yo' can't tell um from one ob dose rose bush in de park.

ARCHDALE. I'm sorry, Porgy. But you must find another place.

FRAZIER. Good-morning', Misteh Archdale. I done gib' dis nigger yo' message. (*Sternly to* PORGY.) 'Membuh what I tell yo'—*Mobe on!*

ARCHDALE. All right, Frazier. (*To* PORGY.) If Peter isn't out in a week, let me know. (*Turning to take leave.*) I suppose you're all going to the picnic today.

(*The Negroes nod and smile.* PORGY *looks wistfully at* BESS, *who stands behind him in the doorway.* ARCHDALE *is crossing toward gate.*)

JAKE. Yas, boss. We goin'.

PORGY. Bess, ain't yo' change yo' mind 'bout picnic now yo' gots divo'ce?

(ARCHDALE *catches word "divorce," turns.*)

ARCHDALE. Divorce?

PORGY (*proudly*). Yas, boss, Misteh Frazier jus' sell my 'oman a divo'ce. She an honest 'oman now.

ARCHDALE (*sternly, to* FRAZIER, *who is looking guilty*). Didn't the judge tell you that if you sold any more divorces he'd put you in jail? I've a good mind to report you.

FRAZIER. Mus' be dat judge fergit dat I votes de Democratic ticket.

ARCHDALE. That won't help you now. The gentleman from the North, who has come down to better moral conditions among the Negroes, says you are a menace to morals. He's going to have you indicted if you don't quit.

PORGY (*suspiciously; handing paper to* ARCHDALE). Ain't dis no good as he stan', boss? 'Cause I ain't goin' pay um fo' no more complications. (*As* ARCHDALE *glances over the paper,* PORGY *glares vindictively at* FRAZIER.) Dat nigger come 'round heah in he By-God coat, an' fo' yo' can crack yo' teet', he gone wid yo' las' cent.

ARCHDALE (*reading*). "I, Simon Frazier, hereby divorce Bess and Crown for a charge of one dollar and fifty cents cash. Signed, SIMON FRAZIER." Well, that's simple enough. (*Examines seal.*) "Sealed—Charleston Steamboat Company." Where did you get this seal?

FRAZIER. I done buy um from de junkshop Jew, boss.

ARCHDALE. Don't you know that there is no such thing as divorce in this state?

FRAZIER. I heah tell dere ain't no such er t'ing fuh de w'ite folks; but de nigger need um so bad, I ain't see no reason why I can't make one up whut sattify de nigger. (*His voice breaks.*) Dem divo'ce is keepin' me alibe, boss, an' whut mo', he is keepin' de nigger straight.

ARCHDALE. How's that?

FRAZIER. Dat jedge say de gots to lib togedder anyhow till dey done dead. Dat's de law, he say. But nigger ain't make dat way. I done get my black folks all properly moralize, an' now he say he goin' jail me. Ef I stops now de nigger leabe each odder anyway. Ef it don't cos' de nigger nuttin' to leabe he wife, het ain't goin' keep she er mont'. But when he gots fuh pay dolluh to get way, he goin' t'ink twice 'fore he trabble.

(ARCHDALE *keeps from laughing with difficulty.*)

BESS. Ain't mah divo'ce no good, boss? Porgy done pay one dolluh an' er half fuh it.

ARCHDALE (*looking at paper*). I could hardly say that it is legal.

BESS. Legal! Dat wo'd mean good?

ARCHDALE. Well, sometimes.

PORGY. Plenty ob our frien' is divo'ce', boss.

ARCHDALE (*with accusing look at* FRAZIER, *who cringes*). So I hear. (*Again consults paper.*) You've left this man, Crown, and intend to stay with Porgy?

BESS. Yes, suh.

ARCHDALE. I suppose this makes a respectable woman of you. Um—on the whole—I'd keep it. I imagine that respectability at one-fifty would be a bargain anywhere. (*Hands paper to* BESS. *Turns back to* FRAZIER.) But remember, Frazier: *No more divorces!* Or to jail you go. I won't report you this time. (*The goat sticks its head out door.* PORGY *throws his arm around its neck.* ARCHDALE *turns to go.*) Good morning. (*Crosses toward gate.*)

FRAZIER (*close by* PORGY'S *door. Recovering from his emotion enough to speak*). Gawd bless yo', boss. Good mornin', boss.

PORGY (*imitating* FRAZIER'S *professional manner*). Mobe on, please. Mobe on! I gots er bery polite goat heah whut object to de smell ob de jail bird. (ARCHDALE, *overhearing, laughs suddenly. Goes out gate, his shoulders shaking with laughter.* FRAZIER *moves off, talks to Negroes in background, and soon leaves the court.* BESS *sits by* PORGY *on step.*) Ain't yo' hear de boss laugh?

BESS. Fo' sho' I heah um laugh.

PORGY (*hugging goat*). No, no, buddah, we ain't goin' mobe on. When de nigger make de buckra laugh, he done win. We goin' spend we life under Misteh Archdale's window. Yo' watch!

(*Draws himself up by door frame, goes inside.* BESS *remains on step. St. Michael's chimes the three-quarter hour. Preparations for the picnic are now at their height. One by one the women, when not on stage, have changed to their most gorgeously colored dresses. Men and women are now wearing sashes all bearing the legend: "Repent Ye Saith the Lord." The leaders have also badges de-*

noting their various ranks: "Marshal," etc. Baskets are being assembled in the court. The court is full of bustle and confusion. SPORTING LIFE *saunters over to* BESS, *who is sitting on step wistfully watching the picnic preparations.*)

SPORTING LIFE. 'Lo, Bess! Goin' to picnic?

BESS. No, guess I'll stay home.

SPORTING LIFE. Picnics all right fo' dese small-town nigger', but we is used to de high life. Yo' an' me onderstan' each odder. I can't see fo' de life ob me what yo' hangin' 'round dis place for! Wid yo' looks, Bess, an' yo' way wid de boys, dere's big money fo' you' an' me in Noo Yo'k.

BESS (*quietly*). I can't remembuh eber meet a nigger I likes less dan I does yo'.

SPORTING LIFE (*laughingly*). Oh, come on, now! How 'bout a little touch happy dus' fo' de ole time' sake?

BESS. I t'rough wid dat stuff.

SPORTING LIFE. Come on! Gib me yo' hand.

(*Reaches out and takes her hand, draws it toward him, and with other hand unfolds paper ready to pour powder.*)

BESS (*wavering*). I tells yo' I t'rough!

SPORTING LIFE. Jus' a pinch. Not 'nough to hurt a flea.

(BESS *snatches her hand away.*)

BESS. I done gib' up happy dus'.

SPORTING LIFE. Tell dat to somebody else! Nobody *eber* gib' up happy dus'. (*Again he takes her hand and she does not resist. Gazes fascinated at the powder.* PORGY's *hand reaches suddenly into the open space of the door; seizes* SPORTING LIFE's *wrist in an iron grip.* SPORTING LIFE *looks at the hand in astonishment mixed with a sort of horror.*) Leggo, yo' damn cripple! (*The hand twists* SPORTING LIFE's *wrist till he relinquishes* BESS's *hand and grunts with pain. Then* PORGY's *hand is silently withdrawn.*) Gawd, what a grip fo' a piece ob a man!

BESS (*rising*). Go 'long now.

SPORTING LIFE (*regaining his swagger*). All right! Yo' men friend' come an' dey go. But 'membuh, ole Sportin' Life an' de happy dus' here all along. (*Saunters along—goes out gate.*)

(*From the distance is heard the blare of a discordant band. It is playing "Ain't It Hard to Be a Nigger," though the tune is scarcely recognizable to the audience. The Negroes, however, are untroubled by the discords. One or another sings a line or two of the song. A jumble of voices rises above the music: "Here come de orphans!" "Dere de orphan band down de block!" "Le's we go!" etc.*

A man passes outside the gate, stopping long enough to call in to the occupants of Catfish Row: "Eberybody gettin' in line up de block. You nigger' bes' hurry."

PORGY *comes out on doorstep to watch. Sits.* BESS *stands beside him absorbed in the gay scene.* PORGY *looks at her keenly, troubled.*)

JAKE (*in the midst of his preparations*). Come 'long to de picnic, Bess! (*Does not wait for reply.*)

PORGY (*triumphantly*). Dere! Don' yo' hear Jake ask yo' to' go? Go 'long!

BESS. Plenty ob de mens ask me. Yo' ain't hear none ob de ladies sayin' nuttin'.

PORGY. Bess, yo' can put on my lodge sash an' be just as good as any 'oman in dat crowd.

BESS (*with a little laugh*). Yo' an' me know it take more'n sash.

(*The confusion grows. Picnickers once started on their way come scurrying back for forgotten bundles.* SCIPIO *runs in at gate in high excitement.*)

SCIPIO (*breathless; to* SERENA). Ma, I gots good news fo' yo'.

SERENA. What dat?

SCIPIO. De bandmaster say I can be a orphan! (*The song breaks out in greater volume.*)

"Ain't it hahd to be a nigger!
Ain't it hahd to be a nigger!
Ain't it hahd to be a nigger!
Cause yo' can't git yo' rights when yo' do.
I was sleepin' on a pile ob lumbah
Jus' as happy as a man could be
When a w'ite man woke me from my slumbah
An' he say, 'Yo' gots fo' work now cause yo' free.' "

(*Other voices are calling back and forth: "How dem little nigger' can play!" "Ain't yo' ready! Time fo' go!" "We off fo' Kittiwah!"*

The band plays with more abandon. BESS *wears the expression of a dreamer who sees herself in the midst of the merrymakers. Her feet begin to shuffle in time to the music.* PORGY *does not look up, but his eyes watch the shuffling feet.*)

PORGY (*mournfully*). Yo' can't tell me yo' ain't wants to go.

(*The Negroes troop across the court all carrying their baskets. In twos and threes they go out at the gate. Among the last to go,* MARIA *comes hurrying from her shop carrying a gigantic basket. Turns to follow the others. Sees* PORGY *and* BESS. *Hesitates. As though afraid of being left behind, turns again toward gate. Then resolutely sets down her basket.*)

MARIA. What de mattuh wid you', Sistuh? Ain't yo' know yo' late fo' de picnic?

(*A sudden wave of happiness breaks over* BESS'S *face. She is too surprised to answer.*)

PORGY. Bess says she ain't figgerin' to go.

MARIA (*crosses rapidly to them*). Sho' she goin'! Eberybody goin'. She gots to help me wid my basket. I gots 'nough fo' six. Where yo' hat? (*Reaches hat just inside door and puts it on* BESS'S *head.*)

PORGY (*taking sash from pocket and holding it out to* BESS). Here my sash, Bess.

(MARIA *unties* BESS'S *apron. Throws it through door. Takes sash from* PORGY, *pins it across* BESS'S *breast, jerking her peremptorily about to save time. Then starts for her basket.*)

MARIA. Come 'long now!

BESS (*hesitating*). I hate fo' leabe yo,' Porgy.

PORGY (*happily*). I too happy fo' hab' yo' go.

MARIA. Ain't yo' goin' help me wid dis basket? (BESS *hurries to her and takes one handle of basket.*) See yo' some mo', Porgy! (MARIA *crosses rapidly to gate. To keep her hold on the basket,* BESS *is forced to hurry.*) (*Looking back*). Good-bye, Porgy!

(MARIA, *apparently seeing the others far ahead and anxious not to be left behind, breaks into a lumbering run, dragging* BESS *after her.* BESS *is waving to* PORGY *as she goes.*

The voices of the Negroes grow fainter. Then the last distant crashes of the band are heard, and the court is quiet.

PORGY *sits on his doorstep dreaming, gazing happily into space, rocking a little. Takes pipe from his pocket, knocks out ashes; lights it.*

Across the sunlit walls falls the shadow of the buzzard flying lazily over the court. PORGY *remains in happy abstraction, oblivious of the bird. Puffs leisurely at his pipe.*

The shadow hovers over his door; then falls across his face. He looks up suddenly and sees the bird. Swift terror sweeps into his face.)

PORGY (*frantically*). Get out ob here! Don' yo' light! Lef' it! Yo' hear me! Lef' it! (*He waves futile arms at it. The bird continues to hover above him.*) Get out! Somebody bring broom! Don' yo' light on my door, yo' debil! Help! Somebody help me! Oh, Gawd! (*He struggles down the steps and at last reaches the brick. The shadow wings of the bird close as it comes to rest directly over* PORGY'S *door. Grasping the brick, he again looks up to take aim. His fingers slowly relax, and the brick falls to the ground.*) 'Tain't no use now. 'Tain't no use. He done lit.

(PORGY *regains his seat on step and sits looking up at the bird with an expression of hopelessness as the curtain falls.*)

CURTAIN

SCENE II

Kittiwah Island. Moonlight revealing a narrow strip of sand backed by a tangled palmetto thicket. In the distance (right) the band is playing "Ain't It Hard to Be a Nigger." JAKE, MINGO, *and several others troop across stage from left to right, swinging apparently empty baskets.*

MINGO. Dis been some picnic, but, Lor', I tired!

JAKE (*swinging his basket in a circle*). Dis basket some lighter fo' carry dan when we come out.

(*Breaks into song: "Ain't It Hard," etc. The others join in. They go off right, their song growing fainter in distance.* SERENA *and* LILY *enter, followed a moment later by* BESS *and* MARIA. MARIA *is puffing, out of breath.*)

MARIA. I ain't no han' fo' walk so fas' on a full stomach. (*Stops abruptly. Looks about her on ground.*)

SERENA. Yo' goin' miss de boat ef yo' ain't hurry, Sistuh.

MARIA. It was jus' about heah I los' my pipe. I 'membuh dere was palmetto sort ob twisted like dat.

LILY. How come yo' lose yo' pipe?

MARIA (*searching ground. The others help her*). I was sittin' under de tree a-smokin', an' I see a Plat-eye ha'nt a-lookin' at me t'rough de palmetto leaf. An', 'fo yo' can crack yo' teet', I is gone from heah, but my pipe ain't gone wid me.

LILY. Plat-eye ha'nt! What was he like?

MARIA. Two big eye' like fireball a-watchin' me.

SERENA (*scornfully*). Plat-eye ha'nt! Yo' ain't read nuttin' in de Bible 'bout Plat-eye is yo'?

MARIA. I ain't needs to read 'bout 'em. I sees 'em lookin' at me t'rough de palmetto leaf.

SERENA. Jus' like yo' hab' buzzard set on yo' table two day ago, an' yo' hab' mighty ha'd time a-thinkin' up some bad luck to lay to um.

MARIA. Bad luck! Ain't I lose my pipe dat I smoke dese twenty yeah', an' my mudder smoke um befo' me?

LILY. I ain't partial to sleepin' out wid de rattlesnake'. Les' we go or de boat go widout us.

MARIA. Ef dat boat go without me, dey's goin' to be some sick nigger' in Catfish Row when I gets back. (*Steamboat whistles off right.* MARIA *answers it.*) Hold yo' halt! I ain't goin' till I gets my pipe.

BESS. Yo' bes' go along, Maria, and le's we whut is de fas' walker' look fo' um a bit.

MARIA (*pointing left*). It might hab' been a little farder back dat way I lose um. (BESS *begins to search at left and wanders off left, her eyes combing the ground.*) An' it might hab' been a little farder dese way. (*Goes off right searching.* LILY *follows.* SERENA *continues her search on stage.*)

LILY (*off right*). I ain't see um nowheres. Le's we go.

MARIA (*farther in distance*). I goin' fin' um.

(*From the blackness of the thicket two eyes can be seen watching* SERENA. *As she turns in her quest, she sees them. For a moment, she is motionless; then her breath catches in a shuddering gasp of horror, and she flees swiftly off right. A snatch of the song rises suddenly in distance and quickly dies down again.* BESS *comes on from left, her head bent, still searching. A great black hand creeps slowly out among the palmetto branches and draws them aside.* BESS *hears the sound. Straightens, stands rigid, listening.*)

BESS (*in a low, breathless voice*). Crown?

CROWN. Yo' know bery well dis Crown. (*She turns and looks at him. He partly emerges from the thicket, naked to the waist, his cotton trousers frayed away to the knees.*) I seen yo' land, an' I been waitin' all day fo' yo'. I mos' dead on dis damn islan'!

BESS (*looks at him slowly*). Yo' ain't look mos' dead. Yo' bigger'n eber.

CROWN. Oh, plenty bird' egg, oyster, an' t'ing. But I mos' dead ob lonesome wid not a Gawd's person fo' swap a word wid. Lor' I'se glad yo' come!

BESS. I can't stay, Crown, or de boat go widout me.

CROWN. Got any happy dus' wid you'?

BESS. No.

CROWN. Come on! Ain't yo' gots jus' a little?

BESS. No, I ain't. I done gib up dope. (CROWN *laughs loudly.*)

CROWN. It sho' do a lonesome man good to hab' he 'oman come an' swap a couple joke wid um.

BESS. Dat's de Gawd's trut'. An' 'sides—I gots sompen fo' tell yo'.

CROWN. Yo' bes' listen to whut I gots fo' tell yo'. I waitin' here til de cotton begin comin' in. Den libin' 'll be easy. Davy 'll hide yo' an' me on de ribber boat fur as Savannah. Who yo' libin' wid now?

BESS. I libin' wid de cripple Porgy.

CROWN (*laughing*). Yo' gots de funny tas' in men. But dats yo' business. I ain't care who yo' takes up wid while I'm away. But 'membuh whut I tol' yo'! He's temporary! I guess it be jus' couple ob week' now 'fo' I comes fo' yo'!

BESS (*with an effort*). Crown, I got sompen fo' tell yo'.

CROWN. What dat?

BESS. I—I sort ob change' my way'.

CROWN. How yo' change'?

BESS. I—I libin' wid Porgy now—an' I libin' decent.

CROWN. Yo' heah whut I tol' yo'? I say in couple week I coming' fo' yo', an' yo' goin' tote fair 'less yo' wants to meet yo' Gawd. Yo' gits dat?

BESS. Crown, I tells yo' I change'. I stayin' wid Porgy fo' good (*He seizes her by the arm and draws her savagely toward him. The steamboat whistles.*) Take yo' han' off me. I goin' miss dat boat!

CROWN. Dere's anudder boat day atter tomorruh.

BESS. I tells yo' I means what I says.

Porgy my man now.

CROWN (*jeering at her*). I ain't had a laugh in weeks.

BESS. Take yo' hot han' off me. I tells yo' I stayin' wid Porgy for keeps.

CROWN. Yo' is tellin' me yo' radder hab' dat crawlin' cripple dan Crown?

BESS (*taking a propitiatory tone*). It like dis, Crown—I de only 'oman Porgy eber hab'. An' I thinkin' how it goin' be if all dese odder nigger' goes back to Catfish Row tonight, an' I ain't come home to um. He be like a little chil' dat los' its ma. (CROWN, *still holding her, throws back his head and laughs.* BESS *begins to be frightened.*) Yo' can laugh, but I tells yo' I change'!

CROWN. Yo' change' all right. Yo' ain't neber been so funny.

(*The boat whistles. She tries to pull away. He stops laughing and holds her tighter with lowering look. Draws her nearer.*)

BESS. Lemme go, Crown! Yo' can get plenty odder women.

CROWN. What I wants wid odder women? I gots a 'oman. An' dats yo'. See?

BESS (*trying flattery*). Yo' know how it always been wid yo', Crown—yo' ain't neber want for a 'oman. Look at dis chest, an' look at dese arm' yo' got! Dere's plenty better-lookin' gal dan me. Yo' know how it always been wid yo'. Dese five year 'now I been yo' 'oman—yo' could kick me in de street, an' den, when yo' ready fo' me back, yo' could whistle fo' me, an' dere I was again a-lickin' yo' han'. What yo' wants wid Bess? She gettin' ole now. (*She sees that her flattery has failed and is terrified.*) Dat boat goin' widout me! Lemme go! Crown, I'll come back fo' see yo'. I swear to Gawd I'll come on de Friday boat. Jus' lemme go *now!* I can't stop out here all night. I 'fraid! Dere's t'ings movin' in de t'icket—rattlesnake, an' such! Lemme go, I tells yo'. Take yo' han' off me!

CROWN (*holding her and looking steadily at her*). No man ever take my 'oman from me. It goin' to be good joke on Crown ef he lose um to one wid no leg' an' no gizzard. (*Draws her closer.*) So yo' is change, is yo'? (*Grips her more tightly. Looks straight into her eyes.*) Whut yo' say now?

BESS (*summoning the last of her resolution*). I stayin' wid Porgy fo' good.

(*His jaw shoots forward, and his huge shoulder muscles bulge and set. Slowly his giant hands close round her throat. He brings his eyes still closer to hers. The boat whistles long and loud, but neither gives sign of hearing it. After a moment,* CROWN *laughs with satisfaction at what he sees in* BESS*'s eyes.*

His hands leave her throat and clasp her savagely by the shoulders. BESS *throws back her head with a wild hysterical laugh.*)

CROWN. I knows yo' ain't change'! Wid yo' an' me, it always goin' be de same. See?

(*He swings her about and hurls her face forward through an opening in the thicket. Then, with a low laugh, he follows her. She regains her balance and goes on ahead of him. The band is still playing, but growing faint in the distance.*)

CURTAIN

ACT THREE

SCENE I

ST. MICHAEL'S *chimes the half hour. Curtain. The court before dawn. Lights in a few windows:* MARIA'S, JAKE'S, PORGY'S.

The fishermen are preparing for an early departure.

JAKE (*coming from his door*). Dat all de breakfas' I time fo'. (*Calls to men in* MARIA'S *shop.*) Come on yo' mens! It almost light. (CLARA *comes from their room, the baby in her arms. Her eyes are anxious and reproachful, but she says nothing.*)

JIM (*coming from* MARIA'S *shop, wiping his mouth*). Yo' ready, Jake? We bes' be off.

JAKE. Let's we go!

(MARIA *appears in her doorway, wiping hands on her apron.*)

MARIA. Good-bye, boys! Hope yo' has de same good luck today!

(JAKE *quickly takes baby from* CLARA'S *arms, kisses it hurriedly, and returns it to* CLARA.)

JAKE. 'Bye, big boy!

(BESS'S *voice is heard from her room, droning in delirium. All the Negroes stop suddenly to listen.*)

BESS. Eighteen mile to Kittiwah—eighteen mile—palmetto bush by de sho'—rattlesnake an' such.

(JAKE *crosses to* PORGY'S *window.*)

JAKE. How Bess dis mornin'?

(PORGY *appears at window.*)

PORGY. She no better.

JAKE. She still out she head?

(PORGY *nods.*)

BESS. Bess goin' fin' um fo' yo'. Dat all right, Maria, Bess goin' fin' um . . .

(JAKE *shakes his head sadly. Hurriedly recrosses to the other men. They go toward gate together,* CLARA *following.*)

JIM. I bet dat catch we made yesterday de bigges' catch eber make 'round dese parts.

NELSON. We bes' make de mores ob today. Look to me like de las' good day we goin' hab'. Gots a wet tas' to um.

JAKE. Don' yo' know dat ain't de kin' ob talk to talk 'fore my 'oman? Ain't yo' hears de raggin' I gits ebery day? (*Laughs.*) But, see! I gots 'er trained now. She ain't sayin' a word. So long, Clara!

(JAKE *gives* CLARA *a hurried, affectionate pat and follows the other men as they troop out the gate, talking and laughing. The gate clangs shut behind them.* CLARA *goes silently into her room, closes door.*)

BESS, Mus' be right heah on de groun'. Bess goin' fin' um . . . (BESS's *voice drones on.*)

(MARIA, *in her doorway, listens a moment. Then crosses to* PORGY's *door; hesitates, awed by the mystery of delirium.* SERENA *silently crosses the court and joins* MARIA. *They listen a moment longer.*)

SERENA (*in a low voice*). She still out she head? (MARIA *nods. They stand silent.*)

BESS (*from the room*). Eighteen mile to Kittiwah—Palmetto bush by de sho'. Eighteen mile to Kittiwah . . .

(PETER *appears outside the gate. He seems older and feebler, but his face is joyful. Pushes gate open, comes into court, looking eagerly about. Sees the two women and crosses toward them.*)

PETER. How eberybody?

(*They turn and see him.*)

MARIA (*joyfully*). Ef it ain't ole Peter!

SERENA. Heah Daddy Peter home again. Hey, yo' Lily! Heah yo' ole man. Lordy, we is glad fo' see yo'!

(LILY *comes running from her door. Hurries to* PETER *and greets him joyfully.*)

LILY. Ef it ain't my ole gran'daddy!

PETER. I begin fo' t'ink mebby I ain't eber see Catfish Row——

(BESS's *voice rises in a sudden wail. The women turn awestricken faces toward* PORGY's *door.* PETER, *who has not heard, is mystified by their expressions. His words die away. He looks questioningly from one to another.* BESS *again takes up her monotonous refrain.*)

BESS. Palmetto bush sort ob twisted like —rattlesnake an' t'ing . . .

PETER. Whut de mattuh?

MARIA (*shouting into his ear*). Porgy's 'oman bery sick.

LILY (*shouting*). She out she head.

PETER. How long she been like dat?

MARIA. More'n a week now. Eber since we hab de picnic on Kittiwah.

SERENA. She wander off by sheself an' git lost in de palmetto t'icket. She ain't come home fo' two day.

BESS. Dat's right, Maria, I goin' fin' um—eighteen mile to Kittiwah—eighteen mile . . .

PORGY (*within room, soothingly*). Das all right, Bess. Yo' here wid Porgy now.

BESS (*monotonously*). Palmetto bush by de sho' . . .

(MARIA, SERENA, *and* PETER *stand wide-eyed, looking in at the door. They do not go too near.*)

PORGY. Yo' right here wid Porgy an' nuttin' can't hurt yo'. Soon de cool wedder comin' an' chill off dese febers.

PETER (*shaking his head*). Dat 'oman bery sick. (*The women nod.*)

PORGY. Ain't yo' remembuh how de cool win' come to town wid de smell ob pine tree, an' how de stars is all polishin' up like w'ite folks silber? Den eberybody git well. Ain't yo' know? Yo' jus' keep still an' watch what Porgy say.

(*Silence in the room.* CLARA *comes from her door carrying her baby, crosses to the gate and stands looking out toward the sea.*

After a moment, PORGY *comes from his door, softly closes it behind him.*)

PORGY. I t'ink mebby she goin' sleep now. (*Sinks wearily on to step.*) (*Dully.*) Dat yo' Peter? A whole week gone, now, an' she ain't no better! What I goin' do? (*A moment of silence.*)

PETER. Ef yo' wants to listen to me, I advise yo' to send she to de w'ite folks' hospital.

(*Blank consternation.* MARIA *is first to find her voice.*)

MARIA (*speaking into his ears*). Fo' Gawd's sake, Peter! Ain't yo' know dey lets nigger' die dere so dey can gib um to de student'? I say dey gib um to de student'.

PETER. De student' ain't gits um till he done dead. Ain't dat so? Den he can't hurt um none. Ain't dat so too? An' I gots dis to say. One ob my w'ite folks is a nurse to de hospital. An' dat lady is a pure angel wid de sick nigger. Ef I sick to-morruh I goin' to she, an' what she say is good wid me. I wants dis carcass took care ob w'ile he is alibe. When he done dead, I ain't keer.

LILY (*shouting*). Yo' ain't keer wedder yo' is cut up an' scatter, 'stead ob bein' bury in Gawd's own grabeyahd!

PETER. Well, mebby I ain't say I jus' as lief. But I t'ink Gawd onderstan' de succumstance an' make allowance.

PORGY (*moaning*). Oh, Gawd! Don't let um take Bess to de hospital!

SERENA (*in injured tone*). Mus' be yo' is all fergit how I pray Clara's baby out ob de convulsion. Dey ain't nebber been a sick pusson or corpse in Catfish Row dat I has refuse' my prayers. Dey is fo' de righteous an' fo' de sinner all two.

PORGY. Dat's right, Sistuh. Yo' pray ober um. Dat can't hurt um none.

(SERENA *closes her eyes and begins to sway.*)

SERENA. Oh, Jedus who done trouble de watuh in de Sea ob Gallerie—

PORGY. Amen!

SERENA. —an' likewise who done cas' de debil out ob de afflicted time an' time again—

PETER. Oh, Jedus! (*Begins to sway.*)

SERENA. —what make yo' ain't lay yo' han' on dis sistuh' head—

LILY. Oh, my Fadder!

SERENA. —an' sen' de debil out ob she, down a steep place into de sea, like yo' used to do, time an' time again.

PORGY. Time an' time again.

SERENA. Lif' dis poor cripple up out ob de dus'—

PETER. Allelujah!

SERENA. —an' lif' up he 'oman an' make she well, time an' time again.

(*They sway a moment in silence. Then* SERENA *silently rises and departs. After a moment,* PETER *and* LILY *follow her.*)

MARIA (*in a low voice*). Listen to me. Yo' wants dat 'oman cure up, ain't yo'?

PORGY. Yo' knows I does.

MARIA. Bery well, den. Why ain't yo' sen' to Lody?

PORGY. Fo' make conjur'?

MARIA. Yo' gots two dollah? (PORGY *nods.*) Den yo' bes' waste no time. Yo' go quick to Lody an' gib she de two dollah an' tell she to make conjur' fo' cas' de debil out ob Bess.

(MINGO *has sauntered in and taken a seat at the table by* MARIA'S *door.*)

PORGY. How I goin' leabe Bess?

MINGO. Hey, Marie! How 'bout a little serbice?

MARIA. Here, yo' Mingo, come here! (*He crosses to them.*) Yo' do little job fo' Porgy an' I gib yo' de free breakfas' when yo' gits back. Yo' know Lody, de conjur' 'oman?

MINGO. Who don't know Lody!

MARIA. Yo' go to Lody an' tell she fo' make conjur' fo' cas' de debil out ob Porgy's Bess. He goin' gib' yo' two dollah fo' she.

(PORGY *has taken out his money bag and is counting out pennies.*)

MINGO. Dat long way to Lody's 'fore breakfus'.

MARIA. Listen to de nigger! Ef yo' wa'n't dead on yo' feet, yo' could get dere an' back in ten minute.'

MINGO. Whut yo' gots fo' breakfus'?

MARIA. I gots de butts meat fo' grease yo' mout', an' de corn bread an' 'lasses fo' sweet yo' mout'.

MINGO. How 'bout er little shark steak?

MARIA. Listen to me, nigger! I ain't serbe no free breakfus' alley cat.

MINGO (*belligerently*). Who you callin' alley cat?

MARIA (*despairingly*). Dis nigger ain't know nuttin'! Get dis! I decides fo' my customer' whut dey goin' hab', but ain't yo' neber been in one ob dem stylish rest'rant where de name ob all de victual' is writ up on de wall, an' you can pick an' choose 'mong um? Dat's alley cat.

PORGY. I goin' gib yo' quarter fo' goin'.

MINGO. Ah! He ain't so far now!

PORGY (*handing him money*). Here de two dollah fo' Lody an' de quarter fo' yo'self.

(MINGO *starts for gate.*)

MARIA. Dat breakfas' I promise yo' goin' be on de table in ten minute'. Ef yo' ain't hurry, he'll be cold.

MINGO. I be back fo' yo' can crack yo' teet'.

(*Goes out gate and off to left. St. Michael's chimes the three-quarter hour.*)

MARIA. Quarter till five. Eben dat lazy nigger can't spend more'n ten minute' *gittin'* to Lody's. By fib o'clock sure, she goin' hab she conjur' make.

PORGY (*eagerly*). Yo' t'ink dat cure she?

MARIA. I ain't t'ink. I know. Yo' watch what I say, my brudder. Bess good as cure right now. Yo' gots jus' a quartuh hour to wait. Come five o'clock, dat 'oman well. (*Crosses to her shop. Goes about her work.*)

(SERENA *has gone to work at her tubs. She now calls to* CLARA, *who still stands gazing out through gate.*)

SERENA. What yo' stan' dere fo', Clara? Boats must be out ob sight by now.

CLARA. Dey been out ob sight fo' long time now.

MARIA (*working at her table*). Yo' ain't gots no call fo' worry 'bout yo' man. Dis goin' be a fine day.

CLARA. I neber see de watuh look so black.

MARIA. Well, has yo' eber see it look so still?

CLARA. No. He too still. An' somet'ing in my head keep a-listenin' fo' dat hurricane bell. (*Crosses to* SERENA. *Sits on bench.*) Let me sit here wid yo', an' yo' talk a lot.

MARIA (*who has crossed to pump with kettle*). I got a feelin'——

SERENA. What yo' gots a feelin' 'bout?

MARIA. I got a feelin' when dat 'oman of Porgy's got lost on Kittiwah Islan' she done been wid Crown.

SERENA (*her face darkening*). Yo' t'ink dat nigger on Kittiwah?

MARIA. I always figger he been dere in dem deep palmettuhs, an' when I hear de t'ings dat 'oman keep sayin' in she sickness, I sure ob two t'ing'—one, dat he is dere, and two, dat she been wid um.

CLARA. Yo' beliebe she still run wid dat nigger!

MARIA. Dem sort ob mens ain't need to worry 'bout habin' women.

SERENA. Bess goin' stay wid Porgy ef she know what good fo' she!

MARIA. She know all right, an' she lobe Porgy. But, ef dat nigger come after she, dey ain't goin' be nobody 'round here but Porgy an' de goat.

(*As* MARIA *speaks,* PORGY *comes from his door. The other women sign to* MARIA *to be careful. Seeing* PORGY, *she drops the subject and returns to her shop.*)

SERENA (*piling clothes in basket*). Come on, Clara, lend me a han' wid dese clothes.

(CLARA, *holding baby on one arm, takes one handle of basket.* SERENA *lifts the other. They carry it through* SERENA'S *door.* PORGY *sits on his doorstep, his face tense, waiting.* DADDY PETER *comes from his door followed by* LILY, *who carries the honey tray. She places it on his head and returns to room, closing the door.* PETER *crosses toward gate, beginning instantly to chant.*)

PETER. I gots honey.—Has yo' gots honey.—Yes, ma'am, I gots honey.—You gots honey cheap?

(*A woman leans from an upper window and calls.*)

THE WOMAN. Oh, honey man! Honey man!

PETER (*going on*). Yes, ma'am, my honey cheap.

THE WOMAN. Hey, dere! I wants some honey!

(PETER *goes out gate and off to the right.*)

PETER. You gots honey in de comb?—Yes, ma'am, I gots honey in de comb.—Heah comes de honey man!—I gots honey.

(PORGY *sits waiting. St. Michael's begins to chime the hour.* PORGY *grows suddenly rigid. As the chimes continue,* MARIA *comes to her doorway and stands motionless, also listening. She and* PORGY *gaze at each other across court with tense, expectant faces. The chimes cease.*)

PORGY (*in a low, vibrant voice*). Now de time! Oh, Gawd!

(*St. Michael's strikes five. As* PORGY *and* MARIA *still wait motionless,* BESS'S *voice is heard, weakly.*)

BESS. Porgy! (PORGY *and* MARIA *are both electrified by the sound. They gaze at each other with joyful faces, but for a second neither moves.*) Porgy! Dat yo' dere, ain't it? Why yo' ain't talk to me?

PORGY (*with a half-laugh that breaks in a sob*). T'ank Gawd! T'ank Gawd!

(BESS *appears in the doorway in her white nightgown. She is very weak.*)

BESS. I lonesome here all by myself.

(MARIA *crosses to her quickly. Gently assists her as she lowers herself to seat beside* PORGY.)

BESS. It hot in dere. Let me sit here a while in de cool.

MARIA. I'll get yo' blanket.

PORGY. Maria, ain't she ought to go back to bed?

MARIA (*going past them into room*). Let she be. What I done tell yo'? Ain't dat conjur' cured she?

BESS. I been sick, ain't it?

PORGY. Oh, Bess! Bess!

BESS. What de mattuh?

PORGY (*almost sobbing with relief*). Yo' been bery sick! T'ank Gawd de conjur cure yo'! (MARIA *reappears with blanket, which she wraps about* BESS.)

MARIA. I ain't goin' let yo' set here bery long. (*Returns to her shop.*)

PORGY. I got yo' back, Bess!

BESS. How long I been sick, Porgy?

PORGY. Jus' a week. Yo' come back from Kittiwah wid yo' eye like fireball, an' Maria git yo' in de bed. An' yo' ain't know me! (BESS *suddenly catches her breath in a stifled sob*). What de mattuh, Bess?

BESS. I guess I ain't know nuttin' wid de feber—or I ain't come back at all!

PORGY. Yo' ain't come back to Porgy? (*She begins to moan hysterically.*)

BESS. No, I ain't ought to come back!

PORGY (*soothingly*). Dat all right. Don' yo' worry none, Bess. I knows yo' been wid Crown. (BESS *draws in her breath sharply, then speaks in a whisper.*)

BESS. How yo' know?

PORGY. Yo' been talk 'bout um while yo' out ob yo' head.

BESS. What I say?

PORGY. Yo' ain't say nuttin' 'cept crazy stuff, but Gawd gib cripple to know many t'ing' he ain't gib strong men.

BESS. Yo' ain't want me go away?

PORGY. No, I ain't want yo' go, Bess. (*Looks at her keenly.*) (*A moment of silence.*) Yo' neber lie to me, Bess.

BESS. No, I neber lie to yo'. Yo' gots to gib me dat. (*Another silence.*)

PORGY. How t'ings stan' 'tween yo' an' Crown?

BESS (*after a pause*). He comin' for' me when de cotton come to town.

PORGY. Yo' goin'?

BESS. I tell um—yes. (PORGY *turns his head from her and sits looking straight before him. After a moment,* BESS *reaches out timidly and lays her hand on his arm. Then she tries to encircle it with her fingers.*) Porgy! Gawd! Yo' gets de arm like stebedore! Why yo' muscle pulls up like dat? (*He looks at her, his face set and stern. She cowers, her hand still on his arm.*) It makes me 'fraid!

(*A pause.*)

PORGY. Yo' ain't gots nuttin' fo' be 'fraid of. I ain't try to keep no 'oman what don' want to stay. Ef yo' wants to go wid Crown, dat fo' yo' to say.

BESS. I ain't wants to go, Porgy.

(PORGY *looks at her with hope.*)

BESS. But I ain't yo' kin'. When Crown put he hand on me dat day, I run to he like watuh. Some day again he goin' put he han' on my throat. It goin' be like dyin', den. But I gots to talk de trut' to yo'. When dem time come, I goin' to go. (*Silence.*)

PORGY (*in a whisper*). Ef dey wa'n't no Crown, Bess! Ef dey was only jus' yo' an' Porgy, what den?

(*She looks into his face with an expression of yearning. Then, suddenly, the weakness of her illness sweeps down upon her and she breaks out hysterically, trembling with fear.*)

BESS. Oh, fo' Gawd's sake, Porgy! Don' let dat man come an' handle me! Ef yo' is willin' to keep me, den lemme stay! (*Her voice rises hysterically, broken by sobs.*) Ef he jus' don' put dem hot han' on me, I can be good! I can 'membuh! I can be happy! (*The sobs overcome her.*)

PORGY. Dere, dere, Bess. (*Pats her arm soothingly, waiting for the storm to spend itself. She grows suddenly quiet, except for occasional silent, rending sighs.*) Yo' ain't need to be afraid. Ain't yo' gots yo' man? Ain't yo' gots Porgy fo' take care ob yo'? What kin' ob nigger yo' tinks yo' gots anyway, fo' let anudder nigger carry he 'oman? No, suh! Yo' gots yo' man now! Yo' gots Porgy! (BESS *has become quiet. A pause.*) Dere, now. Yo' been set up too long. Let Porgy help yo' back to bed.

(*He draws himself up by the door frame.* BESS *rises unsteadily and, with a hand on his arm, they make their way into the room.* PORGY *closes the door behind them.* MINGO *appears outside the gate, steadies himself against it, then staggers through and crosses to* MARIA's *table. Slumps into chair. Pounds on table, then buries head in his hands.* MARIA *comes to doorway.*)

MARIA. Oh, dat yo', Mingo! Gawd A'mighty, how yo' gits drunk so fas'! (*Goes into shop and immediately returns with breakfast things on a tray. Begins putting them before him.*) I bet yo' drink dat rot-gut stuff straight! Ain't yo' know nuff to pollute yo' whisky wid watuh?

MINGO (*pushing dishes away*). Don' want dat stuff. Wants de shark steak.

MARIA (*hands on hips*). So yo' don' want dat stuff! Bery well! Yo' wants de shark steak! Yo' t'ink I gibin' shark steak wid de free breakfas'?

MINGO. I tells yo' I wants de shark steak. (*With uncertain movements, draws a handful of change from pocket.*)

MARIA (*mollified*). Ob course, ef yo' goin' pay fo' um! (MINGO *spills the money in a pile on table. It is all pennies.* MARIA *stares at it, then at him. Her eyes are suddenly filled with suspicion.*) Where yo' gits dat money? (MINGO *looks up at her stupidly. She speaks in a ferocious whisper.*) Where yo' gits dat money? (MINGO *seems to try to recollect.*) He all pennies —jus' like Porgy gits fo' beggin'! (*She suddenly seizes him, jerks him to his feet.*) Dats Porgy's money, I tells yo', what he gibe yo' fo' Lody! (MINGO *opens his mouth to protest, searching wildly for words.*)

MARIA. Don' yo' lie to me, nigger!

MINGO. I jus' take 'nough fo' li'l' drink. (MARIA *gives him a savage shake which seems to spill out further words.*) I t'ink Lody must habe move'. I can't find she. (*With weak bravado.*) Leggo me, ole lady! (*Tries to shake off her grip.*)

(MARIA *holds him tighter and brings her face close to his. His eyes suddenly meet hers, and he sees a look of such cold ferocity that he quails and sobs with terror.*)

MINGO. Oh, Jedus.

MARIA. Yo' low, crawlin' houn'! Yo' drink up de conjur' money ob a poor dyin' 'oman, an' ain't leabe she nuttin' but de Christian prayers! You listen to me, nigger! (*Slowly and impressively.*) Fo' yo' own good, I goin' lock yo' up in my coset till yo' sober nuff to keep yo' mout' shut. Den mebby I lets yo' loose. But I goin' to where I can git my han' on yo' again! Ef yo' eber tell Porgy—or any libin' pusson—dat yo' ain't deliber dat message to Lody, I goin' hab nigger blood on my soul when I stan' at de Jedgment. Now, yo', gots dat straight in yo' head? (MINGO, *unable to speak, nods. She swings him suddenly about, hurls him into her room, and closes the door on him. Wipes her face on apron, looks with mystified expression toward* PORGY's *closed door. Baffled.*) Mus' hab' been Jedus done cure Bess after all. (*Considers a moment. Takes a few steps toward* PORGY's *door. Then stops, with decision.*) No, I be damn ef He did. He ain't gots it in um. (*Goes into her room. Bangs door behind her.*)

(*For a moment, the court is empty and silent. Suddenly, the silence is broken by the deep, ominous clang of a bell, very different from the silver tone of St. Michael's.*

Instantly, every resident of Catfish Row, excepting MINGO *and* BESS, *is in the court or leaning from his window. Having come, they now stand motionless, scarcely breathing, listening to the bell.*

CLARA, *with her baby, has come from* SERENA's *door, her eyes bright with terror.*)

MARIA. Mus' be de bell fo' a hot wave. Yo' see! He ain't goin' ring more'n twelbe.

LILY (*who has been counting half audibly*).—ten—eleben—twelbe——

(*For a moment no one breathes. Then the bell rings on. Every face is suddenly rigid with horror.*)

CLARA (*wildly*). Twenty! (*She runs to the gate and looks off left.*)

SERENA (*following and seeking to comfort her*). Dat bell mus' be mistake! Ain't yo' membuh de las' hurricane? How he take two day' fo' blow up?

ANNIE. Now eberyt'ing quiet. Not a breaf ob air.

(*All the Negroes have gone to the gate and are gazing off to left.*)

PORGY (*from his window*). How de Custom House flag?

SERENA. He right dere on de pole, jus' like always.

MARIA (*seeing it too, relieved*). Don' yo' see dat flag dere, Clara?

SERENA (*reassuringly to* CLARA). Dat ain't no hurricane signal, is it?

MARIA. Ain't yo' know long as de American flag wabin' ober de Custom House dat mean eberyt'ing all right, jus' like——

(*They are all gazing off left at the distant flag. Suddenly, a new wave of horror sweeps simultaneousy over every face.* MARIA's *speech breaks off with her lips still parted.*)

LILY (*in a low, awed voice*). Gawd! Dey take um down! (*They continue to gaze, fascinated, but* CLARA *turns away, back into the court. Her terror has given way to dull hopelessness.*)

CLARA. Dey don' hab' to run up no hurricane signal to tell me nuttin'. My head stop listenin' fo' um now.

PORGY. De mens goin' see de signal an' come home quick.

CLARA. Dey can't see dat signal from de Blackfish Banks, an' dey dere by his time.

ANNIE (*hysterically*). How dey goin' come back wid no win' fo' de sail?

MARIA (*sternly silencing her*). Dey can row in 'fo' dis storm come. He ain't here yet, is he?

PORGY. No, he ain't here yet.

LILY. I ain't fo' worryin' 'bout t'ing dat mightn't happen 'tall.

(*There is a general babble of voices: "Time 'nough fo' worry when de storm come!" "Mebby by to-morruh we habe li'l' storm!" etc.*

While they reassure themselves, the sea is darkening. The shutters of Catfish Row begin to flap back and forth in a sudden wind. CLARA *stands watching the swinging shutters.*)

CURTAIN

Scene II

BEFORE *the rise of the curtain the sound of wind and water begins and swiftly swells and rises. Through the wind the chimes and bell of St. Michael's are heard, sometimes rising clear and strong as the wind lulls, then lost completely in a sudden gust.*

The curtain rises on SERENA's *room, dim and shadowy in the light of guttering kerosene lamps. The Negroes are huddled together in groups. A few have found seats on the chairs and bed. Others sit on the floor. A small group at right, including* SERENA *and* PETER, *are on their knees, swaying and singing the monotonous chant of "The Judgment Day Spiritual."*

PORGY *and* BESS *sit together on the floor at left front.* CLARA *stands motionless at window, her baby in her arms. Every face is filled with fear. They shudder and draw closer together as the wind rises.*

THE SINGERS.

"We will all sing togedduh on dat day,
We will all sing togedduh on dat day,
An' I'll fall upon my knees an' face de risin' sun,
Oh, Lord, hab' mercy on me!"

MARIA (*speaking above the monotonous chant*). What yo' stand ere all de time a-lookin' out fo', Clara? Yo' can't see nuttin' in de dark.

CLARA (*gazing out between slats of closed shutters; in a flat, dull voice*). I t'ink I see a little light now 'round de edge ob dis storm. He mus' be mos' daytime.

(*In a sudden silence of the wind, a faint, distant sound is heard.*)

ANNIE. What dat? Sound like a whinny.

CLARA. Somebody's poor horse in de watuh.

PORGY. (*moaning*). My poor li'l' goat. He goin' to dead. Dat goat's my leg, I can't neber walk again!

MARIA. Dat's right sma't goat, Porgy. He goin' to climb on yo' bed an' keep he head out ob de watuh. Yo' watch whut I say!

PETER. Yo' bes' come sing wid me, Clara. Dat make yo' feel better.

CLARA (*suddenly hysterical*). I mos' lose my min' wid yo' singin'. Yo' been singin' de same speritual since daylight yesterday!

SERENA (*severely*). Ain't we want to be ready when de grabe gib up de dead an' Gabriel sound he trumpet?

SPORTING LIFE. I ain't so sure dis de Jedgment Day. We hab bad storm 'fore.

SERENA. Not like dis.

MINGO. I 'membuh my ma tell me, when dey hab' de earthquake here, all day de nigger' sing dat Jedgment Day speritual, waiting fo' de sound ob de trumpet. But he ain't de Jedgment Day den, an' mebby he ain't now.

SERENA. Dat may be so, but dis ain't no time fo' takin' chances. (*Bursts again into song. Her group joins her.*)

(*The shutters suddenly fly apart and flap violently in the wind, drowning out the singing. The Negroes cower and draw closer together. Some of the men struggle to capture the flying shutters.* BESS *sits calm, gazing straight ahead of her.* PORGY *is watching her thoughtfully.*)

PORGY (*in a brief moment of quiet*). Yo' ain't 'fraid, Bess? (BESS *shakes her head. A pause.*) What make yo' ain't say nuttin'?

BESS. I jus' t'inkin'. (*The men finally lash the shutters together with rope.*) Yo' know whut I t'inkin' 'bout, Porgy.

PORGY. Yo' t'inkin' whut storm like dis mus' be like out on de sea islands.

(BESS *nods.*)

BESS. Wabe' like dese mus' wash clean across Kittiwah.

(*After a moment, she lays her hand on his arm.* PORGY *looks keenly into her eyes.*)

PORGY. Yo' sorry?

BESS. I sorry fo' any man lef' out in storm like dis. But I can stop a-listenin' now fo' his step a-comin'. (*Puts her hand in his.*) I guess yo' gots me fo' keeps, Porgy.

PORGY. Ain't I tells yo' dat all 'long.

(*A distant roar is heard, coming steadily nearer.*)

LILY (*terror-stricken*). Here he come now!

SERENA. Oh, Masteh! I is ready!

(*The crash and roar sweep by.*)

MARIA. Yo' can see um, Clara?

CLARA. He somebody's roof goin' by.

ANNIE. Gawd A'mighty!

PETER. Oh, Jedus, hab' a little pity!

SERENA. Le's we sing!

(SERENA'S *group begins to sing, but before they have completed a single line* CLARA *cries out loudly.*)

CLARA. Fo' Gawd's sake, sing somet'ing else!

(*The singers are startled into silence. A blank pause. Then* BESS *begins to sing, "Somebody's Knockin' at de Door," and one by one the others join her till the whole room is singing.*)

ALL.

"Dere's somebody knockin' at de do'.
Dere's somebody knockin' at de do'.
Oh, Mary, oh, Mart'a,
Somebody knockin' at de do'.

It's a-moaner, Lord,
Somebody knockin' at de do'.
"It's a moaner, Lord,
Somebody knockin' at de do'.
Oh, Mary, oh, Mart'a,
Somebody knockin' at de do'.

"It's a sinnuh, Lord," etc.
"It's my preachuh, Lord," etc.
"It's my Jedus, Lord," etc.

(*The spiritual swells and gains in tempo; the rhythm of the patting and swaying grows. A few begin to shout.*)

PETER. I hear death knockin' at de door. (*Looks fearfully at door.*)

(*His haunted expression draws the attention of the others. One by one, they stop singing.*)

ANNIE. What yo' say, Daddy Peter?

(*The singing stops, but the rhythm continues.*)

PETER. I hear death knockin' at de do'.

(*A horrified silence. All eyes turn to door.*)

LILY (*in an awed whisper*). It mus' be death, or Peter can't hear um.

MINGO. He ain't hear nuttin'. Nobody knock.

LILY. Yes, dey is! Somebody dere!

PETER. Death is knockin' at de do'.

MARIA. Open de do' an' show um nobody ain't dere.

MINGO. Open um yo'self.

(MARIA *rises and starts toward door.*)

LILY (*wildly*). I tells yo' dere is somebody dere! An' Peter can't hear no libbin' person!

(MARIA *hesitates. A loud knock is heard. The Negroes immediately burst into a pandemonium of terror. There are cries of "Oh, Gawd, hab' me'cy!" "Don't let um come in!"*

The knock is repeated, louder. Some begin to pray, but the more energetic begin piling furniture in front of door. "Bring dat dresser!" "Wedge um under de knob," etc. The door is shaken violently.)

BESS. Dat ain't no use. Ef he death, he comes in, anyway.

MARIA (*now the most terrified of all*). Oh, Gawd! Gawd! Don't let um in!

(*With a sucking sound of the wind, the door slowly opens, pushing away the flimsy furniture. Shrieks of terror and prayers fill the room.*

CROWN, *bent double against the wind, enters. As one by one they gain courage to look toward the door, the prayers die away. For a moment, the Negroes stare at him in silence. Then there are cries of "Crown!" "Gawd, it's Crown!"* BESS *sits silent, rigid.* PORGY *gazes at her searchingly.*)

CROWN. Yo' is a nice pa'cel ob nigger! Shut a frien' out in a storm like dis!

SERENA. Who' frien' is yo'?

CROWN. I yo' frien', Sistuh. Glad fo' see yo'! Still mopin' or has yo' got anudder man?

SERENA. I prayin' Gawd to hold back my han'.

CROWN (*laughing*). Well, he'll hold it, all right. Better try de police.

MARIA. Yo' know bery well Serena too decent to gib' a nigger away to de w'ite folks.

CROWN (*to* SERENA). Well, between yo' Gawd an' yo' manners, yo' sho' makes t'ings soft fo' a hard nigger! (*Sees* BESS). Oh, dere's who I'm lookin' fo'! Why ain't yo' come say hello to yo' man?

BESS. Yo' ain't my man.

CROWN. It's sho' time I was comin' back! Dere jus' ain't no 'oman a man can leabe! (*Looking at* PORGY.) Yo' ain't done much fo' yo'self while I been gone. Ain't dere no whole ones left?

BESS (*rising and facing him*). Keep yo' mout' off Porgy!

CROWN. Well, fo' Gawd's sake! Dem humn-whiners got yo' too?

BESS. I tol' yo' I ain't goin' wid yo' no more. I stayin' wid Porgy fo' good.

CROWN. 'Oman! Do yo' want to meet yo' Gawd? Come here!

BESS (*holding her ground*). Porgy my man now.

CROWN (*laughing*). Yo' call dat a man! Don' yo' min'. I gots de forgivin' nature, an' I goin' take yo' back. (*Reaches for her.* BESS *violently repulses him.*)

BESS. Keep yo' han' off me!

SERENA (*to* CROWN). Ef yo' stick 'round here, yo' sure to get killed sooner or later. Den de w'ite folks goin' figger I done um. Dey gots it in de writin' now dat I been Robbins' wife. An' dey goin' lock me up fo' um anyway. So I might as well do um.

(BESS *returns to her seat by* PORGY.)

CROWN (*laughing*). What makes yo' t'ink I goin' get killed? Ef Gawd want to kill me, he got plenty ob chance 'tween here an' Kittiwah Islan'. Me an' Him been havin' it out all de way from Kittiwah; first Him on top, den me. Dere ain't nuttin' He likes better'n a scrap wid a man! Gawd an' me frien'!

(*A terrific roar of wind.*)

SERENA (*terror-stricken*). Yo' fool! Ain't yo' gots more sense dan talk 'bout Gawd like dat in a storm like dis! (*Another sudden gust.*)

CROWN. Gawd's laughin' at yo'!

PETER. It bery dangerous fo' we all to hab' dat blasphemin' nigger 'mong us. Le's we sing unto de Lord!

(*A woman's voice leads the spiritual, "Got to Meet de Jedgment."*)

THE WOMEN. "All I know—

SEVERAL MEN. I got to meet de Jedgment.

THE WOMEN. "All I know—

THE MEN. Got to meet de Jedgment.

THE WOMEN. "All I know—

THE MEN. Got to meet de Jedgment.

TOGETHER. All I know, All I know, All I know—

THE WOMEN. "All I moan—

THE MEN. I got to meet de Jedgment. . . ."

(*As the wind subsides, the spiritual rises strong and clear. The Negroes sing and sway for a moment uninterrupted.*)

CROWN (*his voice rising above the singing*). Yo' folk mus' t'ink de Lord bery easy pleased ef yo' t'ink he like to listen to dat. (*They sing on.*) Ef it affec' Him de way it do me, yo' is gibin' um de lonesome blues. (*They continue to sing.* CROWN *shouts above singing.*)

CROWN. Here, here! Cut dat! I didn't come all de way from Kittiwah to sit up wid no corpses! Dem as is in such a hurry fo' de Jedgment, all dey gots fo' do is to kiss demselves good-bye an' step out dat door. Yo', Uncle Peter, here's yo' chance. The Jim Crow's leabin' an' yo' don' need no ticket! (*Turning to* SERENA.) How 'bout yo', Sistuh? All abo'd! What, dey ain't no trabbelers?

(*A roar of wind.*)

CROWN. Dere go de train! An' yo' miss yo' chance! (*The wind rises above the singing.* CROWN *shouts up at ceiling.*) Dat's right, drown um out! Don' yo' listen to um sing! Dey don' gib' yo' credit fo' no taste in music. How 'bout dis one, Big Frien'? (*Sings.*)

"Rock in de mountain,
Fish in de sea,
Dere neber was a nigger
Take an 'oman from me."

LILY. Jedus! He goin' call down Gawd' wrath on we all! (*The wind rises to its highest pitch. The Negroes huddle together in terror. They begin to sway and moan.* CROWN *stands in middle of room, his arms thrown wide. His voice rises above the wind.*)

CROWN. Don' yo' hear Gawd A'mighty —laughing up dere? Dat's right, Ole Frien'! Gawd laugh, an' Crown laugh back! (*Throws back his head and laughs. The wind shrieks above his laugh.*) Dat's right! Yo' like um, Gawd? I'll gib' yo' anudder verse! (*Sings.*)

"I ain't no doctor,
No' doctor' son,
But I can cool yo' feber
Till de doctor come."

(*While he is singing, the wind suddenly ceases. The Negroes look at one another, appalled by the suddenness of the change.*)

BESS. Mus' be de storm ober.

PORGY. He jus' takin' a res'. When de wind lull like dis, he come back soon, worse'n eber.

CROWN. Ain't I tell yo' Gawd like um? He quiet now fo' listen. (*He bursts again into song.*)

"I laugh in de country,
I laugh in de town,
'Cause a cripple t'ink he goin'
Take an 'oman from Crown."

(*Then begins to shuffle.*) Come on, Bess! Yo' ain't one ob dese spiritual-whimperin' niggers. What, ain't yo' got no guts! Come 'long! Yo' used to be de bes' dancer in Charleston. Ef yo' don' want to dance wid Crown, mebby yo' new man'll dance wid yo'! (*Roars with laughter.* BESS *is silent. He dances a few more steps.*) Come 'long, Maria! Yo' can't tell me dese Gawd-f'arin' whiners has got yo'! (MARIA *hesitates,* CROWN *dances on. Laughs.*) Dis ole lady too fat fo' dance!

MARIA (*Indignantly*). Who say I'm too fat!

(*Gets lumberingly to her feet and begins to shuffle.* MINGO *begins to clap for them.*)

CROWN (*dancing*). How 'bout ole Sportin' Life? (SPORTING LIFE *joins in the dancing.* PETER *begins to clap.*)

LILY. Stop dat, yo' ole fool!

CROWN (*dancing near* PETER *and shouting in his ear*). Dis nigger too ole fo' dance!

PETER (*indignant, puffing out his chest*). Who say I too ole! (*Gets laboriously to his feet and begins a feeble shuffle.*)

(*A group are now forgetting their terror in song and dance in the middle of the room. Another group, including* SERENA, *are looking on disapprovingly and with fear in their faces.* CLARA *pays no attention to it all, gazes steadily from window.* PORGY *and* BESS *sit together, absorbed in each other. Every now and then* CROWN *cuts a pigeon wing before* BESS. *She ignores him. He laughs and dances away. A wild crescendo shriek cuts across the sound of merriment. The dancers stop in their places. Everyone turns to* CLARA, *who is pointing from the window, her eyes wild and horror-stricken. They all rush to the window.* SERENA *and* ANNIE *are already trying to comfort* CLARA.)

ANNIE. Course it's a boat upside down, but 'tain't de *Sea Gull.*

CLARA. It got red gunnels same as *Sea Gull.*

SERENA. Don' yo' know *Sea Gull* gots bird wid spread wing on he bow.

MINGO (*pointing*). He goin' come up ober dere now.

SERENA. You'll see! He gots no bird! Dere! Watch um! See he——

(*She breaks off suddenly with widening eyes.* CLARA *cries out.*)

MINGO. Gawd! It de *Sea Gull* fo' true!

CLARA (*shaking off* SERENA'S *arm*). Lemme go!

PETER. What yo' goin' do?

SERENA (*holding her*). Yo' wait now, Clara!

CLARA. Lemme go! (*Breaks from* SERENA'S *hold. Runs frantically to the door. Then turns back suddenly to* BESS.) Bess, yo' keep my baby till I come back. (*Thrusts the baby into* BESS'S *arms. Wrests the door open while the Negroes call protests after her.*)

BESS. Clara! Don' go!

(CLARA *rushes out. The door bangs shut behind her. A startled moment of silence. They all stand looking at closed door.*)

MINGO. Dat 'oman t'ink she goin' find Jake *alibe!*

BESS. Clara oughtn't to be out dere by sheself.

SPORTING LIFE. Eberyt'ing quiet now.

PORGY. Dat storm comin' back any minute.

BESS. Somebody go fo' Clara. Don' leabe she out dere alone! (*No one moves.*)

SPORTING LIFE. What de fool 'oman go fo'!

MARIA. Dey ain't nobody in here got de guts ob a chicken.

MINGO. Go 'long yo'self, Auntie. Dere ain't no wabe big nough fo' drown yo'.

PETER (*starting for door*). Who goin' wid me?

BESS (*holding him back*). Yo' ain't goin', Daddy Peter! Yo' too ole. (*Looking scornfully over the room.*) Ain't dere no *man* 'round here?

CROWN. Yes! Where all dem nigger been wantin' to meet de Jedgment? Go 'long! Yo' been askin' fo' somet'ing, an' yo' ain't got de gizzards to go an' get um. Now's yo' chance. (*Laughs. Goes and stands before* BESS, *looking sideways to see effect on her.*) Porgy, what yo' sittin' dere fo'? Ain't yo' hear yo' 'oman calling fo' a *man?* Yes, looks to me like only *one man* 'round here! (*Again glances toward* BESS; *then runs to door, throwing up his arms and calling. Calls the men by name: "Go 'long, Sam!" etc.*) All right, Ole Frien' up dere! We's on fo' annudder bout! (*Jerks door open and runs out.*) (*A moment of silence. The stage has grown perceptibly lighter. All the Negroes crowd to the window, looking over each other's *shoulders through slats of the closed shutters.)*

PETER. Dere Clara almost to de wharf already.

BESS. De watuh deep?

SERENA. Almost to she waist.

SPORTING LIFE. Gawd! How Crown splash t'rough dat watuh!

(They watch a moment in silence. A roar of wind and water. The stage darkens suddenly. With a swift, sucking sound, the shutters fly apart. Confused cries of "Oh, Jedus! Hab' a little me'cy!" "Gawd A'might'! De storm come back!" "Ain't I tell yo' he comin' worser'n eber.")

SERENA (*kneeling center*). Gawd answerin' Crown!

(Others kneel with her, shrinking close together, moaning with terror.)

MINGO (*at window, his voice rising high in horror*). De wharf goin'! Gawd A'mighty!

BESS (*screaming futilely against the wind*). Clara! Clara!

(Wild shrieks of horror from all the Negroes at window. Then a terrific roar, accompanied by the splintering of timber. Then a sudden awed silence in the room. PETER *turns the women from the window, blocking further view. They huddle together in the center of the room around* SERENA'S *group.* BESS *crosses to* PORGY. *Sits beside him, the baby in her arms. All the others fall upon their knees as with one accord they begin to sing the "Jedgment Day Spiritual."*

BESS *does not sing, but sits holding the baby close, with a rapt look in her eyes.)*

"We will all pray togedduh on dat day,
We will all pray togedduh on dat day,
An' I'll fall upon my knees an' face de risin' sun.
Oh, Lord, hab' mercy on me!
"We will drink wine togedduh on dat day.
We will drink wine togedduh on dat day," etc.
"We will eat bread togedduh on dat day,
We will eat bread togedduh on dat day,
An' I'll fall upon my knees an' face de risin' sun.
Oh, Lord, hab' mercy on me!"

DADDY PETER (*in the midst of the singing*). Allelujah! Gawd hab' mercy on de souls ob Clara an' Crown!

*(*BESS *turns and looks directly at* PORGY. *With an expression of awe in his face, he reaches out a timid hand and touches the baby's cheek.*

The roar increases. The shutters fly back and forth. With fear-stricken eyes, the Negroes sway and pat and sing, their voices sometimes rising above the roar of the wind and sometimes drowned by it.

BESS *continues silent, looking straight ahead of her, tenderness, yearning, and awe in her face.* PORGY *sits watching her. The shutters crash more violently. The roar of wind and water increases. The Negroes huddle closer and sing on.)*

CURTAIN

ACT FOUR

SCENE I

CHIMES, *St. Michael's strikes one. Curtain. The court, dark except for lights around the closed shutters of a second story room at back left and the glow from* MARIA'S *open door.*

PORGY *is at his window but is only vaguely seen in the darkness. He holds the shutters partly closed so as to screen himself, while he is able to look out.*

From the second-story room comes the sound of a spiritual muffled by the closed shutters.

Door to stairway at back left open and SERENA *comes out. Through the open door the spiritual is heard more plainly. It is sung by women's voices—a slow, mournful dirge.*

"Nelson, Nelson, don' let yo' brudder condemn yo'.
Nelson, Nelson, don't let yo' brudder condemn yo'.
Nelson, Nelson, don't let yo' brudder condemn yo'.
Way down in dat lonesome grabeyahd."

*(*SERENA *closes door, muffling the chant. She crosses toward her room; sees the light from* MARIA'S *door and pauses.)*

SERENA. Yo' still up, Maria? How come yo' ain't sing wid we women fo' de dead in de storm?

MARIA (*coming to her doorway*). Some ob dose nigger' liable to sing all night, I too tired clearin' t'ing up. My stove been wash' clean 'cross de street. An' 'sides, it break my heart to hear dese 'omans mourning fo' de mens dat provide um wid bread and what was dey lover' too. All dem fine, strong mens, dead in de storm!

(*In lower voice.*) It gib' me de creeps, Serena, to t'ink how many ghost' must be listenin' 'round dis court to-night.

SERENA (*nervously*). I ain't no patience wid yo' talk 'bout ghost'.

(PORGY *softly moves his shutter.* SERENA *starts.*) What's dat?

MARIA. Jus' Porgy watchin' at he window. (*Draws* SERENA *farther from* PORGY's *window and lowers her voice ominously.*) What's he watchin' for?

SERENA (*impatiently*). How I know?

MARIA. He been dere all day. He ain't gone out on de street to beg like he always does. An' he ain't gone up wid Bess to sing for de dead in de storm.

SERENA. What ob dat?

MARIA. Crown dead, ain't he? (*Lowers voice still further.*) Mus' be he t'ink Crown' ghost is a-comin' for trouble', Bess. (SERENA *gives a scornful grunt.*) Bery well, Sistuh. But I knows dis—Gawd gib' dat cripple to see many t'ing yo' an' me can't see—an' if he is watch for sompen, den dere is sompen for watch for.

(BESS, *the baby in her arms, opens door at left back. The spiritual is again heard clearly.* BESS *does not close door, but stands listening, holding baby close.* MARIA *and* SERENA *move over to listen.*)

WOMEN'S VOICES.

"Jake, Jake, don't let yo' brudder condemn yo'
Jake, Jake, don' let yo' brudder condemn yo' . . ."

BESS. Dey singin' for Jake an' Clara now. I couldn't stay. (*The three women listen a moment in silence.*)

VOICES. "Clara, Clara, don't let yo' sistuh condemn yo'
Way down in dat lonesome grabeyahd . . ."

(BESS *softly closes door, muffling the singing. Turns toward her own door.*)

SERENA. What we all goin' to do wid dat poor mudderless baby?

BESS (*stopping short. Turns slowly back*). Mus' be Clara has come back already.

SERENA (*looks fearfully about her*). What yo' means?

BESS. Mus' be Clara has come back an' say sompen to yo' I ain't hear. I ain't hear her say nuttin' 'bout "we." She say, "Bess, yo' keep dis baby for me till I comes for um."

SERENA. Somebody oughts to make sure de poor chile gets a proper Christian raisin'.

BESS. Clara ain't say nuttin' to me 'bout dat, an', until she do, I goin' stan' on she las' libbin' word an' keep she baby for she till she do come back. (*Again starts toward her door. Again turns back impulsively.*) Oh, let me be, Serena. Can't yo' see I ain't de same 'oman what used to run wid Crown? Gawd wouldn't ha' let Clara gib' me dis baby if He hadn't seen I was different inside. He wouldn't ha' gib' me Porgy if he didn't want to gib me my chance. (*Looking down at baby.*) See! He t'ink already dat I he ma. I gots de big brightness all inside me today. I can't stan' not to hab' eberybody kind to me to-day! (*Holds baby out to* SERENA.) Look at um now, Serena—hold um a minute. Tell um he gots a good ma what goin' stan' by um!

(SERENA *takes the baby reluctantly, but responds when it touches her bosom. She rocks it in her arms.*)

SERENA. Yes—I reckon yo' gots a good ma now. She gots Gawd in she heart at las'. Yo' ain't gots no cause for fret (*Hands baby back to* BESS, *who draws it close.*)

BESS. Ain't yo' see, Serena, how he scroogin' down? Dis baby know already dat he done git back home. (*Turns to go.*)

SERENA. Good-night, Sistuh.

(BESS *pauses slightly, as though taken by surprise.*)

BESS. Good-night—Sistuh.

(*Goes into her room. A dim light appears in the room. The shutters are closed from within.*

SERENA *goes to her room.* MARIA *begins to shut up her shop for the night. Several women carrying lanterns come from the funeral room, leaving the door open. They go out of the gate.*

The spiritual is again heard.)

THE SINGERS. "Ummmmm, Ummmmm, yeddy ole Egypt duh yowlin'
Way down in dat lonesome grabeyahd.
"Crown, Crown, don't let yo' brudder condemn yo',
Crown, Crown, don't let yo' brudder condemn yo' . . ."

(*There is a sudden raucous laugh in the darkness.* MARIA *starts; then turns and peers into the shadows under* SERENA's *stairs.*)

MARIA. Yo' low-live skunk! What yo'

hidin' 'round here for?

SPORTING LIFE (*sauntering into the light from* MARIA's *window*). Jus' listenin' to de singin'. Nice happy little tune dat. Now dey's stowin' my ole frien' Crown. (*Laughs again.*)

(MARIA *crosses quickly; closes the door, muffling the singing.*)

MARIA (*returning to* SPORTING LIFE). Yo' ain't gots no shame—laughin' at dem poor 'omans singin' for dere dead mens!

SPORTING LIFE. I ain't see no sense makin' such a fuss ober a man when he dead. When a gal's man done gone, dere's plenty mens still libin' what likes good-lookin' gals.

MARIA. I know it ain't dem gals yo' is atter. Ain't yo' see Bess gots no use for yo'? Ain't yo' see she gots a man?

SPORTING LIFE. I see more'n dat, Auntie. (*Laughs as though at a joke all his own.*)

MARIA. What yo' means?

SPORTING LIFE. I see she gots two mens—an' when a 'oman gots two mens—pretty soon she ain't got none at all!

MARIA (*threateningly*). What yo' means by dat—Bess gots two mens?

SPORTING LIFE. What make yo' all so sure Crown dead?

MARIA. Ain't we see de wharf wash' away under um?

SPORTING LIFE. Ain't he tell yo' Gawd an' he frien'?

MARIA (*alarmed*). Yo' is tellin' me Crown ain't dead?

SPORTING LIFE (*nonchalantly*). I ain't tellin' yo' nuttin', Auntie.

MARIA (*advancing on him threateningly*). Yes, yo' is. Yo' tellin' me ebery-t'ing yo' knows, an' damn quick! (*Corners him.*)

SPORTING LIFE. Ob course he dead! Ain't we hear um singin' he funeral song?

MARIA (*grabbing his arm and bringing her face close to his*). Yo' has seen um?

SPORTING LIFE. How can I seen um if he dead? Mus' be he ghos' I seen hangin' 'round here.

MARIA (*meditatively*). So yo' has seen um. (*Menacingly*). Well, if Bess gots two mens, dat sho' count' yo' out.

(SPORTING LIFE *laughs at her. While they talk,* PORGY's *shutter opens inch by inch.*)

SPORTING LIFE. Dat jus' where I comes in. When a 'oman gots jus' one man, mebby she gots um for keep. But when she gots two mens—dere's mighty apt to be carvin'!—An' de cops takes de leabin's.

MARIA (*warningly*). Dere ain't nobody in dis court would gib' a nigger 'way to de cops.

SPORTING LIFE. *Oh, no,* Auntie! But dem cops is bery smart, an' dey gots it in fo' Crown, remembuh! An', when dat time comes, yo' can tell Bess for me dat little ole Sportin' Life is still on de premises.

MARIA (*starting for him*). Well, he ain't goin' stay bery long on my premises!

SPORTING LIFE (*hurriedly withdrawing, but not forgeting his swagger*). Dat's all right, ole lady! I was jus' leabin'. (*Saunters toward gate.*)

(MARIA *turns back to the closing of her shop.* SPORTING LIFE *glances at her over his shoulder. Sees her engaged in barring her windows. Steps swiftly into the darkness under* SERENA's *stairs.* MARIA *finishes her work. Looks about court. Sees it's apparently empty. Goes into her shop. Locks door. A child's whimper is heard from* BESS's *room, then* BESS's *voice singing in the darkness.*)

"Hush, little baby, don' yo' cry,
Hush, little baby, don' yo' cry,
Hush, little baby, don' yo' cry,
Mother an' fadder born to die.

"Heard a thunder in de sky,
Heard a thunder in de sky,
Heard a thunder in de sky,
Mus' be Jedus passin' by.

"Heard a rumblin' in de groun',
Heard a rumblin' in de groun',
Heard a rumblin' in de groun',
Mus' be Satan turnin' 'roun'.
"Hush, little baby, don' yo' cry,
Mother an' fadder born to die."

(*Her voice trails off sleepily and is silent. During her lullaby, the last singers have come from the funeral room and crossed to their own rooms or gone out at gate. The light in the funeral room goes out.* MARIA's *light goes out.*
A moment of complete darkness and silence in Catfish Row; then the sudden flash of a match in the darkness reveals SPORTING LIFE *about to light a cigarette. He hears something at gate and hurriedly extinguishes match, with cigarette unlit. Against the gray background beyond the gate a gigantic figure can be seen. The gate opens very slowly and noiselessly.*

CROWN *comes stealthily into court; very gently closes gate behind him. Picks his way slowly and silently across court. Stops to listen. Silence. Goes on to* PORGY'S *door. Again listens. Puts his hand on knob and softly tries door. Opens it very cautiously, inch by inch. When it is wide enough, he stealthily slips through. Inch by inch, the door closes. A full minute of absolute silence.* MARIA *is in her wrapper; opens her door and stands listening. Satisfied, she is turning back.*

A muffled thud sounds from PORGY'S *room,* MARIA *stops short. Stands motionless. Suddenly* PORGY'S *laugh is heard, deep, swelling, lustful. The baby cries out.)*

BESS (*within room. Horror in her voice*). Fo' Gawd' sake, Porgy! What yo' laughin' 'bout?

PORGY (*triumphantly*). Dat all right, honey. Don' yo' be worryin'. Yo' gots Porgy now, an' he look atter he 'oman. Ain't I don' tell yo'? Yo' gots a *man* now!

(MARIA *crosses the court swiftly. Opens* PORGY'S *door, goes in, and closes it behind her.*

Again the flash of a match in the shadows. SPORTING LIFE *lights his cigarette and continues his vigil.)*

CURTAIN

SCENE II

ST. MICHAEL'S *chimes and strikes six. The curtain rises on the court, silent and apparently deserted.*

After a moment, three white men appears outside the gate. One is the DETECTIVE *who arrested* PETER. *The second is the* CORONER, *a fat, easy-going, florid man. The third is a* POLICEMAN.

DETECTIVE (*to* POLICEMAN, *pointing off right*). Bring the wagon 'round to the corner, Al, and wait for us there. (*The* POLICEMAN *goes off right. The* DETECTIVE *and* CORONER *come in at gate.*) This is the joint. I'd like to get something on it this time that would justify closing it up as a public nuisance and turning the lot of 'em into the street. It's alive with crooked niggers.

CORONER (*looking around him*). Looks pretty dead to me.

DETECTIVE. Dead, hell! If you was on the force, 'stead of sitting down in the coroner's office, you'd know we don't make a move that isn't watched by a hundred pair of eyes. (*The* CORONER *looks exceedingly uncomfortable. Glances apprehensively about him.*) There! Did you catch that? (*Points at a window.* CORONER *starts.*) They're gone now.

CORONER. Don't know as I have much business, after all. Just to get a witness to identify the body at the inquest. Maybe you'll bring one along for me when you come.

DETECTIVE. Like hell I will! You stay and get your own witness, and I'll learn you something about handling niggers, too. Now, let's see—got several leads here! The widow of Robbins, the fellow Crown killed. That's her room there. And then there's the corpse's woman. She's living with the cripple in there now.

CORONER. What makes you think the buck was killed here?

DETECTIVE (*pointing toward sea*). Found right out there.

CORONER. Found at flood tide. Might have been washed in from miles out.

DETECTIVE. A hell of a lot you know about niggers. Come on! I'll show you. (CORONER *nods and follows* DETECTIVE. *They stop at door leading to* SERENA'S *room.* DETECTIVE *kicks it open, and shouts up the stairs.*)

DETECTIVE. Come on down, Serena Robbins, and make it damn quick!

(*There is silence for a moment, then the shutters of* SERENA'S *window are slowly opened, and* ANNIE *looks out.*)

ANNIE. Serena been sick in she bed three day, an' I been here wid she all dat time.

DETECTIVE. The hell she has! Tell her, if she don't come down, I'll get the wagon and run her in.

ANNIE. She bery sick, boss. She can't leabe she bed.

DETECTIVE. She'll leave it damn quick if she knows what's good for her. (ANNIE *disappears. A loud moaning is heard. Then* ANNIE *reappears accompanied by another woman. Between them they support* SERENA. *She wears a voluminous white nightgown, and her face and head are bound in a towel. She collapses across the window sill with a loud groan.*) Drop that racket. (SERENA *is silent.*) Where were you last night?

SERENA (*slowly and as though in great pain*). I been sick in dis bed now three day an' night.

ANNIE. We been sittin' wid she an' nursin' she all dat time.

THE OTHER WOMAN. Dat's de Gawd's trut'.

CORONER. Would you swear to that?

SERENA, ANNIE, AND OTHER WOMAN (*in unison, as though answer had been learned by rote*). Yes, boss, we swear to dat.

CORONER (*to* DETECTIVE). There you are —an airtight alibi. (DETECTIVE *regards* CORONER *with scorn.*)

DETECTIVE (*to* SERENA). You know damn well you were out yesterday. I've a good mind to send for the wagon and carry you in. (*The women are silent.* DETECTIVE *waits, then shouts abruptly.*) Well?

THE THREE WOMEN (*again unison*). We swear to Gawd we been in dis room three day'.

DETECTIVE (*bluffing*). Ah-hh, that's what I wanted! So you swear you were in last night, eh? (*The women are frightened and silent.*) And just two months ago—right here—Crown killed your husband, didn't he? (*No answer.*) Answer me! (DETECTIVE *runs halfway upstairs.*) You'll either talk here or in jail. Get that! Did Crown kill Robbins? Yes or no! (SERENA *nods her head.*) Exactly. And last night Crown got his right here—didn't he? (*Women are silent except* SERENA, *who groans as though in pain.* DETECTIVE *pretends to construe groan as assent—triumphantly.*) Yes, and how do you know he was killed if you didn't see it?

WOMEN (*in unison*). We ain't see nuttin', boss. We been in here t'ree day an' night, an' de window been closed.

DETECTIVE (*shouting*). Look at me, Robbins! Do you mean to tell me that the man who killed your husband was bumped off right here, under your window, and you didn't know?

WOMEN (*in unison*). We ain't see nuttin', boss. We been in here——

DETECTIVE (*interrupting*). —three days and nights with the window closed. You needn't do that one again. (*Turning away disgustedly.*) Oh, hell! You might as well argue with a parrot cage, but you'll never break them without your own witnesses, and you'll never get 'em. (*The three women leave the window, closing shutters.*) Well, come along. Let's see what's here. (*Goes to* LILY'S *and* PETER'S *door. Throws it open.*) Come on out here, you! (LILY *comes to door.*) What's your name?

LILY (*seeing* CORONER). Do, Lord! Ef it ain't Mr. Jennings!

CORONER. Well, Lily! So you live here? (*To* DETECTIVE.) I'll answer for this woman. She worked for us for years.

DETECTIVE. That don't prove she don't know anything about this murder, does it? (*To* LILY.) What's your name?

LILY (*stubbornly*). I don' know nuttin' 'bout um.

DETECTIVE (*shouting at her*). I didn't ask you whether——

CORONER. Let me question her. (*Kindly to* LILY.) What's your name?

LILY. Do, Mr. Jennings! You ain't 'membuh my name is Lily Holmes?

CORONER. I know your name was Lily Holmes, but you left us to get married. What's your name now?

LILY. Lord, Mr. Jennings! I de same Lily Holmes. You ain't t'ink I goin' be responsible for no ole nigger' name? No, suh! An' I ain't gib' um my name, nedder!

DETECTIVE (*looking through door*). That your husband? (*Calling into room.*) Come on out here, you!

LILY. I'll fetch um. (*Goes into room. Returns with* PETER.)

CORONER. Why, it's the old honey man! (PETER *is terror-stricken at sight of* DETECTIVE.)

DETECTIVE (*recognizing him*). Oh, so it's you, is it? Well, Uncle, do you want to go back to jail or are you going to come clean?

LILY (*appealing to* CORONER). Ain't no use to ask him nuttin'. He deaf, an' 'sides, he ain't got good sense nohow.

CORONER. But, Lily, you didn't marry the old honey man?

LILY (*surveying* PETER). Whut wrong wid um?

CORONER. He's not a suitable age.

LILY (*puzzled*). Whut he ain't?

CORONER. Do you think he's the right age?

LILY. Sho he de right age. He eighty-two.

CORONER. An old man like that's apt to linger on your hands.

(DADDY PETER, *hearing nothing of con-*

versation, but feeling that he is its subject, is nodding and smiling with self-appreciation.)

LILY. No, boss. Ef I is marry to young man an' he took sick, mebbe *he* linger on my hand. But—(*Points to* PETER, *who smiles more amiably.*) He ain't linger on my han'. He took sick—he gone.

CORONER. What did you marry him for?

LILY. Why, yo' see, boss, he like dis. Ain't yo' 'membuh how I used to hab' dem crazy fits ob misery in my stomach? I wake up in de night wid 'em. De doctor say to me, "Lily Holmes, one ob dese nights yo' goin' dead in yo' bed all by yo'self." So I t'ink I bes' marry dat nigger so as I won't go dead all by myself. But since I marry um, I gets well ob my misery, an' I ain't got no furder use for 'um.

DETECTIVE (*to* CORONER). Say, are you investigating a murder or just paying social calls? (*To* LILY *and* PETER.) That'll do for you two. Get inside.

(LILY *and* PETER *hurriedly return to their room.*)

CORONER. Well, seems to me I get as much out of them as you do.

DETECTIVE. Come on, let's put the cripple and his woman through. I have a hunch that's where we'll find our bacon. (*Crosses toward* PORGY'S *door.* CORONER *follows.*)

CORONER. All right. Go ahead. I'm watching you handle them.

DETECTIVE. You won't find the cripple much of a witness. I tried to break him in the Robbins case but he wouldn't come through. (*Kicks the door open with a bang.*) Come on out, both you niggers. Step lively now!

(BESS *helps* PORGY *to seat on doorstep. Then she stands by him, the baby in her arms.* DETECTIVE *enters room.*)

CORONER (*to* PORGY). What is your name?

(PORGY *looks at him keenly, then, reassured, smiles.*)

PORGY. Jus' Porgy. You knows me, boss. Yo' done gib' me plenty ob pennies on Meetin' Street.

CORONER. Of course! You're the goat man. I didn't know you without your wagon. Now, this nigger Crown—you knew him by sight, didn't you?

PORGY (*as though remembering with difficulty*). Yes, boss—I 'membuh um when he used to come here, long ago.

CORONER. You could identify him, I suppose. (PORGY *looks blank.*) You'd know him if you saw him again, I mean.

PORGY (*slowly*). Yes, boss, I'd know um. (*With dawning apprehension.*) But I ain't care none 'bout see um.

(CORONER *laughs. Makes note in notebook. Puts it in pocket. Calls to* DETECTIVE.)

CORONER. Well, I'm through. Let's pull freight.

DETECTIVE (*appears in doorway; looks knowingly at* PORGY *and* BESS). Mighty clean floor in there. Funny it got its first scrubbing in twenty years this morning.

BESS. I scrubs my floor ebery week. You can ask these people here 'bout um.

CORONER (*sneering*). Oh, yes! More witnesses! (*Then triumphantly.*) But you missed the blood under the bed this time. (*Jerks out his gun, covers* PORGY, *shouts.*) Come, out with it! You killed Crown, didn't you? Speak up, or I'll hang you sure as hell! (PORGY *and* BESS *sit silent, with eyes lowered.*) Well?

BESS. I ain't understan', boss. Dere ain't no blood dere, an' nobody ain't kill Crown in our room.

CORONER (*drawing* DETECTIVE *aside*). For God's sake, Duggan, let's call it a day. The cripple couldn't kill a two-hundred-pound buck and tote him a hundred yards.

DETECTIVE. You don't know much about niggers, do you?

CORONER (*turning toward gate*). Anyway, *I'm* through, and I've got to get along. It's 'most time for my inquest.

(BESS *and* PORGY *go swiftly inside. Close door.*)

DETECTIVE (*following* CORONER *reluctantly*). Got your witness?

CORONER. Yeh.

(*They go out gate and off to left.
Again the court is deserted and silent. For a moment, there is no sound or movement. Then, in one of the rooms, a voice is raised singing.*)

VOICE. "Ain't it hard to be a nigger!
Ain't it hard to be a nigger!"

(*Another voice joins, then another. In a moment, the empty court is ringing with the song, sung mockingly, triumphantly. Another moment, and doors and shutters begin to fly open. The Negroes come from their doors or lean from their windows, and the court is quickly filled with life and movement. They are all singing.*

SERENA's *door flies open, and she comes out singing. She is fully dressed and carries a great basket of clothes, which she begins to hang on line while she sings.*

BESS *helps* PORGY *on to the doorstep and sits beside him, the baby in her arms. Both are singing.* LILY *comes out carrying the honey tray.* PETER *follows. She balances it on his head.* SCIPIO *drives* PORGY'S *goat cart in through archway.*

Then someone breaks into a wilder tune, and all the others instantly change to the new song.)

"Sit down! I can't sit down!
Sit down! I can't sit down!
My soul's so happy dat I can't sit down!"

(*A Negro near the gate looks out, suddenly gives a loud hiss and waves his arms—in a warning gesture.*

The song ceases abruptly. SERENA *grabs her wash from the line. The Negroes return swiftly and silently to their rooms. Doors and shutters close stealthily.*

BESS *attempts to help* PORGY *to his feet, but, seeing that they have no time, he sinks down again on his doorstep and pretends to doze.* BESS *goes inside, closes door.* SCIPIO *drives the goat back through archway.*

The court is again silent, and deserted by all but PORGY.

A POLICEMAN *enters from left. Comes in at gate. Looks about court. Sees* PORGY, *who is apparently oblivious of him. Crosses to* PORGY.)

POLICEMAN. Hey, you! (PORGY *opens his eyes.*) You're Porgy, aren't you? I've got something for you. (*Holds out paper.* PORGY *looks at it in alarm.* POLICEMAN *speaks kindly.*) You needn't be afraid to take it. It's just a summons as a witness at the coroner's inquest. All you've got to do is view the body and tell the coroner who it is.

(PORGY *is suddenly terror-stricken. His voice shakes.*)

PORGY. I gots to go an' look on Crown's face?

POLICEMAN. Yes, that's all.

PORGY. Wid all dem w'ite folks lookin' at me?

POLICEMAN. Oh, cheer up! I reckon you've seen a dead nigger before. It'll be all over in a few minutes.

(BESS *appears in doorway, listening, her eyes wide with horror.*)

PORGY. Dere ain't goin' to be no nigger in dat room 'cept me?

POLICEMAN. Just you and Crown—if you still call him one. (*Turns away.*)

PORGY (*scarcely able to speak for terror*). Boss—I couldn' jus' bring a 'oman wid me? I couldn't eben carry my—my 'oman?

POLICEMAN (*slightly impatient*). No, you can't bring anyone. Say, you're the cripple, aren't you? I'll get the wagon and carry you down. And as soon as you've seen Crown, you can come home. (*Starts for gate.*)

PORGY (*desperately*). Boss——

POLICEMAN. Now, listen, I've summoned you, and you've got to go, or it's contempt of court. I'll call the wagon for you. (*Goes out gate and off to left.*)

(*As soon as he has gone, doors open stealthily. The Negroes come out and gather about* PORGY, *speaking in low, frightened tones.*)

PORGY. Oh, Gawd! Whut I goin' to do?

BESS. Yo' got to go, Porgy. Mebby yo' can jus' make like to look at um an' keep yo' eye shut.

MARIA. Yo' goin' be all right, Porgy. Yo' jus' goin' to be a witness.

SPORTING LIFE. I ain't so sure ob dat. (*They all look at him in alarm.*) I don' know who done de killin'. All I knows is, when de man what done um goes in dat room, Crown' wounds begin to bleed.

PORGY (*terror-stricken*). Oh, Jedus!

SPORTING LIFE. Dat's one way de cops got ob tellin' who done um.

PORGY (*in a panic, moaning*). I can't look on he face! Oh, Gawd! Whut I goin' to do!

SPORTING LIFE (*taking command of the situation*). Listen to me! Yo' do jus' as I say an' yo' won't hab' to look on he face.

PORGY. What I do, Sporting Life?

SPORTING LIFE. Get busy, yo' niggers. We gots to get Porgy out ob here! Get de goat, Scipio. Here, Mingo! Yo' stan' by to gib' me a han' wid Porgy.

BESS. Don' yo' go, Porgy! He can't get away!

SPORTING LIFE. He gots to get away or dey'll hang um sure.

PORGY. Oh, Gawd!

(SCIPIO *has brought the goat cart.* SPORTING LIFE *and* MINGO *are lifting* PORGY *in while he moans with terror and mutters uninterrigibly.*)

SPORTING LIFE. No, listen! Make straight for Bedens Alley. When yo' gets dere, turn in an' lie low.

MINGO. Bedens Alley too far. He'll neber make it.

SPORTING LIFE. Shut up, Mingo. I'm runnin' dis. All right, Porgy, light out!

MARIA. Quick! Start um!

BESS. Make um run!

(*The clang of the patrol wagon bell is heard approaching rapidly. The Negroes stand as though paralyzed with terror.*)

MINGO. Here dey is!

BESS. Oh, Gawd! It's too late now!

SPORTING LIFE. No, it ain't. Here, yo' niggers, get um in dere!

(*Directs them to the archway. They drive the goat through, then mass in front of archway, hiding* PORGY *from view.*

SPORTING LIFE *saunters across the court as though he had nothing to do with the affair, and awaits developments.*

The patrol bells rings more slowly as the wagon slows down, then comes to a stop at left of gate just out of view.

The POLICEMAN *again comes in at gate. Looks toward* PORGY's *door. Crosses to it abruptly. Throws it open.*)

POLICEMAN. Hey, you there! (*Runs to gate. Calls.*) Jim! The fool's trying to make a get-away! Come on! (*Turns to the Negroes.*) Where did he go? (*They look at him with blank faces.*) All right! (*Starts for* PORGY's *door.*) (*The* SECOND POLICEMAN *enters from left.*) You take that side, Jim. I'll take this. (*Goes into* PORGY's *room.*)

(SECOND POLICEMAN *goes through* SERENA's *door. As soon as both* POLICEMEN *are out of sight, the Negroes beckon to* PORGY, *who drives from archway and quickly toward gate.*

The shutters of an upper window are thrown open, and the FIRST POLICEMAN *looks out.*)

POLICEMAN. Hey, you! What d'you think you're doing? (PORGY *leans forward and wrings the goat's tail. The astonished animal leaps forward and goes out gate at a run.*) Jim! (*The* SECOND POLICEMAN *throws open shutters of room opposite and leans from window.*) Look there! (*Points to* PORGY *as he disappears off left.*)

(*Both* POLICEMEN *burst itno peals of laughter.*

The Negroes follow to gate, pushing it shut, looking out through bars.)

SECOND POLICEMAN. He must want to have a race.

(*The two* POLICEMEN *leave the windows and a minute later come running from doors.*)

FIRST POLICEMAN. Racing the wagon! That's good!

(*They start toward gate.*)

SECOND POLICEMAN (*laying a hand on the other's arm*). Say, let him get a start. (*They double up with laughter.*) This is going to be good!

FIRST POLICEMAN. Here, you niggers! Get away from the gate. (*The Negroes stand back. He opens gate.*) Come on now! We're off!

(*They run out gate, still shouting with laughter. They run off right. The Negroes press close about gate to watch.*

The clang of the patrol wagon bell is heard as the vehicle sets off at top speed.)

ANNIE. Oh, Gawd! Dey'll get um!

MARIA. Ef he can jus' git 'round de corner!——

LILY. —Mebby dey won't fin' um.

BESS (*turning hopelessly away*). 'Tain't no use. (*The tension in the crowd of watchers suddenly relaxes, and their faces assume hopeless expressions.*) Dey got um?

LILY. Yeh. Dey got um.

SERENA. Dey putting him an' de goat all two in de wagon.

(BESS *sits hopelessly on her doorstep. The other Negroes return to their various rooms and tasks.* SPORTING LIFE *saunters across court and sits down on step by* BESS.

The stage is darkening. A light appears in a window.)

BESS. Oh, Gawd! Dey goin' carry um to look on Crown' face!

SPORTING LIFE (*laughing*). Don' yo' worry none 'bout dat, Sistuh. Dat nigger ain't a witness now. Dey goin' lock um up in de jail.

MINGO (*at gate*). Dat's de trut'. Dey done turn de wagon 'round toward de jail.

BESS. Well, dat better'n makin' um look on Crown. (*Fearfully.*) Not for long, Sportin' Life?

SPORTING LIFE (*sympathetically*). No, not for long. Jus' a yeah, mebby.

BESS. A yeah.

SPORTING LIFE. Contempt ob court—dat's a serious offence. (BESS *drops her face into her hands.*) Jus' like I tol' yo'. Nobody home now but Bess an' ole Sportin' Life.

BESS. I ain't gots no time fo' yo'.

SPORTING LIFE (*laughing*). Fo' sho' yo' has. Yo' jus' gots nice little vacation now fo' play 'round wid yo' ole frien'. Contempt ob court—dat serious offence. Dat nigger ain't be back heah fo' a yeah.

BESS (*alarmed*). Sportin' Life, yo' ain't t'ink dey puts Porgy up fo' a yeah?

SPORTING LIFE. A yeah for sho'. Cheer up, Sistuh! Gib' me yo' han'. (*He takes her hand. She is too preoccupied to resist.*) Ole Sportin' Life got de stuff fo' scare away de lonesome blues.

(*Pours powder into her hand.* BESS *looks down at it.*)

BESS. Happy dus'! (*Gazes at the powder with fascinated horror.*) I ain't want none ob dat stuff, I tells yo'.

SPORTING LIFE. Ain't nuff ter hurt er flea.

BESS. Take dat stuff away, nigger! (*But she continues to hold it in her hand.*)

SPORTING LIFE. Jus' a little touch fo' ole time' sake. (BESS *suddenly claps her hand over her face. When she takes it away, it is empty.* SPORTING LIFE *smiles with satisfaction.*) Dat de t'ing, ain't it? An' 'membuh, dere's plenty more where dat come from. Dere's a boat to Noo Yo'k tomorruh an' I'm goin'. (*Pauses significantly.* BESS *says nothing.*) Why yo' such a fool, Bess? What yo' goin' to do a whole yeah here by yo'self? Now's yo' chance.

(BESS *leaps to her feet, her eyes blazing. She glares at* SPORTING LIFE *with contempt and hatred.*)

BESS. Yo' low, crawlin' houn'! Git 'way from my door, I tell you'! Lef it, yo'! Rattlesnake! Dat's whut yo' is! Rattlesnake!

(*While she berates him,* SPORTING LIFE *lights a cigarette, continues to sit on step.*)

SPORTING LIFE. Rave on, Sistuh! But I'll be right here when yo' is wantin' dat second shot.

(BESS *runs suddenly past him into her room. Slams door behind her.* SPORTING LIFE *sits smiling to himself and leisurely blowing smoke rings.*)

(MARIA *comes to her doorway. Sees him. Crosses to him.*)

MARIA (*contemptuously*). What yo' waitin' 'round here for?

SPORTING LIFE. Jus' waitin'. (*Smokes contentedly.*)

MARIA. What yo' t'ink yo' goin' to get?

SPORTING LIFE (*with shrug of shoulders*). Uummmmmm—jus' waitin'.

MARIA (*turning scornfully away*). Yo' don' know Bess. (*Recrosses to her shop.*)

(SPORTING LIFE *watches her till she has reached her doorstep.*)

SPORTING LIFE (*in a low voice, not intended for* MARIA *to hear*). You don' know happy dus'.

(MARIA *does not hear. Goes into shop; closes door.* SPORTING LIFE *continues to wait. St. Michael's chimes the half hour.*)

CURTAIN

SCENE III

CHIMES. *Two o'clock. The court is as usual, except that* PORGY'S *door and shutters are closed. Negroes are coming and going about their tasks.*

PETER, LILY, *and* MINGO *sit at* MARIA'S *table. She is busy serving them.* SCIPIO *is playing near the gate.* SERENA *sits near her door rocking a baby in her arms and singing, "Hush little baby, don't you cry."* MARIA *goes into her shop.*

PORGY *drives up outside the gate and calls softly to* SCIPIO. *His air is one of mystery.*

PORGY. Here, Scipio! Here Porgy back from jail. Open de gate an' don't make no noise.

(SCIPIO *goes reluctantly to gate, opens it, and leads the goat inside.* SERENA *looks up, sees* PORGY, *stops singing in the middle of a bar, and hunches over the baby as though to hide it. Various Negroes about the court look up, see him, and go silently into their rooms.*

PORGY *is too preoccupied with his secret to notice anything. He drives over and stops beside* MARIA'S *table,* LILY, PETER, *and* MINGO *half rise, then see that it is too late to escape, and resume their seats.*)

PORGY (*in a joyous but guarded voice*). Shhh, don't nobody let on yet dat I is home again. I gots a surprise for Bess, an' I ain't want she to know till I gots eberyt'ing ready. (*He does not notice that the others are silent and embarrassed, and, reaching into the wagon, commences to remove packages, talking volubly all the time. He unwraps a harmonica and hands it to* SCIPIO.) Here, boy. T'row away dat ole mout' organ you gots an' start in on dis one. See, he gots picture ob brass band on um. Work on dat, an' fus' t'ing dat yo' know, yo'll be playin' wid de orphans. (*He turns to* LILY.) Here, gal, hol' up yo' head. Dat's right. I nebber did like dem ole funeral bonnet Peter buy fo' yo'. (*Unwraps a gorgeous, feather-trimmed hat and hands it to her.*) Now get underneat' dat, an' make all de red bird and de blue jay jealous.

(LILY *takes hat, but is unable to speak her thanks.* PORGY *is hurrying on, and does not notice this. He opens a package and shakes out a gay dress, then lays it on the table.*)

Now, dat's de style for Bess. She is one gal what always look good in red. (*He opens a hat and places it beside the dress.*) I reckon I is de fus' nigger anybody roun' here ebber see what go to jail po', an' leabe dere rich. But Porgy' luck ridin' high now. Ain't nuttin' can stop um. When de buckra search me in de jail, I all de time gots my lucky bones in my mout'—see! an time I get settle' in my new boardin' house, I start to go right t'rough dem odder crap-shootin' nigger' like Glory Hallelujah.

(*He takes a package from the cart, opens it, and holds up a baby dress.*)

Now, ain't dis de t'ing! Course, de baby ain't really big 'nough for wear dress yet, but he goin' grow fas'. You watch, he goin' be in dat dress by de fus' frost. (*Continues his story.*) Yes, suh! dere warn't no stoppin' dem bones. Dey jus' gone whoopin' right t'rough dat jail, a-pullin' me after 'em. And den, on de las' day, de big buckra guard hear 'bout it, an' he come an' say I gots to gib up de bones. But I been seein' um roll wid de jailer in de watch house, an' I know he weakness. I ask dat buckra if he ain't likes me to teach um how to sing lucky to de bones 'fore I gib' dem up, an' 'fore he git 'way I done gone t'rough um for t'ree dollar an' seben cent an' dis shirt. (*He proudly exhibits shirt that he is wearing. His purchases are now all spread out on the table, and he looks from them to the faces of the Negroes.*)

Now it time to call Bess. Oh, Bess. Here Porgy come home.

(*There is a moment of absolute silence.* LILY *gets to her feet, buries her face in her hands, and runs to her room.* PETER *starts to follow.* MINGO *rises and goes toward* MARIA'*s door.*)

Here, Lily, Peter, Mingo, where you all goin'? What de hell kin' ob a welcome dis for a man what been in jail for a week, an' for de contemp' ob court at dat. Oh, now I see. Well, yo' ain't gots to min' Bess an' me. All de time we wants to hab we frien' wid us. Eben now, we ain't wants to be jus' by weself.

(*They continue to withdraw. He looks about him in growing surprise, and discovers* SERENA *hunched up silently over the baby.*)

Why, hello! Dere's Serena. Yo' sho' work fas', Sistuh. I ain't been gone a week, an' yo' done gots a new baby. (SERENA *rises hurriedly, exposing baby for first time.*) Here, hold on. Let me see dat chile. Dat's Bess's baby, ain't it? Where yo' get um? Where Bess, anyhow? She ain't answer me.

SERENA (*calling*). Maria, come out dat cookshop. Here Porgy come home. *You* gots to talk wid um.

(PORGY *drives to his own door.*)

PORGY. Bess! Ain't yo' dere, Bess? (MARIA *comes to her doorway.* PORGY *turns to her, his eyes wide with alarm.*) Where's Bess? (MARIA *sits on her doorstep.* PORGY *turns his goat and drives over to her.*) Tell me quick. Where's Bess? (MARIA *does not answer.*) Where? Where?

MARIA (*trying to put on a bold face*). Ain't we tell yo' all along, Porgy, dat 'oman ain't fit for yo'?

PORGY (*frantically*). I ain't ask yo' opinion. Where's Bess? (*They all shrink from telling him. Each evades, trying to leave it to the others.*)

MARIA. Dat dirty dog Sportin' Life make us all t'ink yo' is lock up for a yeah.

PORGY. Won't somebody tell me, where Bess?

SERENA. Bess very low in she min' 'cause she t'ink yo' is gone for a yeah. (*Pauses, unable to come to the point.*)

PORGY. But I home *now*. I want to tell she I is here.

SERENA. She gone back to de happy dus' an' de red eye. She been very drunk two day'.

PORGY. But where she now? I ain't care if she was drunk. I want she now.

LILY. Dat houn' Sportin' Life was foreber hangin' 'round and gettin' she to take more dope.

PORGY (*driving again to his own door. Calls*). Bess! Bess! Won't nobody tell me——

MARIA (*following him*). Ain't we tellin' yo'? Dat Houn' Sportin' Life——

PORGY (*desperately*). I ain't ask 'bout Sportin' Life. Where Bess?

SERENA. She gone, Porgy. An' I done take dis chile to gib um a Christian raisin'——

PORGY. *Where* she gone?

SERENA. Dat gal ain't neber had Gawd in she heart, an' de debil get um at last.

MARIA. 'Tain't de debil. De happy dus' done for um.

PORGY (*wildly*). You—Bess?—Yo' ain't means Bess dead?

SERENA. She worse dan dead.

LILY. Sportin' Life carry she away on de Noo Yo'k boat. (*They are all silent, gazing at* PORGY. *He, too, is silent for a moment.*)

PORGY. Where dat dey take she?

MINGO. Noo Yo'k.

MARIA. Dat's way up Nort'.

PORGY (*pointing*). It dat way?

MARIA. It take two days by de boat. Yo' can't find um.

PORGY. I ain't say I can find um. I say, where it is?

MARIA. Yo' can't go after she. Ain't yo' hear we say yo' can't find um.

ANNIE. Ain't yo' know Noo Yo'k mos' a t'ousand mile' from here?

PORGY. Which way dat?

LILY (*pointing*). Up Nort'—past de Custom House.

(PORGY *turns his goat and drives slowly with bowed head toward the gate.*)

MARIA. Porgy, I tells yo' it ain't no use!

LILY. Dat great big city. Yo' can't find um dere!

SERENA. Ain't we tells you'——

(*But* PORGY *is going on toward gate as if he did not hear, and they cease to protest and stand motionless watching him. As* PORGY *reaches the gate,* SCIPIO *silently opens it.* PORGY *drives through and turns to left, as* LILY *pointed. St. Michael's chimes the quarter hour. The gate clangs shut.*)

CURTAIN

The Front Page

BY BEN HECHT AND CHARLES MAC ARTHUR

First produced at the Times Square Theatre, New York City, by Jed Harris, on August 14, 1928. Following is the original cast:

WILSON, *American* ...... Vincent York
ENDICOTT, *Post* .... Allen Jenkins
MURPHY, *Journal* .... Willard Robertson
McCUE, *City Press* ...... William Foran
SCHWARTZ, *Daily News* .. Tammany Young
KRUGER, *Journal of Commerce* .... Joseph Spurin-Calleia
BENSINGER, *Tribune* .... Walter Baldwin
MRS. SCHLOSSER ...... Violet Barney
WOODENSHOES EICHORN .... Jay Wilson
DIAMOND LOUIE ...... Eduardo Cianelli
HILDY JOHNSON, *Herald-Examiner* ...... Lee Tracy
JENNIE .... Carrie Weller
MOLLY MALLOY .... Dorothy Stickney
SHERIFF HARTMAN .... Claude Cooper
PEGGY GRANT .... Frances Fuller
MRS. GRANT .... Jessie Cromette
THE MAYOR .... George Barbier
MR. PINCUS .... Frank Conlan
EARL WILLIAMS .... George Leach
WALTER BURNS .... Osgood Perkins
CARL, A DEPUTY ..... Mathew Cromley
FRANK, A DEPUTY .... Gene West
A POLICEMAN .... Larry Doyle
A POLICEMAN .... George T. Fleming

The scene is the Press Room in the Criminal Courts Building, Chicago.

ACT I

Eight-thirty o'clock on a Friday night.

ACT II

Shortly afterward.

ACT III

A few minutes later.

ONE of the lustiest productions of the Broadway market and a contribution of a sort to Americana was flung upon the stage when Jed Harris produced *The Front Page* by Ben Hecht and Charles MacArthur. It was not the only play to celebrate the more flamboyant and racy aspects of popular journalism (Louis Weitzenkorn's *Five Star Final* was a quite noisy sequel), but it was one of the most madcap farces of the period. True to its genre, the play made a lather of romance, melodrama, farce, and exposé that was unmistakably Broadway at the peak of its irreverence. Nothing in the organized activities of a community quite escaped a scornful snort from its authors, and their scorn seemed not altogether unmerited in the eyes of a public familiar with widely advertised corruptions in municipal government and with the antics of the press. The farce, then, commended itself also as realism of a kind that suited the debunking spirit of the times, although it was actually too carefree to provide any pertinent analysis or to make any show of indignation. In the field of popular farce in which it scored its loud and vivacious triumph, mockery was enough, and of this commodity *The Front Page* had a sufficient quantity.

Its authors were ideally equipped to give this type of play all the verisimilitude and all the pyrotechnics they needed to overcome lethargy and overwhelm fastidiousness. They were both well acquainted with popular journalism and of the areas under its observation. They were both able and energetic reporters with a flair for bravura, plain speaking, and muckracking. They also made a specialty of vivacious cynicism.

Ben Hecht (born in New York City in 1894) was a reporter in 1912 on the Chicago Daily News when he started writing short plays and even contributed a piece to the art-loving Washington Square Players, *The Hero of Santa Mariá*. In 1923 he had a full-length play *The Egoist* on the boards. Charles MacArthur (born in Scranton, Pa., in 1895), the nephew of the playwright Edward Sheldon and the son of a Unitarian clergyman, had been a student for two years in a theological seminary before he joined the Hearst press. Taking to journalism with uncommon zest, he became a successful feature writer, and he resumed his newspaper career after returning from war service in the then famous Rainbow Division. His overture in the theatre was a collaboration with Edward Sheldon, *Lulu Belle,* 1926. Next he collaborated with Sidney Howard on an exposé of sorts, *Salvation Nell* (1928). In 1928 Hecht and MacArthur put their lively heads together to give the Broadway stage *The Front Page,* and it proved to be a long-lived and much acclaimed play.

Their collaboration continued with *20th Century* (1933), and with the super-spectacle *Jumbo* (1935). Mr. Hecht also collaborated with another former gentleman of the press, Gene Fowler, on *The Great Magoo* (1932). Independently, he wrote many stories and several novels, such as *Erik Dorn* (1921) and *A Jew in Love* (1930), a work of considerable penetration as well as the vivid tract on culture and politics, *A Guide to the Bedevilled* (1945). Independently, he also wrote a serious play *To Quito and Back* (1937) which was more provocative than successful. He has also been a prolific and highly prized scenarist for Hollywood, and is perhaps best known for the motion picture *The Scoundrel.* He resumed collaboration with Mr. MacArthur, who has also been a well regarded screen writer, in *Ladies and Gentlemen* (1939), and *Swan Song* (1946). Mr. MacArthur assumed the editorship of the combined Theatre Arts and Stage magazine in 1947.

ACT ONE

This is the press room in the Criminal Courts Building, Chicago; a chamber set aside by the City Fathers for the use of journalists and their friends.

It is a bare, disordered room, peopled by newspapermen in need of shaves, pants pressing and small change. Hither reporters are drawn by an irresistible lure, the privilege of telephoning free.

There are seven telephones in the place, communicating with the seven newspapers of Chicago.

All are free.

An equally important lure is the continuous poker game that has been going on now for a generation, presumably with the same deck of cards.

Here is the rendezvous of some of the most able and amiable bums in the newspaper business; here they meet to gossip, play cards, sleep off jags and date up waitresses between such murders, fires, riots and other public events as concern them.

The furniture is the simplest; two tables, an assortment of chairs, spittoons and waste baskets, a water cooler, etc.—two dollars worth of dubious firewood, all told.

There is one elegant item, however; a huge, ornate black walnut desk, the former property of Mayor Fred A. Busse, deceased about 1904. It now belongs to ROY BENSINGER, *feature writer for the Chicago Tribune and a fanatic on the subject of hygiene.*

Despite MR. BENSINGER's *views, his desk is the repository for soiled linen, old sandwiches, empty bottles and other items shed by his colleagues.*

The two tables serve as telephone desks, gaming boards and (in a pinch) as lits d'amour.

The electric lights are naked of shades.

The walls, unpainted since the building was erected in 1885, sport a frieze of lithographs, hand painted studies, rotogravure cuttings and heroic pencil sketches, all on the same theme: Woman. The political unrest of the journalists is represented by an unfavorable picture of Kaiser Wilhelm II, hand drawn.

At the stage left is a door, labelled "Gents."

At the back is a double door, opening on the main corridor of the building.

At the stage right are two high, old-fashioned windows overlooking the Cook County jail.

It is eight-thirty at night.

Four men are playing poker at the main table in the center of the room. They are MURPHY *of the Journal,* ENDICOTT *of the Post,* SCHWARTZ *of the News and* WILSON *of the American; four braves known to their kind as police reporters. Katatonic, seedy Paul Reveres, full of strange oaths and a touch of childhood.*

Off by himself in a chair sits ERNIE KRUGER, *a somnolent reporter for the Journal of Commerce.* ERNIE *is gifted beyond his comrades. He plays the banjo and sings. He is dreamily rendering his favorite piece, "By the Light of the Silvery Moon," as the poker game progresses.*

MC CUE *of the City News Bureau is telephoning at* BENSINGER's *desk through the gamblers' chatter. He is calling all the police stations, hospitals, etc. on behalf of his companions, in a never-ending quest for news. His reiterations, whined in a manner intended to be ingratiating, have in them the monotonous bally-hoo wail of the Press.*

And so:

THE CARD PLAYERS. Crack it for a dime. . . . By me. . . . I stay. . . . Me too. . . . I'm behind again. . . . I was even a couple of minutes ago. . . . Papers? . . . Three. . . . Two. . . . Three to the dealer.

MC CUE (*into phone*). Kenwood three four hundred. . . . (*Another telephone rings.*) Hey, take that, one of you guys. Ernie, you're not doing anything. (*They pay no attention. With a sigh,* MC CUE *props one telephone receiver against his ear; reaches over and answers the other phone.*) What's the matter with you guys? Are you all crippled or something? (*Into second phone.*) Press room! (*Suddenly he gives attention to the first phone.*) Hello, Sarge . . . McCue. Hold the line a minute. (*Back to second phone.*) No, I told you it was the press room. (*Hangs up; takes first phone again.*) Anything doing, Sarge? . . . All right. Thank you, Sarge. (*Hangs up.*)

THE CARD PLAYERS. What are you waiting for? How'd I know you were out? Two Johns. Ladies, *etc.*

MC CUE. Robey four five hundred. . . . .

MURPHY. Ernie! Take that mouth organ in the can and play it!

(*The music swells a little in reply.*)

ENDICOTT. These cards are like wash-rags.

WILSON. Let's chip in for a new deck.

SCHWARTZ. These are good enough—I'm eighty cents out already!

MC CUE (*into phone*). Is this the home of Mrs. F. D. Margolies?

MURPHY. I'd like a deck with some aces in it.

MC CUE (*cordially, into phone*). This is Mr. McCue of the City News Bureau. . . . Is it true, Madame, that you were the victim of a Peeping Tom?

KRUGER. Ask her if she's worth peeping at.

WILSON. Has she got a friend?

MC CUE (*into phone*). Now, that ain't the right attitude to take, Madame. All we want is the facts. . . . Well, what did this Peeping Tom look like? I mean, for instance, would you say he looked like a college professor?

ENDICOTT. Tell her I can run up for an hour.

KRUGER. I'll accommodate her if she'll come down here.

SCHWARTZ. By me.

MC CUE (*into phone*). Just a minute, Madame. Is it true, Mrs. Margolies, that you took the part of Pocahontas in the Elks' Pageant seven years ago? . . . Hello. (*To the others.*) She hung up.

MURPHY. The hell with her! A dime. (*The fire-alarm box, over the door, begins to ring.*)

ENDICOTT. Where's that fire?

WILSON. Three-two-one!

SCHWARTZ. Clark and Erie.

KRUGER (*wearily as he strums*). Too far.

MC CUE (*into phone*). Harrison four thousand.

SCHWARTZ (*rises, stretching; ambles over and looks out the window*). Oh, Christ!—what time is it, anyway?

WILSON. Half past eight. (*Rises; goes to the water cooler.*)

MURPHY (*drawing cards*). One off the top.

WILSON. How's the wife, Ed? Any better?

SCHWARTZ. Worse.

WILSON. That's tough.

SCHWARTZ. Sitting here all night, waiting for 'em to hang this bastard! (*A gesture toward the jail.*)

KRUGER. It's hard work, all right.

MC CUE (*into phone*). Hello, Sarge? McCue. Anything doing? . . . Yeah? That's swell . . . . (*The players pause.*) A love triangle, huh? . . . Did he kill her? . . . Killed em *both!* Ah! . . . Was she good looking? . . . (*A pause. With vast disgust*) What? Oh, Niggers! (*The players relax.*)

KRUGER. That's a *break*.

MC CUE. No, never mind—thank you, Sarge. (*Jiggles receiver.*) Englewood, six eight hundred. (*The Examiner phone rings. It is on the main table.* ENDICOTT *answers.*)

ENDICOTT (*into phone*). Criminal Courts press room. . . . No, Hildy Johnson ain't here. . . . Oh, hello, Mr. Burns. . . . No, he ain't here yet, Mr. Burns. (*Hangs up.*) Walter Burns again. Something must have happened.

SCHWARTZ. I'm telling you what's happened. Hildy quit.

MURPHY. What do you mean, quit? He's a fixture on the Examiner.

KRUGER. Yeh! He goes with the woodwork.

SCHWARTZ. I got it from Bert Neeley. I'm *telling* you—he's gettin' married.

MURPHY. Walter wouldn't let him get married. He'd kidnap him at the altar.

MC CUE (*into phone*). Hello, Sarge. McCue. Anything doing?

ENDICOTT. Remember what he did to Bill Fenton, when he wanted to go to Hollywood? Had him thrown into jail for arson.

MURPHY. Forgery.

MC CUE. Shut up! . . . (*Into phone.*) Anybody hurt? . . . Oh, fine! What's his name? . . . Spell it. . . . S. . . . C . . . . Z. . . . J. . . . Oh, the hell with it. (*Hangs up.*)

ENDICOTT. A guy ain't going to walk out on a job when he's drawing down seventy bucks a week.

SCHWARTZ. Yeah? Well, if he ain't quit, why ain't he here covering the hanging?

MC CUE (*into phone*). Give me rewrite.

ENDICOTT. Walter sounded like he was having a hemorrhage.

MC CUE (*into phone*). Hello, Emil. Nothing new on the hanging. But here's a big scoop for you.

SCHWARTZ. I wish to God *I* could quit.

KRUGER. You'd think he'd come in and

say goodbye.

MURPHY. That Swede bastard!

MC CUE. Shut up, fellas. (*Into phone.*) Ready, Emil? (*He intones.*) Dr. Irving Zobel—Z for zebra—O for onion—B for baptize—E for anything and L for lousy—

CARD PLAYERS. Pass. . . . By me. . . . Crack it for a dime. . . . Stay.

MC CUE (*into phone*). Yes, Zobel! That's right! With offices at sixteen-o-eight Cottage Grove Avenue. Well, this bird was arrested to-night on complaint of a lot of angry husbands. They claim he was treating their wives with electricity for a dollar a smack.

MURPHY. Is the Electric Teaser in again?

MC CUE (*intoning into phone*). He had a big following, a regular army of fat old dames that was being neglected by their husbands. So they was visiting this Dr. Zobel in their kimonos to get electricity.

ENDICOTT. I understand he massages them too.

MC CUE (*into phone*). Anyhow, the Doctor is being held for mal-practice and the station is full of his patients who claim he's innocent. But from what the husbands say it looks like he's a Lothario. All right. (*Hangs up; jiggles receiver.*)

MURPHY. Hey, Ernie, why don't you go in for electricity instead of the banjo?

(BENSINGER *enters. He is a studious and slightly neurotic fellow who stands out like a sore thumb owing to his tidy appearance.*)

KRUGER. It's got no future.

MC CUE (*into phone*). Sheridan two thousand.

BENSINGER (*with horror*). What the hell, Mac! Is that the only telephone in the place?

MC CUE. It's the only one with a mouthpiece on it. (*This is true.*)

MURPHY (*putting down his hand*). Read 'em and weep. (*Takes the pot. Prepares to deal.*)

BENSINGER. (*howling*). How many times have I got to tell you fellows to leave my phone alone? If you've got to talk through a mouthpiece go *buy* one, like I did!

MURPHY. Aw, shut up, Listerine.

MC CUE (*at another phone*). Sheridan two thousand.

BENSINGER. My God, I'm trying to keep this phone clean and I'm not going to have you fellows coughing and spitting in it, either, or pawing it with your hands!

SCHWARTZ. What is this—a hospital or something?

ENDICOTT. How's that pimple coming along, Roy?

BENSINGER (*pulling a suit of dirty underwear from a drawer of his desk*). And you don't have to use this desk for a toilet!

MURPHY. Yeah? Well, suppose you quit stinking up this place with your God-damn antiseptics for a change! (*Removing a mouldy piece of pie from a desk drawer.*)

BENSINGER (*wailing*). Ain't you guys got any self-respect?

MC CUE (*into phone*). Hello, Sarge! . . . McCue. Congratulations on that Polack capture, Sarge. I hear you're going to be promoted. Anything doing?

THE CARD PLAYERS. Nickel. . . . Up a dime. . . . Drop. . . . Stay.

MC CUE (*into phone*). Yeah? . . . Just a second, Sarge. . . . (*To the players.*) Nice little feature, fellas. Little kid, golden curls, everything, lost out near Grand Crossing. The cops are feeding her candy.

MURPHY. What else are they doing to her?

MC CUE. Don't you want it?

SCHWARTZ. No!

ENDICOTT. Stick it!

WILSON. All yours. (*Starts to deal a new hand.*)

MC CUE (*into phone*). Never mind, Sarge. Thank you, Sarge. (MC CUE *hangs up.*)

SCHWARTZ. Anything new on the hanging, Bensinger?

WILSON (*dealing*). My deal, ain't it?

MURPHY. Hey! Zonite!

BENSINGER. What is it?

MURPHY. Question before the house: Gentleman wants to know what's new on the hanging.

BENSINGER. Nothing special.

KRUGER (*with a yawn*). Did you see the sheriff?

BENSINGER (*bitterly*). Why don't you get your own news?

KRUGER (*philosophically*). Somebody ought to see the sheriff.

ENDICOTT. Anyhow, this looks like the last hanging we'll ever have to cover.

SCHWARTZ. Yeah. Can you imagine their

putting in an electric chair? That's awful.

ENDICOTT. Going to toast them, like Lucky Strikes.

MURPHY. Who opened?

SCHWARTZ. What's the matter? Got a hand?

(MRS. SCHLOSSER *enters. She is the wife of* HERMAN SCHLOSSER, *of the Examiner.* MRS. S. *once used to go to dances, movies and ice cream parlors and she is still pretty, although shop-worn. If she is a bit acidulated, tight-lipped and sharp-spoken, no one can blame her, least of all these bravos of the press room, who have small respect for themselves or each other as husbands, fathers and lovers.*)

ENDICOTT (*as guiltily as if he were the errant* MR. SCHLOSSER). Hello, Mrs. Schlosser. Herman hasn't been in yet.

MC CUE. Hello, Mrs. Schlosser. Have you tried the Harrison Street Station? (*Helpfully.*) He may be sleeping in the squad room.

SCHWARTZ (*bitterly*). What became of that rule about women coming into this press room?

MURPHY. Yeah—I don't let my *own* wife come in here.

MRS. SCHLOSSER (*inexorably*). Did he have any money left when you saw him?

MC CUE. Well, I didn't exactly see him. Did you, Mike?

ENDICOTT. No, I didn't really see him either.

MRS. SCHLOSSER (*like twenty wives*). Oh, you didn't? Well, was he still drinking?

MC CUE (*with unconvincing zeal*). I tell you what, I'll call up the grand jury room if you want. Sometimes he goes to sleep up there.

MRS. SCHLOSSER. Don't trouble yourself! I notice Hildy Johnson ain't here either. I suppose the two of them are out sopping it up together.

SCHWARTZ. Now, you oughtn't to talk that way, Mrs. Schlosser. Hildy's reformed—he's gettin' married.

MRS. SCHLOSSER. Married? Well, all I can say is, God help his wife!

MURPHY. Come on—are we playing cards or aren't we?

MRS. SCHLOSSER. I suppose you've cleaned Herman out.

WILSON (*a nervous husband in his own right*). Honest, Mrs. Schlosser, we ain't seen him.

MRS. SCHLOSSER (*bitterly*). He can't come home. I kept dinner waiting till eleven o'clock last night and he never even called up.

ENDICOTT. Well, why pick on us?

KRUGER. Yeah—we're busy. (*A phone rings.*)

ENDICOTT (*answering it*). Press room!

MRS. SCHLOSSER. You know where he is. You're covering up for him.

MC CUE. Honest to God, Mrs. Schlosser—

ENDICOTT (*into phone*). . . No, Mr. Burns, Hildy ain't showed up yet.

MRS. SCHLOSSER. Is that Walter Burns? Let me talk to him!

ENDICOTT (*into phone*). Just a minute, Mr. Burns. Herman Schlosser's wife wants to talk to you.

MRS. SCHLOSSER (*taking the phone; honeyed and polite*). Hello, Mr. Burns.

MURPHY. Come on—who opened?

ENDICOTT. Check it.

MURPHY. A dime.

MRS. SCHLOSSER. This is Mrs. Schlosser. . . . Oh, I'm very well, thank you. . . . Mr. Burns, I was just wondering if you knew where Herman was. He didn't come home last night, and you know it was pay day. . . . (*Tearfully.*) But it won't be all right. I'm just going crazy. . . . I've done that, but the cashier won't give it to me. . . . So I thought maybe if you gave me some sort of order—oh, will you, Mr. Burns? That's awfully nice of you. . . . I'm sorry to have to do a thing like that, but you know how Herman is about money. Thank you ever so much. (*Hangs up; turns on the reporters viciously.*) You're all alike, every one of you! You ought to be ashamed of yourselves!

MURPHY. All right, we're ashamed. (*To* WILSON.) A dime's bet.

MRS. SCHLOSSER. Sitting around like a lot of dirty, drunken tramps! Poker! (*She grabs* MURPHY's *cards.*)

MURPHY (*leaping up in fury*). Here! Gimme those! What the hell!

MRS. SCHLOSSER. You know where he is, and I'm going to stay right here till I find out!

MURPHY. He's at Hockstetter's, that's where he is! Now give me those cards!

MRS. SCHLOSSER. Where?

WILSON. The Turkish Bath on Madison Street!

ENDICOTT. In the basement!

MURPHY. Give me those!

MRS. SCHLOSSER. So! You did know. (MURPHY *nervously awaits his cards.*) Liars! (*She throws the cards face up on the table.*)

MURPHY (*as she throws them*). Hey! (*They spread out on the table.*)

MRS. SCHLOSSER. You're a bunch of gentlemen, I must say! Newspapermen! Bums! (*Exits.*)

MURPHY (*almost in tears*). Look! The second straight flush I ever held.

ENDICOTT. Jesus!

MURPHY. Eight, nine, ten, jack, and queen of spades. If I was married to that dame I'd kick her humpbacked.

BENSINGER (*having cleansed his telephone with a dab of absorbent cotton and a bottle of antiseptic: into phone*). City Desk!

ENDICOTT (*gathering the cards together*). I don't know what gets into women. I took Bob Brody home the other night and his wife broke his arm with a broom.

BENSINGER (*having collected his notes, and thoroughly protected himself from contagion by wrapping a piece of paper around the handle of his telephone*). Shut up, you fellows! (*Into phone.*) This is Bensinger. Here's a new lead on the Earl Williams hanging. . . . Yeah, I just saw the sheriff. He won't move the hanging up a minute. . . . I don't care *who* he promised. . . . All right, I'll talk to him again, but it's no use. The execution is set for seven o'clock in the morning.

KRUGER (*to the tune of "Three O'Clock in the Morning"; sings*). Seven o'clock in the morning—

BENSINGER. Shut up Ernie. . . . (*Into phone.*) Give me a rewrite man.

KRUGER (*morose*). Why can't they jerk these guys at a reasonable hour, so we can get some sleep?

BENSINGER (*to the room*). I asked the sheriff to move it up to five, so we could make the City Edition. Just because I asked him to, he wouldn't.

MURPHY. That guy wouldn't do anything for his mother.

KRUGER. He gives a damn if we stay up all night!

ENDICOTT. You've got no kick coming. I've had two dinners home in the last month.

BENSINGER (*into phone*). Hello. Jake? . . . New lead on the Williams hanging. And listen—don't put Hartman's name in it. Just say "the Sheriff." (*The* REPORTERS *listen.*) Ready? . . . The condemned man ate a hearty dinner. . . . Yeah, mock turtle soup, chicken pot pie, hashed brown potatoes, combination salad, and pie a la mode.

KRUGER. Make mine the same.

BENSINGER (*into phone*). No—I don't know *what* kind of pie.

MURPHY. Eskimo!

MC CUE (*wistfully*). I wish I had a hamburger sandwich.

BENSINGER (*into phone*). And, Jake, get this in as a big favor. The whole dinner was furnished by Charlie Apfel. . . . Yeah—Apfel. A for adenoids, P for psychology, F for Frank, E for Eddie, and L for—ah—

MURPHY. Lay an egg.

BENSINGER. Proprietor of the Apfel—wants—to—see—you—restaurant.

WILSON. That means a new hat for *some*body. (*A soft cadenza from the banjo.*)

MURPHY. I better catch the fudge, fellas. (*Without dropping his cards,* MURPHY *picks up a telephone. He pantomimes for three cards.*)

BENSINGER (*into phone*). Now here's the situation on the eve of the hanging. The officials are prepared for a general uprising of radicals at the hour of execution, but the Sheriff still refuses to be intimidated by the Red menace.

MURPHY (*into his phone, while accepting three cards*). Give me a rewrite man, will you? . . . Yeah. Some more crap on the Earl Williams hanging.

BENSINGER (*into phone, as the reporters listen*). A double guard has just been thrown around the jail, the municipal buildings, railroad terminals and elevated stations. Also, the Sheriff has just received four more letters threatening his life. He is going to answer these threats by a series of raids against the Friends of American Liberty and other Bolshevik organizations. Call you later. (*Hangs up.*)

SCHWARTZ. Bet a dime.

MURPHY (*into phone*). Ready? . . . Sheriff Hartman has just put two hundred more relatives on the payroll to protect the city against the Red army, which is leaving Moscow in a couple of minutes. (*Consults his hand.*) Up a dime. (*Back to phone.*) And to prove to the voters that the Red menace is on the square, he has just wrote himself four more letters threatening his life. I know he wrote them on account of the misspelling.

ENDICOTT. Drop.

MURPHY (*into phone*). That's all, except the doomed man ate a hearty dinner. As follows: Noodle soup, rustabiff, sweet a-potat', cranberry sauce, and pie-a-la mud.

SCHWARTZ. I raise another dime.

MURPHY (*consults his cards*). Wait a minute. Up again. (*Back to phone.*) Statement from who? The Sheriff? . . . Quote him for anything you want—*he* can't read. (*Hangs up.* BENSINGER'S *phone rings.*)

THE CARD PLAYERS. Call. . . Three bullets. . . . Pay at this window. . . . Shuffle that deck. . . . I get the same hand every time.

BENSINGER (*answering his phone*). What? (*To* MC CUE, *as* SCHWARTZ *starts to shuffle.*) Didn't you send that in about the new alienist?

MC CUE (*flat on his back on the smaller table*). I got my hands full with the stations.

BENSINGER (*into phone*). All right, I'll give you what I got. Dr. Max J. Eglehofer. From Vienna. There's a dozen envelopes on him in the morgue. . . . Well, he's going to examine Williams at the request of—ah—wait a minute— (*Shuffles through his notes.*)—the United Federation for World Betterment.

KRUGER. I'm for that.

BENSINGER. Sure—He's one of the biggest alienists in the world. He's the author of that book, "The Personality Gland."

MC CUE. And where to put it.

BENSINGER (*modestly into phone*). He just autographed it for me.

MURPHY. Did he bite his initials in your pants, too? . . . Nickel.

KRUGER (*into phone lazily*). Give me the City Desk!

BENSINGER (*into phone*). All right. He's going to examine him in about fifteen minutes. I'll let you know. (*He hangs up and resumes his study of "The Personality Gland."*)

KRUGER (*very tired*). Kruger calling! Nothing new on the hanging.

SCHWARTZ. Say, how about roodles on straights or better? I want to get some of my dough back.

WILSON. Hey, I thought we weren't going to give them alienists any more free advertising.

ENDICOTT. That's the fourteenth pair of whiskers they called in on this God-damned case.

MURPHY. Them alienists make me sick. All they do is goose you and send you a bill for five hundred bucks.

MC CUE (*into phone*). This is McCue. . . . Looks like the hanging's coming off at seven all right. . . . Yeah, the Governor's gone fishing and can't be found. . . . No, fishing. (*From the direction of the jail comes a sudden whirr and crash.*) They're testing the gallows now. . . . Yeah—testing 'em, with sandbags. . . . Maybe you can hear 'em. (*He holds up phone towards window and laughs pleasantly. Then, bitterly.*) What? The same to you! (*Hangs up. Another whirr and crash.*)

SCHWARTZ. I wish they'd quit practising. It makes me nervous.

WILSON. Up a dime.

KRUGER (*yelling out of window*). Hey, Jacobi! Quit playing with that gallus! How do you expect us to do any *work?*

VOICE FROM JAIL YARD. Cut that yelling, you God damned bums!

MC CUE. Ain't much respect for the press around here. (*The fire alarm sounds the same number as before.*)

MC CUE. That's a second alarm, ain't it?

MURPHY. Who cares?

KRUGER (*motionless*). Probably some orphanage.

MURPHY. Maybe it's another cat-house. Remember when Big Minnie's burned down, and the Mayor of Galesburg came running out? (*A phone rings.*)

THE CARD PLAYERS. Dime. . . . I call. . . . Two sixes, *etc.*

MC CUE (*answering phone*). What? The Mayor's office! (*To the rest.*) Maybe a statement.

KRUGER. Tell 'em we're busy.

MC CUE (*into phone*). Hello. (*Then exuberantly.*) Hello, you God-damn Swede! (*To the others.*) It's Hildy.

MURPHY. What's he doing in the Mayor's office?

MC CUE (*into phone*). What? What's that? What? (*To the others.*) He's stinko! (*Into phone.*) What are you doing with the Mayor?

MURPHY. If he's got any left tell him to bring it over.

MC CUE (*into phone*). Huh? Kissing him good-bye?

ENDICOTT. Tell him to come over and kiss us.

MURPHY. I'm getting ready.

MC CUE (*into phone*). Well hurry up. (*To the room.*) He's stepping high.

MURPHY. What did he say?

KRUGER. Is he coming over?

MC CUE. That's what he said.

THE CARD PLAYERS. Pass. . . . By me. . . . Take a deal, *etc.*

(WOODENSHOES EICHHORN *enters. He is a big, moon-faced, childish and incompetent German policeman.*)

BENSINGER. Hello, Woodenshoes. Got any news?

WOODENSHOES (*solemnly*). I just been over to the death house. Did you hear what Earl Williams said to the priest?

ENDICOTT. Aw, forget it!

MURPHY. The paper's full of the hanging now. We ain't got room for the ads.

BENSINGER (*looking up from his book*). What did he say, Woodenshoes?

WOODENSHOES (*awed*). He says to the priest that he was innocent.

MURPHY. Do you know any more jokes?

WOODENSHOES. Well, I'm just telling you what he says.

MURPHY. I suppose that copper committed suicide. Or maybe it was a love pact.

WOODENSHOES. Well, Williams has got a very good explanation for that.

ENDICOTT (*derisively, to the reporters*). He'll start crying in a minute. (*To* WOODENSHOES.) Why don't you send him some roses, like Mollie Malloy?

SCHWARTZ. Yeah. She thinks he's innocent, too.

WOODENSHOES. You fellas don't understand. He admits killing the policeman, but he claims they're just using that as an excuse to hang him, on account he's a radical. But the thing that gets me—

MC CUE. Before you go on, Woodenshoes, would you mind running down to the corner and getting me a hamburger sandwich?

WOODENSHOES (*patiently*). Personally, my feeling is that Earl Williams is a dual personality type on account of the way his head is shaped. It's a typical case of psychology. (*The card game goes on.*) Now you take the events leading up to the crime; his hanging a red flag out of the window on Washington's Birthday. That ain't normal, to begin with. The officer ought to have realized when he went up there that he was dealing with a lunatic. I'm against having colored policemen on the force, anyway. And I'll tell you why—

ENDICOTT (*suddenly*). Make that two hamburgers, will you, Woodenshoes, like a good fellow?

WOODENSHOES (*hurt*). I thought you fellas might be interested in the psychological end of it. None of the papers have touched that aspect.

MURPHY (*profound, but casual*). Listen, Woodenshoes, this guy Williams is just a bird that had the tough luck to kill a nigger policeman in a town where the nigger vote is important.

KRUGER. Sure! If he'd bumped him off down South they'd have given him a banquet and a trip to Europe.

MC CUE. Oh, the South ain't so bad. How about Russia, where they kill all the Jews and nobody says anything?

MURPHY. Williams was a bonanza for the City Hall. He gets hung—everybody gets elected on a law and order platform.

ENDICOTT. "Reform the Reds with a Rope."

(WILSON *makes an unprintable sound.*)

MURPHY. When that baby drops through the trap tomorrow, it's a million votes. He's just a divine accident. Bet a dime.

WOODENSHOES (*blinking through the above*). That's it—an accident. He didn't know it was a policeman, even. Why, when this officer woke him up—

MC CUE (*tolerantly*). Sure. You're right, Woodenshoes. And ask 'em to put a lot of ketchup on one of them sandwiches, will you?

WILSON (*sore*). I haven't filled a hand all night.

(DIAMOND LOUIE, *a ham gunman, enters. He is sleek, bejewelled and sinister to everybody but the caballeros of the press room, who knew him when he ran a fruit stand. He is greeted with unction.*)

LOUIE. Hello, fellows.

SCHWARTZ. Well, well, well! Diamond Louie!

MURPHY. If it ain't the Kid himself! Oooh! Look at the pop bottles!

MC CUE. Hurry up, Woodenshoes! I'm starving!

KRUGER. Get one for me, Woodenshoes!

BENSINGER. Make mine a plain lettuce

—on gluten bread.

WOODENSHOES (*blinking*). Where am I gonna get the dough for all these eats?

MC CUE. Charge it.

MURPHY. You got a badge, ain't you? What's it good for?

WOODENSHOES (*shuffling out*). Four hamburgers and a lettuce.

DIAMOND LOUIE. Where's Hildy Johnson?

ENDICOTT (*rudely*). Up in Minnie's room.

MURPHY. Who wants to know?

KRUGER. Say, Louie, I hear your old gang is going to bump off Kinky White.

DIAMOND LOUIE (*with sinister reticence*). Is that so?

MURPHY. Better wait till after election or you won't make the front page.

ENDICOTT. Yeah. We had to spike that Willie Mercer killing.

DIAMOND LOUIE. Well, I'll tell you. I'm off that racket. I don't even associate with them fellas, any more.

MURPHY. Go on! You gotta kill somebody every day or you don't get any supper.

DIAMOND LOUIE. No. No kiddin'. I'm practically retired, you know what I mean?

SCHWARTZ. Retired from what? You never carried anything but a bean blower!

DIAMOND LOUIE. All joking aside. Honest. I'm one of you fellas now. I'm in the newspaper game.

MURPHY (*with scorn*). You're what?

ENDICOTT. He's gettin' delusions of grandeur.

DIAMOND LOUIE. Yeah. That's right. I'm a newspaperman . . . working for Walter Burns.

WILSON. What!

ENDICOTT (*very politely*). What you doin' for Burns? A little pimping?

MURPHY. He's marble editor.

DIAMOND LOUIE (*with dignity*). I'm assistant circulation manager for de nort' side.

WILSON. Got a title and everything.

ENDICOTT. Burns'll be hiring animal acts next.

SCHWARTZ. What d'ye want Hildy for? Tailing him for Walter?

ENDICOTT. What do you know about that, Louie. We hear he's quit the Examiner.

MC CUE. Yeah. What's the dope, Louie?

DIAMOND LOUIE. Well, I don't think it's permanent, you know what I mean?

SCHWARTZ. What the hell happened?

ENDICOTT. They must of murdered each other, the way Walter sounded.

DIAMOND LOUIE. Naaaa! Just a little personal argument. Nothin' serious.

MC CUE. Come on . . . what's the dirt?

DIAMOND LOUIE. I don't know a single thing about it.

MC CUE. Should we tell Hildy you were lookin' for him?

DIAMOND LOUIE (*with affected nonchalance*). No. Never mind. (*Again the whirr and crash of the gallows.* LOUIE *looks.*) What's that?

ENDICOTT. They're fixin' up a pain in the neck for somebody.

DIAMOND LOUIE (*with a genteel lift of his eyebrows*). Hah! Mr. Weeliams!

MURPHY. They'll be doing that for you some day.

DIAMOND LOUIE (*very flattered*). Maybe. (*To the players.*) Well—keep your eye on the dealer. (*He starts to leave.*)

MURPHY (*turning from the card game for the first time*). Wait a second, Louie. (DIAMOND LOUIE *pauses politely.*) Come here. (*As* DIAMOND LOUIE *approaches.*) Where do you keep your cap pistol? . . . Here? (*He gooses* DIAMOND LOUIE.)

DIAMOND LOUIE (*with a leap*). Hey! For God's sake! Look out, will you! Jesus, that's a hell of a thing to do! . . . (*He exits angrily.*)

ENDICOTT (*calling after him*). Call again, Louie.

MURPHY. Any time you're in the building.

KRUGER. And don't bump off anybody before election day.

MURPHY (*sadly*). Louie hasn't got much self control.

ENDICOTT. What do you know about Hildy? Looks like he's quit, all right.

WILSON. Yeah. . . . What do you think of that?

ENDICOTT. There won't be any good reporters left after awhile.

MURPHY (*gently*). No. Mossie Enright getting stewed and falling down the elevator shaft. And poor old Larry Malm.

SCHWARTZ. And Carl Pancake that disappeared. (*A phone rings.*)

ENDICOTT (*answering it*). Hello . . . Oh hello, Mr. Burns. Why, he was in the mayor's office a few minutes ago . . . (HILDY JOHNSON *enters. He is a happy-go-lucky Swede with a pants-kicking sense of humor. He is barbered and tailored like a normal citizen—a fact which at once excites the wonder and mirth of his colleagues.* HILDY *is of a vanishing type—the lusty, hoodlumesque half-drunken caballero that was the newspaperman of our youth. Schools of journalism and the advertising business have nearly extirpated the species. Now and then one of these boys still pops up in the profession and is hailed by his editor as a survival of a golden age. The newspapermen who have already appeared in this press room are in reality similar survivals. Their presence under one roof is due to the fact that Chicago is a sort of journalistic Yellowstone Park offering haven to a last herd of fantastic bravos that once roamed the newspaper offices of the country.* MR. JOHNSON *carries a new suitcase, two paper parcels and—a cane! A rowdy outburst follows his entrance.*)

MURPHY (*loudly*). Ooh! Lookit the cane! What are you doing? Turning fairy?

MC CUE. Yum, yum! Kiss me!

WILSON. Where the hell you been?

ENDICOTT. Walter Burns on the wire, Hildy.

HILDY. What's that?

MC CUE. What's the matter, Hildy? My God! He's got a shave!

SCHWARTZ. Jesus! Look at the crease in his pants!

ENDICOTT. It's Walter Burns, Hildy. Will you talk to him for God's sake?

HILDY. Tell that paranoiac bastard to take a sweet kiss for himself! . . . Come on Ernie! . . . (*Sings. "Goodbye, Forever . . ."*)

ENDICOTT. Say, listen, Hildy. Will you do me a personal favor and talk to Walter? He knows you're here.

MC CUE. He's calling up about nine million times.

KRUGER. All we do is answer that Goddamn phone . . .

MURPHY. What's the matter? Scared of him?

HILDY. I'll talk to that maniac—with pleasure. (*Into phone, with mock formality.*) Hello, Mr. Burns. . . . What's that, Mr. Burns? . . . Why, your language is shocking, Mr. Burns . . . Now, listen, you lousy baboon. Get a pencil and paper and take this down: Get this straight because this is important. It's the Hildy Johnson curse. The next time I see you—no matter where I am or what I'm doing—I'm going to walk right up to you and hammer on that monkey skull of yours until it rings like a Chinese gong. . . .

MC CUE. Oh, boy!

ENDICOTT. That's telling him!

HILDY (*holding sizzling receiver to the nearest reporter*). Listen to him! (*Into phone.*) No, I ain't going to cover the hanging! I wouldn't cover the last supper for you! Not if they held it all over again in the middle of Clark Street. . . . Never mind the Vaseline, Jocko! It won't do you any good this time! Because I'm going to New York like I told you, and if you know what's good for you you'll stay west of Gary, Indiana! A Johnson never forgets! (*He hangs up.*) And that, boys, is what is known as telling the managing editor. (*The reporters agree loudly.*)

BENSINGER. Can't you guys talk without yelling?

HILDY (*his song rising again. "Goodbye, Forever!"*)

VOICE (*from jail yard*). Hey, cut the yodeling! Where do you think you are!

HILDY (*moving toward the window, takes out his pocket flask*). Hey, Jacobi! Pickle-nose! (*He takes a final drink from the flask, then aims and throws it out the window. A scream of rage arises from the jail yard.*)

HILDY (*smiles and salutes his victim*). On the button! (*Turns to* ERNIE, *resumes his song.*)

BENSINGER (*pleading*). Oh, shut up!

WILSON. What did you quit for, Hildy?

SCHWARTZ. We hear you're going to get married?

HILDY. I'm getting married, all right. (*Shows tickets.*) See that? Three tickets to New York! Eleven-eighteen tonight!

WILSON. Tonight!

MC CUE. Jesus, that's quick.

MURPHY. What do you mean three?

HILDY. Me and my girl and her Goddamn ma!

ENDICOTT. Kinda sudden, ain't it?

SCHWARTZ. What the hell do you want to get married for?

HILDY. None of your business!

MURPHY. Ooooh! He's in love! Tootsie-wootsie!

MC CUE. Is she a white girl?

ENDICOTT. Has she got a good shape?

WILSON. Does Walter know you're getting married?

HILDY. Does he know I'm getting married? He congratulated me! Shook hands like a pal! Offered to throw me a farewell dinner even.

ENDICOTT. That's his favorite joke—farewell dinners.

MURPHY. He poisons people at them.

HILDY. He gets me up to Polack Mike's—fills me full of rotgut—I'd have been there yet if it hadn't been for the fire escape!

SCHWARTZ. That's what he done to the Chief of Police!

HILDY. Can you imagine? Trying to bust up my marriage! After shaking hands! . . . (*Anxiously.*) Say, my girl didn't call up, did she, or come in looking for me? What time is it, anyway?

SCHWARTZ. Quarter past nine.

MC CUE. Eighteen minutes after.

HILDY (*starting to take off his coat*). I got to be at this house at seven.

ENDICOTT. What house?

HILDY. Somebody giving a farewell party to my girl.

WILSON. At seven tonight?

HILDY. Yeah?

MURPHY. You got to run like hell.

HILDY. Oh, that's all right. Fellow doesn't quit a job every day. Especially when it's Walter Burns. The lousy baboon—

ENDICOTT. When's the wedding, Hildy?

HILDY. It's in New York, so you guys ain't going to have any fun with it. None of them fake warrants or kidnapping the bride, with me! (HILDY *folds his old shirt and puts it in* BENSINGER'S *drawer.*)

BENSINGER. Aw, for God's sake! Cut that out! (*Throws the shirt on the floor.*)

WILSON. Everybody's getting this New York bug. It's just a rube town for mine.

SCHWARTZ. I was on a New York paper once—the Times. You might as well work in a bank.

MURPHY. I hear all the reporters in New York are lizzies.

MC CUE. Remember that fellow from the New York World?

ENDICOTT. With the derby?

MURPHY (*presumably mimicking a New York journalist*). Could you please instruct me where the telegraph office is? (*Makes a rude noise.*) You'll be talking like that, Hildy.

HILDY. Yeah?

ENDICOTT. Which one of them sissy journals are you going to work for?

HILDY. None of them! Who the hell wants to work on a newspaper? A lot of crumby hoboes, full of dandruff and bum gin they wheedle out of nigger Aldermen.

MURPHY. That's what comes of stealing a cane.

ENDICOTT. What are *you* going in for—the movies?

HILDY. I am not. Advertising business. One hundred and fifty smackers a week.

MC CUE. Yeah?

ENDICOTT. One hundred and fifty *what?*

SCHWARTZ (*a sneer*). A hundred and fifty!

HILDY. Here's the contract. (*Hands it to* MC CUE, *who starts to look through it. They crowd around this remarkable document.*) I was just waiting to get it down in black and white before I walked in and told Walter I was through.

MC CUE (*with contract*). Jesus, it *is* a hundred and fifty!

WILSON. Was Walter sore?

HILDY. The lousy snake-brain! The God-damn ungrateful ape! Called me a traitor, after ten years of sweating my pants off for practically nothing. Traitor to what? What did he or anybody else in the newspaper business ever do for me except try to make a bum out of me! Says "You can't quit without notice!" What the hell does he think I am? A hired girl? Why, one more word and I'd have busted his whiskey snout for him!

KRUGER. Why didn't you?

MURPHY. Who's going to cover the hanging for the Examiner?

MC CUE. Why the hell didn't you tell a fellow?

WILSON. Yeah—instead of waiting till the last day?

HILDY. And have Walter hear about it? I've always wanted to walk in and quit just like that! (*A snap of the fingers.*) I been planning this for two months—packed up everything yesterday, and so did my girl! Furniture and all. (*The fire signal has been sounding through the last few words.* HILDY *looks up.*) Hey, fellows, that's Kedzie and Madison ain't it? The Washington Irving School's out there.

MURPHY. Who the hell's in school this time of night?

MC CUE. What do you care, anyhow? You've quit.

HILDY (*laughs, chagrined*). Just thought it might be a good fire, that's all. (*Again the whirr and crash of the gallows.*)

KRUGER. For Christ's sake! (*At the window.*) Ain't you got anything else to do? Hey! You Jacobi!

BENSINGER. Hey, fellows. I'm trying to read.

WILSON (*also near window*). They're changing the guards down there. Look—they've got sixteen of them. (*Voices come up from the courtyard—"Hey!" "Hurry up." "Get a move on, Carl!" etc.*)

MC CUE (*hands back the contract*). You're going to miss a swell hanging, Hildy.

HILDY. Yeah? You can stick it.

MURPHY. So you're going into the advertising business, eh? Writing poetry about Milady's drawers.

ENDICOTT. Going to wear an eye shade?

WILSON. I'll bet he has a desk with his name on it, and a stenographer.

MURPHY. You'll be like a firehorse tied to a milk wagon.

ENDICOTT (*to* MURPHY). I don't know what gets into these birds. Can you imagine punching a clock, and sitting around talking like a lot of stuffed shirts about statistics?

HILDY. Yeah—sour grapes, that's all it is. Sour grapes.

MURPHY. I got a dumb brother went in for business. He's got seven kids and a mortgage, and belongs to a country club. He gets worse every year. Just a fat-head.

HILDY. Listen to who's talking. Journalists! Peeking through keyholes! Running after fire engines like a lot of coach dogs! Waking people up in the middle of the night to ask them what they think of Mussolini. Stealing pictures off old ladies of their daughters that get raped in Oak Park. A lot of lousy, daffy buttinskis, swelling around with holes in their pants, borrowing nickels from office boys! And for what? So a million hired girls and motormen's wives'll know what's going on.

MURPHY. Your girl must have handed you that line.

HILDY. I don't need anybody to tell me about newspapers. I've been a newspaperman fifteen years. A cross between a bootlegger and a whore. And if you want to know something, you'll all end up on the copy desk—gray-headed, humpbacked slobs, dodging garnishees when you're ninety.

SCHWARTZ. Yeah, and what about you? How long do you think you'll last in that floosie job?

ENDICOTT. You'll get canned cold the minute your contract's up, and then you'll be out in the street.

KRUGER. Sure—that's what always happens.

HILDY. Well, it don't happen to me. And I'll tell you why, if you want to know. Because my girl's uncle owns the business, that's why.

WILSON. Has he got a lot of jack?

HILDY. It's choking him. You know what he sent us for a wedding present?

MURPHY. A dozen doilies.

HILDY. I wouldn't tell you bums, because it's up in high finance and you wouldn't understand it.

ENDICOTT. Probably gave you a lot of stock in the company, that you can't sell.

KRUGER. I know them uncles.

HILDY. The hell he did! He gave us five hundred in cash, that's what he gave us.

MC CUE. Go on!

SCHWARTZ. There *ain't* five hundred in cash.

HILDY. Yeah? (*Pulling out a roll.*) Well, there it is—most of it, except what it costs to get to New York.

MC CUE. Jees, let's see.

HILDY. Oh, no!

MURPHY. How about a finif till tomorrow?

HILDY (*mimicking an androgyne*). I won't be here tomorrow. And that reminds me. (*Takes out a little book.*) It comes to— (*Consults book.*) eight dollars and sixty-five cents altogether, Jimmie. Eight dollars and sixty-five cents.

MURPHY. What does?

HILDY. That includes the four bucks in front of the Planter's Hotel, when you were with that waitress from King's.

MURPHY. I thought I paid that.

HILDY. No. (*Reading from notes.*) Herman Schlosser . . . altogether twenty dollars and . . .

MC CUE. Ha! Ha! Ha!

ENDICOTT. Ho! Ho! Ho!

HILDY. All right. I guess I might as well call it off, all around. I should have known better than to try to collect, anyhow. (*Tears out the page and throws it at* MURPHY.) You might say thanks.

MURPHY. Not after that waitress.

SCHWARTZ. About that fifty bucks, Hildy. If you want a note—

HILDY. What fifty bucks? Aw, forget it.

SCHWARTZ. You see, it wasn't only the

wife taking sick, but then besides . . . (JENNIE, *a slightly idiotic scrubwoman, enters. She receives an ovation. "Yea, Jennie!" "Jennie!" "Well, if it ain't Jennie," all delivered in various dialects with intended comedy effect.*)

KRUGER. I hear you just bought another apartment house, Jennie!

MURPHY. I hear you've fallen in love again, Jennie!

JENNIE (*giggling*). Can I wash up now, please?

BENSINGER. Yeah, for God's sake do! This place smells like a monkey cage.

HILDY. Go on! You don't want to wash up on a night like this! This is a holiday! I'm going away, Jennie! Give us a kiss! (*He embraces her.*)

JENNIE (*squealing*). Now you Hildy Johnson, you keep away from me! I'll hit you with this mop! I will!

HILDY (*tickling her*). What's the matter? Ain't I your fellow any more? I'll tell you what we'll do, Jennie! You and I'll go around and say goodbye! Everybody in the building!

MC CUE. Hey, the warden called you up. Wants to see you before you go!

HILDY. There you are, Jennie! We're *invited!* He invited Jennie, didn't he? You bet he did!

JENNIE. Now you know he didn't.

HILDY (*lifting pail of water*). Only we can't carry this all over! *I* know! (*At window.*) Hey! Jacobi! Look! (*Throws water out.* JENNIE *giggles hysterically.*)

VOICE (*off*). Who did that?

SCHWARTZ. Better shut off them lights. Somebody's liable to come up.

HILDY (*to* JENNIE). Come on, Jennie! We'll say good-bye to the warden! (*He embraces her again.*)

JENNIE (*struggling*). No, no! You let go of me! The warden'll be mad! He'll *do* something!

HILDY. To hell with him! *I* own this building! Come on! (*Pausing in the door.*) If my girl calls up, tell her I'm on my way! (*Exits with* JENNIE, *singing "Waltz Me Around Again, Jennie." Coy screams from* JENNIE, *and the banging of a pail as it is kicked down the corridor.*)

BENSINGER. Thank God *that's* over!

KRUGER. What's the Examiner going to do with Hildy off the job?

WILSON. It must be great to walk into a place and quit.

MC CUE. Yeah. (*He moves sadly away and uses one of the phones on the long table.*) Diversey three two hundred.

ENDICOTT (*sentimentally*). I got an offer from the publicity department of the stock yards last year. I shoulda took it.

SCHWARTZ. What I'd like would be a job on the side.

MC CUE (*a lump in his throat*). A desk and a stenographer. That wouldn't be so bad. I wouldn't mind a nice big blonde.

MURPHY (*outlining a voluptuous bust*). With a bozoom! (*Phone on small table rings.*)

MC CUE (*sighs, then into his own phone*). Hello, Sarge. McCue. Anything doing?

WILSON (*answering other phone*). What's that? (*His tone becomes slightly formal.*) Yes, ma'am. . . . No, Hildy ain't here just now, madam. He left a message for you, though. . . . Why, he said he was on his way. . . . No, he didn't say where —just that he was on his way. . . . All right, I'll tell him, ma'am. (*Hangs up.*) Oooh! Is *she* sore?

SCHWARTZ. Hildy oughtn't to do that. She's a swell kid.

MC CUE (*into phone*). All right! Thank you, Sarge! (*Hangs up.*) A hundred and fifty bucks a week! Can you imagine?

KRUGER. Probably gets Saturdays and Sundays off, too.

WILSON (*sadly*). And Christmas.

MC CUE. I wonder who Walter'll send over here in Hildy's place. (MOLLIE MALLOY *enters. She is a North Clark Street tart, cheap black sateen dress, red hat and red slippers run over at the heels. She is a soiled and gaudy houri of the pavement. Despite a baleful glare on* MOLLIE'S *part, the boys brighten visibly. They are always glad to see whores.*)

MURPHY (*warmly*). Hello, Mollie!

ENDICOTT. Well, well! Nookie!

WILSON. Hello, kid! How's the old tomato-can?

MC CUE (*feeling himself to be a Chauncey Olcott*). Shure, and how are yez, Mollie?

MOLLIE (*in a tired, banjo voice*). I've been looking for you bastards!

MURPHY. Going to pay a call on Williams?

SCHWARTZ. He's just across the courtyard!

KRUGER. Better hurry up—he hasn't got all night.

MC CUE. Yes, he has!

ENDICOTT (*formally*). Say, Mollie, those were pretty roses you sent Earl. What do you want done with them tomorrow morning?

MOLLIE (*tensely*). A lot of wise guys, ain't you? Well, you know what I think of you—all of you.

MURPHY. Keep your pants on, Mollie.

MOLLIE (*to* MURPHY). If you was worth breaking my fingernails on, I'd tear your puss wide open.

MURPHY. What you sore about, sweetheart? Wasn't that a swell story we give you?

MOLLIE. You cheap crumbs have been making a fool out of me long enough!

ENDICOTT. Now what kind of language is that?

BENSINGER. She oughtn't to be allowed in here! I caught her using the drinking cup yesterday!

MOLLIE (*flaring*). I never said I loved Earl Williams and was willing to marry him on the gallows! You made that up! And all that other crap about my being his soul mate and having a love nest with him!

MC CUE. Well, didn't you?

ENDICOTT. You've been sucking around that cuckoo ever since he's been in the death house! Everybody knows you're his affinity!

MOLLIE (*blowing up*). That's a lie! I met Mr. Williams just once in my life, when he was wandering around in the rain without his hat and coat on like a sick dog. The day before the shooting. And I went up to him like any human being would and I asked what was the matter, and he told me about bein' fired after working at the same place twenty-two years and I brought him up to my room because it was warm there.

ENDICOTT. Did he have the two dollars?

MURPHY. Aw, put it on a Victrola.

MOLLIE. Just because you want to fill your lying papers with a lot of dirty scandal, you got to crucify him and make a bum out of me!

ENDICOTT. Got a match, Mollie?

MOLLIE (*heedless*). I tell you he just sat there talking to me . . . all night . . . just sat there talkin' to me . . . and never once laid a hand on me! In the morning he went away and I never saw him again till the day at the trial!

ENDICOTT. Tell us what you told the jury!

(*They laugh reminiscently.*)

MOLLIE. Go on, laugh! God damn your greasy souls! Sure I was his witness—the only one he had. Yes, me! Mollie Malloy! A Clark Street tart! I was the only one with guts enough to stand up for him! And that's why you're persecuting me! Because he treated me decent, and not like an animal, and I said so!

ENDICOTT. Why didn't you adopt him instead of letting him run around shooting policemen?

SCHWARTZ. Suppose that cop had been your own brother?

MOLLIE. I wish to God it had been one of you!

MURPHY (*finally irritated*). Say, what's the idea of this song and dance, anyhow? This is the press room. We're busy.

SCHWARTZ. Go on home!

MURPHY. Go and see your boy friend, why don't you?

MC CUE. Yeah—he's got a nice room.

ENDICOTT (*with a wink at the rest*). He won't have it long. He's left a call for seven A. M.

MOLLIE (*through her teeth*). It's a wonder a bolt of lightning don't come through the ceiling and strike you all dead! (*Again the sound of the gallows.*) What's that? Oh, my God! (*She begins to cry.*)

BENSINGER (*rising*). Say, what's the idea?

MOLLIE. Talking that way about a fellow that's going to die.

ENDICOTT (*uncomfortable at this show of grief*). Don't get hysterical.

MOLLIE (*sobbing*). Shame on you! Shame on you!

MC CUE (*to the rest*). It wasn't my fault. *I* didn't say anything.

MOLLIE (*hysterically*). A poor little crazy fellow that never did any harm. Sitting there alone this minute, with the Angel of Death beside him, and you cracking jokes.

MURPHY (*getting up meaningly*). Listen, if you don't shut up, I'll give you something *good* to cry about!

MOLLIE (*savage*). Keep your dirty hands off me!

MURPHY (*in a short and bitter struggle with her*). Outside, *bum!*

MOLLIE (*shooting through the door*). You dirty punks! Heels! Bastards! (*Exit.*)

MURPHY (*slams the door. A pause*). The nervy bitch!

MC CUE. Whew!

MURPHY. You guys want to play some more poker?

ENDICOTT. What's the use? *I* can't win a pot.

MURPHY. I'm the big loser.

WILSON. Me too. I must be out three dollars, anyhow.

ENDICOTT. It's God-damn funny who's got it.

SCHWARTZ. Don't look at me. I started in with five bucks, and I got two-eighty left.

MC CUE (*who has taken up the phone again*). Michigan eight thousand.

(SHERIFF HARTMAN *enters briskly, bitter words forming on his lips. He is a diabetic and overwrought little fellow, an incompetent fussbudget. He has come to raise hell, but an ovation checks him. "Ah, Sheriff!" "Hello, Pinky!" "How's the old statesman?"* BENSINGER *puts down his book;* MC CUE *abandons his telephoning.*)

ENDICOTT. Any news, Sheriff?

SHERIFF (*briefly*). Hello, fellas. (*In another tone.*) Now, who dumped that bucket of water out the window?

KRUGER. What bucket of water?

SHERIFF. Who threw it out the window is what I asked, and I want to know!

MURPHY. Judge Pam threw it out.

SHERIFF. I suppose Judge Pam threw that bottle!

ENDICOTT. Yeah. That was Judge Pam, too.

MURPHY. He was in here with his robes on, playing fireman.

SHERIFF. Come on now, fellas, I know who it was. (*Wheedling.*) It was Hildy Johnson, wasn't it? Where is he?

MC CUE. Out with a lady.

ENDICOTT. Hildy's quit, Sheriff. Didn't you hear?

SHERIFF. Well, I'm glad of it. It's good riddance! Now personally, I don't give a God damn, but how do you suppose it looks to have a lot of hoodlums yelling and throwing things out of windows? (*In a subdued voice*) Besides there's somebody *in* that death house. How do you suppose he feels, listening to all this re*vel*-ery?

MURPHY. A hell of a lot you care how he feels!

SCHWARTZ. Keep your shirt on, Pinky.

SHERIFF. Wait a minute, you! I don't want to hear any more of that Pinky stuff. I got a name, see? Peter B. Hartman.

MURPHY. What's the matter with Pinky?

MC CUE (*taking the cue*). He's all right.

THE REPORTERS (*lustily*). Who's all right?

SHERIFF (*desperate*). Now stop! (*Whining.*) Honest, boys, what's the idea of hanging a name like that on me? Pinky Hartman! How's that look to the voters? Like I had sore eyes or something.

MURPHY. You never heard of Bathhouse John kicking, did you?

WILSON. Or Hinky Dink?

ENDICOTT. It's made you famous!

SHERIFF. I swear *I* don't know what to do about you fellows. You abuse every privilege you get. I got a damn good notion to take this press room away from you.

MURPHY. That would be a break.

ENDICOTT. Yeah. The place is so full of cockroaches you can't walk.

BENSINGER (*rising*). Wait a minute, fellows. Now listen, Pete, this is the last favor I'm ever going to ask you, and it ain't me that's asking it. Get me? *You* know who's asking it—a certain party is asking it. Once and for all, how about hanging this guy at five o'clock instead of seven? It ain't going to hurt you and we can make the City Edition.

SHERIFF (*sincerely*). Aw, now, Roy, that's kind of raw. You can't hang a fella in his sleep, just to please a newspaper.

MURPHY. No, but you can reprieve him twice so the hanging'll come three days before election! So you can run on a law-and-order ticket! You can do that all right!

SHERIFF. I had nothing whatsoever to do with those reprieves. That was entirely up to the Governor.

ENDICOTT. And who told the Governor what to do?

SCHWARTZ. How do we know there won't be another reprieve tonight? For all I know I'm hanging around here for nothing! When I've got a sick wife!

WILSON. Yeah, with another alienist getting called in!

MURPHY. This Wop gooser!

SCHWARTZ. Sure—what's all that about? Suppose he finds he's insane or something?

SHERIFF. He *won't* find he's insane. Because he isn't. This ruse of reading the Declaration of Independence day and night is pure fake. But I've got to let this doctor see him, on account of his being sent by these Personal Liberty people, or whatever they call themselves. You and I know they're nothing but a bunch of Bolsheviks, but a hanging is a serious business. At a time like this you want to please everybody.

ENDICOTT. Everybody that can vote, anyhow.

SHERIFF. Now he's going to look him over in my office in a couple of minutes, and then you'll know all about it. Besides, there's nothing he *can* find out. Williams is as sane as I am.

SCHWARTZ. Saner!

SHERIFF. The hanging's going to come off exactly per schedule. And when I say "per schedule" that means seven o'clock and not a minute earlier. There's such a thing as being humane, you know.

BENSINGER. Just wait till *you* want a favor.

SHERIFF (*to change the subject*). Now here are the tickets. Two for each paper.

MC CUE. What do you *mean,* two for each paper?

SHERIFF (*stung*). What do you want to do—take your family?

SCHWARTZ. Now listen, Pete. I promised a pair to Ernie Byfield. He's never seen a hanging.

WILSON. The boss wants a couple for the advertising department.

SHERIFF (*passing out tickets*). This ain't the "Follies," you know. I'm tired of your editors using these tickets to get advertising accounts.

ENDICOTT. You got a lot of nerve! Everybody knows what *you* use 'em for—to get in socially.

MURPHY. He had the whole Union League Club over here last time.

ENDICOTT. Trying to suck in with Chatfield-Taylor. I suppose you'll wear a monocle tomorrow morning.

SHERIFF (*melting*). Now that ain't no way to talk, boys. If any of you want a couple of extra tickets, why I'll be more than glad to take care of you. Only don't *kill* it.

SCHWARTZ. Now you're talking!

WILSON. That's more like it.

SHERIFF. Only you fellas got to lend a hand with us once in a while. We got a big job on our hands, smashing this Red menace—

ENDICOTT. We gave you four columns yesterday. What do you want?

SHERIFF (*always the boy for a speech*). That ain't it. The newspapers got to put their shoulders to the wheel. They've got to forcibly impress on the Bolsheviks that the death-warrant for Earl Williams is a death-warrant for every bomb-throwing un-American Red in this town. This hanging means more to the people of Chicago today— (*To* MURPHY, *who is reading a comic supplement.*) This is a *statement,* Jimmie. What's the matter with you?

MURPHY. Aw, go home.

SHERIFF. All right, you'll just get scooped. Now we're going to reform these Reds with a rope. That's our slogan. Quote me if you want to: "Sheriff Hartman pledges that he is going to reform the Reds with a rope."

ENDICOTT. Oh, for Christ's sake, Pinky! We've been printing that chestnut for weeks! (*He goes into the can.*)

SHERIFF. Well, print it once more, as a favor to me.

WILSON. You don't have to worry about the election. You're as good as in now, with the nigger vote coming around.

SHERIFF (*Lafayette, at least*). I was never prejudiced against the Negro race in any shape, manner, or form.

MURPHY. Are *you* still talking?

SHERIFF (*suddenly querulous*). During the race riots I just had to do my duty, that's all. And of course I was misunderstood.

KRUGER. Go on! You're a Southern gentleman, and you know it. (*Phone rings.*)

SHERIFF. Now, boys!

MURPHY. Shoah! (*In bogus Negro dialect.*) Massa Hartman, of the Vahginia Hartmans. (*Phone on small table rings.* MC CUE *heads for it.*)

ENDICOTT (*in the can, his voice rising above the plumbing*). I hear you used to own slaves.

SCHWARTZ (*answering phone*). Press room! (*Into phone.*) Who? Yeah, he's here. . . . For you, Sheriff.

SHERIFF. Me? (*Into phone—very businesslike.*) Sheriff Hartman talking. . . . (*An eagle falling out of the clouds.*) Oh, hello, dear.

KRUGER. Sounds like the ball and chain.

SHERIFF. Why, no, I didn't figure on coming home at all. . . . Well, you see on account of the hanging being so early—

MURPHY. Tell her she's getting a break when you don't go home.

SHERIFF (*winningly*). But you see this is business, dear. You don't think a hanging's any fun for me!

ENDICOTT. Music for this, Ernie!

SHERIFF (*agitatedly motions for silence*). But I have a whole lot to do first —getting things ready.

MURPHY. Why don't you take him out to your house and hang him?

SHERIFF (*fishhooks in his pants*). I'll call you up later, Irma—I'm not in my own office, now. Besides, I've got to meet an alienist. . . . No—alienist. No. Not for me. For Williams.

(HILDY *re-enters, bringing back* JENNIE'S *mop.*)

HILDY (*throwing the mop across the room*). Boy, we cleaned up!

SHERIFF (*hurriedly*). I'll call you later, dear. (*He hangs up; turns on* HILDY.) Now Johnson, what the hell do you mean? Throwing things out of windows. Who do you think you are?

(*During the quieter moments of the remainder of this act,* HILDY *is opening his parcels and putting the contents into his suitcase.*)

HILDY. Who wants to know?

SHERIFF. You think you and Walter Burns are running this town! Well, I'm going to send a bill to the Examiner tomorrow for all the wreckage that's been committed around here in the past year! How do you like that?

HILDY. I think that's swell! You know what else you can do?

SHERIFF (*belligerently*). What?

HILDY. Guess.

SHERIFF. You stick your nose in this building tomorrow and I'll have you arrested!

HILDY. It's damn near worth staying for!

SHERIFF. And I'll tell you another thing, and you can pass it on to Walter Burns! The Examiner don't get any tickets for this hanging after the lies they been printing! You can make up your story like you do everything else—out of whole cloth.

HILDY. Listen, you big pail of lard! If I wanted to go to your God-damn hanging I'd go! See? And sit in a box!

SHERIFF. The hell you would!

HILDY. And I'd only have to tell *half* of what I know, at that!

SHERIFF. You don't know *any*thing.

HILDY. No? Tell me, Mr. Hartman, where'd you spend the night before that last hanging! At the Planter's Hotel with that librarian. Room Six Hundred and Two. And I got two bell boys and a night manager to prove it!

SHERIFF. If I didn't have to go and see that alienist I'd tell *you* a few things. (*Exits.*)

HILDY (*calling after him*). And if I were you I'd get two tickets for the hanging over to Walter Burns pretty fast, or he's liable to come over here and stick a firecracker in your pants!

WILSON. Hey! Hildy! Your girl called up.

HILDY (*stricken*). My girl? When? (*Starts for the telephone.*)

WILSON. Just after you went out. And if you take my advice, you'll call her back.

HILDY. Jesus! Why didn't you tell a fellow!

(WOODENSHOES *re-enters with sandwiches and a bottle of ketchup.*)

MC CUE. *Yea!* Sandwiches.

HILDY (*at phone*). Edgewater two-one-six-four. (*To the rest.*) Was she mad at me?

MC CUE. Did you bring the ketchup?

(*They are crowding about* WOODENSHOES.)

BENSINGER. How about my plain lettuce?

ENDICOTT. A hamburger for me!

SCHWARTZ. I ordered one, didn't I?

KRUGER. You did not! This way, Woodenshoes!

(*They are taking their sandwiches from* WOODENSHOES—ENDICOTT *tosses one at* KRUGER.)

HILDY (*into phone*). Hello, Peggy? . . . Hello. . . . (*His voice becomes romantic.*)

MC CUE. Attaboy! God, I'm starved.

HILDY (*into phone*). Why, darling, what's the matter?

BENSINGER. For God's sake, I said gluten bread.

HILDY (*into phone*). But there isn't anything to cry about.

MURPHY. The service is geting terrible around here.

HILDY (*into phone*). But listen, darling! I had business to attend to. I'll tell you all about it the minute I see you . . . Aw, darling, I just dropped in here for one second. . . . Because I *had* to. I couldn't go away without saying goodbye to the fellows. (*To the others.*) Will you guys talk or something? (*Back to *phone.*) But listen! Sweetheart! . . . Yes, I . . . Of *course* I handed in my resignation . . . Yes, I've got a taxi waiting . . . Right outside.

WOODENSHOES (*uneasily*). Go easy on that ketchup. I'm responsible for that.

HILDY (*into phone*). I've got them right in my pocket, honey . . . Three on the eleven-eighteen. I'm bringing 'em right out, mile a minute.

WOODENSHOES. She says you fellows have got to pay something soon.

HILDY (*into phone*). Aw, darling, if you talk like that I'm going to go right out and jump in the lake. I swear I will, because I can't stand it. Listen! (*He looks around to see if it is safe to continue.*)

KRUGER. We're listening.

HILDY (*trying to lower his voice. With his mouth pasted to the mouthpiece, the following speeches are gargled into phone*). Darling . . . I love you. (*Appropriate music by* KRUGER.) I said . . . I love you. (*Music again.*)

SCHWARTZ. Aw, give him a break, Ernie.

(KRUGER *stops playing.*)

HILDY (*into phone*). That's more like it.

WOODENSHOES. Are you finished with this? (*Reaching for ketchup.*)

MC CUE (*operating the bottle*). No.

HILDY (*into phone*). Feel better now? . . . Well, smile. And say something . . . You know what I want to hear.

SCHWARTZ (*a Cinderella*). Give me a half a one, somebody!

ENDICOTT. Nothing doing.

HILDY (*into the phone*). That's the stuff. That's better . . . Are you all packed? . . . Oh, swell . . .I'll be right there.

WOODENSHOES. You fellas ought to pay her a little something on account. (*Exits.*)

WILSON (*answering Examiner phone*). What do you want?

HILDY. Listen, darling, will you wear that little blue straw hat?

WILSON (*into phone*). Wait a minute—I'll see.

HILDY (*into phone*). And are you all happy now? . . . I bet you're not as happy as I am. Oh, I'll bet you anything you want . . . All right . . . All right . . . I'm on my way . . . Not more than fifteen minutes. *Really* this time . . . Bye. (*Hangs up.*)

WILSON (*his hand over the mouthpiece*). Jesus Christ, Hildy—here's Walter again! Tell him to give us a rest, will you?

HILDY. Oh, bollacks! (*Into phone.*) You're just making a God-damn nuisance of yourself! . . . What's the idea of calling up all the time! . . . *No!* I'm through with newspapers! I don't give a God damn what you think of me! I'm leaving for New York tonight! Right now! This minute! (*Hangs up. Phone rings again. He tears it from the wall and throws it out the window.*)

KRUGER (*calmly*). Wrong number.

MC CUE (*nervous*). For God's sake, Hildy!

SCHWARTZ (*putting out the lights*). You'll get us in a hell of a jam!

BENSINGER. Haven't you got any sense?

HILDY (*yelling out the window*). Tell Pinky to stick that among his souvenirs! (*To the rest.*) If that lunatic calls up again tell him to put it in writing and mail it to Hildebrand Johnson, care of the Waterbury-Adams Corporation, Seven Thirty-five Fifth Avenue, New York City . . .

MURPHY. Put it on the wall, Mike.

ENDICOTT (*going to the rear wall*). Waterbury what?

MC CUE. Adams.

HILDY (*opening a parcel and showing a pale pair of gloves*). How do you like those onions? Marshall Field!

MC CUE. Very individual.

HILDY. Where's my cane?

ENDICOTT. What cane?

HILDY (*suddenly desperate*). Come now, fellas. That ain't funny, who's got my cane?

MURPHY (*in a Central Office manner*). Can you describe this cane?

HILDY (*frantic*). Aw, for God's sake! Now listen, fellas—

KRUGER (*solicitous*). Are you sure you had it with you when you came into the room?

WILSON. Was there any writing on it?

HILDY (*diving into* BENSINGER'S *desk*). Come on! Cut the clowning! Where is it?

BENSINGER. Keep out of my desk! Of all the God-damn kindergartens!

HILDY. Jesus! I only got fifteen minutes. Now, cut the kidding! My God, you fellows have got a sense of humor!

MURPHY. Aw, give him his fairy wand!

ENDICOTT (*a Uranian for the moment,*

he produces cane from trouser leg). Here it is, Gladys.

HILDY. God! You had me worried. (*He picks up his suitcase. Bravura.*) Well, good-bye, you lousy wage slaves! When you're crawling up fire escapes, and getting kicked out of front doors, and eating Christmas dinner in a one-armed joint, don't forget your old pal, Hildy Johnson!

ENDICOTT. Good-bye, Yonson.

MC CUE. So long, Hildy.

MURPHY. Send us a postcard, you big stewbum.

KRUGER. When'll we see you again, Hildy?

HILDY. The next time you see me I'll be riding in a Rolls-Royce, giving out interviews on success-y.

BENSINGER. Good-bye, Hildy.

WILSON. Good-bye.

SCHWARTZ. Take care of yourself.

HILDY. So long, fellows! (*He strikes a Sidney Carton pose in the doorway; starts on a bit of verse.*) "And as the road beyond unfolds—" (*He is interrupted by a terrific fusillade of shots from the courtyard. A roar of voices comes up from the jail yard. For a tense second everyone is motionless.*)

VOICES (*in the courtyard*). Get the riot guns! Spread out, you guys! (*Another volley.*)

WILSON. There's a jail break!

MURPHY (*at window, simultaneously*). Jacobi! What's the matter? What's happened?

VOICES (*in the jail yard*). Watch the gate! He's probably trying the gate! (*A huge siren begins to wail.*)

SCHWARTZ (*out the window*). Who got away? Who was it?

VOICE (*outside*). Earl . . . Wilson!!!

THE REPORTERS. Who? Who'd he say? Earl Williams! It was Earl Williams! He got away!

MC CUE. Holy God! Gimme that telephone! (*He works hook frantically.*) Hurry! Hurry up! Will you? This is important. (*Others are springing for the telephones as searchlights sweep the windows from the direction of the jail.*)

SCHWARTZ. Jeez, this is gonna make a bum out of the Sheriff!

(HILDY *stands paralyzed, his suitcase in his hand. There is a second rifle volley. Two window panes crash within the room. Some plaster falls. Gongs sound above the siren.*)

MC CUE (*screaming*). Look out!

MURPHY (*out of the window*). Where you shooting, you God-damn fools? For Christ's sake! (*Another pane goes.*) Look out where you're aiming, will you?

SCHWARTZ. There's some phones in the state's attorney's office!

KRUGER. Yeah!

(*There is a general panic at the door. The* REPORTERS *leave as if a bomb had broken in a trench.* HILDY *is left alone, still holding his suitcase. It falls. He moves back into the room, absently trailing a chair. Another shot.*)

HILDY. Ahh, Jesus Christ! (*He lets go of the chair and takes one of the telephones.*) Examiner? Gimme Walter Burns! Quick! (*Very calmly he sits on one of the long tables, his back against the wall. Then, quietly.*) Hello, Walter! Hildy Johnson! Forget that! Earl Williams just lammed out of the County Jail! Yep . . . yep . . . yep . . . don't worry! I'm on the job! (*There is a third volley.* HILDY *sails his hat and coat into a corner and is removing his overcoat as the curtain falls.*)

ACT TWO

THE SCENE *is the same as Act I—It is twenty minutes later. Searchlights play outside the windows.* JENNIE, *the scrubwoman, is on stage, sweeping up broken glass and doing a little miscellaneous cleaning.* WOODENSHOES *enters.*

WOODENSHOES. Where are all the reporters? Out looking for him?

JENNIE. They broke all the windows, and pulled off a telephone. Aiiy, those newspaper fellows! They're worse'n anything.

WOODENSHOES. There wasn't any excuse for his escaping. This sort of thing couldn't ever happen, if they listened to me.

JENNIE. Oooh, they'll catch him. Those big lights.

WOODENSHOES. What good will that do Society? The time to catch 'em is while they're little kids. That's the whole basis of my crime prevention theory. It's all going to be written up in the papers soon.

JENNIE. Ooooh, what they print in the papers! I never seen anything like it.

(*She is sweeping.* ENDICOTT *enters and makes for a phone.* WOODENSHOES *watches him.*)

WOODENSHOES. Has anything happened, Mr. Endicott?

ENDICOTT (*into phone*). Endicott calling. Gimme a rewrite man.

WOODENSHOES. You know, this would be just the right time for you to print my theory of crime prevention, that you said you were going to. (*Pulling out a sheaf of documents.*)

ENDICOTT (*into phone, waving him off as if he were a horsefly*). Well, hurry it up.

WOODENSHOES. Now here I got the city split up in districts. I got them marked in red.

ENDICOTT. What? For God's sake, can't you see I'm— (*Into phone.*) Hello! Gill?

WOODENSHOES. But you been promising me you'd—

ENDICOTT (*snatches papers*). All right—I'll take it home and study it. Now for God's sake stop annoying me—I got to work! I can't sit around listening to you! Get out of here and stop bothering me! (*Back to phone.*) Ready, Gill? . . . Now, here's the situation so far.

WOODENSHOES (*to* JENNIE). He's going to take it home and study it. You'll see it in the paper before long. (*Exits.*)

ENDICOTT (*into phone*). Right! . . . At ten minutes after nine Williams was taken to the Sheriff's private office to be examined by this Professor Eglehofer, and a few minutes later he shot his way out . . . No—nobody knows where he got the gun. Or if they do they won't tell . . . Yeah . . . Yeah . . . He run up eight flights of stairs to the infirmary, and got out through the skylight. He must have slid down the rainpipe to the street . . . Yeah . . . No, I tell you nobody knows where he got it. I got hold of Jacobi, but he won't talk. (MURPHY *enters.*)

MURPHY (*crossing to phone*). Outside, Jennie! Outside!

ENDICOTT. They're throwing a dragnet around the whole North Side. Watching the railroads and Red headquarters. The Chief of Police has ordered out every copper on the force and says they'll get Williams before morning.

MURPHY (*into phone*). Hello, sweetheart. Give me the desk, will you?

ENDICOTT (*into phone, after a final look at his notes*). The Crime Commission has offered a reward of ten thousand dollars for his capture . . . Yeah. I'm going to try to get hold of Eglehofer. He knows what's happened, if I can find him. Call you back. (*Hangs up and exits swiftly.*)

MURPHY. For Chris' sake, Jennie! Every time we turn our backs you start that God-damn sweeping.

JENNIE (*picking up her traps*). All right. Only it's dirty. I get scolded.

MURPHY (*into phone*). Murphy talking . . . No clue yet as to Earl Williams' whereabouts. Here's a little feature, though. . . . A tear bomb . . . *tear* bomb . . . criminals cry for it . . .

(SHERIFF HARTMAN *appears in the doorway. He has been running around, shouting a million orders, nervous, bewitched and sweating like a June bride. He is in his shirt sleeves, and his diamond-studded badge of office is visible.*)

MURPHY (*into phone*). Yeh; Tear bomb.

SHERIFF (*as he enters, speaking to someone in the corridor*). To hell with the Mayor! If he wants me he knows where I am.

MURPHY (*into phone*). A tear bomb went off unexpectedly in the hands of Sheriff Hartman's bombing squad.

SHERIFF (*stunned*). What went off?

MURPHY (*into phone*). The following deputy sheriffs were rushed to Passavant Hospital: . . .

SHERIFF. A fine fair-weather friend you are!

MURPHY (*remorselessly, into phone*). Philip Lustgarten . . .

SHERIFF. After all I've done for you!

MURPHY (*phoning*). Herman Waldstein . . .

SHERIFF. Putting stuff like that in the papers!

MURPHY (*phoning*). Sidney Matsburg . . .

SHERIFF. That's gratitude for you! (*He exits.*)

MURPHY (*phoning*). Henry Koo . . .

JENNIE (*going toward door*). Ain't that terrible?

(KRUGER *enters and goes to a phone.*)

MURPHY (*phoning*). Abe Lefkowitz . . .

JENNIE. All those fellows! (*Exits.*)

KRUGER (*at his phone*). Give me rewrite.

MURPHY (*phoning*). And William Gilhooly. Call you back. (*Hangs up and exits.*)

KRUGER (*into phone*). Ready? . . . A man corresponding to Earl Williams' description was seen boarding a southbound Cottage Grove Avenue car at Austen Avenue by Motorman Julius L. Roosevelt. (MC CUE *enters.*) Yeah—Roosevelt. I thought it would make a good feature on account of the name.

MC CUE (*phoning*). McCue talking. Give me the desk.

KRUGER (*phoning*). All right, I'll go right after it. Call you back. (*Exits.*)

MC CUE (*into phone*). Hello. Is that you, Emil? Are you ready? . . . Sidelights on the man hunt . . . Mrs. Irma Schlogel, fifty-five, scrublady, was shot in the left leg while at work scrubbing the eighth floor of the Wrigley Building by one of Sheriff Hartman's special deputies. (*There is a fusillade of shots in the distance.* HILDY JOHNSON *enters.*)

HILDY. There goes another scrublady. (*Goes to phone, but starts arranging notes.*)

MC CUE (*phoning*). No, just a flesh wound. They took her to Passavant Hospital. (*Hangs up. To* HILDY.) Any dope on how he got out?

HILDY. From all I can get they were playing leap frog.

MC CUE. How about Jacobi? Did he say anything to you?

HILDY. Not a word. (MC CUE *goes.*)

HILDY (*quickly picks up his receiver*). Gimme Walter Burns. (*He gets up and closes the door carefully; comes back to his phone.*) Walter? Say, listen. I got the whole story from Jacobi and I got it exclusive . . . That's right, and it's a pip. Only listen. It cost me two hundred and sixty bucks, see? . . . Just a minute—I'll *give* you the story. I'm telling you first I had to give him all the money I had on me and it wasn't exactly mine. Two hundred and sixty bucks, and I want it back. (*Yells.*) Well, did you hear what I said about the money? . . . All right, then here's your story. It's the jail break of your dreams . . . Dr. Max J. Eglehofer, a profound thinker from Vienna, was giving Williams a final sanity test in the Sheriff's office—you know, sticking a lot of pins in him to get his reflexes. Then he decided to re-enact the crime exactly as it had taken place, so as to study Williams' powers of co-ordination. . . . Well, I'm coming to it, God damn it. Will you shut up? . . . Of course he had to have a gun to reenact with. And who do you suppose supplied it? . . . Peter B. Hartman . . . "B" for brains. . . . I tell you, I'm *not* kidding. Hartman gave his gun to the Professor, the Professor gave it to Earl, and Earl shot the Professor right in the belly . . . Ain't it perfect? If the Sheriff had unrolled a red carpet like at a Polish wedding and loaned Williams an umbrella, it couldn't have been more ideal . . . Eglehofer? No, not bad. They spirited him away to Passavant Hospital . . . No, we got it exclusive. Now listen, Walter. It cost me two hundred and sixty bucks for this story, and I want it back . . . I had to give it to Jacobi before he'd cough up his guts. Two hundred and sixty dollars—the money I'm going to get married on . . . Never mind about fine work—I want the money . . . No, I tell you, I'm not going to cover anything else—I'm going away. (PEGGY *appears in the doorway. She is a pretty girl of twenty.* HILDY *has his back to the door.*) Listen, you lousy stiff. I just did this as a personal favor. Now I'm leaving town and I gave Jacobi every cent I got, and I want it back right away! . . . *When* will you send it over? . . . Well, see that you do or I can't get married! . . . All right, and tell him to run. I'll be waiting right here in the press— (*He hangs up and sees* PEGGY. *With a guilty start.*) Hello, Peggy.

PEGGY. What was that, over the telephone?

HILDY. Nothing. I was just telling Walter Burns I was all through, that's all. Hello, darling.

(PEGGY, *despite her youth and simplicity, seems overwhelmingly mature in comparison to* HILDY. *As a matter of fact,* PEGGY *belongs to that division of womanhood which dedicates itself to suppressing in its lovers or husbands the spirit of D'Artagnan, Roland, Captain Kidd, Cyrano, Don Quixote, King Arthur or any other type of the male innocent and rampant. In her unconscious and highly noble efforts to make what the female world calls "a man" out of* HILDY, PEGGY *has neither the sympathy nor acclaim of the authors, yet —regarded superficially, she is a very sweet and satisfying heroine.*)

PEGGY. You haven't done something foolish with that money? Our money!

HILDY. No. No!

PEGGY. You still *have* got the rest of it?

HILDY. Of course. Gee, darling, you

don't think for a minute—

PEGGY. I think I'd better take care of it from now on!

HILDY. Now listen, honey, I can look after a couple of hundred dollars all right. . . .

PEGGY. Hildy, if you've still got that money I want you to give it to me.

HILDY. Now, sweetheart, it's going to be perfectly all right. . . .

PEGGY (*she divines, alas, her lover's failing*). Then you haven't got it.

HILDY. Not—this minute, but I—

PEGGY. You *did* do something with it!

HILDY. No, no. He's sending it right over—Walter, I mean. It'll be here any minute.

PEGGY (*her vocabulary is reduced to a coal of fire*). Oh, Hildy!

HILDY (*a preposterous fellow*). Listen, darling, I wouldn't have had this happen for the world. But it's going to be all right. Now here's what happened: I was just starting out to the house to get you when this guy Williams broke out of jail. You know, the fellow they were going to hang in the morning.

PEGGY (*intolerant of the antics of the Cyrano sex*). Yes, I know.

HILDY. Ah now, listen, sweetheart, I *had* to do what I did. And—and the same thing when it came to the money— (*She turns away.*) Peggy! Now listen. I shouldn't tell you this, but I haven't got any secrets from you. Do you know how this guy escaped? He was down in the Sheriff's office when Hartman—that's the Sheriff—and Eglehofer—that's this fellow from Vienna—

PEGGY. Hildy!

HILDY. Aw, now I can't tell you if you won't listen. I *had* to give him the money so he wouldn't give the story to anybody else. Jacobi, I mean. That's the assistant warden. I got the story exclusive—the biggest scoop in years, I'll bet.

PEGGY. Do you know how long mother and I waited, out at that house?

HILDY. Aw, Peggy, listen. You ain't going to be mad at me for this. I couldn't help it. You'd have done the same thing yourself. I mean, the biggest story in the world busting, and nobody on the job.

PEGGY. I might have known it would happen again.

HILDY. Aw, listen—

PEGGY. Every time I've ever wanted you for something—on my birthday, and New Year's Eve, when I waited till five in the morning—

HILDY. But a big story broke; don't you remember.

PEGGY. It's always a big story—the biggest story in the world, and the next day everybody's forgotten it, even you!

HILDY. What do you mean forgotten? That was the Clara Hamon murder—on your birthday. Now for God's sake, Peggy, it won't hurt to wait five more minutes. The boy's on his way with the money now.

PEGGY. Mother's sitting downstairs waiting in a taxicab. I'm just ashamed to face her, the way you've been acting. If she knew about that money—it's all we've got in the world, Hildy. We haven't even got a place to sleep in, except the train, and—

HILDY. Aw, gee, I wouldn't do anything in the world to hurt you, Peggy. You make me feel like a criminal.

PEGGY. It's all that Walter Burns. Oh, I'll be so glad when I get you away from him.—You simply can't resist him.

HILDY. For God's sake, Peggy, I've told you what I think of him. I wouldn't raise a finger if he was dying. Honest to God.

PEGGY. Then why did you loan him the money?

HILDY. I didn't! You see, you won't listen to me, or you'd know I didn't. Now, listen. I had to give the money to Jacobi, the assistant—

(WOODENSHOES *ushers in* MRS. GRANT. MRS. GRANT *is a confused little widow who has tried her best to adjust her mind to* HILDY *as a son-in-law.*)

WOODENSHOES. Here they are, ma'am. (*Exits immediately.*)

HILDY. Oh, hello, Mrs. Grant—mother. I was just explaining to Peggy—

PEGGY. Mother, I thought you were going to wait in the cab.

MRS. GRANT (*a querulous yet practical soul*). Well, I just came up to tell you the meter's gone to two dollars.

HILDY. Yeah, sure. But that's all right. . . .

MRS. GRANT (*with the wandering egoism of age*). I had a terrible time finding you. First I went into a room where a lot of policemen were playing cards.

HILDY. Yeah—that was—now, I'll tell you what we'll do.

MRS. GRANT. Then I met that policeman and I asked him where Mr. Johnson's office was, and he brought me here.

PEGGY. Now listen, mother, I think you'd better go downstairs and we'll come as soon as we can.

MRS. GRANT (*inspecting*). You've got a big room, haven't you? Where do you sit?

HILDY. Now, I tell you what you do. You and Peggy go on over to the station and get the baggage checked . . . now here's the tickets.

PEGGY. Now, Hildy.

HILDY. I'll be along in fifteen minutes —maybe sooner.

MRS. GRANT. How do you mean—that you aren't going?

HILDY. Of course I am. Now, I'll meet you at the Information Booth—

PEGGY. Come, mother. Hildy has to wait here a few minutes. It's something to do with the office—he's getting some money.

MRS. GRANT (*on familiar ground*). Money?

HILDY. Yeah—they're sending over—it's my salary. They're sending over my salary.

MRS. GRANT (*the voice of womankind*). Your salary? At this hour?

HILDY. They were awful busy, and I couldn't disturb them very well.

MRS. GRANT. The trouble is you're too easy with people—letting them wait till this hour before paying you your salary. How do you know they'll give it to you at all?

PEGGY. Mother, we'll go on over. Hildy'll be along.

MRS. GRANT. Do you know what I'm beginning to think?

HILDY (*apprehensive*). What?

MRS. GRANT. I think you must be a sort of irresponsible type or you wouldn't do things this way. It's just occurred to me you didn't do one blessed thing to help our getting away.

PEGGY. Now you stop picking on my Hildy, mother.

MRS. GRANT. Why, I had to sublet the apartment, and pack all the wedding presents— (MC CUE *enters. Goes to phone, with side glances at the others.*) Why, that's work a man ought to do. You weren't even there to put things in the taxi—I had to give the man fifty cents. And now here you are standing here with the train leaving any minute—

HILDY. Now, mother, I never missed a train in my life. You run along with Peggy—

MC CUE (*into phone*). Hello. McCue talking.

PEGGY. Come on, mother. We're disturbing people.

HILDY. This is my girl, Mac, and her mother. Mr. McCue.

MC CUE (*tipping his hat*). Pleased to meet you. (*Into phone.*) Here's a hell of a swell feature on the man hunt. (*To the ladies.*) Excuse my French! (*Into phone.*) Mrs. Phoebe De Wolfe, eight-sixty-one and a half South State Street, colored, gave birth to a pickaninny in a patrol wagon, with Sheriff Hartman's special Rifle Squad acting as midwives.

MRS. GRANT. Mercy!

MC CUE (*pleased at having interested her*). You oughta have seen 'em, ma'am.

PEGGY. Come on, mother.

HILDY. Listen, mother, you better run along. I'll put my suitcase in the cab.

MC CUE (*phoning*). Well, Phoebe was walking along the street when all of a sudden she began having labor pains. No! Labor pains! Didn't you ever have labor pains? Righto! She was hollering for her husband, who's been missing for five months, when the police seen her. And Deputy Henry Shereson, who's a married man, saw what her condition was. So he coaxed her into the patrol wagon and they started a race with the stork for Passavant Hospital.

HILDY (*to* MC CUE, *as he goes out*). If a boy comes here for me hold him. I'll be right back! (*They are gone.*)

MC CUE (*into phone*). Listen—when the pickaninny was born the Rifle Squad examined him carefully to see if it was Earl Williams, who they knew was hiding somewhere. (*Laughs at his own joke.*) They named him Peter Hartman De Wolfe in honor of the Sheriff, and they all chipped in a dollar apiece on account of it being the first baby ever born in a man hunt. (*The Mayor enters.*) Wait a minute—here's the Mayor himself. Maybe there's a statement. (*Under ordinary circumstances the* MAYOR *is a bland, unruffled soul, full of ease and confidence; a bit stupid, walking as if he were on snowshoes and carrying an unlighted cigar with which he gestures as if it were a wand. The events of the last hour have unhinged him. He is eager for news—even the worst.*)

MAYOR. Don't pester me now, please, I got a lot on my mind.

MC CUE (*into phone*). The Mayor won't say anything. (*He hangs up.*)

MAYOR. Have you seen Sheriff Hartman?

MC CUE. Been in and out all night, your Honor . . .

(MURPHY *and* ENDICOTT *enter.*)

MURPHY. Now listen, your Honor. We've got to have a statement. . . .

ENDICOTT. We go to press in twenty minutes.

MAYOR. I can't help that, boys. I have nothing to say—not at this time.

MURPHY. What do you mean—"not at this time?" Who do you think you are, Abraham Lincoln?

ENDICOTT. Come on, cut the statesman stuff! What do you know about the escape? How'd he get out?

MURPHY. Where'd he get the gun?

MAYOR. Wait a minute, boys . . . Not so fast!

ENDICOTT. Well, give us a statement on the election, then.

MURPHY. What effect's all this going to have on the colored voters?

MAYOR. Not an iota. In what way can an unavoidable misfortune of this sort influence the duty of every citizen, colored or otherwise?

MURPHY. Baloney. . . .

ENDICOTT. Listen here, Mayor. *Is* there a Red Menace or ain't there? And how did he get out of that rubber jail of yours?

MC CUE. Are you going to stand the gaff, Mayor? Or have you picked out somebody that's responsible?

MURPHY (*innocently*). Any truth in the report that you're on Trotsky's payroll?

ENDICOTT. Yeah— the Senator claims you sleep in red underwear.

MAYOR. Never mind the jokes. Don't forget that I'm Mayor of this town and that the dignity of my office . . .

(HARTMAN *enters—the* MAYOR *turns abruptly on him.*) Hartman! I've been looking for you. . . .

ENDICOTT (*leaping at the* SHERIFF). What's the dope, Pinky? How did he get out?

MC CUE. What was he doing in your office?

MURPHY. What's this about somebody gettin' shot?

ENDICOTT. Where did he get the gun?

SHERIFF (*jotting notes on a piece of paper with the hope that he will seem busy*). Just a minute, fellas.

MURPHY. For God's sake, cut the stallin'! Who engineered the getaway?

ENDICOTT. Was it the Reds?

SHERIFF. Just a minute, I tell you. We've got him located!

MURPHY. Who? Williams!

ENDICOTT. Where?

MC CUE. Where is he?

SHERIFF. Out to the place where he used to live . . . on Clark Street . . . Just got the tip.

ENDICOTT. Holy God!

MC CUE. Why didn't you say so?

SHERIFF. The Rifle Squad is just going out.

ENDICOTT. Where are they?

SHERIFF. Downstairs. All the boys are with them.

MURPHY. For the love of God! (MURPHY, ENDICOTT *and* MC CUE *rush out.*)

ENDICOTT (*in the hall*). Hey, there, Charlie!

SHERIFF (*calling into the corridor*). Report to me, Charlie, the minute you get there! I'll be in the building!

MAYOR. Pete, I want to talk to you!

SHERIFF. I ain't got time, Fred—honest. I'll see you after.

MAYOR. Pete, there's one thing I've got to know. Did you yourself actually give Williams that gun?

SHERIFF (*wailing*). The Professor asked me for it. I didn't know what he wanted it for. I thought it was something scientific.

MAYOR. Now listen, Fred— (KRUGER *enters, whistling. Both statesmen become silent and self-conscious.*)

KRUGER (*heading for phone*). Hello, your Honor. Any statement on the Red uprising tomorrow?

MAYOR. What Red uprising?

SHERIFF. There'll be no Red uprising!

KRUGER. The Senator claims the situation calls for the militia.

MAYOR. You can quote me as saying that anything the Senator says is a tissue of lies.

KRUGER (*at phone*). Kruger calling.

SHERIFF. Why aren't you with the Rifle Squad? They've just gone out.

KRUGER. We've got a man with them. (*Into phone.*) Here's a red-hot statement from the Senator. Ready? . . . He says the City Hall is another Augean Stables . . . Augean! . . . Oh, for God's sake!

(*Turns.*) He don't know what Augean means.

MAYOR. The Senator don't know either.

KRUGER. Well, take the rest, anyhow. (*Into phone.*) The Senator claims that the Mayor and the Sheriff have shown themselves to be a couple of eight-year-olds playing with fire. Then this is quote: "It is a lucky thing for the city that next Tuesday is Election Day, as the citizens will thus be saved the expense of impeaching the Mayor and the Sheriff." That's all—call you back. (*Hangs up.*) How are you, Mayor? (*Exits, whistling.*)

MAYOR (*closing the door*). I've got a mighty unpleasant task to perform, Pete—

SHERIFF (*beside himself*). Now listen, Fred, you're just gonna get me rattled.

MAYOR (*inexorably*). Two years ago we almost lost the colored vote on account of that coon story you told at the Dixie Marching Club . . . Mandy and the traveling salesman. . . .

SHERIFF. Why harp on that *now?* . . .

MAYOR. Now you come along with another one of your moron blunders . . . The worst of your whole career.

SHERIFF (*frantic*). Listen, Fred. Stop worrying, will you? Just do me a favor and stop worrying! I'm doing everything on God's green earth! I've just sworn in four hundred deputies!

MAYOR. Four hundred! Do you want to bankrupt this administration?

SHERIFF (*pleadingly*). I'm getting them for twelve dollars a night.

MAYOR. Twelve dollars—! For those God damn uncles of yours? What do you think this is—Christmas Eve?

SHERIFF (*with dignity*). If you're talking about my brother-in-law, he's worked for the city fifteen years.

MAYOR (*bitterly*). I know. Getting up fake tag days! . . . Pete, you're through!

SHERIFF (*stunned*). What do you mean —through?

MAYOR. I mean I'm scratching your name off the ticket Tuesday and running Czernecki in your place. It's nothing personal. . . . And Pete—it's the only way out. It's a sacrifice we all ought to be glad to make.

SHERIFF (*David to Jonathan*). Fred!

MAYOR. Now, Pete! Please don't appeal to my sentimental side. . . .

SHERIFF. I don't know what to say. A thing like this almost destroys a man's faith in human nature. . . .

MAYOR. I wish you wouldn't talk like that, Pete. . . .

SHERIFF. Our families, Fred. My God, I've always looked on Bessie as my own sister.

MAYOR (*wavering and desperate*). If there was any way out . . .

SHERIFF (*as a phone rings*). There is a way out. I've got this Williams surrounded, haven't I? What more do you want? Now if you just give me a couple of hours— (*Into phone.*) Hello. . . . Yes. . . . Hello! (*Wildly.*) Four hundred suppers! Nothing doing! This is a man hunt —not a banquet! . . . The twelve dollars includes everything! . . . Well, the hell with them! Earl Williams ain't eating, is he? (*He hangs up.*) That gives you an idea of what I'm up against!

MAYOR (*hotly*). We're up against a lot more than that with that nutty slogan you invented. "Reform the Reds with a rope." (SHERIFF *winces.*) There ain't any God damn Reds and you know it!

SHERIFF. Yeah, but why go into that now, Fred?

MAYOR. The slogan I had was all we needed to win—"Keep King George Out of Chicago!"

SHERIFF. My God, I ain't had a bite to eat since this thing happened.

MAYOR. Pete, two hundred thousand colored votes are at stake! And we've got to hang Earl Williams to get them.

SHERIFF. But we're *going* to hang him, Fred. He can't get away. (*A knock on the door.*)

MAYOR. What do you mean he can't get away! He *got* away, didn't he? Now look here, Pete— (*Knocking louder.*) Who's out there? . . .

A VOICE (*outside*). Is Sheriff Hartman in there?

SHERIFF (*starts for door; relieved*). Ah! It's for me! (*Opens the door. A small man named* PINCUS *stands there.*) I'm Sheriff Hartman. Do you want me?

PINCUS (*a very colorless and uneffectual person*). Yes, sir. I've been looking all over for you, Sheriff. You're certainly a hard fellow to find.

MAYOR (*annoyed*). What do you want?

PINCUS (*taking a document from his pocket and proffering it to the* SHERIFF. *He smiles in a comradely fashion*). From the Governor.

MAYOR. What's from the Governor?

SHERIFF. Huh?

PINCUS. The reprieve for Earl Williams.

SHERIFF (*stunned*). For *who?*

PINCUS (*amiably*). Earl Williams. The reprieve. (*A ghastly pause.*) I thought I'd never find you. First I had a helluva time getting a taxi—

MAYOR. Wait—a minute. (*Getting his bearings.*) Is this a joke or something?

PINCUS. Huh?

SHERIFF (*bursting out*). It's a mistake —there must be a mistake! The Governor gave me his word of honor he wouldn't interfere! Two days ago!

MAYOR. And you fell for it! Holy God, Pete! It frightens me what I'd like to do to you! Wait a minute! Come here, you! Who else knows about this?

PINCUS. They were all standing around when he wrote it. It was after they got back from fishing.

MAYOR. Get the Governor on the phone, Hartman.

PINCUS. They ain't got a phone. They're duck-shooting now.

MAYOR. A lot of God-damn nimrods.

SHERIFF (*who has been reading the reprieve*). Can you beat that? Read it! (*Thrusts the paper into* MAYOR's *hands.*) Insane, he says! (*Striding over to the messenger.*) He knows God damn well that Earl Williams ain't insane!

PINCUS. Yeah! But I—

SHERIFF. This reprieve is pure politics and you know it! It's an attempt to ruin us!

MAYOR (*reading*). Dementia praecox! My God!

SHERIFF. We got to think fast before those lying reporters get hold of this. What'll we tell 'em?

MAYOR. What'll you tell 'em? I'll tell you what you can tell 'em! You can tell 'em your damn relatives were out there shooting everybody they see, for the hell of it!

SHERIFF. Now Fred, you're just excited. (*Phone rings;* SHERIFF *starts for the phone, talking as he goes.*) We aren't going to get any place, rowing like this.

MAYOR. And you can tell 'em the Republican Party is through in this state on account of you.

SHERIFF (*into phone*). Hello! This is Hartman.

MAYOR (*apoplectic*). And you can add as an afterthought that I want your resignation now.

SHERIFF (*from the phone*). Sssh. Wait, Fred. (*Excitedly, into phone.*) What? Where? . . . Where? My God!

MAYOR. What is it?

SHERIFF. They got him! (*Back to phone.*) Wait a minute—hold the wire. (*To the* MAYOR.) They got Earl Williams surrounded . . . the Rifle Squad has . . . in his house.

MAYOR. Tell 'em to hold the wire.

SHERIFF. I did. (*Into phone.*) Hold the wire.

MAYOR. Cover up that transmitter! (SHERIFF *does so.* MAYOR *faces* PINCUS.) Now listen! You never arrived here with this—whatever it is. Get that?

PINCUS (*blinking*). Yes, I did.

MAYOR. How much do you make a week?

PINCUS. Huh?

MAYOR (*impatiently*). How much do you make a week? What's your salary?

PINCUS (*reluctantly*). Forty dollars.

SHERIFF (*into phone*). No—don't cut me off.

MAYOR. How would you like to have a job for three hundred and fifty dollars a month? That's almost a hundred dollars a week!

PINCUS. Who? Me?

MAYOR. Who the hell do you think? (PINCUS *is a little startled; the* MAYOR *hastens to adopt a milder manner.*) Now listen. There's a fine opening for a fellow like you in the City Sealer's office.

PINCUS. The what?

MAYOR. The City Sealer's office!

PINCUS. You mean here in Chicago?

MAYOR (*foaming*). Yes, yes.

SHERIFF (*at phone*). Well, wait a minute, will you? I'm in conference.

PINCUS (*a very deliberate intellect*). No, I couldn't do that.

MAYOR. Why not?

PINCUS. I couldn't work in Chicago. You see, I've got my family in Springfield.

MAYOR (*desperate*). But you could bring 'em to Chicago! We'll pay all your expenses.

PINCUS (*with vast thought*). No, I don't think so.

MAYOR. For God's sake, why not?

PINCUS. I got two kids going to high school there, and if I changed them from one town to another they'd probably lose a grade.

MAYOR. No, they wouldn't—they'd gain

one! They could go into any class they want to. And I guarantee that they'll graduate with highest honors!

PINCUS (*lured*). Yeah?

MAYOR. And the Chicago school system is the best in the world. (*To* SHERIFF.) Isn't it?

SHERIFF. Far and away! (*Into phone.*) Hold your horses—will you, Mittelbaum. Hurry up, Fred!

MAYOR. Now what do you say?

PINCUS. What did you say this job was?

MAYOR. In the City Sealer's office!

PINCUS. What's he do?

MAYOR (*jumping*). Oh, for God's sake!

SHERIFF. He has charge of all the important documents. He puts the City seals on them.

MAYOR. That's about on a par with the rest of your knowledge! The City Sealer's duty, my friend, is to see that the people of Chicago are not mulcted by unscrupulous butchers and grocers.

SHERIFF. That's what I meant.

MAYOR. It's his duty to go around and test their scales.

PINCUS. Yeah?

MAYOR. But only twice a year.

PINCUS. This puts me in a hell of a hole.

MAYOR. No it doesn't. . . . (*Hands him the reprieve.*) Now remember. You never delivered this, whatever it is. You got caught in the traffic or something. . . . Now get out of here and don't let anybody see you. . . .

PINCUS. But how do I know . . .

MAYOR. Come in and see me in my office tomorrow. What's your name?

PINCUS. Pincus.

MAYOR. All right, Mr. Pincus, all you've got to do is lay low and keep your mouth shut. Here! (*He hands him a card.*) Go to this address. It's a nice homey little place, and you can get anything you want. (*He sees* PINCUS *through the door.*) Just tell 'em Fred sent you. (PINCUS *goes.*)

SHERIFF (*into phone, desperately*). Will you wait, for God's sake? I'll tell you in a minute! (*He turns to the* MAYOR *with a gesture of appeal.*)

MAYOR (*huskily*). All right. Tell 'em to shoot to kill.

SHERIFF. What?

MAYOR. Shoot to kill, I said.

SHERIFF. I don't know, Fred. There's that reprieve if they ever find out.

MAYOR. Nobody reprieved that policeman he murdered. Now do as I tell you.

SHERIFF (*into phone*). Hello, Mittelbaum . . . Listen. (*His voice is weak.*) Shoot to kill. . . . That's the orders—pass the word along. . . . No! We don't want him! And listen, Mittelbaum—five hundred bucks for the guy that does the job. . . . Yes, I'll be right out there. (*Hangs up.*) Well, I hope that's the right thing to do. (*There is a great kicking on the door.*)

HILDY (*outside*). Hey! Who's in there? Open that door!

MAYOR (*en route to the door*). For God's sake take that guilty look off your face. And stop trembling like a horse. (*The* SHERIFF *starts whistling, "Ach, du Lieber Augustine" in what he imagines is a care-free manner. The* MAYOR *opens the door;* HILDY *enters.*)

HILDY. Oh, it's you two! Well, what's the idea of locking the door? Playing post-office? (*Going to phone.*)

SHERIFF (*with elaborate unconcern, as he walks toward the door*). Oh, hello, Hildy.

MAYOR. Come on, Hartman.

HILDY (*into the phone*). Gimme Walter Burns. (*To the others.*) Was there a fellow in here asking for me?

SHERIFF. Did you hear we've got Williams surrounded?

HILDY. Yeah. I heard you only let him out so he could vote for you on Tuesday.

MAYOR. Hartman! (*He pulls* SHERIFF *out of the room.*)

HILDY (*into phone*). Hello, Duffy . . . this is Hildy.Listen, where's Walter? Well, where did he go? God damn it, Duffy, I'm waitin' here for the boy to bring over my money . . . the two hundred and sixty dollars he owes me. . . . Yeah . . . in the press room. He told me the boy was on his way. . . . What the hell are you laughin' about? . . . Listen, Duffy, has that maniac started the money over or not? . . . No, I ain't got time to come over to the office. I'll miss the train. . . . Oh, for God's sake! . . . that double-crossing louse! (*He hangs up.*)

(WOODENSHOES *enters.*)

WOODENSHOES. The trouble is, nobody's using the right psychology. Now you take this aspect of the situation: you got a man named Earl Williams who has escaped . . .

HILDY (*seizing at a straw*). Have you got two hundred and sixty dollars on you?

WOODENSHOES. What?

HILDY. Have you got two hundred and sixty dollars?

WOODENSHOES. No, but I got a way of making it, and more. I know how we can get ten thousand dollars, if you'll just listen. (*Pointing his finger at* HILDY *in the manner of a man letting the cat out of the bag.*) Serchay la femme!

HILDY. What?

WOODENSHOES (*inexorably—for him*). Who is it that's been defendin' this feller Williams right along? Who is it that was hangin' around his room just before the escape happened?

HILDY. O, for God's sake! I ain't got time, Woodenshoes. I got to get two hundred and sixty dollars in the next five minutes!

WOODENSHOES. It's gonna take longer than five minutes. I know where Earl Williams is!

HILDY. He's out at Clark and Fullerton, getting his head blown off. But that don't get me any money.

WOODENSHOES. Earl Williams is with that girl, Mollie Malloy! *That's* where he is!

HILDY (*despairing*). Can you imagine —this time tomorrow I'd have been a gentleman. (DIAMOND LOUIE *enters.* HILDY *leaps for him.*) Thank God! Have you got the dough?

LOUIE. Huh?

WOODENSHOES. She sent him a lot of roses, didn't she?

HILDY. God damn it—the hell with your roses. Gimme the dough. I'm in a hell of a hurry, Louie.

LOUIE. What are you talkin' about?

WOODENSHOES. I'll betcha I'm right. (*Exits.*)

HILDY. Listen, Louie! Do you mean to say Walter didn't give you the dough he owes me?

LOUIE. Walter's pretty sore. You better come over and see him.

HILDY. But that's all settled! Walter and I are like this! (*He illustrates with two twined fingers.*) I just did a swell favor for him—scooped the whole town! We're pals again! I'm telling you.

LOUIE. He just told me be sure and get you, you know what I mean?

HILDY (*frantically*). I tell you that's fixed! By God, Louie, do you think I'd try to put something over on you?

LOUIE. What do you mean fixed? He wants to talk to you. I been looking all over—

HILDY. But I did talk to him! Everything's all right! I swear to you!

LOUIE (*weakening*). Jesus, Hildy, I don't know.

HILDY. Certainly! My God, he *wants* me to go! Now listen, Louie—you've always got a lot of money—will you help me out? This two hundred and sixty bucks—Walter's sending a boy with it, but I can't wait! I gotta catch a train, see? Now—

LOUIE. What two hundred and sixty bucks?

HILDY. The money I spent on the story! He's sending it over, but I want *you* to take *that* and give *me* the money *now!*

LOUIE. Oh! You want two hundred and sixty dollars—*now.*

HILDY. *YES!*

LOUIE. Well, that's a lot of money, you know what I mean?

HILDY. You can get it from Walter, I'll give you my I. O. U.

LOUIE. Lis'en, Hildy, I'd like to help you out. But I've been stung on so many I. O. U.'s lately that I made myself a promise.

HILDY. But this ain't an I. O. U. . . . It's money comin' to me from the paper!

LOUIE. What have you got to show for it?

HILDY. Louie, listen! My whole future is dependent on this. My girl's waitin' at the train. I've just got fifteen minutes to get there. If you'll help me out, I swear . . . Honest to God . . .

LOUIE (*interrupting*). Two hundred and sixty dollars . . . that's a big gamble!

HILDY. It's no gamble at all. I'll write out a note to Walter sayin' for him to give you the money he owes me.

LOUIE. Well, I'll tell you what I'll do with you. I'll take a chance.

HILDY (*as he writes out note*). That's the stuff!—You're a white man, Louie, you're a real white man. God—I knew I could depend on you.

LOUIE. I tell you what I'll do. I'll give you a hundred and fifty dollars for the debt.

(HILDY *stares at him.*)

HILDY. That's just takin' advantage, Louie.

LOUIE. That's the best I can do.

HILDY. Well, Christ! I lose almost a hundred bucks by that.

LOUIE. All right. (*Puts money back in*

his pocket.) Have it your own way.

HILDY. Make it two hundred.

LOUIE. One hundred and fifty!

HILDY. All right, give me the dough. (DIAMOND LOUIE *takes the paper that* HILDY *has written out and reads it very carefully, folds it, puts it in his pocket and then proceeds to count out the money, as* HILDY *is looking for his hat and coat.*)

LOUIE. Here you are. (HILDY *grabs the money and begins to count it.*) Well, good-bye and good luck. I'll look you up in New York—if there's anything wrong with this. (LOUIE *exits.*)

HILDY (*counting the money*). Ten, twenty, thirty, thirty-five, forty-five—(*Gets confused; starts again.*) Ten, twenty, thirty, forty, forty-five, fifty-five—(*In trouble again; he gives up.*) The hell with it. Anyway, I get out of this lousy place. They can take their story now and— (HILDY *pockets the money and starts hurriedly to pick up his parcels, including his old felt hat in a paper bag. As he starts for the door he is arrested by a sound at the window. The sound is caused by* EARL WILLIAMS *falling through the window into the room.* MR. WILLIAMS *is a little harmless-looking man with a mustache. He is coatless and is shod with death-house sneakers. He carries a large gun. He is on the verge of collapse and holds on to a chair for support. He talks in an exhausted voice.* HILDY, *at the sight of him, drops his packages and stands riveted.*)

EARL. They're after me with search lights . . .

HILDY. Put—put down that gun!

EARL (*supporting himself*). It ain't loaded. I fired all the bullets already.

HILDY. Holy God Almighty! . . .

EARL (*weakly—handing* HILDY *the gun*). I surrender. . . . I couldn't hang off that roof any longer.

HILDY. Holy God!— Get away from that window. (EARL *obeys.* HILDY *strides to the door and locks it. He comes back and stands staring at* EARL *and scratches his head.*) Well, for God's sake . . .

EARL. I'm not afraid to die. I was tellin' the fella that when he handed me the gun.

HILDY. Shut up a second! (*He locks the door.*)

EARL (*babbling on*). Wakin' me up in the middle of the night . . . talking to me about things they don't understand. Callin' me a Bolshevik. I ain't a Bolshevik. I'm an anarchist. (HILDY *is pulling down the blinds and putting out the lights.*) It's got nothin' to do with bombs. It's the one philosophy that guarantees every man freedom. (*Weakly.*) All those poor people being crushed by the System. And the boys that were killed in the war. And in the slums—all those slaves to a crust of bread—I can hear 'em cryin'—

HILDY. Be quiet! The hell with that. Shut up! . . . will you? (*He is hunting for a hiding place.*)

EARL. Go on . . . take me back and hang me . . . I done my best. . . . (*He crumples and falls to the floor.* HILDY *stands for a second, desperate. His eye falls on the toilet door. He considers, picks up* WILLIAMS *and hurriedly dumps him inside the toilet. He closes the door and springs for the telephone.*)

HILDY (*into phone*). Hello. . . . Gimme Walter Burns, *quick!* (*Second phone rings.* HILDY *hesitates, then answers it, propping first receiver between ear and shoulder.*) Hello! . . . Hello! . . . Oh, hello, Peggy. . . . Listen, for God's sake have a heart, will you? Something terrific has happened! (*Into first phone.*) Walter? Hildy . . . No, the hell with that. Listen—come right over here. . . . Come over here *right away*. . . . Wait a minute. (*Into second phone.*) For God's sake, Peggy, quit bawling me out, will you? I'm in a hell of a jam! (*Back to* WALTER.) Walter! Get this—I only want to say it once. . . . I got Earl Williams. . . . Yes! . . . Here in the press room! . . . Honest to God! . . . For God's sake, hurry! I need you. . . . I will. (*Hangs up. Into* PEGGY'S *phone again.*) Listen, darling, this is the biggest thing that ever happened. . . . Now, wait! Don't cry. Wait till I tell you. (*Lowers his voice.*) I just captured Earl Williams! (*In an intense whisper.*) Earl Williams . . . the murderer! I got him. . . . For God's sake, don't tell anybody. . . . Aw, Peggy . . . Peggy . . . I can't. . . . I can't now! . . . Good Lord! Don't you realize . . . I *know,* but Peggy . . . (*She has hung up.*) Hello, Peggy . . . Peggy! (HILDY *hangs up the phone dejectedly. During the last few speeches, there has been a knocking on the door.* HILDY *glares apprehensively and holds himself ready for fight. He moves to the door, and as he approaches it, cries.*) Who is it? (*There is no answer.* HILDY *opens the door cautiously.* MOLLIE *bounds in like a wildcat. He seizes her and wrestles with her.*) Wait a minute! What the hell do *you* want?

MOLLIE (*wildly*). Where they gone? You know where they are.

HILDY. Get outa here, Mollie!

MOLLIE. They got him surrounded. They're gonna shoot him—like a dog.

HILDY. Listen! They're lookin' for you, too! If you're smart, you'll get outa here.

MOLLIE. For God's sake, tell me where they've gone. I ain't afraid of them, the yella murderers . . .

HILDY. I'll tell you where they are. They're out at Clark Street! That's where they are! Clark and Fullerton!

MOLLIE. Where? Where? . . . (*The toilet door opens and* EARL WILLIAMS *appears, dazed and blinking.* MOLLIE *sees him.*) Oh! (*A knock on the outer door is heard.*)

HILDY (*with a desperate look at the door*). Oh, for Christ's—! . . . Sh—! (*With a desperate gesture for silence, and tiptoeing towards the door.*) Who is it?

WOODENSHOES (*outside*). It's me.

HILDY. What do you want, Woodenshoes?

WOODENSHOES (*outside*). I got some important information for you . . . a clue . . .

HILDY. I'll be right with you. I'm making a personal call. . . . (*Turning to the two, tensely.*) Get back in there! (*Indicating toilet.*)

MOLLIE. What's this . . . a double cross?

HILDY. Damn it! I'm trying to save him. . . .

WOODENSHOES (*outside*). This is very important.

MOLLIE (*to* EARL). What are *you* doing here?

HILDY (*to* MOLLIE.) Keep him *quiet!* It's a cop! (*On his way to the door.*) I'll get rid of him . . . (*He opens the door cautiously and steps quickly into the hall, leaving his arm behind him, his hand on the inside knob of the door. Loud and friendly.*) Hello, Woodenshoes! What's on your mind?

(*During the ensuing scene a hardly audible conversation takes place between* HILDY *and* WOODENSHOES. HILDY's *shoulder is visible in the door.*)

EARL. Thank you for those roses . . .

MOLLIE. How did you get here? Does anybody know?

EARL. I came down the rainpipe. I didn't mean to shoot him. I don't know what happened.

MOLLIE. But what are you going to do? You can't stay here! They'll get you!

EARL. I don't care any more.

MOLLIE. You've got to hide! You've got to hide somewhere! The rats!

EARL. No. Don't do anything. I'm ready to go. I don't care. It's better to die for a cause than the way most people die—for no reason.

MOLLIE. You won't die. They'll never get you.

EARL. I ain't important. It's humanity that's important, like I told you. Humanity is a wonderful thing, Mollie.

MOLLIE. No, it ain't. They're just dirty murderers. Look what they done to you . . . and to me . . .

EARL. That's because they don't know any better.

MOLLIE. You're too good for 'em . . . that's why.

EARL. You're good, too.

MOLLIE (*with wonder*). Me?

EARL. Yeah, I think you're wonderful. . . . I wrote out a statement today and left it with Mr. Jacobi, so that when I was dead people would understand what I meant. There was a lot about you in it. I said you were the most beautiful character I ever met.

MOLLIE (*blinking and dazed*). Yeah?

HILDY (*entering, indicating toilet*). Get back in there! The fellows are coming down the hall now! (*He locks the door.*)

MOLLIE. They'll find him there!

HILDY. Well, there isn't any place else. (*He looks helplessly around the room; at that moment someone tries the door knob.*)

MOLLIE. There's somebody!

HILDY. Sssh!

ENDICOTT (*outside*). Who locked the door?

HILDY. Coming right away, Mike. (*Whispers to* MOLLIE.) He's got to go in there!

ENDICOTT (*outside*). Well, for God's sake, hurry.

MOLLIE. Oh, my God!

HILDY. Wait a minute! I got an idea! (*Springs and opens the desk.*) Can you get in this desk?

WILSON (*outside*). What the hell's going on in there? (*Starts to pound on door.*)

EARL. What good'll it do?

HILDY. We'll get you out in ten minutes.

WILSON (*outside*). *Open up* there, will you?

HILDY. All right, all right. God damn it!

EARL. Please, don't talk like that in front of her.

MOLLIE (*to* EARL). Go on! Please! Please!

EARL. They'll find me, anyhow. (*More pounding.*)

HILDY. All right, I'm coming! (*To* EARL.) Keep dead quiet. Don't even breathe.

MOLLIE. I'll be right here. I won't leave you.

ENDICOTT (*outside, shouting*). Hey, what the God-damn hell?

HILDY. Keep your shirt on! (*He opens the door.*) What are you trying to do! Kick down the building? (ENDICOTT *and* WILSON *enter. Head for phones at back.*)

ENDICOTT. Kind of exclusive, ain't you? (*Sees* MOLLIE.) Oh! (*Elaborately.*) I beg your pardon.

WILSON. City desk, please! What's the idea of locking the door?

HILDY. I was interviewing her.

ENDICOTT (*at phone*). Gimme the city desk. . . . What was he doing to her?

WILSON. With the blinds down. (MURPHY *enters.*)

MURPHY. Where the hell you been, Hildy? There's the damnedest Hallowe'en going on—the whole police force standing on its ear. (*At phone.*) Murphy talking. Gimme the desk.

WILSON (*into phone*). Wilson speaking. No luck yet on Williams. Call you back! (KRUGER *enters.*)

KRUGER. God, I never was so tired in my life.

HILDY. Any news?

MURPHY (*into phone*). This is Murphy. . . . Well, they surrounded the house, only Williams wasn't there.

KRUGER. Gimme a rewrite man.

(MC CUE *enters.*)

MC CUE (*entering*). Jesus, what a chase!

MURPHY (*into phone*). Wait a minute. They shot somebody, anyhow. Here you are! Ready? Herman Schulte, the Sheriff's brother-in-law. He was leading the squad through the house and was looking under a bed when Deputy John F. Watson came in the room and mistook him for Earl. Shot him right in the pants. Yeah. A bull's eye. Right. (*Hangs up.*)

HILDY (*on edge*). He always had lead in his pants.

MC CUE (*at his phone*). McCue talking. Gimme the desk.

KRUGER (*phoning*). This is Kruger, out with Hartman's deputies. . . . Yeah? . . . I'm in the drug store at Clark and Fullerton. Well, call me back if you don't believe me. (*Hangs up.*)

MC CUE (*into phone*). That so? I'll check on it. (*Hangs up.*) There's something doing at Harrison Street Station. (*Into phone.*) Gimme Harrison 2500. Hurry it, will you please?

KRUGER (*to* MOLLIE, *who is in the swivel chair in front of the desk*). What's the idea, Mollie? Can't you flop somewhere else?

MURPHY. Yeah, parking her fanny in here like it was a cathouse. (*Takes a sniff of the air.*) Fleur de Floosie, she's got on.

KRUGER (*neighing like a horse*). Makes me passionate!

MURPHY. Go on, Mollie, put it somewhere else. Go out and stink up Clark Street.

MOLLIE (*nervous and twitching*). You lay off me!

MC CUE. Look out—she'll start bawling again. (*Into phone.*) I'll hold the wire. Only don't forget me.

HILDY. Let her alone, fellas. She's not doing anything.

MURPHY (*to* HILDY). What the hell are you two so chummy about?

ENDICOTT. Yeah, they were locked in here together when we come along.

WILSON. Wouldn't open the door.

MC CUE. You'll be out of training for your honeymoon—playing pinochle with this baby.

MURPHY. I thought you were going to catch a train.

KRUGER. He was running around here ten minutes ago with his pants on fire about going to New York.

ENDICOTT. Told us he was interviewing her.

MURPHY. What are you trying to do? Scoop us?

HILDY. I'm waiting here for Walter. He's coming over with some dough.

MC CUE (*phoning*). Hello, Sarge. McCue. I hear you got a tip on Williams.

WILSON. Look, she's got the shakes. What the hell you making faces about?

ENDICOTT (*singing childishly*). She's jealous because Hildy's going to be married.

HILDY. Go on— Show 'em you can smile through your tears. Relax.

MOLLIE. You let me alone—all of you. (SCHWARTZ *enters.*)

MC CUE (*into phone*). Yeah! What's the address!

SCHWARTZ. Hello, fellas. What the hell, Hildy? You still here?

ENDICOTT. Yeah, and trying to hang something on us, if you ask me. What's the low-down, Hildy?

SCHWARTZ. Who the hell pulled these shades down?

MC CUE (*turning from phone*). Hey! this looks good. An old lady just called up the detective bureau and claims Williams is hiding under her piazza.

ENDICOTT. Tell her to stand up.

MURPHY. Who you got there?

MC CUE. The Captain.

MURPHY. Let me talk to him. (*Taking the phone.*) Hello, Turkey. . . . How's your gussie mollie? . . . I hear this guy Williams is hiding in your mustache. . . . Yeah? Well, get your nose out of the way. (*Hangs up. Points to* MOLLIE's *crossed and highly visible legs.*) Oooh! Lookit! Pike's Peak!

MC CUE. Listen, fellows, that sounds like a pretty good tip. What do you say?

HILDY. If you boys want to get out I'll cover this end for you.

ENDICOTT. Aw, the hell with chasing around any more. I spent a dollar forty on taxis already.

KRUGER (*flat on his back*). Don't let's do any more going out.

SCHWARTZ (*who has gone to the window*). If you ask me, I got a hunch Williams ain't anywhere they been looking for him.

WILSON. How do you mean?

SCHWARTZ. Well, I just been talking to Jacobi about that roof he's supposed to have jumped off of. Look! Now there's that skylight he got out of.

ENDICOTT. Where?

MC CUE (*looking out*). Jesus, how could he get from there to the ground?

SCHWARTZ. That's just the point. Jacobi's gone up there with a couple of cops to look over the whole roof.

MC CUE (*leaning out*). I tell you what he could have done, though. Look! He could have jumped over to this roof. That's only about four feet.

ENDICOTT. Yeah, he could have done that, all right.

KRUGER (*wearily*). I'm pretending there ain't no Earl Williams.

SCHWARTZ. And that's why I'm telling you guys that I don't think this guy Williams is anywhere they been looking for him. I got a stinking hunch he's right in this building.

HILDY (*derisive*). Hanging around like a duck in a shootin' gallery, I suppose! You're a lot of bright guys. . . .

MC CUE (*still looking*). It'd be easy, once he got on this roof. . . .

HILDY (*with nervous hilarity*). Hey— Sherlock Holmes, what correspondence school did you graduate from?

SCHWARTZ. What's the matter with that? He could come down the rainpipe and crawl into any one of these windows on this side. . . .

KRUGER. Well if the story's going to walk right in the window—!

HILDY. The master minds at work! Why don't you guys go home—he'll probably *call* on you. . . .

(BENSINGER *enters and approaches his desk.* MOLLIE, *sitting in his chair, is hidden from him at the moment by one or two of the* REPORTERS.)

BENSINGER. Hello, Hildy. Thought you were going to New York. (HILDY *has sprung into action with* BENSINGER's *entrance.* BENSINGER *sees* MOLLIE.) For God's sake, what's she doing in my chair? (MOLLIE *springs up.*) Is that the only place you can sit? That's my property and I don't want anybody using it!

HILDY (*leaning against the closed desk*). Nobody's using it, Roy. Everything's all right.

BENSINGER (*anxiously*). Any of you fellows got some aspirin?

ENDICOTT. No, sweetheart, but I got some nice cyanide.

BENSINGER (*sitting down*). Cut the kidding, fellows. I tell you I'm sick.

SCHWARTZ. How about a good truss? I'll sell it to you cheap.

HILDY. What's the matter, Roy? Off your feed?

BENSINGER. If I haven't got a good case of grippe coming, I miss my guess. (*Reaching for desk cover.*) Get out of the way, will you?

HILDY (*not moving*). I hope you didn't get it off me.

BENSINGER. I got it off somebody. Everybody using my phone all the time—it's a wonder I ain't caught anything worse. (*Pushing* HILDY *slightly.*) Look out, I got to get my cup.

HILDY (*doubling up as if with a violent cramp*). Wait a minute, will you?

BENSINGER (*frightened*). What's the matter?

HILDY (*faintly*). I don't know, oh—

BENSINGER. Don't you feel all right?

HILDY. No. (*Coughs violently in* BENSINGER'S *face.*)

BENSINGER. Don't do that!

HILDY (*weakly*). Do what?

BENSINGER. Cough on a guy! Jesus!

HILDY. Well, I don't know what's the matter. I suddenly got a pain right—(*Vaguely indicates his throat*) and a kind of rash on my chest. (*Opening his shirt.*)

BENSINGER (*recoiling*). What? You've probably got some disease!

MURPHY. Sure! He's got the pazooza!

HILDY (*advancing on* BENSINGER, *tries to take his hand*). Feel! Ain't that fever?

BENSINGER (*retreating from the desk*). Hey, cut it out! It may be diphtheria!

HILDY. I woke up this morning, and had yellow spots all over my stomach.

BENSINGER. That ain't funny!

KRUGER. For God's sake, Roy, can't you see he's kidding you. (HILDY *following* BENSINGER, *seizes him.*)

BENSINGER. Let go of me! You may have something contagious! If you're sick go to a hospital! (HILDY *coughs in his face.*) For the love of God!

MURPHY. It's no worse than a bad cold, Roy.

HILDY (*opening his mouth*). Can you see anything in there? Aaah!

BENSINGER. Listen, fellows! You ain't got any sense, letting him hang around here. We'll all catch it, whatever it is! (*They all laugh.*) All right, laugh! But I'm going to get this place fumigated!

MURPHY. The hell you are!

BENSINGER (*furiously*). The hell I ain't. We got to breathe this air. I'm gonna get Doc Springer and clean this whole place up! You God-damn maniacs. (*Exits.* HILDY *leans weakly up against the desk and laughs hysterically.*)

ENDICOTT. What's the idea, Hildy? Now he'll be burning sulphur for a week like last time. . . .

MC CUE. Yeah, you're leavin', but we gotta work here, with all them stink pots. . . . What a sense of humor you got.

SCHWARTZ. Now look here. What about Williams? Let's get the cops and search the building. What do you say?

ENDICOTT. I could use that reward.

MURPHY. What the hell could you do with ten grand? . . .

ENDICOTT. You could have a girl in every room at the Sherman Hotel for that. . . .

MURPHY. You'd never get past the basement.

MC CUE. It would be funny if we found him right here in the building.

SCHWARTZ. What do you say? Should we get the cops?

MURPHY. Call up Lieut. Callahan, Mac. Tell him we got a hot tip.

HILDY. Wait! What do you want to call the cops for? Suppose he *is* in the building. They'll grab all the reward and you guys won't get a smell.

SCHWARTZ. Huh?

WILSON. That's right.

HILDY. Listen! Each of us take a floor and whoever finds him, we split it up. What do you say?

WILSON. That's not a bad idea.

KRUGER. I'll stay here.

HILDY. Two grand apiece! Why we could retire for life! You could pay off all those loan sharks, Jimmie, and have enough left to stay stinko forever!

MC CUE. I don't know, getting my can blown off.

HILDY. What else is it good for? . . . Besides, he can't hurt anybody. . . . What do you say? Do you want to try it?

MRS. GRANT (*enters, in a very righteous mood*). Well!

HILDY (*stricken*). Now—now, listen, mother—

MRS. GRANT. Don't you mother me! If you've got anything to say for yourself you come downstairs and say it to Peggy.

HILDY. Listen, mother, tell Peggy I'll be downstairs in five minutes, will you? Will you go down and tell her that?

MRS. GRANT. No, sir—I don't move out of here without you.

HILDY. Listen, mother, you don't understand. Now I told Peggy—

MRS. GRANT. I know what you told her! A lot of gibberish about a murderer!

HILDY. No—no!

MRS. GRANT. I don't care if you *did* catch him, you come with me this minute!

THE REPORTERS. I knew something stunk around here. Who says he caught him? What's going on. What do you mean caught a murderer? *etc.* (*In the midst of this babel,* WOODENSHOES *enters; stands listening.*)

HILDY. No, No! I don't know what she's talking about! I didn't tell her any such thing.

MRS. GRANT. Yes, you did!

MOLLIE. He never told her that!

HILDY. I said I was *trying* to catch one, that's all! You got it balled up, mother!

MURPHY (*to* MOLLIE). What do *you* know about it? How do you know he didn't?

MOLLIE. Let go of my arm!

ENDICOTT. Hildy and that tart were in here together!

WOODENSHOES. Yah! Yah! She's the one that knows! Ask *her!*

MURPHY (*wheeling on him*). What do you mean she knows?

WOODENSHOES. Serchay la femme! (*To* MOLLIE.) Where's Earl Williams?

MOLLIE. How the hell should I know?

WOODENSHOES. Where have you got him hid?

MURPHY (*viciously*). Who you holding out on, Hildy? Come clean, or God damn it, we'll knock it out of you! (*The* REPORTERS *surround* HILDY *menacingly.*)

MC CUE. Yeah. What the hell! Sock him, Jimmie!

ENDICOTT. You dirty double-crosser.

MOLLIE (*wildly*). Wait! You God damn stool pigeons! He don't know where Earl Williams is. I'm the one that knows.

ENDICOTT. What do you mean you know? (*The* REPORTERS *turn on* MOLLIE.)

WOODENSHOES. Where is he?

MOLLIE. Go find out, you lousy heels. You don't think I'm gonna tell!

WOODENSHOES. You'll tell all right! We'll make you . . .

MOLLIE (*slowly backing toward the door*). Yeah? . . . Yeah . . . the hell I will.

HILDY (*who has remained riveted to the desk*). Let her alone . . . she's goofy! (MOLLIE *lunges suddenly for the door.*)

THE REPORTERS. Look out! . . . Close that door . . . For Chris' sake! Don't let her get away. (*She is headed off at the door.*)

MC CUE. You ain't gettin' out o' here, Mollie.

ENDICOTT. Now where is he? In the building?

MC CUE. Where you hidin' him?

MOLLIE. I ain't gonna squeal! I ain't gonna squeal!

MURPHY (*approaching her slowly*). Come on, you lousy tart! Before we kick your teeth out!

ENDICOTT. D'ye want us to call the cops and give you the boots?

MURPHY. Go on, Woodenshoes. Slap it out of her!

WOODENSHOES (*reaching for her*). Come on now. Where is he before I hurt you?

MOLLIE (*tearing away from him, wild and blubbering*). Take your hands off me, you God-damn kidney foot! (*She snatches at a chair and swings it at the slowly advancing circle of men.*) Let me alone or I'll knock your God-damn heads off. . . .

ENDICOTT. Put down that chair!

SCHWARTZ. Get around—get on the side of her.

MOLLIE (*backing away, swinging her chair*). No you don't! You bastards! Keep away from me!

KRUGER. Grab her.

MOLLIE (*with a last wild look at the circling foe*). You'll never get it out of me. . . . (*She hurls the chair at their heads and screams.*) I'll never tell! Never! (*She leaps for the open window and disappears. Her scream of terror and exultation is heard as she drops through the darkness to the ground. The* REPORTERS *stand riveted for an instant, powerless before the tragedy. Then they rush forward. An assortment of awed and astonished oaths rise from them. They lean out of the window.* WOODENSHOES *the Theorist stands sick at heart. His body is doubled up with pain for a moment. Through the babble of cries his voice comes thickly.*)

WOODENSHOES. Oh! I never thought she'd do that! That's terrible. . . .

MRS. GRANT (*coming out of a trance*). Take me out of here! Take me out of here! Oh, my God! (*She collapses in a chair.*)

THE REPORTERS (*at the window*). She ain't killed. . . . No. . . . She's moving. . . . Get the cops, Woodenshoes. . . . Come on fellas. . . .

HILDY. Holy God—the poor kid. . . .

the poor kid.

(*Voices come from the jail yard—"Hey Carl. . . . Get a doctor! What the hell! Who is it? What happened?" etc. The* REPORTERS *rush out to get to* MOLLIE. HILDY *stands dazed, looking out of the window.* MRS. GRANT *moans through her hands. As the vibrations subside a newcomer is standing in the door. This is* MR. WALTER BURNS, *the Managing Editor. Beneath a dapper and very citizen-like exterior lurks a hobgoblin, perhaps the Devil himself. But if* MR. BURNS *is the Devil he is a very naif one. He is a Devil with neither point nor purpose to him—an undignified Devil hatched for a bourgeois Hallowe'en. In less hyperbolic language* MR. BURNS *is that product of thoughtless, pointless, nerve-drumming unmorality that is the Boss Journalist—the licensed eavesdropper, trouble maker, bombinator and Town Snitch, misnamed The Press. At this moment* MR. BURNS, *in the discharge of his high calling, stands in the door, nerveless and meditative as a child, his mind open to such troubles as he can find or create.*)

HILDY (*seeing him*). Walter! My God—did you see that?

WALTER (*quietly*). Yes. Where is he?

HILDY. She jumped out of the window.

WALTER. I know. . . . Where is he, I said?

HILDY (*looking out of the window*). She's moving! Thank God she ain't killed herself!

WALTER. Come to, Hildy! Where have you got Williams?

HILDY (*still absorbed in the* MOLLIE *matter*). Huh? He's—he's in the desk. (*As* WALTER *goes to desk.*) Thank God she ain't dead. (WALTER *opens desk a crack.*)

EARL (*muffled*). Let me out, I can't stand it!

WALTER. Keep quiet! You're sitting pretty.

MRS. GRANT (*staring at the Editor*). What's the matter?

WALTER (*he wheels*). Who the hell is that?

HILDY. It's my girl's mother.

MRS. GRANT. What are you doing? Oh, my God!

WALTER. Shut up!

MRS. GRANT. I won't shut up! That girl killed herself. Oh! You're doing something wrong. What's in there? (DIAMOND LOUIE *appears in the doorway.*)

HILDY. Now, mother, please!

WALTER. Take her out of here, will you?

MRS. GRANT. What did you say?

HILDY. Now look here, Walter—

WALTER. Louie, take this lady over to Polack Mike's, and lock her up. See that she don't talk to anyone on the way!

MRS. GRANT. What's that? What's that?

HILDY (*startled*). Aw, now, Walter, you can't do that!

LOUIE (*calls*). Hey, Tony!

MRS. GRANT. Don't you touch me!

WALTER. Tell 'em it's a case of delirium tremens.

LOUIE. Tony, give me a hand with this lady.

HILDY (*helplessly*). Listen, Walter, this'll get me in a hell of a jam. . . . (*To* MRS. GRANT *who, a hand over her mouth, is being dragged off, her heels trailing.*) Now don't worry, mother, this is only temporary. . . . Honest to God, Walter . . .

MRS. GRANT (*vaguely heard*). Peggy, Peggy! Oh, my God! (*Exit* TONY, LOUIE *and* MRS. GRANT. HILDY *starts out.*)

WALTER (*grabs his arm*). Where the hell do you think you're going?

HILDY. Let go of me! I gotta get my girl! She's downstairs in a cab all alone.

WALTER. Your girl! Good God, what are you? Some puking college boy! Why, in time of war you could be shot for what you're doing—for less than you're doing!

HILDY. To hell with you—there's your story—locked up in that desk! Smear it all over the front page— Earl Williams caught by the Examiner—and take all the credit. . . . I covered your story and I covered it God damn right. . . . Now I'm gettin' out. . . .

WALTER. You drooling saphead . . . What do you mean—a story? You've got the whole city by the seat of the pants!

HILDY. I know all about that, but . . .

WALTER. You know hell—You got the brains of a pancake. . . . Listen, Hildy, if I didn't have your interests at heart would I be wastin' time now arguin' with you! You've done somethin' big—you've stepped into a new class . . .

HILDY (*D'Artagnan never gave Richelieu an ear more startled or more innocent*). Huh?

WALTER. Listen, we'll make such monkeys out of these ward heelers that *nobody* will vote for them—not even their *wives.*

HILDY. Expose 'em, huh . . .

WALTER. Expose 'em! Crucify 'em! We're gonna keep Williams under cover till morning so's the Examiner can break the story exclusive. . . . Then we'll let the Senator in on the capture—share the glory with him.

HILDY. I see—I see! (*Blinking and warming up.*)

WALTER. You've kicked over the whole City Hall like an applecart. You've got the Mayor and Hartman back against a wall. You've put one administration out and another in. . . . This ain't a newspaper story—it's a career. And you standin' there bellyachin' about some girl. . . .

HILDY. Jesus, I— I wasn't figuring it that way, I guess. We'll be the white-haired boys, won't we?

WALTER. Why, they'll be naming streets after you. Johnson Street! You and I and the Senator are going to *run* this town. . . . Do you understand that?

HILDY. Yeah. . . . Yeah! But—wait a minute—we can't leave Williams here. . . . . One of those reporters'll . . .

WALTER. We're going to take him over to my private office right away . . . Where's the Examiner phone?

HILDY. That one. The red one. How the hell you gonna do it? They'll see him!

WALTER. Not if he's inside the desk. We'll carry the desk over. (*Into phone.*) Hello! Examiner. Give me Duffy. . . . I'd have had him there now if you hadn't give me such an argument.

HILDY. You can't take that out. It's crawling with cops outside.

WALTER. We'll lower it out of the window with pulleys. Quit stallin'. (*To* HILDY.) Hildy! Get that machine and start pounding out a lead, will you. . . . Come on—snap into it. . . .

HILDY. How much you want on it? . . .

WALTER. All the words you got. . . .

HILDY. Where the hell is there some paper?

WALTER (*into phone*). Hello. . . . Hello!

HILDY (*moving for* BENSINGER's *desk*). Can I call the Mayor an animal at bay?

WALTER. Call him a nigger if you want to! Come on! Come on!

HILDY. How about that time he had his house painted by the fire department.

WALTER. Give him the works. . . . (*Into phone.*) Hello, Duffy. Get set! We got the biggest story in the world. Earl Williams caught by the Examiner . . . exclusive. . . . (HILDY *has opened the drawers of* BENSINGER's *desk and in a frantic search for paper is tossing play manuscripts, syringes, patent medicines and old socks in the air.*)

WALTER (*continuing into phone*). Duffy! Send down word to Butch McGuirk I want ten huskies from the circulation department to lam right over here—press room criminal courts building. That's what I said—Butch McGuirk. (*To* HILDY.) He'll get that desk out—nothin' ever stopped those boys yet. (HILDY *has unearthed a full package of* BENSINGER's *personal stationery. He now picks up the typewriter.*) What if they start shootin'?

WALTER. Fine! (*Into phone.*) Now listen, Duffy. I want you to tear out the whole front page. . . . That's what I said—the whole front page . . . out . . . (*Into phone*). Johnson's writing the lead. . . .

(PEGGY *enters—a desperate and strident antagonist.*)

PEGGY. Hildy!

WALTER. What the hell do you want?

PEGGY. Hildy!

HILDY (*holding the typewriter in his arms. Dazed*). What?

WALTER. Listen, Miss, you can't come in here! (*Into phone.*) To hell with the Chinese earthquake! . . . What's that?

HILDY. Listen, darling—

PEGGY. Where's mother?

WALTER (*into phone*). I don't care if there's a *million* dead.

HILDY. Peggy, I got to ask you to do something! A big favor!

PEGGY. You're not coming!

WALTER (*into phone*). What? I don't hear you.

HILDY. Now don't get sore and fly off the handle, darling. What happened was—

PEGGY. You're *not! Are* you? Tell me, Hildy! Tell me the truth!

WALTER (*into phone*). Take all those Miss America pictures off Page 6. Wait a minute, Duffy. (*Turns.*) Now look here, little girl—

PEGGY (*wheels on* WALTER). You're doing this to him! He was going and you stopped him!

HILDY. Something terrific's happened,

Peggy! Wait till I tell you! I couldn't—

WALTER. You'll tell her nothing! She's a woman, you damn fool!

PEGGY. Well, I'm not going to let you do it! You're coming right now! With me!

WALTER. Holy God!

HILDY. But it's the biggest chance of my life. Now listen, darling—

WALTER (*frenzied*). Shut up, will you?

PEGGY. You don't *want* to marry me! That's all!

HILDY (*putting down the typewriter*). That ain't true! Just because you won't listen you're saying I don't love you when you know I'd cut off my hands for you! I'd do anything in the world for you! Anything!

WALTER (*into phone*). Hello, Duffy! What? . . . What's that? . . . To hell with the League of Nations! Spike it!

PEGGY. You never intended to be decent and live like a human being! You were lying all the time!

HILDY. Peggy, don't keep saying that!

WALTER (*into phone*). What's that? What?

PEGGY. Lying! That's what you were! Just lying!

HILDY (*his tortured male spirit takes refuge in hysteria*). All right! If that's what you think!

WALTER (*shouting at the lovers*). H. Sebastian God! I'm trying to concentrate!

PEGGY. I see what you are now! You're just a bum! Like him— (*Indicates* WALTER) and all the rest!

HILDY. Sure! That's what I am!

WALTER (*into phone*). No! Leave the rooster story alone—that's human interest!

PEGGY. You're just a heartless selfish animal without any feelings! (*To* WALTER.) And you're worse! It's all your fault and if you think I'm going to put up with it—

WALTER. Shut up, will you? . . . (*Into phone.*) Duffy, let me talk to Butch—

HILDY. Shut up, will you? Yeah! That's what I am! A bum! Without any feelings! And that's all I want to be!

WALTER (*into phone*). Get a hold o' Butch as fast as you can.

PEGGY. You never did love me or you couldn't talk to me like that! (*The desk top opens slowly and* EARL WILLIAMS *sticks his head out.*)

WALTER (*screaming across the room*). Get back in there—you God-damn turtle . . . (*The desk top falls, the fugitive disappears within and* PEGGY, *her heartbreak audible in her sobs, moves blindly toward the door.*)

HILDY (*sitting before his typewriter calls after her, his voice tormented but his egoism intact*). If you want me you'll have to take me as I am instead of trying to turn me into some lah de dah with a cane! I'm no stuffed shirt writing peanut ads. . . . God damn it—I'm a newspaper man. . . . (PEGGY *exits, her sobs filling the room and corridor.*)

WALTER. Shut up! (*Into phone as the curtain is falling.*) Hello, Duffy! The edition gone in yet? . . . Well don't. . . . Never mind the mail trains. . . . You ain't working for the advertising department. . . . The hell with Marshall Field's! Stick on this wire!

HILDY (*has started typing. The click of the keys stops suddenly and he rips the piece of copy paper from the machine. He is not quite himself—he has made an error in his lead*). . . . God damn it——

CURTAIN

ACT THREE

The same scene, five minutes later. HILDY *is typing furiously.* WALTER *is pacing up and down. He finally picks up the receiver, which has been standing on the table. Into phone, with moderate excitement.*

WALTER. Duffy. . . . Duffy! (*To* HILDY.) God damn it! I told him to stay on that phone. If I had a few people who did what they were told I could get something accomplished. . . . I bet he never told 'em to take taxis. . . . Butch and the gang are probably *walking* over here. . . . (*Looking out of the window.*) Oh, for Chris' sake . . . Now the *moon's* out! (HILDY *types on.* WALTER *skitters to the desk and taps three times.* EARL *taps back three times from within.*) Fine! Three taps is me! Don't forget! . . . You're sitting pretty now. Got enough air? (*He raises the roll top an inch or two and fans air in with his hand.*) Is that better? (*Closing the desk and going to phone.*) Lam into 'em, Hildy! Below the belt! Every punch! (*Into phone, with great sarcasm.*) Hello! . . . Duffy! Where the hell you been? Well, the hell with your diabetes! You stick on this phone! Listen, did you impress it on Butch to take a taxi—that every minute counts? Who's he bringing with him? What do you mean, you don't know? But you told Butch it was life and death, huh? All right, stick on the wire! (*Putting down receiver.*) Duffy's getting old. . . . Well, Butch is on the way, Hildy. All we got to do is hold out for fifteen minutes.

HILDY (*over his typing*). The boys'll be back. They'll be coming in to phone.

WALTER. I'll handle them. It's that three-toed Sheriff I'm worrying about. If he starts sticking his snoot into this . . . (*Cudgeling his brain*) I wonder if we could arrest him for anything? (HILDY *has never ceased his typing.*) Did you ever get the dope on that stenographer he seduced?

HILDY (*over his shoulder*). That was the coroner.

WALTER. Haven't we got *any*thing on him—besides graft?

HILDY (*thoughtfully*). He's got an idiot kid in the asylum.

WALTER (*depressed*). I don't see how we can use that against him. (*Brightening.*) Wait a minute! Idiot kid. Idiot kid. . . . (*He meditates, then sighs.*) No, that's impractical . . . (*Approaching* HILDY.) What's your lead?

HILDY (*with authorly pride*). "While hundreds of Sheriff Hartman's paid gunmen stalked through Chicago shooting innocent bystanders, spreading their reign of terror, Earl Williams was lurking less than twenty yards from the Sheriff's office where . . ."

WALTER. That's *lousy!* Aren't you going to mention the Examiner? Don't we take *any* credit?

HILDY. I'm putting that in the second paragraph. . . .

WALTER. Who the hell's going to read the second paragraph? Ten years I've been telling you how to write a newspaper story—My God, have I got to do everything? Get the story? Write the story? . . .

HILDY. Listen, you bastard! I can blow better newspaper stories out of my nose than you can write!

WALTER (*cackling*). "While hundreds of paid gunmen are out taking a walk . . ." God, that stinks! You ought to go back to chasing pictures!

HILDY. Yeah?

WALTER. You were *good* at that!

HILDY. You ungrateful bastard! Who wrote the Fitzgerald confession? Who wrote Ruth Randall's diary? How about the Dayton flood? Even the telegraph operator was crying!

WALTER. All right, make me cry now! (*Into phone.*) Duffy! Listen, Duffy. What's the name of that religious editor of ours? The fellow with the dirty collar? Sipper what? Well, tell the Reverend Sipperly I want to see him right away! . . . (*To* HILDY.) Do you know what I'm gonna do?

HILDY. Shut up, or I'll throw this typewriter at your head!

WALTER (*happily*). I'm going to get the Reverend Sipperly to make up a prayer for the City of Chicago—right across the top of the paper! . . . "Our Father Who art in Heaven—There were four hundred and twenty-one murders in Chicago last year!" All in religious lingo, see? Eight columns Old English Boldface! The God-damnedest prayer you ever heard. . . . (*Awed at his own resourcefulness.*) Christ, what an idea!

HILDY. You better pray that this desk will float out of the window over to the paper.

WALTER. Wait a minute, Hildy. . . . (*The Pentecostal fire upon him.*) Wait, wait! . . . I got an inspiration! Now take this down, just as I say it! (*He yanks a page from the typewriter.*)

HILDY (*leaping*). Some day you're going to do that, Walter, and I'm gonna belt you in the jaw . . .! You God-damn Know-it-all!

WALTEP (*chanting*). Here's your lead: "The Chicago Examiner again rode to the rescue of the city last night in the darkest hour of her history! (*Lowering his voice.*) Earl Williams—Earl Williams, the Bolshevik Tiger, who leaped snarling from the gallows upon the flanks of the city, was captured . . ."

HILDY. I got you! I got you! . . .

WALTER. Go on from *there!* (HILDY *is hurriedly putting another sheet into the machine as the door knob is rattled. A pause.*)

HILDY. What do you want to do?

BENSINGER'S VOICE (*outside*). What's the idea of locking that door?

HILDY. That's Bensinger. That's his desk.

WALTER. What's his name again? (*The door knob is rattled violently.*)

HILDY. Bensinger. Reporter for the Tribune. . . . Covers the building.

BENSINGER'S VOICE. Open this door, will you? Who's in there?

WALTER. I'll handle him! The Tribune, eh? Watch me. (*He opens the door.* BENSINGER *appears.*)

BENSINGER (*entering*). Ain't you got any more sense than to . . . (*Sees* WALTER. *Is overcome at this visitation.*) Oh, hello, Mr. Burns. . . . Why, quite an honor, having you come over here.

WALTER (*casually*). Hello, Bensinger.

BENSINGER. Excuse me. I just want to— (*Starts for the desk.*)

WALTER (*blocking his path*). Quite a coincidence, my running into you tonight. . . . Isn't it, Hildy?

HILDY. Yeah.

BENSINGER. How do you mean?

WALTER. I was having a little chat about you just this afternoon—with Mr. Duffy.

BENSINGER. Is that so? (*Essaying a pleasantry.*) Nothing detrimental, I hope.

WALTER. I should say not! That was one swell story you had in the paper this morning.

BENSINGER (*deeply moved*). Well, I'm glad you think so, Mr. Burns. Did you care for the poem?

WALTER. The poem? . . . The poem was great! I got a big kick out of that.

BENSINGER (*blinking at these sweet words*). Did you like the ending? (*He recites.*)

"... And all is well, outside his cell
But in his heart he hears
The hangman calling and the gallows falling
And his white-haired mother's tears . . ."

WALTER (*overcome*). Heartbreaking! Isn't it, Hildy? Bensinger, how would you like to work for me?

BENSINGER. What!

WALTER. I mean it. We need somebody like you. All we got now is a lot of lowbrows and legmen. Like Johnson, here. (*Pushing* BENSINGER *farther from the desk.*) I tell you what you do. Go over and talk to Duffy now. I just had him on the phone. You'll catch him if you hurry.

BENSINGER. You mean seriously, Mr. Burns?

WALTER. I'll show you how serious I am. . . . (*Clinging to* BENSINGER'S *pants, he takes him to the phone. Into phone.*) Duffy! I'm sending Bensinger over to see you. (*To* BENSINGER) Marvin, isn't it?

BENSINGER. No. Roy. Roy V.

WALTER. Funny I should forget that! (*Into phone.*) Roy Bensinger, the poet. Put him right on the staff!

BENSINGER. Right away, you mean?

WALTER (*into phone*). Never mind what doing . . . He'll tell you. No, I'll talk salary with him right here. (*To* ROY.) How much you getting on the Tribune, Roy?

BENSINGER. Seventy-five.

WALTER. Bensinger, I'll give you a hundred and a by-line. (*Into phone.*) He's to get a hundred and a by-line, Duffy. Tell the cashier. Let him have everything he wants. He can use the big desk in the corner. (*To* BENSINGER, *dropping receiver.*) Now hustle right over to the office and tell Duffy I've—I've assigned you to write the human interest side of the man hunt. I want it from the point of view of the escaped man. (*Acting it out.*) He hides, cowering . . . afraid of every light, of every sound . . . hears footsteps . . . his heart going like that . . . And all the time they're closing in . . . get the sense of an animal at bay!

BENSINGER. Sort of a Jack London style?

WALTER. Exactly. Now you ain't got a minute to lose. Hop right over to the office.

BENSINGER. Well, I don't know about quitting the Tribune that way, Mr. Burns. It's not quite ethical. . . .

WALTER. What did they ever do for you? . . . They've never considered your interests—that is, from what I hear. . . .

BENSINGER. Well, between you and me they have given me a pretty rotten deal. The way they handle my copy's a shame —just butcher it.

WALTER. Your copy will be sacred on the Examiner. I guarantee that personally. . . . (*He edges* BENSINGER *toward the door.*)

BENSINGER (*the artist*). You can't lop off the end of a story and get the same effect. The whole *feeling* goes . . .

WALTER. Of course. Now I want a real Bensinger story tomorrow morning, with a crackerjack poem on the side. (*He has him nearly to the door.*)

BENSINGER (*indicating his desk*). I got my rhyming dictionary in . . .

WALTER. It don't have to rhyme! Now duck!

BENSINGER. Gee, I'm terribly grateful, Mr. Burns. (*Pausing in the doorway.*) Do you suppose there might be an opening some time as foreign correspondent? I parlay a little French, you know.

WALTER (*shaking hands with him and pushing him out*). That'll all depend on yourself. I'll keep you in mind.

BENSINGER (*on his way to Garcia*). Well, au revoir, mon capitaine!

WALTER (*never at a loss in any language*). Bon jour! (WALTER *closes the door and skips to the phone. Into phone.*) Duffy! Listen. Now get this! A God damn Tribune sneak is coming over to get a job. Yeah, Bensinger, the fellow I told you about. Now listen, handle him with kid gloves and tell him to get busy writing poetry. No . . . no! We don't want him. But wait till he gets through. Then tell him his poetry stinks and kick him down the stairs. . . . (*Lays receiver down. To* HILDY.) His white-haired mother's tears! (*Picks up* HILDY'S *copy.*) Come on, Hildy, tear into it! Don't sit there like a frozen robin!

HILDY (*coming out of the ether*). You've just bitched up my whole life! That's what you've done!

WALTER (*oblivious to this mood*). Listen, Hildy. We ought to have our plans all set when Butch gets here. All we can look for out of that guy is pure, peasant strength . . . A mental blank. (*Sentimentally.*) But he'd go through hell for me!

HILDY. What a fine horse's bustle I turned out to be!

WALTER (*as before*). The window's *out*. . . . We'll have him pick it up and walk right out of the building with it. With ten guys it'll be a cinch.

HILDY. She was the most wonderful girl I'll ever know . . . (WALTER *looks at him in horror and disgust.*) She had spirit, brains, looks . . . everything!

WALTER. Who the hell you talking about?

HILDY. My girl! God damn it! Who do you think?

WALTER. What are you going to do? Start mumbling about your girl *now?* You got a story to write!

HILDY. I practically told her to go to hell—like she was some waitress!

WALTER. You acted like a man for the first time in your life! Now, don't start crawling now!

HILDY. I'll never love anybody else again! They don't come like that twice in a man's life.

WALTER. You'll sleep it off. Now listen, Hildy. I got enough on my mind!

HILDY. When she was sick in the hospital and you sent me on that wild goose chase all over Kentucky for three weeks she never even complained. . . .

WALTER. Ha, ha. Sick in the hospital!

HILDY. Damn it, she was! She nearly died!

WALTER. I see. She didn't complain, but she just nearly died! That's all!

HILDY (*almost to himself*). I would have been on the train now . . . I would have been . . .

WALTER (*confidentially*). Listen, Hildy. *I* was in love once—with my third wife. I treated her white—let her have a maid and everything! I was sweet to her!

HILDY. Who cares about your God damned wife?

WALTER. I trusted her. Then I let her meet a certain party on the Tribune and what happened? One night I came home unexpectedly—I let myself in through the bathroom window—and there they were! In bed.

HILDY. I don't want to hear about your troubles. I got enough. . . .

WALTER (*interrupting ecstatically*). The very next morning, what do I find in the Tribune, all over the front page? *My traction story,* I'd been saving for two months!

HILDY. You know a lot about women! You and your God-damn stable of tarts! You never met a decent woman! You wouldn't know what to *do* with a pure girl! . . .

WALTER (*owlishly*). Oh, yes I would!

HILDY. You take that back!

WALTER (*deciding to reason with his young friend*). What do you think women are? Flowers? Take that dame that shot the dentist! And Mrs. Vermilya! Husband comes home all worn out, hungry, takes a spoonful of soup and falls dead! Arsenic! And Mrs. Petras! Burning her husband up in a furnace! When you've been in this business as long as I have you'll know what women are! Murderers! Borgias!

HILDY. My God, I'm a sap! Falling for your line of crap . . . ! Naming streets after me!

WALTER. Now, listen, Hildy. You've had a good rest. Get back on the story. That's all you got to do. . . . (*Hands him a pocket flask.*) Here. You're just nervous.

HILDY. *I'll* take that! . . . (*Goes to the water cooler. Pouring.*) I'll get stewed tonight, and I'm gonna stay stewed for the rest of my life! Yeah, I'll be a newspaperman! Right in your class! (*The door knob is tried.*)

WALTER (*whispering*). Shut up!

HILDY. On my pratt in a monkey cage!

WALTER. Shut up, you *fathead!* (HILDY *drinks.* WALTER *approaches the door.*) If that's Bensinger again, we'll crown him and throw him in the can for keeps! (*To the door.*) Who is it?

DIAMOND LOUIE (*outside*). Hello, Boss.

WALTER. It's Louie. . . . (*He opens the door.* DIAMOND LOUIE *appears, bearing some evidence of a mishap. His hat is crushed, face bruised, clothes torn.* WALTER *sees this with alarm.*) My God, what's the matter!

HILDY (*frantically*). Where's the old lady?

WALTER. What did you do with her?

HILDY. What the hell happened?

WALTER. You been in a fight?

LOUIE (*still out of breath*). Down Wentworth Avenue. We were going sixty-five miles an hour, you know what I mean?

WALTER. Take the mush out of your mouth!

HILDY. Where's the old lady!

LOUIE. I'm *telling* you! We run smack into a police patrol. You know what I mean? We broke it in half!

HILDY. My God! Was she hurt?

WALTER. Where is she? Tell me! . . .

HILDY. For God's sake, Louie! . . .

LOUIE. I'm *telling* you. Can you imagine bumping into a load of cops? They come rolling out like oranges!

HILDY (*seizing him*). What did you *do* with her, God damn you!

WALTER. What became of her, I'm asking you!

LOUIE. Search me! When I come to I was running down Thirty-fifth Street! Get me?

HILDY. You were with her! You were in the *cab,* weren't you!

LOUIE (*exposing his bruised scalp*). *Was* I! Tony got knocked cold!

WALTER. You God-damn butter-fingers! I give you an old lady to take somewhere and you hand her over to the cops!

LOUIE. What do you mean, I hand her? The patrol wagon was on the wrong side of the street!

WALTER (*bitterly*). Oh, my God! She's probably squawking her head off in some police station! Now everything is *fine.*

LOUIE (*holding his head*). I don't think she's talking much, you know what I mean! (*He winks reassuringly.*)

HILDY. My God! Was she killed?

WALTER (*hopefully*). Was she? Did you notice?

LOUIE. Say, with that alky rap and the bank job and the big blow on my hip! I should stick around asking questions from a lot of cops!

HILDY (*overcome*). Oh, my God! Dead! That finishes me! . . .

WALTER. Listen, Hildy. That's Fate. What will be, will be!

HILDY (*wildly*). What am I going to say to Peggy, for God's sake! What'll I *tell* her? . . .

WALTER. You're never going to see her again. Snap out of it! Would you rather have the old dame dragging the whole police force in here? . . .

HILDY. I killed her! I did it! Oh, my God, what can I do *now?* How can I ever face her? . . .

WALTER (*becoming the entire Foreign Legion*). Listen, Hildy, if it was my own mother, I'd carry on, you know I would!

HILDY. You God-damn murdering bastard!

WALTER (*crescendo*). No matter how I felt! If my heart was breaking! I'd carry on! For the paper!

HILDY (*to* LOUIE). Where was it? I'll go out!

WALTER. You stay here! I'll find out everything! (*Into phone*) Duffy! . . . Just a minute. . . . (*To* LOUIE.) Where was it?

LOUIE. Wentworth and Thirty-fourth . . . near the corner . . .

WALTER (*into phone*). Call up the Thirty-fifth Street station and ask Nick Gallagher if he's got a report on any old lady that was in a smash-up at Thirty-fourth and Wentworth. . . . (*To* HILDY.) What's her name?

HILDY (*brokenly*). Mrs. Amelia Grant.

WALTER (*into phone*). Millie Grant. About . . . fifty-seven? (*With an enquiring look at* HILDY.) Refined. White hair.

Blue eyes. Black cotton stockings. She was wearing rubbers. (*To* HILDY, *pleased.*) How's that for noticing?

HILDY (*grabbing a phone*). Gimme an outside wire.

WALTER. Never *mind*. We'll get the dope right here . . . in two minutes! (*Another phone rings.*)

HILDY (*into phone*). Gimme Wentworth, Four, five, five, seven! . . .

WALTER (*answering the other telephone in guarded tones*). Hello. Hello. Who? (*Wildly.*) Hello, Butch! Where are you!!

HILDY (*into phone*). Passavant Hospital? Gimme the Receiving Room, will you?

WALTER. Hotel? You mean *you're* in a hotel? What are you doing there! Ain't you even *started?!*

HILDY (*into phone*). Hello, Eddie, Hildy Johnson. Was there an old lady brought in from an auto smashup? . . .

WALTER (*panic*). Oh, for . . . (*Screaming.*) H. Sebastian God! Butch! Listen, it's a matter of life and death, Butch! *Listen!*

HILDY (*into phone.*) Nobody? (*Jiggles hook.*) Archer three one two four. . . .

WALTER (*into phone*). I can't hear you! You got who? Speak up! A What?!!! . . . Holy God, you can't stop for a dame *now!*

HILDY (*into phone*). Is this the German Deaconess Hospital?

WALTER (*howling*). I don't care if you've been trying to make her for six years! Now, listen, Butch! Our whole lives are at stake! Are you going to let some blonde pushover ruin everything? . . . What do you mean—an hour? It'll be too late in an hour!

HILDY (*into phone*). Hello, Max. Hildy Johnson. Was there an old lady . . .

WALTER. *Butch!!* I'd put my arm in the fire for you up to here! (*Indicates up to where.*) I'd go through hell for you! Now you ain't gonna double cross me.... She does? All right—put her on the wire. *I'll* talk to her. . . . *Hello!* . . . Oh, hello, Madam! Now listen here, you God-damn bum . . . You can't keep Butch away from his duty! . . . What! *What!!!* . . . What kind of language is that! Hello, hello . . . (*Turning to* LOUIE *hanging up the telephone.*) That tub of guts! Lousy whore-headed flannel mouth! (*Into phone.*) Duffy! (*To* HILDY.) I'll *kill* 'em—both of them! I'll butter this town with their brains! (*Into phone.*) Duffy! (*To the world.*) Mousing around with some big blonde Annie! *That's* co-operation! (*Screaming into Examiner phone.*) Duffy!

HILDY (*to* WALTER). Shut up, will you? (*Into phone.*) You sure! Nobody?

WALTER (*a howl*). Duffy! (*Throwing the receiver to the desk.*) I ought to know better than hire anybody with a disease! (*To* LOUIE, *panting.*) Louie! It's up to you!

LOUIE (*loyally*). Anything you want, boss.

WALTER. Beat it out and get me hold of some guys, will you?

LOUIE. Who do you want?

WALTER (*trembling*). I want anybody with hair on their chests! Get them off the streets—anywhere! Offer them anything —only get them! (*Confidentially.*) Listen, Louie. We got to get this desk out of here!

LOUIE (*surveys the desk calmly.*) Is it important?

WALTER. Is it important!!! Louie, you're the best friend I got. I'd go through hell for you and I know you won't fail me. Get me enough people to move it! Do you understand that? Now, beat it! And remember, I'm relying on you!

LOUIE (*departing*). You know me. The shirt off my back.

WALTER (*yelling after him*). Don't bump into anything! (*He locks the door.*)

HILDY (*emotionally, into phone*). Calumet two one hundred . . .

WALTER. That lousy immigrant'll flop on me! I know it. (*Bitterly.*) Can you imagine Butch laying up with some whisker at the Revere House! At a time like this! Listen, Hildy . . . (*Confidentially.*) If Louie don't come back in five minutes, we'll get it out alone! There's millions of ways! We can start a fire and get the firemen to carry it out in the confusion!

HILDY. Do anything you damn please! . . . (*Into phone.*) Ring that number, will you?

WALTER (*very excited*). We don't even have to do that. We'll get the Chicago Historical Society to claim it as an antique. We can move it out in a decent normal manner ourselves! Just the two of us!

HILDY. I don't give a God damn what you do!

WALTER. Come on, Hildy! Come here and see if we can move it!

HILDY (*into phone*). Hello! Hello! Is this the Lying-in Hospital? Did you have an auto accident in the last hour?

WALTER. Will you come here?

HILDY (*into phone*). Oh, I see. I beg your pardon.

WALTER. Right when I'm surrounded, with my back against the wall, you ain't going to lie down on me!

HILDY (*jiggling the phone hook*). I'm going to lay down on you and spit in your eye, you murderer!

WALTER. Scared, huh? Yellow running out of your collar!

HILDY. I don't care what you think! I'm going to find my girl's mother! (*Madly jiggling the hook.*) Oh, for God's sake!

WALTER. Your girl! You and Butch McGuirk! Woman lovers!

HILDY (*hangs up phone with a bang*). God damn it! I'm going to go *out* and find her! (*Starts for door. At that instant there comes a loud knock.*)

WALTER. Who's that? Don't open that!

HILDY. The hell I won't! I'm going to the morgue! To . . . look! . . . (*He flings the door open. The* SHERIFF, *accompanied by two Deputies*—CARL *and* FRANK—*surrounded by* MC CUE, KRUGER *and* MURPHY, *bar his exit.*)

THE REPORTERS. Oh, there he is! Say Hildy! Wait a second, *etc.* (HILDY *is struggling past them. The* SHERIFF *grabs him.*)

SHERIFF. Just a minute, Johnson!

HILDY. Let go of me! What the hell's the idea?

THE REPORTERS. What's your hurry? We want to see you! *etc.*

HILDY. Take your God damn paws off me!

SHERIFF. Hold him, boys!

WALTER (*to the* SHERIFF). Who the hell do you think you are, breaking in here like this?

SHERIFF. You can't bluff me, Burns! I don't care who you are or what paper you're editor of!

HILDY. God damn it! Let me go! (*Hysterically.*) Let me go, fellas! Something's happened to my girl's mother!

SHERIFF. Hang on to him!

THE REPORTERS. We know what you're up to! Going out to get Williams, probably! The door was locked! He and Mollie were talking! They know where he is! *etc.*

HILDY (*retreating back into the room before* HARTMAN *and his deputies.*) Listen, guys! I don't know anything, I tell you! There's been an accident—I just been calling up the hospitals! I was just going out to the morgue to see if she was there! Now . . .

SHERIFF. Johnson, there's something very, very peculiar going on. . . .

HILDY. Listen, Pinky! You can send somebody *with* me if you want to! If you don't believe me!

SHERIFF. I wasn't born yesterday, Johnson. Now the boys tell me you and Mollie . . .

HILDY. Nobody's trying to put anything over on you! Now, I'm getting out of here and you can't stop me!

MURPHY. You're not going anywhere! He's got the story sewed up, Pete! He and his God damn boss. That's why he's here!

WALTER (*purring*). If you've got any accusations to make, Hartman, make them in the proper manner! Otherwise I'll have to ask you to get out!

SHERIFF (*pop-eyed*). You'll ask me to *what?*

WALTER. I'll ask you to get out.

SHERIFF (*to his deputies*). Close that door! Don't let anybody in or out!

MURPHY. Come on, Pinky! Give him a little third degree!

SHERIFF. Johnson, I'm going to the bottom of this! Now then, come clean! What do you know about Williams? Are you going to talk or aren't you?

HILDY. What the hell do *I* know about Williams?

SHERIFF. All right, boys! Take him along. I got ways of making him talk. (HILDY *struggles.*)

HILDY. Look out, you . . . !

MC CUE. What's the use of fighting, Hildy? (THE REPORTERS *swarm around* HILDY. *Shouts of "I got him." "No, you don't!" "Hey, what you doing?" "Paste him!" "Aw, Hildy! What the hell!" etc.* HILDY'S *voice rises out of the din.*)

HILDY. Say what the hell's the idea?

THE DEPUTIES. He's got a gun on him! Look out! He's got a gun! He's got a gun!

HILDY. No, you don't! Hey, Walter!

WALTER. What is it? Here!

SHERIFF. Gimme that! (*Takes the gun.*)

HILDY (*resisting*). That's mine! . . .

MURPHY. Jesse James, huh! The drug store cowboy!

MC CUE. He's been going to the movies. Two-gun Johnson!

KRUGER. The terror of Wilson Avenue

beach!

SHERIFF (*frozen, looking at the gun*). Where did you get this?

HILDY. I got a right to carry a gun if I want to.

SHERIFF. Not *this* gun!

WALTER (*easily*). I can explain that, Hartman. He was having some trouble with the Durkin story and I gave it to him . . . to defend himself!

SHERIFF. Oh, you *did!* . . . Well, that's very, *very i*nteresting! This *happens* to be the gun that Earl Williams shot his way out with!

THE REPORTERS. What? What's that? *etc.*

WALTER (*to* HARTMAN). Are you trying to make me out a liar?

SHERIFF (*wildly*). I know my own gun, don't I?

MURPHY (*bitterly to* HILDY). Getting married, huh!

KRUGER. Maybe Williams was gonna be his best man.

SHERIFF (*trembling*). Where is he? Where you got him?

WALTER (*sympathetically*). You're barking up the wrong tree, Hartman.

SHERIFF. I'll give you three minutes to tell me where he is!

HILDY. He went over to the hospital to call on Professor Eglehofer!

SHERIFF. What!!!

HILDY. With a bag of marshmallows. (*The* SHERIFF *stands silent, a gypsy; then streaks wildly for the toilet and throws open the door.*)

WALTER. Take a magazine along.

THE REPORTERS. Come on, Hildy. Where is he? That's a hell of a trick, Hildy. I thought we were friends! *etc.*

SHERIFF (*rushing back from the toilet*). By God, I'll show you!

THE REPORTERS. Look here, Pete! What about Mr. Burns? Ask the Master Mind! Yeah. What's *he* doing over here? *etc.*

SHERIFF (*grabbing* WALTER's *arm*). Speak up, Burns! What do you know about this?

WALTER (*gently but firmly disengaging his arm*). Listen, Hartman . . .

MURPHY. The hell with that! Where is he?

WALTER (*continuing*). The Examiner is not obstructing justice or aiding criminals. You ought to know that!

CARL (*pointing to the Examiner phone*). Look! Somebody was talking on there! The receiver is off! (MC CUE *jumps for the phone.*)

MC CUE. I'll find out who it is . . .

SHERIFF (*also jumping*). Leave that alone! *I'm* in charge here!

HILDY. Walter, listen! If I don't get out of here . . .

SHERIFF. Quiet, everybody! I'll handle this. It may be Earl Williams.

HILDY. Tell him to come on over.

SHERIFF. Sssh! (*Into phone, swallowing, then elaborately disguising his voice.*) Hello, Earl!

WALTER (*smiling*). Scotland Yard.

SHERIFF (*to* MC CUE, *in a whisper*). Trace this call—quick! (MC CUE *jumps for another phone.*) Yes, this is Walter.

MC CUE (*into another phone*). Trace the call on twenty-one! In a hurry!

SHERIFF (*into Examiner phone*). What? You gotta do what? Who is this?!!!

WALTER. You're talking to the Examiner, Hawkshaw!

(*The* SHERIFF *wheels.*)

MC CUE. That's right, Sheriff!

SHERIFF. Johnson, you're under arrest! You too, Burns!

WALTER (*calmly, without moving from his post at the desk*). Who's under arrest? . . . Listen, you pimple-headed German spy, do you realize what you're doing?

SHERIFF. We'll see about this. Get the Mayor, Carl! Ask him to come over here! (*As* CARL *goes to the telephone the door opens and* MRS. GRANT, *disheveled, with her hat over one ear, enters with two policemen.*)

FIRST POLICEMAN (*entering*). . . . In here, Madam?

HILDY (*leaping forward, happily*). Mother!

MRS. GRANT (*to* POLICEMAN). That man there! With the gray necktie! (*She points accusingly at* WALTER.)

HILDY (*hugging her*). Mother! Oh, my God, I'm glad to see you! Are you all right? Tell me! (MRS. GRANT *indignantly shakes* HILDY *off.*)

SHERIFF. What's the idea here?

POLICEMAN. This lady claims she was kidnapped!

SHERIFF. What?!!

MRS. GRANT. They dragged me all the way down the stairs—I tried to get help and they began to pinch me—I'm black and blue all over! Then they ran into another automobile and I was nearly killed!

SHERIFF. Just a minute? What did this

man have to do with it, lady? (*He points at* WALTER.)

MRS. GRANT. He was the one in charge of everything! He told them to kidnap me!

WALTER (*amazed*). Are you referring to *me*, Madam?

MRS. GRANT (*to* WALTER). You know you did! You told them to take me out of here!

SHERIFF. What about this, Burns! Kidnapping, eh?

WALTER (*round-eyed*). It's beyond *me*. Who is this woman?

MRS. GRANT. Oh! Oh, what a thing to say! I was standing right there . . . after the girl jumped out of that window!

SHERIFF. Did you get the Mayor? Was he in?

A DEPUTY. He's coming over.

WALTER (*to* MRS. GRANT). Now, Madam, be honest, if you were out joy-riding—drunk! . . . and got in some scrape . . . why don't you *admit* it instead of accusing innocent people!

MRS. GRANT (*beginning to doubt her senses*). You ruffian! You unprincipled man! How dare you say a thing like that!

HILDY. Please, Mother! He's just crazy! Don't! . . .

MRS. GRANT. I'll tell you something more, officer! I'll tell you why they did it!

WALTER (*fidgeting*). Come on, Sheriff. We've got to get bail.

MRS. GRANT (*continuing crescendo*). I was in here and they had some kind of a murderer—hiding him! (*This is a bombshell. The room is electrified by the old lady's announcement.*)

SHERIFF. Hiding him! Hiding him! In here?

MURPHY. Hiding him where?

HILDY. Mother!

THE REPORTERS. Where was he? Where did they have him? *etc.*

WALTER (*with superb indignation*). Madam, you're a God-damn liar! (*To emphasize his righteousness* WALTER *pounds on the desk three times—and then stands horrified. He remembers, too late, the signal.*)

THE REPORTERS. For God's sake, tell us where he was! Did they tell you where? Tell us! *etc.*

SHERIFF. Shut up, everybody! Now! where was he? Tell me where he was!

MRS. GRANT. Well, I was sitting right in this chair.

(*Three answering knocks come from* WILLIAMS. *The* SHERIFF *leaps as if the desk had bitten him.*)

SHERIFF (*whispering*) What was that?

THE REPORTERS. My God, he's in the desk! For the love of Christ! Holy God, he's in there! *etc.*

SHERIFF. *Aha! I thought so!* Stand back, everybody!

DEPUTY. Look out, Sheriff! He may shoot!

SHERIFF. Get your guns out! (*The police all take out guns.*)

HILDY. He's harmless, for God's sake!

SHERIFF. Don't take any chances! Shoot through the desk!

HILDY. He can't hurt anybody! You got his gun!

MRS. GRANT (*panic-stricken*). Oh, dear! Oh, dear!

WALTER (*to* MRS. GRANT). You gray-haired old Judas!

MRS. GRANT. Let me out! Let me out of here! (*Streaks for the door; exits.* THE REPORTERS *are going for the telephones.*)

MURPHY (*into phone*). City desk! Quick!

SHERIFF (*to* POLICEMAN). Close the door. You stand there. You cover the windows. (*Indicates with his gun.*)

MURPHY. Look out where you're pointing that gun, Pinky!

MC CUE (*into phone*). Gimme Emil.

KRUGER (*into phone*). Gimme the city desk.

MURPHY. Hold the wire! I've got a flash for you.

WALTER (*to* HILDY). Call Duffy.

SHERIFF. No, you don't!

WALTER. Do you want us to get scooped?

MC CUE. (*into phone*). Emil? Hang on for a second.

SHERIFF. Now then! Everybody aim right at the centre. And when I say three—

HILDY. God damn it! That's murder!

SHERIFF. Carl! Frank! One of you get on each side of the desk. Take hold of the cover. Now then! We got you covered, Williams—don't try to move. *Now!* Everybody quiet and ready for any emergency. I'm going to count three.

MURPHY (*phoning in the silence*). I'll have it in a minute . . .

SHERIFF. One! . . .

KRUGER. Right away now!

SHERIFF. Two! . . . (DIAMOND LOUIE *enters, accompanied by three people he has picked up in the street. One is a boy in short pants, the second is a sailor, the third is a seedy old man of the Trader Horn type.)*

POLICEMAN *(at the door, opposing them)*. What do you want? (WALTER *waves violently,* LOUIE *and his assistants disappear.)*

SHERIFF *(wheeling)*. Who was that?

WALTER *(white with rage)*. Double crossing Sicilian!

SHERIFF. Shut up!

KRUGER *(into phone)*. Keep holding it!

SHERIFF. Now then! Keep everybody out of here! I want quiet! . . . There's a dozen guns on you, Williams! You can't escape! Do you surrender or not?

WALTER *(into phone)*. Duffy!

SHERIFF. Are you ready, boys?

CARL. Yah. . . .

SHERIFF. All right. Now everybody aim right at the centre. *(Looking around)*. Are you all ready? *(To the men at the desk.)* You boys? *(From the* DEPUTIES *comes a whispered "Yes.")* Ready back there? *(This to the men at the door and windows; they give quick nods in reply.)* All right. Now then—up with it. (CARL *and* FRANK *raise the cover. The* SHERIFF *waits a discreet distance until he sees there is no danger.* WILLIAMS *is cowering in the desk, his hands over his face. The* SHERIFF *rushes on him, jabbing his gun into him.)*

WILLIAMS *(a wail)*. Go on—shoot me!

SHERIFF. Got you, Williams!

THE POLICE AND DEPUTIES. Grab him there! That's him! That's him! Don't let him shoot! Stick 'em up, you! Clout him! Give him the boots! Hold his arm! *(Through this* THE REPORTERS *are telephoning in. As they talk, the police drag the screaming little anarchist out. The* SHERIFF *follows them.)*

MURPHY *(into phone)*. Earl Williams was just captured in the press room o' the Criminal Courts Building hiding in a desk.

MC CUE *(into phone)*. The Sheriff just caught Williams in a roll top right here in the room.

KRUGER *(into phone)*. Just nabbed Williams hiding in a desk, Criminal Court press room.

MC CUE *(into phone)*. Williams put up a desperate struggle but the police overpowered him.

MURPHY *(into phone)*. Williams tried to shoot it out with the cops but his gun wouldn't work.

KRUGER *(into phone)*. Williams was unconscious when they opened the desk.

WALTER *(into phone)*. Duffy! The Examiner just turned Earl Williams over to the Sheriff . . .

(The SHERIFF *rushes back.)*

SHERIFF *(indicating* WALTER *and* HILDY). Just a minute! Put the cuffs on those two! *(The police obey.)* Harboring a fugitive from justice!

MURPHY *(into phone)*. A well dressed society woman tipped off the cops. Call you back in a minute . . .

KRUGER *(into phone)*. An old sweetheart of Williams double crossed him . . . Call you back . . .

MC CUE *(into phone)*. More in a minute.

THE REPORTERS. Where's that old lady? Hey madam! . . . Wait a minute! . . . Where's the old dame? *(They exit in a hurry.)*

SHERIFF *(into phone)*. Hello, girlie! Gimme Jacobi! Quick! . . .

WALTER. Hartman . . . you're going to wish for the rest of your life you'd never been born!

(The MAYOR *enters.)*

MAYOR. Fine work, Pete! You certainly delivered the goods! I'm proud of you!

SHERIFF *(over his shoulder as he phones)*. Look kind of natural, don't they, Fred? *(Referring to the handcuffs.)*

MAYOR *(happily.)* A sight for sore eyes! Well, it looks like you boys stepped in something up to your neck!

HILDY *(to His Honor)*. Go on! Laugh! You big tub of guts!

MAYOR. That's pretty, isn't it? Aiding an escaped criminal, huh?

SHERIFF *(rolling in catnip)*. And a little charge of kidnapping I'm looking into! *(Into phone.)* That's the jail! There must be *some*body over there!

MAYOR. Well! Looks like about ten years apiece for you birds.

WALTER. Does it? Well, whenever you think you've got the Examiner licked, that's a good time to get out of town.

HILDY. On a hand car.

MAYOR. Whistling in the dark, eh? Well, it isn't going to help you. You're through.

WALTER. Yeah? The last man that told me that was Barney Schmidt . . . a week before he cut his throat.

MAYOR. Is that so?

WALTER. And remember George T. Yorke, blowing his head off with a shotgun? We've been in worse jams than this—haven't we, Hildy? But something seems to watch over the Examiner. (*He raises his eyebrows.*)

HILDY. Yeah. When that minister sued us—remember? False arrest?

WALTER. Oh, yes . . . (*Coolly to the* MAYOR.) The Reverend J. B. Godolphin sued the Examiner once for . . . a hundred thousand dollars. It seems that we'd called him a fairy. Well, the day of the trial came and the Reverend was on his way to court . . .

HILDY. With all his lawyers and medical witnesses.

WALTER (*orgiastic*). Drowned by God! Drowned in the river! With their automobile, their affidavits and their Goddamn law books! And I got the same feeling right now that I had five minutes before that accident!

MAYOR. Your luck ain't with you now.

SHERIFF (*into telephone*). Jacobi? . . . I caught him. Williams. Singlehanded. . . . Yeah. They're bringing him right over. Notify everybody. We're going to proceed with the hanging per schedule. (*Wiggles telephone for another call.*)

WALTER (*to the* MAYOR). You're going to be in office for exactly two days more and then we're pulling your big nose out of the feed bag and setting you out on your fat can!

SHERIFF. Give me the state's attorney's office.

HILDY. And when you're walking up and down North Avenue with blue eyeglasses selling lead pencils, we're not going to forget you, either!

SHERIFF (*merrily*). We're going to be selling lead pencils, eh?

MAYOR. Don't even answer him.

THE SHERIFF. Well, I'll tell you what you'll be doing. Making *brooms* in the state penitentiary. . . . (*Into phone.*) Hello, Pyrstalski? This is Hartman. Come right over to my office, will you? I've just arrested a couple of important birds. I want you to take their confessions. (*Hangs up.*)

WALTER (*seizing the Examiner phone*). Duffy! Get Clarence Darrow!!!!

MAYOR. Get anybody you want! All the Darrows in the world aren't going to help you!

WALTER. Schmidt, Yorke, Godolphin. . . . You're next, Fred.

MAYOR. The power of the press, huh? Well, it don't scare me! Not an iota!

SHERIFF. It's a big windbag! That's all it is! Take 'em along, Carl!

WALTER. Bigger men than you have found out what it is! Presidents! Yes . . . and Kings!

(PINCUS, *the governor's messenger, reels in, stewed.*)

PINCUS (*woozy*). Here's your reprieve.

MAYOR (*seeing him, in panic*). Get out of here!

PINCUS. You can't bribe me!

SHERIFF. Get out of here, you!

PINCUS. I won't! Here's your reprieve!

HILDY. What's that?

PINCUS. I don't want to be City Sealer.

MAYOR. Who *is* this man?

SHERIFF (*frenzied*). Throw him out, Frank!

HILDY (*seizing* PINCUS *with his free hand*). Who was bribing you? (WALTER *also seizes* PINCUS, *already being pulled out of shape.*)

PINCUS. They wouldn't take it! . . .

MAYOR. You're insane!

WALTER. What did I tell you? An unseen power. What's your name?

PINCUS. Irving Pincus!

MAYOR. You drunken idiot! Arrest him! The idea of coming in here with a cock-and-bull story like that.

SHERIFF. It's a frameup! That's what it is! Some impostor!

HILDY. Wait a minute! (*To the* DEPUTIES.) Let go there!

WALTER. Murder, huh?

HILDY. Hanging an innocent man to win an election!

SHERIFF. That's a lie!

MAYOR. I never saw him before in my life!

WALTER (*to* PINCUS). When did you deliver this first?

HILDY. Who did you talk to?

PINCUS. They started right in bribing me!

HILDY. Who's "they"?

PINCUS (*indicating the* MAYOR *and* SHERIFF). Them!

MAYOR. That's absurd on the face of it, Mr. Burns! He's talking like a child!

WALTER (*really impressed*). An unseen power.

MAYOR. Certainly! He's insane or drunk or something! Why, if this unfortunate man Williams has really been reprieved,

I personally am tickled to death! Aren't you, Pete?

HILDY. Go on, you'd kill your mother to get elected!

MAYOR (*shocked*). That's a hell of a thing to say, Johnson, about anybody! Now, look here, Walter, you're an intelligent man . . .

WALTER (*stopping the* MAYOR). Just a minute. (*To* PINCUS.) All right, Mr. Pincus. Let's have your story.

PINCUS. Well, I've been married for nineteen years . . .

WALTER. Skip all that.

MAYOR (*loudly*). Take those handcuffs off the boys, Pete. That wasn't at all necessary. . . .

SHERIFF (*springing to obey*). I was just going to. . . .

MAYOR. I can't tell you how badly I feel about this, Walter. There was no excuse for Hartman flying off the handle.

SHERIFF (*busy with the handcuffs*). I was only doing my duty. There wasn't anything personal intended.

HILDY. You guys had better quit politics and take in washing. (*They are set free.*)

MAYOR. Sheriff. . . . (*He is looking over the reprieve.*) This document is authentic! Earl Williams, thank God, has been reprieved, and the commonwealth of Chicago has been spared the painful necessity of shedding blood.

WALTER. Save that for the Tribune.

MAYOR (*to* PINCUS). What did you say your name was—Pincus?

PINCUS. That's right. (*Shows a locket.*) Here's a picture of the wife.

MAYOR (*trapped*). A very fine-looking woman.

PINCUS (*mysteriously angered*). She's good enough for me.

(PEGGY *enters.*)

HILDY. I'll bet she is.

MAYOR. A real character.

PEGGY. Hildy, what's the matter? What are they going to do? Mother said—

HILDY (*seeing her*). Peggy, don't bawl me out now.

WALTER. Nobody's going to do anything to anybody. .

MAYOR. Of course not. My good friend Walter Burns and I understand each other perfectly, I trust.

SHERIFF (*eager*). And so do I.

MAYOR. So do you *what,* you God damn hoodoo! And now, Mr. Pincus, if you'll come with us we'll take you over to the Warden's office and deliver that reprieve.

PEGGY. But Hildy, mother said that they'd arrested you . . .

PINCUS (*being escorted out by the* MAYOR.) If I was to go home and tell my wife—

MAYOR. The hell with your wife!

PINCUS (*drunkenly loyal to his mate.*) She *loves* me. (*Exit* PINCUS *and the* MAYOR.)

SHERIFF (*pauses. His eyes lower. He speaks winningly*). By the way, Walter . . . We were going to have a little feed after the hanging . . . a sort of buffet breakfast. . . .

MAYOR (*calling from the corridor*). Hartman!

SHERIFF (*nervously*). I'm coming, Fred. (*Coyly, as* WALTER *stares.*) What do you say we eat it now? . . . Hmm? (*Still the dead pan from* WALTER.) Delicious ham . . . and some of Mrs. Hartman's own preserves. . . .

MAYOR (*loudly from the hall*). Hartman!!!

(*The* SHERIFF *sighs. A plaintive shrug indicates that he has a great deal to contend with. He leaves.*)

WALTER (*dreamily*). Wait till those two Greeks read the Examiner tomorrow! (*Back to life.*) Hildy, I'll tell you what I want you to do.

HILDY. What?

WALTER. I want you to get this guy Pincus over to the office tomorrow—

HILDY. Nothing doing, Walter. I'm all washed up. I mean it this time, Walter.

PEGGY. Oh, Hildy, if I only thought you did.

HILDY. Listen, Peggy,—if I'm not telling you the absolute truth may God strike me dead right now. I'm going to New York with you to-night—if you give me this one last chance! I'll cut out drinking and swearing and everything connected with the God-damn newspaper business. I won't even *read* a newspaper.

WALTER. Listen, Hildy, I got an idea.

HILDY (*to* WALTER). There's nothing you can say can make me change my mind. This time I'm through, and I *mean* it. I know I don't deserve you, Peggy. I've done everything in the world to prove that, I guess.

PEGGY. Hildy, please! Don't say things like that.

HILDY. I've gotta hell of a nerve to ask

you to marry me. I'm a prize package, all right. But if you'll take me, here I am.

PEGGY. Darling, don't talk that way. I want you just the way you are. (*Anyway* PEGGY *will always remember that she said this and always forget that she didn't mean it.*)

WALTER. God, Hildy, I didn't know it was anything like this. Why didn't you *say* something? I'd be the last person in the world to want to come between you and your happiness.

HILDY (*staggered*). What?

WALTER. You ought to know that. . . . (*As* HILDY *continues to blink.*) I love you, you crazy Swede! (*To* PEGGY.) You're getting a great guy, Peggy.

HILDY. Never mind the Valentines. Goodbye, you lousy bohunk. (*They shake hands.*)

WALTER. You're a great newspaperman, Hildy. I'm sorry to see you go. Damn sorry.

HILDY. Well, if I ever come *back* to the business . . . (*To* PEGGY.) Which I won't . . . (*To* WALTER, *his arm around* PEGGY.) There's only one man I'd work for. You know that, don't you?

WALTER. I'd kill you if you ever worked for anybody else.

HILDY. Hear that, Peggy? That's my diploma. (*He hesitates.*) Well, Walter . . . I don't know what to say . . . except I'm going to miss you like hell.

WALTER. Same here, son.

HILDY (*to* PEGGY). Twelve years we've been knocking around together . . . before you were born . . . (*To* WALTER, *his face lighting up.*) Remember the time we hid the missing heiress in the sauerkraut factory?

WALTER. Do I! (*To* PEGGY.) Get him to tell you some time about how we stole Old Lady Haggerty's stomach . . . off the coroner's physician. We *proved* she was poisoned. . . .

HILDY (*laughing*). We had to hide for a week!

PEGGY. Darling . . .

HILDY (*back to life*). What?

PEGGY. You don't want to go to New York . . . down deep.

HILDY. Aw . . . what do you mean? I was just talking. (*With a nervous laugh.*) I'd feel worse if I stayed, I guess. . . .

PEGGY. Hildy, if I thought you were going to be unhappy—I mean, if you really wanted to— (*Firmly.*) No. No. It's your chance to have a home and be a human being—and I'm going to make you take it.

WALTER (*to* PEGGY). Why, I wouldn't let him stay. . . . Go on, Hildy, before I make you city editor.

HILDY (*starting*). Hurry up, Peggy. He means it.

WALTER (*as* PEGGY *follows*). Any objection to my kissing the bride?

HILDY (*stopping*). It's O.K. with me. (*He looks at* PEGGY. *She smiles.*) Go ahead, Mrs. Johnson.

WALTER (*removing his hat and kissing her chastely*). Thank you. . . . What time does your train go?

PEGGY. There's another one at twelve-forty. (*To* HILDY.) We came awfully near going without you.

WALTER. New York Central, eh? (*To* HILDY.) I wish there was time to get you a little wedding present . . . but it's awful short notice.

PEGGY (*straining to be gone*). Thank you, Mr. Burns, but Hildy's all the wedding present I want. . . . (*Laughing a little.*) If I've really got him.

HILDY. Ah, forget it, Walter. (*He, too, is leaving.*)

WALTER. Hold on! I want you to have something to remember me by. You can't just leave like this. . . . (*Thoughtfully reaching for his watch.*) And I know what it's going to be. . . . (*Produces the watch.*)

HILDY (*embarrassed*). Aw, Jesus, no, Walter! You make me feel like a fairy or something!

WALTER (*with affected brusqueness*). Shut up! You're going to take it, I tell you! It was a present from the Big Chief himself! And if you'll look inside . . . (*Opening the watch.*) You'll find a little inscription: "To the Best Newspaperman I know." . . . When you get to New York, you can scratch out my name and put yours in its place, if you want to. . . .

HILDY. You know I wouldn't do that. . . .

WALTER. Here. . . . (*Giving him the watch.*)

HILDY. Aw, Walter! It's too good for me! I can't take it!

WALTER. You got to! (*To* PEGGY.) *Make* him!

PEGGY. Go on, Hildy . . . if Mr. Burns

wants you to. You don't want to hurt his feelings. . . .

(HILDY *takes it.* WALTER *pats him on the shoulder, his face averted.*)

HILDY (*a lump in his throat*). Well, this is the first and last thing I ever got from a newspaper. . . .

PEGGY. Goodbye, Mr. Burns. . . . I always had a queer opinion of you, Mr. Burns. I *still* think you're a little peculiar, but you're all right . . . underneath. I mean I think you're a peach.

WALTER (*winningly*). So are you! You look just like a little flower!

HILDY (*ushering* PEGGY *out*). Goodbye, you big baboon. . . .

PEGGY. Goodbye. . . . (*They exit.*)

WALTER (*calling after, leaning against the door*). Goodbye, Johnson! Be good to yourself . . . and the little girl. . . .

HILDY'S VOICE. The same to you and many of them!

(WALTER *waits till* HILDY *and* PEGGY *are out of sight and earshot, then closes the door. He walks slowly to the telephone. The receiver is still off the hook, the obedient* DUFFY *still on the other end.* WALTER *hesitates sentimentally, the receiver in his hand. Then he heaves a huge sigh and speaks.*)

WALTER. Duffy! . . . (*He sounds a bit tired.*) Listen. I want you to send a wire to the Chief of Police of La Porte, Indiana. . . . That's right. . . . Tell him to meet the twelve-forty out of Chicago . . . New York Central . . . and arrest Hildy Johnson and bring him back here. . . . Wire him a full description. . . . The son of a bitch stole my watch!

CURTAIN

ONE of the most unusual plays of the twenties, *Machinal,* appeared on the stage in the very last year of that decade, almost as if it had been deliberately produced to sum up trends in the theatre of that period. In *Machinal* were to be found formal experimentalism, recognition of the machine age and concern with individual struggles viewed against a general background of modern life in America, and vague protest against the blight of materialism. Formally, it belonged to the main theatrical adventure of the twenties, the telegraphic imaginative style which reached its frantic, discordant apogee in Central Europe and was known as *expressionism.* Among American playwrights, O'Neill had familiarized playgoers with it in *The Emperor Jones, The Hairy Ape, All God's Chillun Got Wings,* and *The Great God Brown,* Elmer Rice in *The Adding Machine,* and Kaufman and Connelly in *Beggar on Horseback.* Sophie Treadwell's use of this subjective style of distortion and depersonalization was, however, quite unique. In her play, expressionism, although applied to a sensational murder, was subdued and was given a muted musical function, being used as a sort of obligato to the heroine's failure. Her first numb state of mind, her awakening to love, her desperation, and her defeat found a theatrical translation in the automatic movement, sound, and speech of the play. There was, in short, a very high degree of artistry in *Machinal* that not everybody was able to recognize in a theatre which had accustomed its public to expect detonating emphases.

In this play, Miss Treadwell was able to convey a rare compassion for her character as an individual and yet make her story representative of many lives; and this in spite of the unusual murder of the climax. In the process, besides, *Machinal* managed to project the mechanical essence of a world in which private frustrations and heartbreaks can seem only half real in spite of their acuteness. If the author had poured the same story into the mold of the ordinary three-act realistic play, it would have been quite unremarkable. By giving the story an expressive form, Miss Treadwell transfigured the commonplaces of adultery and murder we encounter in newspapers and popular fiction into something considerably more humanly meaningful and socially suggestive.

Sophie Treadwell was born in California, and is of Spanish and English ancestry. She assisted the famous Polish actress Helena Modjeska (1844-1909) in the composition of her memoirs. Her early plays on Broadway were *Gringo* (1922) and *Oh, Nightingale* (1925). After *Machinal* came *Ladies Leave* (1929), *Lone Valley* (1933), the Edgar Allen Poe biography *Plumes in the Dust* (1936), and *Hope for a Harvest,* a Theatre Guild production of the 1941-42 season.

Machinal, which appears to have been suggested by one of the sensational courtroom trials of the period, the Ruth Snyder-Judd Grey murder case, aroused considerable attention. Its topical matter and its dramatic form attracted the European theatre. It ran for about a year in Moscow's Kamerny Theatre, which specialized in stylized production techniques.

Machinal

BY SOPHIE TREADWELL

First produced by Arthur Hopkins at the Plymouth Theatre, New York City, on September 7, 1928, with the following cast:

YOUNG WOMAN	Zita Johann
TELEPHONE GIRL	Millicent Green
STENOGRAPHER	Grace Atwell
FILING CLERK	Leopold Badia
ADDING CLERK	Conway Washburn
MOTHER	Jean Adair
HUSBAND	George Stillwell
BELLBOY	Otto Frederick
NURSE	Nancy Allen
DOCTOR	Monroe Childs
YOUNG MAN	Hal K. Dawson
GIRL	Zenaide Ziegfield
MAN	Jess Sidney
BOY	Clyde Storke
MAN	Clark Gable
ANOTHER MAN	Hugh M. Hite
WAITER	John Hanley
JUDGE	Tom Waters
LAWYER FOR DEFENSE	John Connery
LAWYER FOR PROSECUTION	James Macdonald
COURT REPORTER	Otto Frederick
BAILIFF	John Hanley
REPORTER	Conway Washburn
SECOND REPORTER	Hugh M. Hite
THIRD REPORTER	Hal K. Dawson
JAILER	John Hanley
MATRON	Mrs. Chas. Willard
PRIEST	Charles Kennedy

Episode I. To Business.
Episode II. At Home.
Episode III. Honeymoon.
Episode IV. Maternal.
Episode V. Prohibited.
Episode VI. Intimate.
Episode VII. Domestic.
Episode VIII. The Law.
Episode IX. A Machine.

THE PLOT is the story of a woman who murders her husband—an ordinary young woman, any woman.

THE PLAN is to tell this story by showing the different phases of life that the woman comes in contact with, and in none of which she finds any place, any peace. The woman is essentially soft, tender, and the life around her is essentially hard, mechanized. Business, home, marriage, having a child, seeking pleasure—all are difficult for her—mechanical, nerve nagging. Only in an illicit love does she find anything with life in it for her, and when she loses this, the desperate effort to win free to it again is her undoing.

The story is told in nine scenes. In the dialogue of these scenes there is the attempt to catch the rhythm of our common city speech, its brassy sound, its trick of repetition, etc.

Then there is, also, the use of many different sounds chosen primarily for their inherent emotional effect (steel rivetting, a priest chanting, a Negro singing, jazz band, etc.), but contributing also to the creation of a background, an atmosphere.

THE HOPE is to create a stage production that will have "style," and at the same time, by the story's own innate drama, by the directness of its telling, by the variety and quick changingness of its scenes, and the excitement of its sounds, to create an interesting play.

SCENICALLY this play is planned to be handled in two basic sets (or in one set with two backs)

The first division—(The first Four Episodes)—needs an entrance at one side, and a back having a door and a large window. The door gives, in

Episode 1—to Vice President's office.
" 2— " hall.
" 3— " bathroom.
" 4— " corridor.

And the window shows, in

" 1—An opposite office.
" 2—An inner apartment court.
" 3—Window of a dance casino opposite.
" 4—Steel girders.

(Of these, only the casino window is important. Sky could be used for the others.)

The second division—(the last Five Episodes)—has the same side entrance, but the back has only one opening—for a small window (barred).

Episode 5, window is masked by electric piano.
" 6, " " disclosed (sidewalk outside).
" 7, " " curtained.
" 8, " " masked by Judge's bench.
" 9, " " disclosed (sky outside).

There is a change of furniture, and props for each episode—(only essential things, full of character).

For Episode 9, the room is closed in from the sides, and there is a place with bars and a door in it, put straight across stage down front (back far enough to leave a clear passageway in front of it.)

LIGHTING concentrated and intense.—Light and shadow—bright light and darkness.—This darkness, already in the scene, grows and blacks out the light for dark stage when the scene changes are made.

OFFSTAGE VOICES

Characters in the Background
Heard, but Unseen

A Janitor
A Baby
A Boy and a Girl
A Husband and Wife
A Husband and Wife
A Radio Announcer
A Negro Singer

MECHANICAL
OFFSTAGE SOUNDS

A small jazz band
A hand organ
Steel rivetting
Telegraph instruments
Aeroplane engine

MECHANICAL
OFFSTAGE SOUNDS

Office Machines (Typewriters, telephones, etc.)
Electric piano.

CHARACTERS

In the Background
Seen, Not Heard

(*See, off the main set; i.e., through a window or door*)

Couples of men and women dancing
A Woman in a bathrobe
A Woman in a wheel chair
A Nurse with a covered basin
A Nurse with a tray
The feet of men and women passing in the street.

EPISODE ONE

TO BUSINESS

SCENE: *An Office.*
A Switchboard
Filing Cabinet
Adding Machine
Typewriter and Table
Manifold Machine

SOUNDS: *Office Machines.*
Typewriters
Adding Machine
Manifold
Telephone Bells
Buzzers

CHARACTERS AND THEIR MACHINES:

A YOUNG WOMAN (*Typewriter*)
A STENOGRAPHER (*Typewriter*)
A FILING CLERK (*Filing cabinet and manifold*)
AN ADDING CLERK (*Adding Machine*)
TELEPHONE OPERATOR (*Switchboard*)

(BEFORE THE CURTAIN—*Sounds of Machines going. They continue throughout the scene, and accompany the Young Woman's thoughts after the scene is blacked out*)

(AT THE RISE OF THE CURTAIN: *All the Machines are disclosed, and all the characters with the exception of* THE YOUNG WOMAN)

Of these characters, THE YOUNG WOMAN, *going any day to any business. Ordinary. The confusion of her own inner thoughts, emotions, desires, dreams cuts her off from any actual adjustment to the routine of work. She gets through this routine with a very small surface of her consciousness. She is not homely and she is not pretty. She is preoccupied with herself—with her person. She has well kept hands, and a trick of constantly arranging her hair over her ears.*

The STENOGRAPHER *is the faded, efficient woman office worker. Drying, dried.*

The ADDING CLERK *is her male counterpart.*

The FILING CLERK *is a boy not grown. callow adolescence.*

The TELEPHONE GIRL, *young, cheap and amorous.*

Lights come up on office scene. Two desks R. *and* L. *Telephone booth back* R.C. *Filing cabinet back of* C. *Adding machine back* L.C.

ADDING CLERK (*in the monotonous voice of his monotonous thoughts; at his adding machine*). 2490, 28, 76, 123, 36842, 1, ¼, 37, 804, 23½, 982.

FILING CLERK (*in the same way—at his filing desk*). Accounts—A. Bonds—B. Contracts—C. Data—D. Earnings—E.

STENOGRAPHER (*in the same way—Left*). Dear Sir—in re—your letter—recent date—will state—

TELEPHONE GIRL. Hello—Hello—George H. Jones Company good morning—hello hello—George H. Jones Company good morning—hello.

FILING CLERK. Market—M. Notes—N. Output—O. Profits—P.—! (*Suddenly.*) What's the matter with Q?

TELEPHONE GIRL. Matter with it—Mr. J.—Mr. K. wants you— What you mean matter? Matter with what?

FILING CLERK. Matter with Q.

TELEPHONE GIRL. Well—what is? Spring 1726?

FILING CLERK. I'm asking yuh——

TELEPHONE GIRL. WELL?

FILING CLERK. Nothing filed with it——

TELEPHONE GIRL. Well?

FILING CLERK. Look at A. Look at B. What's the matter with Q?

TELEPHONE GIRL. Ain't popular. Hello—Hello—George H. Jones Company.

FILING CLERK. Hot dog! Why ain't it?

ADDING CLERK. Has it personality?

STENOGRAPHER. Has it Halitosis?

TELEPHONE GIRL. Has it got it?

FILING CLERK. Hot dog!

TELEPHONE GIRL. What number do you want? (*Recognizing but not pleased.*) Oh—hello—sure I know who it is—tonight? Uh, uh— (*Negative, but each with a different inflection.*)—you heard me—No!

FILING CLERK. Don't you like him?

STENOGRAPHER. She likes 'em all.

TELEPHONE GIRL. I do not!

STENOGRAPHER. Well—pretty near all!

TELEPHONE GIRL. What number do you want? Wrong number. Hello—hello—

George H. Jones Company. Hello, hello—

STENOGRAPHER. Memorandum—attention Mr. Smith—at a conference of——

ADDING CLERK. 125—83¾—22—908—34—¼—28593——

FILING CLERK. Report—R, Sales—S, Trade—T.

TELEPHONE GIRL. Shh—! Yes, Mr. J.—? No—Miss A. ain't in yet—I'll tell her, Mr. J.—just the minute she gets in.

STENOGRAPHER. She's late again, huh?

TELEPHONE GIRL. Out with her sweetie last night, huh?

FILING CLERK. Hot dog.

ADDING CLERK. She ain't got a sweetie.

STENOGRAPHER. How do you know?

ADDING CLERK. I know.

FILING CLERK. Hot dog.

ADDING CLERK. She lives alone with her mother.

TELEPHONE GIRL. Spring 1876? Hello—Spring 1876. Spring! Hello, Spring 1876? 1876! Wrong number! Hello! Hello!

STENOGRAPHER. Director's meeting semi-annual report card.

FILING CLERK. Shipments—Sales—Schedules—S.

ADDING CLERK. She doesn't belong in an office.

TELEPHONE GIRL. Who does?

STENOGRAPHER. I do!

ADDING CLERK. You said it!

FILING CLERK. Hot dog!

TELEPHONE GIRL. Hello—hello—George H. Jones Company—hello—hello—

STENOGRAPHER. I'm efficient. She's inefficient.

FILING CLERK. She's inefficient.

TELEPHONE GIRL. She's got J. going.

STENOGRAPHER. Going?

TELEPHONE GIRL. Going and coming.

FILING CLERK. Hot dog.

(*Enter* JONES.)

JONES. Good morning, everybody.

TELEPHONE GIRL. Good morning.

FILING CLERK. Good morning.

ADDING CLERK. Good morning.

STENOGRAPHER. Good morning, Mr. J.

JONES. Miss A. isn't in yet?

TELEPHONE GIRL. Not yet, Mr. J.

FILING CLERK. Not yet.

ADDING CLERK. Not yet.

STENOGRAPHER. She's late.

JONES. I just wanted her to take a letter.

STENOGRAPHER. I'll take the letter.

JONES. One thing at a time and that done well.

ADDING CLERK (*yessing*). Done well.

STENOGRAPHER. I'll finish it later.

JONES. Hew to the line.

ADDING CLERK. Hew to the line.

STENOGRAPHER. Then I'll hurry.

JONES. Haste makes waste.

ADDING CLERK. Waste.

STENOGRAPHER. But if you're in a hurry.

JONES. I'm never in a hurry— That's how I get ahead! (*Laughs. They all laugh.*) First know you're right—then go ahead.

ADDING CLERK. Ahead.

JONES (*to* TELEPHONE GIRL). When Miss A. comes in tell her I want her to take a letter. (*Turns to go in—then.*) It's important.

TELEPHONE GIRL (*making a note*). Miss A.—important.

JONES (*starts up—then*). And I don't want to be disturbed.

TELEPHONE GIRL. You're in conference?

JONES. I'm in conference. (*Turns—then*) Unless its A.B.—of course.

TELEPHONE GIRL. Of course—A.B.

JONES (*starts—turns again; attempts to be facetious*). Tell Miss A. the early bird catches the worm.

(*Exit* JONES.)

TELEPHONE GIRL. The early worm gets caught.

ADDING CLERK. He's caught.

TELEPHONE GIRL. Hooked.

ADDING CLERK. In the pan.

FILING CLERK. Hot dog.

STENOGRAPHER. We beg leave to announce——

(*Enter* YOUNG WOMAN. *Goes behind telephone booth to desk* R.)

STENOGRAPHER. You're late!

FILING CLERK. You're late.

ADDING CLERK. You're late.

STENOGRAPHER. And yesterday!

FILING CLERK. The day before.

ADDING CLERK. And the day before.

STENOGRAPHER. You'll lose your job.

YOUNG WOMAN. No!

STENOGRAPHER. No?

(WORKERS *exchange glances.*)

YOUNG WOMAN. I can't!

STENOGRAPHER. Can't?

(*Same business.*)

FILING CLERK. Rent—bills—installments—miscellaneous.

ADDING CLERK. A dollar ten—ninety-five—3.40—35—12.60.

STENOGRAPHER. Then why are you late?

YOUNG WOMAN. Why?

STENOGRAPHER. Excuse!

ADDING CLERK. Excuse!

FILING CLERK. Excuse.

TELEPHONE GIRL. Excuse it, please.

STENOGRAPHER. Why?

YOUNG WOMAN. The subway?

TELEPHONE GIRL. Long distance?

FILING CLERK. Old stuff!

ADDING CLERK. That stall!

STENOGRAPHER. Stalled?

YOUNG WOMAN. No——

STENOGRAPHER. What?

YOUNG WOMAN. I had to get out!

ADDING CLERK. Out!

FILING CLERK. Out?

STENOGRAPHER. Out where?

YOUNG WOMAN. In the air!

STENOGRAPHER. Air?

YOUNG WOMAN. All those bodies pressing.

FILING CLERK. Hot dog!

YOUNG WOMAN. I thought I would faint! I had to get out in the air!

FILING CLERK. Give her the air.

ADDING CLERK. Free air—

STENOGRAPHER. Hot air.

YOUNG WOMAN. Like I'm dying.

STENOGRAPHER. Same thing yesterday. (*Pause.*) And the day before.

YOUNG WOMAN. Yes—what am I going to do?

ADDING CLERK. Take a taxi!

(THEY *laugh.*)

FILING CLERK. Call a cop!

TELEPHONE GIRL. Mr. J. wants you.

YOUNG WOMAN. Me?

TELEPHONE GIRL. You!

YOUNG WOMAN (*rises*). Mr. J.!

STENOGRAPHER. Mr. J.

TELEPHONE GIRL. He's bellowing for you!

(YOUNG WOMAN *gives last pat to her hair —goes off into door—back.*)

STENOGRAPHER (*after her*). Get it just right.

FILING CLERK. She's always doing that to her hair.

TELEPHONE GIRL. It gives a line—it gives a line—

FILING CLERK. Hot dog.

ADDING CLERK. She's artistic.

STENOGRAPHER. She's inefficient.

FILING CLERK. She's inefficient.

STENOGRAPHER. Mr. J. knows she's inefficient.

ADDING CLERK. 46-23-84-2-2-2-1,492—678.

TELEPHONE GIRL. Hello—hello—George H. Jones Company—hello—Mr. Jones? He's in conference.

STENOGRAPHER (*sarcastic*). Conference!

ADDING CLERK. Conference.

FILING CLERK. Hot dog!

TELEPHONE GIRL. Do you think he'll marry her?

ADDING CLERK. If she'll have him.

STENOGRAPHER. If she'll have him!

FILING CLERK. Do you think she'll have him?

TELEPHONE GIRL. How much does he get?

ADDING CLERK. Plenty—5,000—10,000—15,000—20,000—25,000.

STENOGRAPHER. And plenty put away.

ADDING CLERK. Gas Preferred—4's--steel —5's—oil—6's.

FILING CLERK. Hot dog.

STENOGRAPHER. Will she have him? Will she have him? This agreement entered into—party of the first part—party of the second part—will he have her?

TELEPHONE GIRL. Well, I'd hate to get into bed with him. (*Familiar melting voice.*) Hello—humhum—hum—hum—hold the line a minute—will you—hum hum. (*Professional voice.*) Hell, hello—A.B., just a minute, Mr. A.B.—Mr. J.? Mr. A.B.—go ahead, Mr. A.B. (*Melting voice.*) We were interrupted—huh—huh —huh-huhuh—hum—hum.

(*Enter* YOUNG WOMAN—*she goes to her chair, sits with folded hands.*)

FILING CLERK. That's all you ever say to a guy—

STENOGRAPHER. Hum—hum—or uh huh — (*Negative.*)

TELEPHONE GIRL. That's all you have to. (*To phone.*) Hum—hum—hum hum—hum hum—

STENOGRAPHER. Mostly hum hum.

ADDING CLERK. You've said it!

FILING CLERK. Hot dog.

TELEPHONE GIRL. Hum hum huh hum humhumhum—tonight? She's got a date —she told me last night—humhumhuh—hum—all right. (*Disconnects.*) Too bad—my boy friend's got a friend—but my girl friend's got a date.

YOUNG WOMAN. You have a good time.

TELEPHONE GIRL. Big time.

STENOGRAPHER. Small time.

ADDING CLERK. A big time on the small time.

TELEPHONE GIRL. I'd ask you, kid, but you'd be up to your neck!

STENOGRAPHERS. Neckers!

ADDING CLERK. Petters!

FILING CLERK. Sweet papas.

TELEPHONE GIRL. Want to come?

YOUNG WOMAN. Can't.

TELEPHONE GIRL. Date?

YOUNG WOMAN. My mother.

STENOGRAPHER. Worries?

TELEPHONE GIRL. Nags—hello—George H. Jones Company—Oh hello—

(YOUNG WOMAN *sits before her machine—hands in lap, looking at them.*)

STENOGRAPHER. Why don't you get to work?

YOUNG WOMAN (*dreaming*). What?

ADDING CLERK. Work!

YOUNG WOMAN. Can't.

STENOGRAPHER. Can't?

YOUNG WOMAN. My machine's out of order.

STENOGRAPHER. Well, fix it!

YOUNG WOMAN. I can't—got to get somebody.

STENOGRAPHER. Somebody! Somebody! Always somebody! Here, sort the mail, then!

YOUNG WOMAN (*rises*). All right.

STENOGRAPHER. And hurry! You're late.

YOUNG WOMAN (*sorting letters*). George H. Jones & Company—George H. Jones Inc. George H. Jones—

STENOGRAPHER. You're always late.

ADDING CLERK. You'll lose your job.

YOUNG WOMAN (*hurrying*). George H. Jones—George H. Jones Personal—

TELEPHONE GIRL. Don't let 'em get your goat, kid—tell 'em where to get off.

YOUNG WOMAN. What?

TELEPHONE GIRL. Ain't it all set?

YOUNG WOMAN. What?

TELEPHONE GIRL. You and Mr. J.

STENOGRAPHER. You and the boss.

FILING CLERK. You and the big chief.

ADDING CLERK. You and the big cheese.

YOUNG WOMAN. Did he tell you?

TELEPHONE GIRL. I told you!

ADDING CLERK. I told you!

STENOGRAPHER. I don't believe it.

ADDING CLERK. 5,000—10,000—15,000.

FILING CLERK. Hot dog.

YOUNG WOMAN. No—it isn't so.

STENOGRAPHER. Isn't it?

YOUNG WOMAN. No.

TELEPHONE GIRL. Not yet.

ADDING CLERK. But soon.

FILING CLERK. Hot dog.

(*Enter* JONES.)

TELEPHONE GIRL (*busy*). George H. Jones Company—Hello—Hello.

STENOGRAPHER. Awaiting your answer—

ADDING CLERK. 5,000—10,000—15,000—

JONES (*crossing to* YOUNG WOMAN—*puts hand on her shoulder,* ALL *stop and stare*). That letter done?

YOUNG WOMAN. No. (*She pulls away.*)

JONES. What's the matter?

STENOGRAPHER. She hasn't started.

JONES. O.K.—want to make some changes.

YOUNG WOMAN. My machine's out of order.

JONES. O.K.—use the one in my room.

YOUNG WOMAN. I'm sorting the mail.

STENOGRAPHER (*sarcastic*). One thing at a time!

JONES (*retreating—goes back* C.). O.K. (*To* YOUNG WOMAN.) When you're finished. (*Starts back to his room.*)

STENOGRAPHER. Haste makes waste.

JONES (*at door*). O.K.—don't hurry. (*Exits.*)

STENOGRAPHER. Hew to the line!

TELEPHONE GIRL. He's hewing.

FILING CLERK. Hot dog.

TELEPHONE GIRL. Why did you flinch, kid?

YOUNG WOMAN. Flinch?

TELEPHONE GIRL. Did he pinch?

YOUNG WOMAN. No!

TELEPHONE GIRL. Then what?

YOUNG WOMAN. Nothing!— Just his hand.

TELEPHONE GIRL. Oh—just his hand— (*Shakes her head thoughtfully.*) Uhhuh. (*Negative.*) Uhhuh. (*Decisively.*) No! Tell him no.

STENOGRAPHER. If she does she'll lose her job.

ADDING CLERK. Fired.

FILING CLERK. The sack!

TELEPHONE GIRL (*on the defensive*). And if she doesn't?

ADDING CLERK. She'll come to work in a taxi!

TELEPHONE GIRL. Work?

FILING CLERK. No work.

STENOGRAPHER. No worry.

ADDING CLERK. Breakfast in bed.

STENOGRAPHER (*sarcastic*). Did Madame ring?

FILING CLERK. Lunch in bed!

TELEPHONE GIRL. A double bed! (*In phone.*) Yes, Mr. J. (*To* YOUNG WOMAN.) J. wants you.

YOUNG WOMAN (*starts to get to her feet—but doesn't*). I can't—I'm not ready—In a minute. (*Sits staring ahead of her.*)

ADDING CLERK. 5,000—10,000—15,000—

FILING CLERK. Profits — plans — purchase—

STENOGRAPHER. Call your attention our prices are fixed.

TELEPHONE GIRL. Hello—hello—George H. Jones Company—hello—hello—

YOUNG WOMAN (*thinking her thoughts aloud—to the subdued accompaniment of the office sounds and voices*). Marry me —wants to marry me—George H. Jones—George H. Jones and Company—Mrs. George H. Jones—Mrs. George H. Jones. Dear Madame—marry—do you take this man to be your wedded husband—I do—to love honor and to love—kisses—no—I can't—George H. Jones—How would you like to marry me—What do you say —Why Mr. Jones I—let me look at your little hands—you have such pretty little hands—let me hold your pretty little hands —George H. Jones—Fat hands—flabby hands — don't touch me — please — fat hands are never weary—please don't—married—all girls—most girls—married—babies—a baby—curls—little curls all over its head—George H. Jones—straight—thin—bald—don't touch me—please—no —can't—must—somebody—something——no rest—must rest—no rest—must rest —no rest—late today—yesterday—before —late — subway — air — pressing—bodies pressing—bodies—trembling—air—stop—air — late — job — no job — fired — late——alarm clock—alarm clock—alarm clock —hurry—job—ma—nag—nag—nag—ma —hurry—job—no job—no money—installments due — no money — money — George H. Jones—money—Mrs. George H. Jones—money—no work—no worry—free!—rest—sleep till nine—sleep till ten —sleep till noon—now you take a good rest this morning—don't get up till you want to—thank you—oh thank you—oh don't!—please don't touch me—I want to rest—no rest—earn—got to earn—married —earn—no—yes—earn—all girls — most girls—ma—pa—ma — all women — most women—I can't—must—maybe—must—somebody—something—ma—pa—ma—can I, ma? Tell me, ma—something—somebody.

BLACK OUT

(*The sounds of the office machines continue until the scene lights into Episode 2,—and the office sounds become the sound of a radio* [*offstage*].)

EPISODE TWO

At Home

SCENE: *A Kitchen.*
Table—chairs—plates and food—Garbage can—a pair of rubber gloves.
The door at the back now opens on a hall—the window, on an apartment house court.

CHARACTERS:

YOUNG WOMAN
MOTHER

OUTSIDE VOICES: *Characters heard, but not seen:*

A JANITOR
A BABY
A MOTHER AND A SMALL BOY
A YOUNG BOY AND YOUNG GIRL
A HUSBAND AND A WIFE
ANOTHER HUSBAND AND A WIFE

SOUNDS:

Buzzer
Radio (*Voice of Announcer*)
(*Music and Singer*)

AT RISE:

YOUNG WOMAN *and* MOTHER *eating—Radio offstage—Radio stops.*

YOUNG WOMAN. Ma—I want to talk to you.

MOTHER. Aren't you eating a potato?

YOUNG WOMAN. No.

MOTHER. Why not?

YOUNG WOMAN. I don't want one.

MOTHER. That's no reason. Here! Take one.

YOUNG WOMAN. I don't want it.

MOTHER. Potatoes go with stew—here!

YOUNG WOMAN. Ma, I don't want it!

MOTHER. Want it! Take it!

YOUNG WOMAN. But I—oh, all right. (*Takes it—then.*) Ma, I want to ask you something.

MOTHER. Eat your potato.

YOUNG WOMAN (*takes a bite—then*). Ma, there's something I want to ask you —something important.

MOTHER. Is it mealy?

YOUNG WOMAN. S'all right. Ma—tell me.

MOTHER. Three pounds for a quarter.

YOUNG WOMAN. Ma—tell me—

(*Buzzer.*)

MOTHER (*her dull voice brightening*). There's the garbage. (*Goes to door—or dumbwaiter—opens it.*)

(*Stop radio.*)

JANITOR'S VOICE (*offstage*). Garbage.

MOTHER (*pleased—busy*). All right. (*Gets garbage can—puts it out.* YOUNG WOMAN *walks up and down.*) What's the matter now?

YOUNG WOMAN. Nothing

MOTHER. That jumping up from the table every night the garbage is collected! You act like you're crazy.

YOUNG WOMAN. Ma, do all women—

MOTHER. I suppose you think you're too nice for anything so common! Well, let me tell you, my lady, that it's a very important part of life.

YOUNG WOMAN. I know, but, Ma, if you—

MOTHER. If it weren't for garbage cans where would we be? Where would we all be? Living in filth—that's what! Filth! I should think you'd be glad! I should think you'd be grateful!

YOUNG WOMAN. Oh, Ma!

MOTHER. Well, are you?

YOUNG WOMAN. Am I what?

MOTHER. Glad! Grateful.

YOUNG WOMAN. Yes!

MOTHER. You don't act like it!

YOUNG WOMAN. Oh, Ma, don't talk!

MOTHER. You just said you wanted to talk.

YOUNG WOMAN. Well now—I want to think. I got to think.

MOTHER. Aren't you going to finish your potato?

YOUNG WOMAN. Oh, Ma!

MOTHER. Is there anything the matter with it?

YOUNG WOMAN. No—

MOTHER. Then why don't you finish it?

YOUNG WOMAN. Because I don't want it.

MOTHER. Why don't you?

YOUNG WOMAN. Oh, Ma! Let me alone!

MOTHER. Well, you've got to eat! If you don't eat—

YOUNG WOMAN. Ma! Don't nag!

MOTHER. Nag! Just because I try to look out for you—nag! Just because I try to care for you—nag! Why, you haven't sense enough to eat! What would become of you I'd like to know—if I didn't nag!

(*Offstage—a sound of window opening—all these offstage sounds come in through the court window at the back.*)

WOMAN'S VOICE. Johnny—Johnny—come in now!

A SMALL BOY'S VOICE. Oh, Ma!

WOMAN'S VOICE. It's getting cold.

A SMALL BOY'S VOICE. Oh, Ma!

WOMAN'S VOICE. You heard me! (*Sound of window slamming.*)

YOUNG WOMAN. I'm grown up, Ma.

MOTHER. Grown up! What do you mean by that?

YOUNG WOMAN. Nothing much—I guess. (*Offstage sound of baby crying.* MOTHER *rises, clatters dishes.*) Let's not do the dishes right away, Ma. Let's talk—I gotta.

MOTHER. Well, I can't talk with dirty dishes around—you may be able to but—(*Clattering—clattering.*)

YOUNG WOMAN. Ma! Listen! Listen!—There's a man wants to marry me.

MOTHER (*stops clattering—sits*). What man?

YOUNG WOMAN. He says he fell in love with my hands.

MOTHER. In love! Is that beginning again! I thought you were over that!

(*Offstage* BOY'S VOICE—*whistles*—GIRL'S VOICE *answers.*)

BOY'S VOICE. Come on out.

GIRL'S VOICE. Can't.

BOY'S VOICE. Nobody'll see you.

GIRL'S VOICE. I can't.

BOY'S VOICE. It's dark now—come on.

GIRL'S VOICE. Well—just for a minute.

BOY'S VOICE. Meet you round the corner.

YOUNG WOMAN. I got to get married, Ma.

MOTHER. What do you mean?

YOUNG WOMAN. I gotta.

MOTHER. You haven't got in trouble, have you?

YOUNG WOMAN. Don't talk like that!

MOTHER. Well, you say you got to get married—what do you mean?

YOUNG WOMAN. Nothing.

MOTHER. Answer me!

YOUNG WOMAN. All women get married, don't they?

MOTHER. Nonsense!

YOUNG WOMAN. You got married, didn't you?

MOTHER. Yes, I did!

(*Offstage voices.*)

WOMAN'S VOICE. Where you going?

MAN'S VOICE. Out.

WOMAN'S VOICE. You were out last night.

MAN'S VOICE. Was I?

WOMAN'S VOICE. You're always going out.

MAN'S VOICE. Am I?

WOMAN'S VOICE. Where you going?

MAN'S VOICE. Out.

(*End of offstage voices.*)

MOTHER. Who is he? Where did you come to know him?

YOUNG WOMAN. In the office.

MOTHER. In the office!

YOUNG WOMAN. It's Mr. J.

MOTHER. Mr. J.?

YOUNG WOMAN. The Vice-President.

MOTHER. Vice-President! His income must be— Does he know you've got a mother to support?

YOUNG WOMAN. Yes.

MOTHER. What does he say?

YOUNG WOMAN. All right.

MOTHER. How soon you going to marry him?

YOUNG WOMAN. I'm not going to.

MOTHER. Not going to!

YOUNG WOMAN. No! I'm not going to.

MOTHER. But you just said—

YOUNG WOMAN. I'm not going to.

MOTHER. Are you crazy?

YOUNG WOMAN. I can't, Ma! I can't!

MOTHER. Why can't you?

YOUNG WOMAN. I don't love him.

MOTHER. Love!—what does that amount to! Will it clothe you? Will it feed you? Will it pay the bills?

YOUNG WOMAN. No! But it's real just the same!

MOTHER. Real!

YOUNG WOMAN. If it isn't—what can you count on in life?

MOTHER. I'll tell you what you can count on! You can count that you've got to eat and sleep and get up and put clothes on your back and take 'em off again—that you got to get old—and that you got to die. That's what you can count on! All the rest is in your head!

YOUNG WOMAN. But Ma—didn't you love Pa?

MOTHER. I suppose I did—I don't know—I've forgotten—what difference does it make—now?

YOUNG WOMAN. But then!—oh Ma, tell me!

MOTHER. Tell you what?

YOUNG WOMAN. About all that—love!

(*Offstage voices.*)

WIFE'S VOICE. Don't.

HUSBAND'S VOICE. What's the matter—don't you want me to kiss you?

WIFE'S VOICE. Not like that.

HUSBAND'S VOICE. Like what?

WIFE'S VOICE. That silly kiss!

HUSBAND'S VOICE. Silly kiss?

WIFE'S VOICE. You look so silly—oh I know what's coming when you look like that—and kiss me like that—don't—go away—

(*End of off stage voices.*)

MOTHER. He's a decent man, isn't he?

YOUNG WOMAN. I don't know. How should I know—yet.

MOTHER. He's a Vice-President—of course he's decent.

YOUNG WOMAN. I don't care whether he's decent or not. I won't marry him.

MOTHER. But you just said you wanted to marry—

YOUNG WOMAN. Not him.

MOTHER. Who?

YOUNG WOMAN. I don't know—I don't know—I haven't found him yet!

MOTHER. You talk like you're crazy!

YOUNG WOMAN. Oh, Ma—tell me!

MOTHER. Tell you what?

YOUNG WOMAN. Tell me— (*Words suddenly pouring out.*) Your skin oughtn't to curl—ought it—when he just comes near you—ought it? That's wrong, ain't it? You don't get over that, do you—ever, do you or do you? How is it, Ma—do you?

MOTHER. Do you what?

YOUNG WOMAN. Do you get used to, it—so after a while it doesn't matter? Or don't you? Does it always matter? You ought to be in love, oughtn't you, Ma? You must be in love, mustn't you, Ma? That changes everything, doesn't it—or does it? Maybe if you just like a person it's all right—is it? When he puts a hand on me, my blood turns cold. But your blood oughtn't to run cold, ought it? His hands are—his hands are—fat, Ma—don't you see—his hands are fat—and they sort of press—and they're fat—don't you see?—Don't you see?

MOTHER (*stares at her bewildered*). See what?

YOUNG WOMAN (*rushing on*). I've always thought I'd find somebody—somebody young—and—and attractive—with wavy hair—wavy hair—I always think of children with curls—little curls all over their head—somebody young—and attractive—that I'd like—that I'd love— But I haven't found anybody like that yet—I haven't found anybody— I've hardly known anybody—you'd never let me go with anybody and—

MOTHER. Are you throwing it up to me that—

YOUNG WOMAN. No—let me finish, Ma! No—let me finish! I just mean I've never found anybody—anybody—nobody's ever asked me—till now—he's the only man that's ever asked me— And I suppose I got to marry somebody—all girls do—

MOTHER. Nonsense.

YOUNG WOMAN. But, I can't go on like this, Ma—I don't know why—but I can't—it's like I'm all tight inside—sometimes I feel like I'm stifling!— You don't know—stifling. (*Walks up and down.*) I can't go on like this much longer—going to work—coming home—going to work—coming home—I can't— Sometimes in the subway I think I'm going to die—sometimes even in the office if something don't happen—I got to do something—I don't know—it's like I'll all tight inside.

MOTHER. You're crazy.

YOUNG WOMAN. Oh, Ma!

MOTHER. You're crazy!

YOUNG WOMAN. Ma—if you tell me that again I'll kill you! I'll kill you!

MOTHER. If that isn't crazy!

YOUNG WOMAN. I'll kill you— Maybe I am crazy— I don't know. Sometimes I think I am—the thoughts that go on in my mind—sometimes I think I am—I can't help it if I am— I do the best I can—I do the best I can and I'm nearly crazy! (MOTHER *rises and sits.*) Go away! Go away! You don't know anything about anything! And you haven't got any pity—no pity—you just take it for granted that I go to work every day—and come home every night and bring my money every week—you just take it for granted—you'd let me go on forever—and never feel any pity—

(*Offstage* RADIO—*a voice singing a sentimental Mother song or popular home song.*)

(MOTHER *begins to cry—crosses to chair Left—sits.*)

YOUNG WOMAN. Oh Ma—forgive me! Forgive me!

MOTHER. My own child! To be spoken to like that by my own child!

YOUNG WOMAN. I didn't mean it, Ma—I didn't mean it!

(*She goes to her mother—crosses to Left.*)

MOTHER (*clinging to her hand*). You're all I've got in the world—and you don't want me—you want to kill me.

YOUNG WOMAN. No—no, I don't, Ma! I just said that!

MOTHER. I've worked for you and slaved for you!

YOUNG WOMAN. I know, Ma.

MOTHER. I brought you into the world.

YOUNG WOMAN. I know, Ma.

MOTHER. You're flesh of my flesh and—

YOUNG WOMAN. I know, Ma, I know.

MOTHER. And—

YOUNG WOMAN. You rest, now, Ma—you rest—

MOTHER (*struggling*). I got to do the dishes.

YOUNG WOMAN. I'll do the dishes— You listen to the music, Ma—I'll do the dishes.

(MA *sits.*)

(YOUNG WOMAN *crosses to behind screen.*) (*Takes a pair of rubber gloves and begins to put them on.*)

(*The* MOTHER *sees them—they irritate her—there is a return of her characteristic mood.*)

MOTHER. Those gloves! I've been washing dishes for forty years and I never wore gloves! But my lady's hands! My lady's hands!

YOUNG WOMAN. Sometimes you talk to me like you're jealous, Ma.

MOTHER. Jealous?

YOUNG WOMAN. It's my hands got me a husband.

MOTHER. A husband? So you're going to marry him now!

YOUNG WOMAN. I suppose so.

MOTHER. If you ain't the craziest—

(*The scene blacks out.*)

(*In the darkness, the* MOTHER *song goes into jazz—very faint—as the scene lights into*)

EPISODE THREE

Honeyman

SCENE: *Hotel Bedroom.*
Bed, chair, mirror.
The door at the back now opens on a bathroom; the window, on a dancing casino opposite.

CHARACTERS:
YOUNG WOMAN
HUSBAND
BELLBOY

OFFSTAGE:
Seen but not heard—MEN *and* WOMEN *dancing in couples.*

SOUNDS:
A small jazz band (violin, piano, saxaphone—very dim, at first, then louder).

AT RISE:
Set dark.
BELLBOY, HUSBAND, *and* YOUNG WOMAN

enter. BELLBOY *carries luggage. He switches on light by door.*

Stop music.

HUSBAND. Well, here we are.

(*Throws hat on bed.*)

(BELLBOY *puts luggage down, crosses to window, raises shade three inches, opens window three inches.*)

(*Sounds of jazz music louder. Offstage.*)

BELLBOY (*comes to man for tip*). Anything else, Sir?

(*Receives tip. Exits.*)

HUSBAND. Well, here we are.

YOUNG WOMAN. Yes, here we are.

HUSBAND. Aren't you going to take your hat off—stay a while? (YOUNG WOMAN *looks around as though looking for a way out, then takes off her hat, pulls the hair automatically around her ears.*) This is all right, isn't it? Huh? Huh?

YOUNG WOMAN. It's very nice.

HUSBAND. Twelve bucks a day! They know how to soak you in these pleasure resorts. Twelve bucks! (*Music.*) Well——we'll get our money's worth out of it all right. (*Goes toward bathroom.*) I'm going to wash up. (*Stops at door.*) Don't you want to wash up? (YOUNG WOMAN *shakes head "No".*) I do! It was a long trip! I want to wash up! (*Goes off—closes door. Sings in bathroom.* YOUNG WOMAN *goes to window—raises shade—sees the dancers going round and round in couples. Music is louder. Re-enter* HUSBAND.) Say, pull that blind down! They can see in!

YOUNG WOMAN. I thought you said there'd be a view of the ocean!

HUSBAND. Sure there is.

YOUNG WOMAN. I just see people—dancing.

HUSBAND. The ocean's beyond.

YOUNG WOMAN (*desperately*). I was counting on seeing it!

HUSBAND. You'll see it tomorrow—what's eating you? We'll take in the boardwalk— Don't you want to wash up?

YOUNG WOMAN. No!

HUSBAND. It was a long trip. Sure you don't? (YOUNG WOMAN *shakes her head "No".* HUSBAND *takes off his coat—puts it over chair.*) Better make yourself at home. I'm going to. (*She stares at him—moves away from the window.*) Say, pull down that blind! (*Crosses to chair down* L.—*sits.*)

YOUNG WOMAN. It's close—don't you think it's close?

HUSBAND. Well—you don't want people looking in, do you? (*Laughs.*) Huh—huh?

YOUNG WOMAN. No.

HUSBAND (*laughs*). I guess not. Huh? (*Takes off shoes.* YOUNG WOMAN *leaves the window, and crosses down to the bed.*) Say—you look a little white around the gills! What's the matter?

YOUNG WOMAN. Nothing.

HUSBAND. You look like you're scared.

YOUNG WOMAN. No.

HUSBAND. Nothing to be scared of. You're with your husband, you know. (*Takes her to chair, left.*)

YOUNG WOMAN. I know.

HUSBAND. Happy?

YOUNG WOMAN. Yes.

HUSBAND (*sitting*). Then come here and give us a kiss. (*He puts her on his knee.*) That's the girlie. (*He bends her head down, and kisses her along the back of her neck.*) Like that? (*She tries to get to her feet.*) Say—stay there! What you moving for? —You know—you got to learn to relax, little girl— (*Dancers go off. Dim lights. Pinches her above knee.*) Say, what you got under there?

YOUNG WOMAN. Nothing.

HUSBAND. Nothing! (*Laughs*). That's a good one! Nothing, huh? Huh? That reminds of the story of the pullman porter and the—what's the matter—did I tell you that one?

(*Music dims off and out.*)

YOUNG WOMAN. I don't know.

HUSBAND. The pullman porter and the tart?

YOUNG WOMAN. No.

HUSBAND. It's a good one—well—the train was just pulling out and the tart—

YOUNG WOMAN. You did tell that one!

HUSBAND. About the—

YOUNG WOMAN. Yes! Yes! I remember now!

HUSBAND. About the—

YOUNG WOMAN. Yes!

HUSBAND. All right—if I did. You're sure it was the one about the—

YOUNG WOMAN. I'm sure.

HUSBAND. When he asked her what she had underneath her seat and she said—

YOUNG WOMAN. Yes! Yes! That one!

HUSBAND. All right— But I don't believe I did. (SHE *tries to get up again, as* HE *holds her.*) You know you have got something under there—what is it?

YOUNG WOMAN. Nothing—just—just my

garter.

HUSBAND. Your garter! Your garter! Say did I tell you the one about—

YOUNG WOMAN. Yes! Yes!

HUSBAND (*with dignity*). How do you know which one I meant?

YOUNG WOMAN. You told me them all!

HUSBAND (*pulling her back to his knee*). No, I didn't! Not by a jugful! I got a lot of 'em up my sleeve yet—that's part of what I owe my success to—my ability to spring a good story— You know— you got to learn to relax, little girl—haven't you?

YOUNG WOMAN. Yes.

HUSBAND. That's one of the biggest things to learn in life. That's part of what I owe my success to. Now you go and get those heavy things off—and relax.

YOUNG WOMAN. They're not heavy.

HUSBAND. You haven't got much on—have you? But you'll feel better with 'em off. (*Gets up.*) Want me to help you?

YOUNG WOMAN. No.

HUSBAND. I'm your husband, you know.

YOUNG WOMAN. I know.

HUSBAND. You aren't afraid of your husband, are you?

YOUNG WOMAN. No—of course not—but I thought maybe—can't we go out for a little while?

HUSBAND. Out? What for?

YOUNG WOMAN. Fresh air—walk—talk.

HUSBAND. We can talk here—I'll tell you all about myself. Go along now. (YOUNG WOMAN *goes toward bathroom door—gets bag.*) Where are you going?

YOUNG WOMAN. In here.

HUSBAND. I thought you'd want to wash up.

YOUNG WOMAN. I just want to—get ready.

HUSBAND. You don't have to go in there to take your clothes off!

YOUNG WOMAN. I want to.

HUSBAND. What for?

YOUNG WOMAN. I always do.

HUSBAND. What?

YOUNG WOMAN. Undress by myself.

HUSBAND. You've never been married till now—have you? (*Laughs.*) Or have you been putting something over on me?

YOUNG WOMAN. No.

HUSBAND. I understand—kind of modest —huh? Huh?

YOUNG WOMAN. Yes.

HUSBAND. I understand women— (*Indulgently.*) Go along. (*She goes off—starts to close door.* YOUNG WOMAN *exits.*) Don't close the door—thought you wanted to talk. (*He looks around the room with satisfaction—after a pause— Rises—takes off his collar.*) You're awful quiet—what are you doing in there?

YOUNG WOMAN. Just—getting ready—

HUSBAND (*still in his mood of satisfaction*). I'm going to enjoy life from now on— I haven't had such an easy time of it. I got where I am by hard work and self denial—now I'm going to enjoy life—I'm going to make up for all I missed—aren't you about ready?

YOUNG WOMAN. Not yet.

HUSBAND. Next year maybe we'll go to Paris. You can buy a lot of that French underwear—and Switzerland—all my life I've wanted a Swiss watch—that I bought right there— I coulda' got a Swiss watch here, but I always wanted one that I bought right there— Isn't that funny—huh? Isn't it? Huh? Huh?

YOUNG WOMAN. Yes.

HUSBAND. All my life I've wanted a Swiss watch that I bought right there. All my life I've counted on having that some day—more than anything—except one thing—you know what?

YOUNG WOMAN. No.

HUSBAND. Guess.

YOUNG WOMAN. I can't.

HUSBAND. Then I'm coming in and tell you.

YOUNG WOMAN. No! Please! Please don't.

HUSBAND. Well hurry up then! I thought you women didn't wear much of anything these days—huh? Huh? I'm coming in!

YOUNG WOMAN. No—no! Just a minute!

HUSBAND. All right. Just a minute!

(YOUNG WOMAN *is silent.*)

HUSBAND (*laughs and takes out watch*). 13—14— I'm counting the seconds on you —that's what you said, didn't you—just a minute! —49—50—51—52—53—

(*Enter* YOUNG WOMAN.)

YOUNG WOMAN (*at the door*). Here I am.

(*She wears a little white gown that hangs very straight. She is very still, but her eyes are wide with a curious, helpless, animal terror.*)

HUSBAND (*starts toward her—stops. The room is in shadow except for one dim light by the bed. Sound of* GIRL *weeping*). You crying? (*Sound of weeping.*) What you crying for? (*Crosses to her.*)

YOUNG WOMAN (*crying out*). Ma! Ma!

I want my mother!

HUSBAND. I thought you were glad to get away from her.

YOUNG WOMAN. I want her now—I want somebody.

HUSBAND. You got me, haven't you?

YOUNG WOMAN. Somebody—somebody—

HUSBAND. There's nothing to cry about. There's nothing to cry about.

BLACK OUT

(*The music continues until the lights go up for* EPISODE FOUR.)

(*Rhythm of the music is gradually replaced by the sound of steel riveting for* EPISODE FOUR.)

EPISODE FOUR

MATERNAL

SCENE: *A room in a hospital. The door in the back now opens on a corridor; the window on a tall building going up.*
Bed. Chair.

CHARACTERS IN THE SCENE:
- YOUNG WOMAN
- DOCTORS
- NURSES
- HUSBAND

OUTSIDE—CORRIDOR LIFE:

CHARACTERS SEEN BUT NOT HEARD:
- WOMAN IN WHEEL CHAIR
- WOMAN IN BATHROBE
- STRETCHER WAGON
- NURSE WITH TRAY
- NURSE WITH COVERED BASIN

SOUNDS:
(*outside window*)
Riveting.

AT RISE:
YOUNG WOMAN *lies still in bed.*
The door is open.
In the corridor, a stretcher wagon goes by.
Enter NURSE.

NURSE. How are you feeling today? (*No response from* YOUNG WOMAN.) Better? (*No response.*) No pain? (*No response.* NURSE *takes her watch in one hand,* YOUNG WOMAN'S *wrist in the other—stands, then goes to chart at foot of bed—writes.*) You're getting along fine. (*No response.*) Such a sweet baby you have, too. (*No response.*) Aren't you glad it's a girl? (YOUNG WOMAN *makes sign with her head, "No".*) You're not! Oh, my! That's no way to talk! Men want boys—women ought to want girls. (*No response.*) Maybe you didn't want either, eh? (YOUNG WOMAN *signs "No". Riveting machine.*) You'll feel different when it begins to nurse. You'll just love it then. Your milk hasn't come yet—has it? (*Sign—"No".*) It will! (*Sign—"No".*) Oh, you don't know Doctor! (*Goes to door—turns.*) Anything else you want? (YOUNG WOMAN *points to window.*) Draft? (*Sign—"No".*) The noise? (YOUNG WOMAN *signs "Yes".*) Oh, that can't be helped. Hospital's got to have a new wing. We're the biggest Maternity Hospital in the world. I'll close the window, though. (YOUNG WOMAN *signs "No".*) No?

YOUNG WOMAN (*whispers*). I smell everything then.

NURSE (*starting out the door—Riveting machine*). Here's your man!

(*Enter* HUSBAND *with large bouquet. Crosses to bed.*)

HUSBAND. Well, how are we today?

(YOUNG WOMAN—*no response.*)

NURSE. She's getting stronger!

HUSBAND. Of course she is!

NURSE (*taking flowers*). See what your husband brought you.

HUSBAND. Better put 'em in water right away. (*Exit* NURSE.) Everything O.K.? (YOUNG WOMAN *signs "No".*) Now see here, my dear, you've got to brace up, you know! And—and face things! Everybody's got to brace up and face things! That's what makes the world go round. I know all you've been through but— (YOUNG WOMAN *signs "No".*) Oh, yes I do! I know all about it! I was right outside all the time! (YOUNG WOMAN *makes violent gesture of "No". Ignoring.*) Oh yes! But you've got to brace up now! Make an effort! Pull yourself together! Start the uphill climb! Oh I've been down—but I haven't stayed down. I've been licked but I haven't stayed licked! I've pulled myself up by my own bootstraps, and that's what you've got to do! Will power! That's what conquers! Look at me! Now you've got to brace up! Face the music! Stand the gaff! Take life by the horns! Look it in the face! —Having a baby's natural! Perfectly natural thing—why should—

(YOUNG WOMAN *chokes—points wildly to door. Enter* NURSE *with flowers in a vase.*)

NURSE. What's the matter?

HUSBAND. She's got that gagging again

—like she had the last time I was here.

(YOUNG WOMAN *gestures him out.*)

NURSE. Better go, sir.

HUSBAND (*at door*). I'll be back.

(YOUNG WOMAN *gasping and gesturing.*)

NURSE. She needs rest.

HUSBAND. Tomorrow then. I'll be back tomorrow—tomorrow and every day—goodbye.

(*Exits.*)

NURSE. You got a mighty nice husband, I guess you know that? (*Writes on chart.*) Gagging.

(*Corridor life*—WOMAN IN BATHROBE *passes door. Enter* DOCTOR, YOUNG DOCTOR, NURSE *wheeling surgeon's wagon with bottles, instruments, etc.*)

DOCTOR. How's the little lady today? (*Crosses to bed.*)

NURSE. She's better, Doctor.

DOCTOR. Of course she's better! She's all right—aren't you? (YOUNG WOMAN *does not respond.*) What's the matter? Can't you talk?

(*Drops her hand—takes chart.*)

NURSE. She's a little weak yet, Doctor.

DOCTOR (*at chart*). Milk hasn't come yet?

NURSE. No, Doctor.

DOCTOR. Put the child to breast. (YOUNG WOMAN—*"No—no!"—Riveting machine.*) No? Don't you want to nurse your baby? (YOUNG WOMAN *signs "No".*) Why not? (*No response.*) These modern neurotic women, eh, Doctor? What are we going to do with 'em? (YOUNG DOCTOR *laughs.* NURSE *smiles.*) Bring the baby!

YOUNG WOMAN. No!

DOCTOR. Well—that's strong enough. I thought you were too weak to talk—that's better. You don't want your baby?

YOUNG WOMAN. No.

DOCTOR. What do you want?

YOUNG WOMAN. Let alone—let alone.

DOCTOR. Bring the baby.

NURSE. Yes, Doctor—she's behaved very badly every time, Doctor—very upset—maybe we better not.

DOCTOR. I decide what we better and better not here, Nurse!

NURSE. Yes, Doctor.

DOCTOR. Bring the baby.

NURSE. Yes, Doctor.

DOCTOR (*with chart*). Gagging—you mean nausea.

NURSE. Yes, Doctor, but—

DOCTOR. No buts, nurse.

NURSE. Yes, Doctor.

DOCTOR. Nausea!— Change her diet!— What is her diet?

NURSE. Liquids.

DOCTOR. Give her solids.

NURSE. Yes, Doctor. She says she can't swallow solids.

DOCTOR. Give her solids.

NURSE. Yes, Doctor. (*Starts to go.*)

(*Riveting machine.*)

DOCTOR. Wait—I'll change her medicine. (*Takes pad and writes prescription in Latin. Hands it to* NURSE.) After meals. (*To door.*) Bring her baby.

(*Exit* DOCTOR, *followed by* YOUNG DOCTOR *and* NURSE *with surgeon's wagon.*)

NURSE. Yes, Doctor.

(*Exits.*)

YOUNG WOMAN (*alone*). Let me alone—let me alone—let me alone—I've submitted to enough—I won't submit to any more—crawl off—crawl off in the dark—Vixen crawled under the bed—way back in the corner under the bed—they were all drowned—puppies don't go to heaven—heaven—golden stairs—long stairs—long—too long—long golden stairs—climb those golden stairs—stairs—stairs—climb—tired—too tired—dead—no matter—nothing matters—dead—stairs—long stairs—all the dead going up—going up to be in heaven—heaven—golden stairs—all the children coming down—coming down to be born—dead going up—children coming down—going up—coming down—going up—coming down—going up—coming down—going up—stop—stop—no—no traffic cop—no—no traffic cop in heaven—traffic cop—traffic cop—can't you give us a smile—tired—too tired—no matter—it doesn't matter—St. Peter—St. Peter at the gate—you can't come in—no matter—it doesn't matter—I'll rest—I'll lie down—down—all written down—down in a big book—no matter—it doesn't matter—I'll lie down—it weighs me—it's over me—it weighs—weighs—it's heavy—it's a heavy book—no matter—lie still—don't move—can't move—rest—forget—they say you forget—a girl—aren't you glad it's a girl—a little girl—with no hair—none—little curls all over his head—a little bald girl—curls—curls all over his head—what kind of hair has God? no matter—it doesn't matter—everybody loves God—they've got to—got to—got to love God—God is love—even if he's bad they got to love him—even if he's got fat hands—fat hands—no no—he wouldn't be God—His hands make you well—He lays on his hands—well — and happy — no matter—doesn't matter — far — too far—tired—too tired Vixen crawled off under bed—eight—there were eight—a woman crawled off under the bed—a woman has one—two three four—one two three four—one two three four—two plus two is four—two times two is four—two times four is eight Vixen had eight—one two three four five six seven eight—eight—Puffie had eight—all drowned — drowned — drowned in blood—blood— oh God! God—God never had one—Mary had one—in a manger—the lowly manger—God's on a high throne—far—too far—no matter—it doesn't matter—God Mary Mary God Mary—Virgin Mary—Mary had one—the Holy Ghost—the Holy Ghost—George H. Jones—oh don't—please don't! Let me rest—now I can rest—the weight is gone—inside the weight is gone—it's only outside—outside—all around—weight—I'm under it—Vixen crawled under the bed—there were eight—I'll not submit any more—I'll not submit—I'll not submit—

(*The scene* BLACKS OUT. *The sound of riveting continues until it goes into the sound of an electric piano and the scene lights up for* EPISODE FIVE.)

EPISODE FIVE

PROHIBITED

SCENE: *Bar — Bottles — Tables — Chairs — Electric piano.*

SOUND: *Electric piano.*

CHARACTERS:

MAN *behind the bar*

POLICEMAN *at bar*

WAITER

At Table 1. A MAN *and a* WOMAN

At Table 2. A MAN *and a* BOY

At Table 3. TWO MEN *waiting for* TWO GIRLS, *who are*

TELEPHONE GIRL *of Episode One and* YOUNG WOMAN.

AT RISE. *Everyone except the* GIRLS *on. Of the characters, the* MAN *and* WOMAN *at Table 1 are an ordinary man and woman.* THE MAN *at Table 2 is a middle-aged fairy; the* BOY *is young, untouched. At Table 3,* 1ST MAN *is pleasing, common, vigorous. He has coarse wavy hair.* 2ND MAN *is an ordinary salesman type.*

1ST MAN (*at Table 3*). I'm going to beat it.

2ND MAN. Oh, for the love of Mike.

1ST MAN. They ain't going to show.

2ND MAN. Sure they'll show.

1ST MAN. How do you know they'll show?

2ND MAN. I tell you you can't keep that baby away from me—just got to—(*Snaps fingers.*)—She comes running.

1ST MAN. Looks like it.

2ND MAN (*to* WAITER—*makes sign "2", with his fingers.*) The same.

(WAITER *goes to the bar.*)

MAN (*at Table 2*). Oh, I'm sorry I brought you here.

BOY. Why?

MAN. This Purgatory of noise! I brought you here to give you pleasure—let you taste pleasure. This sherry they have here is bottled—heaven. Wait till you taste it.

BOY. But I don't drink.

MAN. Drink! This isn't drink! Real amontillado is sunshine and orange groves—it's the Mediterranean and blue moonlight and—love? Have you ever been in love?

BOY. No.

MAN. Never in love with—a woman?

BOY. No—not really.

MAN. What do you mean—really?

BOY. Just—that.

MAN. Ah! (*Makes sign to* WAITER.) Two—you know what I want—Two.

(WAITER *goes to the bar.*)

MAN (*at Table 1*). Well, are you going through with it, or ain't you?

WOMAN. That's what I want to do—go through with it.

MAN. But you can't.

WOMAN. Why can't I?

MAN. How can yuh? (*Silence.*) It's nothing—most women don't think anything about it—they just—Bert told me a doctor to go to—gave me the address—

WOMAN. Don't talk about it!

MAN. Got to talk about it—you got to get out of this. (*Silence*—MAN *makes sign to* WAITER.) What you having?

WOMAN. Nothing—I don't want anything. I had enough.

MAN. Do you good. The same?

WOMAN. I suppose so.

MAN (*makes sign "2" to* WAITER.) The same.

(WAITER *goes to the bar.*)

(*At Table 3.*)

1ST MAN. I'm going to beat it.

2ND MAN. Oh say, listen! I'm counting

on you to take the other one off my hands.

1ST MAN. I'm going to beat it.

2ND MAN. For the love of Mike have a heart! Listen—as a favor to me—I got to be home by six—I promised my wife—sure. That don't leave me no time at all if we got to hang around—entertain some dame. You got to take her off my hands.

1ST MAN. Maybe she won't fall for me.

2ND MAN. Sure she'll fall for you! They all fall for you—even my wife likes you—tries to kid herself it's your brave exploits, but I know what it is—sure she'll fall for you.

(*Enter two girls*—TELEPHONE GIRL *and* YOUNG WOMAN.)

GIRL (*coming to Table.*) Hello—

2ND MAN (*grouch*). Good night.

GIRL. Good night? What's eatin' yuh?

2ND MAN (*same*). Nothin's eatin' me—thought somethin' musta swallowed you.

GIRL. Why?

2ND MAN. You're late!

GIRL (*unimpressed*). Oh—(*Brushing it aside.*)—Mrs. Jones—Mr. Smith.

2ND MAN. Meet my friend, Mr. Roe. (*They all sit. To the* WAITER.) The same, and two more.

(WAITER *goes.*)

GIRL. So we kept you waiting, did we?

2ND MAN. Only about an hour.

YOUNG WOMAN. Was it that long?

2ND MAN. We been here that long—ain't we, Dick?

1ST MAN. Just about, Harry.

2ND MAN. For the love of God what delayed yuh?

GIRL. Tell Helen that one.

2ND MAN (*to* YOUNG WOMAN). The old Irish woman that went to her first race? Bet on the skate that came in last—she went up to the jockey and asked him, "For the love of God, what delayed yuh?"

(*All laugh.*)

YOUNG WOMAN. Why, that's kinda funny!

2ND MAN. Kinda!—What do you mean kinda?

YOUNG WOMAN. I just mean there are not many of 'em that are funny at all.

2ND MAN. Not if you haven't heard the funny ones.

YOUNG WOMAN. Oh I've heard 'em all.

1ST MAN. Not a laugh in a carload, eh?

GIRL. Got a cigarette?

2ND MAN (*with package*). One of these?

GIRL (*taking one*). Uhhuh.

(*He offers the package to* YOUNG WOMAN.)

YOUNG WOMAN (*taking one*). Uhhuh.

2ND MAN (*to* 1ST MAN). One of these?

1ST MAN (*showing his own package*). Thanks—I like these. (*He lights* YOUNG WOMAN'S *cigarette.*)

2ND MAN (*lighting* GIRL'S *cigarette*). Well—baby—how they comin', huh?

GIRL. Couldn't be better.

2ND MAN. How's every little thing?

GIRL. Just great.

2ND MAN. Miss me?

GIRL. I'll say so—when did you get in?

2ND MAN. Just a coupla hours ago.

GIRL. Miss me?

2ND MAN. Did I? You don't know the half of it.

YOUNG WOMAN (*interrupting reslessly*). Can we dance here?

2ND MAN. Not here.

YOUNG WOMAN. Where do we go from here?

2ND MAN. Where do we go from here! You just got here!

1ST MAN. What's the hurry?

2ND MAN. What's the rush?

YOUNG WOMAN. I don't know.

GIRL. Helen wants to dance.

YOUNG WOMAN. I just want to keep moving.

1ST MAN (*smiling*). You want to keep moving, huh?

2ND MAN. You must be one of those restless babies! Where do we go from here!

YOUNG WOMAN. It's only some days—I want to keep moving.

1ST MAN. You want to keep moving, huh? (*He is staring at her smilingly.*)

YOUNG WOMAN (*nods*). Uhhuh.

1ST MAN (*quietly*). Stick around a while.

2ND MAN. Where do we go from here! Say, what kind of a crowd do you run with, anyway?

GIRL. Helen don't run with any crowd—do you, Helen?

YOUNG WOMAN (*embarrassed*). No.

1ST MAN. Well, I'm not a crowd—run with me.

2ND MAN (*gratified*). All set, huh?—Dick was about ready to beat it.

1ST MAN. That's before I met the little lady.

(WAITER *serves drinks.*)

1ST MAN. Here's how.

2ND MAN. Here's to you.

GIRL. Here's looking at you.

YOUNG WOMAN. Here's—happy days.

(*They all drink.*)

1ST MAN. That's good stuff!

2ND MAN. Off a boat.

1ST MAN. Off a boat?

2ND MAN. They get all their stuff here—off a boat.

GIRL. That's what *they* say.

2ND MAN. No! Sure! Sure they do! Sure!

GIRL. It's all right with me.

2ND MAN. But they do! Sure!

GIRL. I believe you, darling!

2ND MAN. Did you miss me?

GIRL. Uhhuh. (*Affirmative.*)

2ND MAN. Any other daddies?

GIRL. Uhhuh. (*Negative.*)

2ND MAN. Love any daddy but daddy?

GIRL. Uhhuh. (*Negative.*)

2ND MAN. Let's beat it!

GIRL (*a little self-conscious before* YOUNG WOMAN). We just got here.

2ND MAN. Don't I know it—Come on!

GIRL. But—(*Indicates* YOUNG WOMAN.)

2ND MAN (*not understanding*). They're all set—aren't you?

1ST MAN (*to* YOUNG WOMAN). Are we? (*She doesn't answer.*)

2ND MAN. I got to be out to the house by six—come on—(*Rising—to* GIRL.) Come on, kid—let's us beat it! (GIRL *indicates* YOUNG WOMAN.) (*Now understanding—very elaborate.*) Business is business, you know! I got a lot to do yet this afternoon—thought you might go along with me—help me out—how about it?

GIRL (*rising, her dignity preserved*). Sure—I'll go along with you—help you out.

(*Both rise.*)

2ND MAN. All right with you folks?

1ST MAN. All right with me.

2ND MAN. All right with you? (*To* YOUNG WOMAN.)

YOUNG WOMAN. All right with me.

2ND MAN. Come on, kid. (*They rise.*) Where's the damage?

1ST MAN. Go on!

2ND MAN. No!

1ST MAN. Go on!

2ND MAN. I'll match you.

YOUNG WOMAN. Heads win!

GIRL. Heads I win—tails you lose.

2ND MAN (*impatiently.*) He's matching me.

1ST MAN. Am I matching you or you matching me?

2ND MAN. I'm matching you. (*They match.*) You're stung!

1ST MAN (*contentedly*). Not so you can notice it. (*Smiles at* YOUNG WOMAN.)

GIRL. That's for you, Helen.

2ND MAN. She ain't dumb! Come on.

GIRL (*to* 1ST MAN). You be nice to her now. She's very fastidious. —Goodbye.

(*Exit* 2ND MAN *and* GIRL.)

YOUNG WOMAN. I know what business is like.

1ST MAN. You do—do yuh?

YOUNG WOMAN. I used to be a business girl myself before—

1ST MAN. Before what?

YOUNG WOMAN. Before I quit.

1ST MAN. What did you quit for?

YOUNG WOMAN. I just quit.

1ST MAN. You're married, huh?

YOUNG WOMAN. Yes—I am.

1ST MAN. All right with me.

YOUNG WOMAN. Some men don't seem to like a woman after she's married—

(WAITER *comes to the table.*)

1ST MAN. What's the difference?

YOUNG WOMAN. Depends on the man, I guess.

1ST MAN. Depends on the woman, I guess. (*To* WAITER, *makes sign of "2".*) The same.

(WAITER *goes to the bar.*)

(*At Table 1.*)

MAN. It don't amount to nothing. God! Most women just—

WOMAN. I know—I know—I know.

MAN. They don't think nothing of it. They just—

WOMAN. I know—I know—I know.

(*Re-enter* 2ND MAN *and* GIRL. *They go to Table 3.*)

2ND MAN. Say, I forgot—I want you to do something for me, will yuh?

1ST MAN. Sure—what is it?

2ND MAN. I want you to telephone me out home tomorrow—and ask me to come into town—will yuh?

1ST MAN. Sure—why not?

2ND MAN. You know—business—get me?

1ST MAN. I get you.

2ND MAN. I've worked the telegraph gag to death—and my wife likes you.

1ST MAN. What's your number?

2ND MAN. I'll write it down for you. (*Writes.*)

1ST MAN. How is your wife?

2ND MAN. She's fine.

1ST MAN. And the kid?

2ND MAN. Great. (*Hands him the card.*) Come on, kid. (*To* GIRL. *Turns back to*

YOUNG WOMAN.) Get this bird to tell you about himself.

GIRL. Keep him from it.

2ND MAN. Get him to tell you how he killed a couple a spig down in Mexico.

GIRL. You been in Mexico?

2ND MAN. He just came up from there.

GIRL. Can you teach us the tango?

YOUNG WOMAN. You killed a man?

2ND MAN. Two of 'em! With a bottle! Get him to tell you—with a bottle. Come on, kid. Goodbye.

(*Exit* 2ND MAN *and* GIRL.)

YOUNG WOMAN. Why did you?

1ST MAN. What?

YOUNG WOMAN. Kill 'em?

1ST MAN. To get free.

YOUNG WOMAN. Oh.

(*At Table 2.*)

MAN. You really must taste this—just taste it. It's a real amontillado, you know.

BOY. Where do they get it here?

MAN. It's always down the side streets one finds the real pleasures, don't you think?

BOY. I don't know.

MAN. Learn. Come, taste this! Amontillado! Or don't you like amontillado?

BOY. I don't know. I never had any before.

MAN. Your first taste! How I envy you! Come, taste it! Taste it! And die.

(BOY *tastes wine—finds it disappointing.*)

MAN (*gilding it*). Poe was a lover of amontillado. He returns to it continually, you remember—or are you a lover of Poe?

BOY. I've read a lot of him.

MAN. But are you a lover?

(*At Table 3.*)

1ST MAN. There were a bunch of bandidos—bandits, you know, took me into the hills—holding me there—what was I to do? I got the two birds that guarded me drunk one night, and then I filled the empty bottle with small stones—and let 'em have it!

YOUNG WOMAN. Oh!

1ST MAN. I had to get free, didn't I? I let 'em have it—

YOUNG WOMAN. Oh—then what did you do?

1ST MAN. Then I beat it.

YOUNG WOMAN. Where to—?

1ST MAN. Right here. (*Pause*). Glad?

YOUNG WOMAN (*nods.*) Yes.

1ST MAN (*makes sign to* WAITER *of "2"*). The same.

(WAITER *goes to bar.*)

(*At Table 1.*)

MAN. You're just scared because this is the first time and—

WOMAN. I'm not scared.

MAN. Then what are you for Christ's sake?

WOMAN. I'm not scared. I want it—I want to have it—that ain't being scared, is it?

MAN. It's being goofy.

WOMAN. I don't care.

MAN. What about your folks?

WOMAN. I don't care.

MAN. What about your job? (*Silence.*) You got to keep your job, haven't you? (*Silence.*) Haven't you?

WOMAN. I suppose so.

MAN. Well—there you are!

WOMAN (*silence—then*). All right—let's go now— You got the address?

MAN. Now you're coming to.

(*They get up and go off.*)

(*Exit* MAN *and* WOMAN.)

(*At Table 3.*)

YOUNG WOMAN. A bottle like that? (*She picks it up.*)

1ST MAN. Yeah—filled with pebbles.

YOUNG WOMAN. What kind of pebbles?

1ST MAN. Pebbles! Off the ground.

YOUNG WOMAN. Oh.

1ST MAN. Necessity, you know, mother of invention. (*As* YOUNG WOMAN *handles the bottle.*) Ain't a bad weapon—first you got a sledge hammer—then you got a knife.

YOUNG WOMAN. Oh. (*Puts bottle down.*)

1ST MAN. Women don't like knives, do they? (*Pours drink.*)

YOUNG WOMAN. No.

1ST MAN. Don't mind a hammer so much, though, do they?

YOUNG WOMAN. No—

1ST MAN. I didn't like it myself—any of it—but I had to get free, didn't I? Sure I had to get free, didn't I? (*Drinks.*) Now I'm damn glad I did.

YOUNG WOMAN. Why?

1ST MAN. You know why. (*He puts his hand over hers.*)

(*At Table 2.*)

MAN. Let's go to my rooms—and I'll show them to you—I have a first edition of Verlaine that will simply make your mouth water. (*They stand up.*) Here—there's just a sip at the bottom of my glass— (BOY *takes it.*) That last sip that's sweetest— Wasn't it?

BOY (*laughs*). And I always thought that was dregs.

(*Exit* MAN *followed by* BOY.)

(*At Table 3.*)

(*The* MAN *is holding her hand across the table.*)

YOUNG WOMAN. When you put your hand over mine! When you just touch me!

1ST MAN. Yeah? (*Pause.*) Come on, kid, let's go!

YOUNG WOMAN. Where?

1ST MAN. You haven't been around much, have you, kid?

YOUNG WOMAN. No.

1ST MAN. I could tell that just to look at you.

YOUNG WOMAN. You could?

1ST MAN. Sure I could. What are you running around with a girl like that other one for?

YOUNG WOMAN. I don't know. She seems to have a good time.

1ST MAN. So that's it?

YOUNG WOMAN. Don't she?

1ST MAN. Don't you?

YOUNG WOMAN. No.

1ST MAN. Never?

YOUNG WOMAN. Never.

1ST MAN. What's the matter?

YOUNG WOMAN. Nothing—just me, I guess.

1ST MAN. You're all right.

YOUNG WOMAN. Am I?

1ST MAN. Sure. You just haven't met the right guy—that's all—a girl like you—you got to meet the right guy.

YOUNG WOMAN. I know.

1ST MAN. You're different from girls like that other one—any guy'll do her. You're different.

YOUNG WOMAN. I guess I am.

1ST MAN. You didn't fall for that business gag—did you—when they went off?

YOUNG WOMAN. Well, I thought they wanted to be alone probably, but—

1ST MAN. And how!

YOUNG WOMAN. Oh—so that's it.

1ST MAN. That's it. Come along—let's go—

YOUNG WOMAN. Oh, I couldn't! Like this?

1ST MAN. Don't you like me?

YOUNG WOMAN. Yes.

1ST MAN. Then what's the matter?

YOUNG WOMAN. Do—you—like me?

1ST MAN. Like yuh? You don't know the half of it—listen—you know what you seem like to me?

YOUNG WOMAN. What?

1ST MAN. An angel. Just like an angel.

YOUNG WOMAN. I do?

1ST MAN. That's what I said! Let's go!

YOUNG WOMAN. Where?

1ST MAN. Where do you live?

YOUNG WOMAN. Oh, we can't go to my place.

1ST MAN. Then come to my place.

YOUNG WOMAN. Oh I couldn't—is it far?

1ST MAN. Just a step—come on—

YOUNG WOMAN. Oh I couldn't—what is it—a room?

1ST MAN. No—an apartment—a one-room apartment.

YOUNG WOMAN. That's different.

1ST MAN. On the ground floor—no one will see you—coming or going.

YOUNG WOMAN (*getting up*). I couldn't.

1ST MAN (*rises*). Wait a minute—I got to pay the damage—and I'll get a bottle of something to take along.

YOUNG WOMAN. No—don't.

1ST MAN. Why not?

YOUNG WOMAN. Well—don't bring any pebbles.

1ST MAN. Say—forget that! Will you?

YOUNG WOMAN. I just meant I don't think I'll need anything to drink.

1ST MAN (*leaning to her eagerly*). You like me—don't you, kid?

YOUNG WOMAN. Do you me?

1ST MAN. Wait!

(*He goes to the bar.* SHE *remains, her hands outstretched on the table staring ahead.*)

(*Enter a* MAN *and a* GIRL. *They go to one of the empty tables. The* WAITER *goes to them.*)

MAN (*to* GIRL). What do you want?

GIRL. Same old thing.

MAN (*to the* WAITER). The usual. (*Makes a sign "2".*)

(*The* 1ST MAN *crosses to* YOUNG WOMAN *with a wrapped bottle under his arm.* SHE *rises and starts out with him. As they pass the piano,* HE *stops and puts in a nickel—the music starts as they exit.*)

BLACK OUT

(*The music of the electric piano continues until the lights go up for* EPISODE SIX, *and the music has become the music of a hand organ, very very faint.*)

EPISODE SIX

INTIMATE

SCENE: *A dark room.*
SOUNDS: *A hand organ. Footbeats, of passing feet.*
CHARACTERS:
MAN
YOUNG WOMAN
AT RISE:
DARKNESS. *Nothing can be discerned. From the outside comes the sound of a hand organ, very faint, and the irregular rhythm of passing feet.*
The hand organ is playing "Cielito Lindo," that Spanish song that has been on every hand organ lately.

MAN. You're awful still, honey. What you thinking about?

WOMAN. About sea shells. (*The sound of her voice is beautiful.*)

MAN. Sheshells? Gee! I can't say it!

WOMAN. When I was little my grandmother used to have a big pink sea shell on the mantle behind the stove. When we'd go to visit her they'd let me hold it, and listen. That's what I was thinking about now.

MAN. Yeah?

WOMAN. You can hear the sea in 'em, you know.

MAN. Yeah, I know.

WOMAN. I wonder why that is?

MAN. Search me. (*Pause.*)

WOMAN. You going?

(*He has moved.*)

MAN. No. I just want a cigarette.

WOMAN (*glad, relieved*). Oh.

MAN. Want one?

WOMAN. No. (*Taking the match.*) Let me light it for you.

MAN. You got mighty pretty hands, honey. (*The match is out.*) This little pig went to market. This little pig stayed home. This little pig went—

WOMAN (*laughs*). Diddle diddle dee. (*Laughs again.*)

MAN. You got awful pretty hands.

WOMAN. I used to have. But I haven't taken much care of them lately. I will now— (*Pause. The music gets clearer.*) What's that?

MAN. What?

WOMAN. That music?

MAN. A dago hand organ. I gave him two bits the first day I got here—so he comes every day.

WOMAN. I mean—what's that he's playing?

MAN. Cielito Lindo.

WOMAN. What does that mean?

MAN. Little Heaven.

WOMAN. Little Heaven?

MAN. That's what lovers call each other in Spain.

WOMAN. Spain's where all the castles are, ain't it?

MAN. Yeah.

WOMAN. Little Heaven—sing it!

MAN (*singing to the music of the hand organ*). De la sierra morena viene, bajando viene, bajando; un par de ojitos negros—cielito lindo—da contrabando.

WOMAN. What does it mean?

MAN. From the high dark mountains.

WOMAN. From the high dark mountains—?

MAN. Oh it doesn't mean anything. It doesn't make sense. It's love. (*Taking up the song.*) Ay-ay-ay-ay.

WOMAN. I know what that means.

MAN. What?

WOMAN. Ay-ay-ay-ay.

(*They laugh.*)

MAN (*taking up the song*). Canta non llores— Sing don't cry—

WOMAN (*taking up song*). La-la-la-la-la-la-la-la-la-la—Little Heaven!

MAN. You got a nice voice, honey.

WOMAN. Have I?

(*Laughs—tickles him.*)

MAN. You bet you have—hey!

WOMAN (*laughing*). You ticklish?

MAN. Sure I am! Hey! (*They laugh.*) Go on, honey, sing something.

WOMAN. I couldn't.

MAN. Go on—you got a fine voice.

WOMAN (*laughs and sings.*)

Hey, diddle, diddle, the cat and the fiddle,
The cow jumped over the moon
The little dog laughed to see the sport

And the dish ran away with the spoon—(*Both laugh.*) I never thought that had any sense before—now I get it.

MAN. You got me beat.

WOMAN. It's you and me.—La—lala lalalala — lalalalalalala — Little Heaven. You're the dish and I'm the spoon.

MAN. You're a little spoon all right.

WOMAN. And I guess I'm the little cow that jumped over the moon. (*A pause.*) Do you believe in sorta guardian angels?

MAN. What?

WOMAN. Guardian angels?

MAN. I don't know. Maybe.

WOMAN. I do. (*Taking up the song again.*) Lalalalala-lalalalala-lalalala—Little Heaven. (*Talking.*) There must be something that looks out for you and brings you your happiness, at last—look at us! How did we both happen to go to that place today if there wasn't something!

MAN. Maybe you're right.

WOMAN. Look at us!

MAN. Everything's us to you, kid—ain't it?

WOMAN. Ain't it?

MAN. All right with me.

WOMAN. We belong together! We belong together! And we're going to stick together, ain't we?

MAN. Sing something else.

WOMAN. I tell you I can't sing!

MAN. Sure you can!

WOMAN. I tell you I hadn't thought of singing since I was a little bit of a girl.

MAN. Well sing anyway.

WOMAN (*singing*). And every little wavelet had its night cap on—its night cap on—its night cap on—and every little wave had its night cap on—so very early in the morning. (*Talking.*) Did you used to sing that when you were a little kid?

MAN. Nope.

WOMAN. Didn't you? We used to—in the first grade—little kids—we used to go round and round in a ring—and flop our hands up and down—supposed to be the waves. I remember it used to confuse me—because we did just the same thing to be little angels.

MAN. Yeah?

WOMAN. You know why I came here?

MAN. I can make a good guess.

WOMAN. Because you told me I looked like an angel to you! That's why I came.

MAN. Jeez, honey, all women look like angels to me—all white women. I ain't been seeing nothing but Indians, you know, for the last couple a years. Gee, when I got off the boat here the other day—and saw all the women—gee I pretty near went crazy—talk about looking like angels—why—

WOMAN. You've had a lot of women, haven't you?

MAN. Not so many—real ones.

WOMAN. Did you—like any of 'em—better than me?

MAN. Nope—there wasn't one of 'em any sweeter than you, honey—not as sweet—no—not as sweet.

WOMAN. I like to hear you say it. Say it again—

MAN (*protesting good humoredly*). Oh—

WOMAN. Go on—tell me again!

MAN. Here! (*Kisses her.*) Does that tell you?

WOMAN. Yes. (*Pause*). We're going to stick together—always—aren't we?

MAN (*honestly*). I'll have to be moving on, kid—some day, you know.

WOMAN. When?

MAN. Quien sabe?

WOMAN. What does that mean?

MAN. Quien sabe? You got to learn that, kid, if you're figuring on coming with me. It's the answer to everything—below the Rio Grande.

WOMAN. What does it mean?

MAN. It means—who knows?

WOMAN. Keen sabe?

MAN. Yep—don't forget it—now.

WOMAN. I'll never forget it!

MAN. Quien sabe?

WOMAN. And I'll never get to use it.

MAN. Quien sabe.

WOMAN. I'll never get—below the Rio Grande—I'll never get out of here.

MAN. Quien sabe.

WOMAN (*change of mood*). That's right! Keen sabe? Who knows?

MAN. That's the stuff.

WOMAN. You must like it down there.

MAN. I can't live anywhere else—for long.

WOMAN. Why not?

MAN. Oh—you're free down there! You're free!

(*A Street Light is lit outside. The outlines of a window take form against this light. There are bars across it, and from outside it, the sidewalk cuts across almost at the top.* [*It is a basement room.*] *The constant going and coming of passing feet,* [*mostly feet of couples*] *can be dimly seen. Inside, on the ledge, there is a lily blooming in a bowl of rocks and water.*)

WOMAN. What's that?

MAN. Just the street light going on.

WOMAN. Is it as late as that?

MAN. Late as what?

WOMAN. Dark.

MAN. It's been dark for hours—didn't you know that?

WOMAN. No!—I must go! (*Rises.*)

MAN. Wait—the moon will be up in a little while—full moon.

WOMAN. It isn't that! I'm late! I must go! (SHE *comes into the light. She wears a white chemise that might be the tunic of a dancer, and as she comes into the light she fastens about her waist a little skirt. She really wears almost exactly the clothes that women wear now, but the finesse of their cut, and the grace and ease with which she puts them on, must turn this episode of her dressing into a personification, an idealization of a woman clothing herself. All her gestures must be unconscious, innocent, relaxed, sure and full of natural grace. As she sits facing the window pulling on a stocking.*) What's that?

MAN. What?

WOMAN. On the window ledge.

MAN. A flower.

WOMAN. Who gave it to you?

MAN. Nobody gave it to me. I bought it.

WOMAN. For yourself?

MAN. Yeah—why not?

WOMAN. I don't know.

MAN. In Chinatown—made me think of Frisco where I was a kid—so I bought it.

WOMAN. Is that where you were born—Frisco?

MAN. Yep. Twin Peaks.

WOMAN. What's that?

MAN. A couple hills—together.

WOMAN. One for you and one for me.

MAN. I bet you'd like Frisco.

WOMAN. I know a woman went out there once!

MAN. The bay and the hills! Jeez, that's the life! Every Saturday we used to cross the Bay—get a couple nags and just ride—over the hills. One would have a blanket on the saddle—the other, the grub. At night, we'd make a little fire and eat—and then roll up in the old blanket and—

WOMAN. Who? Who was with you?

MAN (*indifferently*). Anybody. (*Enthusiastically.*) Jeez, that dry old grass out there smells good at night—full of tar weed—you know—

WOMAN. Is that a good smell?

MAN. Tar weed? Didn't you ever smell it? (*She shakes her head, "No".*) Sure it's a good smell! The Bay and the hills. (*She goes to the mirror of the dresser, to finish dressing. She has only a dress to put on that is in one piece—with one fastening on the side. Before slipping it on, she stands before the mirror and stretches. Appreciatively but indifferently.*) You look in good shape, kid. A couple of months riding over the mountains with me, you'd be great.

WOMAN. Can I?

MAN. What?

WOMAN. Some day—ride mountains with you?

MAN. Ride mountains? Ride donkeys!

WOMAN. It's the same thing!—with you!—Can I—some day? The high dark mountains?

MAN. Who knows?

WOMAN. It must be great!

MAN. You ever been off like that, kid?—high up? On top of the world?

WOMAN. Yes.

MAN. When?

WOMAN. Today.

MAN. You're pretty sweet.

WOMAN. I never knew anything like this way! I never knew that I could feel like this! So,—so purified! Don't laugh at me!

MAN. I ain't laughing, honey.

WOMAN. Purified.

MAN. It's a hell of a word—but I know what you mean. That's the way it is—sometimes.

WOMAN (*she puts on a little hat, then turns to* HIM). Well—goodbye.

MAN. Aren't you forgetting something? (*Rises.*)

WOMAN (*she looks toward him, then throws her head slowly back, lifts her right arm—this gesture that is in so many statues of women [Volupte]— He comes out of the shadow, puts his arm around her, kisses her. Her head and arm go further back,—then she brings her arm around with a wide encircling gesture, her hand closes over his head, her fingers spread. Her fingers are protective, clutching. When he releases her, her eyes are shining with tears. She turns away. She looks back at him—and the room—and her eyes fasten on the lily*). Can I have that?

MAN. Sure—why not?
(*She takes it—goes. As she opens the door, the music is louder. The scene blacks out.*)

WOMAN. Goodbye. And— (*Hesitates.*) And—thank you.

MUSIC—CURTAIN—BLACK OUT

(*The music continues until the Curtain goes up for* EPISODE SEVEN— *It goes up on silence.*)

EPISODE SEVEN

DOMESTIC

SCENE: *A Sitting Room* (*A divan—a telephone—a window.*)

CHARACTERS:

HUSBAND

YOUNG WOMAN

They are seated on opposite ends of the divan. They are both reading papers—to themselves.

HUSBAND. Record production.

YOUNG WOMAN. Girl turns on gas.

HUSBAND. Sale hits a million—

YOUNG WOMAN. Woman leaves all for love—

HUSBAND. Market trend steady—

YOUNG WOMAN. Young wife disappears—

HUSBAND. Owns a life interest— (*Phone rings.* YOUNG WOMAN *looks toward it.*) That's for me. (*In phone.*) Hello—oh hello, A.B. It's all settled?—Everything signed? Good. Good! Tell R.A. to call me up. (*Closes phone—to* YOUNG WOMAN.) Well, it's all settled. They signed!—aren't you interested? Aren't you going to ask me?

YOUNG WOMAN (*by rote*). Did you put it over?

HUSBAND. Sure I put it over.

YOUNG WOMAN. Did you swing it?

HUSBAND. Sure I swung it.

YOUNG WOMAN. Did they come through?

HUSBAND. Sure they came through.

YOUNG WOMAN. Did they sign?

HUSBAND. I'll say they signed.

YOUNG WOMAN. On the dotted line?

HUSBAND. On the dotted line.

YOUNG WOMAN. The property's yours?

HUSBAND. The property's mine. I'll put a first mortgage. I'll put a second mortgage and the property's mine. Happy?

YOUNG WOMAN (*by rote*). Happy.

HUSBAND (*going to her*). The property's mine! It's not all that's mine! (*Pinching her cheek—happy and playful.*) I got a first mortgage on her—I got a second mortgage on her—and she's mine! (YOUNG WOMAN *pulls away swiftly.*) What's the matter?

YOUNG WOMAN. Nothing—what?

HUSBAND. You flinched when I touched you.

YOUNG WOMAN. No.

HUSBAND. You haven't done that in a long time.

YOUNG WOMAN. Haven't I?

HUSBAND. You used to do it every time I touched you.

YOUNG WOMAN. Did I?

HUSBAND. Didn't know that, did you?

YOUNG WOMAN (*unexpectedly*). Yes. Yes, I know it.

HUSBAND. Just purity.

YOUNG WOMAN. No.

HUSBAND. Oh, I liked it. Purity.

YOUNG WOMAN. No.

HUSBAND. You're one of the purest women that ever lived.

YOUNG WOMAN. I'm just like anybody else only— (*Stops.*)

HUSBAND. Only what?

YOUNG WOMAN (*a pause*). Nothing.

HUSBAND. It must be something.

(*Phone rings.*)

(*She gets up and goes to window.*)

HUSBAND (*in phone*). Hello—hello, R.A. —well, I put it over—yeah, I swung it—sure they came through—did they sign? On the dotted line! The property's mine. I made the proposition. I sold them the idea. Now watch me. Tell D.D. to call me up. (*Hangs up.*) That was R.A. What are you looking at?

YOUNG WOMAN. Nothing.

HUSBAND. You must be looking at something.

YOUNG WOMAN. Nothing—the moon.

HUSBAND. The moon's something, isn't it?

YOUNG WOMAN. Yes.

HUSBAND. What's it doing?

YOUNG WOMAN. Nothing.

HUSBAND. It must be doing something.

YOUNG WOMAN. It's moving—moving— (*She comes down restlessly.*)

HUSBAND. Pull down the shade, my dear.

YOUNG WOMAN. Why?

HUSBAND. People can look in. (*Phone rings.*) Hello—hello D.D.—Yes—I put it over—they came across—I put it over on them—yep—yep—yep—I'll say I am—yep—on the dotted line— Now you watch me—yep. Yep yep. Tell B.M. to phone me. (*Hangs up.*) That was D.D. (*To* YOUNG WOMAN *who has come down to davenport and picked up a paper.*) Aren't you listening?

YOUNG WOMAN. I'm reading.

HUSBAND. What you reading?

YOUNG WOMAN. Nothing.

HUSBAND. Must be something. (*He sits and picks up his paper.*)

YOUNG WOMAN (*reading*). Prisoner escapes—lifer breaks jail—shoots way to freedom—

HUSBAND. Don't read that stuff—listen—here's a first rate editorial. I agree with this. I agree absolutely. Are you listening?

YOUNG WOMAN. I'm listening.

HUSBAND (*importantly*). All men are born free and entitled to the pursuit of happiness. (YOUNG WOMAN *gets up.*) My, you're nervous tonight.

YOUNG WOMAN. I try not to be.

HUSBAND. You inherit that from your mother. She was in the office today.

YOUNG WOMAN. Was she?

HUSBAND. To get her allowance.

YOUNG WOMAN. Oh—

HUSBAND. Don't you know it's the *first.*

YOUNG WOMAN. Poor Ma.

HUSBAND. What would she do without me?

YOUNG WOMAN. I know. You're very good.

HUSBAND. One thing—she's grateful.

YOUNG WOMAN. Poor Ma—poor Ma.

HUSBAND. She's got to have care.

YOUNG WOMAN. Yes. She's got to have care.

HUSBAND. A mother's a very precious thing—a good mother.

YOUNG WOMAN (*excitedly*). I try to be a good mother.

HUSBAND. Of course you're a good mother.

YOUNG WOMAN. I try! I try!

HUSBAND. A mother's a very precious thing— (*Resuming his paper.*) And a child's a very precious thing. Precious jewels.

YOUNG WOMAN (*reading*). Sale of jewels and precious stones. (YOUNG WOMAN *puts her hand to throat.*)

HUSBAND. What's the matter?

YOUNG WOMAN. I feel as though I were drowning.

HUSBAND. Drowning?

YOUNG WOMAN. With stones around my neck.

HUSBAND. You just imagine that.

YOUNG WOMAN. Stifling.

HUSBAND. You don't breathe deep enough—breathe now—look at me. (*He breathes.*) Breath is life. Life is breath.

YOUNG WOMAN (*suddenly*). And what is death?

HUSBAND (*smartly*). Just—no breath!

YOUNG WOMAN (*to herself*). Just no breath. (*Takes up paper.*)

HUSBAND. All right?

YOUNG WOMAN. All right.

HUSBAND (*reads as she stares at her paper. Looks up after a pause*). I feel cold air, my dear.

YOUNG WOMAN. Cold air?

HUSBAND. Close the window, will you?

YOUNG WOMAN. It isn't open.

HUSBAND. Don't you feel cold air?

YOUNG WOMAN. No—you just imagine it.

HUSBAND. I never imagine anything. (YOUNG WOMAN *is staring at the paper.*) What are you reading?

YOUNG WOMAN. Nothing.

HUSBAND. You must be reading something.

YOUNG WOMAN. Woman finds husband dead.

HUSBAND (*uninterested*). Oh. (*Interested.*) Here's a man says "I owe my success to a yeast cake a day—my digestion is good—I sleep very well—and— (*His wife gets up, goes toward door.*) Where you going?

YOUNG WOMAN. No place.

HUSBAND. You must be going some place.

YOUNG WOMAN. Just—to bed.

HUSBAND. It isn't eleven yet. Wait.

YOUNG WOMAN. Wait?

HUSBAND. It's only ten-forty-six—wait! (*Holds out his arms to her.*) Come here!

YOUNG WOMAN (*takes a step toward him—recoils*). Oh—I want to go away!

HUSBAND. Away? Where?

YOUNG WOMAN. Anywhere—away.

HUSBAND. Why, what's the matter?

YOUNG WOMAN. I'm scared.

HUSBAND. What of?

YOUNG WOMAN. I can't sleep—I haven't slept.

HUSBAND. That's nothing.

YOUNG WOMAN. And the moon—when it's full moon.

HUSBAND. That's nothing.

YOUNG WOMAN. I can't sleep.

HUSBAND. Of course not. It's the light.

YOUNG WOMAN. I don't see it! I feel it! I'm afraid.

HUSBAND (*kindly*). Nonsense—come here.

YOUNG WOMAN. I want to go away.

HUSBAND. But I can't get away now.

YOUNG WOMAN. Alone!

HUSBAND. You've never been away alone.

YOUNG WOMAN. I know.

HUSBAND. What would you do?

YOUNG WOMAN. Maybe I'd sleep.

HUSBAND. Now you wait.

YOUNG WOMAN (*desperately*). Wait?

HUSBAND. We'll take a trip—we'll go to Europe—I'll get my watch—I'll get my Swiss watch—I've always wanted a Swiss watch that I bought right there—isn't that funny? Wait—wait. (YOUNG WOMAN *comes down to davenport—sits.* HUSBAND *resumes his paper.*) Another revolution below the Rio Grande.

YOUNG WOMAN. Below the Rio Grande?

HUSBAND. Yes—another—

YOUNG WOMAN. Anyone—hurt?

HUSBAND. No.

YOUNG WOMAN. Any Prisoners?

HUSBAND. No.

YOUNG WOMAN. All free?

HUSBAND. All free.

(*He resumes his paper.*)

(YOUNG WOMAN *sits, staring ahead of her—The music of the hand-organ sounds off very dimly, playing Cielito Lindo. Voices begin to sing it—'Ay-ay-ay-ay'—and then the words—the music and voices get louder.*)

THE VOICE OF HER LOVER. They were a bunch of bandidos—bandits you know—holding me there—what was I to do—I had to get free—didn't I? I had to get free—

VOICES. Free—free—free—

LOVER. I filled an empty bottle with small stones—

VOICES. Stones—stones—precious stones—millstones—stones—stones—millstones—

LOVER. Just a bottle with small stones.

VOICES. Stones—stones—small stones—

LOVER. You only need a bottle with small stones.

VOICES. Stones—stones—small stones—

VOICE OF A HUCKSTER. Stones for sale—stones—stones—small stones—precious stones—

VOICES. Stones—stones—precious stones—

LOVER. Had to get free, didn't I? Free?

VOICES. Free? Free?

LOVER. Quien sabe? Who knows? Who knows?

VOICES. Who'd know? Who'd know? Who'd know?

HUCKSTER. Stones—stones—small stones—big stones—millstones—cold stones—head stones—

VOICES. Head stones—head stones—head stones.

(*The music,—the voices—mingle—increase—the* YOUNG WOMAN *flies from her chair and cries out in terror.*)

YOUNG WOMAN. Oh! Oh!

(*The scene* BLACKS OUT—*the music and the dim voices, "Stones—stones—stones," continue until the scene lights for* EPISODE EIGHT.)

EPISODE EIGHT

THE LAW

SCENE: *Courtroom.*

SOUNDS: *Clicking of telegraph instruments offstage.*

CHARACTERS:

JUDGE
JURY
LAWYERS
SPECTATORS
REPORTERS
MESSENGER BOYS
LAW CLERKS
BAILIFF
COURT REPORTER
YOUNG WOMAN

The words and movements of all these people except the YOUNG WOMAN *are routine—mechanical— Each is going through the motions of his own game.*

AT RISE: ALL *assembled, except* JUDGE.

(*Enter* JUDGE.)

BAILIFF (*mumbling*). Hear ye—hear ye—hear ye!

(ALL *rise.* JUDGE *sits.* ALL *sit.*)

(LAWYER FOR DEFENSE *gets to his feet—He is the verbose, 'eloquent'—typical criminal defense lawyer.*)

(JUDGE *signs to him to wait—turns to* LAW CLERKS, *grouped at foot of the bench.*)

1ST CLERK (*handing up a paper—routine voice*). State versus Kling—stay of execution.

JUDGE. Denied.

(1ST CLERK *goes.*)

2ND CLERK. Bing vs. Ding—demurrer.

(JUDGE *signs.*)

(2ND CLERK *goes.*)

3RD CLERK. Case of John King—habeas corpus.

(JUDGE *signs.*)

(3RD CLERK *goes.*)

(JUDGE *signs to* BAILIFF.)

BAILIFF (*mumbling*). People of the State of——versus Helen Jones.

JUDGE (*to* LAWYER FOR THE DEFENSE). Defense ready to proceed?

LAWYER FOR DEFENSE. We're ready, your Honor.

JUDGE. Proceed.

LAWYER FOR DEFENSE. Helen Jones.

BAILIFF. HELEN JONES!

(YOUNG WOMAN *rises.*)

LAWYER FOR DEFENSE. Mrs. Jones, will you take the stand?

(YOUNG WOMAN *goes to witness stand.*)

1ST REPORTER (*writing rapidly*). The defense sprang a surprise at the opening of court this morning by putting the accused woman on the stand. The prosecution was swept off its feet by this daring defense strategy and—

(*Instruments get louder.*)

2ND REPORTER. Trembling and scarcely able to stand, Helen Jones, accused murderess, had to be almost carried to the witness stand this morning when her lawyer—

BAILIFF (*mumbling—with Bible*). Do you swear to tell the truth, the whole truth and nothing but the truth—so help you God?

YOUNG WOMAN. I do.

JUDGE. You may sit.

(*She sits in witness chair.*)

COURT REPORTER. What is your name?

YOUNG WOMAN. Helen Jones.

COURT REPORTER. Your age?

YOUNG WOMAN (*hesitates — then*). Twenty-nine.

COURT REPORTER. Where do you live?

YOUNG WOMAN. In prison.

LAWYER FOR DEFENSE. This is my client's legal address. (*Hands a scrap of paper.*)

LAWYER FOR PROSECUTION (*jumping to his feet*). I object to this insinuation on the part of counsel on any illegality in the holding of this defendant in jail when the law—

LAWYER FOR DEFENSE. I made no such insinuation.

LAWYER FOR PROSECUTION. You implied it—

LAWYER FOR DEFENSE. I did not!

LAWYER FOR PROSECUTION. You're a—

JUDGE. Order!

BAILIFF. Order!

LAWYER FOR DEFENSE. Your Honor, I object to counsel's constant attempt to—

LAWYER FOR PROSECUTION. I protest—I—

JUDGE. Order!

BAILIFF. Order!

JUDGE. Proceed with the witness.

LAWYER FOR DEFENSE. Mrs. Jones, you are the widow of the late George H. Jones, are you not?

YOUNG WOMAN. Yes.

LAWYER FOR DEFENSE. How long were you married to the late George H. Jones before his demise?

YOUNG WOMAN. Six years.

LAWYER FOR DEFENSE. Six years! And it was a happy marriage, was it not? (YOUNG WOMAN *hesitates.*) Did you quarrel?

YOUNG WOMAN. No, sir.

LAWYER FOR DEFENSE. Then it was a happy marriage, wasn't it?

YOUNG WOMAN. Yes, sir.

LAWYER FOR DEFENSE. In those six years of married life with your late husband, the late George H. Jones, did you EVER have a quarrel?

YOUNG WOMAN. No, sir.

LAWYER FOR DEFENSE. Never one quarrel?

LAWYER FOR PROSECUTION. The witness has said—

LAWYER FOR DEFENSE. Six years without one quarrel! Six years! Gentlemen of the jury, I ask you to consider this fact! Six years of married life without a quarrel. (*The* JURY *grins.*) I ask you to consider it seriously! Very seriously! Who of us—and this is not intended as any reflection on the sacred institution of marriage—no—but!

JUDGE. Proceed with your witness.

LAWYER FOR DEFENSE. You have one child—have you not, Mrs. Jones?

YOUNG WOMAN. Yes, sir.

LAWYER FOR DEFENSE. A little girl, is it not?

YOUNG WOMAN. Yes, sir.

LAWYER FOR DEFENSE. How old is she?

YOUNG WOMAN. She's five—past five.

LAWYER FOR DEFENSE. A little girl of past five. Since the demise of the late Mr.

Jones you are the only parent she has living, are you not?

YOUNG WOMAN. Yes, sir.

LAWYER FOR DEFENSE. Before your marriage to the late Mr. Jones, you worked and supported your mother, did you not?

LAWYER FOR PROSECUTION. I object, your honor! Irrelevant—immaterial—and—

JUDGE. Objection sustained!

LAWYER FOR DEFENSE. In order to support your mother and yourself as a girl, you worked, did you not?

YOUNG WOMAN. Yes, sir.

LAWYER FOR DEFENSE. What did you do?

YOUNG WOMAN. I was a stenographer.

LAWYER FOR DEFENSE. And since your marriage you have continued as her sole support, have you not?

YOUNG WOMAN. Yes, sir.

LAWYER FOR DEFENSE. A devoted daughter, gentlemen of the jury! As well as a devoted wife and a devoted mother!

LAWYER FOR PROSECUTION. Your Honor!

LAWYER FOR DEFENSE (*quickly*). And now, Mrs. Jones, I will ask you—the law expects me to ask you—it demands that I ask you—did you—or did you not—on the night of June 2nd last or the morning of June 3rd last—kill your husband, the late George H. Jones—did you, or did you not?

YOUNG WOMAN. I did not.

LAWYER FOR DEFENSE. You did not?

YOUNG WOMAN. I did not.

LAWYER FOR DEFENSE. Now, Mrs. Jones, you have heard the witnesses for the State—They were not many—and they did not have much to say—

LAWYER FOR PROSECUTION. I object.

JUDGE. Sustained.

LAWYER FOR DEFENSE. You have heard some police and you have heard some doctors. None of whom was present! The prosecution could not furnish any witness to the crime—not one witness!

LAWYER FOR PROSECUTION. Your Honor!

LAWYER FOR DEFENSE. Nor one motive.

LAWYER FOR PROSECUTION. Your Honor —I protest! I—

JUDGE. Sustained.

LAWYER FOR DEFENSE. But such as these witnesses were, you have heard them try to accuse you of deliberately murdering your own husband, this husband with whom, by your own statement, you had never had a quarrel—not one quarrel in six years of married life, murdering him, I say, or rather they say, while he slept, by brutally hitting him over the head with a bottle—a bottle filled with small stones —Did you, I repeat this, or did you not?

YOUNG WOMAN. I did not.

LAWYER FOR DEFENSE. You did not! Of course you did not! (*Quickly.*) Now, Mrs. Jones, will you tell the jury in your own words exactly what happened on the night of June 2nd or the morning of June 3rd last, at the time your husband was killed.

YOUNG WOMAN. I was awakened by hearing somebody—something—in the room, and I saw two men standing by my husband's bed.

LAWYER FOR DEFENSE. Your husband's bed—that was also your bed, was it not, Mrs. Jones?

YOUNG WOMAN. Yes.

LAWYER FOR DEFENSE. You hadn't the modern idea of separate beds, had you, Mrs. Jones?

YOUNG WOMAN. Mr. Jones objected.

LAWYER FOR DEFENSE. I mean you slept in the same bed, did you not?

YOUNG WOMAN. Yes.

LAWYER FOR DEFENSE. Then explain just what you meant by saying 'my husband's bed.'

YOUNG WOMAN. Well—I—

LAWYER FOR DEFENSE. You meant his side of the bed, didn't you?

YOUNG WOMAN. Yes. His side.

LAWYER FOR DEFENSE. That is what I thought, but I wanted the jury to be clear on that point. (*To the* JURY.) Mr. and Mrs. Jones slept in the same bed. (*To her.*) Go on, Mrs. Jones. (*As she is silent.*) You heard a noise and—

YOUNG WOMAN. I heard a noise and I awoke and saw two men standing beside my husband's side of the bed.

LAWYER FOR DEFENSE. Two men?

YOUNG WOMAN. Yes.

LAWYER FOR DEFENSE. Can you describe them?

YOUNG WOMAN. Not very well—I couldn't see them very well.

LAWYER FOR DEFENSE. Could you say whether they were big or small—light or dark, thin or—

YOUNG WOMAN. They were big dark looking men.

LAWYER FOR DEFENSE. Big dark looking men?

YOUNG WOMAN. Yes.

LAWYER FOR DEFENSE. And what did you do, Mrs. Jones, when you suddenly awoke and saw two big dark looking men standing beside your bed?

YOUNG WOMAN. I didn't do anything!

LAWYER FOR DEFENSE. You didn't have time to do anything—did you?

YOUNG WOMAN. No. Before I could do anything—one of them raised—something in his hand and struck Mr. Jones over the head with it.

LAWYER FOR DEFENSE. And what did Mr. Jones do?

(SPECTATORS *laugh.*)

JUDGE. Silence.

BAILIFF. Silence.

LAWYER FOR DEFENSE. What did Mr. Jones do, Mrs. Jones?

YOUNG WOMAN. He gave a sort of groan and tried to raise up.

LAWYER FOR DEFENSE. Tried to raise up!

YOUNG WOMAN. Yes!

LAWYER FOR DEFENSE. And then what happened?

YOUNG WOMAN. The man struck him again and he fell back.

LAWYER FOR DEFENSE. I see. What did the men do then? The big dark looking men.

YOUNG WOMAN. They turned and ran out of the room.

LAWYER FOR DEFENSE. I see. What did you do then, Mrs. Jones?

YOUNG WOMAN. I saw Mr. Jones was bleeding from the temple. I got towels and tried to stop it, and then I realized he had—passed away—

LAWYER FOR DEFENSE. I see. What did you do then?

YOUNG WOMAN. I didn't know what to do. But I thought I'd better call the police. So I went to the telephone and called the police.

LAWYER FOR DEFENSE. What happened then.

YOUNG WOMAN. Nothing. Nothing happened.

LAWYER FOR DEFENSE. The police came, didn't they?

YOUNG WOMAN. Yes—they came.

LAWYER FOR DEFENSE (*quickly*). And that is all you know concerning the death of your husband in the late hours of June 2nd or the early hours of June 3rd last, isn't it?

YOUNG WOMAN. Yes sir.

LAWYER FOR DEFENSE. All?

YOUNG WOMAN. Yes sir.

LAWYER FOR DEFENSE (*to* LAWYER FOR PROSECUTION). Take the witness.

1ST REPORTER (*writing*). The accused woman told a straightforward story of—

2ND REPORTER. The accused woman told a rambling, disconnected story of—

LAWYER FOR PROSECUTION. You made no effort to cry out, Mrs. Jones, did you, when you saw those two big dark men standing over your helpless husband, did you?

YOUNG WOMAN. No sir. I didn't. I—

LAWYER FOR PROSECUTION. And when they turned and ran out of the room, you made no effort to follow them or cry out after them, did you?

YOUNG WOMAN. No sir.

LAWYER FOR PROSECUTION. Why didn't you?

YOUNG WOMAN. I saw Mr. Jones was hurt.

LAWYER FOR PROSECUTION. Ah! You saw Mr. Jones was hurt! You saw this—how did you see it?

YOUNG WOMAN. I just saw it.

LAWYER FOR PROSECUTION. Then there was a light in the room?

YOUNG WOMAN. A sort of light.

LAWYER FOR PROSECUTION. What do you mean—a sort of light? A bed light?

YOUNG WOMAN. No. No, there was no light on.

LAWYER FOR PROSECUTION. Then where did it come from—this sort of light?

YOUNG WOMAN. I don't know.

LAWYER FOR PROSECUTION. Perhaps—from the window.

YOUNG WOMAN. Yes—from the window.

LAWYER FOR PROSECUTION. Oh, the shade was up!

YOUNG WOMAN. No—no, the shade was down.

LAWYER FOR PROSECUTION. You're sure of that?

YOUNG WOMAN. Yes. Mr. Jones always wanted the shade down.

LAWYER FOR PROSECUTION. The shade was down—there was no light in the room—but the room was light—how do you explain this?

YOUNG WOMAN. I don't know.

LAWYER FOR PROSECUTION. You don't know!

YOUNG WOMAN. I think where the window was open—under the shade—light came in—

LAWYER FOR PROSECUTION. There is a street light there?

YOUNG WOMAN. No—there's no street light.

LAWYER FOR PROSECUTION. Then where did this light come from—that came in under the shade?

YOUNG WOMAN (*desperately*). From the moon!

LAWYER FOR PROSECUTION. The moon!

YOUNG WOMAN. Yes! It was bright moon!

LAWYER FOR PROSECUTION. It was bright moon—you are sure of that!

YOUNG WOMAN. Yes.

LAWYER FOR PROSECUTION. How are you sure?

YOUNG WOMAN. I couldn't sleep—I never can sleep in the bright moon. I never can.

LAWYER FOR PROSECUTION. It was bright moon. Yet you could not see two big dark looking men—but you could see your husband bleeding from the temple.

YOUNG WOMAN. Yes sir.

LAWYER FOR PROSECUTION. And did you call a doctor?

YOUNG WOMAN. No.

LAWYER FOR PROSECUTION. Why didn't you?

YOUNG WOMAN. The police did.

LAWYER FOR PROSECUTION. But you didn't?

YOUNG WOMAN. No.

LAWYER FOR PROSECUTION. Why didn't you? (*No answer.*) Why didn't you?

YOUNG WOMAN (*whispers*). I saw it was —useless.

LAWYER FOR PROSECUTION. Ah! You saw that! You saw that—very clearly.

YOUNG WOMAN. Yes.

LAWYER FOR PROSECUTION. And you didn't call a doctor.

YOUNG WOMAN. It was—useless.

LAWYER FOR PROSECUTION. What did you do?

YOUNG WOMAN. It was useless—there was no use of anything.

LAWYER FOR PROSECUTION. I asked you what you did?

YOUNG WOMAN. Nothing.

LAWYER FOR PROSECUTION. Nothing!

YOUNG WOMAN. I just sat there.

LAWYER FOR PROSECUTION. You sat there! A long while, didn't you?

YOUNG WOMAN. I don't know.

LAWYER FOR PROSECUTION. You don't know? (*Showing her the neck of a broken bottle.*) Mrs. Jones, did you ever see this before?

YOUNG WOMAN. I think so.

LAWYER FOR PROSECUTION. You think so.

YOUNG WOMAN. Yes.

LAWYER FOR PROSECUTION. What do you think it is?

YOUNG WOMAN. It think it's the bottle that was used against Mr. Jones.

LAWYER FOR PROSECUTION. Used against him—yes--that's right. You've guessed right. This neck and these broken pieces and these pebbles were found on the floor and scattered over the bed. There were no fingerprints, Mrs. Jones, on this bottle. None at all. Doesn't that seem strange to you?

YOUNG WOMAN. No.

LAWYER FOR PROSECUTION. It doesn't seem strange to you that this bottle held in the big dark hand of one of those big dark men left no mark! No print! That doesn't seem strange to you?

YOUNG WOMAN. No.

LAWYER FOR PROSECUTION. You are in the habit of wearing rubber gloves at night, Mrs. Jones—are you not? To protect—to soften your hands—are you not?

YOUNG WOMAN. I used to.

LAWYER FOR PROSECUTION. Used to—when was that?

YOUNG WOMAN. Before I was married.

LAWYER FOR PROSECUTION. And after your marriage you gave it up?

YOUNG WOMAN. Yes.

LAWYER FOR PROSECUTION. Why?

YOUNG WOMAN. Mr. Jones did not like the feeling of them.

LAWYER FOR PROSECUTION. You always did everything Mr. Jones wanted?

YOUNG WOMAN. I tried to—Anyway I didn't care any more—so much—about my hands.

LAWYER FOR PROSECUTION. I see—so after your marriage you never wore gloves at night any more?

YOUNG WOMAN. No.

LAWYER FOR PROSECUTION. Mrs. Jones, isn't it true that you began wearing your rubber gloves again—in spite of your husband's expressed dislike—about a year ago—a year ago this spring?

YOUNG WOMAN. No.

LAWYER FOR PROSECUTION. You did not suddenly begin to care particularly for your hands again—about a year ago this spring?

YOUNG WOMAN. No.

LAWYER FOR PROSECUTION. You're quite sure of that?

YOUNG WOMAN. Yes.

LAWYER FOR PROSECUTION. Quite sure?

YOUNG WOMAN. Yes.

LAWYER FOR PROSECUTION. Then you did

not have in your possession, on the night of June 2nd last, a pair of rubber gloves?

YOUNG WOMAN (*shakes her head*). No.

LAWYER FOR PROSECUTION (*to* JUDGE). I'd like to introduce these gloves as evidence at this time, your Honor.

JUDGE. Exhibit 24.

LAWYER FOR PROSECUTION. I'll return to them later—now, Mrs. Jones—this nightgown—you recognize it, don't you?

YOUNG WOMAN. Yes.

LAWYER FOR PROSECUTION. Yours, is it not?

YOUNG WOMAN. Yes.

LAWYER FOR PROSECUTION. The one you were wearing the night your husband was murdered, isn't it?

YOUNG WOMAN. The night he died,—yes.

LAWYER FOR PROSECUTION. Not the one you wore under your peignoir—I believe that is what you call it, isn't it? A peignoir? When you received the police—but the one you wore before that—isn't it?

YOUNG WOMAN. Yes.

LAWYER FOR PROSECUTION. This was found—not where the gloves were found—no—but at the bottom of the soiled clothes hamper in the bathroom—rolled up and wet—why was it wet, Mrs. Jones?

YOUNG WOMAN. I had tried to wash it.

LAWYER FOR PROSECUTION. Wash it? I thought you had just sat?

YOUNG WOMAN. First—I tried to make things clean.

LAWYER FOR PROSECUTION. Why did you want to make this—clean—as you say?

YOUNG WOMAN. There was blood on it.

LAWYER FOR PROSECUTION. Spattered on it?

YOUNG WOMAN. Yes.

LAWYER FOR PROSECUTION. How did that happen?

YOUNG WOMAN. The bottle broke—and the sharp edge cut.

LAWYER FOR PROSECUTION. Oh, the bottle broke and the sharp edge cut!

YOUNG WOMAN. Yes. That's what they told me afterwards.

LAWYER FOR PROSECUTION. Who told you?

YOUNG WOMAN. The police—that's what they say happened.

LAWYER FOR PROSECUTION. Mrs. Jones, why did you try so desperately to wash that blood away—before you called the police?

LAWYER FOR DEFENSE. I object!

JUDGE. Objection overruled.

LAWYER FOR PROSECUTION. Why, Mrs. Jones?

YOUNG WOMAN. I don't know. It's what anyone would have done, wouldn't they?

LAWYER FOR PROSECUTION. That depends, doesn't it? (*Suddenly taking up bottle.*) Mrs. Jones—when did you first see this?

YOUNG WOMAN. The night my husband was—done away with.

LAWYER FOR PROSECUTION. Done away with! You mean killed?

YOUNG WOMAN. Yes.

LAWYER FOR PROSECUTION. Why don't you say killed?

YOUNG WOMAN. It sounds so brutal.

LAWYER FOR PROSECUTION. And you never saw this before then?

YOUNG WOMAN. No sir.

LAWYER FOR PROSECUTION. You're quite sure of that?

YOUNG WOMAN. Yes.

LAWYER FOR PROSECUTION. And these stones—when did you first see them?

YOUNG WOMAN. The night my husband was done away with.

LAWYER FOR PROSECUTION. Before that night your husband was murdered—you never saw them? Never before then?

YOUNG WOMAN. No sir.

LAWYER FOR PROSECUTION. You are quite sure of that!

YOUNG WOMAN. Yes.

LAWYER FOR PROSECUTION. Mrs. Jones, do you remember about a year ago, a year ago this spring, bringing home to your house—a lily, a Chinese water lily?

YOUNG WOMAN. No—I don't think I do.

LAWYER FOR PROSECUTION. You don't think you remember bringing home a water lily growing in a bowl filled with small stones?

YOUNG WOMAN. No—No I don't.

LAWYER FOR PROSECUTION. I'll show you this bowl, Mrs. Jones. Does that refresh your memory?

YOUNG WOMAN. I remember the bowl—but I don't remember—the lily.

LAWYER FOR PROSECUTION. You recognize the bowl then?

YOUNG WOMAN. Yes.

LAWYER FOR PROSECUTION. It is yours, isn't it?

YOUNG WOMAN. It was in my house—yes.

LAWYER FOR PROSECUTION. How did it come there?

YOUNG WOMAN. How did it come there?

LAWYER FOR PROSECUTION. Yes—where did you get it?

YOUNG WOMAN. I don't remember.

LAWYER FOR PROSECUTION. You don't remember?

YOUNG WOMAN. No.

LAWYER FOR PROSECUTION. You don't remember about a year ago bringing this bowl into your bedroom filled with small stones and some water and a lily? You don't remember tending very carefully that lily till it died? And when it died you don't remember hiding the bowl full of little stones away on the top shelf of your closet—and keeping it there until—you don't remember?

YOUNG WOMAN. No, I don't remember.

LAWYER FOR PROSECUTION. You may have done so?

YOUNG WOMAN. No—no—I didn't! I didn't! I don't know anything about all that.

LAWYER FOR PROSECUTION. But you do remember the bowl?

YOUNG WOMAN. Yes. It was in my house—you found it in my house.

LAWYER FOR PROSECUTION. But you don't remember the lily or the stones?

YOUNG WOMAN. No—No I don't!

(LAWYER FOR PROSECUTION *turns to look among his papers in a brief case.*)

1ST REPORTER (*writing*). Under the heavy artillery fire of the State's attorney's brilliant cross-questioning, the accused woman's defense was badly riddled. Pale and trembling she—

2ND REPORTER (*writing*). Undaunted by the Prosecution's machine-gun attack, the defendant was able to maintain her position of innocence in the face of rapid-fire questioning that threatened, but never seriously menaced her defense. Flushed but calm she—

LAWYER FOR PROSECUTION (*producing paper*). Your Honor, I'd like to introduce this paper in evidence at this time.

JUDGE. What is it?

LAWYER FOR PROSECUTION. It is an affidavit taken in the State of Guanajato, Mexico.

LAWYER FOR DEFENSE. Mexico? Your Honor, I protest. A Mexican affidavit! Is this the United States of America or isn't it?

LAWYER FOR PROSECUTION. It's properly executed—sworn to before a notary—and certified to by an American Consul.

LAWYER FOR DEFENSE. Your Honor! I protest! In the name of this great United States of America—I protest—are we to permit our sacred institutions to be thus—

JUDGE. What is the purpose of this document—who signed it?

LAWYER FOR PROSECUTION. It is signed by one Richard Roe, and its purpose is to refresh the memory of the witness on the point at issue—and incidentally supply a motive for this murder—this brutal and cold-blooded murder of a sleeping man by—

LAWYER FOR DEFENSE. I protest, your Honor! I object!

JUDGE. Objection sustained. Let me see the document. (*Takes paper which is handed up to him—looks at it.*) Perfectly regular. Do you offer this affidavit as evidence at this time for the purpose of refreshing the memory of the witness at this time?

LAWYER FOR PROSECUTION. Yes, your Honor.

JUDGE. You may introduce the evidence.

LAWYER FOR DEFENSE. I object! I object to the introduction of this evidence at this time as irrelevant, immaterial, illegal, biased, prejudicial, and—

JUDGE. Objection overruled.

LAWYER FOR DEFENSE. Exception.

JUDGE. Exception noted. Proceed.

LAWYER FOR PROSECUTION. I wish to read the evidence to the jury at this time.

JUDGE. Proceed.

LAWYER FOR DEFENSE. I object.

JUDGE. Objection overruled.

LAWYER FOR DEFENSE. Exception.

JUDGE. Noted.

LAWYER FOR DEFENSE. Why is this witness himself not brought into court—so he can be cross-questioned?

LAWYER FOR PROSECUTION. The witness is a resident of the Republic of Mexico and as such not subject to subpoena as a witness to this court.

LAWYER FOR DEFENSE. If he was out of the jurisdiction of this court how did you get this affidavit out of him?

LAWYER FOR PROSECUTION. This affidavit was made voluntarily by the deponent in the furtherance of justice.

LAWYER FOR DEFENSE. I suppose you didn't threaten him with extradition on some other trumped-up charge so that—

JUDGE. Order!

BAILIFF. Order!

JUDGE. Proceed with the evidence.

LAWYER FOR PROSECUTION (*reading*). In

the matter of the State of—— vs. Helen Jones, I Richard Roe, being of sound mind, do herein depose and state that I know the accused, Helen Jones, and have known her for a period of over one year immediately preceding the date of the signature on this affidavit. That I first met the said Helen Jones in a so-called speak-easy somewhere in the West 40s in New York City. That on the day I met her, she went with me to my room, also somewhere in the West 40s in New York City, where we had intimate relations—

YOUNG WOMAN (*moans*). Oh!

LAWYER FOR PROSECUTION (*continues reading*). —and where I gave her a blue bowl filled with pebbles, also containing a flowering lily. That from the first day we met until I departed for Mexico in the Fall, the said Helen Jones was an almost daily visitor to my room where we continued to—

YOUNG WOMAN. No! No!

(*Moans.*)

LAWYER FOR PROSECUTION. What is it, Mrs. Jones—what is it?

YOUNG WOMAN. Don't read any more! No more!

LAWYER FOR PROSECUTION. Why not?

YOUNG WOMAN. I did it! I did it! I did it!

LAWYER FOR PROSECUTION. You confess?

YOUNG WOMAN. Yes—I did it!

LAWYER FOR DEFENSE. I object, your Honor.

JUDGE. You confess you killed your husband?

YOUNG WOMAN. I put him out of the way—yes.

JUDGE. Why?

YOUNG WOMAN. To be free.

JUDGE. To be free? Is that the only reason?

YOUNG WOMAN. Yes.

JUDGE. If you just wanted to be free—why didn't you divorce him?

YOUNG WOMAN. Oh I couldn't do that!! I couldn't hurt him like that!

(*Burst of laughter from* ALL *in the court. The* YOUNG WOMAN *stares out at them, and then seems to go rigid.*)

JUDGE. Silence!

BAILIFF. Silence!

(*There is a gradual silence.*)

JUDGE. Mrs. Jones, why— (YOUNG WOMAN *begins to moan—suddenly—as though the realization of her enormity and her isolation had just come upon her. It is a sound of desolation, of agony, of human woe. It continues until the end of the scene.*) Why—?

(YOUNG WOMAN *cannot speak.*)

LAWYER FOR DEFENSE. Your Honor, I ask a recess to—

JUDGE. Court's adjourned.

(SPECTATORS *begin to file out. The* YOUNG WOMAN *continues in the witness box, unseeing, unheeding.*)

1ST REPORTER. Murderess confesses.

2ND REPORTER. Paramour brings confession.

3RD REPORTER. I did it! Woman cries!

(*There is a great burst of speed from the telegraphic instruments. They keep up a constant accompaniment to the* WOMAN'S *moans.*

The scene BLACKS OUT *as the courtroom empties and* TWO POLICEMEN *go to stand by the woman.*)

BLACK OUT

(*The sound of the telegraph instruments continues until the scene lights into* EPISODE NINE—*and the prayers of the* PRIEST.)

EPISODE NINE

A MACHINE

SCENE: *A Prison Room. The front bars face the audience. (They are set back far enough to permit a clear passageway across the stage.)*

SOUNDS: *The voice of a Negro singing. The whir of an aeroplane flying.*

CHARACTERS:

YOUNG WOMAN
A PRIEST
A JAILER
TWO BARBERS
A MATRON
MOTHER
TWO GUARDS

AT RISE:

In front of the bars, at one side, sits a MAN; *at the opposite side, a* WOMAN. (*The* JAILER *and the* MATRON).

Inside the bars, a MAN *and a* WOMAN. (*The* YOUNG WOMAN *and a* PRIEST). *The* YOUNG WOMAN *sits still with folded hands. The* PRIEST *is praying.*

PRIEST. Hear, oh Lord, my prayer; and let my cry come to Thee. Turn not away Thy face from me; in the day when I am in trouble, incline Thy ear to me. In what day soever I shall call upon Thee, hear me speedily. For my days are vanished like smoke; and my bones are grown dry, like fuel for the fire. I am smitten as grass, and my heart is withered; because I forgot to eat my bread. Through the voice of my groaning, my bone hath cleaved to my flesh. I am become like to a pelican of the wilderness. I am like a night raven in the house. I have watched and become as a sparrow all alone on the housetop. All the day long my enemies reproach me; and they that praised me did swear against me. My days have declined like a shadow, and I am withered like grass. But Thou, oh Lord, end rest forever. Thou shalt arise and have mercy, for it is time to have mercy. The time is come.

(*Voice of* NEGRO *offstage—Begins to sing a Negro spiritual.*)

PRIEST. The Lord hath looked upon the earth, that He might hear the groans of them that are in fetters, that He might release the children of—

(VOICE OF NEGRO *grown louder.*)

JAILER. Stop that nigger yelling.

YOUNG WOMAN. No, let him sing. He helps me.

MATRON. You can't hear the Father.

YOUNG WOMAN. He helps me.

PRIEST. Don't I help you, daughter?

YOUNG WOMAN. I understand him. He is condemned. I understand him.

(THE VOICE OF THE NEGRO SINGER *goes on louder, drowning out the voice of the* PRIEST.)

PRIEST (*chanting in Latin*). Gratiam tuum, quaesumus, Domine, metibus nostris infunde, ut qui, angelo nuntiante, Christifilii tui incarnationem cognovimus, per passionem eius et crucem ad ressurectionis gloriam perducamus. Per eudem Christum Dominum nostrum.

(*Enter* TWO BARBERS. *There is a rattling of keys.*)

1ST BARBER. How is she?

MATRON. Calm.

JAILER. Quiet.

YOUNG WOMAN (*rising*). I am ready.

1ST BARBER. Then sit down.

YOUNG WOMAN (*in a steady voice*). Aren't you the death guard come to take me?

1ST BARBER. No, we ain't the death guard. We're the barbers.

YOUNG WOMAN. The barbers.

MATRON. Your hair must be cut.

JAILER. Must be shaved.

BARBER. Just a patch. (*The* BARBERS *draw near her.*)

YOUNG WOMAN. No!

PRIEST. Daughter, you're ready. You know you are ready.

YOUNG WOMAN (*crying out*). Not for this! Not for this!

MATRON. The rule.

JAILER. Regulations.

BARBER. Routine. (*The* BARBERS *take her by the arms.*)

YOUNG WOMAN. No! No! Don't touch me—touch me! (THEY *take her and put her down in the chair, cut a patch from her hair.*) I will not be submitted—this indignity! No! I will not be submitted!—Leave me alone! Oh my God am I never to be let alone! Always to have to submit—to submit! No more—not now—I'm going to die—I won't submit! Not now!

BARBER (*finishing cutting a patch from her hair*). You'll submit, my lady. Right to the end, you'll submit! There, and a neat job too.

JAILER. Very neat.

MATRON. Very neat.

(*Exit* BARBERS.)

YOUNG WOMAN (*her calm shattered*). Father, Father! Why was I born?

PRIEST. I came forth from the Father and have come into the world—I leave the world and go into the Father.

YOUNG WOMAN (*weeping*). Submit! Submit! Is nothing mine? The hair on my head! The very hair on my head—

PRIEST. Praise God.

YOUNG WOMAN. Am I never to be let alone! Never to have peace! When I'm dead, won't I have peace?

PRIEST. Ye shall indeed drink of my cup.

YOUNG WOMAN. Won't I have peace tomorrow?

PRIEST. I shall raise Him up at the last day.

YOUNG WOMAN. Tomorrow! Father! Where shall I be tomorrow?

PRIEST. Behold the hour cometh. Yea, is now come. Ye shall be scattered every man to his own.

YOUNG WOMAN. In Hell! Father! Will I be in Hell?

PRIEST. I am the Resurrection and the Life.

YOUNG WOMAN. Life has been hell to me, Father!

PRIEST. Life has been hell to you, daughter, because you never knew God! Gloria in excelsis Deo.

YOUNG WOMAN. How could I know Him, Father? He never was around me.

PRIEST. You didn't seek Him, daughter. Seek and ye shall find.

YOUNG WOMAN. I sought something—I was always seeking something.

PRIEST. What? What were you seeking?

YOUNG WOMAN. Peace. Rest and peace. Will I find it tonight, Father? Will I find it?

PRIEST. Trust in God.

(*A shadow falls across the passage in the front of the stage—and there is a shirring sound.*)

YOUNG WOMAN. What is that? Father! Jailer! What is that?

JAILER. An aeroplane.

MATRON. Aeroplane.

PRIEST. God in His Heaven.

YOUNG WOMAN. Look, Father! A man flying! He has wings! But he is not an angel!

JAILER. Hear his engine.

MATRON. Hear the engine.

YOUNG WOMAN. He has wings—but he isn't free! I've been free, Father! For one moment—down here on earth—I have been free! When I did what I did I was free! Free and not afraid! How is that, Father? How can that be? A great sin—a mortal sin—for which I must die and go to hell—but it made me free! One moment I was free! How is that, Father? Tell me that?

PRIEST. Your sins are forgiven.

YOUNG WOMAN. And that other sin—that other sin—that sin of love— That's all I ever knew of Heaven—heaven on earth! How is that, Father? How can that be—a sin—a mortal sin—all I know of heaven?

PRIEST. Confess to Almighty God.

YOUNG WOMAN. Oh, Father, pray for me—a prayer—that I can understand!

PRIEST. I will pray for you, daughter, the prayer of desire. Behind the King of Heaven, behold Thy Redeemer and God, Who is even now coming; prepare thyself to receive Him with love, invite him with the ardor of thy desire; come, oh my Jesus, come to thy soul which desires Thee! Before Thou givest Thyself to me, I desire to give Thee my miserable heart. Do Thou accept it, and come quickly to take possession of it! Come my God, hasten! Delay no longer! My only and Infinite Good, my Treasure, my Life, my Paradise, my Love, my all, my wish is to receive Thee with the love with which—

(*Enter the* MOTHER. *She comes along the passage way and stops before the bars.*)

YOUNG WOMAN (*recoiling*). Who's that woman?

JAILER. Your mother.

MATRON. Your mother.

YOUNG WOMAN. She's a stranger—take her away—she's a stranger.

JAILER. She's come to say goodbye to you—

MATRON. To say goodbye.

YOUNG WOMAN. But she's never known me—never known me—ever— (*To the* MOTHER.) Go away! You're a stranger! Stranger! Stranger! (MOTHER *turns and starts away. Reaching out her hands to her.*) Oh Mother! Mother!

(*They embrace through the bars.*)

(*Enter* TWO GUARDS.)

PRIEST. Come, daughter.

1ST GUARD. It's time.

2ND GUARD. Time.

YOUNG WOMAN. Wait! Mother, my child; my little strange child! I never knew her! She'll never know me! Let her live, Mother. Let her live! Live! Tell her—

PRIEST. Come, daughter.

YOUNG WOMAN. Wait! wait! Tell her—

(*The* JAILER *takes the* MOTHER *away*).

GUARD. It's time.

YOUNG WOMAN. Wait! Wait! Tell her! Wait! Just a minute more! There's so much I want to tell her— Wait—

(*The* JAILER *takes the* MOTHER *off.*)

(*The* TWO GUARDS *take the* YOUNG WOMAN *by the arms, and start through the door in the bars and down the passage, across stage and off.*

The PRIEST *follows; the* MATRON *follows the* PRIEST; *the* PRIEST *is praying.*

The scene BLACKS OUT.

The voice of the PRIEST *gets dimmer and dimmer.*

PRIEST. Lord have mercy—Christ have mercy—Lord have mercy—Christ hear us! God the Father of Heaven! God the Son, Redeemer of the World, God the Holy Ghost—Holy Trinity one God—Holy Mary—Holy Mother of God—Holy Virgin of Virgins—St. Michael—St. Gabriel—St. Raphael—

(*His voice dies out.*)

(*Out of the darkness come the voices of* REPORTERS.)

1ST REPORTER. What time is it now?

2ND REPORTER. Time now.

3RD REPORTER. Hush.

1ST REPORTER. Here they come.

3D REPORTER. Hush.

PRIEST (*his voice sounds dimly—gets louder—continues until the end*). St. Peter pray for us—St. Paul pray for us—St. James pray for us—St. John pray for us—all ye holy Angels and Archangels—all ye blessed orders of holy spirits—St. Joseph—St. John the Baptist—St. Thomas—

1ST REPORTER. Here they are!

2ND REPORTER. How little she looks! She's gotten smaller.

3RD REPORTER. Hush.

PRIEST. St. Phillip pray for us. All ye Holy Patriarchs and prophets—St. Phillip—St. Matthew—St. Simon—St. Thaddeus—All ye holy apostles—all ye holy disciples—all ye holy innocents—Pray for us—Pray for us—Pray for us.—

1ST REPORTER. Suppose the machine shouldn't work!

2ND REPORTER. It'll work!—It always works!

3RD REPORTER. Hush!

PRIEST. Saints of God make intercession for us—Be merciful—Spare us, oh Lord—be merciful—

1ST REPORTER. Her lips are moving—what is she saying?

2ND REPORTER. Nothing.

3RD REPORTER. Hush!

PRIEST. Oh Lord deliver us from all evil—from all sin—from Thy wrath—from the snares of the devil—from anger and hatred and every evil will—from—

1ST REPORTER. Did you see that? She fixed her hair under the cap—pulled her hair out under the cap.

3RD REPORTER. Hush!

PRIEST. —Beseech Thee—hear us—that Thou would'st spare us—that Thou would'st pardon us—Holy Mary—pray for us—

2ND REPORTER. There—

YOUNG WOMAN (*calling out*). Somebody! Somebod—

(*Her voice is cut off.*)

PRIEST. Christ have mercy—Lord have mercy—Christ have mercy—

CURTAIN

Maxwell Anderson, who had revealed strong if undoctrinaire social sympathies in *What Price Glory?*, in the hobo drama *Outside Looking In* (1925), and in *Saturday's Children* (1927), was sufficiently aroused by the Sacco-Vanzetti case to merge his indignation with that of the journalist Harold Hickerson and write *Gods of the Lightning*. It is the strongest drama of social protest produced in the nineteen twenties. As such, it helps to round out our survey of the period.

The play is indicative of the difference between the protestant drama of the twenties and that of the next decade. It is not a faithful rendition of the Sacco-Vanzetti case and indulges in some questionable speculation on what the facts may have been, introducing a line of action through the romantic criminal Suvorin which bears doubtfully on the evidence. The underlying social framework is, moreover, romantic by comparison with the closely analytical quality of the later social drama. Its inspiration comes neither from Marx nor Lenin but from Bakunin, Sorel, and Kropotkin, the philosophers of anarchism and syndicalism whom the Marxists regarded as confused idealists. The character Suvorin looks like a twentieth century edition of Balzac's arch-criminal Vautrin in *Father Goriot*.

The play also reflects Anderson's highly individual attitude toward society, and connects with the later poetic plays from *Elizabeth the Queen*, through *Winterset*, to the *Masque of Kings* and *Knickerbocker Holiday*. Like these works, *Gods of the Lightning* takes a dim view of all governments and a pessimistic one of all attempts to make justice prevail. Mr. Anderson's obvious spokesman Suvorin tells the idealists: "There is no government--only brigands in power who fight always for more power! It has always been so. It will always be so." All uplifters are believers in pap, for the world never changes for the better and always belongs to the hard-hearted, which is about the same statement that Elizabeth makes in *Elizabeth the Queen* when she declares that the valiant and admirable go down in their prime and that "the rats inherit the earth." For this reason Anderson was outspokenly sceptical of efforts to alter the world by revolutionary action and gave the impression for a time that it was even futile to try to resist evil—an impression he modified in *Valley Forge* (1934) and corrected in *Key Largo* (1939) and later war-time plays.

Mr. Anderson was to pay a penalty for his outlook, which was to destroy the effectiveness of *Winterset* after the second act. It caused *High Tor* to taper off as an elegiac mood after its high reaches of satire and fantastic humor. It immobilized the *Masque of Kings,* which might have been one of his best plays if he had not channeled his writing into a circular tunnel of half-hearted and futile rebellion by Rudolph of Hapsburg. He also pays a penalty in *Gods of the Lightning,* where he may be seen straining to shift the emphasis on to Suvorin, the proponent of negativism. It is curious how the "Sacco" and "Vanzetti" characters, who should have stood in the center of this drama if it was to have maximum emotion as well as relevance to the case, are overshadowed and given an essentially passive role.

Nevertheless, *Gods of the Lightning* communicates pity and anger, crackles with contempt for connivance and time-serving, and flagellates the coward heart and the mean spirit. If the author's vision of the world is jaundiced (and plainly it *is* jaundiced if only because the historical case roused many men of good will to appeal to reason or protest against injustice), he, nevertheless, affirmed humanity through his very capacity for indignation. He happily contradicted Suvorin's pessimism through the very nature of the play and through the fact of his being moved to write it—as well as by giving us Suvorin's heroic stand toward the end. Not until the playwright came to write the second act of *Winterset* in 1935, did he create scenes as powerful as those in the prosecuting attorney's office and the courtroom. Here, as in later plays, it is evident that Mr. Anderson is never so superbly the dramatist as when his anger and scorn are aroused. If romanticism is his forte, it is not, as a rule, the romanticism of the "blue flower," of dreams and self-pity. It is charged with some of the lightning of the twentieth century. And in *Gods of the Lightning* the thunder, too, is very audible.

Gods of the Lightning

BY MAXWELL ANDERSON AND HAROLD HICKERSON

First produced by Hamilton MacFadden and Kellogg Gary at the Little Theatre, New York City, on October 24, 1928, with the following cast:

SUVORIN	Leo Bulgakov
PETE	Arthur Peterson
HEINE	Jules Artfield
ROSALIE	Sylvia Sydney
WARD	Barton MacLane
MACREADY	Charles Bickford
ANDY	Thomas Kelly
IKE	Sam Silverbush
MILKIN	Ian Wolfe
SOWERBY	Sam Coit
SPIKER	Morris Ankrum
BAUER	Jules Ferrar
CAPRARO	Horace Braham
SALVATION LASSIE	Molly Ricardel
JERUSALEM SLIM	Moss Fleisig
POLICE SERGEANT	Lloyd Sabine
POLICEMAN	Benjamin Fessenden
SALTER	Robert Brister
HASLET	Willard Dashiell
JUDGE VAIL	Douglas Wood
ASSISTANT TO DISTRICT ATTORNEY	Del Cleveland
MRS. LUBIN	Eva Condon
BARTLET	Harry Bliven
GLUCKSTEIN	John R. Hamilton
LUBIN	Maynard Burgess
CLERK OF THE COURT	Edward Cutler
SHERIFF HENRY	Henry Engel

ACT I

Lyceum Restaurant.

ACT II

Scene 1. District Attorney's office.
Scene 2. Court room of the Supreme Court.

ACT III

Same as Act I.

ACT ONE

SCENE.—*The scene is the restaurant in the Labor Lyceum building of a city on the eastern seaboard.*

At the right is a large window facing on the street, and at the right rear an outside entrance. At the left a door leads to an inner hall and the stairway to the upper floors. Along about half of the rear wall at the right runs a counter with a coffee urn and the usual display of quick lunch foods. A swinging door back of the counter leads to a small kitchen. There are folding doors in the rear wall at the left, opening on a hall used for labor meetings. There are tables and chairs for the customers of the restaurant. In the left rear corner there is a table covered with books and pamphlets and another which holds a chess-board. A large clock hangs on the rear wall. The hands point to ten-twenty. It is dark outside.

PETE, *the counter-man, swabs off the top of his counter and goes into the kitchen.* SUVORIN, *a solid bulk of a man, with a satanic, dominating face, sits in the left rear corner, his chair tilted against the wall. His eyes are fixed on the floor.* HEINE, *a disreputable figure enters from the street and looks furtively about him, glancing back at the window.*

SUVORIN (*without moving*). What are you doing here?

HEINE. Am I going to leave town without getting mine?

SUVORIN. You'll get yours fast enough if you hang around here.

HEINE. How much was it?

SUVORIN. $28,000.

HEINE. Where's mine?

SUVORIN. That's half.

HEINE. How much?

SUVORIN. Fourteen. Take it and get out. You'd better beat it into Canada and stay there. You're a fool and a bungler. If you'd followed instructions you'd have been safe.

HEINE. I had to do it. He was jumping at me.

SUVORIN. Take your money and to hell with you. You're a fool. Are they trailing you?

HEINE. No.

SUVORIN. You wouldn't know.

HEINE. Jesus, I'd know that.

SUVORIN. Don't go out that way. Go upstairs and out the back. There's an alley into Clark Street. Cross the line and for God's sake use your head.

HEINE (*going to lefthand door*). Goodbye, Sport.

SUVORIN. Get out.

(HEINE *goes out. Before the door has quite closed,* ROSALIE *enters from the left, evidently passing* HEINE. *She is a beautiful girl with a childlike Russian face.*)

ROSALIE. Who was that? Has he any business here?

(SUVORIN, *seating himself, pays no attention to the question. One of the folding doors opens and* WARD *enters and closes the door.*)

WARD. Mac here yet?

SUVORIN. No.

WARD. Hell! Have you seen him this evening, Rosalie?

ROSALIE. No.

WARD. Oh, that's right, you—

ROSALIE. Yes?

WARD. Never mind.

(*He goes back through the doors.* MAC *enters from the street.*)

ROSALIE. Oh, Mac, where were you? I've been terrified!

MAC (*thrusting a revolver into her hands*). Hello, kid. Put that away for me, will you, kid?

ROSALIE. But—whose is it?

MAC. That's all right—I don't want to carry it—that's all.

(WARD *re-enters, cramming his hat on.*)

WARD. Say, Mac, I thought you'd been picked up.

MAC. Do you need me in there yet?

WARD. You'd better come in just so they'll know you're here.

MAC. How's it going?

WARD. They're scared. Three men killed and about fifty in the hospital. You might be able to hold 'em if you put it to 'em just right. Otherwise we're licked.

MAC. Oh, no. We've got another card up our sleeves. Is Andy in there?

WARD. He's waiting for you. Listen—there's some talk about a raid tonight—maybe more than one—

ROSALIE. Say, Ward—if that'll keep I want to talk to Mac a minute. Do you mind?

WARD. All right. I'll tell Andy you're here.

(*He goes. Again part of a speech is heard.*)

THE SPEAKER. And now they ask us to vote another five thousand for relief! Where are we going to get five thousand? (*The door closes.*)

ROSALIE. Now then—

MAC. Now then—

ROSALIE. This is no place for you tonight.

MAC. I knew it was coming.

ROSALIE. And you're to beat it and stay under cover till they forget about this afternoon—

MAC. What do you know about this afternoon?

ROSALIE. I read about it—and my opinion is that you've done enough for one day. They can get along without you here.

MAC. It just happens they can't get along without me.

ROSALIE. You won't be much good to them in jail—

MAC. I'm not going to jail—so get that out of your head—

ROSALIE. Mac, you're a child—

MAC. You're pretty young yourself, you know. (ANDY *enters.*) Hello, Andy.

ANDY. Looks like they was going to vote us down.

MAC. And then what?

ANDY. What do you say?

MAC. If you boys'll stay with me you know what we can do.

ANDY. I'll tell you how it is, Mac. We want to stay, see? I saw two or three of the boys before the meeting. They aren't scared worth a damn, because we licked the company once before and we can do it again. They can't operate without engineers.

MAC. I knew we could count on you.

ANDY. Well, wait a minute, Mac. Get us right. If the longshoremen go back tomorrow and we stay out it'll take 'em a couple of weeks to pick up enough engineers to get along, see?

MAC. Right.

ANDY. All right. But in a couple of weeks they could do it—and we'd be left holding the bag. See? So we figure this way. The mills are holding a strike meeting tonight. If the mills go out and the engineers stay out, why the longshoremen they won't be much good around the docks, and they'll walk out again. But if the mills keep going, we don't want to try it alone.

MAC. Don't worry. The mills are going out.

ANDY. Can I tell the boys you said that?

MAC. I want you to tell them I said it.

ANDY. All right. We'll have a meeting upstairs right after this jamboree's over in here, see? Will you wait for me here?

MAC. Yeah.

(ANDY *goes out.*)

ROSALIE. Now you'll have to wait here—right where they'll be looking for you—

MAC. I've got to hold the thing together.

ROSALIE. But use your head—

MAC. I am using it. I know it's a risk to be here, but if I can pull this strike through it's worth it—

ROSALIE. Let them lose their strike—

MAC. Be reasonable—

ROSALIE. Anthing you can do somebody else could do for you! I'll get rid of the gun for you—and you'll disappear for a couple of weeks! Do you think it's reasonable for you to wander in here with a gun in your pocket and half the police in town laying for you?

MAC. You certainly do feel old tonight, don't you, kid?

ROSALIE. It's enough to make anybody feel old. I've lived about a thousand years today—I wish this strike had never started, or it was over, or we could get away somewhere—

MAC. That wouldn't help. Everywhere I go there's a strike. I seem to take 'em with me. You'll have to get used to that.

ROSALIE. Can't you play safe, just this once? Can't you do that much for me?

MAC. You heard what I said to Andy. The company thinks it's got us in a corner and I'm going to prove it's wrong, that's all. (*He stoops and kisses her briefly as the folding doors open and* WARD *looks in.*)

WARD. You'd better come on in. Spiker isn't going so well.

MAC. Yeah. Don't worry, kid. We'll be all right.

(*The voice of Spiker is heard.*)

SPIKER (*inside*). I'll tell you what I think—I think you're too easy—

A HECKLER (*inside*). When did you ever work on the docks?

(MAC *and* WARD *enter the hall just as* IKE

and MILKIN *emerge, evidently shoved out of the meeting.*)

IKE (*as the door closes on him*). Long live the freedom of loose talk! Why should they put me out? I was a longshoreman before most of those guys cut their first knee-pants! They wasn't even alive in '97. They ain't never seen hard times. I was born during the glorious second administration of General Grant, the most stupendous period of graft and prosperity this country has ever seen—with the solitary and luminous exception of Warren Gamaliel Harding! (*He goes to the counter with* MILKIN.) Where's Pete? (*He addresses the hole in the wall through which food is pushed out from the kitchen.*) Hey, cuckoo, cuckoo, we want coffee!

PETE (*looking out*). What you want?

IKE. A slug of coffee, cuckoo!

PETE. We don't cash checks.

IKE. You pay this time, Milkin. I lent all my money to a comrade. You can't trust these revolutionists.

MILKIN. You didn't have no money.

IKE. I had fifty cents this morning, and I gave it to a guy under guise of introducing me to a jane. But he weasled me, at that.

MILKIN. Dat's all right. Only don't try to fool me.

IKE. You mean I was lying?

MILKIN. I can see right into your mind. I can see what you're thinking.

PETE. Yeah?

IKE. Yes, sir. And if you don't hurry up and give us coffee we'll put the black art on you.

PETE. I lost tree dollar on you for a check.

MILKIN (*laying a bill on the counter*). Dat's all right. (PETE *draws coffee for two.*) We wouldn't put no black art on you. We wouldn't do nothing like that.

IKE. No, we wouldn't do that. Only we could, see? I could, too.

MILKIN. I don't tink you could. Not widout de cabalistic sign.

IKE. You gave me the sign, mystic?

MILKIN. Yeah, but you don't know how to apply it!

IKE. Yes, sir—it comes natural to me. I can handle the black art sign like a plate of beans, and right after you give it to me I could tell any man in the street what he was thinking. Just like that! Won't that be good when we get it working in politics? Jeez, that's a highly mystical sign!

MILKIN. Only remember, if you got it you don't work it for nutting but de best interests of de State.

IKE. Sure, the best interest of the State—

MILKIN (*with emphasis*). And wait! Wait! Bide your time. And when you find a man in high office what don't belong dere, level your finger at him and say to him— "Come down from dere—come down from dere!"

(*As he says this he points a finger at an imaginary personage and by accident levels it at the street door, through which* SOWERBY *is entering.* SOWERBY *is a tall, lean, academic person, very threadbare and even frayed. He carries a high pile of books, a small bundle, and a coat. On top of the pile of books are perched two slippers.*)

SOWERBY. Yes, gentlemen, I'll come down. I've already come down considerably. In fact I've been shaken down again.

IKE. Put you out, huh?

SOWERBY. A recurrence of an old malady of mine, gentlemen. Landlady trouble. Don't let anybody tell you there's no housing shortage in this city. The housing problem is acute at this moment. I missed paying the rent just once—just once, mind you—and I'm on the street. Now that's a situation that should never arise. And it occurs, not once, not twice, but over and over again. (*He comes to the counter.*)

IKE. You ought to be a mystic.

SOWERBY. If that would help I'll be one. In fact, I am one.

IKE. It'll help you to a cup of coffee.

MILKIN. Sure ting. Give us another coffee.

(PETE *does so.*)

IKE. Listen, you was going to tell me about that second sign, you know—I never saw that one.

MILKIN. Yeah, you seen it all right, but you didn't recognize it. (*He reaches for pencil and paper.* IKE *casually puts the change in his pocket.*) See dat! Dat's de second one! Oh, boy, dat is a sign!

IKE. What can you do with it?

MILKIN. Dat is a sign! Dat's a black art sign! You wait!

SOWERBY. What do you mean, a black art sign?

IKE. We mean a black art sign, see? We're mystics. Me and him.

SOWERBY. Tell me about it.

IKE. You wouldn't know, see, you wouldn't know.

MILKIN. We got de numbers, dat's all.

IKE. See, we got the numbers.

MILKIN. We got de whole world's number. We got three, five, seven, and nine, see, and one more.

IKE. And one more, see? That's the real one.

SOWERBY. You can tell fortunes, I presume?

MILKIN. Dat's de amateur game.

SOWERBY. All right. Tell me how the strike's coming out.

MILKIN (*scribbling rapidly*). I'll tell you. Look at dat! See dat? It don't look so good for de strike.

SOWERBY (*pointing*). What's that?

MILKIN (*impressively*). See dat? (*To* IKE.) He picks dat one out. Dat's de sign of three. And dat's de sign of seven. And when dey comes togedder—it means deat'.

SOWERBY. Debt? I'm pretty deep in debt myself.

MILKIN. Deat'! Deat' the leveller, deat' the radical, deat' the end of worldly glory!

SOWERBY. Death? Who's going to die?

MILKIN. I can't tell dat. Dat ain't fair.

SOWERBY. But you know?

IKE. Sure we know.

MILKIN. I know. He don't know. Not yet.

SOWERBY. You know, gentlemen, the older I become the less seriously I regard the deaths of other people—or even of myself. The fact that I have no place to sleep tonight bothers me a good deal, but if I were only going to die tonight—that is, without discomfort—I shouldn't mind it in the least. The idea of death, philosophically regarded, is welcome to the mature mind.

(*There is a sudden crash against the folding doors.* SOWERBY *drops instantly under the table, and all eyes turn toward the disturbance. The doors open and* SPIKER *can be heard speaking above the cries of "Put him out!" "Who told him he could talk?" "That's all!" "He's a Red!" "Back to Russia!"*)

SPIKER. You're compromisers, you're lick-spittles, you're wage-slaves, you're finks—you haven't got enough guts to demand what's yours! I tell you—

A VOICE. Will you get the hell out?

SPIKER. I will not! I'm a member in good standing!

A VOICE. Back to Russia!

ANOTHER VOICE. All right, Mac!

(SPIKER *is thrust into the restaurant and the door is closed. He tries it futilely.*)

IKE. This is the overflow meeting. Come on in. (SPIKER *turns to glare at* IKE, *then sits gloomily alone.*) Lost anything?

SOWERBY (*rising*). My—dignity.—Let me see—where was I? (*He seats himself and picks up a tabloid paper.*) Where was I?

IKE. You was saying before you got under the table that death was a matter of indifference to you.

SOWERBY. Exactly—exactly. And in a civilization such as ours that is as it should be. What does any one human life amount to? Look at this headline, for instance. "Paymaster killed, robbers escape with $28,000 belonging to Northfield Dock Company!"

(*All eyes are suddenly turned toward* SOWERBY.)

MILKIN. I told you!

IKE. What's that? That means the scabs didn't get their pay today! Hey? (*He picks up the paper.*) Hey, do they know that in there? (*He tries the doors.*) The scabs don't get their pay this week! (*There is a sound of cheering from within.*) That's Mac talking. Hey, Mac—the scabs had bad luck!

(*The door opens in* IKE'S *face and a voice exclaims at him.*)

THE VOICE. Sh! Shut up, will you?

IKE. Hey! All right! Jeez, it certainly was a swell afternoon for a holdup—all the cops were beating up the strikers. (*He returns.*) I wonder who got away with that $28,000?

SOWERBY. You ought to know. I thought you were a mystic.

IKE. I ain't got to that. He knows.

SOWERBY (*to* MILKIN). Who was it?

MILKIN. Oh, no. Dat wouldn't be for the best interest. To tell dat.

SOWERBY. I thought not.

(*The folding doors open a crack, and* BAUER, *a self-important busybody, looks out, then emerges and closes it. While he holds the door open a fragment of* MAC'S *speech drifts out. He listens, shakes head, shows disapproval.*)

MAC (*within*). Compromise? Why certainly, when it's necessary. Capitulate to Northfield? Why certainly, when he's got us where he wants us! But, for God's sake, why compromise now, when you don't have to? Why capitulate when we've got him on the run? Don't you know the

mills are going out tomorrow? Within a week there won't be a loom running!
(*The door shuts off the rest.*)

BAUER. It's the last time Mac talks in there, if he knows it or not.

ROSALIE. What do you mean?

BAUER. Never mind. There was a little caucus before he came. He is just a little too wild. Also, Mr. Suvorin, we have had a meeting of the house committee this afternoon. You hear that? (SUVORIN *looks up at him without changing his expression.*) We had a meeting of the house committee. It will affect you somewhat. The lyceum has given desk room to certain radical groups, without pay. Well, we have changed all that. No more desk room without pay. And—*and* no more desk room for radicals, for any price. No more I.W.W.'s, no more anarchists, only straight union activities.

SUVORIN. I understand.

BAUER. Also, Mr. Suvorin, in the past it has been the custom for radicals to meet here in your restaurant and talk. Well, this is a restaurant. It is open to the public. We cannot stop that. But it has been allowed for some time that they put literature on the shelf there—Macready and Bardi and Capraro—they have you all filled up with I.W.W. stuff and anarchist stuff—syndicalism, that sort. We want it out. And we want it out before closing time tonight. You see?

SUVORIN. I do.

BAUER. You will tell them?

SUVORIN. That's your business, not mine.

ROSALIE. I'll tell them, Mr. Bauer.

BAUER. Thank you, Miss Suvorin. We want that literature out of here tonight, tell 'em. We want nothing in this building but straight union literature. You never know when there's going to be a raid. They raided the Zeitung right across the street. Well, why wouldn't they raid you here if you're distributing anarchist literature? (*He goes to the shelf in the corner and picks up a book.*) Here's one. Liberty, Equality, Fraternity for Humanity! Is that I.W.W. or Anarchist?

SOWERBY. That goes back to the French Revolution.

BAUER. Revolution, huh?

SOWERBY. French Revolution.

BAUER. Anyway, we've had too much talk of revolution, no matter if it's French. This should be a labor lyceum, not a hatchery for revolutions. (*He takes up another book.*) Here is a heavy one. (*He reads.*) "Certain Positive Aspects of the Negative Outcome of Philosophy." Oh, I see.

SOWERBY. You'll find some copies of the Declaration of Independence there. Dangerous stuff, too. Highly inflammatory. Suppressed by the police of Los Angeles and Boston.

BAUER. You would not kid me, for instance?

SOWERBY. Oh, no.

BAUER (*looking at* SOWERBY'S *books*). What's this?

SOWERBY. If you will pardon me, these are my effects.

BAUER. Your effects?

SOWERBY. My, as it were, personal effects.

BAUER. Think of that now. (*To* IKE.) How about you—have you got desk room in the building?

IKE (*turning away loftily and tapping with his foot*). No, my good man, no.

BAUER. What!

IKE (*looking down his nose at* BAUER). No, my good man, no! (*Bursting with rage,* BAUER *slams down one of* SOWERBY'S *books and returns to his examination of the radical shelf.*) Personally, I'd rather be a bum. I'd rather be an auctioneer. (*He picks up* BAUER'S *hat, watching* BAUER *narrowly.*) Ladies and gentlemen, before the regular auctioneer returns from lunch, what am I offered for this indescribable object? (BAUER *turns, and* IKE *puts down the hat and quickly substitutes one of* SOWERBY'S *slippers.*) Ladies and gentlemen, in all my years as a broker in rare and curious objects, I have never—never—in fact— (*He smells the slipper.*) We withdraw that exhibit—we are forced to withdraw that exhibit—and we offer in its place this rare and original manuscriptum —(*he takes up* SOWERBY'S *manuscript*) being the first and only extant draft of Sowerby's History of—what was it you said you was writing a history of, Mr. Sowerby?

SOWERBY. I am writing a history, sir, of irrelevant and unimportant details.

IKE. Yes—of irrelevant and unimportant details. Would you mind describing a irrelevant detail, Mr. Sowerby? Mr. Sowerby, ladies and gentlemen, will now appear in person, describing a irrelevant detail! Mr. Sowerby!

(*There is a sudden crash of applause,*

mingled with cheers and the stamping of feet from the auditorium. SOWERBY, *about to speak, instead slides under the table, rising at once when he realizes there is no danger. Voices are heard above the din yelling "The strike's over! The strike's over! Make it unanimous!"* MACREADY, WARD, *and* ANDY *come through the folding doors, with a group of longshoremen, who pass through and out to the street, talking.*)

WARD. I knew they'd do it!

MAC. We had to make a play for it anyway.

SPIKER. So it's over, huh?

MAC. They think so.

ANDY. Yeah—they think so.

MAC. That's the way it goes. You win a strike for 'em—have it all wrapped up and laid on the table like a Christmas present—and they're afraid to take it! You've got to feed 'em higher wages like horse-medicine!

SPIKER. I guess that stops us.

MAC. No. Sorry they handled you rough, Spiker. I didn't expect that.

SPIKER. What are you doing now?

MAC. Ask Andy. (*He glances meaningly at* BAUER.)

ANDY. I can tell you better later. I'm going upstairs.

MAC. Good. (ANDY *goes out by the hall door.*) Engineers are meeting.

SPIKER. I get you.

BAUER. I see you have a little trouble, Mr. Macready.

MAC. That's news to me. What's the matter?

BAUER. I guess they blocked the strike for you, huh?

MAC (*to* WARD, *paying no attention to* BAUER). By the way, can I get hold of Benny?

WARD. He's going to call you here.

MAC. Good.

BAUER. I wish to speak to you, Mr. Macready.

MAC. Well, then, I'll bet you do it.

BAUER. There was a meeting of the house committee this afternoon—

MAC. Yes?

BAUER. And it was decided to give the radical organizations no more desk room.

MAC. Well, well.

BAUER. It was decided you would have to go out—I.W.W.'s and Syndicalists—everybody but straight A.F. of L.

MAC. Who holds the mortgage on this building?

BAUER. That has nothing to do with it.

MAC. I thought not.

BAUER. So you will pardon me if I tell you we want you to take your literature and move out. I told the committee you would be out tonight.

MAC. I'm busy tonight.

BAUER. I said tonight. I told the committee tonight.

MAC. You said you'd put me out?

BAUER. I did.

MAC. Do you know I'm a longshoreman?

BAUER. You're an I.W.W. You have been in this union two years and you have made nothing but trouble since you came. You are not a union man—and Bardi is not, and Capraro is not. You are out to make trouble. When one strike is over you start another, you three. And we have had enough of you!

MAC. I'll tell you, Mr. Bauer, this looks to me like the start of a long conversation, and as I said, I'm busy—

BAUER. You will find out! You saw the way the vote went on your strike. Well, you were not here earlier in the evening. That was decided before hand. And we have talked about you and Bardi and Capraro. Capraro is an anarchist. I have heard him say so. And he is going out of the union. And your literature must be taken away tonight.

MAC. You throw it out. If you're scared of a raid, throw it out. I hope they raid you and find enough Rights of Man around here to give the Department of Justice the heebie-jeebies.

BAUER. You will not take it away?

MAC. No.

BAUER. Very well. I will. (*He goes out.*)

IKE. Personally, I'd rather be a bum.

MAC. Where's Capraro? Hasn't he been around?

ROSALIE. No.

MAC. Nor Bardi?

ROSALIE. No.

MAC. That's funny. Maybe they ran them in. We'd better find out.

ROSALIE. Don't you know they've got warrants out for all of you? For instigating a riot?

WARD. That's a good joke.

ROSALIE. It's not a joke.

MAC. Well, no, not exactly. They didn't mean it that way.

IKE. It's in the paper. And did you

know the scabs didn't get paid today?

MAC. No, why? (WARD *looks at the paper.*)

IKE. Payroll was robbed. That's in the paper, too.

MAC. Hell, Ike can read. When did this happen?

IKE. This afternoon. Got clean away with the money.

WARD. That's good. That soaks Northfield and the scabs, too. Say, they killed old Kendall.

SPIKER. Who's Kendall?

WARD. Paymaster.

MAC. Good day for a holdup. They had every policeman in town guarding the docks, and riot guns all up and down the harbor front.

ROSALIE. Mac, what did happen this afternoon?

MAC. Nothing. Only we tried to re-establish our picket lines, and somebody had squealed to the chief of police, so he met us with a young army. They started shooting over the boys' heads and naturally there was hell to pay.

ROSALIE. But Mac, there were some policemen hurt—and the way the papers have it they blame everything on you—

MAC. I was hardly in it. I was a sort of an in-and-outer. Capraro and I were riding with Waterman in his car. We had to have him there so they couldn't rush the boys off to jail without seeing a lawyer, and they've been trying to get Waterman, so he wouldn't come unless he was guarded. And they tried to take him away from us, you see. That's how I happened to grab the gun. They had it all planned. A cop jumps on the running board and tosses a gun into the car and then they start to arrest the bunch for carrying concealed weapons. I've seen that tried before, so I picked up the gun and beat it. That's all.

ROSALIE. Then they made up the story about your starting it by knocking a policeman down.

MAC. I ran into him by accident.

ROSALIE. You could have let them arrest Waterman.

MAC. They were going to pull all three of us! We'd have been through the third degree by now and stretched out on the iron floor like so much sirloin steak. The way it is we're all out of it. We're all out of it—we can carry the strike right over to the mills tomorrow.

IKE. Maybe you didn't hear that Bardi was hurt.

MAC. Bardi?

IKE. You didn't hear that?

MAC. No.

SPIKER. He wasn't hurt much. I saw him leaning up against the gates, and he said he'd be all right in a minute.

IKE. Oh, no. He was hurt bad.

MAC. Who told you?

IKE. Some fellow in there. He said Bardi was shot.

MAC. What?

IKE. Yeah, I thought you knew that.

MAC. Where did they take the boys that were hurt?

(*He rises.*)

WARD. I don't know.

(CAPRARO, *a gentle young Italian, enters quietly from the street.*)

MAC. Hello, Cappie. We were just talking about Bardi.

CAPRARO (*after a pause*). Bardi is dead.

MAC. He is?

CAPRARO. I just came from the hospital.

MAC. Hell. So it had to happen to Bardi. Was he shot?

CAPRARO. Yes. They were careful to hit him where it would kill. He asked me to tell you good-bye for him. He was so sorry to die that way—in a hospital. He said—it means nothing this way. He said, please tell you all good-bye.

MAC. I see.

ROSALIE. And don't you see pretty soon it will be your turn? Everybody knows what Northfield has said about all of you—

MAC. So it had to happen to little Bardi.

IKE. He was a good scout.

(*A Salvation Army group begins to play and sing outside.*)

THE ARMY.

There's a land that is fairer than day,
And by faith we can see it afar,
For the Father waits over the way
To prepare us a dwelling-place there.

In the sweet bye and bye,
We shall meet on that beautiful shore,
In the sweet bye and bye,
We shall meet on that beautiful shore.

(IKE, *who is standing at the window, sings the next stanza with them, beginning in a low tone.*)

IKE.

Those preachers come out every night
To tell us what's wrong and what's right.

If you ask them for something to eat,
They answer in voices so sweet—
(*He raises his voice so that the words are heard.*)
You will eat, bye and bye,
In your beautiful home beyond the sky.
Watch and pray, live on hay,
You'll get pie in the sky bye and bye.

WARD. Aw, shut up, Ike.

(*The door opens and a pretty Salvation lass passes the tambourine while the band goes on singing. Nobody pays any attention to her.* JERUSALEM SLIM, *wearing a Salvation uniform, enters behind her and stands near the door.*)

THE ARMY.
We shall sing on that beautiful shore
The melodious songs of the blest,
And our spirits shall sorrow no more,
Not a sigh for the blessings of rest.

In the sweet, etc.

(*The* LASSIE *comes last to* IKE, *who looks inquisitively into the tambourine, then gravely holds out his cap to her.*)

IKE. I'm in the same line myself, sister.

THE LASSIE. Jesus will save you.

IKE. Not if I see him first, he won't. I'm a Southern Jew, and Jesus himself wouldn't touch a Southern Jew, sister. He might be willing to do something for one of those New York Jews, but I never met anybody that didn't draw the line at an Israelite hill-billy.

THE LASSIE. Have you tried Him?

IKE. Sister, I get saved regular every winter, whenever my shoes wear out. I've got a groove wore in my back from backsliding.

THE LASSIE. "Come unto me all ye who labor and are heavy-laden." You'll never find rest till you find Him.

IKE. Sister, if you're speaking for yourself, I'll come, but if you're speaking for the Kingdom of Heaven, I've been to Florida and these summer resorts ain't what they're cracked up to be in the prospectus. You're too pretty to go round distributing the word of God. You're liable to create a false impression. Heaven ain't like that. Why don't you speak for yourself, kid?

THE LASSIE (*stepping back*). I'm safe in His arms, brother.

IKE. You'd be a lot more comfortable in mine.

(*The* LASSIE *goes out. As she passes through the door, a shrill voice is heard testifying.*)

THE VOICE. I was on the street and Jesus saved me. My sins fell from me and left my soul as pure as the driven snow.

(*The door closes, cutting off the words.*)

WARD. That was no accident, you know, about Bardi.

MAC. No, probably not.

WARD. They had it in for him, after last year.

SPIKER. You think they planned that?

WARD. I do.

CAPRARO. It is they that have red hands. The murderer loses in the end.

MAC. The kind of murderer that killed Bardi dies mostly of old age.

SLIM. You have all forgotten something. You have forgotten that God is love.

WARD (*angrily*). Christ, I thought that one was dead!

MAC. Oh, God is love, is he? Well, how much does He love the guy that instructed somebody to get Bardi?

SLIM. Judge not that ye be not judged.

SPIKER. Throw him out.

MAC. You! You're a pious fraud. You're one of them. The net effect of all you've got to say is to support their capitalistic system! That's what your army says, and that's why business supports you. Teach 'em temperance so they'll work steadier, teach 'em to turn the other cheek, so they won't make trouble when they're robbed, teach 'em to judge not, so we can jail 'em and murder 'em without a come-back. Make 'em all good slaves in the name of Jesus Christ. That's what you stand for!

SLIM. Would you do violence for higher wages?

MAC. No, but if I had my hands on the man that shot Bardi, I wouldn't answer for him.

CAPRARO. You would be wrong. When you take violence into your hands, you lower yourself to the level of government, which is the origin of crime and evil.

MAC. Go on! The government's nothing so important. It's a police system, to protect the wealth of the wealthy. And Slim there, he stands for the priests of the world, going around advising everybody to knuckle under so the bankers can keep all they've got! That's why the boys voted to end the strike in there. They've been taught to be slaves till they don't know enough to take what's their own. We had the strike all won for them, and they throw it all away because they owe a little money at the corner grocery and they're scared of the police! Capraro and I talk ourselves blue in the face for them, and Bardi gets himself killed for them, and it's all coming their way, and then what do they do? They decide they can't stand it any longer and they take their wage cut and go back to work! No wonder the Rockefellers are good Baptists!

ROSALIE. Then isn't it all useless, Mac?

MAC. By God, they're going to know they've been in a fight before they put me away! What else does Northfield own besides mills and docks? I'll have them all out on him! I'll bleed him till he can't pay his private dicks!

WARD. Good boy!

(*The telephone rings.* ROSALIE *answers it.*)

ROSALIE. Yes, he's here. Mac.

(MAC *takes the phone.*)

MAC. Hello. Hello, Ben. What? Wait a minute. They're *not* going back to work! I know they voted it down but they're not going back because the engineers are staying out. Did you get that? And now get this, too. The engineers are staying out on my word that the mills are going out in sympathy, and you've got to work it for me. No, I've got to wait here till the meeting's over. You can pull that through for me. (*A pause.*) Well, can you do this? Can you hold them half an hour till I can get there? Put on a show. Make it dramatic, and I'll be over as soon as I hear from Andy. You're damn right we'll have the longshoremen out again! We'll make them eat that vote and like it! All right! (*He hangs up, and turns to* WARD.) What was that you heard about raids tonight?

WARD. I got it from old Bauer.

MAC. Well, there may be something in it, from what Benny says. They've got a posse mobilized over at the mills.

ROSALIE. Then you won't go over there?

MAC. I've got to. It's probably only the regular guard. They call out the State Militia every time a couple of mill-workers shake hands. (*He takes down the receiver.*) Give me the committee room. Hello. Hello, Andy. I know you're not alone. You don't need to talk. You can give it to me yes or no. Are they waiting to hear from the mills? Well, the mills are waiting to hear from you, so for God's sake shove them over. Yes. Benny says they will. And move fast or I won't be in time. I'm going over there. (*He comes over to* ROSALIE.) You've got to be a sport, sweetheart, you've got to.

ROSALIE. I can't do it any more. I've done it all I can. (*She is set and stern.*)

MAC. It's the only chance the strike's got, Rosalie. If I go down there with the news that the engineers are going out I'm pretty sure I can stampede them.

ROSALIE. You'd better go then. Only don't ask me to be a sport about it. I'm not going to try any more. I'm not going to be interested any more.

MAC. What do you want me to do? Put on a white collar and sit in an office and push a pen around all day?

ROSALIE. You could do anything—anything you wanted to—only you don't want to do anything but—save humanity or something like that—I don't know what! All I know is they aren't worth it— and they don't care how much you do for them!

MAC. They're the only people who are worth anything. I admit they're lunkheads and you've got to tell them. By God, somebody's got to do the telling.

ROSALIE. Get wise to yourself, Mac. They sit around here and guzzle coffee and yes you one day and then go in there and vote you down the next! And they aren't worth it and you don't get anything out of it!

MAC. I get a hell of a lot of fun out of it.

ROSALIE. I thought so. You start strikes because you like to be in a fight and you run them because you like to act like a tin Napoleon—that's all!

MAC. Thanks!

ROSALIE. That's that—there's nothing more to say—go ahead with your strike —do anything you like but don't count on me.

MAC. Does that mean you are walking out on me?

ROSALIE. It does. Don't touch me and don't come near me. I'm through, Mac, through. I don't want to see you again and I hope— (ROSALIE *runs out.*)

SPIKER. "Tin Napoleon," eh? Getting soft, Mac? Never knew you to take anything like that before.

MAC. You try it on, fella, and see what'll happen to you. (*Phone rings.* MAC *answers.*) Hello. What? Who is this? How do you know that? I've just been talking to Benny. They did! Ah, Christ! Can't you round them up? Can't you get another hall? You don't have to let them get away with that! Who have you got with you? (*A long pause.*) All right. All right. Well, it certainly lets us down over here. Where are you going to be? I'll call you there. (*He hangs up.*) That settles it.

WARD. What's up?

MAC. Police broke up the mill meeting, wrecked the hall, and scattered the crowd. They won't vote tonight. Anyway, they're licked. And I guess we are. What do you say, Cappie?

CAPRARO. We must call Andy.

MAC. I wish I thought the engineers would go out alone.

CAPRARO. They will not. Anyway, you must tell them.

MAC. You tell 'em, Cappie.

CAPRARO (*going to telephone*). Give me the committee room.

SPIKER. So they go back tomorrow.

MAC. Looks like it.

CAPRARO. Hello, Andy. It's all off. Police raided the mill-workers. Oh, no, no, no! We must not do that! Yes, so am I. (*He hangs up.*)

SPIKER. You'd let the longshoremen go back to work tomorrow—after that?

MAC. Not if I saw my way out of it.

SPIKER. What kind of guts have we got in this crowd, anyway? We can't let 'em get away with that! Don't you see it? They get away with that and we're licked for good—the whole labor crowd's licked?

MAC. Pretty damn near it.

SPIKER. Look here, Mac. I never knew you to go soft before. What's the matter with you? Do you want a vacation?

MAC. I didn't ask for one, but I guess I'm going to get it.

SPIKER. Ward, what's the matter with you? I don't understand this bunch. Are we going to lie down? God, there's got to be something to do!

WARD. There's got to be, all right, but I can't think of it.

SPIKER. I'll tell you what I'd do if anybody had the guts to go with me—I'd fix it so nobody could go to work, scabs or union. I'd blow the docks to hell!

WARD. There wouldn't be any sense to that.

SPIKER. Christ, what a crowd!

MAC. Be logical, man, be logical. I'll do anything that'll get us anywhere. Only that wouldn't. Not this time.

SPIKER. Now's the time it would do some good. And why not? They've used everything on us.

WARD. Well, I'd like to see it.

SPIKER. Only you won't touch it—oh, no! You wanted to know what you could do about the strike—and I told you that's all—and do I get volunteers? I do not. Well, I'll tell you what I'll do. I'm going alone.

MAC. Are you joking?

SPIKER. I don't joke with nitroglycerine. (SUVORIN *has silently risen and come over behind* SPIKER. *He lays his hand on* SPIKER'S *shoulder.* SPIKER *jumps.*) What do you want?

SUVORIN. You asked for a man.

SPIKER. Well?

SUVORIN. Will I do?

SPIKER. Will you come with me?

SUVORIN. Who are you?

SPIKER. Who the hell are you?

SUVORIN. You know me. I run this restaurant.

SPIKER. You're no longshoreman.

SUVORIN. You asked for a man.

SPIKER. All right. Who else is coming?

SUVORIN. And now, who are you?

SPIKER. Say, bohunk, I guess you know who I am.

SUVORIN. I do not.

SPIKER. Well, I don't know as I can help you then.

MAC. He's all right, Suvorin. He's been working with us three months. He's a California wobbly. They grow wild out there.

SPIKER. Anybody else game to go along?

MAC. You wouldn't go into that?

SUVORIN. If he will tell me who he is.

SPIKER. Damn it, Mac told you who I am!

SUVORIN. How long were you in California?

SPIKER. Is this a third degree?

SUVORIN. Why not answer me?

MAC. Tell him, Spiker. He's all right. There's nobody here you need be afraid of.

SPIKER. Three years.

SUVORIN. And before that?

SPIKER. Do you want my life history?

SUVORIN. This is a serious matter.

SPIKER. All right. I've been an I.W.W. organizer over four years. Before that I was in Pittsburgh.

SUVORIN. What was your trade?

SPIKER. Iron-worker.

SUVORIN. You've never been an iron-worker.

SPIKER. Are you calling me a liar?

SUVORIN. I am. Look at that hand. Look at that wrist. (*He holds up* SPIKER'S *hand.*) Where do you wear it?

SPIKER. What are you getting nasty about?

SUVORIN. I said where do you wear it? On your underwear?

SPIKER. What do you mean?

SUVORIN. Your badge!

SPIKER. I don't wear any badge. Do I look like a dick?

SUVORIN. You do. (*He seizes* SPIKER'S *shirt and turns the collar down.*)

SPIKER. Take your lousy paws off me.

SUVORIN. There it is. (*He withdraws his hand with a detective's badge in it.*)

SPIKER. You planted that on me!

SUVORIN. Oh, no.

MAC (*rising*). Look, here, Spiker!—

SPIKER (*his hands on a gun in his pocket*). Let go of me!

(SOWERBY *slides under the table and stays there.*)

SUVORIN. Certainly.

(SPIKER, *released, backs to the street door, his eyes on* MAC.)

MAC. Spiker, is that true? (SPIKER, *nearing the door, makes no answer.*) You're a rat, then, are you? (SPIKER *disappears.*) Why, God damn his soul, he's been sitting in with us all through the strike! (*He makes a sudden dash for the cash drawer, takes out the gun and makes for the door.*)

ROSALIE. Mac!

(SUVORIN *blocks* MAC'S *way and pinions him,* WARD *takes the gun.*)

MAC. All right, all right. I'm letting go. Only that's the nearest I ever came to bumping anybody off.

(WARD *replaces the gun.*)

SUVORIN. Sit there and think it over! And when next you wish to do a thing like that do it well, with forethought to save your skin, not like a fool! (*He looks over the group.*) How many years have I sat here listening to fools' talk? Five, ten—many years. And what have I learned from you? I have learned that you know nothing—that you learn nothing! Uplifters, you are, reformers, dreamers, thinking to make over the earth. I know you all, and you are all fools but Ike, who is a pan-handler. That is sensible. . . . The earth is old. You will not make it over. Man is old. You will not make him over. You are anarchists, maybe, some of you socialists, some of you wobblies, you are all believers in pap. The world is old, and it is owned by men who are hard. Do you think you can win against them by a strike? Let us change the government, you say. Bah! They own this government, they will buy any government you have. I tell you there is no government—there are only brigands in power who fight for more power! It has always been so. It will always be so. Till you die! Till we all die! Till there is no earth!

This Spiker you have here, you believe him, he looks right to you. How do I know him? I have a test for him. All my life I listen among men for a man who has hell in him, as I have. All my life I listen for one rebel, and when I have thought to find him I have looked under his lapel for the badge. When I find him he is a spy—always! There is only one man with enough hell in him to be dangerous—enough hell and cunning and power—and it is I alone! I came here from tyranny to find a free country, and this country set out to break me in its prisons because I believed in its liberty. You should know what it is to wear iron to your bone! I can tell you of liberty! I can tell you of justice! There is none! There are men with whips and there are whipped men! That is all. And you are whipped. Because you are fools.

WARD. Who's whipped?

SUVORIN. You are. You are whipped before you start. The government sets a little game for you, and you play it with them, and the government wins because it is their game. Then they put you in prison till you have tuberculosis. That is the end of you. It is an easy way. You are children in their hands. You have not even bothered to get money to fight them, you have not even learned to break from a prison, you do not even learn their tricks. Bah! They have cheap little tricks to hold you—handcuffs, bars—do you think they could hold me again with handcuffs and bars?—Yes, but you are happier so. You have not gone bad inside—and that is why you are not dangerous. That is why—you are not dangerous. (*He sits, his head in his hands.*) Play your game. They are safe from you.

(*The door opens and a* POLICEMAN *and* SERGEANT *enter.* SPIKER *stands in the doorway.* MAC *and* WARD *rise.*)

SERGEANT. Sit still, sit still. Just got warrants for a couple of arrests here, that's all.

MAC. Who do you want?

SERGEANT. James Macready and Dante Capraro.

ROSALIE. They're not here.

SPIKER. Oh, yes, they are.

WARD. Hello, rat.

SPIKER. Those two.

SERGEANT (*to* MAC). What's your name?

MAC. Macready.

SERGEANT. Well, you're wanted. What's yours?

CAPRARO. Capraro.

SERGEANT. You two come along. That's all.

MAC. Wait a minute, wait a minute. Where's your warrant?

SERGEANT. Oh, I see. Constitutional rights and everything, huh? Well, here you are.

MAC. Wait. Let me read it.

SERGEANT. Sure, read it.

MAC (*reading*). Do you mean you're arresting us for a murder?

SERGEANT. That's what it says, ain't it?

MAC. You can't arrest us for any murder.

SERGEANT. I guess I can.

ROSALIE. What murder?

MAC. Kendall, the paymaster. Listen, we know nothing about that. We were having troubles of our own this afternoon.

POLICEMAN. We don't know anything about that.

ROSALIE. But you can't do this. It isn't right.

SERGEANT. I don't want any argument about it.

SPIKER (*coming in*). You'd better search the place for weapons, sergeant. Look in the cash drawer.

MAC. You lousy fink, is this your affair?

SPIKER. And look them over for guns.
(MAC *suddenly hits* SPIKER *in the jaw.* SPIKER *goes down. The* SERGEANT *grabs* MAC, *who wrestles with him to get at* SPIKER. *The other policeman gets him from behind.* ROSALIE *tries to help and is shoved away. The* SERGEANT *turns to* CAPRARO.)

SERGEANT. How about you?

CAPRARO. I know nothing of a murder.

SERGEANT. Put out your hands.

CAPRARO. I will not.
(*He is handcuffed.* SPIKER *finds the gun in the cash drawer.*)

SPIKER (*to* SUVORIN). Whose is this?

SUVORIN. I do not know.

ROSALIE. It's mine. I put it there.

SERGEANT. How long have you had it?

ROSALIE. I don't know. I've always had it.

SERGEANT. I'll take it. (SPIKER *hands it over.*) That's a service revolver.

ROSALIE. Mac!

SERGEANT. You say this is yours?

ROSALIE. Yes.

SERGEANT. You can't talk to him, you know. What's your name?

ROSALIE. Rosalie Suvorin.

SERGEANT. That's all. We're going.

ROSALIE. Wait just a minute—please!

SERGEANT. You can't go along, you know.

ROSALIE. Can't I speak to him a minute?

SERGEANT. No.

MAC. Don't worry, kid. I've been pinched before.
(*He and the* SERGEANT *go out, following* CAPRARO *and the other* POLICEMAN. SPIKER *hits* MAC *outside the door.*)

SERGEANT (*at the door*). By the way, I don't think so much of the crowd you keep in here.

SUVORIN. Neither do I.
(*Exit* SERGEANT. WARD *goes to the door.* MILKIN *is scribbling on a napkin.*)

MILKIN (*to* IKE). See dat? Dat don't look so good. Dat's de wrong sign.

CURTAIN

ACT TWO

SCENE I

SCENE.—*Office of District Attorney* SALTER *in the court-house.*

There is a window, partly ivy-covered, at the right, and a door at the rear communicating with the JUDGE'S *chambers. A door at the left opens on a hallway. The rear and left-hand walls are almost covered with a legal reference library, mostly in yellow leather bindings. There are two desks, one for* SALTER, *one for his secretary. A couple of padded chairs are placed to front the attorney's desk. The desks are piled with stacks of letters and 'script.*

SALTER, *a thin, keen, and rather weary person, enters from the hall, tosses a hat on the rack, and begins to search through a mass of papers. He finds what he wants and sits at his desk.*

There is a tap at the door and HASLET *enters. He is a well-dressed, middle-aged business man.*

It is after lunch.

SALTER. Oh, hello, Arthur.

HASLET. How's our little trial coming?

SALTER. It's all right.

HASLET. Going to convict?

SALTER. Oh, yes.—Want to let 'em off?

HASLET. I do not.

SALTER. Thought maybe somebody had changed his mind.

HASLET. Good God, man, those two Bolsheviks have raised more hell in this town the last two years than you'd get out of a dozen reform administrations. Every time we turn around they start something new on us.

SALTER. Damned unpleasant.

HASLET. They've turned my hair grey, and they've cost the Northfield company a couple of millions, one time and another.

SALTER. It's rather hard to make it look as if they had anything to do with the murder—

HASLET. Why is it?

SALTER. Lord, there's no evidence.

HASLET. It looks like a pipe to me.

SALTER. I wish you had the job. And the next time the boys want to pin something on a couple of radicals I wish you'd call in a little expert advice before you start.

HASLET. You, for instance?

SALTER. Me, for instance. It might make it a damn sight easier.

HASLET. Not that I tried to pin anything on them. But I think it was a damned good idea.

SALTER. Well, so far as I'm concerned it's a mess. And devilish uncomfortable.

HASLET. How about that bomb last night?

SALTER. That helps. By the way, who set that bomb?

HASLET. How would I know? Some of their black-hand friends, I suppose.

SALTER. Oh, no. They know better than that. Even a foreigner knows better than to set a bomb under a juryman's front porch. Is Spiker still working for the company?

HASLET. You think Spiker did it?

SALTER. Well, I bet he knows who did.

HASLET. It was all news to me.

SALTER. Spiker's got it in for Macready and Capraro. He'll do more than he's paid for. It wasn't necessary at that. Not with this jury. It's a hundred and forty proof Shriners and Chamber of Commerce.

HASLET. What are you kicking about then?

SALTER. The way it looks, that's all. It's the God-damnedest flimsiest case I ever had on my hands, yes, and the most sickening bunch of welching witnesses I ever had to deal with. We're going to convict and it's going to look like a frame-up. If I had it to do over again I'd see Northfield and his docks and mills in hell before I'd handle it.

HASLET. You're nervous, Will. What's the matter with you? Don't you own any stock?

SALTER. I need some evidence to show up in the newspapers. You told me your operatives had an air-tight case, and they said the same thing, and your witnesses are trying to back out all along the line. And who has to hold them to it? I do. It's a rotten job. I'd like to know how Spiker got that original bunch of affidavits. He must have had everybody chloroformed.

HASLET. Those two Bolsheviks have got it coming. I don't give a damn so long as we don't lose.

SALTER. You may wish you had, that's all. The town's crawling with reporters sending in front page stuff. It's going to make a stink you can smell from here to Siberia.

HASLET. What does the judge think about it?

SALTER. When did a judge ever think? He's paid not to. By the way, this Spiker person of yours, whom I dislike intensely, was in here this morning. He tells me the defense have a surprise witness to spring after I get all through.

HASLET. Who is it? The girl?

SALTER. The girl's father.

HASLET. What of it?

SALTER. Well, Spiker thinks he's got something on the old boy, that's all. He's looking up his record and if they put him on the stand he wants to spring something. I rather wish Spiker was up for murder. I'd take a passionate delight in railroading a crook, just for a change.

(JUDGE VAIL *enters from the rear; he is fastening his robe.*)

HASLET. How are you, Judge?

VAIL. How are you? I'm excellent, excellent, thanks. You in court today?

HASLET. I'll have to get back to town—just dropped in on my way. What's the news?

VAIL. It's all in the papers. They're printing us verbatim this time. Great honor. I wanted to ask you, Will—as things are going now, are you likely to conclude your case today or will you require another session?

SALTER. I'm putting on my two last witnesses this afternoon. I don't know what the defense will do.

VAIL. I fear it's likely to drag on for some days.

HASLET. Are you betting on the results, Judge?

VAIL. I daresay they'll be found guilty. And no doubt they are. No doubt they are. I long ago gave up trying to decide who was innocent and who was guilty. That's the jury's business. In this case we have an intelligent jury. (*He goes to the door, then turns to deliver a dry joke.*) But not too intelligent—not too intelligent. (*He goes out.*)

HASLET. He's all right.

SALTER. Yeah. He's been dead from the neck up for twenty-five years. And from the neck down for about forty—otherwise he's fine.

HASLET. By the way, can we do anything for you?

SALTER. Sure, I want a steam yacht and a villa overlooking the Mediterranean. And I'm going to need 'em when I'm through with this. No, you big swine, run along and sell your papers. I'm incorruptible. Anyway, you don't need to corrupt me. I've got to win this case now or retire. I just wish to God I'd never got into it. That's what makes me sore.

HASLET. You're made, man, you're made.

SALTER. I suppose you think I'll be the next governor.

HASLET. Why not? So long, Will!

SALTER. So long, Arthur.

(HASLET *goes out left.* SALTER *pushes a bell. A* COURT ATTENDANT *enters.*)

ATTENDANT. Yes, sir.

SALTER. Got that woman waiting?

ATTENDANT. Yes, sir.

SALTER. Bring her in.

(*The* ATTENDANT *opens the door at the left and ushers in* MRS. LUBIN, *a woman of fifty or so.*)

MRS. LUBIN. Yes, Mr. Salter.

SALTER. I got your letter this morning. Sit down.

MRS. LUBIN (*sitting*). Yes, sir.

SALTER. You say you've changed your mind, you aren't sure of what you saw and you can't testify?

MRS. LUBIN. Yes, sir.

SALTER. Don't you think it's pretty late in the day to change your mind?

MRS. LUBIN. Yes, sir—but—

SALTER. Do you remember what you said in your affidavit? (*He taps the paper in his hand.*) You said you were standing at the front window of your apartment at four-fifteen on the afternoon of April second and you saw Macready shoot Kendall from the front seat of a Buick touring car. That's pretty definite, isn't it? You swore to that, didn't you?

MRS. LUBIN. Yes, sir—but—he was the only man in the room.

SALTER. Who was?

MRS. LUBIN. Macready. When I identified him.

SALTER. Well, what of it? You identified him, didn't you? You don't deny that?

MRS. LUBIN. They told me I had to.

SALTER. Who did?

MRS. LUBIN. The men. The detectives.

SALTER. Now, you're going to forget about this letter, you understand? You're going to forget about all that and testify to the story you told in your affidavit.

MRS. LUBIN. Mr. Salter, I really couldn't identify him. I was too far away. And I've—Mr. Salter, I've been looking from that window,—and—I—couldn't have seen the shooting at all. I heard the shot, but I couldn't see where it was. And—Mr. Gluckstein knows that—

SALTER. How does he know?

MRS. LUBIN. He came to the apartment.

SALTER. So you've been talking to the defense?

MRS. LUBIN. I didn't know who he was then. He came and asked if he could look out the window, and he asked me where the shooting was. I'd said the shooting was on the other side of the track, and you can't see the street there because there's a railroad tower in the way—and anyway—

SALTER. When you made this statement did you know you couldn't see that part of the street from your window?

MRS. LUBIN. No, sir. I thought I could. I didn't really see the shooting. I looked out after I heard the shot.

SALTER. Now get this straight, Mrs. Lubin. You're not conducting this prosecution. I'll take care of any little discrepancies between what you saw and what you couldn't see. I want only one thing of you and that one thing I'm going to get. I want you to tell your story on the stand exactly as you told it before the magistrate.

MRS. LUBIN. I tell you I can't.

SALTER. You'll find you can. Tell me, Mrs. Lubin, why did you swear to this in the first place? Do you remember?

MRS. LUBIN. They told me I had to.

SALTER. Was there any special reason why you had to?

MRS. LUBIN. No.

SALTER. I have your record here, Mrs. Lubin. You have a grown son up-state, haven't you?

MRS. LUBIN. Yes, sir.

SALTER. Does your son know that in 1915 you conducted a certain type of house at 54 Charles Street?

MRS. LUBIN. Oh, God, are you going over that again?

SALTER. Not unless I have to. There are a good many things in this paper which have never come to the ears of your son. Shall I read it to you?

MRS. LUBIN (*hopelessly*). No.

SALTER. Very well. We'll forget that. I think you've failed to realize the extent to which the state is interested in this case, and also the extent to which the state is interested in you. You are a citizen of this country, Mrs. Lubin. Do you believe in the constitution?

MRS. LUBIN. Yes.

SALTER. Do you reverence the flag?

MRS. LUBIN. Yes.

SALTER. Then why do you change your testimony to shield anarchists? You'll find that very hard to explain, Mrs. Lubin.

MRS. LUBIN. I don't—I—

SALTER. Perhaps you are yourself an anarchist, Mrs. Lubin. Perhaps you have been bought off by the defense.

MRS. LUBIN. I'm not being paid—

SALTER. I don't say you are. I'm just saying it might look that way. To a jury. The question is, would a jury believe you? It looks like perjury, and if it came to a perjury trial how much of your past would you be able to conceal from your son?

MRS. LUBIN (*deciding*). Very well.

SALTER. I give you my word, Mrs. Lubin, it is your duty as a citizen to stick to your story.

MRS. LUBIN. Very well, I will.

SALTER. Exactly as in the affidavit?

MRS. LUBIN. Yes, sir. Is that all?

SALTER. That's all.

(MRS. LUBIN *goes out. The* ATTENDANT *appears.*)

ATTENDANT. Bartlet's here, sir.

SALTER. Bartlet?

ATTENDANT. Yes, sir.

SALTER. Send him in. (*The* ATTENDANT *ushers in* BARTLET, *a youth of eighteen with a sodden face. He slumps in a chair.*) Well, sir, what have you got to say to me?

BARTLET. Me? They said you wanted to see me.

SALTER. Stand up! When I want you to sit down I'll tell you.

(BARTLET *rises.*)

BARTLET. All right.

SALTER. I've heard about you. You couldn't wait to get to court to give your testimony. You had to spread yourself all over town. Tell me what you've been saying.

BARTLET. What I've been saying?

SALTER. You heard me.

BARTLET. I haven't been saying much.

SALTER. Don't lie to me! Sit down! (BARTLET *sits.*) Did you identify Capraro?

BARTLET. Well—I—

SALTER. Did you identify Capraro?

BARTLET. What if I did? I guess I was —I guess I was mistaken.

SALTER. Listen to me, Bartlet. When you start swearing to evidence there's only one safe thing to do—and that's tell one story and stick to it. Now you've told your story and if you stick to it you'll be protected—

BARTLET. Yeah, but—

SALTER. But you start talking in court the way you've been talking down at the mill and you're going to talk yourself into enough trouble to make you look sick the rest of your life. You said last spring that Capraro looked like the man you saw in the car—

BARTLET. Yeah, but I couldn't say it was him—

SALTER. You don't have to say it was him. I wouldn't want you to. You'll say it was the dead image of him. Can you remember that? The dead image of him.

BARTLET. Maybe that wouldn't be right.

SALTER. It's true, isn't it? It looked like Capraro. All right, say that.

BARTLET. It looked like Capraro, all right.

SALTER. Certainly it did. It was the dead image of him. And mind you, that doesn't mean it was Capraro. That means it looked like him. Can you remember that?

BARTLET. Yeah, I guess that'd be all right.

SALTER. Can you remember it?

BARTLET. The dead image of him, sure.

SALTER. And if you aren't going to stay with it you'd better tell me now.

BARTLET. All right.

SALTER (*changing tone*). You know, Bartlet, there's a good many of us taking an interest in you around here. Some of us haven't been quite sure whether you'd turn yellow or come through like a man. It isn't as if these birds weren't guilty, you know. We know they're guilty. Why, damn it, they believe in murder. It's part of their platform. Do you know why you thought Capraro looked like the man in the car?

BARTLET. No.

SALTER. Well, I'll tell you. Because he was the man in the car. Talk about the dead image of him! It was Capraro!

BARTLET. Yes, sir, it was the dead image of him.

SALTER (*under his breath*). Jesus Christ! (*He goes back to his desk.*) All right, Bartlet. You'll be called this afternoon. And we're depending on you.

BARTLET. Yes, sir. (*He goes out.*)

(*There is a knock at the door.*)

SALTER. Come in. (GLUCKSTEIN *enters.*) Why, hello, Gluckie. How's the Soviet today?

GLUCKSTEIN. Pretty well, thanks. How's the White Guard?

SALTER. A bit shaky, but game.

GLUCKSTEIN. Listen, Salter—just man to man, now— you know my boys aren't guilty, don't you?

SALTER. You're a man of high principles, Gluckie, if they weren't innocent you wouldn't defend 'em—not for a minute.

GLUCKSTEIN. But seriously now, Salter. I don't mind telling you I'm worried. I know you haven't any case. I know you haven't any evidence. I know the boys aren't guilty. I know the case looks as if it was going against you. But if you keep on playing up the Bolshevik business to that jury—why, it's plain murder. You tell that jury a man's a radical and the whole twelve will vote to hang him. And do you think they're guilty?

SALTER. That's what we're here to find out, friend. That's what the jury's for.

GLUCKSTEIN. Well—maybe it's too much to ask.

SALTER. I guess it is.

GLUCKSTEIN. You wouldn't consider playing the game fair?

SALTER. Old man, I'm a District Attorney. I'm paid to play the game. I'm supposed to win if I can.

GLUCKSTEIN. Well, but, for God's sake, have a little decency about it. That bomb last night, for instance.—That's dirty, you know.

SALTER. Your clients have amusing little friends.

GLUCKSTEIN. *My* clients!

SALTER. You don't think we'd do that—?

GLUCKSTEIN. Well—

SALTER. Well, God knows I don't know. Why the foreman of a jury should hitch a bomb under his front porch. It's just my good luck, that's all.

GLUCKSTEIN. And why are my witnesses shadowed, Salter? And why am I shadowed?

SALTER. I don't know about the witnesses.

GLUCKSTEIN. Then how about me? Is it fair to put plain-clothes men on my trail?

SALTER. You mean you've been followed?

GLUCKSTEIN. You know I have.

SALTER. Gluckie, you've been followed by nothing but your own bad conscience. You mean you've had detectives following my detectives? Gluckie, that isn't right!

GLUCKSTEIN. I know the men and I know who pays them.

SALTER. It's none of my doing, Gluckie. I'll tell you the truth about that, though. Somebody was tipped off by somebody that there was a woman somewhere in your spotless young life. That's all.

GLUCKSTEIN. But that's—that's contemptible.

SALTER. Certainly it is. I wouldn't use anything of the sort. But as a matter of fact I'd advise you to watch your step, Gluckie. Not all the members of my club are men of conscience, like me.

GLUCKSTEIN. I see.

SALTER. Then there's something in it?

GLUCKSTEIN. No.

SALTER. No? Well—it might be better on the whole if you didn't win the case, you see? That is, as far as you're concerned personally.

GLUCKSTEIN. That's blackmail, isn't it?

SALTER. Well, not legally. And you have nothing to worry about, anyway. Because I don't think you can win, Gluckie. I don't think you've got a chance in the world. I almost wish you had. That's straight.

GLUCKSTEIN. Well—we'll see.

SALTER. Sure, we'll see.

(GLUCKSTEIN *goes out.* SALTER *goes wearily to the telephone, takes it up, thinks a minute, then takes the receiver off the hook.*) Get me Spiker, will you? Hello, hello! Hello, Spiker—say, listen, Spiker, this is Salter. Wait a minute, listen to me. You're a low-down crook and I hate your guts and I could win this case without you, do you get that? All right, many of them—but if you want that guy Henry in court when the old man testifies you'd better bring him along this afternoon, just to make sure. Yeah? Well, now listen to me some more. I think you're all set to queer this case with your under-cover stuff. If this is Department of Justice information it's probably crooked and it's probably dirty, because I've played with them before. (*A silence.*) Well, damn it, when do I get my data? I've got to talk, you know. I'm no moving picture. All right. Have him up near the stand. Well, you can explain it to him, can't you? If he used to be a sheriff he ought to know that much. (*The* ATTENDANT *enters.*) I haven't got time. The session starts at one.

ATTENDANT. Are you ready, Mr. Salter?

SALTER (*in the phone*). Yeah, I think they will. I don't know whether he knows it or not. Oh, it's a pleasure, a pleasure! (*He hangs up.*) No brains, that's all, no brains. (*He picks up his manuscript and makes for the door.*)

CURTAIN

SCENE II

SCENE.—*The court room with the court in session.* JUDGE VAIL *is on the bench; the jury sits back opaque and weary;* GLUCKSTEIN *waits nervously;* SALTER *is examining* MRS. LUBIN, *who is on the witness stand;* MACREADY *and* CAPRARO *sit in irons, with guards on either side;* ROSALIE, SUVORIN, BARTLET *and* MRS. LUBIN'S *son wait to be called as witnesses. Attendants right and left of* BENCH SERGEANT *at door left.*

SALTER. Now from that point will you tell the story in your own words, Mrs. Lubin?

MRS. LUBIN. From the time I went to the window?

SALTER. Yes.

MRS. LUBIN. I was looking out and I noticed there wasn't much traffic for a Saturday afternoon, and—

SALTER. Go on.

MRS. LUBIN. Then I noticed there was a train on the track and the gates were down, but the engine was backing up again—well, there were only two automobiles south of the tracks and they could have gone on, but they didn't because there was some kind of a fight there. One of the cars was a Ford and the other was a larger car, a Buick, I thought—

SALTER. Open or closed?

MRS. LUBIN. Open. Then there was a shot and I saw a man jump into the large car. He was carrying something I couldn't see. And then the car went up the street around the corner. But the Ford stayed there and people came running.

SALTER. You say there was a shot, Mrs. Lubin. Did you see who fired that shot?

MRS. LUBIN (*looking down*). Yes, sir.

SALTER. Who was it?

MRS. LUBIN. Macready.

SALTER. Where was he when he fired the shot?

MRS. LUBIN. At the steering wheel.

SALTER. And the other man, the one that jumped into the car, do you know who it was?

MRS. LUBIN. No, sir. His back was toward me.

SALTER. Do you see Macready in this room, Mrs. Lubin.

MRS. LUBIN. Yes, sir.

SALTER. Where is he?

MRS. LUBIN. He is one of the defendants. The tall one.

SALTER. Thank you, Mrs. Lubin.

(MRS. LUBIN *starts to rise.*)

JUDGE VAIL. Does the defense wish to examine?

GLUCKSTEIN. I do.

JUDGE VAIL. You may take the witness.

GLUCKSTEIN. There is one point in your story which I wish you would explain in greater detail, Mrs. Lubin. You say you saw this shooting from the front window of your apartment on the third floor?

MRS. LUBIN. Yes, sir.

GLUCKSTEIN. On which side of the railroad track were these two cars when the shooting occurred?

MRS. LUBIN. On the south side.

GLUCKSTEIN. Now isn't it true, Mrs. Lubin, that there is a signal tower between your apartment windows and the tracks which entirely shuts off your view of the street south of the railroad?

MRS. LUBIN. Not entirely.

GLUCKSTEIN. Almost entirely?

MRS. LUBIN. Not so much as that.

GLUCKSTEIN. You have a son, haven't you, Mrs. Lubin?

MRS. LUBIN. Yes, sir.

GLUCKSTEIN. Do you see him in court?

MRS. LUBIN. Yes, sir.

GLUCKSTEIN. Had you expected to see him here?

SALTER. I don't see what that has to do with it!

GLUCKSTEIN. One moment.

MRS. LUBIN. No, sir.

GLUCKSTEIN. Has your son ever visited you in your apartment?

MRS. LUBIN. Yes, sir.

GLUCKSTEIN. Is he familiar with the details of it?

MRS. LUBIN. Yes, sir.

GLUCKSTEIN. Now, Mrs. Lubin, can you look your son in the eyes and say again that it was possible to see that shooting where you said it was—?

SALTER. I object to that. She answered that!

JUDGE VAIL. Objection sustained. Strike out the question.

GLUCKSTEIN. Very well. That is all. (*He sits down.*)

JUDGE VAIL. Call the next witness.

(MRS. LUBIN *leaves the stand.*)

SALTER. Jerome Bartlet.

ATTENDANT. Jerome Bartlet will take the stand.

(BARTLET *goes up to the stand.*)

ATTENDANT. Do you swear to tell the truth and nothing but the truth, so help you God?

BARTLET. Yes, sir.

MACREADY. Ha! Ha!

(*The* JUDGE *raps for order.*)

SALTER. How old are you, Mr. Bartlet?

BARTLET. Twenty-four.

SALTER. Where are you employed?

BARTLET. At the mill. The planing mill on Front Street.

SALTER. Where were you at four-fifteen on the afternoon of April second of this year?

BARTLET. I was going home from work along the docks along Front Street.

SALTER. And did anything especial occur on that afternoon as you were going home?

BARTLET. Yes, sir.

SALTER. Tell us what it was, please.

BARTLET. Just before I got to the railroad track I heard a shot and I thought I'd better get out of the way, so I—

SALTER. Tell us what else you saw.

BARTLET. I saw a man fall over a wheel in a Ford by the tracks. The Ford was standing still because the gates was down. And then I saw a man jump away from the Ford and get in another car—

SALTER. And then what—?

BARTLET. Then the gates was coming up, so the car went up Front Street and turned off, and then I saw a policeman jumping in a car—and it went after them—

SALTER. And the Ford stayed there?

BARTLET. Yes, sir, the man was shot.

SALTER. Did you see who did the shooting?

BARTLET. No, sir.

SALTER. Did you see the face of the man who jumped into the other car after the shooting occurred?

BARTLET. Yes, sir.

SALTER. Have you seen him since?

BARTLET. Yes, sir.

SALTER. Did you identify him?

BARTLET. Yes, sir.

SALTER. Who was he?

BARTLET. I said he looked like Capraro.

SALTER. Oh, he looked like Capraro. How much did he look like him?

GLUCKSTEIN. I object to that.

JUDGE VAIL. Overruled.

SALTER. Would you say it was Capraro?

BARTLET. It was the dead image of him.

SALTER. That is all, your Honor. The prosecution rests.

JUDGE VAIL. The defense may take the witness.

GLUCKSTEIN. Where did you say you were, Mr. Bartlet, at four-fifteen on the afternoon of April second?

BARTLET. I was—I was watching the—robbery. I was going home from work.

GLUCKSTEIN. And how do you fix the

time in your mind? How do you know it was four-fifteen?

BARTLET. I get out of the mill at four—on Saturdays, I do.

GLUCKSTEIN. And how do you know it was April second?

BARTLET. Well, it was the day the murder happened, because I saw it.

GLUCKSTEIN. Where were you standing when you saw it?

BARTLET. Right near the gate to the pier there.

GLUCKSTEIN. Were you on the south or the north side of the tracks?

BARTLET. The south side.

GLUCKSTEIN. On which side of the tracks did the murder occur?

BARTLET. The south side—where I was.

GLUCKSTEIN. You say you heard the shooting and then saw a man jump into a car which drove away?

BARTLET. Yes, sir.

GLUCKSTEIN. Did you see the shooting or only hear it?

BARTLET. I heard it.

GLUCKSTEIN. And you saw this man who jumped into the car?

BARTLET. Yes, sir.

GLUCKSTEIN. And you say he looked like Capraro?

BARTLET. Yes, sir.

GLUCKSTEIN. Do you say he was Capraro?

BARTLET. No, sir. It was the dead image of him.

GLUCKSTEIN. Oh, it was not Capraro. It was the dead image of him?

BARTLET. Yes, sir.

GLUCKSTEIN. What do you mean by the dead image of him?

BARTLET. Well, it looked like him.

GLUCKSTEIN. Do you mean it was a dead image that looked like him?

SALTER. Objection.

JUDGE VAIL. Sustained. You need not answer that question.

GLUCKSTEIN. Your Honor, this witness quite evidently has no notion of the meaning of the phrase "dead image." It is my belief that his use of it will mislead the jury unless we hear an explanation of it from his own lips.

JUDGE VAIL. You must allow the jury to decide what he means, Mr. Gluckstein. (GLUCKSTEIN *bows.*)

GLUCKSTEIN. When you identified Capraro as the man who leaped into the murder car, Mr. Bartlet, what was the procedure followed? Were there other men in the room, or was Capraro there alone?

SALTER. Objection.

JUDGE VAIL. Sustained. The method of identification should not concern us here. We assume that every precaution was taken by the police against the possibility of error.

GLUCKSTEIN. I do not assume that, your Honor.

JUDGE VAIL. Then you have not properly prepared for the question. We are not investigating the methods of identification customary in this state.

GLUCKSTEIN. Your Honor, my point is that the methods of identification employed by the State in securing evidence for this trial were arbitrary, unusual, and deliberately pre-arranged to incriminate the defendants.

JUDGE VAIL. You have witnesses to that effect?

GLUCKSTEIN. The prosecution is well aware that every possible hindrance has been put in the way of my obtaining such evidence!

SALTER (*on his feet*). If you have evidence of anything like that!—

JUDGE VAIL. The objection is sustained. You may proceed.

GLUCKSTEIN. I enter an exception. (*The* JUDGE *bows.* GLUCKSTEIN *turns to* BARTLET.) What do you mean by dead image, Mr. Bartlet?

BARTLET. I mean it looked like him. Short and dark.

SALTER. Objection! I object to that! That question has been answered!

JUDGE VAIL. You are a little late, Mr. Salter, nevertheless the objection is sustained. Strike out the question and answer.

GLUCKSTEIN. May I point out to your Honor that his second answer does not tally with the first—

JUDGE VAIL. The second question is not admissible in the record. Proceed.

GLUCKSTEIN. In that case, I have finished with the cross-examination.

JUDGE VAIL. You have a number of witnesses to call in rebuttal, I understand? (BARTLET *leaves the stand.*)

GLUCKSTEIN. Yes, your Honor. Harry Lubin.

ATTENDANT. Harry Lubin to the stand. (MRS. LUBIN's *son comes forward. He is a young countryman of twenty-two or thereabout.*) Do you swear to tell the truth, the whole truth, and nothing but the truth, so help you God?

LUBIN. I do.

GLUCKSTEIN. How old are you, Mr. Lubin?

LUBIN. Twenty-two.

GLUCKSTEIN. Where are you employed?

LUBIN. I've been working on a farm up north.

GLUCKSTEIN. Are you the son of Mrs. Lubin, who testified a few moments ago?

LUBIN. Yes, sir.

GLUCKSTEIN. Have you lived at your mother's home recently?

LUBIN. No, sir. Not since I can remember. I've always lived on my uncle's farm up-state.

GLUCKSTEIN. You have visited your mother in the apartment she now occupies?

LUBIN. Yes, sir. Quite often.

GLUCKSTEIN. How often?

LUBIN. Maybe once or twice a year.

GLUCKSTEIN. And she has lived there how long?

LUBIN. About ten years.

GLUCKSTEIN. Did you find anything strange about your mother's testimony?

SALTER. I object to that.

JUDGE VAIL. You will reframe your question.

GLUCKSTEIN. Have you ever looked out the front windows of your mother's apartment on Front Street?

LUBIN. Yes, sir. Often.

GLUCKSTEIN. Is it possible to see the street south of the tracks from those windows?

LUBIN. Very little of it.

GLUCKSTEIN. In case you were looking out from the front of that apartment and the gates were down across the tracks, would it be possible to see the face of the driver of a car on the south side of the tracks.

LUBIN. Not usually.

GLUCKSTEIN. It would sometimes?

LUBIN. Yes, sir. If a car happened to be standing at the far side of the street.

GLUCKSTEIN. Would it be possible to see the face of a driver of more than one car at the same time?

LUBIN. I've never been able to.

GLUCKSTEIN. You have tried it?

LUBIN. Yes, sir.

GLUCKSTEIN. When?

LUBIN. After my mother identified one of the men in the robbery.

GLUCKSTEIN. And did you ask her how she happened to be able to see the face of the man in the car?

LUBIN. Yes, sir.

GLUCKSTEIN. Do you remember her answer?

SALTER. Objection. This court is hardly interested in hearsay.

JUDGE VAIL. The question is relevant, Mr. Salter. Answer the question.

LUBIN. At first she said the car was on the far side of the street—but it couldn't have been there because that was where the Ford was standing, so she finally—

GLUCKSTEIN. Yes?

LUBIN. She finally said she didn't see the robbery at all. She said she looked out after the shot was fired.

GLUCKSTEIN. Did you ask her anything else?

SALTER. Objection!

JUDGE. Answer the question.

LUBIN. I asked her why she identified Macready if she couldn't see him, and she said she had a reason she couldn't tell me. And then she said—

(MRS. LUBIN *is sobbing quietly.*)

SALTER. Your Honor, will you allow this to continue?

JUDGE VAIL. It is quite relevant.

LUBIN. She said she'd take it back—she wouldn't identify him in the trial.

GLUCKSTEIN. Do you know why she has changed her mind again?

LUBIN. No, sir. I can't understand it.

GLUCKSTEIN. Thank you, Mr. Lubin. That is all.

JUDGE VAIL. Has the State any question?

SALTER. No questions.

JUDGE VAIL. The witness is excused.

(LUBIN *goes back to his place. His* MOTHER *looks up at him, then looks away.* LUBIN *puts his arm about her for a moment. Then sits.*)

GLUCKSTEIN. Call Miss Rosalie Suvorin.

ATTENDANT. Miss Suvorin to the stand. (ROSALIE *comes to the witness chair.*) You understand the value of an oath, Miss Suvorin?

ROSALIE. I do.

ATTENDANT. Do you swear to tell the truth, the whole truth, and nothing but the truth, so help you God?

ROSALIE. I do.

GLUCKSTEIN. I have only a few questions to ask you, Miss Suvorin.

ROSALIE. Yes, sir.

GLUCKSTEIN. Where were you on the evening of April second of this year?

ROSALIE. The Lyceum restaurant on Laden Street.

GLUCKSTEIN. Did you during that evening see either of the defendants?

ROSALIE. I saw both of them.

GLUCKSTEIN. Did you have any conversation with Mr. Macready?

ROSALIE. Yes, sir.

GLUCKSTEIN. Will you give us the substance of what was said?

ROSALIE. We talked about where he had been that afternoon—and about—whether it wasn't foolish for him to get mixed up in strikes.

GLUCKSTEIN. Did Mr. Macready tell you what part he had taken in the strike that afternoon?

ROSALIE. Yes, sir.

GLUCKSTEIN. Do you know what Macready did with the gun he took from the car?

ROSALIE. He gave it to me.

GLUCKSTEIN. Did you look at it?

ROSALIE. No, sir, I put it in the cash drawer.

GLUCKSTEIN. Do you know whether any of the chambers had been fired when he gave it to you?

ROSALIE. No, sir.

GLUCKSTEIN. Now, I'm going to ask you a personal question, Miss Suvorin, because if I don't ask it, it will be asked by the prosecution. What were your relations with Mr. Macready?

ROSALIE. We—are engaged to be married—

GLUCKSTEIN. You are still engaged to be married?

ROSALIE (*looking at* MACREADY). Yes, sir.

GLUCKSTEIN. Did you encourage him to take part in the strike?

ROSALIE. No, sir. I asked him not to. We quarreled about that.

GLUCKSTEIN. Was it a serious quarrel?

ROSALIE. Yes, sir. I told him I wouldn't marry him. But I would now.

GLUCKSTEIN. Have you seen him since that evening?

ROSALIE. No, sir. They wouldn't let me.

GLUCKSTEIN. Why not?

ROSALIE. They said I was a material witness.

GLUCKSTEIN. But you are still engaged to marry him?

ROSALIE. I think so. I'm—I'm in love with him. And I'm telling him now because it's the only chance I have—

SALTER. Objection.

GLUCKSTEIN. Quite right. I thank you, Miss Suvorin.

JUDGE VAIL. Has the prosecution any questions?

SALTER. A very few, your honor. I also, Miss Suvorin, have only a few questions I wish to ask you. Were you present, Miss Suvorin, on the evening of the robbery when Mr. Macready was arrested?

ROSALIE. Yes, I was.

SALTER. As you remember it, what was Mr. Macready's attitude toward the arrest?

ROSALIE. His attitude?

SALTER. Yes, did he resist the arrest?

ROSALIE. No, sir.

SALTER. There has been evidence here, my dear, that Mr. Macready struck a detective. You don't remember that?

ROSALIE. Yes, but the detective had pretended he was an I.W.W. He'd been in the strike with them.

SALTER. Then Mr. Macready did strike the detective?

ROSALIE. Yes, sir.

SALTER. Then he did resist arrest?

ROSALIE. He didn't want to be arrested.

SALTER. No. Certainly not. Now, is it true, Miss Suvorin, that you ran to him and took part in the struggle?

ROSALIE. I don't remember. I think so.

SALTER. Were you trying to save him from something when you did that?

ROSALIE. Yes, sir.

SALTER (*menacing*). Were you trying to save him from death in the electric chair for the murder of Kendall?

ROSALIE. No, sir.

SALTER. Mr. Macready had come to you and given you this weapon and asked you to hide it.

ROSALIE. He didn't ask me to hide it!

SALTER. Then why did you say you knew nothing about the weapon when the police found it?

ROSALIE. I was afraid.

SALTER. What were you afraid of?

ROSALIE. I was afraid they wouldn't believe what he'd told me about it.

SALTER. You mean that you two had made up a story about this weapon and that you were afraid it wasn't good enough?

ROSALIE. No, sir—we hadn't made—

SALTER. Yes or no is enough.

ROSALIE. No.

SALTER. Do you mean to tell this court that you come here to give unbiased testimony in favor of the defendants?

ROSALIE. I'm telling the truth.

SALTER. Did you tell the truth to the detectives about the gun you had in the cash drawer?

ROSALIE. No.

SALTER. When did you make up your mind to change your story?

ROSALIE. I don't know.

SALTER. You're in love with Macready, aren't you? You'd say anything to save him?

ROSALIE. I—

GLUCKSTEIN. I object to that!

JUDGE VAIL. Strike out the question.

SALTER. That's all.

JUDGE VAIL. Will you call your next witness, Mr. Gluckstein? (*He looks at his watch.*)

GLUCKSTEIN. James Macready.

(MACREADY *is led to the stand by an officer.*)

ATTENDANT. Do you swear to tell the truth, the whole truth, and nothing but the truth?

MAC. Now just for a change from the prosecution's witnesses, I do.

GLUCKSTEIN. Will you tell me, Mr. Macready, where were you at four-fifteen on the afternoon of the murder of Kendall?

MAC. I was walking north along Front Street.

GLUCKSTEIN. You left the scene of the rioting?

MAC. Yes, sir. After I got away with that gun I thought I'd better not go back. They knew I had it, and they'd have pulled me for having it.

GLUCKSTEIN. How far was the scene of the rioting from the tracks where the crime was committeed?

MAC. All of a mile.

GLUCKSTEIN. The time of the rioting has been fixed by many witnesses at about four o'clock. Would it have been possible for you to reach the scene of the crime by four-fifteen?

MAC. Well, the mix-up had been going on about fifteen minutes before I left.

GLUCKSTEIN. Then you started north at about four-fifteen?

MAC. I think so.

GLUCKSTEIN. If you had walked south you'd have been going toward the scene of the robbery?

MAC. Yes, sir.

GLUCKSTEIN. But you walked north?

MAC. Yes. Well, at first I was running, you know; later I slowed down.

GLUCKSTEIN. Where were you going?

MAC. I went to Capraro's room. We always went there, and I thought he'd telephone as soon as he got loose from the police.

GLUCKSTEIN. Did he telephone?

MAC. No.

GLUCKSTEIN. Do you know why not?

MAC. He was taking care of Nick, Nick Bardi. Nick was shot by the police, died that evening.

GLUCKSTEIN. When did you leave the room?

MAC. About seven I went over to my room to see if Capraro was there. I hadn't heard any news and I thought we'd have dinner together.

GLUCKSTEIN. Was Capraro there?

MAC. No.

GLUCKSTEIN. Where did you go after that?

MAC. I went to Suvorin's restaurant in the Lyceum and looked in and there were two policemen eating there, so I went and ate at Joe's. Then I went to a movie to kill time.

GLUCKSTEIN. At what time did you return to the Lyceum?

MAC. About ten-thirty.

GLUCKSTEIN. Why did you go there?

MAC. There was a strike meeting called —and I was one of the speakers. And then I wanted to see Rosalie.

GLUCKSTEIN. For any especial reason?

MAC. No, just wanted to see her.

GLUCKSTEIN. How did you happen to give her the revolver?

MAC. I didn't want to carry it around.

GLUCKSTEIN. How did that revolver come into your possession?

MAC. A policeman threw it into the car we were riding in, and I grabbed it up and jumped out of the car.

GLUCKSTEIN. And what was your motive in that?

MAC. To prevent the police planting evidence on Mr. Waterman.

GLUCKSTEIN. Did you ever fire that revolver?

MAC. No.

GLUCKSTEIN. Did you know, while it was in your possession, that one chamber had been fired?

MAC. Yes, I looked at it in Capraro's room.

GLUCKSTEIN. Did that mean anything to you?

MAC. Not a thing. It was just a service revolver, with one cartridge empty. Only now I think that cartridge killed Bardi.

GLUCKSTEIN. Were you present at the holdup of Kendall?

MAC. No.

GLUCKSTEIN. Did you shoot Kendall with that service revolver?

MAC. No. I've never shot at anybody—at any time.

GLUCKSTEIN. One more question. Are you engaged to marry Rosalie Suvorin?

MAC. She said she wouldn't marry me because I got into too much trouble. But if she will, I'm certainly engaged to her.

GLUCKSTEIN. Are you in love with her?

MAC (*leaning forward*). Why drag that in? From the day it started I knew this trial was a railroad train. I took one look at the jury and I knew what they came in here for. Now I've listened to about a thousand phoney witnesses, lying like hell, and my impression is they got by a hundred per cent. It won't make any difference whether I'm in love with a girl or not—not to them. And at that, it's nobody's business but the girl's.

GLUCKSTEIN. Very well. Thank you, Mr. Macready.

JUDGE VAIL. Does the State wish to question?

SALTER. Yes, your Honor. So you believe, Mr. Macready, that you are going to be convicted?

MAC. If it can be fixed it will be.

SALTER. What makes you so pessimistic, Mr. Macready?

MAC. I've been around in this country some, and I've seen the courts work. When you get a red or an agitator in court the custom is to soak him.

SALTER. Have you ever been convicted of a crime?

MAC. Well, I've been convicted of belonging to the I.W.W. out in California, if you call that a crime.

SALTER. Were you guilty?

MAC. I was of being an I.W.W.

SALTER. What are the principles of the I.W.W.?

MAC. One big union, organized to break the capitalistic stranglehold on natural resources.

SALTER. Does the I.W.W. advocate violence?

MAC. Only when expedient, which is seldom.

SALTER. When does it consider violence expedient?

MAC. Listen, we're taking up time here. If you're interested in the I.W.W. I've got a book I'd like to lend you. You can read it in fifteen minutes, and when you get through, you'll know something about economics.

SALTER. Thank you. But do you advocate violence?

MAC. I never have.

SALTER. You would if you thought it expedient?

MAC. I would. So would you. So does everybody.

SALTER. And you don't think the workers get justice in this country?

MAC. No. Do you? Did you ever hear of a policeman hitting a capitalist over the head?

SALTER. Do you believe in our constitution?

MAC. I believe it was made by a little group of hogs to protect their own trough. Anyway, why bring up the constitution when you don't even enforce the bill of rights? The whole damn thing's a dead letter except the eighteenth amendment, and the only reason we make a play for enforcing that is because there's graft in it! You use the courts and the constitution and the flag and the local police to protect capital and keep the working man in his place! Whenever there's a law that might be to the working man's advantage, you forget that one! That's why you forget the bill of rights! And when some law gets passed by accident that might hamper capital, you forget that! You forgot the Sherman Act till some of you figured out how you could apply it to the Labor Unions! And then, Jesus Christ, how quick you put it on 'em!

(JUDGE VAIL's *gavel falls.*)

JUDGE VAIL. Have you no respect for the courts, sir?

MAC. Certainly not. The courts are the flunkies of the rich.

JUDGE VAIL. You realize that you are on trial in this court for your life?

MAC. Do you think you can scare me into respecting you?

JUDGE VAIL. I merely wish to warn you, sir, that in this frame of mind you make an exceedingly poor witness in your defense.

MAC. It's my usual frame of mind.

SALTER. So you don't advocate violence?

MAC. No. If I did I wouldn't work through the unions.

SALTER. Isn't it true that you and Capraro and a man named Nick Bardi, who was killed, organized the attack on the police on the afternoon of the murder?

MAC. We didn't attack the police. They attacked us. We did nothing we didn't have a right to do under that constitution you're talking about.

SALTER. But you knew there would be violence?

MAC. We knew the police could always be trusted to start something.

SALTER. You had been warned not to try to reestablish your picket lines?

MAC. We had. By a corporation judge.

SALTER. Now, Mr. Macready, isn't it true that you and Capraro started this riot to draw the police and make it easy to get away after robbing the payroll?

GLUCKSTEIN. I object.

MAC. I'll answer it. No, it is not true.

SALTER. Why did you resist arrest?

MAC. I hit Spiker because he double-crossed me.

SALTER. Did you make no other resistance?

MAC. Maybe I did. I didn't like the idea of being arrested.

SALTER. Have you ever heard of such a thing as the consciousness of guilt?

MAC. I didn't feel it.

SALTER. Why did you turn away from the restaurant when you saw two policemen inside?

MAC. That's a childish question. What would you do if you'd just been in a brush with the police?

SALTER. When you leaped from the car, you knocked a policeman down. Was that because you don't believe in violence?

MAC. He was in my way.

SALTER. You have no respect for authority?

MAC. Respect for authority is a superstition. And the sooner everybody gets over it, the better.

SALTER. Where were you during the war?

MAC. I was in Bisbee, Arizona, at the time of the deportations. I was in Everett at the time of the I.W.W. massacre. You heard about that, I suppose? When the gallant business men of Everett came out and shot down wobblies in cold blood?

SALTER. You were a pacifist and an agitator during the war?

MAC. I was, and I am proud of it. What were you in the war?

SALTER. Do you have respect for that flag?

MAC. What does it stand for? If it stands for the kind of government we've got in Washington and for you and your kind, all right, I've got as much respect for it as I've got for the government in Washington—and for you and your kind! Who killed Salsedo?

SALTER. I think I understand you—and I think the court and the jury understand you. That's all, Mr. Macready.

(*There is a brief silence. Then the* FOREMAN *of the jury rises slowly, a long finger stretched out at* MACREADY.)

FOREMAN. There's one thing I'd like to ask. There was a bomb set off under my house last night. Now I don't want to do anybody an injustice, but I was under the impression Mr. Macready believed in violence. If he don't I'd like to know where that bomb came from!

(*The* JUDGE'S *gavel falls.*)

JUDGE VAIL. You are out of order, Mr. Schaler.

FOREMAN. All right. (*He starts to sit down.*)

MAC (*rising*). If anybody wants to know who sets bombs in this state—

SALTER (*to the guards*). Hold that man.

(*The* GUARDS *leap on* MAC, *who submits smiling.*)

MAC. What's the matter, kid? Are you afraid of me?

(*They haul him to his chair.*)

GLUCKSTEIN. Your Honor, I move to call this a mistrial. The Foreman of the jury has displayed open prejudice.

JUDGE VAIL. I will take your motion under advisement. Meanwhile let us proceed with the evidence. Is it your intention to place the other defendant on the stand?

GLUCKSTEIN. One moment. (*He bends over and speaks low to* CAPRARO.) Mr. Capraro will take the stand.

(CAPRARO *does so.*)

ATTENDANT. Do you swear to tell the truth, the whole truth, and nothing but the truth?

CAPRARO. As near as I can.

JUDGE VAIL. There are two possible answers to that question: I do, or I do not.

CAPRARO. You must excuse me. I do.—As near as I can.

JUDGE VAIL. Do you mean that you will

tell the truth to the best of your knowledge and belief?

CAPRARO. If you like that phrase better—yes, I do. But I would not wish you to believe that I would know the truth better than other men, for it seems to me that no man would know the truth exactly. (JUDGE VAIL *smiles frigidly.*)

GLUCKSTEIN. The court is aware of that, Mr. Capraro. We expect only that you tell the truth as you see it.

CAPRARO. I will try, Mr. Gluckstein.

GLUCKSTEIN. I want you to tell me first, Mr. Capraro, where you were at four-fifteen on the day of the murder of the paymaster.

CAPRARO. I think I was taking care of Nick Bardi.

GLUCKSTEIN. How did that happen?

CAPRARO. After they throw the gun in the car and Mac runs away with it, I am sitting at the wheel while they arrest Mr. Waterman, the lawyer. They seem to pay no attention to me at first, and when they leave me alone in the car there is a great deal of excitement and I just drive away. (*He smiles.*)

GLUCKSTEIN. Where did you drive?

CAPRARO. I drove around the block and leave the car there. I am planning to wait there until Mr. Waterman will wish me to drive him somewhere—police station—home—somewhere.

GLUCKSTEIN. And where did you go after leaving the car?

CAPRARO. I went back where the fight was and then I saw Nick Bardi trying to get up off the ground. He said he was shot at the first but he didn't know it was bad till he fell down. So I help and we went to the car and go to his house. When the doctor comes he says to take Nick to the hospital and before long he is dead in the hospital, and I take the car to the garage where Mr. Waterman keeps it. Then I walk to the restaurant in the Lyceum.

GLUCKSTEIN. At what time did you reach the restaurant?

CAPRARO. Maybe eleven o'clock.

GLUCKSTEIN. Did you make any resistance when arrested?

CAPRARO. Not much. But I am not used to it. (*He smiles.*)

GLUCKSTEIN. Were you present when Kendall was shot?

CAPRARO. No, I could not be.

GLUCKSTEIN. When did you first learn that he had been killed?

CAPRARO. In the newspaper, in Suvorin's.

GLUCKSTEIN. Is it true that after you drove away from the pier you picked up Macready and drove south to carry out the holdup of the paymaster?

CAPRARO. No. To that I can say I am very sure. No.

GLUCKSTEIN. That is all, Mr. Capraro. Thank you.

JUDGE VAIL. The prosecution may take the witness.

SALTER. How much money have you in the bank, Mr. Capraro?

CAPRARO. I do not know. Not exactly. But not much.

SALTER. Do you remember depositing five thousand dollars in the City Bank on April second?

CAPRARO. That was not my money. That was relief funds.

SALTER. You could draw checks on it, couldn't you?

CAPRARO. Only the committee.

SALTER. Is it true that the holdup occurred on April second and on that same day you deposited five thousand dollars?

CAPRARO. Yes.

SALTER. The City Bank stays open in the evening, doesn't it?

CAPRARO. Yes, sir.

SALTER. You might have robbed the paymaster at four-fifteen and had plenty of time to put money in that bank the same day? It was possible?

CAPRARO. No, it was not possible for me. I put that money in the bank in the morning.

SALTER. Do you believe in capitalism?

CAPRARO. No.

SALTER. You believe that all property should belong to the workers?

CAPRARO. Property should belong to those who create it.

SALTER. You are a communist?

CAPRARO. I am an anarchist.

SALTER. What do you mean by that?

CAPRARO. I mean, government is wrong. It creates trouble.

SALTER. You would destroy all government?

CAPRARO. It will not be necessary. I would rather wait till it was so rotten it would rot away. That would not be so long now. (*He smiles.*)

SALTER. You are an anarchist?

CAPRARO. Yes.

SALTER. You are against this government

of ours?

CAPRARO. Against all governments.

SALTER. Have you ever thrown a bomb?

CAPRARO. No, I would leave that for the other side.

SALTER. In 1917 you left your home to avoid the draft, didn't you?

CAPRARO. Yes.

SALTER. You opposed the war?

CAPRARO. It was a war for business, a war for billions of dollars, murder of young men for billions.

SALTER. You broke the law in evading the draft?

CAPRARO. Yes.

SALTER. You don't mind breaking the law?

CAPRARO. Sometimes not.

SALTER. Who decides for you what laws you will break and what laws you'll keep?

CAPRARO. I decide it.

SALTER. Oh, you decide it!

CAPRARO. Every man decides for himself.

SALTER. There was nothing to prevent you from deciding to kill a paymaster and putting the money in the bank?

CAPRARO. No, only I. I would decide against it.

SALTER. Do you honor that flag?

CAPRARO. I did before I came to this country. Now I know it is like all the other flags. They are all the same. When we are young boys we look on a flag and believe it is the flag of liberty and happy people—and now I know it is a flag to carry when the old men kill the young men for billions. Now I look at that flag and I hear it saying to me, "How much money have you? If you have plenty of money—then I promise you paradise—I will give you more—I will give you the justice and freedom of your neighbours! But if you are poor I am not your flag at all."

SALTER. What is your religion, Mr. Capraro?

CAPRARO. I have none.

SALTER. You are an atheist?

CAPRARO. Yes.

SALTER. You are then an outlaw, bowing neither to the standards of God nor men?

CAPRARO. I have committed no crime.

SALTER. And do you expect us to believe that, Mr. Capraro? What, in all solemnity, in the name of God, prevents you from committing crime?

CAPRARO. Myself. My own heart.

SALTER. You set yourself above God, above all law, above all control?

CAPRARO. I have met nobody I would trust to decide for my own soul.

SALTER. Your Honor, we have stumbled here upon a subject more serious than robbery, more serious than murder. If I had known where my questions were leading, I should have hesitated before asking them. Perhaps I should apologize—

MAC. You're goddam right you should! (*The gavel falls.*)

CAPRARO. Is there any reason in your constitution why I should not believe as I think? Is there any reason in your constitution why I should worship your God or your flag?

SALTER. That is all, your Honor.

MAC. For Christ's sake, Amen.

(CAPRARO *leaves the stand.*)

JUDGE VAIL. Does this conclude your case, Mr. Gluckstein?

GLUCKSTEIN. No, your Honor. I have one more witness I should like to call.

JUDGE VAIL. Very well.

GLUCKSTEIN. Michael Suvorin.

ATTENDANT. Michael Suvorin. To the stand. (SUVORIN *rises, seats himself in the witness chair.* SHERIFF HENRY, *an elderly, hard-faced man, enters and sits quietly in the rear of the witnesses.* SPIKER *takes a memorandum to* SALTER, *who studies it.*) Do you swear to tell the truth, the whole truth, and nothing but the truth? so help you God?

SUVORIN. I do.

GLUCKSTEIN. What is your occupation, Mr. Suvorin?

SUVORIN. I am the keeper of the Lyceum restaurant on Laden Street.

GLUCKSTEIN. How long have you been in business there?

SUVORIN. Ten or twelve years.

GLUCKSTEIN. Where were you at four-fifteen on the afternoon of April second of this year?

SUVORIN. Near the railroad tracks on Front Street.

GLUCKSTEIN. How did you happen to be there?

SUVORIN. It is on the way to the produce markets. I was buying supplies for the restaurant.

GLUCKSTEIN. Did you witness the murder of Kendall?

SUVORIN. I did.

GLUCKSTEIN. Did you see the men who committed the crime?

SUVORIN. I did.

GLUCKSTEIN. Did you see the shot fired?

SUVORIN. I did.

GLUCKSTEIN. Could you identify the bandits?

SUVORIN. I could.

GLUCKSTEIN. Did you see Capraro there?

SUVORIN. No.

GLUCKSTEIN. Did you see Macready there?

SUVORIN. No.

GLUCKSTEIN. If they had been there, would you have seen them?

SUVORIN. Yes.

SALTER. I object, your Honor. I wasn't informed of this.

JUDGE VAIL. Do you wish a postponement?

SALTER. No. I merely wish to call the attention of the court to the somewhat arbitrary methods of the defense.

JUDGE VAIL. Proceed.

GLUCKSTEIN (*smiling*). That is all, your Honor.

JUDGE VAIL (*to* SALTER). Do you wish to question?

SALTER. Well—a few questions. (*Haltingly.*) Your name is Suvorin?

SUVORIN. Yes.

SALTER. You are the father of Rosalie Suvorin?

SUVORIN. Yes.

SALTER. Isn't it a little strange, Mr. Suvorin, that you, the father of Miss Suvorin, should have happened to be passing along Front Street at so opportune a moment for your prospective son-in-law?

SUVORIN. It was strange, yes.

SALTER. Isn't it strange, also, that you have so far said nothing about the fact?

SUVORIN. No. One does not testify unless necessary.

SALTER. How long have you lived in this country?

SUVORIN. Thirty years.

SALTER. Have you spent all of that time in this city?

SUVORIN. I was in the West for twenty years.

SALTER. The West?

SUVORIN. Illinois, West Virginia.

SALTER. What was your occupation?

SUVORIN. Coal miner.

SALTER. Have you ever been convicted of a crime?

SUVORIN. No.

SALTER. Are you a citizen of this country?

SUVORIN. No.

SALTER. Of what country?

SUVORIN. None.

SALTER. You came from what country?

SUVORIN. Russia.

SALTER. Why have you not altered your citizenship?

SUVORIN. I have no interest in politics.

SALTER. You witnessed the murder of Kendall?

SUVORIN. Yes.

SALTER. Had you ever witnessed a crime before?

SUVORIN. Not that I remember.

SALTER. You would not remember then, perhaps?

SUVORIN. I think so.

SALTER (*turns away as if baffled, then returns*). Did you ever work in the mills in this state?

SUVORIN (*pausing*). No.

SALTER. I have just been handed the record of a man named Gregorin who worked in the Falltown mills in 1892. You are not that man?

SUVORIN. No.

SALTER. The man of whom I speak was one of a radical group of workers who led a strike in which considerable property was destroyed. He was convicted of sabotage and sentenced to twenty years in the federal penitentiary. Before his sentence was complete he escaped. You are not that Gregorin?

SUVORIN. No.

SALTER. This man escaped, finding it necessary to murder a guard, as you may remember. He was caught, tried, and sentenced to hang. He escaped once more on the way to prison. You are not the man?

SUVORIN. No.

SALTER. If the court will pardon me, I have here also the record of a man named Thievenen who was apprehended in Colorado last year as one of two bandits who robbed a mail truck of $170,000. He escaped from the Denver jail, but not until after he had been finger printed and photographed. You are not by any chance that man Thievenen?

SUVORIN. No!

SALTER. I think you are! Mr. Henry, I think this is your prisoner. (HENRY *rises.*) Your Honor, I am distressed to interrupt the session.

(HENRY *comes forward.* SUVORIN *rises.*)

SUVORIN. I'm not your man yet. I saw you here. You won't take me till I'm ready.

JUDGE VAIL (*to* HENRY). You have a warrant for his arrest?

HENRY. Right here.

JUDGE VAIL. Then if the prosecution has finished with the witness—

SUVORIN (*speaking slowly and heavily*). He'll wait for me. You'll all wait. (*To* SALTER.) You thought it somewhat strange that I should have been so opportunely at the scene of the murder of Kendall. I'll explain that. The man who shot down Kendall was killed in White Plains a month ago, by a federal officer. He was what you call a rum-runner in his spare time. So am I—in my spare time. When he needed cash he took it—where he could get it. So do I. We took Kendall's twenty-eight thousand. We divided it between us. I ought to know. I planned it. I carried it out.

SALTER. Are you, by any chance, confessing to participation in this crime?

SUVORIN (*menacing*). Are you slow in the head? What do you think I'm doing? You asked Macready if he planned the rioting to make his opportunity for the holdup. He did not. But I knew the plans of the longshoremen. I overheard them. And I am guilty and they are not. That may not interest you but it interests me. You would rather they were guilty. You would rather pin this crime on a radical than on a criminal. It suits your plans better. The radicals are not criminals. They are young fools who think they are saving humanity. They think they will change the government and bring in the millennium.

SALTER. Who killed Kendall, if you don't mind telling us?

SUVORIN. Heine, the Gat.

JUDGE VAIL. Mr. Gluckstein, were you aware of this person's record?

GLUCKSTEIN. No, your Honor.

JUDGE VAIL. Why was he called?

GLUCKSTEIN. He told me the story he told first in Court.

JUDGE VAIL (*to* SUVORIN). What did you say your occupation was, sir?

SUVORIN. I came to this country a young man. I came believing in it; and I worked in your mines and your mills and I set myself to establish justice to the workers. I was a fool. I believed in Justice. They found me guilty of sabotage and sent me to prison. I studied you there. I knew you there for what you are. I tasted your justice. I drank it deep. I bear its marks on my body and I bear them on my brain. My wife died and I had loved her. She died after fifteen years of your justice and I swore by the bleeding Christ you would pay me! You have paid me.

JUDGE VAIL. I asked you a question.

SUVORIN. I say you have paid me! I have had my day with you! You have felt me when you least knew it. You have puzzled over me and I have laughed at you. Fifteen years I had my way with you and you'd never have caught me if I hadn't tried to save innocent men! I have had my revenge—and it was little enough for a woman dead when I could not even say good-bye to her; too little—oh damn you —too little—!

SALTER. This man's confession is an obvious fraud. He is under sentence of death. He has nothing to lose. His daughter is to marry Macready. The man on whom he fixes the crime is dead. This story has been concocted to save the defendants.

SUVORIN. What!

SALTER. This story has been concocted to save the defendants.

SUVORIN. I have confessed to this crime—!

SALTER. Oh, no—you've confessed that Heine, the Gat did it—and Heine's dead. I say it's a fraud—

SUVORIN. You do not believe this?

SALTER. No, I tell you. You've got nothing to lose. There's a murder in your record already.

SUVORIN. That would be like you, too! To kill us all three, innocent and guilty together—burn us in your little hell to make your world safe for your bankers—you kept Judge, of a kept nation, you dead hand of the dead.

(*Several jurors rise. The* JUDGE *thunders with his gavel.* SUVORIN *puts out his hands for the waiting handcuffs. General confusion.*)

CURTAIN

Scene III

SCENE.—*The court room.*

There is no jury present; the JUDGE *is on the bench, the* ATTENDANTS *in place, and* MACREADY *and* CAPRARO *face the judge. Aside from the lawyers* ROSALIE *is the sole spectator.*

GLUCKSTEIN. If the court please I should like to move for a new trial before sentence is pronounced. My motion is based on the depositions of four witnesses. Your Honor has these depositions before you.

JUDGE VAIL. I have read them.

GLUCKSTEIN. I shall make only a brief summary of the evidence they disclose. Mrs. Lubin, a chief witness for the prosecution, swears that her identification of Macready was obtained under duress. She retracts that identification. Her son, a witness for the defense, corroborates that retraction by evidence tending to show that his mother was threatened with the exposure of certain facts in her history of which he himself had been ignorant. Jerome Bartlet, the only witness to identify Capraro as at the scene of the crime, retracts that identification—

SALTER. You will find that he has retracted that retraction, Mr. Gluckstein—

GLUCKSTEIN. I know nothing of that. No doubt the attorney for the prosecution has seen him again—

SALTER. I have.

GLUCKSTEIN. The other affidavit is signed by the ballistic expert, Mr. Howard, who appeared in the trial. He states that his answers to the State's questions were pre-arranged to mislead the jury—

SALTER. Pre-arranged?

GLUCKSTEIN. Pre-arranged between himself and the district attorney—that he did not intend to say that the mortal bullet was fired from the pistol in the possession of Macready, but only that it might have been fired from that weapon.

JUDGE VAIL. Does this affidavit indicate that Mr. Howard committed perjury during the trial?

GLUCKSTEIN. No, your Honor. It merely amplifies the statements made during the trial, which were so worded as to create a false impression.

JUDGE VAIL. If the witness amplifies but does not alter his statements his affidavit cannot be accepted as basis for a new trial. Such a motion strikes at the jury's competence to decide.

GLUCKSTEIN. But the jury was deliberately misled.

JUDGE VAIL. Can it be proved that it was misled? Even if there was intention to mislead?

GLUCKSTEIN. Your Honor, I believe this addition to the expert testimony of sufficent importance to rank as new evidence. And it appears incontrovertible that the identifications are rendered null by the first three affidavits.

JUDGE VAIL. I have considered the additions to the ballistic evidence and I find them in entire accordance with the evidence already in the record. As for the identifications, it does not astonish me that the identification witnesses have withdrawn their testimony. It was obvious to me, and was no doubt obvious to the jury, that the identifications were completely discredited by the defense. The verdict of guilty was brought in on other grounds. In my opinion those grounds must have been the defendant's consciousness of guilt, as shown by their actions after the crime, and, furthermore, the general principles of the defendants, tallying, as they did, with the circumstantial evidence. These affidavits do not attack those grounds for the verdict, and the motion is therefore denied.

GLUCKSTEIN. Does your Honor mean that these men were convicted on circumstantial evidence and consciousness of guilt—?

JUDGE VAIL. There was no other evidence which was not disposed of most ably during the trial.

GLUCKSTEIN. But in that case, your Honor— (*He pauses.*)

JUDGE VAIL. Yes?

GLUCKSTEIN. In that case there was no real evidence against these men! And you make that fact the basis for denying a new trial!

JUDGE VAIL. There was sufficient evidence to convict. —If you have no further motion we will proceed to the sentence.

THE CLERK. James Macready, have you anything to say why sentence of death should not be passed upon you?

MAC. Well—no, I guess not. The only reason I can think of is that I'm not guilty of the murder, and that doesn't seem to have anything to do with this case. I'm not guilty as charged but I am guilty—I'm guilty of being a radical—and that's what I was convicted for and that's what you're sentencing me for. I'm guilty of thinking like a free man and talking like a free man and acting like a free man—and the jury didn't like it and you don't like it—and so the logical thing is to put me where I can't do it any more. I'm guilty of spreading unrest among the slaves and raising hell with slave morality. I'm guilty of exercising my rights under the constitution and I guess the constitution's gone out in this country. It isn't being done. So you go right ahead and sentence me, and don't let your conscience bother you at all, because you're doing exactly what you were put there for.

JUDGE VAIL. You have quite finished?

MAC. Oh, quite.

THE CLERK. Dante Capraro, have you anything to say why sentence of death should not be passed upon you?

CAPRARO. What I say is that I am innocent, not only of this crime but of all crimes. I have worked, I have worked hard, and those who know these two hands will tell you they have never needed to kill to earn bread. I have earned by labor what I wanted to live, and I have refused to be a member of any class but the working class, even when it could have been, because to be in business is to take profits, to be a parasite, to take what you have not deserved, and that I could not do. All my life I have worked against crime, against the murder of war, against oppression of the poor, against the great crime which is government—. Do not do this thing, Judge Vail. It has been a long time and I have suffered too much to be angry. I know that you have been an unjust judge to us, that you have fear for us, and therefore hate for us—that you have wanted us dead and have taken advantage to kill us. You have ruled to help us in the little things so that you could safely rule against us at the last. But you are an old man, and wearier than we, even if we have been in prison; and you too will die sometime, even if you kill us first. So I say to you, do not do this thing, not because the world looks at us and knows that you are wrong, but because if you do it you will prove that I was right all the time. If you kill us in this one-time free city, in this one-time free country, kill us for no wrong we have done but only for passion of prejudice and greed, then there is no answer to me, no answer to the anarchist who says the power of the State is power for corruption, and in my silence I will silence you.

JUDGE VAIL. Under the law the jury says whether a defendant is guilty or innocent. The court has nothing to do with that question. It is considered and ordered by the court that you, James Macready, and you, Dante Capraro,—

CAPRARO. I am innocent!

MAC. You know he's innocent! You couldn't listen to him without knowing that!

CAPRARO. One more moment, your Honor,—I want to speak to Mr. Gluckstein.

GLUCKSTEIN. It's too late, Capraro.

JUDGE VAIL. I think I should pronounce the sentence. That you, James Macready, and you, Dante Capraro, suffer the punishment of death by the passage of a current of electricity through your body within the week beginning on Monday, the tenth day of August, in the year of our Lord one thousand nine hundred and twenty-seven. This is the sentence of the law.

CURTAIN

ACT THREE

SCENE.—*The restaurant as in the first act.*

PETE, *the counter-man, is leaning on his elbows, reading a paper. The clock points to 11:30.*

It is dark outside. The murmur of a crowd is heard for a moment and dies away.

MILKIN, *bent, grey, and more wizened, enters from the street and looks questioningly about.*

MILKIN. Miss Rosalie here?

PETE. No.

MILKIN. Give me coffee. (*He pays for the coffee and sits gloomily without touching it.*)

PETE (*grudgingly*). She's seeing the governor.

MILKIN. She don't get no sleep.

PETE. You think they're going to bump 'em off?

MILKIN. I couldn't say dat.

PETE. Tonight, I mean?

MILKIN. De signs is wrong. Dey might. De signs is bad.

(BAUER *enters from the left, a paper folded in his hand. He goes directly across to the window.*)

BAUER. I'll bet money they get themselves raided over at the Zeitung. They've got a sheet up to flash bulletins of the executions. They kept it dark till the last minute.

PETE. Yeah?

BAUER. And what the hell is all the row about, anyway? Some rough guys get caught for murder and when they start to put 'em through all the radicals and poets in the country begin marching around the jail. You'd think nobody ever got it before.

(*A* POLICEMAN *enters.*)

PETE. Yeah, that's the truth.

BAUER. Look here, officer, you see what they're doing over at the Zeitung? They're all ready to flash bulletins.

OFFICER. Yeah, I saw it. We haven't got any orders about that. We're just watching the street here. (*He lowers his voice.*) Where's the girl, do you know? (IKE *appears in the doorway.*)

BAUER. She's seeing the governor again.

OFFICER. They'll have to hurry if they're going to stop it now. (*He glances at the clock.*)

BAUER. Think it's going through this time?

OFFICER. Sure, it's going through. They put it off once and that's enough. (*He goes out.*)

PETE. Everybody comes in here looks at that damn clock. It makes me feel queer.

IKE. Any news?

(BAUER *goes out left.*)

PETE. No.

IKE. Then I guess there won't be any. Not till twelve o'clock.

PETE. Maybe not.

(SOWERBY *enters as in the first act, with his pile of books and the slippers.*)

IKE. Meanwhile, life goes on as usual. Where are you living now?

SOWERBY. It's extraordinary how economic difficulties manage to catch one at the most embarrassing moments. (*He puts down his things.*) You've noticed that, I suppose?

IKE. In my walk of life I couldn't miss it. What's the trouble?

SOWERBY. Simple enough. Lack of funds.

IKE. Milkin'll stake you to something. Hey, Milkin, ain't you going to eat?

MILKIN. Naw. Dere ain't no use eating.

IKE. I can't get him to eat any more.

SOWERBY. What's the matter? That? (*He points to the clock.*)

IKE. Yeah, he won't eat at all.

PETE. I don't eat so good myself.

IKE. Yeah, but he's got a special worry, see? You know that theory about putting the number on them—by the cabalistic system? Well, he put it on 'em.

SOWERBY. Yeah?

IKE. Yeah, he put the number on the judge and said, "Come down from dere!" and the judge didn't come down.

SOWERBY. I daresay that hit him pretty hard.

NEWSBOY. Extra! Extra—

IKE. Jeez, it busted him up. You been over in the square?

SOWERBY. No.

IKE. There's about a million people there.

SOWERBY. Any fights?

IKE. No, sir. Nobody said a word to the police. They've got machine guns trained right on them. Down by the jail you can't even walk past. There was a bright little girl down there making a speech. They took her away. This ain't a favorable time for speeches. Personally I prefer a ham sandwich. You paying, Milkin?

MILKIN. Sure ting—if you can eat.

SOWERBY. Indeed I could eat.

MILKIN. Wid dat going on out dere?

SOWERBY. You mean the crowds?

MILKIN. I mean what dey're doing to Mac and Capraro and de old man.

SOWERBY. They won't do it. I have never for one moment believed they would carry it out.

MILKIN. Oh, yes, dey will. If somebody don't get de numbers on 'em and do it quick. And dere ain't much time.

SOWERBY. My friend, I am something of a historian, and I have made a specialty of labor developments. Never within my memory has there been a plutocracy which did not play the game with an eye to the future. Now they feel like executing Mac and Capraro. That feeling pervaded the trial and swayed the jury. On the other hand, it would be a gigantic error, from a tactical point of view to kill these men now when the whole world is watching them. They will pursue a safer and more dastardly course of action. They will execute Suvorin and commute the sentences of Mac and Capraro to life imprisonment. They will do this and then they will sit back and laugh at us, having drawn the sting from all our arguments. That was what they did in the Mooney case. Trust any government to choose the safe and dastardly course.

MILKIN. Not dis time.

SOWERBY. I think so.

MILKIN. How about de stars? How about de numbers? Dey don't come out dat way. Dey come out— (*He turns down an expressive thumb.*)

SOWERBY. If the government wishes the friendship of other nations, if it wishes the respect of its own citizens, it will take, as I said, the safe and dastardly course.

(WARD *enters.*)

WARD. Have you seen the cheap story that's out in the *Herald*—about the governor going to hold it up? (*He shows a paper.*)

SOWERBY. And why not?

WARD. They're all crazy fighting for papers up in the avenue. I had to battle for this one.

SOWERBY. Is it definite?

WARD. Read it. All the news it's safe to print.

SOWERBY (*reading*). "Macready-Capraro Reprieve Likely."

IKE. About as definite as the price of clothes in a one-price second-hand store.

SOWERBY (*reading*). "The correspondent of this paper learned from an inside official source this evening that the governor had practically made up his mind to issue a stay of execution pending further investigation into the Macready-Capraro case. This will probably mean that the executions set for midnight will be postponed another ten days." That means the governor will act.

WARD. Like hell it does! It means he's stringing us along till he gets 'em good and dead and it's too late to say anything. He knows nobody cares but the radicals, and he's playing them for suckers. Why should he worry about the crowd over in the square? There's several million around here going to bed and going to sleep as usual. Why shouldn't they? There's nothing unusual happening. This isn't a miscarriage of justice! It is justice! The government's putting away some bad boys the way governments always put away the boys that won't play the game! You ask any honest citizen what he thinks about it and he'll say, "Hell, they killed a paymaster, didn't they? Anyway, they're anarchists, ain't they? I should worry!" And he should. They won't bother him as long as he's a fat-head! (ROSALIE *enters from the left. The men rise.*) Oh, Rosalie! I thought you were seeing the governor.

ROSALIE. I was. I just got back. (*To* PETE.) Has anybody telephoned for me here?

PETE. No, Miss Suvorin.

ROSALIE. Oh, but there must be a mistake! (*She takes up the phone.*) Will you get me Mr. Gluckstein's office—right away?

WARD. What did he say, Rosalie?

ROSALIE. He said he couldn't decide. He —he was weighing the evidence. He had stacks of letters on both sides, and he was reading them. Oh, God—if it were anything else it would be just—funny. To think such a fool should decide if Mac will live or die. (*In the phone.*) Hello—yes, yes—. But he must be. Yes, I see. Yes, yes—but he must hurry. And tell him to call me—please—no, at the Lyceum. (*She hangs up the receiver.*) I thought there might be news here. Everywhere I go I think maybe there's news somewhere else.

SOWERBY. There's something in the *Herald*.

ROSALIE. I've quit trying to read about it.

SOWERBY. It says there's going to be a reprieve.

ROSALIE. Oh, but why didn't he tell me then?— (*She looks at the paper.*)

SOWERBY. It's been very unlikely from the beginning that they'd carry out the sentence. I don't know that it's much better if they commute to life imprisonment, —still—they might be pardoned, if we ever get a decent governor in office.

ROSALIE (*looking up*). Yes—they might. They might. I haven't allowed myself to think it, since they turned down the appeals.

SOWERBY. That was only the judge, my dear. We know where the judge stands and where the governor's committee stands, but nobody else has spoken. The governor doesn't have to act as his committee advises. And even if the governor failed to act there's a supreme court justice waiting with a writ of certiorari—and everything in his record indicates that he'll come forward if necessary.

ROSALIE. But where is he? Here it's the last—my God—the last few minutes, and Gluckstein hasn't even answered!

(ROSALIE, *who has been dry-eyed, looks round her at the group, then sinks into a chair and begins to sob.*)

WARD. I don't know as I'd do that, Rosalie.

(*Two* POLICEMEN *enter casually.*)

FIRST OFFICER. What's going on?

IKE. Not a thing.

FIRST OFFICER. What's she crying about?

IKE. Her? Oh, she had a sweetheart killed over in France. And every once in a while she gets thinking about it, see?

FIRST OFFICER. Don't kid me, big boy.

IKE. I wouldn't think of it.

(*The* POLICEMEN *go out.*)

MILKIN. Christ, when I look at dem—when I look at dem—de paid hirelings of de unjust—I kin feel strengt' coming back in me, de strengt' I lost! If I was worthy to do it I could break dem all—I could break dem and bring dem down. It ain't knowledge I lack. It ain't courage! It's being worthy! Worthy to rise above self! (*He snatches a paper napkin and marks it feverishly with a pencil, then rises, stretching up his arms to full length, the napkin clutched in the right.*) On dis paper I have set down de sign of One, de great cabalistic sign, wit' powers over Earth and Heaven and all de Hells! Dat is de sign which de powers has said will sway de tides and draw aside de stars from deir paths in de infinite! It is de power over all powers, de invisible *signum monstrum, de gloria cœlis, gloria mundi!* And by dis sign I conjures you in dis moment out of de endless of eternity—strike down dat judge—palsy de hands dat would lay demselves on does two men—by all dat is cognate under dis abstraction—strip dem of deir powers for good and evil, make dem as little children—and dis by de sign of One—by de sign of de mystery! (*For a moment he holds his pose, then sits again, staring gloomily before him.*) It don't work. I ain't worthy. Dat's de second time.

(ANDY *enters.*)

ANDY. A couple of telegrams for you, Ward.

WARD. Thanks.

ANDY. Anything else happened?

(*Crowd offstage. "They've escaped," etc.*)

WARD. No. Just a few more helpful friends asking us why in God's name we don't do something.

(JERUSALEM SLIM *flings open the street door and enters hastily in great excitement. A burst of cheering is heard.*)

JERUSALEM SLIM. I knew it would happen! I knew it would happen—if I prayed for it! The women are all crying out there—and Rosalie's crying—but don't cry any more—don't cry any more! Haven't you heard it? Haven't you heard it?

IKE. What?

JERUSALEM SLIM. They've escaped.

IKE. Who's escaped?

JERUSALEM SLIM. The men! Mac and Cappie and Suvorin! They're gone and nobody knows where they are!

WARD. Escaped? Out of the death-house!

JERUSALEM SLIM. Yes! It's in the papers.

SOWERBY. You're crazy, Slim!

(*A newsboy passes shouting.*)

JERUSALEM SLIM. Everybody says so.

(WARD *makes a dash for the door and goes out.*)

IKE. What paper's it in?

JERUSALEM SLIM. I don't know.

(WARD *enters with a paper. He looks at it in astonishment.*)

WARD. "Break from death-house reported!" They must be doing it to sell papers.

(*Crowd dies away.* ROSALIE *looks at the paper.*)

ROSALIE. Ward—could it be true?

WARD. I—I don't think so, Rosalie. It's never happened. I wish it might. But it couldn't possibly.

(*The* SALVATION LASS *enters from the street, looking at* ROSALIE *expectantly. The news is written in her face.*)

SOWERBY. However, it's extraordinary that the *Gazette* should print it—if there's nothing in the story.

WARD. It says it's reported—any kind of rumor could get about. There's no use hoping for anything like that. If it did happen, they'd just take them back again.

(*An elderly priest enters from the street and goes to the counter. The group fails to notice him.*)

THE PRIEST. Give me same coffee, please.

(*At the sound of his voice,* ROSALIE *recognizes* SUVORIN *in the priest. She turns toward him.*)

ROSALIE. Then—it is true! Oh, God, it is true!

WARD. What is it?

ROSALIE. It's—my father. Don't you see? Dad—Dad!

(SUVORIN *makes an almost imperceptible motion for silence. The words freeze on* ROSALIE'S *lips. A* POLICEMAN *enters and walks to the counter.*)

THE OFFICER. Coffee, old man, and fill it up with milk. I've got to drink fast. Evening, father.

(PETE *serves him.* SUVORIN *and the* POLICEMAN *sip their coffee elbow to elbow. The* POLICEMAN *goes out without a word.*)

ROSALIE. But—dad—then it's true! You

got away!

SUVORIN. Yes.

ROSALIE. Why are you here?

SUVORIN. I had to come back for some money. I'll go out the other way. (*Goes toward door at left.*)

ROSALIE. Then—where are the others?

SUVORIN. The others?

ROSALIE. Cappie—and Mac?

SUVORIN. I couldn't help them. I'm sorry.

ROSALIE. Oh—

SUVORIN. They couldn't hold me. I knew they couldn't. But I couldn't help anybody else. I'm sorry.

ROSALIE. You mean—you left Mac—there?

SUVORIN. I couldn't help him.

ROSALIE. No. (SUVORIN *goes out left.*) But—they won't go ahead now—now that one of them's escaped! They won't, will they, Ward?

WARD. I don't know.

ROSALIE. No—no! Say they won't! What are we doing here! Oh, don't you see it's nearly time! Why do we wait for other people to do something! It will be too late soon—and then we'll think of what we might have done! They're going to kill Cappie—and—and Mac—don't you know it? They're going to kill them—and we've had all day to help—we've had days and weeks—and years! We've let it go on till—till it's almost too late. Oh, dear God, don't they know Mac couldn't be guilty? They know it! They can't kill him! (*The phone rings.* ROSALIE *looks at it, clenching her hands, staring wildly.*)

WARD. I'll answer it. (*He goes to the phone.*) Hello. Yes. Yes, this is Ward. Yes. I can take a message. (*He waits.*) I didn't hear that. (*He listens, then turns toward* ROSALIE *apprehensively.* ROSALIE *is looking away. The men watch him. He makes a downward sign for silence.*) Yes, we know that. Thank you. Yes, sure. (*He hangs up, slowly. It is obvious that the news was bad.*)

ROSALIE. Was it Gluckstein?

WARD. Yes. It's not decided yet. They're still—trying everything.

ROSALIE. Oh, are they truly, Ward—or are you lying to me? Because, you see—he's warm and alive now—and if they'd only wait till I could tell them again—No, no, we've told them over and over—and they listened to us—and went on killing them. Because they know they're innocent—and they don't care.

(IKE *looks out the window and turns to pick up* SOWERBY *and* WARD *with a glance. They look out.* IKE *whispers. The crowd murmurs outside.*)

IKE. Capraro goes first.

(*They watch in silence, then* IKE *whispers again.*)

ROSALIE. Don't!—Don't!—Don't whisper any more! What is it? (*She sees the clock. The hands point to one minute of twelve.*) There's still time! There's still time! Oh, my dear, my dear, one minute more time in all your world—only one minute more of time and I can do nothing! (*The hands click to midnight!* WARD *returns to* ROSALIE.) You lied to me, Ward, they're killing them now. What does it say over there? Tell me what it says. Ike, you can tell me.

IKE. It says "Capraro Murdered."

(ROSALIE *drops her hands, frozen. One of the* OFFICERS *enters, looks around casually, then looks out of the window.* SOWERBY *speaks low to* IKE.)

ROSALIE. Don't whisper it! Don't whisper it! Didn't you hear me say not to whisper any more? That's what they'll want you to do—whisper it—keep quiet about it—say it never happened—it couldn't happen—two innocent men killed—keep it dark—keep it quiet— No! No! Shout it! They're killing them! (*There is a cry from the crowd. The* POLICEMAN *looks at* ROSALIE. *The* MEN *at the window stir uneasily. Cry from crowd—woman shrieks. Crowd silent.*) What does it say now, Ike? (IKE *makes no answer.*) I know what it says! It says "Macready Murdered." Mac—Mac—my dear—they have murdered you—while we stood here trying to think of what to do they murdered you! Just a moment ago you had a minute left—and it was the only minute in the whole world—and now—now this day will never end for you—there will be no more days! (*The crowd is heard again.*) Shout it! Shout it! Cry out! Run and cry! Only—it won't do any good—now.

CURTAIN

Elmer Rice had already left his mark on the theatre on two occasions when his *Street Scene* brought to fruition the various genuine and factitious strivings toward realism that a playgoer could encounter every season. He had given a new fillip to melodrama with *On Trial* (1914) by employing the flashback method of the motion pictures, and he had presented the theatre of the twenties with one of its best expressionist plays, *The Adding Machine,* in 1923. Nothing much else from this prolific author had quite made an impression, but then nothing much else of importance had been attempted by him. Although competently written, *For the Defense* in 1919 was still melodrama of the old dispensation, and other pieces had been collaborations (*Wake Up Jonathan,* with Hatcher Hughes, 1921; *Close Harmony,* with Dorothy Parker, 1924; *Cock Robin,* with Philip Barry, 1928). But *Street Scene* was eventful as a "slice of life" or rather, to vary the naturalists' formula, a *cross-section* of life, executed with distinct authenticity of speech and local color. The author had, logically enough, ventured to treat the people of the city slum areas with the same painstaking attention to local detail that regionalists and proponents of folk drama lavished on the people of the soil. Compassion and an awareness of social reality enriched the local description; and if Mr. Rice resorted to a rather stereotyped melodrama to give the play a plot, his fateful triangle of husband, wife, and the milkman was just the sort of complication that accorded with the round of little lives under observation. Not until seven years later in *Awake and Sing* (1935) was the stage to have a comparable picture of urban life, and then, since conversions to radical ideology were in vogue, the picture could no longer be allowed to stand alone and speak for itself.

Mr. Rice's life had sharpened his eyes for the details of *Street Scene.* He was born in New York City in 1892 and scored some sort of record for roots, with which New Yorkers are not conspicuously endowed, by spending the first quarter of a century within about two miles of the house he was born in. He tried business and failed, and then practiced law for about five years without developing a liking for it or winning any success in the profession. His first play, *On Trial,* released him from bondage to the law and although he was not to have a success again for a number of years, facing public apathy with two pacifistic plays during the first World War, he remained loyal to the theatre. He had better fortune with another melodrama *For the Defense* (1919) and then struggled with variable success to the pinnacle of Broadway fortune and a Pulitzer Prize with *Street Scene* in 1929.

He had two other productions that year *The Subway* and *See Naples and Die* without adding to his prestige, but returned to the limelight in 1931 with a sensible comedy on expatriation, *The Left Bank,* and the vivid character drama and picture of the law business, *Counsellor-at-Law.* Jolted by the depression and the conflicts of the thirties, he next wrote the two impassioned pleas *We, the People* (1933) and *Judgment Day* (1934), the first on unemployment, the second on the Reichstag Fire Trial. In 1934 also came his conversation piece concerning capitalist and communist attitudes, *Between Two Worlds.* None of these plays, which he produced himself, succeeded and Mr. Rice retired from Broadway for a while, contenting himself with the writing of a novel and with productions by the London Stage Society and the Pasadena Theatre of his ingenious play about the theatre *No Time for Children* (1935, 1936). He assumed charge of the Federal Theatre relief project in New York for a time in 1935, and did not return to the professional theatre until 1938 when he joined Sherwood, Anderson, Howard, and Behrman in The Playwrights Company, directing and writing for that organization. Since then he has written the social problem fantasy *American Landscape* (1938), the pleasant romantic comedy *Two on an Island* (1939), the somewhat philosophical anti-Nazi drama *Flight to the West* (1940), *A New Life* (1943), the highly successful fantastic comedy *Dream Girl* (1945), and the book for the often affecting Kurt Weill musical version of *Street Scene* (1947).

Street Scene

BY ELMER RICE

First produced by William A. Brady, Ltd., at the Playhouse, New York City, on January 10, 1929, with the following cast:

ABRAHAM KAPLAN	Leo Bulgakov
GRETA FIORENTINO	Eleanor Wesselhoeft
EMMA JONES	Beulah Bondi
OLGA OLSEN	Hilda Bruce
WILLIE MORAN	Russell Griffin
ANNA MORAN	Mary Servoss
DANIEL BUCHANAN	Conway Washburne
FRANK MORAN	Robert Kelly
GEORGE JONES	T. H. Manning
STEVE SANKEY	Joseph Baird
AGNES CUSHING	Jane Corcoran
CARL OLSEN	John M. Qualen
SHIRLEY KAPLAN	Anna Kostant
FILIPPO FIORENTINO	George Humbert
ALICE SIMPSON	Emily Hamill
LAURA HILDEBRAND	Frederica Going
MARY HILDEBRAND	Eileen Smith
CHARLIE HILDEBRAND	Alexander Lewis
SAMUEL KAPLAN	Horace Braham
ROSE MORAN	Erin O'Brien-Moore
HARRY EASTER	Glenn Coulter
MAE JONES	Millicent Green
DICK McGANN	Joseph Lee
VINCENT JONES	Matthew McHugh
DR. JOHN WILSON	John Crump
OFFICER HARRY MURPHY	Edward Downes

ACT ONE

SCENE.—*The exterior of a "walk-up" apartment house, in a mean quarter of New York. It is of ugly brownstone and was built in the '90's. Between the pavement of large, gray flagstones and the front of the house, is a deep and narrow "areaway," guarded by a rusted, ornamental iron railing. At the right, a steep flight of rotting wooden steps leads down to the cellar and to the janitor's apartment, the windows of which are just visible above the street level. Spanning the areaway is a "stoop" of four shallow, stone steps, flanked on either side by a curved stone balustrade. Beyond the broad fourth step, another step leads to the double wooden outer doors of the house; and as these are open, the vestibule, and the wide, heavy glass-panelled entrance door beyond are visible. Above the outer doors, is a glass fanlight, upon which appears the half-obliterated house number. At the left side of the doorway is a sign which reads: "Flat To-Let. 6 Rooms. Steam Heat."*

On either side of the stoop are the two narrow windows of the ground-floor apartments. In one of the windows, at the left, is a sign bearing the legend: "Prof. Filippo Fiorentino. Music for all occasions. Also instruction." Above, are the six narrow windows of the first-floor apartments, and above that, the stone sills of the second-floor windows can just be seen.

To the left of the house, part of the adjoining building is visible: the motor entrance to a storage warehouse. Crude boarding across the large driveway and rough planks across the sidewalk and curb indicate that an excavation is in progress. On the boarding is painted in rude lettering: "Keep Out"; and at the curb is a small barrel bearing a sign with the words: "Street Closed." To the wall of the warehouse is affixed a brass plate, bearing the name: "Patrick Mulcahy Storage Warehouse Co. Inc."

To the right of the house, scaffolding and a wooden sidewalk indicate that the house next door is being demolished. On the scaffolding is a large, wooden sign reading: "Manhattan House-Wrecking Corp." In the close foreground, below the level of the curb, is a mere suggestion of the street.

At rise, the house is seen in the white glare of an arc-light, which is just offstage to the right. The windows in the janitor's apartment are lighted, as are also those of the ground-floor apartment, at the right, and the two windows at the extreme left of the first-floor. A dim, red light is affixed to the boarding of the excavation at the left.

In the lighted ground-floor window, at the right of the doorway, ABRAHAM KAPLAN *is seated in a rocking-chair, reading a Yiddish newspaper. He is a Russian Jew, well past sixty: clean-shaven, thick gray hair, hooked nose, horn-rimmed spectacles. To the left of the doorway,* GRETA FIORENTINO *is leaning out of the window. She is forty, blonde, ruddy-faced, and stout. She wears a wrapper of light, flowered material and a large pillow supports her left arm and her ample, uncorseted bosom. In her right hand is a folding paper fan, which she waves languidly.*

Throughout the act and, indeed, throughout the play, there is constant noise. The noises of the city rise, fall, intermingle: the distant roar of "L" trains, automobile sirens, and the whistles of boats on the river; the rattle of trucks and the indeterminate clanking of metals; fire-engines, ambulances, musical instruments, a radio, dogs barking and human voices calling, quarrelling, and screaming with laughter. The noises are subdued and in the background, but they never wholly cease.

A moment after the rise of the curtain, an elderly man enters at the right and walks into the house, exchanging a nod with MRS. FIORENTINO. A MAN, *munching peanuts, crosses the stage from left to right.*

A VOICE (*off-stage*). Char-lie!

(EMMA JONES *appears at the left. She is middle-aged, tall, and rather bony. She carries a small parcel.*)

MRS. FIORENTINO (*she speaks with a faint German accent*). Good evening, Mrs. Jones.

MRS. JONES (*stopping beneath Mrs. Fiorentino's window*). Good evenin', Mrs. F. Well, I hope it's hot enough for you.

MRS. FIORENTINO. Ain't it joost awful? When I was through with the dishes, you could take my clothes and joost wring them out.

MRS. JONES. Me, too. I ain't got a dry

stitch on me.

MRS. FIORENTINO. I took off my shoes and my corset and made myself nice and comfortable, and tonight before I go to bed, I take a nice bath.

MRS. JONES. The trouble with a bath is, by the time you're all through, you're as hot as when you started. (*As* OLGA OLSEN, *a thin, anemic Scandinavian, with untidy fair hair, comes up the cellar steps and onto the sidewalk.*) Good evenin', Mrs. Olsen. Awful hot, ain't it?

MRS. OLSEN (*coming over to the front of the stoop*). Yust awful. Mrs. Forentiner, my hoosban' say vill you put de garbage on de doom-vaider?

MRS. FIORENTINO. Oh, sure, sure! I didn't hear him vistle. (*As* MRS. JONES *starts to cross to the stoop.*) Don't go 'vay, Mrs. Jones.

(*She disappears from the window.*)

MRS. OLSEN (*pushing back some wisps of hair*). I tank is more cooler in de cellar.

MRS. JONES (*sitting on the stoop and fanning herself with her parcel*). Phew! I'm just about ready to pass out.

MRS. OLSEN. My baby is crying, crying all day.

MRS. JONES. Yeah, I often say they mind the heat more'n we do. It's the same with dogs. My Queenie has jes' been layin' aroun' all day.

MRS. OLSEN. The baby get new teet'. It hurt her.

MRS. JONES. Don't tell me! If you was to know what I went t'roo with my Vincent. Half the time, he used to have convulsions.

(WILLIE MAURRANT, *a disorderly boy of twelve, appears at the left, on roller skates. He stops at the left of the stoop and takes hold of the railing with both hands.*)

WILLIE (*raising his head and bawling*). Hey, ma!

MRS. JONES. (*disapprovingly*). If you want your mother, why don't you go upstairs, instead o' yellin' like that?

WILLIE (*without paying the slightest attention to her, bawls louder.*) Hey, ma!

MRS. MAURRANT (*appearing at one of the lighted first-floor windows*). What do you want, Willie?

(*She is a fair woman of forty, who looks her age, but is by no means unattractive.*)

WILLIE. Gimme a dime, will ya? I wanna git a cone.

MRS. MAURRANT. (*to* MRS. OLSEN *and* MRS. JONES). Good evening.

MRS. OLSEN *and* MRS. JONES. Good evenin', Mrs. Maurrant.

MRS. MAURRANT (*to* WILLIE). How many cones did you have today, already?

WILLIE (*belligerently*). I'm hot! All de other guys is havin' cones. Come on, gimme a dime.

MRS. MAURRANT. Well, it's the last one. (*She disappears.*)

MRS. JONES. You certainly don't talk very nice to your mother. (*To* MRS. OLSEN.) I'd like to hear one o' mine talkin' that way to me!

MRS. MAURRANT (*appearing at the window*). Remember, this is the last one.

WILLIE. Aw right. T'row it down.

(MRS. FIORENTINO *reappears and leans out of the window again.*)

MRS. MAURRANT. Catch it!

(*She throws out a twist of newspaper.* WILLIE *scrambles for it, hastily extracts the dime, drops the newspaper on the pavement and skates off, at the left.*)

MRS. FIORENTINO (*twisting her neck upwards*). Good evening, Mrs. Maurrant.

MRS. MAURRANT. Good evening, Mrs. Fiorentino. (*Calling after* WILLIE.) And don't come home too late, Willie!

(*But* WILLIE *is already out of earshot.*)

MRS. FIORENTINO. Why don't you come down and be sociable?

MRS. MAURRANT. I'm keeping some supper warm for my husband. (*A slight pause.*) Well, maybe I will for just a minute.

(*She leaves the window. The lights in her apartment go out.*)

MRS. FIORENTINO. She has her troubles with dot Willie.

MRS. JONES. I guess it don't bother her much. (*Significantly.*) She's got her mind on other things.

MRS. OLSEN (*looking about cautiously and coming over to the left of the stoop between the two women*). He vas comin' again today to see her.

MRS. JONES (*rising excitedly, and leaning over the balustrade*). Who—Sankey?

MRS. OLSEN (*nodding*). Yes.

MRS. FIORENTINO. Are you sure, Mrs. Olsen?

MRS. OLSEN. I seen him. I vas doostin' de halls.

MRS. FIORENTINO. Dot's terrible!

MRS. JONES. Wouldn't you think a woman her age, with a grown-up daughter——!

MRS. OLSEN. Two times already dis veek, I see him here.

MRS. JONES. I seen him, meself, one day last week. He was comin' out o' the house, jest as I was comin' in wit' de dog. "Good mornin', Mrs. Jones," he says to me, as if butter wouldn't melt in his mouth. "Good mornin'," says I, lookin' him straight in the eye—(*Breaking off suddenly, as the vestibule door opens.*) Be careful, she's comin'.

(MRS. MAURRANT *comes out of the house and stops, for a moment, on the top step.*)

MRS. MAURRANT. Goodness, ain't it hot! I think it's really cooler upstairs.

(*She comes down the steps to the sidewalk.*)

MRS. JONES. Yeah, jes' what I was sayin', meself. I feel like a wet dish-rag.

MRS. MAURRANT. I would have liked to go to the Park concert tonight, if Rose had got home in time. I don't get much chance to go to concerts. My husband don't care for music. But Rose is more like me—just crazy about it.

MRS. JONES. Ain't she home yet?

MRS. MAURRANT. No. I think maybe she had to work overtime.

MRS. JONES. Well, all mine ever comes home for is to sleep.

MRS. FIORENTINO. The young girls nowadays——!

MRS. OLSEN. My sister was writin' me in Schweden is same t'ing——

MRS. JONES. It ain't only the young ones, either.

(*A baby is heard crying in the cellar.*)

OLSEN'S VOICE. (*From the cellar.*) Ol-ga!

(*A* MAN, *in a dinner jacket and straw hat, appears at the left, whistling a jazz tune. He crosses the stage and goes off at the right.*)

MRS. OLSEN (*hurrying to the right*). I betcha the baby, she's cryin' again.

OLSEN'S VOICE. Ol-ga!

MRS. OLSEN. Yes. I come right away.

(*She goes down the cellar steps.*)

MRS. JONES. What them foreigners don't know about bringin' up babies would fill a book.

MRS. FIORENTINO (*a little huffily*). Foreigners know joost as much as other people, Mrs. Jones. My mother had eight children and she brought up seven.

MRS. JONES (*tactfully*). Well, I'm not sayin' anythin' about the Joimans. The Joimans is different—more like the Irish. What I'm talkin' about is all them squareheads an' Polacks—(*with a glance in* KAPLAN'S *direction*)—an' Jews.

BUCHANAN'S VOICE (*from a third story window*). Good evening, ladies.

THE WOMEN (*in unison, looking upward*). Oh, good evening, Mr. Buchanan.

BUCHANAN'S VOICE. Well, is it hot enough for you?

MRS. JONES. I'll say!

BUCHANAN'S VOICE. I was just saying to my wife, it's not the the heat I mind as much as it is the humidity.

MRS. JONES. Yeah, that's it! Makes everything stick to you.

MRS. MAURRANT. How's your wife feeling in this weather?

BUCHANAN'S VOICE. She don't complain about the weather. But she's afraid to go out of the house. Thinks maybe she couldn't get back in time, in case—you know.

MRS. JONES (*to the other women*). I was the same way with my Vincent—afraid to take a step. But with Mae, I was up an' out till the very last minute.

MRS. FIORENTINO (*craning her neck upward*). Mr. Buchanan, do you think she would eat some nice minestrone—good Italian vegetable-soup?

BUCHANAN'S VOICE. Why, much obliged, Mrs. F., but I really can't get her to eat a thing.

MRS. JONES (*rising and looking upward*). Tell her she ought to keep up her strength. She's got two to feed, you know.

BUCHANAN'S VOICE. Excuse me, she's calling.

MRS. JONES (*crossing to the railing, at the left of* MRS. FIORENTINO). You'd think it was him that was havin' the baby.

MRS. MAURRANT. She's such a puny little thing.

MRS. FIORENTINO (*with a sigh*). Well, that's the way it goes. The little skinny ones have them and the big strong ones don't.

MRS. MAURRANT. Don't take it that way, Mrs. Fiorentino. You're a young woman, yet.

MRS. FIORENTINO (*shaking her head*). Oh, well!

MRS. JONES. My aunt, Mrs. Barclay, was forty-two—(*Breaking off.*) Oh, good evenin', Mr. Maurrant!

(FRANK MAURRANT *appears, at the left, with his coat on his arm. He is a tall, powerfully-built man of forty-five, with a rugged, grim face.*)

MRS. FIORENTINO. Good evening, Mr. Maurrant.

MAURRANT. 'Evenin'. (*He goes to the stoop and seats himself, mopping his face.*) Some baby of a day!

MRS. MAURRANT. Have you been working all this while, Frank?

MAURRANT. I'll say I've been workin'. Dress-rehearsin' since twelve o'clock, with lights—in this weather. An' to-morra I gotta go to Stamford for the try-out.

MRS. MAURRANT. Oh, you're going to Stamford tomorrow?

MAURRANT. Yeah, the whole crew's goin'. (*Looking at her.*) What about it?

MRS. MAURRANT. Why, nothing. Oh, I've got some cabbage and potatoes on the stove for you.

MAURRANT. I just had a plate o' beans at the Coffee Pot. All I want is a good wash. I been sweatin' like a horse all day.
(*He rises and goes up the steps.*)

MRS. FIORENTINO. My husband, too; he's sweating terrible.

MRS. JONES. Mine don't. There's some people that just naturally do, and then there's others that don't.

MAURRANT (*to* MRS. MAURRANT). Is anybody upstairs?

MRS. MAURRANT. No. Willie's off playing with the boys. I can't keep him home.

MAURRANT. What about Rose?

MRS. MAURRANT. I think maybe she's working overtime.

MAURRANT. I never heard o' nobody workin' nights in a real-estate office.

MRS. MAURRANT. I thought maybe on account of the office being closed to-morrow—— (*To the others.*) Mr. Jacobson, the head of the firm, died Tuesday, and tomorrow's the funeral, so I thought maybe——

MRS. JONES. Yeah. Leave it to the Jews not to lose a workin' day, without makin' up for it.

MAURRANT (*to* MRS. MAURRANT). She shouldn't be stayin' out nights without us knowin' where she is.

MRS. MAURRANT. She didn't say a word about not coming home.

MAURRANT. That's what I'm sayin', ain't it? It's a mother's place to know what her daughter's doin'.

MRS. FIORENTINO (*soothingly*). Things are different nowadays, Mr. Maurrant, from what they used to be.

MAURRANT. Not in my family, they're not goin' to be no different. Not so long as I got somethin' to say.

A GIRL'S VOICE (*off-stage*). Red Rover! Red Rover! Let Freddie come over!
(GEORGE JONES, *a short, rather plump, red-faced man, cigar in mouth, comes out of the house, as* MAURRANT *enters the vestibule.*)

JONES. Hello, Mr. Maurrant.

MAURRANT (*curtly*). 'Evenin'.
(*He enters the house.* JONES *looks after him in surprise for a moment.* MRS. MAURRANT *seats herself on the stoop.*)

JONES. Good evenin', ladies.

MRS. FIORENTINO *and* MRS. MAURRANT. Good evening, Mr. Jones.

JONES (*seating himself on the left balustrade*). What's the matter with your hubby, Mrs. Maurrant? Guess he's feelin' the heat, huh?

MRS. MAURRANT. He's been working till just now and I guess he's a little tired.

MRS. JONES. Men are all alike. They're all easy to get along with, so long as everythin's goin' the way they want it to. But once it don't—good night!

MRS. FIORENTINO. Yes, dot's true, Mrs. Jones.

JONES. Yeah, an' what about the women?

MRS. MAURRANT. I guess it's just the same with the women. I often think it's a shame that people don't get along better together. People ought to be able to live together in peace and quiet, without making each other miserable.

MRS. JONES. The way I look at it, you get married for better or worse, an' if it turns out to be worse, why all you can do is make the best of it.

MRS. MAURRANT. I think the trouble is people don't make allowances. They don't realize that everybody wants a kind word now and then. After all, we're all human, and we can't just go along by ourselves, all the time, without ever getting a kind word.
(*While she is speaking,* STEVE SANKEY *appears at the right. He is in the early thirties, and is prematurely bald. He is rather flashily dressed, in a patently cheap, light-gray suit and a straw hat with a plaid band. As he appears,* MRS. JONES *and* MRS. FIORENTINO *exchange a swift, significant look.*)

SANKEY (*stopping at the right of the stoop and removing his hat*). Good evening, folks! Is it hot enough for you?

THE OTHERS. Good evening.

MRS. MAURRANT (*self-consciously*). Good evening, Mr. Sankey.

(*Throughout the scene,* MRS. MAURRANT *and* SANKEY *try vainly to avoid looking at each other.*)

SANKEY. I don't know when we've had a day like this. Hottest June fifteenth in forty-one years. It was up to ninety-four at three P. M.

JONES. Six dead in Chicago. An' no relief in sight, the evenin' paper says.

(MAURRANT *appears at the window of his apartment and stands there, looking out.*)

MRS. FIORENTINO. It's joost awful!

SANKEY. Well, it's good for the milk business. You know the old saying, it's an ill wind that blows nobody any good.

MRS. MAURRANT. Yes. You hardly get the milk in the morning, before it turns sour.

MRS. JONES. I'm just after pourin' half-a-bottle down the sink.

(MAURRANT *leaves the window.*)

MRS. FIORENTINO. You shouldn't throw it away. You should make—what do you call it?—schmier-käs'.

SANKEY. Oh, I know what you mean—pot-cheese. My wife makes it, too, once in a while.

MRS. MAURRANT. Is your wife all right again, Mr. Sankey? You were telling me last time, she had a cold.

(MRS. JONES *and* MRS. FIORENTINO *exchange another look.*)

SANKEY. Was I? Oh, sure, sure. That was a couple weeks ago. Yes, sure, she's all right again. That didn't amount to anything much.

MRS. JONES. You got a family, too, ain't you?

SANKEY. Yes. Yes, I have. Two little girls. Well, I got to be going along. (*He goes to the left of the stoop and stops again.*) I told my wife I'd go down to the drug-store and get her some nice cold ginger-ale. You want something to cool you off in this kind of weather.

MRS. JONES (*as* SANKEY *passes her*). If you ask me, all that gassy stuff don't do you a bit of good.

SANKEY. I guess you're right, at that. Still it cools you off. Well, good-night, folks. See you all again.

(*He strolls off, at the left, with affected nonchalance; but when he is almost out of sight, he casts a swift look back at* MRS. MAURRANT. *A dowdy* WOMAN, *wheeling a dilapidated baby carriage, appears at the left, and crosses the stage.*)

JONES. What's his name—Sankey?

MRS. JONES. Yeah—Mr. Sankey.

MRS. MAURRANT. He's the collector for the milk company.

(AGNES CUSHING *comes out of the house. She is a thin, dried-up woman, past fifty.*)

MISS CUSHING (*coming down the steps*). Good evening.

THE OTHERS. Good evening, Miss Cushing.

MRS. MAURRANT. How is your mother today, Miss Cushing?

MISS CUSHING (*pausing at the left of the stoop*). Why, she complains of the heat. But I'm afraid it's really her heart. She's seventy-two, you know. I'm just going down to the corner to get her a little ice-cream.

(*As she goes off at the left,* OLSEN, *the janitor, a lanky Swede, struggles up the cellar steps with a large, covered, tin garbage-barrel. The others look around in annoyance as he bangs the garbage barrel upon the pavement.*)

OLSEN. Phew! Hot!

(*He mops his face and neck with a dingy handkerchief, then lights his pipe and leans against the railing.*)

MRS. JONES (*significantly, as she crosses to the center of the stoop and sits*). Between you and I, I don't think her mother's got long for this world. Once the heart starts goin' back on you—!

MRS. FIORENTINO. It's too bad.

MRS. MAURRANT. Poor soul! She'll have nothing at all when her mother dies. She's just spent her whole life looking after her mother.

MRS. JONES. It's no more than her duty, is it?

MRS. FIORENTINO. You could not expect that she should neglect her mother.

A VOICE (*off-stage*). Char-lie!

MRS. MAURRANT. It's not a matter of neglecting. Only—it seems as if a person should get more out of life than just looking after somebody else.

MRS. JONES. Well, I hope to tell you, after all I've done for mine, I expect 'em to look after me in my old age.

MRS. MAURRANT. I don't know. It seems to me you might just as well not live at all, as the way she does. (*Rising, with affected casualness.*) I don't know what's become of Willie. I think I'd better walk down to the corner and look for him. My husband don't like it if he stays out late.

(*She goes off at the left. They all watch her, in dead silence, until she is out of earshot. Then the storm breaks.*

MRS. JONES (*rising excitedly*). Didja get that? Goin' to look for Willie! Can ya beat it?

MRS. FIORENTINO. It's joost terrible!

JONES. You think she's just goin' out lookin' for this guy Sankey?

MRS. JONES (*scornfully*). Ain't men the limit? What do you think he come walkin' by here for? (*Mincingly.*) Just strolled by to get the wife a little ginger-ale. A fat lot he cares whether his wife has ginger-ale!

MRS. FIORENTINO. Two little girls he's got, too!

JONES. Yeah, that ain't right—a bird like that, wit' a wife an' two kids of his own.

MRS. FIORENTINO. The way he stands there and looks and looks at her!

MRS. JONES. An' what about the looks she was givin' him! (*Seating herself again.*) You'd think he was the Prince of Wales, instead of a milk-collector. And didja get the crack about not seein' him for two weeks?

MRS. FIORENTINO. And joost today he was upstairs, Mrs. Olsen says.

(OLSEN *approaches the stoop and removes his pipe from his mouth.*)

OLSEN (*pointing upwards*). Some day, her hoosban' is killing him.

(*He replaces his pipe and goes back to his former position.*)

MRS. FIORENTINO. Dot would be terrible!

JONES. He's li'ble to, at that. You know, he's got a wicked look in his eye, dat baby has.

MRS. JONES. Well, it's no more than he deserves, the little rabbit—goin' around breakin' up people's homes. (*Mockingly.*) Good evenin', folks! Jes' like Whozis on the radio.

JONES. D'ya think Maurrant is wise to what's goin' on?

MRS. JONES. Well, if he ain't, there must be somethin' the matter with him. But you never can tell about men. They're as blind as bats. An' what I always say is, in a case like that, the husband or the wife is always the last one to find out.

(MISS CUSHING, *carrying a small paper bag, hurries on, at the left, in a state of great excitement.*)

MISS CUSHING (*breathlessly, as she comes up the left of the stoop*). Say, what do you think! I just saw them together—the two of them!

MRS. JONES (*rising excitedly*). What did I tell you?

MRS. FIORENTINO. Where did you see them, Miss Cushing?

MISS CUSHING. Why, right next door, in the entrance to the warehouse. They were standing right close together. And he had his hands up on her shoulders. It's awful, isn't it?

JONES. Looks to me like this thing is gettin' pretty serious.

MRS. JONES. You didn't notice if they was kissin' or anythin', did you?

MISS CUSHING. Well, to tell you the truth, Mrs. Jones, I was so ashamed for her that I hardly looked at all.

JONES (*sotto voce, as the house door opens*). Look out! Maurrant's comin'.

(*A conspirators' silence falls upon them as* MAURRANT, *pipe in month, comes out of the house.*)

MISS CUSHING (*tremulously*). Good evening, Mr. Maurrant.

MAURRANT (*on the top step*). 'Evenin'. (*To the others.*) What's become of me wife?

MRS. JONES. Why, she said she was goin' around the corner to look for Willie.

MAURRANT (*grunts*). Oh.

MRS. JONES. They need a lot of lookin' after when they're that age.

(*A momentary silence.*)

MISS CUSHING. Well, I think I'd better get back to my mother.

(*She goes up the steps.*)

MRS. JONES, MRS. FIORENTINO, *and* JONES. Good night, Miss Cushing.

MISS CUSHING. Good night. (*As she passes* MAURRANT.) Good night, Mr. Maurrant.

MAURRANT. 'Night.

(*She looks at him swiftly, and goes into the vestibule.*)

A BOY'S VOICE (*Off-stage*). Red Rover! Red Rover! Let Mary come over!

(*As* MISS CUSHING *enters the house,* SHIRLEY KAPLAN *appears at the ground-floor window, at the extreme right, with a glass of steaming tea in her hand. She is a dark, unattractive Jewess, past thirty. She wears a light house-dress.* KAPLAN *goes on reading.*)

SHIRLEY (*to the neighbors outside; she speaks with the faintest trace of accent*). Good evening.

THE OTHERS (*not very cordially*). Good

evenin'.

SHIRLEY. It's been a terrible day, hasn't it?

JONES *and* MRS. JONES. Yeah.

SHIRLEY (*going to the other window*). Papa, here's your tea. Haven't you finished your paper yet? It makes it so hot, with the lights on.

KAPLAN (*lowering his newspaper*). Oll right! Oll right! Put it out! Put it out! There is anahoo notting to read in de papers. Notting but deevorce, skendal, and moiders.

(*He speaks with a strong accent, overemphatically, and with much gesticulation. He puts his paper away, removes his glasses, and starts to drink his tea.*)

(*No one answers.* SHIRLEY *goes away from the window and puts out the lights.*)

SHIRLEY. There doesn't seem to be a breath of air anywhere.

MRS. JONES (*sotto voce*). You wouldn't think anybody would want to read that Hebrew writin', would ya? I don't see how they make head or tail out of it, meself.

JONES. I guess if you learn it when you're a kid——

MRS. JONES (*suddenly*). Well, will you look at your hubby, Mrs. F.! He's sure got his hands full!

(*She looks towards the left, greatly amused.* SHIRLEY *reappears at the window at the extreme right, and seats herself on the sill.*)

MRS. FIORENTINO (*leaning far out*). Joost look at him! (*Calling.*) Lippo, be careful you don't drop any!

LIPPO (*off-stage*). 'Allo, Margherita!

(*They all watch in amusement, as* FILIPPO FIORENTINO, *a fat Italian, with thick black hair and moustache, comes on at the left. He is clutching a violin in his left arm and balancing five ice-cream cones in his right hand.*)

LIPPO (*shouting*). Who wantsa da ice-cream cone? Nice fresha ice-cream cone!

MRS. FIORENTINO. Lippo, you will drop them!

MRS. JONES (*going up to him*). Here, gimme your violin.

(*She relieves him of the violin and he shifts two of the cones to his left hand.*)

LIPPO (*as* MRS. JONES *hands the violin to* MRS. FIORENTINO). T'ank you, Meeses Jones. 'Ere's for you a nica, fresha ice-cream cone.

(MRS. FIORENTINO *puts the violin on a chair behind her.*)

MRS. JONES (*taking a cone*). Why thank you very much, Mr. F.

LIPPO (*going up to the window*). Meeses Fiorentino, 'ere's for you a nica, fresha ice-cream cone.

MRS. FIORENTINO (*taking the cone*). It makes me too fat.

LIPPO. Ah, no! Five, ten poun' more, nobody can tell da deef!

(*He laughs aloud at his own joke and crosses to the stoop.*)

MRS. JONES (*enjoying her cone*). Ain't he a sketch, though?

LIPPO. Meester Jones, you eata da cone, ha?

JONES. Why, yeah, I will at that. Thanks. Thanks.

LIPPO. Meester Maurrant?

MAURRANT. Naw; I got me pipe.

LIPPO. You lika betta da pipe den da ice-cream? (*Crossing the stoop.*) Meesa Kaplan, nica, fresha cone, yes?

SHIRLEY. No, thanks. I really don't want any.

LIPPO. Meester Kaplan, yes?

KAPLAN (*waving his hand*). No, no! Tenks, tenks!

MRS. JONES (*to* JONES). You oughta pay Mr. F. for the cones.

JONES (*reluctantly reaching into his pocket*). Why, sure.

LIPPO (*excitedly*). Ah, no, no! I don' taka da mon'. I'm treata da whole crowd. I deedn' know was gona be such a biga crowd or I bringa doz'. (*Crossing to* OLSEN.) Meester Olsen, you lika da cone, ha?

OSLEN. Sure. Much oblige'.

(*He takes the pipe from his mouth and stolidly licks the cone.*)

LIPPO (*seating himself on the stoop, with a long sigh of relaxation*). Aaah! (*He tastes the cone and smacking his lips, looks about for approval.*) Ees tasta good, ha?

JONES (*his mouth full*). You betcha!

MRS. JONES. It cools you off a little.

LIPPO. Sure. Dassa right. Cool you off. (*He pulls at his clothing and sits on the stoop.*) I'ma wat, wat—like I jus' come outa da bad-tub. Ees 'ota like hal in da Park. Two, t'ree t'ousan' people, everybody sweatin'—ees smal lika menageria.

(*While he is speaking,* ALICE SIMPSON, *a tall, spare spinster, appears at the right. She goes up the steps, enters the vestibule, and is about to push one of the buttons on the side wall.)*

MRS. JONES (*sotto voce*). She's from the Charities. (*Coming over to the stoop and calling into the vestibule.*) If you're lookin' for Mrs. Hildebrand, she ain't home yet.

MISS SIMPSON (*coming to the doorway*). Do you know when she'll be back?

MRS. JONES. Well, she oughta be here by now. She jus' went aroun' to the Livingston. That's the pitcher-theayter.

MISS SIMPSON (*Outraged*). You mean she's gone to a moving-picture show?

OLSEN (*calmly*). She's comin' now.

LIPPO (*rising to his feet and calling vehemently*). Mees Hil'brand! Hurry up! Hurry up! Ees a lady here.

(*He motions violently to her to hurry.* LAURA HILDEBRAND *appears at the right, with her two children,* CHARLIE *and* MARY. *She is a small, rather young woman, with a manner of perpetual bewilderment. Both children are chewing gum, and* MARY *comes on skipping a rope and chanting: "Apple, peach, pear, plum, banana."* CHARLIE *carefully avoids all the cracks in the sidewalk.*)

MISS SIMPSON (*coming out on the steps*). Well, good evening, Mrs. Hildebrand!

MRS. HILDEBRAND (*flustered*). Good evening, Miss Simpson.

MISS SIMPSON. Where have you been?—to a moving-picture show?

MRS. HILDEBRAND. Yes, ma'am.

MISS SIMPSON. And where did you get the money?

MRS. HILDEBRAND. It was only seventy-five cents.

MISS SIMPSON. Seventy-five cents is a lot, when you're being dispossessed and dependent upon charity. I suppose it came out of the money I gave you to buy groceries with.

MRS. HILDEBRAND. We always went, Thursday nights, to the pictures when my husband was home.

MISS SIMPSON. Yes, but your husband isn't home. And as far as anybody knows, he has no intention of coming home.

KAPLAN (*leaning forward out of his window*). Ees dis your conception of cherity?

SHIRLEY. Papa, why do you interfere?

MISS SIMPSON (*to* KAPLIN). You'll please be good enough to mind your own business.

KAPLAN. You should go home and read in your Bible de life of Christ.

MRS. JONES (*to* MRS. FIORENTINO). Will you listen to who's talkin' about Christ!

MISS SIMPSON (*turning her back on* KAPLAN *and speaking to* MRS. HILDEBRAND). You may as well understand right now that nobody's going to give you any money to spend on moving-picture shows.

LIPPO. Ah, wotsa da matter, lady? (*He thrusts his hand into his pocket and takes out a fistful of coins.*) 'Ere, you taka da mon', you go to da pitcha, ever' night. (*He forces the coins into* MRS. HILDEBRAND'S *hand.*) An' here's for da bambini. (*He gives each child a nickel.*)

MRS. FIORENTINO (*to* MRS. JONES). Dot's why we never have money.

MRS. HILDEBRAND (*bewildered*). I really oughtn't to take it.

LIPPO. Sure! Sure! I got plenta mon'.

MISS SIMPSON (*disgustedly*). We'd better go inside. I can't talk to you here, with all these people.

MRS. HILDEBRAND (*meekly*). Yes, ma'am.

(*She follows* MISS SIMPSON *into the house, her children clinging to her.*)

MRS. JONES. Wouldn't she give you a pain?

LIPPO. I tella you da whola troub'. She's a don' gotta nobody to sleepa wit'.

(*The men laugh.*)

MRS. JONES (*to* MRS. FIORENTINO). Ain't he the limit!

MRS. FIORENTINO (*greatly pleased*). Tt!

LIPPO. Somebody go sleepa wit' her, she's alla right. Meester Jones, 'ow 'bout you?

(*Shirley, embarrassed, leaves the window.*)

JONES (*with a sheepish grin*). Naw, I guess not.

LIPPO. Wot'sa matter? You 'fraid you' wife, ha? Meester Maurrant, how 'bout you?

(MAURRANT *emits a short laugh.*)

MRS. FIORENTINO (*delighted*). Lippo, you're joost awful.

LIPPO (*enjoying himself hugely*). Alla ri'. Ahma gonna go myself!

(*He laughs boisterously. The others laugh too.*)

MRS. JONES (*suddenly*). Here's your wife now, Mr. Maurrant.

(*A sudden silence falls upon them all, as* MRS. MAURRANT *approaches at the left. A swift glance appraises her of* MAURRANT'S *presence.*)

LIPPO. 'Allo, Meeses Maurrant. Why

you don' come to da concerto?

MRS. MAURRANT. Well, I was waiting for Rose, but she didn't get home. (*To* MAURRANT, *as she starts to go up the steps.*) Is she home yet, Frank?

MAURRANT. No, she ain't. Where you been all this while?

MRS. MAURRANT. Why, I've been out looking for Willie.

MAURRANT. I'll give him a good fannin', when I get hold of him.

MRS. MAURRANT. Ah, don't whip him, Frank, please don't. All boys are wild like that, when they're that age.

JONES. Sure! My boy Vincent was the same way. An' look at him today—drivin' his own taxi an' makin' a good livin'.

LIPPO (*leaning on the balustrade*). Ees jussa same t'ing wit' me. W'en Ahm twelva year, I run away—I don' never see my parent again.

MAURRANT. That's all right about that. But it ain't gonna be that way in my family.

MRS. MAURRANT (*as* MISS SIMPSON *comes out of the house*). Look out, Frank. Let the lady pass.

MISS SIMPSON. Excuse me.

(*They make way for her, as she comes down the steps.* MRS. MAURRANT *seats herself on the stoop.*)

LIPPO. Meeses Hil'brand, she gotta de tougha luck, ha? To-morra, dey gonna t'row 'er out in da street, ha?

MISS SIMPSON (*stopping at the right of the stoop and turning towards him*). Yes, they are. And if she has any place to sleep, it will only be because the Charities find her a place. And you'd be doing her a much more neighborly act, if you helped her to realize the value of money, instead of encouraging her to throw it away.

LIPPO (*with a deprecatory shrug*). Ah, lady, no! I give 'er coupla dollar, maka 'er feel good, maka me feel good—dat don' 'urt nobody.

(SHIRLEY *reappears at the window.*)

MISS SIMPSON. Yes it does. It's bad for her character.

KAPLAN (*throwing away his cigarette and laughing aloud*). Ha! You mek me leff!

MISS SIMPSON (*turning, angrily*). Nobody's asking your opinion.

KAPLAN. Dot's oll right. I'm taling you wit'out esking. You hoid maybe already dot poem:

"Orgenized cherity, measured and iced,
In der name of a kushus, stetistical Christ."

MISS SIMPSON (*fiercely*). All the same, you Jews are the first to run to the Charities.

(*She strides angrily off at the right.* LIPPO, *affecting a mincing gait, pretends to follow her.*)

KAPLAN (*leaning out of the window*). Come back and I'll tal you somet'ing will maybe do good your kerecter.

MRS. FIORENTINO. Lippo!

MRS. JONES (*highly amused*). Look at him, will ya?

LIPPO (*laughing and waving his hand*). Goodabye, lady!

(*He comes back to the stoop.*)

KAPLAN (*to the others*). Dey toin out in de street a mudder vit' two children, and dis female comes and preaches to her bourgeois morelity.

MRS. JONES (*to* MRS. FIORENTINO). He's shootin' off his face again.

SHIRLEY. Papa, it's time to go to bed!

KAPLAN (*irritably*). Lat me alone, Shoiley. (*Rising and addressing the others.*) Dees cherities are notting but anudder dewise for popperizing de verking-klesses. W'en de lendlords steal from de verkers a million dollars, dey give to de Cherities a t'ousand.

MAURRANT. Yeah! Well, who's puttin' her out on the street? What about the lan'lord here? He's a Jew, ain't he?

MRS. JONES. I'll say he's a Jew! Isaac Cohen!

KAPLAN. Jews oder not Jews—wot has dis got to do vit' de quastion? I'm not toking releegion, I'm toking economics. So long as de ke*pit*alist klesses——

MAURRANT (*interrupting*). I'm talkin' about if you don't pay your rent, you gotta move.

MRS. MAURRANT. It doesn't seem right, though, to put a poor woman out of her home.

MRS. FIORENTINO. And for her husband to run away—dot vos not right either.

LIPPO. I betcha 'e's got 'nudder woman. He find a nice blonda chicken, 'e run away.

MRS. JONES. There ought to be a law against women goin' around, stealin' other women's husbands.

MRS. FIORENTINO. Yes, dot's right, Mrs. Jones.

MAURRANT. Well, what I'm sayin' is, it ain't the landlord's fault.

KAPLAN. Eet's de folt of our economic system. So long as de institution of priwate property exeests, de verkers vill be at de moicy of de property-owning klesses.

MAURRANT. That's a lot o' bushwa! I'm a woikin' man, see? I been payin' dues for twenty-two years in the Stage-Hands Union. If we're not gettin' what we want, we call a strike, see?—and then we get it.

LIPPO. Sure! Ees same wit' me. We gotta Musician Union. We getta pay for da rehears', we getta pay for da overtime——

SHIRLEY. That's all right when you belong to a strong union. But when a union is weak, like the Teachers' Union, it doesn't do you any good.

MRS. JONES (*to* MRS. FIORENTINO). Can y' imagine that?—teachers belongin' to a union!

KAPLAN (*impatiently*). Oll dese unions eccomplish notting wotever. Oll dis does not toch de fondamental problem. So long as de tuls of industry are in de hands of de ke*pit*alist klesses, ve vill hev exploitation and sloms and——

MAURRANT. T' hell wit' all dat hooey! I'm makin' a good livin' an' I'm not doin' any kickin'.

OLSEN (*removing his pipe from his mouth*). Ve got prosperity, dis coontry.

JONES. You said somethin'!

KAPLAN. Sure, for de reech is plenty prosperity! Mister Morgan rides in his yacht and upstairs dey toin a woman vit' two children in de street.

MAURRANT. And if you was to elect a Socialist president to-morra, it would be the same thing.

MRS. FIORENTINO. Yes, dot's right, Mr. Maurrant.

JONES. You're right!

KAPLAN. Who's toking about electing presidents? Ve must put de tuls of industry in de hends of de vorking-klesses and dis ken be accomplished only by a sushal revolution!

MAURRANT. Yeah? Well, we don't want no revolutions in this country, see?

(*General chorus of assent.*)

MRS. JONES. I know all about that stuff—teachin' kids there ain't no Gawd an' that their gran'fathers was monkeys.

JONES (*rising, angrily*). Free love, like they got in Russia, huh?

(KAPLAN *makes a gesture of impatient disgust, and sinks back into his chair.*)

MAURRANT. There's too goddam many o' you Bolshevikis runnin' aroun' loose. If you don't like the way things is run here, why in hell don't you go back where you came from?

SHIRLEY. Everybody has a right to his own opinion, Mr. Maurrant.

MAURRANT. Not if they're against law and order, they ain't. We don't want no foreigners comin' in, tellin' us how to run things.

MRS. FIORENTINO. It's nothing wrong to be a foreigner. Many good people are foreigners.

LIPPO. Sure! Looka Eetalians. Looka Cristoforo Colombo! 'E'sa firs' man discov' America—'e's Eetalian, jussa like me.

MAURRANT. I'm not sayin' anythin' about that——

OLSEN (*removing his pipe*). Firs' man is Lief Ericson.

LIPPO (*excitedly, going towards* OLSEN). Wassa dat?

OLSEN. Firs' man is Lief Ericson.

LIPPO. No! No! Colombo! Cristoforo Colomb'—'e'sa firs' man discov' America—ever'body knowa dat!

(*He looks about appealingly.*)

MRS. JONES. Why, sure, everybody knows that.

JONES. Every kid learns that in school.

SHIRLEY. Ericson was really the first discoverer——

LIPPO (*yelling*). No! Colomb'!

SHIRLEY. But Columbus was the first to open America to settlement.

LIPPO (*happily, as he goes back to the stoop*). Sure, dassa wot Ahm say—Colomb' is firs'.

OLSEN. Firs' man is Lief Ericson.

(LIPPO *taps his forehead, significantly.*)

LIPPO. Looka wot Eetalian do for America—'e build bridge, 'e build railroad, 'e build subway, 'e dig sewer. Wit'out Eetalian, ees no America.

JONES. Like I heard a feller sayin': the Eye-talians built New York, the Irish run it an' the Jews own it.

(*Laughter.*)

MRS. FIORENTINO (*convulsed*). Oh! Dot's funny!

JONES (*pleased with his success*). Yep; the Jews own it all right.

MAURRANT. Yeah, an' they're the ones that's doin' all the kickin'.

SHIRLEY. It's no disgrace to be a Jew, Mr. Maurrant.

MAURRANT. I'm not sayin' it is. All I'm sayin' is, what we need in this country is a little more respect for law an' order. Look at what's happenin' to people's homes, with all this divorce an' one thing an' another. Young girls goin' around smokin' cigarettes an' their skirts up around their necks. An' a lot o' long-haired guys talkin' about free love an' birth control an' breakin' up decent people's homes. I tell you it's time somethin' was done to put the fear o' God into people!

MRS. JONES. Good for you, Mr. Maurrant!

JONES. You're damn right.

MRS. FIORENTINO. Dot's right, Mr. Maurrant!

MRS. MAURRANT. Sometimes, I think maybe they're only trying to get something out of life.

MAURRANT. Get somethin' huh? Somethin' they oughtn't to have, is that it?

MRS. MAURRANT. No; I was only thinking——

MAURRANT. Yeah, you were only thinkin', huh?

KAPLAN (*rising to his feet again*). De femily is primerily an economic institution.

MRS. JONES (*to* MRS. FIORENTINO). He's in again.

KAPLAN. W'en priwate property is ebolished, de femily will no longer hev eny reason to exeest.

SHIRLEY. Can't you keep quiet, papa?

MAURRANT (*belligerently*). Yeah? Is that so? No reason to exist, huh? Well, it's gonna exist, see? Children respectin' their parents an' doin' what they're told, get me? An' husbands an' wives, lovin' an' honorin' each other, like they said they would, when they was spliced—an' any dirty sheeny that says different is li'ble to get his head busted open, see?

MRS. MAURRANT (*springing to her feet*). Frank!

SHIRLEY (*trying to restrain* KAPLAN). Papa!

KAPLAN. Oll right! I should argue vit' a low-kless gengster.

MAURRANT (*raging*). Who's a gangster? Why, you goddam——!

(*He makes for the balustrade.*)

MRS. MAURRANT (*seizing his arm*). Frank!

JONES (*seizing the other arm*). Hey! Wait a minute! Wait a minute!

MAURRANT. Lemme go!

SHIRLEY (*interposing herself*). You should be ashamed to talk like that to an old man!

(*She slams down the window.*)

MAURRANT. Yeah? (*To* MRS. MAURRANT *and* JONES.) All right, lemme go! I ain't gonna do nothin'.

(*They release him.* SHIRLEY *expostulates with* KAPLAN *and leads him away from the window.*)

MRS. JONES (*who has run over to the right of the stoop*). Maybe if somebody handed him one, he'd shut up with his talk for a while.

LIPPO. 'E talka lika dat een Eetaly, Mussolini's gonna geeve 'eem da castor-oil.

MRS. JONES (*laughing*). Yeah? Say, that's a funny idea!

(*Still chuckling, she goes back to the railing at the left of the stoop.*)

JONES. No kiddin', is that what they do?

MRS. FIORENTINO. Yes, dot's true. My husband read it to me in the Italian paper.

MRS. MAURRANT. Why must people always be hurting and injuring each other? Why can't they live together in peace?

MAURRANT (*mockingly*). Live in peace! You're always talkin' about livin' in peace!

MRS. MAURRANT. Well, it's true, Frank. Why can't people just as well be kind to each other?

MAURRANT. Then let 'im go live with his own kind.

JONES (*coming down the steps*). Yeah, that's what I say. (*As* MRS. JONES *laughs aloud.*) What's eatin' you?

MRS. JONES. I was just thinkin' about the castor-oil.

(MAURRANT *seats himself on the right balustrade.*)

LIPPO. Sure, 'esa funny fell', Mussolini. (*Doubling up in mock pain.*) 'E geeve 'em da pain in da belly, dey no can talk. (*Suddenly.*) Look! 'Eresa da boy. 'Esa walk along da street an' reada da book. Datsa da whola troub': reada too much book.

(*While* LIPPO *is speaking,* SAMUEL KAPLAN *appears at the left. He is twenty-one, slender, with dark, unruly hair and a sensitive, mobile face. He is hatless, and his coat is slung over one shoulder. He walks along slowly, absorbed in a book. As he approaches the stoop,* SHIRLEY, *in a kimono, appears at the closed window, opens it, and is about to go away again, when she sees* SAM.)

SHIRLEY (*calling*). Sam!

SAM (*looking up*). Hello, Shirley.

SHIRLEY. Are you coming in?

SAM. No, not yet. It's too hot to go to bed.

SHIRLEY. Well, I'm tired. And papa's going to bed, too. So don't make a noise when you come in.

SAM. I won't.

SHIRLEY. Good night.

SAM. Good night.

(SHIRLEY *goes away from the window.*)

SAM (*to the others, as he seats himself on the curb to the right of the stoop*). Good evening!

SEVERAL. 'Evening.

LIPPO (*approaching* SAM). 'Ow you lika da concerto? I see you sittin' in da fronta seat.

SAM. I didn't like it. Why don't they play some real music, instead of all those Italian organ-grinder's tunes?

LIPPO (*excitedly*). Wotsa da matter? You don't lika da Verdi?

SAM. No, I don't. It's not music!

LIPPO. Wot you call music—da Tschaikov,' ha?

(*He hums derisively a few bars from the first movement of the Symphonie Pathétique.*)

SAM. Yes, Tschaikovsky—and Beethoven. Music that comes from the soul.

MRS. MAURRANT. The one I like is——

(*She hums the opening bars of Mendelssohn's Spring Song.*)

LIPPO. Dotsa da Spreeng Song from da Mendelson.

MRS. MAURRANT. Yes! I love that.

(*She goes on humming softly.*)

MRS. FIORENTINO. And the walzer von Johann Strauss.

(*She hums the Wienerwald Waltz.*)

MRS. JONES. Well, gimme a good jazz band, every time.

LIPPO (*protesting*). Ah no! Ees not music, da jazz. Ees breaka your ear.

(*He imitates the discordant blaring of a saxophone.*)

JONES (*bored*). Well, I guess I'll be on me way.

MRS. JONES. Where are you goin'?

JONES. Just around to Callahan's to shoot a little pool. Are you comin' along, Mr. Maurrant?

MAURRANT. I'm gonna wait awhile.

(*A* MAN, *with a club-foot, appears at the right and crosses the stage.*)

MRS. JONES (*as* JONES *goes toward the right*). Don't be comin' home lit, at all hours o' the mornin'.

JONES (*over his shoulder*). Aw, lay off dat stuff! I'll be back in a half-an-hour.

(*He goes off at the right.*)

A VOICE (*off-stage*). Char-lie!

MRS. JONES. Him an' his pool! Tomorra he won't be fit to go to work again.

SAM (*who has been awaiting a chance to interrupt*). When you hear Beethoven, it expresses the struggles and emotions of the human soul.

LIPPO (*waving him aside*). Ah, ees no good, da Beethoven. Ees alla time sad, sad. Ees wanna maka you cry. I don' wanna cry, I wanna laugh. Eetalian music ees make you 'appy. Ees make you feel good.

(*He sings several bars of Donna è mobile.*)

MRS. MAURRANT (*applauding*). Yes, I like that, too.

LIPPO. Ah, ees bew-tiful! Ees maka you feela fine. Ees maka you wanna dance.

(*He executes several dance steps.*)

MRS. FIORENTINO (*rising*). Vait, Lippo, I vill give you music.

(*She goes away from the window. The lights go on, in the Fiorentino apartment.*)

LIPPO (*calling after her*). Playa Puccini, Margherita! (*He hums an air from Madame Butterfly. Then as* MRS. FIORENTINO *begins to play the waltz from La Bohème on the piano.*) Ah! La Bohème! Bew-tiful! Whosa gonna dance wit' me? Meeses Maurrant, 'ow 'bout you?

MRS. MAURRANT (*with an embarrassed laugh*). Well, I don't know.

(*She looks timidly at* MAURRANT, *who gives no sign.*)

LIPPO. Ah, come on! Dansa wit' me!

(*He takes her by the hand.*)

MRS. MAURRANT. Well, all right, I will.

LIPPO. Sure, we hava nica dance.

(*They begin to dance on the sidewalk.*)

LIPPO (*to* MAURRANT). Your wife ees dansa swell.

MRS. MAURRANT (*laughing*). Oh, go on, Mr. Fiorentino! But I always loved to dance!

(*They dance on.* SANKEY *appears, at the left, carrying a paper-bag, from which the neck of a ginger-ale bottle protrudes.* MAURRANT *sees him and rises.*)

MRS. JONES (*following* MAURRANT'S *stare and seeing* SANKEY). Look out! You're blockin' traffic!

SANKEY (*stopping at the left of the stoop*). I see you're having a little dance.

(MRS. MAURRANT *sees him and stops dancing.* LIPPO *leans against the right balustrade, panting. The music goes on.*)

SANKEY. Say, go right ahead. Don't let me stop you.

MRS. MAURRANT. Oh, that's all right. I guess we've danced about enough.

(*She goes up the steps, ill at ease.*)

SANKEY. It's a pretty hot night for dancing.

MRS. MAURRANT. Yes, it is.

SANKEY (*going towards the right*). Well, I got to be going along. Good night, folks.

THE OTHERS (*except* MAURRANT). Good night.

LIPPO (*as he seats himself at the left of the stoop*). Stoppa da music, Margherita! (*The music stops.*)

(SANKEY *goes off at the right.* MRS. MAURRANT *goes quickly up the steps.*)

MAURRANT (*stopping her*). Who's that bird?

MRS. MAURRANT. Why, that's Mr. Sankey. He's the milk-collector.

MAURRANT. Oh, he is, is he? Well, what's he hangin' around here for?

MRS. MAURRANT. Well, he lives just down the block somewhere.

MRS. JONES. He's just been down to the drug-store, gettin' some ginger-ale for his wife.

MAURRANT. Yeah? Well, what I want to know is, why ain't Rose home yet?

MRS. MAURRANT. I told you, Frank——

MAURRANT. I know all about what you told me. What I'm sayin' is, you oughta be lookin' after your kids, instead of doin' so much dancin'.

MRS. MAURRANT. Why, it's the first time I've danced in I don't know when.

MAURRANT. That's all right about that. But I want 'em home, instead o' battin' around the streets, hear me?

(*While he is speaking,* WILLIE *appears sobbing at the left, his clothes torn and his face scratched. He is carrying his skates.*)

MRS. MAURRANT (*coming down the steps*). Why, Willie, what's the matter? (*Reproachfully, as* WILLIE *comes up to her, sniffling.*) Have you been fighting again?

WILLIE (*with a burst of indignation*). Well, dat big bum ain't gonna say dat to me. I'll knock da stuffin's out o' him, dat's what I'll do!

MAURRANT (*tensely, as he comes down the steps*). Who's been sayin' things to you?

WILLIE. Dat big bum, Joe Connolly, dat's who! (*Blubbering.*) I'll knock his goddam eye out, next time!

MRS. MAURRANT. Willie!

MAURRANT (*seizing* WILLIE'S *arm*). Shut up your swearin', do you hear?—or I'll give you somethin' to bawl for. What did he say to you, huh? What did he say to you?

WILLIE (*struggling*). Ow! Leggo my arm!

MRS. MAURRANT. What difference does it make what a little street-loafer like that says?

MAURRANT. Nobody's askin' you! (*To* WILLIE.) What did he say? (*He and* MRS. MAURRANT *exchange a swift involuntary look; then* MAURRANT *releases the boy.*) G'wan up to bed now, an' don't let me hear no more out o' you. (*Raising his hand.*) G'wan now. Beat it!

(WILLIE *ducks past* MAURRANT *and hurries up the steps and into the vestibule.*)

MRS. MAURRANT. Wait, Willie, I'll go with you. (*She goes up the steps, then stops and turns.*) Are you coming up, Frank?

MAURRANT. No I ain't. I'm goin' around to Callahan's for a drink, an' if Rose ain't home when I get back, there's gonna be trouble.

(*Without another glance or word, he goes off at the right.* MRS. MAURRANT *looks after him for a moment with a troubled expression.*)

MRS. MAURRANT (*entering the vestibule*). Well, good night, all.

THE OTHERS. Good night.

(SAM *rises. As* MRS. MAURRANT *and* WILLIE *enter the house,* MRS. FIORENTINO *reappears at the window.*)

MRS. FIORENTINO. Lippo!

(*She sees that something is wrong.*)

MRS. JONES. Say, you missed it all!

(SAM, *about to go up the steps, stops at the right of the stoop.*)

MRS. FIORENTINO (*eagerly*). Vat?

MRS. JONES (*volubly*). Well, they were dancin', see? An' who should come along but Sankey!

MRS. FIORENTINO. Tt!

(*A light appears in the Maurrant apartment.*)

MRS. JONES. Well, there was the three o' them—Mr. Maurrant lookin' at Sankey as if he was ready to kill him, an' Mrs. Maurrant as white as a sheet, an' Sankey as innocent as the babe unborn.

MRS. FIORENTINO. Did he say something?

MRS. JONES. No, not till after Sankey was gone. Then he wanted to know who he was an' what he was doin' here. "He's the milk-collector," she says.

MRS. FIORENTINO. It's joost awful.

MRS. JONES. Oh, an' then Willie comes home.

LIPPO. Da boy tella 'eem 'is mamma ees a whore an' Weelie leeck 'im.

MRS. JONES. Well, an' what else is she?

SAM (*unable longer to restrain himself*). Stop it! Stop it! Can't you let her alone? Have you no hearts? Why do you tear her to pieces like a pack of wolves? It's cruel, cruel!

(*He chokes back a sob, then dashes abruptly into the house.*)

LIPPO (*rising to his feet and yelling after him*). Wotsa matter you?

MRS. JONES. Well, listen to him, will you! He must be goin' off his nut, too.

LIPPO. 'Esa reada too mucha book. Ees bad for you.

MRS. FIORENTINO. I think he is loving the girl.

MRS. JONES. Yeah? Well, that's all the Maurrants need is to have their daughter get hooked up wit' a Jew. It's a fine house to be livin' in, ain't it, between the Maurrants upstairs, an' that bunch o' crazy Jews down here.

(*A* GIRL *appears at the left, glancing apprehensively, over her shoulder, at a* MAN *who is walking down the street behind her. They cross the stage and go off at the right.*)

MRS. JONES (*as* MRS. OLSEN *comes up the cellar steps and over to the stoop*). Well, good night.

MRS. FIORENTINO. Good night, Mrs. Jones.

LIPPO. Goo' night, Meeses Jones.

MRS. JONES. Wait a minute, Mrs. Olsen. I'll go with you.

(MRS. JONES *and* MRS. OLSEN *enter the house.* OLSEN *yawns mightily, knocks the ashes from his pipe, and goes down the cellar steps.* WILLIE MAURRANT *leans out of the window and spits into the areaway. Then he leaves the window and turns out the light. A* POLICEMAN *appears, at the right, and strolls across the stage.*)

LIPPO (*who has gone up the steps*). Margherita, eef I ever ketcha you sleepin' wit' da meelkaman, Ahm gonna breaka your neck.

MRS. FIORENTINO (*yawning*). Stop your foolishness, Lippo, and come to bed!

(LIPPO *laughs and enters the house.* MRS. FIORENTINO *takes the pillow off the windowsill, closes the window, and starts to pull down the shade.* ROSE MAURRANT *and* HARRY EASTER *appear at the left.* ROSE *is a pretty girl of twenty, cheaply but rather tastefully dressed.* EASTER *is about thirty-five, good-looking, and obviously prosperous.*)

MRS. FIORENTINO. Good evening, Miss Maurrant.

ROSE (*as they pass the window*). Oh good evening, Mrs. Fiorentino.

(ROSE *and* EASTER *cross to the stoop.* MRS. FIORENTINO *looks at them a moment, then pulls down the shade and turns out the lights.*)

ROSE (*stopping at the foot of the steps*). Well, this is where I live, Mr. Easter. (*She extends her hand.*) I've had a lovely time.

EASTER (*taking her hand*). Why, you're not going to leave me like this, are you? I've hardly had a chance to talk to you.

ROSE (*laughing*). We've been doing nothing but talking since six o'clock.

(*She tries gently to extricate her hand.*)

EASTER (*still holding it*). No, we haven't. We've been eating and dancing. And now, just when I want to talk to you—(*He puts his other arm around her.*) Rose——

ROSE (*rather nervously*). Please don't, Mr. Easter. Please let go. I think there's somebody coming.

(*She frees herself as the house-door opens and* MRS. OLSEN *appears in the vestibule. They stand in silence, as* MRS. OLSEN *puts the door off the latch, tries it to see that it is locked, dims the light in the vestibule and comes out on the stoop.*)

MRS. OLSEN (*as she comes down the steps*). Goot evening, Miss Maurrant.

(*She darts a swift look at* EASTER *and crosses to the cellar steps.*)

ROSE. Good evening, Mrs. Olsen. How's the baby?

MRS. OLSEN. She vas cryin' all the time. I tank she vas gettin' new teet'.

ROSE. Oh, the poor little thing! What a shame!

MRS. OLSEN (*as she goes down the steps*). Yes, ma'am. Goot night, Miss Maurrant.

ROSE. Good night, Mrs. Olsen. (*To* EASTER.) She's got the cutest little baby you ever saw.

EASTER (*rather peevishly*). Yeah? That's great. (*Taking* ROSE'S *hand again.*) Rose, listen——

ROSE. I've really got to go upstairs now, Mr. Easter. It's awfully late.

EASTER. Well, can't I come up with you for a minute?

ROSE (*positively*). No, of course not!

EASTER. Why not?

ROSE. Why, we'd wake everybody up. Anyhow, my father wouldn't like it.

EASTER. Aren't you old enough to do what you like?

ROSE. It's not that. Only I think when you're living with people, there's no use doing things you know they don't like. (*Embarrassed.*) Anyhow, there's only the front room and my little brother sleeps there. So good night, Mr. Easter.

EASTER (*taking both her hands*). Rose—I'm crazy about you.

ROSE. Please let me go now.

EASTER. Kiss me good-night.

ROSE. No.

EASTER. Why not, hm?

ROSE. I don't want to.

EASTER. Just one kiss.

ROSE. No.

EASTER. Yes!

(*He takes her in his arms and kisses her.* ROSE *frees herself and goes to the right of the stoop.*)

ROSE (*her bosom heaving*). It wasn't nice of you to do that.

EASTER (*going over to her*). Why not? Didn't you like it? Hm?

ROSE. Oh, it's not that.

EASTER. Then what is it, hm?

ROSE (*turning and facing him*). You know very well what it is. You've got a wife, haven't you?

EASTER. What of it? I tell you I'm clean off my nut about you.

ROSE (*nervously, as the house-door opens*). Look out! Somebody's coming.

(EASTER *goes to the other side of the stoop and they fall into a self-conscious silence, as* MRS. JONES *comes out of the house, leading an ill-conditioned dog.*)

MR. JONES (*as she comes down the steps*). Oh, good evenin'.

(*She stares at* EASTER, *then goes towards the right.*)

ROSE. Good evening, Mrs. Jones. It's been a terrible day, hasn't it?

MRS. JONES. Yeah. Awful. (*Stopping.*) I think your father's been kinda worried about you.

ROSE. Oh, has he?

MRS. JONES. Yeah. Well, I gotta give Queenie her exercise. Good night.

(*She stares at* EASTER *again, then goes off at right.*)

ROSE. Good night, Mrs. Jones. (*To* EASTER.) I'll soon have all the neighbors talking about me.

EASTER (*going over to her again*). What can they say, hm?—that they saw you saying good-night to somebody on the front door-step?

ROSE. They can say worse than that—and what's more, they will, too.

EASTER. Well, why not snap out of it all?

ROSE. Out of what?

EASTER (*indicating the house*). This! The whole business. Living in a dirty old tenement like this; working all day in a real-estate office, for a measly twenty-five a week. You're not going to try to tell me you like living this way, are you?

ROSE. No, I can't say that I like it especially. But maybe it won't always be this way. Anyhow, I guess I'm not so much better than anybody else.

EASTER (*taking her hand*). Do you know what's the matter with you? You're not wise to yourself. Why, you've got just about everything, you have. You've got looks and personality and a bean on your shoulders—there's nothing you haven't got. You've got It, I tell you.

ROSE. You shouldn't keep looking at me, all the time, at the office. The other girls are beginning to pass hints about it.

EASTER (*releasing her hand, genuinely perturbed*). Is that a fact? You see, that shows you! I never even knew I was looking at you. I guess I just can't keep my eyes off you. Well, we've got to do something about it.

ROSE (*nervously snapping the clasp of her handbag*). I guess the only thing for me to do is to look for another job.

EASTER. Yes, that's what I've been thinking, too. (*As she is about to demur.*) Wait a minute, honey! I've been doing a little thinking and I've got it all doped out. The first thing you do is throw up your job, see?

ROSE. But——

EASTER. Then you find yourself a nice, cozy little apartment somewhere. (*As she is about to interrupt again.*) Just a minute, now! Then you get yourself a job on the stage.

ROSE. How could I get a job on the stage?

EASTER. Why, as easy as walking around the block. I've got three or four friends in the show-business. Ever hear of Harry Porkins?

ROSE. No.

EASTER. Well, he's the boy that put on Mademoiselle Marie last year. He's an old pal of mine, and all I'd have to say to him is: (*Putting his arm around her shoulder.*) "Harry, here's a little girl I'm interested in," and he'd sign you up in a minute.

ROSE. I don't think I'd be any good on the stage.

EASTER. Why, what are you talking about, sweetheart? There's a dozen girls, right now, with their names up in electric lights, that haven't got half your stuff. All you got to do is go about in the right way—put up a little front, see? Why, half the game is nothing but bluff. Get yourself a classy little apartment, and fill it up with trick furniture, see? Then you doll yourself up in a flock of Paris clothes and you throw a couple or three parties and you're all set. (*Taking her arm.*) Wouldn't you *like* to be on Broadway?

ROSE. I don't believe I ever could be.

EASTER. Isn't it worth trying? What have you got here, hm? This is no kind of a racket for a girl like you. (*Taking her hand.*) You do like me a little, don't you?

ROSE. I don't know if I do or not.

EASTER. Why, sure you do. And once you get to know me better, you'd like me even more. I'm no Valentino, but I'm not a bad scout. Why, think of all the good times we could have together—you with a little apartment and all. And maybe we could get us a little car——

ROSE. And what about your wife?

EASTER (*letting go her hand*). The way I figure it is, she doesn't have to know anything about it. She stays up there in Bronxville, and there are lots of times when business keeps me in New York. Then, in the Summer, she goes to the mountains. Matter of fact, she's going next week and won't be back until September.

ROSE (*shaking her head and going towards the stoop*). I don't think it's the way I'd want things to be.

EASTER. Why, there's nothing really wrong about it,

ROSE. Maybe there isn't. But it's just the way I feel about it, I guess.

EASTER. Why, you'd get over that in no time. There's lots of girls——

ROSE. Yes, I know there are. But you've been telling me all along I'm different.

EASTER. Sure, you're different. You're in a class by yourself. Why, sweetheart——

(*He tries to take her in his arms.*)

ROSE (*pushing him away*). No. And you mustn't call me sweetheart.

EASTER. Why not?

ROSE. Because I'm not your sweetheart.

EASTER. I want you to be——

(*A sudden yell of pain is heard from upstairs. They both look up, greatly startled.*)

EASTER. My God, what's that—a murder?

ROSE. It must be poor Mrs. Buchanan. She's expecting a baby.

EASTER. Why does she yell like that? God, I thought somebody was being killed.

ROSE. The poor thing! (*With sudden impatience she starts up the steps.*) I've got to go now. Good night.

EASTER (*taking her hand*). But, Rose——

ROSE (*freeing her hand quickly*). No, I've got to go. (*Suddenly.*) Look, there's my father. There'll only be an argument, if he sees you.

EASTER. All right, I'll go.

(*He goes toward the left, as* MAURRANT *appears at the right.*)

ROSE (*going up to the top step*). Good night.

EASTER. Good night.

(*He goes off at the left.* ROSE *begins searching in her hand-bag for her latch-key.*)

ROSE (*as* MAURRANT *approaches*). Hello, pop.

MAURRANT (*stopping at the foot of the steps*). Who was that you was talkin' to?

ROSE. That's Mr. Easter. He's the manager of the office.

MAURRANT. What's he doin' here? You been out wit' him?

ROSE. Yes, he took me out to dinner.

MAURRANT. Oh, he did, huh?

ROSE. Yes, I had to stay late to get out some letters. You see, pop, the office is closed tomorrow, on account of Mr. Jacobson's funeral——

MAURRANT. Yeah, I know all about that. This is a hell of a time to be gettin' home from dinner.

ROSE. Well, we danced afterwards.

MAURRANT. Oh, you danced, huh? With a little pettin' on the side, is that it?

ROSE (*rather angrily, as she seats herself on the left balustrade*). I don't see why you can never talk to me in a nice way.

MAURRANT. So you're startin' to go on pettin' parties, are you?

ROSE. Who said I was on a petting party?

MAURRANT. I suppose he didn't kiss you or nothin', huh?

ROSE. No, he didn't! And if he did——

MAURRANT. It's your own business, is that it? (*Going up the steps.*) Well, I'm gonna make it my business, see? Is this bird married? (ROSE *does not answer.*) I t'ought so! They're all alike, them guys—all after the one thing. Well, get this straight. No married men ain't gonna come nosin' around my family, get me?

ROSE (*rising agitatedly as the house-door opens*). Be quiet, pop! There's somebody coming.

MAURRANT. I don't care!

(BUCHANAN *hurries out of the house. He is a small and pasty young man—a typical "white-collar slave." He has hastily put on his coat and trousers over his pajamas and his bare feet are in slippers.*)

BUCHANAN (*as he comes down the steps*). I think the baby's coming!

ROSE (*solicitously*). Can I do anything, Mr. Buchanan?

BUCHANAN (*as he hurries towards the left*). No, I'm just going to phone for the doctor.

ROSE (*coming down the steps*). Let me do it, and you go back to your wife.

BUCHANAN. Well, if you wouldn't mind. It's Doctor John Wilson. (*Handing her a slip of paper.*) Here's his number. And the other number is her sister, Mrs. Thomas. And here's two nickels. Tell them both to come right away. She's got terrible pains. (*Another scream from upstairs.*) Listen to her! I better go back.

(*He dashes up the steps and into the house.*)

ROSE. Oh, the poor woman! Pop, tell ma to go up to her. Hurry!

MAURRANT. Aw, all right.

(*He follows* BUCHANAN *into the house.* ROSE *hurries off at the left, just as* MAE JONES *and* DICK MCGANN *appear.* MAE *is a vulgar shop-girl of twenty one;* DICK, *a vacuous youth of about the same age.* MAE *is wearing* DICK'S *straw hat and they are both quite drunk.*)

MAE (*to* ROSE). Hello, Rose. What's your hurry?

ROSE (*without stopping*). It's Mrs. Buchanan. I've got to phone to the doctor. (*She hurries off.*)

DICK (*as they approach the stoop*). Say, who's your little friend?

MAE. Oh, that's Rose Maurrant. She lives in the house.

DICK. She's kinda cute, ain't she?

MAE (*seating herself on the stoop*). Say, accordin' to you, anythin' in a skirt is kinda cute—providin' the skirt is short enough.

DICK. Yeah, but they ain't any of 'em as cute as you, Mae.

MAE (*yawning and scratching her leg*). Yeah?

DICK. Honest, I mean it. How 'bout a little kiss?

(*He puts his arms about her and plants a long kiss upon her lips. She submits with an air of intense boredom.*)

DICK (*removing his lips*). Say, you might show a little en-thoo-siasm.

MAE (*rouging her lips*). Say, you seem to think I oughta hang out a flag every time some bozo decides to wipe off his mouth on me.

DICK. De trouble wit' you is you need another little snifter.

(*He reaches for his flask.*)

MAE. Nope! I can't swaller any more o' that rotten gin o' yours.

DICK. Why, it ain't so worse. I don't mind it no more since I had that brass linin' put in me stomach. Well, happy days!

(*He takes a long drink.*)

MAE (*rising indignantly*). Hey, for God's sake, what are you doin'—emptyin' the flask?

DICK (*removing the flask from his lips*). I t'ought you didn't want none.

MAE. Can't you take a joke?

(*She snatches the flask from him and drains it, kicking out at* DICK, *to prevent his taking it from her.*)

DICK (*snatching the empty flask*). Say, you wanna watch your step, baby, or you're li'ble to go right up in a puff o' smoke.

MAE (*whistling*). Phew! Boy! I feel like a t'ree alarm fire! Say, what de hell do dey make dat stuff out of?

DICK. T'ree parts dynamite an' one part army-mule. Dey use it for blastin' out West.

MAE (*bursting raucously into a jazz tune*). Da-da-da-da-dee! Da-da-da-da-dee! (*She executes some dance steps.*)

DICK. Say, shut up, will ya? You'll be wakin' the whole neighborhood.

MAE (*boisterously*). What the hell do I care? Da-da-da-da-dee! Da-da-da-da-dee! (*Suddenly amorous, as she turns an unsteady pirouette.*) Kiss me, kid!

DICK. I'll say!

(*They lock in a long embrace.* SAM, *coatless, his shirt-collar open, appears at the window, watches the pair for a moment, and then turns away, obviously disgusted. They do not see him.*)

DICK (*taking* MAE's *arm*). Come on!

MAE. Wait a minute! Where y' goin'?

DICK. Come on, I'm tellin' ya! Fred Hennessy gimme de key to his apartment. Dere won't be nobody dere.

MAE (*protesting feebly*). I oughta go home. (*Her hand to her head.*) Oh, baby! Say, nail down dat sidewalk, will ya?

DICK. Come on!

(*Rose appears at the left.*)

MAE. Sweet papa! (*She kisses* DICK *noisily; then bursts into song again.*) Da-da-da-da-dee! Da-da-da-da-dee! (*As they pass* ROSE.) Hello, Rose. How's de milkman?

DICK (*raising his hat with drunken politeness*). Goo' night, sweetheart.

(*They go off at the left,* MAE's *snatches of song dying away in the distance.* ROSE *stands still, for a moment, choking back her mortification.*)

BUCHANAN's VOICE. Miss Maurrant, did you get them?

ROSE (*looking up*). Why yes, I did. The doctor will be here right away. And Mrs. Thomas said it would take her about an hour.

(VINCENT JONES *appears at the right and stops near the stoop. He is a typical New York taxicab driver, in a cap.* ROSE *does not see him.*)

BUCHANAN's VOICE. She's got terrible pains. Your mother's up here with her. (MRS. BUCHANAN *is heard calling faintly.*) I think she's calling me.

(ROSE *goes towards the stoop and sees* VINCENT.)

VINCENT. Hello, Rosie.

ROSE. Good evening.

(*She tries to pass, but he blocks her way.*)

VINCENT. What's your hurry?

ROSE. It's late.

VINCENT. You don't wanna go to bed, yet. Come on, I'll take you for a ride in me hack.

(*He puts his arm about her.*)

ROSE. Please let me pass.

(SAM *appears at the window. They do not see him.*)

VINCENT (*enjoying* ROSE's *struggle to escape*). You got a lot o' stren'th, ain't you? Say, do you know you're gettin' fat? (*He passes one hand over her body.*)

ROSE. Let me go, you big tough.

SAM (*simultaneously*). Take your hands off her!

(*He climbs quickly out of the window and onto the stoop.* VINCENT, *surprised, releases* ROSE *and steps to the sidewalk.* ROSE *goes up the steps.* SAM, *trembling with excitement and fear, stands on the top step.* VINCENT *glowers up at him.*)

VINCENT. Well, look who's here! (*Mockingly.*) Haster gesehn de fish in de Bowery? (*Menacingly.*) What de hell do you you want?

SAM (*chokingly*). You keep your hands off her!

VINCENT. Yeah? (*Sawing the air with his hands.*) Oi, Jakie! (*He suddenly lunges forward, seizes* SAM's *arm, pulls him violently by the right hand down the steps and swings him about, so that they stand face to face, to the left of the stoop.* ROSE *comes down between them.*) Now what o' ya got t' say?

ROSE. Let him alone!

SAM (*inarticulately*). If you touch her again——

VINCENT (*mockingly*). If I touch her again——! (*Savagely.*) Aw, shut up, you little kike bastard!

(*He brushes* ROSE *aside and putting his open hand against* SAM's *face, sends him sprawling to the pavement.*)

ROSE (*her fists clenched*). You big coward.

VINCENT (*standing over* SAM). Get up, why don't you?

ROSE (*crossing to* SAM). If you hit him again, I'll call my father.

VINCENT (*as* MRS. JONES *and the dog appear at the right*). Gee, don't frighten me like dat. I got a weak heart.

(*He is sobered, nevertheless.* SAM *picks himself up.*)

VINCENT (*as* MRS. JONES *approaches*). Hello, ma.

MRS. JONES (*with maternal pride*). Hello, Vincent. What's goin' on here?

VINCENT. Oh, just a little friendly argument. Ikey Finkelstein don't like me to say good evenin' to his girl friend.

ROSE. You'd better keep your hands to yourself hereafter.

VINCENT. Is dat so? Who said so, huh?

MRS. JONES. Come on, Vincent. Come on upstairs. I saved some stew for you.

VINCENT. All right, I'm comin'. (*To* ROSE.) Good night, dearie.

(*He makes a feint at* SAM, *who starts back in terror.* VINCENT *laughs.*)

MRS. JONES. Aw, let 'im alone, Vincent.

VINCENT (*as he goes up the steps*). Who's touchin' him? A little cockroach like dat ain't woit' my time. (*To* ROSE.) Some sheik you picked out for yourself! (*He enters the vestibule and opens the door with his latchkey.*)

MRS. JONES (*going up the steps*). You seem to have plenty of admirers, Miss Maurrant. (*Passing on the top step.*) But I guess you come by it natural.

(ROSE *does not reply.* MRS. JONES *follows* VINCENT *into the house.* ROSE *averts her head to keep back the tears.* SAM *stands facing the house, his whole body quivering with emotion. Suddenly he raises his arms, his fists clenched.*)

SAM (*hysterically, as he rushes to the foot of the stoop*). The dirty bum! I'll kill him!

ROSE (*turning and going to him*). It's all right, Sam. Never mind.

SAM (*sobbing*). I'll kill him! I'll kill him!

(*He throws himself on the stoop and, burying his head in his arms, sobs hysterically.* ROSE *sits beside him and puts her arm about him.*)

ROSE. It's all right, Sam. Everything's all right. Why should you pay any attention to a big tough like that? (SAM *does not answer.* ROSE *caresses his hair and he grows calmer.*) He's nothing but a loafer, you know that. What do you care what he says?

SAM (*without raising his head*). I'm a coward.

ROSE. Why no, you're not, Sam.

SAM. Yes, I am. I'm a coward.

ROSE. Why, he's not worth your little finger, Sam. You wait and see. Ten years from now, he'll still be driving a taxi and you—why, you'll be so far above him, you won't even remember he's alive.

SAM. I'll never be anything.

ROSE. Why, don't talk like that, Sam. A boy with your brains and ability. Graduating from college with honors and all that! Why, if I were half as smart as you, I'd be just so proud of myself!

SAM. What's the good of having brains, if nobody ever looks at you—if nobody knows you exist?

ROSE (*gently*). I know you exist, Sam.

SAM. It wouldn't take much to make you forget me.

ROSE. I'm not so sure about that. Why do you say that, Sam?

SAM. Because I know. It's different with you. You have beauty—people look at you—you have a place in the world—

ROSE. I don't know. It's not always so easy, being a girl—I often wish I were a man. It seems to me that when you're a man, it's so much easier to sort of—be yourself, to kind of be the way you feel. But when you're a girl, it's different. It doesn't seem to matter what you are, or what you're thinking or feeling—all that men seem to care about is just the one thing. And when you're sort of trying to find out just where you're at, it makes it hard. Do you see what I mean? (*Hesitantly.*) Sam, there's something I want to ask you——

(*She stops.*)

SAM. (*turning to her*). What is it, Rose?

ROSE. I wouldn't dream of asking anybody but you. (*With a great effort.*) Sam, do you think it's true—what they're saying about my mother?

(SAM *averts his head, without answering.*)

ROSE (*wretchedly*). I guess it is, isn't it?

SAM (*agitatedly*). They were talking here, before—I couldn't stand it any more! (*He clasps his head and, springing to his feet, goes to the right of the stoop.*) Oh, God, why do we go on living in this sewer?

ROSE (*appealingly*). What can I do, Sam? (SAM *makes a helpless gesture.*) You see, my father means well enough, and all that, but he's always been sort of strict and—I don't know—sort of making you freeze up, when you really wanted to be nice and loving. That's the whole trouble, I guess; my mother never had anybody to really love her. She's sort of gay and happy-like—you know, she likes having a good time and all that. But my father is different. Only—the way things are now—everybody talking and making remarks, all the neighbors spying and whispering —it sort of makes me feel—— (*She shudders.*) I don't know——!

SAM (*coming over to her again*). I wish I could help you, Rose.

ROSE. You do help me, Sam—just by being nice and sympathetic and talking things over with me. There's so few people you can really talk to, do you know what I mean? Sometimes, I get the feeling that I'm all alone in the world and that——

(*A scream of pain from* MRS. BUCHANAN.)

ROSE (*springing to her feet*). Oh, just listen to her!

SAM. Oh, God!

ROSE. The poor thing! She must be having terrible pains.

SAM. That's all there is in life—nothing but pain. From before we're born, until we die! Everywhere you look, oppression and cruelty! If it doesn't come from Nature, it comes from humanity—humanity trampling on itself and tearing at its own throat. The whole world is nothing but a blood-stained arena, filled with misery and suffering. It's too high a price to pay for life—life isn't worth it!

(*He seats himself despairingly on the stoop.*)

ROSE (*putting her hand on his shoulder*). Oh, I don't know, Sam. I feel blue and discouraged sometimes, too. And I get a sort of feeling of, oh, what's the use. Like last night. I hardly slept all night, on account of the heat and on account of thinking about—well, all sorts of things. And this morning, when I got up, I felt so miserable. Well, all of a sudden, I decided I'd walk to the office. And when I got to the Park, everything looked so green and fresh, that I got a kind of feeling of, well, maybe it's not so bad, after all. And then, what do you think?—all of a sudden, I saw a big lilac-bush, with some flowers still on it. It made me think about the poem you said for me—remember?—the one about the lilacs.

SAM (*quoting*).

"When lilacs last in the dooryard bloom'd
And the great star early droop'd in the western sky in the night,
I mourn'd and yet shall mourn, with ever-returning Spring."

(*He repeats the last line.*)

I mourn'd and yet shall mourn, with ever-returning Spring? Yes!

ROSE. No, not that part. I mean the part about the farmhouse. Say it for me, Sam. (*She sits at his feet.*)

SAM. "In the door-yard, fronting an old farm-house, near the white-washed palings,
Stands the lilac-bush, tall-growing, with heart-shaped leaves of rich green,
With many a pointed blossom, rising delicate, with the perfume strong I love,
With every leaf a miracle—and from this bush in the door-yard,
With delicate-color'd blossoms and heart-shaped leaves of rich green,
A sprig with its flower I break."

ROSE (*eagerly*). Yes, that's it! That's just what I felt like doing—breaking off a little bunch of the flowers. But then I thought, maybe a policeman or somebody would see me, and then I'd get into trouble; so I didn't.

BUCHANAN'S VOICE. Miss Maurrant! Miss Maurrant!

(SAM *and* ROSE *spring to their feet and look up.*)

ROSE. Yes?

BUCHANAN'S VOICE. Do you mind phoning to the doctor again? She's getting worse.

ROSE. Yes, sure I will. (*She starts to go.*) Wait! Maybe this is the doctor now.

BUCHANAN'S VOICE (*excitedly as* DR. WILSON *appears at the left*). Yes, that's him. Mrs. Maurrant! Tell her the doctor's here! Doctor, I guess you're none too soon.

DR. WILSON (*a seedy, middle-aged man in a crumpled Panama*). Plenty of time. Just don't get excited.

(*He throws away his cigarette and enters the vestibule. The mechanical clicking of the door-latch is heard as* DR. WILSON *goes into the house.*

ROSE. I hope she won't have to suffer much longer.

MAURRANT (*appearing at the window, in his undershirt*). Rose!

ROSE (*rather startled*). Yes, pop, I'll be right up.

MAURRANT. Well, don't be makin' me call you again, d'ya hear?

ROSE. I'm coming right away.

(MAURRANT *leaves the window.*)

ROSE. I'd better go up now, Sam.

SAM. Do you have to go to bed when you're told, like a child?

ROSE. I know, Sam, but there's so much wrangling goes on all the time, as it is, what's the use of having any more? Good night, Sam. There was something I wanted to talk to you about, but it will have to be another time.

(*She holds out her hand.* SAM *takes it and holds it in his.*)

SAM (*trembling and rising to his feet*). Rose, will you kiss me?

ROSE (*simply*). Why, of course I will, Sam.

(*She offers him her lips. He clasps her in a fervent embrace, to which she submits but does not respond.*)

ROSE (*freeing herself gently*). Don't be discouraged about things, Sam. You wait and see—you're going to do big things some day. I've got lots of confidence in you.

SAM (*turning away his head*). I wonder if you really have, Rose?

ROSE. Why, of course, I have! And don't forget it! Good night. I hope it won't be too hot to sleep.

SAM. Good night, Rose.

(*He watches her, as she opens the door with her latch-key and goes into the house. Then he goes to the stoop and seating himself, falls into a reverie. A* POLICEMAN *appears at the right and strolls across, but* SAM *is oblivious to him. In the distance, a home-comer sings drunkenly. A light appears in the* MAURRANT *hall-bedroom, and a moment later* ROSE *comes to the window and leans out.*)

ROSE (*calling softly*). Hoo-hoo! Sam! (SAM *looks up, then rises.*) Good night, Sam.

(*She wafts him a kiss.*)

SAM (*with deep feeling*). Good night, Rose dear.

(*She smiles at him. Then she pulls down the shade.* SAM *looks up for a moment, then resumes his seat. A scream from* MRS. BUCHANAN *makes him shudder. A deep rhythmic snoring emanates from the Fiorentino apartment. A steamboat whistle is heard. The snoring in the* FIORENTINO *apartment continues.* SAM *raises his clenched hands to heaven. A distant clock begins to strike twelve.* SAM'S *arms and head drop forward.*)

THE CURTAIN FALLS SLOWLY

ACT TWO

Daybreak, the next morning. It is still quite dark and comparatively quiet. The rhythmic snoring in the FIORENTINO *apartment is still heard, and now and then a distant "L" train or speeding automobile. A moment after the rise of the curtain,* JONES *appears, at the right on his way home from the speakeasy. He reels slightly, but negotiates the steps and entrance-door without too much difficulty. It grows lighter—and noisier. The street-light goes out. The* OLSEN *baby begins to cry. An alarm clock rings. A dog barks. A canary begins to sing. Voices are heard in the distance. They die out and other voices are heard.*

The house-door opens and DR. WILSON *comes out, passing* JONES *at the top of the stoop.* DR. WILSON *stands on the steps and yawns the yawn of an over-tired man. Then he lights a cigarette and goes towards the left.*

BUCHANAN'S VOICE. Doctor!

DR. WILSON (*stopping and looking up*). Well?

BUCHANAN'S VOICE. What if she does wake up?

DR. WILSON (*sharply*). She won't, I've told you! She's too exhausted. The best thing you can do is lie down and get some sleep yourself.

(*As he goes off at the left,* MAE *and* DICK *appear. They walk slowly and listlessly and far apart.*)

DICK (*as they reach the stoop*). Well, goo' night.

MAE (*with a yawn, as she finds her latch-key*). Goo' night. (*Going up the steps and looking towards the Fiorentino apartment.*) Aw, shut up, you wop!

DICK (*his dignity wounded*). How 'bout kissin' me good-night?

MAE (*venomously, from the top step*). For God's sake, ain't you had enough kissin' for one night!

(*She enters the vestibule and puts the key in the lock. The ringing of an alarm clock is heard.*)

DICK (*raising his voice*). Well, say, if that's the way you feel about it——

MAE. Aw, go to hell!

(*She enters the house. The alarm clock has stopped ringing.*)

DICK. You dirty little tart!

(*He stands muttering to himself for a moment, then goes off at the right, passing the* POLICEMAN, *who looks at him suspiciously. The sounds of a Swedish quarrel are heard from the janitor's apartment. The baby is still crying. As the* POLICEMAN *goes left, a* MILKMAN *ap-*

pears, whistling and carrying a rack of full milk-bottles.)

THE POLICEMAN. Hello, Louie.

(*The snoring in the Fiorentino apartment stops.*)

THE MILKMAN. Hello, Harry. Goin' to be another scorcher.

THE POLICEMAN. You said it.

(*He goes off at the left.*)

(*The* MILKMAN *crosses to the cellar steps.* MAE *appears, at the hall bedroom window of the Jones apartment, and removes her dress over her head.* THE MILKMAN, *about to go down the steps, sees her and stops to watch.* MAE, *about to slip out of her step-in, sees him, throws him an angry look and pulls down the shade. The* MILKMAN *grins and goes down the cellar steps.* CHARLIE HILDEBRAND *comes out of the house. He is chewing gum and as he comes out to the top of the stoop, he scatters the wrappings of the stick of gum on the stoop. Then he jumps down the four steps of the stoop in one jump, and goes off at the left, pulling the chewing-gum out in a long ribbon, and carefully avoiding all the cracks in the pavement. A* YOUNG WORKMAN, *carrying a kit of tools and a tin lunch-box, appears at the left, extinguishes the red light on the excavation, and opening the door, goes in. A* TRAMP *comes on at the right and shuffles across. He sees a cigar butt on the pavement, picks it up and pockets it, as he exits at the left.* ROSE, *in her nightgown, appears at the window, yawns slightly and disappears. It is daylight now. The baby stops crying.* MRS. OLSEN *comes up the cellar steps. She goes up the stoop, turns out the light in the vestibule, and takes the door off the latch. The* MILKMAN *comes up the cellar steps, his tray laden with empty bottles and goes off, whistling, at the left.* SAM, *coatless, a book in his hand, appears at the window. He looks out for a moment, then climbs out on the stoop, looks up at* ROSE'S *window, then seats himself and begins to read.* WILLIE *comes out of the house.*)

WILLIE (*chanting, as he comes down the steps*). Fat, Fat, the water-rat, Fifty bullets in his hat.

SAM. Hello, Willie. Is Rose up yet?

WILLIE (*without stopping or looking at him*). Yeah. I don't know. I guess so.

(*He turns a somersault and goes off at left, continuing his chanting.* SAM *glances up at* ROSE'S *window again, then resumes his book.* MRS. JONES *and her dog come out of the house.*)

MRS. JONES (*haughtily, as she comes down the steps*). Mornin'.

SAM (*scarcely looking up from his book*). Good morning.

(MRS. JONES *and the dog go off at the right. A middle-aged workman, carrying a large coil of wire, appears at the left and goes to the door of the excavation.* MRS. OLSEN *comes out of the house and exits into the basement.*)

THE WORKMAN (*calling*). You down there, Eddie?

A VOICE (*from the depths*). Yeah!

THE WORKMAN. All right!

(*He climbs down into the excavation.* ROSE *comes to window and pulls up the shade.* WILLIE *and* CHARLIE *can be heard, offstage left, engaged in an earnest conversation.*)

CHARLIE (*offstage*). He could not!

WILLIE (*offstage*). He could so!

(*They appear at left. Each has under his arm a paper-bag, from which a loaf of bread protrudes.*)

CHARLIE. I'll betcha he couldn't.

WILLIE. I'll betcha he could.

CHARLIE. I'll betcha a million dollars he couldn't.

WILLIE. I'll betcha five million dollars he could. Hold that! (*He hands* CHARLIE *his loaf of bread and turns a cart-wheel.*) Bet you can't do it.

CHARLIE. Bet I can.

(*He puts both loaves of bread on the pavement, attempts a cart-wheel and fails.*)

WILLIE (*laughing raucously*). Haw-haw! Told you you couldn't!

CHARLIE. Can you do this?

(*He turns a back somersault.*)

WILLIE. Sure—easy! (*He turns a back somersault. They pick up their loaves again.* WILLIE'S *drops out of the bag, but he dusts it with his hand and replaces it.*) How many steps can you jump up?

CHARLIE. Three.

(*He jumps up three steps.*)

WILLIE. I can do four.

CHARLIE. Let's see you.

(WILLIE, *the bread under his arm, jumps up the four steps, undisturbed by* SAM'S *presence. He drops the bread, and is about to replace it in the bag, but gets a better idea. He inflates the bag and explodes it with a blow of his fist.* CHARLIE *looks on, in admiration and envy.*)

ROSE (*appearing at the window*). Willie, we're waiting for the bread.

WILLIE (*holding it up*). All right! Cantcha see I got it?

(*He enters the house, followed by* CHARLIE.)

SAM (*rising*). Hello, Rose.

ROSE. Hello, Sam.

SAM. Come down.

ROSE. I haven't had breakfast yet. (*Calling into the room.*) Yes! He's on his way up.

MISS CUSHING (*coming out of the house*). Good morning.

(*She looks inquiringly from* SAM *to* ROSE.)

SAM (*impatiently*). Good morning.

(*A middle-aged nun appears at the right, accompanied by a scrawny child of about fourteen. They walk across the stage.*)

ROSE. I'm going to Mr. Jacobson's funeral. (*Calling into the room.*) Yes, I'm coming. (*To* SAM.) Breakfast's ready. I'll be down as soon as the dishes are done.

(*She disappears.* SAM *looks up at the window for a moment, then begins to read again.* MRS. FIORENTINO *appears at the window, at the extreme left, with a double armful of bedding, which she deposits upon the window-sill. Then she goes away again.*)

SHIRLEY (*appearing at the window*). Sam, breakfast is ready.

SAM. I don't want any breakfast.

SHIRLEY. What do you mean, you don't want any breakfast? What kind of a business is that, not to eat breakfast?

SAM. Do I have to eat breakfast, if I don't want to?

SHIRLEY. You've got your head so full of that Rose Maurrant upstairs that you don't want to eat or sleep or anything any more.

SAM. If I don't feel like eating, why should I eat? (*Bursting out.*) You're always telling me: "Eat!" "Don't eat!" "Get up!" "Go to bed!" I know what I want to do, without being told.

SHIRLEY. I don't see, just when you're graduating from college, why you want to get mixed up with a little batzimer like that!

SAM. It's always the same thing over again with you. You never can get over your race prejudice. I've told you a hundred times that the Jews are no better than anybody else.

SHIRLEY. I'm not talking about that! Look at the kind of family she comes from. What's her father? Nothing but an illiterate rough-neck. And her mother——

SAM (*indignantly*). Are you starting, too?

KAPLAN'S VOICE. Shoi-ley!

SHIRLEY. Wait a minute, papa's calling. (*Into the room.*) All right, papa! (*To* SAM.) Come in, Sam, or papa will be making long speeches again.

SAM (*impatiently*). All right! All right! I'll come.

(*A young shopgirl, smiling to herself, appears at the right and walks across the stage.* SAM *rises and goes into the house.* SHIRLEY *leaves the window.* BUCHANAN, *emerging from the house, collarless and unshaven, encounters* SAM *in the vestibule.*)

BUCHANAN (*eagerly*). Good morning!

SAM (*abruptly*). Good morning.

(*He enters the house.* BUCHANAN *looks back at him, then comes down the steps.* MRS. FIORENTINO *raises the drawn shade and opens the window.*)

MRS. FIORENTINO. Good morning, Mr. Buchanan.

BUCHANAN. Oh, good morning, Mrs. Fiorentino. (*Going over to the left balustrade.*) I guess you know that the baby came last night, don't you?

MRS. FIORENTINO. No! I did not hear a vord about it.

BUCHANAN. Why, I thought she'd wake up the whole neighborhood, the way she was yelling. Three-thirty this morning the baby came. I been up the whole night.

(*An old* LETTER-CARRIER, *coatless, appears at the right.*)

MRS. FIORENTINO. A boy, is it?

BUCHANAN. No, it's a little girl. I guess we'll call her Mary, after my mother.

LETTER-CARRIER (*going up the steps*). Mornin'.

MRS. FIORENTINO. Good morning. Any letters for me?

LETTER-CARRIER (*from the top of the steps*). No, not a thing.

BUCHANAN (*turning toward him*). I was just telling Mrs. Fiorentino, I had a little addition to my family last night.

LETTER-CARRIER. Your first, is it?

BUCHANAN (*hastening to explain*). Well, we've only been married a little over a year.

LETTER-CARRIER. Well, I've had seven, an' I'm still luggin' a mail-bag at sixty-two.

(*He goes into the vestibule and puts the

mail into the letter-boxes.)

MRS. FIORENTINO. How is your wife?

BUCHANAN. Well, she had a pretty hard time of it. Her sister's up there with her. And Mrs. Maurrant was up, nearly all night. I don't know what we'd have done without her.

LETTER-CARRIER (*coming down the steps*). It don't pay to let 'em have their own way too much. That's where I made my mistake.

(*As the* LETTER-CARRIER *goes off at the left,* LIPPO *appears at the window behind his wife, and tickles her.*)

MRS. FIORENTINO (*startled*). Lippo!

BUCHANAN. Morning. I was just telling your wife——

MRS. FIORENTINO. Lippo, what do you think? Mr. Buchanan has a little girl!

LIPPO. Ah, dotsa fine! Margherita, why you don' have da baby, ha?

MRS. FIORENTINO (*abruptly*). I must go and make the coffee.

(*She goes away from the window.* OLSEN *comes half-way up the steps and leans against the railing, smoking his pipe.*)

A VOICE (*offstage left*). Oh-h! Corn! Sweet corn!

LIPPO. Ees funny t'ing. You gotta de leetle, skeeny wife and she's hava da baby. My Margherita, she's beeg an' fat an' she no can hava da baby.

BUCHANAN. Well, that's the way o' the world, I guess.

(*As he goes off, at the left, an* ICE-MAN *appears, trundling a three-wheeled cart, filled with ice.*)

LIPPO. Buon giorno, Mike.

MIKE. Buon giorno, signore. Come sta?

LIPPO. Benissimo. Fa molto caldo ancora, oggi.

MIKE. Si, si, signore. Bisognera abbastanza ghiaccio. Twen'y fi' cent, ha?

LIPPO. No, no, è troppo.

MIKE. Twen'y cent? Eesa melta fas'.

LIPPO. Alla right. Gimme twen'y cent.

MIKE. Si, si, signore. Sure.

(*As he wheels the cart to the cellar-entrance and begins to chop a block of ice, a man in shirt-sleeves strides in from the left and stops at the curb, as though seeing someone in a house across the street.*)

THE MAN (*angrily*). Well, what about it? We've been waiting a half an hour!

A VOICE. I'll be right over!

THE MAN. Yeah? Well, make it snappy!

(*He strides off at the left, muttering angrily.* ROSE *comes out of the house and stands in the doorway, looking for* SAM. *Then she comes out on the stoop and peers into the* KAPLAN *apartment. As she turns away, she sees* LIPPO.)

ROSE (*crossing to the left of the stoop*). Good morning.

LIPPO. Gooda mornin', Meesa Maurrant.

(MIKE *goes down into the cellar, with a chunk of ice.*)

ROSE. It's awful hot again, isn't it?

LIPPO. You don' like?

ROSE. I don't sleep very well, when it's so hot.

LIPPO. No? Ahm sleepa fine. Een Eetaly, where Ahm born, is much more 'ot like 'era. Een summer, ees too 'ot for workin'. Ees too 'ot only for sleepin'. W'en Ahm leetla boy, Ahm sleepa, sleepa, whola day. I don't wear no clo's—nawthin' only leetle short pair pants. I lay down on groun' under da lemon-tree, Ahm sleepa whola day.

ROSE. Under a lemon-tree! That must have been nice.

LIPPO. Ees smella sweet, lemon-tree. Where Ahm born ees t'ousan' lemon-tree. Lemon an' olive an' arancia.

ROSE. Oh, that must be lovely!

LIPPO. Ah, ees bew-tiful! Ees most bew-tiful place in whole worl'. You hear about Sorrent', ha?

ROSE. No, I don't think I ever did.

LIPPO (*incredulously*). You never hear about Sorrent'?

ROSE. No, I don't know much about geography. Is it a big place?

LIPPO. Ees not vera beeg—but ever'body know Sorrent'. Sorrento gentile! La bella Sorrento! You hear about Napoli—Baia di Napoli?

ROSE. Oh yes, the Bay of Naples! Is it near there?

LIPPO. Sure, ees on Bay of Napoli. Ees bew-tiful! Ees alla blue. Sky blue, water blue, sun ees shine alla time.

ROSE. Oh, how lovely.

(MIKE *comes up the cellar-steps, chops another block of ice, and goes down the cellar-steps with it.*)

LIPPO. An' ees Vesuvio, too. You hear about Vesuvio?—ees beeg volcano.

ROSE. Oh yes, sure. I saw a picture once, called The Last Days of Pompeii, and it showed Mount Vesuvius, with smoke coming out of the top.

LIPPO. Da's right. An' night-time, ees fire come out, maka da sky red.

ROSE. Didn't it frighten you?

LIPPO. Ah no, ees nawthin' to be afraid. Ees jus' volcano.

ROSE. I'd love to go to Italy. It must be awfully pretty. But I don't suppose I ever will.

LIPPO. W'y sure! Some day you gonna marry reech fella; 'e's take you Eetaly—ever'where.

ROSE. I guess there's not much chance of that. Rich fellows aren't going around looking for girls like me to marry. Any-how, I don't think money is everything, do you?

LIPPO. Ees good to hava money. Da's w'y Ahm come to America. Een Eetaly, ees bewtiful, but ees no money. 'Ere ees not bewtiful, but ees plenty money. Ees better to 'ave money.

(*An elderly* MAN, *in the gray uniform of a special officer, comes out of the house, filling his pipe from a tobacco-box.*)

THE MAN. Good mornin'.

ROSE. Good morning, Mr. Callahan. (*The* MAN *drops the empty tobacco-tin on the sidewalk and goes off slowly at the left.*) I don't think I'd be happy, just marrying a man with money, if I didn't care for him, too.

LIPPO (*laughing*). Wotsa matter, ha? You lova da leetla kike, ha?

ROSE. Why no, I don't. I don't love any-body—at least, I don't think I do. But it's not on account of his being a Jew.

LIPPO. No, ees no good—Jew. 'E's only t'ink about money, money—alla time money.

ROSE. But Sam isn't like that, a bit. He's only interested in poetry and things like that.

(*The* ICE-MAN *comes up out of the cellar and trundles off his cart at the right*).

MRS. FIORENTINO (*calling*). Lippo! Breakfast!

LIPPO (*calling*). Alla right, Margherita! (*To* ROSE.) You marry fella wit' lot o' money. Ees much better.

(*He goes away from the window as* MISS CUSHING *appears at the left, carrying a paper-bag.*)

ROSE. How's your mother today, Miss Cushing?

MISS CUSHING. She's not feeling so good today.

ROSE. It's too bad she's not feeling well.

MISS CUSHING. I'm afraid it's her heart. At her age, you know——!

(*As she enters the house,* TWO COLLEGE GIRLS *of nineteen appear at the right.*)

FIRST GIRL (*as they appear*). I don't understand it.

SECOND GIRL. Convex is this way; and concave is this way.

FIRST GIRL. That I know.

SECOND GIRL. When you're near-sighted, they give you convex glasses, and when you're far-sighted, they give you concave.

FIRST GIRL. That I didn't know.

SECOND GIRL. Of course, you know it. Didn't we have it in psychology?

FIRST GIRL (*as they disappear at the left*). I don't remember.

(WILLIE *comes out of the house on his way to school. He is hatless, and carries his books under his arm.*)

ROSE (*intercepting him at the top of the stoop*). Why, Willie, the way you look! Your collar's all open.

WILLIE. I know it! De button came off.

ROSE. Why didn't you ask ma to sew it on for you?

WILLIE. She ain't dere. She's up at Buchanan's.

ROSE. Well, wait till I see if I have a pin. (*She searches in her hand-bag.*)

WILLIE (*starting down the steps*). Aw, it's all right de way it is.

ROSE (*following him to the sidewalk*). No, it isn't. You can't go to school like that. (*Producing a safety-pin.*) Now, hold still while I fix it.

WILLIE (*squirming*). Aw, fer de love o' Mike——!

ROSE. You'll get stuck, if you don't hold still. There, that looks better now. And you didn't comb your hair, either.

WILLIE (*trying to escape*). Say, lemme alone, cantcha?

ROSE (*taking a comb out of her hand-bag and combing his hair*). You can't go to school looking like a little street-loafer.

WILLIE. Aw, you gimme a pain in de——

ROSE. You're getting big enough to comb your own hair, without being told. There! Now, you look very nice.

WILLIE. So's your old man!

(*He runs towards the left kicking the empty tobacco tin ahead of him, then stops, turns, and deliberately rumples his hair.*)

ROSE (*indignantly, as* WILLIE *runs off*). Why, Willie!

(MRS. JONES *and the dog appear at right.*

OLSEN *knocks the ashes out of his pipe and goes down into the cellar.* MRS. MAURRANT *comes out of the house.*)

ROSE. Hello, ma.

MRS. JONES (*at the steps*). Good mornin'.

ROSE *and* MRS. MAURRANT. Good morning, Mrs. Jones.

MRS. JONES. How's little Mrs. Buchanan gettin' on?

MRS. MAURRANT. Well, she's sleeping now, poor thing. She was so worn out she just went off into a sound sleep. I really didn't think, last night, she'd have the strength to pull through it.

MRS. JONES. Well, it's somethin' we all got to go through. I been through enough with mine, I hope to tell you. Not that they didn't turn out all right.

MRS. MAURRANT. I wouldn't give up having mine for anything in the world.

MRS. JONES. Well, after all, what more does any woman want than watchin' her kids grow up an' a husband to look out for her?

MRS. MAURRANT. Yes, that's true.

MRS. JONES. Yes, and the world would be a whole lot better off, if there was more that lived up to it. (*Starting up the steps*). Well, I gotta get my Mae up out o' bed. Gawd knows what time she got in this mornin'. (*She enters the vestibule, then stops and turns.*) If you don't mind my bein' so bold, Mrs. Maurrant—an' I don't mind sayin' it in front of your daughter, either—I'd think twice before I'd let any child o' mine bring a Jew into the family.

ROSE (*with a show of temper*). I don't see what it has to do with you, Mrs. Jones.

MRS. JONES. There's no need to get huffy about it. I'm only advisin' you for your own good. I'm sure it don't make no difference to me what you do. Come on, Queenie.

(*She goes into the house.*)

ROSE. Well, of all the nerve I ever heard in my life——! She and those wonderful children of hers!

MRS. MAURRANT (*coming half way down the steps*). The best way is not to pay any attention to her. There's lots of people like that in the world—they never seem to be happy, unless they're making trouble for somebody. Did Willie go to school?

ROSE. Yes, he did. It's awful the way he goes around, looking like a little tough. And the language he uses, too.

MRS. MAURRANT. I know. I just don't seem able to manage him any more.

ROSE. I sometimes wonder if it wouldn't be better for us all, if we moved out to the suburbs somewhere—you know, some place in Jersey or Staten Island.

MRS. MAURRANT. I don't think pop would do it. (*As* MAURRANT *comes out of the house, carrying a much-battered satchel.*) Are you leaving now, Frank?

MAURRANT (*from the top of the stoop*). Looks like it, don't it? Where you been all this while?

MRS. MAURRANT. Why, you know where I've been, Frank—up to Mrs. Buchanan's.

MAURRANT. Yeah? An' where you goin' now?

MRS. MAURRANT. Just around to Kraus's to get a chicken. I thought I'd make her some chicken-soup, to give her strength.

MAURRANT. Say, how about lookin' after your own home an' lettin' the Buchanans look after theirs.

MRS. MAURRANT. All I'm trying to do is to be a little neighborly. It's the least anybody can do, with the poor thing hardly able to lift her hand.

MAURRANT. That's all right about that! (*Coming down the steps.*) A woman's got a right to stay in her own home, lookin' after her husband an' children.

MRS. MAURRANT (*going towards him*). What else have I been doing all these years, I'd like to know?

MAURRANT. Well, just see that you don't forget it, that's all—or there's li'ble to be trouble.

MRS. MAURRANT (*putting her hand on his arm*). All right, Frank. Don't say any more, please. When will you be back—to-morrow?

MAURRANT. I don't know when I'll be back. Whenever I'm t'roo wit' me work—that's when. What are you so anxious to know for, huh?

MRS. MAURRANT. Why, I just asked, that's all.

MAURRANT. Oh, you just asked, huh? Just in case somebody wanted to come aroun' callin', is that it?

MRS. MAURRANT. No, it isn't. It isn't anything of the kind. You got no right to talk to me like that in front of my own daughter. You got no right. No, you haven't!

(*She turns away and hurries off abruptly at the left.*)

ROSE. Ma!

(*She starts to run after her mother.*)

MAURRANT (*imperiously*). Come back here, you! (ROSE *hesitates.*) Come back, hear me? (ROSE *turns and comes slowly back.*) You stay right here.

(*He puts down his satchel and takes a flask from his pocket.*)

ROSE. Why do you talk to her like that?

MAURRANT. Nobody's askin' you.

ROSE. If you were only a little nicer to her, maybe everything would be different.

MAURRANT. Yeah? Where's she got any kick comin'? Ain't I always been a good husband to her? Ain't I always looked after her?

(*He takes a drink.*)

ROSE. It's not that, pop. It's somebody to be sort of nice to her that she wants—sort of nice and gentle, the way she is to you. That's all it is.

MAURRANT (*turning to her*). So she's got you headed the same way, has she? Goin' out nights with married men, huh?

ROSE. You don't need to worry about me, pop. I can take care of myself, all right.

MAURRANT. No daughter o' mine ain't gonna go that way. I seen too many o' those kind around the theayter.

ROSE. Things are different nowadays, pop. I guess maybe you don't realize that. Girls aren't the way they used to be—sort of soft and helpless. A girl nowadays knows how to look out for herself. But not her, pop; she needs somebody to look after her.

MAURRANT. Aw, can all that talk! You been listenin' to them bolshevikis, that's the trouble. But I'm gonna keep you straight, by God, or I'll know the reason why.

ROSE. I guess I've got a right to think about things for myself.

MAURRANT. Yeah? Well, don't let me ketch that other bozo comin' around here, either—that's all I got to say.

ROSE (*hesitantly, going up to him*). Pop, listen—couldn't we get a little house somewhere—Queens or somewhere like that?

MAURRANT. What's the idea?

ROSE. Well, I don't know. I sort of thought it would be nice for all of us. And maybe if ma had a nice little home and some real nice neighbors—do you see what I mean?

MAURRANT. This place suits me all right.

ROSE. You can get some real nice little houses that don't cost such an awful lot. And I wouldn't mind helping to pay for it. And once we had it all fixed up——

MAURRANT. Forget it! I don' know when I'll be back. (*As he starts to go right.*) An' remember what I tol' you, hear?

MRS. JONES (*appearing at her window with a tin dust-pan*). Good mornin', Mr. Maurrant. You off on a little trip?

MAURRANT (*curtly*). Yeah.

(*He goes off.* MRS. JONES *empties the dust-pan out of the window and goes away.* KAPLAN *comes out of the house, a bundle of newspapers under his arm. He walks slowly and painfully, with the aid of a heavy stick.*)

KAPLAN (*at the foot of the steps*). Vy do you look so sed, hm?

ROSE (*turning and sitting on the right balustrade.*) Oh, good morning, Mr. Kaplan.

KAPLAN. A young girl, like you, should not look so sed.

ROSE. I'm not sad, especially, only——

KAPLAN. You got troubles, hm?

ROSE. I don't know. It's just sort of everything.

KAPLAN. Velt-schmerz you got, hm? Vit' my boy Sem is de same t'ing. Dees vay you feel only ven you are young. Ven you gat old like me, you tink only: "Moch longer I von't be here."

ROSE. Why should things be the way they are, Mr. Kaplan? Why must people always be fighting and having troubles, instead of just sort of being happy together?

KAPLAN. My dear young leddy, ef I could enser dis quastion, I would be de greatest benefactor thet de verld hes ever known. Dees is som't'ing, vich all de philosophers hev been unable to enser. De ones thet believe in God, say de davil is responsible; and de ones thet don't believe in God, say 'uman nature is responsible. It is my opinion thet most unheppiness can be traced to economic cosses and thet——

(CHARLIE *and* MARY HILDEBRAND *have come out of the house, carrying their school-books.*)

MARY. Hello.

ROSE. Hello, Mary. Hello, Charlie.

CHARLIE. Hello.

MARY (*chattily, as they reach the sidewalk*). We're going to be dispossessed today.

ROSE. What a shame!

MARY. Yes, ma'am. My father went away and so we couldn't pay the rent.

CHARLIE (*tugging at her arm*). Aw, come on, Mary.

ROSE. Have you another place to live, Mary?

MARY. No ma'am. But Miss Simpson, from the Charities, says she'll find us a place. She says we must learn to be less extravagant.

CHARLIE. Come ahead, will you?

MARY. I'm going to school now. Good-bye.

ROSE. Good-bye.

(*The children go off, at the left.*)

KAPLAN. More trobles!

ROSE. I know. Isn't it awful to think of them being turned out in the street like that?

KAPLAN. In a ciwilized verld, soch t'ings could not heppen.

ROSE. You mean if there were different laws?

KAPLAN. Not laws! We got already too many laws. Ve must hev ection, not laws. De verking-klesses must t'row off de yoke of ke*pit*alism, and ebolish wage-slavery.

ROSE. But wouldn't people still be unkind to each other and fight and quarrel among themselves?

KAPLAN. My dear young leddy, so long as ve keep men in slevery, dey vill behave like sleves. But wance ve establish a verld based upon 'uman needs and not upon 'uman greed——

ROSE. You mean people will begin being nice to each other and making allowances and all?

KAPLAN. All dees vill come. Wot ve hev now is a wicious soicle. On de one hend, ve hev a rotten economic system——

ROSE. Excuse me, here's my mother.

(*She goes towards the left as* MRS. MAURRANT *approaches, a paper package in her hand.* KAPLAN *goes off at the right.*)

MRS. MAURRANT (*as* ROSE *comes up to her*). Did he go?

(*They stop on the pavement, at the left of the stoop.*)

ROSE. Yes.

MRS. MAURRANT. I got a little chicken, to make Mrs. Buchanan some soup.

ROSE. He had a flask with him, ma. I hope he doesn't start drinking.

MRS. MAURRANT. What did he say—anything?

ROSE. No, only the way he always talks. I tried to talk to him about buying a house somewheres, but he wouldn't listen.

MRS. MAURRANT. No, I knew he wouldn't.

ROSE. It doesn't seem to be any use trying to get him to listen to anything.

MRS. MAURRANT. It's always been that way. I've always tried to be a good wife to him, Rose. But it never seemed to make any difference to him.

ROSE. I know, ma.

MRS. MAURRANT. And I've tried to be a good mother, too.

ROSE. I know, ma. I know just the way you feel about it.

MRS. MAURRANT (*appealingly*). Do you, Rose?

ROSE. Yes, ma, I do. Honest I do.

MRS. MAURRANT. I've always tried to make a nice home for him and to do what's right. But it doesn't seem to be any use.

ROSE. I know, ma. (*Hesitantly.*) But it's on account of——

(*She stops.*)

MRS. MAURRANT. Are you going to start, too? Are you going to start like all the others?

(*She turns away and bursts into tears.*)

ROSE (*fondling her*). Don't, ma. Please don't.

MRS. MAURRANT. I thought you'd be the one that would feel different.

ROSE. I do, ma—really I do.

MRS. MAURRANT. What's the good of being alive, if you can't get a little something out of life? You might just as well be dead.

ROSE. Look out, ma. Somebody's coming.

(*A smartly-dressed girl, with one side of her face covered with cotton and adhesive tape, appears at the left and crosses the stage. At the same time,* JONES *comes out of the house.* ROSE *and* MRS. MAURRANT *stand in awkward silence, as he comes down the stoop and approaches them.*)

JONES. Well, is it hot enough for you today?

ROSE. It's awful, isn't it?

JONES (*as he goes towards the left*). You said it. Still along about January, we'll all be wishin' we had a little o' this weather.

(*He exits.* MRS. MAURRANT *goes towards the stoop.*)

ROSE. Ma, listen. If I say something, will

you listen to me?

MRS. MAURRANT. Yes, sure I will, Rose. I'll listen to anything you say, only——

ROSE. Well, what I was thinking was, if he didn't come around here so much, maybe. Do you see what I mean, ma?

MRS. MAURRANT (*constrainedly*). Yes, Rose.

ROSE (*putting her arm around her*). It's on account of all that's going around—everybody in the whole house. You see what I mean, don't you, ma?

MRS. MAURRANT. Every person in the world has to have somebody to talk to. You can't live without somebody to talk to. I'm not saying that I can't talk to you, Rose, but you're only a young girl and it's not the same thing.

ROSE. It's only on account of pop. I'm scared of what he's likely to do, if he starts drinking.

MRS. MAURRANT. Well, I'll see, Rose. Sometimes I think I'd be better off if I was dead.

ROSE. If there was only something I could do.

MRS. MAURRANT. There isn't anything anybody could do. It's just the way things are, that's all.

(BUCHANAN *appears at the left. They turn and face him as he approaches.*)

MRS. MAURRANT. Oh, Mr. Buchanan, I got a little chicken, so that I could make her some good, nourishing soup.

BUCHANAN. Well, say, you got to let me pay you for it.

MRS. MAURRANT. Oh, never mind about that. We'll have the chicken for supper tonight. Did you have her medicine made up?

BUCHANAN. Yes, I got it right here. I called up the office and they told me not to come down today.

MRS. MAURRANT. Well, that's very nice. It'll be a comfort to her to have you around.

BUCHANAN. Yes, that's what I thought, too. Well, I'd better be getting upstairs.

(*He goes up the steps.*)

MRS. MAURRANT. I'll be up later, with the soup.

BUCHANAN. Well, thanks. (*Stopping at the top of the stoop and turning to her.*) You've been a mighty good neighbor, Mrs. Maurrant.

(*He enters the house.*)

MRS. MAURRANT He's an awful nice young feller—so nice and gentle. And he's always trying to be so helpful. It makes you feel sort of sorry for him.

(SHIRLEY *comes out of the house, carrying a large wicker bag, which contains her lunch and school-books. She takes a post-card out of the mail-box.*)

MRS. MAURRANT (*going up the steps*). Well, I'd better go and start this chicken. Are you coming home for lunch, Rose?

ROSE. Yes. I'll be back as soon as the funeral's over.

MRS. MAURRANT. Oh, all right. (*As she sees* SHIRLEY.) Good morning.

SHIRLEY (*coming out of the vestibule, reading the post-card*). Good morning.

ROSE. Good morning.

(MRS. MAURRANT *goes into the house. The shade of* MAE's *window flies up and she is seen, for an instant, dressed only in her step-in. She yawns noisily and turns away from the window.*)

ROSE (*seating herself on the stoop*). It's another awful day, isn't it?

SHIRLEY. Yes, and when you have to keep forty children quiet—! Well, thank goodness, in two weeks, school closes. Otherwise, I think I'd go crazy.

ROSE. Well, you get a nice long vacation, anyhow.

SHIRLEY. Not much vacation for me. I'm taking Summer courses at Teachers' College. (*She looks at* ROSE *a moment, hesitates, and then comes down the steps.*) Miss Maurrant, if you don't mind, I want to talk to you about my brother, Sam.

ROSE. Why certainly, Miss Kaplan.

SHIRLEY. I guess you know he's only finishing college this month——

ROSE. Yes, of course, I do.

SHIRLEY. Then he has to go three years to law-school and pass the bar examination, before he can be a full-fledged lawyer.

ROSE. Yes, it takes a long time.

SHIRLEY. A long time and lots of money. And before a young lawyer begins to make his own living, that takes a long time, too. It will be ten years, maybe, before he's making enough to support himself and a family. (*Looking away.*) Then it's time enough for him to think about marriage.

ROSE. You don't mean me and Sam, Miss Kaplan?

SHIRLEY. Yes, that's just what I mean.

ROSE. Why, we're just good friends, that's all.

SHIRLEY. I know how it is with a boy

like Sam, Miss Maurrant. He thinks he's a man already; but he's nothing but a boy. If you're such a good friend, you shouldn't take his mind away from his work.

ROSE. But I haven't meant to, Miss Kaplan—honest I haven't.

SHIRLEY. I've had to work hard enough to get him as far as he is. And I have my father to take care of, too. The few dollars he makes, writing for the radical papers, don't even pay the rent. Believe me, every dollar I make goes.

ROSE. I know. Sam's often told me how much he owes to you.

SHIRLEY. He doesn't owe me anything. I don't care about the money. Only he should be thinking about his work and not about other things.

ROSE. Yes, he should be thinking about his work. But don't you think there are other things in the world, too, besides just work?

SHIRLEY. Don't you think I know that? I know that just as well as you do. Maybe you think I'm only an old-maid schoolteacher, without any feelings.

ROSE. Oh, I don't—really I don't!

SHIRLEY (*turning her head away*). Maybe I'm not a movie vamp, with dimples—but I could have had my chances, too. Only, I wanted to give Sam an education.

ROSE. I haven't tried to vamp Sam, honestly I haven't. We just seemed sort of naturally to like each other.

SHIRLEY. Why must you pick out Sam? You could get other fellows. Anyhow, it's much better to marry with your own kind. When you marry outside your own people, nothing good ever comes of it. You can't mix oil and water.

ROSE. I don't know. I think if people really care about each other——

SHIRLEY. He's nothing but a baby. He sees a pretty face and, right away, he forgets about everything else.

ROSE (*with a flash of temper*). I know I haven't as much brains as Sam, or as you, either, if that's what you mean.

SHIRLEY (*contritely, going towards her*). I didn't mean to hurt your feelings. I haven't got anything against you. Only, he's all I've got in the world. What else have I got to live for?

SAM (*appearing at the extreme right window, with a cup of coffee and a piece of coffee-cake*). Hello, Rose.

ROSE. Hello, Sam.

SHIRLEY (*in a low tone*). Please don't tell him what I said.

(SAM *goes to the other window.*)

ROSE. Oh no, I won't.

(SHIRLEY *hurries off at the left.*)

ROSE (*rising and turning towards* SAM). Sam——

SAM (*holding out the coffee-cake*). Want some coffee-cake?

ROSE. No. (*Going up the steps.*) Sam, there's something I want to ask you, before I forget. Is there any special way you have to act in a synagogue?

SAM (*eating throughout*). In a synagogue?

ROSE. Yes. The funeral I'm going to is in a synagogue, and I thought there might be some special thing you have to do. Like in church, you know, a girl is always supposed to keep her hat on.

SAM. I don't know. I've never in my life been in a synagogue.

ROSE. Didn't you ever go to Sunday-school, or anything like that?

SAM. No.

ROSE. That's funny. I thought everybody went once in a while. How about when your mother died?

SAM. She was cremated. My parents were always rationalists.

ROSE. Didn't they believe in God or anything?

SAM. What do you mean by God?

ROSE (*puzzled*). Well—you know what I mean. What anybody means—God. Somebody that sort of loves us and looks after us, when we're in trouble.

SAM (*sitting on the window-sill*). That's nothing but superstition—the lies that people tell themselves, because reality is too terrible for them to face.

ROSE. But, Sam, don't you think it's better to believe in something that makes you a little happy, than not to believe in anything and be miserable all the time?

SAM. There's no such thing as happiness. That's an illusion, like all the rest.

ROSE. Then, what's the use of living?

SAM (*brushing the last crumbs off his hands*). Yes, what is the use?

ROSE. Why, you oughtn't to talk like that, Sam—a person with all the talent and brains that you've got. I know things aren't just the way you want them to be. But they aren't for anybody. They aren't for me, either.

SAM. Then, why don't we get out of it,

together?

ROSE. I don't see just how we could do that, Sam.

SAM. It would be easy enough—ten cents' worth of carbolic acid.

ROSE. Why, Sam, you don't mean kill ourselves!

SAM. Is your life so precious to you that you want to cling to it?

ROSE. Well, yes. I guess it is.

SAM. Why? Why? What is there in life to compensate for the pain of living?

ROSE. There's a lot. Just being alive—breathing and walking around. Just looking at the faces of people you like and hearing them laugh. And seeing the pretty things in the store-windows. And rough-housing with your kid brother. And—oh, I don't know—listening to a good band, and dancing—Oh, I'd hate to die! (*Earnestly.*) Sam, promise you won't talk about killing yourself, any more.

SAM. What difference would it make to you, if I did?

ROSE. Don't talk like that, Sam! You're the best friend I've ever had.

(*She puts her hand on his.*)

SAM. I can't think of anything but you.

ROSE. There's something I want to ask your advice about, Sam. It's about what I started to tell you about, last night. A man I know wants to put me on the stage.

SAM (*releasing her hand and drawing back*). What man?

ROSE. A man that works in the office. He knows a manager and he says he'll help me get started. You see, what I thought was, that if I could only get out of here and have a decent place to live and make a lot of money, maybe everything would be different, not only for me, but for ma and pop and Willie.

SAM. But don't you know what he wants, this man?

ROSE. Nobody gives you anything for nothing, Sam. If you don't pay for things in one way, you do in another.

SAM. Rose, for God's sake, you mustn't!

(VINCENT JONES *comes out of the house.*)

ROSE. (*seeing* VINCENT *in the vestibule*). Look out, Sam, here's that tough from upstairs.

(*She goes over to the left of the stoop.*)

VINCENT (*in the doorway*). Hello, Rosie. Been here all night, talkin' to the little yid?

(ROSE *does not answer.*)

VINCENT (*turning to* SAM). Hello, motzers! Shake!

(*He leans over the balustrade and seizes* SAM's *hand in a crushing grip.*)

SAM (*writhing with pain*). Let me go!

ROSE. Let him alone!

(VINCENT *gives* SAM's *hand another vicious squeeze and then releases him.* SAM *cowers back in the window, nursing his hand.*)

VINCENT (*waving his hand about in mock pain*). Jesus, what a grip dat little kike's got! I'd hate to get into a mix-up wit' him. (*To* ROSE.) Got a date to-night, kid?

ROSE. Yes, I have.

VINCENT. Yeah? Gee, ain't dat too bad. I'll give you two dollars, if you let me snap your garter.

ROSE. Shut up, you!

(VINCENT *laughs.* SAM *makes an inarticulate sound.*)

VINCENT (*threateningly*). Whadja say? I tought I hoid you say sumpin.

(*He makes a threatening gesture.* SAM *shrinks back.*)

VINCENT (*with a loud laugh, as he goes down the steps*). Fightin' Kaplan, de pride o' Jerusalem! (*He looks at them both, then laughs again.*) Fer cryin' out loud!

(*He goes off at the left.*)

ROSE. Oh, if there was only some way of getting out of here! (SAM *puts the back of his hand to his forehead and turns away.*) I sometimes think I'd just like to run away.

SAM (*without turning*). Yes!

ROSE. Anywhere—it wouldn't matter where—just to get out of this.

SAM (*turning*). Why shouldn't we do it?

ROSE (*rather startled, coming over to the right balustrade*). Would you go with me, Sam?

SAM. Yes—anywhere.

ROSE. I've heard that people are much nicer and friendlier, when you get outside of New York. There's not so much of a mad rush, other places. And being alone, you could sort of work things out for yourself. (*Suddenly.*) Only, what would you do, Sam?

SAM. I could get a job, too.

ROSE. And give up your law-work?

SAM. I'd give up everything, to be with you.

ROSE. No. I wouldn't let you do that, Sam. It's different with me——

(EASTER *appears at the right.*)

EASTER (*stopping at the right of the stoop*). Good morning, Miss Maurrant.

(*Startled,* ROSE *turns and sees him, for the first time.*)

ROSE (*none too pleased*). Oh, good morning, Mr. Easter. What brings you in this neighborhood?

EASTER (*not very plausibly*). Well, I just happened to have a little business right around the corner. So, I thought as long as you were going to the funeral, we might just as well go together.

ROSE. Well, I hardly expected to see you around here. (*An awkward pause.*) Oh, I'd like you to meet my friend, Mr. Kaplan.

EASTER. How do you do, Mr. Kaplan? Glad to know you.

(SAM *murmurs something inaudible. An awkward silence.*)

ROSE (*to* SAM). Mr. Easter is the manager of the office.

(SAM *does not reply. Another silence.*)

ROSE (*to* EASTER). It's awful hot again, isn't it?

EASTER. Worse than yesterday. (*Approaching the stoop.*) Tell you what I was thinking. I was thinking that after the funeral, we might take a run down to the beach, somewhere, and cool off a little.

ROSE. I can't today. I've got a lot of things I want to do.

EASTER. Oh, you can do 'em some other day.

ROSE. No, really, I can't. (*Looking at her watch.*) Well, I guess it's time we got started.

(*She comes down the steps.*)

EASTER. Yes, it is. We'll pick up a cab at the corner.

(MRS. MAURRANT *appears at her window, looks out, and sees* ROSE *and* EASTER.)

ROSE. Why, I thought I'd walk. It's not far.

EASTER. Too hot today for any walking.

ROSE (*starting to go towards the left*). Not if you keep in the shade.

EASTER. Much more comfortable taking a cab.

ROSE. I'd rather walk.

EASTER. Well, whatever you say. Good morning, Mr. Kaplan. Glad to have met you.

(SAM *murmurs an inaudible reply.*)

ROSE. Good-bye, Sam, I'll see you later.

(SAM *does not answer.* ROSE *and* EASTER *go towards the left, in silence.* SAM *watches them intently, trembling with jealousy.* MRS. MAURRANT, *surprised and disturbed, watches* ROSE *and* EASTER.)

ROSE (*to* EASTER, *as they disappear*). It's a lucky thing my father wasn't around.

(SAM *suddenly turns and disappears into the house.* MRS. MAURRANT *remains at the window, looking out with obvious expectancy.*)

A DISTANT VOICE. (*Off-stage left.*) *Straw*-berries! Straw-*berries!*

(*An anemic girl of eighteen, with a music-roll under her arm, appears at the left. She enters the house and pushes one of the buttons in the vestibule, then goes to the entrance-door and waits. A moment later* MRS. FIORENTINO *appears hastily at the window, and whisks away the bed-clothes. After another moment the latch clicks and the girl enters the house.*)

THE VOICE (*a little nearer*). Oh-h! *Straw*-berries! Straw-*berries!*

(SANKEY *appears at the right. He carries a pencil behind his ear, wears a round cap with a metal name-plate and a stiff visor, and carries a large black-covered bill-holder. He and* MRS. MAURRANT *see each other and both become tense with excitement.* MRS. MAURRANT *beckons to him and he comes over to the railing under her window.*)

MRS. MAURRANT (*in a low, tense voice*). Come up.

SANKEY (*looking about nervously*). Now?

MRS. MAURRANT. Yes. I got to talk to you.

SANKEY. Is it all right?

MRS. MAURRANT. Yes. He's gone to Stamford.

SANKEY. How about later?

MRS. MAURRANT. No. Rose'll be home in an hour. She's not working today.

SANKEY. All right.

(*He looks about again, then goes quickly towards the steps.* SAM *appears at the entrance-door. He is about to step out, when he sees* SANKEY. *He stops and looks at him.* SANKEY *sees* SAM, *hesitates a moment, then goes quickly into the house. Meanwhile,* MRS. MAURRANT *has closed both windows and pulled down the shades.* SAM *takes a periodical out of the mail-box, then comes out of the house and down the steps. He looks up at the* MAURRANT *windows, sees the drawn shades, and looks about in perturbed perplexity, not knowing what to do. At length, he sits down on the steps of the stoop, tears the wrapper off the periodical—The Nation —and begins to read. The girl in* LIPPO'S *apartment begins playing the piano. This continues throughout the scene. Two untidy and rather coarse-looking men appear at the left and approach the stoop:* JAMES HENRY, *a city-marshal, and* FRED CULLEN, *his assistant. They stop in front of the house.* SAM *pays no attention to them.*)

THE MARSHAL (*crossing to the left of the stoop, and taking a paper from his pocket*). Dis is it. (*To* SAM.) Hildebrand live here?

SAM (*startled*). What?

THE MARSHAL. I'm askin' you if Hildebrand lives here.

SAM. Yes. Fourth floor.

THE MARSHAL. Better give de janitor a buzz, Fred.

(FRED *goes up the steps and rings the janitor's bell, then leans over the left balustrade.*)

FRED (*bawling*). Hey, janitor.

OLSEN (*below*). Vell?

FRED. Come on out a minute. (*As* OLSEN *appears below.*) We got a warrant for Hildebrand.

OLSEN. Fourt' floor—Hildebrand.

FRED. Yeah, I know. We got a warrant for her.

THE MARSHAL. I'm City Marshal Henry. We got a dispossess warrant.

OLSEN (*coming up the steps*). Oh, sure. You gonna put 'em out?

THE MARSHAL. Yeah, dat's it. Has she got anybody to take de foinicher away?

OLSEN (*with a shrug*). I don't know.

THE MARSHAL. Well, we'll have t' dump it on de side-walk, den. Go ahead, Fred.

(*They enter the house.* OLSEN *leans his elbows on the coping, and smokes his pipe.* SAM *sits on the steps, deep in troubled thought. A grocery boy, with a full basket, appears at the right, and goes down the cellar-steps.* MAE JONES *comes out of the house. She stands on the top step, yawns noisily, and goes off at left. She and* SAM *do not pay the slightest attention to each other.*)

A VOICE (*a little nearer*). *Straw*-berries! Straw-*berries!*

(MRS. OLSEN *comes up the cellar-steps with a heavy pail of water.* OLSEN *leans forward to make room for her. She staggers over to the stoop, almost dropping the pail, and goes up the steps into the vestibule.* OLSEN *yawns and goes down into the cellar.* MRS. JONES *appears at the window, her hair wet and stringy, a towel pinned about her shoulders, and leans out to dry her hair.*)

AN OLD-CLOTHES MAN (*appearing at left*). I kesh ko! I kesh ko!

(*He wears a battered derby and carries a folded newspaper under his arm.* MRS. OLSEN, *on her knees, begins washing up the vestibule.* FRED *comes out of the house, carrying a worn chair and a large gilt-framed picture, which he deposits on the side-walk, against the railing to the left of the stoop.*)

AN OLD-CLOTHES MAN (*as if to someone across the street*). Kesh ko? (*To* SAM.) Any old klose, mister?

(SAM *pays no attention to him.* FRED *re-enters the house.*)

THE OLD-CLOTHES MAN (*to* MRS. JONES). Any ol' klose, leddy?

MRS. JONES. Naw, nawthin'.

THE OLD-CLOTHES MAN. Hets? Shoes? Ol' stockings?

MRS. JONES. Nawthin', I tell you.

(*As the* OLD-CLOTHES MAN *goes off at the right,* MAURRANT *appears, still carrying his satchel.*)

MRS. JONES. Why, hello, Mr. Maurrant. (MAURRANT *looks up without replying and comes over to the stoop.*) I thought you was off to Stamford.

MAURRANT. I changed me——

(*He stops, to the right of the stoop, and looks up at the drawn shades of his apartment.* SAM *rises, slowly and rigidly, his eyes glued in fascination upon* MAURRANT. MAURRANT'S *movements take on a lithe and cat-like quality. Then, slowly and deliberately, he goes towards the steps, his back arched, like a tiger ready to spring.*)

SAM (*suddenly blocking the steps*). No! No! For God's sake——!

MAURRANT (*raging*). Out o' me way, you goddam little rat!

(*He flings* SAM *violently aside, almost knocking him down.* MRS. OLSEN, *terrified, rises and shrinks into a corner as* MAURRANT *with swift stealthiness enters the house.* MRS. JONES *leans out to see what is wrong.* SAM *rushes down the steps and stands under the* MAURRANT *windows. The* MARSHAL *comes out of the house, carrying a wash-boiler filled with pots.*)

SAM (*hysterically*). Mrs. Maurrant! Mrs. Maurrant!

MRS. JONES. What's the matter?

(*The* MARSHAL *puts the wash-boiler on the balustrade and looks on in amazement.*)

SAM (*to* MRS. JONES). Quick! Run and tell her! Quick!

MRS. JONES. What is it? (*Suddenly.*) Oh, Gawd, is he in there?

(*She leaves the windows hastily.*)

SAM. Yes! Mrs. Maurrant! Mrs. Maurrant!

(*A scream of terror is heard from the* MAURRANT *apartment.*)

MRS. MAURRANT'S VOICE. Frank! Frank!

(*Two shots are heard, in quick succession, and then a heavy fall.* MRS. OLSEN *runs out of the vestibule and down into the cellar.* SANKEY'S *voice is heard, inarticulate with fear. Then one of the shades shoots up, and* SANKEY *appears at the window, coatless, his face deformed by terror. He tries to open the window, but succeeds only in shattering the pane with his elbow.* MAURRANT *appears behind him and pulls him away from the window. Then another shot is heard.*)

THE MARSHAL. For Chris' sake, what's happenin'? Get an ambulance, you!

(*He pushes* SAM *towards the left, then hurries off at the right. As* SAM *runs off, a crowd begins to form.* OLSEN *comes up from the cellar, followed by the* GROCERY-BOY. *The two workmen come up out of the excavation. Two or three of the workmen from the demolished building run on at the right.*)

A WORKMAN. What's happening?

A MAN. What is it? A murder?

(*Still others join the crowd: A huckster, a janitor from a neighboring house, a mulatto girl, six or eight women of the neighborhood, some in street-dresses, others in house-dresses or dingy wrappers.* LIPPO'S *pupil appears at the window, badly frightened. The crowd surges about uncertainly, not knowing what has happened, and buzzing with questions which nobody can answer. While the crowd is still forming,* FRED, *the* MARSHAL'S *assistant, appears at the broken window.*)

FRED (*excitedly*). Grab dat boid! He's comin' down!

A WORKMAN. What boid?

A MAN. Here he is, now!

(*The crowd murmurs with excitement and surges about the stoop as the house-door opens and* MAURRANT *appears. His coat is open and his shirt is torn almost to shreds. His face, hands, and clothing are covered with blood. He stands in the door-way for a moment, surveying the crowd, his eyes glaring.*)

FRED. Grab him! Don't let him get away!

(*As the crowd makes a concerted movement towards* MAURRANT, *he whips out an automatic revolver and levels it. The crowd shrinks back. Some of the women scream.*)

MAURRANT. Git back! Git back, all o' you!

(*The crowd falls back towards the left to make way for him. With his back to the balustrade, he comes quickly down the steps, and still leveling his revolver at the crowd, retreats backwards to the cellar steps. A man, approaching at the right, comes stealthily up behind him, but* MAURRANT *senses his presence in time, wheels quickly, menaces the man with his revolver, then rushes down the cellar steps. While all this is happening, the other shade in the* MAURRANT *apartment flies up and* MISS CUSHING *opens the window and leans out.*)

MISS CUSHING. Hurry up! Get an ambulance!

(*No one pays any attention to her, as they are all watching* MAURRANT. *As* MAURRANT *runs down the cellar steps, the crowd surges forward to the railing on both sides of the stoop and leans over. A scream from* MRS. OLSEN *is heard from the basement.* FRED *goes away from the window.*)

MISS CUSHING. Get an ambulance, somebody!

(*Unable to attract anyone's attention, she leaves the window.*)

OLSEN. Olga!

(*He hurries down the cellar steps.*)

A MAN (*calling*). Here's a cop! (*The crowd looks to the right.*) Hey! Hurry up!

(*A* POLICEMAN *runs on from the right.*)

THE POLICEMAN. Where is he?

VOICES IN THE CROWD. He's down the cellar! He ran down the cellar! He went down the steps!

THE POLICEMAN. Get out of the way!

(*The* POLICEMAN *and two* MEN *in the crowd go down the cellar steps.*)

VOICES IN THE CROWD. Watch yourself! Look out, he's got a gun! He's a big guy with his shirt torn!

(*The rest of the crowd peers over the railing.*)

MISS CUSHING (*leaning out of* ROSE'S *window*). Hey, don't you hear me? Get an ambulance!

ANOTHER MAN (*looking up*). What's de matter? You want de ambulance?

MISS CUSHING. Yes! Right away!

ANOTHER MAN (*to the* GROCERY-BOY). Run aroun' de corner to de horspital, Johnny, an' tell 'em to send de ambulance!

THE GROCERY-BOY. Sure!

MISS CUSHING. Run!

(*The* GROCERY-BOY *runs off swiftly at the left.* MISS CUSHING *leaves the window. Meanwhile, as the* POLICEMAN *and the two* MEN *have gone down the cellar steps, the* MARSHAL *has run on from the right, panting.*)

THE MARSHAL (*as the* GROCERY-BOY *runs off*). Did dey git 'm?

A MAN. He beat it down de cellar.

A WORKMAN. De cop's gone after him.

THE MARSHAL. Why de hell didn' you stop 'im?

(FRED *comes out of the house.*)

A WORKMAN. He had a gun.

FRED. Did somebody go for de ambulance?

A MAN. Yeah. De kid went.

A WOMAN. It's only aroun' de corner.

ANOTHER MAN. Dey'll be here, right away.

(*The crowd moves over towards* FRED.)

THE MARSHAL (*pushing his way through the crowd and up the steps*). What de hell happened, Fred?

FRED (*as the crowd moves toward the stoop*). It's a moider. Dis boid's wife an' some other guy. Jesus, you oughta see de blood.

(*Another* POLICEMAN *runs up at the left, closely followed by* SAM.)

FRED. Upstairs, officer! Dere's two of 'em got shot.

THE POLICEMAN (*elbowing his way through the crowd*). Look out o' de way, youse! (*He goes up the stoop and crosses to the door.*) Where's de guy dat did it?

VOICES IN THE CROWD. Down de cellar! He beat it down de steps!

FRED. Dere's another cop after 'im. You better look after dem upstairs. Foist floor.

SAM (*agonized*). Are they dead?

(*No one pays any attention to him.*)

THE MARSHAL (*stopping the* POLICEMAN, *and exhibiting his badge*). I'm City Marshal Henry. Kin I do anythin'?

POLICEMAN. Don' let anybody in or out! Hear?

THE MARSHAL. Yeah, sure!

(*The* POLICEMAN *exits quickly into the house.*)

SAM. Are they dead?

(*No one notices him. The* MARSHAL *takes up his position in the doorway.*)

BUCHANAN (*appearing at the* MAURRANT *window*). Where's the ambulance?

THE MARSHAL. It'll be here right away. Dere's a cop on his way up.

SAM. Mr. Buchanan! Mr. Buchanan! Are they dead?

(*But* BUCHANAN *has already disappeared. The two* MEN *who followed the first* POLICEMAN *into the cellar now come up the steps. The crowd moves over to the railing at the right.*)

THE MARSHAL. Did you get him, boys?

ONE OF THE MEN. He must be hidin' somewheres. De cop's lookin' for 'im.

ANOTHER MAN. Somebody better call de resoives.

(SAM *runs up the steps and tries to enter the house.*)

THE MARSHAL (*seizing him roughly*). You can't get in now! Get back dere!

(*He pushes* SAM *back into the crowd at the foot of the steps.*)

THE POLICEMAN (*appearing at the* MAURRANT *window*). Hey, call up headquarters an' tell 'em to send the resoives. Make it quick!

(*He goes away from the window.*)

THE MARSHAL. You go, Fred.

FRED. Sure!

A MAN. Dere's a phone in de warehouse.

(*An ambulance bell is heard at the left, as* FRED *goes quickly towards the left. Another spectator hurries on and joins the crowd.*)

VOICES IN THE CROWD. Dere it is! Dere's de ambulance now! Here dey come!

(*The crowd moves over towards the left.*)

A MAN. Dey won't be able to git past.

THE POLICEMAN (*reappearing at the window*). Is dat de ambulance?

THE MARSHAL. Yeah.

(BUCHANAN *and* MRS. JONES *crowd to the window, behind the* POLICEMAN, *and at the other window,* LIPPO, MISS CUSHING, *and* MRS. HILDEBRAND *appear. A hospital interne and an ambulance-driver come on at the left.*)

THE POLICEMAN. Hurry up, doc! She's still breathin'.

THE INTERNE (*forcing his way through the crowd*). All right! Better bring the stretcher, Harry.

THE AMBULANCE-DRIVER. Yes, sir.

(*He hurries off at the left. The* INTERNE

goes quickly into the house. The crowd attempts to follow, several of its members going up the steps.)

THE MARSHAL (*pushing them back*). Keep back, now! Back off de stoop, everybody!

(*The crowd forms a compact mass about the foot of the steps. The persons at the* MAURRANT *windows have disappeared.* FRED *hurries on at the left.)*

FRED (*pushing his way through the crowd and up the steps*). I got 'em. Dey'll be right up. Anudder cop jes' wen' in t'roo de warehouse cellar.

THE MARSHAL. Dey'll git 'im all right. (*Looking at his watch.*) Better git busy wit' dat foinicher, Fred. We got two udder jobs today.

FRED. Yeah, sure, Jimmy.

(*He enters the house. The* AMBULANCE-DRIVER *appears at the left, carrying a canvas stretcher.)*

THE AMBULANCE-DRIVER. Get out o' the way!

THE MARSHAL. Git back, can't youse? What de hell's de matter wit' youse?

(*He comes down the steps and violently pushes the crowd back. The* AMBULANCE-DRIVER *enters the house.)*

THE POLICEMAN (*at the window*). Are dey bringin' dat stretcher?

THE MARSHAL. On de way up! (*To the crowd.*) Keep back!

(*The* POLICEMAN *leaves the window.* LIPPO'S PUPIL, *her music-roll under her arm, appears timidly in the doorway.)*

THE MARSHAL (*grabbing her arm roughly*). Where you goin'?

THE GIRL (*nervously*). I'm going home.

THE MARSHAL. Home? Where do you live?

THE GIRL. Ninety-first Street.

THE MARSHAL. What are you doin' here?

THE GIRL. I just came for a music-lesson, that's all.

THE MARSHAL. Yeah? Well, you can't go now.

THE GIRL (*beginning to whimper*). I want to go home.

THE MARSHAL. You can't go now. Nobody can't leave de house now.

THE POLICEMAN (*coming out of the house*). Who's dis kid?

THE MARSHAL. Says she come here to take a music-lesson an' she wants to go home.

THE POLICEMAN (*to the girl*). Do you know anythin' about this killin'?

THE GIRL. No, I don't. I just heard some shooting, that's all. My mother will be worried, if I don't come home.

THE POLICEMAN. Well, you can't go now. Get inside dere, out o' de way. Dey'll be bringin' her down in a minute.

(*He pushes the girl inside the house and comes down the steps.)*

THE POLICEMAN. Come on, git back from dem steps! Back now, all o' youse!

(*He and the* MARSHAL *push the crowd back to the right of the stoop, leaving the steps and the side-walk in front of them clear. Then he goes up the steps again.)*

THE MARSHAL. What did he do? Shoot two of 'em?

THE POLICEMAN. I'll say he did! His wife an' her sweetie. A guy named Sankey. He was dead when I got up dere.

THE MARSHAL. I seen him tryin' to climb out t'roo de winder. An' dis guy grabs 'im an' pulls 'im back.

THE INTERNE (*from the* MAURRANT *window*). Officer! Come on up!

(*He leaves the window, as the* POLICEMAN *exits into the house. Suddenly* SAM *utters an exclamation of anguish and, pushing his way out of the crowd, hurries over to the left.)*

THE MARSHAL. Hey, you! Where you goin'?

(SAM *ignores him and hurries on.)*

A WOMAN. Look! There's the Maurrant girl!

ANOTHER WOMAN. Who?

A WOMAN. It's her daughter.

(*The crowd murmurs excitedly, as* ROSE *comes on quickly at the left.)*

ROSE. What's the matter, Sam? What's the ambulance for? Did anybody get hurt?

SAM. Go away, Rose. Go away.

ROSE. Who is it, Sam? What's the matter? Is it my mother? It's not my mother, is it? (*Clinging to him.*) Sam, is it?

SAM. There's been an accident. Go away. Rose.

(*He tries to force her away.)*

ROSE. Tell me what's happened! Tell me!

MISS CUSHING (*appearing at the window*). They're bringing her down!

ROSE (*with a cry*). It *is* my mother!

MISS CUSHING (*seeing her*). Oh, my God, there's Rose!

(MRS. FIORENTINO, MRS. JONES, MRS. HILDEBRAND, LIPPO, *and* BUCHANAN *crowd to the* MAURRANT *windows.)*

SAM. Rose! Go away!

(*She pays no attention to him, but stands watching the door, transfixed. The* INTERNE *comes briskly out of the house.*)

THE INTERNE (*to the* MARSHAL). Hold the door open, will you?

(*He comes down the steps.*)

THE MARSHAL. Sure, doc!

(*He hurries into the vestibule.*)

THE INTERNE (*to the crowd*). Keep back, now!

ROSE (*seizing the* INTERNE's *arm*). Doctor! Is she dead?

THE INTERNE. Who are you? Her daughter?

ROSE. Yes, sir. I'm her daughter.

THE INTERNE. She's pretty badly hurt. Step aside, now!

(*They step aside, as the* AMBULANCE-DRIVER *and the* POLICEMAN *come out of the house, carrying* MRS. MAURRANT *on the stretcher. There is a low murmur from the crowd.*)

THE AMBULANCE-DRIVER. Easy, now.

THE POLICEMAN. All right.

(*They come down the steps and go towards the left.*)

ROSE (*running forward and gripping the side of the stretcher*). Mother! Mother!

MRS. MAURRANT (*opening her eyes, feebly*). Rose!

(*She tries to lift her hand, but it falls back.*)

THE INTERNE (*pulling* ROSE *back*). You mustn't talk to her now.

(SAM *takes her about the shoulders. They and the* INTERNE *follow the stretcher off at the left. The crowd swarms after them.* FRED *comes out of the house, carrying one end of an iron bedstead.*)

CURTAIN

ACT THREE

Mid-afternoon of the same day. At the left of the stoop is a large roll of bedding. Before the rise of the curtain, and continuing faintly thereafter, a woman can be heard singing scales. OLSEN, *pipe in mouth, is leaning against the railing. Two* MEN, *furniture-movers, appear at the left.*

ONE OF THE MEN (*picking up the bedding*). All right. Dat's all, Charlie!

(*The* MEN *exit left. A* POLICEMAN *comes out of the house, carrying the blood-stained dress of* MRS. MAURRANT, *and* SANKEY's *coat, cap, and bill-holder. He comes down the steps, and exits at the right. At the left, two young* NURSE-MAIDS, *in smart uniforms, appear, each wheeling a de-luxe baby-carriage.*)

FIRST NURSE-MAID (*seeing the house-number*). This must be the place, right here—346.

(*They stop, under the* MAURRANT *windows.*)

SECOND NURSE-MAID. Yes, I guess it is.

FIRST NURSE-MAID. Yes, this is it, all right. (*Looking up.*) Must be right up there, on the first floor, see?

SECOND NURSE-MAID. Yes, sure. (*Excitedly.*) Say, look! You can see where the glass is out of the window. That's where this feller What's-his-name tried to climb out.

FIRST NURSE-MAID. Oh, yes, I see it! Say, what do you know about that!

SECOND NURSE-MAID (*taking a pink tabloid newspaper from under the hood of the baby-buggy*). Wait! There's a picture of it somewhere. (*Turning the pages.*) Here it is. (*They excitedly examine it together, as she reads.*) "Composograph showing Sankey, scantily clad, in a last vain attempt to escape the vengeance of the jealousy-crazed husband whose home he had destroyed." And there's Maurrant pulling him back. And Mrs. Maurrant trying to get the pistol away from him, see? Look at the blood running down her face, will you?

FIRST NURSE-MAID. It's worse than awful! Can you *imagine* what those two must have felt like, when he walked in on them like that?

SECOND NURSE-MAID. Well, he just happened to be one of the ones that finds out! Believe me, there's lots and lots of husbands that don't know the half of what goes on up-town, while they're down-town making a living.

FIRST NURSE-MAID. Say, you're not telling me, are you? If I was to spill all I know, there'd be many a happy home busted up. I wonder if they caught him.

SECOND NURSE-MAID (*as her* BABY *begins a thin wailing*). Oh, God, he's in again! (*To the unseen* BABY) Shut up a little while, can't you?

(*She shakes the carriage.*)

A POLICEMAN (*appearing at the* MAURRANT *windows, a tabloid in his hand*). Keep movin', ladies. No loiterin' aroun' here.

FIRST NURSE-MAID (*eagerly*). Say, have they caught him yet?

THE POLICEMAN. Why, ain't you hoid? He was last seen flyin' over Nova Scotia, on his way to Paris.

FIRST NURSE-MAID. Who are you trying to string, anyhow?

SECOND NURSE-MAID (*coquettishly*). Say, will you let us come up and look around?

THE POLICEMAN. Why, sure, sure! Bring de babies, too. De commissioner is soivin' tea up here at four-thoity.

SECOND NURSE-MAID. You're awful smart, aren't you?

THE POLICEMAN. Yeah, that's why dey put me on de entertainment committee. I'm Handsome Harry Moiphy, de boy comedian o' Brooklyn.

FIRST NURSE-MAID (*looking at her watch*). Oh, say, I ought to be getting back. (*Turning her carriage.*) Clarice darling would throw a duck-fit, if she knew I brought her precious Dumplings to a neighborhood like this.

SECOND NURSE-MAID (*turning her carriage*). There's not so much to see, anyhow. It's nothing but a cheap, common dump.

(*They go towards the left.*)

THE POLICEMAN. Over de river, goils. See you in de funny paper.

SECOND NURSE-MAID. Don't you get so fresh.

THE POLICEMAN. Drop in again, when you're in de neighborhood. An' tell Mrs. Vanderbilt, Harry was askin' for her.

(*As the* NURSE-MAIDS *go off at the left,* EASTER *hurries on at the right, several folded newspapers under his arm.*)

EASTER (*to the* POLICEMAN, *going to the left of the stoop*). Is Miss Maurrant up there, officer?

THE POLICEMAN. No. There ain't nobody up here but me.

EASTER. You don't happen to know where she is, do you?

THE POLICEMAN. No, I don't. Are you a reporter?

EASTER. Who, me? I'm just a friend of hers. I've got to see her.

THE POLICEMAN. Well, I ain't seen her since she went off to the horspital this mornin'. She ain't been back since.

(*He starts to leave the window.*)

EASTER. Oh, officer!

THE POLICEMAN. Yeah?

EASTER. Have they caught him yet?

THE POLICEMAN. Naw, not yet. But we'll get 'im, all right!

(*He leaves the window.* EASTER *remains at the left of the stoop, uncertain whether to go or not.* MRS. JONES *appears, at the right, carrying several newspapers.*)

MRS. JONES (*to* OLSEN). Have they caught him yet?

OLSEN (*shaking his head*). No.

MRS. JONES. I been down at Police Headquarters all this while—(*Breaking off, as she notices* EASTER.) Say, what's he want here?

(OLSEN *shrugs his shoulders.*)

EASTER (*approaching them*). Pardon me, but maybe you can tell me where I can find Miss Maurrant?

(OLSEN *shakes his head.*)

MRS. JONES. Why no, I can't. I jus' this minute got back from Police Headquarters. Maybe she's aroun' at the horspital.

EASTER. No, I just came from there.

MRS. JONES. Well, I really couldn't say where she is. Was there somethin' special you wanted to see her about?

EASTER. I'm a friend of hers——

MRS. JONES. Yeah, I noticed you talkin' to her last night, when I took the dog out. (*Staring at him.*) Well, I guess she'll need all the friends she's got, now. Imagine a thing like that happenin' right here in this house, at ten o'clock in the mornin'! Everythin' goin' on just as usual, and then, all of a sudden, before you know it, there's two people murdered.

OLSEN. I tal everybody some day he kill her.

MRS. JONES. Well, I ain't sayin' it's right to kill anybody, but if anybody had a reason, he certainly had. You oughta heard some o' the questions they was askin' me down at the Police. I could feel myself gettin' redder an' redder. "Say," I says, "how do you expect me to know things like that?" (*Suddenly, as she looks left.*) Here's Rose now!

EASTER. Where?

(*He turns quickly and hurries to the left, as* ROSE *appears, carrying four or five packages.*)

MRS. JONES (*to* OLSEN). He seems to take a pretty friendly interest in her.

(OLSEN *nods.*)

ROSE (*anxiously, as she comes up to* EASTER *at the left of the stoop*). Have they caught him yet?

EASTER. Why no, they haven't. I just asked the officer upstairs.

ROSE. Oh, I hope he got away! If they get him, there's no telling what they'll do to him. And what would be the good of that? He never would have done it, if he'd been in his right mind.

EASTER. I only heard about it a little while ago. So I went right around to the hospital. But they said you'd left.

ROSE (*going to the steps*). She never opened her eyes again. They did everything they could for her, but it didn't help.

EASTER. Here, let me take your bundles.

ROSE. No, it's all right. I think I'll just sit down for a minute.

(*She sits on the stoop and puts the packages beside her.*)

EASTER. Can't I get you something? A drink or something?

ROSE. No, I'm all right. It's so hot. (*She puts her hand to her head.*) And all those people asking me a lot of questions.

MRS. JONES (*approaching the stoop*). Are you feelin' dizzy or anythin'?

ROSE. No, I'll be all right in a minute.

MRS. JONES. Well, I was gonna say, if you want to go up to my flat an' lay down for a minute——

ROSE. No, thanks; I don't want to lie down. I've got to go upstairs to get some things.

EASTER. Why, say, you don't want to go up there!

ROSE. I've got to; there's some things I need.

EASTER. Well, let me get them for you. Or this lady here.

MRS. JONES. Yeah, sure. The place is a sight up there. You're li'ble to go into a faint or somethin'.

ROSE. I guess nothing can be any worse than what's happened already. (*Indicating the bundles.*) I got to change my dress. I bought a white dress for her. And white silk stockings. I want her to look pretty.

MRS. JONES. Yeah, white is the nicest.

ROSE. She looks so quiet and natural. You'd think she was asleep.

MRS. JONES. It was the same way with my mother. You'd of thought she was gonna get up the next minute. (*Starting to go up the steps.*) Well, I gotta go up an' get me some lunch. Between everythin' happenin' an' goin' down to Police Headquarters an' all, I ain't had a bite to eat since breakfast. (*Stopping on the top step, and looking from* ROSE *to* EASTER.) Well, you certainly never know, when you get up in the mornin', what the day is gonna bring.

(*She enters the house.*)

ROSE (*rising*). Well, I'd better be going up, too. There's a lot of things to attend to.

EASTER. You better let me come up with you.

ROSE. Why thanks, Mr. Easter. But I'd rather go alone, if you don't mind.

EASTER. But, listen here—you can't go through all this alone—a kid like you. That's why I came around. I knew you'd be needing a helping hand.

ROSE. That's awfully nice of you, Mr. Easter. But I don't need any help, honest I don't.

(*She opens one of the packages.*)

EASTER. Why, you can't handle everything yourself! What about a place to live and all that?

ROSE (*taking a rosette of black crape out of the package*). Well, I don't exactly know, yet. I'll have to find some place where Willie and I can live. I'd like it to be some place where he wouldn't be running around the streets all the time. You see, there's nobody but me to look out for him now.

(OLSEN *crosses to the cellar.* MRS. JONES *appears at her window and furtively peeps out at* ROSE *and* EASTER.)

ROSE (*as she sees that* OLSEN *is about to descend the cellar steps*). Oh, Mr. Olsen!

OLSEN (*stopping*). Yes, ma'am.

ROSE. Would you mind lending me a hammer and some tacks? I want to put up this crape.

OLSEN. Yes, ma'am; I bring 'em right away.

(*He goes down into the cellar.* MRS. JONES *leaves the window.*)

EASTER (*insistently*). But why won't you let me help you out?

ROSE. It's terribly nice of you, Mr. Easter. But I'll be able to manage alone, really I will. It isn't as if I wasn't young and strong and able to take care of myself. But as it is, I'd sort of rather not be under obligations.

EASTER. Why, you wouldn't be under any obligations. I just mean it in a friendly way, that's all.

ROSE. You've been very nice to me and all that, Mr. Easter. But—well, I've been sort of thinking things over—you know, about what we talked about last night and all. And I honestly don't think I'd care about going on the stage.

EASTER. Say, you've got me all wrong, Rose! Just forget all about that, will you? I just want to help you out, that's all. (*Taking a step towards her.*) I think you're one swell kid, and I want to do something for you. I'm not trying to put anything over on you.

(SHIRLEY *appears, at the left, carrying her school-bag, from which a newspaper protrudes.*)

ROSE. Well, that's nice and friendly of you, Mr. Easter. And if I ever do need any help——

SHIRLEY (*catching sight of* ROSE). Rose! You poor thing! (*She runs up to* ROSE *and throws her arms about her.*) It's terrible—terrible!

ROSE. Yes, it is. But I sort of had a feeling, all along, that something terrible was going to happen.

(OLSEN *comes up the steps, with a hammer and a box of tacks.*)

SHIRLEY. How could he do such a thing! I couldn't believe it when I read it.

ROSE. He was out of his mind, when he did it. Oh, I only hope he got away! (*As* OLSEN *approaches.*) Oh, thanks, Mr. Olsen.

OLSEN. I do it.

ROSE (*giving him the crape*). Oh, would you, please? Right up there, I think.

(*She indicates the left of the doorway.*)

OLSEN (*going up the steps*). Sure.

ROSE (*going to* EASTER *and extending her hand*). Thanks for coming around, Mr. Easter. I don't know when I'll be able to get back to the office.

EASTER. Why, that's all right about that. Only, in the meantime, I wish——

ROSE. If I need any help, I'll let you know. (*With a tone of finality in her voice.*) Good-bye.

EASTER. All right; but don't forget. (*He hesitates, then decides to go.*) Well, good-bye.

(*He goes off at left.*)

ROSE. I've got to go up and get some things that Willie and I need. Sam went to call for him at school and take him around to my aunt's. You see, I didn't want him coming back here. He's only a little kid, after all.

SHIRLEY. Oh, it's such a terrible thing! can't believe it yet.

OLSEN (*holding up the crape*). Dis vay?

ROSE. Yes, like that. (*Hesitantly, as she picks up her bundles.*) Miss Kaplan, it's sort of silly of me, I guess. But I'm kind of afraid to go up there alone. I wonder if you'd mind coming up with me.

(OLSEN *tacks up the crape.*)

SHIRLEY. Anything I can do for you, poor child!

(*She and* ROSE *go up the steps.*)

ROSE. Thanks ever so much. (*To* OLSEN.) Thanks, Mr. Olsen. It's awfully nice of you.

(*She and* SHIRLEY *enter the house.* OLSEN *exits down the cellar steps.* KAPLAN *appears at his window, and seating himself, begins to read a newspaper. An undersized* MAN *and a tall, athletic* WOMAN *appear at the right. They are dressed for tennis, and carry tennis-rackets.*)

MAN (*as they cross*). He *would* say that.

WOMAN. So I just looked at him for a moment, without saying anything. And then, I said: "My dear boy," I said. "What do you expect anyhow, in this day and age?" I said, "Why even Frankl has to do a black bathroom occasionally," I said.

MAN (*as they disappear at the left*). Exactly! And what did he say to that?

(BUCHANAN *comes out of the house, and, seeing* KAPLAN *at the window, stops at the right balustrade.*)

BUCHANAN. Well, there's been *some* excitement around here to-day.

KAPLAN (*looking up from his paper*). Dees is a terrible t'ing vich hes heppened.

BUCHANAN. I'll say it is! You know, the way I look at it, he didn't have a right to kill the both of them like that. Of course I'm not saying what she did was right, either.

KAPLAN. How ken ve call ourselves ciwilized, ven ve see thet sax jealousy hes de power to avaken in us de primitive pessions of de sevege?

BUCHANAN (*rather bewildered by this*). Yes, that's true, too. Of course, you can't expect a man to stand by and see his home broken up. But murdering them, like that, is going a little too far. Well, I got to go and phone the doctor. This thing's given my wife a kind of a *re*lapse. She thought a lot of Mrs. Maurrant.

(*He goes down the steps, and off at the left, as* LIPPO *appears at the right.*)

LIPPO (*stopping in front of* KAPLAN's *window*). Dey don' ketcha Maurrant, ha?

KAPLAN. I hevn't hoid anyt'ing foider.

LIPPO. He'sa gonna gat da 'lectricachair, ha?

KAPLAN. De blood-lust of our enlightened population must be setisfied! De Chreestian state will kerry out to de last letter de Mosaic law.

LIPPO. Eef Ahm ketcha my wife sleepin' wit' 'nudder man, Ahm gonna kella 'er, too.

(SAM *hurries on at the left.*)

KAPLAN. So you t'ink thet merriage should give to de hosband de power of life and det' and thet——

SAM (*going up the steps*). Papa, is there any news of Maurrant?

KAPLAN. I hev heard notting.

SAM. The police are going to make me testify against him. What can I do, papa?

KAPLAN. You ken do notting.

SAM. How can I send a man to the electric-chair? How can I? I tried to stop him, papa. I tried to warn her—— (*He stops short, as several shots are heard off-stage at the left.*) What's that?

LIPPO (*excitedly*). Dey finda 'im!

(*He runs off at the left, followed by* SAM. KAPLAN *leans out of the window. At the same moment,* MRS. JONES *leans out of her window and, a moment later,* MRS. FIORENTINO *out of hers. In the* MAURRANT *apartment, the* POLICEMAN *leans out and* ROSE *and* SHIRLEY *appear in the hall bedroom window.* ROSE *is wearing a mourning-dress.* OLSEN *comes up the cellar steps and runs off at the left.* MRS. OLSEN *comes up the steps. Several* MEN *and* WOMEN *appear at the right, and run off at the left.*)

ROSE (*agitatedly*). Is that him?

THE POLICEMAN. Must be!

(*Voices are heard shouting in the distance, and then another shot. The* POLICEMAN *leaves the window.*)

ROSE. Oh, God! They wouldn't shoot him, would they?

(*She leaves the window.*)

SHIRLEY (*following her*). Rose!

(*Two or three more persons appear at the right and run off at the left. The* POLICEMAN *runs out of the house, as* BUCHANAN *appears at the left.*)

BUCHANAN (*excitedly*). They got him!

(*The* POLICEMAN *runs off at the left.* SHIRLEY *reappears at the* MAURRANT *window.*)

MRS. JONES (*calling*). Have they got him?

BUCHANAN. Yes! He was hiding in the furnace down at 322. (*As* ROSE *comes out of the house.*) They found him, Miss Maurrant!

ROSE (*her hand to her heart*). Oh! Is he hurt?

BUCHANAN. I don't know. He fired at the cops and they fired back at him. I was just passing the house when it happened.

MRS. JONES (*leaning far out*). Here they come!

(*She leaves the window. The low murmur of the approaching crowd can be heard, off-stage left.*)

ROSE. Where? (*She comes down the stoop and looks off at the left.*) Oh!

(*She covers her eyes and turns away.*)

MRS. FIORENTINO. You better come inside.

SHIRLEY. Come up, Rose.

BUCHANAN. Yes, you better.

(*He takes her by the arm.*)

ROSE (*resisting*). No. No. Please let me alone. I want to see him.

(*She leans against the railing. Meanwhile, the murmur and tramp of the approaching crowd has grown nearer and nearer.*)

MRS. FIORENTINO. Look at him, vill you!

(MISS CUSHING *comes out of the house and stands on the stoop, followed a moment later by* MRS. JONES. MAURRANT *appears at the left, between two policemen. Behind him a third* POLICEMAN *holds back a swarming crowd, which includes* SAM *and* LIPPO. MAURRANT'S *clothes are torn, and his right arm is in a crude sling. Sweat, blood, and grime have made him almost unrecognizable. The* POLICEMEN, *too, show evidences of a struggle.*)

ROSE (*running forward*). Pop! Are you hurt?

MAURRANT (*seeing her for the first time*). Rose!

ONE OF THE POLICEMEN (*to whom* MAURRANT *is manacled*). Keep back, miss!

MAURRANT. It's me daughter! Fer Chris' sake, boys, lemme talk to me daughter! Maybe I'll never be seein' her again!

FIRST POLICEMAN. Give 'im a woid wit' her.

(*He is the* OFFICER *who was on duty in the Maurrant apartment.*)

SECOND POLICEMAN (*after a moment's hesitation*). Well, all right. (*Savagely to* MAURRANT.) But don't try to pull nothin', hear?

(*There is a forward movement in the crowd.*)

FIRST POLICEMAN (*to the crowd*). Keep back, youse!

MAURRANT. Rose! You're wearin' a black dress, Rose!

ROSE. Oh, pop, why did you do it? Why did you?

MAURRANT. I must o' been out o' me head, Rose. Did she say anythin'?

ROSE. She never opened her eyes again.

MAURRANT. I'd been drinkin', Rose—see what I mean?—an' all the talk that was goin' around. I just went clean off me nut, that's all.

ROSE. What'll they do to you, pop?

MAURRANT. It's the chair for me, I guess. But I don't care—let 'em give me the chair. I deserve it all right. But it's her I'm thinkin' of, Rose—the way she looked at me. I oughtn't to done it, Rose.

ROSE. She was always so good and sweet.

MAURRANT. Don't I know it? I ain't no murderer—you ought to be the one to know that, Rose. I just went out o' me head, that's all it was.

SECOND POLICEMAN. All right, that's all now. Come on!

MAURRANT. Gimme a minute, can't you? She's me daughter. Gimme a chance, can't you? What's gonna happen to you, Rose?

ROSE. I'll be all right, pop. You don't need to worry about me.

MAURRANT. I ain't been a very good father, have I?

ROSE. Don't worry about that, pop.

MAURRANT. It ain't that I ain't meant to be. It's just the way things happened to turn out, that's all. Keep your eye on Willie, Rose. Don't let Willie grow up to be a murderer, like his pop.

ROSE. I'm going to do all I can for him, pop.

MAURRANT. You're a good girl, Rose. You was always a good girl.

ROSE (*breaking down*). Oh, pop!

(*She throws her arms about his neck and buries her head against him.* MAURRANT *sobs hoarsely.*)

FIRST POLICEMAN (*gently*). Come on now, miss.

(*He and* SAM *take* ROSE *away from* MAURRANT.)

SECOND POLICEMAN. All right. Come on, Charlie.

(THEY *go towards the right, the crowd swarming behind them. Straggling along at the very end of the crowd is an unkempt* WOMAN, *wheeling a ramshackle baby-carriage.* MRS. JONES *and* MISS CUSHING *fall in with the crowd.* ROSE *gradually recovers her self-control, and stands at the stoop with* SAM *beside her. The others watch the receding crowd for a moment. Then* KAPLAN *and* MRS. FIORENTINO *leave their windows. The* FIRST POLICEMAN *enters the house, followed by* LIPPO. MRS. OLSEN *goes to the cellar.* SHIRLEY *looks down at* ROSE *and* SAM *for a moment, then abruptly leaves the window.*)

SAM (*taking* ROSE *by the arm*). Rose, you better come inside.

ROSE. No, I'm all right again, Sam—honestly I am. (*Trying to regain her self-composure.*) What about Willie, Sam?

SAM. I told him an accident had happened.

ROSE. It's better to break it to him that way. But I'll have to tell him, I guess. He'd only find it out himself to-morrow, with the papers all full of it. I saw Mrs. Sankey down at Police Headquarters. It's terrible for her, with two little children.

SHIRLEY (*appearing at the* MAURRANT *window, a covered pot in her hand*). Rose!

ROSE (*looking up*). Yes, Miss Kaplan?

SHIRLEY. There's a chicken here that I found on the gas-stove.

ROSE. A chicken?

SHIRLEY. Yes. The policeman says he smelt it cooking this morning, so he turned out the gas.

ROSE. Oh, I remember, now. My mother said she was going to make some soup for poor Mrs. Buchanan, upstairs.

SHIRLEY. It won't keep long, in this weather.

ROSE. No. I really think Mrs. Buchanan ought to have the good of it.

SHIRLEY. All right. I'll take it up to her.

ROSE. Thanks ever so much, Miss Kaplan. (SHIRLEY *leaves the window.*) It's only a few hours ago that she was standing right here, telling me about the chicken. And then she went upstairs, and the next I saw of her, they were carrying her out. (*Abruptly, as she starts to go up the steps.*) Well, I've got to go up and get my things.

SAM. I must talk to you! What are you going to do, Rose?

ROSE. Well, I haven't really had any time to do much thinking. But I really think the best thing I could do, would be to get out of New York. You know, like we were saying this morning—how things might be different, if you only had a chance to breathe and spread out a little. Only when I said it, I never dreamt it would be this way.

SAM. If you go, I'll go with you.

ROSE. But, Sam dear——

SAM. I don't care anything about my career. It's you—you—I care about. Do you think I can stay here, stifling to death, in this slum, and never seeing you? Do you think my life means anything to me without you?

ROSE. But, Sam, we've got to be practical about it. How would we manage?

SAM. I don't care what I do. I'll be a day-laborer; I'll dig sewers—anything. (*Taking her passionately in his arms.*) Rose, don't leave me!

ROSE. I like you so much, Sam. I like you better than anybody I know.

SAM. I love you, Rose. Let me go with you!

ROSE. It would be so nice to be with you. You're different from anybody I know. But I'm just wondering how it would work out.

SAM. If we have each other, that's the vital thing, isn't it? What else matters but that?

ROSE. Lots of things, Sam. There's lots of things to be considered. Suppose something was to happen—well, suppose I was to have a baby, say. That sometimes happens, even when you don't want it to. What would we do, then? We'd be tied down then, for life, just like all the other people around here. They all start out loving each other and thinking that everything is going to be fine—and before you know it, they find out they haven't got anything and they wish they could do it all over again—only it's too late.

SAM. It's to escape all that, that we must be together. It's only because we love each other and belong to each other, that we can find the strength to escape.

ROSE (*shaking her head*). No, Sam.

SAM. Why do you say no?

ROSE. It's what you said just now—about people belonging to each other. I don't think people ought to belong to anybody but themselves. I was thinking that if my mother had really belonged to herself, and that if my father had really belonged to himself, it never would have happened. It was only because they were always depending on somebody else for what they ought to have had inside themselves. Do you see what I mean, Sam? That's why I don't want to belong to anybody, and why I don't want anybody to belong to me.

SAM. You want to go through life alone?—never loving anyone, never having anyone love you?

ROSE. Why, of course not, Sam! I want love more than anything else in the world. But loving and belonging aren't the same thing. (*Putting her arms about him.*) Sam dear, listen. If we say good-bye now, it doesn't mean that it has to be forever. Maybe some day, when we're older and wiser, things will be different. Don't look as if it was the end of the world, Sam!

SAM. It *is* the end of my world.

ROSE. It isn't, Sam! If you'd only believe in yourself a little more, things wouldn't look nearly so bad. Because once you're sure of yourself, the things that happen to you aren't so important. The way I look at it, it's not what you do that matters so much; it's what you are. (*Warmly.*) I'm so fond of you, Sam. And I've got such a lot of confidence in you. (*Impulsively.*) Give me a nice kiss!

(SAM *takes her in his arms and kisses her passionately. A gawky* GIRL *of seventeen—one of* LIPPO'*s pupils, appears at the left, and looks at them, scandalized. Then she goes into the vestibule and rings the bell. The door clicks and she enters the house, as* SHIRLEY *comes out, carrying a wicker suit-case.* SHIRLEY *looks at* SAM *and* ROSE.)

ROSE (*to* SHIRLEY). I was just telling Sam that I think I'll soon be going away from New York.

(SAM *looks at her for a moment, in agony, then goes abruptly into the house.*)

SHIRLEY. I put your things in this suit-case.

(*She comes down to the pavement. The* GIRL, *in the Fiorentino apartment, begins tuning her violin.*)

ROSE (*taking the suit-case*). You've been awfully nice to me. Don't worry about Sam, Miss Kaplan. Everything will be all right with him.

SHIRLEY. I hope so.

(*From the Fiorentino apartment come the strains of Dvorák's "Humoresque," jerkily played on a violin.*)

ROSE. Oh, I just know it will! (*Extending her hand.*) Good-bye, Miss Kaplan.

SHIRLEY. Good-bye, Rose. (*Impulsively.*) You're a sweet girl!

(*She hugs and kisses her.*)

ROSE. I hope I'll see you again.

SHIRLEY (*crying*). I hope so, Rose.

(ROSE *takes up the suit-case and goes off at the left.* SHIRLEY *stands watching her.*)

KAPLAN (*re-appearing at his window*). Shoiley, vot's de metter again vit Sem? He's crying on de bed.

SHIRLEY. Let him alone, papa, can't you?

(*She turns and enters the house.* KAPLAN *sighs and, seating himself at the window, opens a newspaper. A shabby, middle-aged* COUPLE *appear at the right, and approach the stoop.*)

THE MAN (*reading the To-Let sign*). Here's a place. Six rooms. Want to take a look at it?

(A GROUP OF CHILDREN *off-stage left begin singing "The Farmer in the Dell." This continues until after the curtain is down.*)

THE WOMAN. All right. No harm lookin'. Ring for the janitor. (*The* MAN *goes up the stoop and rings the janitor's bell.*) Somebody must o' just died.

THE MAN. Yeah, maybe that's why they're movin' out. (*Wiping his face with a handkerchief.*) Phoo! Seems to be gettin' hotter every minute.

(MRS. FIORENTINO *seats herself at her window, a sewing-basket in her lap.* MRS. JONES *and* MISS CUSHING *appear at the right, busily engaged in conversation.*)

MISS CUSHING. The poor little thing!

MRS. JONES (*as they go up the steps*). Well, you never can tell with them quiet ones. It wouldn't surprise me a bit, if she turned out the same way as her mother. She's got a gentleman friend, that I guess ain't hangin' around for nothin'. I seen him late last night, and this afternoon, when I come home from the police——

(*She is still talking, as they enter the house.* MRS. OLSEN *comes up the cellar steps.* A SAILOR *appears at the left with two girls, an arm about the waist of each. They stroll slowly across.*)

CURTAIN

Born in Chicago in 1898 and adopted three years later by his stepfather, Solomon Sturges, who apparently took a considerable interest in travel and education, Preston Sturges received an extensive education during his childhood in Paris, Normandy, Lausanne, Dresden, Berlin and Naples. But he plunged quite soon into the workaday world—first into his mother's cosmetic business, then into the brokerage business as a runner. Subsequently he became an inventor of sorts and a song writer (1927-28), and finally entered the theatre as assistant stage manager for Brock Pemberton. This step carried Mr. Sturges into the arduous profession of playwriting, and he turned out several plays—*The Guinea Pig* (1928), *Strictly Dishonorable* (1929), *Recapture* (1930), *Well of Romance* (1930), and *Child of Manhattan* (1932). Of these only *Strictly Dishonorable,* produced by Brock Pemberton, won unqualified acclaim and success.

Inevitably Mr. Sturges gravitated to the motion picture industry, where he became that remarkable phenomenon, a screen writer who can have his say on celluloid and can practice the fine art of satire with little restraint. Perhaps the reason for this, however, is to be found in the author's ability to skate lightly on the surface of reality, which is no mean accomplishment in his particular case since he has a special flair for humor and oddity. In Hollywood, he also came to direct his own scenarios, which is an advantage to a writer of his unconventional calibre. The results of this good fortune are to be seen at their best perhaps in *The Great McGinty* (1940), an Academy Award winner, in *The Miracle of Morgan's Creek* (1943), and in *Hail the Conquering Hero,* 1944.

Strictly Dishonorable, which ran continuously for over 550 performances, proved to be a thoroughly delightful comedy set in the speakeasy *milieu* of Manhattan. Mingled with genial sophistication and casual irreverence, it is a vivid, if unassuming, comedy of manners. The play was also quite unique in departing from the dominantly strenuous style that was normally applied to the prohibition era. It forms a marked contrast to *Broadway* and to some of the Kaufman farce-comedies.

Strictly Dishonorable

BY PRESTON STURGES

First produced by Brock Pemberton at the Avon Theatre, New York City, on September 18, 1929, with the following cast:

GIOVANNI	John Altieri
MARIO	Marius Rogati
TOMASO ANTIOVI	William Ricciardi
JUDGE DEMPSEY	Carl Anthony
HENRY GREENE	Louis Jean Heydt
ISABELLE PARRY	Muriel Kirkland
COUNT DI RUVO	Tullio Carminati
PATROLMAN MULLIGAN	Edward J. McNamara

ACT I

The speakeasy of Tomaso Antiovi on West 49th St.—11:41 P.M.

ACT II

A rear apartment upstairs over the speakeasy—12:40 A.M.

ACT III

Same apartment upstairs over the speakeasy—10:00 A.M.

ACT ONE

SCENE.—*An Italian speakeasy in West 49th Street. About midnight, a Saturday evening in Autumn.*

Door R.2 leads into kitchen. Door U.R. leads into hall which runs from R. to L., connecting with the kitchen off R. and the street door off L. Arch U.L. leads into hallway stairs to apartments, upstairs can be seen through arch. Two windows in R. wall, but they are covered with heavy drapes and cannot be seen. Bar down R. Stool behind bar; stool in front of bar upstage end. Small door U.R. and Arch U.L. Mirror between two windows. Two tables before banquette. Chair R. of Table R. Chair below Table L. Wall telephone R. of banquette. Hall rack in hall. R. and between rack and stairs, small chair. Slot machine U.L. Portable phonograph on stool just above mirror. Radio R. of Arch. Table and 3 chairs L.C.

At Rise: MARIO, *a waiter, is reading tabloid newspaper at table U.L.C. The radio is playing.* GIOVANNI *is seated in hall listening to music.*

GIOVANNI. La musica é una gran bella cosa.

(MARIO *turns off radio angrily, then reads.* GIOVANNI *enters, puzzled, then turns on radio. He goes back to seat.*)

MARIO. Come é possible sentire a questa robaccia.

(*Turns off radio.* GIOVANNI *rises and comes into room.*)

GIOVANNI. Che diavolo succede. Bada di non toccare niente. (*Turns on radio and hides behind arch R. side.* MARIO *tears paper in rage, then turns off radio just as* GIOVANNI *looks in and catches him by wrist.*) A lazzarone! Ti hó detto. Di non toccare.

MARIO. Questo maledetto radio mi fá venire inervi.

GIOVANNI. Ma io hó l'ostesso diritto di sentire il radio come tu di leggere il giornale.

(TOM *enters R.2 and crosses between them.*)

TOM. Silenzio! What's a matter with you people? You make all noise when it's near to close. E questa tavola qui senza sparecchiare.

(GIOVANNI *goes into hall. The iron gate is heard to slam and he goes off L. to answer it.* MARIO *folds napkins and orders table, then sits upstage and pulls tabloid from pocket and begins to read.*)

GIOVANNI (*off L.*) Good evening, Mister Judge.

(JUDGE *enters, starting to stairs as* TOM *stops him.* GIOVANNI *sits in hall.*)

TOM (*goes upstage toward arch*). Oh, Mister Judge, could you come in one minute, please?

JUDGE. I'm pretty tired, Tom. I want to get upstairs to bed.

TOM. Only just one little minute.

JUDGE (*entering to R. of* TOM). What is it?

TOM. I make you one drink, huh? Then you no feel tired.

JUDGE. No. I've had a devil of a siege in court today and I'm tired and weak.

TOM. I make one little Old Fashioned. (*He crosses* JUDGE *and starts to bar;* JUDGE *follows to front of bar upstage end.*)

JUDGE. I know your Old Fashioneds; don't make more than one.

TOM (*behind bar*). All right, Mister Judge—all right. (*Starts to mix drink.*) Judge, I got today a bigga trouble. I gotta paper.

JUDGE. What sort of a paper?

TOM. I don't know, Mister Judge. A man leava dis paper—(*Takes summons from pocket.*) Suh—suh—summons to appear before the presiding mag—magistrato. I don't understand. I no do nothing. (*Hands* JUDGE *summons.*)

JUDGE. Let me see it. (*Reads summons.*) Why—this is for contempt of court!

TOM. Me?

JUDGE. Sure. Tomaso Antiovi.

TOM. Corpo di Bacco! Contempt of court? Why, I do nothing. What means contempt for court, Mister Judge?

JUDGE. Contempt? Why, it means you have no respect for the court—that you—ah—spit on it.

TOM. I spit? Cristo Santo! Never could I do such a thing, Mister Judge. I spit on the court? I do not even spit on the floor. I have admiration for the court. I love the court and all the fine judges—like you, Mister Judge.

JUDGE. Yeah—I know. Well now, let me see—you were summoned to appear on Tuesday. Why didn't you go instead of being in contempt?

TOM. I have no contempt. Why must I go last Tuesday?

JUDGE. Because you were caught speeding on Sunday.

TOM. It say that?

JUDGE. Sure it does.

(WAITER *rises guiltily and starts to straighten table, moving around slowly to L. and downstage as scene progresses.*)

TOM. Me make too much money to go joy ride. I no use the car on Sunday, Mister Judge.

JUDGE. You didn't lend your car to anybody, did you?

TOM. Lend my—?

(*Looks at* MARIO *and crosses to him.* MARIO *comes part way to him from front of table and they meet at L.C.*)

Mario—Mario! You took my automobile—

MARIO. Si l'hó preso, ma non é successo niente.

TOM (*turning to* JUDGE). Yes, Mister Judge, he took the automobile, but he say nothing happen.

JUDGE. Did any policeman give you a paper?

MARIO. No, Mister Judge—only one small very little ticket.

TOM (*mimicking him*). Only one very little ticket—

JUDGE. Were you speeding?

MARIO. No, Mister Judge, no. I went so slow—like a snails I went—a sick snails.

JUDGE (*returning to bar*). You must have been obstructing traffic. Well, I guess it'll be all right.

(*Gives* TOM *summons.*)

TOM (*returning to behind bar*). You fix it up, Mister Judge?

(MARIO *picks up glasses and bottles from table.*)

JUDGE. Yes, I'll fix it up.

TOM. Thank you, Mister Judge—I'm very sorry.

GIOVANNI (*appearing in arch, mimicking* MARIO). I went slow—like a snails, Mister Judge. Animale!

MARIO. Tartaruge! Lumacha!

TOM. Piano! Ssh! Ssh! (*They stop abruptly.* GIOVANNI *returns to chair in hall;* MARIO *exits U.R. The telephone rings.*) This is a SPEAKEASY. You make it sound like a LOUDSPEAKER! (*He answers phone.*) Allo. Yes. His excellency no come in yet, Miss Lilli. No. . . . No. . . . No. . . . I don't know. . . . Any time now. . . . Yes, Miss Lilli. You call again . . . all right. Goodbye. (*Hangs up and goes to table U.R.C. Takes pencil and makes note of call.*) Alla time—alla time—womens call up—Miss Lilli—Mimi—Miss Katie — Susie — Tessy — alla time — too much for a singer!

JUDGE. Is Di Ruvo singing tonight?

TOM (*coming down slightly*). No—no sing tonight. Sing last night. Pagliacci. I go. Ah, Dio mio! The whole Metropolitan. Everybody, he weep like an onions when he sing—(*Sings.*) Ri di Pagliacci. (*At finish of a snatch of song.*) Ah, he is grand!

JUDGE. Where is he? I want to congratulate him.

TOM. He go on big party, but he should be home now. (*Looks at watch.*) He stay out too late. No good.

JUDGE. Why shouldn't he stay out late if he wants to? He isn't a child.

TOM. Ah, to me, il Signorino is always a child—a little child. I remember in Sorrento when he first arrive—when the stork bring him and his father, il Signor Conte, come all smiles and tell us servants: Open the wine, my good friends, and drink to the health of my son who just now, this minute, I have the pleasure to meet.

JUDGE. Yes, but he's grown up now.

TOM. Ah, grown up. To me who see him so—and so—and so—well, now he is so. But still he is not grown up. When I tell him instructions from his mother, La Signora Contessa, you know what he do—he laugh at me. (*Bell rings.* GIOVANNI *rises and exits L. in hall.* TOM *looks at watch again, shakes his head sadly as he returns behind bar.*) Ah, too late—too late!

JUDGE. Nonsense, nonsense!

TOM. No nonsense, Judge—no good.

JUDGE. He can take care of himself.

GIOVANNI (*appearing in arch and holding up small card*). Customers, Signor Tomaso.

TOM. Who are they?

GIOVANNI. Man and a lady—no come before.

TOM. They got card?

GIOVANNI. Yeah.

TOM. All right.

(GIOVANNI *exits R. in hall.* JUDGE *starts to arch.*)

JUDGE. I guess I'd better disappear. (HENRY *appears in arch and looks in room.*) Oh.

(JUDGE *returns and sits below bar.* HENRY *not pleased with place starts to leave.*)

TOM. Come in, Mister—come in.

HENRY (*turns to go; meets* ISABELLE).

Naw. I'll come back some other time.

(*Sound of Gate off L. and* ISABELLE *appears in arch and enters room slightly, looking around.*)

TOM. What's the matter? You no like?

ISABELLE (*R. side of arch*). What a lovely place, Henry. And look at that quaint little bar. Can we sit down?

(TOM *exits R.2.*)

HENRY. No. This isn't the place I thought it was. This is dead. I guess I got the cards mixed.

ISABELLE (*crossing to L. end of table U.L.C.*). I—I like it here, Henry.

HENRY. I tell you the other place is the one we're looking for. The whole gang from the office goes there. They'll be there with their wives.

ISABELLE. Let's not bother. It took an hour to park the car this time. (*Goes to chair R. of table L.C.*) Let's sit down for a minute, anyway.

HENRY (*coming down slightly*). I tell you if you saw the other place . . .

ISABELLE. I wouldn't even know the difference, Henry. I've never been in a speakeasy before and I'm afraid if we leave this one, you'll just carry me home.

HENRY (*comes L. of table L.C. and sits*). Oh—all right. But we'd be better off if we were home.

ISABELLE (*sits R. of table L.C.*). Aw, no, we wouldn't. You gotta have a little fun sometimes.

(*She opens pocketbook, takes out mirror and looks at herself. Powders nose. Leaves pocketbook open with* HENRY's *list easily accessible.*)

HENRY. What's the matter with home? (TOM *enters R.2 with bottle of cherries, placing them on bar.*) Don't you like it there?

ISABELLE. Of course I do, Henry.

HENRY. Well, don't—talk that way about it then. (*To* TOM.) Hey, there—how about some service?

TOM (TOM *rings bell.* MARIO *enters U.R.*). In a moment.

MARIO (*crossing to table*). You like a drink?

HENRY (*mimicking*). Yes, I like a drink. What do you think I came here for? Bring me a double Scotch! What do you want, Izzy—a liqueur?

ISABELLE. Whatever you say, Henry. It's all the same to me.

HENRY. And a crême de mint!

WAITER (*as he crosses to upper end of bar*). One double Scotch—and one benedictine.

HENRY. I . . . SAID . . . CRÊME . . . DEE . . . MINT! Now get it straight!

MARIO. No got any. S'alla same, anyway.

TOM. Maybe I got!

(TOM *exits R.2.* MARIO *starts to read tabloid.*)

HENRY. Well, make it snappy!

ISABELLE. Don't get angry, Henry. You never used to get cross so easily. Why . . . when . . . when I first knew you, you were always smiling and . . . and sweet. What's the matter with you, getting cross all the time?

HENRY. You didn't think I was going to be as sappy all my life as when I first met you, did you?

ISABELLE. Well, I hoped so. You said you'd be always like that and I'd . . . learn to love you 'cause you were going to be so good to me. You weren't just making believe, were you?

HENRY. Of course I wasn't. But when a fellow's courting a girl, naturally . . . he puts his best foot forward . . . and . . . puts up with a whole lot of damned nonsense he . . . he wouldn't stand for all his life. Now when I sell bonds—

ISABELLE. You . . . you're not going to be nice to me any more?

HENRY. Of course I am, Isabelle. But you've got to be more SERIOUS. LIFE is serious. You Southerners are all alike. You think the sun shines just to make a nice day for you to go picnicking. It doesn't! It shines to germinate the wheat kernels to make your bread. It shines so you can have vegetables—fresh squash, beans, spinach—

ISABELLE. I hate spinach!

(TOM *enters R.2.*)

HENRY. Well, you don't eat the right food. But you will! (*To* TOM.) Say, do I have to wait here all night?

TOM. Just a minute, Mister. I got other customer. Must serve him first.

HENRY. You seem to be taking a long time about it.

TOM. An Old Fashioned take a lot of stuff.

ISABELLE. We're not in any hurry, Henry.

HENRY. Who said we're not? I want to get home.

ISABELLE. Not just yet, please. You know . . . New York thrills me so, I'm happy . . . just to be in it.

HENRY. Yeah? Well, it doesn't thrill me. (*Drums table and looks over at* TOM.) Hey!

TOM. In a moment, sir.

ISABELLE. Could we—could we have our drinks at the bar, Henry?

HENRY. The bar is for men; you'd better stay at the table.

ISABELLE. Oh, but I wanted to . . . (*Resignedly.*) Oh, all right.

JUDGE (*to* TOM). They must be married.

ISABELLE. Not yet. (*To* JUDGE.) But this is part of my trousseau.

JUDGE. Take your time, young woman, take your time. S'like going to jail: S'easy to get in, but hard to get out. I know. I'll tell you how I know. . . .

(*Rises and starts toward them.* HENRY *scowls at him menacingly.*)

HENRY. Yeah?

JUDGE (*crosses to bar*). Some other time, my dear, some other time.

TOM. Mario!

MARIO. Subito!

(*Picks up tray of drinks, crosses to table and serves them—then exits U.R. to kitchen.*)

HENRY (*in an ugly mood*). Well, it's about time . . . and say! Tell your friend the jailbird to keep away from this table.

JUDGE (*crossing to C*). Jailbird! Are you referring to me?

TOM. Ssh! Ssh! Ssh!

JUDGE (*in a voice like thunder*). Answer my question!

ISABELLE (*looks up at him and makes a pleading little gesture with her hands*). Please. . . .

JUDGE. At your service, Madam. (*Turns to* TOM.) You know, Tom, I seem to be the only sober person in this place—(*Turns to* ISABELLE *and bows.*) And you, Madam—and you. And this is no place for a sober man. (*Starts to door U.R.*) I'm going into the kitchen—(*Turns at door.*)—where the eggs aren't boiled so hard.

(*He exits.* TOM *exits R.2.*)

ISABELLE (*rising*). I suppose we'd better get out of here, Henry.

(*She starts getting her things together.*)

HENRY (*sullenly*). There's no hurry. That old . . . Turk isn't going to drive me away!

ISABELLE. No, Henry . . . (*Coaxingly.*) . . . But let's go anyway . . . and not have any more rows this evening.

(HENRY *pounds table.* TOM *enters R.2.*)

HENRY. Bring me another Scotch.

TOM. S'pretty late . . . Well . . . one more maybe . . . all right.

HENRY. Don't do me any favors.

TOM (*framed in doorway*). Don't worry, Mister, I won't.

ISABELLE. Really, Henry, I'd much rather go. (TOM *rings bell.*)

HENRY (*harshly*). Well, I'd rather stay. (MARIO *enters U.R. and goes to upper end of bar.*) I suppose I'm in the wrong again. (TOM *exits R.2.*)

ISABELLE. No, you aren't!

HENRY. I suppose I should have let that old booze-hound get away with that stuff. . . .

ISABELLE (*sitting R. of table L.C.*). No, Henry. You were perfectly right . . . (MARIO *starts across to serve drink.*) I mean it . . . but sometimes I . . .

HENRY. But sometimes you what?

ISABELLE (*desperately*). I mean . . . (MARIO *serves a double Scotch.*) Thank you very much. . . . Now let's be happy. Here's to you, Henry. Here's to us.

(MARIO *exits U.R.*)

HENRY (*doggedly*). Sometimes you what?

ISABELLE. Huh? Oh, I don't remember. (*Sweetly.*) Let's forget about it.

HENRY. Let's *not.* If you've got any private thoughts about me, I'd rather know them . . . BEFORE we're married. If I had any private thoughts or criticisms of you, I'd tell you about them.

ISABELLE. I'm sure you would, dear, you're so . . . frank.

HENRY. Well, you be frank, too!

ISABELLE. It's nothing really, except that I'm not used to all the ways up here.

HENRY. Well, the people are different.

ISABELLE. Oh, not really, I guess, but . . . down home everybody's sort of friendly like . . . that's all.

HENRY. That's only because it's a little town. You'll find the same thing once we're settled in West Orange. . . .

ISABELLE. I . . . I don't think we'll find it in West Orange, Henry.

HENRY. What's the matter with West Orange?

ISABELLE. Oh, nothing.

HENRY. Isn't everybody there friendly to you? The family's certainly been nice to you, hasn't it?

ISABELLE. Of course, Henry. Naturally everybody I've *met* has been nice. That isn't what I'm talking about. It's the whole *feeling* out there that isn't . . . cordial. Don't you see?

HENRY. Frankly, I don't.

ISABELLE. No . . . I don't suppose you do. But . . . but . . . that's why I don't want to live in New Jersey.

HENRY (*facing her across table*). You . . . you . . . don't . . . want . . . to . . . live . . . in . . . New Jersey!

ISABELLE. No, Henry, I don't.

HENRY. But that's . . . ridiculous! I've never *lived* anywhere else. I've never *considered* living anywhere else.

ISABELLE. I know, dear.

HENRY. All my family's lived there always. I was born there. Why, it's *beautiful* in New Jersey.

ISABELLE. Yes, Henry . . . But I don't like it.

HENRY. I suppose you're going to tell me Yoakum, Mississippi, is a better town than West Orange. That little dump!

ISABELLE. I never said I wanted to live in Yoakum all my life. . . . I don't boast about it.

HENRY. You don't bo . . . Well, I should say you wouldn't. Good Lord! You come from Yoakum to West Orange. . . .

ISABELLE. From Hell to Heaven?

HENRY. Well, I wouldn't have said it. . . .

ISABELLE. Of course not, dear, you're too polite. (*She smiles at him quizzically.*) Aw, listen to me, Henry. I'm not ungrateful. It was sweet of your mother to ask me to visit you all and give me those two pretty dresses. I think you're all just as nice as you can be: sweet and thoughtful and . . . and very elegant and . . . and . . . honorable and . . . and . . . (*She makes a hopeless gesture.*) . . . But I don't want to live in New Jersey, Henry.

HENRY. Where *do* you want to live?

ISABELLE. Couldn't we have a tiny little apartment here? I've seen pictures in "House and Garden" of such cunning ones . . . with little kitchenettes and . . . and . . . built-in wash-tubs and things. Couldn't we afford that, Henry?

HENRY. Of course I could afford it . . . but you couldn't run it. You can't even take care of your own stuff, let alone manage a whole apartment!

ISABELLE. I could manage it.

HENRY. No, you couldn't! (*Takes list from her pocketbook.*) How about this little list of things I asked you to do yesterday?

ISABELLE. I did 'em.

HENRY. Yeah? (*Reading from list.*) "Purchase six white broadcloth shirts for Henry. Size fifteen and 34 inch sleeve. . . .

ISABELLE. I got 'em.

HENRY. Yeah . . . you got 'em! Thirty-five and a half inch sleeves so Mother had to sit up half the night shortening them . . . you can't even sew.

ISABELLE. I can embroider.

HENRY. That's practical! And another thing . . . did you go to the Insulex Office and get their booklet on heating an eight-room house all winter on a ton of coal?

ISABELLE. I don't think you can.

HENRY. Never mind what you think, did you?

ISABELLE. I . . . I forgot.

HENRY. Check! (*Checks off item.*) Now did you go up and look at that lot?

ISABELLE. Uh-huh.

HENRY. Well?

ISABELLE. I don't like it.

HENRY. What are you talking about? Why, that's one of the finest lots in town. In the heart of a restricted neighborhood, near a playground . . . for the kiddies, only a block from Mother's, a block and a half from the church . . . what's the matter with it?

ISABELLE. It hasn't got any trees on it.

HENRY. Good! What are trees good for, anyway—except for a lot of damned birds to roost in and wake you up at four o'clock in the morning!

ISABELLE. Oh, Henry. . . .

HENRY. Besides, you'll be a lot better off near Mother, so she can show you how to manage things.

ISABELLE. I want to live here, Henry.

HENRY. I've already told you I don't like New York . . . rotten, dirty place. I want to be some place where I can exercise and take long walks, where I've got room to BREATHE.

ISABELLE. Don't you think you could do that here? Everybody looks as if they breathed all right.

HENRY. Yeah—carbon monoxide!

ISABELLE. I don't know anything about that, but I read in a paper where people out in the country die much sooner than people in a big city.

HENRY. That's not statistics!

ISABELLE. Well, it said so in the paper. (*She looks away despondently.*) Aw, Henry, couldn't we live here for a while anyway?

HENRY (*disagreeably*). Well, you can live where you like . . . but *I'm* going to live in West Orange.

ISABELLE (*after a pause*). Then I will too, Henry. . . . (*She smiles with an effort.*) . . . And . . . and maybe it'll be very nice.

HENRY. You bet it will! (*Patronizingly.*) Well now, that's settled! You just leave your happiness to me, and you won't have a thing to worry about.

ISABELLE. I . . . I know I won't, Henry.

HENRY (*pompously*). That's the way to talk. (ISABELLE *rises and starts towards the bar.*) Where are you going?

ISABELLE (*stopping C.*). Just over here. I . . . I want to put my foot on the rail.

HENRY. I think you'd better stay at the table.

ISABELLE (*over her shoulder*). Please, Henry. Let me do a little bit what I like—till we get married.

(*She goes to bar, putting foot on rail and laughing. Her arm hits bell accidentally. She laughs and rings bell again, then pounds twice on bar.* TOM *enters R.* HENRY *rises—goes up to Victrola and starts to wind it.*)

TOM. Yessir?

ISABELLE (*pretending to be an old souse*). Gimme a drink.

TOM (*smilingly*). Yessir, what you want?

ISABELLE. What've you got?

TOM. Baccardi, Manhattan, Bronx, Silver Fizz, Golden Fizz . . . Old Fashioned.

ISABELLE. Ooh! I think I'll go back to my boyhood days and have an Old Fashioned.

TOM. Yessir.

ISABELLE. Will you join me, Henry?

HENRY (*crossing to center*). No, thanks—I've got a Scotch. You'd better stick to Crême de Mint.

ISABELLE. But that just tastes like sugar-water. Henry, I'd like to have something real while we're here.

HENRY. You want to get drunk, huh?

ISABELLE. Course I don't—it's only an Old Fashioned—and old-fashioned people never got drunk—leastways, that's what I always heard.

HENRY. By the way . . . who's paying for this?

ISABELLE (*looking in pocketbook*). Oh, I forgot, I haven't any money, Mister.

TOM. Don't you worry, young lady—no pretty girl has to go thirsty in Tom's place.

ISABELLE (*toward* HENRY). There, Henry. You see? That's what I call friendly. Thank you, Tom, very much.

TOM. 'S all right, lady. Any time.

HENRY (*back to Victrola*). Oh, I'll pay for it.

ISABELLE. No, Henry. (*Back to bar.*) We couldn't allow that. Could we, Tom?

TOM. Yes, mam.

(*He puts the completed drink before her.*)

ISABELLE. You should say no.

TOM. Yes, mam.

ISABELLE. Well, anyway . . . Here's to you, Tom. (*She drinks.*) That was *delicious.*

TOM (*in a whisper*). You want another one?

ISABELLE. Yes.

JUDGE (*enters U.R., going to bar*). Say, Tom . . . (*He sees* ISABELLE.) Make me one of those too.

ISABELLE (*is feeling slightly emancipated already*). They're mostly fruit-juice, anyway.

TOM (*smiling wickedly*). Mos'ly.

HENRY (*looks up and sees his enemy, the* JUDGE, *behind the bar; he stiffens*). Haven't you been at the bar about long enough?

ISABELLE. No, Henry,—I'm having a lovely time.

(*She sits on stool, upper end of bar.*)

JUDGE (*goes to table U.R.C.*). Whyn't you get wise to yourself, Henry? I'm not trying to swipe your girl.

HENRY (*meets* JUDGE *center*). You'd have a swell chance.

JUDGE (*comes C. slightly*). Well . . . well, I guess you're right. There is something about your manner that . . . ah . . . must be very fascinating . . . to some people.

HENRY. You're very quick on the repartee, aren't you?

JUDGE. No . . . not quick, Henry . . . but sincere, Henry. Come on—let's bury the hatchet—come and have a drink.

ISABELLE. Come on, Henry.

HENRY. Oh . . . all right. (*They cross to bar.*) But we'll make this the last.

(HENRY *goes to lower end of bar.*)

JUDGE. Nonsense. Who's tired? Make that three, Tom . . . on my bill. What do you want to go home for? It's early.

HENRY. Well, it may be early for you,

but it's pretty late out in New Jersey.

JUDGE. Why? Do they have different time out there?

HENRY. Of course not. But we live pretty far away. And we might be locked out.

JUDGE (*to* ISABELLE). Oh, do they lock you out, too?

ISABELLE (*head of bar*). Why . . . I'm . . . living with him.

JUDGE. But you said you weren't married.

HENRY. We're not, but—

JUDGE. But you're living in the same house?

HENRY. Yes, but—

JUDGE (*in horror*). Slightly irregular—

HENRY. Not at all—not at all!

JUDGE. Now let's get this straight; you're living together in New Jersey, aren't you?

HENRY. Yes, but . . .

JUDGE. Just a minute. . . . Under the same roof?

ISABELLE. Oh, yes.

JUDGE (*crosses L. slightly*). Well? There y'are. S'all right. S'none o' my business. (*Turns.*) Say! You must think I'm drunk. Ha, ha, ha.

HENRY (*coldly*). You're quite right. However, since you *will* mix into other people's affairs . . . Listen carefully: This young lady is engaged to marry me. She is living with my parents in West Orange, New Jersey. Is that clear?

JUDGE (*bowing low to Isabelle*). I beg your pardon . . . a thousand times.

ISABELLE. That's all right.

JUDGE (*turns to* HENRY). And whom are *you* living with?

HENRY (*somewhat startled*). Why, I live with them too. Naturally.

JUDGE. What do you mean: Naturally? I don't live with my parents. Tom, here, doesn't live with his parents. The young lady don't live with her parents. (*Down to* HENRY.) Why should YOU live with YOUR parents?

HENRY. Well, I do.

JUDGE. Very suspicious. (*To himself.*) Very suspicious.

HENRY. Time we were home.

JUDGE (*to* HENRY). Say, Henry, how is everything out there? Huh? How're the crops?

HENRY. The what?

JUDGE (*sits on edge of table U.R.C.*). The waving wheat fields—the waving onion fields, all the little radishes—and things like that. SAY! What do you want to live in a place like that for, anyway? S'terrible!

ISABELLE (*crossing to him*). That's just what I was saying.

JUDGE. Whassa name?

ISABELLE. West Orange.

JUDGE. Wes' Orange. S'awful. (*He mimics.*) Where d'ya live? I live in Wes' Orange. Where's that? Why, it's just beyond South Banana before y' get to Eas' Pineapple. Nothin' but fruit stands. All Greeks.

HENRY. Yeah? Well, it was good enough for the men who fought the Revolution.

JUDGE. Certainly it was good enough for 'em. Anybody'd start a revolution if he lived in Pineapple, New Jersey. I'd start one myself—throw fruit at everybody—that's what I'd do. Say, now I'm beginning to understand, he's a revolutionist—dangerous character. You want to be very careful of a man with whiskers.

ISABELLE (*laughing*). But Henry hasn't got any whiskers.

JUDGE. Oh, yes, he has, he's fooling you. Shaved 'em off. Probably got a pocketful of bombs. (*Picks up drink at bar.*) Well, here's to a merry life in West Orange—New Jersey!

(*Bell off L. rings.* JUDGE *goes below bar and sits.*)

HENRY (*starting to table L.C.*). We'd better get started.

ISABELLE (*crosses L. back of table to mirror*). Please, not yet, Henry. I'm having a beautiful time.

HENRY. You know the family will expect us to go to church in the morning.

ISABELLE. Oh, yes—I'd forgotten . . . still, let's stay a little bit longer.

HENRY. Well, make up your mind. A few moments ago you said you wanted to leave.

ISABELLE. That was when you were cross. But now I'd like to stay. Sometimes you're very sweet, Henry.

GIOVANNI (*off L.*). Buona sera, Signor Conte.

HENRY. That's more like it. (*Goes up to slot machine.*)

GUS. Buona sera. (AUGUSTINO CARAFFA, *Count of Ruvo, appears in arch. The sound of the gate closing is heard.*) Good evening.

(MARIO *appears in arch, takes* GUS's *coat and muffler,* ISABELLE *is at mirror and sees* GUS. HENRY *starts to play slot machine at intervals throughout scene. On* GUS's *entrance he looks over shoulder at him.* TOM *crosses to center to welcome* GUS.)

TOM. Oh! Eccellenza . . . COSI TARDI! (*He looks at his watch and holds out his arms in a supplicating gesture.*) E le raccomandazioni della Signora Contessa? Cosa posso scrivere alla Signora Contessa. . . . BUGIE!

GUS (*crosses to* TOM *at center. Placatingly*). Andiamo, Tomaso! (*He points to his own watch.*) Non é encora mezza notte!

TOM (*grumbling*). E ma peró. . . .

GUS (*holding up his hand*). Oh, falla finita.

JUDGE. What's the matter?

GUS (*crossing to L. slightly*). It appears, my dear Judge, that I am very wicked . . . because I stay out too late.

JUDGE (*looking at his own watch*). Well . . . I think he's right.

GUS. What!

JUDGE (*puzzled, he looks at the watch again, then listens to it. He starts to wind it*). Well, I think he's right anyway.

GUS. This is a conspiracy. . . . You're all against me. How are you, Judge?

JUDGE. Never felt better in my life—I'm on the wagon. Not drinking anything except a few Old Fashioneds.

GUS. Oh—just a few lemonades. (*He turns again to* TOMASO.) Tomaso, did any letters come for me?

TOM (*crossly*). No, Eccellenza . . . but a call from Miss Lilli,—and some packages. . . . No BUY so much. Spenda too mucha money!

(TOM *exits U.R.*)

GUS (*to the* JUDGE). Maybe my old Tomaso will forgive me when he sees what I have in the packages.

JUDGE. Why? What did you get?

GUS. Some surprises for him.

TOM (*entering*). Here are the packages for you.

(*He carries two packages, placing them on table U.R.C.*)

GUS (*crossing to L. of* TOMASO). Not for me, Tomaso, but for you.

TOM (*opens packages*). Come?

GUS. Yes! For you, old brontolone.

(*Gives stick and hat to* MARIO, *who exits up steps with them.*)

TOM (*pointing to himself and smiling*). For me?

GUS. Yes. And never again let me hear you complain about your rheumatism.

TOM (*opens box with violet ray lamp. Puzzled, he picks it up*). Cos' é questo?

JUDGE. What's that?

GUS (*taking lamp from* TOMASO). You shine it so. . . . (*He demonstrates on* TOMASO.) . . . where it hurts . . . and then it doesn't hurt any more.

(ISABELLE *drifts to L. of table L.C.*)

TOM (*beaming*). Oh . . . Grazie, Eccellenze, ma perche spenda so mucha money per me?

GUS. Never mind that . . . now look in the other box. (*Toward* JUDGE *slightly.*) Now watch him . . . he will be like a cat with a . . . catnips.

TOM (*opens box and discovers it is full of India Figs, a sort of cactus*). Ah, SANTO DIO! . . . FICHI D'INDIA! (*Displays them to* JUDGE.) You—you like to eat some with me?

JUDGE. What—a cactus? Never!

TOM (*he licks his lips greedily*). Good! I go eat 'em right away to your health, Eccellenza.

(*He exits U.R.* GUS *goes to door, watching him* ISABELLE *is R. of table L.C.*)

GUS. Yes, but think of YOUR health, and don't eat them too much. Funny old man . . .

(HENRY *goes up to arch and gets change from* GIOVANNI) . . . but very nice. Now we are friends again.

JUDGE (*rising*). Gus, I want you to meet a very old friend of mine. This charming little lady is Miss . . . ah . . . Miss . . . what's your name?

(GUS *looks at* ISABELLE *and starts toward her slowly.*)

ISABELLE (*crosses down to front of table*). Isabelle . . . Isabelle Parry.

JUDGE. Of course, Miss Isabelle Parry. The flower of the South, Gus. Miss Parry, the Count Di Ruvo.

(JUDGE *goes behind bar.*)

GUS (*facing* ISABELLE). How do you do, Miss Parry.

(*He bows low.*)

ISABELLE (*looking intently as if trying to place him*). How do you do?

GUS (*turning to* JUDGE *and crossing to C.*). Judge, this is most unkind of you.

(HENRY *returns to slot machine.*)

JUDGE. HUH?

GUS. I mean, a true friend, as you pretend to be, would not have kept anyone so charming and beautiful all for himself. It was very selfish of you not to give me this great pleasure before.

JUDGE. I want you to meet her fortunate

escort, Mr.—ah—Henry.

(HENRY *drops down several steps.*)

GUS. Oh, how do you do?

ISABELLE. Oh, Henry.

GUS. Not my favorite author, O. Henry?

HENRY. I'm not an author and my name is Greene. How do you do?

GUS. I am well, thank you.

(HENRY *exits to hall, speaks to* GIOVANNI, *then exits R. in hallway.*)

JUDGE (*back of bar*). Have a drink, Gus.

GUS (*crossing to C.*). Since when have you taken up bartending, Judge? The Bar Association should see you now.

JUDGE. SH! Don't remind me of my duties. (ISABELLE *looks at him in astonishment.*) You'll spoil the evening.

ISABELLE (*crosses to front of chair R. of table*). Are you a *real* Judge?

GUS. Why, certainly—

JUDGE. Certainly not, my dear, certainly not. That's only the courtesy title. I'm a . . . I'm . . . a . . . a . . . judge at the dogshow.

ISABELLE (*sits R. of table*). But you said—

GUS. Oh—but, Miss Parry—didn't you know? He's a famous expert—the World famous expert on Pekinese—Oh, he *loves* dogs!

JUDGE (*coming from behind bar to R.C.*). Yessir! You can't fool me on a Pekinese—or a Bulldog—or a Collie— or a—

GUS (*sitting edge of table U.R.C.*). Or a Schnauzer.

JUDGE. What's that?

GUS. Schnauzer.

JUDGE. What?

GUS. Well, take it a Spitz then.

JUDGE. Take it yourself!

GUS. I mean, Judge, there is a dog also called the Spitz.

JUDGE. Is that so! Well, the way these new dogs spring up over night! They don't give you time to brush up on the old ones. (*As he goes to bar and sits on stove.*) Anyway, I know my Pekinese.

(*Telephone rings.*)

GUS. I think we should offer a toast to such an expert and to our beautiful guest. (*Telephone rings again.* TOMASO *enters U.R.*). Tomaso must find some champagne to celebrate the presence here of—someone so lovely. And some Italian chocolates.

(MARIO *enters U.R. and goes to phone.*)

TOM (*as he exits U.R.*). Subito, Eccellenza—I go downstairs.

MARIO (*at phone*). Allo—yes—One minute, please.

(MARIO *crosses down to* GUS.)

GUS (*crosses to* ISABELLE). Do you like some champagne, Miss Parry?

ISABELLE. I've never had any.

GUS. You've never had any!

MARIO. Eccellenza la Signorina Lilli al telephone.

GUS (*angrily, pantomime as* GUS *goes to telephone and* MARIO *exits U.R. At telephone*). Hello—Hello—Who?—Oh, hello, Lilli—Not just now—I am in conference —No, don't come—I explain to you tomorrow—All right. I call you back in half an hour—good-bye.

(*Hangs up.* ISABELLE *rises and crosses to L.C.*)

ISABELLE. But, Mister Count—

GUS (*down to her*). Di Ruvo.

ISABELLE. I know I've seen you before—it was recently. I'm sure we've met—I wonder where it was.

GUS. No, Miss Parry. I'm sorry to say we have not met. I wish we had.

ISABELLE. Thank you. But I know I've seen you—

JUDGE (*chair foot of bar*). I guess it was in the Lucky Strike advertisement.

ISABELLE. The Lucky—? Of course—that was it.

GUS. Such is fame. (HENRY *appears in arch from R.*) But we've never met. If we had—how could I have forgotten?

(TOMASO *enters U.R.* ISABELLE *goes L. above table L.C.* TOMASO *goes to table U.R.C. and places champagne there.*)

TOM. Here is the champagne.

ISABELLE (*seeing* HENRY *in mirror as he comes down to chair L. of table L.C.*). Henry, you've seen those Lucky Strike advertisements.

HENRY. I don't like that guy!

(*He sits L. of table L.C.*)

GUS (*toward* ISABELLE *as far as center with box of chocolates*). Will you have some Italian chocolates, Miss Parry?

ISABELLE. Thank you.

TOM. There! One bottle of happiness! It turns your tears into laughter—makes you forget all your troubles. The sunshine of Italy in a bottle of Chinzano.

(*He takes glass and crosses L. to* HENRY. GUS *goes up to tray and takes a glass for himself and* ISABELLE. JUDGE *gets glass of champagne and returns to bar.*)

JUDGE. Let's have some music, Tom—something romantic.

TOM. Sure, Judge—what do you want—something hot?

JUDGE. Play a love song.

TOM (*to phonograph*). Sure.

ISABELLE. Are you romantic, Judge?

GUS (*crossing to her and giving her champagne*). How could he help to be—this evening.

(ISABELLE *sits back of table L.C. Phonograph starts and plays "La Maison Blanche" from Manon.*)

ISABELLE. That sounds like Caraffa. It is Caraffa, isn't it?

GUS (*at table U.L.C.*). Yes. . . . I think so. How do you like the chocolates?

HENRY. That's a good phonograph.

ISABELLE (*closing her eyes*). What a heavenly voice. There's nobody else like him.

JUDGE. So you have heard him?

ISABELLE. Oh, yes, I've been to the Metropolitan three times to hear him sing.

GUS. Did you like him?

ISABELLE. He was marvelous. It was such a thrill! Of course I couldn't see him very well from where I sat . . . (*She points to the ceiling.*) . . . but they say . . .

GUS. Perhaps it is just as well you couldn't see him . . . so you can keep your illusions. Most of the singers are a little . . . débordant. Only the birds can sing . . . and keep their shape.

(*They all listen in silence till the record ends.*)

TOM (*stands lost in the music and then comes to with a start and shuts off the machine. Then he turns and speaks to* GUS *with pride*). Ah, my little Signorino, how you sing! I could listen to you all night. (*To* ISABELLE.) He's some singer, huh?

ISABELLE (*dumbfounded. She stares at* GUS). YOU! . . . But that's Caraffa!

GUS (*giving* TOM *a dirty look*). Yes.

JUDGE. Oh, yes, he sings a little . . . when he isn't posing for Luckies.

(*He smiles sardonically at* HENRY.)

ISABELLE (*still staring fascinatedly at* GUS). But I thought you said Caraffa . . .

GUS (*very quietly*). I am Tino Caraffa That is my stage-name.

ISABELLE (*rises—crosses to back of chair R. of table*). You! How wonderful!

GUS (*slightly embarrassed*). Thank you very much. . . . May I give you a little more champagne?

(GUS *goes to table U.R.C.*)

ISABELLE (*crosses to L.C. Still in the land of dreams*). If you please.

GUS (*serving her champagne at L.C.*). Have you still . . . some illusions?

ISABELLE. More than ever.

HENRY (*who has not been enjoying this*). Don't drink too much of that stuff, Isabelle.

(GUS *puts glass on table U.L.C.*)

JUDGE (*in mock surprise*). Oh, there you are, Henry! (*Bell.*) I thought you were lost.

HENRY (*with meaning*). I stick around pretty well.

JUDGE. Yes. . . .

GUS. Put on some jazz, Tom.

TOM. Si, Signor Conte—right away—

(GIOVANNI *enters from L. in hall and beckons to* TOM.)

GIOVANNI. Signor Tomaso—

(TOM *and* GIOVANNI *exit off L. in hall.*)

ISABELLE (*to* GUS). I didn't know opera singers liked jazz.

GUS. Why, it's new, interesting, courageous! I think young people should like jazz.

JUDGE. How about old people who like it?

GUS. It shows they're still young, Judge.

HENRY. Yeah? Well, how about young people who DON'T like jazz?

GUS. The conclusion is obvious, Mr. Greene.

HENRY. Is that so! Well, let me tell you . . .

TOM. Excuse me—(*Entering to above table L.C.*) Nobody here got a car outside with a Jersey license, have they?

(ISABELLE *puts drink on table L.C.*)

HENRY. I have. What about it?

TOM. The policeman outside wants to see you.

(*Goes to arch.*)

JUDGE (*steps forward slightly*). Perhaps if I . . .

HENRY (*rising*). I can manage all right, thank you. (*To* TOM.) How much do I owe you?

TOM (*back above table*). Two Scotch—one-fifty, one benedictine fifty cents—altogether two dollars.

(*Returns L. side of arch.*)

HENRY. You mean to say you charge seventy-five cents for that lousy Scotch?

JUDGE. That's all right, Tom—this is my party.

HENRY. Here you are. (*Hands* TOM *a bill.*) Leave the change on the table.

(*Goes into hall and gets hat.* TOM *puts change on table.*)

HENRY. Come on, Isabelle.

ISABELLE (*below table*). Oh, please, let's stay a little longer, Henry. I'm having such a nice time. See if you can fix it up with the—

JUDGE (*crossing to U.L.C.*). If you'll allow me to say a word to the policeman . . .

HENRY (*returning U.L.C.*). I don't need ANY HELP . . . from you.

JUDGE. But I think if I spoke to—

HENRY. There's nothing you could do, I couldn't do.

JUDGE. This isn't West Orange, you know.

HENRY (*picking up his change*). I'll say it isn't. Come on, Isabelle!

ISABELLE (*coaxingly*). Oh, Henry, please! Just a little . . .

(*Then seeing that he is adamant, she shrugs and begins slowly to gather her things. The bell rings violently three times. Someone bangs the gate.*)

TOM. You better hurry, Mister. I think Mulligan is getting mad.

HENRY. To hell with that guy!

ISABELLE. You'd better go, Henry!

HENRY (*looks furiously at* ISABELLE *who is still taking her time*). All right. . . . But I'm coming right back. And then we're going home. Do you understand?

(*He stalks out—followed by* TOM. *There is an embarrassed silence after he goes.*)

ISABELLE (*looks at the two men pleadingly. She is ashamed*). He isn't . . . always that way.

GUS (*crosses to front of table L.C. Consolingly*). Of course not, my dear. We understand.

JUDGE (*returns, top end of bar*). A charming fellow . . . at heart.

ISABELLE. Oh, yes, he really is, but—

(TOM *enters in arch, coming R.C.*)

TOM. They're having a lovely argument. The car is sitting in front of a . . . water faucet.

(*He exits at once to L. in hall.*)

ISABELLE (*goes up to arch*). Perhaps we could help.

JUDGE. He said he didn't need any help. He's so sure of himself. Aw, he'll get out of it all right.

ISABELLE (*returning to table L.C. for cape and bag*). Goodbye! It's been mighty nice to meet you both. I never met anybody famous before—I thought it would be different—

GUS. But why?

ISABELLE. Oh, I don't know. I thought a famous person would be very grand . . . and . . . and . . . but you're just . . . like the people I like.

GUS. I am very glad you like such people . . . because I . . . like you . . . very much.

ISABELLE. Thank you.

GUS (*crossing to phonograph*). Do you think we could dance once before you go? Or would Mr. Henry object?

JUDGE. Oh, Henry would be delighted.

ISABELLE (*backs up to table U.L.C.*). Well, Henry's outside . . . he isn't here . . . and I'd like to dance with you.

GUS. Will you then?

(*She nods. He starts phonograph. They meet and dance.*)

JUDGE (*as he exits U.R.*). Playing with dynamite—playing with dynamite.

GUS. You are very lovely!

ISABELLE. You shouldn't say that.

GUS. Why not?

ISABELLE. Because it isn't true.

GUS. But aren't you beautiful?

ISABELLE. No.

GUS. Very well. (*He laughs.*) I . . . I love to dance with you, because you are very ugly. Is that better?

ISABELLE. I'm not so terribly ugly.

GUS (*in feigned astonishment*). Aren't you?

ISABELLE. No. . . . I'll get by.

GUS. Really!

ISABELLE. Oh, yes. But I'm not beautiful.

GUS. To me, Miss Parry, you are more beautiful than . . . than . . .

ISABELLE. Than what?

GUS. Than I could ever imagine anyone to be.

ISABELLE. You shouldn't say that to me.

GUS. You are right. I shouldn't.

ISABELLE. And I ought not to like to hear it.

GUS. No.

ISABELLE. But I do. (*They both laugh.*) Aren't we wicked? (*She trips and hurts her ankle.*) Oh! (*She looks down at it.*)

GUS. Oh, my dear, did you hurt yourself?

ISABELLE. It's all right.

GUS. We must not let anything happen to something . . . so adorable. (*He is kneeling; kisses finger tips and touches them to ankle.*) There. Now, it is well again.

ISABELLE. I think you are a very bad man.

GUS. I? A bad man? But why?

ISABELLE. Well . . .

GUS. Do you really dislike me?

ISABELLE. I . . . I don't know. (*Tries to walk; ankle causes her to limp slightly.*) Oh—

GUS. It still hurts? I'm so sorry.

(*Gets chair R. of table L.C. and places it about C.*)

ISABELLE (*sitting in chair*). I think if I take my weight off—it'll be all right.

GUS (*R. of* ISABELLE). There.

(*Pause.*)

ISABELLE. Who is Lilli?

GUS. Who?

ISABELLE. Lilli—the girl you spoke to on the telephone. Is she a singer?

GUS. No . . . no . . . she's a cousin of mine. (*Laughs.*) How observing you are! Was your papa on the police force? A detective, maybe?

ISABELLE. No, no—papa never did any work. Work irritated him terribly.

GUS. But how did you live?

ISABELLE. Plantation. Cotton, you know.

GUS. Oh, yes—I know. I sing some plantation songs.

ISABELLE. They're pretty, aren't they?

GUS. Beautiful.

ISABELLE. I love to hear darkies sing 'em at night. Funny people! Don't have thing . . . never did have anything . . . never will have anything. And just as happy. . . . You ever been to Mississippi?

GUS. Where?

ISABELLE. Mississippi.

GUS. Mississippi?

ISABELLE. Yes.

GUS. Is that near Buffalo?

ISABELLE. You've never been there. We used to have a nice place. And then, just when cotton got high, women stopped wearing underwear.

GUS. Did women wear cotton underwear?

ISABELLE. Silk underwear is immoral. That's what papa always said. He tried to get us all to wear cotton stockings, too, but we wouldn't do it.

GUS. I don't blame you. . . . Ah—were you a large family?

ISABELLE. No, just an ordinary family—four boys and seven girls.

GUS. Salute!

ISABELLE. Oh, that isn't big. Down home when they raise families, they raise FAMILIES.

GUS. And how!

ISABELLE. Well, they don't have much else to do.

GUS. And you are the most beautiful of the seven Parry sisters.

ISABELLE. Oh, no—they're all better looking—except one. One is uglier than me.

(HENRY *and* GIOVANNI'S *voices are heard in alteration off L.* ISABELLE *rises, goes to table U.R.C. and picks up bag.*) But Mother is more beautiful than any of them.

(HENRY *rushes into room, followed by* TOM *and* GIOVANNI. *Door in hall left open. He goes L.C.* TOM *goes above table L.C.* GIOVANNI *remains in arch, leaning against it at Left. Gate is heard to slam.* JUDGE *enters R.2 and goes behind bar, sitting on stool and watching fight progress.*)

HENRY (*coming L.C.*). Just what I thought! A grafting cop sees a New Jersey car parked near a hydrant, so he pushes it up in front of it, and then works a little blackmail.

JUDGE. How do you know he pushed it?

HENRY. Because I know he did! (*To* ISABELLE.) And you want me to live in this rotten town! Come on, let's get out of here!

(*Goes to downstage side of table L.C. and picks up money, then goes upstage.*)

TOM (*L.C.*). You like to stay and dance before you go?

HENRY (*U.L.C.*). No! Who wants to dance?

TOM. The young lady—she dances good.

HENRY (*downstage slightly*). What! (*No reply.*) What!

GUS (*to* TOM, *reprehensively*). Tomaso!

HENRY. Oh! So that's what you do the minute my back's turned?

ISABELLE. Please, Henry. . . .

HENRY. That's why you wanted me to go out, huh? So you could make a fool out of me. . . .

GUS (*R.C. throughout scene*). But, Mr. Henry—we only—

HENRY (*looking her up and down*). What a fine wife you'd make!

ISABELLE. But, Henry! I didn't do anything.

HENRY (*sneering*). Oh, no. Maybe it isn't anything where YOU come from. But the women in MY family don't pick up with the drunken bums they meet in a speakeasy.

ISABELLE (*aghast*). Henry . . . PLEASE!
(MARIO *appears in arch.*)

HENRY. You heard me. It's a good thing I wasn't gone longer. What do you MEAN by dancing with that lousy Wop?
(MARIO *and* GIOVANNI *go forward angrily. Talk in Italian.*)

GUS (*jumping to his feet*). You—

ISABELLE (*turning to* GUS *and the* JUDGE *with a helpless gesture*). I'm . . . I'm sorry.

GUS (*bowing to* ISABELLE). It's perfectly all right.
(*Then to* MARIO *and* GIOVANNI *who are talking angrily.*) No, no, ragazzi. That was for me. (*He waves them back.*)

HENRY. Yeah, that was for you, you Dago! (*He starts to cross and bumps against the chair at C. He falls to his hands and knees.* MARIO *and* GIOVANNI *laugh loudly. Beside himself.*) Shut us! You rats.
(ISABELLE *intervenes, coming L.C.*)

GUS (*perfectly calm*). Why not address your remarks to me?—Mr. Greene!

HENRY. Did you think you weren't included? What I say goes for everybody.

GUS. Splendid!

HENRY. Yes . . . you're very brave, aren't you?

GUS. No . . . not unusually so.

HENRY. I'll say you're not!

GUS. You say so.

HENRY. YES! And I'll tell you something else, you greaser!

GUS. Continue, please . . . don't hesitate.

HENRY (*advances menacingly. Then he looks back at the two and hesitates*). If there weren't so many Dagoes around here to stick knives in my back, I'd give you something to remember me by.
(MARIO *and* GIOVANNI *threaten* HENRY.)

GUS. One moment, Mr. Greene. (*He turns to* TOM.) Tomaso, porta via i ragazzi—(MARIO *and* GIOVANNI *exit R. in hallway, followed by* TOM *who goes off L.*) You see? . . . Now, Mr. Greene, I am at your service—you have only *one* Dago —to face.

HENRY. Yeah! I'm apt to trust you and your gangster friends. (ISABELLE *goes up to table U.R.C.*) Come on. Get your things and get out of here. (ISABELLE *looks around helplessly, then begins to gather her things very slowly. Savagely.*) Do you hear me? (*He goes upstage and turns.* ISABELLE *clenches her fists and doesn't move.*) Do you hear me? Get your stuff together and come on or, by God, I'll . . .

ISABELLE. You'll what?

HENRY (*toward her*). I'll teach you to behave like a little tart!

ISABELLE (*furious*). You'll WHAT?

HENRY. You heard me. I'll give you one more chance. Now, snap into it or you can stay—for good! (ISABELLE *puts bag on table U.R.C. defiantly. Somewhat less blusteringly.*) You—you know what this means?

ISABELLE. Perfectly.

HENRY. If you don't come now . . .

ISABELLE. I understand.

HENRY. I . . . won't come back. . . .

ISABELLE. I know everything you're thinking; that I have no money . . . to go home . . . and that . . . that my Mother . . . hasn't any to send me. It's all right. I'm glad. I'll . . . manage without you. Now . . . (*She takes off her engagement ring.*) . . . take your ring. (*Crosses to* HENRY, *hands him ring.*) Take it, I say! (*Dazedly, he does so.*)

HENRY. Now, wait a minute!

ISABELLE (*working herself into a frenzy*). Now, go back to *West Orange* . . . and tell them about me. That I wasn't good enough for you. And while you're at it, you can tell them I'd rather scrub floors than be married to such a . . . such a . . . GENTLEMAN.

HENRY. Yes, and it would suit you better too. You and all the other lazy white trash like you.
(*He strides to the door and exits.*)

ISABELLE. Thank you, Henry. (*The iron gate clangs.*) Well . . . now I've done it. (*She starts to laugh hysterically. Turns back to audience.*)

GUS (*rushes to her side*). I'm very sorry —Miss Parry—I feel so guilty about this.

TOM (*coming in from L.*). Nice fella. (*Straightens chair R. of table and exits L.*)

JUDGE (*rises and stands behind bar*). Everything will blow over. Things like that always do. Don't be unhappy.

ISABELLE (*facing front*). Who's unhappy?
(*She breaks into a peal of laughter.*)

JUDGE. There, there. (*She continues to laugh.*) Now, now. (*Still she laughs.*) Everything will be all right.

GUS. We must make it all right.

ISABELLE. Everything *is* all right. Hooray! (*Crosses to bar.*) Oh, Lordy, give me a drink! (JUDGE *serves her with a soft drink.*) Do you know, there's been something the matter with me for months, and I've just this minute found out what it was.

GUS (*going R. slightly*). What was it?

ISABELLE. It was Henry! Entirely too much Henry. And that family in West Orange. Oh, Lordy, give me another drink.

GUS. Please don't drink too much.

JUDGE (*displaying soft drink*). It's all right.

GUS. I'm afraid we've made you a lot of trouble, Isabelle.

ISABELLE. Trouble? You darling—you've saved me from trouble—and a lifetime of boredom. I thank you.

(*She kisses* JUDGE *as* GIOVANNI *and* MARIO *appear in arch, dressed for street.*)

MARIO. Good night. That fellow no mean any harm.

GIOVANNI. After all, he's not a bad fellow.

MARIO (*going L. and making exit*). Buona notte ragazzi.

GIOVANNI (*as he exits L.*). Buona notte.

ISABELLE. Good night. (*The gate clangs.*) Now, that's what I call friendliness. Like we have down home. The Darkies say: "How do, Miss Isabelle, this sholy is a pow'ful fine day." It don't mean anything, but it sounds nice.

JUDGE. I think we can easily arrange to send you home.

GUS (*crossing to her*). But, not right away—I hope. We must talk these things over. I cannot lose you so soon.

(*Is now at bar.*)

ISABELLE (*crossing L. to R. of table L.C. in front of* GUS). He seemed so different from everybody down there that I thought he was different than they were. And I just this minute woke up. They were lazy and he was industrious. They liked to make love, gamble and likker up. Oh, they were bad all right and compared to them he was upright and honorable. But I guess honor isn't everything—do you think so, Judge?

JUDGE. Well, now, let me see. Speaking ex officio, I should say that honor . . . or righteousness . . . should be tempered with the milk of human kindness—that is if you can temper anything with milk. But I think too much honor is apt to curdle the milk.

TOM (*enters arch from L.*). That fella come back. He wanta talk to you. I no let him in.

(ISABELLE *moves up to* TOM *slightly.*)

ISABELLE (*to the other two*). Shall I talk to him?

GUS (*table U.L.C.*). Do you want to?

ISABELLE (*to* TOM, *with great finality*). Tell him to go away.

(*Leans on chair R. of table L.C. She smiles triumphantly at her companions.* TOM *exits L. in hallway.*)

JUDGE (*sits on stool behind bar, back to audience*). Cruel woman.

ISABELLE. Tell me I was right, Gus.

GUS. I am afraid that I could not give an honest opinion. I want so much for you to stay. . . .

ISABELLE (*looking at him sweetly*). Oh!

GUS. Yes.

ISABELLE. That's nice of you to say so.

GUS. I would not say so if it were not true.

ISABELLE. Do you always tell the truth?

GUS. Well—nearly always.

ISABELLE. I wonder.

TOM (*reappearing U.L. in arch*). He's mad as Hell. I tell him to go away. He say No . . . he stay. I say all right, Good night. He say: Listen, you Wop, you, I break down the door. I say: I ain't no Wop, go ahead and try. He say: All right, then, you Dago, I go get an officer and make you all arrest for a-kidnap the young lady. So I say I ain't no Dago, I'm Siciliano and I poosh the door in his face. That's what I do!

(*He exits U.L.*)

ISABELLE (*running to bar*). Do you suppose Henry will get an officer?

GUS (*going C.*). Now, Judge, we're in your hands.

TOM (*appears in arch*). He's out there with Mulligan the cop. Mulligan says what's goin' on here. What'll I do, Judge?

JUDGE (*rises*). Just a minute. (*He thinks, then speaks to the other two.*) Gus, you take Isabelle in the dining room, and keep quiet. (*They rise, and exit U.R. She takes all her things.*) Now, Tom, bring Mulligan in here, but leave the young man outside. If he asks you why, tell him he isn't a member of this club.

(*Puts bottle of Scotch and two glasses on bar, then comes front of bar.*)

TOM (*as he exits U.L. to door*). All right, Judge.

MULLIGAN (*appears in arch at C.* TOM *follows, standing L. of him*). Where is she?

TOM. Who?

MULLIGAN. The young lady.

TOM. No lady come to my speakeasy.

MULLIGAN. Don't use that word! How many times do I have to tell you I don't know what this place is?

TOM. I'll tell you.

MULLIGAN. Shut up! Now, where is she?

TOM. I don't know!

JUDGE (*turns*). Officer! What are you doing in a speakeasy?

MULLIGAN (*crossing to C.*). Well, bless my soul if it isn't my old friend Judge Dempsey. Shure, your honor, I'm here in pursuance of my duty.

(TOM *exits hall to Right.* JUDGE *starts toward* MULLIGAN.)

JUDGE. And what duty are you pursuing?

MULLIGAN. I'm pursuin' a kidnapper, your honor.

JUDGE (*meeting* MULLIGAN *at C.*). Are you sure, now, that you're not pursuing an alcoholic beverage?

MULLIGAN. Shure, Judge, my tongue is hangin' out a foot, but I'm on the trail of a dangerous kidnapper.

JUDGE. A dangerous kidnapper, huh? My, what a wicked world. And who is this kidnapper?

MULLIGAN (*toward* JUDGE, *slightly*). Ther're two of thim, your honor. One of thim is a young Eyetalian, and the other one is an old, broken-down barfly, a regular bum.

JUDGE (*starting*). Huh?

MULLIGAN. That's what the other fellow said. And they've stolen a girl!

JUDGE (*slightly vexed*). Huh! Is that so? And where did you get this information?

MULLIGAN. The young fellow who lost the girl is outside. Shall I bring him in?

JUDGE. Don't bother. He's outside, huh? Well, well. And why does he suspect that the damsel is secreted in this establishment?

MULLIGAN (*puzzled*). Yes—indade—to be sure.

JUDGE. I'm asking you: Why does he think the girl is here?

MULLIGAN. Oh! He says he lost her here. He was here earlier in the evening.

JUDGE (*puzzled*). Oh, he was!

MULLIGAN. Yeah!

JUDGE. What does he look like? Was he a tall man, with a beard?

MULLIGAN. No, your honor, he's clean shaven.

JUDGE. With a broken nose?

MULLIGAN. No, not atall, he wears glasses.

JUDGE (*thinking hard*). With glasses, huh? . . . Oh! THAT fellow—that Orangeman.

MULLIGAN. That what?

JUDGE. That Orangeman!

MULLIGAN (*stiffening*). Oh, is he, now?

JUDGE. Oh, yes. He was talking about it all the time he was in here.

MULLIGAN. And I thought he was a dacent young fella.

JUDGE. You never can tell.

MULLIGAN. That's a fact.

(*He eyes the bottle surreptitiously.*)

(JUDGE (*crosses to bar, lower end*). Would you like a little drink, Mulligan?

MULLIGAN. Shure, your honor, an' me tongue is like blottin' paper, but I never touch a drop whilst pursuin' a criminal.

JUDGE. And a very good rule too. How about a little ginger ale, out of a nonrefillable bottle? That's what I'm having.

MULLIGAN (*crosses to top of bar—eyeing the bottle*). Oh, ginger ale! With pleasure, your honor. (*The* JUDGE *pours two stiff drinks.*) Well, here's to Prohibition, sor: a noble law.

JUDGE. Experiment.

MULLIGAN. Whatever it is. (*They drink.*) And what a wonderful improvement they've made in these soft drinks since the law went in.

JUDGE. That's progress for you.

MULLIGAN (*he thinks a second, then scowls*). An Orangeman, huh? And makin' all that trouble. (*He pounds on the bar.*) They ALWAYS make trouble.

JUDGE (*tapping his forehead*). I think he's crazy.

MULLIGAN. Naturally, your honor.

JUDGE. He was a terrible nuisance in here, always losing things.

MULLIGAN. Besides the girl, what else did he lose?

JUDGE. Well . . . well, first, he lost a dog.

MULLIGAN. You're sure it wasn't a horse?

JUDGE. No, it was a dog! That's what he said, and we believed him.

MULLIGAN. Never believe an Orangeman.

JUDGE. Of course not. But we didn't know he was one then.

MULLIGAN. I'll bet there wasn't any dog.

JUDGE. That's what I suspect.

(JUDGE *goes U.C.*)

MULLIGAN. Just a liar.

JUDGE (*starts to arch, slightly*). Yes, and when he came back from the street HE TOLD such a STORY, such a PREPOSTEROUS, RIDICULOUS, UNBELIEVABLE story, that we *knew* he was a liar.

(*Comes back to* MULLIGAN.)

MULLIGAN. What did he say?

JUDGE. HE SAID . . . Well, he said, the OFFICER on this *beat* . . .

MULLIGAN (*thinks this over. Suddenly he frowns*). HUH!

JUDGE. Yes, the officer on this beat had deliberately, and with malice aforethought, pushed his car—

MULLIGAN. Pushed his car—

JUDGE. In front of a Municipal hydrant.

MULLIGAN. With malice aforethought—

JUDGE. And then—you won't believe your ears, Mulligan—had tried to extract from him a certain amount of United States currency, in other words, held him up for a bribe—not to arrest him.

MULLIGAN. Oh, he said that, did he? Well, he'll be lucky this night if he doesn't lose some of his teeth!

JUDGE. Of course, after that, we didn't believe anything he said.

(*Bell and pounding heard off L. Also* HENRY'S *voice.*)

MULLIGAN. I think I hear a disturbance on the public highway. (*Crosses* JUDGE *as he starts toward arch.*) Some drunk, no doubt. Perhaps a few hours in the cooler. Well, good night, sir, and many thanks for the ginger ale.

JUDGE (*center stage*). Don't mention it. Oh—and Mulligan!

MULLIGAN (*stopping middle of arch*). Yes, sir?

JUDGE. Observe the Law!

MULLIGAN. To the letter, your honor.

(*Starts off, stops.*)

JUDGE (*crossing to* MULLIGAN). You go ahead—but I'm coming right out to see that no murders are committed.

MULLIGAN. All right. But you could trust me to do the right thing.

JUDGE (*L.C.*). That's just what I'm afraid of. And Mulligan! (MULLIGAN *stops.*) Don't use that stick!

MULLIGAN. Only in case of a tie.

(*He exits to L. in hallway. Gate is heard closing.* JUDGE *calls off R.*)

JUDGE. Gus! Isabelle! It's all right. Come on back.

(*They enter.*)

ISABELLE (*to R.C.*). What's happened?

GUS. (*to Center*). I am sorry to have made such complications.

ISABELLE. Are we to be arrested?

JUDGE (*L.C.*). I don't think so. In fact, I think by now Henry has probably changed his mind. Almost certainly has changed his mind.

ISABELLE. I guess he's cooled off.

JUDGE. I think Mulligan did say something about the cooler—

(*Goes up to arch.*)

ISABELLE. The what?

JUDGE. Nothing—nothing. But I'll just go out and see that Mulligan doesn't get too excited.

ISABELLE (*up to table U.L.C.*). I'm sorry to be such a nuisance.

JUDGE (*as he exits to L. in hall*). It's no nuisance—it's a pleasure.

GUS (*crossing to* ISABELLE). Isabelle—may I call you Isabelle?

(*She turns and faces* GUS.)

ISABELLE. Uh-huh.

GUS. Can you possibly forgive me? I'm terribly sorry for you, but very happy for me. To think—you are alone—with me. Do you know that you are adorable?

ISABELLE. Am I?

GUS (*very passionately*). Yes. (*They start dancing and he kisses her. She fights a little, but not much.*) I am mad about you.

ISABELLE. You're very convincing.

GUS. But, now, where are you going for tonight?

ISABELLE (*crosses down front of table L.C.*). I . . . I don't know.

GUS (*follows her*). You must . . . stay here.

ISABELLE. Huh?

GUS. With me.

ISABELLE (*looking into his eyes*). What do you mean?

GUS (*slightly ill at ease, looks away*). I mean, I . . . I hope you will accept my hospitality—until you find what you wish to do.

ISABELLE. For tonight?

GUS. For so long as you will honor me as my guest.

ISABELLE (*very slowly*). But . . . have you room for me?

GUS. Certainly! In my living room is a divan so comfortable . . . so embracing —so soft—it longs for somebody to repose on it.

ISABELLE. Somebody like me?

GUS. Nobody else, Isabelle.

ISABELLE. But I don't want to be any more bother.

GUS. You—bother? Sweet child—will you be my guest?

(*Gate is heard off L. Then* JUDGE *enters through arch to center, speaking as he comes.*)

JUDGE. Well, Mulligan pointed things out to Henry very clearly. (*Comes to C.*) And now, young lady, to find a place for you.

ISABELLE. Well, he just said—he was kind enough to offer me—he said I could stay in the living room of his apartment for tonight.

JUDGE. But you're not going to?

ISABELLE. Yes—I am.

JUDGE (*glancing from one to the other*). Well, in that case, I wish you a very good night then.

(*Goes up to arch on way to staircase.* ISABELLE *follows to front of table U.L.C.*)

ISABELLE. Judge!

(*He stops and turns.*)

JUDGE. Yes?

ISABELLE (*hesitating*). Good night.

JUDGE (*mumbling indistinctly*). Good night.

(*He goes upstairs. She watches him a moment, then comes down to* GUS.)

ISABELLE. The Judge is afraid for me.

GUS. Yes.

ISABELLE. What are your intentions toward me?

GUS (*smiling*). Strictly dishonorable, Isabelle.

CURTAIN

ACT TWO

SCENE: *The living room of* GUS's *apartment, upstairs over the speakeasy. It is a few minutes later.*

French windows and window seat R. wall. Covered canary cage hung upstage section of window. U.R.C. door leading to hallway of building. U.C., door to bath. U.L.C., door to bedroom. Grand piano and stool R. Keyboard set slightly upstage and to R. Music on same. Props to dress. Love Seat set in curve of piano, nearly parallel with footlight trough. Table just L. of this with Teddy Bear and picture of woman in frame. Down R., a small stand with drawers. Stockings in boxes in drawers. Book case R. of door U.R.C. Table between doors U.C. and U.L.C. On table, phonograph and telephone. Screen L. of door U.L.C. Small bed table below this and against L. Wall. Small bed lamp on same. Lamps on piano and on phonograph. Switch plate L. of door U.R.C. in wall. Large arm chair just L. of C. Divan, with cover, and fully made up with sheets and pillows, down R., head against L. wall. Foot of divan, small cushioned seat. Bathroom fixtures in bath, chest of drawers in bedroom.

AT RISE.—*Stage is dark, except for moonlight coming through French windows. Door U.R.C. is opened and* GUS *enters, coming downstage slightly, turning and calling Up.*

GUS. Come in, Isabelle. Are you afraid?

ISABELLE (*in doorway*). Put on the light, please.

GUS (*switching on lights*). Certainly. There.

(*He crosses to bed table and turns on light.*)

ISABELLE (*entering to L.C.*). So this is what it's like.

GUS. What what is like?

ISABELLE. A man's apartment.

GUS (*closes door U.R.C. and hooks chain*). Yes . . . it is not so terrible . . . is it?

ISABELLE. No, it's lovely. Is this your own furniture—or do you rent it?

GUS (*closes curtains on upstage window*). No, it is mine. Tomaso—he is my landlord, you know—his taste in furniture is different.

ISABELLE. I suppose it is.

GUS (*comes around back piano to R. of chair L.C.*). Yes. He likes . . . ah . . . massive mahogany . . . carved very elegantly with lions' heads and such things . . . and covered in green . . . how you say . . . ploosh?

ISABELLE. I know. We've got that kind down home . . . in the parlor. But ours was red plush.

GUS. In red it's more beautiful, no doubt.

ISABELLE. I think it's awful.

GUS. Do you? I am very glad then. (*They laugh.*) Will you give me your things, please?

ISABELLE (*she hands him cape and bag, which he places on upstage edge of piano. She crosses to Love Seat, kneeling one knee on L. end. She notes Teddy Bear*). Oh, what a darling Teddy Bear.

GUS (*turns R. of arm chair*). It was given to me for Luck—and right away I meet you.

(*He drifts down C.*)

ISABELLE (*picking up hair pin below R. end of Love Seat*). I didn't know women used hairpins any more.

GUS. Probably my cleaning woman dropped it.

ISABELLE. Probably. (*Crosses to small stand D.R.*) Is she blonde?

GUS. I . . . ah . . . never noticed. . . . She wears a dust cap.

(*While* ISABELLE *is examining ash tray, he sees photograph of woman on table L. of Love Seat. He turns it down quickly.*)

ISABELLE (*pushing cigarette end from tray*). Well, you ought to tell her to stop smoking your cigarettes. It doesn't look nice to see the ashtrays all full of cigarette-butts with . . . lip rouge on them.

GUS (*crosses to Love Seat. Kneels one knee on R. end*). Darling—are you jealous?

ISABELLE. Me? No, just neat. You get that way when you've got four big brothers tearing 'round the house and up-setting things.

GUS (*sits*). You say your brothers are . . . LARGE?

ISABELLE (*R. of Love Seat*). Oh . . . not large. Why, the biggest one is only six feet two, and Charley, the baby, I don't think he's even quite six feet.

GUS. Practically . . . a midget.

ISABELLE. No, but papa always said he'd be puny.

GUS. What a man. Your papa.

ISABELLE. Papa was a real man and when he died it took ten men to carry him.

GUS. I'm sorry. (*Telephone rings. He smiles nervously, rises.*) Er—excuse me just a moment. (*He goes to telephone. She goes to window and looks out.*) Allo. . . . Oh, yes, Lilli. I am still in conference. . . . We moved upstairs. . . . I don't know, probably very late. We are hardly beginning . . . no, I wouldn't come . . . it would not amuse you. . . . Yes, dear . . . yes . . . yes . . . yes . . . I do . . . I do . . . I do . . . very much . . . yes . . . good night.

ISABELLE (*closing window*). Your cousin again?

GUS (*down to L.C.*). Oh, yes. . . . She . . . ah . . . she is one of those women who wastes much time on the telephone . . . other people's time.

ISABELLE (*crossing in front of Love Seat*). What is she like?

GUS. I don't know. She's really very charming. You must forgive my telling lies, but she wishes always to talk about family matters. . . . (*Crosses to* ISABELLE.) —and I do not like to talk about family matters . . . tonight. (*He embraces her.*)

ISABELLE. Uh-huh.

GUS. Yes. How lovely you are . . . so young . . . so pliant . . . so intoxicating. . . . So sweet—so gentle—

ISABELLE (*breaking away slightly*). I'm so pleased to hear you say nice things.

GUS. Darling, I'm so happy to have you alone with me—all alone.

(*She breaks away from him nervously to R. end of Love Seat.*)

ISABELLE. Uh-huh, uh-huh, uh-huh—

(*She is at downstage end of keyboard. She looks at a piece of music.*) Oh—this is your music?

GUS. Yes, darling.

ISABELLE. Will you—sing something for me?

GUS (*sitting on Love Seat*). No, no, Isabelle.

ISABELLE. Why not?

GUS. Because, I am not Caraffa now. I am only me, Di Ruvo, Gus, who—who is so happy to be alone—with you.

ISABELLE. But I—

GUS. No, no, no. Caraffa belongs to everybody. He is hanging in his dressing room with his costumes. He waits for his sweethearts—for Mimi, for Tosca, for Manon. He is not lonely. It is Di Ruvo—Gus—who *was* lonely—until he found his Isabelle.

ISABELLE (*R. end of Love Seat*). Is it like that to be famous?

GUS. Yes, it is like that to be alone, nearly always. To own a talent like singing is like to own maybe a trained bear that dances to make people laugh. The owner, he is nobody, but the bear, he is everybody. The poor man is invited to a party. What happen? So soon he arrives, they say: Did you bring the bear? Or: Will you sing for us a song? It is the bear, the talent, they want. For him they care nothing.

(*She crosses to his R. and stands there. He takes her hand.*)

ISABELLE. I never thought of that.

GUS. (*draws her to him slightly*). No. Nobody thinks of it. But what do I care. Perhaps you like a little Di Ruvo, huh?

A little bit?

(*There is a pounding coming from floor above. They break in alarm, and she turns toward window.*)

ISABELLE. What's that?

GUS. It is the Judge—signaling to me from upstairs.

(*More pounding, then the* JUDGE *calls down.*)

JUDGE. Gus. Gus.

(GUS *rises and crosses to window.*)

GUS (*as he crosses to window*). Proprio al momento opportuna. (*Calling out window.*) Hello.

JUDGE. Say, what's the date today?

GUS. The day?

(ISABELLE *kneels L. end of Love Seat, listening.*)

JUDGE. The date.

GUS (*looking at watch*). Sunday—since half an hour—already.

JUDGE. What?

GUS. Sunday. (*Turns to* ISABELLE.) What is the matter with him?

JUDGE. No, no—not the day—the date.

GUS (*to* ISABELLE). What date is today? (*Calls out window.*) The ninth.

JUDGE. Thanks.

(*He slams window.*)

GUS (*crossing to foot of divan angrily. Back to R.C.*). Seccatore, noioso.

ISABELLE (*watching* GUS). I wonder what he wants so badly.

GUS. Oh, he probably suffers from curiosity.

ISABELLE. I like him. I wish he weren't angry with me.

GUS (*crossing to L.C.*). I wish he would mind his own business. They are all the same—these busybodies. Tomaso tells me how to live; the Judge would tell me how to love. And neither knows—they have already forgotten. (*He crosses to her.*) Believe me, darling—believe me and you will know happiness.

(*Footsteps heard outside U.R.C.*)

ISABELLE. I wonder what that is? Do you suppose Henry—

GUS. Ssh.

(*Three raps on door U.R.C.*)

JUDGE (*off U.R.C.*). Say, Gus—

(GUS *takes chain off door.* ISABELLE *turns upstage and as* JUDGE *enters goes to R. of Love Seat.* GUS *goes L. of arm chair angrily.*) May I come in? (*Comes down to U.R.C.*) Say, are you positive this is the ninth?

GUS. Absolutely.

JUDGE. S'my birthday. What do you know about that?

ISABELLE. Many happy returns of the day.

GUS. Congratulations.

JUDGE. Thank you—thank you both. (*Crosses and sits in Love Seat.*) And now—now I'm going to save you both from a very dull evening. We're going to celebrate.

GUS. Here?

JUDGE. Now, don't apologize—this is good enough for me. I'm an old-fashioned man—don't like anything fancy. Tom will be right up with the champagne.

GUS. You—ah—told Tom to bring the champagne here?

JUDGE. Yeah, I telephoned down to him.

(GUS *laughs mirthlessly.*)

GUS. Oh.

JUDGE. This is my party. I'm taking care of everything. (GUS *laughs again.*) You—ah—didn't mind my giving a party here, did you, Gus?

GUS. Of course not, my dear Judge—I'm delighted.

(*He laughs again and sits angrily in small seat foot of divan.*)

ISABELLE. Me, too.

JUDGE. Good. Let's have some music. You know, a party without music is like an egg without salt.

(*He goes up to phonograph, but before he can get it in readiness,* TOM *enters with champagne and glasses.*)

TOM. Here is the champagne, Mister Judge. I am sorry it take so long, but that fellow come back.

(*Leaves door open and places tray on small table L. of Love Seat.*)

ISABELLE (*downstage slightly in alarm*). Who? Henry?

TOM. The policeman—Mulligan.

JUDGE (*down back of arm chair*). What does he want?

TOM. He look for somebody.

GUS (*rising—up to L. of arm chair*). Who is he looking for, Tomaso?

TOM. Looking for la Signorina.

GUS. La Signorina?

TOM. Yes. Il sus capolo há mandato a cercare e dice che il signore di West Orange e qui, e va di la di qua, di su, di giu.

GUS. Calma. Calma, Tomaso. It would seem that Mr. Henry also told the sergeant that Isabelle has been kidnapped, so the officer—

JUDGE. Mulligan—

GUS. —has come back again with orders to search the house.

JUDGE. Oh, he has, has he? Tom!

ISABELLE (*returns to R. of Love Seat*). What shall I do?

TOM. Hide in the Judge's room.

JUDGE (*alarmed*). Not on your life! (*Turns to* TOM.) Where is Mulligan?

TOM. When I come upstairs, he say he go look in the yard—behind the house in the back-house.

(*He points to window and crosses above piano to it.*)

JUDGE (*crossing to window below piano*). I'll get rid of him all right. (*Calling out window.*) Mulligan! Mulligan! Mulligan.

(GUS *follows* JUDGE *to window.* ISABELLE *is behind* GUS *to L.* MULLIGAN *enters U.R.C. and comes downstage several steps to left slightly. He watches them at window.*)

ISABELLE (*starting toward window*). Do you suppose he'll find me?

GUS (*holding her back*). No, darling, never! But don't show yourself at the window.

ISABELLE. Could he come up here?

TOM. If he do, I kill him!

JUDGE. I'll have him broken!

GUS. He wouldn't dare.

(JUDGE *almost falls out window.*)

ISABELLE. Catch him, Gus.

GUS (*holding* JUDGE *back*). I've got him.

TOM. Me, too.

JUDGE. It's all right. I see him. Do you see him, Tom?

TOM. Yes.

JUDGE. That thing that looks like a horse over there?

TOM. Yes—like a horse.

ISABELLE (*turns and sees* MULLIGAN). Oh! (*She recovers.*) Fancy seeing you here. (*She nudges* GUS.)

MULLIGAN. Fancy!

GUS (*turning*). Oh. (*He laughs nervously and nudges* JUDGE, *who turns.*)

JUDGE. Oh—you!

MULLIGAN. Yes—the horse, himself.

TOM (*crossing to* MULLIGAN). I no mean to kill you, Mr. Mulligan.

(GUS *and* ISABELLE *are R. of Love Seat.* JUDGE *crosses up to R. of* MULLIGAN.)

JUDGE. What are you doing in here again?

MULLIGAN. The desk sergeant sent me back here to find her.

JUDGE (*crosses L. of* MULLIGAN). To find whom?

MULLIGAN. The young lady I was looking for.

JUDGE. It seems to me, Mr. Mulligan, you're always running after young ladies when you should be pounding your beat.

MULLIGAN. Judge!

JUDGE. Very suspicious. Very suspicious. I think you're lascivious.

MULLIGAN. Well—er—only on rainy days.

JUDGE. What about this young lady?

MULLIGAN. Your honor, it's just like I told you. I'm pursuing a dangerous—

JUDGE. Stop! Remember the straw that broke the camel's back—remember the heel of Achilles!

MULLIGAN. I will! I've got fallen arches, myself. But I'm looking for a young lady held against her will by villains!

JUDGE (*back of arm chair*). Do you see any young lady being held against her will by villains?

MULLIGAN. Not a sign of one, your honor.

JUDGE. You didn't think for a moment it was this young lady, did you? Come here, my dear— (ISABELLE *goes up between* MULLIGAN *and* JUDGE.) —show the officer your wrists and ankles aren't tied.

MULLIGAN. Ah, the Judge is having his little joke.

ISABELLE (*to* GUS). Perhaps the officer would like some of your Italian chocolates.

GUS (*front of Love Seat*). I think he much rather have a drink. Tomaso!

(TOMASO *starts to pour champagne.*)

ISABELLE. But policemen never drink on duty!

MULLIGAN. It just seems like never.

(GUS *takes drink from table and returns to position before Love Seat.* ISABELLE *hands drink to* JUDGE *and one to* MULLIGAN.)

GUS. Here's to the police!

MULLIGAN. And here's to the people that send the police out on false clues. Bless their little hearts!

JUDGE (*to* MULLIGAN *significantly*). And here's to a long farewell.

(*They all drink and put glasses down.*)

MULLIGAN. Well, thanks very much for the ginger ale. And excuse me coming in like this—it was orders.

(*Starts to leave;* JUDGE *stops him.*)

JUDGE. You'd better run around to all the other speakeasies and see if you can find any kidnappers there.

MULLIGAN. All the other speakeasies? What do you take me for—Paul Revere? (*He exits U.R.C.* ISABELLE *comes R. of arm chair.* JUDGE *sits upstage end of foot of divan.*)

TOM. I go let him out. (*Comes down to* ISABELLE.) Oh—la Signorina like tea or coffee?

ISABELLE. What?

GUS (*sitting Love Sea*). Do you like tea or coffee?

ISABELLE (*nodding toward champagne*). Why can't I have that?

GUS. For breakfast.

ISABELLE. Oh. . . . Oh . . . coffee . . . please.

TOM. Grapefruit?

ISABELLE. No, thank you.

TOM. And an egg.

ISABELLE. No, thank you.

TOM, Sausage?

GUS (*reprovingly*). Tomaso.

TOM. No hungry, huh? Tt. Tt. Too bad. You get sick. What time you want?

GUS. Finiscilla di parlare, Tomaso!

TOM. Va bene eccellenza. Good nigh', good nigh'. . . . Buona notte a tutti! Sleep good.

(*He exits U.R.C.*)

ISABELLE (*sitting R. arm of arm chair*). He's nice. Have you known him long, Gus?

GUS. All my life. He was what you call . . . chamber valet . . . in my father's house.

ISABELLE. Chamber valet?

GUS. Yes. You know . . . he makes the beds and dusts . . . with a feather.

JUDGE. Housemaid?

GUS. The same work. But later he came to America. He's a rich man now. The food in his restaurant is famous.

JUDGE. That's why I never moved out of the house when he bought it and opened up his café.

ISABELLE. I see! It was very nice of you to come and live with him.

GUS. Well, my mother wanted me to. She's funny, my mother. Every month she writes a long letter to Tomaso, telling him what I should eat, and how it must be cooked and am I wearing my flannels and, I suppose, do I brush my teeth.

ISABELLE. How sweet of her.

GUS. Ah, well, to our mothers we are always little children, also when we get old.

JUDGE. Don't talk about being old on my birthday.

TOM (*knocking, then entering hurriedly*). Eccellenza, eccellenza! Signor Conte!

GUS. Ma cosa c'è?

TOM (*in a whisper*). La signorina Lilli. (*Describes her presence downstairs with pantomime.*)

GUS (*starting to door U.R.C.*). Ah, I must go downstairs . . . excuse me a moment.

JUDGE (*stops him*). Has Henry—

GUS. No, it is not Henry this time.

ISABELLE. Your cousin again?

GUS. Yes, Lilli—

ISABELLE. Why don't you ask her to come up?

GUS (*going to door U.R.C.*). No. She is too old. You know—two flights of stairs is—

(*He exits.* JUDGE *rises, crosses to table, fills glass and crosses to Love Seat.*)

JUDGE. Now we can celebrate. Here's to you, my dear—look well before the leap. (*Sits on Love Seat.*)

ISABELLE. Judge—I'm in love with him. (*Crosses down to L. of and level with* JUDGE.)

JUDGE. Isn't this rather sudden?

ISABELLE. I don't know. I've never been in love before.

JUDGE. But—but this other fellow?

ISABELLE. Henry?

JUDGE. Yes.

ISABELLE. I didn't love Henry.

JUDGE. Was that quite—fair?

ISABELLE. I told him I didn't love him.

JUDGE. Oh.

ISABELLE. He said I'd learn to love him —little by little.

JUDGE. Oh—an optimist.

ISABELLE. I think he read it in a book somewhere. I never heard of anybody learning to love little by little, like it was playing the piano or something. Did you?

JUDGE. I—ah—never studied the piano.

ISABELLE. I always thought it was *bang* —all at once, or not at all. And now, I know it's bang.

JUDGE. A big bang.

ISABELLE (*upstage slightly—looks at door U.R.C.*). Uh-huh. So much so that nothing else matters very much.

JUDGE. How did you ever get engaged to Henry—although it's none of my business.

ISABELLE (*down to arm chair—sitting*). *Well,* I had to get married some time; and my sisters all got the pick of the boys 'cause they were prettier—

JUDGE. Aw—

ISABELLE. Oh, yes, they were. So that only left Willie Borelle and Chet Lee when it came my turn to pick, and Willie's got the jitters—

JUDGE. Jitters?

ISABELLE. You know, he makes faces all the time—like this. (*She distorts her face.*)

JUDGE. Oh, my God.

ISABELLE. And both Chet's parents died in the State Asylum, and he said if I didn't marry him he'd shoot me, so I didn't marry him.

JUDGE. You were very brave.

ISABELLE. Well, he'd already told that to all my sisters, so I reckoned he was pretty safe. Besides, poppa always said: Never let anybody bluff you.

JUDGE. Your father was right.

ISABELLE. Uh-huh—he played poker that way. By the time he died our plantation was so small, we didn't know whether to try and grow cotton on it, or turn it into a croquet grounds.

JUDGE. And then along came Henry.

ISABELLE. Uh-huh—in a big shiny Buick. He was visiting over at the Sawyers'. Went to college with Buck. He liked me right away.

JUDGE. Can't blame him for that.

ISABELLE. Thank you. Had to carry me up to show me to his parents right off. They're all right—if you like that kind of people. Think they're better than my family. He was so sweet to me down home and then, soon's he got me North you'd 'a' thought I belonged to him. (*She rises—goes up toward door and looks at it as if waiting for* GUS *to return.*) And I know now I couldn't belong to anybody—unless I loved him.

JUDGE. And you think you're in love with him?

ISABELLE (*turning downstage slightly*). I don't think, Judge. When I heard that record and I saw him standing there like a bashful little boy, I said: Woman, prepare to see your dreams come true.

JUDGE (*rises—looks at her a moment, then goes up to phonograph table*). Young woman— (*She turns up to him.*) Tonight you're going to a hotel—to the Martha Washington! And tomorrow you're going home!

ISABELLE (*backing toward R. a step or two*). No, I'm not!

JUDGE (*goes to piano and picks up her wrap and bag, then putting them down again*). Do you hear me? Put on your things!

ISABELLE (*backs D.R. several more steps*). I won't.

JUDGE. You will!

ISABELLE. I won't.

JUDGE. You're very unreasonable. (*She smiles at him.*) I'll have you arrested.

ISABELLE (*front of Love Seat*). You can't do that.

JUDGE. Oh, CAN'T I?

ISABELLE. No. You haven't got a warrant.

JUDGE. Ha-ha! I'll *show* you. . . . (*He starts for secretary U.R.*) . . . Just give me a fountain pen and a piece of paper, and I'll . . .

ISABELLE. You can't fool me. You're not a real JUDGE.

JUDGE (*down to above L. end of Love Seat*). I'm not, hah? Well, by GOD. . . .

ISABELLE. It's just a . . . courtesy title.

JUDGE. Oh, it is, is it? Well, there are a lot of people in Sing Sing right this minute who'd be glad to hear that . . . (*To Left, and return during laugh.*) . . . to wish I hadn't shown them so much courtesy.

ISABELLE (*sitting R. end of Love Seat*). Judge!

JUDGE (*very suspicious*). What is it?

ISABELLE. Even if you are a real judge, come and sit here . . . beside me.

JUDGE (*starts to sit—checks himself*). No, no! You can't weaken me with THAT STUFF. No bribes. That's been tried before. They're all in jail!
(*Crosses to L.C.*)

ISABELLE (*sniffles*). I think . . . I'm going to cry

JUDGE (*going below chair to U.R.*). Has no effect on me whatsoever! (ISABELLE *sobs.*) Women's tears leave me cold. (*Down to and above L. end of Love Seat.*) I hate women! (*Goes U.R.C.*) I like to see them cry. I enjoy it! (*Down slightly to back of Love Seat.*) For God's sake, stop it!

ISABELLE (*still sobbing*). Come here!

JUDGE (*going C.*). I will not! (*She sobs again as he starts R. He stops.*) All right—stop it! (*Crossing and sitting L. of her.*) Stop it, I say! (*Pats her.*) There, there. (*She stops crying as he pats her, looks up at him with a broad smile. He realizes she has deceived him.*)

ISABELLE. I wonder where Gus is.

JUDGE. I don't want you to see him again!

ISABELLE. You can't send me home!

JUDGE. But I tell you—

ISABELLE. But, darling, you don't understand.

JUDGE. What! I don't understand WHAT!

ISABELLE. That I CAN'T go home. I went away to be MARRIED.

JUDGE. What of it?

ISABELLE. *I* can't go back like—*damaged goods.* YOU can't *do that* in a little town, no matter how innocent you are. They'd think there was something WRONG with me. Why, the whole of Yoakum would sit with its eyebrows up in the air for nine months just waiting and hoping for the worst.

JUDGE. They could wait as long as they liked—nothing would happen.

ISABELLE. Then they'd say nothing could happen. (*She laughs.*) I know my own home town.

JUDGE. Then what ARE you going to do?

ISABELLE. Gonna stay here . . . with Gus.

JUDGE. But . . .

ISABELLE. He SAID I could stay . . . as long as I liked.

JUDGE. Of course you know he won't marry you.

ISABELLE (*placidly*). I don't expect him to marry me.

JUDGE. He'll never marry!

ISABELLE. He's probably right.

JUDGE (*pounding cushion of Love Seat*). I . . . won't . . . have . . . it!

ISABELLE. Now don't start again, darling. If I want to be foolish, let me be foolish . . . for once. I've always been sensible and good . . . you know it isn't much fun to be a girl . . . sometimes . . . and now I'd just like to drift with the current and not struggle any more . . . and for a little while . . . be happy.

JUDGE. I think you're immoral.

ISABELLE. Well, I read in a book of psycho-analysis that nothing is immoral except—

JUDGE. Except what?

ISABELLE. Oh, Lordy—I've plumb forgotten.

GUS (*entering U.R.C. and crossing to bedroom*). Ah, forgive me—that Lilli—she makes me tired and hot. Women are so illogical—

ISABELLE. Oh!

GUS (*at door U.R.C.*). Except you, darling—except you.

(*He exits U.R.C.*)

JUDGE (*rises, goes to L. of arm chair and stops, turning to her and pointing his finger at her*). And suppose you *do* have a baby!

ISABELLE (*very amiably*). And SUPPOSE . . . I don't. They're not compulsory, you know.

JUDGE. What! Why . . .

ISABELLE. In the movies, darling. Only in the movies.

JUDGE. Where did you learn such things?

ISABELLE. Well . . . I've got five married sisters.

JUDGE (*starts to door, stops above chair*). Well . . . REMEMBER . . . I WARNED YOU!

ISABELLE (*rises, backs D.R. slightly*). Of what? You haven't warned me about anything.

JUDGE (*indignantly*). WHAT? (*He comes back to center.*) Didn't I TELL YOU that you're taking the first downward step . . . didn't I tell you that you're treading . . . THE ROAD TO HELL?

ISABELLE. Why, NO. You didn't say anything about it . . . you must have forgotten. (*Crosses down to L. of divan. Crossing toward* JUDGE *as far as L. end of chair.*) Judge! You're a darling . . .

JUDGE. Forgive me. I'm just an old busybody. I've no right to tell you how to find happiness . . . When I never was able to find it for myself.

ISABELLE. Do you think I will be unhappy, Judge?

JUDGE. I don't know. You always hear of these things ending up . . . in sorrow.

ISABELLE. Maybe you don't hear about them when they end happily.

JUDGE. Maybe.

ISABELLE. You see, I've never been very happy, Judge. I mean like I am now, because I never felt about anybody, like I do about Gus. Don't you think, it's better to be very happy for a little while . . . than never to be happy at all?

JUDGE. I don't know. (*Goes above arm chair.*) I don't know anything about it. All I know is you've spoiled my birthday—

ISABELLE (*wheels to R. side of arm chair*). I'm sorry.

JUDGE (*meets* ISABELLE *at C.*). But I

wish you'd give it a little more thought—will you?

ISABELLE (*R. of arm chair*). I will, Judge. (*He goes to door U.R.C. She follows upstage slightly.*) Good night.

(JUDGE *opens door.*)

JUDGE. Good night. (*Starts out door and turns.*) But if you do have a baby, I'll adopt it.

(JUDGE *exits U.R.C. She trails him to door, lingers, then comes down to upstage side of piano and picks up cape and bag. She looks toward bedroom door, then starts to door U.R.C. as* GUS *enters. She puts her things back quickly and starts to R.C.* GUS *is in pyjamas and lounging suit.*)

GUS (*coming L. of arm chair*). Where's the Judge?

ISABELLE (*coming down R.C.*). Gone to bed.

GUS. Good! What was he talking about so long?

ISABELLE (*about C. downstage*). Oh, happiness—and things like that. He—he wanted me to go away from you.

GUS. And you?

ISABELLE. I didn't want to go. (*Pause.*) But I think I'd better.

GUS (*down to her at C.*). Darling!

ISABELLE (*warding him off*). Don't you think I'd better?

GUS. Yes—I think you had.

ISABELLE. But I don't want to.

GUS. Come here!

ISABELLE. If I stayed—would you promise not to say sweet things to me?

GUS (*holding her hands*). But, darling, I won't say sweet things to you if you don't want me to.

ISABELLE. But I do want you to! (*He starts to embrace her.*) Gus, couldn't you overpower me?

GUS (*backs away a step in surprise*). What!

ISABELLE. Then it wouldn't be my fault.

GUS. Darling, you must not say such things.

ISABELLE. But I think 'em.

GUS. Listen to me, darling! A great man once said: "Thought is the eternal rival of love." When you love, don't think—just drift with the current of your heart.

ISABELLE. But that's just it. I'm a little frightened.

(*Starts to back R. slowly through next speech.*)

GUS. Frightened? You? A great big girl like you? Who came from Missis—well, where you said—here to New Jersey to live with those cold storage family—and after weeks with these ice boxes, you had the courage to face Mister Henry. You are not frightened; I'll not let you be frightened.

(ISABELLE *is downstage end of piano keyboard R.*)

ISABELLE. Stop scolding me—stop it, I say. I won't let you scold me. (*Defensively, she picks up music from downstage end of piano. She looks at it.*) Oh, it's in Italian. I always wanted to travel. Sing it for me!

GUS (*crossing above piano to piano stool*). You're trying to be clever to avoid me.

ISABELLE. No, I'm not—honest! Please sing it for me.

GUS. Do you think you will understand? (*She smiles.*) Perhaps you will like Caraffa then—better than Di Ruvo (*Takes music, sits at piano and sings. She is down extreme right, listening to him.*) Donna Vorrei Morir! Donna Vorrei Morir! (GUS *rises and crosses down to her, taking her hands. He draws her over to a position below R. end of Love Seat.*)

ISABELLE. What does it mean, Gus?

GUS (*taking her in arms*). It means I adore you!

ISABELLE. I wonder why that sounds so nice—even if it isn't true.

GUS. But it is true! Isabelle, kiss me! (*They kiss and break.*)

ISABELLE. Don't lie to me, Gus. The thing I like best about you is you've told the truth.

GUS. You are a strange little girl—I'm not sure I understand you.

ISABELLE (*up to R. of arm chair*). I'm not sure I understand myself. I only know—that I'm happy to be here.

GUS. Thank you.

ISABELLE (*pointing to divan*). Is that where the guest sleeps?

GUS (*crossing to lower side and head of divan*). Yes, darling. It's more comfortable than my bed and it's all ready— (*Pulls cover back, disclosing bed made up.*) —See! (*He crosses around foot of divan going to upstage end.*)

ISABELLE (*front of arm chair*). Pink sheets, ruffles and everything. Always made up . . . in case of emergency!

GUS (*upstage end of divan, fixing sheets*). Sometimes a friend may want to stay . . . if he misses a train.

ISABELLE. And have you pyjamas for the friends who miss trains?

GUS (*down foot of divan. Solemnly*). I think I can find a very nice pair of pyjamas . . . that shrunk in the wash . . . they should be just about right.

ISABELLE. And SLIPPERS?

GUS (*pensively*). I think it is just possible . . . YES! when my sister was here she forgot a pair . . .

ISABELLE (*merrily*). I THOUGHT you probably could find some. SOMEBODY must have forgotten some sometime.

GUS (*looking at her feet*). What adorable feet! . . . You must wear about size three.

ISABELLE (*back R. several steps*). Good heavens! Have you them in different SIZES? WHAT a man!

GUS (*crossing to embrace her*). DARLING! You must not say such things . . .

ISABELLE. I wouldn't have you any different. (*He puts arms around her. She holds him off.*) Now, go and get the pygies and things.

(*He exits bedroom. She starts to untie belt of dress as she moves around from R. to L. side of arm chair. He enters with pyjamas and a pair of slippers. She puts belt of dress on L. arm of arm chair.*)

GUS (*coming L. of* ISABELLE). Here are the pygies and things. May I help you?

ISABELLE. Uh-huh.

GUS (*looking dress over*). Where does it unbutton?

ISABELLE. You see where it unbuttons.

GUS. Shall I then?

ISABELLE. Uh-huh. (*He starts to unhook dress. When she lifts dress over shoulders, she starts to speak.*) I used to love to have my clothes taken off when I was too little to know how. (*He takes dress and hangs it on screen U.L. She is now in Teddies, stockings and shoes. She sits on L. arm of arm chair, dropping stockings to below knees. He comes down, sits on seat foot of divan and takes shoes and stockings off.*) I used to wear a lot more clothes when I was little . . . and Mama wore more than I did . . . and Gramma wore more than all of us put together. (*Stockings, garters and shoes are laid upstage end of small seat at foot of divan. He puts on slippers. As* GUS *puts slippers on.*) Gramma said when she was a young girl, she wore three times as much as when I knew her—

GUS. Really.

(*Rises. She drops straps of Teddy over her shoulders. He takes top of pyjamas and puts it over her head. Teddy drops at her feet.*)

ISABELLE. I'll bet the men back in Gramma's day used to get awfully impatient waiting for the women to get undressed . . . (*She picks Teddies up and places them on back of chair. Then she sits on arm of chair again.*) to go swimming. But maybe they didn't swim much in those days— (GUS *has pyjama pants. She slips her feet into them as he draws them up and over pyjama coat.*) I used to wear things like that when I was a little girl only they had feet in 'em. (*Pyjamas on, she rises, fixes her hair, then looks down at herself, slapping thighs of legs in protest.*) No, no, no—the top goes on the outside.

GUS (*drawing top out of pyjama pants and laughing*). I must patent this. (*He goes between foot of divan and small seat; she ties belt of pyjama coat. He holds his arm out to her.*) Ah, Isabelle—my lovely Isabelle—come and sit beside me.

(*He sits foot of divan, she sits on small seat, reclining in his arms.*)

GUS. Piccolo amore caro, tell me—what can you see in this ugly old opera singer?

ISABELLE. You're not ugly.

GUS. Do you like me a little?

ISABELLE. More than a little.

GUS. Why?

ISABELLE. I don't know— don't think any woman knows. But it's like heaven to be near you—just your hand on my arm is like—I can't explain what it's like—

GUS. Don't explain. Words cannot explain such things. Words are only good for "How do you do?"—"Will you have some sugar in your tea?" Only for things that do not matter. No one must ever try to explain miracles with words. Darling! (*Kisses her.*) I am mad about you.

(*Kisses her again.* ISABELLE *rises, a little bewildered. She crosses to table L. of Love Seat. He follows her.*)

ISABELLE. I guess I—I'd like a little more champagne. (*She hands him glass of champagne*). Here's to you.

GUS. Here's to you!

(*They drink. Then put glasses down. He tries to take her in arms. She breaks away defensively.*)

ISABELLE. Now—put out the lights. (GUS *goes up to switch. Lamps on piano and table between bath and bedroom doors go out. He starts L. to bed lamp; she stops him. Going to front of chair.*) Except that one.

GUS (*starting to her*). Angel!

ISABELLE (*meeting him L. of chair in embrace*). Oh, Gus, I am happy!

GUS. It is I who am so happy.

ISABELLE. I love you.

GUS. But, darling, you are trembling. Are you then so afraid?

ISABELLE. I'm a little bit afraid.

GUS. But you must not be. Life is beautiful . . . and its most beautiful moments are called . . . love. They are very rare, my Isabelle, such moments as this . . . to be accepted tenderly . . . and without fear.

ISABELLE. Don't ever let me go.

GUS. No, no—let you go? I'll hold you close—close to me. My baby—like a child —(*She breaks into sobs.*) But you are crying. (*They break.*) But you are a baby! (GUS *backs upstage slightly as she crosses to L. end of Love Seat, her back to him and still sobbing.*)

ISABELLE. No, I'm not . . . don't girls usually cry?

GUS. Yes.

ISABELLE. Well . . . I'm no different from anybody else. (*Then, out of a clear sky.*) Do you think I'm pretty?

GUS. Hein?

ISABELLE. Do you think I'm pretty?

GUS. Of course I think you're pretty. You're lovely.

ISABELLE. Well, why don't you say so, then? (*Turns to him angrily.*) Isn't this the time to say sweet things to me? What are you staying over there for? Don't you like me?

GUS (*rather emotionally*). It is because I like you so much . . . that I'm staying here. You little . . . foolish! (*Suddenly he makes up his mind.*) Now come here! (*Crossing to her and taking her hand.*) Come here, I say! (*Leads her to divan.*) Now get into bed! (*She gets into bed and he stands over her upstage side. Angrily.*) Now listen to me: Never in my life before . . . have I done anything so stupid as now I am about to do . . . Do you understand? Never! Not once . . . I . . . I cover myself with ridicule . . . and I am . . . positive . . . that I will regret it forever. ALL MY LIFE. I will be angry for this moment. I . . . I . . . am CRAZY! (*He strides over to table and picks up Teddy Bear. He returns to the bed and puts it down beside her.*) THERE! So you won't be frightened.

ISABELLE (*clutching at the Teddy Bear*). I'm not frightened.

GUS (*with an effort*). Now . . . GOOD NIGHT.

ISABELLE. What do you mean?

GUS. I mean . . . I will sleep tonight in the Judge's apartment. And You . . . YOU are going home tomorrow. Where your Mama can take care of you.

ISABELLE. I won't. (*Then she sobs.*) Oh, Gus, you're horrid.

GUS (*at the door*). Yes, I knew you would thank me. Good night. (*Goes up to door.*) Come here! Come here!

ISABELLE (*she crosses to him, dragging Teddy Bear*). What do you want?

GUS (*picking up chain on door*). So soon as I have gone, you will place this end of the chain in this receptacle . . . do you see? (*He indicates it.*) . . . So if I change my mind, if I weaken, this chain will be stronger . . . than my resolutions. Do you understand?

ISABELLE (*mulishly*). I won't do it. I hate you.

GUS. You are a very bad girl. Good night.

ISABELLE. Aren't you even going to kiss me?

GUS. No.

ISABELLE. Aren't you going to put me to bed?

GUS. No!

ISABELLE. Then I'll scream!

(*She starts to scream. He picks her up and starts to divan.*)

GUS. Am I a nurse-maid that I have to take care so of babies? (*Puts her on divan.*) Good night.

ISABELLE. Now kiss me!

GUS. Just a little one. (*He leans over. She grabs him and kisses him soundly. With difficulty, he breaks away.*) *Now*—hook the chain on the door, Baby!

(*He starts for door, U.R.C. She picks up Teddy Bear and throws it on floor, crying as she does so.*)

ISABELLE. I'm not a baby! I'm not a baby!

CURTAIN

ACT THREE

SCENE—*Same as Act Two, except that the hangings on the center section of French windows have been drawn. It is the next morning and the sunlight can be seen stealing through the curtains from off R.*

At Rise: ISABELLE *is lying on divan, sleeping. There is a soft rap on door and* TOM *enters, dressed in the uniform of a valet de chambre. He carries a breakfast tray, which he places on table L. of Love Seat. He picks up tray with champagne and glasses and exits U.R.C. He returns at once, crosses to French windows and pulls drapes open. Then he takes cover off canary cage. The bird whistles. He silences bird. He crosses to divan, picking up Teddy Bear from floor and placing it at her side. He goes to arm chair, takes chemise and places it over small seat foot of divan. He looks at stockings on arm of chair and finding a hole, he crosses to small stand D.R. Opens drawer, takes out several boxes, looking at them until he gets right size. Throws old stockings in drawer, crosses to chair and puts new ones on arm of chair. Goes to bedroom door, then down to bed, touching it to see if* GUS *is there. She wiggles her feet. Returns to bedroom door, raps. No reply, looks puzzled. Raps on bathroom door. No reply. Opens it and looks in. Enters, turning on light. Looks at shower curtains to see if* GUS *is behind them, then turns on water. Enters leaving door open. Calls softly:*

TOM. Signorina — signorina — signorina. (*She pulls cover over her head. He goes to phonograph and plays record— "Stars and Stripes Forever." She sits up angrily and throws Teddy Bear on floor. He picks it up and places it on piano, then closes phonograph.*) Good morning, Signorina.

ISABELLE. Good morning.

TOM (*to upstage head of divan*). I no see his Eccellency . . . any place.

ISABELLE. He's not here.

TOM. Not here?

ISABELLE. No.

TOM. That's very funny.

ISABELLE. He's sleeping in the Judge's apartment.

TOM (*crossing to table L. of Love Seat*). Well, chi va piano, va seno, e va lontano.

ISABELLE. Please don't play the piano.

TOM. No, I no play the piano. I go get your breakfast.

ISABELLE. I'll like a cup of coffee, if it isn't too much trouble.

TOM. No trouble—(*Takes tea to her.*) I got for you a nice cup of tea.

ISABELLE. Are you going to boss me too? (*He hands her a cup of plain tea.*) I'd like some cream and sugar, please.

TOM. No, no. No cream and sugar . . . make you sick. Taka plain. Maka stomach swell up . . . maka room for the eggs.

ISABELLE. I HATE eggs. I won't eat any eggs.

TOM. Very good for you. You eat eggs, and I give you sausage to poosh 'em down. THEN you feel fine.

(*Canary starts to sing.*)

ISABELLE. Oh, Lawdy, couldn't you tell him to sing a little later?

TOM. You no like music?

ISABELLE. Not just now . . . PLEASE.

TOM. I turn him off. (TOM *crosses to cage.*) Silenzio! Ssh! Ssh! (*Canary stops. A cat begins to meow. He hurries to table L. of Love Seat and fills saucer with milk.*) Ah, poosy, poosy, poosy.

ISABELLE (*in despair*). Bring him in. Bring him in. Let's have a party.

TOM. He's hungry.

ISABELLE. Well, for heaven's sake, give him those sausages. I hope he chokes on 'em.

TOM. I give him a little cream. Here, poosy, poosy, poosy! (*Puts cream out window. Cat stops. Then he looks at her a moment.*) Ah, Cristoforo Columbo—what's the matter with you? You getting fat again, huh? (*As he crosses toward bathroom door.*) It won't be long, it won't be long. (*Suddenly he rushes into bathroom.*) Every morning I forget. (*Turns off water and re-enters.*) The bath tub ready, Signorina.

ISABELLE. I'll take a shower later.

TOM. Si, Signorina.

ISABELLE. You're not going to wash me, I hope!

TOM. No, no—no. (*Takes tooth brush from drawer in table U.L.C.*) I got for you a nice tooth brush. (*Crosses to her with it.*)

ISABELLE. It's not Lilli's, I hope.

TOM (*hands her tooth brush*). No, it's a new one. You will find all different tooth paste in the bathroom. Well, I go wake up Mr. Augustino now, g'bye.

(*Takes her tea cup and crosses tray on table L. of Love Seat. Puts it on tray and goes to door. She stops him at door.*)

ISABELLE. Tom!

TOM. Yes, Signorina.

ISABELLE. Do—many young ladies come

here?

TOM. No—just a few cousins and aunts. (*He exits. She rises, crosses to C. Cat has begun to meow.*)

ISABELLE. Hello, Cristoforo Columbus. (*Cat meows. She crosses to window and looks out.*) You happy? (*Cat meows.*) You're going to have a lot of little pussies, huh? (*Cat meows.*) How many you going to have? (*Three short meows.*) You're going to have a whole family. (*Turning to L.*) Gee, you're lucky. (*Cat meows. Rap on door. She goes up R. of door.*) Who is it?

JUDGE (*off U.R.C.*). It's I!

ISABELLE. Come in. (*He enters and sees her in pyjamas. He is about to leave at once.*) Oh, I don't mind. (*She goes to R. of piano.*)

JUDGE. Well! And how is our little guest this morning?

ISABELLE (*listlessly*). M'all right . . . thank you.

JUDGE (*at door*). I was glad . . . mighty glad . . . to learn that you had come to your senses last night . . . but I always knew you would. You can't fool me on CHARACTER . . . that's my business.

ISABELLE. I guess it would be hard . . . to fool you.

JUDGE. IMPOSSIBLE! . . . practically. And when Gus knocked on my door and told me that you had sent him away . . . I wasn't a BIT surprised . . . HE was, but *I* wasn't . . . because I always KNEW you would.

ISABELLE. Did you?

JUDGE (*down to R. of arm chair*). OH, yes! You know . . . there's something about a decent girl that . . . shows in the eyes.

ISABELLE (*moves to R. of Love Seat*). Is there?

JUDGE. OH, MY, yes. To an expert, there is no mistaking the good . . . for the bad.

ISABELLE. I guess you know quite a lot about women.

JUDGE. Yes . . . ah . . . I do. (*And he adds hastily.*) About GOOD women.

ISABELLE (*crosses to L. end of Love Seat*). Judge, maybe good women are good because . . . because it takes two to be bad . . . and they can't find anybody . . .

JUDGE (*angry, up to door then to phonograph table*). Rubbish!

ISABELLE. Well, of course you KNOW, Judge.

JUDGE. Yes, yes. Of course. (*Starts down to her with ticket.*) I took a little walk down to Grand Central this morning, heh heh. (*He laughs nervously and produces an envelope.*) . . . And while there, heh heh, I . . . ah . . . I bought you this little present. (*He hands it to her.*)

ISABELLE (*hardly audible*). Thank you, Judge . . . I . . . I . . . thank you.
(*She fumbles with the envelope and pulls out about a yard of green ticket, starts to look at it.*)

JUDGE. I think you'll find it all there. There's quite a lot of it, isn't there? Yoakum must be at some distance from here. You know your home must be very beautiful this time of the year. The fleecy clouds, the giant red woods, the sparkling Pacific—

ISABELLE. Oh!
(*She drops down into Love Seat.*)

JUDGE (*crosses to R. of her*). Now, now, Isabelle . . . be reasonable.

ISABELLE (*through her tears*). How *can* I be reasonable . . . I don't want to go to Oregon when I live in Mississippi. You're just trying to get rid of me.
(*She throws ticket on Love Seat.*)

JUDGE (*picking up the ticket and looking at it*). Is it possible there can be TWO places with such a name. S'ridiculous!

ISABELLE. You don't have to insult me. Is it my fault, where I was born?

JUDGE. Now, now, Isabelle, I didn't mean that. The mistake is easily rectified. (*He stuffs the tickets in his pocket.*) Now be a good girl and get dressed, and we'll go down there together, in a nice taxicab, and we'll fix it all up.

ISABELLE (*rises*). Does . . . Gus know that you're sending me home?

JUDGE. It was he who told me to get the tickets.

ISABELLE. Gus!

JUDGE. Yes. I forgot to mention it—it's a little present from both of us.

ISABELLE. Oh—oh, yes.

JUDGE. Yes.

ISABELLE (*after a pause*). I . . . I don't want to go home, Judge. I . . . I can't go home. I told you so last night.

JUDGE (*up to her. Distressed*). What ARE you going to do then?

ISABELLE. I don't know. I guess I'd better get dressed though.

JUDGE (*up to door U.R.C.*). Yes . . . Yes. And in the meanwhile I'll see if I can think of something. Don't be long.
(*He exits U.R.C.*)

ISABELLE (*walks into the bathroom. She re-enters and goes to phone slowly, not knowing whether to answer it*). Hello . . . Yes . . . Yes, this is Mr. Caraffa's apartment . . . Oh! . . . Oh, hello . . . Henry . . . how did you find it? . . . Oh, in the 'phone book . . . that was right smart of you . . . Yes . . . Yes . . . Yes . . . you certainly were . . . I think you'd better quit drinking . . . all right . . . all right . . . I'll see you. (*For the last word she drops her voice.*) . . . all right. (*She hangs up very slowly.*)

JUDGE (*off U.R.C.*). Isabelle?

ISABELLE (*going to bathroom door*). What is it?

JUDGE (*entering*). Isabelle, I've been thinking and really the best thing you can do is to go home to your mother.

ISABELLE. You won't have to worry about me any more, Judge. I've made up my mind.

(*Goes into bathroom and* JUDGE *crosses to foot of divan. Rap on door U.R.C. It is* GUS.)

GUS. Isabelle! Isabelle! (*Enters hurriedly U.R.C. Sees* JUDGE.) Oh—you are here. (*Looking around the room.*) Where's the child? (GUS *down to R. of arm chair.*)

JUDGE. She's dressing.

(*He indicates the bathroom.*)

GUS (*smiling happily at the bathroom door*). I can't wait to see her. Oh, Judge! Congratulate me, felicitate me, shake me by the hand, kiss me on both cheeks, I'M IN LOVE!

JUDGE. HUH?

GUS (*ecstatically*). Oh! It's WONDERFUL, it's MARVELOUS!

JUDGE. When did this happen?

GUS. This morning. About two o'clock. I couldn't sleep. I couldn't think. I got up, I listened to you snoring, STILL I couldn't sleep. I thought I was going crazy. I thought: Am I SICK? No. Am I HUNGRY? No. THIRSTY? No. Well, what DO I want? (*He smiles languorously.*) And *then,* Judge, THEN I knew. OH, IT'S WONDERFUL to feel such a PAIN in the heart.

JUDGE (*sourly*). It must be.

GUS. So THEN, what do I do? I take the telephone, I say give me Western Union, I say take a cable, please. And to my Mother I say: Mama Mia, I am in LOVE. With the most beautiful, adorable, enchanting, exquisite, lovely, pure, intelligent, remarkable, educated . . .

JUDGE. At fifty cents a word?

GUS. It was on your telephone. (JUDGE *sits on divan.*) Faithful, obedient and irreplaceable maiden in the entire world and I humbly beg your permission to marry her. Answer immediately. Urgent. The answer should be here now . . . let me see: Two o'clock here is . . . seven o'clock in the morning in Italy . . . The cable would get there about nine . . . Mama would faint once with excitement . . . that takes about an hour . . . then she composes her answer . . . that takes another hour . . . then Giulio goes down to the telegraph office with the message . . . it isn't far, but he's old . . . that's another hour . . . then two hours for transmission, that makes nine o'clock . . . What time is it?

JUDGE (*looking at his watch*). Eleven minutes past ten.

GUS (*crosses R.*). Aie . . . Santo Deo. One hour and eleven minutes . . . late. They have *no* consideration. It would be quicker to send a *letter*. Or to go by street car—

(*Goes U.R.C.*)

JUDGE (*rises, crosses to C.*). Now don't get excited, it'll be here. Hold your horses.

GUS (*crossing down to* JUDGE). What do I want with horses? I want telegraphs.

JUDGE. There, there. Go and get dressed. It'll be here by the time you're ready. You're not going to propose in that, are you?

GUS (*hugs* JUDGE). I'm a little bit excited . . . OH, IT'S MARVELOUS.

JUDGE. Suppose she refuses you?

GUS. My God, I never thought of that. I must look my best. (*He starts up to bedroom, singing. Enters.* JUDGE *goes up to R. of phonograph table.* GUS *returns with clothes. Shower increases in volume. He goes to door U.R.C. Stops. Hears shower and comes toward bathroom door slightly.*) Oh! She's in my little bath tub.

JUDGE. Well, go and use mine. (*Shower stops.*)

GUS. Thank you. (*Starts to go—stops.*) And, Judge—if she comes out—don't tell her anything—let me surprise her.

JUDGE. You can trust me.

(GUS *exits.* JUDGE *comes D.C. then returns to bathroom door and raps.*)

ISABELLE (*offstage in bath*). Don't come in.

JUDGE. Isabelle!

ISABELLE. What is it?

JUDGE. I've been thinking . . .

ISABELLE. So early?

JUDGE. I say I've been thinking . . .

ISABELLE. Just a minute. (*She opens the door a little.*) What did you say?

JUDGE. I say I've been thinking . . .

ISABELLE. Drinking?

JUDGE. No! Thinking . . . with the brains . . . about you.

ISABELLE. Would you pass me that pink thing up there? What have you been thinking with your brains about me?

JUDGE. Well . . . after much thought, I've come to the conclusion that perhaps you may be right.

ISABELLE. And now the stockings, please. (*He gets stockings.*) Don't forget the garters! (*Picks up garters, returns to door and hands them in.*) These aren't my stockings.

JUDGE. Well, it's a cinch they aren't mine!

ISABELLE. I guess they must be Lilli's. They're very nice though.

JUDGE. I have come to the conclusion . . .

ISABELLE. The what?

JUDGE (*shouting*). The CONCLUSION . . . THE END.

ISABELLE. The end? Have you finished?

JUDGE (*paces back and forth front of door*). No!

ISABELLE. Then why do you stop?

JUDGE (*tearing his hair*). Oh, GOD!

ISABELLE. What?

JUDGE. Nothing. Now listen carefully . . .

ISABELLE. Will you pass me my dress?

JUDGE (*looks around room for dress*). Dress? Dress? (*Sees it on screen and takes it.*) Dress! (*Takes it to bathroom.*) Here you are.

ISABELLE. Thanks. Now go right on—don't let me interrupt.

JUDGE (*L. of door. Wearily*). Well, as I was saying . . .

ISABELLE. Yes, go on.

JUDGE. I have been thinking, and . . .

ISABELLE. Just a second, darling, would you please—

JUDGE (*anticipating her*). All right—I'll get them.

(*Gets slippers from upstage end of divan and hands them in to her. Then starts to Love Seat, exhausted.*)

ISABELLE. Now, go on.

JUDGE. No, I'll wait until you're finished. (*Sitting.*)

ISABELLE. What did you say?

JUDGE (*wearily*). I said . . .

ISABELLE. What?

JUDGE. God give me strength!

ISABELLE (*enters dressed. Comes R. of chair. Stepping into the room*). THERE! That didn't take long, did it?

JUDGE. Noooooo! Not when you think of all the things I handed you.

ISABELLE. You were sweet. Would you . . . would you hook me up?

JUDGE (*rising*). Certainly. (*Goes up behind her and hooks her up with difficulty.*) There! You should have zippers on here. (*Crosses to L. of chair.*)

ISABELLE. Thank you. (*Goes R. and below chair.*) Now what were you trying to say while I was in there?

JUDGE. What I was trying to convey, with remarkably little success, was, that after thinking matters over carefully, I've decided you were right.

ISABELLE. Of course I was right. What about?

JUDGE. About going home.

ISABELLE. You think I'd better not go?

JUDGE. To put it in a nutshell, yes.

ISABELLE. But if I don't go home, what WILL I do?

JUDGE. STAY HERE AND GET MARRIED.

ISABELLE (*crosses to window*). That's what *I* thought. (*After a long pause.*) Even if I don't love him? . . .

JUDGE. Great Guns! What's happened now?

ISABELLE. Maybe you're right. There doesn't seem much else to do.

JUDGE. He would be flattered if he heard you.

ISABELLE. I don't care . . . I don't care about anything.

TOM (*knocking and coming right in*). Signorina . . . That young man . . . who come with you last night . . . he's downstairs . . . insists he wants to see you. I no tell him you're here yet.

ISABELLE (*L. end Love Seat. Sighs*). Tell him to come up.

JUDGE. What! (*Above chair.*)

TOM (*exiting*). Yes, Signorina.

ISABELLE. I don't think Gus would mind . . .

JUDGE. What do you mean — he wouldn't mind—he'd be furious.

ISABELLE (*crossing to divan downstage side*). No, he wouldn't.

JUDGE (*crossing to upstage side of

divan). He would—(*They start to straighten cover of chair.*) He would.

ISABELLE. I know.

JUDGE. Oh, I don't understand anything any more.

(ISABELLE *crosses to Love Seat.* JUDGE *puts two pillows on divan. He is about to get others when she turns and sees him as she sits.*)

ISABELLE. Never mind about that. (*Rap on door.*) Come in.

(HENRY *enters.* JUDGE *brushes by him with a snort and exits.* HENRY *comes R. of arm chair.*)

HENRY. I . . . I came to apologize . . . Isabelle.

ISABELLE. That's all right, Henry.

HENRY. I said some rotten things. I'm sorry.

ISABELLE. I said things, too.

HENRY. I was pretty drunk, I guess.

ISABELLE. I guess so.

HENRY (*eyeing the room surreptitiously*). Did you . . . sleep . . . here?

ISABELLE. Yes, Henry. THERE!

(*She points to the divan.*)

HENRY (*from the chair*). Nice apartment . . . in a flashy way.

ISABELLE. Do you think it's flashy?

HENRY (*L. slightly*). Yes—ostentatious.

ISABELLE. What's the matter with it?

HENRY. Ostentatious—Woppish.

ISABELLE. Well, I like it and the Count Di Ruvo said I could stay as long as I liked.

HENRY (*viciously*). Damn nice of him. And where would HE stay?

ISABELLE. I didn't ask him that.

HENRY. No . . . you wouldn't. But I can tell you where he'd stay, if you're anxious to know.

ISABELLE. I'm not.

HENRY. Where did he stay last night?

ISABELLE (*smiling slightly and looking at him*). Where did YOU stay?

HENRY. Never mind where *I* stayed . . . where was HE?

ISABELLE. With the judge . . . your friend.

HENRY. How do I know he was?

ISABELLE. You don't . . . you never will.

HENRY (*toward her slightly*). What do you mean?

ISABELLE. Just that! If you don't believe me NOW, you never will, that's all. About THIS, or anything else.

HENRY (*narrowing his eyes*). If I thought . . .

ISABELLE. You can think anything you like. I know how your mind works.

HENRY. Naturally I . . .

ISABELLE. I STILL have my virginity, if that's what's worrying you.

HENRY (*shocked*). ISABELLE!

ISABELLE. Don't be a hypocrite . . . that's what you were thinking . . . though why they make so much fuss about it is more than I can understand.

HENRY (*thunderstruck*). FUSS ABOUT IT!

ISABELLE. You heard me. As if it mattered to anybody but me. By the way, I forgot to ask you! Are *you* pure?

HENRY. WHAT? Why . . .

ISABELLE. You needn't bother to answer. I'm not curious.

HENRY. It's ENTIRELY different anyway.

ISABELLE. Well, I don't REALLY know anything about it, so you may be right.

HENRY. Now you're being sensible. (*Smiles—several steps toward her.*) I . . . ah . . . hope you didn't take our little lovers' quarrel . . . too seriously. (ISABELLE *looks away, but says nothing.*) We're . . . still engaged, I mean. (ISABELLE *remains silent. Edging closer.*) Aren't we?

TOM (*is heard pounding up the stairs yelling*). Signor Conte, Signor Conte.

(*He bursts into the room with a cable in his hand. He stands panting and looking around.*)

ISABELLE. I guess he's in the Judge's apartment, Tom.

TOM. Thank you, I look.

(*He rushes out.*)

HENRY (*watches him go, then*). Isabelle!

ISABELLE. Yes?

HENRY. You didn't answer my question.

ISABELLE (*vaguely*). Huh?

HENRY. Are you still my fiancée?

ISABELLE (*moving D.R. listlessly*). I . . . I suppose so.

HENRY (*follows to R. end of Love Seat*). I knew you didn't mean it . . . you couldn't. (ISABELLE *turns and looks at him without a trace of a smile. Advancing.*) Well, aren't you . . . aren't you going to kiss me?

ISABELLE. Yes, Henry. (*She is taken in his arms and kissed.*)

GUS (*off U.R.C.*). Isabelle! (*Bursts into room with cable. Sees* HENRY *kissing her. She backs up against piano.* GUS *comes to R. of chair and stops.*) I beg your pardon. The Judge said you wanted to see me.

HENRY (*up to R. of* GUS. *All smiles*). It's

quite all right, Count. It's OUR fault. By the way, Count, I want to thank you for turning over your rooms to my fiancée last night. It was very kind of you. I appreciate it.

GUS. I was only too happy.

HENRY. I also want to straighten out our little difference. I'm afraid I was intoxicated.

GUS (*stiffly*). It is not necessary to mention it, sir.

HENRY. Well, then I guess . . . that's all. (*Turns to* ISABELLE.) Are you ready, Isabelle?

ISABELLE. Yes, Henry. (HENRY *goes to door U.R.C. and opens it. She picks up cape and bag, sadly, crosses L toward* GUS *to L. end of Love Seat.*) Good-bye, Gus.

GUS (*bowing*). Good-bye, Miss Parry.

HENRY. Well, so long.

(ISABELLE *starts to go, and is stopped by* GUS'S *words.*)

GUS. If you please . . . I would like to speak with you . . . for one minute.

HENRY. Well, the fact is . . . we're in pretty much of a hurry . . .

ISABELLE. What is it, Gus?

HENRY (*coming to R. of* GUS). Well, I suppose we CAN spare a couple of minutes.

GUS (*to* ISABELLE). Alone.

HENRY (*belligerently*). SAY! What's the idea?

ISABELLE (*turning coldly to* HENRY). This gentleman has shown me the greatest courtesy, Henry. More than you can possibly realize. You have nothing to fear in leaving me alone with him.

HENRY. I didn't mean that.

ISABELLE (*still in the same level tone*). Will you wait for me in the car, please?

HENRY. Yeah, but—

ISABELLE. Are you going to start all over again, Henry?

HENRY (*going to door W.R.C.*). Oh—all right. (*Turns.*) But it's a damn funny idea.

(*He exits, leaving door open.*)

ISABELLE (*looking at* GUS *uneasily*). What is it, Gus?

GUS (*closing door. Very gravely*). I came here just now . . . to ask you to marry me. (*Goes down to R. and below chair.*)

ISABELLE. Oh!

(*She turns to R., away from him.*)

GUS. Yes.

ISABELLE. When did you get that idea?

GUS. This morning . . . after I left you. I couldn't sleep. I lay in bed wondering . . . wondering.

ISABELLE. What to do with me?

GUS. Yes.

ISABELLE. Then you thought of this . . . solution.

GUS. Yes. Always you see, I thought marriage was not for me. For a woman, such life would be . . . Hell. Here a few months, then quick to Milan, a week at La Scala, then two, maybe three days at home, then a rotten trip to Spain . . . (ISABELLE, *who has been only to Excelsior Springs, West Orange, N. J., and New York, listens to this itinerary breathlessly. She dreamily contemplates the wonders of such a trip.*) . . . one week in Barcelona, one week in Madrid, then off to South America for the season. IT'S TERRIBLE!

ISABELLE. Yes . . . it must be.

GUS. IT IS. IT'S AWFUL. So always I put behind me thoughts of marriage, so that some poor woman would not have to . . . share my sufferings.

ISABELLE. That was very thoughtful of you.

GUS. But bad as it would be for the woman, think what it would mean for the children.

ISABELLE (*turns to him*). Yes, I suppose it would be hard for the children.

GUS (*toward her slightly*). TERRIBLE! But I will NOT be separated from my wife and children. I am, by nature, a family man. All my ancestors, on both sides, had families.

ISABELLE (*looking front, wistfully*). I guess mine did too.

GUS. So can you see what it would be like . . . to travel? Nurses, valets, governesses, maids, toys, animals . . . Tutors, little boys, little girls . . . it would be like traveling with a menagerie!

ISABELLE. How many children did you expect to have?

GUS. I haven't decided yet.

ISABELLE. Oh!

GUS. But then this morning, I said, what the Hell, we only live once . . . if I can travel, the family can travel. So I put on my best suit, and came to tell you. And I find—(*He extends his arm towards where she stood with* HENRY. ISABELLE *looks away from him.*) So now . . . before you go . . . out of my life into the arms of . . . a younger man, I want you please to remember that I loved you, Isabelle.

ISABELLE. You don't.

GUS (*unheeding*). . . . that I loved you. Very real . . . very fine . . . very honorable love. And when I lose you, I am losing something . . . (*He taps his heart.*) . . . of me. Something . . . I am afraid I will not find any more. (*In a more matter-of-fact tone.*) Something I did not deserve, Isabelle, because I have been a very wicked man. But that is no consolation for me now. You must go now. (*He turns L. slightly.*) You must not keep Henry waiting . . . the wife must be obedient and thoughtful. (*Looks around at her.*) But if sometimes you hear me sing . . . you will know I am singing for you, Isabelle, only for you, and . . . and . . . that is all.

ISABELLE (*up to R. of chair. Facing him*). You don't love me.

GUS (*L. of chair facing her*). Would I then have asked you to marry me? The only time in my life I ask anybody.

ISABELLE. And you were sure I'd say "Yes," weren't you?

GUS. No, Isabelle, but I hoped.

ISABELLE. Oh, yes, you were.

GUS. No, my child.

ISABELLE. You were sure I'd say yes because I couldn't do anything else. You felt sorry for me, and out of the kindness of your heart, you said, well, nobody else wants her, she's in trouble. I'LL take her. Well, I don't want your charity. I won't have it, yours or anybody else's.

GUS. But, I love you, baby—

ISABELLE. No, you don't.

GUS. But, Isabelle.

ISABELLE. You don't, you don't.

(*She is practically sobbing by now.*)

GUS. I do . . . and you know it.

ISABELLE. You don't. YOU DON'T. If you did you wouldn't have left me . . . last night, with that stuffed Teddy Bear.

(*She goes up to door and opens it.*)

GUS (*putting up his hands*). Baby!

ISABELLE. You're just trying to make me unhappy by telling me this now. That's what you're doing. Well . . . it's too late. I DON'T love you . . . I . . . I love Henry. You saw me kissing him just now. You know what that means? It means . . . that for the rest of my life . . . I'm going to live . . . in WEST ORANGE . . . New Jersey!

(*She exits.* JUDGE *appears in door, watching* ISABELLE *leave. Then he enters and comes down to R. of* GUS. GUS *passes cable to* JUDGE, *who looks at it a moment, then hands it back.*)

JUDGE. What does it say?

GUS (*below arm chair and L. Reading*). Figlio mio: tu hoi il permesso e la mia beneizioned . . . (JUDGE *interrupts.*) Oh —excuse me—(*Translates.*) My son—you have my permission and my blessing but . . . there cannot be no such person . . . you must be dreaming. (*Looks up.*) I guess she is right . . . my mother. I was dreaming. (*The canary begins to sing. He crosses to front of Love Seat, back to audience. Throws cable down.*) You can sing, Caruso, but I . . . I will never sing again. (*Canary stops singing.*)

JUDGE. Oh, for God's sake, let's have a drink. (*Phone starts to ring as he starts up to door U.R.C.*) I have something in my room.

(*He exits.* GUS *goes to telephone reluctantly.*)

GUS. Yes? Who? Oh, hello, Lilli, but the conference has just ended. No, it was not a success. I had hoped it would mean a long contract, but it was a complete failure . . . Yes, Lilli . . . No, Lilli, I cannot see you.

(JUDGE *enters, leading* ISABELLE. GUS *sees her and puts receiver on phone. Then he rushes down to her to R.C.*)

JUDGE. Gus! Gus! Look what I found crying in my room! Isabelle!

ISABELLE (*R.C. Down C.*). It wasn't true. I lied to you. I do love you.

(*Telephone starts ringing in jerks, then begins to ring regularly. They embrace and break.*)

GUS. But I warn you—I must have four sons and seven daughters—

JUDGE (*L. of door U.R.C. starting to exit*). In that case I'll tell Henry not to wait.

CURTAIN

Berkeley Square

BY JOHN L. BALDERSTON

First produced by Gilbert Miller and Leslie Howard at the Lyceum Theatre, New York City, on November 4, 1929, with the following cast:

MAID	Irene Howard
TOM PETTIGREW	Brian Gilmour
KATE PETTIGREW	Valerie Taylor
THE LADY ANNE PETTIGREW	Alice John
MR. THROSTLE	Traver Penna
HELEN PETTIGREW	Margalo Gillmore
THE AMBASSADOR	Fritz Williams
MRS. BARWICK	Lucy Beaumont
PETER STANDISH	Leslie Howard
MARJORIE FRANT	Ann Freshman
MAJOR CLINTON	Charles Romano
MISS BARRYMORE	June English
THE DUCHESS OF DEVONSHIRE	Louise Prussing
LORD STANLEY	Henry Warwick
H.R.H. THE DUKE OF CUMBERLAND	Robert Greig

The action throughout takes place in the morning room of a house of the Queen Anne period in Berkeley Square, London, in the years 1784 and 1928.

ACT I

Scene 1. Five o'clock, October 23, 1784.
Scene 2. Five o'clock, October 23, 1928.
Scene 3. Continuous with Scene 1.

ACT II

Night—a few days later, 1784.

ACT III

Scene 1. Afternoon in 1784, a week later.
Scene 2. Continuous with Scene 1, but in 1928.

ALTHOUGH fantasy, except in conjunction with satirical extravaganza, as in *Beggar on Horseback,* was not in vogue during the worldly twenties, the period brought forth one excursion, *Berkeley Square,* which was not equalled in kind either before or after in the American theatre. It was gentle by the standards of the Broadway stage but reflective, ironic, and rather touching. It has been a favorite in the amateur theatre ever since it won affectionate attention in New York.

Its author John Lloyd Balderson was born in Germantown, Pa., in 1889. That he was of British descent could have surprised no one who knew the play, but it is a curious biographical detail that his great-great-grandmother made the first American flag, no doubt to the great distress of the portion of his family that remained stubbornly Tory and loyal to George III. After studying at Columbia University, between 1911 and 1914, and working on the U.S. Government Committee on Public Information in 1918-1919, he started his career as a playwright with the war drama *The Genius of the Marne* (1919), published with a preface by George Moore but not produced.

He published a second play in 1920 both in New York and London, *A Morality for the Leisure Class* (1924), but again without achieving production. It was followed by *Tongo* in 1924, which also failed to make an impression in the theatre. But his persistence was amply rewarded when he adapted the melodrama *Dracula* (1927) and when he wrote *Berkeley Square.* It was produced with success in England and then in a somewhat modified version in New York. His last produced play on Broadway was the unsuccessful *Red Planet* (1934). Mr. Balderston was also editor of "The Outlook" in London between 1920 and 1923 and chief London correspondent for the New York World between 1923 and 1931. He was active in the American defense movement after 1940, and he wrote many scenarios.

ACT ONE

Scene I

October the 23rd, 1784. The morning-room of a Queen Anne house in Berkeley Square. It is panelled and painted a creamy white. There are two long recessed windows at the back, with pelmets and curtains of rose-coloured Italian brocade that fall to the window seats. They look out into the trees of the enclosed garden, now drenched with rain. The backdrop shows houses across the Square. In the right wall, well front stage, a door opens inwards. Tall Queen Anne walnut writing-bureau, closed, with a pair of brass candlesticks on the candle-slides, stands against the right wall back stage, with a needlework-covered walnut stool in front of it. Between the door and the writing-bureau, a walnut chair. In the centre panel of the rear wall hangs a tapestry; under this, a delicately modelled gilt console table, with a Chelsea group upon it. An armchair a little to the front and right of the table. The large fireplace, set at an angle across the corner between the left window and a double door in the left wall, has bolection moulding around the fire, and a painted landscape let into the panel above. Small table, folded, against the back wall between left window and fire; and on each side of the double door, a walnut cabriole-leg chair. Mirror and bell pull on the wall between fireplace and door; low walnut stool before fireplace. A small settee is placed left centre; to the right of this a walnut cabriole-leg table, with drawers, used as a work table. Occupying the centre of the stage, a section of an oval rug, yellow, with a Chinese design in blue and rose. Parquetry stagecloth on part of floor not covered by rug. The room is lit by five glass sconces of two lights each, one between writing-bureau and door, one to the right of the right window, one to the left of left window, one on each side of the double door.

As the curtain rises, five full deep notes are heard from a grandfather clock—off stage, on the landing outside the door right. It is dusk. The fire is burning. Candles on left of stage are lit as the curtain rises. MAID, *wearing a blue-grey dress with frilled mobcap, is discovered with taper lighting candles right. She blows out the taper, and as she is drawing the curtains, the sound of a horse's hoofs is heard. The horse stops outside. She hurries out right. She reenters right, carrying a letter in her hand.* TOM PETTIGREW *follows. He is a youth in his twenties, clothed as a town buck of the period. He has aristocratic features; mouth normally twisted into a sneer; naturally coarse, brutal, disagreeable under the veneer of good breeding. He is, very slightly, tipsy.*

TOM. What have you there?

MAID. For her ladyship, sir.

TOM. Give it to me.

MAID. But 'tis for her ladyship.

TOM (*scowling*). Give it to me!

(MAID *reluctantly lets him take the letter. He stoops to kiss her.*)

MAID. No, please, Mr. Tom!

TOM. Gad's life, Wilkins, when did you turn prude?

MAID. I told you I'm to be married, sir.

TOM. Ay, but to whom, my love? Some lusty great footman, what? (*As thought strikes him.*) And if we found him—(*Leers at her*)—we could tell him something.

MAID (*terrified*). Oh, Mr. Tom, you'd never—

TOM (*seizing her*). We're more reasonable now, ain't we? (*Enter* KATE PETTIGREW, L., *carrying needlework. She is twenty-five, dressed fashionably, cool, competent, handsome, self-assured. She stops at door.* TOM *releases* MAID) Damme, you shouldn't sling about. (KATE *makes a gesture of dismissal to* MAID, *who exits by door* R.)

KATE (*contemptuously*). Are not maids difficult enough to find, at the beggarly wage we can afford, without your making the keeping of them impossible?

TOM (*trying to recover his poise*). 'Tis me you should thank, Kitty, that they seek our employment at all.

KATE. Foh! Your tastes are those of a stableboy!

TOM. Your tongue is worse than Helen's great staring eyes when she looks through a man. An agreeable pair of sisters! I'll not endure it. While my father's at sea, am I not his deputy here?

KATE. A pretty deputy! I hope you'll repeat that remark to our mother.

TOM. And why not, pray? Where is her ladyship?

KATE (*puts her work in drawer of small table* L. *front*). You had best avoid her.

Your latest follies have set her beside herself.

TOM (*importantly*). She will forget such trifles when she hears my news.

KATE (*mockingly*). Is it so important? Has Miss Sinclair taken pity upon you at last?

TOM. 'Tis a lie! I never asked her.

KATE. How many malicious tongues there are in town—'tis said she is the sixth to refuse you.

TOM. Damn them all, no woman nowadays will look at a man without money—until after she's married a man who's got it!

KATE. If you realize you've no money, why must you gamble as though you'd a fortune?

TOM (*mysteriously*). Ah, Fortune! Perhaps Fortune is but now knocking at our door. I come as Fortune's herald.

KATE. I *thought* you were tipsy.

TOM. If Helen were here she'd interpret my oracle, and not carp like a Covent Garden orange wench.

KATE (*curious but haughty*). Why so classical today? First a herald, now an oracle?

TOM. Helen could read my riddle. Helen could see through the wall with those damned eyes of hers—and what d'you think she'd see? Fortune approaching this house, now in the flesh. Fortune—wearing breeches, no doubt very badly cut. (*Teasingly.*) Now. Three guesses, Kate.

KATE (*intensely excited*). Is he—has Cousin Peter arrived from America?

TOM. Faith, you have guessed it in one!

KATE (*holding herself in*). If you are the first Pettigrew he's met, we are unfortunate!

TOM. He has not had that honor.

KATE (*impatiently*). Then how do you know he's in London?

TOM. Met Bill Clinton in St. James's Street not an hour since. He came with him from New York in the *General Wolfe*. (KATE *starts to go out* L.) So you've no interest in my further news? (*Waves letter tantalizingly.*)

KATE (*turning*). From him?

TOM (*scrutinizing it*). I judge so!

KATE. Give it to me!

TOM (*affecting to be shocked*). When 'tis directed, as is proper, to her ladyship?

KATE (*turns, pulls bellcord*). And you have kept it all this time?

TOM. I thought to find your Yankee already here. He can't be so eager as his letters have made you suppose.

KATE. He sends an intimation before him, as any gentleman would.

TOM (*sneering*). Gentleman! From New York! Now look'ee, Kitty. Hook this Colonial and there need be no more talk of beggary in this family. (*The* MAID *enters* R.)

KATE. Find out her ladyship and give her this letter. (TOM *gives* MAID *letter*, MAID *exits* L.) I know what you've in mind. He is not to know of your debts.

TOM. D'you think all the benefits from this arrangement are to be yours?

KATE. I know of no arrangement.

TOM. I suppose there's been no suggestion of a settlement of fifteen thousand pounds?

KATE. I've not said I'll have him.

TOM (*dryly*). You will.

(*Enter* LADY ANNE L., *carrying letter open. She wears the high wig in fashion a few years earlier. She is fifty—stout, high-nosed, determined; rather a dragon.*)

LADY ANNE. Kate! Thomas! He's arrived. Cousin Peter is in London! (*Waves letter, comes to settee.*)

KATE. Read it, ma'am! (KATE *sits by her mother.* TOM *leans over back of settee.*)

LADY ANNE (*fumbles with lorgnette*). Let me see. Ah, "October 23rd, 17 and 84. Honored madam. Having arrived within the hour——"

TOM. Where'd he send this from?

LADY ANNE (*fumbles again and peers*). The Blue Boar in Jermyn Street.

TOM. Lodges in that old stable, when he's ten thousand a year.

KATE. Go on, ma'am.

LADY ANNE. "—within the hour, traveling by post from Plymouth, I make haste to dispatch you this intimation that I shall do myself the honor to wait upon yourself, my fair cousins, and Mr. Pettigrew, at a half after five this evening, in Berkeley Square. I subscribe myself, Madam, your most obedient cousin and humble servant, Peter Standish. To the Lady Anne Pettigrew."

KATE. Our cousin's letter is well-bred.

LADY ANNE. Mr. Standish's letters from New York have already vouched for his parts.

TOM. And Messrs. Baring's discreet replies, for his substance.

LADY ANNE (*surveying* KATE *thoughtfully*). You look charming, my child.

TOM. Such blushes, too. Art or nature?

KATE. More natural than wit in you.

TOM. Your husband will find you sharp of tongue, my lass. (*Clock outside on landing strikes once.* TOM *looks at his watch.*) A quarter after five o'clock. The cavalier should be here ere long.

LADY ANNE (*after a moment's thought*). Tom, you will greet him below and bring him here. (*To* KATE.) And you will welcome him on my behalf.

KATE. Not—alone? Surely you will present him to me?

TOM. My sister fears that she would make herself cheap.

LADY ANNE. Hold your tongue! (*To* KATE.) You will do as I tell you. When I return I shall know——

TOM. The baggage is bashful! Where learnt you this trick, Kate? Gad's blood, if only he'll have you!

LADY ANNE. He wants an English wife, and he commends Kate's miniature. Where else could he aspire to such a connection?

TOM. Our mother is ingenious. If you fail to please in person as you did by post, there's still another daughter——

LADY ANNE. What insolence is this?

TOM (*a bit cowed, but pressing on*). My poor friend Throstle's fifteen hundred a year is scarcely to be set against ten thousand——

LADY ANNE. Enough of your crude jesting. You will know whom Helen is to marry.

KATE. But Helen's disposition, ma'am. (*Sits by mother on settee.*)

LADY ANNE. You may safely leave Helen's fancies to me, and trust her mother to act in her interests.

TOM (*to* KATE). Ay, and in ours, too. And as for your prejudice against my friend Throstle——

KATE. Your friend, while you can borrow from him!

TOM. Gad, even tailors have to be paid somehow.

KATE. The disgusting little man!

LADY ANNE. Kate!

TOM. What's wrong with him? Teeth none too good, perhaps, but an artist, a man of parts, not without generosity.

KATE. Such as you hope to find in Mr. Standish! (*To* LADY ANNE.) He'll ruin everything! (*To* TOM.) I wish you'd go racing at Newmarket for the week.

TOM. And who then would dry-nurse Master Colonial?

LADY ANNE. You are not to say Colonial. The Colonists are now independent.

TOM. Yankee puppy, then.

LADY ANNE. Peter Standish is your cousin!

TOM. What was his father? A fur dealer, a tradesman!

LADY ANNE. His grandfather built this house.

TOM. And lost his money—fled to America with the scum o' the country and married God knows whom there.

KATE. Dry-nurse indeed! You think to find him drink, women and cards, so that he pay for yours.

TOM. I shall. But I will get you your husband.

LADY ANNE. You grow offensive, sir!

KATE. And is it likely that such a man as our cousin will put himself in your hands?

TOM. Such a man! His polite letters have foxed you, Kitty.

LADY ANNE. What do you know of him?

TOM (*mischievously*). Bill Clinton told me he's a devil of a temper. Got cashiered from the rebel army for insubordination.

LADY ANNE (*anxiously*). Every woman likes a man of spirit. What else did Clinton say?

TOM (*laughing*). That he can drink any two men of us here under the table. That the mothers in the Yankee villages locked up their daughters when Captain Peter Standish was looking for billets.

LADY ANNE (*angrily, anxiously looking toward* KATE). These are monstrous lies!

KATE. He thinks to disturb me, ma'am, with absurd inventions.

TOM (*indignant*). Inventions! (*Laughs again.*) I leave those to your Yankee! Clinton says he's always inventing things——

KATE (*indifferently*). Our cousin has written me of his hobbies.

TOM (*embarrassed*). I had thought to put him down at White's, ma'am. We might lighten this load of dollars there. But at the moment that attention is beyond me.

LADY ANNE (*suspiciously*). Indeed? And why?

TOM. Because of a slight put upon me by the committee.

KATE. He's been posted at his club.

TOM (*sheepishly*). If I am to show him proper civility, I must beg a hundred pounds of you, ma'am.

LADY ANNE. You had fifty but Tuesday!

KATE. Gambling again!

TOM. I'm a gentleman and do as my equals. Am I to parade our wretched poverty before the town?

KATE. Need you scatter months of our pin money in an evening?

TOM (*to* KATE). Think you I'd grudge you a hundred pounds had I a settlement of fifteen thousand all but in my hands?

LADY ANNE. You are insupportable. I know not where to turn for money.

TOM. After this once, ma'am, I'll not need to trouble you more.

KATE. He means to rob our cousin.

TOM (*snarling, turning on her*). Rob! How dare you!

KATE. Rook, then.

TOM. D'you mean I play unfairly, wench?

LADY ANNE. Kate! Thomas!

(*Enter* MAID R.,—*announcing.*)

MAID. Mr. Throstle, your ladyship.

(THROSTLE *enters* R. *A dandified, fussy, precious little man of forty odd. The* MAID *goes out.* LADY ANNE *and* KATE *rise. Bows and curtsies exchanged.*)

THROSTLE. Your servant, Lady Anne! Miss Pettigrew! Your servant, sir! (LADIES *resume seats.*)

LADY ANNE. Even the rain cannot keep faithful Mr. Throstle away. (TOM *sits in chair by door* R.; *reads newspaper.*)

THROSTLE. Madam, I learned at the Bull that a certain coach has borne a precious freight to London——

LADY ANNE (*smiling at him*). She will be down directly, sir; she stays only to change her gown.

THROSTLE. Miss Helen indeed comes first in my thoughts, even when my curiosity is so lively respecting your Croesus of a cousin—whose arrival—

TOM (*puts down paper*). Does anything ever happen that you don't hear of it in the instant, Throstle?

LADY ANNE. He'll be with us at any moment now.

THROSTLE. Mr. Standish, I gather, has never been in England? If I can be of assistance, in effecting introductions——

LADY ANNE. Oh, sir, we shall indeed make bold to enlist your help.

TOM. And we'll need it, Throstle! If only he'll imitate his better, but these Yankees! 'Twan't worth our trouble to catch and hang the lot, so they say they won the war!

LADY ANNE. You are not to mention the late war with America!

TOM. You don't know these Yankees. 'Twon't be I who'll mention it.

(*Enter* HELEN L. *A girl of about twenty. A wistful, sensitive face. She is in all respects a contrast to her polished, worldly sister.*)

THROSTLE (*kissing her hand*). Your most devoted, faithful slave, now as always, dear Miss Helen.

HELEN (*curtseys*). I am your servant, sir.

THROSTLE. The week of your absence has been to me a desert.

HELEN (*absently*). Thank you, sir.

KATE (*bursts out to* HELEN). Cousin Peter's in London!

HELEN. He's on his way to us now?

TOM. Helen! Observe Kate's maidenish agitation! Mother has contrived that she's to meet him first, and alone.

HELEN. Mother! What *will* Cousin Peter think?

LADY ANNE (*severely*). Think? What should he think? Our cousin has written, Mr. Throstle, that he would buy a town house, a country estate——

TOM. And a wife!

HELEN. Oh, Tom!

THROSTLE (*interposing*). The lady upon whom Mr. Standish prevails then need not exchange our civilized society for Mr. Washington's crude democracy?

LADY ANNE. What Miss of quality would leave London for the Colonies?

TOM. Now who said Colonies?

HELEN. I hear a coach.

(*Noise of coach—it stops.* TOM *hurries to window* R.; *draws back curtains.* KATE *and* LADY ANNE *go to window* L., *peer into street.*)

LADY ANNE. 'Tis he! Look, Kate! A most elegant young man!

TOM (*with faint sneer*). His back is most elegant.

LADY ANNE (*turning*). Now, Tom, downstairs to him.

TOM. Good luck with your savage, Kate!

KATE. Savage or not, there's to be no sneering.

TOM. You'll need those blushes now. (*Exits* R.)

LADY ANNE. Come, come into the drawing-room. (*She waves* THROSTLE *out* L. *He goes out.*) He is the handsomest man, Kate!

KATE (*hysterically*). This is too much,

ma'am! Would you have me sell myself to pay our debts?

LADY ANNE. Kate, dear Kate, I meant no such thing. You're to have no man who does not please you. (*Noise of coach turning outside.*) Come, Helen! (*Exit* L.)

KATE (*turns to* HELEN). Oh, Helen! Mother presses me so. Oh, Helen, will he be as we pictured him?

HELEN (*playfully*). How indeed can I know? I've not even seen his back.

KATE. Tom has heard dreadful things—

HELEN. I believe he will be—all that you could wish for.

KATE. Then he may not care for me!

HELEN. He will, dearest, he will!

KATE. Why must Mother make it so hard——

HELEN. I know. But only be yourself, Kate. (*In tenderly chaffing tones.*) Our cousin will not eat you. (KATE *smiles at her gratefully. Exit* HELEN, *closing door.* KATE, *left alone, shows her extreme tension by crossing to window* L., *looks out, looks in mirror, glances at door* R., *then as though in sudden panic goes to door* L., *pulls herself together, walks* C. *expectantly. Knock at door* R. KATE *faces it, holding herself together.*)

KATE. Enter!

(*Enter* TOM. *Kate shows surprise and disappointment. He looks around, laughs, puzzled.*)

TOM. Where's your Yankee?

KATE. What have you done with him?

TOM. I thought he must have let himself in. Wilkins says there was no knock.

KATE. She did not hear it for the rain. He's on the doorstep!

TOM. Gad, then he must be fetched to you quickly, or this rain will cool him off. (*Exit* TOM R., *laughing, leaving door slightly ajar.* KATE *again walks about nervously, turns quickly as* TOM *enters* R., *closing door after him.*) Damned if I can find him!

KATE. (*exasperated*). We saw him, at the door!

TOM. I looked—there was no one there.

KATE. Then *someone* has let him in!

TOM (*thinks a moment; laughs*). He's gone round to the servants' door. Knows his place. (*As he walks rapidly* L. *and goes out chuckling.*) I'll bring him up the back stairs!

(KATE'S *nervousness increases. Noise of wind and rain, which has been slightly audible since* HELEN *left* KATE *alone, rises to greater intensity.* KATE, *with quick, nervous glances about her, stands* C., *then walks slowly to settee, sits on it, arranging her dress and folding her hands in attractive pose. Clock strikes without, twice. Door* R. *commences to open slowly.* KATE *jumps up and walks* R.C., *just beyond table. It then opens more rapidly, and as the shadow of a man is thrown upon the wall* L., KATE *curtseys slowly. As she starts to curtsey the lights commence to dim and the curtain starts coming down slowly. Just as she has reached the floor the lights are out and the curtain is down.*)

SCENE II

The same room, at the same time, on the same day, in 1928. Most of the furniture remains, but the tone of time has settled upon it, and there are some changes. The windows now have curtains and different shaped pelmets of flowered linen. The curtains are open and the windows shut. A copy of a Georgian pattern on a blue ground, and between them, in place of the tapestry, is a three-quarter length portrait of a young man in eighteenth century costume, by Sir Joshua Reynolds. Through the windows are bare trees of the Square, seen in pale, rain-washed windows. A plain panel replaces the landscape above the fire. The writing-bureau is open, littered with papers and books, and has a lamp on it and an Egyptian antique, a Crux Ansata in blue faience, about four inches high, mounted on small ebony block. No candles on candle-slides. The low tea-table, which before stood folded between window and fireplace, now stands in place of the walnut cabriole-leg table at the L.C. *of the stage; it is open; holds another litter of pipes, papers, books, matches and a brass candlestick. To* R. *of table, an over-stuffed armchair. To* L. *of table an over-stuffed couch, both covered with the same material as the curtains. Back of the couch stands the old cabriole-leg table (now hidden), and on this a large electric lamp. The console table remains where it was, but it is now bare. The stools have gone, and one of the walnut chairs stands before writing bureau.*

As the curtain rises the clock on the landing strikes five, a wheezy, feeble chime, distinct from the full-throated strokes of the clock in the previous scene. MRS. BARWICK, *an elderly housekeeper, dressed in grey with a white apron, opens door* R. *and stands aside to admit the* AMBASSADOR. *The* AMBASSADOR *is elderly, distinguished, suave, urbane, sensitive.*

MRS. BARWICK (*with exaggerated deference*). If you'll wait here, Your Excellency, I'll tell Mr. Standish. I'm not sure he's dressed, sir.

AMBASSADOR. Isn't he well?

MRS. BARWICK (*doubtfully*). Oh, yes, sir. I think so, sir. (*She turns to go* R.)

AMBASSADOR. One moment. Miss Frant has been telling me how you take such good care of Mr. Standish.

MRS. BARWICK (*flattered*). I do my best for him, sir.

AMBASSADOR. Just between ourselves, Miss Frant's a little worried about him.

MRS. BARWICK. He's a bit of a quiet one, Your Excellency. I'm sure I hope there's nothing to worry about, begging your pardon, sir. I mean he's a gentleman of moods. Yes, sir, a gentleman of moods.

AMBASSADOR (*smiling*). You mean he has good moods—and bad ones?

MRS. BARWICK. Oh, no, sir, I didn't mean it that way. But there are times when he does seem, well, just a bit jumpy.

AMBASSADOR. Really?

MRS. BARWICK (*gossiping*). Oh, nothing you could put your finger on, Your Excellency. But it does seem a pity he should stay around the house so much.

AMBASSADOR. Well, it's quite true that I haven't seen him about at all lately, come to think of it. Tell me, how does he spend his time cooped up here?

MRS. BARWICK. Well, sir, he seems to me to spend most of his time reading. When he isn't just walking about. I keep hearing him in the night, sir. It seems he's found some old books and papers in the house here. Of course, sir, I don't exactly know, but I sometimes think——

(*Enter* PETER STANDISH, R. *nervous, sensitive, a man of about twenty-six. He wears a long, black dressing-gown. His manner is feverish; his impatience at being disturbed by an unwelcome visit is tempered by respect for his visitor.*)

PETER. Mr. Ambassador! I heard the bell, but I didn't expect such an honor. Excuse me. I'll just run and put my coat on.

AMBASSADOR. Nonsense, Mr. Standish. Don't do that. (*They shake hands.* MRS. BARWICK *draws curtains.*) It's a very becoming dressing-gown.

PETER. But I can't receive an Ambassador like this. I ought to be wearing something—well—more respectful.

AMBASSADOR. Don't worry. The Foreign Secretary once received me in pyjamas.

(PETER *snaps switch by door* R., *lighting lamp on desk, lamp on table* L., *lamp over portrait.* AMBASSADOR *sits on settee.*)

PETER. Did he? Well, I'll go put mine on if that would seem more appropriate. I'm not up on how to receive Ambassadors. I don't know that one ever called on me before, but I can manage to give you some tea if you like.

AMBASSADOR. How quickly we Yankees take to that, over here.

PETER. Tea, please, Mrs. Barwick. (*She goes out* R. PETER *walks about nervously.*) Yes, it doesn't take long to get to like tea, does it? I don't mean the tea itself, but what it stands for, that we don't get at home—sort of charming rest period, general let-up and all that sort of thing.

AMBASSADOR. But they tell me that even here those dreadful cocktails will soon have sent tea packing from the drawing-room.

PETER. Yes, cocktails, jazz and one universal traffic block—London's just like New York. (*Lights cigarette from case in pocket of dressing-gown.*)

AMBASSADOR. Excepting the weather, which is infinitely worse.

PETER. Has it been bad? I hardly realize there's been any weather.

AMBASSADOR. Haven't been going out much, eh?

PETER. Not a great deal, no.

AMBASSADOR. You're feeling fit, aren't you, Standish?

PETER. Oh, pretty much as usual. What makes you ask?

AMBASSADOR. Nothing in particular. I just wondered why I haven't seen you anywhere all these weeks.

PETER. Well, this house has really been taking all my time.

AMBASSADOR (*not looking at him*). Yes, indeed, it is a delightful place. I read about it in *The Times.* (PETER *pauses before portrait, looking up at it.*) You're really going to settle down here?

PETER. I wouldn't live anywhere else in the world.

AMBASSADOR. Well, I don't blame you. I couldn't make out from the article why your remote English cousin left you the place. Your family didn't know him, from what I gather?

PETER (*wandering about nervously, back stage*). No, but old Standish Pettigrew read a paper of mine on architecture and wrote me about this Queen Anne house. That's how we came to meet. It turned out a Standish ancestor of mine had built the place.

AMBASSADOR. The first Standish who went to America?

PETER. Yes, about 1730. (*Points to partrait.*) His grandfather.

AMBASSADOR. Hm! I suppose everybody comments on the likeness? You might have sat for it yourself.

PETER (*constrained*). Oh, yes; curious, isn't it? His name happens to have been Peter Standish, too.

AMBASSADOR. And that's still more curious. (*Looking up at picture and then at* PETER.) Perhaps what impressed your cousin was the coincidence—the likeness, and then the name. (PETER, *about to speak, checks himself.* MRS. BARWICK *enters* R. *to table with tea-tray; arranges tea.*) And the house itself is as strange as the legacy—two hundred years old, and yet apparently just as it was, furniture, everything!

PETER. Yes, old Mr. Pettigrew left nearly every stick as he found it.

AMBASSADOR (*picks up Crux Ansata from desk*). But what about this thing? Surely this is Egyptian!

PETER. It's the Crux Ansata, the symbol of life.

AMBASSADOR. Yes, but the symbol of Isis, not of Queen Anne. What's it doing here?

PETER. I don't know. It came with the house.

AMBASSADOR (*puts it down, walks to teatable.*) Wedgwood! That came with the house, too?

PETER. Everything did. Even Mrs. Barwick there. (MRS. BARWICK *smiles on them as she goes out* R.) Milk and sugar?

AMBASSADOR. Both, please. (PETER, *after pouring tea and handing cup, pours out cup for himself; does not take it; instead, lights cigarette from case, puffs nervously.* AMBASSADOR *sips tea; eats muffin.*) I suppose you'll entertain here a good deal?

PETER (*resumes walking up and down*). I couldn't afford to.

AMBASSADOR. But when you're married——

PETER. Oh, then! You'll have to ask Marjorie that.

AMBASSADOR. Charming girl! How lucky for you that she wants to live over here.

PETER. Oh, she loves the house, too. We're going to do it over.

AMBASSADOR. Do it over? Well, *you* can be trusted not to spoil it.

PETER. There's a new roof needed, and things like that. That'll all be her doing. You know I've no money.

AMBASSADOR. Marjorie was worried, I thought, that you didn't come to the Embassy reception last night. She came—(*Glances at him.*)—alone.

PETER. Did she? I told her I—didn't feel up to it.

AMBASSADOR. But I thought you said——H'm. It's too bad she's off to America tomorrow.

PETER (*coming towards him*). She's coming right back; it's just some family affair; the wedding isn't postponed. I mean, our plans aren't changed.

AMBASSADOR. So she told me. We had quite a talk.

PETER (*sits in armchair; looks at* AMBASSADOR; *politely challenging*). Yes?

AMBASSADOR (*after pause*). And I may as well admit I didn't come here, Standish, only to see the house.

PETER (*dryly*). I *had* flattered myself that what you really came to see was *me*.

AMBASSADOR. And of course you must think me a meddling old busybody.

PETER. Oh, please, Mr. Ambassador! I do appreciate your kindness. But, you see, there's nothing wrong with me at all!

AMBASSADOR. Who said there was anything wrong? I suppose what you meant just now was that I'd come in to—look you over. Nobody likes being looked over, when there's no need for it.

PETER (*smiling*). Still less, when there is, I suppose.

AMBASSADOR. Any way, you won't mind my suggesting that London is a very fascinating place.

PETER (*enthusiastically*). The most fascinating place in the world!

AMBASSADOR. Ah, good! Everybody's talking about the legacy; everybody'd be delighted to meet you. One thing an American Ambassador can do in London is open doors—and such interesting doors, Standish.

PETER (*ill at ease; rises; goes over to bureau; speaks as he moves*). I see what you're getting at. It's very thoughtful of you, but I'm very busy just now. Going through some old papers. (*Fumbles with papers on desk.*)

AMBASSADOR. Too many old papers, Standish. People get morbid and musty when they shut themselves up in old houses. Marjorie is really quite disturbed about you.

PETER. I wish she wouldn't be. I can't go out just now. I've most important work to do here.

AMBASSADOR. The eighteenth century is fascinating, no doubt, but surely your studies are not so pressing——

PETER. But I've just got to stay here in the house.

AMBASSADOR (*perplexed*). Well, I mustn't bore you with questions. But you *are* making your friends a bit uneasy. Of course—if there were anything I could do—though if you *will* make a hermit of yourself there probably isn't——

PETER (*walks to tea-table*). Well, as a matter of fact—— (*Stops.*)

AMBASSADOR (*encouragingly*). Yes?

PETER. Well, if you could possibly manage to drop in here two or three times a week, regularly, while Marjorie is gone, I'd appreciate it enormously. Oh, but now I've said it I realize that for *me* to ask such a thing of *you* would be impertinent. And you probably haven't the time, anyway.

AMBASSADOR (*puzzled*). But why shouldn't *you* come and see *me?* And make it as often as you like.

PETER (*struggling to avoid saying too much*). Thanks, but, well, I don't know if I could. I mean, I might not want to.

AMBASSADOR (*really shocked*). But surely——

PETER. Oh, I simply can't make it any clearer just now. (*Sits in armchair.*)

AMBASSADOR. Look here, Standish. Don't you think you ought to get away for a bit?

PETER (*a little wildly*). Ah! Getaway! It would be great to get away, really away, into the blue, wouldn't it? You think I'm a bookworm, don't you? But there still are adventures, inconceivable adventures——

AMBASSADOR (*after pause*). Won't you tell *me* what's the trouble?

PETER. I'd like to—it *isn't* trouble—it's—it's wonderful! (*Rises.*) Oh, I'd like there to be someone here who *knows*—but I *can't.* We can't talk without using words, so what's the use of talking when there are no words? I understood it all till just now, when you asked me about it, and *now* I don't understand anything about it at all. (*Sits beside him on settee.*) Now look here. Here's an idea. Suppose you are in a boat, sailing down a winding stream. You watch the banks as they pass you. You went by a grove of maple trees, upstream. But you can't see them now, so you saw them in the *past,* didn't you? You're watching a field of clover now; it's before your eyes at this moment, in the *present.* But you don't know yet what's around the bend in the stream there ahead of you. There may be wonderful things, but you can't see them until you get around the bend in the *future,* can you? (AMBASSADOR *nods; he listens politely.*) Now remember, *you're* in the boat. But *I'm* up in the sky above you, in a plane. I'm looking down on it all. I can see *all at once!* So the past, present, and future to the man in the boat are all *one* to the man in the plane. Doesn't that show how all Time must really be one? Real Time—real Time is nothing but an idea in the mind of God!

(PETER *is panting and excited. Clock without strikes once.* AMBASSADOR *rises, consults watch. Turns, looks at* PETER *reflectively.*)

AMBASSADOR. I suppose that old grandfather clock came with the house, too?

PETER. Yes, it's ticked away five generations—and it's ticking away now, back in that other time!

AMBASSADOR (*replaces watch*). H'm. Other time. (*Walks towards picture, looking at it.*) A quarter past five already. Wasn't Marjorie coming to tea?

PETER (*tense, half-turned around on settee, watching him closely.*) Oh, yes, I think she was. She told you?

AMBASSADOR (*warily*). That portrait now. (PETER'S *head comes up.*) One might almost think that—— (PETER *looks excitedly at the* AMBASSADOR.) Of course, none of us believes in ghosts at home, but over here, in these old houses——

PETER (*interrupting*). Who said anything about ghosts? (*Jumps up.*) He isn't a ghost. He's alive, alive, alive! I don't mean now; he's dead now, of course; I mean then. I mean back there in his own time, back there where that clock's ticking, just as it's ticking here, now. (*Hurries excitedly to window* L., *throwing back curtains.*) How would you like to walk the quiet streets of London in the eighteenth century? And breathe pure air, instead of gasoline! And ride in sedan-chairs, instead of taxicabs? (*Coming down to* AMBASSADOR.) See Sheridan at the first night of "The School for Scandal" or hear Dr. Johnson say the things Boswell wrote —(*Turning glances at portrait.*)—or watch Reynolds at work on—— (*Turns again and stops, meeting* AMBASSADOR's *grave, steady look.*)

AMBASSADOR (*gently taking* PETER's *arm*). Yes, Standish, it does sound attractive, but it isn't a thing we'd really do, even if we could. And if we felt anything like *that* coming on, we'd clear out—even out of a wonderful house like this.

PETER (*impatiently throws off his arm*). Oh, I'd like to see anybody try to clear me out, *now!*

AMBASSADOR. If we *could* get back, we'd seem worse than ghosts to all the people in the other time; we'd seem to them things that hadn't even been born yet!

PETER. They wouldn't know.

AMBASSADOR. They'd find us out, Standish—we'd make *slips*.

PETER. Oh, no, we wouldn't, we couldn't, don't you see, because what happened back there is real, does really happen, of course, it *has* happened. So if anybody *could* change places with somebody back there, it would only be a charade; he'd have to do all the things that the other fellow had done. He couldn't change anything in the eighteenth century that really *had happened* in the eighteenth century, could he?

AMBASSADOR. H'm. Change places.

PETER (*excitedly*). Yes, *change places!* Oh, but I was a fool to tell you. And now I suppose you'll go and call up a specialist.

AMBASSADOR (*ignoring this*). I still don't see what credentials we could take back into the past that would make them accept us as even human.

PETER (*triumphantly*). Ah, credentials! (*Rummages among papers; comes back waving small book above his head.*) Here's my passport!

AMBASSADOR. What's that?

PETER. It's *his* diary! (*Sits by him on settee, opening leaves; speaks with feverish rapidity.*) He's put everything down! I've learned it almost word for word. That's what I've been doing! (*Looks in diary.*) His trip from New York took twenty-seven days, in a barque called the *General Wolfe*. No wonder he calls the trip "dreary." He fought under Washington. The war was just over, but he made friends with an English Major Clinton on the boat. Peter was an inventor, when all that was just beginning, that's why he wants to see into our wonderful new age of machinery that he senses ahead of him. (*Turning leaves.*) It says Reynolds wouldn't finish the portrait. (*Turns to picture.*) But he did finish it. It's obviously all Reynolds'! Look! (*Points to passages.*) He married the elder sister, you see! Kate —that's Kate Pettigrew. They lived in this house. I've other papers about them—they had children, who died here. See! There was a younger sister, Helen. Her people tried to force her into a marriage she hated. The diary stops before that was settled. Look! There's even something about a Kashmir shawl that Helen's aunt in the country gave her just before Peter came over. Minute details about everything, you see! (*Drops diary beside* AMBASSADOR *on settee.*) And I've got his letters, courting Kate before he'd ever seen her. (*Dashes to desk; sits; rummages.*) They were in a secret drawer here. I've got the letter Peter wrote Lady Anne— the girl's mother—when he'd just arrived from New York. (*Jumps up.*) Oh, damn! I know where I left it! You *must* see that! (PETER *hurries out* L.)

(AMBASSADOR *looks after him intently, then rises and crosses slowly to picture, stands looking up at it.* MRS. BARWICK *opens door* R. MARJORIE FRANT *enters. An attractive girl in the late twenties, dressed with sensible good taste.* MRS. BARWICK *goes out.*)

MARJORIE. Mr. Ambassador! (*He turns.*) What a surprise! Isn't Peter here?

AMBASSADOR (*they shake hands*). He'll be back in a minute, Marjorie.

MARJORIE (*takes off hat; puts it on table* L.; *walks to settee as she says*). You came because of what I said last night, and I'm so grateful for your sympathy and your——

AMBASSADOR (*follows her. Interrupts; speaks gravely and quickly*). I'm going to leave you together.

MARJORIE (*alarmed at his tone*). Why, what's the matter?

AMBASSADOR. If you have to sail tomorrow, try your very best to persuade him to go with you. But whatever happens, he must be got out of this house! When you leave him come to me at the Embassy. There's no time now to explain. Sh!

(*Turns; moves* R.)

(MARJORIE *sits on settee.* PETER *enters* L., *reading letter, walks to* AMBASSADOR.)

PETER. Here it is. Read it.

AMBASSADOR. "From the Blue Boar in Jermyn Street, October 23rd, 1784."

PETER (*triumphantly*). October 23rd! That's today!

AMBASSADOR (*looks up, then reads, half to himself*). "October 23rd, 1784. Honored Madam: Having arrived within the hour, traveling by post from Plymouth, I make haste to dispatch you this intimation that I shall do myself the honor to wait upon yourself, my fair cousins, and Mr. Pettigrew, at a half after five this evening, in Berkeley Square. I subscribe myself, Madam, your most obedient cousin and humble servant, Peter Standish. To the Lady Anne Pettigrew." (*He hands the letter back to* PETER.)

PETER. The paper's yellow, and the ink faded—and yet Lady Anne is just reading that letter, *now!*

MARJORIE (*who has risen*). Peter!

PETER (*starts, and faces* MARJORIE). How long have you been here?

MARJORIE. Only a minute.

PETER. Oh—I do hope you have a nice crossing—you're sailing tomorrow—isn't it? (MARJORIE'S *lips tremble.*)

AMBASSADOR (*looking at watch*). You've made me forget an appointment. Goodbye, Marjorie. (PETER *follows him to door* R.) No, don't come down. (*Meaningly.*) I'll drop in here, Peter, as you suggested.

PETER. Oh, thank you! (*Exit* AMBASSADOR, *leaving door ajar.*)

MAJORIE. Peter, what made you speak to me that way?

PETER (*turns; walks to her before armchair*). Was I rude? Forgive me. (*Kisses her.*) I was thinking of something else.

MARJORIE. What?

PETER (*crosses up to desk; handles papers*). Only a job I've got to do. (*Lights cigarette from case.*)

MARJORIE. What were you talking about?

PETER. Just some eighteenth-century people.

MARJORIE (*sits on settee*). You're so nervous! Smoking too much, dear. (PETER *crushes out cigarette.*) Only a month now till I'll be living here to look after you. And you need it, Peter!

PETER (*walking to armchair*). You don't want to marry me, Marjorie dear. You want only to look after me.

MARJORIE. One goes with the other, doesn't it?

PETER. You're so patient with me, so good, so kind.

MARJORIE. Peter, I want you to do something specially nice for me. I don't want to leave you. I want to be with you. Pack up and sail with me tomorrow—we'll come right back.

PETER (*startled*). Oh, no, I can't. I'd rather be here.

MARJORIE. Rather be here than with me? You do care more for this old house than—— If you love me you will come!

PETER. I can't!

MARJORIE. You won't, you mean. Peter, darling, I don't know what's the matter, but you're not well; you're not yourself. Well—if you won't come, then I won't go. I'm going to stay in London.

PETER (*distressed*). You told me you *had to* go!

MARJORIE. You want to get rid of me! You're so strange, you hold me off from you!

PETER. I must have this month here alone. Trust me.

MARJORIE. But, Peter, dear—you're so strange, you've never been like this. Why won't you tell me what it is? I *will* trust you, if you'll just tell me—

PETER (*distressed. Turns from her*). But I can't. You'd—— No, no—you mustn't ask it—— (*Stops; listens. Noise of coach. In a low, tense whisper.*) What's that? (*He crosses rapidly to window* R. *and holds back curtains.*)

MAJORIE. What's what? (*Faint noise of wind and rain.*)

PETER (*turns at window*). Sounded like a wagon rattling over cobblestones. It seemed to stop here. (*Looking up at portrait.*) But there's only your car at the door.

MARJORIE. I didn't hear anything. Cobblestones, in Berkeley Square? Why, they've had wood blocks for ages; it's quieter even than our asphalt in New York. Peter, what's the matter with you? (*The electric lights go out. Noise of wind and rain increases.*) Oh, dear!

PETER. I'll light a candle. (*Lights candle on tea-table.*)

MARJORIE. Darling, your hand's shaking! Ring, Peter. Get somebody to fix the lights!

(*Enter* MRS. BARWICK R., *carrying candle.*

She stops a few steps inside door. PETER *faces her behind tea-table, holding candle.*)

MRS. BARWICK. A gentleman to see you, sir. Just as he came in the lights went out all over the house. He's all muffled up.

MARJORIE. Who is he?

MRS. BARWICK. When I asked his name he only said again, "Mr. Peter Standish." I've shown him into the study. (PETER *walks slowly to door* R. *as if in a trance.*)

MARJORIE. Peter, who is it? (*He walks on, unheeding.*) Peter, it's my very last evening.

PETER (*speaking in a dead cold voice*). There's no time. No time!

(*Exit* PETER, *closing door behind him.*)

MARJORIE (*hysterical*). Who is this man?

MRS. BARWICK. I don't know, miss.

MARJORIE (*crying*). He heard noises in the street when there were no noises.

MRS. BARWICK. He's not himself, miss. I'll get a lamp and then see to the lights. (*She goes out* L.)

(*Door* R. *opens slowly. Pale light from candle carried by the man who is opening the door. Wind and rain heard more loudly again. Clock on landing strikes twice.* MARJORIE *runs to door with a cry of recognition.*)

MAJORIE. Peter! (MARJORIE *stops suddenly, face to face with man at door, who is invisible to audience. Steps back.*) Peter! I'm afraid of you! (*Little nervous laugh.*) Isn't it absurd, to be afraid of my Peter! (*Another step back.*)

QUICK CURTAIN

(*The instant the curtain is down,* MARJORIE *screams.*)

Scene III

The room in the past. Clock is heard to strike twice, an instant before the curtain goes up. The curtain rises at the exact moment when it fell upon Scene I. Noise of wind and rain. The lights fade in slowly.

KATE *discovered at* C., *just going to curtsey. Noise of wind and rain stops, as* PETER *enters slowly, in the costume of the man in the portrait. Dazed, he stares at her, shrinking back against the door, his hand on the knob. Staring at him, she curtseys again.*

KATE. Your servant, sir. (*Pause.*) At your service, cousin.

PETER (*at length*). Who—are you?

KATE. Kate Pettigrew.

PETER (*in awe and wonder*). Kate—Pettigrew!

(KATE *walks toward him; extends her hand to be kissed.* PETER *takes step forward doubtfully, as though not quite sure whether* KATE *is really flesh and blood. At length he takes her hand, awkwardly, bows and kisses it, then retreats two steps toward door.*)

KATE. I bid you welcome, on Mother's behalf.

PETER. Your mother. The Lady Anne. I trust she is well?

KATE. Indeed yes, I thank you. (*Awkward silence.*)

PETER. It's raining awfully hard.

KATE (*still extremely nervous*). Yes, the weather has been wretched. But you'll find it nearly always so in London.

PETER. You have a great many fogs, haven't you?

KATE. Indeed, yes, there was one last week that lasted three days. And they're getting worse than they used to be, with people burning more sea coal.

PETER (*at length, to cover his own lack of resource*). You seem a little embarrassed, cousin.

KATE (*with nervous laugh*). You are not exactly at your ease yourself.

PETER. You've never seen me before, have you?

KATE. That seems a strange question.

PETER. I mean, am I—different from what you expected?

KATE. Indeed, I think you are, cousin. We were led to look for a bold, forward fellow.

PETER. I'm a little surprised, too—I thought that Kate would be—well——

KATE (*with a touch of spirit*). Not so timid? I trust you will find me not always such a ninny, and my conversation not limited to the weather. But I'm sure you've had a tiring journey after your voyage. Come, sit down and tell me about it. (KATE *sits on settee.* PETER *remains standing.*) You said nothing of your voyage in your letter.

PETER. My letter!

KATE (*surprised*). To my mother, from the "Blue Boar," where I hope they have made you comfortable.

PETER. My letter from the "Blue Boar"!

(*Looking to her for confirmation.*) Of course. I went there when the coach came in, and I've just come over from America.

KATE (*surprised*). We did not think you had come from Poland.

PETER. In the *General Wolfe*.

KATE. Really! In the packet? Did you not swim across?

PETER (*now reassured, laughs with her*). In the *General Wolfe*—it took twenty-seven dreary days.

KATE. I suppose the sea is always dreary, but you had a swift passage.

PETER (*after pause*). Yes, the wind was with us all the way; we must have almost beat the record.

KATE. Record?

PETER. Oh, that's an American word. I'm afraid you'll find that I use a lot of strange phrases. We're developing a new language over there.

KATE. You must instruct me in it.

PETER (*goes to settee, sits by her awkwardly, still a little afraid*). Kate, forgive me for being such a boor.

KATE (*nervous, but coquettish since she likes him*). Your manners have been unexceptionable.

PETER. But hardly appropriate for a man who has just met his betrothed for the first time.

KATE. Are we betrothed? I had not heard of it.

PETER. Come, don't tease me. It's been practically all arranged in our letters. (*Clumsily steals a kiss.*)

KATE (*shrinking back*). There's nothing settled yet, and this is more in keeping with what I have heard of your rough ways at home, sir.

PETER (*taking his cue from her coquettish tone, and rather awkwardly attempting to act as he imagines his role demands*). Come, Kate, don't call me sir. I'll certainly not call you miss. (*Seizes her arm.*) Call me Peter! Say it!

KATE (*protestingly*). Sir! Cousin! (PETER *makes to hold her hands. She escapes, laughing.*) Peter, then! You'll think me a brazen creature to laugh at your clowning, but I'll have no more of it!

PETER. Come, Kate, it's all arranged. The settlement was to be fifteen thousand pounds, wasn't it? That's all for the lawyers. We two needed only a kiss to make sure.

KATE. I vow you are the most abrupt man! You are but the audacious fellow I told Helen we must expect.

PETER. Helen? Oh, yes, your sister.

KATE. You've not even asked Mother's permission to pay your addresses.

PETER. Must I do that?

KATE. Is it not invariably done?

PETER. Er—not in New York.

KATE (*chaffing*). This is London. These are strange manners you bring us from the United States. And do visitors in New York walk into people's houses without so much as a by your leave?

PETER (*disturbed*). I rang the bell.

KATE. Bell? What bell?

PETER. I mean, the knocker.

KATE. We saw you alight from your coach, but—who let you in?

PETER. The door was ajar. I walked in—to get out of the rain.

KATE (*accepting this*). We wondered—— But your clothes are dry!

PETER. I wore a cloak.

KATE. Even your boots are dry! (PETER, *disturbed and at a loss, turns from her, fumbling for cigarette case in waistcoat pocket. Absent-mindedly opens and extends silver case to her. Looking at case.*) I had no miniature of *you*, although I wrote and asked you for one.

PETER (*looks at miniature, astonished; puts it back in pocket, fumbling in other pocket*). Well, I preferred to present myself in the flesh. (*Brings jewelled bracelet out of pocket.*)

KATE. Oh, what is that? (PETER *gallantly hands it to* KATE.) Most charming. But—is this not a little premature?

PETER (*puzzled*). Premature?

KATE (*sits on settee*). Does not this signify, in New York, what it does here?

PETER (*understanding*). Of course. If you will have the declaration formal, I know how it was done—how it is done. (*Goes on one knee before her.*) Miss Pettigrew, fair cousin, will you be my wife?

KATE (*laughing*). You go much too fast.

PETER. You'll not dislike me for that.

KATE. I've not said that I mislike you! (*She lets him slip the bracelet over her wrist.* LADY ANNE *enters* L. PETER *springs up and back in alarm and confusion.* KATE *also rises.*) Ma'am, I present our cousin, Mr. Peter Standish. (PETER *stares at her.* LADY ANNE *curtseys. They both advance, and he kisses her hand.*)

LADY ANNE. Welcome, ten thousand welcomes, dear, dear cousin.

PETER. Lady Anne, forgive me. Kate's

beauties have quite deprived me of my wits and speech.

KATE. A deceiving tongue you've brought with you from New York—Peter. (LADY ANNE *looks from one to the other. After sigh of satisfaction, walks to settee; sits.* HELEN *enters, rather quickly and disturbed, followed closely by* THROSTLE.)

LADY ANNE. Can you take your eyes from Kate to spare a nod for your cousin Helen? (PETER *and* HELEN *stare and step toward each other.* KATE *sits in chair extreme* L. *front.* HELEN *curtseys.* PETER *advances and kisses her hand.* TOM *slouches in* L.)

HELEN. Your servant, sir.

LADY ANNE. And our dear friend, Mr. Throstle, Mr. Standish. (*They bow.*)

PETER. Mr. Throstle, of the Academy of Painters in Water Color?

THROSTLE. I had not supposed a name so insignificant——

PETER. Oh, I have—been reading about you.

LADY ANNE. And your cousin Tom.

TOM (*sniggers as they bow*). The jest is against me, sir. I had thought to call a tailor in to you before you could face the town.

PETER (*surveys his clothes uneasily.*) I'm afraid the jest is against me.

TOM. No, 'pon my oath; your coat's a better fit than mine, and your scarf's perfection, sir. Eh, Kate? Eh, Mother? Isn't he in the tone? (*They laugh as* PETER *turns to them.*)

LADY ANNE. This sudden storm, cousin, so unusually violent for the time of year—I hope you were not incommoded.

KATE. His clothes were dry!

PETER. Oh, I was already in the coach when it really started to pour—I think it's clearing—— (*Crosses to window; glances out; exclaims involuntarily.*) Oh, four lackeys with a sedan-chair! (*He turns quickly, realizing his mistake.*)

HELEN. You speak, sir, as though you'd never before seen a sedan chair.

PETER. I don't believe I'd noticed one.

THROSTLE. Sir, I passed a dozen but now, and so must have you, on your way hither from the "Blue Boar."

PETER. I didn't see them.

LADY ANNE. Are the New York quality not borne abroad in their chairs?

PETER. No—they ride in—coaches.

LADY ANNE. Sit here by Kate, cousin. (PETER *sits by* LADY ANNE *on settee.* TOM *sits before desk.* THROSTLE *brings up chair from beside console table for* HELEN. THROSTLE *walks near* TOM.) Your boxes shall be fetched. Of course you remain with us.

PETER. If you will have me.

LADY ANNE. *If* we will have you! And had you an agreeable voyage, dear cousin?

PETER. A dreary twenty-seven days in the *General Wolfe*.

KATE. My brother has but now met with a shipmate of yours.

PETER (*nervous and alert*). Indeed? Who was that?

TOM. Major Clinton.

PETER. Oh, yes, of course, a most agreeable fellow.

TOM. Clinton told me of your ingenious inventions, sir. (*Laughs.*) Now that you're rid of us, you seem to think you're going to do great things in the Col—the United States.

PETER. Oh, I suppose we are (*A little unnerved.*) Our forefathers—I mean we—have brought forth on that continent a new nation, conceived in liberty and dedicated to the proposition that all men are created equal.

LADY ANNE (*astonished*). All men—created equal!

PETER. That is the proposition.

THROSTLE. But, sir, that proposition is absurd.

PETER. Of course it is absurd! (THROSTLE *turns to* TOM. *They laugh together at* PETER.)

KATE. I'm fascinated by your strange theories that life in the future is all going to be so changed—and so exciting——

TOM (*with a faint sneer*). Especially in the United States.

PETER. Exciting? Oh, very, for people who like bustle, and efficiency, but I'm sure people like—ourselves, in a hundred years, would give their eyes to get back here again!

TOM (*rises; walks* C). We shall be damnably mouldy in a hundred years. But if the present interests you, sir, I'm your man—Cousin Tom will show you the town!

PETER (*it bursts out*). Oh, yes!

TOM. Where shall I take him first? Cox's Museum and Ranelagh and Vauxhall——

PETER (*eagerly*). I want to see everything!

THROSTLE. Should your tastes prove

more sober than Mr. Tom's, sir, my poor services as cicerone——

LADY ANNE. Yes, the exhibition at the Royal Academy!

TOM (*disgusted*). Gad's life! (*Turns and leans on door.*)

THROSTLE. Sir, should you care to join me there tomorrow, I should be glad to present you to the President of the Academy, Sir Joshua.

PETER. Reynolds! (*Rises, glances at panel where picture hangs in 1928.*) Do you think he would paint my portrait?

TOM. Ay—at a hundred guineas.

PETER. Five hundred dollars—a Reynolds!

LADY ANNE. Indeed, a monstrous price! But he's the fashion.

PETER (*resumes seat. To* THROSTLE). Oh, thank you! Of course I'll come. My curiosity will wear you all out. But I mustn't make myself a nuisance—(*Turns to* KATE.)—except to my cousins——

TOM. You may regard our friend Throstle, cousin, as one of the family.

PETER. Indeed?

TOM. I think I may go so far as to say, as a prospective brother-in-law. Eh, Throstle? (HELEN *rises in mingled shame and anger.* THROSTLE *turns protestingly to* TOM. *General constraint.* PETER *looks at her, rising abruptly.*)

HELEN (*choking back her tears. Smiles sourly at* PETER). Poor Tom is always putting his foot in it!

(PETER *tactfully gets up, walks behind settee towards console table.*)

PETER (*handling china*). What a magnificent piece! Finest old Chelsea!

KATE (*laughing*). Five and sixpence, in the Shepherd's Market!

PETER. Forgive my ignorance. (*Looking around room.*) I've been admiring your Queen Anne chairs, Lady Anne.

LADY ANNE. Ay, to our shame, it is so; the wars have impoverished so many of us here, dear cousin, alas, we cannot afford to rid ourselves of our old rubbish. (*There is an awkward silence.* PETER *resumes seat.*)

KATE. Do you dance, cousin?

PETER. Why, of course.

KATE (*pleased*). I could not have endured you else.

TOM. Our cousin has all the talents.

LADY ANNE. Helen's birthday, indeed, comes at a most opportune moment, cousin.

KATE. Yes, there's to be a ball here next week.

PETER. Er—what do you dance, in London?

KATE. Why, what everybody dances. Gavottes, minuets.

PETER. I fear I shall disgrace you. (*He has been looking at* HELEN.) Your birthday dance, cousin! Then your aunt's gift is your birthday present!

LADY ANNE. Gift! What gift, Helen?

PETER. Why, the Kashmir shawl.

KATE. Oh, Helen, you sly puss!

HELEN (*rises. Bewildered, to* PETER). Is it a shawl?

LADY ANNE (*to* HELEN). Why, pray, have you kept this from us?

HELEN. Aunt Willoughby gave me a parcel for my birthday, but I wasn't to open it until then. I haven't opened it. I don't know what's in it. (*All but* PETER *make some exclamation. There is a pause.* HELEN *goes out quickly* L. TOM *rises; comes down front.* THROSTLE *moves down.*)

TOM. Damme, what conjuror's trick is this?

PETER (*embarrassed, worried*). Why all this fuss about a shawl?

KATE. But how did you know about Helen's present?

LADY ANNE. How do you know it's a shawl?

KATE (*wagging finger*). I believe 'tis an American joke.

PETER. Joke? (HELEN *re-enters with Kashmir shawl; stops behind small table, showing it to them all.* THROSTLE *fingers it.*)

TOM. A shawl, so it is, by Gad!

KATE. Cousin, how did you know?

LADY ANNE. Indeed, how, cousin? Come, come, sir.

PETER. I'm heartily sorry. I got muddled somehow.

TOM. Muddled, sir, muddled! 'Tis not you who are muddled!

KATE. Have pity on us, you tricksy man.

HELEN. Indeed, cousin, plague us no more. (PETER *is silent.*)

TOM. 'S life, you make rare sport of us, sir.

THROSTLE. My friend, Mr. Boswell, says such feats as this are common in Scotland.

LADY ANNE. Come, we'll take no refusal. How did you know?

PETER. I've forgotten.

LADY ANNE. How can you be so teasing? Come, come!

TOM. Here's a rival for you, Helen.

HELEN. I'm sure 'tis very strange. (*Puts shawl down on small table.*)

TOM. Lookee, cousin, can you read thoughts?

PETER. Of course not!

HELEN. It wasn't reading thoughts. *I* didn't know.

KATE. Pray solve us your riddle, Peter!

PETER. I must have heard about the shawl. I told you I'd forgotten where.

LADY ANNE. Sir, you but now reached London from America.

HELEN. I'm afraid Cousin Peter is not well.

PETER (*rises; looks at her gratefully*). No, I'm not. I can't think. The truth is, I suppose it's the trip. I've rather a tiresome headache.

LADY ANNE. Your poor head. Oh, you must rest, after so long a journey.

PETER. Yes—a very long journey.

KATE (*rises*). I'll fetch you a compress. (TOM *goes to window* R.; *looks out, as* THROSTLE *comes to* LADY ANNE; *kisses her hand.*)

THROSTLE. I must take my leave (*Kisses* HELEN's *hand. Bows to* PETER.) Command me, sir, if and when Tom's more full-blooded entertainment palls.

PETER (*bowing*). Indeed I shall.

TOM (*at window*). The rain has stopped, Throstle. Come to the stables and see my new smoker from Newmarket.

THROSTLE. If you'll come to Duke Street and see my new aquatint——

TOM (*as they go out* R. *together*). Damn your aquatints!

THROSTLE (*tittering*). Damn your horses, then!

LADY ANNE (*to* PETER). I must see to your room, sir. (PETER *walks* L. *and holds door open for* LADY ANNE. *As she goes out, curtseys.*) We are so, so happy to greet you here, dear, dear cousin. (PETER *bows, turns and finds himself facing* HELEN, *who has crossed above settee as though to go out. They look at one another for a moment.*)

HELEN. Won't you sit down, cousin?

PETER. Thanks so much for helping me out.

HELEN (*smiling*). There wasn't anything really the matter with your head, was there?

PETER. No, not exactly, but you were the only one who saw—or, at any rate, you made them stop bothering me.

HELEN. I didn't see how you could know about my shawl.

PETER. Please be an angel and don't ask me any more about the confounded thing.

HELEN (*sits on settee*). If you wish.

PETER. Oh, thank you. Just as soon as I saw you I felt, "here's someone I can talk to." You'll help me out here, won't you? (*Sits beside her.*)

HELEN. How can *I* help you, cousin?

PETER. It's all so strange.

HELEN. Strange?

PETER. All this.

HELEN. England? London?

PETER. Yes. I didn't think it would, but it makes me—uncomfortable. You see that. I see that you see it. I—I feel like a fish out of water.

HELEN. Kate will soon put you at your ease.

PETER. I'm sure she'll try. Oh, there's so much I want to ask you, I don't know where to begin.

HELEN (*looks at him*). We're all most anxious to make you feel at home here.

PETER. Helen—are you really engaged to Mr.—Mr.——

HELEN. Mr. Throstle.

PETER. Forgive me. It's none of my business. But I thought your brother said——

HELEN (*flashing. Turning from him*). He had no *right* to say it!

PETER. I thought so! I could see that you weren't in love with him.

HELEN (*turns back to him*). Do you think that's reason enough not to marry him?

PETER. Of course. Well, Helen, we'll make a bargain. You help me out and I'll back you up.

HELEN (*rising and speaking eagerly*). Will you?

PETER (*rising*). Yes, I will! But—— I'd forgotten. I can't interfere with things that happen, that really *do* happen. (*Lamely.*) My position here is so—so unusual.

HELEN. Oh, but you can. You don't realize yet what your position here is. They'll do anything you wish.

PETER. Yes, but—— Oh, you can't understand this—— Perhaps you really *do* marry him, after all.

HELEN. Never!

PETER. That's the spirit! I don't like the little fellow. And, anyway, I'm sure there isn't anybody good enough—— Why do you look at me like that?

HELEN. I don't know.

PETER (*earnestly*). Is there anything strange, or wrong, about me?

HELEN. Strange, or wrong?

PETER. I'm an American, you know. Just come into this new world. That's why I'm nervous.

HELEN. Is it? (*Picks up shawl.*) My sister will join you in a moment. (*Turns to go* R.)

PETER (*following her, pleadingly*). Don't go. Just to see you steadied me. I've nothing in common with all the others.

HELEN (*turning to him at door. Meaningly*). *All* the others? (*Exits* R., *closing door.*)

(PETER *moves quickly as though to open door and follow her; checks himself. He stands a moment, disheartened and afraid; walks* C.; *looks around the room. He goes up to the writing-desk as to an old friend, strokes it, looks at familiar chairs and the carpet. Standing back stage, he pulls out miniature case, opens it again absent-mindedly, snaps it shut in disappointment. Then he opens it again and gazes at the miniature. He looks at the door* L. *through which* KATE *has gone out, then, slowly putting case back in his pocket, at the door* R. *Musing a moment, he turns again, sees himself in the mirror beside the fireplace, touches wig and his collar, passes his hand over his coat. He goes up 1o the tapestry suspended over console table where the picture hangs in 1928, and as he is gazing at it the chimes from a neighboring church tower are heard.* PETER *hears them; walks to window* L.; *slowly opens curtains and raises the window. The chimes are louder.* PETER *looks out into Berkeley Square for some time, motionless.*)

PETER (*the thrill of the adventure, and all his appreciation of what he sees, in his voice*). Berkeley Square! I thought it would look like this!

(*The chimes continue to play. The curtain falls slowly.*)

ACT TWO

Late at night. The room in the Past brilliantly lit by the candles. A string orchestra is playing music in the drawing-room L., *and the double doors are open. An easel bearing canvas is propped in the corner between the writing-bureau and the rear wall. Some of the furniture has been rearranged. The settee has been pushed back and to the* R.C.; *the tea-table, folded again, stands against* L. *end of settee, and the stool that was before the writing-bureau is placed to* L. *of settee at such an angle that two people sitting on settee and stool respectively appear in profile to audience. The armchair has been placed before the* L. *window and the pair of walnut chairs are downstage* L. *at right angles to each other, as though placed in position by two people who had been talking. The fire stool and the cabriole table have been removed.*

MISS BARRYMORE *and* MAJOR CLINTON, *in uniform, enter* L.

CLINTON. I trust that dancing has given you an appetite, Miss Susan.

MISS BARRYMORE. Perhaps a glass of sherry and a biscuit—

CLINTON. There's a very large banquet spread below tonight; indeed, a novelty in *this* house.

MISS BARRYMORE. The cousin from the Colonies will pay. Ah, Major Clinton, *you* can tell us how much money he *really* has. Some say, twenty-five thousand a year!

CLINTON. I'll wager there can be no such fortune in the whole of Yankeedoodle-dom.

MISS BARRYMORE. Scoff as you will, Kate Pettigrew has made a splendid match.

CLINTON (*looks through door* L.). She might have fared worse. Have you noticed her younger sister? 'Tis pity she's so odd and distant.

MISS BARRYMORE. The Pettigrew Cinderella?

CLINTON. Cinderella at the ball, tonight! (*Both start to exit* R.) She's dancing with the fairy prince! (*They go out as* DUCHESS OF DEVONSHIRE *enters from the drawing-room, magnificently dressed, beautiful and distinguished, aged twenty-seven, followed by* LADY ANNE.)

LADY ANNE (*agitated*). 'Tis full twenty minutes, Duchess, since I sent my son down to entice His Royal Highness upstairs.

DUCHESS (*fanning herself*). Compose yourself, Lady Anne, these fat German princelings poison any entertainment. Be content with the honor of his presence among your bottles.

LADY ANNE. His presence anywhere is

small honor beside that of the Duchess of Devonshire.

DUCHESS. Who would not come, my dear, to meet your dazzling Yankee? His success tonight will be the talk of the town tomorrow.

LADY ANNE (*delighted*). Oh, Duchess!

DUCHESS. His manner, his voice, his wit, have captivated the least impressionable of our sex, and disarmed the most critical of his own. Or so I am informed. I would appraise for myself this odd *je ne sais quoi*——

LADY ANNE. Oh, Duchess, our cousin is *not* odd!

DUCHESS. I hear what I hear. I *also* hear that your Kate has not danced so much as once with her Peter. They might be already married.

LADY ANNE (*flustered*). Indeed no, Madam, they *dote* upon one another.

DUCHESS (*laughing*). Now pray remember, you have promised me a *tete-a-tete* with your cousin.

(*Enter* TOM R., *in conversation with* LORD STANLEY, *Under-Secretary of the Foreign Office, a man of about fifty, who wears an order.*)

TOM. He drank "vun more," and then "anuzzer" swamped him.

STANLEY. I heard the Royal snore. But let sleeping princes lie, Pettigrew, and contrive for me a word with Mr. Standish.

TOM (*as they cross stage*). If the women will let you get near him.

DUCHESS. Ah, Lord Stanley! Why do you never come to my Thursdays? (STANLEY *and* TOM *bow.* STANLEY *and* DUCHESS *go out* L.)

STANLEY. The outbreak of peace—my dear Duchess, has redoubled our labors at the Foreign Office.

LADY ANNE (*to* TOM). Why have you not brought up the Duke as I bade you?

TOM. Would you have me carry him up, ma'am? He's snoring by the punch bowl.

LADY ANNE. Then, Thomas, someone *must* wake him.

TOM (*shocked*). What, ma'am? Shake a prince of the blood by the collar?

LADY ANNE (*agitated*). The Duke does not so much as come up the stairs to greet his hostess. 'Tis noticed how Kate dances with every Tom, Dick and Harry but not with Peter. Helen will not be commonly civil to Mr. Throstle. Oh, I am distracted! (*Looks out door* L.) There's Miss Sinclair. Ask her for a dance.

TOM. She's an heiress; she'll not look at me. (THROSTLE *enters* L., *comes to* LADY ANNE, *before settee, points* L., *as* TOM *goes out.*)

LADY ANNE. Surely, sir, you would have Helen be civil to her cousin?

THROSTLE. Any woman here would gladly relieve her of that task. Excepting Miss Pettigrew, who seems to avoid him.

LADY ANNE (*disturbed*). Nonsense. Kate is fulfilling her social duties. And if Helen is coy and shy, 'tis merely that she would tease you, dear sir. But I will speak to her. (LADY ANNE *goes off* L.)

(*Enter* TOM L.)

TOM (*walking up to* THROSTLE, *grumbling*). Did you see that, Throstle? Some insolent Scotch puppy whipped her off right in front of my very nose! But 'tis all one, for I could never bring myself to bed with that Sinclair filly, had she twice five thousand a year. (*Points* L.) My God, Throstle, look at him! Now the dance has stopped they all crowd around him—a levee, by God, a levee!

THROSTLE. Mr. Standish, sir, is a man of rare parts.

TOM. Too rare, by half. 'Tis no small honor for a Yankee to enter White's Club. He patronizes all the bucks, sir. Told me the best quality in England were vulgar, brutal and dirty. He turned his back on the Prince of Wales! Thank God 'twas thought an accident!

THROSTLE. Why did he do so?

TOM. Because His Highness blew his nose with his fingers.

THROSTLE. Sir, the first gentleman of Europe, in his cups, is something coarse.

TOM. So, but he's the Prince!

THROSTLE. How the man bewilders me! His strange zest for things we despise, his aversions! They are pulling down some houses built in the dark ages, on the old city wall, near Moorgate. Mr. Standish would have them preserved! I informed him these are eyesores, since the taste of our ancestors was in all respects barbarous. He was angry. He said, "How the future will curse you!" (TOM *yawns.*) "Whatever the taste of the future," I replied, " 'twill not be for the works of our half-savage forbears." A neat retort, I think.

TOM. We make him pay for his airs, at the gaming tables.

THROSTLE. And his ignorance of all the petty details of everyday life, and his nice disgust with so many of them!

TOM. Disgust! The young rebel!

THROSTLE. We affect him as a tribe of barbarians would affect us. Yet he's an American, a Colonial—'tis the most absurd paradox.

TOM. The most absurd impudence. And his damned superiority! Every morning two maids have to carry buckets of hot water up three pairs of stairs for Master Colonial to wash himself.

THROSTLE. Wash himself all over?

TOM. Every morning.

THROSTLE (*wonderingly*). Washes himself all over, every morning!

(KATE *and* LADY ANNE *enter* L. MAJOR CLINTON *enters* R. TOM *and* THROSTLE *turn up to window* R.)

LADY ANNE. Ah, Major Clinton! Kate, this is Peter's dear friend, Major Clinton; Mr. Throstle, Major Clinton. (KATE *curtseys;* CLINTON *bows,* KATE *comes to him at settee as he exchanges bows with* THROSTLE.)

CLINTON. All my congratulations, Miss Pettigrew. You have monopolized Standish so that I have seen nothing of him since we landed. (KATE *sits* L. *on settee.* CLINTON *sits* R. TOM *comes behind settee as he speaks.*)

TOM. This is too good to waste on you—they must all hear it. You haven't heard this one, ma'am, nor you, Kate. Yesterday, after dinner at White's, he said he couldn't afford to lose a hundred and twelve guineas at a sitting. He'd never lost more than fifty! Last night three of us sat down at ecarte, and when the reckoning came—zounds, it gave me a turn!

KATE. He'd lost the hundred and twelve guineas.

TOM. How did you guess? Exactly a hundred and twelve! And he paid us off with a damned sheepish smile at me, as if to say he was sorry he'd mentioned it *before* it happened.

LADY ANNE (*irritated*). A truce to these childish riddles and puzzles.

CLINTON. You appear distressed, Miss Pettigrew. 'Twas but a prank; he seems to be playing some singular charade here on London.

TOM (*mockingly*). A woman may well mislike to live with a man who knows what she's going to do the day after tomorrow, eh, Kate? (*Exit* TOM R.)

LADY ANNE (*indignantly*). Thomas! (*Speaks in undertone with* THROSTLE *as she goes to fireplace with him.*) Mr. Throstle, I must tell you—— (*Goes into whisper.*)

CLINTON (*to* KATE). Standish has made a model of an engine that he says will drive looms by water power. He will transform England, if this be true.

(*Enter* PETER *with* LORD STANLEY. *As* STANLEY *talks, they walk* L.C. *and stop.* KATE *and* CLINTON *listening.*)

STANLEY. Well, well, sir, I trust you can sympathize with the feelings of Englishmen who have been obliged to sign away a continent.

PETER. Do not grudge us our poor stretches of wilderness, my lord, you upon whose Empire the sun never sets!

STANLEY (*greatly impressed*). Sir, that is the most magnificent compliment ever paid to Great Britain!

PETER. It's not a bad phrase, is it? Though it might sound hackneyed if you'd heard it a hundred times before. (*Exeunt* LADY ANNE *and* THROSTLE L.)

STANLEY. Were it not your own, sir, we should all have heard it before. After all, why did we quarrel about tea? We would have yielded the tax to end the fighting—I cannot understand why you went on with the war.

PETER (*at a loss for a moment*). Why, my lord, to make the world safe for democracy! (*Moving over to* KATE. *Exit* STANLEY L. CLINTON *rises; steps back* R. *of settee.*) We haven't danced yet, Kate. Do you think you could bear with my clumsy steps?

CLINTON (*hearty, but astonished*). What, no word for me? (PETER *looks at him blankly.*)

KATE. Surely, Peter, you remember Major Clinton?

PETER. Oh, of course.

CLINTON. Another of his jests. My friend of twenty-seven days in the *General Wolfe* pretends he doesn't know me!

PETER (*hastily*). When you put off your service uniform and dress like a peacock, your own mother wouldn't know you, Clinton. You don't seem the same man ashore.

CLINTON (*gaping*). You took the very words out of my mouth. *You* don't seem the same man, on shore.

PETER. I've been getting my land legs. (PETER *steps to* KATE, *offers his arm. She rises as though to take it, then impulsively turns to* CLINTON, *saying:*)

KATE. Forgive me, Peter, I promised this dance to Major Clinton. (CLINTON *looks at her, astonished, then offers his arm and they go off* L. PETER, *much disturbed, standing before settee staring after them.* LADY ANNE *appears in doorway* L. *with the* DUCHESS.)

LADY ANNE (*calls*). Peter! (PETER *crosses to them.*) The Duchess of Devonshire, Mr. Peter Standish. (LADY ANNE *curtseys as the* DUCHESS *crosses her; and exits immediately.* PETER *bows.* DUCHESS *curtseys; she turns as if to go into drawing-room.*)

PETER. Ah, Duchess, I'm afraid I have already disgraced myself as a dancer. And I had three lessons! (DUCHESS *laughs; turns from door. They move across to* R. *as she says chaffingly:*)

DUCHESS. What was it you said about your American "steps"?

PETER. Oh, we have forgotten your polite measures; *our* dances are modelled on those of the—Red Indians.

DUCHESS. If you are to take my scalp it must be by your wit, which they say is better than your dancing. I am told, sir—(*Sits settee.*)—that you seem to regard this country as a museum, and ourselves as specimens in glass cases.

PETER. Oh, I cannot leave you with that absurd impression.

DUCHESS. Do your best to make another, then. But, please, no politics; I should be no match for you there. You have overwhelmed Lord Stanley.

PETER. Upon one theme, in *your* company, I might do justice to what Lady Anne expects of me.

DUCHESS. Your tone of voice identifies the theme! If we are not to speak of sentiment, let me congratulate you. Miss Pettigrew will make you a devoted wife.

PETER. There is nothing in the world like the devotion of a married woman. It's a thing no married man knows anything about.

DUCHESS. What! A cynic about marriage before you have reached the altar?

PETER. What is a cynic, Duchess?

DUCHESS. One who sneers at love, at romance.

PETER. Yes; one who knows the price of everything, and the value of nothing! But we should face the facts. (*Sits on stool*) In love one first deceives oneself and then others—and that is what is called romance.

DUCHESS. Sir, such views of romance are commonly entertained by that most ignoble work of God, a faithless husband.

PETER. Fidelity is a strange thing! When we are young we try to be faithful, and cannot; when we are old we try to be faithless——

DUCHESS (*delighted*). And cannot! Oh, a delightful aphorism, sir! Your American pyrotechnics make me feel as stupid as a schoolgirl at her first ball. I can scarcely believe that I am—well, who I am——

PETER (*rises and with a deep bow*). Georgiana, Duchess of Devonshire!

DUCHESS. You roll it out as though you were announcing me at Court.

PETER (*with real but wholly impersonal enthusiasm*). All the charm of the period seems to center in that name!

DUCHESS. Flatterer! Admit that in America you had never heard of me!

PETER. What barbarian has not heard of the Fifth Duchess? (*Sits again on stool.*) Your name in English social history is the finest flower of the age of elegance. We know your face from—— (*Anxiously.*) Gainsborough *has* painted you, hasn't he? (*She nods.*) All the legend and beauty of the age cling about you. All one's dreams of the time have you for their central figure—your receptions, those dinners at Devonshire House—as powerful in politics as irresistible in love. What can the eighteenth century offer that—(*Breaks off, alarmed, continues self-consciously.*)—that can compare with——

DUCHESS. You speak of me so strangely. (*With a little laugh.*) I find your overwhelming compliments—a little disturbing. You're talking about me as we two might talk about Madame de Maintenon. In the past tense!

PETER. Oh, no, Duchess, I never once used the past tense! (*He rises.*)

DUCHESS. You have been *thinking* of me in the past tense. (*She rises.*) Now I know what it is! You've been talking about me—as though—— (*She steps back.*)—as though I were already dead!

PETER (*discouraged*). And I tried so hard to make an impression.

DUCHESS (*controlling herself and smiling*). Sir, *you* have made an—indescribable impression. (*The* DUCHESS *curtseys, turns, exits* R. THROSTLE *enters* L. *and crosses to* PETER.)

THROSTLE. Sir, my compliments upon your success tonight.

PETER. My success with the Duchess has been devastating. Is Major Clinton in there?

THROSTLE. He's dancing again with Miss Pettigrew.

PETER. Oh, damn the meddler! I wish they'd order him abroad again.

THROSTLE. Sir, you appear distressed. Ah, believe me, I've known Miss Pettigrew these five years; 'tis but a mood.

PETER. Your assurance is most comforting.

THROSTLE. And I entirely understand about Miss Helen.

PETER. What do you mean?

THROSTLE. Merely that I take no exception to your marked attentions to the lady to whom I offer the devotion of a lifetime.

PETER (*angry*). Come, Throstle, you're not fifty. I advise you not to offer any young girl the devotion of a lifetime until you're over seventy.

THROSTLE (*paling*). Your self-assurance, sir, is magnificent. Are you so confident that Miss Pettigrew is not almost of a mind to break with you?

PETER (*laughing, with a touch of nervous hysteria*). Kate, break with me! (*Rises.*) Listen, Throstle! We're going to get married and have three children—one of them dies of smallpox at the age of seven and is buried in St. Mark's Churchyard! That's absurd, isn't it? But you believe it, don't you?

THROSTLE (*keeps composure with difficulty*). Since you can read Miss Pettigrew's future, perhaps you'll inform me as to Miss Helen's?

PETER (*staggered*). Helen's future. No, I don't know that! (*With forced jocularity.*) Look here, Throstle, can't you take a joke? I don't know any more about the future than you do.

THROSTLE (*takes snuff; turns away*). My reason, sir, tells me as much.

TOM (*enters* R.). Gad's life, Throstle, he's still asleep!

PETER. Who's asleep?

TOM. His Royal Highness!

PETER. Why not let him sleep?

THROSTLE. Ah, you wouldn't know, sir; etiquette permits no guest to leave any assembly before Royalty.

PETER (*laughs*). Then this ball will have to go on all night?

TOM. 'Tis no laughing matter, sir. (PETER *walks back to portrait; looks at it; looks out of* R. *window.* CLINTON *enters* L., *talking to* STANLEY. *They turn to fireplace.*)

CLINTON. Gad, sir, as I tried to force myself through the press, I saw a fellow running away with a piece of charred bone.

THROSTLE (*walks up to them*). Charred bone?

CLINTON. Did any of you see that woman burned before Newgate this morning?

PETER (*startled. Comes down stage*). What woman burned?

CLINTON. One Phoebe Harris, for coining. There's not been such a crush for years—I paid three guineas for a seat in a window.

THROSTLE (*with a faint sneer*). Those who fancy the odor of burning flesh may observe the roasting of an ox in the Smithfields Market any morning gratis.

PETER (*exploding*). You paid three guineas for a seat in a window to see a woman burned alive? And that can happen in London?

TOM. They strangle 'em before they put the fire to the wood.

PETER (*to* CLINTON). I hope you enjoyed the spectacle! Did you take your mother and sisters?

TOM (*shocked*). Sir, women of quality do not attend executions.

CLINTON (*with faint sneer*). Americans appear squeamish people—when they're not at home——

THROSTLE (*interrupting tactfully, to* PETER). I trust, sir, our great lexicographer did not disappoint you when you called upon him this afternoon?

CLINTON (*to* PETER). I saw Doctor Johnson this morning, at the spectacle which so offends you.

PETER. So he was there too, was he? God!

TOM. What did the old bear say to you?

PETER. Oh, he thundered out a few platitudes. Really, his friends ought to stop him from dribbling food and snuff all over his waistcoat. And he'd be none the worse for a bath.

TOM. Bath! You and your everlasting baths!

PETER. Bathing hasn't always been an eccentricity—you admire the Romans; the Romans bathed.

THROSTLE. Only excessively, sir, when they became degenerate. The virile fathers of the Republic——

PETER (*interrupting impatiently*). Were as dirty as you are? I suppose you're right.

TOM. 'Struth, sir, you speak of the best

of us here as no better than a litter of lousy Irishmen.

CLINTON. What in the devil's name is all this about baths? You took but one bath in the *General Wolfe,* and you talked about that for a week beforehand.

PETER (*at fault for a moment*). I can't stand salt water. (*Walks toward window* R., *looks at portrait, turns and comes front, meeting* HELEN *as she enters* R.)

CLINTON (*as they move to door* L., THROSTLE *behind* TOM *and* CLINTON). What *have* you done to him here?

TOM. There's no fine lady so finicky as this Colonial. You didn't tell me he was like this, Clinton!

CLINTON (*explosively*). Gad, sir, he wasn't. London has made another man of him. It is altogether incredible!

(TOM *and* CLINTON *exeunt talking.* THROSTLE *turns at the door and watches* PETER *and* HELEN. LORD STANLEY *appears door* L. *and talks to* THROSTLE.)

PETER (*standing with* HELEN *before settee*). He's been annoying you again. If only I could *do* something about it.

HELEN. But you do *do* something, just by feeling as you *do.* Are we going to dance again? (DUCHESS *enters* R., *crossing to* STANLEY) All the other women will be so jealous!

PETER. The Duchess tells me I dance so badly.

DUCHESS. I'm bored beyond all endurance, Stanley, and I've sent for my carriage.

(*Exit* THROSTLE.)

STANLEY. But His Highness!

DUCHESS. Oh, I've no desire to make scandal by leaving before Royalty, so there's naught for it but to wake up the drunken old pig and get him out of the house. Come, lend me your countenance! (*The* DUCHESS *exits* R., *ignoring* PETER *and* HELEN, *followed by* LORD STANLEY.)

HELEN. What *have* you been saying to the Duchess, Peter? She's been repeating such wicked, hard, cruel things downstairs——

PETER. Come and talk to me. (HELEN *sits on settee.*) Your mother begged me to impress the Duchess—(*Sitting on stool.*)—so I dazzled her with some cheap epigrams made up by a fellow named Oscar Wilde.

HELEN. A friend of yours in New York?

PETER. Oh, no. He's dead. At least he's not been —— Well, never mind. It's rather complicated.

HELEN. You did indeed dazzle the Duchess, Peter. But somehow you seem to have made her almost afraid of you, too!

PETER. I know. They all like me at first. But then I say something—wrong. I see it in their eyes. (*Intensely.*) Are you afraid of me?

HELEN. I couldn't be afraid of somebody I'm sorry for.

PETER. Why are you sorry for me?

HELEN. Oh, because I think you're unhappy with us, though you're so brave, and you try to hide it. You feel so strange here——

PETER. Yes, I do.

HELEN. I can't imagine what America's like. It's so far away. But I suppose everything's so different. And the people, too.

PETER. Yes, that's it. Everything's different. Oh, you are so kind!

HELEN. And as for what worries you so, people being afraid of you, I mean—that's only—only——

PETER. Only what?

HELEN. You know, Peter. It's because you look through us, you seem to know what we think, even what we're going to do next. (*Slowly*). I don't understand you. And I wish I could help you.

PETER. Oh, but you do! Just by your sympathy, even though you can't know how much I need it. The days are all right. I go about your old London—that's the most wonderful experience that ever came to a living man! But when I lie in bed and think! It all seems nightmare, until I remember you. You're not like the others. You're—real—— (*Seizes her hand.*)

HELEN (*withdrawing hand*). I am Kate's sister!

PETER (*humbly*). Forgive me.

(LORD STANLEY *enters* R. *and crosses the stage hurriedly; as he goes out* L., *the voices of the* DUKE *and* DUCHESS *are heard.* PETER *and* HELEN *rise as they enter* R. *The* DUKE *is elderly, many-chinned, amiable. He wears the Garter with ribbon and star.*)

DUKE (*laughing*). The Duke of Cumberland must not be known as the Duke of Slumberland. (LADY ANNE *enters hurriedly* L. *immediately followed by* LORD STANLEY. DUKE *and* DUCHESS *stop.*) Zo, goot efening, Laty Anne.

LADY ANNE (*curtseys*). Your Royal Highness confers a great honor upon us. (*Enter* L. KATE, CLINTON, THROSTLE *and*

TOM, *gradually spreading out in a semicircle,* TOM *and* KATE L., *downstage.*)

DUKE. Your bunch iss fery goot. I haf stayed too long, below. I asg your pardon. (LADY ANNE *curtseys again. Looking over company.*) I had hert mine ald vrent Sir Choshwa Reynolds vas here.

LADY ANNE (*embarrassed*). He was suddenly taken ill, Your Highness.

DUKE. So? I am sorry. And vere iss diss American gousin off whom I haf hert? (LADY ANNE *gestures to* PETER, *who advances and bows.*)

LADY ANNE. Your Royal Highness, Mr. Peter Standish.

DUKE. You marry Miss Pettigrew, Mr. Standish?

PETER. Yes, Your Highness.

DUKE. Vere iss she? (LADY ANNE *moves* L. KATE *advances* L. *front.*)

LADY ANNE. My daughter, Your Royal Highness. (KATE *curtseys.*)

DUKE. Zo! A fine bair of lofers. All my gongratulations. (*To* PETER.) You haf gum a long joorney—Amerigans are great dravellers. You haf drabbled mooch, Mr. Standish?

PETER (*casually*). Oh, from time to time. (DUCHESS, *who has been standing to* R., *rear of* DUKE L., *moves toward him and signals him a reminder with her fan.*)

DUKE (*taking the hint, with a laugh*). Zo! Laty Anne, the Tuchess has tolt me it is fery late. I must dake my leaf. (LADY ANNE *curtseys; the* DUKE *bows to her and to the others; turns; takes* PETER's *arm*) You trink mooch in Ameriga—an Indian trink, I haf hert. (*As the* DUKE *walks* PETER *out* L. *everyone curtseys.*)

PETER. Oh, you mean corn whisky, Your Highness. I found a bottle in my boxes, if you care to try it.

DUKE. And how did you get it t'rough the gustoms?

(*Exeunt* DUKE *and* PETER L., LADY ANNE *immediately following, with all the others excepting* HELEN *and* KATE. *As* KATE *turns to follow them,* HELEN *detains her.*)

HELEN. What is it, Kate? We always tell one another everything.

KATE. Helen dear, I don't know myself. I *meant* to dance with him—I was rude, ill-bred, anything you like—but I *couldn't.*

HELEN. He cannot understand why you slight him.

KATE. Then you were talking of me as you danced. (*Ironically.*) I suppose he complained of my cruelty.

HELEN. He doesn't seem to take your behavior—so seriously as I do.

KATE. Oh, so he doesn't take me seriously?

HELEN. *He says there* can't be any *real* disagreement. It isn't possible, because of course you *will* marry.

KATE. So; he thinks I *must* marry him, because we must have the money!

HELEN. Oh, Kate, you *know* such a thought could never cross his mind!

KATE. How do you know what thoughts cross his mind? About you, for instance? You're too good, Helen, to suspect anybody.

HELEN. Suspect Peter? of what?

KATE. Oh, it doesn't matter.

HELEN (*earnestly*). I want to compose this—estrangement. I shall be miserable until everything is settled—and over.

KATE. You think I'm being very unfair. But there's such a thing as instinct, Helen.

HELEN. Oh, Kate, just because he sees and knows things, strangely——

KATE (*interrupts*). I can't help it, Helen. When I'm with him he makes me afraid. (*Rises*) And when you're with him—I'm afraid for you!

LADY ANNE (*enters* L., *followed by* THROSTLE). The dear, dear Duchess! Had she not awakened him, he might have slept on for hours, everyone cooped up here, and our ball the laughing-stock of London!

THROSTLE (*with bow to* KATE). Miss Pettigrew, your lover has the town at his feet.

LADY ANNE. Oh, dear, kind sir, your partiality—

THROSTLE. Has not obscured my judgment. (*With veiled irony.*) None of your guests could credit our late Colonies with such a product.

TOM (*enters* L., *yawning*). Look ye, Throstle, 'twas you took my cousin to Sir Joshua.

THROSTLE. I did, sir.

TOM. Sir Joshua sends Mr. Standish his compliments by me, and would have Mr. Standish destroy the portrait; he'll paint him no more!

LADY ANNE. What can Sir Joshua mean? Our cousin was to sit for him here tomorrow.

TOM. Then he may sit and admire himself, for there will be no painter.

KATE. I wonder why?

TOM. A hundred guineas they compounded for, and now the man throws the picture and money too into Standish's face.

HELEN. Something has occurred between them.

THROSTLE. Some fault in the portrait has displeased the artist.

TOM. Fault in the portrait, eh? (*As* THROSTLE *drags out easel from behind writing desk, and turns it around, showing half-finished portrait,* TOM *continues.*) (*Mimicking* REYNOLDS.) "Something in his face eludes me. I thought, at first, it was irony. And yet, I fancy I know irony." (KATE *rises, walks up behind* THROSTLE.)

THROSTLE. The work is in the artist's best manner.

KATE (*gazing intently at picture*). I wonder why!

THROSTLE (*taking snuff*). This is not like Sir Joshua.

KATE (*to* TOM). What exactly *did* Sir Joshua say?

TOM (*mimicking*). "There is a quality in his every look, when I take up my brushes and fasten my eyes on his face, beyond all *my* experience of human nature."

KATE (*slowly*). Painters have good eyes.

TOM. He had no mind to set his on Peter again.

KATE (*as to herself*). What did he see? (*Sits on stool by settee.*)

HELEN (*rising and taking her arm*). Sister, what is it?

LADY ANNE. Kate, Kate, what is amiss with you?

TOM. Vapours, vapours.

THROSTLE (*disturbed*). None of us understands him.

HELEN (*with spirit*). I understand him —he's strange here. He feels just the same way, about us, that some of us do about him.

TOM. Why shouldn't he understand us? We are but ordinary people of quality.

KATE. God knows what he is.

LADY ANNE (*angrily*). Shame, shame, to speak so of your lover!

TOM. 'Tis no matter; perhaps Yankees get like that.

HELEN. Oh, Tom!

KATE. While you can pigeon him at White's you'll choke it down. But what of me?

LADY ANNE (*rising*). Kate! This is disgraceful!

KATE. So his bank account be sound, naught else matters to anyone—but me.

HELEN (*distressed*). Kate, Kate, don't you see that he's unhappy, too?

LADY ANNE (*interrupts, to* KATE). I forbid you to discuss your lover so.

MAID (*appears in door* L. *with candle-snuffer*). The musicians, my lady.

LADY ANNE (*sweeping* L.) Tom, this is your mischief, with your tales to fright scullery maids! (LADY ANNE *walks out with* MAID L., *giving directions.*)

KATE. How did he first get into this house?

TOM. I'll engage his legs carried him.

KATE. He walked in here. No one saw him below. You remember the rain. His boots were dry.

HELEN. Kate, dear, what *do* you mean?

KATE. I don't know what I mean. I think I'm going out of my senses.

HELEN. There's no reason to be afraid of him.

KATE. There's no reason to be afraid of a graveyard at midnight.

THROSTLE. And we're living in the eighteenth century! (*Takes snuff.*) The age of reason, the age of Voltaire!

HELEN. What if he does see things—ahead of other people?

KATE (*more intensely.*) How did he get into this house?

HELEN. Oh, that again!

KATE. Nobody answers me.

HELEN. Kate, dearest, you *shall* be happy. Ask him about whatever troubles you!

KATE. I loved him, when he kissed me that first day. And now I'd rather die than ask him—anything!

PETER (*enters* R.; *stops at door*). Hello, what's the picture doing out here?

TOM. Sir Joshua would have you destroy his portrait.

THROSTLE. Sir, I propose to wait upon Sir Joshua tomorrow.

PETER (*without surprise*). Pray do not disturb yourself.

HELEN. You do not seem affronted, cousin.

PETER. He's entitled to paint whom he chooses.

KATE (*with an effort*). You expected this?

PETER. Now that it's happened, I'm not surprised.

HELEN. 'Tis most uncivil of him, cousin.

PETER (*vaguely, as though to himself; slowly, as he walks to easel, looks at por-*

trait). The picture shall not be destroyed, and Sir Joshua will complete it.

TOM (*languidly*). Damnation, sir, men have sent their seconds for less than this!

LADY ANNE (*enters* L.) What! Still harping on that portrait! An old man's vagary, dear cousin; he'll no doubt send you his apologies; but, if not, Mr. Gainsborough will do you a better likeness. Thomas, put the ugly thing back where it came from.

TOM. Gad's life! All these frenzies about a lump of paint! (TOM *lugs easel back and stows it behind writing-bureau.*)

LADY ANNE. Cousin, I've had no time for a morsel of supper, nor, I am sure, have you. Come below. 'Tis late. Come, Mr. Throstle. Come down with Helen.

(*Exit* THROSTLE *and* HELEN R. TOM *stops at door, looks from* KATE *to* PETER, *goes out, leaving door open.* PETER *goes to door, closes it, turns and faces* KATE.)

PETER. Kate, what's the matter? You've been avoiding me all the evening.

KATE. You have not been avoiding my sister.

PETER. That fellow Clinton's been upsetting you, hasn't he? I know what he told you.

KATE. Of course you know what he told me.

PETER. You see, Kate——

KATE (*interrupting*). You know what he told me. You know what I am thinking now. You know what is going to happen next.

PETER (*steps nearer*). This is just a mood, Kate; it will pass. (KATE *shudders; moves back.*) There's nothing to be afraid of.

KATE. You attracted me; *I thought I loved you.*

PETER (*definitively*). You mustn't talk like that. We're going to be married.

KATE. So, I am to marry you, when I am put to it to force myself to remain alone with you!

PETER. Oh, this is that cursed picture—— (*Moves up toward easel.*)

KATE. Sir Joshua saw it! (*Moves toward door* R.)

PETER. Go to bed, Kate; you'll be yourself again in the morning.

KATE (*turns at door*). In the morning I shall post to Budleigh. I cannot stay in this house with you. (*Tries to slip bracelet from wrist.*)

PETER (*coming toward her*). Kate, you mustn't break our engagement. (*Confidently.*) You can't do that!

KATE. Oh, I *can't* do that. How smugly you say it! So you think there are no limits to what a wizard can do with a woman? The women all press after you, don't they? But no woman wishes to dance with you twice—excepting Helen! I was never so afraid of anything in my life as I am of you—(*Laughs wildly.*)—And you think you can make me marry you when I fear you as I fear the devil! (*Throws bracelet on floor.*)

PETER. This can't be!

KATE. I leave London in the morning, and I'll not return while you are in this house. I hope I may never set eyes on you again. In God's name, go back to—to America, if that's where you come from!

PETER. But things *can't* happen that *didn't* happen.

KATE. You speak words without sense. Only God and the devil know what they mean.

PETER. Oh, Kate, be reasonable. (*Picks up bracelet.*) Please. I only mean it's all arranged. I've come over to marry you—

KATE. Sir, your self-assurance is almost ridiculous.

PETER. Oh no, Kate, if you only knew, I haven't got any self-assurance at all. I wish I had. But we are going to be married, and have children, and live in this house. That *happens!* (*Pleadingly.*) You must feel that just as I do, don't you? It's *true!*

KATE. I've only this to say to you: I shall not return from Budleigh while you are in this house! (*Turns, to open door.*)

PETER (*advancing towards her. Hysterically*). No, Kate, don't go! (*She turns to him.*) We'll be happy together, and this marriage *has* to be. It *is!* (*Holding out bracelet.*) *This, this* is impossible! You *can't* do that! It *didn't happen* that way!

KATE (*advancing to him*). Whatever you mean, I've a woman's simple answer to your "can't do that." Since that first day I've been afraid to look in your eyes. But now, look in mine and tell me that you love me!

PETER (*turns away, hand to head*). Kate, that will be all right; we'll be happy together. (*She turns to door.*) Kate! You won't go to Budleigh to-morrow, for when you meet me in the morning I shall be —different. I won't seem the same man. I may feel differently about Helen and Throstle—promise me now that you'll stand by Helen against them all, even against—me. Help her, Kate! She'll be alone, and she'll need your help—

KATE. She will indeed need help, if *you* take such an interest in her!

LADY ANNE (*enters* R. PETER *walks out* L.). Kate, Kate, what is amiss?

KATE (*curtseys*). Ma'am, I post to Budleigh in the morning.

LADY ANNE. To Budleigh! I forbid you. (*Enter* HELEN *and* THROSTLE R.)

KATE. Madam, I have always obeyed you; but I cannot stay in the same house with that man!

LADY ANNE. What rebellion is this? (*To the others.*) She's mad. She won't have her cousin.

HELEN (*an involuntary ejaculation*). Oh! (*She comes* R. *front and listens intently, motionless, during following.*)

LADY ANNE. Kate, what devil has got into you? Oh, Mr. Throstle! The catch of the year! The town mad about him! I shall never survive it!

THROSTLE. Dear Madam, this is no time—— (*He advances as if to kiss her hand in farewell, but she pays no attention to him.*)

LADY ANNE. Oh, oh, was ever such a perverse occurrence!

TOM (*enters* R.) Hell's fury, what's wrong here? What is it, ma'am? (LADY ANNE *moans.*)

THROSTLE. Miss Pettigrew and Mr. Standish, sir—

TOM (*interrupting, to* KATE). He's thrown you over? Now I must fight the scoundrel, though I know damned well he can kill me if he's half a mind to it.

KATE. He can kill you by looking at you if he's half a mind.

THROSTLE. Miss Pettigrew, sir, believes her cousin to be an arch-angel or demon —I'm not certain which!

LADY ANNE (*moaning*). She's out of her senses.

TOM. I'll have this out with him.

KATE (*contemptuously*). Don't get yourself killed on my account, I did it.

TOM. *You* did it?

THROSTLE. This is no time for the presence of the most devoted friend. (*Kisses* LADY ANNE'S *hand.*)

(KATE *and* HELEN *whisper.*)

LADY ANNE. Oh, sir, we know you are discretion itself.

THROSTLE. Count upon me always, honoured madam.

(*Advances to kiss the hands of* KATE *and* HELEN. *They ignore him, he bows to* TOM *and goes out* R.)

TOM. No, look'ee, Kate, you shall have him, if I've to post the banns myself!

LADY ANNE. Tom, leave this to me! Helen, Kate, go to your beds.

(HELEN *and* KATE *go out* R.)

TOM. This must not be! Fifteen thousand in settlement!

LADY ANNE. All my pains for nothing, and here's an end.

TOM. Hell and damnation!

LADY ANNE (*after long pause significantly*). Helen shall compose him, in the morning.

TOM (*comprehending*). Helen!

LADY ANNE. And why not, pray?

TOM. 'Tis all one, so the money be not lost. But what of Throstle?

LADY ANNE (*contemptuously, as she goes out* R.). Oh, Throstle!

(MAID *enters* L. *carrying candle snuffer. She yawns, snuffs candle to* L. *of door; as she is snuffing candles between door and fireplace,* TOM *pinches her.*)

MAID. Oh, please, Mr. Tom.

TOM (*stepping back and cocking head*). And how's Master Galton?

MAID (*terrified*). Oh!

TOM. I told you I'd find out who he was! A fine handsome fellow in his scarlet plush and gold buttons! You're a lucky girl, Wilkins!

MAID (*pleadingly*). Mr. Tom, you couldn't be so cruel—he'd never marry me if he knew.

TOM. Who's cruel? 'Tis you who are cruel. Come, a good kiss like old times, and you shall have a golden guinea for Tom Pettigrew's wedding gift. (MAID *turns to him,* TOM *hugs her, whispers.*) And remember, not a word from me if you're sensible!

(PETER *walks out of the now dark drawing room, wholly abstracted.* TOM *hastily disengages, turns sheepishly to* PETER, *but* PETER *does not see him, walks mechanically to the fire stool and sits.*)

TOM. 'Tis late, I'm for bed.

(PETER *pays no attention.* TOM *turns with a shrug and goes out* R. *with a yawn which he stifles as he glances back uneasily at* PETER. MAID *goes hesitatingly to fireplace to snuff candles in sconce to right of fireplace. She seems afraid to approach* PETER, *but* PETER *walks past her, not noticing her, but looking up at tapestry panel again as he passes it, goes to window* R. *and looks out.* MAID *snuffs sconce, then turns, moves hesitatingly to snuff other sconces, but* PETER *turns from window and looks through her. She is afraid of him and she turns and goes out* L. *looking back at him over her shoulder from door.* PETER *walks to easel, looks at portrait again, then walks before tapestry panel, half raising his arms as though in invocation. Then he turns and walks, slowly and stiffly, as though dazed, towards door* R. *It opens suddenly and* HELEN *enters, flurried, as though she had been running. He stops. She closes door and stands with her back to it.*)

HELEN. Peter!

PETER (*at length, in dazed voice*). You know?

HELEN. We all know. (*He turns; walks away.*) Kate's not herself tonight. You mustn't think hardly of her, cousin.

PETER (*turns*). Oh, it isn't Kate's fault.

HELEN. That's generous of you, Peter. I want you to tell me what all this mystery means, so that I can go to Kate——

PETER. No, I can't; you'd be afraid of me, too.

HELEN (*with quiet dignity and force*). That's not true!

PETER. Oh, if I could only believe that!

HELEN (*gently pressing*). How can you speak of things that haven't happened yet, as though they had happened? How can you know things you couldn't know? First, about my shawl. And since, so many things? (*He sits on stool by settee,* HELEN *standing by him.*) Tell me! (*Pause.*)

PETER. The border-line between what's just happened, and what's just going to is —shadowy, for me. Things of tomorrow often seem as real as things of yesterday. And so, in fact, they are.

HELEN. Then it's true! You do see ahead!

PETER. You believe, when it's incredible, against nature?

HELEN. Can you see ahead just a day or two, or months and years?

PETER. Many months, and many years.

HELEN. I love life so! I want to see ahead, because I love it so.

PETER. So you're in love with the future, as I was in love with the—— (*He breaks off.*) It's better just to dream about what's ahead—to dream *your* dreams—than really to know.

HELEN (*sits on settee*). But, Peter, I want to make Kate understand about these powers of yours; I want to make her see how proud and happy she should be, instead of afraid.

PETER. She'd only be still more afraid. It wouldn't be any use. But I could tell you about things that are going to happen, just for yourself, if you really want so much to know.

HELEN (*eagerly*). Oh, yes, Peter, please! Things you've seen!

PETER. Things I've seen. Where shall I begin? Helen, you see the candle there? Well, long after us, this room—Berkeley Square, all London outside, will be lit by one movement of a man's hand.

HELEN. By magic? But—what will it be like, Peter?

PETER (*helplessly*). I can't tell you; you wouldn't understand; there aren't any words that could make you understand.

HELEN (*their eyes meet and she continues to look at him fixedly*). No words. There aren't any words because these things come to your mind in visions, Peter, and I think I could see them, too— through your eyes. Will you let me try?

PETER. But that isn't possible.

HELEN. Let me look! (*Gazes intently into his eyes.*)

PETER. Helen! Your eyes burn mine!

HELEN (*in low voice*). 'Tis this room. It blazes with your magic lights, Peter! There's your portrait, on the wall, finished! You said it would be.

PETER. The veil is thin, for you!

HELEN. A man and a girl. They are dressed—so queerly. The man turns to her; he kisses her. I can't see his face, but he's like you, Peter.

PETER (*wrenches his head away*). No, no!

HELEN. Yes, show me, I *will* see!

PETER. Not that, the wonders of the future—ah, *now* look! (*Turns head back to her.*)

HELEN (*looking in his eyes again.*) Sunshine, white clouds, three great birds, bigger than a hundred eagles——

PETER. Machines, with men in them.

HELEN. And below them, water! The ocean! That great floating mountain there! A ship? No sails! No masts! And beyond —a great cluster of towers. They climb into the clouds. Oh, Peter, is it heaven?

PETER. Only a city across the sea.

HELEN. A fairy dream city. It fades. (*Sinking back.*) Is the future all poetry, beauty? They fly like birds, crush the ocean, their houses pierce the sky. They'll conquer evil. They'll be angels, not men.

PETER (*murmurs ironically*). "Angels, not men." (PETER *turns his head as* HELEN *again peers into his eyes.*) No—you'd see other pictures now, things that you mustn't see.

HELEN (*grasps his shoulders*). I will see!

PETER (*moans, but turns his head to her*). You cannot bear it!

HELEN. Monsters—no, men, in masks over their heads—a yellow mist around them—they fall, they twist in the mud——

PETER (*with great effort*). If you *must* see, let it be by night!

HELEN. Lights, dancing, flashing, everywhere! But this is most beautiful of all.

PETER. The fireworks of hell.

HELEN. Oh! A great flame opens like a flower.

PETER. A dump of shells that blew a score of men to pieces.

HELEN (*unheeding*). Curving streams of fire—

PETER. Pumped out of hoses to shrivel men up like insects!

HELEN (*shrinks back; covers face with hands*). Oh!

PETER (*leaping up and back*). We should have stopped with your fairy city.

HELEN. Devils, demons, not men! (*She rises; turns from him.*) 'Tis not true! God would never have put us here to suffer, for a race of fiends like that to come after us.

PETER (*embraces her*). Helen, dear Helen, what were we doing?

HELEN. The mystery, behind your eyes!

PETER. You saw the future there. (*Pause.*)

HELEN. But there was something else, more wonderful than that! (*They disengage; he turns away; She half turns away, then turns to him again.*) And now I will go to Kate and tell her that I have shared your vision, and why it is that people are afraid——

PETER. No, you mustn't tell her. She won't be afraid tomorrow. Nobody will be afraid any more. I'll be different then.

HELEN (*walks toward door* R.—*then turns*). But I don't understand why I mustn't talk to Kate——

PETER. You think she threw me over tonight just because she was afraid of me? It's more hopeless than that, Helen. She's found out that I don't love her.

HELEN (*after pause*). But you want to marry her.

PETER. Don't let's talk about that. I had to go on with it, that was all.

HELEN. Then you don't love Kate any more than she loves you now, and it isn't about Kate you're unhappy, but because you feel lost here, and strange, and because people are afraid of you——

PETER. Yes, and as everything has closed in around me, your sympathy has kept me from going mad.

HELEN. You make me very happy.

PETER. You know how I feel. You must know. But try to believe, even though you can never understand why, that the beauty that is with us and about us now, though it's more lovely than all the real things that ever were, *isn't* real, Helen. It's only a mirage. It's like a vision of heaven. It couldn't exist in this world at all, or in any real world. It's—it's unnatural!

HELEN. Unnatural!

PETER. Yes, and impossible, *not real,* Helen. You must forget it all and forget me, for your own dear sake.

HELEN. You know I can't do that, Peter.

PETER (*in agony and remorse*). Oh, what have I done?

HELEN (*bewildered*). Peter, you know the future! Tell me ours!

PETER. Our future! No, I don't know that. Oh, Helen, try to understand. I come to you from—somewhere else. Another world.

HELEN. I know. It's all so different, here.

PETER. But I'm not—one of you!

HELEN. I've always felt that, Peter. Peter, it's something you've done that's like a wild beast in your mind. Peter! What price have you paid for the splendor about you? You've not sold your soul to——

PETER. No, my soul's not damned, not what you mean by damned. (*Embraces her.*) I love you. Oh, God, help us both! I love you!

HELEN (*quietly and proudly*). I loved you before I ever saw you, in my first dream of you, coming with a candle, from somewhere far away, to meet me.

PETER. Oh, but, Helen, I'm not playing my part now. (*Breaks from her.*) I'm myself, you see. I'm *myself,* and I'm muddling everything up! This isn't possible, this isn't my world—or yours. It isn't my life—or yours!

HELEN. Then take me away with you, Peter.

PETER. I can't! I can't!

HELEN (*runs to him; clings to him*). Then don't leave me!

PETER. I won't! (*Looks wildly behind him to where the picture hangs in the modern scene.*) When I kissed Kate, that was *his* kiss, to his betrothed! (*Straining her to him.*) But there's never been a kiss like *that* since the world began!
(*A long kiss.*)

CURTAIN

ACT THREE

Scene I

The room in the Past. Late afternoon—a week later. The scene is set as in Act I, Scenes I and III.

MAID *shows in* THROSTLE R., *curtseys and exits* L. *Enters* LADY ANNE, L. THROSTLE *turns, bows to* LADY ANNE, *she curtseys.*

THROSTLE. Your faithful servant, madam.

LADY ANNE (*embarrassed*). A pleasure, indeed a pleasure, dear Mr. Throstle! (*During this* TOM *has entered* L. *He and* THROSTLE *bow.* TOM *strolls to fireplace; leans on elbow against it.*)

TOM (*nonchalantly*). 'Pon my oath, Throstle, you haven't been near us in a week.

THROSTLE. I have been with you in thought.

LADY ANNE. We had hoped, sir, that your visits, so welcome always, were not now to be discontinued.

THROSTLE. In the altered circumstances, you would say, Lady Anne?

TOM. Things do turn out in devilish queer fashions.

LADY ANNE (*sharply*). I know of nothing, Thomas, that has turned out queerly in this house.

TOM (*smiling*). Mr. Throstle would scarcely agree with you there, ma'am.

LADY ANNE (*reprovingly*). Thomas!

THROSTLE. Nevertheless, there can be no choice between my fifteen hundred and your cousin's ten thousand a year.

TOM (*approvingly*). You know the world, sir!

THROSTLE. One corner of it, fairly well.

LADY ANNE. Dear, dear friend, such tact, such breeding—had it been anyone else—— (*Not looking at him.*) But indeed 'twas evident from the first that Helen and Mr. Standish were made for each other.

THROSTLE. I have come to lay at Miss Helen's feet the felicitations of a rejected suitor.

LADY ANNE (*hurriedly. Turns to him*). Pray, do not do that, sir!

THROSTLE. But, ma'am, I have ears, I have eyes, and so indeed have others. What motive can there be for reticence?

TOM. What indeed! Every tongue in London must be wagging, ma'am. Does he not avoid everyone since the ball? Are they not seen together every day?

LADY ANNE (*constrained again*). When we have news, Mr. Throstle, you shall be the first to hear.

THROSTLE. Am I then to understand that Mr. Standish has made as yet no formal application—— (HELEN *enters* R., *followed by* PETER. PETER *is in riding costume and carries a riding-crop.* PETER'S *face is paler and more drawn than in Act Two; he seems to have aged; he is much more nervous.*) Miss Helen, it has been a week since I have been able to ask after your health.

HELEN (*abstractedly*). Has it been so long, Mr. Throstle? Forgive me, I thank you.

THROSTLE (*to* PETER). I trust, sir, that your first impressions of England have been confirmed by your—rides about our countryside?

PETER. I love England, sir.

THROSTLE. Such an unequivocal declaration warms one's heart. Some men are more backward in confessing their affections.

LADY ANNE (*hastily, coming to him; with forced lightness*). Dear Mr. Throstle, now do come into the drawing-room and tell me all the gossip. I always count on you for that! (THROSTLE *bows to* HELEN *and* PETER, *turns with* LADY ANNE L.)

THROSTLE. All the gossip that I hear, ma'am, seems confined to one topic.

LADY ANNE (*as they go out* L.). I've not stirred from the house these three days. (PETER *walks to console table, puts down whip.* TOM *walks* L., *turns at door, looks from* PETER *to* HELEN, *laughs and raises his hand to* PETER *as though drinking to him. Exit.*)

PETER (*comes down stage*). I'd like to wring the little sneak's neck for him.

HELEN. But, Peter, we don't really care about what they say.

PETER. Of course we're always together, Lady Anne keeps expecting me to say something—

HELEN (*a little strained*). You *are* happy with me, Peter?

PETER (*embracing her*). Divinely happy! This morning, in those enchanted Richmond woods——

HELEN. The sun on the red leaves!

PETER. Helen, dearest, forgive me. I don't want to drag in everyday, practical things into this dreamland we've been living in—

HELEN (*pleadingly*). Then don't, Peter! (*Turns, walks to window* R., *looking out.*) Come out into the Square. We mustn't lose even the twilight of this day that was made just for us!

PETER. That Throstle—they're *all* talking about us, now! We can't go on like this. Why did you make me promise not to tell them we love each other?

HELEN. You try to keep away from them all. And they know you do, Peter. (*She comes down* C. *from window.*)

PETER. Of course I try to keep away from them—to be with you. That's natural, isn't it?

HELEN. When you do have to talk to them you say things you shouldn't. Sometimes I'm afraid you'll even tell them—tell them the truth. (*Sits on settee.*)

PETER. Oh, Helen, don't bring back the thoughts that are a nightmare! Do you think I'm going out of my head? (*With laugh, sits* L. *of* HELEN.) If I did tell them, it would certainly send *them* out of theirs.

HELEN (*sadly*). Can't you think of it as I do, as a fairy story, and not as a nightmare? Don't you see the difference? They're both impossible, but fairy stories are beautiful and nightmares are ugly.

PETER. What is the end of every fairy tale?

HELEN (*murmurs*). And so they lived happily ever afterwards.

PETER. Then make this a *true* fairy story! Let me go to Lady Anne!

HELEN. How can I when, even though you love me, your mind and body ache to get back?

PETER. They don't, Helen, they don't; I adore the peace of old things, the quiet and the charm——

HELEN. You don't deceive me. 'Tis true that you were fond of what's left in your world of our poor little London that is here now. But I feel the loathing and contempt in your heart, and the fear! Your whole soul yearns for your own life.

PETER. Helen, how can it matter to me where I am or what world I'm in, if I have you with me?

HELEN. You're like an angel who should put off his wings and give up his heaven to live on earth with a girl who loves him.

PETER. Heaven! I thought of it when I lived in it as all raw nerves and clatter and ugliness.

HELEN. But you don't think that now as you look back on it, Peter. Oh, I've watched you, and you've let things slip. When you were talking of the thrill of speed you said we all live here with chains on our feet—and you said, if I thought your city was Paradise by day, I ought to see it in the winter evenings, when the lights come on—and even in the woods at Richmond you said you wished you had a cigarette!

PETER. Oh, curse cigarettes! Give me yourself and I can forget it all and be happy in our love.

HELEN (*suddenly*). Peter, did you sleep last night?

PETER (*taken aback*). Do people really *sleep,* in the eighteenth century?

HELEN (*distressed*). Oh, my love, I knew it!

PETER. Why, that's nothing at all, Helen. I shall be all right when I really have *you!*

HELEN (*sadly, doubtfully, murmurs—turns away*). When you have me.

PETER. My darling—the way you say that, as though it would never happen!—you make me afraid—tell me that you never think of this as a love of ghost for ghost! Even though you love me so, don't you think of me sometimes as a phantom who hasn't been born yet, as a shadow?

HELEN (*kisses him passionately*). Dear shadow!

PETER. Your kisses! You seem all spirit and white fire, not flesh and blood at all, excepting when you kiss me, and then I know that you want me as I want you, and that whatever else of terror and mystery there may be, our love is the old everlasting love of man and girl——

HELEN. Something more! (*Rises; turns from him.*) Perhaps something less!

PETER (*rises*). Not something less! We're going to live out our lives here together!

HELEN (*turns to him; embraces him*). I want to believe it. Peter! Make me believe it!

PETER. I will, Helen; I can and I will! I'll go to Lady Anne right away. (*Noise of coach.*) That's what I need: to feel that I've taken the plunge, that it's settled! And you want me, you need me too! Why else has this wonder happened? (*Door opens* L. *They disengage.* TOM *enters; looks from one to the other uneasily.*)

TOM. Too occupied to hear it, I suppose?

PETER. What do you mean?

TOM. Oh, a coach has stopped at the door. Someone has got out, that's all.

HELEN. Kate!

TOM (*chaffingly*). Gad, a fellow can't tell *you* two anything you don't already know! I wish I had second sight! (*Seriously.*) Better go in there and let me talk to her. She'll need a little preparation, eh, cousin? (HELEN *and* PETER *go out together.* TOM *strolls to mirror, adjusts cravat, humming, "Let schoolmasters puzzle their brains." Enter* KATE R. *in hat and traveling costume.* TOM, *affecting surprise.*) Gad's life! You! Better be scared to death in town than bored to death in the country, eh, sister? You'd never believe the luck I've had at White's the week you've been at Budleigh!

KATE. I know what has happened.

TOM. Oh, indeed? News travels fast, it seems. You've not developed second sight, too, by any chance?

KATE. Where is Mr. Standish?

TOM. *Mr.* Standish, is it now? Now look'ee, sister! I'd blame no woman for not having our Yankee mystery-monger. But, thank God, for all our sakes, there's someone who doesn't feel as you do, and now you're back, you *must* be civil to him.

KATE. Where is he?

TOM. He's where and with whom he should be. (*Looks out of window and exclaims with surprise.*) Gad's life, now the cat's come home the mice have scampered off! So, he opens the gate! The fountain plays in the Square! (*Mimicking* DUKE.) "A fine bair ov lofers!" (KATE *goes to window* R., *looks, turns, covers her face with hands.*) Eh, what's wrong with you?

KATE. This shall never be.

TOM (*angrily*). Who says so?

KATE. I say so!

TOM. Hell and damnation! First you put aside the settlement and ten thousand a year yourself; now, a week later, you post to town to stop Helen from bringing it into the family! (KATE *tugs bell-pull sharply. He follows her.*) Now, Kate, no mischief. 'Tis no more your affair.

KATE. I came back to save her. I'd rather see Helen in her coffin than the wife of Peter Standish!

TOM. 'Slife, if you set her against him!

KATE. So, because you've had his money and can't pay if we break with him, you'd see your sister damned!

TOM (*furious, but confused*). See my sister damned! You're my sister, and I say damn you— for not minding your own business. (*Enter* MAID R.)

KATE. Mr. Standish is walking in the Square with Miss Helen. Ask him to come here to me.

MAID. Yes, madam. (*Exits* R.)

TOM (*with ugly laugh*). We'll see what Mother has to say to your pretty scheme!

KATE. You think you're but selling Helen for money, as girls are sold every day.

TOM. Sell, indeed! The girl dotes on him!

KATE. Then she's bewitched, as I was!

TOM. As you *are,* you mean! There's to be no meddling, you hear me, no meddling!

LADY ANNE (*enters* L., *followed by* THROSTLE). Thomas! What, Kate, you here! (KATE *curtseys.* THROSTLE *bows.* LADY ANNE *turns to* THROSTLE, *expecting him to take his leave.*) Mr. Throstle——

KATE. Mr. Throstle, don't go—help me to save her! (KATE *sits on* L. *end of settee.* THROSTLE *bows and stays.*)

LADY ANNE (*angrily, to* KATE). What, have you not repented of your folly?

TOM (*speaks to* LADY ANNE). No, and she would commit worse folly. Won't have Peter herself, and now has him fetched here to tell him he shan't have Helen.

LADY ANNE (*to* THROSTLE). Dear sir, pray return to us when we are not in turmoil. (THROSTLE *bows uncertainly.*)

TOM (*suspiciously, to* KATE). Where did you hear all this?

KATE. Oh, Mr. Throstle, *you* understand —stay and help me!

THROSTLE. Madam, is ten thousand a year worth the loss of Miss Helen's happiness?

LADY ANNE. Eh, what's this, Mr. Throstle? Who speaks of loss of happiness?

TOM (*to* LADY ANNE). He's a party to

this; he's been writing to her about Helen!

LADY ANNE. Is this true, Mr. Throstle?

THROSTLE. Madam, Mr. Standish is no fit mate for any mortal woman.

KATE. You *know*, you *know!*

THROSTLE. God will not permit it.

LADY ANNE. What treachery is this, Mr. Throstle?

KATE (*crying*). I must open your eyes, ma'am. I came back to save her, and she's out there now—(*Gesture to window*)—with *that!* Oh, my poor sister! (*Sits on settee.*)

LADY ANNE (*turning to* TOM). Flight, and now conspiracy—my rebel daughter returns to ruin all our hopes, and all our prospects.

TOM (*in half whisper*). Throstle is concerned in this, ma'am. Be high with her, pack her off again, or she'll bedevil everything.

LADY ANNE. Leave her to me, Thomas.

TOM. Ma'am, with this Yankee—my God, anything might happen. They must marry at once.

(THROSTLE *walks to window* L.)

LADY ANNE. Helen fobs me off with distant answers.

TOM. I'd another hundred out of him last night. He'd not have lent me more, after Kate broke with him, had he not meant to have Helen. Press him, ma'am, press him!

LADY ANNE. Be calm, Thomas. This is in my hands. (*Advancing toward* KATE.) Kate, if you cannot master this strange perversity, you must return to Budleigh. (*Turns to* THROSTLE.) Sir, I beg you to carry your plots and stratagems elsewhere. (THROSTLE *bows; walks* L. *toward doors.*)

KATE. This marriage must not be!

LADY ANNE. What, hussy—"must not be"?

TOM. Now you see, ma'am! (*Sits before desk.*)

LADY ANNE (*walks up to* KATE *with dignity, before settee*). You will beg my pardon, miss, for this unheard-of insolence.

KATE (*stands her ground*). I told you I'd not have him, did I not love him. I did love him; he cast his spell on me, but God took pity and saved me.

LADY ANNE. More of this and I will have physicians to you.

(*Enter* MAID R. *announcing:*)

MAID. Major Clinton.

(*Enter* CLINTON R. *Looks about him in surprise, bows. Exit* MAID.)

LADY ANNE (*frigidly*). To what do we owe this wholly unexpected honour?

KATE. I asked him to come.

TOM. What's this, Clinton, are you in this damned conspiracy?

CLINTON. I know of no conspiracy, sir. Miss Pettigrew called at my house and asked me to follow her here.

LADY ANNE. For what purpose did she ask you to come, sir?

CLINTON. Miss Pettigrew insisted. But she made no mention of a general company. I could scarcely disoblige a lady, but I am conscious 'tis an absurd errand.

LADY ANNE. This fooling grows tedious, sir. What is your errand?

(*Enter* PETER R.)

KATE. Major Clinton, will you be good enough to ask your questions now?

LADY ANNE. Questions, what questions?

PETER (*walks up stage* R., *turns, looks about him like a man in a trap*). Ah, so the questions seem to have been agreed between you.

CLINTON. If I might speak but a word alone with Mr. Standish, I could then reassure Miss Pettigrew—

TOM. Gad's bones! Reassure her of what?

CLINTON (*much embarrassed*). Since I am forced to say it, that Mr. Standish is—that this gentleman is—my friend of the *General Wolfe*.

(LADY ANNE *and* TOM *leap up.*)

LADY ANNE. What lunacy is this?

PETER. It seems that my identity is challenged.

CLINTON. Not by me, sir, for all your strange behaviour since we landed.

LADY ANNE. You dare to come here, as the accomplice of this mad daughter of mine, to insult—

TOM (*interrupts*). Sir, you shall give me satisfaction, after Mr. Standish has called you to account!

CLINTON. If I'm to fight you, sir, you must invent another quarrel; I'll be no butt for the town wits.

LADY ANNE. You call yourself a gentleman—you wear the King's uniform—

CLINTON (*interrupts*). I'd rather face a Yankee battery than this hornet's nest—

PETER (*coming down stage between* CLINTON *and* TOM. *With hysterical laugh*). Or is it a mare's nest?

KATE. Question him!

CLINTON (*to* PETER). I intended only to set her mind at rest, by which I thought to earn your thanks. Miss Pettigrew, I protest I've not earned this treatment.

KATE. You white livered coward!

LADY ANNE. Take yourself off, sir!

CLINTON. My most abject apologies, madam.

(CLINTON *bows.* TOM *opens door for him, closes it behind him,* PETER *laughing hysterically.* THROSTLE *walks to window* R., *looks out.*)

KATE (*in front of settee*). Mr. Standish! When you came into this house, though the door was shut and locked, *did* you come from America?

LADY ANNE (*turning on her, furiously*). To your room! To your room, I say!

KATE (*to* LADY ANNE). I remain till I've had my answer. (*To* PETER.) Sir, do you *really* come from America?

PETER (*much upset by* KATE'S *direct attack*). I do. That's true. But, Kate——

KATE (*laughing hysterically*). I made a list of ten of his phrases. He said they were used in New York. On my way home I stopped at the Legation in Grosvenor Square. Should not the American Minister, Mr. Adams, know what words are used in New York?

PETER. He's from Massachusetts.

KATE. I asked him. He had never heard one of the ten! So you see, those words are not used in America! They are not used in England! They are not used in this world! (*Violently.*) The devils use them, in hell!

TOM. Hark'ee, Kate, you mad wench! That Throstle skulking over there, who is as mad as you now, spoke to Mr. Adams, and the Yankee Minister knew Peter in New York.

KATE. Peter Standish came from New York in the *General Wolfe*—his body stands there—(*To* PETER.)—but what have you done with *him?*

LADY ANNE. Poor abused cousin!

KATE (*turns on her*). In the old days he'd have been burned, he'd have been burned at the stake!

PETER. Why not now? You burn people still—you burn women!

LADY ANNE. Physicians, restraint, *confinement! Straps!*

PETER (*suddenly beside himself*). Yes, *and whips!* Whip her, if she's crazy, flog her in public, as you flog lunatics at Bedlam, flog them in public, with a crowd of your gaping Londoners looking on—you savages!

KATE. You have stolen his body, but what have you done with his *soul?*

PETER (*laughing hysterically*). "His soul goes marching on! John Brown's body lies a-mouldering in the grave."

TOM (*behind* PETER). She's out of her head. Never mind what she thinks about you!

PETER (*turning on him quickly*). And what do *you* think about me? (TOM *steps back.*) You daren't look me in the eyes, yet you'd marry me to your sister. D'you think I don't know why? You—a gentleman! Insolence, ignorance and dirt! Making a beast of yourself with drink and debauching servant girls! And you're no worse than your Prince—you are a typical English gentleman of your time—God! What a time! You and your friends know it all, don't they, Throstle? So you despise your rude barbarian forbears, do you? Well, we who know better, love them and despise you! No warmth in your blood, no soul in your art! God! What a Period! Dirt, disease cruelly, smells! A new fire of London, that's what's needed here; yes, and a new plague, too! God, how the Eighteenth Century stinks! You, Kate, may be a fool, but you're the best of the lot, for you're trying in your silly way to help Helen now, and I love you for it! (*Advances toward* LADY ANNE.) Madam, I've seen you in Sheridan's plays; I've read you in Jane Austin's novels. You know what you want, and you plough straight ahead over everything, through everything, like a tank, lumbering through the mud! (*Laughs wildly.*) You hear that, Kate! Like a tank lumbering through the mud. That's your eleventh word from the Lexicon of Beelzebub. Go to the American Legation and ask Charles Francis Adams what "tank" means! No, it's not Charles Francis Adams who's minister here now, it's his grandfather, John Adams, second President of the United States. Charles Francis Adams isn't born yet; he won't be born until the Civil War in 1861. What's one blunder among so many? Peter Standish came from New York to Plymouth in the *General Wolfe,* did he? Peter Standish came from New York to Plymouth in the *Mauretania!* Shall I make a few more blunders for you to gibber at? Shall I drive you back to Budleigh in my car, fifty miles an hour? No, not on a broomstick! (*To* LADY ANNE.) Shall I sell that portrait for you in America, madam, for thirty thousand pounds? (*Shouts as he turns and rushes up to tapestry.*) The Americans buy all the Reynoldses! (*Stops dead, arms outstretched, gazing at tapestry. The others exchange glances.* LADY ANNE *steps forward as though to go to him when he turns, shrinking back against console table.*) What do I care about you? You're all over and done with! (*Sidles along rear wall, afraid, grasping curtain of window for support.*) You're all dead—you've all rotted in your graves—you're all ghosts, that's what you are—ghosts! (KATE *turns quickly; exits* L., *followed by* LADY ANNE)

TOM (*runs after them*). God, she's going to Helen!

THROSTLE. Sir, a word with you! You have won her affections, as you could win those of any woman who did not fear you.

PETER. What the devil do you mean?

THROSTLE. Sir, you do not even intend to make her your wife?

PETER. You dead and buried little pipsqueak—— (*Seizes whip from console table, advancing on* THROSTLE, *who hastily turns, seizes candlesticks from desk.*) You dare to soil with your dirty mind——

THROSTLE (*turns as* PETER *is about to strike him, holding candlesticks in the form of the Cross*). Retro me, Sathanas.

THROSTLE. Adjuro ergo te, draco nequissime, in nomine agni immaculati. Adjuro ergo te, omnis immundissime spiritus, omne phantasma, omnis incursio satanae.

Exi ergo, impius, exi scelerate, exi cum omni fallacia tua, quia hominum templum suum esse voluit Deus——

Exi ergo, transgressor. Exi seductor, plene omnis doli et fallaciae, virtutis inimicus, innocentium prosecutor!

PETER (*stops, whip poised in midair, laughs hysterically; slings whip across room*). Ha! Exorcism! Throstle casts out the devil! Banned by bell, book and candle! You've got *two* candles, but where's your book, where's your bell? Most irregular! (*Pauses.* THROSTLE'S *phrases are heard alone for a moment. More violently.*) So you send me back to hell where I came from, do you? I'm to vanish in a clap of thunder, am I? (*Stands on toes, fingers crooked, towering over* THROSTLE *like Mephisto.*) Smell the brimstone, Throstle. Can't you smell the brimstone? Shall I take off my shoe and show you the cloven hoof? I'll set ten devils on you, damn your soul!

(*During latter part of scene,* THROSTLE *has retreated few steps toward door* R. PETER *wrenches away candlesticks, throws them to floor behind settee.* THROSTLE *with a hoarse scream, pulls door open, exits.*)

PETER (*turns, walks few steps almost to small table, then, head in hand, staggers to window, looks out. After pause. Quietly, voice shaking*). And I was in love with the past! (*Turns, walks to settee*) Is that a crime? Is it as bad as murder? It must be, for see what my sentence is—— imprisonment for life, for life, for life—— (*Sinks on settee, buries head in hands.*) in this filthy little pigsty of a world!

HELEN (*after pause, enter* HELEN L. *She sees* PETER'S *back; stops*). Peter! Is it you? (*He rises, back to her.*) Say you are not the other! (PETER *turns to her. She runs to him. They embrace before settee.*) I was afraid *he* had come.

PETER. He isn't here. He can't be. It takes us both to do it! (*Reproachfully.*) So you thought I might have *sneaked* back!

HELEN. No, no!

PETER. Then you've heard. You thought I'd do it while I was out of my head. Even if I *were* mad, I'd never leave you! I told them it's for life—for life! Let them stay there and be damned. I've made my choice.

HELEN. 'Tis beyond your strength.

PETER. You do not know my strength. Oh, Helen, Kate *knows* and Throstle——

HELEN. I know, Peter, they baited you. You told them how you hate their world, my world——

PETER. I was blaspheming, since you are part of it.

HELEN. You told them how you feel buried alive—among the dead. And now, you can never see them again.

PETER. We'll go away together! To

America!

HELEN. People would hate and fear you, anywhere.

PETER. Why should they hate me?

HELEN. They hate what they fear, just as you fear and hate them, my changeling.

PETER. I can face them all, for you belong to me, not them. Kiss me.

HELEN (*gently repulses him*). I'm strong now. Don't make me weak again! (*Sinks on settee.*) Each night I've said, "He must go back!" But each morning, when we'd ride away together, I'd think, "Let me have only one more day!"

PETER. No, we're going to tell them—— (*Sits by her.*) You agreed, Helen!

HELEN. My darling, I've known that you must go. Except when to be with you made me a coward again, when I let you convince me, only because I *wanted* to be convinced. But *after this*——

PETER. Don't Helen! I was a fool, a weakling. It won't happen again. I couldn't face my own life without you.

HELEN. What life is this for you? Be brave, Peter, and listen! My life, my London, are nightmares to you. No sad thoughts now, my Peter. We two alone have been chosen for this wonder out of all the millions of lovers since time began. Our love is against nature, you said, and so it can't be real; but it *is* real, more real, Peter, than if you had been born in my world, or I in yours, because—it is a miracle. Think of what has been given us, not of what is taken away!

PETER. Nothing can be taken away; that we have come together at all, doesn't that prove that we weren't meant to lose each other?

HELEN. Yes, yes, and we shall be together always, Peter—not in my time, nor in yours, but in God's.

PETER. Yes, but Helen, I want you *now* —this is our one life on earth!

HELEN. *Our* life on earth? Oh, Peter, think more clearly!

PETER (*turns to her*). You can't want me to go back! You love me!

HELEN. With all my soul.

PETER. Then I stay here!

HELEN (*rises*). Stay, then, Peter! "For life—for life"—a life of nightmare that never ends! So that I may watch you in torment, when I cannot help you! So that you may live on in my world, in a living death, *mad!* (*Kneels beside him.*) Because you love me, you condemn me to *that?* (PETER *buries his face on her shoulder.*) You *do* see it! Leave me, while our love is still beautiful! I ask it for *my* sake. (*She rises. Pause.* PETER *rises; turns slowly; takes a few mechanical steps toward the panel where the picture hangs in 1928. He stops, then goes up to console table, extends his hands to the panel, in gesture of surrender.*)

PETER (*turns, leaning against console table*). But now *he* will be here, in my place, with my body! How can *you* bear *that?*

HELEN. Love will give me strength. (*Turns away, head in hands, as he walks slowly down front, looking out. She speaks half over her shoulder.*) You've your life to live out in the future, Peter. Don't be too sad there about a girl who's been dead so long. (*Turns to face him.*) As I grow old, your youth will seem to me eternal youth, for you *will* come, won't you, young as I see you now, to my grave in St. Mark's churchyard? To you, that will be tomorrow. And yet, 'twill be generations after I am dead. I'll ask for a stone with the letters cut deep, so they won't wear away, before you come to me. And you must come—alone.

PETER. Alone?

HELEN (*turns away*). But if you love that girl, you must marry her.

PETER. Don't, don't!

HELEN (*turns to him again*). You *can't* live in this house with only that old woman to look after you. When that happens I shall be—— And yet, I *am* jealous, even though I *will* be dead.

PETER. I love you only, now and in my own time and in whatever other times may come. (HELEN *takes three steps toward him, coming to just beyond small table.*)

HELEN. I believe. Forgive me. (*The afternoon light has been gradually dimming. Clock on landing strikes once. They both start; he steps back; stops as* HELEN *speaks.*) If only you could take back with you just one thing that was mine! (*Turns, opens drawer in small table, takes out Crux Ansata.*) Father got this in Egypt, while the fleet was there. In some strange way it has meant so much to me. (PETER *looks up slowly.*)

PETER (*overwhelmed*). The Crux Ansata!

HELEN (*during this they are separated by four feet*). What is it?

PETER. The symbol of Life, and of

Eternity!

HELEN. Then that's why I loved it so.

PETER. Helen! This was mine—long ago!

HELEN. Yours—long ago?

PETER (*points*). It was standing over there, when I first entered this room—in the Future. (*It has now grown dusk.*)

HELEN. This little thing—has crossed the great darkness between us. Mine while I live, yours in the world that I shall never see. (PETER *steps toward her; she holds out the Crux Ansata as though to ward him off, and takes step backward.*) *This* was our parting! (PETER *walks backward toward door* R., *slowly and mechanically. Door opens.* LADY ANNE *enters, stops and exclaims violently on seeing* PETER. *She is terrified, and for the first time.*)

LADY ANNE. Eh—what—*you here!* I saw you as I came up, drinking with Tom in the study! How, then, are you here before me?

PETER (*slowly as in a trance—still looking at* HELEN). I passed you on the stairs as you turned your head.

LADY ANNE (*accepting his explanation*). I vow you run like a cat. (PETER *backs out* R., *as* LADY ANNE *is crossing to settee and picking up candlesticks.* PETER *closes door as she puts them on the table. She closes drawer in table; sits.* HELEN *still motionless.*) Why have you brought out that ugly old Egyptian thing?

HELEN (*walks up stage to* L. *of window* R., *turns, holds Crux Ansata in front of her against her breast and looks fixedly out front.*) No more, dear shadows! (LADY ANNE *glances at* HELEN.)

LADY ANNE. Frenzy from them, moonshine from you! He seemed quiet. Are his wits then restored? (*Pause.* HELEN *standing looking fixedly before her.*) Are you not well, child? (*Pause.* TOM *enters* R.; *looks from one to the other importantly. Stops near door.*)

TOM. God's life, what an afternoon! Two lunatics in one house are too many for any man's stomach. God knows what devilment Kate will concoct when she's up to it again, but I've one piece of good news for you he's just been telling me in the study, poor devil. He's been ill, ever since he came here. (*Tapping forehead.*) Can't remember a thing that's happened. Didn't even remember me. Gaped at me and said, "Mr. Pettigrew, I presume?"

LADY ANNE (*up and comes* C. *front.* TOM *meets her* C.). Oh, then his wits must be quite, quite gone!

TOM. But no, ma'am; they've come back! He's cured! That frenzy in here was but the end of a fever. 'Twas only the fever made his brain work oddly, so that everyone feared him—he's like one of us now. (*Pauses, turns and looks out, puzzled.*) That's it—*one of us!*

LADY ANNE (*relieved*). Ah! And now may God's mercy remember Kate as well! (*Comes* L. *to doors.*) I said all along 'twas superstitious gabble. (*As she goes out* L.) A fever, poor dear man!

TOM. I never could make the fellow swallow above half a bottle. And now he's laid me five guineas—he'll drink me under the table! (*Looks out door* R.) Here he comes upstairs!

HELEN. Leave *me* alone with him!

TOM. *You!* 'Tis Kate he wants to see! (*Exits* R., *closing door, calling in boisterous chaff.*) You Yankee mystery-monger!

HELEN (*repeats mechanically*). One of us—now! (*The doorknob* R. *turns. The door opens slowly.* HELEN *turns to door; curtseys slowly as the curtain falls.*)

SCENE II

The curtain rises in 1928 at the relative moment when it fell on the preceding scene in 1784. Scene set as in Act I, Scene II. Portrait hangs as before. Curtains closed. One candle burning on desk; two on small table between couch and armchair. No other lights, excepting from the fire. Light switch hangs from wall near door R. *by torn wires. Crux Ansata on writing-table.*

MARJORIE *and* AMBASSADOR *are shown in* R. *by* MRS. BARWICK, *who is talking volubly as she enters.*

MRS. BARWICK. —but it wasn't anything definite he said, miss; it was the tone of his voice and the way he looked at me when he was going out, sir, as though he was seeing the last of me. That was why I took the liberty of telephoning the Embassy, your Excellency.

AMBASSADOR (*interrupting*). Quite right, too, Mrs. Barwick, even if it turns out a false alarm. You've had the patience of Job, and nobody will appreciate it so much as Mr. Standish when he's well again. But why are you using candles all over the house. Can't we talk this over better if we have some real light?

MRS. BARWICK. It's no good, your Excellency, the lights aren't working.

MARJORIE (*impatiently*). Oh, dear, what does that matter?

MRS. BARWICK. He did it himself, sir; he tore out this fitting last night—(*Handles broken and dangling light switch.*)—Then he smashed the main switchboard downstairs.

AMBASSADOR. But when this thing first came on him he was *fascinated* by the light. Kept turning it on and off.

MARJORIE. Oh, Mr. Ambassador, we didn't come here to talk about electric light! We've got to find him right away before anything can happen to him.

AMBASSADOR. There, there, my dear, I'm sure he's all right, wherever he is.

MARJORIE. Now pull yourself together, Mrs. Barwick—(AMBASSADOR *sits in armchair.*)—and try and be clear and definite. How long has he been gone?

MRS. BARWICK. I heard the clock strike the quarter, miss, as he went downstairs and out the front door.

MARJORIE (*sits on settee*). This is terrible; it was wicked to leave him alone here when he was so ill; we ought to have sent him where he can be taken care of.

AMBASSADOR. My dear, I've been in touch with Sir William Briggs all along, but Peter has been one too many for us. He won't give himself away to the doctors—

MARJORIE. Won't give himself away! Why, those drunken scrapes, when he shouts old curses and drinking songs, his gambling and scattering I O U's all over London, telling people that he's ten thousand pounds a year but some other man has got hold of all his money—*surely,* any doctor with a grain of sense——

AMBASSADOR. Ah, no, Marjorie, of course we who know Peter—but to convince others there must be some definite symptoms.

MARJORIE. Anyway, we've got to find him now; we must follow him!

AMBASSADOR. But we haven't anything to go on yet. You mustn't be so upset, Marjorie. Of course he'll come back. Where could he go? And he didn't even say he wasn't coming back. Now, Mrs. Barwick, has anything in particular happened since I was here?

MRS. BARWICK. Well, sir, some people came from a night club. He was shouting at them, sir. I—I listened, sir. I thought it my duty, sir, so I could tell you, sir.

AMBASSADOR. Oh, quite right, Mrs. Barwick.

MRS. BARWICK. He yelled at them, sir. He said they weren't alive and they wouldn't be born for another hundred years. And when they laughed at him he hit one of them and then they went away and I found him drunk on the floor, Miss. (*Cries.*)

(*Door* R. *opens slowly.* PETER *comes in carrying a sheet of paper. He wears a lounge suit. He looks pale and dazed and, without seeing the others, lays the paper down on writing-bureau, placing the Crux Ansata on it.*)

PETER (*turns*). Mr. Ambassador!

AMBASSADOR. I just thought I'd look in, Peter. I've taken the liberty of bringing a great friend of mine——

PETER (*goes toward settee*). Marjorie!

MARJORIE (*steps toward him*). Peter! You know me! (*Holds up her face for him to kiss.* PETER *kisses her hand.*)

PETER. Of course. (*To* MRS. BARWICK.) Mrs. Barwick, I'm afraid—Peter Standish—has been giving you a lot of trouble.

MRS. BARWICK (*delighted*). Oh, sir, it's all right now! (*She goes out.*)

PETER (*to* AMBASSADOR). So you think I'm still the other man?

AMBASSADOR (*looks at portrait, back again to* PETER). I'm blessed if I know what I think.

MARJORIE (*overjoyed*). It's all right *now,* Mr. Ambassador!

PETER. Mr. Ambassador, all my thanks for your kindness! If you'll forgive me, I must talk to Marjorie now.

AMBASSADOR (*disturbed*). Don't you think perhaps——

PETER. You may take it that I'm myself again.

AMBASSADOR. I'll go over in the corner with a book.

MARJORIE. Please go; you understand, you—if you weren't an Ambassador I'd call you old darling.

AMBASSADOR (*reluctantly, to* MARJORIE). I'll wait downstairs.

(*Exit* AMBASSADOR R. *A pause.*)

PETER. We were going to be married. It seems so very long ago.

MARJORIE (*happily*). You remember!

PETER (*his head turns toward portrait*). The Ambassador came here and found—

MARJORIE. He found my poor Peter

ill, but now he's cured.

PETER. I'm incurable.

MARJORIE. You *are* cured. If you remember me, you can't think any longer that—(*Gesture to portrait.*)—you're—*him*.

PETER (*distressed*). You couldn't marry me after this, could you?

MARJORIE. Never mind that now, Peter. I'm here to take care of you.

PETER. Marjorie! Something has happened, something you could never believe. And now I must live here—alone.

MARJORIE (*after a pause, turns away, her voice shaking*). In this house, with only your old woman? Why, the place can't even be kept clean.

PETER. I'll shut up most of it.

MARJORIE. Peter, you know you can't afford it.

PETER. No—but I'll keep this room—(*As though to himself*) —just as it was, *always*.

MARJORIE. Even when you're well you can't look after yourself. (*She sees his distress and begins again in a different voice.*) Never mind, Peter. But I can't break an old habit. I shall go on looking after you, even if it's from a long way off.

PETER. I feel such a beast.

MARJORIE (*sure of herself by now*). It's all right. (*Crosses to desk.*) Tell me about your work. (*Crosses to writing-bureau.*) This used to be over there. (*She takes the Crux Ansata, walks with it towards console table.* PETER *turns, almost snatches it from her, comes down to small table; puts it down; sits in armchair.* MARJORIE, *astonished and hurt.*) Why, Peter, what's the matter? (*Then turns and ruffles papers on writing-bureau.*) Is this the draft for your new architecture book? May I look? (*Picks up paper.*) Why, here's an epitaph.

PETER. I copied it, just now, from a tombstone in St. Mark's churchyard.

MARJORIE (*coming to him with a paper*). Whose epitaph is it?

PETER. A girl who died one hundred and forty-one years ago.

MARJORIE. Who was she?

PETER. A cousin of Peter Standish.

MARJORIE (*looking at paper*). It's Latin. What's it all mean? (*Extends paper to him.* PETER *takes it mechanically.*) Peter! You're crying! Who was that girl who's been dead for ages? Peter, speak to me! (*Turns away; turns again to him.*) Don't you know me, Peter? (*Moves toward door* R., *hesitates, turns to him again.*) You want me to go?

PETER. "Here lies, in the confident hope of the blessed resurrection, and life eternal, Helen Pettigrew, beloved younger daughter of Sir William Pettigrew, K.B., Vice-Admiral of the Blue, and the Lady Anne Pettigrew, who departed this life June the fifteenth, 1787, aged twenty-three years—" (*His voice breaks down. The paper falls to the floor.* PETER *remains motionless in the same pose for some moments before the curtain falls slowly.*)

In America the one-act play was not taken seriously until the rise of the little theatres. Until about 1910 one-acters, it is true, were played, but they were used only as curtain-raisers or added to a play in order to lengthen the evening; and naturally, they had a place in vaudeville. But in this lowly estate they had to be either farcical or melodramatic, and in neither case were they expected to have dramatic distinction of any sort. It was sufficient if they were funny or thrilling enough for the trade. Edward Harrigan wrote at least seventy-five low-comedy pieces for the Harrigan and Hart variety shows during the 1870's. Only occasionally did a serious playwright try his hand, as did Bronson Howard in *Old Love Letters* back in 1878, Augustus Thomas (although his dozen contributions have made no impression as dramatic literature), Clyde Fitch who wrote three one-acters in the 1890's (*Frederick Lemaître, Betty's Finish, The Harvest*), Brander Matthews, William Gillette, Richard Harding Davis, and the novelist William Dean Howells, who found a place for his brief compositions in *The Atlantic Monthly* and *Harper's*. Some of the latter, especially *The Mouse Trap* and *The Garroters,* alone have some standing as literature.

It was otherwise across the Atlantic, where one-acters had been cultivated for a long time and received considerable literary attention. When the modern movement developed, one-acters were freely used by Antoine in the *Théâtre Libre,* and that great pioneer of modernity August Strindberg even made a specialty of the short form in the interests of concentration upon the essence of his type of drama, which highlighted character conflict. Chekhov, Schnitzler, and Maeterlinck mastered the one-act form. Modern Irish theatre was largely weaned on the one-act play through the varied exertions of William Butler Yeats, Lady Gregory, and John Millington Synge.

The little theatres followed suit, and the number of American one-acters would fill at least fifty volumes. Among the important pioneering collections are two volumes of *Harvard Dramatic Club Plays* (1918-1919), four of *Plays of the 47 Workshop* (1918-25), and *Wisconsin Plays,* 1914, 1918. George Pierce Baker's classes turned out numerous one-acters, and so did the classes of all his successors, particularly those of Frederick H. Koch at the University of North Carolina and Professor A. M. Drummond at Cornell University. The programs of the Provincetown Players and the Washington Square Players at first consisted of foreign and domestic playlets, the latter specially written for the company by its members. For the Provincetown, O'Neill, Susan Glaspell, Edna St. Vincent Millay, Alfred Kreymborg, and many others wrote unique short pieces, as different in type and style as O'Neill's *Ile* and Millay's *Aria da Capo*.

O'Neill's *Ile* (1917) is inferior to the best of his sea-pieces *The Long Voyage Home* and *The Moon of the Caribbees* (1918), but it proved to be his most powerful independent one-acter. The other two, combined with *Bound East for Cardiff* (1916) and *In the Zone* (1917), were collectively produced on Broadway under the title of *S.S. Glencairn*. A rather frantic effort, indicative of his melodramatic bent, was *Where the Cross Is Made,* while *The Dreamy Kid,* in 1919, was an affecting play and foreshadowed his full-length Negro dramas. O'Neill even tried a monologue in the Strindberg manner, *Before Breakfast,* in 1916. It is significant of O'Neill's fascination with the one-act art form, perhaps under the influence of Strindberg and undoubtedly because of the unity of atmosphere and concept the form could provide for his fertile imagination, that even his full-length play *Emperor Jones* is, technically, a one-act play. And, fundamentally, so is *The Hairy Ape*.

Edna St. Vincent Millay's allegiance was, of course, to her poetry. But in addition to *Aria da Capo* she wrote one other effective playlet for the Provincetown, *Two Slatterns and a King,* and her fellow-poet Alfred Kreymborg turned out the highly original *Lima Beans* and *Manikin and Minikin.*

Particularly effective as a one-act writer among the Provincetown pioneers was Susan Glaspell (1882-1946) whose *Trifles* became a classic of the little theatre here and abroad. Her other pieces for the group were *Suppressed Desires* and *Tickless Time,* written with the Provincetown director George Cram Cook. Later Miss Glaspell was to write a number of full-length dramas, among them *The Verge* (1921) and *Chains of Dew* for the Provincetown, *The Inheritors,* which was successfully produced in 1927 by Eva Le Gallienne's Civic Repertory Theatre, and the Emily Dickinson drama *Alison's House,* another Le Gallienne production which won the Pulitzer Prize in 1931. Miss Glaspell also published novels, the first in 1909, and her playwriting career appears to have been primarily the result of her activity as a co-founder of the Provincetown Players on Cape Cod.

Equally hospitable to the short play, the Washington Square Players inspired Lawrence Langner's *Licensed* and *Another Way Out,* Philip Moeller's historical spoof *Helena's Husband,* Alice Gerstenberg's psychological, split-personality comedy *Overtones,* and *The Clod* by Lewis Beach, who published four one-acters in 1921 and later won a popular success with the full-length comedy *The Goose Hangs High.*

Remarkably fruitful in the one-act field was the regional theatre throughout the country. One of its best products was the novelist Zona Gale's touching, if somewhat overextended piece *Neighbors,* produced by the Wisconsin Players and published in their first volume in 1914. And as late as 1928 the Mid-West could engender the talent of E. P. Conkle, associate of E. C. Mabie at the University of Iowa and now professor at the University of Texas. Mr. Conkle's *Minnie Field,* with its acute understatement and affecting economy, is a masterpiece, but his entire volume of one-acters, *Crick Bottom Plays,* constitutes high artistry. Mr. Conkle, a Baker graduate from Yale, has also written a number of long folk plays produced in local theatres. He graduated to Broadway with two honorable plays, *Two Hundred Were Chosen* and the Abraham Lincoln drama *Prologue to Glory,* produced in the late 30's.

The most important regional one-act practitioner, however, has been Paul Green, who is, of course, not limited to that practice. A student of Frederick H. Koch, as well as a teacher of philosophy at the University of North Carolina and a native son of that state (he was born on a farm near the village of Lillington in 1894), Mr. Green drew dramatic sustenance from the land. *White Dresses* is only one of his many one-acters (a number of them were published under the title of *The Lonesome Road* and *In the Valley,* 1928), but it well represents his humane concern with the common people's sufferings and aspirations. Another small masterpiece of his is *The No 'Count Boy,* which won the Belasco trophy in the Little Theatre Tournament of 1925. Paul Green's absorption in the one-act form is even evident in his first full-length Broadway production. *In Abraham's Bosom,* with which he won the Pulitzer Prize of 1927, is a chronicle of Negro life told in a series of episodes, each of which is a completed one-act drama. Inspired by his love of folk theatre, Mr. Green wrote a number of dance-dramas, one of which nearly won the calloused heart of Broadway (*Roll Sweet Chariot*), and wrote several pageants on Southern historical themes like *The Lost Colony* and *The Highland Call* that became regional events of great interest. His second play for Broadway, *The Field God,* did not fare well, but his drama of social stress in the South, *The House of Connelly,* was a memorable production of the 1931-32 season, his treatment of a pacifistic idealist's disillusionment *Johnny Johnson* was in this writer's opinion the most original and moving play of the 1936-37 season, and his later dramatization of Richard Wright's novel *Native Son* was equally noteworthy. Faithful, nevertheless, to the one-act play, Mr. Green gave us one of the most powerful short plays in the English language, *Hymn to the Rising Sun,* a chain-gang drama almost unbearably painful and nevertheless poetic in the writing. This excoriation of a social evil reached the Civic Repertory Theatre in New York in 1936. In fine, Mr. Green is a superb artist and a good man to have in any country.

The devotee of the one-act play will, of course, have to take note of many other writers who cannot even be mentioned here. But this report cannot close without drawing attention to the many compositions of George Middleton (*Embers,* 1911; *Tradition,* 1913; *Possession,* 1915; *Masks,* 1920) and Percival Wilde (*Dawn and Other Plays,* 1915, etc.). Individual playlets widely performed are Austin Strong's *The Drums of Oude* and *The Valiant* by Hall and Middlemass. George Kelly's *Poor Aubrey* is particularly important as the first sketch for the same author's comedy *The Show-Off,* but it is also a self-contained superior example of one-act farce, here written on a level of satire rarely attained by the little farces of an earlier American period.

The short play continued to be composed with distinction, as well as in profusion, after 1930, and it even acquired modifications in form and tone, as in *Waiting for Lefty, Bury the Dead,* and *The Cradle Will Rock.* The authors, Clifford Odets, Irwin Shaw, and Marc Blitzstein, owed their introduction as professional playwrights to off-Broadway productions of these strident, multi-scene, and semi-expressionist one-acters—repeating the experiences of O'Neill, Green, and Susan Glaspell. The seeds planted by the little theatre movement have obviously borne fruit, and even Broadway gleaned some of the harvest.

The Clod

BY LEWIS BEACH

First produced and staged by The Harvard Dramatic Club on March 31, 1914.

CHARACTERS

THADDEUS TRASK
MARY TRASK
A NORTHERN PRIVATE
A SOUTHERN SERGEANT
A SOUTHERN PRIVATE

SCENE.—*The kitchen of a farmhouse on the borderline between the Northern and Southern states. It is ten o'clock in the evening, September, 1863.*

The back wall is broken at stage left by the projection at right angles of a partially enclosed staircase; the four steps leading to the landing cut into the room. Underneath the enclosed part of the stairway, a cubby-hole; in front of it a small table which partially hides the door. To the left of the table a kitchen chair. A door, leading to the yard, is the centre of the unbroken wall, back. To the right of the door, a cupboard; to the left, a small cooking-stove. Two windows in the right wall. Between them a bench on which a pail and a tin dipper stand. Above the bench a towel hanging on a nail, and above the towel a double-barrelled shotgun suspended on two pegs. Well downstage left, a closed door leading to a second room. In the centre of the kitchen a large table; straight-backed chairs to the right and left of it. A lighted candle on this table.

The moon shines into the room through the windows, but at no time is the kitchen brightly lighted. The characters appear as silhouettes except when they stand near the candle or the lantern, and then the lights throw huge shadows on the roughly plastered walls. When the door, back, is opened one sees a bit of the farmyard, desolate even in the moonlight.

(*As the curtain rises,* THADDEUS TRASK, *a man of sixty odd years, short and thickset, slow in speech and action, yet in perfect health, sits at the left of the centre table. He is pressing tobacco into his corncob pipe. He lights it with the candle.*

After a moment, MARY TRASK, *a tired, emaciated woman, whose years equal her husband's, enters from the yard carrying a heavy pail of water and a lighted lantern. She puts the pail on the bench and hangs the lantern above it; then crosses to the stove.*)

MARY. Ain't got wood 'nough fer breakfast, Thad.

THADDEUS. I'm too tired t' go out now. Wait 'til mornin'.

(*Pause.* MARY *lays the fire in the stove.*)

THADDEUS. Did I tell yuh that old man Reed saw three Southern troopers pass his house this mornin'?

MARY (*takes coffee-pot from stove, crosses to bench, fills pot with water*). I wish them soldiers would git out o' the neighborhood. Whenever I see 'em passin', I have t' steady myself 'gainst somethin' or I'd fall. I couldn't hardly breathe yesterday when them Southerners came after fodder. I'd died if they'd spoke t' me.

THADDEUS. Yuh needn't be afraid o' Northern soldiers.

MARY (*carries coffee-pot to stove*). I hate 'em all,—Union or Southern. I can't make head or tail t' what all this fightin's 'bout. An' I don't care who wins, so long as they git through, an' them soldiers stop stealin' our corn an' potatoes.

THADDEUS. Yuh can't hardly blame 'em if they're hungry, ken yuh?

MARY. It ain't right that they should steal from us poor folk. (*Lifts a huge gunny sack of potatoes from the table, and begins setting the table for breakfast, getting knives, forks, spoons, plates, cups and saucers,—two of each, from the cupboard.*) We have hard 'nough times t' make things meet now. I ain't set down onct today 'cept fer meals. An' when I think o' the work I got t' do t'morrow, I ought t' been in bed hours ago.

THADDEUS. I'd help if I could, but it ain't my fault if the Lord seed fit t' lay me up so I'm always ailin'. (*Rises lazily.*) Yuh better try an' take things easy t'morrow.

MARY. It's well enough t' say, but them apples is got t' be picked an' the rest o' the potatoes sorted. If I could sleep at night it'd be all right, but with them soldiers 'bout, I can't.

THADDEUS (*crosses right; fondly handles his gun*). Jolly, wish I'd see a flock o' birds.

MARY (*nervously*). I'd rather go without than hear yuh fire. I wish yuh didn't keep it loaded.

THADDEUS. Yuh know I ain't got time t' stop an' load when I see the birds. They don't wait fer yuh. (*Hangs gun on wall, drops into his chair; dejectedly.*) Them pigs has got t' be butchered.

MARY. Wait 'til I git a chance t' go t' sister's. I can't stand it t' hear 'em squeal.

THADDEUS (*pulling off his boots: grunting meanwhile*). Best go soon then, 'cause they's fat as they'll ever be, an' there ain't no use in wastin' feed on 'em. (*Pause, rises.*) Ain't yuh most ready fer bed?

MARY. Go on up.

(THADDEUS *takes the candle in one hand, his boots in the other, and climbs the stairs.* MARY *speaks when he reaches the landing.*)

MARY. An' Thad, try not t' snore t'night.

THADDEUS. Poke me if I do. (*Disappears.*)

(MARY *fills the kettle with water and puts it on the stove; closes the door, back; takes the lantern from the wall and tries twice before she succeeds in blowing it out. Puts the lantern on the table before the cubby-hole. Slowly drags herself up the stairs, pausing a moment on the top step for breath before she disappears. There is a silence. Then the door, back, is opened a trifle and a man's hand is seen. Cautiously the door is opened wide and a young* NORTHERN PRIVATE *stands silhouetted on the threshold. He wears a dirty uniform, and a bloody bandage is tied about his head. He is wounded, sick, and exhausted. He stands at the door a moment, listening intently; then hastily moves to the centre table looking for food. He bumps against a chair and mutters an oath. Finding nothing on the table, he hurries to the cupboard. Suddenly the galloping of horses is heard in the distance. The* NORTHERNER *starts. Then rushes to the window nearer the audience. For a moment the sound ceases, then it begins again, growing gradually louder and louder. The* NORTHERNER *hurries into the room at the left. Horses and voices are heard in the yard, and almost immediately heavy, thundering knocks sound on the door, back. The men at the door grow impatient and push the door open. A large, powerfully built* SOUTHERN SERGEANT, *and a smaller, younger* TROOPER *of the same army enter.* THADDEUS *appears on the stairs, carrying a candle.*)

SERGEANT (*to* THADDEUS; *not unkindly*). Sorry, my friend, but you were so darn slow 'bout openin' the door that we had to walk in. Has there been a Northern soldier round here today?

THADDEUS (*timidly*). I ain't seed one. (*Comes down the stairs.*)

SERGEANT. Have you been here all day?

THADDEUS. I ain't stirred from the place.

SERGEANT. Call the rest of your family down.

THADDEUS. My wife's all there is. (*Goes to foot of stairs, and calls loudly and excitedly.*) Mary! Mary! Come down. Right off!

SERGEANT. You better not lie to me or it'll go tough with you.

THADDEUS. I swear I ain't seed no one.

(MARY *comes downstairs slowly. She is all atremble.*)

THADDEUS. Say, Mary, you was here—

SERGEANT. Keep still, man. I'll do the talkin'. (*To* MARY.) You were here at the house all day?

(MARY *is very frightened and embarrassed, but after a moment manages to nod her head slowly.*)

SERGEANT. You didn't take a trip down to the store?

(MARY *shakes her head slowly.*)

SERGEANT. Haven't you got a tongue?

MARY (*with difficulty*). Y-e-s.

SERGEANT. Then use it. The Northern soldier who came here a while ago was pretty badly wounded, wasn't he?

MARY. I—I—no one's been here.

SERGEANT. Come, come, woman, don't lie.

(MARY *shows a slight sign of anger.*)

SERGEANT. He had a bad cut in his forehead, and you felt sorry for him, and gave him a bite to eat.

MARY (*haltingly*). No one's been near the house t'day.

SERGEANT (*trying a different tone*). We're not going to hurt him, woman. He's a friend of ours. We want to find him, and put him in a hospital, don't we, Dick? (*Turning to his companion.*)

DICK. He's sick and needs to go to bed for a while.

MARY. He ain't here.

SERGEANT. What do you want to lie for?

MARY (*quickly*). I ain't lyin'. I ain't seed no soldier. (*She stands rooted to the spot where she stopped when she came downstairs. Her eyes are still fixed on the* SERGEANT.)

SERGEANT. I reckon you know what'll happen to you if you are hidin' the spy.

THADDEUS. There ain't no one here. We both been here all day, an' there couldn't no one come without our knowin' it. What would they want round here anyway?

SERGEANT. We'll search the place, Dick.

MARY (*quickly*). Yuh ain't got no—

SERGEANT (*sharply*). What's that, woman?

MARY. There ain't no one here, an' yer keepin' us from our sleep.

SERGEANT. Your sleep? This is an affair of life and death. Get us a lantern.

(THADDEUS *moves to the small table and lights the lantern with the candle which he holds in his hand. He gives the lantern to the* SERGEANT.)

SERGEANT (*noticing the door to the cubby-hole*). Ha! Tryin' to hide the door, are you, by puttin' a table in front of it? You can't fool me. (*To* THADDEUS.) Pull the table away and let's see what's behind the door.

THADDEUS. It's a cubby-hole an' ain't been opened in years.

SERGEANT (*sternly and emphatically*). I said to open the door.

(THADDEUS *sets the candle on the larger table, moves the smaller table to the right, and opens the door to the cubby-hole.* MARY *is angry. The* SERGEANT *takes a long-barrelled revolver from his belt and peers into the cubby-hole.*)

SERGEANT (*returning his revolver to his belt.*) We're goin' to tear this place to pieces 'til we find him. You might just as well hand him over now.

MARY. There ain't no one here.

SERGEANT. All right. Now we'll see. Dick, you stand guard at the door.

(DICK *goes to the door, back, and stands gazing out into the night,—his back to the audience.*)

SERGEANT (*to* THADDEUS). Come along, man. I'll have to look at the upstairs. (*To* MARY.) You sit down in that chair. (*Points to chair at right of centre table, and feels for a sufficiently strong threat.*) Don't you stir or I'll—I'll set fire to your house. (*To* THADDEUS.) Go on ahead.

(THADDEUS *and the* SERGEANT *go upstairs.* MARY *sinks lifelessly into the chair. She is the picture of fear. She sits facing left. Suddenly she leans forward. She opens her eyes wide, and draws her breath sharply. She opens her mouth as though she would scream, but makes no sound. The* NORTHERNER *has opened the door. He enters slowly and cautiously, his gun pointed at* MARY. (DICK *cannot see him because of the jog in the wall.*) MARY *only stares in bewilderment at the* NORTHERNER, *as he, with eyes fixed appealingly on her, opens the door to the cubby-hole and crawls inside.*)

DICK. Woman!

MARY (*almost with a cry, thinking that* DICK *has seen the* NORTHERNER). Yes.

DICK. Have you got an apple handy? I'm starved.

(MARY *rises and moves to the cupboard. The* SERGEANT *and* THADDEUS *come downstairs. The* SERGEANT, *seeing that* MARY *is not where he left her, looks about rapidly and discovers her at the cupboard.*)

SERGEANT. Here, what did I tell you I'd do if you moved from that chair?

MARY (*terrified*). Oh, I didn't—I only —he wanted—

DICK. It's all right, Sergeant. I asked her to get me an apple.

SERGEANT. Take this lantern and search the barn.

(DICK *takes the lantern from the* SERGEANT *and goes out, back.*)

SERGEANT (*to* THADDEUS). Come in here with me.

(*The* SERGEANT *picks up the candle. He and* THADDEUS *move toward the door, left. As though in a stupor,* MARY *starts to follow.*)

SERGEANT. Sit down!

(MARY *drops into the chair at the right of the table. The* SERGEANT *and* THADDEUS *go into the room, left. They can be heard moving furniture about.* MARY *sees a pin on the floor. She stoops, picks it up, and fastens it in her belt. The* SERGEANT *and* THADDEUS *return.*)

SERGEANT. If I find him now after all the trouble you've given me, you know what'll happen. There's likely to be two dead men and a woman, instead of only the Yankee.

DICK (*bounding into the room*). Sergeant!

SERGEANT. What is it?

(DICK *hurries to the* SERGEANT *and says something to him in a low voice.*)

SERGEANT (*satisfaction showing on his face*). Now, my good people, how did that horse get here?

THADDEUS. What horse?

DICK. There's a horse in the barn with a saddle on his back. I swear he's been ridden lately.

THADDEUS (*amazed*). There is?

SERGEANT. You know it. (*To* MARY.) Come, woman, who drove that horse here?

MARY (*silent for a moment, her eyes on the floor*). I don't know. I didn't hear nothin'.

THADDEUS (*moving toward the door*). Let me go an' see.

SERGEANT (*pushing* THADDEUS *back*). No, you don't. You two have done enough to justify the harshest measures. Show us the man's hiding place.

THADDEUS. If there's anybody here, he's,

he's come in the night without our knowin' it. I tell yuh I didn't see anybody, an' she didn't, an—

SERGEANT (*has been watching* MARY) Where is he?

(*His tone makes* THADDEUS *jump. There is a pause, during which* MARY *seems trying to compose herself. Then slowly she lifts her eyes and looks at the* SERGEANT.)

MARY. There ain't nobody in the house 'cept us two.

SERGEANT (*to* DICK). Did you search all the outbuildings?

DICK. Yes. There's not a trace of him except the horse.

SERGEANT (*wiping the perspiration from his face; speaks with apparent deliberation at first, but becomes very emphatic*). He didn't have much of a start of us, and I think he was wounded. A farmer down the road said he heard hoof-beats. The man the other side of you heard nothin', *and the horse is in your barn.* (*Slowly draws his revolver and points it at* THADDEUS.) There are ways of making people confess.

THADDEUS (*covering his face with his hands*). For God's sake, don't I know that horse looks bad, but as I live, I ain't heard a sound, or seen anybody. I'd give the man up in a minute if he was here.

SERGEANT (*lowering his gun*). Yes, I guess you would. You wouldn't want me to hand you and your wife over to our army to be shot down like dogs.

(MARY *shivers.*)

SERGEANT (*swings round sharply and points the gun at* MARY). Your wife knows where he's hid.

MARY (*breaking out in irritating, rasping voice*). I'm sure I wish I did. I'd tell yuh quick an' git yuh out o' here. 'Tain't no fun fer me t' have yuh prowlin' all over my house, trackin' it up with yer dirty boots. Yuh ain't got no right t' torment me like this. Lord knows how I'll git my day's work done, if I can't have my sleep out.

SERGEANT (*has been gazing at her in astonishment; lowers his gun*). Good God! Nothing but her own petty existence. (*In different voice to* MARY.) I'll have to ask you to get us some breakfast. We're famished.

(*With relief but showing some anger,* MARY *turns to the stove. She lights the fire and puts more coffee in the pot.*)

SERGEANT. Come, Dick, we better give our poor horses some water. They're all tired out. (*In lower voice.*) The man isn't here. If he were he couldn't get away while we're in the yard. (*To* THADDEUS.) Get us a pail to give the horses some water in. (*Sees the pails on the bench. Picks one of them up and moves toward the door.*)

MARY. That ain't the horses' pail.

SERGEANT (*to* THADDEUS). Come along. You can help.

MARY (*louder*). That's the drinkin' water pail.

SERGEANT. That's all right.

(*The* SERGEANT, THADDEUS, *and* DICK,—*carrying the lantern, go out back.* MARY *needs more wood for the fire, so she follows in a moment. When she has disappeared, the* NORTHERNER *drags himself from the cubby-hole.* MARY *returns with an armful of wood.*)

MARY (*sees the* NORTHERNER. *Shows no sympathy for him in this speech nor during the entire scene*). Yuh git back! Them soldiers'll see yuh.

NORTHERNER. Some water. Quick. (*Falls into chair at left of table.*) It was so hot in there.

MARY (*gives him water in the dipper*). Don't yuh faint here! If them soldiers git yuh, they'll kill me an' Thad. Hustle an' git back in that cubby-hole. (*Turns quickly to the stove.*)

(*The* NORTHERNER *drinks the water. Puts the dipper on the table. Then, summoning all his strength, rises and crosses to* MARY. *He touches her on the sleeve.* MARY *is so startled that she jumps and utters a faint cry.*)

NORTHERNER. Be still or they'll hear you. How are you going to get me out of here?

MARY. Yuh git out! Why did yuh come here, a bringin' me all this extra work, an' maybe death?

NORTHERNER. I couldn't go any farther. My horse and I were ready to drop. Won't you help me?

MARY. No, I won't. I don't know who yuh are or nothin' 'bout yuh, 'cept that them men want t' ketch yuh. (*In a changed tone of curiosity.*) Did yuh steal somethin' from 'em?

NORTHERNER. Don't you understand? Those men belong to the Confederacy, and I'm a Northerner. They've been chasing me all day. (*Pulling a bit of crumpled paper from his breast.*) They want this paper. If they get it before tomorrow morning it will mean the greatest disaster that's ever come to the Union army.

MARY (*with frank curiosity*). Was it yuh rode by yesterday?

NORTHERNER. Don't you see what you can do? Get me out of here and away from those men, and you'll have done more than any soldier could do for the country,—for *your* country.

MARY. I ain't got no country. Me an' Thad's only got this farm. Thad's ailin' an' I do most the work, an'—

NORTHERNER. The lives of thirty thousand men hang by a thread. I must save them. And you must help me!

MARY. I don't know nothin' 'bout yuh, an' I don't know what yer talkin' 'bout.

NORTHERNER. Only help me get away.

MARY (*angrily*). No one ever helped me or Thad. I lift no finger in this business. Why yuh come here in the first place is beyond me,—sneakin' in our house, spoilin' our well-earned sleep. If them soldiers ketch yuh, they'll kill me an' Thad. Maybe you didn't know that.

NORTHERNER. What's your life and your husband's compared to thirty thousand? I haven't any money or I'd give it to you.

MARY. I don't want yer money.

NORTHERNER. What do you want?

MARY. I want yuh t' git out. I don't care what happens t' yuh. Only git out o' here.

NORTHERNER. I can't with the Southerners in the yard. They'd shoot me like a dog. Besides, I've got to have my horse.

MARY (*with naive curiosity*). What kind o' lookin' horse is it?

NORTHERNER (*dropping into the chair at left of centre table in disgust and despair*). Oh, God! If I'd only turned in at the other farm. I might have found people with red blood. (*Pulls out his gun and hopelessly opens the empty chamber.*)

MARY (*alarmed*). What yuh goin' t' do with that gun?

NORTHERNER. Don't be afraid. It's not load—

MARY. I'd call 'em if I wasn't—

NORTHERNER (*leaping to the wall, left, and bracing himself against it*). Go call them in. Save your poor skin and your husband's if you can. Call them in. You can't save yourself. (*Laughs hysterically.*) You can't save your miserable skin. 'Cause if they get me, and don't shoot you, *I will.*

MARY (*leaning against the left side of the table for support; in agony*). Oh!

NORTHERNER. You see? You've got to help me whether you want to or not.

MARY (*feeling absolutely caught*). I ain't done nothin'. I don't see why yuh an' them others come here a threatenin' t' shoot me. I don't want nothin'. I don't want t' do nothin'. I jest want you all t' git out o' here an' leave me an' Thad t' go t' sleep. Oh, I don't know what t' do. Yuh got me in a corner where I can't move. (*Passes her hand back along the table. Touches the dipper accidentally, and it falls to the floor. Screams at the sound.*)

NORTHERNER (*leaping toward her*). Now you've done it. They'll be here in a minute. You can't give me up. They'll shoot you if you do. They'll *shoot.* (*Hurries up the stairs and disappears.*)

(MARY *stands beside the table, trembling terribly. The* SERGEANT, DICK, *and* THADDEUS *come running in.*)

SERGEANT. What did you yell for?

(MARY *does not answer.*)

SERGEANT (*seizing her by the arm*). Answer!

MARY. I knocked the dipper off the table. It scared me.

SERGEANT (*dropping wearily into chair at left of centre table*). Well, don't drop our breakfast. Put it on the table. We're ready.

MARY (*stands looking at the* SERGEANT). It ain't finished.

SERGEANT (*worn out by his day's work and* MARY'S *stupidity, from now on absolutely brutish*). You've had time to cook a dozen meals. What did you do all the time we were in the yards?

MARY. I didn't do nothin'.

SERGEANT. You good-for-nothin'—. Get a move on and give us something fit to eat. Don't try to get rid of any left-overs on us. If you do, you'll suffer for it.

(MARY *stands looking at him.*)

SERGEANT. Don't you know anything, you brainless farm-drudge? *Hurry,* I said.

(MARY *picks up the dipper and turns to the stove.* THADDEUS *sits in the chair at left of smaller table.*)

DICK. What a night. My stomach's as hollow as these people's heads. (*Takes towel which hangs above the bench, and wipes the barrel of his gun with it.*)

MARY. That's one of my best towels.

DICK. Can't help it.

SERGEANT. 'Tend to the breakfast. That's

enough for you to do at one time.

(DICK *puts his gun on the smaller table, and sits at the right of the larger.*)

SERGEANT (*quietly to* DICK). I don't see how he gave us the slip.

DICK. He knew we were after him, drove his horse in here, and went on afoot. Clever scheme, I must admit.

THADDEUS (*endeavoring to get them into conversation*). Have yuh rid far t'night, Misters?

DICK (*shortly*). Far enough.

THADDEUS. Twenty miles or so?

DICK. Perhaps.

THADDEUS. How long yuh been chasin' the critter?

SERGEANT. Oh, shut up! Don't you see we don't want to talk to you? Take hold and hurry, woman. My patience 's at an end.

(MARY *puts a loaf of bread, some fried eggs, and a coffee-pot on the table.*)

MARY. There! I hope yer satisfied.

(DICK *and the* SERGEANT *pull their chairs up and begin to eat.*)

SERGEANT. Is this all we get? Come, it won't do you any good to be stingy.

MARY. It's all I got.

SERGEANT. It isn't a mouthful for a chickadee! Give us some butter.

MARY. There ain't none.

SERGEANT. No butter on a farm? God, the way you lie.

MARY. I—

SERGEANT. Shut up!

DICK. Have you got any cider?

SERGEANT. Don't ask. She and the man probably drank themselves stupid on it. (*Throws fork on floor.*) I never struck such a place in my life. Get me another fork. How do you expect me to eat with that bent thing?

(MARY *stoops with difficulty and picks up the fork. Gets another from the cupboard and gives it to the* SERGEANT.)

SERGEANT. Now give me some salt. Don't you know that folks eats it on eggs?

(MARY *crosses to the cupboard; mistakes the pepper for the salt and puts it on the table.*)

SERGEANT (*sprinkles pepper on his food*). I said salt, woman! (*Spelling.*) *S-a-l-t.* Salt! Salt!

(MARY *gets the salt and gives it to the* SERGEANT. *Almost ready to drop, she drags herself to the window nearer the back and leans against it, watching the* SOUTHERNERS *like a hunted animal.* THADDEUS *is nodding in the corner. The* SERGEANT *and* DICK *go on devouring the food. The former pours the coffee. Puts his cup to his lips, takes one swallow; then, jumping to his feet and upsetting his chair as he does so, he hurls his cup to the floor.*)

SERGEANT (*bellowing and pointing to the fluid trickling on the floor*). Have you tried to poison us, you God damn hag?

(MARY *screams and the faces of the men turn white. It is the cry of an animal goaded beyond endurance.*)

MARY (*screeching*). Break my cup? Call my coffee poison? Call me a hag, will yuh? I'll learn yuh! I'm a woman, but yer drivin' me crazy. (*She has snatched the gun from the wall and pointed it at the* SERGEANT. *Fires.*)

(*The* SERGEANT *falls to the floor.* MARY *keeps on screeching.* DICK *rushes for his gun.*)

THADDEUS. Mary! Mary!

MARY (*aiming at* DICK *and firing*). I ain't a hag. I'm a woman, but yer killin' me.

(DICK *falls just as he reaches his gun.* THADDEUS *is in the corner with his hands over his ears. The* NORTHERNER *stands on the stairs.* MARY *continues to pull the trigger of the empty gun. The* NORTHERNER *is motionless for a moment; then he goes to* THADDEUS *and shakes him.*)

NORTHERNER. Go get my horse. Quick!

(THADDEUS *hurries out. The* NORTHERNER *turns to* MARY. *She gazes at him but does not understand a word he says.*)

NORTHERNER (*with great fervor*). I'm ashamed of what I said. The whole country will hear of this, and you. (*He takes her hand and presses it to his lips; then turns and hurries out of the house.*)

(MARY *still holds the gun in her hand. She pushes a strand of grey hair back from her face, and begins to pick up the fragments of the broken cup.*)

MARY (*in dead, flat tone*). I'll have to drink out the tin cup now.

(*The hoof-beats of the* NORTHERNER'*s horse are heard.*)

CURTAIN

Trifles

BY SUSAN GLASPELL

First performed by the Provincetown Players at the Wharf Theatre, Provincetown, Mass., on August 8, 1916.

CHARACTERS

GEORGE HENDERSON, County Attorney
HENRY PETERS, Sheriff
LEWIS HALE, a Neighboring Farmer
MRS. PETERS
MRS. HALE

SCENE.—*The kitchen in the now abandoned farmhouse of* JOHN WRIGHT, *a gloomy kitchen, and left without having been put in order—unwashed pans under the sink, a loaf of bread outside the bread-box, a dish-towel on the table—other signs of incompleted work. At the rear the outer door opens and the* SHERIFF *comes in followed by the* COUNTY ATTORNEY *and* HALE. *The* SHERIFF *and* HALE *are men in middle life, the* COUNTY ATTORNEY *is a young man; all are much bundled up and go at once to the stove. They are followed by the two women—the* SHERIFF'S *wife first; she is a slight wiry woman, a thin nervous face.* MRS. HALE *is larger and would ordinarily be called more comfortable looking, but she is disturbed now and looks fearfully about as she enters. The women have come in slowly, and stand close together near the door.*

COUNTY ATTORNEY (*rubbing his hands*). This feels good. Come up to the fire, ladies.

MRS. PETERS (*after taking a step forward*). I'm not—cold.

SHERIFF (*unbuttoning his overcoat and stepping away from the stove as if to mark the beginning of official business*). Now, Mr. Hale, before we move things about, you explain to Mr. Henderson just what you saw when you came here yesterday morning.

COUNTY ATTORNEY. By the way, has anything been moved? Are things just as you left them yesterday?

SHERIFF (*looking about*). It's just the same. When it dropped below zero last night I thought I'd better send Frank out this morning to make a fire for us—no use getting pneumonia with a big case on, but I told him not to touch anything except the stove—and you know Frank.

COUNTY ATTORNEY. Somebody should have been left here yesterday.

SHERIFF. Oh—yesterday. When I had to send Frank to Morris Center for that man who went crazy—I want you to know I had my hands full yesterday. I knew you could get back from Omaha by today and as long as I went over everything here myself—

COUNTY ATTORNEY. Well, Mr. Hale, tell just what happened when you came here yesterday morning.

HALE. Harry and I had started to town with a load of potatoes. We came along the road from my place and as I got here I said, "I'm going to see if I can't get John Wright to go in with me on a party telephone." I spoke to Wright about it once before and he put me off, saying folks talked too much anyway, and all he asked was peace and quiet—I guess you know about how much he talked himself; but I thought maybe if I went to the house and talked about it before his wife, though I said to Harry that I didn't know as what his wife wanted made much difference to John—

COUNTY ATTORNEY. Let's talk about that later, Mr. Hale. I do want to talk about that, but tell now just what happened when you got to the house.

HALE. I didn't hear or see anything; I knocked at the door, and still it was all quiet inside. I knew they must be up, it was past eight o'clock. So I knocked again, and I thought I heard somebody say, "Come in." I wasn't sure, I'm not sure yet, but I opened the door—this door. (*Indicating the door by which the two women are still standing.*) And there in that rocker—(*pointing to it*) sat Mrs. Wright.

(*They all look at the rocker.*)

COUNTY ATTORNEY. What—was she doing?

HALE. She was rockin' back and forth. She had her apron in her hand and was kind of—pleating it.

COUNTY ATTORNEY. And how did she—look?

HALE. Well, she looked queer.

COUNTY ATTORNEY. How do you mean—queer?

HALE. Well, as if she didn't know what she was going to do next. And kind of done up.

COUNTY ATTORNEY. How did she seem to feel about your coming?

HALE. Why, I don't think she minded—one way or other. She didn't pay much attention. I said, "How do, Mrs. Wright, it's cold, ain't it?" And she said, "Is it?"—and went on kind of pleating at her apron. Well, I was surprised; she didn't ask me to come up to the stove, or to set down, but just sat there, not even looking at me, so I said, "I want to see John." And then she—laughed. I guess you would call it a laugh. I thought of Harry and the team outside, so I said a little sharp: "Can't I see John?" "No," she says, kind o' dull like. "Ain't he home?" says I. "Yes," says she, "he's home." "Then why can't I see him?" I asked her, out of patience. " 'Cause he's dead," says she. *"Dead?"* says I. She just nodded her head, not getting a bit excited, but rockin' back and forth. "Why—where is he?" says I, not knowing what to say. She just pointed upstairs—like that (*Himself pointing to the room above.*) I got up, with the idea of going up there. I walked from there to here—then I says, "Why, what did he die of?" "He died of a rope round his neck," says she, and just went on pleatin' at her apron. Well, I went out and called Harry. I thought I might—need help. We went upstairs and there he was lyin'—

COUNTY ATTORNEY. I think I'd rather have you go into that upstairs, where you can point it all out. Just go on now with the rest of the story.

HALE. Well, my first thought was to get that rope off. It looked . . . (*Stops, his face twitches.*) . . . but Harry, he went up to him, and he said, "No, he's dead all right, and we'd better not touch anything." So we went back downstairs. She was still sitting that same way. "Has anybody been notified?" I asked. "No," says she, unconcerned. "Who did this, Mrs. Wright?" said Harry. He said it business-like—and she stopped pleatin' of her apron. "I don't know," she says. "You don't *know?"* says Harry. "No," says she. "Weren't you sleepin' in the bed with him?" says Harry. "Yes," says she, "but I was on the inside." "Somebody slipped a rope round his neck and strangled him and you didn't wake up?" says Harry. "I didn't wake up," she said after him. We must 'a' looked as if we didn't see how that could be, for after a minute she said, "I sleep sound." Harry was going to ask her more questions but I said maybe we ought to let her tell her story first to the coroner, or the sheriff, so Harry went fast as he could to Rivers' place, where there's a telephone.

COUNTY ATTORNEY. And what did Mrs. Wright do when she knew that you had gone for the coroner?

HALE. She moved from that chair to this one over here (*pointing to a small chair in the corner*) and just sat there with her hands held together and looking down. I got a feeling that I ought to make some conversation, so I said I had come in to see if John wanted to put in a telephone, and at that she started to laugh, and then she stopped and looked at me—scared. (*The* COUNTY ATTORNEY, *who has had his notebook out, makes a note.*) I dunno, maybe it wasn't scared. I wouldn't like to say it was. Soon Harry got back, and then Dr. Lloyd came, and you, Mr. Peters, and so I guess that's all I know that you don't.

COUNTY ATTORNEY (*looking around*). I guess we'll go upstairs first—and then out to the barn and around there. (*To the* SHERIFF.) You're convinced that there was nothing important here—nothing that would point to any motive.

SHERIFF. Nothing here but kitchen things.

(*The* COUNTY ATTORNEY, *after again looking around the kitchen, opens the door of a cupboard closet. He gets up on a chair and looks on a shelf. Pulls his hand away, sticky.*)

COUNTY ATTORNEY. Here's a nice mess.

(*The women draw nearer.*)

MRS. PETERS (*to the other woman*). Oh, her fruit; it did freeze. (*To the* LAWYER.) She worried about that when it turned so cold. She said the fire'd go out and her jars would break.

SHERIFF. Well, can you beat the women! Held for murder and worryin' about her preserves.

COUNTY ATTORNEY. I guess before we're through she may have something more serious than preserves to worry about.

HALE. Well, women are used to worrying over trifles.

(*The two women move a little closer together.*)

COUNTY ATTORNEY (*with the gallantry of a young politician*). And yet, for all their worries, what would we do without the ladies? (*The women do not unbend. He goes to the sink, takes a dipperful of water from the pail and pouring it into a basin, washes his hands. Starts to wipe them on the roller towel, turns it for a cleaner place.*) Dirty towels! (*Kicks his foot against the pans under the sink.*) Not much of a housekeeper, would you say, ladies?

MRS. HALE (*stiffly*). There's a great deal of work to be done on a farm.

COUNTY ATTORNEY. To be sure. And yet (*with a little bow to her*) I know there are some Dickson county farmhouses which do not have such roller towels.

(*He gives it a pull to expose its full length again.*)

MRS. HALE. Those towels get dirty awful quick. Men's hands aren't always as clean as they might be.

COUNTY ATTORNEY. Ah, loyal to your sex, I see. But you and Mrs. Wright were neighbors. I suppose you were friends, too.

MRS. HALE. (*shaking her head*). I've not seen much of her of late years. I've not been in this house—it's more than a year.

COUNTY ATTORNEY. And why was that? You didn't like her?

MRS. HALE. I liked her all well enough. Farmers' wives have their hands full, Mr. Henderson, And then—

COUNTY ATTORNEY. Yes—?

MRS. HALE (*looking about*). It never seemed a very cheerful place.

COUNTY ATTORNEY. No—it's not cheerful. I shouldn't say she had the homemaking instinct.

MRS. HALE. Well, I don't know as Wright had, either.

COUNTY ATTORNEY. You mean that they didn't get on very well?

MRS. HALE. No, I don't mean anything. But I don't think a place'd be any cheerfuller for John Wright's being in it.

COUNTY ATTORNEY. I'd like to talk more of that a little later. I want to get the lay of things upstairs now.

(*He goes to the left, where three steps lead to a stair door.*)

SHERIFF. I suppose anything Mrs. Peters does'll be all right. She was to take in some clothes for her, you know, and a few little things. We left in such a hurry yesterday.

COUNTY ATTORNEY. Yes, but I would like to see what you take, Mrs. Peters, and keep an eye out for anything that might be of use to us.

MRS. PETERS. Yes, Mr. Henderson.

(*The women listen to the men's steps on the stairs, then look about the kitchen.*)

MRS. HALE. I'd hate to have men coming into my kitchen, snooping around and criticizing.

(*She arranges the pans under sink which the* LAWYER *had shoved out of place.*)

MRS. PETERS. Of course it's no more than their duty.

MRS. HALE. Duty's all right, but I guess that deputy sheriff that came out to make the fire might have got a little of this on. (*Gives the roller towel a pull.*) Wish I'd thought of that sooner. Seems mean to talk about her for not having things slicked up when she had to come away in such a hurry.

MRS. PETERS (*who has gone to a small table in the left rear corner of the room, and lifted one end of a towel that covers a pan*). She had bread set. (*Stands still.*)

MRS. HALE (*eyes fixed on a loaf of bread beside the bread box, which is on a low shelf at the other side of the room. Moves slowly toward it*). She was going to put this in there. (*Picks up loaf, then abruptly drops it. In a manner of returning to familiar things.*) It's a shame about her fruit. I wonder if it's all gone. (*Gets up on the chair and looks.*) I think there's some here that's all right, Mrs. Peters. Yes —here; (*Holding it toward the window.*) this is cherries, too. (*Looking again.*) I declare I believe that's the only one. (*Gets down, bottle in her hand. Goes to the sink and wipes it off on the outside.*) She'll feel awful bad after all her hard work in the hot weather. I remember the afternoon I put up my cherries last summer.

(*She puts the bottle on the big kitchen table, center of the room. With a sigh, is about to sit down in the rocking-chair. Before she is seated realizes what chair it is; with a slow look at it, steps back. The chair which she has touched rocks back and forth.*)

MRS. PETERS. Well, I must get those things from the front room closet. (*She goes to the door at the right, but after looking into the other room, steps back.*) You coming with me, Mrs. Hale? You could help me carry them.

(*They go in the other room; reappear,* MRS. PETERS *carrying a dress and skirt,* MRS. HALE *following with a pair of shoes.*)

MRS. PETERS. My, it's cold in there.

(*She puts the clothes on the big table, and hurries to the stove.*)

MRS. HALE (*examining the skirt*). Wright was close. I think maybe that's why she kept so much to herself. She didn't even belong to the Ladies' Aid. I suppose she felt she couldn't do her part, and then you don't enjoy things when you feel shabby. She used to wear pretty clothes and be lively, when she was Minnie Foster, one of the town girls singing in the choir. But that—oh, that was thirty years ago. This all you was to take in?

MRS. PETERS. She said she wanted an apron. Funny thing to want, for there isn't much to get you dirty in jail, goodness knows. But I suppose just to make her feel more natural. She said they was in the top drawer in this cupboard. Yes, here. And then her little shawl that always hung behind the door. (*Opens stair door and looks.*) Yes, here it is.

(*Quickly shuts door leading upstairs.*)

MRS. HALE (*abruptly moving toward her*). Mrs. Peters?

MRS. PETERS. Yes, Mrs. Hale?

MRS. HALE. Do you think she did it?

MRS. PETERS (*in a frightened voice*). Oh, I don't know.

MRS. HALE. Well, I don't think she did. Asking for an apron and her little shawl. Worrying about her fruit.

MRS. PETERS (*starts to speak, glances up, where footsteps are heard in the room above. In a low voice*). Mr. Peters says it looks bad for her. Mr. Henderson is awful sarcastic in a speech and he'll make fun of her sayin' she didn't wake up.

MRS. HALE. Well, I guess John Wright didn't wake when they was slipping that rope under his neck.

MRS. PETERS. No, it's strange. It must have been done awful crafty and still. They say it was such a—funny way to kill a man, rigging it all up like that.

MRS. HALE. That's just what Mr. Hale said. There was a gun in the house. He says that's what he can't understand.

MRS. PETERS. Mr. Henderson said coming out that what was needed for the case was a motive; something to show anger, or—sudden feeling.

MRS. HALE (*who is standing by the table*). Well, I don't see any signs of anger around here. (*She puts her hand on the dish towel which lies on the table, stands looking down at table, one half of which is clean, the other half messy.*) It's wiped to here. (*Makes a move as if to finish work, then turns and looks at loaf of bread outside the bread-box. Drops towel. In that voice of coming back to familiar things.*) Wonder how they are finding things upstairs. I hope she had it a little more red-up up there. You know, it seems kind of *sneaking*. Locking her up in town and then coming out here and trying to get her own house to turn against her!

MRS. PETERS. But Mrs. Hale, the law is the law.

MRS. HALE. I s'pose 'tis. (*Unbuttoning her coat.*) Better loosen up your things, Mrs. Peters. You won't feel them when you go out.

(MRS. PETERS *takes off her fur tippet, goes to hang it on hook at back of room, stands looking at the under part of the small corner table.*)

MRS. PETERS. She was piecing a quilt.

(*She brings the large sewing basket and they look at the bright pieces.*)

MRS. HALE. It's a log cabin pattern. Pretty, isn't it? I wonder if she was goin' to quilt it or just knot it?

(*Footsteps have been heard coming down the stairs. The* SHERIFF *enters followed by* HALE *and the* COUNTY ATTORNEY.)

SHERIFF. They wonder if she was going to quilt it or just knot it!

(*The men laugh, the women look abashed.*)

COUNTY ATTORNEY (*rubbing his hands over the stove*). Frank's fire didn't do much up there, did it? Well, let's go out to the barn and get that cleared up.

(*The men go outside.*)

MRS. HALE (*resentfully*). I don't know as there's anything so strange, our takin' up our time with little things while we're waiting for them to get the evidence. (*She sits down at the big table smoothing out a block with decision.*) I don't see as it's anything to laugh about.

MRS. PETERS (*apologetically*). Of course they've got awful important things on their minds.

(*Pulls up a chair and joins* MRS. HALE *at the table.*)

MRS. HALE (*examining another block*). Mrs. Peters, look at this one. Here, this is the one she was working on, and look at the sewing! All the rest of it has been so nice and even. And look at this! It's all over the place! Why, it looks as if she didn't know what she was about!

(*After she has said this they look at each other, then start to glance back at the door. After an instant* MRS. HALE *has pulled at a knot and ripped the sewing.*)

MRS. PETERS. Oh, what are you doing, Mrs. Hale?

MRS. HALE (*mildly*). Just pulling out a stitch or two that's not sewed very good. (*Threading a needle.*) Bad sewing always made me fidgety.

MRS. PETERS (*nervously*). I don't think we ought to touch things.

MRS. HALE. I'll just finish up this end. (*Suddenly stopping and leaning forward.*) Mrs. Peters?

MRS. PETERS. Yes, Mrs. Hale?

MRS. HALE. What do you suppose she was so nervous about?

MRS. PETERS. Oh—I don't know. I don't

know as she was nervous. I sometimes sew awful queer when I'm just tired. (MRS. HALE *starts to say something, looks at* MRS. PETERS, *then goes on sewing.*) Well, I must get these things wrapped up. They may be through sooner than we think. (*Putting apron and other things together.*) I wonder where I can find a piece of paper, and string.

MRS. HALE. In that cupboard, maybe.

MRS. PETERS (*looking in cupboard*). Why, here's a bird-cage. (*Holds it up.*) Did she have a bird, Mrs. Hale?

MRS. HALE. Why, I don't know whether she did or not—I've not been here for so long. There was a man around last year selling canaries cheap, but I don't know as she took one; maybe she did. She used to sing real pretty herself.

MRS. PETERS (*glancing around*). Seems funny to think of a bird here. But she must have had one, or why would she have a cage? I wonder what happened to it?

MRS. HALE. I s'pose maybe the cat got it.

MRS. PETERS. No, she didn't have a cat. She's got that feeling some people have about cats—being afraid of them. My cat got in her room and she was real upset and asked me to take it out.

MRS. HALE. My sister Bessie was like that. Queer, ain't it?

MRS. PETERS (*examining the cage*). Why, look at this door. It's broke. One hinge is pulled apart.

MRS. HALE (*looking too*). Looks as if someone must have been rough with it.

MRS. PETERS. Why, yes.

(*She brings the cage forward and puts it on the table.*)

MRS. HALE. I wish if they're going to find any evidence they'd be about it. I don't like this place.

MRS. PETERS. But I'm awful glad you came with me, Mrs. Hale. It would be lonesome for me sitting here alone.

MRS. HALE. It would, wouldn't it? (*Dropping her sewing.*) But I tell you what I do wish, Mrs. Peters. I wish I had come over sometimes when *she* was here. I—(*Looking around the room.*)—wish I had.

MRS. PETERS. But of course you were awful busy, Mrs. Hale—your house and your children.

MRS. HALE. I could've come. I stayed away because it weren't cheerful—and that's why I ought to have come. I—I've never liked this place. Maybe because it's down in a hollow and you don't see the road. I dunno what it is, but it's a lonesome place and always was. I wish I had come over to see Minnie Foster sometimes. I can see now—

(*Shakes her head.*)

MRS. PETERS. Well, you mustn't reproach yourself, Mrs. Hale. Somehow we just don't see how it is with other folks until—something turns up.

MRS. HALE. Not having children makes less work—but it makes a quiet house, and Wright out to work all day, and no company when he did come in. Did you know John Wright, Mrs. Peters?

MRS. PETERS. Not to know him; I've seen him in town. They say he was a good man.

MRS. HALE. Yes—good; he didn't drink, and kept his word as well as most, I guess, and paid his debts. But he was a hard man, Mrs. Peters. Just to pass the time of day with him— (*Shivers.*) Like a raw wind that gets to the bone. (*Pauses, her eye falling on the cage.*) I should think she would 'a' wanted a bird. But what do you suppose went with it?

MRS. PETERS. I don't know, unless it got sick and died.

(*She reaches over and swings the broken door, swings it again, both women watch it.*)

MRS. HALE. You weren't raised round here, were you? (MRS. PETERS *shakes her head.*) You didn't know—her?

MRS. PETERS. Not till they brought her yesterday.

MRS. HALE. She—come to think of it, she was kind of like a bird herself—real sweet and pretty, but kind of timid and—fluttery. How—she—did—change. (*Silence; then as if struck by a happy thought and relieved to get back to every day things.*) Tell you what, Mrs. Peters, why don't you take the quilt in with you? It might take up her mind.

MRS. PETERS. Why, I think that's a real nice idea, Mrs. Hale. There couldn't possibly be any objection to it, could there? Now, just what would I take? I wonder if her patches are in here—and her things.

(*They look in the sewing basket.*)

MRS. HALE. Here's some red. I expect this has got sewing things in it. (*Brings out a fancy box.*) What a pretty box. Looks like something somebody would give you. Maybe her scissors are in here.

(*Opens box. Suddenly puts her hand to her nose.*) Why— (MRS. PETERS *bends nearer, then turns her face away.*) There's something wrapped up in this piece of silk.

MRS. PETERS. Why, this isn't her scissors.

MRS. HALE (*lifting the silk*). Oh, Mrs. Peters—it's—

(MRS. PETERS *bends closer.*)

MRS. PETERS. It's the bird.

MRS. HALE (*jumping up*). But, Mrs. Peters—look at it! Its neck! Look at its neck! It's all—other side *to.*

MRS. PETERS. Somebody—wrung—its—neck.

(*Their eyes meet. A look of growing comprehension, of horror. Steps are heard outside.* MRS. HALE *slips box under quilt pieces, and sinks into her chair. Enter* SHERIFF *and* COUNTY ATTORNEY. MRS. PETERS *rises.*)

COUNTY ATTORNEY (*as one turning from serious things to little pleasantries*). Well, ladies, have you decided whether she was going to quilt it or knot it?

MRS. PETERS. We think she was going to—knot it.

COUNTY ATTORNEY. Well, that's interesting, I'm sure. (*Seeing the bird-cage.*) Has the bird flown?

MRS. HALE (*putting more quilt pieces over the box*). We think the—cat got it.

COUNTY ATTORNEY (*preoccupied*). Is there a cat?

(MRS. HALE *glances in a quick covert way at* MRS. PETERS.)

MRS. PETERS. Well, not *now*. They're superstitious, you know. They leave.

COUNTY ATTORNEY (*to* SHERIFF PETERS, *continuing an interrupted conversation*). No sign at all of anyone having come from the outside. Their own rope. Now let's go up again and go over it piece by piece. (*They start upstairs.*) It would have to have been someone who knew just the—

(MRS. PETERS *sits down. The two women sit there not looking at one another, but as if peering into something and at the same time holding back. When they talk now it is in the manner of feeling their way over strange ground, as if afraid of what they are saying, but as if they cannot help saying it.*)

MRS. HALE. She liked the bird. She was going to bury it in that pretty box.

MRS. PETERS (*in a whisper*). When I was a girl—my kitten—there was a boy took a hatchet, and before my eyes—and before I could get there— (*Covers her face an instant.*) If they hadn't held me back I would have— (*Catches herself, looks upstairs where steps are heard, falters weakly.*)—hurt him.

MRS. HALE (*with a slow look around her*). I wonder how it would seem never to have had any children around. (*Pause.*) No, Wright wouldn't like the bird—a thing that sang. She used to sing. He killed that, too.

MRS. PETERS (*moving uneasily*). We don't know who killed the bird.

MRS. HALE. I knew John Wright.

MRS. PETERS. It was an awful thing was done in this house that night, Mrs. Hale. Killing a man while he slept, slipping a rope around his neck that choked the life out of him.

MRS. HALE. His neck. Choked the life out of him.

(*Her hand goes out and rests on the bird-cage.*)

MRS. PETERS (*with rising voice*). We don't know who killed him. We don't *know.*

MRS. HALE (*her own feeling not interrupted*). If there'd been years and years of nothing, then a bird to sing to you, it would be awful—still, after the bird was still.

MRS. PETERS (*something within her speaking*). I know what stillness is. When we homesteaded in Dakota, and my first baby died—after he was two years old, and me with no other then—

MRS. HALE (*moving*). How soon do you suppose they'll be through looking for the evidence?

MRS. PETERS. I know what stillness is. (*Pulling herself back.*) The law has got to punish crime, Mrs. Hale.

MRS. HALE (*not as if answering that*). I wish you'd seen Minnie Foster when she wore a white dress with blue ribbons and stood up there in the choir and sang. (*A look around the room.*) Oh, I *wish* I'd come over here once in a while! That was a crime! That was a crime! Who's going to punish that?

MRS. PETERS (*looking upstairs*). We mustn't—take on.

MRS. HALE. I might have known she needed help! I know how things can be —for women. I tell you, it's queer, Mrs. Peters. We live close together and we live far apart. We all go through the same things—it's all just a different kind of the same thing. (*Brushes her eyes, noticing the bottle of fruit, reaches out for it.*) If I was you I wouldn't tell her her fruit was gone. Tell her it *ain't.* Tell her it's all right. Take this in to prove it to her. She—she may never know whether it was broke or not.

MRS. PETERS (*takes the bottle, looks about for something to wrap it in; takes petticoat from the clothes brought from the other room, very nervously begins winding this around the bottle. In a false voice*). My, it's a good thing the men couldn't hear us. Wouldn't they just laugh! Getting all stirred up over a little thing like a—dead canary. As if that could have anything to do with—with—wouldn't they *laugh!*

(*The men are heard coming downstairs.*)

MRS. HALE (*under her breath*). Maybe they would—maybe they wouldn't.

COUNTY ATTORNEY. No, Peters, it's all perfectly clear except a reason for doing it. But you know juries when it comes to women. If there was some definite thing. Something to show—something to make a story about—a thing that would connect up with this strange way of doing it—

(*The women's eyes meet for an instant. Enter* HALE *from outer door.*)

HALE. Well, I've got the team around. Pretty cold out there.

COUNTY ATTORNEY. I'm going to stay here a while by myself. (*To the* SHERIFF.) You can send Frank out for me, can't you? I want to go over everything. I'm not satisfied that we can't do better.

SHERIFF. Do you want to see what Mrs. Peters is going to take in?

(*The* LAWYER *goes to the table, picks up the apron, laughs.*)

COUNTY ATTORNEY. Oh, I guess they're not very dangerous things the ladies have picked out. (*Moves a few things about, disturbing the quilt pieces which cover the box. Steps back.*) No, Mrs. Peters doesn't need supervising. For that matter, a sheriff's wife is married to the law. Ever think of it that way, Mrs. Peters?

MRS. PETERS. Not—just that way.

SHERIFF (*chuckling*). Married to the law. (*Moves toward the other room.*) I just want you to come in here a minute, George. We ought to take a look at these windows.

COUNTY ATTORNEY (*scoffingly*). Oh, windows!

SHERIFF. We'll be right out, Mr. Hale.

(HALE *goes outside. The* SHERIFF *follows the* COUNTY ATTORNEY *into the other room. Then* MRS. HALE *rises, hands tight together, looking intensely at* MRS. PETERS, *whose eyes make a slow turn, finally meeting* MRS. HALE'S *A moment* MRS. HALE *holds her, then her own eyes point the way to where the box is concealed. Suddenly* MRS. PETERS *throws back quilt pieces and tries to put the box in the bag she is wearing. It is too big. She opens box, starts to take bird out, cannot touch it, goes to pieces, stands there helpless. Sound of a knob turning in the other room.* MRS. HALE *snatches the box and puts it in the pocket of her big coat. Enter* COUNTY ATTORNEY *and* SHERIFF.)

COUNTY ATTORNEY (*facetiously*). Well, Henry, at least we found out that she was not going to quilt it. She was going to—what is it you call it, ladies?

MRS. HALE (*her hand against her pocket*). We call it—knot it, Mr. Henderson.

CURTAIN

Ile

BY EUGENE O'NEILL

First produced by the Provincetown Players at the Provincetown Playhouse, New York City, on November 30, 1917.

CHARACTERS

BEN, the cabin boy
THE STEWARD
CAPTAIN KEENEY
SLOCUM, second mate
MRS. KEENEY
JOE, a harpooner

Members of the crew of the steam whaler *Atlantic Queen*.

SCENE—CAPTAIN KEENEY'S *cabin on board the steam whaling ship* Atlantic Queen—*a small, square compartment about eight feet high with a skylight in the center looking out on the poop deck. On the left (the stern of the ship) a long bench with rough cushions is built in against the wall. In front of the bench, a table. Over the bench, several curtained portholes.*

In the rear, left, a door leading to the captain's sleeping quarters. To the right of the door a small organ, looking as if it were brand new, is placed against the wall.

On the right, to the rear, a marble-topped sideboard. On the sideboard, a woman's sewing basket. Farther forward, a doorway leading to the companion way, and past the officer's quarters to the main deck.

In the center of the room, a stove. From the middle of the ceiling a hanging lamp is suspended. The walls of the cabin are painted white.

There is no rolling of the ship, and the light which comes through the skylight is sickly and faint, indicating one of those gray days of calm when ocean and sky are alike dead. The silence is unbroken except for measured tread of some one walking up and down on the poop deck overhead.

It is nearing two bells—one o'clock—in the afternoon of a day in the year 1895.

At the rise of the curtain there is a moment of intense silence. Then the STEWARD *enters and commences to clear the table of the few dishes which still remain on it after the* CAPTAIN'S *dinner. He is an old, grizzled man dressed in dungaree pants, a sweater, and a woolen cap with ear flaps. His manner is sullen and angry. He stops stacking up the plates and casts a quick glance upward at the skylight; then tiptoes over to the closed door in rear and listens with his ear pressed to the crack. What he hears makes his face darken and he mutters a furious curse. There is a noise from the doorway on the right and he darts back to the table.*

BEN *enters. He is an over-grown, gawky boy with a long, pinched face. He is dressed in sweater, fur cap, etc. His teeth are chattering with the cold and he hurries to the stove, where he stands for a moment shivering, blowing on his hands, slapping them against his sides, on the verge of crying.*

THE STEWARD (*in relieved tones—seeing who it is*). Oh, 'tis you, is it? What're ye shiverin' 'bout? Stay by the stove where ye belong and ye'll find no need of chatterin'.

BEN. It's c-c-cold. (*Trying to control his chattering teeth—derisively.*) Who d'ye think it were—the Old Man?

THE STEWARD (*makes a threatening move*—BEN *shrinks away*). None o' your lip, young un, or I'll learn ye. (*More kindly.*) Where was it ye've been all o' the time—the fo'c's'tle?

BEN. Yes.

THE STEWARD. Let the Old Man see ye up for'ard monkeyshinin' with the hands and ye'll get a hidin' ye'll not forget in a hurry.

BEN. Aw, he don't see nothin'. (*A trace of awe in his tones—he glances upward.*) He just walks up and down like he didn't notice nobody—and stares at the ice to the no'the'ard.

THE STEWARD (*the same tone of awe creeping into his voice*). He's always starin' at the ice. (*In a sudden rage, shaking his fist at the skylight.*) Ice, ice, ice! Damn him and damn the ice! Holdin' us in for nigh on a year—nothin' to see but ice—stuck in it like a fly in molasses!

BEN (*apprehensively*). Ssshh! He'll hear ye.

THE STEWARD (*raging*). Aye, damn him, and damn the Arctic seas, and damn this stinkin' whalin' ship of his, and damn me for a fool to ever ship on it! (*Subsiding as if realizing the uselessness of this outburst—shaking his head—slowly, with deep conviction.*) He's a hard man—as hard a man as ever sailed the seas.

BEN (*solemnly*). Aye.

THE STEWARD. The two years we all signed up for are done this day. Blessed Christ! Two years o' this dog's life, and no luck in the fishin', and the hands half starved with the food runnin' low, rotten as it is; and not a sign of him turnin' back for home! (*Bitterly.*) Home! I begin to doubt if ever I'll set foot on land again. (*Excitedly.*) What is it he thinks he's goin' to do? Keep us all up here after our time is worked out till the last man of us is starved to death or frozen? We've grub enough hardly to last out the voyage back if we started now. What are the men goin' to do 'bout it? Did ye hear any talk in the fo'c's'tle?

BEN (*going over to him—in a half whisper*). They said if he don't put back south for home today they're goin' to mutiny.

THE STEWARD (*with grim satisfaction*). Mutiny? Aye, 'tis the only thing they can do; and serve him right after the manner he's treated them—'s if they wern't no better nor dogs.

BEN. The ice is all broke up to s'uth'ard. They's clear water 's far 's you can see. He ain't got no excuse for not turnin' back for home, the men says.

THE STEWARD (*bitterly*). He won't look nowheres but no'th'ard where they's only the ice to see. He don't want to see no clear water. All he thinks on is gittin' the ile—'s if it was our fault he ain't had good luck with the whales. (*Shaking his head.*) I think the man's mighty nigh losin' his senses.

BEN (*awed*). D'you really think he's crazy?

THE STEWARD. Aye, it's the punishment o' God on him. Did ye ever hear of a man who wasn't crazy do the things he does? (*Pointing to the door in rear.*) Who but a man that's mad would take his woman—and as sweet a woman as ever was—on a stinkin' whalin' ship to the Arctic seas to be locked in by the rotten ice for nigh on a year, and maybe lose her senses forever—for it's sure she'll never be the same again.

BEN (*sadly*). She useter be awful nice to me before— (*His eyes grow wide and frightened.*) She got—like she is.

THE STEWARD. Aye, she was good to all of us. 'Twould have been hell on board without her; for he's a hard man—a hard, hard man—a driver if there ever was one. (*With a grim laugh.*) I hope he's satisfied now—drivin' her on till she's near lost her mind. And who could blame her? 'Tis a God's wonder we're not a ship full of crazed people—with the damned ice all the time, and the quiet so thick you're afraid to hear your own voice.

BEN (*with a frightened glance toward the door on right*). She don't never speak to me no more—jest looks at me 's if she didn't know me.

THE STEWARD. She don't know no one—but him. She talks to him—when she does talk—right enough.

BEN. She does nothin' all day long now but sit and sew—and then she cries to herself without makin' no noise. I've seen her.

THE STEWARD. Aye, I could hear her through the door a while back.

BEN (*tiptoes over to the door and listens*). She's cryin' now.

THE STEWARD (*furiously—shaking his fist*). God send his soul to hell for the devil he is! (*There is the noise of some one coming slowly down the companionway stairs. The* STEWARD *hurries to his stacked up dishes. He is so nervous from fright that he knocks off the top one, which falls and breaks on the floor. He stands aghast, trembling with dread.* BEN *is violently rubbing off the organ with a piece of cloth which he has snatched from his pocket.* CAPTAIN KEENEY *appears in the doorway on right and comes into the cabin, removing his fur cap as he does so. He is a man of about forty, around five-ten in height but looking much shorter on account of the enormous proportions of his shoulders and chest. His face is massive and deeply lined, with gray-blue eyes of a bleak hardness, and a tightly clenched, thin-lipped mouth. His thick hair is long and gray. He is dressed in a heavy blue jacket and blue pants stuffed into his seaboots. He is followed into the cabin by the* SECOND MATE, *a rangy six-footer with a lean weather-beaten face. The* MATE *is dressed about the same as the captain. He is a man of thirty or so.*)

KEENEY (*comes toward the* STEWARD*—with a stern look on his face. The* STEWARD *is visibly frightened and the stack of dishes rattles in his trembling hands.* KEENEY *draws back his fist and the* STEWARD *shrinks away. The fist is gradually lowered and* KEENEY *speaks slowly*). 'Twould be like hitting a worm. It is nigh on two bells, Mr. Steward, and this truck not cleared yet.

THE STEWARD (*stammering*). Y-y-yes, sir.

KEENEY. Instead of doin' your rightful work ye've been below here gossipin' old woman's talk with that boy. (*To* BEN, *fiercely.*) Get out o' this, you! Clean up the chart room. (BEN *darts past the* MATE *to the open doorway.*) Pick up that dish, Mr. Steward!

THE STEWARD (*doing so with difficulty*).

Yes, sir.

KEENEY. The next dish you break, Mr. Steward, you take a bath in the Bering Sea at the end of a rope.

THE STEWARD (*trembling*). Yes, sir. (*He hurries out. The* SECOND MATE *walks slowly over to the* CAPTAIN.)

MATE. I warn't 'specially anxious the man at the wheel should catch what I wanted to say to you, sir. That's why I asked you to come below.

KEENEY (*impatiently*). Speak your say, Mr. Slocum.

MATE (*unconsciously lowering his voice*). I'm afeard there'll be trouble with the hands by the look o' things. They'll likely turn ugly, every blessed one o' them, if you don't put back. The two years they signed up for is up to-day.

KEENEY. And d'you think you're tellin' me somethin' new, Mr. Slocum? I've felt it in the air this long time past. D'you think I've not seen their ugly looks and the grudgin' way they worked?

(*The door in rear is opened and* MRS. KEENEY *stands in the doorway. She is a slight, sweet-faced little woman primly dressed in black. Her eyes are red from weeping and her face drawn and pale. She takes in the cabin with a frightened glance and stands as if fixed to the spot by some nameless dread, clasping and unclasping her hands nervously. The two men turn and look at her.*)

KEENEY (*with rough tenderness*). Well, Annie?

MRS. KEENEY (*as if awakening from a dream*). David, I—— (*She is silent. The* MATE *starts for the doorway.*)

KEENEY (*turning to him—sharply*). Wait!

MATE. Yes, sir.

KEENEY. D'you want anything, Annie?

MRS. KEENEY (*after a pause, during which she seems to be endeavoring to collect her thoughts*). I thought maybe—I'd go up on deck, David, to get a breath of fresh air. (*She stands humbly awaiting his permission. He and the* MATE *exchange a significant glance.*)

KEENEY. It's too cold, Annie. You'd best stay below to-day. There's nothing to look at on deck—but ice.

MRS. KEENEY (*monotonously*). I know—ice, ice, ice! But there's nothing to see down here but these walls. (*She makes a gesture of loathing.*)

KEENEY. You can play the organ, Annie.

MRS. KEENEY (*dully*). I hate the organ. It puts me in mind of home.

KEENEY (*a touch of resentment in his voice*). I got it jest for you.

MRS. KEENEY (*dully*). I know. (*She turns away from them and walks slowly to the bench on left. She lifts up one of the curtains and looks through a porthole; then utters an exclamation of joy.*) Ah, water! Clear water! As far as I can see! How good it looks after all these months of ice! (*She turns round to them, her face transfigured with joy.*) Ah, now I must go up on deck and look at it, David.

KEENEY (*frowning*). Best not to-day, Annie. Best wait for a day when the sun shines.

MRS. KEENEY (*desperately*). But the sun never shines in this terrible place.

KEENEY (*a tone of command in his voice*). Best not to-day, Annie.

MRS. KEENEY (*crumbling before this command—abjectly*). Very well, David. (*She stands there staring straight before her as if in a daze. The two men look at her uneasily.*)

KEENEY (*sharply*). Annie!

MRS. KEENEY (*dully*). Yes, David.

KEENEY. Me and Mr. Slocum has business to talk about—ship's business.

MRS. KEENEY. Very well, David. (*She goes slowly out, rear, and leaves the door three-quarters shut behind her.*)

KEENEY. Best not have her on deck if they's goin' to be any trouble.

MATE. Yes, sir.

KEENEY. And trouble they's goin' to be. I feel it in my bones. (*Takes a revolver from the pocket of his coat and examines it.*) Got your'n?

MATE. Yes, sir.

KEENEY. Not that we'll have to use 'em—not if I know their breed of dog—jest to frighten 'em up a bit. (*Grimly.*) I ain't never been forced to use one yit; and trouble I've had by land and by sea 's long as I kin remember, and will have till my dyin' day, I reckon.

MATE (*hesitatingly*). Then you ain't goin'—to turn back?

KEENEY. Turn back! Mr. Slocum, did you ever hear o' me pointin' s'uth for home with only a measly four hundred barrel of ile in the hold?

MATE (*hastily*). No, sir—but the grub's gittin' low.

KEENEY. They's enough to last a long time yit, if they're careful with it; and they's plenty o' water.

MATE. They say it's not fit to eat—what's left; and the two years they signed on fur is up to-day. They might make trouble for you in the courts when we git home.

KEENEY. To hell with 'em! Let them make what law trouble they kin. I don't give a damn 'bout the money. I've got to git the ile! (*Glancing sharply at the* MATE.) You ain't turnin' no damned sea lawyer, be you, Mr. Slocum?

MATE (*flushing*). Not by a hell of a sight, sir.

KEENEY. What do the fools want to go home fur now? Their share o' the four hundred barrel wouldn't keep 'em in chewin' terbacco.

MATE (*slowly*). They wants to git back to their folks an' things, I s'pose.

KEENEY (*looking at him searchingly*). 'N you want to turn back, too. (*The* MATE *looks down confusedly before his sharp gaze.*) Don't lie, Mr. Slocum. It's writ down plain in your eyes. (*With grim sarcasm.*) I hope, Mr. Slocum, you ain't agoin' to jine the men again me.

MATE (*indignantly*). That ain't fair, sir, to say sich things.

KEENEY (*with satisfaction*). I warn't much afeard o' that, Tom. You been with me nigh on ten year and I've learned ye whalin'. No man kin say I ain't a good master, if I be a hard one.

MATE. I warn't thinkin' of myself, sir—'bout turnin' home, I mean. (*Desperately.*) But Mrs. Keeney, sir—seems like she ain't jest satisfied up here, ailin' like—what with the cold an' bad luck an' the ice an' all.

KEENEY (*his face clouding—rebukingly but not severely*). That's my business, Mr. Slocum. I'll thank you to steer a clear course o' that. (*A pause.*) The ice'll break up soon to no'th'ard. I could see it startin' to-day. And when it goes and we git some sun Annie'll perk up. (*Another pause—then he bursts forth:*) It ain't the damned money what's keepin' me up in the Northern seas, Tom. But I can't go back to Homeport with a measly four hundred barrel of ile. I'd die fust. I ain't never come come back home in all my days without a full ship. Ain't that truth?

MATE. Yes, sir; but this voyage you been icebound, an'——

KEENEY (*scornfully*). And d'you s'pose any of 'em would believe that—any o' them skippers I've beaten voyage after voyage? Can't you hear 'em laughin' and sneerin'—Tibbots 'n' Harris 'n' Simms and the rest—and all o' Homeport makin' fun o' me? "Dave Keeney what boasts he's the best whalin' skipper out o' Homeport comin' back with a measly four hundred barrel of ile?" (*The thought of this drives him into a frenzy, and he smashes his fist down on the marble top of the sideboard.*) Hell! I got to git the ile, I tell you. How could I figger on this ice? It's never been so bad before in the thirty year I been acomin' here. And now it's breakin' up. In a couple o' days it'll be all gone. And they's whale here, plenty of 'em. I know they is and I ain't never gone wrong yit. I got to git the ile! I got to git it in spite of all hell, and by God, I ain't agoin' home till I do git it! (*There is the sound of subdued sobbing from the door in rear. The two men stand silent for a moment, listening. Then* KEENEY *goes over to the door and looks in. He hesitates for a moment as if he were going to enter—then closes the door softly.* JOE, *the harpooner, an enormous six-footer with a battered, ugly face, enters from right and stands waiting for the captain to notice him.*)

KEENEY (*turning and seeing him*). Don't be standin' there like a gawk, Harpooner. Speak up!

JOE (*confusedly*). We want—the men, sir—they wants to send a depitation aft to have a word with you.

KEENEY (*furiously*). Tell 'em to go to—— (*Checks himself and continues grimly.*) Tell 'em to come. I'll see 'em.

JOE. Aye, aye, sir. (*He goes out.*)

KEENEY (*with a grim smile*). Here it comes, the trouble you spoke of, Mr. Slocum, and we'll make short shift of it. It's better to crush such things at the start than let them make headway.

MATE (*worriedly*). Shall I wake up the First and Fourth, sir? We might need their help.

KEENEY. No, let them sleep. I'm well able to handle this alone, Mr. Slocum. (*There is the shuffling of footsteps from outside and five of the crew crowd into the cabin, led by* JOE. *All are dressed alike—sweaters, seaboots, etc. They glance uneasily at the* CAPTAIN, *twirling their fur caps in their hands.*)

KEENEY (*after a pause*). Well? Who's to speak fur ye?

JOE (*stepping forward with an air of bravado*). I be.

KEENEY (*eyeing him up and down coldly*). So you be. Then speak your say and be quick about it.

JOE (*trying not to wilt before the* CAPTAIN's *glance and avoiding his eyes*). The time we signed up for is done to-day.

KEENEY (*icily*). You're tellin' me nothin' I don't know.

JOE. You ain't pintin' fur home yit, far 's we kin see.

KEENEY. No, and I ain't agoin' to till this ship is full of ile.

JOE. You can't go no further no'th with the ice afore ye.

KEENEY. The ice is breaking up.

JOE (*after a slight pause during which the others mumble angrily to one another*). The grub we're gittin' now is rotten.

KEENEY. It's good enough fur ye. Better men than ye are have eaten worse. (*There is a chorus of angry exclamations from the crowd.*)

JOE (*encouraged by this support*). We ain't agoin' to work no more less you puts back for home.

KEENEY (*fiercely*). You ain't, ain't you?

JOE. No; and the law courts'll say we was right.

KEENEY. To hell with your law courts! We're at sea now and I'm the law on this ship. (*Edging up toward the harpooner.*) And every mother's son of you what don't obey orders goes in irons. (*There are more angry exclamations from the crew.* MRS. KEENEY *appears in the doorway in rear and looks on with startled eyes. None of the men notice her.*)

JOE (*with bravado*). Then we're agoin' to mutiny and take the old hooker home ourselves. Ain't we, boys? (*As he turns his head to look at the others,* KEENEY's *fist shoots out to the side of his jaw.* JOE *goes down in a heap and lies there.* MRS. KEENEY *gives a shriek and hides her face in her hands. The men pull out their sheath knives and start a rush, but stop when they find themselves confronted by the revolvers of* KEENEY *and the* MATE.)

KEENEY (*his eyes and voice snapping*). Hold still! (*The men stand huddled together in a sullen silence.* KEENEY's *voice is full of mockery.*) You've found out it ain't safe to mutiny on this ship, ain't you? And now git for'ard where ye belong, and—— (*He gives* JOE's *body a contemptuous kick.*) Drag him with you. And remember the first man of ye I see shirkin' I'll shoot dead as sure as there's a sea under us, and you can tell the rest the same. Git for'ard now! Quick! (*The men leave in cowed silence, carrying* JOE *with them.* KEENEY *turns to the* MATE *with a short laugh and puts his revolver back in his pocket.*) Best get up on deck, Mr. Slocum, and see to it they don't try none of their skulkin' tricks. We'll have to keep an eye peeled from now on. I know 'em.

MATE. Yes, sir. (*He goes out, right.* KEENEY *hears his wife's hysterical weeping and turns around in surprise—then walks slowly to her side.*)

KEENEY (*putting an arm around her shoulder—with gruff tenderness*). There, there, Annie. Don't be afeard. It's all past and gone.

MRS. KEENEY (*shrinking away from him*). Oh, I can't bear it! I can't bear it any longer!

KEENEY (*gently*). Can't bear what, Annie?

MRS. KEENEY (*hysterically*). All this horrible brutality, and these brutes of men, and this terrible ship, and this prison cell of a room, and the ice all around, and the silence. (*After this outburst she calms down and wipes her eyes with her handkerchief.*)

KEENEY (*after a pause during which he looks down at her with a puzzled frown*). Remember, I warn't hankerin' to have you come on this voyage, Annie.

MRS. KEENEY. I wanted to be with you, David, don't you see? I didn't want to wait back there in the house all alone as I've been doing these last six years since we were married—waiting, and watching, and fearing—with nothing to keep my mind occupied—not able to go back teaching school on account of being Dave Keeney's wife. I used to dream of sailing on the great, wide, glorious ocean. I wanted to be by your side in the danger and vigorous life of it all. I wanted to see you the hero they make you out to be in Homeport. And instead—— (*Her voice grows tremulous.*) All I find is ice and cold—and brutality! (*Her voice breaks.*)

KEENEY. I warned you what it'd be, Annie. "Whalin' ain't no ladies' tea party," I says to you, and "you better stay to home where you've got all your woman's comforts." (*Shaking his head.*) But you was so set on it.

MRS. KEENEY (*wearily*). Oh, I know it isn't your fault, David. You see, I didn't believe you. I guess I was dreaming about the old Vikings in the story books and I thought you were one of them.

KEENEY (*protestingly*). I done my best to make it as cozy and comfortable as could be. (MRS. KEENEY *looks around her in wild scorn.*) I even sent to the city for that organ for ye, thinkin' it might be soothin' to ye to be playin' it times when they was calms and things was dull like.

MRS. KEENEY (*wearily*). Yes, you were very kind, David. I know that. (*She goes to left and lifts the curtains from the porthole and looks out—then suddenly bursts forth:*) I won't stand it—I can't stand it—pent up by these walls like a prisoner. (*She runs over to him and throws her arms around him, weeping. He puts his arm protectingly over her shoulders.*) Take me away from here, David! If I don't get away from here, out of this terrible ship, I'll go mad! Take me home, David! I can't think any more. I feel as if the cold and the silence were crushing down on my brain. I'm afraid. Take me home!

KEENEY (*holds her at arm's length and looks at her face anxiously*). Best go to bed, Annie. You ain't yourself. You got fever. Your eyes look so strange like. I ain't never seen you look this way before.

MRS. KEENEY (*laughing hysterically*). It's the ice and the cold and the silence—they'd make any one look strange.

KEENEY (*soothingly*). In a month or two, with good luck, three at the most, I'll have her filled with ile and then we'll give her everything she'll stand and pint for home.

MRS. KEENEY. But we can't wait for that—I can't wait. I want to get home. And the men won't wait. They want to get home. It's cruel, it's brutal for you to keep them. You must sail back. You've got no excuse. There's clear water to the south now. If you've a heart at all you've got to turn back.

KEENEY (*harshly*). I can't, Annie.

MRS. KEENEY. Why can't you?

KEENEY. A woman couldn't rightly understand my reason.

MRS. KEENEY (*wildly*). Because it's a stupid, stubborn reason. Oh, I heard you talking with the second mate. You're afraid the other captains will sneer at you because you didn't come back with a full ship. You want to live up to your silly reputation even if you do have to beat and starve men and drive me mad to do it.

KEENEY (*his jaw set stubbornly*). It ain't that, Annie. Them skippers would never dare sneer to my face. It ain't so much what any one'd say—but—— (*He hesitates, struggling to express his meaning.*) You see—I've always done it—since my first voyage as skipper. I always come back—with a full ship—and—it don't seem right not to—somehow. I been always first whalin' skipper out o' Homeport, and—— Don't you see my meanin', Annie? (*He glances at her. She is not looking at him but staring dully in front of her, not hearing a word he is saying.*) Annie! (*She comes to herself with a start.*) Best turn in, Annie, there's a good woman. You ain't well.

MRS. KEENEY (*resisting his attempts to guide her to the door in rear*). David! Won't you please turn back?

KEENEY (*gently*). I can't, Annie—not yet awhile. You don't see my meanin'. I got to git the ile.

MRS. KEENEY. It'd be different if you needed the money, but you don't. You've got more than plenty.

KEENEY (*impatiently*). It ain't the money I'm thinkin' of. D'you think I'm as mean as that?

MRS. KEENEY (*dully*). No—I don't know—I can't understand—— (*Intensely.*) Oh, I want to be home in the old house once more and see my own kitchen again, and hear a woman's voice talking to me and be able to talk to her. Two years! It seems so long ago—as if I'd been dead and could never go back.

KEENEY (*worried by her strange tone and the far-away look in her eyes*). Best go to bed, Annie. You ain't well.

MRS. KEENEY (*not appearing to hear him*). I used to be lonely when you were away. I used to think Homeport was a stupid, monotonous place. Then I used to go down on the beach, especially when it was windy and the breakers were rolling in, and I'd dream of the fine free life you must be leading. (*She gives a laugh which is half a sob.*) I used to love the sea then. (*She pauses; then continues with slow intensity:*) But now—I don't ever want to see the sea again.

KEENEY (*thinking to humor her*). 'Tis no fit place for a woman, that's sure. I was a fool to bring ye.

MRS. KEENEY (*after a pause—passing her hand over her eyes with a gesture of pathetic weariness*). How long would it take us to reach home—if we started now?

KEENEY (*frowning*). 'Bout two months, I reckon, Annie, with fair luck.

MRS. KEENEY (*counts on her fingers—then murmurs with a rapt smile*). That would be August, the latter part of August, wouldn't it? It was on the twenty-fifth of August we were married, David, wasn't it?

KEENEY (*trying to conceal the fact that her memories have moved him—gruffly*). Don't *you* remember?

MRS. KEENEY (*vaguely—again passes her hand over her eyes*). My memory is leaving me—up here in the ice. It was so long ago. (*A pause—then she smiles dreamily.*) It's June now. The lilacs will be all in bloom in the front yard—and the climbing roses on the trellis to the side of the house—they're budding. (*She suddenly covers her face with her hands and commences to sob.*)

KEENEY (*disturbed*). Go in and rest, Annie. You're all wore out cryin' over what can't be helped.

MRS. KEENEY (*suddenly throwing her arms around his neck and clinging to him*). You love me, don't you, David?

KEENEY (*in amazed embarrassment at this outburst*). Love you? Why d'you ask me such a question, Annie?

MRS. KEENEY (*shaking him—fiercely*). But you do, don't you, David? Tell me!

KEENEY. I'm your husband, Annie, and you're my wife. Could there be aught but love between us after all these years?

MRS. KEENEY (*shaking him again—still more fiercely*). Then you do love me. Say it!

KEENEY (*simply*). I do, Annie.

MRS. KEENEY (*gives a sigh of relief—her hands drop to her sides.* KEENEY *regards her anxiously. She passes her hand across her eyes and murmurs half to herself*): I sometimes think if we could only have had a child. (KEENEY *turns away from her, deeply moved. She grabs his arm and turns him around to face her—intensely.*) And I've always been a good wife to you, haven't I, David?

KEENEY (*his voice betraying his emotion*). No man has ever had a better, Annie.

MRS. KEENEY. And I've never asked for much from you, have I, David? Have I?

KEENEY. You know you could have all I got the power to give ye, Annie.

MRS. KEENEY (*wildly*). Then do this this once for my sake, for God's sake—take me home! It's killing me, this life—the brutality and cold and horror of it. I'm going mad. I can feel the threat in the air. I can hear the silence threatening me—day after gray day and every day the same. I can't bear it. (*Sobbing.*) I'll go mad, I know I will. Take me home, David, if you love me as you say. I'm afraid. For the love of God, take me home! (*She throws her arms around him, weeping against his shoulder. His face betrays the tremendous struggle going on within him. He holds her out at arm's length, his expression softening. For a moment his shoulders sag, he becomes old, his iron spirit weakens as he looks at her tear-stained face.*)

KEENEY (*dragging out the words with an effort*). I'll do it, Annie—for your sake—if you say it's needful for ye.

MRS. KEENEY (*with wild joy—kissing him*). God bless you for that, David! (*He turns away from her silently and walks toward the companionway. Just at that moment there is a clatter of footsteps on the stairs and the* SECOND MATE *enters the cabin.*)

MATE (*excitedly*). The ice is breakin' up to no'the'ard, sir. There's a clear passage through the floe, and clear water beyond, the lookout says.

(KEENEY *straightens himself like a man coming out of a trance.* MRS. KEENEY *looks at the* MATE *with terrified eyes.*)

KEENEY (*dazedly—trying to collect his thoughts*). A clear passage? To no'-the'ard?

MATE. Yes, sir.

KEENEY (*his voice suddenly grim with determination*). Then get her ready and we'll drive her through.

MATE. Aye, aye, sir.

MRS. KEENEY (*appealingly*). David!

KEENEY (*not heeding her*). Will the men turn to willin' or must we drag 'em out?

MATE. They'll turn to willin' enough. You put the fear o' God into 'em, sir. They're meek as lambs.

KEENEY. Then drive 'em—both watches.

(*With grim determination.*) They's whale t'other side o' this floe and we're going to git 'em.

MATE. Aye, aye, sir. (*He goes out hurriedly. A moment later there is the sound of scuffling feet from the deck outside and the* MATE's *voice shouting orders.*)

KEENEY (*speaking aloud to himself—derisively*). And I was agoin' home like a yaller dog!

MRS. KEENEY (*imploringly*). David!

KEENEY (*sternly*). Woman, you ain't adoin' right when you meddle in men's business and weaken 'em. You can't know my feelin's. I got to prove a man to be a good husband for ye to take pride in. I got to git the ile, I tell ye.

MRS. KEENEY (*supplicatingly*). David! Aren't you going home?

KEENEY (*ignoring this question—commandingly*). You ain't well. Go and lay down a mite. (*He starts for the door.*) I got to git on deck. (*He goes out. She cries after him in anguish:*) David! (*A pause. She passes her hand across her eyes—then commences to laugh hysterically and goes to the organ. She sits down and starts to play wildly an old hymn.* KEENEY *reënters from the doorway to the deck and stands looking at her angrily. He comes over and grabs her roughly by the shoulders.*)

KEENEY. Woman, what foolish mockin' is this? (*She laughs wildly and he starts back from her in alarm.*) Annie! What is it? (*She doesn't answer him.* KEENEY's *voice trembles.*) Don't you know me, Annie? (*He puts both hands on her shoulders and turns her around so that he can look into her eyes. She stares up at him with a stupid expression, a vague smile on her lips. He stumbles away from her, and she commences softly to play the organ again.*)

KEENEY (*swallowing hard—in a hoarse whisper, as if he had difficulty in speaking*). You said—you was a-goin' mad—God! (*A long wail is heard from the deck above.*) Ah bl-o-o-o-ow! (*A moment later the* MATE's *face appears through the skylight. He cannot see* MRS. KEENEY.)

MATE (*in great excitement*). Whales, sir—a whole school of 'em—off the star'b'd quarter 'bout five mile away—big ones!

KEENEY (*galvanized into action*). Are you lowerin' the boats?

MATE. Yes, sir.

KEENEY (*with grim decision*). I'm a-comin' with ye.

MATE. Aye, aye, sir. (*Jubilantly.*) You'll git the ile now right enough, sir. (*His head is withdrawn and he can be heard shouting orders.*)

KEENEY (*turning to his wife*). Annie! Did you hear him? I'll git the ile. (*She doesn't answer or seem to know he is there. He gives a hard laugh, which is almost a groan.*) I know you're foolin' me, Annie. You ain't out of your mind—(*Anxiously.*) Be you? I'll git the ile now right enough—jest a little while longer, Annie—then we'll turn hom'ard. I can't turn back now, you see that, don't ye? I've got to git the ile. (*In sudden terror.*) Answer me! You ain't mad, be you? (*She keeps on playing the organ, but makes no reply. The* MATE's *face appears again through the skylight.*)

MATE. All ready, sir. (KEENEY *turns his back on his wife and strides to the doorway, where he stands for a moment and looks back at her in anguish, fighting to control his feelings.*)

MATE. Comin', sir?

KEENEY (*his face suddenly grown hard with determination*). Aye. (*He turns abruptly and goes out.* MRS. KEENEY *does not appear to notice his departure. Her whole attention seems centered in the organ. She sits with half-closed eyes, her body swaying a little from side to side to the rhythm of the hymn. Her fingers move faster and faster and she is playing wildly and discordantly as*)

THE CURTAIN FALLS

Aria Da Capo

BY EDNA ST. VINCENT MILLAY

First produced by the Provincetown Players at the Provincetown Playhouse, New York City, on December 15, 1919.

CHARACTERS

PIERROT
COLUMBINE
COTHURNUS
CORYDON
THYRSIS

SCENE: A STAGE

The curtain rises on a stage set for a Harlequinade, a merry black and white interior. Directly behind the footlights, and running parallel with them, is a long table, covered with a gay black and white cloth, on which is spread a banquet. At the opposite ends of this table, seated on delicate thin-legged chairs with high backs, are PIERROT *and* COLUMBINE, *dressed according to the tradition, excepting that* PIERROT *is in lilac, and* COLUMBINE *in pink. They are dining.*

COLUMBINE. Pierrot, a macaroon! I cannot *live*
Without a macaroon!
PIERROT. My only love,
You are *so* intense! . . . Is it Tuesday, Columbine?—
I'll kiss you if it's Tuesday.
COLUMBINE. It is Wednesday,
If you must know. . . . Is this my artichoke,
Or yours?
PIERROT. Ah, Columbine,—as if it mattered!
Wednesday. . . . Will it be Tuesday, then, tomorrow,
By any chance?
COLUMBINE. To-morrow will be—Pierrot,
That isn't funny!
PIERROT. I thought it rather nice.
Well, let us drink some wine and lose our heads
And love each other.
COLUMBINE. Pierrot, don't you love
Me now?
PIERROT. La, what a woman!—how should I know?
Pour me some wine: I'll tell you presently.
COLUMBINE. Pierrot, do you know, I think you drink too much.
PIERROT. Yes, I dare say I do. . . . Or else too little.
It's hard to tell. You see, I am always wanting
A little more than what I have,—or else
A little less. There's something wrong. My dear,
How many fingers have you?
COLUMBINE. La, indeed,
How should I know?—It always takes me one hand
To count the other with. It's too confusing.
Why?
PIERROT. Why?—I am a student, Columbine;
And search into all matters.
COLUMBINE. La, indeed?—
Count them yourself, then!
PIERROT. No. Or, rather, *nay*.
'Tis of no consequence. . . . I am become
A painter, suddenly,—and you impress me—
Ah, yes!—six orange bull's-eyes, four green pin-wheels,
And one magenta jelly-roll,—the title
As follows: *Woman Taking in Cheese from Fire-Escape*.
COLUMBINE. Well, I like that! So that is all I've meant
To you!
PIERROT. Hush! All at once I am become
A pianist. I will image you in sound. . . .
On a new scale. . . . Without tonality. . . .
Vivace senza tempo senza tutto. . . .
Title: *Uptown Express at Six o'clock*. . .
Pour me a drink.
COLUMBINE. Pierrot, you work too hard.
You need a rest. Come on out into the garden,
And sing me something sad.
PIERROT. Don't stand so near me!
I am become a socialist. I love
Humanity; but I hate people. Columbine,
Put on your mittens, child; your hands are cold.
COLUMBINE. My hands are *not* cold!
PIERROT. Oh, I am sure they are.
And you must have a shawl to wrap about you,
And sit by the fire.
COLUMBINE. Why, I'll do no such thing!
I'm hot as a spoon in a teacup!
PIERROT. Columbine,
I'm a philanthropist. I know I am,
Because I feel so restless. Do not scream,
Or it will be the worse for you!
COLUMBINE. Pierrot,
My vinaigrette! I cannot *live* without
My vinaigrette!
PIERROT. My only love, you are
So fundamental! . . . How would you like to be
An actress, Columbine?—I am become
Your manager.
COLUMBINE. Why, Pierrot, I can't act.
PIERROT. Can't act! Can't act! La, listen to the woman!
What's that to do with the price of furs?—You're blonde,

Are you not?—you have no education, have you?—
Can't act! You under-rate yourself, my dear!

COLUMBINE. Yes, I suppose I do.

PIERROT. As for the rest,
I'll teach you how to cry, and how to die,
And other little tricks; and the house will love you.
You'll be a star by five o'clock . . . that is,
If you will let me pay for your apartment.

COLUMBINE. *Let* you?—well, that's a good one!
Ha! Ha! Ha!
But why?

PIERROT. But why?—well, as to that, my dear,
I cannot say. It's just a matter of form.

COLUMBINE. Pierrot, I'm getting tired of caviar
And peacocks' livers. Isn't there something else
That people eat?—some humble vegetable,
That grows in the ground?

PIERROT. Well, there are mushrooms.

COLUMBINE. Mushrooms!
That's so! I had forgotten . . . mushrooms . . . mushrooms. . .
I cannot *live* with. . . . How do you like this gown?

PIERROT. Not much. I'm tired of gowns that have the waist-line
About the waist, and the hem around the bottom,—
And women with their breasts in front of them!—
Zut and ehè! Where does one go from here!

COLUMBINE. Here's a persimmon, love.
You always liked them.

PIERROT. I am become a critic; there is nothing
I can enjoy. . . . However, set it aside;
I'll eat it between meals.

COLUMBINE. Pierrot, do you know,
Sometimes I think you're making fun of me.

PIERROT. My love, by yon black moon, you wrong us both.

COLUMBINE. There isn't a sign of a moon, Pierrot.

PIERROT. Of course not.
There never was. "Moon's" just a word to swear by.
"Mutton!"—now *there's* a thing you can lay the hands on,
And set the tooth in! Listen, Columbine:
I always lied about the moon and you.
Food is my only lust.

COLUMBINE. Well, eat it, then,
For Heaven's sake, and stop your silly noise!
I haven't heard the clock tick for an hour.

PIERROT. It's ticking all the same. If you were a fly,
You would be dead by now. And if I were a parrot,
I could be talking for a thousand years!

(*Enter* COTHURNUS.)

PIERROT. Hello, what's this, for God's sake?—What's the matter?
Say, whadda you mean?—get off the stage, my friend,
And pinch yourself,—you're walking in your sleep!

COTHURNUS. I never sleep.

PIERROT. Well, anyhow, clear out.
You don't belong on here. Wait for your own scene!
Whadda you think this is,—a dress-rehearsal?

COTHURNUS. Sir, I am tired of waiting. I will wait
No longer.

PIERROT. Well, but whadda you going to do?
The scene is set for me!

COTHURNUS. True, sir; yet I
Can play the scene.

PIERROT. Your scene is down for later!

COTHURNUS. That, too, is true, sir; but I play it now.

PIERROT. Oh, very well!—Anyway, I am tired
Of black and white. At least, I think I am.

(*Exit* COLUMBINE.)

Yes, I am sure I am. I know what I'll do!—
I'll go and strum the moon, that's what I'll do. . . .
Unless, perhaps . . . you never can tell. . . . I may be,
You know, tired of the moon. Well, anyway,
I'll go find Columbine. . . . And when I find her,
I will address her thus: "*Ehè,* Pierrette!"—
There's something in that.

(*Exit* PIERROT.)

COTHURNUS. You, Thyrsis! Corydon!
Where are you?

THYRSIS (*off stage*). Sir, we are in our dressing-room!

COTHURNUS. Come out and do the scene.

CORYDON (*off stage*). You are mocking

us!—
The scene is down for later.
COTHURNUS. That is true;
But we will play it now. I am the scene.
(*Seats himself on high place in back of stage.*)

(*Enter* CORYDON *and* THYRSIS.)

CORYDON. Sir, we are counting on this little hour.
We said, "Here is an hour,—in which to think
A mighty thought, and sing a trifling song,
And look at nothing."—And, behold! the hour,
Even as we spoke, was over, and the act begun,
Under our feet!

THYRSIS. Sir, we are not in the fancy
To play the play. We had thought to play it later.

CORYDON. Besides, this is the setting for a farce.
Our scene requires a wall; we cannot build
A wall of tissue-paper!

THYRSIS. We cannot act
A tragedy with comic properties!

COTHURNUS. Try it and see. I think you'll find you can.
One wall is like another. And regarding
The matter of your insufficient mood,
The important thing is that you speak the lines,
And make the gestures. Wherefore I shall remain
Throughout, and hold the prompt-book. Are you ready?

CORYDON-THYRSIS (*sorrowfully*). Sir, we are always ready.

COTHURNUS. Play the play!

(CORYDON *and* THYRSIS *move the table and chairs to one side out of the way, and seat themselves in a half-reclining position on the floor.*)

THYRSIS. How gently in the silence, Corydon,
Our sheep go up the bank. They crop a grass
That's yellow where the sun is out, and black
Where the clouds drag their shadows. Have you noticed
How steadily, yet with what a slanting eye
They graze?

CORYDON. As if they thought of other things.
What say you, Thyrsis, do they only question
Where next to pull?—Or do their far minds draw them
Thus vaguely north of west and south of east?

THYRSIS. One cannot say. . . . The black lamb wears its burdocks
As if they were a garland,—have you noticed?
Purple and white—and drinks the bitten grass
As if it were a wine.

CORYDON. I've noticed that.
What say you, Thyrsis, shall we make a song
About a lamb that thought himself a shepherd?

THYRSIS. Why, yes!—that is, why,—no.
(I have forgotten my line.)

COTHURNUS (*prompting*). "I know a game worth two of that."

THYRSIS. Oh, yes. . . . I know a game worth two of that!
Let's gather rocks, and build a wall between us;
And say that over there belongs to me,
And over here to you!

CORYDON. Why,—very well.
And say you may not come upon my side
Unless I say you may!

THYRSIS. Nor you on mine!
And if you should, 'twould be the worse for you!

(*They weave a wall of colored crêpe paper ribbons from the centre front to the centre back of the stage, fastening the ends to* COLUMBINE'S *chair in front and to* PIERROT'S *chair in the back.*)

CORYDON. Now there's a wall a man may see across,
But not attempt to scale.

THYRSIS. An excellent wall.

CORYDON. Come, let us separate, and sit alone
A little while, and lay a plot whereby
We may outdo each other.

(*They seat themselves on opposite sides of the wall.*)

PIERROT (*off stage*). *Ehè,* Pierrette!

COLUMBINE (*off stage*). My name is Columbine! Leave me alone!

THYRSIS (*coming up to the wall*). Corydon, after all, and in spite of the fact
I started it myself, I do not like this
So very much. What is the sense of saying
I do not want you on my side the wall?

It is a silly game. I'd much prefer
Making the little song you spoke of making,
About the lamb, you know, that thought himself
A shepherd!—what do you say?
(*Pause.*)

CORYDON (*at wall*). (I have forgotten the line.)

COTHURNUS (*prompting*). "How do I know this isn't a trick?"

CORYDON. Oh, yes. . . . How do I know this isn't a trick
To get upon my land?

THYRSIS. Oh, Corydon,
You *know* it's not a trick. I do not like
The game, that's all. Come over here, or let me
Come over there.

CORYDON. It is a clever trick
To get upon my land. (*Seats himself as before.*)

THYRSIS. Oh, very well!
(*Seats himself as before.*) (*To himself.*)
I think I never knew a sillier game.

CORYDON (*coming to wall*). Oh, Thyrsis, just a minute!—all the water
Is on your side the wall, and the sheep are thirsty.
I hadn't thought of that.

THYRSIS. Oh, hadn't you?

CORYDON. Why, what do you mean?

THYRSIS. What do I mean?—I mean
That I can play a game as well as you can.
And if the pool is on my side, it's on
My side, that's all.

CORYDON. You mean you'd let the sheep
Go thirsty?

THYRSIS. Well, they're not my sheep. My sheep
Have water enough.

CORYDON. *Your* sheep! You are mad, to call them
Yours—mine—they are all one flock! Thyrsis, you can't mean
To keep the water from them, just because
They happened to be grazing over here
Instead of over there, when we set the wall up?

THYRSIS. Oh, can't I?—wait and see!—and if you try,
To lead them over here, you'll wish you hadn't!

CORYDON. I wonder how it happens all the water
Is on your side. . . . I'll say you had an eye out
For lots of little things, my innocent friend,
When I said, "Let us make a song," and you said,
"I know a game worth two of that!"

COLUMBINE (*off stage*). Pierrot,
D'you know, I think you must be getting old,
Or fat, or something,—stupid, anyway!—
Can't you put on some other kind of collar?

THYRSIS. You know as well as I do, Corydon,
I never thought anything of the kind.
Don't you?

CORYDON. I *do* not.

THYRSIS. Don't you?

CORYDON. Oh, I suppose so.
Thyrsis, let's drop this,—what do you say?—it's only
A game, you know . . . we seem to be forgetting
It's only a game . . . a pretty serious game
It's getting to be, when one of us is willing
To let the sheep go thirsty for the sake of it.

THYRSIS. I know it, Corydon.
(*They reach out their arms to each other across the wall.*)

COTHURNUS (*prompting*). "But how do I know—"

THYRSIS. Oh, yes. . . . But how do I know this isn't a trick
To water your sheep, and get the laugh on me?

CORYDON. You can't know, that's the difficult thing about it,
Of course,—you can't be sure. You have to take
My word for it. And I know just how you feel.
But one of us has to take a risk, or else,
Why, don't you see?—the game goes on forever! . . .
It's terrible, when you stop to think of it. . . .
Oh, Thyrsis, now for the first time I feel
This wall is actually a wall, a thing
Come up between us, shutting you away
From me. . . . I do not know you any more!

THYRSIS. No, don't say that! Oh, Corydon, I'm willing
To drop it all, if you will! Come on over
And water your sheep! It is an ugly game.

I hated it from the first. . . . How did it start?

CORYDON. I do not know . . . I do not know . . . I think
I am afraid of you!—you are a stranger!
I never set eyes on you before! "Come over
And water my sheep," indeed!—They'll be more thirsty
Than they are now before I bring them over
Into your land, and have you mixing them up
With yours, and calling them yours, and trying to keep them!

(*Enter* COLUMBINE.)

COLUMBINE (*to* COTHURNUS). Glummy, I want my hat.

THYRSIS. Take it, and go.

COLUMBINE. Take it and go, indeed! Is it my hat,
Or isn't it? Is this my scene, or not?
Take it and go! Really, you know, you two
Are awfully funny!
(*Exit* COLUMBINE.)

THYRSIS. Corydon, my friend,
I'm going to leave you now, and whittle me
A pipe, or sing a song, or go to sleep.
When you have come to your senses, let me know.
(*Goes back to where he has been sitting, lies down and sleeps.*)
(CORYDON, *in going back to where he has been sitting, stumbles over bowl of colored confetti and colored paper ribbons.*)

CORYDON. Why, what is this?—Red stones—and purple stones—
And stones stuck full of gold!—The ground is full
Of gold and colored stones! . . . I'm glad the wall
Was up before I found them!—Otherwise,
I should have had to share them. As it is,
They all belong to me. . . . Unless— (*He goes to wall and digs up and down the length of it, to see if there are jewels on the other side.*) None here—
None here—none here—They all belong to me! (*Sits.*)

THYRSIS (*awakening*). How curious! I thought the little black lamb
Came up and licked my hair; I saw the wool
About its neck as plain as anything!
It must have been a dream. The little black lamb
Is on the other side of the wall, I'm sure.
(*Goes to wall and looks over.* CORYDON *is seated on the ground, tossing the confetti up into the air and catching it.*)
Hello, what's that you've got there, Corydon?

CORYDON. Jewels.

THYRSIS. Jewels?—And where did you ever get them?

CORYDON. Oh, over here.

THYRSIS. You mean to say you found them,
By digging around in the ground for them?

CORYDON (*unpleasantly*). No, Thyrsis,
By digging down for water for my sheep.

THYRSIS. Corydon, come to the wall a minute, will you?
I want to talk to you

CORYDON. I haven't time.
I'm making me a necklace of red stones.

THYRSIS. I'll give you all the water that you want,
For one of those red stones,—if it's a good one.

CORYDON. Water?—what for?—what do I want of water?

THYRSIS. Why, for your sheep!

CORYDON. My sheep?—I'm not a shepherd!

THYRSIS. Your sheep are dying of thirst.

CORYDON. Man, haven't I told you
I can't be bothered with a few untidy
Brown sheep all full of burdocks?—I'm a merchant.
That's what I am!—And if I set my mind to it
I dare say I could be an emperor!
(*To himself.*) Wouldn't I be a fool to spend my time
Watching a flock of sheep go up a hill,
When I have these to play with?—when I have these
To think about?—I can't make up my mind
Whether to buy a city, and have a thousand
Beautiful girls to bathe me, and be happy
Until I die, or build a bridge, and name it
The Bridge of Corydon,—and be remembered
After I'm dead.

THYRSIS. Corydon, come to the wall,
Won't you?—I want to tell you something.

CORYDON. Hush!
Be off! Be off! Go finish your nap, I tell you!

THYRSIS. Corydon, listen: if you don't want your sheep,
Give them to me.
CORYDON. Be off! Go finish your nap.
A red one—and a blue one—and a red one—
And a purple one—give you my sheep, did you say?—
Come, come! What do you take me for, a fool?
I've a lot of thinking to do,—and while I'm thinking,
The sheep might just as well be over here
As over there. . . . A blue one—and a red one—
THYRSIS. But they will die!
CORYDON. And a green one—and a couple
Of white ones, for a change.
THYRSIS. Maybe I have
Some jewels on my side.
CORYDON. And another green one—
Maybe, but I don't think so. You see, this rock
Isn't so very wide. It stops before
It gets to the wall. It seems to go quite deep,
However.
THYRSIS (*with hatred*). I see.
COLUMBINE (*off stage*). Look, Pierrot, there's the moon!
PIERROT (*off stage*). Nonsense!
THYRSIS. I see.
COLUMBINE (*off stage*). Sing me an old song, Pierrot,—
Something I can remember.
PIERROT (*off stage*). Columbine.
Your mind is made of crumbs,—like an escallop
Of oysters,—first a layer of crumbs, and then
An oystery taste, and then a layer of crumbs.
THYRSIS (*searching*). I find no jewels . . . but I wonder what
The root of this black weed would do to a man
If he should taste it . . . I have seen a sheep die,
With half the stalk still drooling from its mouth.
'Twould be a speedy remedy, I should think,
For a festered pride and a feverish ambition.
It has a curious root. I think I'll hack it
In little pieces . . . First I'll get me a drink;
And then I'll hack that root in little pieces
As small as dust, and see what the color is
Inside. (*Goes to bowl on floor.*) The pool is very clear. I see
A shepherd standing on the brink, with a red cloak
About him, and a black weed in his hand. . . .
'Tis I. (*Kneels and drinks.*)
CORYDON (*coming to wall*). Hello, what are you doing, Thyrsis?
THYRSIS. Digging for gold.
CORYDON. I'll give you all the gold
You want, if you'll give me a bowl of water.
If you don't want too much, that is to say.
THYRSIS. Ho, so you've changed your mind?—It's different,
Isn't it, when you want a drink yourself?
CORYDON. Of course it is.
THYRSIS. Well, let me see . . . a bowl
Of water,—come back in an hour, Corydon.
I'm busy now.
CORYDON. Oh, Thyrsis, give me a bowl
Of water!—and I'll fill the bowl with jewels,
And bring it back!
THYRSIS. Be off, I'm busy now.
(*He catches sight of the weed, picks it up and looks at it, unseen by* CORYDON.)
Wait!—Pick me out the finest stones you have . . .
I'll bring you a drink of water presently.
CORYDON (*goes back and sits down, with the jewels before him*).
A bowl of jewels is a lot of jewels.
THYRSIS. I wonder if it has a bitter taste.
CORYDON. There's sure to be a stone or two among them
I have grown fond of, pouring them from one hand
Into the other.
THYRSIS. I hope it doesn't taste
Too bitter, just at first.
CORYDON. A bowl of jewels
Is far too many jewels to give away
And not get back again.
THYRSIS. I don't believe
He'll notice. He's too thirsty. He'll gulp it down
And never notice.
CORYDON. There ought to be some way
To get them back again. . . I could give him a necklace,
And snatch it back, after I'd drunk the water,

I suppose. . . Why, as for that, of course, a *necklace*. . .

(*He puts two or three of the colored tapes together and tries their strength by pulling them, after which he puts them around his neck and pulls them, gently, nodding to himself. He gets up and goes to the wall, with the colored tapes in his hands.*)

(THYRSIS *in the meantime has poured the powdered root—black confetti—into the pot which contained the flower and filled it up with wine from the punch-bowl on the floor. He comes to the wall at the same time, holding the bowl of poison.*)

THYRSIS. Come, get your bowl of water, Corydon.

CORYDON. Ah, very good!—and for such a gift as that
I'll give you more than a bowl of unset stones.
I'll give you three long necklaces, my friend.
Come closer. Here they are.

(*Puts the ribbons about* THYRSIS' *neck.*)

THYRSIS (*putting bowl to* CORYDON'S *mouth*). I'll hold the bowl
Until you've drunk it all.

CORYDON. Then hold it steady.
For every drop you spill I'll have a stone back
Out of this chain.

THYRSIS. I shall not spill a drop.

(CORYDON *drinks, meanwhile beginning to strangle* THYRSIS.)

THYRSIS. Don't pull the string so tight.

CORYDON. You're spilling the water.

THYRSIS. You've had enough—you've had enough—stop pulling
The string so tight!

CORYDON. Why, that's not tight at all . . .
How's this?

THYRSIS (*drops bowl*). You're strangling me! Oh, Corydon!
It's only a game!—and you are strangling me!

CORYDON. It's only a game, is it?—Yet I believe
You've poisoned me in earnest!

(*Writhes and pulls the strings tighter, winding them about* THYRSIS' *neck.*)

THYRSIS. Corydon! (*Dies.*)

CORYDON. You've poisoned me in earnest. . . . I feel so cold. . . .
So cold . . . this is a very silly game. . . .
Why do we play it?—let's not play this game
A minute more . . . let's make a little song
About a lamb . . . I'm coming over the wall,
No matter what you say,—I want to be near you. . . .

(*Groping his way, with arms wide before him, he strides through the frail papers of the wall without knowing it, and continues seeking for the wall straight across the stage.*)

Where is the wall? (*Gropes his way back, and stands very near* THYRSIS *without seeing him; he speaks slowly.*) There isn't any wall,
I think. (*Takes a step forward, his foot touches* THYRSIS' *body, and he falls down beside him.*)
Thyrsis, where is your cloak?—just give me
A little bit of your cloak! . . . (*Draws corner of* THYRSIS' *cloak over his shoulders, falls across* THYRSIS' *body, and dies.*)

(COTHURNUS *closes the prompt-book with a bang, arises matter-of-factly, comes down stage, and places the table over the two bodies, drawing down the cover so that they are hidden from any actors on the stage, but visible to the audience, pushing in their feet and hands with his boot. He then turns his back to the audience, and claps his hands twice.*)

COTHURNUS. Strike the scene! (*Exit* COTHURNUS.)

(*Enter* PIERROT *and* COLUMBINE.)

PIERROT. Don't puff so, Columbine!

COLUMBINE. Lord, what a mess
This set is in! If there's one thing I hate
Above everything else,—even more than getting my feet wet—
It's clutter!—He might at least have left the scene
The way he found it . . . don't you say so, Pierrot?

(*She picks up punch bowl. They arrange chairs as before at ends of table.*)

PIERROT. Well, I don't know. I think it rather diverting
The way it is. (*Yawns, picks up confetti bowl.*) Shall we begin?

COLUMBINE (*screams*). My God!
What's that there under the table?

PIERROT. It is the bodies
Of the two shepherds from the other play.

COLUMBINE (*slowly*). How curious to strangle him like that,
With colored paper ribbons.

PIERROT. Yes, and yet
I dare say he is just as dead. (*Pauses. Calls.*) Cothurnus!
Come drag these bodies out of here! We can't
Sit down and eat with two dead bodies lying
Under the table! . . . The audience wouldn't stand for it!

COTHURNUS (*off stage*). What makes you think so?—Pull down the tablecloth
On the other side, and hide them from the house,
And play the farce. The audience will forget.

PIERROT. That's so. Give me a hand here, Columbine.

(PIERROT *and* COLUMBINE *pull down the table cover in such a way that the two bodies are hidden from the house, then merrily set their bowls back on the table, draw up their chairs, and begin the play exactly as before.*)

COLUMBINE. Pierrot, a macaroon,—I cannot *live*
Without a macaroon!

PIERROT. My only love,
You are *so* intense! . . . Is it Tuesday, Columbine?—
I'll kiss you if it's Tuesday. (*Curtains begin to close slowly.*)

COLUMBINE. It is Wednesday,
If you must know . . . Is this my artichoke
Or yours?

PIERROT. Ah, Columbine, as if it mattered!
Wednesday. . . Will it be Tuesday, then, to-morrow,
By any chance? . . .

CURTAIN

Poor Aubrey

BY GEORGE KELLY

First presented at the Palace Theatre, New York City, and was played in the principal Keith and Orpheum Theatres for two years. It was produced by the Little Theatre of Mobile, Alabama, on April 18, 1929.

CHARACTERS

AUBREY PIPER
AMY (his wife)
MRS. FISHER (Amy's Mother)
MRS. COLE (a friend of Amy's)

The scene is the sitting room in Mrs. Fisher's house, about four o'clock of a Saturday afternoon in February.

AMY *enters briskly through the portières at the right, carrying a fancy cushion, which she sets in the armchair at the back of the room; then continues on over to an arched doorway at the left and draws the curtains together. She is a dark-haired, trim-looking woman, in her late twenties, dressed in black—a very pretty dress, of black crêpe, with a graceful side sash of the goods, piped with buff-colored silk. She has on black slippers and stockings, and wears a string of buff-colored beads—quite large. Her general manner suggests a quality of intelligent definiteness; something of which is even evident in the arrangement of her hair. While she is engaged at the curtains, the portières over at the right are brushed aside, and her husband swings into the room, and stands preening himself near the table. He is fearfully and wonderfully gotten up!—a perfect flash of cross-barred gray and brilliantine. Poor* AUBREY! *He is painfully arrayed, even to the toupee; a feature that, as Dickens remarked of Sairey Gamp's transformation, could scarcely be called false, it is so very innocent of anything approaching to deception. And the quantities of brilliantine that have obviously been employed upon it only serve to heighten its artificiality. He is wearing a glistening white vest and a shiny gold watchchain, a necktie of living green, with a rather large horseshoe tie-pin of imitation diamonds, and a very high collar. He has a flashily bordered silk handkerchief set forth in the breast pocket of his coat, and there is a pair of heavy-rimmed nose-glasses depending from his neck on a black tape.*

AUBREY (*touching his toupee gingerly*). Does this thing look all right?

AMY. What?

AUBREY. This toupee. (*She glances over her right shoulder indifferently.*) I put some of that brilliantine on it.

AMY (*resuming her arrangement of the curtains*). It's all right.

AUBREY (*turning to the little wall mirror just below the portières at the right*). You don't seem very enthusiastic about it.

AMY (*turning from the curtains and crossing quickly to the table—an oblong table, in the middle of the room, and towards the back*). Because I don't think you need it.

(*She picks up a small folded cover from the table, shakes it out, and tosses it across her left shoulder; then commences to gather up the scattered books and put them into the little table-rack.*)

AUBREY (*settling the toupee at the mirror*). What do you want your friend to think, that you married an old man?

AMY. Why, a man doesn't look old simply because he hasn't a big head of hair.

AUBREY. Well, mine's pretty thin here on top.

AMY. Well, that's nothing; lots of young men haven't much.

AUBREY (*turning to her*). Why, it was you that suggested my getting a toupee in the first place!

AMY (*stopping, and resting her hands on the table; and speaking directly to him*). I know very well it was; because I knew I'd never have a minute's peace till you'd get one. All I heard morning, noon and night was something about your hair coming out. You might think nobody ever heard of anybody being baldheaded.

AUBREY (*turning back to the mirror*). Well, a man's got to make the most of himself.

AMY. Well, if you think that thing's adding anything to *your* appearance, you've got another think. (*She starts towards the tabourette in front of the bay-window over at the left.*) Lift up this plant here for me, I want to put this cover on. (*She picks up a dead leaf or two from the floor and tosses them out the window. He remains standing at the mirror, looking at the toupee very critically from various angles.*) Aubrey!

AUBREY (*without moving, and with a touch of irritation*). All right, all right!

AMY. Well, hurry up!—I want to change these covers. (*He withdraws lingeringly from the mirror.*) You'll keep fooling with that wig till there isn't a hair left on it.

AUBREY (*crossing to her*). It isn't a wig, now, Amy! I've told you that half a dozen times!

AMY (*raising her hand quietly, to silence him*). Well, a toupee then, dearie,—don't get excited.

AUBREY. I'm not getting excited at all!

AMY (*indicating the plant with an authoritative gesture*). Lift up this plant and shut up. (*He lifts up the plant and holds it, till she has changed the covers.*) There.

(*He sets the plant down again, and she settles it more precisely.*)

AUBREY (*starting back across the room, in front of the sofa*). You just call it a wig because you know it makes me mad!

AMY (*straightening up and looking after him, with one hand on her hip*). I don't know why it should make you so mad, to have it called a wig.

AUBREY (*turning to her sharply*). Because it *isn't* a wig! It's a toupee!

AMY (*turning to the plant again and giving it a final touch*). Well, it's pretty, whatever it is.

AUBREY. It isn't even a toupee; it's just a patch!

AMY (*starting across to the back of the center table, carrying the soiled cover*). It's a young *wig*, that's what it is. (*He turns and glares at her. She settles the scarf on the center table.*) And if it were only a half as big as it is, anybody that'd look at it a mile away'd know that it never grew on you.

(*She goes quickly out through the portières at the right, and he returns to the mirror and preens himself generally. Immediately she comes back into the room again, carrying a big, dark dust-cloth, with which she commences to dust the center table; while he struts across the room in front of the table, settling his cuffs and whistling the opening bars of the chorus of "I'm Forever Blowing Bubbles."*)

AUBREY (*as he approaches the bay-window*). What do you say about putting a couple of these plants out on the front porch?

AMY. What for?

AUBREY. I think it adds a lot to the appearance of the house as you come up the street.

AMY. Oh, don't be silly, Aubrey!

AUBREY (*wheeling around and looking at her in astonishment*). What do you mean, don't be silly?

AMY (*pausing in her dusting*). Why, who ever heard of anybody putting plants on a front porch in February!

AUBREY. I don't mean to leave them out there! We could bring them in again as soon as she goes.

AMY (*starting for the little corner table down at the right*). Yes, and she'd go away thinking we were both crazy. (*She arranges the few magazines on the table, and then commences to dust it.*)

AUBREY (*sauntering back to the center table, where he proceeds to take the books which she has just arranged out of the little rack, and stand them on their ends*). Oh, everybody's thinking you're crazy, with you!

AMY (*turning to him and speaking emphatically*). Well, I know that's exactly what *I'd* think, if I were to come along and see plants on an open porch in the middle of winter.

AUBREY (*occupied with the book arrangement, and without looking up*). Well, I've seen *lots* of plants on front porches in the winter.

AMY (*returning to her work of dusting the table*). Well, if you did, they were *enclosed* porches. (*She finishes the dusting, and starts back towards the center table; but comes to a dead stop upon seeing the arrangement of the books, and her husband's intense absorption in it. There is a slight pause.*) What are you doing with those books?

AUBREY (*still busy*). I'm just standing them up this way, so you can see what they are.

AMY. Can't you see what they are in the rack?

AUBREY. Certainly you can; but I think they show up better this way.

AMY (*stepping towards him and pushing him out of the way*). Go away! and let them alone!

(*She hurriedly commences to gather them up and restore them to the rack.*)

AUBREY (*wandering towards the arched doorway at the left*). That's the way they have them in all the store windows.

(*He proceeds to push the curtains back at the arched doorway.*)

AMY. Well, this isn't a store window. (*She glances at what he's doing, and starts towards him.*) And don't push those curtains back that way, Aubrey! I just fixed them.

(*She pushes him towards the back of the room. He wanders around her and comes forward at the left.*)

AUBREY. They cover up the Victrola, that way.

AMY (*settling the curtains*). That doesn't matter. These doors look too bare with the curtains pushed back. (*She starts back towards the center table to complete her rearrangement of the books.*) Now, let things alone, for heaven's sake! She can see the Victrola when she goes in there.

AUBREY (*sauntering a little towards the right, in front of the center table*). She may not *go* in there.

AMY (*addressing him, as she crosses to the portières at the right, taking the dust cloth with her*). Well, I guess she's seen Victrolas before, even if she *doesn't* go in there. (*She goes out through the portières. He stands for a second fixing himself, then breaks into "I'm Forever Blowing Bubbles" again. The detection of a speck of dust on his left shoe brings his whistling to a close; and, whipping out the eloquent handkerchief from his breast pocket, he leans over it flick it off. The effort dislodges the toupee, which drops to the floor in front of him. He snatches it up frantically, and claps it back upon his head; thrusts his handkerchief back into his pocket, and, with a panic-stricken glance over his right shoulder, in the direction of the portières, bolts to the bay-window, at the left, holding the toupee in place with his left hand.* AMY *hurries in from the right carrying a small vase, which she takes to the little stand down at the right.*) Any sign of her?

AUBREY (*adjusting the toupee, and pretending to look out the window*). I don't see any sign of her yet.

AMY (*turning from the little stand and moving towards the front of the center table*). Maybe her train's late.

(*She glances about the room, to see that everything is all right.*)

AUBREY. I don't know why it *should* be; there wasn't any hold-up along the line to-day that *I* heard of.

AMY (*settling her sash*). She said in her telegram that she'd get into Broad Street at three o'clock sharp, and that she'd come right out here—Because she had to leave again on the Bridge train at four-fourten.

AUBREY (*turning from the window and coming towards her*). Too bad she didn't know, she could have gotten right off here at North Philadelphia—And then she could have gotten that Bridge train right there again at—a—four-twenty-seven.

(*He finishes his remarks with an explanatory gesture, and stands looking at his wife. She is still settling her sash. There is a fractional pause. Then she finishes and looks up at him. Then there is another pause, during which her eyes shift to his toupee, which is on askew,—a bit over the left eye.*)

AMY (*with a kind of wearied impatience*). Fix your toupee.

AUBREY (*putting his hand to it, and with a note of challenge in his voice*). What's the matter with it?

AMY. Why, it's all over the place.

AUBREY. Is that so!

AMY. Well, look at it!

AUBREY. Well, I fixed it that way!

(*He emphasizes the remark with a little bob of his head, and starts up around the center table towards the mirror.*)

AMY. Well, it's pretty.

AUBREY. To let the air get to my scalp.

AMY. Well, for Heaven's sake, don't have it fixed that way when Marion comes! (*Fixing the lace at her left cuff.*) You look as though your head were lopsided.

(*He turns from the mirror, and gives her a withering look. But she is occupied with her cuff.*)

AUBREY (*turning back to the mirror*). How is it you didn't put on your other dress?

AMY. What other dress?

AUBREY. The one with all the beads.

AMY (*looking at him*). Why, this is my good dress.

AUBREY. I think that other one's more of a flash.

AMY (*turning away again and settling the front of her dress*). Oh, don't be such a show-off, Aubrey!

AUBREY (*turning sharply and looking at her*). Show-off!

AMY. That's what I said.

AUBREY. I don't know how you figure *that's* showing off!—Because I want you to *look* good.

AMY (*looking at him stonily, and speaking in a level key*). You want me to look good because I'm *your* wife. And you want this friend of mine to *see* me looking good; just as you want her to see that Victrola in there—(*She indicates the arched door on the left with a slight nod.*) that isn't half paid for.

(*She looks out*).

AUBREY (*coming towards her a step or two*). I suppose *you'd* rather have her think you married some poor thing!

AMY. Listen, Aubrey—It won't make the least bit of difference *what* we want her to think—She's a very smart girl; and all she'll have to do is glance around this room, and she'll know *exactly* what I married.

(*She looks straight out again.*)

AUBREY (*mimicking her tone*). Is that so! (*She simply emphasizes her remarks with a slow and very positive nod.*) Well, now, you listen to me for a minute, Amy! You know I can beat it right over to the barber shop (*She breaks into a rather tired little laugh.*) and stay there, till this friend of yours has gone, (*He moves over towards the little stand at the right.*) if you're so awfully afraid that I'm going to show up so badly in front of her!

AMY (*looking after him with a very knowing expression*). No fear of your beating it over to the barber shop.

AUBREY. No?

AMY. You'll be strutting around here in front of her if she stays till midnight.

AUBREY (*very nettled, and securing his tie and tie-pin*). All right.

AMY (*taking a step or two towards him*). And, by the way, Aubrey—When Marion comes—I want you to do me a little favor; and don't be giving her a lot of big talk,—the way you were doing to that insurance man the other night; (*He turns and looks at her in astonished indignation.*) for I don't want her to think you're silly.

AUBREY. When was I doing any big talk to any insurance man?

AMY. The other night when you were talking to that man about the price of a fifty-thousand dollar policy.

AUBREY. Well, what about it?

AMY. Nothing; only that he was just laughing up his sleeve at you.

AUBREY. Is that so!

AMY. Well now, what else *could* he do, Aubrey? He knew you hadn't the slightest intention of taking any such policy.

AUBREY. How do you know he did?

AMY. Because he knows you're only a clerk. And that you don't get enough salary in six months to pay one year's premium on a policy like that. So when Marion comes, please don't be trying to impress her. (*She turns away from him rather slowly and moves up at the right of the center table.*) For she's a very sensible woman.

AUBREY (*turning and going up to the mirror*). I won't have anything to say to the woman at all.

AMY (*standing above the center table glancing through a magazine*). Oh, yes, you will, dearie.

AUBREY. She's not coming to see me.

AMY. That doesn't make any difference to you.

AUBREY. No reason why I should stand around *gabbing* to her.

AMY. Well, you'll stand around gabbing, if you can get anybody to listen to you.

AUBREY. Well, now, you watch me.

AMY. I've been watching you; and listening to you too; for nearly four years.

AUBREY (*turning to her from the mirror, very peevishly, and holding up his right hand*). All right, I'll raise my hand,—if I want to say anything. (*He moves forward at the right.*)

AMY. I know what you'll do, if you get the chance; I've heard you before.

(*There is a slight pause, during which he frets a bit, down at the right. Then his mood shifts and he breaks into whistling his familiar "I'm Forever Blowing Bubbles." But this dies gradually as he becomes conscious of the little vase which Amy brought in for the stand at his right. He tilts his head a bit to one side and looks at it with critical disapproval.*)

AUBREY. You know, it's too bad we haven't got something flashier for this stand here.

AMY (*just lifting her eyes over the top of the magazine*). There's that vase up in mother's room.

AUBREY. Is she up there now?

AMY. She was when I came down.

AUBREY (*with a gesture of finality, and starting across in front of the center table*). Well, *that's* out.

AMY. Why, she wouldn't mind my taking it.

AUBREY (*turning to his left and speaking emphatically*). It isn't that! But if she sees you taking anything out of her room, she'll get an idea there's something going on down here, and she'll be right down for the rest of the night and you won't be able to chase her!

(*He turns to his right and looks out the bay-window.*)

AMY. Why, she knows that Marion Brill is coming here this afternoon.

AUBREY (*turning to her sharply, with a distressed expression*). Did you tell her?

AMY. Certainly I told her.

AUBREY (*despairingly, and crossing over again in front of the center table*). Good night!

AMY. Why, I want her to *meet* Marion! She's never *met* her!

AUBREY. Well, if your mother ever gets *talking,* this friend of yours'll know everything from *your* age to *my* salary! (*He turns away to his right.*) Now, I'm telling you!

AMY (*with a glance towards the portières at the right, and speaking in an emphatic but subdued manner*). I don't care whether she does or not.

AUBREY. Well, I *do.*

(AMY *glances quickly towards the bay-window at the left; then, dropping the magazine, she steps eagerly towards it.*)

AMY. There's a taxi, now.

(*She draws the curtain aside and looks keenly out.*)

AUBREY (*whirling round and striding towards the bay-window,—holding on to his toupee with his left hand*). Is it stopping?

AMY (*suddenly, and in a tone of suppressed excitement*). *There* she is! (*She runs to the door at the back of the room and vanishes into the hallway.*) She's looking for the number!

(AUBREY *peers eagerly through the bay-window, then steps quickly up to the door at the back.*)

AUBREY. Don't stand out there talking, now, Amy, without something around you!

(*He rushes across at the back, still holding on to the toupee and, after a fleeting glance through the portières at the right, reaches the mirror, where he gives himself a hasty and critical survey. Then the laughter and greetings of his wife and* MRS. COLE *reach him from the front door; so, with a glance in that direction, he struts forward at the right and strikes a pose,—swinging his nose-glasses carelessly back and forth, and looking away off.*)

AMY (*out at the left*). I knew you through the window of the taxi!

MRS. COLE. Well, you know, I was thinking all the way out, "Now, I wonder if Amy got my wire."

AMY. I got it yesterday morning.

MRS. COLE and AMY (*together*).

(MRS. COLE). Because, you know, I couldn't wait to hear from you.

(AMY). But I said to Aubrey, "There's no use in my sending any word now, for she's already left Chicago by this time."

(*The front door closes.*)

MRS. COLE. Well, you see, dear I didn't know *definitely—*

MRS. COLE and AMY (*together*).

(MRS. COLE). Up until Thursday night that I was coming. (AMY, *appearing in the hall door*). Oh, well, it doesn't matter! (*Coming into the room.*) Just so long as I get to see you.

(*She glances at her husband, then turns and faces the hall door. There is a second's pause; then* MRS. COLE *enters the room; and, glancing about, stops just inside the door. She is a bit older than* AMY, *—probably three or four years, and considerably lighter in coloring. And very smart.* AMY *said she was, and she is—extremely so. It's in the clearness of her eye, and the peculiarly deft coördination of her general movement. Her clothes are smart too; and by the looks of them, she must have married rather well; they are quite gorgeous. A fine seal coat, full length, with a cape effect, and an enormous muff made of black fox; rather large hat of black lace over black satin, faced with pale coral, and black slippers and stockings. She doesn't remove her coat, but when she opens it, there is a glimpse of a light coral-colored dress, heavily trimmed with steel beads, a long neck-scarf in steel silk, and a lovely-looking necklace of pale jade. She is wearing white kid gloves and carries a fancy bag made of jade and coral beads on her left wrist.*)

MRS. COLE. What an attractive house you have, Amy.

AMY (*smiling, and indicating her husband*). There's the principal attraction, over there.

(AUBREY *acknowledges the compliment by melting slightly.*)

MRS. COLE (*smiling graciously and passing down at the left of the center table, towards* AUBREY). Is this *him?*

(*He advances.*)

AMY (*coming forward at the left of the center table*). That's him.

MRS. COLE. I'm *so* glad to meet you, Mr. Piper.

AUBREY (*with a touch of condescension*). How do you do.

(*They shake hands.*)

MRS. COLE. You know, I've always been enormously *curious* to see Amy's husband.

AUBREY. That so?

AMY (*looking straight out, and securing a hairpin in the right side of her head*). There he is.

MRS. COLE (*tilting her head a bit to the left side and looking at* AUBREY *with a smile*). He's terribly good-looking.

AMY (*turning away*). Oh!

(MRS. COLE *turns her head sharply and looks at her, still smiling.*)

AUBREY (*addressing his wife*). You hear *that?*

(MRS. COLE *turns again to* AUBREY.)

AMY. Please don't tell him that, Marion! he's bad enough as it is.

MRS. COLE. I don't know how you managed it, Amy. I could never do it. You should see *my* husband, Mr. Piper. I don't suppose he's any *older* than Mr. Piper, but, my dear, he *looks* old enough to be your father. (AMY *gives a little laugh of incredulity, and* MRS. COLE *turns suddenly to her.*) Really! (*Then she turns suddenly again to* AUBREY.) He's almost bald!

(AUBREY'S *smile freezes.*)

AMY. Let me take your coat, Marion.

(AUBREY *turns quietly around to the right, touching his toupee with his right hand, and moves up to the mirror, where he takes a reassuring peep at it, unobserved.*)

MRS. COLE. I don't think I'll bother, dear, really; that taxicab's waiting out there for me. You see, I've got to get that Bridge train out of Broad Street at four-fourteen.

AUBREY (*coming forward at the right*). I was just saying to Amy, it's too bad you didn't know, you could have gotten right off here at North Philadelphia, and wouldn't have had to go downtown at all.

AMY. You know, that Bridge train makes a stop here, Marion, at North Philadelphia, on the way to Atlantic City.

MRS. COLE. Oh, does it!

AMY. Get's there at four-twenty-seven.

MRS. COLE. Isn't it too bad I didn't know that.

AUBREY. Well, you won't have to go back downtown now, as it is, will you, Mrs. Cole?

MRS. COLE. Yes, I've checked my grip at Broad Street.

AMY. Oh, isn't that too bad!

MRS. COLE. Well, it doesn't matter! Just so long as I got to see you.

AMY. That's about all you'll be able to do.

MRS. COLE. Well, sometime I'm going to invite myself to spend a few days with you, and then we'll have lots of time to talk.

AMY. I wish you could spend them now.

MRS. COLE. So do I, dear child; but what can a poor woman do with a sick husband on her hands.

AMY. How is he, Marion?

MRS. COLE. Why, he's pretty good, now.

AMY. Sit down.

(*She picks up the cushion from the right end of the sofa to make a place for* MRS. COLE.)

MRS. COLE (*stepping over to the sofa and unfastening her coat*). I must unfasten this coat. (AMY *sits at the left end of the sofa; then* MRS. COLE *sits down.*) You know he had quite an attack of the flu last winter; and, I don't know, he never seemed to really get over it.

(AUBREY *has assumed a position over at the right of the center table, and is listening with a general expression of heavy consequence.*)

AMY. So many people didn't.

AUBREY. One of the bookkeepers down at my office was telling me the other day that the flu has left him with a weak heart.

MRS. COLE. Yes, I've heard of that, too. But with my husband, it all seems to be in his nerves. That's the reason he's at Atlantic City now.

AMY. How long has he been there, Marion?

MRS. COLE. Since the week after New Year's.

AUBREY. They say Atlantic City's a great place for the nerves.

MRS. COLE. Well, Ralph says he feels ever so much better. I had a letter from him on Tuesday, and he said he was only going to stay another week. So I thought I'd better just run down there myself and see how he is before he starts that long trip back to Chicago.

AMY. That flu was a dreadful thing, wasn't it?

MRS. COLE. Dreadful! My dear, you've never seen anything change a person the way it has changed my husband. (*She turns suddenly to* AUBREY.) He's even lost his hair. (*She coughs a little, and uses her handkerchief; while* AUBREY *glides to the mirror again, touching his toupee discreetly.*

AMY (*picking up the muff from* MRS. COLE'S *lap*). I love this muff, Marion.

MRS. COLE. Do you know how long I've had that?

AMY. How long?

MRS. COLE. Three years last Christmas.

AMY. Really!

MRS. COLE. Ralph gave it to me the first Christmas we were married.

AMY (*holding it out on her left arm*). It's beautiful!

(AUBREY *comes forward again.*)

AUBREY. What kind of fur *is* that, Mrs.

Cole?

MRS. COLE. Fox.

AUBREY. Makes a nice looking fur.

MRS. COLE (*turning and looking at it*). It was pretty when I first got it. (*Turning again to* AUBREY.) But it's getting old now; (*looking back to the muff*) the hair's commencing to fall out. (*He turns and drifts to the back of the room.*) I was so sorry to hear about your father, Amy.

AMY. Yes, it was so sudden.

MRS. COLE. How is your mother, Amy? (AUBREY *turns and looks towards his wife.*)

AMY. She keeps pretty well.

MRS. COLE. That's good.

AMY. She's here with us, you know. (AUBREY *makes a despairing gesture.*)

MRS. COLE. Oh, is she?

AMY. Yes.

MRS. COLE. Living with you, you mean?

AMY (*getting up, and going round back of the sofa*). Hum-hum. I must tell her you're here.

MRS. COLE. Well, now, don't bother her, Amy, if she's doing anything.

AMY (*crossing to the portières at the right*). Not a thing—She's crazy to see you.

MRS. COLE and AMY (*together*).

(MRS. COLE). I don't want to bother her.

(AMY). I told her I'd call her as soon as you came. (*Going out through the portières.*) I'll be down in a second.

(AUBREY, *standing up at the back of the room, glances after his wife, then turns and looks at* MRS. COLE. *She is settling her muff beside her on the sofa. He glances at himself in the mirror, and then comes forward at the right, rather grandly, flipping the nose-glasses back and forth.*)

MRS. COLE. Isn't it nice that Amy can have her mother here with her.

AUBREY. Yes; I've had her here ever since Mr. Fisher died.

MRS. COLE. She must be so much company for you.

AUBREY. Yes; a person'd never be lonesome.

MRS. COLE. I often say to *my* husband, I wish there were some one like that with us; I get so lonesome sometimes in the house during the day.

AUBREY. Well, when my father-in-law died, I thought Amy's mother might just as well come here with us. She was alone; and we had plenty of room; so I said, "Come ahead! (*He makes a rather magnificent gesture with his right hand.*) The more the merrier!"

MRS. COLE. This *is* rather a large house, isn't it?

AUBREY. Yes, it is. Quite a wonderfully made house, too. They were put up by the McNeil people out here at Jenkintown. They're considered to build the best dwelling-house of anybody in the country. They just put up the twenty of them, as kind of sample houses—ten on that side, and ten on this. Of course, these on this side have the southern exposure; so a person's got to have quite a little pull to get hold of one of these. (*He catches his thumbs in the armholes of his vest, and, tilting his head a bit to the left side, looks away out and off, tapping his fingers on his chest.*) But I have a friend—that's one of the biggest real estate men here in town, and he was able to fix it for me.

MRS. COLE. You were very lucky, weren't you?

AUBREY. Yes, I *was* pretty lucky in a way. Although I'd like to have gotten hold of one of the corner ones.

MRS. COLE. Are they a much larger house than these?

AUBREY. They're a fifteen-thousand-dollar house; these are only ten. (*He moves across in front of her, with ever so slight a suggestion of strut.*)

MRS. COLE. I see.

AUBREY (*with a casual glance out of the bay-window*). I'm very anxious to get hold of one of them. I told this friend of mine to keep his eye open, and if there's a chance, I'll go as high as twenty thousand. Then, of course, I could always rent this.

MRS. COLE. It's an awfully nice street.

AUBREY. Nice in summer.

MRS. COLE. I was so surprised when I saw it, because the taxicab driver didn't know where it was when I asked him. (AUBREY *looks at her, with a quick movement of his head.*)

AUBREY. Didn't know where Cresson Street was?

MRS. COLE. He said not.

AUBREY (*shaking his head from side to side and smiling with heavy amusement*). He must be an awful rube.

MRS. COLE. He had to ask the traffic officer down on Broad Street.

AUBREY. Well, I'll tell you—I don't suppose they *have* many calls for taxis out this way. You see, most everybody in through here has his own car.

MRS. COLE. Oh, I see.

AUBREY. Some of them have a half a dozen, for that matter. (*He laughs consequentially, and she reflects his amusement faintly.*) I was saying to Amy, when we got your wire yesterday, it was too bad *my* car was laid up, I could have picked you up at the station to-day.

MRS. COLE. Oh, that didn't matter.

AUBREY. But I've been working it pretty hard lately, and I had to turn it in Thursday to have the valves ground.

MRS. COLE. There's always something to be done to them, isn't there?

AUBREY. I should say so. Funny thing, too,—people have an idea if they get hold of a high-priced car their trouble's over. (*She smiles and shakes her head from side to side in appreciation of that illusion.*) I swear, I've had just as much trouble with my *Pierce Arrow* as I ever had with my Buick.

(*They both laugh, and* AUBREY *looks out the window.*)

AMY (*coming in through the portières at the right*). Mother says she was just coming down to inquire how it was you hadn't come. (AUBREY *turns and looks at his wife, then turns around to his right and moves towards the back of the room.* MRS. FISHER *comes in through the portières, and* MRS. COLE *rises.*) *This* is Mrs. Cole, Mother—Marion Brill that you've heard so much about.

MRS. FISHER (*coming forward at the right of the center table*). Well, indeed I have.

MRS. COLE (*advancing*). I'm *so* glad to meet you, Mrs. Fisher.

MRS. FISHER (*shaking hands with her*). How do you do. I'm certainly pleased to meet you, too.

MRS. COLE. Thank you.

MRS. FISHER. For I think I've heard your name more than any other girl's name I ever heard in this house.

MRS. COLE. Well, Amy and I worked beside each other so long.

MRS. FISHER. All I used to hear morning, noon and night was, "Marion Brill said so and so" (MRS. COLE *and* AMY *laugh.*) *or,* "Marion Brill is going to do so and so." (MRS. FISHER *laughs.*)

AMY (*standing at her mother's right*). I'm afraid that's about all we did was talk, wasn't it, Marion?

(*She laughs again.*)

MRS. COLE. It's about all *I* used to do.

(*She laughs.*)

MRS. FISHER (*indicating the sofa*). Won't you sit down, Mrs. Cole?

MRS. COLE (*turning to her right, towards the sofa*). Thanks.

AMY (*indicating the armchair at the right of the center table*). Sit here, Mother.

MRS. FISHER (*passing to the armchair, in front of* AMY). Amy, why didn't you ask Mrs. Cole to take off her coat?

MRS. COLE (*sitting on the sofa*). She did, Mrs. Fisher.

(MRS. FISHER sits down.)

AMY (*sitting on the edge of the center table*). Marion can't stay, Mother.

MRS. COLE. I've got to go almost immediately, Mrs. Fisher.

MRS. FISHER. It's too bad you can't stay for a cup of tea, anyway.

MRS. COLE. I'd love it, Mrs. Fisher, but I really haven't time.

MRS. FISHER. You're going to Atlantic City, aren't you?

MRS. COLE. Yes.

MRS. FISHER (*as though admitting a weakness in herself*). I wish I was going with you.

(*She laughs shyly. And when she laughs she's pretty. She must have been a rather pretty girl; for there are traces of it yet; even after nearly thirty years as the wife of a poor man. Her husband was a wage-earner, always; and it was only by dint of vigilance and excessive scrimping that they were able to purchase and pay for the house in which she now lives. But the economic strain has told upon her, in many ways; perhaps, most obviously, in the developing of a certain plainness of personal quality,—a simplicity that is at once pathetic and, in a way, quaint. And her manner of dressing and the arrangement of her hair rather heighten this impression. She looks old-fashioned. But her hair is quite lovely; it's thick and silvery, with the loveliest wave in it; and she has it simply parted in the middle and drawn back over her ears. She must have been a decided blonde. Her dress, which looks as though she might have made it herself, a long time ago, has no particular pattern; simply a plain, brown poplin dress, without a bit of trimming except a little ruffle of the goods, about two inches deep, around the hem of the skirt. This skirt is one of the old-fashioned, full kind,—touching all the way round. She is wearing a deep lace collar, probably to re-*

lieve the almost basque-like tightness of the body, and an enormous breastpin, featuring a very vague likeness of a delicate-looking gentleman in a straw hat; presumably, MR. FISHER.)

MRS. COLE. Do you like Atlantic City, Mrs. Fisher?

(*She nods, still smiling.*)

AMY. Yes, mother's always been crazy about Atlantic City.

MRS. FISHER. I like the bathing.

MRS. COLE. Yes, wonderful, isn't it?

MRS. FISHER. I used to go in sometimes twice a day.

(*She laughs a little again.*)

MRS. COLE. You must have liked it.

MRS. FISHER (*with an instant change to seriousness of expression and voice*). Of course, that was before my operation.

(AUBREY, *who has been standing at the back of the room watching her with an expression of contemptuous pity, makes an impatient gesture and turns to the bay-window.* AMY *feels the movement, and, under the pretext of touching her hair, glances towards him.*)

MRS. COLE. It certainly is a wonderful place.

MRS. FISHER. I haven't been there now since my husband died.

MRS. COLE. Is that so?

MRS. FISHER. Yes; it'll be four years the seventeenth of next October. He died the day Amy was twenty-five. (AUBREY *turns from the bay-window and looks daggers at her.*) Died on her birthday. Didn't he, Amy?

AMY. Yes.

(*She glances towards* AUBREY *again, and he says voicelessly to her, but with very eloquent gestures, "Didn't I tell you!" and goes towards the back of the room again.*)

MRS. COLE. And you haven't been to Atlantic City *since* then?

MRS. FISHER. No, not since then. But before that, we used to spend two days there every single summer. (AUBREY *turns at the back of the room and looks at her stonily.*) Go down on Saturday morning, and come up Sunday night. Of course, it didn't cost us anything, you know, 'cept our fares; because we used to carry our lunch with us (AUBREY *begins to boil.*) And in those days, they used to allow the excursionists to sleep under the board walk, if you remember.

(AUBREY *raises his hand in the hope of attracting her attention and silencing her; but she is oblivious of him. He's away up in the left-hand corner of the room, out of range of* MRS. COLE's *eye.*)

MRS. COLE. Yes, I remember.

MRS. FISHER. Dear me, I used to look forward to those two days the whole year round. (*She laughs a little.*) I was just saying to Amy the other day, that if I could see my way clear to do it, I believe I'd enjoy a day down there now, just as much as ever I did.

MRS. COLE. Well, I don't see why you shouldn't, Mrs. Fisher.

MRS. FISHER (*with another instantaneous shift to seriousness*). Well, of course, since my operation.

(AUBREY *makes a movement of excessive irritation, and* AMY *gets it; and thinks it wise to interrupt her mother.*)

MRS. FISHER and AMY (*together*).

(MRS. FISHER). I've got to be more careful. I can't do the things—that —I—

(AMY, *turning suddenly to* MRS. COLE). *You* haven't been in Atlantic City since you were married, have you, Marion?

MRS. COLE. No, it's five years since I've been there.

MRS. FISHER. Are you going to stay there for any length of time, Mrs. Cole?

MRS. COLE. No, I'm not, Mrs. Fisher; I just want to see how my husband it.

MRS. FISHER. Has he consumption?

(AUBREY *snaps with irritation.*)

MRS. COLE. No-o, he had the flu last winter; (MRS. FISHER *folds her lips in, shakes her head slowly from side to side, and looks at the floor in front of her.*) and he's never been exactly himself since.

MRS. FISHER. They never do much good after that flu.

(AMY *rises and crosses towards the left, above the sofa.*)

AMY. I suppose it depends upon how bad a person's had it, Mother.

(*As soon as she passes out of the range of* MRS. COLE's *vision,* AUBREY *appeals to her to know if there isn't something she can do to shut her mother up. She simply dismisses him with a deft gesture; and, with a sharp nod of her head, indicates the immediate presence of* MRS. COLE.)

MRS. FISHER (*unaware of the situation*). Well, now, this doctor that tended me during my operation (AUBREY *whirls round and goes to the hall door, at the back, and* AMY *comes around and sits down on the sofa, to* MRS. COLE's *left.*) Doctor Stainthorpe—she's a lady doctor—she was telling me that the flu is like scarlet fever; if it don't leave you with one thing, it'll leave you with something else.

MRS. COLE. Well, Mr. Cole seems pretty good, most of the time, but occasionally he has a spell of sort of—nervous exhaustion.

(AUBREY *wanders over and stands resting his right hand on the left end of the center table, listening to* MRS. COLE.)

MRS. FISHER. Maybe he works too hard.

MRS. COLE. No, I don't think it's that; (*Speaking directly to* AUBREY.) his work is easy enough. (*Shifting her eyes again to* MRS. FISHER.) He's just a wig-maker. (AUBREY *drifts towards the mirror.*) Makes all kinds of hair goods, you know.

MRS. FISHER. Oh, yes.

AMY. I don't think I ever knew your husband's business, Marion.

MRS. COLE. Didn't I ever tell you?

AMY. You *may* have, but I've forgotten. (*With a glance at his toupee in the mirror,* AUBREY *glides down at the right of* MRS. FISHER.)

MRS. COLE. That's what he does— Makes all these toupees that you see,— (AUBREY *turns quietly away to the right and glides up again towards the back of the room.*) And switches and—patches— All that kind of thing.

MRS. FISHER. Did you have any trouble finding the house, Mrs. Cole?

MRS. COLE. No, not very much.

AMY. Marion came out in a taxi.

MRS. FISHER (*as though coming out in a taxi were quite an experience*). Oh, *did* you!

MRS. COLE (*dropping her handkerchief at her left foot*). Yes, I came right out Broad Street.

AMY (*handing her the handkerchief*). Here's your handkerchief, Marion.

MRS. COLE *and* MRS. FISHER (*together*).

(MRS. COLE). Oh, thanks. Did I drop that?

(MRS. FISHER). Have you any children, Mrs. Cole?

MRS. COLE. What did you say, Mrs. Fisher?

MRS. FISHER. I say, have you any children?

MRS. COLE. No, I haven't, Mrs. Fisher.

MRS. FISHER. Didn't you ever have any? (AUBREY *looks helplessly at his wife, then back to his mother-in-law.*)

MRS. COLE. No.

MRS. FISHER. Well, maybe you're just as well off.

MRS. COLE. Yes, I suppose I am, in a way.

MRS. FISHER (*looking at the floor in front of her, and shaking her head philosophically*). If they never make you laugh, they'll never make you cry.

MRS. COLE. That's true.

MRS. FISHER. I buried a boy, when he was eight years old; and, dear me, it seemed as though I never in this *world* would get over it. But when I read in the newspapers now about all these bandits, and moving-picture people,—I'm kind of glad he went when he did. He might have gotten in with bad company and turned out just as bad as any of the others.

MRS. COLE. It's hard to tell how they'll turn out.

MRS. FISHER. Well, you see, this is such a terrible neighborhood in through here, to bring a boy *up* in. (AUBREY *makes a movement of controlled desperation towards the left.* AMY *glances at him, and he gives her a speaking look.*) So many foreigners.

MRS. COLE. Is that so?

MRS. FISHER. Oh, it's just dreadful. (AUBREY *tries to signal her from the upper left-hand corner of the room, with divers shakes and waves of his hands. But it is utterly lost upon* MRS. FISHER. *She is all set for a good chat; and it will require more than the gesticulations of* MR. PIPER *to distract her. So she goes serenely on; never casting a glance in his direction.*) A body'd be afraid to put their nose outside the door, after dark. Why, right across the street here. (*She extends her arm and hand towards the right.*) In two-twenty-eight, there's a big *Polish* family; and I don't believe there's a soul in that house speaks a word of English. And there's a *colored* organization of some kind has just bought two-forty-nine— (AUBREY *has passed into a state of desperate unconsciousness, and stands glaring at his mother-in-law.*) That's the corner property on this side. (*She points to the right.*) Paid three thousand dollars cash for it, too. So you can see what the neighborhood's coming to.

AMY (*tactfully*). Aubrey,— I wish you'd go down and close the heater; the house is getting cold again, I think.

(*He starts for the portières immediately, and* MRS. COLE *turns and says something to* AMY. *As* AUBREY *crosses the back of the room, he fixes* MRS. FISHER *with an icy glare, which he holds until he passes through the portières. Not knowing wherein she has offended, she turns and looks over her right shoulder after him with an expression of puzzled resentment. Then she turns to* AMY.)

MRS. FISHER. Amy, you'd better go down, too; he'll be locking those grates again, the way he did last week.

AMY (*rising and going around back of the sofa and over towards the portières*). He doesn't need to touch those grates; that fire's all right.

(*Goes out.*)

MRS. FISHER. We have one of those old-fashioned heaters; and when you're raking it, unless you turn it just a certain way, the grates'll lock. It's a perfect nuisance. I often say, I don't wonder people want to live in apartments; where they won't have to be bothered with all this heater business.

MRS. COLE. It is a bother.

MRS. FISHER. Oh, it's a pest.

MRS. COLE. Although I had the hardest time getting used to an apartment when I was first married.

MRS. FISHER. Oh, do you live in an apartment in Chicago, Mrs. Cole?

MRS. COLE. Yes, I've lived in one ever since I've been out there.

MRS. FISHER. Well, you ought to be glad of it.

MRS. COLE. Well, really, it was the only place we could get—there have been so few houses go up in Chicago in the last few years.

MRS. FISHER. That's just the way it's been here. Why, when Amy was married four years ago, she couldn't get a house for love or money. That is, I mean, one that she could afford the rent, you know.

MRS. COLE. Yes, I know.

MRS. FISHER. Of course, she could have gotten plenty at fancy rents; but as I said to her, "How are you going to pay it on his wages?" (*She turns carefully in her chair and glances over her right shoulder towards the portières, for fear* AUBREY *might be within hearing distance. Then she turns back to* MRS. COLE, *and, leaning towards her a bit, speaks in a rather subdued tone.*) He's only a clerk, you know, —down here in the Pennsylvania Freight Office. But she couldn't get a thing. Of course, I'd have liked to have her stay here; because there was only Mr. Fisher and myself; but—a— (*She turns again and glances over her right shoulder, then back again to* MRS. COLE; *this time with even more confidence.*) My husband never liked *him.* (*She indicates* AUBREY *with a nod towards the portières. Then to emphasize the fact, she looks straight at* MRS. COLE *and gives her head a little shake from side to side. But evidently she feels that she hasn't stated the circumstance sufficiently; or that, having mentioned it at all, it implies some measure of elucidation; for she rises gingerly, and, tiptoeing over to the center table, rests her left hand upon it and leans towards* MRS. COLE *in an attitude of extreme caution and confidence.*) Said he was kind of a blatherskite, you know— (*She tiptoes towards the portières, but stops halfway and turns again.*) Very big ideas and very little brains. (*She continues on to the portières and glances out; then returns to the table.*) So—a—finally, they had to take two little rooms over here on Lehigh Avenue. Nine dollars a month, so you can imagine what they were like. But you couldn't *tell* them anything. As I said to them, the night they first told me they were going to be married—I said, "How do you two ever expect to make ends meet on thirty-two dollars a week?" "Oh," he says, "that's only temporary," he says,— "I'll *own* the Pennsylvania Railroad within the next five years." This is the way he's owning it. (*She looks towards the portières; then turns back and says emphatically.*) He's never even gotten a raise. He's been getting thirty-two dollars a week for the last four years. (*She moves stealthily towards the portières again; far enough over to enable her to glance through them; then comes back to the table.*) But—a—as soon as Mr. *Fisher* died, I told Amy she could come here, and I'd take my rent out in board. And then she makes me different things to wear; she's very handy, you know.

MRS. COLE. Yes, she's a wonderful *girl.*

MRS. FISHER. But, you know, you'd think *he* was doing me a favor to *live* here. (MRS. COLE *doesn't know exactly what to say, so she simply shakes her head from side to side and smiles.*) He doesn't like me, you know. Hardly ever speaks to me. I suppose you noticed it, didn't you?

MRS. COLE. No, I didn't, Mrs. Fisher.

MRS. FISHER. He's been *furious* ever since last spring. (*She turns away again and glances towards the portières; then turns hurriedly back, as though she had a particularly incredible item of information to communicate.*) Wanted *me* to put a *mortgage* on this house to get him an automobile. Can you imagine that! He's *crazy* about automobiles. And, Mrs. Cole, I know just as well as I'm standing here, that if he *got* one, he'd only kill himself —for he has no more brains than a rabbit. So I told him. I sez—

(AMY's *voice, out at the right, interrupts her.*)

AMY. Be sure and close this cellar door Aubrey; there's a draught here if you don't.

MRS. FISHER (*tiptoeing back to her chair, with a significant gesture to* MRS. COLE.) Well, I hope you find your husband all right, Mrs. Cole.

(*She sits down.*)

MRS. COLE. I hope so, thanks, Mrs. Fisher. He *seems* pretty good, from his letters.

AMY (*coming through the portières*). I'm sorry, Marion, but I seem to be the only one around here that knows how to tend to that heater.

MRS. COLE (*rising*). Well, you know, you were always able to do everything, Amy.

(*She moves a little towards the front of the center table, fastening her glove.*)

AMY. You don't have to go already, do you, Marion?

MRS. COLE. I'm afraid so, dear. (MRS. FISHER *rises.*) It's getting on to four o'clock. (AUBREY *sways in through the portières, flicking imaginary ashes from himself with the fancy handkerchief.*)

MRS. FISHER. Couldn't you take a later train, Mrs. Cole?

(AUBREY *comes forward at the right.*)

MRS. COLE. Why, I suppose I could, Mrs. Fisher; but I've wired Mr. Cole that I'll be on *that* one.

MRS. FISHER. Oh, I see.

MRS. COLE. And he's so nervous and worrisome since he's been sick, that I'm afraid if I'm *not* on it, he'll be tearing his hair out. (*She turns, laughing a little, which* AMY *and her mother reflect, and goes back to the sofa for her muff.* AUBREY *is feigning a profound absorption in an examination of his finger nails.* AMY *crosses over after* MRS. COLE *and goes up back of the sofa towards the bay-window.*)

MRS. FISHER. Are you going back to the station on the trolley, Mrs. Cole?

MRS. COLE. No, I told the taxi to wait, Mrs. Fisher. I hope he's still out there. Is he, Amy?

AMY (*at the window*). Yes, he's still there.

MRS. FISHER (*hurrying across in front of* MRS. COLE). Oh, I must see it! Pardon me.

MRS. COLE. Certainly. (*Turning around to her right and going up towards the hall door.*) Now, Amy, I *do* hope you're going to write to me occasionally.

AMY (*coming away from the window, towards her*). *You're* the one who never writes.

MRS. COLE (*laughing guiltily*). I know, darling; but I'm going to reform, really.

AMY. Well, now, I'm going to wait and see.

MRS. COLE. But, really, I've been so terribly busy since Mr. Cole's been ill, that I don't seem to be able to—

(*She becomes confidential.*)

MRS. FISHER (*turning, at the window, and addressing* AUBREY, *who is standing directly opposite her at the right, and who happens to be the first one her eye lights upon*). Seems so funny to see an automobile in this street. (AUBREY *is paralyzed; and before he can recover the use of his arm sufficiently to try to silence her, she has turned again to the window; and he stands watching her, frozen with the fear that she may turn again, and sustained only by the hope that* MRS. COLE *did not hear her. His agony is very brief, however, for almost immediately,* MRS. FISHER *turns again and addresses him.*) I don't think I've ever *seen* one in this street before. (AUBREY *makes a frantic gesture to her, and, turning around to his left, strides up to the back of the room, pointing vigorously at* MRS. COLE. MRS. FISHER *is bewildered— She simply stares blankly at the goings-on of her son-in-law; and it is not until he strides forward again at the right, glowering at her savagely, that it occurs to her to speak.*) Why, what's the matter with you!

(AUBREY *suddenly raises his left arm and hand as though he'd like to sweep her from the earth, but the opportune turning of* MRS. COLE *to say good-by to* MRS. FISHER, *restores order.*)

MRS. COLE. Good-by, Mrs. Fisher.

MRS. FISHER (*shaking hands with her*). Good-by, Mrs. Cole.

MRS. COLE. I'm sorry to have to run

away like this.

(AMY *moves around to* MRS. COLE'S *right.*)

MRS. FISHER. Well, I know how you feel.

MRS. COLE (*turning and chucking* AMY *under the chin*). But I *did* want to see my child here. And her husband—probably the *best*-looking man I've seen in Philadelphia so far.

(AMY, *with an exclamation of deprecation, turns to her left and goes laughing out into the hallway.* MRS. FISHER *laughs a little, out of courtesy.*)

AUBREY (*swaggering up at the right of the center table, excessively self-satisfied, and pointing after his wife*). Tell *her* that!

MRS. FISHER. I hope the next time you come this way you'll be able to stay a little longer, Mrs. Cole.

MRS. COLE. Thanks; I hope so, too, Mrs. Fisher. (*She turns to the right to greet* AUBREY, *who has come across above the center table.*) Good-by, Mr. Piper.

AUBREY. Good-by, Mrs. Cole.

(*They shake hands.*)

MRS. COLE (*dropping her glove at her right foot*). I'm *so* glad to have met you. —Oh!

AUBREY (*stooping*). I'll get it.

(*The toupee glides off and falls on to the black, fur rug on which they're standing; but he doesn't observe the circumstance, and restores the glove with a touch of flourish.*)

MRS. COLE. Thanks.

(*She simply takes the glove, without the slightest evidence of an appreciation of the situation. But old* MRS. FISHER *is in a state of siege; and, taking advantage of her position behind* MRS. COLE, *endeavors to communicate to her son-in-law, by means of funny little pointings and movements with her head, some knowledge of his condition. But* AUBREY *is mercifully oblivious of everything, save that he is in the presence of a very attractive woman, who has admitted that she considers him probably the best-looking man she has seen in Philadelphia.*)

AUBREY. Sorry you have to go so soon.

MRS. COLE. I'm sorry, too, Mr. Piper. But if I'm not on that train. (*She turns to* MRS. FISHER.) I'm afraid I'll get scalped. (*She goes out into the hallway.*)

MRS. FISHER (*stepping to the hall door*). Don't let her stand out there in the cold with nothing around her, Mrs. Cole.

MRS. COLE. No, I'll send her right in, Mrs. Fisher.

MRS. FISHER. Good-by.

MRS. COLE. Good-by.

AUBREY (*standing immediately behind* MRS. FISHER, *looking out into the hallway*). Good-by.

MRS. COLE. Amy, your mother says you mustn't stand out here in the cold with nothing around you.

(MRS. FISHER *turns, and, with a glance at* AUBREY, *steps to the bay-window, to watch* MRS. COLE *get into the taxi.* AUBREY *follows her and takes up his position just back of her, looking out.*)

MRS. FISHER (*after a slight pause*). Good-by. (*She waves to* MRS. COLE; *and so does* AUBREY,—*perhaps with a trifle more dignity than the occasion implies. Then the taxi moves away, and they watch it, smiling, down the street. Suddenly* MRS. FISHER *looks sharply in the opposite direction.*) There's the boy with the paper. (*Turning from the window, folding her arms tightly together.*) I've got to get my little woolen shawl. (*She crosses to the right, above the center table.*) This room's too chilly for me.

(*She goes out through the portières at the right. The front door, out at the left, closes; and* AUBREY *turns from the window to the hall door.*)

AMY (*entering briskly through the hall door, carrying the evening paper*). Here's the *Ledger*.

AUBREY. You ought to have something around you.

AMY (*stepping to the bay-window*). I'm not cold. Where's Mother?

AUBREY (*opening the paper, as he strolls across above the center table*). She's gone up for her shawl.

(*He sits in the armchair, down at the right, and* AMY *peers through the bay-window, as though trying to catch a last glimpse of the departing taxi.*)

AMY (*suddenly turning from the window and coming across to the right, above the center table*). Isn't Marion nice?

AUBREY. Yes, she's very pleasant.

AMY (*looking at herself in the mirror*). She's an awfully smart girl, too. She had charge of our entire department when I worked at the Bank.

(*There is a slight pause.*)

AUBREY (*half-turning, and very significantly*). Say, Amy.

AMY. What?

AUBREY. Listen.

(*She turns her head sharply and looks at him. He beckons her to him with a rather mysterious nod, and she comes around to his left.*)

AMY. What?

AUBREY (*in a subdued, level tone*). Did you get your mother telling her your age?

AMY. That's nothing; Marion knows my age.

AUBREY. I *told* you what she'd do.

AMY (*starting towards the portières*). Well, now, it doesn't make the least bit of difference; so don't start anything.

(*She glances through the portières.*)

AUBREY. It's a good thing she didn't have any longer to stay.

MRS. FISHER (*out at the right*). You know, Amy,—

AMY (*turning suddenly to him with a deft gesture*). Sh—sh—

(*She steps to the mirror and pretends to be fixing her hair.*)

AUBREY. Or she'd have told her a whole lot more.

MRS. FISHER (*coming through the portières wearing a rather skimpy-looking white shoulder-shawl and carrying some pale-pink knitting*). I always pictured that girl as a much bigger woman than she is, when you used to talk about her.

(*She walks down between* AUBREY *and the center table and crosses over to the sofa. She appears to be having difficulty in disentangling her yarn.*)

AMY. Don't you think she's a big girl?

MRS. FISHER. Well, *stouter,* I mean.

AMY. No, she never was stout.

MRS. FISHER (*sitting on the sofa, and settling herself*). I'd never know her in the world from that picture you have of her upstairs.

AMY (*turning from the mirror*). Don't you think she's nice?

MRS. FISHER. Very nice.

AMY (*standing at her husband's right*). Give me a piece of that paper.

MRS. FISHER. And very stylish, too.

AMY. Any part'll do.

(*He detaches a section of the paper and gives it to her. She moves a step or two to the right and forward and commences to read.* AUBREY *resumes his reading; and* MRS. FISHER *knits.*)

MRS. FISHER (*after a pause*). I'll bet there was five hundred dollars right on her back there to-day if there was a penny. And that's not counting her hat nor her shoes, either. (*There is another little pause.*) That wig business must be a very good business. (AUBREY *looks over at her stonily; but she's occupied with her knitting.*) I saw a piece in the *North American* the other morning, that a lot of people were wearing wigs now that don't need them at all. (*She looks over at* AMY, *to find* AUBREY *glaring at her.*) That's what it said. (*He snaps his head round and continues reading.*) She was telling me, Amy, that she lives in an apartment there in Chicago. Sez they couldn't *get* a house when they first went there. Sez there hasn't been a house go up in Chicago since before the war. (*She laughs faintly to herself.*) I was telling her about the time you and Aubrey had, when you were first married— (*He looks over at her, with a dangerous squint.*) Trying to get even a couple of rooms somewhere. And the kind they were, when you *did* get them. (*She laughs a little more, at the recollection of them.*) But they had the nerve to charge you nine dollars a month for them, just the same.

(*She smiles and looks at* AUBREY.)

AUBREY (*explosively*). I suppose you told her *that,* too, didn't you!

(AMY *is startled out of her interest in the newspaper.*)

MRS. FISHER (*after a second's amazement*). Told her what?

AUBREY. When were you handing out all this information?

AMY. Now, Aubrey, don't start, please!

AUBREY (*jumping to his feet*). It's enough to *make* (*He slams the piece of newspaper down on to the chair violently.*) a fellow start! (*He thrusts his hands into his trousers' pockets and strides towards the back of the room.*) Trying to make me look like a poor *sap!*

(*He crosses to the hall door and right back again.*)

MRS. FISHER (*looking in bewilderment at* AMY). Why, what's the matter with *him!*

AMY *and* AUBREY (*together*).

(AMY). Nothing at all, Mother.

(AUBREY, *at the upper right-hand corner of the center table*). You know very *well* what's the matter with me!

MRS. FISHER. What?

AUBREY. Handing out a line of *gab* about my *business!* every time you can get anybody to *listen* to you.

MRS. FISHER. Who was handing out any line of gab about your business?

AUBREY. *You* were!—and you're always doing it!

MRS. FISHER. Why, you haven't got any line of business for anybody to hand out any line of gab about—that I ever heard of.

(*She turns away.*)

AUBREY. It doesn't matter whether I have any line of business or not! It isn't necessary for you to be gabbing to perfect strangers about it.

MRS. FISHER. What did you want me to do, sit there lookin' at the woman, like a cow?

AMY. Mother, please.

AUBREY. You don't have to talk about my affairs!

MRS. FISHER (*with vast amusement*). Your affairs—

AUBREY. That's what I said, my affairs! (MRS. FISHER *laughs derisively, and* AUBREY *turns to his wife, desperately.*) You hear her!

MRS. FISHER. That's funny.

AMY. She wasn't talking about you, Aubrey.

AUBREY. She *was* talking about me! That's all she ever *does,* is talk about me! (MRS. FISHER *whirls around.*)

MRS. FISHER. I was talkin' about houses! —that ain't you, is it?

AUBREY. I know what you were talking about, you needn't tell me.

MRS. FISHER. I had to talk about something, didn't I?

AMY. Keep quiet, Aubrey!

AUBREY *and* MRS. FISHER (*together*).

(AUBREY, *whirling around and going towards the hall door*). No, I won't keep quiet!

(MRS. FISHER). You two were down in the cellar fixing the fire! And you can't sit there with your two hands as long as each other when a person's visiting in your house!

AUBREY (*stopping abruptly above the center table, on his way back towards the portières*). I suppose you mentioned *that,* too, didn't you!

MRS. FISHER (*half-turning and listening narrowly*). Mentioned what?

AUBREY. That it was *your* house!

(MRS. FISHER *turns her whole body round to him in a literal bounce.*)

MRS. FISHER (*shrilly*). Well, whose house *would* I mention that it was!

AUBREY (*turning to* AMY *with a broad gesture of his right hand*). You see! Didn't I tell you!

AMY *and* AUBREY (*together*).

(AMY). Well, what of it, Aubrey! What of it!

(AUBREY). Every opportunity she gets she's trying to make me look like a poor thing!

(*He brings his right hand down thunderously upon the center table. Then, thrusting his hands into his trousers' pockets again, strides over to the arched door and back again to the portières.*)

MRS. FISHER (*after a strained pause*). Why, what's the matter with the crazy Jack!

AMY. Pay no attention to him, Mother.

MRS. FISHER. I suppose I won't be able to say this house *is* my own after a while.

AUBREY (*stopping above the center table and rapping his fist upon it*). It isn't necessary for you to be gabbing to perfect strangers about *whose* house it is!

MRS. FISHER (*keenly*). I guess it'd have been all right if I'd told her it was yours, wouldn't it?

AUBREY (*repudiating her remark with a sharp gesture of his left hand*). You don't have to tell anybody *anything!*

(MRS. FISHER *springs to her feet.*)

MRS. FISHER. I suppose that's what's the matter with you, isn't it?

AUBREY *and* MRS. FISHER (*together*).

(AUBREY). There's nothing at all the matter with me!

(*He touches his handkerchief to his forehead.*)

(MRS. FISHER, *taking a few steps towards* AMY). He's very likely been telling this friend of yours, Amy, that this is *his* house! And I guess with a lot of big talk about taking *me* in, and giving *me* a home! Trying to make *me* look like a poor thing!

AMY (*trying to pacify her mother*). Now, he didn't tell her anything of the kind, Mother!

MRS. FISHER (*shaking with wrath*). He did if he got the chance! I know him.

AMY. Well, he didn't *get* the chance; I was only out of the room two minutes.

MRS. FISHER (*returning to the sofa*). Well, that's long enough for him! I've heard *him* before. (*She gathers up her knitting, preparatory to sitting down.*) Blowing his bubbles! (*She sits down, fuming.*) The big blatherskite! (*There is a pause.* AMY *and* AUBREY *look at each other, then at* MRS. FISHER, *who knits violently.*)

I'm very glad now I *did* tell her this was my house!— (*She knits a little more.*) I'm glad I had sense enough! (*More knitting.*) For I know he'd very soon tell her it was *his,* if he got my back turned long enough! (*She draws some yarn from the ball.*) And it wouldn't be mine long, either, if I listened to all his silly blather about stocks, and bonds, and automobiles, and every other thing!— On his thirty-two dollars a week. (AUBREY *looks stonily at her for a second; then she turns sharply and leans on the arm of the sofa towards him.*) I told her *that,* too!

AUBREY (*turning to* AMY, *who is standing back of the armchair*). You see! Didn't I tell you!

(*He passes forward at the right of his wife.*)

MRS. FISHER (*resuming her knitting*). So she'd know how much brains you had!

AMY. It wasn't at all necessary, Mother, for you to tell Marion that.

MRS. FISHER (*without looking up from her work*). Well, I told her; whether it was necessary or not. (*She looks at* AMY *and speaks emphatically.*) It was the truth, anyway. And I guess that's more than can be said for a whole lot that *he* told her. (*She indicates* AUBREY *with a nod; then resumes her work. There is a pause.* AUBREY *is standing fuming down at the right.* AMY *picks up the piece of the paper that he threw on the chair, then extends the piece that she has been reading towards him.*)

AMY. Do you want this?

AUBREY (*half-turning, and with a shade of hauteur*). What is it?

AMY. Why, it's the newspaper of course! what do you think it is?

(*He deigns to take it. She gives him a long look, then opens the other half of the paper and reads.*)

AUBREY (*opening his part of the paper*). A man'd certainly have a swell chance trying to make anything of himself around this *hut!*

MRS. FISHER. I don't see that anybody's trying to *stop* you from making something of yourself.

AUBREY. No, and I don't see that anybody's trying to *help* me any, either. Only trying to make me look like a *pin-head* every chance they get.

MRS. FISHER. Nobody'll have to try very hard to make *you* look like a pin-head. Your own silly talk'll do *that* for you, any time at all.

AUBREY (*turning to her sharply*). I suppose it's silly talk to try to make a good impression.

MRS. FISHER (*looking over at him, and inclining her head conclusively*). Yes— It's silly to try to make an impression of *any* kind; for the only one that'll be made'll be the *right* one; and that'll make itself.

(*She reverts to her work.*)

AUBREY. Well, if you were out in the world as much as I am, you'd very soon see how much easier it is for a fellow to get along if people think he's *got* something.

MRS. FISHER. Well, anybody listen to you very long'd know you *couldn't* have very much.

AUBREY. Is that so.

MRS. FISHER (*quietly*). You heard me. (AUBREY *steps over to the armchair at his left and sits down, looking bitterly at his mother-in-law*). People that are smart enough to be able to make it easier for anybody, are not interested in what you've *got.* (*Looking over at him.*) It's what you've got in your *brains* that they're interested in. And nobody has to tell them that, either. They'll know all about it, if you never opened your mouth.

AMY. Oh, stop talking, Mother.

(*She turns, with a movement of wearied impatience, from the right end of the center table, and crosses over back of the armchair to the right, where she continues to read. There is a quiet pause;* AMY *and* AUBREY *reading, and* MRS. FISHER *knitting. Then* AUBREY *looks up from his paper, thinks for a second, and half turns to his wife.*)

AUBREY. Did you get that remark your friend made, as she was going out?

AMY. What remark?

(MRS. FISHER *looks over.*)

AUBREY (*with a self-satisfied smile*). About the best-looking man in Philadelphia?

MRS. FISHER (*rearranging her knitting*). Oh, dear!

(AUBREY *gives her a narrow look; then turns back to his wife.*)

AUBREY. She made it twice, too.

AMY. I suppose I'll never hear the end of that now.

AUBREY. No, but it made an awful hit with me, after all the talk you made about putting on the toupee.

AMY. Oh, it wasn't the toupee that made her say it; don't flatter yourself.

AUBREY. I don't think it hurt any.

AMY. No, and I don't think you're so crazy about the toupee yourself.

AUBREY. It's better than being baldheaded.

AMY. I notice you got rid of it very quickly, as soon as she went.

(MRS. FISHER *listens.*)

AUBREY. What?

AMY (*without looking up from the paper*). You heard me. (MRS. FISHER *can't resist a glance at* AUBREY; *but realizing that her expression might precipitate another row, she turns away quietly and continues with her knitting.* AUBREY *hasn't grasped the significance of his wife's remark. He turns and looks at her with a puzzled expression; but she is reading; so he turns back again and looks straight out, baffled. Then a thought occurs to him. He reaches up and touches his head. The toupee is off. His brows lift and his mouth falls open, and he sits staring straight ahead for a second. Then he glances furtively at his mother-in-law, but she is studiously avoiding the situation. He gets up, very quietly; and, with a little glance over his right shoulder at his wife, turns and gives a quick look on the armchair and under it. No sign of the toupee. He feels all over his head and around the back of his neck; puts his hand up under his coat, and looks on the floor back of the armchair. All very quietly, and with a pathetic attempt at nonchalance. But the toupee is not to be seen. He saunters up towards the back of the room, steps over and glances at himself in the mirror, then stands looking about the floor in a quandary. His wife observes him out of the corner of her eye, and turns to him.*) What are you looking for?

(*He glances at* MRS. FISHER, *then goes very close to his wife and speaks in a confidential tone.*)

AUBREY. My toupee. Did you see anything of it?

AMY. Where'd you put it?

AUBREY (*with a shade of impatience*). I didn't put it anywhere.

AMY. Well, where did you have it?

AUBREY (*becoming more impatient*). I had it on my head, of course! where'd you think I had it!

AMY. I thought you took it off, when Marion went.

AUBREY. No, I didn't take it off!

AMY. Well, where is it?

AUBREY (*throwing discretion to the winds*). I don't know *where* it is? That's why I'm asking *you!*

(MRS. FISHER *can no longer contain herself, and bursts into unrestrained laughter. They both turn sharply and look at her,* AUBREY *glaring.*) Funny! isn't it!

(AMY *crosses quickly to the center table, in front of her husband.*)

AMY. Did you see anything of it, Mother?

MRS. FISHER (*bursting out afresh*). I saw it *fall off,* that's all *I* know about it.

(*They stand looking at her.*)

AUBREY. You see that! She'd let me walk around here all day with it off, and never tip me off that it was off!

MRS. FISHER. What good was it to tip you off that it was off after it was off! (*Turning back to her knitting.*) The cat was out of the bag, then.

AMY. Where'd it fall off, Mother?

MRS. FISHER. When he was picking that woman's glove up, up there at the hallway. (AMY *turns quickly towards the hall door, glancing about the floor; and* MRS. FISHER *turns to* AUBREY.) It isn't *my* fault if his old *wig* doesn't fit him.

(*He is looking at her with murder in his eye; but she doesn't flinch. If anything, there is a glint of challenge in her look. And it's quite as steady as his own.* AMY *finds the toupee where it fell, and holds it up towards* AUBREY *by one hair.*

AMY. Is this it?

(*But the duel of eyes is still on between* AUBREY *and his mother-in-law; and he is oblivious of both his wife and her question. So the toupee, looking very much like a dead cat, depends from* AMY's *uplifted fingers. Then, suddenly,* AUBREY *snatches it, with a whirling movement to the left, and goes towards the mirror to adjust it.*)

MRS. FISHER (*following him with her eyes*). It just serves him right! That's what he gets for showing off!

AUBREY (*whirling at the mirror, and literally shouting at her*). Shut up, will you!

(*The violence of his turning sends the toupee flying off his head on to the floor, and causes* MRS. FISHER *to start so that her ball of yarn flies four feet into the air.*)

AMY (*taking a step towards her husband*

and lifting her hand to enjoin silence). Sh—sh—sh—

AUBREY (*looking at her with an eye of fire*). I won't stand much more of this, Amy! now, I'm telling you!

AMY. Keep quiet, Aubrey! Marion probably never noticed it at all.

MRS. FISHER. I don't know how she could *help* noticing it. *I* noticed it; and I don't think my eyesight's as good as hers.

AUBREY. Then, why didn't you say something!

MRS. FISHER. Because I knew if I did I'd very likely get snatched baldheaded!

(AUBREY *starts violently, and* MRS. FISHER *snaps back to her knitting.*)

AUBREY (*appealing to his wife*). You hear that! Is it any wonder my nerves are the way they are!

AMY. Oh, keep quiet, Aubrey! for Heaven's sake! (*Pointing to the toupee on the floor, as she steps forward at the right of the center table.*) And pick up your wig.

(*This is too much for* AUBREY. *He literally sways against the portières above the mirror.*)

AUBREY (*recovering himself*). It isn't a wig, now, Amy! I've told you that a half a dozen times!

AMY (*looking up from the paper which she has commenced to read, and in an exhausted tone*). Well, then, pick up your toupee!

(*He picks it up and simply slaps it back on to his head. The effect is weird; for it is quite disheveled from its recent experiences, and, in his temper, he has put it on backwards. He swings forward at the right and sits in the armchair, very sulkily.* AMY *crosses over back of the armchair and stands down near the little table at the right, where she continues to read the evening paper.* MRS. FISHER *knits, and* AUBREY *sits sulking, looking straight ahead. There is a pause. Then, possibly at the recollection of certain of the remarks that his mother-in-law made earlier in the battle,* AUBREY *darts a sudden glare in her direction; only to find that she has been the victim of similar memories. So they sit and scowl at each other; then turn away. Then turn back again, and away again. Then* AUBREY *becomes conscious of his wife; and of the fact that she is reading the evening newspaper; and, by the association of ideas, his thought is diverted into more becoming channels. He half-turns to* AMY, *with something of the self-importance that characterized his earlier manner, and, after a slight pause, addresses her.*)

AUBREY. Have you got the—a—financial page there?

(AMY *hands it to him; and the curtain commences to descend very slowly.*)

MRS. FISHER. Hum!

(*He glares over at her, but she's knitting; so, withdrawing his eyes, he reaches into his vest pocket and brings forth the rimmed nose-glasses, which he settles rather authentically upon his nose. Then he takes a silver pencil from the other vest pocket, and, turning to his wife, accepts the newspaper. Then he crosses his knees, and, spreading the newspaper upon them, proceeds to figure profits in the margin.* AMY *stands looking at him, and* MRS. FISHER *knits.*

THE CURTAIN IS DOWN

White Dresses

BY PAUL GREEN

First produced in Cleveland in February, 1928.

CHARACTERS

GRANNY McLEAN, an old Negro Woman
MARY McLEAN, her granddaughter
JIM MATTHEWS, in love with Mary
HENRY MORGAN, a white man and landlord

Time: The evening before Christmas.
Scene: The home of Granny McLean in eastern North Carolina.

A small fire is burning in the huge fireplace of a Negro cabin on a cold winter night and lighting up with its flickering flames the poverty-stricken interior of a comfortless room. Here and there on the rough-planked walls hang illustrations, which strive in a crude way to beautify the place. A few chairs are in the room and a small eating-table is in the Center. GRANNY MC LEAN, *a big, bony, black old woman, comes in at the rear door, walking with the aid of a cane and carrying several sticks of firewood under her arm. She is dressed in a slat bonnet, which hides her face in its shadows, brogan shoes, a man's ragged coat, checkered apron and dark-colored dress. After much straining and grunting, she puts the wood on the fire and then takes the poker and examines some potatoes cooking in the ashes. Hanging her bonnet on the chair behind her, she takes out her snuffbox and fills her lip. In the firelight her features are discernible—sunken eyes, high cheek bones and big flat nose. On her forehead she wears steel-rimmed spectacles. She sits down in the rocking chair, now and then putting her hand to her head and groaning. For a moment she pats her foot nervously on the floor and then gets up and opens the door. She stands looking out at the gathering dusk. She mutters something to herself and then closes the door and looks restlessly around the room. Hobbling over to a chest, she rakes a pile of newspapers and catalogues to the floor, and taking a key from around her neck, opens the chest and lifts out a small black oblong box. She takes another key from the string around her neck and starts to unlock it. The door at the rear opens quickly and* MARY MC LEAN *comes in with a "turn" of collards and a bundle in her arms. She lays the collards on the floor near the door and puts the bundle on the bed. She is an attractive mulatto girl about eighteen years old, with an oval face and dark straight hair neatly done up. Her dress is shabby but clean.*

GRANNY (*suddenly springing around in confusion*). Oh—mah back! (*She hides the box under her apron.*)

MARY. How you feeling, Granny?

GRANNY. I's tuck in mah kidneys. (*She tries to straighten up.*)

MARY. You hadn't ought to jump so quick; I'm not going to bother you about that old box.

GRANNY. Yeh, yeh, and I dunno. I thought you wa'n't a-coming a good wile yit. (*She locks the box away in the chest and hobbles back to her chair.*)

MARY (*watching her*). Why won't you ever let me see what you got hid in that box?

GRANNY. Hush it, chile! I done told you I'd let you know when de time come. (*Shaking her head*) And I's afea'd de time ain't fur off, nuther.

MARY (*turning from hanging up her shawl*). All the week you been talking about something being not far off. What is it?

GRANNY. Neveh you mind. Go on now and tell me why you stay up dere at Mis' Mawgin's house so late?

MARY (*punching up the fire*). She had such a big ironing and a lot of cleaning up for Christmas, I couldn't get through any quicker.

GRANNY. And me setting hyuh dese las' two hours wid mah haid busting open, and being oneasy 'bout my gal off wukking so ha'd.

MARY. But look what I brought you. (*She opens her hand and shows her a five-dollar bill.*)

GRANNY (*pulling down her spectacles and looking at it*). Five dollahs! Lawd he'p my life!

MARY (*bringing the package from the bed*). And look what Mr.—Mr.—Morgan sent you. (*She undoes the package, revealing sausage, ham and other cooked food.*) He said as 'twas Christmas time, he sent you all these things and the collards there.

GRANNY (*reaches impulsively for the food, but drops her hand and sits blinking at* MARY). Whah'd you git all dese things? (*Suspiciously.*) Whah'd you git dat 'ere money?

MARY (*stammering*). They—they all sent it to you, I said.

GRANNY (*excitedly*). Mr. Mowgin ain't de kind to be making free wid his money. And dey ain't no past Chris'mus he was so good to me lak dat, and you knows it, him a-having his washing done raght up on de evening of de Saviour's birf. (*Sharply.*) Did Mr. Hugh gi'n you dat money?

MARY. It's every bit for you. When I

was washing some of Mr. Hugh's shirts—and they was soft and shiny—he come out and handed me the money and said give it to you.

GRANNY. He'p mah soul and body, de boy said dat! He ain't fo'got his old granny since he gut to gwine off to school 'way yander at de University.

MARY (*handing the money to* GRANNY, *who takes it quickly*). He said maybe when he'd make a lot of money and got rich he'd send you more things than you could shake a stick at, like as not.

GRANNY. De Lawd bless his baby heart! Ain't he a sight to think o' me lak dat? He's a reg'lar Trojas. Allus was a good boy, and he ain't changed since he growed up, nuther. Mind me when I used to nuss him, he'd neveh whimpeh, no, suh. (*She rubs the bill in her hand.* MARY *sits down and looks into the fire.*)

MARY (*after a moment*). I bet he was a purty baby, won't he, Granny?

GRANNY. De fines' gwine. (*Turning with sudden sharpness to look at her.*) Why you ax dat?

MARY. I thought he must have been purty from—from the way he seems—(*She looks at the fire without noticing the old woman's uneasy movement.*)

GRANNY. Listen hyuh. Don't you know you gut no call to be talking 'bout a white boy lak dat?

MARY (*getting up hastily*). Time I was fixing your supper.

GRANNY. Didn't he g'in you nothing a-tall?

MARY. No'm, he didn't give me a thing. (*She suddenly sits down, stifling a sob.*)

GRANNY. Hyuh, putt dis money in de pocketbook. Don't mind whut I's saying. I 'spects I's too keerful 'bout you, I dunno. (*Looking around.*) What ails you, chile?

MARY (*wiping her eyes*). Nothing, nothing. (*She puts the money away, then lights the lamp.* GRANNY *watches her perplexedly.*)

GRANNY (*solicitously*). Mah po' baby's been wukking too much.

MARY. I feel all right now. You want me to fix your supper on the table?

GRANNY. No, suh-ree. Whut betteh do I want'n dis hyuh in mah lap? (*She begins eating greedily. Suddenly she utters a low scream and puts her hand to her head.*)

MARY. It's your head again, ain't it? Now you rest easy. (*And she comes over and begins rubbing her cheeks and forehead.* GRANNY *becomes quiet and goes back to her eating.*) Set still while I git in a turn o' lightwood. It's going to be a cold night and looks like snow. (*She goes just outside the door and returns with an armful of wood which she throws down near the fireplace.*) You feel all right still?

GRANNY. Purty well. Dis hyuh victuals puts new life in me.

MARY. Now, you see, that spell didn't last any time. And it's like I keep telling you, you'll be well and back in the fields with the hoe-hands by spring.

GRANNY (*sharply.*) No, suh, I ain't long foh dis world. I's done my last washing and chopping and leading de gang in de fields.

MARY. You're always talking like that, and you'll live to be a hundred or more.

GRANNY (*licking her fingers*). Dese is good spar' ribs and sa'sages sho' 'nough.

MARY (*sits down again and stares before her with her chin in her hand*). Don't it sorter make you feel lonesome and queer to be setting here tonight, just you'n me, and nobody in the world that cares one thing for us? Up at Mis' Morgan's the children are all having a lot of fun, and——

GRANNY. Whut's dat? Whut's de matteh?

MARY. Oh, nothing.

GRANNY. You's worried. Dey's sump'n on yo' mind, ain't dey? (*With misgiving.*) Mr. Mawgin—he—ain't said nothing else 'bout us having to get out o' this house, has he?

MARY. No'm, no'm—he said—I don't think he said any more about it.

GRANNY (*anxiously*). You sho' 'bout dat?

MARY (*stolidly*). Oh, he said today—he said maybe he'd let us stay right on here. (*Nervously.*) Something like that.

GRANNY (*listening*). Talk louder. Say dat ag'in.

MARY. He said it might be so we could stay as long as we pleased.

GRANNY. He did? (*Joyously.*) Thank de Lawd! Bless His holy name! I knowed Mr. Mawgin gwine do it. I knowed it. (*Soberly.*) But I been pow'ful skeahd he's gwine run us off—when Mr. Hugh gut to taking up foh us. Now I kin res' mah bones raght whah I wants to. (*Uncertainly.*) How come he change lak dat and say we could stay on? How come?

MARY. I dunno—just did, I reckon.

GRANNY (*looking at her keenly*). Is you trying to keep de truf f'om me, hunh?

MARY. Shucks! It's going to be all right. Mr. Morgan didn't exactly say much about it. But Mr. Hugh, he said he'd look out for us, and he will, too. (GRANNY *stops eating and sits in silence.*)

GRANNY (*harshly, after a moment*). Don' you say no mo' 'bout Mr. Hugh—heah me?— You ain't even had nothing t'eat, has you?

MARY. Yes'm, I have, too. They told me not to come off without eating, and I git my supper in the kitchen—and—and I didn't want much. (GRANNY *rakes a potato from the ashes and begins peeling it.* MARY *turns restlessly in her chair. She goes over to the bureau; takes out a piece of pink ribbon and begins arranging her hair.*)

GRANNY (*noticing her movements*). That's right, make yo'self purty. Jim'll be coming round tonight. (*She wraps up the remainder of her food and puts it in the chimney corner.*)

MARY. Yes'm, he'll be coming. (*Scornfully.*) They's no getting away from him and his guitar.

GRANNY (*blowing on her hot potato*). Whut you gut ag'in Jim? Dey ain't no betteh nigger'n Jim is. He's gwaine treat you straight. And it's time you's gitting merried.

MARY. I'm not going to marry anybody, and you know it well enough.

GRANNY. Whut keeps gitting into you? When I was yo' age, yo' mammy was a stropping young 'un pulling at mah breas'. Yessuh, I wants you to git merried. I told you and told you. 'Tain't a good sign when a 'oman old as you ain't thinking o' gitting her a home. I's lak to nuss yo' li'l-uns and sing to 'em fo' I go. Mind me o' de old times.

MARY (*bitterly*). What's Jim Matthews for a husband?

GRANNY. Well, he works ha'd and saves his money. (MARY *finishes her hair and powders her face.* GRANNY *sits silently peeling her potatoes.*)

MARY (*presently*). Granny, you ought to see him since he come back. He's as kind and good to me as he can be.

GRANNY (*looking at her questioningly*). Co'se he's kind and good.

MARY (*softly*). And today he said 'twas a pity I had to work and wash like a dog for a living. He don't treat me like a—like a colored person. He acts same as if I was white.

GRANNY (*staring at her in troubled astonishment*). I knows it, honey. Jim's solid to de bottom. He'll be uh a-one husband for you.

MARY (*vehemently*). I'm not talking about Jim, I tell you!

GRANNY. Whut you mean? Who you talking 'bout?

MARY. Oh, nobody, like as not. (*Appealingly.*) I don't look like a common nigger, do I?

GRANNY. Lawd bless you, you sho' don't. You's purty as dey makes 'em—lak yo' po' mammy whut's daid and gone—(*Softly.*)—'Ceptin' you's—mebbe whiteh.

MARY. I been thinking a whole heap lately. If I was to go 'way off to New York or somewhere, the people there might think I was real white folks, wouldn't they?

GRANNY (*rising from her seat in alarm*). Gohd in heaben, chile! Whut's come oveh you?

MARY. I'm wore out with all—(*Her hands fluttering in a vague gesture.*)—All this. I am, I tell you! Didn't you ever wish you was white?

GRANNY. Hesh, hesh, I says. (*Sitting down and turning her face away.*) Po' thing, po' chile, yo' mammy used to talk lak dat. Don't you say no sech words to me. Lawd Jesus!

MARY. But there's no use of talking. (*Helplessly.*) Talk won't change anything. But I can't stand it—I can't!

GRANNY (*sternly*). Hesh dat! (*Kindly.*) Honey chile, you listen to me. We's bofe niggehs, bawn niggehs and'll die niggehs. De Lawd He made us, and de Lawd He'll take us away, and whut He does is raght. Now you trust in Him and rest easy in yo' trust.

MARY. No, no, I won't. I'll change it somehow, I will! (*A sound of stamping feet is heard outside and a knock at the door.* MARY *brushes her hand across her face and calls out.*) Come in!

GRANNY. Who's dat?

(JIM MATTHEWS *enters. He is a young Negro of twenty-two or three and as black as his African ancestors. He carries a guitar slung over his shoulder, wears an old derby hat, tan shirt with flowing tie, a well-worn blue suit, the coat of which comes nearly to his knees, and shoes slashed along the edges to make room for his feet. As he comes in, he pulls off his hat and smiles genially, showing his big, white teeth.*)

JIM. Good evening, ladies. (*He lays his derby on the bed.*)

GRANNY (*turning in her chair*). Whut does he say?

MARY. He says good evening.

GRANNY. Ah-hah! Good evening, Jim. Take a seat. I's sho' glad you come 'round. Mary's been talking 'bout you. (*He smiles complacently and takes a seat between* MARY *and* GRANNY.)

JIM. Yeb'm, and I's sho' glad to be wid you all. (*Gallantly.*) I's allus glad to be wid de ladies.

GRANNY. Whut does he say?

JIM (*more loudly*). I's glad to be wid you all.

GRANNY. Ah-hah! (JIM *pulls out a large checkered handkerchief from his breast pocket, wipes his forehead and then flips the dust from his shoes. He folds it carefully and then puts it back.*) Any news, Jim?

JIM. Nob'm. Any wid you?

GRANNY. None a-tall. Yo' folks all well?

JIM. Peart and kicking. How you all come on?

GRANNY. Hah? I's purty feeble. (*She groans and rocks to and fro.*)

JIM. Still having dem spells wid her haid, Mary?

MARY (*lowering her voice*). You ought to know, you're here 'most every night. Yes, she has 'em and will till she's laid away in the grave. (*She goes to* GRANNY *and begins rubbing her head again.* GRANNY *waves her off.*)

GRANNY. Ne' mind me now. You chillun go on wid yo co'ting, I's gwine eat my 'taters.

JIM (*looks sheepishly at* MARY *and strums his guitar. He moves his chair nearer to her. She moves mechanically from him*). Uh—Mary, you's looking 'ceeding snatching in dat pink ribbon. Glad to see you's 'specting me 'round. Yeb'm, I tells all de gals you gut 'em beat to a frazzle. (MARY *pays no attention to him.*) F'om heah slam to France and back I ain't seed nobody lak you, and I's a old road niggeh and ought to know. (*He stops and fidgets in his chair.*) Mary, I——

MARY. Jim, I done told you forty times over you needn't come snooping around me. I don't love you, and I'm not going to marry you.

JIM. Now—uh—Mary, honey, I knows des' how you feels. And I ain't gwine give you up. I cain't heah you when you says no. Today I was talking to dat young Hugh Mawgin, and he——

MARY. "Hugh Morgan!" Mr. Hugh Morgan, you mean.

JIM (*hurriedly*). Yeh, yeh, Mr. Hugh.

MARY. What'd you say to him?

JIM. I told him I was calling heah 'casionally, and he said—he said—— (*He wilts before* MARY'*s eyes.*)

MARY (*eying him straightly*). Go on, go on.

JIM. He axed me if I's a-co'ting, and I told him I—uh—mought be.

MARY. Did he seem glad that you was coming?

JIM. He said he 'spected to heah o' us being merried some dese days. (MARY *is silent.*) He 'lowed as how you was most too fine to be wukking yo' eyeballs out, and you needed a man to look adder you. I tuk f'om his talk dat he thought I'd fill de bill.

MARY. Oh, yes, I reckon you thought that.

JIM. He's a eddicated boy, and he sees my worf. Dey teaches him to know a heap 'way out yander at dat college place.

MARY (*springing up*). Jim Matthews, you set there and talk like you owned the whole world and me to boot. Well, I tell you right now you don't! Before I'll marry a smut black nigger like you I'll die stone dead. (JIM *gasps in amazement.* MARY *goes to the window and looks out.*)

GRANNY (*looking up*). Whut ails you chillun making sech a racket? You quit dat corkusing.

MARY. I'm just trying to get Jim to play a piece on his box. (*To* JIM *in a lower voice.*) Play something for her.

JIM (*morosely*). I cain't play nothing.

GRANNY. Whut you say, Jim?

JIM (*shaking his head mournfully and strumming the strings*). I'll play you sump'n, den. (*He plays a few bars and then begins singing, with ohs and ahs thrown in.*)

Oh, whah you gwine, mah loveh?
Gwine on down de road.
Whut make you pale and weeping?
I's carrying a heavy load.

She th'owed her arms around me,
And cast me silveh and gold,
Sing, whah you gwine, mah loveh?
I's a-gwine on down de road.

(MARY *comes back to her chair and sits down.* JIM *stops and speaks softly.*) Mary, why you want to cry lak dat? (*She makes no reply.*)

GRANNY. Whut de matteh wid you, Mary? You's same lak somebody whut's seed de dead.

MARY (*to* JIM). Play her burying piece.

GRANNY. Yeh, yeh, play dat.

JIM (*fits his pocket-knife between his fingers in imitation of the Hawaiians, clears his throat, and strikes another chord*).

Hearse done carried somebody to de graveyard.
Lawd, I know mah time ain't long.
Mary come a-weeping, Martha wailing.
Lawd, I know mah time ain't long.

(*He sings louder, syncopating with his feet.*)

Preacher keep a-preaching, people keep a-dying.
Lawd, I know mah time ain't long.

(GRANNY *begins swaying with the music, clapping her hands, and now and then crying out, "Jesus, Lawdy mah Lawd!" She and* JIM *start singing alternately, he the verses and she the refrain.* MARY *takes off her ribbon and throws it on the bureau.*)

Hammer keep a-ringing on somebody's coffin.

GRANNY. Lawd, I know mah time ain't long.

JIM. Gwine a-roll 'em up lak leaves in de judgment.

GRANNY. Lawd, I know mah time ain't long.

MARY (*turning quickly from the window*). Yes, yes, roll 'em up like leaves in the judgment! (*Bitterly.*) That's the time it's all made right. Yes, God will make it right some day! (*With sharp insistence she sings, with unhappy mockery.*)

Yea, yea, gwine, a-roll 'em up lak leaves in de judgment.

JIM (*stopping his music before her shrill voice*). I dunno ezzactly whut you driving at.

MARY. —And you'll never know—maybe.

GRANNY (*goes on swaying and singing a moment*). Keep on wid dat music, Jim. (*To* MARY.) Jine in wid us once mo' and le's make 'er roll.

(*There is a sudden banging on the door.* MARY *hesitates a moment, and then opens it. A look of fear spreads over her face as* HENRY MORGAN *enters. He is a heavily built man, about fifty years old. A week's growth of frizzled beard darkens his face. He wears a slouch hat, long black shabby overcoat buttoned up to his chin, big black boots, and yarn mittens. He carries a package which he throws contemptuously on the bed. He keeps his hat on.* MARY *closes the door and stands with her back to it.* GRANNY *and* JIM *offer their seats.* JIM's *look is one of servile respect,* GRANNY's *one of trouble.*)

MORGAN (*in a booming voice*). Dad burn you, Jim! Still a-courting, eh? Set down, Granny. I ain't going to stay long.

GRANNY (*querulously*). Whuh does he say?

MARY (*leaving the door and standing by her chair, as she eyes the package*). He says for you to set down. He ain't going to stay long.

GRANNY (*sitting down*). Ah-hah—— Oh, Lawdy, Lawdy!

MORGAN. How you getting on now, Granny?

GRANNY. Po'ly, po'ly, Mr. Mawgin. Ain't gut much longer down hyuh below, ain't much longer.

MORGAN (*laughing*). Aw, come on, come on, cut out your fooling. You ain't half as bad off as you make out. (JIM *moves his chair into the corner and sits down.*)

MARY (*hotly*). She is sick too. She's bad off. (*She twists her apron nervously.*)

MORGAN (*with a touch of anger*). 'Y God, I ain't talking to you right now, Mary.

GRANNY (*whining*). Mr. Mawgin, I sho' is in a bad condition. I hopes you'll neveh have to suffeh lak me.

MORGAN. Well, I may, though. I'll send you some more medicine in a day or two.

GRANNY. Thanky, thanky, Mr. Mawgin.

MORGAN. Never mind the thanks. (*Turning to* MARY.) Have you told her everything?

MARY. Not yet. (*Pleadingly.*) I couldn't tonight, Mr. Morgan.

MORGAN. Unh-hunh, I knowed it. I knowed I'd better come down and make sure. Durn me, you been crying, ain't you? (*Less brusquely.*) What you crying over?

MARY. Nothing. I was just feeling bad or something.

MORGAN (*grimly*). Well, my young lady, you needn't be crying over what I told you today.

GRANNY. What does he say?

MORGAN. Keep quiet, cain't you, Granny? I'm talking to Mary.

GRANNY (*now seeing the package on the bed*). Is it 'bout de package you bring? Is dat bundle foh me or her?

MORGAN. It's hers. Coming down here, I caught up with Zeke. Said he had a Christmas present for Mary. I took and brought it. Wonder what that nigyer's giving her. (*With a chuckle.*) Looks like you'd be jealous, Jim. (MARY *starts toward the bed. He clutches her arm.*) No, you ain't going to see it now, gal. We got a little business to 'tend to first. (GRANNY *begins staring at the bundle on the bed, now and then glancing around to see if any one is watching her. She pays no attention to the conversation.* MARY *stands with head bowed.*) Well, what you going to do about it?

MARY (*stammering*). I—I can't talk about it now, Mr. Morgan.

MORGAN. Keep your mouth shet, then, and I'll talk. (*He turns to* JIM, *who straightens up.*) Jim, I've done my best to make a match for you and get things straightened out. (*To* MARY.) Either marry him or take your duds and grandmuh and git from here. (GRANNY *steals across the room and picks up the package.*)

MARY. Oh, I dunno—I dunno—— (*Piteously.*) Mr. Morgan, Granny couldn't stand to leave here and you know it.

MORGAN (*angrily*). What'n the name o' God do you want me to do—lose money on you till the end of time? You ain't earned enough to keep you in clothes the last three years since Granny got down—

GRANNY (*crying out in a loud voice*). Lawd in Heaben ha' muhcy on us! (*She stands by the bed, holding a white dress up before her.* MORGAN *looks around in perplexity. She throws the dress on the bed and stares at* MORGAN.)

MARY (*running to the bed*). It's for me! It's mine!

GRANNY. Mr. Mawgin, Mr. Mawgin, you knows whut dat dress means! (*She sits down, rocking and mumbling.*)

MARY. He sent it to me! He sent it to me! I knew he wouldn't forget.

MORGAN (*quickly*). Who sent it to you?

MARY. He did.

MORGAN. Who?

MARY. It was him and I don't care if you do know it.

MORGAN (*striding up to her and clutching her arm*). Him who? Who'n the devil you mean?

MARY. Your own boy, that's who. Mr. Hugh—give it to me.

MORGAN. God A'mighty, that's a lie! (MARY *goes to the mirror and holds the dress up in front of her.*) It's a lie, I tell you. Zeke sent you that dress.

MARY. Mr. Hugh done it. He said he was going to remember me and give me something purty. And I knew he would. After all, I've not been working the whole year for nothing. He's got a heart in him if nobody else has.

MORGAN (*almost shouting*). Tell me, gal, what's the meaning of this?

GRANNY (*quivering*). You knows whut it all means, Mr. Mawgin, you knows. (*She groans and shakes her head.*)

MORGAN (*loudly*). Shet up, Granny!—Mary! Mary, you put up that damned dress. Put it up, I say! (*She shrinks back from him, and he snatches the dress from her and throws it on the bed. Then he pushes her out into the room.*) You listen to me. We're going to settle it once and for all right now. Are you going to marry Jim?

MARY. Mr. Morgan, please—I can't marry him. I'll work and hoe and wash day and night. I'll do anything.

MORGAN. Yes, you will! You've told me that time and again. And how much money do you make hoeing and washing? No, you got to say one or the other right here and now. Marry Jim, and everything will be all right. He'll take care of you. If you don't——

MARY. I can't do it, I tell you. I'd rather die. Look at him. He's black, and I hate him. I'll never marry a nigger.

MORGAN (*staring at her*). What in the name of Heaven, gal!

MARY. I hate the ground he walks on.

MORGAN (*turning*). Granny——

MARY. Don't worry her. Don't tell her. I won't see her drove out in the cold like a dog. (GRANNY *sits rocking and gazing into the fire.* JIM, *lost in amazement, fingers his guitar.*) Oh, Mr. Morgan— Mr. Morgan!

MORGAN. I don't want to be too hard on

you, Mary. But use common sense. They ain't a man in this country would have been as good to you all these years.

MARY. He wouldn't let you treat me so hard if he was here. And he said he wouldn't let you run us off.

MORGAN. Who you talking about this time?

MARY. Mr. Hugh's got feelings, he has.

MORGAN. Damn Mr. Hugh! Don't you mention his name again. Thank God he's not here and won't be.

MARY. He said he'd see after us.

MORGAN. The fool, he's got no more sense! But he's gone with a crowd of young folks to Charlotte, and when he gets back there won't be any helping you. I'll see to that.

MARY. He said—he said he'd see me tomorrow and fix it all.

MORGAN. Well, he won't. And ain't you got no shame about you, using my boy's name like a common nigger? What's he to you? (*Pleadingly.*) Listen, Mary, I'm going to talk plain. Are you planning to ruin his life? You know what I mean, too, don't you?

MARY (*sobbing*). There's no use trying to change it. (*Starting back.*) But I won't do it. I won't! Let us starve or freeze, I don't care what. I won't marry Jim.

MORGAN. All right, is that your last word?

MARY. Beat me black and blue, I won't do it.

MORGAN. I'm not going to beat you. (*Turning to the old woman.*) Granny, I got bad news for you. (*She makes no sign that she has heard.*) Mary ain't got no more sense than she was born with, and you might as well get your fixings together and search another place.

GRANNY (*without looking around*). Mr. Mawgin, it don' matteh whut you do to me now. You's done hurt me all you kin. Put me out o' dis house and lemme die quick as I kin.

MORGAN (*turning to* MARY). Are you going to see her suffer for your craziness?

MARY. Yes, make me marry him then. There's nothing to be done about it. I thought it might be changed, but it won't. I'll marry him and raise more children to go through it all like me. No, no, nobody can help me anywhere. (*She sits dejectedly down in her chair.*)

MORGAN (*silent a moment and then speaking more kindly*). All right, Mary. That's sensible. I'll send for the license and preacher in the morning and have him marry you and Jim right here. Does that suit you, Jim?

JIM (*uncertainly*). Yessuh, yessuh, Mr. Mawgin.

MORGAN (*going up to* GRANNY). Well, Granny, things are going to be all right, after all. Mary and Jim's going to tie up. Don't worry no more. (*She makes no answer.* MORGAN *offers* MARY *his hand, but she keeps her head muffled in her apron.*) Mary, I hated to push you along so, but it's all for the best. (*Embarrassed.*) I could mebbe tell you something that'd make you understand what I mean—but —well, I can't now. (*He stands a moment, looking at the floor, then goes out quietly. Presently* JIM *rises and lays more wood on the fire. He comes over to* MARY.)

JIM. Mary, honey, don't take on so. (*He waits patiently, but she says nothing. He strums his guitar and breaks mournfully into song.*)

She th'owed her arm around me
And cast me silver and gold,
Sing, whah you gwine, my loveh?—

Oh, don't worry no mo', Mary, please'm.

MARY. Leave me alone! I promised, but I take it back. (*Starting up.*) And I'll run catch Mr. Morgan and tell him so. (*She moves toward the door.*) I won't marry you, Jim Matthews.

GRANNY (*calling loudly*). Hyuh, hyuh, chile! Don' you go out dat do'! (*She puts out her hand to stop* MARY.) Take dis hyuh key and bring me dat li'l' black box. (MARY *stops.*) Bring me dat box, I say! (*Her threatening voice quavers high.* MARY *comes slowly back, gets the key, and brings the box from the chest and stands wiping the tears from her eyes.*) I's gwine tell you de secret o' dis li'l box. Yo' mammy said tell you if de time eveh come, and it's come. And when I tells you, you'll see why you got to marry Jim. She went th'ough sin and trouble 'at sont her to her death, and I's gwine save you. (GRANNY *opens the box and pulls out a wrinkled white dress, of a generation ago, yellowed with age.* JIM *looks on with open mouth.*) Listen hyuh, po' baby, I's gwine tell you now. Nineteen yeahs ago come dis Christmus dey was a white man gi'n yo' mammy dis heah dress, and dat white man is clost kin to you, and he don' live fur off nuther. Gimme dat udder dress dere on de bed. (MARY *gets it and holds it tightly to her.* GRANNY *snatches at it.*) Gimme dat dress, I tells you.

MARY. It's mine and I'm going to keep it.

GRANNY (*glaring at her*). Gimme. (*She jerks the dress from* MARY. *Hobbling to the fireplace, she lays both of them carefully on the fire.* JIM *makes a movement to save them, but she waves him back with her stick.*) Git back, niggeh, git back! Dis night I's gwine wipe out some o' de traces o' sin. (MARY *sits sobbing. As the dresses burn,* GRANNY *comes over and stands looking down at her.*) And when dey comes tomorrow wid de license, you go on and marry Jim, and you'll live 'spectable. (*She lays her hand on her head.*) I knows yo' feelings, chile, but you's got to smother 'em in, you's got to smother 'em in.

CURTAIN

Minnie Field

BY E. P. CONKLE

First produced by The 47 Workshop at Yale University on May 1, 1928.

CHARACTERS

ALT PAGE
JIM DAY
MEL CLARK
CORNIE YOUNG
TIP FIELDS

SCENE.—*Five men sitting up with* TIP FIELD's *wife's corpse. The men sit in the kitchen; the corpse and coffin are in the spare front-room just off. It is three o'clock in the morning.* JIM DAY *has his feet cocked up on the stove-hearth. He leans back and smokes his pipe.* ALT PAGE *leans against the wall on the other side of the stove.* CORNIE YOUNG *sits at the table nibbling at this and that.* MEL CLARK *stands at the door looking out into the night through the glass pane.* TIP FIELDS *sits in a small rocker with his nose in a newspaper. He reads and rocks and reads and rocks. Things go slowly, quietly.*

ALT. Settin' up with a corpse is like goin' a courtin'.

JIM. How so, Alt?

ALT. A feller'll think-a some-a th' dadblamdest things sometimes.

CORNIE. Don't they, though.

MEL. I reckon Tip's a-thinkin' 'bout Minnie in thur . . . dead. Et's too bad.

CORNIE. You shore got my sympathy, Tip. I don't know what I'd do ef I was t' lose Emmy.

ALT. A man's losin' his wife's 'bout like him a' losin' his best mare.

JIM. Feller cain't break in a new one t' no account.

CORNIE. Leastwise, not one like Minnie was.

MEL. Don't take et too hard, Tip.

TIP. I wonder ef . . . ef that sow's gone an' laid on her pigs.

(*The men glance at one another.*)

JIM. Oh. Well. . . . I ain't heard no squealin'.

TIP. Guess we'd-a heard et if she had-a.

ALT. Them little devils shore does squeal.

CORNIE. Feller cain hear 'em in th' next county on a clear night like this'n.

MEL. I wudn't worry none, Tip. You got s'many other things t' worry over.

TIP. I ain't worryin' none. I was just . . . wonderin'.

(*Silence.*)

CORNIE. Say, fellers . . . here's this card's got t' be wrote on. (*He motions to a card on the table.*)

JIM. What'll we write on et?

ALT. What you think, Tip? Et's your folkses funeral.

TIP. You fellers is payin' for th' flowers. Say what you're a-mind to. You can't hurt me none what you say.

MEL. Say as how th' flowers was given by all th' neighbors to th' diseased.

JIM. Might put in a little verse or so.

CORNIE. Anybody know any verse 't put on?

MEL. Roses is red;
Vi'let is blue;
Sugar is sweet;
So're you.

ALT. That's all th' po'try I know of.

TIP. Et's good enough.

JIM. Might say;
Roses is red;
Vi'lets is blue;
Sugar is sweet;
So *was* you.

. . . since Minnie *ain't* no more.

CORNIE. You ain't got no objections to us callin' Minnie "sweet" have you, Tip?

TIP. I reckon not. They always say nice things 'bout th' dead even when they mayn't be true. Cain't hurt me none.

MEL. Us folks allus thought Minnie was about *it*.

JIM. We all liked Minnie, too. She allus was a doin' somethin' for Amy and th' kids.

ALT. Funny how Minnie come t' die, ain't et?

TIP. Nothin' funny. She just kicked up her heels, passed in her checks, an' died. That's all.

MEL. Minnie was allus a workin' perty hard whenever I seen her.

TIP. That was one thing about Minnie. She went an' killed herse'f-a hard work. I give her credit for that.

CORNIE. Everybody's got to die sooner as later. Some-a 'em got to die a workin'. A feller gets ketched that-a-way sometimes.

JIM. I reckon it won't never ketch you that-a-way, will et, Tip?

TIP. I ain't aimin' fer et to, Jim.

(*The men laugh, except* TIP, *who reads.*)

(*Then the men become conscious of their place and the corpse. Silence.*)

MEL. Et's a funny thing. . . . Death is.

CORNIE. Et strikes when a person ain't lookin' for et.

ALT. And et strikes *where* a feller ain't lookin' fer et, too.

JIM. Et struck Jenny's pa right below th' collar-bone when et struck him. They was a black-an'-blue spot there big as a goose-egg whur et struck him. We all seen et when they was layin' him out.

MEL. Et's like lightnin' strikin' a forked tree.

TIP. Minnie was carryin' up a bucket of warter from th' well at th' foot of th' hill. Ag'in she got ha'f way up, she keeled over an' spilt all th' warter out. That's about all they was to et. I called up th' doc an' he come an' worked on her. I had t' fetch up another bucket-a warter m'se'f.

MEL. Et's too bad, Tip.

TIP. Shore . . . is.

(*Silence.* CORNIE *eats.*)

CORNIE. These yeller t'mater p'serves is fine, Tip.

TIP. Minnie put 'em up for th' winter. She was allus a doin' some durned-fool thing like that. Got a whole cellar-full-a that kinda truck.

CORNIE. Cudn't a been better ef I'd a put 'em up m'se'f, Tip. Yummmm.

JIM. I hear none-a your folks is comin' to th' funeral, Tip.

TIP. I . . . reckon not.

ALT. So *I* heard. How come, Tip?

TIP. They didn't like Minnie none. They said she was allus too smart. She was allus tryin' t' git me t' pull my freight an' git away from 'em. Minnie was plannin' big on that. Th' day she died she got a letter from Montana or somewheres 'bout new land. She even drawed a plan for a new house out there. My folks didn't like that none.

JIM. Well . . . us folks all liked Minnie real well. Mighty well.

ALT. Us folks, too.

MEL. Minnie was allus smilin'. I never seen her when she wasn't smilin'.

TIP. She cudn't tolerate none-a my folks none. I reckon my folks was as good as hern.

JIM (*pointing with his pipe-stem at* TIP). Wasn't nobody good as Minnie, Tip.

TIP. I . . . reckon not.

(*Silence.*)

MEL. Who put that rose on her coffin in thur, Tip?

TIP. She done et herse'f.

JIM. *She* done et?

ALT. How'd *she* do et, Tip?

TIP. Couple-a years ago she set them posies out in th' back yard. An' she says to me: "Ef I ever die when those-there roses are in bloom, Tippy dear, put one of them on my coffin." So . . . her ma went an' done et.

JIM. Et looks mighty perty and simple. Naturally I don't go much on beauty. But that-there was a beautiful idea, I say.

MEL. My Haley's that-a-way, too. Women-folks is durned funny critters.

CORNIE. They shore put th' trimmin's on a feller.

ALT. I didn't 'mount to a durn b'fore I was married.

JIM. Y' don't 'mount t' much more now, do you, Alt?

ALT. I reckon me and you is on a par, ain't we, Jim?

JIM. That suits me, Alt.

(*The men laugh loudly.*)

CORNIE. Oh, hummmm. Kinda sleepy. You reckon th' corpse is all right, in there?

ALT. Take a look, Mel.

MEL. Et makes me creepy t' snoop 'round a corpse. Cornie, you look.

CORNIE. Nothin' to that, Mel. (*He goes to the left door and opens it.*) They ain't nothin' could hurt a person 'bout a corpse.

MEL. Mebby not. But they're like cold mashed p'taters; they ain't got no life to 'em.

CORNIE. Ever'thing's all O.K. 's fur's I can see. Minnie's women-folks is snorin' like all-git-out in th' spare bedroom. Sounds like a hog-pen.

TIP. Et is . . . with *them* in it.

CORNIE (*looking in*). You got a nice front-room in there, Tip. Fixed up a sight better'n ourn is at home.

TIP. Et was . . . her.

CORNIE (*closing the door*). Whur'd you git th' pianner at?

TIP. She got et. She usta thump on et in th' evenings. "In th' Gloamin'" and "Darlin' Nellie Gray" and such.

JIM. Must-a cost a sight. Emmy got a parler-organ and et kept me poverty-struck for five years hand-runnin'.

TIP. Didn't cost *me* nothin'. She got et with her butter 'n egg money. Took seven years. There et is in there now. Doin' nobody no good. She was just thet-a-way.

ALT. You cain cut et up for kindlin' wood, Tip.

CORNIE. Et'd make a good hen-coop for yer little chickens. All you got t' do is t' take out th' works and put a strip-a tar paper on top.

TIP. May do that.

MEL. Well . . . who's goin' t' write out that card? There et is on th' table.

JIM. I cain't write so's a person can read et.

TIP. Don't worry . . . nobody's goin' to read et.

CORNIE. I can't draw my X's so's a person can make 'em out. And my Z's has got curley-cues on 'em. You write et out, Alt.

ALT. I wud . . . but I sprained my ankle an' I'm stiff all over so's I can't even scratch my own back.

JIM. A-course, we couldn't ask Tip t' do et.

TIP. Stick th' durned flowers on without a card. Who cares for style? I been a-gettin' my belly-full-a style fer th' past ten years.

CORNIE. Just's you say, Tip. We just thunk et'd be kind-a nice, that's all.

(MEL *looks out the window.*)

MEL. Et's gettin' daylight out, boys. I got t' be goin' on home.

JIM. Me, too. Them calves got t' be tended to.

(*The men start to put on their coats and hats.*)

TIP. You fellers is comin' back t' carry th' woman to th' grave, ain't you?

CORNIE. I reckon so. We was 'pointed pall-bearers. Won't be hard to carry Minnie. She didn't weigh no more'n a bag-a feathers.

ALT. I guess I orta be hikin' on home, too. I got some chores t' do.

JIM. You goin' my way, Cornie?

CORNIE. Guess I'll cut across the hog pasture—it's shorter.

MEL. Whut'll you do without Minnie to do your milkin' now, Tip?

TIP. Reckon I'll have t' . . . git me another woman.

(*The men stop still.*)

CORNIE. You . . . got anybody . . . in mind, Tip?

TIP. I got Annie Smith in mind.

JIM. Ab Smith's dortor?

TIP. Yeh. I've had her in mind for some time. When I seen Minnie was . . . ailin'.

(*The men look at one another. They say nothing. Silence.*)

ALT. Well . . . I . . . I guess I'll be . . . goin' on, boys.

JIM. Me too, Alt.

TIP. I may need you fellers later t' help me bust up that pianner in there . . . when we git Minnie out of the way.

CORNIE. Any time. *Ef I ain't doin' somethin'.*

ALT. Me, too. Most likely I *won't* be.

MEL. I guess . . . I'll just take another look . . . at Minnie in there . . . b'fore I go.

JIM. Me . . . too.

(MEL *opens the door. The men look in.*)

MEL. Th' sun . . . looks perty . . . shinin' on that . . . rose, Tip.

JIM. Shore . . . does.

ALT. Et's tough luck t' lose a woman like Minnie.

MEL. She was allus smilin' and bright.

TIP. I'll git over et all right. Don't worry none 'bout me.

CORNIE. I reckon . . . we won't . . . much.

(ALT *opens the outside door. The men start out.*)

ALT (*turning toward* TIP). I s'pose th' baby is inside th' coffin with Minnie, ain't it?

TIP. It's layin' on her breast. (*Pause.*) They wa'n't no use wastin' *two* coffins.

(*The men leave.* TIP *resumes his reading and rocking. The sunlight washes out the pale of the lamplight.*)

THE CURTAIN FALLS SLOWLY

A MEMORANDUM ON OTHER PRODUCTIONS IN NEW YORK CITY

AN IMPRESSION that we must avoid creating is that the "little theatres" in New York ended with the big three—the Provincetown, Washington Square, and Neighborhood Playhouse groups. As a matter of fact, amateur groups mushroomed throughout the first half of the twenties. It does not appear that any formal record was made of this activity. But this writer recalls seeing quite a number of productions at the Greenwich Village little Cherry Lane Theatre and other cubbyholes of art between 1924 and 1926. Those that he remembers most gratefully were John Gay's *Polly* (the sequel to *The Beggar's Opera*), Gita Sowerby's grimly realistic family tragedy *Rutherford and Son,* and a simply staged Gluck opera, *Orpheus and Eurydice.* Among less satisfactory, yet valiant, productions were John Ford's late Elizabethan incest tragedy *'Tis Pity She's A Whore* and Shelley's *The Cenci,* the last played uptown with a bewildering assortment of accents by a group calling itself the Lenox Hill Players. (And, it need hardly be said, short-lived little theatre groups have played sporadically in all the boroughs of New York ever since.)

As for the production of modern drama in languages other than English, and not without influence on those who created theatre in English, there is material for several volumes. The "Chinatown" district provided many examples of oriental stylization throughout the years, and Mei Lan-Fang and his company, occupying the Forty-ninth Street Theatre, gave performances of Chinese classics so supremely quintessential theatre that they could be considered, as Stark Young noted in a brilliant tribute (see pages 114-118, *Immortal Shadows,* Scribner's 1948), the highest point in the theatrical season of 1929. Theatre in the Italian language left a profound effect in the fall of 1923 when the unforgettable Duse gave us glimpses of her magic at the Century Theatre in such modern classics as Ibsen's *Ghosts* and *Hedda Gabler* (*ibid.,* 29-32). And still more importantly, a visit by the Moscow Art Theatre in 1923, with plays by Gorky and Chekhov, provided, as Stark Young and others were able to report (*ibid.,* 15-19), our most instructive experience of the art of ensemble acting. The Moscow Art Theatre's musical studio, which visited us two years later, moreover, set us a high lesson in integrated music-drama; its production of a streamlined version of Bizet's opera without "grand opera" pyrotechnics, *Carmencita and the Soldier,* left a deep impression. It is possible to speculate whether it did not plant the seed for the successful Oscar Hammerstein's *Carmen Jones* in the nineteen forties. More esoteric but also unforgettable was the visit of the great Hebrew-speaking Habima Theatre in 1926. The Habima, especially with S. Ansky's *The Dybbuk,* gave the supreme example of stylized theatre. The production had been originally staged by Stanislavski's ablest pupil Vakhtangov, who died shortly thereafter at an early age. Stark Young, who understood style in theatre better than any of us, could write (*ibid.,* 71) that it was the only completely successful instance of extreme stylization he had ever encountered.

Nor may we overlook the contribution of the Jewish theatre on Second Avenue. Among its early practitioners, the stately Jacob Adler provided acting in a classically heroic manner, by comparison with which a good deal of acting on the English-speaking stage seemed mild. Two of Mr. Adler's children, Stella Adler (who played the mother in Clifford Odets' *Awake and Sing*) and Luther Adler (who played Joe Bonaparte in the same author's *Golden Boy*) were later to be co-founders and important actors of New York's Group Theatre in the nineteen thirties. Moreover, Adler and others played modern classics and Jewish equivalents in the form of problem plays by means of which, through acquaintance with Yiddish or German or through English synopses, New Yorkers were familiarized with the theatrical possibilities of modern drama. This was even more the case with Maurice Schwartz and his Jewish Art Theatre, which continued to produce after 1930. Mr. Schwartz favored stylized productions and acting to a degree, and he provided opportunities for us to see modernistic departures from realism, such as Andreyev's

Thought and the expressionist Ernst Toller's *Hinkemann* (given under the title of *Bloody Laughter*), as well as folk plays like *Yoshe Kalb* for which the nearest equivalent in English were *Porgy* and *The Green Pastures.* This art theatre served as a training ground for such contributors to the stage and screen as the actor Paul Muni and the playwright (formerly, actor) John Wexley.

Finally, we must note that as early as 1892 New Yorkers could see many seminal productions given in German at the Irving Place Theatre off Fourteenth Street, near Fourth Avenue, under Heinrich Conried's and later Christian's and Marlow's direction. As late as 1943 the Theatre Guild director Lee Simonson, one of the two leading designers of the twenties, could recall the enterprise with gratitude. He has called it "certainly the most extraordinary repertory theatre this city has had in the last fifty years." (See: *Part of a Lifetime,* Duell, Sloan and Pearce, pp. 2-3, 13.) At the Irving Place Theatre, in addition to seeing the German classics, the New Yorker who understood German could become familiar with many examples of the modern drama on the stage before, as in the case of Shaw's *Pygmalion* (1914) and Arthur Schnitzler's *Light O'Love,* he could see them in the English-speaking theatre; and some of these he was not to see there at all. Among other plays given by Conried and his successors were: Hauptmann's famous symbolist verse play *The Sunken Bell* (1897) and that masterpiece of naturalism *Drayman Henschel* (1899), hardly known in the English-speaking theatre, and what appear to have been first New York productions of Ibsen's *Pillars of Society* (1889), *Hedda Gabler* (1892), Sudermann's *Magda* (*Heimat,* 1893), Gorky's *The Lower Depths* (1902), Maeterlinck's *Monna Vanna* (1903), Oscar Wilde's *Salomé* (1907), and Molnar's *The Guardsman* (*Der Leibgardist,* 1914). The last-mentioned play later became one of the Theatre Guild's outstanding successes and was to start Alfred Lunt and Lynn Fontanne on their meteoric joint career.

SUPPLEMENTARY LIST OF PLAYS *

1. EUGENE O'NEILL: *The Dreamy Kid.* (One-act play.) Produced by the Provincetown Players, 1919.
   S.S. Glencairn. (A series of one-acters, produced individually in different years; and collectively in 1924: *Bound East for Cardiff,* 1916; *In the Zone,* 1917; *The Long Voyage Home,* 1917; *The Moon of the Caribbees,* 1918.)
   Beyond the Horizon. Produced by John D. Williams, 1920.
   The Emperor Jones. Produced by the Provincetown Players, 1920.
   Anna Christie. Produced by Arthur Hopkins, 1921.
   All God's Chillun Got Wings. Produced by the Provincetown Players, 1924.
   The Great God Brown. Produced by Macgowan, Jones, and O'Neill, 1926.
   Marco Millions. Produced by the Theatre Guild, 1928.
   Strange Interlude. Produced by the Theatre Guild, 1928.
2. ELMER RICE: *The Adding Machine.* Produced by the Theatre Guild, 1923.
3. SIDNEY HOWARD: *Lucky Sam McCarver.* Produced by William A. Brady, Jr., Dwight Deere Wiman, and John Cromwell, 1925.
   Ned McCobb's Daughter. Produced by the Theatre Guild, 1926.
   The Silver Cord. Produced by the Theatre Guild, 1926.
4. PAUL GREEN: *In Abraham's Bosom.* Produced by the Provincetown Players, 1926.
5. GEORGE KELLY: *The Show-Off.* Produced by Stewart and French, Inc., 1924. (Compare with *Poor Aubrey* in this book.)
   Behold the Bridegroom. Produced by Rosalie Stewart, 1927. (A failure when produced but a notable anomaly in its time as a deeply moral play!)
6. GEORGE S. KAUFMAN and EDNA FERBER: *The Royal Family.* Produced by Jed Harris, 1928.
7. GEORGE S. KAUFMAN and RING LARDNER: *June Moon.* Produced by Sam H. Harris, 1929.
8. S. N. BEHRMAN: *Serena Blandish.* Produced by Jed Harris, 1929.

* For one-acters, see also pages 686-687.

9. PHILIP BARRY: *Holiday*. Produced by Arthur Hopkins, 1928.
10. JOHN HOWARD LAWSON: *Processional*. Produced by the Theatre Guild, 1925.
11. DAN TOTHEROH: *Wild Birds*. Produced by the Cherry Lane Players, 1929.
12. JOHN WEXLEY: *The Last Mile*. Produced by Herman Shumlin, 1930.
13. EDWIN JUSTIN MAYER: *The Firebrand*. Produced at the Morosco Theatre in 1924.
14. VIRGIL GEDDES: *The Earth Between*. Produced by the Provincetown Players, 1929.
15. MARTIN FLAVIN: *Children of the Moon*. Produced by Jacob A. Weiser in association with A. L. Jones and Morris Green, 1923.

    The Criminal Code. Produced by William Harris, Jr., 1929.
16. JOHN COLTON and CLEMENCE RANDOLPH: *Rain*. Produced in 1922.
17. GILBERT EMERY: *The Hero*. Produced in 1921.
18. ARTHUR RICHMAN: *Ambush*. Produced by the Theatre Guild, 1922.
19. VINCENT LAWRENCE: *Spring Fever*. Produced in 1925.
20. LULU VOLLMER: *Sun-up*. Produced in 1923.
21. MAURINE WATKINS: *Chicago*. Produced at the Music Box in 1926.
22. RACHEL CROTHERS: *Let Us Be Gay*. Produced by John Golden, 1929.
23. WILLIAM JOURDAN RAPP and WALLACE THURMAN: *Harlem*. Produced in 1929.
24. SUSAN GLASPELL: *The Inheritors*. Produced by the Provincetown Players, 1921.
25. ARTHUR GOODRICH and ROSE A. PALMER: *Caponsacchi*. (Dramatization of a part of Robert Browning's *The Ring and the Book*.) Produced by Walter Hampden, 1926.
26. WINCHELL SMITH and FRANK BACON: *Lightnin'*. Produced by Winchell Smith and John Golden, 1918.
27. FRANK CRAVEN: *The First Year*. Produced at the Little Theatre, 1920.
28. OWEN DAVIS: *Icebound*. Produced by Harris, Lewis and Gordon, 1923.
29. HATCHER HUGHES: *Hell-Bent for Heaven*. Produced by the Provincetown Players, 1924.
30. JESSE LYNCH WILLIAMS: *Why Marry?* Produced by Selwyn & Co., 1917.

    Why Not? Produced by the Equity Players—Actors' Company, 1922.
31. KENYON NICHOLSON: *The Barker*. Produced by Charles L. Wagner in association with Edgar Selwyn, 1927.
32. ZOE AKINS: *Déclassé*. Produced by Charles Frohman, 1919.

    The Texas Nightingale. Produced by Charles Frohman, 1922.
33. LANGDON MITCHELL: *The New York Idea*. Produced by Harrison Grey Fiske, 1906.
34. LOUIS KAUFMAN ANSPACHER: *The Unchastened Woman*. Produced by Oliver Morosco, 1915.
35. EUGENE WALTER: *The Easiest Way*. Produced by David Belasco, 1909.
36. CLARE KUMMER: *Good Gracious Annabelle*. Produced by Arthur Hopkins, 1916.
37. PERCY MACKAYE: *The Scarecrow*. Produced by Henry B. Harris, 1911.
38. WILLIAM VAUGHN MOODY: *The Great Divide*. Produced by Henry Miller, 1906.
39. ELEANOR GATES: *The Poor Little Rich Girl*. Produced by Arthur Hopkins, 1913. (Noteworthy for attempt at fantasy.)
40. EDWARD SHELDON: *The Nigger*. Produced in 1909.

    The Boss. Produced in 1911.
41. GEORGE M. COHAN: *Seven Keys to Baldpate*. Produced by Cohan and Sam. H. Harris, 1913.

BIBLIOGRAPHY

STUDENTS can consult the files of *Theatre* and *Theatre Arts* magazines for the years covered by this book, and Burns Mantle's Best Plays volumes of those years (Dodd, Mead & Company), as well as *The Best Plays of 1899-1909* and *The Best Plays of 1909-1919,* edited by Burns Mantle and Garrison P. Sherwood. In the last-mentioned volume will be found synoptic versions of *The Easiest Way, Seven Keys to Baldpate, On Trial, The Unchastened Woman, Good Gracious Annabelle,* and *Why Marry?*

The most penetrating volume of dramatic criticism is *The American Drama since 1938,* by Joseph Wood Krutch (New York: Random House, 1939).

Brilliant notations on the period are scattered in George Jean Nathan's many volumes of dramatic criticism before 1930.

Extremely illuminating reviews of productions of the period appear in *Immortal Shadows,* by Stark Young (New York: Charles Scribner's Sons, 1948), pages 1-118.

Penetrating but politically colored appraisals will be found in Eleanor Flexner's *American Playwrights 1918-1938* (New York: Simon and Schuster, 1938).

The most detailed account of the period after 1900 is in *A History of the American Drama: From the Civil War to the Present Day,* by Arthur Hobson Quinn (New York: F. S. Crofts & Co., 1936). See also: *Revolution in American Drama* by Edmond Gagey (New York: Columbia University Press, 1947), which starts its summary with the year 1912.

Other books to be consulted are:

The American Theatre as Seen by Its Critics. Edited by Montrose J. Moses and John Mason Brown. New York: W. W. Norton & Co., 1934.

The American Theatre, by John Anderson. New York: The Dial Press, 1938. Although the text is brief, the illustrations are numerous.

The Provincetown, by Helen Deutsch and Stella Hanau. New York: Farrar & Rinehart, 1931. A history of the Provincetown Players.

The Theatre Guild: The First Ten Years. Edited by Walter Prichard Eaton, with articles by the Theatre Guild's directors. New York: Brentano's, 1929.

Part of a Lifetime, by Lee Simonson. New York: Duell, Sloan & Pearce, 1943. A personal account of Lee Simonson's association with the Guild as its regular scenic artist and one of its directors.

The One-Act Play Today. Edited by William Kozlenko, with chapters by Glenn Hughes, Barrett Clark, John Gassner, and others. New York: Harcourt, Brace & Co., 1938.

The American Dramatist, by Montrose J. Moses. Boston: Little, Brown & Co. (?), 1925.

The Art Theatre, by Sheldon Cheney. New York: Alfred A. Knopf, 1925.

Many of the plays referred to in the Introduction to this book and in the Supplementary List of Plays will be found in:

Representative American Plays. Edited by Arthur Hobson Quinn. Revised edition. New York: Appleton-Century, 1930.

Representative Plays by American Dramatists. Edited by Montrose J. Moses, Volume III. New York: E. P. Dutton, 1921.

Representative American Dramas, National and Local. Edited by Montrose J. Moses. Boston: Little, Brown & Co., 1925.

For one-act plays, see, among other collections:

Representative One-Act Plays. Edited by Margaret Mayorga. Boston: Little, Brown & Co., 1919.

Twenty American One-Act Plays. Edited by Frank Shay. New York, 1922.